INSTITUTES AND HISTORY

OF

Roman Private Law

WITH

CATENA OF TEXTS.

BY

DR. CARL SALKOWSKI,

ORDINARY PROFESSOR OF LAWS IN THE UNIVERSITY OF KÖNIGSBERG.

TRANSLATED IN FULL AND EDITED

BY

E. E. WHITFIELD, M.A.

OF ORIEL COLLEGE, OXFORD; MEMBER OF THE INCORPORATED LAW SOCIETY.

THE LAWBOOK EXCHANGE, LTD.

Clark, New Jersey

2008

ISBN-13: 978-1-58477-903-2
ISBN-10: 1-58477-903-9

The quality of this reprint is equivalent to the quality of the original work.

THE LAWBOOK EXCHANGE, LTD.
33 Terminal Avenue
Clark, New Jersey 07066-1321

Please see our website for a selection of our other publications and fine facsimile reprints of classic works of legal history:
www.lawbookexchange.com

Library of Congress Cataloging-in-Publication Data

Salkowski, Carl, 1838-1899.
[Lehrbuch der Institutionen und der Geschichte des römischen Privatrechts. English.]
Institutes and history of Roman private law : with catena of texts / by Carl Salkowski ; E.E. Whitfield (translator and editor).
p. cm.
In English and Latin.
Translation of the author's Lehrbuch der Institutionen und der Geschichte des römischen Privatrechts.
Originally published: London : Stevens and Haynes, 1886.
Includes bibliographical references and index.
ISBN-13: 978-1-58477-903-2 (cloth : alk. paper)
ISBN-10: 1-58477-903-9 (cloth : alk. paper)
1. Roman law. 2. Roman law--History. I. Whitfield, E. E. (Edward Elihu), b. 1849. II. Title.
KJA2190.S254 1994
340.5'4--dc22 2008014000

Printed in the United States of America on acid-free paper

INSTITUTES AND HISTORY

OF

Roman Private Law

WITH

CATENA OF TEXTS.

BY

DR. CARL SALKOWSKI,

ORDINARY PROFESSOR OF LAWS IN THE UNIVERSITY OF KÖNIGSBERG.

TRANSLATED IN FULL AND EDITED

BY

E. E. WHITFIELD, M.A.

OF ORIEL COLLEGE, OXFORD; MEMBER OF THE INCORPORATED LAW SOCIETY.

LONDON:

STEVENS AND HAYNES,

Law Publishers,

BELL YARD, TEMPLE BAR.

1886.

Incipientibus nobis exponere iura populi Romani ita maxime videntur posse tradi commodissime, si primo levi ac simplici, post deinde diligentissima atque exactissima interpretatione singula tradantur. Alioquin si statim ab initio rudem adhuc et infirmum animum studiosi multitudine ac varietate rerum oneraverimus, duorum alterum aut desertorem studiorum efficiemus, aut cum magno labore eius, saepe etiam cum diffidentia, quae plerumque iuvenes avertit, serius ad id perducemus, ad quod leniore via ductus sine magno labore et sine ulla diffidentia maturius perduci potuisset.

§ 2, I. de J. et J. 1, 1.

VIRO CLARISSIMO

CAROLO EDVARDO GÜTERBOCK

POTENTISSIMI GERMANIAE IMPERATORIS

A CONSILIIS IUSTITIAE INTIMIS,

IURIS IN ACADEMIA REGIOMONTANA

PROFESSORI PUBLICO ORDINARIO,

HOC OPUS

EX DISCIPLINA BORUSSORUM PROFECTUM,

AUCTORE COLLEGA VOLENTE,

D. D. D.

ICTUS ANGLICANUS INTERPRES.

TRANSLATOR'S PREFACE.

WITHIN the present century an attempt has been made to impart to English Law a scientific character. The first great worker in this field, by his contributions to an accurate English legal terminology, has vindicated the permanent value of ROMAN Law in legal education. Towards the end of John Austin's life was published Mr. (now Lord Justice) Lindley's translation of the General Part of Thibaut's 'System'; which was soon followed by a volume of *Cambridge Essays* containing that by Sir Henry Maine on 'Roman Law and Legal Education' (reprinted in his 'Village Communities'). To be told in 1856, not only that 'texts of Roman Law have been worked into the foundations of our jurisprudence,' but also that 'it is not because our jurisprudence and that of Roman Law were once alike that they ought to be studied together, it is because *they will be alike*,' was for our lawyers to learn, though slowly, the need of radical reform in elementary professional study.

In the year 1872 we find a master of English Case Law speaking of the Roman Law as 'a system that more than any other exhibits the principles which ought to, and to some extent do, underlie the jurisprudence of all nations': so thought the late Lord Justice Mellish. And it seems to be admitted on all sides that an exact knowledge of legal principle—for which the 'Corpus Juris' affords such treasure—should from the beginning of his career be cultivated by every one seeking a place in the legal profession; not least, perhaps, by those to whom will be entrusted the initiative in law-business. The statement, however, of Mr. F. Harrison, that 'an effective knowledge of Roman Law has been introduced into the ordinary education of every lawyer' (*Fortn. Rev.* Jan. 1879), is still subject to so much exception as to afford only slight satisfaction. Mr. Harrison could of course refer alone to the state of things created by such examinations as the Bar Pass, under regulations, at that time, of less than ten years' standing. Of this examination another authority writes: 'The slight knowledge of the subject requisite to pass will have no direct value to the student in his after course, and indeed will probably soon be forgotten.' In the Law Schools of Oxford and Cambridge it is now far otherwise. But Roman Law as yet forms *no* part of the necessary acquisitions of the large body of our 'articled clerks,' provision not having been made for this subject in examinations controlled by the Law Society. Accordingly, no instruction in that Law under official auspices is open to them, no encouragement extended to the student to travel beyond what to him in most cases are 'dry' textbooks of our own Law.

Few would venture to maintain that legal education is at present carried far enough in point of thoroughness. The *history* of each branch of ENGLISH Law should be studied by those who seek to obtain a clear idea of such Law in its present, largely confused, shape. Who can expect to work with comfort at the Law of Real Property without the help of some such book as Mr. Digby's?

As to Common Law, it would be impossible to speak of any portion as dry in the hands of writers like Mr. Justice Holmes or the present Professor of Common Law at the Inns of Court. Again, a distinguished Judge has written a 'History' which no student of the Criminal Law can long leave unread. For LAW as a *study* being second to none, I may perhaps rely upon the striking testimony of Dr. Arnold (Life and Correspondence, vol. ii. p. 81).

A healthy sentiment now happily prevails amongst law-students themselves, which found expression at the Congress, representing some 4,000 of those in England and Wales, in June of last year. Advance in this direction is of primary importance to lawyers as such, for it underlies discussions as to some proposals for administrative reforms of the utmost magnitude. If to such be added that orderly arrangement of English Law towards which our jurists are steadily working, Law as appropriately administered must with us ere long be neither cumbersome nor protracted, and will be not merely cheap but good.

Manuals of Roman Law, for the most part explanatory of its rules represented by, and according to the order—such as it is—of the Institutes of Gaius and Justinian, have during the last thirty years appeared in rapid succession. Whilst Austin was still alive, Mr. Sandars may be said to have led the way with his well-known textbook. Then in the year when the illustrious Savigny died, Sir H. Maine began the publication of a set of works which connect the ideas of ancient and modern life. Dr. Hunter has recently been able to put forth a second edition of his 'Roman Law in the order of a Code'; and in 1884 Mr. Roby enriched the literature with his 'Introduction to the Digest.' By such books as these English students are being left without excuse for their neglect of the subject.

In studying Roman Law I had found that best progress could be made through use of German treatises. That now published in English represents what may be the fifth edition of a book[1] which is recommended by the Oxford Board of Legal Studies. It exhibits a modern arrangement of so much of that Law as is of chief importance to English lawyers.

The plan of the original work I must leave my author to describe in his own words. I have broken up his paragraphs and placed the Latin passages in immediate conjunction with that part of the explanatory text which relates to them; consulting in this the convenience of the English reader. The author's parenthetical references have been here transferred to the margin, and I have, as far as I could, cited authorities rather than the sections (in the original, sub-sections) in which they occur, not having preserved Dr. Salkowski's subdivisions of either text or excerpts. The student will find such passages by reference to the first Index.

The parenthetical notes have in most cases also been placed in the margin, and to these I have added occasional references to approved English manuals, in lieu of the continuous sectional references to German textbooks, as those of Puchta and Böcking, in the original work. For Scotch Law, I have commonly referred the reader to Bell's Dictionary. An English student of Roman Law should not

---

[1] *Lehrbuch der Institutionen und der Geschichte des Römischen Privatrechts, für den akademischen Gebrauch.* Von Dr. Carl Salkowski (Vierte Auflage, 1883).

neglect the large infusion of Roman elements in the Scots' Law, as he may afterwards come across them in practice.

It has been no part of my plan to cite the excerpts always in the same way: beginners should be practised in methods of citation other than those which they may find prevalent in strictly English books on Roman Law. I have cited rubrics at the first occurrence in the particular section of the title affected, and afterwards where they could conveniently, and by way of variety, be cited without the numbers for book and title. This may serve to exercise the student's memory.

I have as far as possible reproduced the Latin text printed in Dr. Salkowski's work, checking mistakes by standard editions. The same as to punctuation.

Responsibility falls to myself alone for the translation of the Latin passages. It has been added in the interest of those for whom this English edition is chiefly intended, the large number of law-students in either branch of the profession who do not resort to the Universities, under conditions very different from those which govern legal education in Germany. Students desirous of further help upon lawyers' Latin would probably find all they need in the sixteenth chapter of Mr. Roby's 'Introduction.' In the rendering of excerpts from the two Roman institutional works I have been frequently indebted to earlier English translations; in that of passages from the Digest, chiefly to Otto, Schilling and Sintenis. The lexicons of Brisson, Dirksen, and Heumann, besides German *Pandekten*, have of course been always at hand.

I must ask the student to make some corrections in the book from the list of Errata.

It gives me great pleasure here to thank the learned author for his supervision of this work, when his valuable book had already gained an assured position in German Universities, and for much kindness.

I have to speak of a very special obligation. It was my privilege from the first to secure the aid of the accomplished author of *Henricus de Bracton und sein Verhältniss zum Römischen Rechte*, to whom the volume is dedicated. His long-continued perusal of English law-books, his special study of our early writers, and the generous manner in which, during his sessional labours of 1884–5, he examined the whole of my MS. translation of the German, render an exaggeration of my debt to him impossible. When I heard him during my holidays in 1884 discourse in his classroom on a topic which has been especially developed by English lawyers, dealing with it not alone as possessed of judicial experience, but by reference to the pages of Bentham and of Best, I was reminded on the one hand of the growing combination amongst ourselves of Science and Practice, and on the other, of our indebtedness in turn to Germany in respect of Roman Law, as of almost every department of study.

Finally, I have had the scholarly help, for the correction of proof-sheets, of my friend Mr. Reginald Broughton, late Fellow of Hertford College.—The assistance I have thus enjoyed may have compensated for defects many and great inherent in work like mine, chiefly performed during the leisure hours of a business life.

132 High Street, Oxford,
January 1886.

AUTHOR'S PREFACE.

THE Roman Law has of old in all the Universities of Germany formed the basis of the study of Law, in such way that in the first (half-yearly) term the lectures upon the Institutes and History of Roman Law impart the Elements and historical development of Roman Private Law; whilst lectures upon the Pandects, to which the second term is devoted, are designed for the exposition of the System of Roman Private Law, and the dogmatical consideration of its details. Then follow exegetical exercises in the sources of Roman Law, especially in the Digest. Though this arrangement of studies find first of all an historical explanation in the fact of the reception of Roman Law, by virtue of which it is still at the present day the dominant Common Private Law in Germany, it is nevertheless before all materially justified by the consideration that it seems to be the only way of accomplishing the task of University study, namely, to make the law-student a real lawyer. That which makes the lawyer is not merely possession of the knowledge of a number of statutes and legal precepts, but thorough scientific penetration into, and intellectual mastery of, the positive Law, and with that at the same time the ability always to apply the Law correctly. And if the acquisition of this mastery and capacity is the object of the study of Law in general, the Roman Law presents itself to us as an incomparable means of education, by help of which the law-student ought to learn a juristic habit of thought both for exactitude and method, an acute apprehension and correct interpretation of laws and legal transactions.

It is true that the growth of the Law of England has not been so closely associated with the Roman Law as that of Germany. Not only did the germ laid, 700 years ago, for the study of Roman Law in England by magister Vacarius, the founder of the Law School at Oxford, fail to develop any promising blossom : it was soon blighted. Traces, nevertheless, of Roman Law have remained in England ; and that it did not lose all influence is shown by modern inquiries, especially those concerning Bracton. And, quite apart from the fact that the Roman Law as a whole has not been received in England, should not the study of it exercise a useful and wholesome influence upon the education of English law-students, and fruitfully affect the science of English Law ? Should not also in England this ideal, intellectual possession, which has come down to us in the Roman LAW as the inheritance of antiquity, in like manner be esteemed and cultivated in a scientific spirit, as the classical remains in other departments of mental culture ? Modern efforts go to prove that more and more is a start being made in comprehending the significance and value of Roman Law for the teaching of Law and for legal education in general on English soil.

The present textbook sets itself the task of grouping and setting forth in the briefest possible and in a precise form the elements of pure Roman Law, as a guide for lectures upon the Institutes, in a comprehensive manner and according to their essential connection. It was not my object to compose a handbook or literary work, which should lay the material before the reader with detailed exposition and in an easily intelligible way, adapted for reception at one's ease, but a textbook by help of which the reader should *learn;* and which on that very account—starting from the principle that we can alone truly call our own what we have ourselves acquired—must make some demand upon independent study and the mental energy of the law-student. My special object was, as far as possible, to make the sources speak for themselves. To these the beginner's attention must be drawn at the outset: he should receive stimulation for self-instruction from the passages which have been transcribed.

I cannot forbear to express my warmest thanks to Mr. Whitfield for the laborious and, having regard to the character of the book, exceedingly difficult work of translating it, by which its sphere of influence will be so largely extended.—May this book succeed in introducing the 'cupida legum iuventus' to the study of Roman Law, and contribute to the knowledge of the importance of that Law so lofty, which was so skilfully elaborated; may they at the same time learn to appreciate it: then our object would be completely attained.

KÖNIGSBERG,
December 29, 1885.

TABLE OF CONTENTS.

INTRODUCTION.

PART I. THE ELEMENTS.

PART II. OUTLINE OF THE HISTORY AND SOURCES OF ROMAN LAW.

THE ROMAN PRIVATE LAW.

BOOK I. THE ORIGINATION OF RIGHTS AND EXERCISE THEREOF.

CHAP. I. COMMENCEMENT AND TERMINATION OF RIGHTS.

CHAP. II. CAPACITY TO ACT.

PART II. JURISTIC PERSONS.

BOOK III. LAW OF PROPERTY ('RES').

PART I. PURE OR SIMPLE LAW OF PROPERTY.

CHAP. I. LAW OF THINGS.

TIT. I.—NOTION AND DIVISION OF THINGS.

(2) Obligationes *ex* *Delicto*.

BOOK IV. (APPENDIX). THE JUDICIAL ENFORCEMENT OF RIGHTS ('ACTIONES').

CHAP. I. THE CONSTITUTION OF THE COURT.

CHAP. II. THE PROCEEDINGS.

ADDENDA ET CORRIGENDA.

ADDENDA.

PAGE

62. Fifth line from bottom, at 'epitome,' *add* note: '[b] By this must not be understood Codification in the modern sense: see art. "Justinian" in the Encyclopaedia Britannica (9th ed.).'

83. Last line but one, *after* 'see,' *add* '"Selden, *Dissertatio ad Fletam*" (tr. by Kelham, 1771).'

84. *After* 'Hunter . . .' *add* 'Scrutton, The Influence of the Roman Law on the Law of England, 1885.'

92. At end of note [a], *add* 'Markby, ss. 691–2.'

93. *After* 'see,' *add* '"Savigny, System," iii., Beilage viii.'

95. Twentieth line from bottom, *after* '9,' *add* 'pr., §.'

137. Sixth line from bottom, *add* comma after 'persons.'

139. Eighteenth line from bottom, *after* '1,' *add* 'pr.'

161. At end of note [b], *add* 'cf. Blackst. i. 130 (Steph. i. 139) cited by Holland.'

163. At end of note [a], *add* 'Holland, pp. 104–6; Dicey, Law of Domicil, pp. 153, *sqq.*'

167. At end of note [a], *add* '; also Blackstone, i. 423-4 (Steph. ii. 226–7).'

172. Seventeenth line from top, *after* 'dominus,' *add* comma.

226. Third line from foot, *before* '§§,' *add* '=.'

229. Thirteenth line from top, *after* 'prohibeatur,' *add* 'D. 23, 2, 38 pr.'

244. Twelfth line from top, *after* 'coemptio,' *add* comma.

248. At end of note, *add* 'Quarterly Review, Jan. 1866 (p. 186).'

277. Sixteenth line from top, *after* 'persona,' *add* 'in.'

282. Sixteenth line from foot, *after* '3,' *add* 'pr.'

284. Sixteenth and twentieth lines from top, *before* the sections, *add* 'iii.'

328. Note, *add* comma *after* 'subject.'

438. Eighth line from top, complete parenthesis at 'interdictum.'

504. Eighth line from top, *add* reference letter [a] *after* 'credendi.'
Fifteenth line from bottom, *after* '12,' *add* 'pr.'

522. Seventh line from top, *after* '72,' *add* 'pr.'

532. Fourth line from top, *after* '45,' *add* '1.'

587. Nineteenth line from bottom, *after* 'pr.,' *add* '§ 1.'

640. Sixteenth line from bottom, *after* 'that,' *add* 'is.'

652. Seventeenth line from top, *after* 'manifestum,' *add* 'furtum.'

657. Thirteenth line from bottom, *after* '*furtum*,' *add* '*conceptum*.'

672. Sixteenth line from top, *before* 'according,' *add* '(2).'

686. Twelfth line from bottom, *before* 'I.,' *add* '§ 1.'

702. Tenth line from top, *after* '173,' *add* 'pr.'

808. Fifteenth line from top, *after* '41,' *add* 'pr.'

939. *Read* note [a] as '§ 40.'

CORRIGENDA.

PAGE

37. Eighth line from bottom, *for* 'vocare' *read* 'vacare.'
62. Eighth line from top, *for* 'Alariciamum' *read* 'Alaricianum.'
67. Fourteenth line from top, *for* διατάζεις *read* διατάξεις.
70. Last line but one, *for* 'c' *read* '=.'
71. Fifth line from bottom, *for* 'ad quirendavel' *read* 'adquirenda vel.'
84. Three first lines, *for* 'History . . . , 1829,' *read* 'Geschichte u. s. w. ii. 159-163, iv. 348, *sqq.*'
89. Sixth line from bottom, *for* 'right' *read* 'rights.'
94. Fourteenth line from bottom, *dele* comma after 'litterarum.'
95. Fourth line from bottom, *for* 'lance' *read* 'plate.'
96. Tenth line from bottom, *for* 'suppose' *read* 'supposed.'
99. Third line from top, *for* 'conditiones' *read* 'condiciones.'
110. Eleventh line from bottom, *for* 'object' *read* 'intention.'
112. Seventeenth line from top, *for* 'mens' *read* 'mens.' (mensis).
Last line, *for* 'the pupil . . . bind,' &c., *read* 'to the ward, he does not put the ward under obligation to.'
115. Seventeenth line from top, *for* '§§' *read* 'll.'
116. Twelfth line from bottom, *for* 'possessionem' *read* 'possessionum.'
119. In last five lines of translation of D. 4, 2, 13, *after* 'him,' *read* 'which was not given to him by the debtor voluntarily, is possessed . . . or has been received by him, and that he has himself,' &c., and *dele* 'he' *before* 'shall forfeit.'
130. Fifth line from bottom, *for* 'venal' *read* 'penal.'
142. Sixth and seventh lines from top, *for* 'may be very different' *read* 'admit of great diversity.'
162. Eleventh line from top, *for* 'by that' *read* 'upon.'
166. Eleventh line from bottom, *dele* 'born.'
169. Fourteenth and thirteenth lines from bottom, *after* 'It is certain that,' *read* 'servile relationships are a hindrance to marriage . . .'
Eighth line from bottom, *for* 'describe' *read* 'demonstrate.'
173. Fourth line from bottom, *dele* 'upon.'
176. Tenth line from top, *for* 'ficti' *read* 'fictio.'
Twentieth line from top, *for* 'revertis set' *read* 'revertisset.'
178. Eighteenth and seventeenth lines from bottom, *after* 'of' *read* 'military service, capital punishment has been abandoned.'
186. In third and second lines from bottom, *read* 'This indulgence, however, it was determined should only be allowed to those whose.'
187. In third line of translation of C. 7, 6, 1, *for* 'taken to him' *read* 'brought forward.'
192. In third line from bottom, *for* 'done an injury' *read* 'insulted.'
195. Fifteenth line from bottom, *for* 'manumittor' *read* 'patron,' and *for* 'by' *read* 'of.'
199. Sixteenth line from bottom, *for* 'Iulia' *read* 'Iunia.'
Seventh line from bottom, *for* 'became' *read* 'become.'
Last line but one, *for* 'they' *read* 'those only.'

PAGE

203. Tenth line from bottom, *for* 'sc.' *read* 'SC.'
212. Fifth line from bottom, *for* 'nomino' *read* 'nomine.'
216. Note [a], *for* 'lapse of a' *read* 'demise of the.'
217. Eighth line from bottom, *dele* 'for these.'
218. Last line, *for* 'reaches' *read* 'approaches.'
224. Thirteenth line from top, *for* 'advantages' *read* 'disadvantages.'
226. Fifth line from top, *for* '58' *read* '59.'
232. Fourth line from top, *dele* second 's' in 'cognoscesbant.'
234. At foot of page, *for* 'if servitude befall' *read* 'other servitude befalling.'
237. Second line from top, *for* 'neo' *read* 'nec.'
Last line, *for* 'take . . . you' *read* 'do business for yourself.'
247. Note [b], *for* 'usurp' *read* 'effect interruption.'
248. Note [b], *for* '15th' *read* '12th.'
250. Twenty-first line from top, for '8' read '8ª.'
Eighth line from bottom, *for* 'kill a disobedient son' *read* 'put a son to death unheard.'
252. Seventeenth line from bottom, *for* 'services' *read* 'as a slave.'
253. Sixteenth line from top, *for* 'ind' *read* 'iud.'
Third line from foot, *for* 'matters of fact' *read* 'upon the case.'
254. Sixteenth line from bottom, *for* 'ius-piciendo' *read* 'in-spiciendo.'
256. Eighth line from top, *for* 'occur' *read* 'come about.'
289. Last line but one, *for* 'pre-' *read* 'pro-'
296. Note [b], *for* 'castrat' *read* 'castrati.'
Eighteenth line from bottom, *for* 'cui' *read* 'qui.'
Fourth and third lines from bottom, *for* 'body but crime' *read* 'body, but vice.'
298. Fourteenth line from bottom, *for* 'vice' *read* 'your vice.'
299. Sixth line from bottom, *for* 'alongside of' *read* 'next to.'
300. Second line from bottom, *for* '*CUBA*' *read* '*CURA*.'
302. Third line from top, *dele* comma.
Eleven lines from bottom, *for* 'Sca' *read* 'Scta.'
Seventh and second lines from bottom, *for* 'curatela' *read* 'cura.'
304. Fourth line from tcp, *for* 'Earlier on' *read* 'At an early period.'
324. Ninth line from top, *for* '196' *read* '195.'
329. Thirteenth line from bottom, *for* 'It being' *read* 'That it should be.'
334. Fifteenth line from top, *for* '29' *read* '27.'
345. First line, *for* 'Planc' *read* 'Plane.'
Seventh line from top, *for* 'morbilis' *read* 'mobilis.'
369. Eighth line from bottom, *for* 'action' *read* 'auction.'
371. Last line before margin, *for* 'donor and donee' *read* 'grantor and grantee.'
407. Ninth line from top, *for* 'rest' *read* 'rests.'
421. Twentieth line from top, *for* 'eod.' *read* 'D. h. t.'
423. First line, *dele* '1, §.'
430. Fourth line from top, *for* '1, 1 pr.' *read* 'l. 1 pr., § 1.'
437. First line, *for* 'Manilia' *read* 'Mamilia.'
444. Eighth line from bottom, *for* 'iure' *read* 'iura.'
455. Seventeenth line from top, *for* 'usufructus' *read* 'usus fructus.'
471. Fourth line from top, *for* 'presentes' *read* 'praesentes.'

PAGE

484. Tenth line from top, *dele* second '4.'
500. Twelfth line from top, *for* 'gb' *read* 'qb.'
517. Fourth line from top, *for* '43' *read* '44.'
524. Tenth line from top, *for* 'utilatas' *read* 'utilitas.'
Thirteenth line from top, *for* 'casual' *read* 'causal.'
535. Twentieth line from top, *for* 'withdrawal' *read* 'deduction.'
550. Tenth line from top, *for* '13' *read* '1, 3.'
554. First line, *for* the semicolon after 'even' *read* a comma.
Nineteenth line from top, *for* 'LI' *read* 'LL.'
Fourteenth line from bottom, *for* 'sanctiori' *read* 'sanction.'
556. Third line from top, *for* 'stipu-lundi' *read* 'stipu-landi.'
574. Second line from top, *for* 'EVERVNT' *read* 'FVERVNT.'
586. Nineteenth line from top, *for* '25' *read* '2, 5.'
587. Note [b], *for* 'fut.' *read* 'fin.'
594. Note [b], *for* 'v.' *read* 'iv.'
600. Nineteenth line from bottom, *for* '3' *read* 'D.'
608. Tenth and eleventh lines from top, *for* 'contract' *read* 'contact.'
609. Eighteenth line from foot, *for* 'conductor' *read* 'conductio.'
623. First line, *for* 'iii.' *read* 'III.'
639. Fourteenth line from top, *for* 'do' *read* 'de.'
640. First line, *for* 'de finirisolet' *read* 'definiri solet.
645. Tenth line from top, *for* '304' *read* '302.'
649. Sixteenth line from top, *for* '—' *read* '=.'
652. Seventh line from top, *for* '134' *read* '184.'
665. Fifth line from top, *for* '20' *read* '21.'
703. Seventeenth line from top, *dele* '(2)'.
736. Ninth line from top, *for* 'eod.' *read* 'D. h. t.'
814. Seventh line from top, *for* 'so as' *read* 'so made as.'
818. Note [c], *for* 'eres' *read* 'heres.'
856. Sixteenth line from top, *for* 'reversely' *read* 'conversely.'
868. Heading of § 173, *for* '*CESSIO TRANSMISSIO*' *read* '*CESSIO* AND *TRANSMISSIO*.'
Fourteenth line from top, *dele* '(1).'
874. Third line from top, *for* 'cohaeredes,' *read* 'coheredes.'
920. Ninth line from top, *for* 'egati' *read* 'legati.'
931. Note [a], *for* 'A. A.' *read* 'H. A.'
957. Last line but one, *for* 'had' *read* 'has.'
963. Last line before margin, *dele* comma before and that after 'in rem.'

WORKS CITED

IN OTHER THAN THE FIRST EDITION.

BLACKSTONE, Commentaries on the Laws of England, 8th ed. 1778.
STEPHEN, Commentaries, 9th ed. 1883.
SAVIGNY, The Right of Possession, 6th ed. translated by PERRY, 1848.
ORTOLAN, Explication Historique des Instituts, 9th ed. 1875.
AUSTIN, Lectures on Jurisprudence, 4th ed. 1873.
SMITH, Leading Cases on Various Branches of the Law, 8th ed. 1879.
ARNDTS, Lehrbuch der Pandekten, 12th ed. 1883.
WESTLAKE, Private International Law, ed. 1880.
MAINE, Ancient Law, 9th ed. 1883.
Village Communities in the East and West, 4th ed. 1881.
Early History of Institutions, 3rd ed. 1880.
LORD MACKENZIE, Studies in Roman Law, 5th ed. 1880.
COULANGES, La Cité Antique, 11th ed. 1885.
POSTE, Elements of Roman Law by Gaius, 2nd ed. 1875.
POLLOCK, Principles of Contract, 4th ed. 1885.
MARKBY, Elements of Law, 3rd ed. 1885.
RIVIER, Introduction Historique au Droit Romain, ed. 1881.
BROWN, Law Dictionary, 2nd ed. 1880.
HUNTER, Roman Law in the Order of a Code, 2nd ed. 1885.
DIGBY, History of the Law of Real Property, 3rd ed. 1884.
HOLLAND, Elements of Jurisprudence, 2nd ed. 1882.

INTRODUCTION.

PART I.

THE ELEMENTS.

§ 1. THE FUNCTION OF THE INSTITUTES.

THE function of the INSTITUTES is, to give a comprehensive, historical and doctrinal account of the pure Roman Private Law, suitable for the beginner, as the basis of the study of Jurisprudence in general and of Roman Law in particular. Thus we shall have to consider the pure Roman Private Law which closes with the legislation of Justinian, the 'classical' especially, exhibited alone in its rudiments. The detailed and complete treatment thereof belongs to the study of the Digest or Pandects.

The several doctrines of Roman Law have at the same time to be described in their historical development, so that the institutions and maxims of law which later on passed away, called *antiquitates iuris,* also fall within the limits of the inquiry.

The study of Roman Law in general reposes not merely upon the fact that it is down to our own day received as the common Municipal Law in certain European States, and as being, partly in form and partly in substance, the basis and essential source of some of the modern Codes, as the Prussian and Austrian, but also upon the high perfection that it attained, especially as worked out by the so-called classical jurists.[a] Their writings stand out incomparably, whether we speak of scientific analysis of the whole substance of Law, or the actual exhibition of legal relations and exactness in the application of legal decisions to the given case; and it is these that have imparted to Roman Law its value as a means of juristic education which has hitherto been unsurpassed.[b]

[a] Cf. §§ 8, 10.

[b] Cf. Austin, 'Lectures on Jurisprudence,' pp. 1114-7 (Student's edn. pp. 153-6); Maine, 'Village Communities,' pp. 330, *sqq*.

§ 2. Law and Jurisprudence.[c]

Law is the sum of the rules, clothed with outward compulsory authority, for the life of individuals living together according to natural requirement, and of their outward actions in a community; whilst MORALITY, which is grounded on Religion, regulates the whole conduct of man, in action as well as in thought, or decision for good or evil, in such wise that compliance with its dictates is under the sole control of personal freedom and the inner consciousness of the individual.[d]

Paulus: Non omne quod licet honestum est.— l. 144 pr., D. de R. J. 50, 17.[e][1]

The basis of Law is, accordingly, the human will and its freedom, or Personality.

[c] See Austin, Lectt. i., v., vi.; Markby, 'Elements of Law,' ch. i.; Holland, 'Elements of Jurisprudence,' chh. i.-iv.; and the art. on 'Law' in the 'Encyclopaedia Britannica' (9th edn. vol. xiv.).

[d] Cf. § 19, ad init.

[e] For methods of citation, see § 10.

Ius in the objective sense (law, rule of law) is the sum of the several rules of law, and imports the will of the community as acknowledging the person himself and his rational will. In the subjective sense (a RIGHT,[f] or legal capacity) it indicates the will of the individual as acknowledged by the will of the community, because corresponding to it—that is, the lawful faculty for a determinate exercise of will, the legal control over an

[f] See Markby, ss. 149-152; Holland, ch. vii.—For the imperfect Roman idea of a legal right, see Maine, 'Early Law and Custom,' pp. 365, *sq*.

---

[1] It is not everything that is allowable which is honourable.

object.[a] Every legal Right correlates with a legal DUTY[b] or Obligation.

The conduct of the individual which answers to the precepts of Law is called *Iustitia*, the opposite of which is *Iniuria*.[c]

> Ulpian.: Iustitia est constans et perpetua voluntas ius suum cuique tribuendi.—Iuris praecepta sunt haec: honeste vivere, alterum non laedere, suum cuique tribuere.—l. 10 pr., § 1, D. de J. et J. 1, 1 (=pr. § 3, I. eod. 1, 1).[d][1]
>
> Idem: Iniuria ex eo dicta est, quod non iure fiat; omne enim quod non iure fit, iniuria dicitur.—D. 47, 10, 1 pr.[2]

[a] Compare definitions collected by Holland, p. 64.

[b] Holland, *ubi supra*; Markby, ss. 147-8, 181-192.

[c] Cf. D. 9, 2, 5, 1; Inst. iv. 4 pr.

[d] See Savigny, 'System des heutigen Römischen Rechts,' i. 407; Austin, 1. pp. 220, *sqq*.

Only the POSITIVE is actual Law, that of a certain State or organically constituted community, to which the power of such State lends external authority. There is no Law the same for all peoples.[e]

The so-called 'Law of Nature,'[f] if we are to understand by that a complete Law, derived merely from principles of Reason by abstract thought, individual caprice *a priori*, or absolute Law—is a nonentity: it exists solely in the consciousness of its author, by whose individual development it is conditioned.[g] Rightly conceived, the function of the Law of Nature or 'Philosophy of Law' is, on the one hand, to develop in general the ultimate ground of Law—that is, the ethical principles which flow from the nature of man as of a being designed for freedom,[h] and to test with such principles the rules of positive law in the light of their morality and rationality; on the other hand, to discover from an historical standpoint the inner connection of positive law with the entire moral, intellectual and social development of the people.[i]

[e] Holl. pp. 35, *sqq*.—Cf. §§ 3, 4.

[f] Austin, Lect. 32; Maine, 'Ancient Law,' chh. iii.-iv.; Mkby. ss. 116-7; Holland, pp. 26-33.

[g] Cf. § 15.

[h] Cf. Inst. i. 2, 11.

[i] Holl. p. 10.

---

[1] Justice is the settled and permanent desire to render to every one his due.—The precepts of Law are as follows: to live virtuously, not to injure another, to render to each his due.

[2] *Iniuria* has been so called because it occurs unlawfully; for whatever occurs unlawfully is called *iniuria*.

Iurisprudentia est divinarum atque humanarum rerum notitia, iusti atque iniusti scientia.[a]—l. 10, § 2, D. de J. et J. (§ 1, I. eod. 1, 1).[1]

[a] Austin, vol. i. *l. c.*

The subject of Jurisprudence is Positive Law in its organic connection; its function is to develop the conceptions of Law from the several legal rules, and, having regard to the whole circumstances of corporate life, to combine all in one system.

Paul.: Regula est, quae rem quae est breviter enarrat; non ex regula ius sumatur, sed ex iure quod est, regula fiat.—D. 50, 17, 1.[2]

Iavolenus: Omnis definitio in iure civili periculosa est; parum est enim, ut non subverti posset.—l. 202 eod.[3]

LEGAL RELATIONS are the concrete relations to one another of men as subjects of will, or 'Persons,' which are regulated by Law. What is called an INSTITUTE of law is the simple sum of the legal relations, regarding what is common to them.

§ 3. ORIGIN AND GROWTH OF POSITIVE LAW.—SOURCES OF LAW.[b]

[b] Cf. Markby, ch. ii.; Holland, ch. v.

Positive Law, as one side of the general culture of a nation, is developed both in it and with it, in conformity with intellectual and moral conditions, and with the co-operation of that people's special external relations; and is also dependent upon the nature, the geographical position and character of the country it inhabits. *The* source from which Law springs is the intellectual individuality of the people, or the popular consciousness; hence its national character.

---

[1] Jurisprudence is the knowledge of divine and human things, the science of right and wrong.

[2] A rule is that which briefly indicates the subject in question; not so that the law is derived from the rule, but so that from the actual law is framed a rule.

[3] Every definition in the *ius civile* is precarious, for it may readily be set aside.

In early times all Law is *ius non scriptum*[a]—*i.e.*, the instinct for Law existing in the people makes itself known immediately in legal usage; hence legal acts, maxims of law, what is called CUSTOMARY Law, or 'mos,' 'mores,' 'consuetudo.'[b] It is not until a later period that Law is formulated and written down, yielding *ius scriptum*, and alongside of the immediate instinct for Law and of its creation is introduced that declared and made known by the constitutional organ of the State—that is, by LEGISLATION.[c] This is the second source of Law; it in the course of things compresses the other into an ever narrower circle, whether of locality, of persons, or of classes in society. On the other hand, with the progressive development and various formation of Law, the knowledge and improvement thereof must fall increasingly to the special function of those skilled in Law—that is, to JURISTS.

[a] See Brown, 'Law Dict.' s. *ius scriptum*, &c.

[b] Cf. Maine, 'Ancient Law,' ch. i., and 'Early Institutions,' ch. ii.; Mkby. ss. 79, *sqq.*; Holl. pp. 45-51.

[c] Cf. 'Anct. Law, pp. 14-20, &c.; Mkby. ss. 61-71; Holl. p. 56.

> Inst. i. 2, 3: Constat ius nostrum aut ex scripto aut ex non scripto. 9: Ex non scripto ius venit quod **usus** comprobavit: nam diuturni mores consensu utentium comprobati legem[d] imitantur.[1]
>
> Ulp.: Mores sunt **tacitus consensus populi** longa consuetudine inveteratus.—Fr. 4.[2]

[d] For *lex*, see Clark, 'Practical Jurisprudence,' pp. 29, *sq.*

Ingrained in the very essence of positive law is, at the same time, its constant variableness and onward development.

> Gell. noct. Att. xx. 1, § 22: Non enim profecto ignoras, legum opportunitates et medelas pro temporum moribus et pro rerum publicarum

---

[1] Our law consists of written and unwritten law.—Law which has been approved by custom is derived from an unwritten source; for long-standing customs resemble law when approved by the consent of those who use them.

[2] Customs are the tacit consent of a people determined by ong-standing habit.

generibus ac pro utilitatum praesentium rationibus mutari atque flecti neque uno statu consistere.[1]

Inst. i. 2, 11: Sed naturalia quidem iura, . . . divina providentia constituta, semper firma atque immutabilia permanent: ea vero, quae ipsa sibi quaeque civitas constituit, saepe mutari solent vel tacito consensu populi vel alia postea lege lata.[2]

STATUTES are the precepts of law declared and made known by the legislative power in the State, and on that account generally binding. The operation of a statute can only commence from the moment of its being made known,—from its publication or promulgation; and it does not extend to earlier cases—that is, to juristic acts perfected under the authority of the earlier law—nor to legal relations already established (acquired rights), unless either the statute attributes to itself retrospective power, or the latter is required by its special nature, its object, or the higher idea of Law, and therefore is to be taken as having been intended by the legislator.[a]

[a] Cf. § 7, s. *lex*.—For *ex post facto* laws, see Blackstone, 'Commentaries,' i. p. 46 (Stephen, i. p. 27); Austin, pp. 502-3 (Student's edn. p. 241).

Imp. Theod.: Leges et constitutiones futuris certum est dare formam negotiis, non ad facta praeterita revocari: nisi nominatim etiam de praeterito tempore et adhuc pendentibus negotiis cautum sit.—C. 1, 14, 7.[3]

---

[1] For you are surely not ignorant that the advantages and remedies of laws are changed and modified according to the customs of the time and to the kinds of States, as well as to reasons of present utilities, and do not remain in one condition.

[2] Laws of nature, appointed by divine ordinance, always remain stable and unchangeable; but such as an individual State has established are wont often to change either by tacit consent of the people, or by the subsequent publication of another law.

[3] It is beyond doubt that *leges* and constitutions only lay down the form of the law for future acts, but cannot be applied to past events, unless something is therein expressly provided concerning past time or matters that are still pending.

CUSTOM is not a source, but—like publication of a statute—phenomenal and originative form of Customary Law, although actual usage will contribute much to the establishment and further development of the Law.[a]

[a] Cf. Puchta, 'Cursus der Institutionen,' i. p. 23. (9th edn.).

> Iulian.: **Inveterata consuetudo** pro lege non immerito custoditur et hoc est ius, quod dicitur moribus constitutum. Nam cum ipsae leges nulla alia ex causa nos teneant, quam quod iudicio populi receptae sunt, merito et ea, quae sine ullo scripto populus probavit, tenebunt omnes: nam quid interest, suffragio populus voluntatem suam declaret, an rebus ipsis et factis?—D. 1, 3, 32, 1.[1]

A customary law is to be acknowledged only if the custom is an established one, evidently by continuity of acts in the Law.

> Hermogenian.: . . . ea quae longa consuetudine comprobata sunt ac per **annos plurimos** observata, veluti tacita civium conventio, non minus quam ea, quae scripta sunt iura, servantur.—l. 35 eod.[2]
>
> Ulp.: Cum de consuetudine civitatis vel provinciae confidere quis videtur, primum quidem illud explorandum arbitror, an etiam contradicto aliquando iudicio consuetudo firmata sit.—l. 34 eod.[3]

---

[1] An immemorial custom is rightly observed as a *lex*, and this is the so-called Customary Law. For since the *leges* themselves are binding upon us for no other reason than because they have been accepted by the will of the people, that also which the people has approved without any written confirmation must rightly be binding upon all: for what difference does it make whether the people declare its will by vote, or by the very matter and act?

[2] That which has been approved by a long-standing custom and has been in force during the course of many years must, as the silent consent of the citizens, be observed just as much as the written Law.

[3] When a person ostensibly appeals to the custom of the city or province, it must, in my opinion, first be ascertained whether it has been actually matter of dispute,[b] and the custom confirmed by a decision.

[b] Taking *contradicto* as absolute, with Clark, cit. p. 217.

Again, if it manifest itself as the expression of an actual legal instinct, *opinio necessitatis,* so-called Rationality of custom.[a]

[a] Cf. Savigny, 'System,' i. § 29, pp. 174, *sq.*

Celsus: Quod non ratione introductum, sed **errore** primum deinde consuetudine obtentum est, in aliis similibus non obtinet.—l. 39 eod.[b] [1]

[b] See also D. 1, 3, 14 and 15.

Imp. Constant.: Consuetudinis ususque longaevi non vilis auctoritas est, verum non usque adeo sui valitura momento, ut aut **rationem** vincat aut legem.—C. 8, 52 (53), 2.[2]

DOCTRINE or *communis doctorum opinio,*[c] and PRACTICE or *usus fori*—judge-made Law[d]—form no source of Law, although worked out, it may be, and developed both by the scientific treatment and application of positive law; but Doctrine, and Practice likewise, often is seen to transmit Customary Law, which becomes known through the legal conviction of jurists as representing the national instinct for Law, and as those in whom is concentrated the knowledge of the actual Law.[e]

[c] Mkby. ss. 101-3; Holl. p. 52.

[d] See Austin, pp. 655-6; Savigny, i. § 20; Mkby. ss. 78, 92, 95, 97; Holl. pp. 51-2.

[e] For the *responsa prudentium,* see § 8.

Callistratus: Imperator noster Severus rescripsit, in ambiguitatibus, quae ex legibus proficiscuntur, consuetudinem aut rerum perpetuo similiter iudicatarum auctoritatem vim legis obtinere debere.—D. 1, 3, 38.[f] [3]

[f] See also l. 37.

Imp. Iustinian.: . . . non exemplis sed legibus iudicandum est.—C. 7, 45, 13.[4]

---

[1] That which is not introduced upon a reasonable ground, but originally by mistake, and then by custom has been upheld, does not hold good in other like cases.

[2] No mean regard attaches to custom and the usage of many years, but its authority must not be stretched so far as that it prevail against a reasonable ground of law or a statute.

[3] Our Emperor Severus has ordained, where doubts arise upon statutes, that custom, or the authority of legal decisions which have been uninterruptedly repeated in similar cases, ought to have the force of *lex.*

[4] Judgment must be given, not according to examples, but according to *leges.*

A rule of law is repealed by statute or custom; the older must give way when conflicting with a later decision.

> Rectissime etiam illud receptum est, ut leges non solum suffragio legislatoris,[a] sed etiam tacito consensu omnium per **desuetudinem** abrogentur. —D. 1, 3, 32, § 1.[1]

[a] Iul.: populi?

The repeal of what has hitherto been a legal decision may be either complete or partial.

> Ulp.: Lex aut **rogatur** i.e. fertur; aut **abrogatur** i.e. prior lex tollitur; aut **derogatur** i.e. pars primae legis tollitur; aut **subrogatur** i.e. adicitur aliquid primae legis; aut **obrogatur** i.e. mutatur aliquid ex prima lege.—Fgm. 3.[2]

§ 4. Branches of Law.

Every individual has not merely a personality of his own, but is daily subject to political ties with others. The sum of the rules which govern the legal relations of individuals as such is PRIVATE Law;[b] those institutions which concern the position and the relations of individuals to one another as members of a State, as well as the legal relations of the State as a body politic, constitute PUBLIC Law.[c] To the latter belong Constitutional Law, Civil Procedure, and Criminal Law.[d]

> Ulp.: Huius studii duae sunt positiones: publicum et privatum. **Publicum** ius est, quod ad statum rei Romanae spectat, **privatum**, quod ad singulorum utilitatem; sunt enim quaedam

[b] *Infra*, Gell. x. 20, 4.

[c] Cf. Holland, pp. 272-4. But see Austin, i. p. 416 (Student's edn. pp. 195-6) with Lect. 44; Markby, ss. 292, *sqq.* Reference may also be made to Bluntschli, 'Theory of the State,' pp. 56, 59 (Engl. Tr.); and, for International Law, to Holl, pp. 96-7.

[d] Cf. *inf.* ad fin. Civil Procedure is by English jurists ranged under the head of Private Law.

---

[1] Quite rightly is it an accepted doctrine that *leges* are repealed, not only by the declaration of the legislator, but also in consequence of the silent consent of the whole community, by reason of their disuse.

[2] A *lex* is either 'rogated,' that is, introduced; or 'abrogated,' that is, the former *lex* is repealed; or 'derogated,' that is, part of the former *lex* is repealed; or 'subrogated,' that is, something is added to the former *lex*; or 'obrogated,' that is, some portion of the former *lex* is altered.

> publice utilia, quaedam privatim. Publicum ius in sacris, in sacerdotibus, in magistratibus consistit.—l. 1, § 2, D. h. t. (= de J. et J. 1, 1).[a][1]

[a] Cf. Inst. i. 1, 4.

Ius scriptum in the Roman sense is the Law declared by one of those organs of the State which are authorised to create Law, and which is made known in the form of writing.[b] *Ius non scriptum* is the Law which springs up by usage, and is founded upon and evidenced partly by Custom, as immediately based upon the national feeling as to Law,[c] and partly by the application imparted to it by the jurists; and is developed by way of interpretation of the written Law (auctoritas prudentium).[d]

[b] § 8.

[c] Inst. i. 2. 3; Dig. 1, 3, 32, 1, and l. 35.

[d] § 7. Cf. Stephen, 'Commentaries,' Introd. s. 3; Austin, Lect. 28; Holl. pp. 56-7.

The Roman jurists distinguish two constituents of Law, called by them *ius civile* and *ius gentium*. The one is Law rigidly national, confined to the legal relations of Roman citizens; the other, Law free from any national peculiarity, which is common to cultivated nations and applicable to all persons, because based on the one hand upon 'naturalis ratio,' or the sense of Law which resides uniformly in all men; on the other, upon positive, universally recognised, practical necessity, whether social or economical. This ultimately quite displaced the old *ius civile proprium Romanorum*.[e]

[e] Cf. §§ 7-9; and Austin, Lect. 31.

> Gai. i. § 1: Omnes populi, qui legibus et moribus reguntur, partim suo proprio, partim communi omnium hominum iure utuntur: nam quod quisque populus ipse sibi ius constituit, id ipsius proprium est vocaturque **ius civile**, quasi ius proprium civitatis; quod vero naturalis ratio inter omnes homines

---

[1] The study of Law falls into two parts, into that of Public and that of Private Law. Public Law is that which relates to the institutions of the Roman Empire; Private Law that which concerns the convenience of individuals; for there are institutions which derive their advantage from public, and those which derive it from private considerations. Public Law relates to religion, the priests and the magistrates.

constituit, id apud omnes populos peraeque custoditur vocaturque **ius gentium,** quasi quo iure omnes gentes utuntur. Populus itaque Romanus partim suo proprio, partim communi omnium hominum iure utitur (=l. 9, D. h. t., § 1, I. h. t. 1, 2).[1]

Ex hoc iure gentium omnes paene contractus introducti sunt, ut emptio venditio, locatio conductio, societas, depositum, mutuum et alii innumerabiles.—§ 2, i. fi. I. h. t.[2]

Ulp.: **Ius civile** est quod neque in totum a naturali vel gentium recedit nec per omnia ei servit: itaque cum aliquid addimus vel detrahimus iuri communi, ius proprium i.e. civile efficimus.—l. 6 pr., D. h. t.[3]

The expression *ius naturale* is used with different meanings. At one time by it is meant the 'ius gentium;'[a] at another, and as a rule, the Law based upon the rational and moral nature of man, and upon universal ethical principles, conflicting, it may be, in certain points with the positive 'ius civile' and 'ius gentium;' occasionally also—as taking the form of a philosophical

[a] Cf. 'Anct. Law,' p. 52.

---

[1] All peoples which are governed by laws and customs make use partly of their own, partly of Law common to all men: for the Law which each people has formed for itself is peculiar to that State, and is called Civil Law, as the Law peculiar to the State itself; but the Law which natural reason has formed amongst all men is observed in like manner amongst all peoples, and is called the Law of Nations, as the Law employed by all nations. The Roman people, accordingly, use not only their own but also the Law common to all men.

[2] From this Law of Nations have almost all contracts been derived, *e.g.*, Purchase and Sale, Hiring, Partnership, Deposit, Loan, and many others.

[3] The Civil Law is that which neither departs entirely from the Law of Nature or of Nations, nor is subject to it in all particulars. Therefore, when we add anything to the common Law or subtract aught from it, we make proper, that is, civil Law.

abstraction—Law rooted in the animal nature of man, and therefore common to all living beings.[a]

[a] Cf. Inst. i. 2, 11 and 32; Dig. 1, 5, 4; 43, 16, 1, 27; 48, 20, 7 pr.; 50, 17, 32 and 206. See also Austin, Lect. 32.

Ulp.: Privatum ius tripertitum est: collectum etenim est ex naturalibus praeceptis, aut gentium, aut civilibus.—Ius **naturale** est, quod natura omnia animalia docuit: nam ius istud non humani generis proprium, sed omnium animalium . . . commune est. Hinc descendit maris atque feminae conjunctio, quam nos matrimonium appellamus, hinc liberorum procreatio, hinc educatio.—l. 1, §§ 2, 3, h. t.[b] [1]

[b] Cf. Inst. i. 1, 4, 2 pr., and Maine, 'Anct. Law,' pp. 52, *sq.*

Paul.: Ius pluribus modibus dicitur: uno modo, cum id, quod semper aequum ac bonum est, ius dicitur, ut est ius naturale.—l. 11 pr. eod.[2]

Ius praetorium s. *honorarium,* in distinction from 'ius civile,' is the sum of the legal maxims put forth by the Praetors in the Edict.[c]

[c] Cf. §§ 7, 8.

Papinian.: Ius civile est, quod ex legibus plebiscitis, senatusconsultis, decretis principum, auctoritate prudentium venit. Ius **praetorium** est quod praetores introduxerunt; . . . quod et honorarium dicitur.—l. 7 pr., § 1, h. t.[3]

The ambiguous expression *aequitas* (Equity)[d] desig-

[d] Austin, Lect. 33; Maine, 'Anct. Law,' pp. 25, 28, 67-72; Mkby. ss. 120, *sqq.*

---

[1] Private Law is threefold; for it is gathered from precepts of Nature, of [all] Nations, and of the [particular] State.—Natural Law is that Law which Nature has taught all living beings: this Law is not one peculiar to the human race, but it is common to all living beings. From it comes the union of man and wife which we call 'marriage;' from it the begetting of children, from it their training.

[2] The word *ius* is used in manifold senses, one sense being when that which is always right and equitable is called *ius;* for instance, *ius naturale.*

[3] The Civil Law is that which has come of statutes, decrees of the People, decrees of the Senate, decrees of the Emperors, the authority of those learned in the Law. Praetorian Law is that which the Praetors have introduced; . . . which is also called *ius honorarium.*

nates, in general, Law constantly accommodated to the actual circumstances, and so, the ideal Law.

First, in legal application 'aequitas' is to be found by regard being had to the particularity of the case in question, whereby the rigid rule of Law is brought into harmony with its natural sentiment. Hence it is said, 'Summum ius summa iniuria.'

Secondly, the demands of 'aequitas' will have found more or less recognition in positive law, so that the contrast of stringent and equitable law (ius strictum, aequum) finds place in it.—*Ius strictum* is Law based upon abstract inference from positive, simple and rigid legal rules, described by the phrases 'iuris *subtilitas, scrupulositas*'—the formal law, unexceptional and absolute; whilst the more liberal and more flexible *ius aequum* endeavours to satisfy the requirements of higher material justice by constant reference to the special, actual elements of the concrete relation and case, as well as to the actual will and the proper legal intention of the persons: *id quod actum est.* From this result 'bonae fidei negotia, actiones,' as distinct from those 'stricti iuris.'[a]

[a] Cf. § 24.

Thirdly, in contrast with ius (civile) as positive law, which by means of some one law-source has already become established, we have Equity regarded as that which answers to the present advanced national ideas of Law, still in an inchoate state; a process of law-making which was in Rome furthered by the Praetorian Edict and by Jurisprudence, and was brought into recognition as positive law by legal decisions.[b] This form of Equity is by no means to be regarded as a mere subjective, indefinite feeling.

[b] Cf. § 30; Austin, Lectt. 34-36; Maine, A. L. pp. 61, *sqq.*; Holl. pp. 53-4.

Cels.: Ius est ars boni et aequi.—l. 1 pr., h. t.[c][1]

[c] Cf. *sup.* Dig. 1, 1, 11 pr.

Paul.: In omnibus quidem, maxime tamen in iure, aequitas spectanda est.—D. 50, 17, 90.[2]

---

[1] Law is the science of what is right and fair.

[2] In everything indeed, but in Law very especially, regard must be had to Equity.

Cels.: Bonus iudex varie ex personis causisque constituet.—D. 6, 1, 38.[1]

Tryph.: Bona fides, quae in contractibus exigitur, aequitatem summam desiderat.—D. 16, 3, 31 pr.[2]

Imp. Constant.: Inter aequitatem iusque interpositam interpretationem nobis solis et oportet et licet inspicere.—C. 1, 14, 1.[a] [3]

[a] Cf. ib. l. 12, § 3.

In contrast with *ius commune*, the general Law equally applicable to all persons and relations, or normal Law, by *ius singulare* is meant—

First, special, for the most part favourable, Law availing for certain classes of persons (*e.g.*, milites, minores, mulieres); of things (*e.g.*, fundus dotalis, property of a ward, res furtivae); and of legal relations,[b] which in the subjective sense is called *privilegium*.[c]

[b] *e.g.*, priority as between pledgees (§ 102), cases of *beneficium competentiae* (§ 139).

[c] Cf. § 8, s. *constitutiones principum.*

Gell. x. 20, 4: Non sunt generalia iussa, . . . sed de singulis concepta; quocirca **privilegia** vocari debent, quia veteres **priva** dixerunt, quae nos singula dicimus.[4]

Cic. p. dom. 17, 43: Vetant XII tabulae leges privatis hominibus irrogari: id est enim privilegium.[5]

Ulp.: Iura non in singulas personas, sed generaliter constituuntur.—D. 1, 3, 8.[6]

---

1 An approved judge will have to decide differently, as taking into account respective persons and causes.

2 The good faith which is required in contracts aims at the highest equity.

3 We alone are empowered and called upon to take into consideration the solution of any doubt between Equity and Law.

4 They are not general commands . . . but are framed about individuals; hence ought to be called *privilegia*, because the things which we speak of as 'individual' the ancients spoke of as 'private.'

5 The Twelve Tables forbid the imposition of statutes upon particular persons; for that is a *privilegium*.

6 *Iura* are established, not for individual persons, but for general application.

Modest.: Privilegia quaedam causae sunt, quaedam personae.—D. 50, 17, 196.[1]

Secondly, the anomalous rules of Law which depart from the unity and sequence of the 'ius commune,' and have arisen from considerations of *utilitas* (with respect to the practical demands of legal intercourse), often also of 'aequitas' (*e.g.*, favore libertatis) for certain cases, and in Roman Law, by the auctoritas prudentium. And so of something it may be said that 'iure singulari, benigne, utilitatis causa receptum, constitutum est.'[a]

[a] For examples, see Dig. 12, 1, 15; 41, 2, 1, 5; ib. 40, 1; 44, 1, 41, 3; 40, 4, 2, 15-16.

Paul.: Ius singulare est, **quod contra tenorem rationis** propter aliquam **utilitatem** auctoritate constituentium introductum est.—D. 1, 3, 16.[2]

Iul.: Multa iure civili **contra rationem disputandi** pro **utilitate communi** recepta esse, innumerabilibus rebus probari potest.—D. 9, 2, 51, 2.[3]

Paul.: Quod contra rationem iuris receptum est, non est producendum ad consequentias—.[4]

Iul.: In his, quae contra rationem iuris constituta sunt, non possumus sequi regulam iuris.—D. 1, 3, 14 sq.[5]

The greatest part of Law leaves to the individual full freedom to make his legal dispositions and to direct his legal relations according to his own judgment, and therefore only comes into application when those

1 Some *privilegia* go with a case, others with a person.

2 Singular law is that which has been introduced by the authority of the framers, against the tenor of reason, for some utility.

3 That many things have been accepted in the *ius civile* against logical argument for the sake of general utility, can be attested by innumerable cases.

4 No conclusion can be drawn from that which has been accepted contrary to legal principle.

5 That which has been established against legal principle cannot be followed as a rule of law.

concerned have arranged nothing otherwise, by its supplementing their imperfectly declared will (voluntatis interpretatio). This is called DISPOSITIVE Law.[a] But there are, besides, other institutions which plainly limit individual will, and exclude every private disposition of a contrary tendency: absolute legal rules, PEREMPTORY Law (ius publicum).[b]

[a] *Naturalia negotia*, § 19.

[b] Cf. Cod. 1, 14, 5.

Papinian.: Ius **publicum** privatorum pactis mutari non potest.—D. 2, 14, 38.[1]

Gai.: Contra iuris civilis regulas pacta conventa rata non habentur.—l. 28 pr. eod.[2]

Paulus: Ex pactis conventis . . . alia ad **voluntatem**, . . . alia ad ius pertinent, . . . in quibus non semper voluntas contrahentium servatur.—D. 23, 4, 12, 1.[3]

The rules of law of the latter kind are, as to their content, either imperative or prohibitive; the prohibitive laws, again, according to their operation (sanctio legis), are leges 'perfectae,' 'imperfectae,' 'minus quam perfectae.'[c]

[c] Cf. § 129, lex Cincia de donis et muneribus; § 182, l. Furia testamentaria.

Modest.: Legis virtus haec est: imperare, vetare, permittere, punire.—D. 1, 3, 7.[4]

Inst. ii. 1, 10: Legum eas partes, quibus poenas constituimus adversus eos, qui contra leges fecerint, **sanctiones** vocamus.[5]

Ulp.: [**Perfecta** lex est, quae vetat aliquid

---

1 The Public Law cannot be varied by the agreements of private persons.

2 Agreements concluded against the rules of the *ius civile* are not upheld.

3 Amongst the bargains that are concluded, some relate to what lies in the will [of the parties], others to what is governed by Law, in which the will of the contracting parties is not always observed.

4 In a statute resides the power to command, to forbid, to permit and to punish.

5 Those parts of statutes in which we have established penalties for the transgressors thereof we call 'sanctions.'

fieri, et si factum sit, rescindit. **Imperfecta** lex est, quae vetat aliquid fieri, et si factum sit, nec rescindit nec poenam iniungit ei, qui contra legem facit.] **Minus quam perfecta** lex est, quae vetat aliquid fieri, et si factum sit, non rescindit, sed poenam iniungit ei, qui contra legem fecit.—Frag. 1, 2.[1]

§ 5. Knowledge and Interpretation of Law.[a]

[a] Cf. Blackstone, i. pp. 59-62, 87, *sqq.* (Steph. i. pp. 71, *sqq.*); Austin, pp. 648, *sqq.*; Markby, ss. 72-77; Clark, pp. 230, *sqq.*

The source of our knowledge of Customary Law is actual legal usage; that of Statute Law, written matter.

1. Like all speech, whether written or by word of mouth, statutes also, as the expression of a thought, require explanation if they are to be understood. This is *interpretatio* in the wider sense. It is, in other words, that mental operation by which one apprehends the meaning of statutes, and accordingly, the will of the legislator expressed in them; their content and scope of application, or 'vis et potestas, voluntas legis.' For the sources of Roman Law, especially of what is called the 'Corpus Iuris,' interpretation acquires a further special meaning in so far as, in particular, is imposed upon the 'interpretatio' the task of first eliciting general maxims of law from the decision of actual cases. To the systematic art of interpretation is given the name HERMENEUTICS. Interpretation itself is grounded upon the

---

[1] [A 'perfect' statute is that which forbids a thing being done, and if it be done, sets it aside. An 'imperfect' statute is that which forbids a thing being done, and if it be done, neither sets it aside nor attaches any penalty to him that infringes the statute.] A 'less than perfect' statute is that which forbids a thing being done, and if it be done, does not set it aside, but attaches a penalty to him that has infringed the statute.

settlement of the text to be explained; which is CRITICISM.

Cels.: **Scire** leges non hoc est, verba earum tenere, sed **vim ac potestatem**.—l. 17, D. h. t. (=de legib. 1, 3).[1]

Ulp.: Quamvis sit manifestissimum edictum praetoris, attamen non est negligenda interpretatio eius.—D. 25, 4, 1, 11.[2]

2. That which interpretation chiefly requires is the consideration in its whole connection of the text to be expounded.

Cels.: Incivile est, nisi tota lege perspecta, una aliqua particula eius proposita iudicare vel respondere.—l. 24, h. t.[3]

3. All interpretation consists of two co-operating elements: the grammatical and the logical.[a] The 'grammatical' side of the interpreter's work has to do with the settlement of the natural meaning of words, and in their connection according to the rules of the language. The 'logical' is directed to the investigation of the sense and the intrinsic ground of the legal rule (ratio, sententia legis[b]) from the inner connection of these, their historical character and position in the legal system; and is at one time explanatory or 'declaratory,' especially in respect of statutes that have been framed obscurely;[c] at another, 'extensive,' in respect of those that have been framed upon too narrow a basis;[d] at other times, 'restrictive,' in respect of those that have been framed upon one too wide.[e]

Paul.: Cum in verbis nulla ambiguitas est,

[a] As Lexicons to the sources there are:—*Brisson* (1743); *Dirksen* (1837); *Heumann* (6th ed. 1884).

[b] Cf. Cod. 1, 14, 5.

[c] Cf. Inst. i. 25, 16: Gai. ii. 29, 8.

[d] Cf. Cic. p. Caec. 19, 54; Dig. 9, 2, 27, 13; 14, 6, 9, 2; 24, 1, 22.

[e] Cf. § 47, ad fin.

---

[1] To know statutes is to master, not their words, but their effect and meaning.

[2] Although the Edict of the Praetor is perfectly clear, yet the interpretation of it must not be neglected.

[3] It is inequitable, unless we take a general view of the statute, to decide or give an opinion according to some small portion of it before us.

non debet admitti voluntatis quaestio.—D. 32, 25, 1.[1]

Cels.: In ambigua voce legis ea potius accipienda est significatio, quae vitio caret, praesertim cum etiam **voluntas legis** ex hoc colligi possit.—l. 19, D. h. t.[2]

Ulp.: Verbum 'ex legibus' sic accipiendum est: tam ex legum sententia quam ex verbis.—D. 50, 16, 6, 1.[3]

Cels.: Nemo existimandus est dixisse, quod non mente agitaverit; . . . prior atque potentior est quam vox, mens dicentis.—D. 33, 10, 7, 2.[4]

Paul.: Non oportere ius civile calumniari neque verba captari, sed qua mente quid diceretur, animadvertere.—D. 10, 4, 19.[5]

Id.: **Contra legem** facit, qui id facit quod lex prohibet: **in fraudem** vero, qui salvis verbis legis sententiam eius circumvenit.—l. 29, D. h. t.[6]

4. Opposed to doctrinal, or that which is based upon scientific work, is the interpretation in Law of a statute by Legislation, or by Customary Law, *i.e.*, respectively 'authentic' and 'usual' interpretation;

---

[1] If in the words there lie no ambiguity, no question of intention ought to be entertained.

[2] In an ambiguous expression of a statute, that acceptation of the meaning is to be preferred which yields nothing false, especially when a conclusion may therefrom be drawn as to the intention of the statute.

[3] The expression 'according to statutes' is to be understood as, both according to the sense and according to the words of the statutes.

[4] It is not to be supposed that a person has said anything which he has not previously contemplated. The purpose of the speaker is anterior to and more important than his language.

[5] That the *ius civile* ought not to be subjected to false interpretation, neither should its words be wrested, but one should note the spirit in which anything is said.

[6] He acts in contravention of a statute who does what is forbidden thereby; whilst he evades the statute who retains its expression and yet applies a subterfuge to its meaning.

in which we have to do also with the decision of controversies.

Imp. Iustinian.: Definimus, omnem **imperatoris** legum interpretationem . . . ratam et indubitatam haberi; si enim in praesenti leges condere soli imperatori concessum est, et leges interpretari solum dignum imperio esse oportet.—C. 1, 14, 12, 3.[1]

Paul.: Si de interpretatione legis quaeratur, in primis inspiciendum est, quo iure civitas retro in eiusmodi casibus usa fuisset; optima enim est legum interpres **consuetudo**.—l. 37, D. h. t.[2]

Id.: Minime sunt mutanda, quae interpretationem certam semper habuerunt.—l. 23 eod.[3]

5. General rules of interpretation have only a relative value.

Iul.: Quotiens idem sermo duas sententias exprimit, ea potissimum excipiatur quae rei gerendae aptior sit.—D. 50, 17, 67.[4]

Gai.: Semper in dubiis benigniora praeferenda sunt.—l. 56 eod.[5]

Modest.: Nulla iuris ratio aut aequitatis benignitas patitur, ut quae salubriter pro utilitate hominum introducuntur, ea nos duriore interpre-

---

[1] We direct that every interpretation of laws proceeding from the Emperor . . . be treated as valid and beyond all doubt; for, if now it is allotted to the Emperor alone to make statutes, the interpretation of them also should be solely his function.

[2] If it be questionable how a statute is to be interpreted, one must first consider what legal maxim the State earlier on employed in like cases; for the best interpreter of statutes is Custom.

[3] Least of all may be altered what has constantly had a fixed interpretation.

[4] Whenever the same phrase expresses a twofold sense, that shall the rather be accepted which suits better the matter to be dealt with.

[5] In doubtful cases the more lenient view is always to be preferred.

tatione contra ipsorum commodum producamus ad severitatem.—l. 25, D. h. t.[1]

From interpretation in the modern sense we have to distinguish Analogy, or *interpretatio* in the proper Roman sense.[a] By it is understood that application to similar cases of a law which, derived from its intrinsic sequence, is according to its essential principles (ratio legis); sometimes taking the form of extensive interpretation,[b] whereby a blank in the law is filled up: 'ubi eadem legis ratio, ibi eadem legis dispositio.'[c]

[a] The *auctoritas prudentium* (§ 7).

[b] *E.g.*, Dig. 47, 8, 7.

[c] See §§ 133, ad fin., 200, ad fin.; but cf. Dig. 1, 3, 39; ib. ll. 14 and 15.

Non possunt omnes articuli singillatim aut legibus aut senatusconsultis comprehendi; sed cum in aliqua causa sententia eorum manifesta est, is qui iurisdictioni praeest **ad similia procedere** atque ita ius dicere debet.—Nam, ut ait Pedius, quotiens lege aliquid unum vel alterum introductum est, bona occasio est, cetera, quae tendunt ad **eandem utilitatem**, vel **interpretatione** vel certe iurisdictione suppleri.—l. 12 (Iul.), l. 13 (Ulp.), D. h. t.[2]

Tertull.: Semper quasi hoc legibus inesse credi oportet, ut ad eas quoque personas et ad

---

[1] Neither legal principle nor the innate mildness of justice permits us, in respect of that which was introduced for the good and convenience of men, to carry interpretation to such a rigid extreme as to violate their interest.

[2] It is impossible that all single cases should be specially comprised in statutes and in decrees of the Senate; but when their sense is clear in respect of some matter, he that is entrusted with the administration of the law must apply the sentence to similar cases, and declare law in accordance therewith. For, as Pedius says, as soon as one thing or another is introduced by the statute, a good opportunity is given for supplying other things that serve the like interest, whether through interpretation or, at least, by the legal functionary.

eas res pertinerent, quae quandoque similes erunt. —l. 27 eod.[1]

On the other hand, the limitation of a statute according to the ground thereof[a]—not to be confounded with restrictive interpretation (*v. sup.*)—is inadmissible, and the maxim 'cessante ratione legis cessat lex ipsa' is erroneous.[b] The application of a statute is not already defeated by the fact that its design is not intrinsically demonstrable; and this whether—

[a] Austin, pp. 648, *sqq.* (Student's edn. pp. 317, *sq.*).

[b] See, *e.g.*, Blackstone, i. p. 61.

(1) it appear to be in general irrational or unsuitable, or

(2) the circumstances giving occasion to it have altered—so long as it has not been displaced by Customary Law (desuetudo)—or that

(3) the principle of the statute may, exceptionally, not hold good for the actual case.

> Non omnium, quae a maioribus constituta sunt, ratio reddi potest.—Et ideo rationes eorum, quae constituuntur, inquiri non oportet; alioquin multa ex his, quae certa sunt, subvertuntur.—l. 20 (Iul.), l. 21 (Nerat.), eod.[2]

§ 6. Systematic Arrangement of the Subject.[c]

[c] See Markby, ch. vii.

Private Law results from the recognition of the individual as a PERSON, being the subject of rights, and regulates the expression of his will in respect of other Persons. The external world is the object of this expression of will: upon it the individual seeks definitely to operate; it is that which he endeavours

---

[1] It must always be supposed that in statutes there is contained the intention, so to speak, that they should concern such persons and circumstances of like kind as shall at any time arise.

[2] We cannot assign the reason of everything that has been decided by our ancestors. And, accordingly, we cannot investigate the grounds of such matters as are decided; otherwise much that is established falls through.

to bring under his control. PROPERTY represents that sovereignty of the will of an individual over objects of the external world which is recognised and protected by Law, *i.e.*, the objective control possessed by the will; in other words, it is the totality of external things by Law subjected to the control of a man's will, or, in general, of his legal relations that bear a monetary value.

> African.: **Bonorum** appellatio universitatem quandam non singulares res demonstrat.—D. 50, 16, 208.[1]
>
> Hermog.: **Pecuniae** nomine non solum numerata pecunia, sed omnes res tam soli quam mobiles et tam corpora quam iura continentur. —l. 222 eod.[2]
>
> Bonorum appellatio aut **naturalis** aut **civilis** est.—Bona intelliguntur cuiusque, quae deducto aere alieno supersunt. — l. 49 (Ulp.), l. 39, § 1 (Paul.), eod.[3]

The arrangement of Private Law, accordingly, divides into the doctrine of Subjects of rights and their natural and legal differences, which is the Law of PERSONS; and into the doctrine of the Objects of rights and the legal control thereof by the individual, which is the Law of PROPERTY.

Both doctrines must, however, be preceded by the doctrine of the origination and exercise of rights in general.

The Law of Persons at the same time comprises FAMILY Law, in the Roman sense,[a] *i.e.*, the doctrine of [a] See Savigny, i. p. 142 n.

[1] The designation 'goods' imports a kind of totality, and not individual things.

[2] Under the name of 'wealth' is comprehended not merely money, but all things, both immovable and movable, and both corporeal objects and rights.

[3] The designation *bona* has either a natural meaning, or that of the *ius civile*.—That is regarded as a man's property which remains over after subtraction of debts.

the legal relations of control and dependence which gather round Persons as members of a *familia*.

Property Law has to do especially with the individual conditions of Property as such—the pure or simple Law of Property. According to the differences herein, we obtain a division into the Law of THINGS (or of real rights [a]) and the Law of OBLIGATIONS. The one relates to the immediate legal control of the individual over objects of external Nature, *i.e.*, of Things; the subject of the other is that partial and transitory control, recognised by Private Law, of the individual over another subject of rights, by virtue of which this latter is under obligation to him in respect of the performance of a definite act bearing a pecuniary value.

[a] Mkby. s. 129; Holl. p. 108.

> Inst. iii. 13 pr.: **Obligatio** est iuris vinculum, quo necessitate adstringimur alicuius solvendae rei, secundum nostrae civitatis iura.[1]

Every obligatory right avails against a certain person who is constrained to a positive operation of will, whilst with the real right of the individual correlates only the legal duty in general of all others to observe a negative attitude towards him, that is, not to interfere with it.[b]

[b] For actions *in rem* and *in personam*, see § 24.

Co-ordinate with the pure or simple Law of Property are the Law of Family Property and the Law of Inheritance, in which property is conceived of as a unit.—The first is concerned with the modifications which the proprietary relations of a subject of rights undergo by reason of his position in a *familia*. The Law of Inheritance finds its subject in property as a whole enduring beyond the life of the previous owner, whose place is taken by another; it is the doctrine of

---

[1] An obligation is the legal bond by which, according to the laws of our State, we are of necessity constrained to the performance of something.

the transfer of the control of property that was possessed by deceased persons to others surviving them (Universal Succession).[a]

> Ulp.: **Bona** autem hic, ut plerumque solemus dicere, ita accipienda sunt: **universitatis** cuiusque **successionem**, qua succeditur in ius demortui suscipiturque eius rei commodum et incommodum. Nam sive solvendo sunt bona sive non sunt, sive damnum habent sive lucrum, sive in corporibus sunt sive in actionibus, in hoc loco proprie bona appellabuntur.—D. 37, 1, 3 pr.[1]

[a] Cf. §§ 17, 153.

We shall therefore have to divide our subject as follows:—

1. The origination and maintenance of Rights.
2. Law of Persons.
3. Property Law.
   (*a*) Pure or simple Property Law: first, the Law of Things, and secondly, that of Obligations.
   (β) The Law of Family Property.
   (γ) The Law of Inheritance.
4. The doctrine of the form of judicial enforcement of rights, or Procedure.

The system followed in the Institutes of Gaius and of Justinian is different from this.[b] There we are told (Gai. i. 8, Just. i. 2, 12) that

> 'Omne autem ius quo utimur vel ad personas pertinet.'—Gai. bk. i.; Just. bk. i.

[b] See Maine, 'Early Law and Custom,' xi.

---

[1] But Inheritance, as we are generally accustomed to take the word, is here to be understood of succession to every whole, whereby there arises a succession to the rights of a deceased person, and the advantages and disadvantages of his property are taken over; for whether the succession admit or not of valuation, bring loss or gain, consist of corporeal objects or of actions, in this connection it will properly be called 'Inheritance.'

'Vel ad res.' — *Singulae res,* see Gai. ii. §§ 1–96, and Just. ii. 1–9; for acquisition by Universal Succession, especially the Law of Inheritance, Gai. ii. § 97–iii. § 87, and Just. ii. 10–iii. 12; for Obligations, Gai. iii. §§ 88–225, Just. iii. 1–iv. 5.

'Vel ad actiones.'—Gai. iv. and Just. iv. 6–17 (tit. 18 de publicis iudiciis).

The Roman institutional works thus present a division into the doctrine of Persons (entirely agreeing with the second part of the following exposition); of the objects of rights corporeal and incorporeal (*i.e.*, obligations), their acquisition—the Law of Inheritance being treated as a form of acquisition—and loss; and of legal remedies.[a]

[a] Cf. Moyle, edn. of Just. Inst. Introd. pp. 67-71.

PART II.

OUTLINES OF THE HISTORY AND THE SOURCES OF ROMAN LAW.[b]

[b] Cf. Puchta, vol. i.; Rivier, 'Introduction historique au droit Romain'; Karlowa, Röm. R. Geschichte.

§ 7. The Republic.

First Period. To the Legislation of the Twelve Tables.[c]

[c] Cf. Clark, 'Early Roman Law,' pp. 136, *sqq.*

Roman Private Law, like the Roman State, developed out of small beginnings. But from the outset the Roman People comes before us as one endowed legally and politically like none other. The strained civil and military discipline, rigidity of thought and action, steadily practical view, clearness in the apprehension of matters within the sphere of Politics and of Law, energy, circumspection and consistency in the pursuit of problems and objects once entertained; in fine, the sharpness of juristic conception and legal arrangement of the relations of life—all these hereditary qualities of the Roman mind give to that nation the appearance of having been predestined to the cultivation of LAW.

According to tradition, the original constitution of Rome was monarchical.[a] After the abolition of royalty, the place of 'rex' was taken by two 'consules,' chosen yearly. Though they were invested with royal authority, their power was limited by the association with them of the Senate (at first composed of the heads of the gentes) in government and the Assembly of the People, or 'comitia curiata, centuriata,'[b] which had legislative functions, and was the Supreme Court in respect of capital offences of Roman citizens. But inasmuch as the governing power was vested alone in the Patricians, or original citizens, and the Plebeians were excluded not merely from the magistracy, but also from the sacral offices commanding influence (especially from the college of the augurs and pontiffs) and from the Senate, there had been in the constitution itself a jar, which evoked the struggle of classes that began in the infancy of the Republic and was for two centuries maintained with great persistency. By it the Plebeians gradually acquired political equality with the Patricians, and finally secured acceptance of the democratic principle in the constitution.

The first result of the contest was the recognition of leaders and officers of the Plebs, the 'tribuni plebis,' upon whom should devolve the defence of that body against encroachment of the consular 'imperium,' as well as against Patrician oppression; and the recognition of separate Plebeian assemblies, the 'comitia plebis' and 'comitia tributa,' whereby the Plebeians were constituted into a special order recognised by Law, and organized as well politically as socially.[c]

A second gain of the Plebeians, in its significance far outlasting the struggle of the orders and the Republic itself, was the legislation of the TWELVE TABLES,[d] which dates from about the year 305 U.C. This was known as the 'Lex XII tabularum,' or

[a] Rivier, pp. 111-125.

[b] See Brown, s. *comitia*; Rivier, pp. 129, *sqq*.

[c] Cf. Maine, 'Ancient Law,' pp. 2-14.

[d] Rivier, pp. 163-182.

simply 'Lex.' Called forth by the endeavour sharply to define the consular imperium, especially as to jurisdiction, by written and ambiguous rules, to put also effectual checks upon Patrician caprice, and to bring about uniformity in the administration of justice, the Law of the Twelve Tables was, and continued to be to the latest times, the firm basis of the national Private Law, or *ius civile*.[a] In clear and definitely conceived commands and prohibitions, it gave formal expression to, and established principles of, the Customary Law[b] until now in vogue, which Law in fact was often unsettled; and at the same time the Private Law, which had continued overgrown with the Public and Sacral Law (ius publicum, sacrum, fas), was raised to a footing of independence.

[a] Cf. Liv. 3, 34, 'velut corpus omnis Romani iuris,' 'fons omnis publici privatique iuris,' and see Maine, *l.c.* pp. 14-20.

[b] Cf. 'Early Roman Law,' pp. 12, *sqq.*

The so-called *leges regiae* which have come down to us in Roman authors contain only long-standing patriarchal and sacral maxims of law, gathered in a collection called 'ius Papirianum.'[c] This probably was derived from the 'commentarii pontificum,' and indeed scarcely existed before the Twelve Tables. Towards the end of the Republic it found a commentator in Granius Flaccus.[d]

[c] Ibid. pp. 1-4.

[d] Cf. D. 50, 16, 144; Bruns, 'Fontes iur. Rom. antiqui,' ed. iv. pp. 1-13.

The Lex XII tabularum, as being the basis of the 'ius civile,' was the subject of many commentaries by jurists down to the latest times; thus we find one by S. Aelius Catus (*c.* 550), and the last was by Gaius, under Antoninus Pius or Marcus Aurelius. Nevertheless, no copy of any continuous portion has come down to us; indirectly through citations and references alone, about one hundred partly imperfect fragments of it have been transmitted.[e]

[e] See Gothfredus, 'Fragm. xii Tab. etc.'; 'Fontes iv. iur. civ.'; Dirksen, 'Uebersicht u. s. w.'; Schöll, 'Leg. xii Tab. reliquiae'; Bruns, pp. 14-35; Voigt, 'Die xii Tafeln.'

Second Period. To the Decline of the Republic.

Rome extended her dominion over all Italy, little by little incorporated its communities, and aimed at world-wide sovereignty. She did this by the subjugation into provinces of the existing civilised States and other territories of independent peoples, and cementing these ties by means of colonies. The extension of the bounds of Roman sovereignty, by which Rome was exalted into the central point of the world's intercourse, was accompanied by an enlargement of her horizon; whilst Hellenic culture began at the same time to make its way into Roman life, and to exercise an influence which gave a new shape to her hitherto contracted views. The finishing touch to the equalisation of the orders was reserved for the first century of this period, when the Plebeians, through the *leges Liciniae Sextiae* (387 U.C.), acquired joint government by a share in the Consulship and, soon afterwards, admission to the newly formed Patrician offices; to the censorship and praetorship, in particular. The constitution did indeed acquire a more democratic basis with the growing significance of the 'comitia tributa,' as resulting from the recognition of the general validity of the 'plebiscita,' ultimately through the *l. Hortensia* (468 U.C.). It led to the 'comitia centuriata' being soon cast into insignificance. Nevertheless, the aristocratic continued long to hold its own against the democratic principle, because the nobility did actually exercise the governing power in the person of the magistrates supplied from their ranks, and by means of the Senate, and offered successful resistance to democratic tendencies. But when, at the beginning of the seventh century, an ever rapidly increasing degeneration of Roman custom and discipline, a moral and political corruption and a far-reaching social disintegration set in, consequent upon the wealth that poured into Rome, and accumulated in the hands of the ruling classes, the balance of power was destroyed in favour of absolute democracy. Whilst the mass of the people laid claim to the highest sovereignty and put no limit upon its exercise, individual masters of power temporarily succeeded in gaining an unconstitutional control of affairs, in the political and social disorders and revolutions which sprang from the intrigues of demagogues, until at last Julius Caesar acquired a position of power bordering on sole imperium, by which the State was certainly preserved from the ruin into which the civil wars threatened to plunge it, and anarchy was disposed of, but the Republic also really ceased to exist, and the groundwork was laid of the monarchy.

The older Private Law fixed by the Twelve Tables, and which alone was in force down to the middle of this period (perhaps to the second Punic War), was an inflexible and rigidly national Law of the City, the 'ius civile proprium Romanorum,' as it suited the simple circumstances in life of a civic community within narrow limits and a settled, and essentially agricultural, population. It is founded on the recognition of the private personality of the independent Roman citizen, the 'paterfamilias,' and his power, originally unlimited, over his whole household—'familia pecuniaque'[a]—and the free persons belonging to him ('patria potestas' and 'manus'), and over his goods, or the 'dominium ex iure Quiritium'; because in certain forms it guaranteed to him the free disposition of each, as also of his own person ('adrogatio,' 'nexum'); and for the maintenance of his rights it established certain judicial processes, the 'legis actiones.' Corresponding to the rigidity and inflexibility of the Law was the stiffness and unwieldiness of legal transactions, which operated by virtue of a few solemn legal forms firmly established in formulae and ceremonies ('gerere'), and especially of a public, partly also of a sacral, character. They were called 'adrogatio,' 'in iure cessio,' 'mancipatio,' 'coemptio,' 'nexum,' 'confarreatio,' 'sponsio': these alone assured full legal effect and protection by 'legis actio.'[b]

From the middle of this period, however, the Law so far in force underwent gradual transformation through the infusion, recognition and increased development of the *ius gentium* as one of the constituents of the Roman Private Law.[c] This 'ius gentium' was

[a] Cf. § 41.

[b] §§ 52, 79 *bis*, 49 *bis*, 116, *sq.*

[c] Cf. § 4.

originally a Law of foreigners, in its application restricted to the legal transactions of the 'peregrini' sojourning at Rome; not merely amongst themselves, but between them and Roman citizens. These were subject to the jurisdiction of the Praetor Peregrinus. The principles of this Law were first learnt in dealings with the 'peregrini'; and were conceived as universal legal truths, contained in the various laws of the non-Roman communities as well as the Roman Law itself. As now the stiff, narrow and formal 'ius civile' could no longer satisfy those needs of legal transactions which increased with the advance of Roman sovereignty, and were dictated by the growth of commerce and the beginnings of intercourse with the world far and wide, or the growing legal conceptions of Roman citizens, the principles of the 'ius gentium' were increasingly recognised also for the legal transactions of Roman citizens with one another. Thus finally did it become an ingredient of the Roman Private Law itself, which by this time, besides the national legal institutions of the 'ius civ. propr. Rom.' available to Roman citizens alone, embraced the more general institutions of the 'ius gentium,' applicable as they were to all persons.

> Cic. de off. iii. 17: Maiores aliud ius gentium, aliud ius civile esse voluerunt: quod civile non idem continuo gentium, quod autem gentium idem civile esse debet.[1]

The reception, and at the same time the wider development, of these new principles was effected by the jurisdiction of the Praetors and by jurisprudence.

The Private Law was, accordingly, not alone shaped,

---

[1] Our ancestors considered that the *i. g.* is one thing, the *i. c.* another: the Civil Law is not always at the same time the Law of Nations, but the Law of Nations must at the same time be Civil Law likewise.

toned down and specialised, so as to be more liberal and more flexible, but the principles of the 'aequum ac bonum'[a] ever acquired more recognition; whilst hitherto it had been only a 'strictum ius.' This development of the Law, by which the basis was everywhere laid for the later Classical Law, amongst other things appeared in the introduction of what is called 'Bonitary' ownership, the creation of an independent Law of Pledge, the protection of possession by the interdicts, the increasing consideration in contracts of the will of the parties as compared with parol,[b] in the recognition of 'bonae fidei contractus' as actionable, the introduction of 'actiones aediliciae,' the beginning of the development of the 'ius dotium' and of 'peculium,' and especially in the new and more liberal procedure 'per formulas,' which took the place of the rigid and cumbersome 'legis actiones.'

[a] See § 4.

[b] 'Voluntas contrahentium, id quod actum est.'

As factors in the formation of Law, we have to notice Legislation, the Praetor's Edict and the 'auctoritas prudentium.'

Lex, in the narrower sense,[c] was every 'iussum' or resolution of the Roman popular assembly that established a rule of law, and consisted in the 'rogatio legis' or acceptance of the proposal of a statute introduced by the presiding magistrate, and submitted for approval in an established form of inquiry.[d] The rogatio legis was regularly preceded by the 'promulgatio legis' or public announcement of the proposed law, which was made for a 'trinundinum'; the 'lex perlata' or law that was accepted, and accordingly became obligatory, was inscribed, and made generally known by being hung up ('legem figere'). 'Lex' originally represented alone the resolution of the whole body of citizens assembled in the comitia centuriata, in contrast with the *plebiscitum*, which was the resolution of the Plebs in the concilia plebis; but this designation, after the recognition of the universally binding power of the plebiscita,[e] was applied also to the popular resolutions proposed by the presiding patrician

[c] Rivier, pp. 190-196.

[d] Cf. § 52.

[e] Lex Publilia Philonis, 415, l. Hortensia, 468 u.c.

magistrate, whether consul or praetor, in the comitia tributa, which by this time comprised the whole of the citizens. 'Plebiscitum,'[a] on the other hand, was the name given alone to the resolution of the tribes, entertained upon the motion and under the presidency of a plebeian official or 'tribunus plebis.'[b]

The number of purely private leges is very small. Amongst them are those relating to suretyship,[c] the lex Aquilia,[d] Cincia,[e] Voconia and Falcidia.[f]

The most important of the leges which have been transmitted directly to our time (by inscriptions), though only in fragmentary form, are—

1. A statute as to *repetundae*,[g] formerly taken to be the lex Servilia, but now known to be the l. Acilia (631 or 632 U.C.).

2. Upon the back of the same fragmentary table a lex agraria[h] (643 U.C.), which formerly was considered to be the l. Thoria.

3. L. Rubria de Gallia Cisalpina.[i] The four tables, which contain chapters 20–22 complete, the end of chap. 19 and the beginning of chap. 23, were discovered in 1760 in the ruins of Veleia, and are now at Parma. This statute regulated the municipal jurisdiction of Gallia Cisalpina after it had in 705 acquired the citizenship, and before it ceased in 712 to be a province. It is important especially because of the forms of pleadings it contains. Perhaps a portion of the same statute is contained in the Fragment discovered at Este in the year 1880.

4. The tabula Heracleensis.[j] The lower portion, or 'aes Neapolitanum,' was discovered in the year 1732; the upper, or 'aes Britannicum,' in 1735; since 1760 both have been preserved, pieced together, at Naples. It contains a Fragment, in thirty chapters, of the l. Iulia municipalis (709 U.C.). This statute is a general ordinance for all the Italic municipalities, and the basis of the whole of the later municipal constitution. The miscellaneous character of its contents—decisions as to the municipal constitution, and purely local and

[a] 'Lex Plebivescitum.'
[b] Gai. 1, 3 (Inst. 1, 2, 4); Gell. x. 20, xv. 27; Liv. 3, 55 and 8, 12.
[c] Cf. § 118.
[d] § 133, and Wordsworth, 'Fragments of Early Latin,' p. 272.
[e] § 129.
[f] § 182, and Wordsw. p. 275.
[g] Wordsw. pp. 176-186.
[h] Ibid. pp. 189-202.
[i] Ibid. pp. 212, *sq.*
[j] Ibid. pp. 213-218.

police-regulations for the City of Rome—is best explained by supposing that the statute was a 'lex satura.'

5. Lex coloniae Iuliae genetivae s. Ursonitana, a 'lex data' [a] (710 U.C.), contains the ordinance for the population of this colony brought out by Caesar, after the destruction of the town of Urso in the province of Baetica. Five tablets [b] were discovered at Osuna in the years 1870 and 1875, which contain chapters 61–82, 91–106, and 123–134 almost perfect.

[a] See § 8.

[b] Mommsen, Ephem. epigraph. vol. ii. pp. 105, *sq.*, 221, *sq.*, vol. iii. pp. 87, *sq.*; Bruns, pp. 50-99, 106-117, Suppl., p. 5.

The Praetors,[c] as the magistrates appointed for civil jurisdiction, in their 'edicta perpetua' issued upon their admission to office, by virtue of their magisterial 'ius edicendi,' regularly made and promulgated rules which would be observed by themselves in the administration of the Law. These rules were sometimes in the form of a binding prescription; sometimes, and commonly, in the form of a promise of certain legal remedies in this or that case described by 'actiones,' 'exceptiones,' 'interdicta,' 'missiones,' 'stipulationes praetoriae.' [d] Arbitrary departure of the Praetors from their own edict once put forth was forbidden by the l. Cornelia (687 U.C.). Whilst a part of the provisions of the Edict only set forth, for practical application by judicial procedure (actiones, exceptiones), legal principles already in force, another portion contained new rules of law called forth by change in the legal ideas of the people, or laid down by the jurists, and answered to the needs of Law which grew with the advance of intercourse.[e] Thus the Praetor's Edict became a main factor in the constant development of the Private Law, by which it was kept in constant progress. As the Praetors possessed no legislative power, the operation of the legal principles contained in the edicts depended indeed solely upon the official power of their authors, and was therefore formally limited to the year of office of the particular praetor that issued the edict. But his

[c] Pr. urbanus, from 387 A.U.C.; Pr. peregrinus, from 512.

[d] Cf. § 193.

[e] See § 4.

successor in the praetorship regularly repeated, though as revised, the edict put forth by the predecessor, and at the same time supplemented it by new additions ('nova edicta,' 'novae clausulae') conformably to the needs of the time and legal transactions. Accordingly, most of the provisions of the edict were impressed with a traditional character ('edicta tralaticia'), and from the separate edicts was developed in time a standing Praetorian Edict ('edictum perpetuum'), which possessed an authority equivalent to Statute Law. In this way was formed, collateral to the ius civile, a special *ius praetorium*, as a second independent constituent of the Private Law; there were some legal institutions and legal claims which existed 'iure civili' and others only 'iurisdictione' s. 'tuitione praetoris,' so that the Private Law itself is seen in many respects to have a twofold character.[a]

[a] Cf., *e.g.*, §§ 75, 96, 100, 154, 161.

Pompon.: Eodem tempore magistratus . . , ut scirent cives, quod ius de quaque re quisque dicturus esset, . . . **edicta** proponebant; quae edicta praetorum ius honorarium constituerunt. **Honorarium** dicitur, quod ab honore praetoris venerat.—D. 1, 2, 2, § 10.[1]

Gai. i. § 6: **Ius** autem **edicendi** habent magistratus populi Romani: sed amplissimum ius est in edictis duorum praetorum, urbani et peregrini, quorum in provinciis iurisdictionem praesides earum habent; item in edictis aedilium curulium.[2]

---

[1] At the same time the magistrates . . . promulgated edicts, that the citizens might know how each should judge of various matters, . . . these edicts of the praetors made up the *i. h.* Everything is called *honorarium* which derived its origin from the praetorship.

[2] The right of declaring the Law lies with the magistrates of the Roman people, but the right is most extensive as exercised in the edicts of the two praetors, the urban praetor and the praetor for foreigners, whose jurisdiction in the provinces is vested in the respective governors. The curule aediles exercise a like right in their edicts.

Papin.: **Ius praetorum** est, quod praetores introduxerunt **adiuvandi vel supplendi vel corrigendi** iuris civilis gratia propter utilitatem publicam.—D. 1, 1, 7, 1.[1]

Marcian: Ius honorarium viva vox est iuris civilis.—l. 8, eod.[2]

Auctoritas prudentium, legal doctrine, Law of the jurists.

Besides the Praetorian Edict, the development of the Law resulted mainly from the work of the jurists, called 'iurisconsulti,' 'iurisperiti,' 'iurisprudentes,' who in the process of interpretation explained the Law formulated in the Twelve Tables, developed it by way of analogy,[a] and adjusted it to the growing exigencies of practical life. This *interpretatio*, eliciting legal maxims from the provisions of the Twelve Tables, led to the formation of a *ius non scriptum* alongside of the written Law of the Twelve Tables. The same result was also in a special way obtained by the *disputatio fori*. It was the discussion of disputed questions and of the legal maxim to be applied *in concreto* by those versed in Law, as legal decision afforded them opportunity.

[a] Cf. § 5.

Pomp.: Proprium **ius civile,** quod sine scripto in sola prudentium interpretatione consistit.—Dig. 1, 2, 2, 12.[3]

Those possessed of legal knowledge were at first and for long the *pontifices*, in whose collegium not only were established and handed down the Calendar, important

---

[1] The Praetorian Law is that which has been introduced by the praetors from general considerations of utility, with the view of aiding, of supplementing, and of improving the Civil Law.

[2] The *i. h.* is the living voice of the *i. c.*

[3] Our own *ius civile* which, unwritten, is made up of the mere interpretation of those skilled in Law.

for legal procedure, and the 'legis actiones' (which were the forms and technicalities required for legal acts, and especially for the judicial prosecution of rights), but the tradition of the ius civile was always handed down.

> Id.: Harum[a] et interpretandi scientia et actiones apud collegium pontificum erant, ex quibus constituebatur, quis quoque anno praeesset privatis; et populus annis prope C[b] hac consuetudine usus est.—§ 6, eod.[1]

[a] Sc. leg. xii. tab.

[b] Until the admission of Plebeians to the praetorship, 417 U.C.

The pontiffs were not deprived of the exclusive possession of such knowledge until after the publication—effected by Cn. Flavius (450 U.C.), though composed by Appius Claudius—of a collection of the judicial calendar and the legis actiones known as the 'ius Flavianum;' and when the coll. pontificum was soon afterwards thrown open to the Plebeians also, knowledge of the Law began to spread by means of teaching and writing. An order of jurists was formed, which attained a very considerable and influential position in the State, and there gradually sprang up a special Science of Law, to the fostering of which later on the ablest men of the nation earnestly devoted themselves. The most eminent of these 'Veteres' or older jurists are—

1. Tib. Coruncanius, the Father of Jurisprudence, first plebeian Pont. Max. (*c.* 500 U.C.).

> Id.: Ante Tib. Cor. publice professum[c] neminem traditur; ceteri ad hunc vel [ut ?] in latenti ius civile retinere cogitabant solumque consultatoribus vocare potius quam discere volentibus se praesta[re vole]bant.—§ 35, eod.[2]

[c] Sc. iuris scientiam.

---

[1] Acquaintance with interpretation of these [*i.e.*, laws of the Twelve Tables] and the forms of action could only be found in the college of the pontiffs, from whom each year one was appointed to superintend private suits. The people adhered to this custom for nearly 100 years.

[2] No one is reported to have come forward as a public teacher

2. S. Aelius (*c.* 550 U.C.), author of the 'ius Aelianum'—a new and enlarged redaction of the ius Flav.—and the 'Tripertita,' containing the 'xii. tab. interpretatio leg. actiones' spoken of by Pomponius as the 'cradles (rudiments) of Law.'[a]

3. M. Porcius Cato (*c.* 600).[b]

4. Publius Mucius Scaevola, M. Junius Brutus, M'. Manilius, 'qui fundaverunt ius civile.'[c] The *Manilianae actiones* were a collection of formulae for contracts of the most diverse kind, especially for those of Sale and of Hiring.

[a] 'Velut cunabula iuris,' D. 1, 2, 2, 38; cf. Coke, Preface to the Commy. on Littleton.

[b] Cf. § 184.

[c] Dig. l.c. § 39; cf. infra, §§ 36, 95.

5. Q. Mucius Scaevola (*c.* 650): 'he was the first to compose a system of the Civil Law, the general principles of which he treated in eighteen books.'[d] With him the customary empirical casuistry was replaced by a more systematic treatment of Law. So late jurists as Gaius and Pomponius wrote commentaries on his 'libri iuris civilis.'

[d] 'Ius civile primus constituit generatim in libros xviii. redigendo' (Dig. l.c. § 41).

6. Aquilius Gallus.[e]

[e] Cf. § 141.

7. Servius Sulpicius (*c.* 700). By the employment of dialectic methods he laid the basis of an 'ars iuris civilis' or scientific theory of Law, and left a great number of writings, amongst which are the 'notata Mucii,' being polemical notes on the system of that jurist. As pupils of Servius were—

8. Alfenus Varus, author of a systematic collection of responsa under the title of *Digesta*, from which extracts appear in Justinian's Digest.

9. Aulus Ofilius, who re-arranged, amongst other things, the Praetorian Edict—at first in detail—and laid the basis for a scientific treatment of the 'ius honorarium,' as well as for the later commentaries on the Edict.

10. C. Trebatius Testa, A. Cascellius, Q. Aelius Tubero.[f]

[f] See generally, Huschke, 'Iurisprudentiae anteiustinianae,' ed. iv. pp. 1-18, 84-104; and Roby, 'Introd. to the Digest,' pp. lxxxiii.-cxxiv.

---

of Law earlier than T. C.; until he did so, the rest were disposed to keep the *ius civile* secret, and did but care rather to lend an ear to clients than to hold out their services to those desirous of instruction.

Not merely by literary labours ('scribere'), but above all by practical work, as iurisconsulti ('respondere'), did the jurists take part in the development of the Law. They thus exercised a great influence upon the administration of Law, through their 'responsa' or opinions taken by private persons, magistrates and judges, who repeatedly resorted to them for advice upon questions of law. Moreover, by skilled composition of formulae for legal matters ('cavere')—formulary and cautelary jurisprudence—they contributed not a little to the development of Private Law itself, because people thus became clearly conscious of the juristic character of their legal transactions and of the consequences that resulted from them.

With the practical work of the jurists was at the same time associated the education ('instructio') of young men for the legal profession; who attended consultations as listeners ('auditores') and received practical instruction.

§ 8. The Period of the Classical Law.

The new and permanent constitution founded by Augustus, the 'principatus,' was a monarchy with republican forms, in which the Emperor—variously called 'Princeps,' 'Imperator,' 'Caesar,' 'Augustus'—united in his person the highest republican powers of office; the republican magistrates (consules, praetores, aediles, tribuni plebis), although in some respects alone nominally, continued alongside of the new imperial functionaries (praefecti praetorio, praef. urbi, praef. vigilum, praef. annonae, etc.); and the sovereignty, in conformity with the constitution, was divided similarly between Emperor and Senate, so that the latter not only was associated with the Emperor in the government, but also, though not for long, retained the superintendence of the public treasury and the finances (aerarium) and the immediate administration of a part of the provinces. And so we find, on the one hand, 'provinciae senatus populique Rom.' administered by 'proconsules,' and on the other, 'provinciae Caesaris,' governed by 'legati Augusti.' Nevertheless, in course of time the Senate was little by little through the power of the Princeps dispossessed of the joint government, and retained only formal rights, until at last the whole power of the State was concentrated in the hand of the Emperor, and the last spark of the republican constitution fully disappeared.

Although during this period the Orbis terrarum, in consequence of its subordination to the imperium of the Emperor, took the form of a politically united and ordered whole, the consolidation into one political body of the many lands and populations subject to Roman sovereignty was not yet accomplished. The provinces were not organically welded to the Roman State; for whilst under the principatus their condition considerably improved and a prosperous time set in for many of them, they remained until towards the end of this period as they had been before, dependent tributary territories of the Empire, which were regarded as 'praedia populi Romani,' and were obliged to contribute to the maintenance of Roman sovereignty itself.

In consequence of the theoretical continuance of the supreme sovereignty of the People, from which the imperial power was derived, the popular assembly also remained provisionally recognised as a factor in legislation, and at the beginning of the imperial period a series of important popular decrees (leges) were still published. But already from the time of Tiberius popular legislation disappeared, and the legislative functions of the comitia were transferred to the Senate, which, however, in its decrees always chanced to be dependent upon the control of the Princeps; until at last, under Septimius Severus, the formal co-operation in legislation of the Senate also came to an end. Senatus-consulta were by this time entirely replaced by *Constitutiones principum*, which gained importance from the time of Hadrian; their legal force, indeed, had always been acknowledged, but until then—in agreement with their nature, as declarations of the highest judicial and administrative authority—it was only in single points that they had more exactly defined and varied the current Law: they had not comprehensively improved and organically re-cast it in legislative form. Only the imperial indulgences in respect of the granting of citizenship (leg. de civitate) and the municipal constitution (leges municipales) had, and formally preserved, the character and the shape of a proper 'lex publ. pop. Rom.,' because they appear as statutes that have been published by commission of the people, in virtue of its legislative power delegated to the Emperor *ad hoc*, *i.e.*, as 'leges datae' in contrast with the 'leges latae,' or laws passed after proposal to the Comitia.

In this period falls the final formation of the Roman Law, which obtains its classical character, especially through the scientific labours of the great, so-called CLASSICAL, jurists. By this is meant the systematic elaboration, and that ideal development of the whole substance of Law, governed by the principles of 'aequitas,' which constantly answers to the concrete arrangement of the relations of life and the needs of legal intercourse. The ius gentium which, by the fostering hand of the jurists—with an especial leaning to the Praetorian Law—was worked out into a perfect system, increasingly displaced in practical application the ius civile propr. Rom., especially as the Peregrini, or Provincials, formed the by far preponderating part of the population of the realm, and because it also alone was adapted to the now widely developed relations of commerce.

The legal sources of this period are—

i. *Leges.*—The most important amongst the private leges are the l. Aelia Sentia[a] and, above all, the l. Iulia (de maritandis ordinibus) et Papia Poppaea (A.D. 4 and 9). Upon this comprehensive statute,[b] supplemented afterwards by some senatus-consulta, deeply penetrating into the whole structure of Law—especially

[a] Cf. §§ 37, *sq.*

[b] Cf. §§ 44, *sq.*, 47, 146, 172, 175.

into the Law of Inheritance—and in many ways destroying the inner unity and symmetry of the legal system, special commentaries were written by the later jurists, as Terentius Clemens, Gaius, Marcellus and Ulpian, by means of which some provisions of this lex have been handed down in the Digest of Justinian.[a]

[a] Attempts at restoration have been made by Heineke and others.

We possess the following leges in their original form :—

(α) Lex Salpensana and l. Malacitana, two municipal laws granted by Flavius Domitianus A.D. 81–84 to the Latin communities of Salpensa and Malaca in Baetica, of each of which a tablet (aes Salp. *cc.* 21–29, aes Mal. *cc.* 51–69) was discovered at Malaga in 1851.[b]

[b] See Mommsen, Die Stadtrechte der lat. Gemeinden (1855), and Bruns, pp. 120-131.

(β) Tabulae honestae missionis, in *diptycha*[c]—so far more than fifty, of the time from Claudius to Diocletian—representing charters of municipal law or grants of conubium to individual veterans, *i.e.*, portions of the respective lex in favour of those so invested, which granted citizenship to the whole body of veterans of the particular legio.[d]

[c] See Smith, Dict. of Antiq. s. 'Tabulae.'

[d] See Bruns, pp. 177-179 and inf. s. 'Inscriptions.'

ii. *Senatus-consulta.*—The decrees of the Senate first appear as a form of legislation in imperial times. The proposal of the senatus-consultum was made by the consul who presided over the meeting of the Senate—after whom the decree was named[e]—later on often by the Emperor in the form of an 'oratio' (principis) read out in the Senate by the quaestor principis and then as a rule accepted by simple acclamation : as this oratio contained the statute, it is itself mostly called the source of Law, instead of the senatus-consultum which followed it.[f] Under Septimius Severus the formal co-operation of the Senate in legislation came to an end.

[e] But comp. § 120.

[f] Cf. §§ 148, 151.

Gai. 1, § 4 : Senatusconsultum est quod senatus iubet atque constituit, idque legis vicem obtinet, quamvis fuerit quaesitum.[1]

---

[1] A *senatus-consultum* is what the Senate orders and establishes,

Only a few senatus-consulta have been handed down directly; amongst them are the SC[a]. Hosidianum and Volusianum (A.D. 41 and 56)—more in verbal extracts.[a]

[a] Cf. §§ 120, 145, 176, 185, and Bruns, pp. 141-143.

iii. *Constitutiones principum.*—A const. princ. was an ordinance proceeding solely from the Emperor, which if it enacted a general and new rule of Law—'generalis constitutio,' in contrast with a 'personalis const.' limited to the actual, special case—had the force of Law. The following distinctions are made:—

Edicta: proclamations by which the Emperor, in virtue of the 'ius edicendi' appertaining to him as the highest magistrate, publicly made known something for observance.

Mandata: instructions to superior officials, especially provincial prefects.[b]

[b] Cf. § 158.

Decreta: decisions and ordinances of the Princeps as the supreme judge in causes which came before him.

Rescripta: these, the most important class in Private Law of the const. princ. in this period, were answers which the Princeps vouchsafed in the form of a special epistula or a 'subscriptio' s. 'adnotatio' put down on the original of inquiries either of parties (libelli; preces, supplications) or of magistrates (relatio, consultatio, suggestio) for instruction as to some doubtful question of law, and as to the legal principle to be applied in the actual case. By the rescript, accordingly, was the legal question decided in the suit, whilst the investigation and examination of the facts in the case requiring decision devolved upon the judge. For the most part only existing legal maxims were brought into application by decrees and rescripts; but they often also contained new principles or decisions of controversies—

---

and it has the force of a *lex*, although this has been subject of dispute.

'authentic' interpretations—and they then availed not merely for the single case, but had general legal effect.—The causes which came before the Princeps were always taken in the 'consilium principis,'[a] which from the time of Hadrian had acquired a standing form and established organisation. Since also its members (consiliarii) included eminent jurists, the representatives of jurisprudence themselves took part in the issue of rescripts and decrees, and in the development of Law which these effected. An official publication and collection of such imperial legal decisions was not made; and further, they were only incidentally handed down in the literary work of jurists or in private collections.[b]

[a] Later on in the 'auditorium.'

[b] *E.g.*, by Papirius Iustus, Constit. l. xx., rescripts of Marcus and Verus; by Paulus, Decretor. l. iii., decrees of Severus.

With the decadence in the third century of the remaining organs of the formation of Law, the legislative acts of the emperors alone continued to exist as sources of Law; in their hands by this time lay the wider development of Law, especially furthered by numberless rescripts, Diocletian's in particular, of whom alone about 1,300 constitutions are known to us.

> Ulp.: Quod principi placuit, legis habet vigorem [nec umquam dubitatum est, quin id legis vicem obtineat, Gai. i. § 5]: utpote cum lege regia, quae de imperio eius lata est, populus ei et in eum omne suum imperium et potestatem conferat. § Quodcumque igitur imperator per epistulam et subscriptionem statuit vel cognoscens decrevit vel de plano interlocutus est vel edicto praecepit, legem esse constat. Haec sunt quas vulgo constitutiones appellamus. § Plane ex his quaedam sunt personales nec ad exemplum trahuntur: nam quae princeps alicui ob merita indulsit vel si quam poenam irrogavit vel si cui sine exemplo subvenit, personam non egreditur. —D. 1, 4, 1.[c][1]

[c] Cf. Inst. i. 2, 6.

[1] The will of the Emperor has the force of a *lex* [and there has never been a doubt as to its having the force of a *lex*] since indeed by the *lex regia*, the statute passed in respect of his

A great part of the const. princ. has been handed down in later collections of constitutions.[a] Those that have been transmitted by inscriptions, or in other authors, are of little significance.[b]

iv. *Edicta magistratum.*—The edictum perpetuum[c] had already acquired its final shape at the beginning of the imperial rule; and although the judicial magistrates retained the ius edicendi, and upon admission to office continued to publish an Edict, no further alterations were admitted into it, except a few additions rendered necessary by the new leges and SCta. The need of a revision of the Edict suited to the times was satisfied by the new redaction thereof (edicti compositio) executed by Julianus[d] at the command of Hadrian, in which the Edict of the praet. urb. and that of the praet. peregrin. were united, arranged and simplified, by the elimination of antiquated provisions; and the Aedilian Edict was added to it. This redaction next, by a senatus-consultum[e] A.D. 131, became legally binding upon the whole empire, and was thenceforth treated scientifically by jurists in comprehensive commentaries and systematic works.

In Justinian's Digest are preserved to us many titular rubrics and a number of more or less complete passages of the Edict from the extracts there made of commentaries upon it, especially that of Ulpian.[f]

v. *Responsa prudentium.*—During the Republic juristic science was not yet a proper source of Law, since the

dignity, the People transfer to him and upon him their whole dignity and power. Whatever, therefore, the Emperor has ordained by a letter or a marginal note, or has purposely decreed, or has declared in an order outside the senate, or has prescribed by a proclamation—that is unqestionably a *lex*. These are what are commonly called 'constitutions.' Some of them clearly are of a personal nature, and ought not to be adduced as precedents; for if the Emperor have shown consideration to any one because of his merits, or inflicted a special punishment upon a person or, without following a definite principle, have given relief to any one, this does not pass beyond the one person.

[a] Cf. §§ 9, 10.

[b] Bruns, pp. 170-177; Haenel, 'Corp. legum' (1857).

[c] Cf. § 7.

[d] See below.

[e] Cf. C. 1, 17, 2, § 18.

[f] For a collection of traditional fragments, see Bruns, pp. 147-170. The first critical attempt to restore the Edict was made by Rudorff ('Ed. perp. quae reliqua sunt 1869'), superseded by the very thorough work of Lenel, 'Edictum Perpetuum,' 1883.

answers given by those learned in the Law (responsa) and the maxims and opinions put forth in their writings possessed merely an intrinsic, though important, authority. Augustus began by introducing as a permanent institution, retained and confirmed by the later emperors, the grant of the 'ius publice (ex auctoritate principis) respondendi' to approved jurists, and by this means a specially select order of AUTHORISED jurists was created (iuris auctores s. conditores) in contrast on the one hand with the *Veteres* of the ante-Augustan times, still held in respect, and on the other with the non-privileged jurists. To their Opinions, given for each case in a certain form, was accorded an external authority, provided they agreed, which was binding upon the judge. The legal value of the 'responsa' extended still further to the opinions and decisions to which these jurists were committed in their writings, so far as an Opinion could be shown to agree with the authorities for the time being (ius certum, receptum), and then in general the influence of the juristic literature upon the development of Law would necessarily continue to increase after the conclusion of the praetorian Edict by the redaction under Hadrian. With the decadence of Law in the third century, the grant of the ius resp. ceased, and resp. prud., accordingly, were not forthcoming; the place of which was by this time practically taken by the 'rescripta princ.' Nevertheless, the authority of the writings of the classical jurists continued to exist to the full extent as a source of Law.

> Gai. i. § 7: Responsa prudentium sunt sententiae et opiniones eorum, quibus permissum est iura condere. Quorum omnium si in unum sententiae concurrant, id quod ita sentiunt legis vicem obtinet; si vero dissentiunt, iudici licet quam velit sententiam sequi; idque rescripto D. Hadriani significatur.[1]

[1] The answers of the learned in the Law are the decisions and

Pomp.: Ante tempora Augusti publice respondendi ius non a principibus dabatur, sed qui fiduciam studiorum suorum habebant, consulentibus respondebant; neque responsa utique signata dabant, sed plerumque iudicibus ipsi scribebant aut testabantur qui illos consulebant. Primus D. Augustus, ut major iuris auctoritas haberetur, constituit, ut ex auctoritate eius responderent: et ex illo tempore peti hoc pro beneficio coepit.—D. 1, 2, 2, 49.[1]

The most fruitful period of Jurisprudence opens already with the beginning of imperial times, when the opposition, lasting for a century and a half, arises between the two Schools of Law—we may say indeed scientific tendencies—of the Proculians and Sabinians, represented respectively by M. Antistius Labeo and by Ateius Capito and Massurius Sabinus. Leading Proculians were Nerva pater, Proculus, Nerva filius, Pegasus, Celsus pater, Celsus filius and Neratius; whilst amongst names of Sabinians we have Sabinus, Cassius, Cael. Sabinus, Iavolenus, Valens, Iulianus, Pomponius, Gaius.[2] This opposition reaches its climax in the period from Hadrian to Alexander Severus, after which

---

opinions of those who are authorised to interpret the laws. If the opinions of all these are unanimous, that which they so hold has the force of a *lex:* but if they disagree, the judge is at liberty to follow which opinion he pleases, as is laid down in a rescript of the late Emperor Hadrian.

[1] Before the time of Augustus the right of giving opinions on the part of the State was not granted by the Emperors, but they who had confidence in their knowledge used to give opinions to such as consulted them; and they did not necessarily give opinions under seal, but themselves[a] generally wrote to the judge, or their clients made an affidavit.[b] The Emperor Augustus, in order to strengthen respect for the Law, was the first to direct that they should give opinions by virtue of his authority; and from that time it began to be sought for as a privilege.

[a] See Roby, p. 102.

[b] *I.e.*, as to the opinion they had obtained. With these *Iurisconsulti* compare conveyancing counsel of the Chancery Division (Order LI. rr. 7-13).

[2] For exx. of controversies, see §§ 19, 26, 55, 60, 74, 83, 86, 88, *sq.*, 112, *sq.*, 119, 122, 125, 129, 139, 167, 173, 179, 183, 185; and cf. Roby, pp. cxxxi.-cl.

sets in a rapid decline of Law. Gifted with an extraordinary intellectual power and in possession of no common culture, the jurists, who were mostly in high official position, evinced in Law a comprehensive and unremitting activity, and in their literary works, which unite theory and practice in a manner not attained before, displayed an incomparable productivity. These many-sided literary performances fall into three main classes:—

1. The treatment by way of commentaries of different sources of Law, as the Praetor's Edict, certain important leges and senatus-consulta, and of fundamental works of earlier authors, as the Libri iur. civ. of Sabinus.

2. Dogmatic treatises on the Law.

(*a*) Of the whole Private Law in manifold shapes, as of complete legal systems, at one time in exhaustive representation of the substance of Law, *Digesta*; at another in elementary treatment, or *Institutiones*; or of summary sketches and developments of formulated maxims and rules—*e.g.*, definitiones, regulae.

(*β*) Particular legal doctrines (monographs).

3. Practical works, as collections of Opinions and Decisions (responsa) or discussions of particular questions of law and the more difficult cases, belonging to the 'ius controversum,' which were often of a didactic nature. Such were opiniones, disputationes, quaestiones.

4. Works of a miscellaneous character, as 'manualia,' 'variae lectiones.'

Legal education was either theoretical and systematic (institutio) or it was practical and technical (instructio). The one, in the form of a connected disquisition of an essentially preparatory nature, was given especially by professional teachers (iuris civilis professores) in the regular law-schools. The other, imparted in the 'stationes ius publice docentium aut respondentium'[a] by approved jurists in connection with their consulting practice, consisted in argumentative discussion of dis-

[a] Gell. xiii. 13.

puted questions of law and of interesting cases, whether actual or imaginary (quaestiones tractare).

> Pomp.: Hi duo primum veluti diversas sectas fecerunt: nam Ateius Capito in his, quae ei tradita fuerant, perseverabat, Labeo ingenii qualitate et fiducia doctrinae, qui et ceteris operis sapientiae operam dederat, plurima innovare instituit.—l. 2, § 47, de O. J.[1]

The most eminent of the classical jurists were—

1. M. Antistius Labeo, under Augustus; of the greatest influence upon the whole wider development of Law and Jurisprudence, through his acute dialectic, as well as by largely progressive, and to a great extent fertile, ideas in almost all branches of the Private Law, and accordingly everywhere often cited by later jurists. Of his writings extracts are given in the Digest from the 'Probabilium' (πειθανῶν) libri viii., as epitomized by Paulus, and from the 'Libri posteriores,' a posthumous work on the Civil Law which was epitomized and elaborated by Javolenus.

2. Massurius Sabinus, under Tiberius and Claudius, wrote a handbook of the Civil Law, 'libri iii. iur. civ.,' in which, upon the established foundations, and in connection with the productions of the *Veteres*, he practically developed the traditional Law grounded upon leges and auct. prud. It remained to later times the foundation of the wider treatment of the ius civile ('libri ad Sabinum').

3. C. Cassius Longinus, from Tiberius to Vespasian, wrote a work upon the ius civile, which was epitomized by Javolenus.

4. Sempronius Proculus, under Claudius and the emperors following, was a pupil of Labeo, and wrote 'Epistularum l. xi.'

---

[1] These two were the first to form different schools: Ateius Capito adhered to that which had been handed down to him, Labeo, in reliance upon his intellectual capacity and his learning having occupied himself with other sciences, began to introduce many innovations.

5. P. Juventius Celsus, from Nerva to Hadrian, was praetor, consul, member of the consil. princ., and was quite the most notable representative of the Proculian school: he was pre-eminent for sagacity, originality and a fundamentally juristic training. His chief work was 'Digestorum l. xxxix.,' the first complete legal system, as comprising both the Praetorian and the Civil Law, and according to the arrangement of the Edict.

6. Neratius Priscus, contemporary with Celsus, and also consul. His chief work was 'Membranarum l. vii.,' 'Regularum l. xv.,' 'Respons. l. iii.'

7. Titius Aristo, a contemporary of the preceding jurist, and member of the council of Trajan,[a] wrote 'notae' to the works of different jurists, and is often cited.

[a] Plin. Ep. i. 22; viii. 14.

8. Plautius, belonging to about the same time, composed a system of law much the subject of commentaries and epitomies.

9. Priscus Javolenus, from Vespasian to Antoninus Pius. His writings (besides those mentioned 1 and 3) were 'Epistularum l. xiv.,' 'Ad Plautium l. v.'

10. Aburnius Valens, under Antoninus Pius, and a member of the cons. princ., wrote 'Fidei-commissorum l. viii.'

11. Salvius Julianus, a pupil of Javolenus, from Hadrian to Marcus Aurelius and Verus (the 'Divi Fratres') was praetor, consul, praef. urbi and member of the cons. princ. He was the most notable jurist of his time, of capital authority for all later time, and thus cited continually, like none other jurists. His chief work was 'Digestorum l. xc.' according to the system of the Edict.

12. S. Pomponius (contemporary with the preceding jurist) wrote, amongst other works, 'Ad Q. Mucium l. xxxix.,' 'Ad Sabinum l. xxxv.,' 'Epistularum l. xx.,' 'Variar. lectionum l. xv.'

13. Gaius, a contemporary of Pomponius, was only a teacher of law, but he was a fruitful author. He

wrote, amongst other things, 'Institutionum commentarii iv.,' 'Rerum quotidianarum (Aureorum) l. viii.,' 'Ad l. xii. tab. l. vi.,' 'Ad l. Pap. Popp. l. xv.,' 'Ad Edict. Praet. urb.,' 'Ad edict. provinciale l. xxxii.'

14. Sextus Caecilius Africanus, a pupil of Julian, and from Hadrian to Antoninus Pius, wrote 'Quaestionum[a] l. ix.,' which became celebrated by their being proverbially hard to understand—the cases treated being difficult—as well as from the profundity and acuteness which characterised the juristic deductions they presented.

[a] For the most part *a Iuliano tractat.*

15. Terentius Clemens: he wrote a Commentary to the l. Papia Poppaea in twenty books.

16. L. Volusius Maecianus was a member of the cons. princ. under Antoninus Pius and Marcus Aurelius, and wrote 'De fideicommissis l. xvi.,' and 'De publicis iudiciis l. xiv.'

17. L. Ulpius Marcellus, under Antoninus, Marcus Aurelius and Commodus, was a member of the council and, besides being a military commander, was one of the most notable and most frequently cited jurists. His chief work was 'Digestorum l. xxx.'

18. Q. Cervidius Severus, from Marcus Aurelius to Septimius Severus, was a coryphaeus of classical Jurisprudence. He wrote 'Responsorum l. vi.' and 'Digestorum l. xl.' (a systematic collection of opinions), which are numbered amongst the most eminent products of the whole casuistical literature of Law,[b] and 'Quaestionum l. xx.' Noteworthy in him is the terseness of treatment, the pregnant brevity of his decisions, and the thoroughness which characterised them.

[b] *I.e.*, Case Law.

19. Claudius Tryphoninus, under Severus and Caracalla, was a member of the council, and wrote 'Disputationum l. xxi.,' which for the most part treat difficult questions of law after a casuistical method. About contemporary with him were—

20. Callistratus, amongst whose works were 'Quaestionum l. ii.,' 'Institutionum l. iii.,' and 'De cognitionibus l. vi.'

21. Venuleius Saturninus : he wrote 'De actionibus l. xv.,' 'De interdictis l. vi.,' and 'Stipulationum l. xix.'

22. Aelius Marcianus: amongst his writings were 'Institutionum l. xvi.,' 'Regularum l. v.,' and 'Ad formulam hypothecariam.'

23. Aemilius Sacer, who wrote 'De appellationibus,' 'De publicis iudiciis,' and 'De re militari.'

24. Florentinus was the writer of 'Institutionum l. xii.'—The following rank as the proper leaders of the classical jurisprudence.

25. Aemilius Papinianus. He was pupil of Cerv. Scaevola, was praefectus praetorio under Severus, and put to death by Caracalla because unwilling to justify the fratricide committed by the emperor. He was regarded by contemporaries and posterity alike as the greatest of all the jurists, and was held in extraordinary regard. His chief works, which likewise were incomparably eminent for juristic depth, acuteness and accuracy of expression, were 'Quaestionum l. xxxviii.' and 'Responsorum l. xix.'

26. Domitius Ulpianus. He was a native of Tyre, assessor under Severus in the auditorium of Papinian, and, after having been banished by Caracalla, was finally praefectus praetorio under Alexander Severus, but was murdered by the Praetorians, 228 A.D. He was one of those jurists of important literary productivity who was in most favour with practising lawyers. His writings are distinguished by great fulness of material and peculiarly practical treatment thereof in a lucid and exhaustive, although also sometimes rather loose, style. His chief works are 'Ad edictum l. lxxxiii.,' 'Ad Salbinum l. li.,' 'Ad l. Pap. Popp. l. xx.,' 'Disputationum l. x.,' 'Opinionum l. vi.,' 'Fideicommissorum l. vi.,' 'Institutionum l. ii.,' 'Regularum l. sing.,' altogether about 250 books.

27. Julius Paulus. He was pupil of Scaevola, assessor in the auditorium of Papinian, and praef. praetorio under Alexander Severus. While of like literary activity, in productive power and depth of

conception surpassing Ulpian, he was that jurist's inferior as regards the charm of the treatment of his matter and apprehension of juristic development, and was often indeed obscure from a compressed style. He wrote altogether about 300 libri, amongst which these deserve special mention: 'Ad Edictum l. lxxx.,' 'Ad Sabinum l. xvii.,' 'Ad Plautium l. xviii.,' 'Ad l. Iuliani et Papiani l. x.,' 'Questionum l. xxvi.,' 'Responsorum l. xxiii.,' and 'Sententiarum l. v.'

28. Herennius Modestinus, a pupil of Ulpian, under the Severi and Gordian, had a reputation not equal to the three last-named, and was the last of the classical jurists. Amongst his writings were 'Excusationum l. vi.' (in Greek), 'Regularum l. x.,' 'Differentiarum l. ix.,' 'Pandectarum l. xiii.,' and 'Responsorum l. xix.'

To speak now of remains of the classical literature of the jurists.[a] In their original purity—by immediate transmission or through other collections of law, in original form or in extracts—we are in possession, though in great part only fragmentarily, of the following:—

1. GAII *institutionum commentarii* iv., discovered by Niebuhr in 1816 in a palimpsest MS. preserved all but three leaves, yet not completely legible; of the library belonging to the Cathedral Chapter at Verona. It has been deciphered by Göschen, Bethmann-Hollweg and Bluhme. A recent and fruitful revision of the text has been executed by Studemund.[b] The Institutes of Gaius altogether constitute the first systematic Manual of the Roman Law intended for elementary legal study: its significance and value are seen in the fact that it remained for all later times the foundation of legal study.[c]

2. *Fragmentum de iure fisci*,[d] discovered at the same time as the Veronese Gaius, and edited by Göschen, next by Böcking.[e]

3. VLPIANI, *lib. singularis regularum* (so-called *fragmenta*) in a Vatican MS.—'tituli ex corpore

[a] See Huschke, 'Iurisprudentiae anteiustinianae quae supersunt,' ed. iv. (1879); Krüger, Mommsen and Studemund: 'Collectio librorum iur. antei.' tom. 1, ed. ii. (1884), 2 (1877). A work still useful for its notes is Schulting, 'Iurisprud. vet. antei. c. not. varior.' (1737).

[b] 'Gaii instit. comm. iv. cod. Veron. denuo coll. apographum' (1874), and edd. by Krüger and Studem. in the 'Collectio' cit. Cf. Huschke, l.c. pp. 148, *sqq.* Earlier edd. were Göschen and Lachmann (1843), Böcking (1866). See further, Huschke, 'Studien d. Röm. Rechts' (1830), pp. 185, *sqq.*; 'Gaius Beitr. z. Krit. u. z. Verstandn. s. Inst.' (1855).

[c] Cf. §6.

[d] Variously attributed to Paul. and Ulp.

[e] For his edn. of Ulp. Last edn. with facsim. of MS. is by Krüger (1868). Cf. Huschke, l.c. pp. 615, *sqq.*; 'Coll.' cit. tom. ii. pp. 162, *sqq.*

Ulpiani,' first discovered and edited by Joh. Tilius (1549).[a] The work of Ulpian is here preserved to us in its purity, but only in the form of an epitome, and fragmentary: the conclusion in particular is wanting, besides perhaps a third part of the whole. Essentially according to the system of the Institutes of Gaius, and also akin to them in matter, this work gives a compressed sketch of the established principles of the Law in force, for didactic purposes—a kind of 'repetitorium'—which has become famous for the clearness and precision of its style.

4. Two small fragments of 'VLPIANI *institutiones*,' discovered by Endlicher at Vienna in 1835.[b]

5. PAVLI *sententiarum* (*receptarum*) *ad filium* l. v., preserved in the lex Romana Visigothorum.[c] This treatise, which has been transmitted in comparative purity, with the omission nevertheless of many parts,[d] contains a collection in outline of the recognised principles of the whole Law, and arranged according to the system of the Edict with the interpolation of matters not adapted for that, and of the later imperial Law. It was for practical use, and later on was invested with unlimited authority.[e]

6. Three small fragments, one indeed from a Commentary on the Edict, the others from Papin. resp. l. v. ix., upon shreds of parchment much mutilated, which were found in Egypt.[f]—In a later and very corrupt recension has been preserved the so-called '*Fragm. veteris Iurisconsulti de iuris partibus et de manumissionibus*,'[g] in the *interpretamenta*—ἑρμηνεύματα—of the Magister Dositheus, a schoolbook designed for instruction in Latin and Greek, with grammar, glossary and passages for translation. The Greek text of the fragment contains a translation of the original, the Latin a translation back made by pupils, which is almost unmeaning.[h]

Not as sources of Law in the proper sense,[i] but in that of sources of knowledge for the ante-Justinian law,

[a] Recent edd. by Böcking (1855), Vahlen (1856), Huschke, l.c. pp. 547; Krüger, l.c. ii. pp. 1, *sqq.*

[b] See above-mentioned edd. of the 'lib. sing.' New revision of the MS. by Krüger, 'Krit. Versuche' (1870), pp. 140, *sqq.*; Huschke, l.c. p. 601; 'Collectio' cit. p. 157; Bremer, 'de Ulp. instit.' (1863).

[c] Cf. § 9.

[d] Which can, however, be supplied from excerpts in Justinian's Digest, &c.

[e] Most recent edd. are—Arndts (1833); Huschke, l.c. p. 434; Krüger, l.c. p. 41.

[f] Deciphered and edited, the first by Mommsen, the others by Krüger, in 'Monatsberichte' of the Berlin Academy (1879, p. 501; 1880, p. 363); and in 'Zschr. d. Savigny-Stiftung, Röm. Abth.' i. p. 93, ii. p 83.

[g] Variously attributed to Gaius, Paulus, Scaevola, Pomponius.

[h] Edd. by Böcking (1832), and in his Ulp. p. 159; Lachmann (1837); Huschke, l.c. p. 422; Krüger in 'Coll.' cit. p. 149. Cf. Dirksen, 'Hinterl. Schriften,' ii. 392, *sqq.*

[i] Cf. § 3.

come further the documents, preserved to us in inscriptions, relating to legal transactions and the like,[a] amongst which the following deserve special attention.

DOCUMENTS *relating to* LEGAL TRANSACTIONS.

(α) Mancipationes:

1. '*Manc. fiduciae causa*,' intended as a mortgage security, but only as a formula; found in Spain, 1867.[b]

2. '*Manc. donationis causa: Donatio Flavii Syntrophi*,' with a preliminary penal proviso regulating the obligations of the donee. 'Don. Fl. Artemidori;' '*Don. Statiae Irenes;*' both with an appended proviso on the part of the donee.[c]

(β) Contracts of purchase, with receipt of the contracting parties and a stipulation appended as to eviction guaranteed by sureties; contracts of loan, and contracts as to locatio operarum, upon *triptycha*,[d] from the 'wax-tablets of Transylvania.' A locatio operis (building contract) in the '*Lex parieti faciendo Puteolana*.'

(γ) Decree of Curia of Puteoli whereby the 'solarium' to be rendered for a plot of ground upon which to build an urban structure is remitted on condition that the right of the superficiary shall lapse on the death of the occupier. It was discovered in 1861.[e]

(δ) *Obligationes praediorum*. To these belong two tablets relating to Trajan's charity-fund for the relief of Italian orphans, in which the ground-owners, in whom the capital of that fund is invested at interest, convey certain pieces of their land by way of mortgage.

1. *Tabula alimentaria Veleias* (103 A.D.), discovered in 1747.

2. *Tab. alim. Baebianorum* (101 A.D.), discovered in 1831.[f]

(ε) *Testamentum Dasumii* (109 A.D.), very frag-

[a] Bruns, pp. 180-234.

[b] Ed. and annot. by Degenkolb, 'Zschr. für Rechtsgesch.' ix. 117; by Rudorff, xi. 52; and by Krüger, 'Krit. Vers.' 41.

[c] Ed. with commy. by Huschke (1838).

[d] See Smith, Dict. of Antiqq. s. 'Tabulae.'

[e] Ed. and explained by Degenkolb, 'Zschr. f. R. G.' iv. 474.

[f] Ed. with commy. by Henzen (1843).

mentary; preserved upon two tablets found at Rome in 1820 and 1830.[a]

[a] Ed. by Rudorff, 'Zschr. f. gesch. R. W.' 301.

STATUTES *and* DECREES OF CORPORATIONS AND SOCIETIES.

(*a*) *Lex collegii funeraticii Lanuvini* (133 A.D.) of a burial society.[b]

(β) Notice of the dissolution of a *coll. fun. Abburnense*, on the part of the magister collegii (167 A.D.); in the 'wax-tablets of Transylvania.'[c]

(γ) Statute of a *coll. aquae*.[d]

(δ) Lex metalli Vipascensis, found in Lusitania in the year 1876: an imperial ordinance as to mining. The part preserved treats of the leasing of all possible industries to be pursued at the place, and for which a monopoly is thereby given.[e]

[b] Ed. and explained by Mommsen, 'De Collegiis,' p. 98 (1843).

[c] Explained by Huschke, 'Zschr. f. gesch. R. W.' xii. 173.

[d] Perhaps an ordinance as to springs of a Roman guild of fullers. Ed. by Rudorff, ibid. xv. 203.

[e] Ed. with commy. by Hübner; Momms., 'Ephem. epigraph.' iii. fasc. 3.

DOCUMENTS *relating to* LAWSUITS.

(*a*) *Sententia Minuciorum* (commissaries of the Roman senate) in frontier-disputes of the town of Genua and of the community of Veturii belonging to it (637 U.C.). It was discovered in 1506.[f]

(β) An award in respect of frontier-disputes of the city Histonium.[g]

(γ) *Lis fullonum* (A.D. 244), found at Rome in 1701, contains a documentary report upon a protracted suit (from 226 to 244) against the Roman fullers' association with regard to the water-rate to be paid by them to the Treasury.[h]

[f] Explained by Rudorff, 'Zschr. f. R. G.' i. 168.

[g] Ed. by Mommsen, 'Stadtrechte,' p. 484.

[h] According to others, the rate to be paid by the *Fiscus* to them. It has been edited by Rudorff, 'Zschr. f. gesch. R. W.' xv. 254; Momms., ibid. p. 326; Bremer, 'Rhein. Museum' for 1866, p. 10.

§ 9. FROM CONSTANTINE TO JUSTINIAN.

The fourth period, which closes with Justinian's legislation, marks the decline of pure Roman Law as a science, and likewise is the time when that Law obtains a cosmopolitan character. The new organization of the State, characterised by centralisation and absolutism, the basis of which was laid by Diocletian and which was completed by Constantine, with its central point transferred to the eastern half of the empire (Constantinople), the introduction of the Christian as the state-religion, the general decline of culture and the dying out of legal productivity, as well as the extinction of Roman nationality,—these together determined also the development of Law. The main task of this we may see in the removal of the obsolete national elements of the Roman Private Law, and accordingly, its extension into a Universal Law, containing the more general legal conceptions of the 'ius gentium'[a] which rendered possible and provided the first step in the transition of the Roman Law to modern times.

[a] Cf., *e.g.*, §§ 39, 74, *sq.*, 81, 150, 166, 170, 181.

The development of Law now depended upon imperial legislation,[b] and that chiefly in the form of *edicta* (leges generales). By Arcadius and Honorius (A.D. 398) the application of 'rescripta' and '*decreta*' beyond the special case was forbidden; nevertheless, according to a provision of Theodosius and Valentinian (426), they were to be of general legal obligation if the Emperor himself had assigned legal effect to them by a special clause, or by the designation of *generalis lex* s. '*edictum*.' By Justinian, on the other hand, the 'decreta' were again declared to be of general obligation. The 'decreta' subscribed by the Emperor took the form either of a communication to the Senate or of a proclamation to his subjects, which as a rule was despatched to a high imperial officer, and was by him then copied and issued by advertisement or otherwise. These were the 'sanctiones pragmaticae.' After the division of the empire the transmission to one part of the laws promulgated in the other was effected by means of publication in that part. Moreover, the later legislation concerned for the most part only the administration; in general, the Criminal Law and Law of Procedure; it was but to a slight extent operative in the department of Private Law, because it did not so much actually develop the Law as simply set aside what was antiquated; and not merely in this, but in

[b] 'Tam conditor quam interpres legum solus imperator.'

the inexactness, obscurity and prolixity, and in the Byzantine bombast of those laws, is plainly reflected the juristic incapacity and ignorance of this period.

In the general substance of the Law a distinction was now made, from the point of view of practical application, between two bodies of Law: *ius* (vetus), *i.e.*, the classical juristic literature—including the imperial constitutions contained in private collections—and *leges* (novae), the laws published since the time of Constantine. As regards the first, thorough study and full practical appreciation of them failed from lack of a scientific frame of mind and juristic aptitude. And further, Practice always increasingly confined itself to some widely spread works of a few especially esteemed jurists. To this relates the so-called 'Law of Citation,' of Valentinian III. (426), which on the one hand was meant to introduce a more liberal use of the whole classical literature of Law, that in practice had mostly fallen into disuse, inasmuch as it at the same time emphasized the limitation of legal authority to the 'Iuris auctores' and the 'Veteres;'[a] whilst, on the other hand, it endeavoured to aid practice so as to settle controversies arising therein, by regulating the external authority of the writings of jurists, as well as by the introduction, suited to the spirit of the times, of the principle of a mechanical balancing of opinions.

[a] Cf. § 8.

Impp. Theodos. et Valentin. AA. ad Senatum urbis Romae.—Papiniani, Pauli, Gaii, Ulpiani atque Modestini scripta universa firmamus ita, ut Gaium quae Paulum, Ulpianum et cunctos comitetur auctoritas, lectionesque ex omni eius opere recitentur. Eorumque quoque scientiam, quorum tractatus atque sententias praedicti omnes eius operibus miscuerunt, ratam esse censemus (ut Scaevolae, Sabini, Iuliani atque Marcelli omniumque quos illi celebrarunt): si tamen eorum libri propter antiquitatis incertum codicum collatione firmentur. Ubi autem diversae sententiae proferuntur, potior numerus vincat auctorum vel si numerus aequalis sit, eius partis praecedat auctoritas, in qua excellentis ingenii vir Papinianus emineat, qui, ut singulos vincit, ita cedit duobus. Notas etiam Pauli atque Ulpiani in Papiniani corpus factas, sicut dudum (a. 321 a Constantino imp. L. i. Th. C. eod.) statutum est, praecipimus infirmari. Ubi autem pares eorum sententiae recitantur, quorum pars censetur auctoritas, quod sequi debeat, eligat moderatio iudicantis.—Pauli quoque sententias semper valere praecipimus.—C. Th. de resp. prud. 1, 4, l. 3.[1]

Legal instruction was now given at public schools of Law by appointed teachers (professores) and according to a fixed plan of teaching.[a] In the first year were taken up 'Gaii institutiones' and four 'libri singu-

[a] Const. *Omnem reip.* § 1.

---

[1] Their imperial majesties Theodosius and Valentinian to the Senate of the City of Rome.—We confirm the whole of the writings of Papinian, Paulus, Gaius, Ulpian and Modestinus, so that the same authority shall attach to Gaius as does to Paulus, Ulpian and all, and let appeal be made to passages from every work of his. The learning also of those whose treatises and opinions the aforesaid persons in general have incorporated with their own works we consider should be upheld (as of Scaevola, Sabinus, Julian and Marcellus, and of all whom they have commemorated): if, however, doubt surround their books by reason of age, let them be confirmed by comparison of copies. But where diverse opinions are expressed, the greater number of authors shall decide, or if the number be equal, the authority of that side shall prevail in which figures Papinian, a man of superior understanding, who while he is worth more than one gives way to two. And, as long since was prescribed by Constantine, we ordain that the notes of Paulus and Ulpian which have been made upon the whole of Papinian are of no authority.[b] But where the opinions of those whose authority is accounted equal are equally balanced,[c] let the moderation of the judge select that which he ought to follow. We also direct that the Sentences of Paulus are of permanent authority.[d]

[b] See Moyle, pp. 59, 60.

[c] *I.e.*, in cases when the voice of Papinian is not available.

[d] 'A general overriding authority being given to the sententiae of P.' Clark, p. 297.

[a] Cf. § 10.

lares'[a] from his commentary on the Edict; in the second year, selections from sectt. 1–3 of the Edict, according to a commentary thereon (perhaps Ulpian's); in the third year, the portions gone over in the previous year of the second and third section of the Edict, and eight books of Papinian's 'Responsa;' in the fourth year, private study of the 'Responsa' of Paulus; and in the fifth year, private study of the Constitutions.

Collections of Law.

Through the requirements of practice, collections were called for of the imperial constitutions, which were scattered, with difficulty accessible, and in great part not published officially.

There were two private collections: 'Gregorianus Codex' (*c.* 300 A.D.) and 'Hermogenianus Codex' (about the middle or towards the end of the fourth century), of both of which only a few fragments are preserved in the 'lex Romana Visigothorum' and in other compilations.

The 'Codex Theodosianus' was an official codification of the imperial constitutions since Constantine the Great, arranged by Theodosius II. and Valentinian III. The order was given for it in A.D. 429, then it was suspended, but recommenced in 435, and completed and published, together with a confirmation of the cod. Greg. and Herm., in 438. The constitutions codified by it underwent much editorial alteration. This collection consists of sixteen books, divided by titles, in which the separate constitutions are arranged chronologically. Books 6–16 are preserved in their original form, but Books 1–5 only in the extracts contained in the lex Rom. Visig.—With this go the collections of constitutions issued later on (novellae leges), of Theodosius II. and his successors.[b]

[b] Ed. by Haenel; the Cod. Theodos., with copious commy. by Gothofred.

As with the decay of jurisprudence the classical literature of Law could no longer be mastered in its full extent, the need of selections and compilations of the Law as treated by the jurists made itself the more felt.

An attempt was made to satisfy this need with the 'libri vi. iuris epitomarum' of Hermogenianus, extracts from which appear in Justinian's Digest. They contain a systematic compilation from various writings of the classical jurists, in which the results—without the source being given—are mostly collected in aphoristic maxims.

A collection of excerpts from the juristic literature and of constitutions is contained in the so-called 'Fragmenta Vaticana,' which were discovered by Angelo Mai (1820) in a palimpsest MS. of the Vatican Library, consisting of 28 leaves, in part cut through lengthwise. This private compilation for use in practice was devoid both of scientific insight and, notwithstanding the division into titles (Purchase, Usufruct, Dos, Excusationes, Donatio, Representation), of scientific method. It dates at any rate from before A.D. 426; according to Mommsen from the time of Constantine, but according to Huschke from that of Honorius. Besides constitutions, it contains extracts almost solely from writings of Papinian, Ulpian and Paulus, in which the respective passages are transmitted in their purity and integrity.[a]

A collection of maxims of the Mosaic and of the Civil Law—indeed with the view of demonstrating the agreement of both, or rather, the priority of the first-mentioned—is found in the 'Collatio legum Mosaicarum et Romanarum s. Lex Dei,' composed about A.D. 400 by a cleric,[b] which in sixteen titles contains extracts from writings of the five jurists recognised by the Law of Citation and from constitutions.[c]

The so-called 'Consultatio veteris ICti,' composed about A.D. 500, contains a series of legal opinions, in which passages are handed down from 'Pauli sententiae' and constitutions.[d]

In the Germanic states founded in the year 476

[a] Ed. by Mommsen (1860) with facsimile of MS., and 1861. Huschke, cit. pp. 688, *sq.*

[b] Possibly Rufinus of Aquileia or Ambrose of Milan.

[c] Ed. by Bluhme, Huschke (pp. 627, *sqq.*), Dirksen (Hinterl. Schrift. ii. 100, *sqq.*), Rudorff (1869), and see 'Zschr. f. gesch. R. W.' x. 298, *sqq.*, 309, and xiii. 1, *sq.*

[d] Ed. by Huschke (pp. 797, *sqq.*).

upon territory of the Western Empire, in which those of German and such as were of Roman nationality—in pursuance of the principle of 'personal laws'—lived each according to the Law of their own stock, collections and records of Law were formed from the beginning of the sixth century.

The most important among the 'leges Romanae' is the 'lex Rom. Visigothorum (Breviarium Alariciamum),' which was composed under Alaric II. in the year 506, and was published exclusively for the Roman subjects of the West-Gothic kingdom. Epitomized in it in the following order, but, with exception of the third, without any change in the text, are: 1. 'Codex Theodosianus' (one-ninth to one-eighth of all the constitutions); 2. 'Novellae Constitutiones'[a] (only about one-third); 3. 'Gaii institutiones,' represented by an abridgement in two books (the so-called 'Gaii epitome'); 4. 'Pauli sententiae l. v.;' 5. 'Codicis Gregoriani l. v.' (only twenty-two Constitutions); 6. 'Hermogeniani Corporis liber' (only two Constitutions); 7. 'Papiniani l. i. responsa' (only one passage).

[a] See above

§ 10. Justinian's Compilation of Law.

In a more broadly comprehensive and happier manner than in earlier attempts—especially as regards the classical literature of Law—Justinian at last, by his collection of Law, solved the problem of his time as to a compilatory arrangement of the existing legal material. This now scarcely admitted of a survey, and was also difficult to make out, and therefore little used. He gave to the Roman Law the form in which it has been received by modern cultivated nations. The plan formed was to codify the practical Law in general, *i.e.*, to make a collection by way of epitome of both the 'leges' and the 'ius.' We must in the first place consider the several parts of Justinian's collection of Law and his legislation.

By the Const. *Haec quae necessario* of February 13th,

528, was appointed a commission of ten superior officials (amongst whom were Tribonian and the professor Theophilus) and advocates, with extensive powers to compile a new *Codex* from the constitutions contained in the three existing Codes and those issued of later date. The work, completed in a year, was confirmed as 'Iustinianus Codex' by the Const. *Summa reipublicae* of April 7th, 529. The three Codes and the various constitutions which were not adopted were at the same time repealed.—Before a start was made with the compilation of the 'ius,' a series of constitutions were issued in which, on the one hand, controversies were decided which arose out of the older Law, on the other, obsolete rules of law were abolished and others were remodelled.

> —permisimus, resecatis tam supervacuis . . . praefationibus quam similibus et contrariis . . . illis etiam quae in desuetudinem abierunt, certas et brevi sermone conscriptas ex tribus codicibus, novellis etiam constitutionibus leges componere et congruis subdere titulis, adiicientes quidem et detrahentes, immo et mutantes verba earum, ubi hoc rei commoditas exigebat.—Const. *Haec quae*, § 2.[1]

By the Const. *Deo auctore* of December 15th, 530, Justinian enjoined a Commission of sixteen members under the presidency of the Quaestor S. Palatii Tribonian, and in which were included the law-professors Theophilus and Cratinus of the school at Constantinople, and Dorotheus and Anatolius of that at Berytus, to make a systematic collection of extracts

[1] . . . We have commissioned them to reject as well superfluous preambles . . . as repetitions and contradictions . . . and also such things as are already obsolete, to compose concise and positive laws from the three Codes and the new constitutions, and reduce them under suitable titles, besides adding or subtracting, altering too the language where this appeared to suit the purpose.

[a] Hence the designation 'Pandecta' (see below).

of whatever was still of practical use[a] from the writings of the recognised 'iuris auctores' without reference to the Valentinian Law of Citation. A discretion was allowed the Commission as well in respect of the elimination of what was superfluous, antiquated and contradictory as with regard to editorial and substantive alteration of the passages adopted—interpolations, so-called 'emblemata Triboniani'—but in other respects these passages were to retain their character as extracts. The source from which they were derived was to be mentioned. At the same time, in order to prevent corruption of the text, and to preclude the repeated growth of a 'ius controversum' in place of the 'ius certum ac receptum,' the use of abbreviations (sigla) as well as the composition and publication of commentaries to the work (after the manner of the libri ad Edictum, Sabinum, etc.) was forbidden for the future under pain of punishment.[b] This somewhat hastily completed body of law, by a proclamation of December 16th, 533 (Const. *Tanta* and Δέδωκεν), received statutory confirmation under the title *Iustiniani iuris enucleati ex omni vetere iure collecti* DIGESTORVM s. *Pandectarum libri.* —An end was at the same time put to the validity of all juristic works.

[b] Cf. § 11.

> —nemo . . . audeat commentarios . . . adnectere: nisi tantum si velit in Graecam vocem transformare sub eodem ordine eaque consequentia, sub qua et voces Romanae positae sunt (hoc quod Graeci κατὰ πόδα dicunt), et si qui forsitan per titulorum subtilitatem adnotare maluerint et ea quae παράτιτλα nuncupantur componere; alias autem legum interpretationes, immo magis perversiones eos iactare non concedimus, ne verbositas eorum aliquod legibus nostris adferat ex confusione dedecus.—Const. *Tanta*, § 21.[1]

---

[1] . . . that no one . . . dare to add commentaries: unless alone he desire to make a Greek translation with the same arrangement, and in that order in which the Latin words are

Excerpts appear in the Digest from thirty-nine jurists,[a] in unequal distribution. The most numerous are those from Ulpian, one third; then from Paulus, one sixth; from Papinian, one eighteenth; from Iulian, one twenty-first; from Pomponius and Cervidius Scaevola, one twenty-fourth; from Gaius, one twenty-eighth; from Modestinus, one forty-fifth; from Marcellus, one sixtieth, or thereabouts. That which has been preserved represents about one twentieth of the whole legal literature extracted.

[a] 'Index Florentinus.'

The Digest, which is in general arranged according to the system of the Edict,[b] is divided into fifty books, and these—with the exception of Bks. 30–32 (de legatis)—into titles, very unequal, with rubrics under which the several excerpts (leges, fragmenta) are gathered, and a statement as to the book from which they are taken.[c] A collateral division, corresponding to the arrangement of the Edict and to legal instruction, is that into seven parts:

[b] Cf. Maine, 'Early Law and Custom,' pp. 369, *sq.*

[c] The division of the extracts into paragraphs was not made until later on.

Pt. i. s. πρῶτα=l. 1–4.
ii. s. de iudiciis=l. 5–11.
iii. s. de rebus sc. creditis=l. 12–19.
iv. s. umbilicus=l. 20–27.
v. s. de testamentis=l. 28–36.
vi. =l. 37–44.
vii. =l. 45–50.

Bks. 20–22 bear the special name of 'Antipapinianus' (in the Byzantine jurists); Bks. 23–36 (in which are treated Marriage and Dowry, Guardianship, Testaments and Legacies) that of 'libri singulares;' Bks. 47–48 (=Delicts and Criminal Law) that of 'libri terribiles.'—The extracts are not arranged by

placed (called by the Greeks κατὰ πόδα); or if any happen to prefer to add a note because of the obscurity of the titles, and to compose what are called παράτιτλα. But we do not permit them to hazard other interpretations, to say nothing of perversions, of the Law, lest their verbosity should bring our laws into disrepute because of confusion.

titles in a systematic manner, but in groups—as discovered by Bluhme[a]—just as the various works had been extracted, the order followed being one observed in legal instruction. This yields the following division into classes or series, in part determined capriciously:—

(α) The Sabinus series, which contains the works upon the 'ius civile,' and is chiefly represented by the 'libri ad Sabinum.'

(β) the Edictal series, to which belong the treatises upon the Praetorian Law, in particular the 'libri ad Edictum' and the 'Digesta' of Celsus and Marcellus.

(γ) the Papinian series, in which are found the casuistical writings headed by the 'Quaest.' and 'Resp.' of Papinian.

(δ) the smaller, so-called 'Appendix' or post-Papinian group, of miscellaneous character, which perhaps contains the writings only discovered later on.[b]

Since the existing hand-books no longer answered to the present state of the Law, a new manual was at Justinian's command composed by Tribonian, Theophilus and Dorotheus, which was designed for elementary instruction. This was in four books, with titles and rubrics, and was derived chiefly from 'Institutiones' and 'res quottidianae' of Gaius, according to the plan of the former,[c] besides being based upon other institutional works, yet with regard to the 'quinquaginta decisiones' or new constitutions. Under the name of *INSTITVTIONES*, it received statutory confirmation by a Const. of November 21, 533 (Proemium instit.), addressed to the 'cupida legum inventus.'[d]

The constitutions which had been issued in the meanwhile rendered necessary a new redaction (repetita praelectio) of the 'Cod. Iustinianus,' which was intrusted to a commission of five members under the

[a] Zschr. f. gesch. R. W. iv. (1820).

[b] Cf. Labittus, 'Index leg. in Dig.,' Wieling, 'Iurisprud. restituta,' Hommel, 'Palingenesia libr. iur. vet.,' and Roby, cit. app. B. and C.

[c] See the 'Syntagma' of Gneist or of Polenaar, and Holland, 'Institt. of Justin., edited as a recension of the Instt. of Gaius.'

[d] Cf. § 6.

presidency of Tribonian. This received confirmation by the Const. *Cordi nobis* of November 16th, 534, when the earlier Code was repealed.

The *CODEX* consists of twelve books, which in general agree with the system of the Digest. Each is divided into titles, among which the constitutions provided with an inscription and a subscription are arranged in chronological order. They contain 4,600 – 700 constitutions; the oldest being of Hadrian, the most recent that of November 4th, 534; in great part Rescripts, and with few exceptions in Latin.

When this collection of Law was finished, a number of *NOVELLAE* sc. constitutiones (νεαραὶ διατάξεις) were issued by Justinian between the years 535 and 564, almost entirely in Greek, but no official collection of them was made. About 166 Novels have been preserved.

By the glossators[a] the Codex and Institutions were augmented by abstracts of the Novels (authenticae); in the former also were ranged some laws of the Emperors Frederic I. and II., either complete or abridged (authenticae Fridericianae): *e.g., Auth. Habita, C. ne filius pro patre*, 4, 13. [a] § 12.

Next as to legal education. The instruction imparted at the public law-schools of Constantinople and Berytus, Justinian reformed with reference to the new law-books, by the Const. *Omnem reipublicae* of December 16th, 533, issued to the professors there, which prescribed a five years' course of instruction and the following plan of study:

First year, 'Institutiones' and 'pars prima Dig.' The students at this stage were styled 'Iustiniani novi.'

Second year, 'pars secunda' or 'tertia Dig.' alternately; four of the 'libri singulares,' one each upon Dos, Tutela, Testaments, Legacies. The students were called 'Edictales.'

Third year, 'pars iii.' or rather 'ii. Dig.;' 'l. xx.–xxii. Dig.' Students were now said to be 'Papinianistae.'

Fourth year, private study of the remaining ten 'libri singulares.' The name of students so engaged was Λύται.

[a] Cf. § 9

Fifth year, private study of the Codex. This was to occupy the 'prolytae.'[a]

We come thirdly to the transmission and editions of Justinian's collection of Law. Since it was not published as a whole, there are only MSS. of the several parts.

As the oldest and most important amongst the MSS. (everywhere numerous) of the 'Institutes' must be distinguished one at Bamberg which is complete, and another at Turin imperfect, both of the ninth or tenth century. There are besides extracts in the 'lex Romana canonice compta' (transferred from it into the Collectio Anselmo dedicata) in MSS. of the same time. The best editions are those of Schrader (with full commentary, 1832), Krueger (1867), Huschke (1868).

[b] Cf. § 11.

The MSS. of the Digests are divided into the Bolognese, accompanied by glosses,[b] or the 'Vulgar' MSS. and the 'Ante-Bolognese,' of which is preserved only an imperfect one, the very celebrated 'Florentine' of the seventh century. The lectio Flor. is, as 'littera Pisana,' used by the Glossators in contrast with the 'litt. communis.' Features common to the MSS. first mentioned are the absence of Inscriptiones and the division into three volumina :

1. Digestum vetus = l. i.–xxiv. tit. 2.

2. Infortiatum = l. xxiv. 3 (tit. soluto matrimonio)–xxxviii.

3. Dig. novum = l. xxxix.–l.

With these go, as further volumina—

4. Codex lib. i.–ix.

5. The so-called 'Volumen [parvum]' containing,

(α) Institutiones.

(β) Authenticum, *i.e.*, the Novellae in nine Collationes, which again are divided into titles.

(γ) Tres libri = Cod. l. x.–xii.

As regards the relation of these MSS. to the Florentine, the copies of the 'Dig. novum' seem to have sprung, directly or indirectly, from it; but the MSS. of the 'Dig. vetus' and 'Infortiatum' some think are derived from a sister MS. of the 'Florentina,' whilst Mommsen is of opinion that they must also themselves have sprung indirectly from this, and then have been only corrected from a particular original. At any rate, the first rank among all the MSS. is taken by the *Florentina*, although it also is not free from mistakes or without lacunae.

The older editions all contain glosses, and are in a tripartite division. The first edition without either glosses or such division is that of Stephanus, 1527–8. Amongst the critical editions should be mentioned: Taurellius, 1553, 2–3 tom. containing a very careful and accurately printed copy of the Flor.; the earlier, and often overvalued, edition of Greg. Haloander (Meltzer), 1529, 3 vols. containing a text (the so-called 'lectio Norica s. Haloandrina') formed from Vulgar MSS. and collations communicated to him of the Flor., often with very good conjectural criticism. The most recent edition, which is based upon a masterly collation of the Flor., and accomplished with rigid philological criticism, is that of Th. Mommsen, 1866–70, 2 vols. See further in Roby, cit. pp. cxxxvi., *sq.*

The complete MSS. of the 'Codex' are Bolognese of the twelfth century, which contain inscriptions and subscriptions, but imperfectly, without any Greek constitutions whatever. Amongst the older, and fragmentary, MSS. the first rank belongs to the Veronese of the eighth, together with the Pistoiensian of the tenth century. The most recent, thoroughly critical, edition is by Krueger, 1873–1877.

Of the Novellae there are three different private collections of MSS.:—

1. The Latin Epitome Iuliani, containing 125 Nov.

2. A collection of 168 (strictly 164) Nov.

3. The collection of 134 Nov., in a Latin translation (Vulgata), which underlies the Authenticum of the Glossators.

Edd. by Haloander, 1531; Osenbrüggen, 1840 (tom. iii. of Kriegel's corp. iur.). The last crit. edd. by Zachariae v. Lingenthal, 2 vols. 1881, containing the Nov., only in the original Greek, and in chronological order; R. Schoell, 1880, still unfinished, containing besides the Text a Latin translation and the Vers. Vulg.; Heimbach, Authenticum, 1846–51; Haenel, Iuliani epit. lat. Nov. 1873.

The first complete edition with the title of '*CORPVS IVRIS CIVILIS*' was that of Dion. Gothofred. (Godefroy), 1583.

Modern edd. by Kriegel, 3 vols. 1833 and often; Mommsen, Krueger, 1872–77, vol. i. (Inst., Dig.), vol. ii. (Codex). The older editions of Godefroy are still useful because of the explanatory parallel passages introduced in the notes, which indeed are contained much more fully in the edd. with glosses of the corp. iur.: the last of such appeared at Leyden in 1627 (6 vols.).

It remains for us to explain the method of citation. The mode of citation most usual with German writers is in the Institutes, Digest and Codex, according to the rubrics of the titles.

(1) pr. [=principium] § 3. I. [=Institutionum] de usucapionibus 2, 6 [lib. 2, tit. 6].

(2) l. [=lex] or fr. [=fragmentum] 22 pr. § 6. D. or ff.[a] [c. Digestorum] mandati 17, 1 [=lib. 17, tit. 1].

[a] 'This has arisen by calligraphic development from a *d* with a line through it' (Roby).

(3) l. or c. [= constitutio] 21 pr. § 5. C. [=Codicis] de testamentis, 6, 23.—Cf. *infra*.

If the title in question contain only a single fragment besides l. [=lex] or c. [constitutio] or fr. [fragmentum], the designation 'un.' [=unica, um] is used, *e.g.*, l. un. § 2 D. de off. cons. 1, 10 l. un. § 9 C. de caduc. toll. 6, 51.

If the immediately preceding passage be from the same title, in place of the rubric of the title, 'eod.' [=eodem sc. titulo] is employed with the one following it, *e.g.*, l. 59 D. pro socio 17, 2, l. 63 § 8 eod. If the title have been mentioned in some previous doctrine, the passages from it are cited with 'h. t.' [hoc titulo], *e.g.*, tit. D. de furtis 47, 2—l. 65 h. t.

The last passage of a title is usually cited as 'ult.' [=ultima] or 'fin.' [=finalis], the last but one sometimes as 'pen.' [=penultima], *e.g.*, l. ult. D. de iure dotium 23, 3, l. fi. C. de novationibus, 8, 42, l. pen. § 1, D. de peculio, 15, 1.

Bks. 30–32 contain only the one title, de legatis, which may be cited thus : l. 3 D. de legatis i. [=in primo] 30, l. 34 pr. D. de legatis ii. 31, l. 99 § 3 eod. iii. 32.

The designation 'D.,' as well as the number of book and title, is very commonly omitted, *e.g.*, l. 22, § 6 mand. [=l. 22, § 6 D. mandati, 17, 1]. The rubric of the title is itself generally much abbreviated, in many titles being confined to the initial letters of the words.[a]

[a] English writers usually omit the rubric altogether.

The most common abbreviations in citation from the Digest are the following :—

de A. E. V.=actionibus empti venditi, 19, 1.

de A. v. A. P. (or de A. P.)=adquirenda vel amittenda possessione, 41, 2.

de A. v. O. H.=ad quirendavel omittenda hereditate, 29, 2.

de A. R. D.=adquirenda rerum dominio, 41, 1.

de B. P.=bonorum possessionibus, 37, 1.

de C. E.=contrahenda emptione, 18, 1.

de C. et D.=condicionibus et demonstrationibus 35, 1.
de D. R. (or R. D.)=divisione rerum, 1, 8.
de H. I.=heredibus instituendis, 28, 5.
de H. P.=hereditatis petitione, 5, 3.
de J. D.=iure dotium, 23, 3.
de J. et J.=iustitia et iure, 1, 1.
de J. F.=iure fisci, 49, 14.
de I. I. R.=in integrum restitutionibus, 4, 1.
de N. G.=negotiis gestis, 3, 5.
de O. J.=origine iuris, 1, 2.
de O. et A.=obligationibus et actionibus, 44, 7.
de R. C.=rebus creditis, 12, 1.
de R. J.=regulis iuris, 50, 17.
de R. N.=ritu nuptiarum, 23, 2.
de R. V.=rei vindicatione, 6, 1.
S. M.=soluto matrimonio, 24, 3.
de S. P. R.=servitutibus praediorum rusticorum, 83.
de S. P. V.=servitutibus praediorum urbanorum, 8, 2.
de V. O.=verborum obligationibus, 45, 1.
de V. S.=verborum significatione, 50, 16.

The Novels are cited according to number, chapter and paragraph, *e.g.*, Nov. 118 praef. c. 4.

Other modes of citation are :

§ 3, I. 2, 6;
l. 22, § 6, D. 17, 1;
c. 21, § 5, C. 6, 23;

and as followed by English writers (in agreement with ancient usage) :

Inst. ii. 6, 3;
Dig. xvii. 1, 22, 6;
Cod. vi. 23, 21, 5.

The custom of the Glossators and their successors is to substitute the first words of the leges for the numbers and paragraphs, *e.g.*:

1. inst. de usucap. § quod autem dictum [=§ 3, I. de usucap. 2, 6].

2. D. (or ff.) mand. l. si mandavero § qui aedem [=l. 22, § 6, mand. 17, 1].

3. Cod. de testamentis l. hac consultissima § si quid autem [=l. 21, § 5 C. de test. 6, 23].

4. Auth. de hered. ab intest. § nullam vero. colla. ix. tit. j. [=Nov. 118 c. 4].[a]

[a] Cf. Roby, pp. ccxlv., *sq.*

§ 11. THE ROMAN LAW IN THE BYZANTINE EMPIRE.

The collection of Law by Justinian, the original of which was certainly always more and more superseded by Greek translations, remained in the Byzantine Empire primarily in full use as a law-book and as the foundation of legal study, upon which it exercised an appreciable influence. And accordingly, as products of lectures at the law-schools, there soon appeared selections, paraphrases and exegetical commentaries upon the law-books, the scientific value of which cannot be denied. The most prominent jurists of Justinian's time were:—

Theophilus, author of a paraphrase of the Institutes, not without importance for the textual criticism and interpretation thereof;[1]

Thalelaeus, writer of a full commentary on the Codex, and

Stephanus, author of a commentary (index) upon the first thirty-six books of the Digest, which contains detailed interpretations of the several passages.[b]

[b] Numerous fragments have been preserved of these two works in the 'Basilica.'

This ephemeral revival, however, was succeeded by a rapid decline of jurisprudence and of the condition of Law itself, so that by the beginning of the eighth century knowledge and comprehension of Justinian's law-works had almost completely disappeared. An endeavour was made to remedy this state of things by a revision of the actual Law, which was begun by Basil the Macedonian, completed by Leo Philosophus (886–910) and published as a Statute-Book under

[1] Paraphrasis graeca institut. ed. Reitz. 1751; ed. Ferrini, 1884.

the title of '*BASILICA*' (*i.e.*, imperial laws). The 'Basilica' contain an abbreviation of Justinian's Books, which was put together from the older selections and paraphrases, according to a peculiar system, but essentially akin to that of the Codex, and in sixty books, which are divided into titles, and again into chapters. The Text was very soon furnished with scholia, which contain references and parallel passages, besides explanatory selections from the commentaries of earlier Byzantine jurists. These and the later scholia to the Text, and to the selections last mentioned, underwent a fresh revision in the twelfth century. The 'Basilica' with scholia are important especially for the criticism of the Text, and as filling up the various lacunae of Justinian's volumes, but also as affording helps to the interpretation of them, to be used with discretion, yet not to be undervalued. Forty-four books have been preserved, of which twenty-nine are almost complete.

The most recent edition is by Heimbach, tom. i.–v. 1833–1850, tom. vi. (Prolegomena and Manuale) 1870, and Zachariae a Lingenthal, supplementum ed. Basil. Heimbach, 1846.

§ 12. THE ROMAN LAW IN THE WEST. IN ITALY: GLOSSATORS AND COMMENTATORS.[a]

[a] See Savigny, 'Gesch. des Röm. Rechts im Mittelalter,' 2. Aufl. 1834–51, 7. Bde.

The downfall of Roman sovereignty in Italy, 568 A.D., which had been re-established a short time before, did not entirely destroy the transmission and validity of the Roman Law; but its continued existence was marred by the very imperfect knowledge there was of it through a limited employment of some few sources, nor was the scientific treatment of the Law any more satisfactory, so that Justinian's works fell into ever greater oblivion.

Of treatises upon the Roman Law, in which the special aim was to arrive at definitions, as well as to establish specific rules, and to make some systematic collection of legal propositions for teaching purposes, there are preserved:—

1. The Turin Gloss on the Institutes, in the Turin MS. of that portion of the Corp. iur.,[a] and of perhaps the sixth or of the ninth century.[b]

2. The 'Brachylogus iuris civilis s. Corpus legum,' a manual of the Roman Law in four books, and with titles according to the system of Justinian's Institutes (but in the fourth book the actiones, or procedure), of the eleventh century.[c]

3. 'Petri Exceptiones legum Romanorum,' belonging to the end of the eleventh century, a manual of the Law as settled by Justinian, in four books.[d]

The Roman Law first awoke to new life by the Law School, dating from *c.* 1100, at Bologna, where the study of Law, based upon the Books of Justinian that had been again brought to light, appeared as a kind of legal revelation, and quickly attained to a high degree of success in the hands of the Glossators. From Bologna the Roman Law was soon spread over Europe. In contrast with their predecessors, the Glossators pursued a new, exact method, by their subjecting the whole of the Justinianean Law to a thorough exegetical treatment, and from their interpreting every single passage by reference to others. In this way they endeavoured at the same time to grasp the systematic connection of the substance of Law. By investigation of the sources, pursued with great intellectual energy and perseverance, they acquired a familiarity with and power over the subject-matter scarcely attained again, and thus prepared the way for the legal science and legal study of after-times. Besides the interpretation of individual passages, which as *Glossae* were attached to the Text—at first 'interlineares,' then 'marginales'—the Glossators also inaugurated the systematic treatment of Law in their *Summae* upon particular titles and whole books of Justinian's collection, besides setting forth the Law of Procedure (ordo iudicarius) and

[a] Cf. § 10.

[b] Last ed. by Krueger (Zschr. f. R. Gesch. vii. 44, *sq.*).

[c] Latest edition by Böcking (1829).

[d] Ed. by Barkow, in Savigny, Gesch. ii. Anh. 1.

publishing collections of 'controversies' and treatises thereon.[a] The most prominent Glossators were:—

Irnerius, the founder of the School.

Bulgarus, Martinus, Jacobus, Hugo, the four so-called 'Doctores,' about the middle of the twelfth century. Contemporary with them was Vacarius, founder of a Law School at Oxford.

Placentius, founder of the Law School at Montpellier, and Johannes Bassianus, towards the end of the twelfth century.

Azo, pupil of the last mentioned, who flourished at the beginning of the thirteenth century; under him the School of Glossators reached their climax.

Franc. Accursius (Accorso), the last Glossator, about the middle of the thirteenth century, who in a rather uncritical and careless manner arranged a compilation of the existing glosses into a new redaction which almost completely superseded the original glosses. This was called 'Glossa ordinaria,' or simply 'Glossa.'

After Accursius, a deep decline of Jurisprudence set in, which is evidenced by the fact that the Gloss soon acquired an inordinate and almost legal authority, and became a kind of source of Law, upon which men even began to write commentaries, the result of which was that the Text of Justinian's law-books was always more and more lost sight of. Under the dominion of the scholastic method an empty formalism came to prevail in Jurisprudence, so that men on the one hand in their treatment of the Law relapsed into a prolix and subtle casuistry in consequence of their misuse of dialectic forms; on the other, in blind reliance upon authority, confined themselves to a spiritless collection of the opinions and interpretations of predecessors upon which they commented. Amongst these commentators the following deserve notice:—

Odofredus, ob. 1265.

Cinus, ob. 1314.

Bartolus, ob. 1357, called 'iuris monarcha,' as the

[a] Ed. by Haenel, 'Dissensiones dominorum,' 1834.

most celebrated of all the commentators, of paramount influence upon the practice of his time and of the centuries following.[a]

Baldus, ob. 1400, second only to the last mentioned in authority.

Fulgosius, ob. 1427, sometimes in exegesis in advance of the rest.

Paulus de Castro, ob. 1441.

Jason de Mayno, ob. 1519.

Their comprehensive works, of scarcely any scientific value, but important through their influence upon the development of practice, consist of 'Commentarii' and 'Lecturae' upon Justinian's Works, and of 'Consilia.'

[a] He was a professor at Pisa and Perugia.

Of relatively greater value are the works of the practical men of this period, of whom the most important was Durantis (author of the 'Speculum iudiciale'), ob. 1296.

§ 13.—The Reception of the Roman Law in Germany.

From the Universities of Italy the knowledge of Roman Law spread to Germany, where, in the form of Justinian's Works, it was in the course of the fourteenth to the sixteenth century 'received,' *i.e.*, taken as Common (though subsidiary) Law. But this was done subject to the limitation received from the Glossators,[b] and by way of usage, although not without manifold opposition, especially to the 'foreign doctors' and the innovations in forensic procedure which rendered it more tedious.

[b] 'Quidquid non agnoscit glossa, nec agnoscit curia.'

The acceptance of the Roman Law finds its explanation—

(1) in its universal character, copiousness and scientific completeness,[c] as compared with the abruptness, insufficiency and clumsiness of the indigenous Law, which was poor in general conceptions and legal principles, and no longer availed to

[c] Cf. §§ 7-9.

satisfy the expanding legal necessities imposed by advance of culture;

(2) in the notion of the Roman as being a Law available for the world in general (ratio scripta);

(3) in the idea and theory of the Middle Ages as to the continuity of the older Roman and the Germanic Empire.[a]

The reception was brought about—

(a) by the teaching of Roman Law at the newly founded German Universities;

(β) by the calling of men learned in the law (doctores iuris) to the higher public offices, to the councils of cities, and to the highest courts of the Empire and the Principalities;

(γ) by the practice of the Spiritual courts; and

(δ) by the rise of a popular literature of a Roman Law, which helped to naturalise it in the circles of unlearned men of business.[b] The immediate validity of Roman Law for Germany found legal expression in the ordinance of 1495 as to the Imperial 'Kammergericht.'[c]

[a] 'The Holy Roman Empire of the German nation.'

[b] Exx. of this were Ulrich Tengler's 'Laienspiegel,' and the 'Klagspiegel,' from 1516 edited by Seb. Brant.

[c] See Bryce, 'Holy Roman Empire,' pp. 172, *sq.*, 396, *sq.*

§ 14. The Reform and Advance of Jurisprudence in the Sixteenth and Seventeenth Centuries.

The revival of Classical studies gradually also gave an incomparable impetus to Jurisprudence, brought a new method into dominance, and led to a more thorough and more elegant treatment of Roman Law, which now first acquired a truly scientific stamp.

Roman Law began to be studied historically, critically and exegetically for its own sake, as a portion of classical antiquity, without immediate reference to practical application; and an endeavour was made to penetrate to the spirit of the classical Roman jurists, because the classical literature in general (especially the then newly discovered remains of the ante-Justinian jurisprudence) was applied to the interpretation of Iustinian's legal system. Pioneers of the new tendency were Andreas Alciatus in Italy (ob. 1550), and Ulrich Zasius in Germany (Recorder and Professor at Freiburg), who was born in 1461 and died in 1535.

The new method was fully developed in the hands of the FRENCH School, with whom the Romanistic jurisprudence reached its climax, and who founded a SECOND epoch in the history of the Roman Law in modern times. The two Coryphaei of this school were—

Jacobus Cujacius (Cujas), born 1522, ob. 1590, He was a professor at Bourges, and the greatest interpreter of the sources of Law—which he expounded thoroughly, and in nearly all parts and passages. He struck out a new path for the critical and historical treatment of the Roman Law. Cujas' chief works are: 'Observationes et emendationes,' in 28 Books, and commentaries on the fragments in the Digests of Africanus, Papinian and Paulus.[a]

Hugo Donellus (Doneau), born 1527. He was a professor at Bourges, Heidelberg, Leyden and Altdorf, and died in 1591. Doneau was a many-sided scientific opponent of Cujas. He introduced the systematic arrangement of Law by his 'Commentarii iuris civilis,' but was also very eminent in exegesis.[b]

The following also must be mentioned—

Franc. Duaren-us, born 1509, ob. 1559. He was teacher of Doneau.

Franc. Hotomanus (Hotman), born 1524, ob. 1590 at Basle. He was an erudite, philological and antiquarian jurist.

Barn. Brisson-ius, born 1531, ob. 1591, was an eminent lexicographer and legal historian with more of an antiquarian tendency.[c]

Jac. Gothofredus (Godefroy), born 1587, ob. 1652, was a legal historian of remarkable learning, although more a philologer and antiquary than a jurist.[d]

The method of the French School wrought a revival in the seventeenth and eighteenth centuries in the Netherlands. The so-called DUTCH School of the

[a] Edd. of his 'Opera omnia,' 1658, 1722, 1757, 1758.

[b] 'Opera omnia,' 1762.

[c] Cf. note to § 5.

[d] See notes to §§ 7, 9.

'elegant jurisprudence' preferred to cultivate jurisprudence on its philological and antiquarian side, and distinguished themselves by painstaking application of the classical literature to the criticism and exegesis of the law-sources and the history of Roman Law, and thus sometimes certainly wasted labour in trifles. The leaders of this school, who were eminent as well for sagacity as for comprehensive learning applied to the sources, were—

Gerhard Noodt, born 1647, ob. 1725. He was a professor at Leyden, celebrated for compressed brevity of style. He has been called 'the Dutch Cujas.'

Ant. Schulting, born 1659, ob. 1734.[a]

[a] See note to § 8.

Corn. v. Bynkershoek, born 1673, ob. 1743. He was President of the Great Council, and a discreet investigator in the different departments of Law.

As noteworthy representatives of the modern scientific tendency to whom also we must call attention are the following:—

In Italy: Ant. Faber, born 1557, ob. 1624. He was President of the Senate and Governor of the Savoy, a jurist highly gifted and learned, but treating the Roman Law with far too great temerity, which became almost proverbial.

In Spain: a teacher of Law in the University of Salamanca—Ramos del Manzano, born 1605, ob. 1683; Suarez de Mendoza, ob. 1681, and Fernandez de Retes, born 1620, ob. 1678. They were celebrated for the thoroughness of their inquiries and many-sided humanistic culture, often paraded by them.

In Germany: Hub. Giphanius (Giffen), born 1534, ob. 1609, was a personal opponent of Doneau in Altdorf. Amongst the German jurists he was the most important leader of the modern school, especially in exegesis. He has been called 'The German Cujas.' To the eighteenth century belongs

Joh. Gottl. Heineccius (Heineke), born 1681, ob. 1741. He was a thoroughly learned master of the Roman as of the German Law, of wide culture, and has rendered good service to the history of Roman Law.

§ 15. The German Practical Jurists.

The rapid advance of Jurisprudence and deepening of legal study wrought by the French School and their successors made little impression upon Germany. The new method gained no footing, and further, men still allowed themselves to be dominated by the authority of commentators.[a] The traditional material of Law alone for immediate practical application, in the form of compendia, commentaries, collections of controversies and the like, was converted into a *usus modernus Pandectarum* (iurisprudentia forensis), in which Roman and German rules of law, ancient and modern ideas, were uncritically thrown together. Contemporaneously with this spiritless practical jurisprudence, a rationalistic Law of Nature [b] held sway. This, with its capricious treatment of the subject, hindered both a correct apprehension of positive law and a grasp of legal relations. Although the dominant jurisprudence had no scientific character, its practical tendency must not hinder the recognition of such merits as it possessed—

(1) as a counterpoise to the method pursued by the French and Dutch Schools, to the danger of confounding jurisprudence with learning that was purely unpractical, philological, antiquarian, and

(2) in its successful effort to shape the Roman Law, in spite of its mistakes and misapprehensions, into a Common Law of practical use for the present time.

[a] Cf. § 12.

[b] Cf. § 2.

§ 16. The Historical School of Law.

The rapid advance of philological and historical studies which dates from the end of the eighteenth century exercised also a lively influence on Jurisprudence. After that Hugo (1764–1844) had in the most express way opposed to the spiritless practical tendency of which we have spoken his historical and systematic method, and had promoted the scientific study of Law for its own sake, the bane of its mechanical treatment, which in Germany was threatening Jurisprudence with complete stagnation, was removed by the epoch-making work of Friedrich Carl von SAVIGNY. He was born in 1779, until 1842 was a professor at Berlin, and after having been Minister of Justice from 1842 to 1848, died there in 1861. Savigny was the greatest jurist of modern times, and for long was generally recognised as the first authority in legal science. The work in question was his treatise upon 'The Law of Possession' (1803). To this we must add the foundation (1814) by him of the HISTORICAL School of jurists, who have endeavoured to comprehend the Roman Law in its purity and its own spirit. The efforts of the Historical School—in agreement with their principle that the Law of every people has sprung from its nationality, and has come into existence historically[a]—were exerted to place Roman Law on the basis of historical investigation, as well as to treat Positive Law as an organism that has grown out of the relationships of life, and is adequate to them. This still dominant method of the Historical School, the foundation of which is to be designated the THIRD epoch of the Roman Law in modern times, has raised to a height before unattained, not only the criticism and exegesis of the sources of Law and legal history, but especially also the systematic arrangement of Roman Law.

[a] Cf. Holland pp. 50-51.

As the most eminent representatives of this school, who by profound labours and by teaching have advanced the Romanistic jurisprudence, we must mention—

Christ. Gottl. Haubold (1766–1824), whose labours in part preceded the foundation of the Historical School. He was a jurist at the same time theoretical and practical; and as an investigator of the sources, and an historian of Law and editor, distinguished by great learning.

Joh. Christ. Hasse (1779–1830).

G. Friedrich Puchta (1798–1846), eminent as a legal historian, but especially as an interpreter, for an acute method and exact development of legal conceptions, as well as by a spirited and elegant style.

C. F. Mühlenbruch (1785–1843).

H. E. Dirksen (1790–1868), legal historian, lexicographer, and original critic of the sources.

Friedrich Ludw. v. Keller (1799–1860), of note as a legal historian, especially for his original treatment of the Roman Civil Procedure; eminent also as an interpreter, and in the exegesis of the sources by sagacity and practical insight.

Carl Ad. v. Vangerow (1808–1870).

Ed. Böcking (1802–1870), distinguished by comprehensive philological learning, as a careful, critical editor of the sources, and as treating the Roman classical Law with originality and depth of thought.

C. Georg v. Wächter (1797–1880), especially an interpreter of Law of a more practical tendency, who has done good service to the scientific depth and many-sided development of the modern Law by the comprehensive value of his penetrating and profound investigations for the shaping of practical legal life.

For a comprehensive survey of the history of Roman Law in various European countries since the Renaissance, and biographical notices, see Rivier, 'Introduction historique au droit Romain,' pp. 555–637. For England see Hale, 'History of the Common Law,' ch. ii.; Reeves, 'History of the

English Law;' Savigny, 'History of the Roman Law during the Middle Ages,' vol. i. ed. by Cathcart, 1829; Spence, 'Inquiry into the origin of the Laws and Political Institutions of Modern Europe,' &c., 1826, and 'Equitable Jurisdiction of the Court of Chancery,' vol. i. 1846; Güterbock, 'Bracton and his relation to the Roman Law,' ed. by Coxe, 1866; Clark, 'Practical Jurisprudence,' pp. 306–310; Hunter, 'Roman Law in the Order of a Code,' 2nd ed. 1885, pp. 107–116. For Scotland see Lord Mackenzie, 'Studies in Roman Law,' pp. 42, *sq.*

Chronological résumé of principal matters noticed in §§ 7–16, from the Decemviral Legislation.[1]

A.U.C.	B.C.	
305	449.	Promulgation of the Twelve Tables.
387	367.	Leges Liciniae Sextiae.
		First Praetor Urbanus.
450	304.	Ius Flavianum.
468	286.	Lex Hortensia.
circ. 500	254.	T. Coruncanius fl.
... 512	242.	Praetor inter peregrinos.
... 550	204.	Ius Aelianum.
... 650	104.	Q. Mucius Scaevola fl.
... 660	94.	M. Porcius Cato "
... 700	54.	S. Sulpicius "
... 705	49.	Lex Rubria.
709	45.	Lex Iulia Municipalis.
725	29–14 A.D.	Octavius Augustus. Labeo fl.
	A.D.	
	4.	Lex Iulia (de maritandis ordinibus).
	9.	Lex Papia Poppaea.
	131.	SCtum giving effect to Edictum Salvianum (Hadrian) Salvius Iulianus, Gaius, etc. fl.

[1] Comp. the comprehensive Tables in Rivier, pp. 129–33, 277–80, 437–40, or Roby, pp. cclxxiv., *sqq.*

A.D.
212. Papinian put to death.
228. Ulpian . . . .
284. Accession of Diocletian.
circ. 300. Gregorianus Codex.
330. Imperial Government transferred to Constantinople.
circ. 350. Hermogenianus Codex.
426. Law of Citations.
438. Publication of Codex Theodosianus.
506. Lex Romana Visigothorum.
527. Accession of Justinian.
529. Publication of Codex vetus.
533. „ „ Institutes.
„ „ „ Digest.
534. „ „ Codex repetitus.
535–564. „ „ Novels.
565. Death of Justinian.
886–910. Publication of *Basilica*.
circ. 1100. Rise of the Law School at Bologna; Glossators.
.... 1150. Vacarius fl. Oxford.
.... 1200. Azo „
.... 1250. Accorso „
.... 1357. Bartolus „
1522–90. Cujas „ French School.
1527–91. Doneau „
1647–1725. Noodt „ Dutch School.
1681–1741. Heineke „
[1748–1832. Bentham.]
1803. Publication of Savigny's treatise on Possession.
1814. Foundation of the German Historical School of Jurisprudence.
[1828–1832. Delivery of Austin's 'Lectures on Jurisprudence': English ANALYTICAL School.[a]
1861. Publication of Sir H. Maine's 'Ancient Law': English HISTORICAL School.[b]]

[a] See 'Fortnightly Review,' Nos. clxxix. pp. 475-487, clxxx. pp. 682, *sqq.*

[b] Ibid., Nos. clxxix. pp. 487-492, clxxx. pp. 114, *sqq.*

A.D.

[1872. New scheme published by the Council of Legal Education: some knowledge of the Roman Civil Law rendered compulsory for Examinations at the Inns of Court.]

THE ROMAN PRIVATE LAW.

BOOK I.

THE ORIGINATION OF RIGHTS AND EXERCISE THEREOF.[a]

[a] See Holland, p. 60 ad fin. (comparing James Mill 'Essay on Jurisprudence,' p. 4); and p. 62 for his definition of a 'legal right.'

CHAPTER I.

COMMENCEMENT AND TERMINATION OF RIGHTS.

§ 17. In General.

Every right supposes a SUBJECT,[b] or Person capable of being subject of rights, an OBJECT which can be governed by Law, and a FACT with a legal basis, *i.e.*, an external act or event by which, in consequence of an existing rule of law, the Object is brought into relation with the Subject, is brought under the control of his will. A right arises, is acquired by a person, when the Object is brought under the legal control of a Subject of rights; it terminates, passes from the person, upon the introduction of a Fact which destroys that control.

[b] Cf. § 6 and Lindley, 'Intn. to Jurisprud.' App. ii.; also the different terminology of Holland, pp. 69, *sqq.*

Every acquisition of a right is either original, immediate, 'primordial,' *i.e.*, the right in question arises altogether for the first time as a new one in the person of the party acquiring (*e.g.*, acquisition of property by occupation or prescription); or it is 'derivative,' *i.e.*, the right already exists in the person

BOOK I. Chapter I.

of another, by whom it is transferred to the party acquiring (*e.g.*, Traditio).[a] That acquisition of a right is called 'Succession' by which an already existing right without change of its content[b] passes from the person of the one hitherto entitled, or 'auctor,' immediately to another Subject by virtue of a juristic relation between the two, which accordingly itself is governed by the earlier right.

[a] The case is similar with the loss of a right.

[b] Cf. Holland, p. 119.

> Ulp.: Nemo plus iuris ad alium transferre potest, quam ipse haberet.—D. 50, 17, 54.[1]
>
> Paul.: Non debeo melioris condicionis esse, quam auctor meus, a quo ius in me transit.—l. 175, § 1 eod.[2]

A distinction is made between 'singular' and 'universal' Succession, according as it has for its object a separate right of property or the totality of the proprietary rights of another as a unit.[c]

[c] Ibid., and see Bell, 'Dicty. of Scotch Law,' s. vv. Cf. §§ 6, 77.

> Pomp.: Heres in omne ius mortui, non tantum singularum rerum dominium succedit.—l. 37, D. de A. v. O. H. 29, 2.[3]

The Fact, to which the Law attaches the commencement or termination of a right for a person, representing the ground of such commencement, acquisition or termination, consists either in an expression of will of such person (as a contract) or in an external event independent of his will (as in lapse of time).[d] In contrast with the voluntary extinction or surrender of a right, which is 'alienatio' in its wider sense, exemplified by Conveyance (or alienatio in its narrower sense), is extinction that is necessary, or not of choice.[e]

[d] Cf. §§ 84, sq., 130.

[e] Cf. §§ 25, 97.

---

[1] No one can make over to another more right than he himself had.

[2] I must not be in a better position than my predecessor from whom the right passes to me.

[3] An heir succeeds to the whole rights of the deceased, not merely to the ownership of the several things.

The Expression of the Will as Ground of the Commencement and Termination of Rights.

§ 18. Nature and Species of Juristic Acts; Legal Transactions in particular.

Juristic Acts are expressions of the Will, positive or negative, which have a legal result, whether this lie in the intention, more or less conscious, of the agent, or take place independently of, even in opposition to, it. To acts of this kind belong Legal Transactions,[a] *i.e.*, the declarations of will which are immediately directed to the commencement, extinction or change of a legal relation, and designed for it. To acts never intended to have a legal result belong those that are disallowed, illegal, 'delicta.'

[a] By Holland named generically 'Juristic Acts,' (p. 85). Cf. Markby, s. 235.

Legal transactions are divided into 'unilateral' (*e.g.*, a disposition by last will) and 'bilateral' or mutual acts (agreements), according as the result intended by them is produced through the declaration of the will of one person, or through the consentient declaration of the will of two or several persons in relation with one another.

> Ulp.: Est **pactio** duorum pluriumve in idem placitum et (?) consensus.—D. 2, 14, 1, 2.[1]

Acts are further divided into 'onerous,' 'gratuitous,' or 'lucrative;' and into those between living persons, or transactions 'inter vivos,' and those on account of death, or transactions 'mortis causa.'

An act with juristic result can be undertaken only by one who is not merely capable of being subject of right, but at the same time has the capacity to act, *i.e.*, possesses the capacity himself actually to exercise the will which attaches to him as a Person.[b]

[b] Upon the grounds of imperfect and limited capacity to act, see §§ 58, *sqq.*

Every legal transaction is composed of two elements

---

[1] A *pactio* is the determination and consent of two or more persons with the same object.

BOOK I. Chapter I.

—the inward one of the direction of the will, and the outward one of its declaration: there must be agreement between these. The legal result of a declaration of will presupposes that the will which is declared is the actual will of the agent. But since the inward element of the direction of will eludes examination, the legal result is already annexed by the provisions of Law to the fact of the declaration, as the outward manifestation of the will; and that which is declared is regarded as having been actually intended, so long as no proof is afforded from external circumstances that free will directed to the substance, or to the legal result of the declaration, has been absent. There must be no 'reservatio mentalis,' *i.e.*, no appeal is admitted to any such consideration as that the declaration was inwardly willed as such, but not its substance.[a] As actual will, Law recognises only that which is outwardly free, that is, self-determining.

[a] But see below, ad fin.

The freedom of the will is infringed, though not completely extinguished, by illegal influence of the determination, especially by—

1. Coercion,[b] 'vis compulsiva,' 'metus,' *i.e.*, illegal menace of a greater evil, which awakens well-founded fear—no matter whether produced by word or by deed—so as to move the other person to a declaration of will. A compulsory transaction in Law is not null from the commencement, but can be disputed by a person that has been under pressure.[c]

[b] Cf. Markby, ss. 254-259.

[c] See §§ 21, 28, 30, 137.

Ulp.: Ait praetor: QVOD METVS CAVSA GESTVM ERIT, RATVM NON HABEBO. Olim ita edicebatur QVOD VI METVSVE CAVSA; vis enim fiebat mentio propter necessitatem impositam contrariam voluntati; . . . sed postea detracta est vis mentio ideo, quia quodcumque vi atroci fit, id metu quoque fieri videtur.—l. 1, D. h. t. = qu, metus, c. 4, 2.[1]

---

[1] The praetor says:—'I will not countenance that which shall have been done out of intimidation.' Formerly the Edict used to run thus:—'That which because of violence or intimi-

Book I. Chapter I.

Paul.: Vis est maioris rei impetus, qui repelli non potest.—l. 2 eod.[1]

Cic. Tusc. iv. 7, 14: Est **metus** opinio impendentis mali quod **intolerabile** esse videatur.[2]

Ulp.: **Metum** accipiendum Labeo dicit non quemlibet timorem, sed **maioris mali.**—l. 5, D. h. t.[3]

Imp. Dioclet.: Nec tamen quilibet metus ad rescindenda ea, quae consensu terminata sunt, sufficit, sed talem metum probari oportet, qui salutis periculum vel corporis cruciatum contineat. —C. 2, 4, 13.[4]

Gai.: Metum autem **non vani** hominis, sed qui merito et in homine constantissimo cadat, ad hoc Edictum pertinere dicemus.—l. 6, h. t.[5]

Ulp.: Metum **praesentem** accipere debemus, non suspicionem inferendi eius; . . . Pomponius ait, metum **illatum** accipiendum, i.e. si illatus est timor ab aliquo.[a]—l. 9 pr. eod.[6]

[a] Cf. § 91.

Paul.: Si metu coactus adii hereditatem, puto

---

dation;' violence, that is, was mentioned with reference to the imposition of necessity against the will; . . . but afterwards the mention of violence was withdrawn, because whatever happens by violent force may also be regarded as happening through intimidation.

[1] *Vis* is the violence of something stronger, which cannot be withstood.

[2] *Metus* is the thought of immediate evil which seems to be unbearable.

[3] Labeo says that *metus* must be taken to be, not any intimidation without distinction, but that of a greater evil.

[4] But not every possible *metus* is enough to set aside matters which have been concluded by agreement, but such *metus* must be proved as embraces danger to life or torture to the body.

[5] Now it is not the fear of a timid man, but what may reasonably befall even the most self-contained man, that we shall have to speak of as connected with this Edict.

[6] We must understand a fear that has already arisen, not the suspicion that it will be awakened. . . . Pomponius says, we must understand the fear to be such as has already been occasioned, *i.e.*, if it has been caused by some person.

Book I. Chapter I.

me heredem effici: quia, quamvis si liberum esset, noluissem, tamen coactus volui.—l. 21, § 5 eod.[1]

Ulp.: Nihil consensui tam contrarium est, . . . quam vis atque metus; quem comprobare, contra bonos mores est.—D. 50, 17, 116 pr.[2]

[a] Cf. Bell, s. v.

2. By Fraud, 'dolus,'[a] 'fraus,' *i.e.*, intentional creation of, or even cherishing, a mistake as to a fact, so as to bring about a declaration of will which is occasioned by this alone. Somewhat wider is the general idea of 'dolus,' as being crafty, dishonest conduct impairing the 'fides' or confidence required by positive law.[b] The result is here the same as with Coercion.[c]

[b] § 115. Cf. §§ 28, 108, 122.

[c] Cf. §§ 28, 137.

Ulp.: **Dolum malum** Servius quidem ita definit: machinationem quandam alterius decipiendi causa, cum aliud simulatur et aliud agitur. Labeo autem, posse et sine simulatione id agi, ut quis circumveniatur; posse et sine dolo malo aliud agi, aliud simulari, sicuti faciunt, qui per eiusmodi dissimulationem deserviant et tuentur vel sua vel aliena: itaque sic definiit, dolum malum esse omnem calliditatem, fallaciam, machinationem ad circumveniendum, fallendum, decipiendum alterum adhibitam. Labeonis definitio vera est.—l. 1, § 2, D. de dolo. 4, 3.[3]

---

[1] If I have entered upon an inheritance under the pressure of intimidation, I am of opinion that I am constituted heir, because although if I had been free I should have refused, nevertheless I consented under coercion.

[2] Nothing is so incompatible with consent . . . as *vis* and *metus*: to sanction such would be contrary to sound morals.

[3] Fraud was indeed thus defined by Servius: 'a certain inveiglement so as to deceive another, when one thing is pretended and another is done.' But by Lab.: 'that it is possible also without pretence to deceive a man; that it is possible also without fraud for one thing to be done, another feigned, as they do who by such a concealment of truth maintain and protect either their own or others' property:' accordingly, he thus defines it: '*dolus malus* is all sharp practice, deceit, device employed to overreach, deceive, delude another.' Labeo's is the right definition.

Id.: Pomponius ait, in pretio emptionis et venditionis naturaliter licere contrahentibus se circumvenire.—D. 4, 4, 16, 4.[1]

On the other hand, bare Mistake as the cause of a declaration of will, or mistake in the motive, as a rule does not affect the juristic result.[a]

Paul.: Id quoque quod ob causam datur, puta quod negotia mea adiuta ab eo putavi, licet non sit factum, quia donare volui, quamvis falso mihi persuaserim, repeti non posse.—D. 12, 6, 65, 2.[2]

Moreover, Mistake and Ignorance have to be considered in many other relations, especially as presupposing the protection of the Law against the disadvantageous results of certain omissions and of the commencement of certain legal relations,[b] and consequently, the distinction becomes important between mistake as to a maxim of Law and mistake as to Fact (ignorantia s. error iuris, facti).[c]

Id.: Regula est **iuris** quidem **ignorantiam** cuique nocere, **facti** vero **ignorantiam** non nocere. . . . Minoribus xxv. annis ius ignorare permissum est, quod et in feminis in quibusdam causis dicitur.—Sed facti ignorantia ita demum cuique non nocet, si non ei summa negligentia obiciatur; quid enim, si omnes in civitate sciant, quod ille solus ignoret?—l. 9 pr. § 2, D. de iur. ign. 22, 6.[3]

[a] 'Falsa causa non nocet,' see Brown, s. vv.

[b] *E.g.*, §§ 80, 135, 171.

[c] See Lindley, App. p. xxi.; Markby, ss. 260-272; Pollock, 'Principles of Contract,' ch. viii.; Brown, s. vv.

---

[1] Pomp. says that in purchase and sale it is naturally allowed the contracting parties to overreach themselves in respect of price.

[2] That also which is given for some reason, as because I have believed my business was promoted by the man, although it has not been so, cannot be recalled, because I have willed to give it, although I have had a false impression.

[3] The rule is that ignorance of Law prejudices a person, but ignorance of Fact does not. . . . Ignorance of the Law by those that are under twenty-five years of age is tolerated; which is said also of women in certain cases. But ignorance of Fact

Book I. Chapter I.

Papin.: Iuris ignorantia non prodest adquirere volentibus, suum vero petentibus non nocet.—I. 7 eod.[1]

The declaration of the will can in general take any possible form; so that there are 'informal' legal transactions; and it may be either express or tacit. An 'express' declaration consists in an intimation that gives immediate and exclusive expression to the will in question, by word or by act; a 'tacit' in an act or a forbearance which by itself has an independent meaning, but nevertheless affords a certain conclusion as to the will—which is an inferred act or one of 'facta concludentia.' Mere silence does not amount to consent.[a]

[a] Cf. §§ 27, 46, 52, 123, and also §§ 97, 103.

Paul.: Sed etiam **tacite** consensu convenire intelligitur. Et ideo si debitori meo reddiderim cautionem, videtur inter nos convenisse, ne peterem.—D. 2, 14, 2.[2]

Id.: Qui tacet, non utique fatetur; sed tamen verum est eum non negare.—D. 50, 17, 142.[3]

For some legal transactions the Law requires the observance of a certain form or solemnity, as in testamentary dispositions. In the older Roman Law the form—gerere, dicere (verborum, litterarum, figura)—was in all transactions an essential element of the declaration of will itself.[b]

[b] Cf. §§ 7, 115.

A declaration which demonstrably does not answer

---

merely does not prejudice a person, unless the highest degree of negligence be imputed to him; for how is it if all in the city know what he alone does not know?

[1] Ignorance of Law is of no advantage to those wishing to acquire, but it does not prejudice those who claim what is their own.

[2] But by an agreement is even understood a silent assent. And therefore it would appear if I have returned the security to my debtor, that we have agreed I should not sue.

[3] A man by his silence makes no absolute admission; but nevertheless it is certain he does not repudiate.

to the will has in Law just as little signification as a will that is not declared at all. The non-agreement of the will with the declaration can be—

(1.) Unintentional, whether the party making the declaration express himself incorrectly—which gives rise to interpretation of the will—or is mistaken as to the substance of his own declaration, as by confusion of persons or objects; or if in contracts each party truly intend something different, where, however, the contract is in fact void by reason of the want of consensus due to the mistake.[a]

[a] Cf. § 120.

Paul.: Qui aliud dicit quam vult, neque id dicit quod vox significat, quia non vult, neque id quod vult, quia id non loquitur.—D. 34, 5, 3.[1]

Ulp.: Quotiens volens alium heredem scribere, alium scripserit in corpore hominis errans, . . . placet, neque eum heredem esse, qui scriptus est, quoniam voluntate deficitur, neque eum, quem voluit, quoniam scriptus non est.—Et si in re quis erraverit utputa dum vult lancem relinquere, vestem leget, neutrum debebitur.—D. 28, 5, 9, 1.[2]

Id.: Non videntur, qui errant, consentire.—D. 50, 17, 116, 2.[3]

Pomp.: In omnibus negotiis contrahendis, . . . si error aliquis intervenit, ut aliud sentiat puta qui emit aut qui conducit, aliud qui cum his contrahit, nihil valet, quod acti sit.—l. 57, D. de O. et A. 44, 7.[4]

---

[1] He who speaks otherwise than he means says neither what the words express, because he does not mean them, nor what he means, because he does not express it.

[2] Whenever he[b] has instituted another as heir than his intention was to do, from mistake as to the person, the opinion is that neither the one whose name is written is heir, because this was not the testator's intention, nor he that was intended, since his name is not that written. And if a person have made a mistake in a thing, for example, whilst he would leave a lance, he bequeaths a garment, neither of these will be binding.

[b] A testator.

[3] They that are mistaken do not appear to consent.

[4] In contracting any matter, if a mistake arise so that, for

Book I. Chapter I.

Ulp.: Si igitur me fundum emere putarem Cornelianum, tu mihi te vendere Sempronianum putasti: quia in corpore dissensimus emptio nulla est.—l. 9 pr. D. de C. E. 18, 1.[1]

(2) Intentional, so that only the declaration as such, not its substance, is willed; sometimes palpably, as when the declaration of will is given as pleasantry, in mirth, and the like; sometimes covertly, but within the knowledge of the other party, as when the transaction which has been concluded is intended only as a nominal transaction, behind which possibly is concealed another that has actually been intended. This is 'simulatio.'[a] From simulatio we must distinguish those nominal transactions—especially a sale 'nummo uno'—in which, for the sake of solemn form, 'dicis gratia,' were embodied certain declarations of will recognised by the ius civile; *e.g.*, mancipatio as intended to transfer ownership, commencement and extinction of the family relationships, and making a testament.[b]

[a] Cf. §§ 120, 148.

[b] Cf. § 79.

Modest.: Contractus imaginarii . . . iuris vinculum non obtinent.—l. 54, D. de O. et A.[2]

Ulp.: Si quis donationis causa minoris vendat, venditio valet: totiens enim dicimus, in totum venditionem non valere, quotiens universa venditio donationis causa facta est.—l. 38, D. de C. E.[3]

---

instance, the purchaser or hirer has intended something else than he who contracts with them, the whole transaction is void.

[1] If, accordingly, I suppose I was purchasing the Cornelian estate, but you that you were selling me the Sempronian, the purchase is void, because we have not been of the same mind upon the object.

[2] Nominal contracts have not the effect of a legal obligation.

[3] If any one in consideration of a gift buys at a lower price, the sale is good; for we only say that the sale is entirely invalid when the whole sale has been effected in consideration of a gift.

Plus valere quod agitur, quam quod simulate concipitur.—Rubr. C. 4, 22.[1]

§ 19. Subject-matter of Legal Transactions. Accessory Provisions.

First, the substance of a legal transaction can in general be all that the individual as a private person can legally intend, with the exception of what naturally or juristically is impossible, as well as what contradicts absolute provisions of the Law,[a] or the dictates of morality and propriety (boni mores), recognised by positive law.[b]

[a] Cf. § 4.

[b] For exx. see §§ 21, 70, 105, 122, 124.

Cels.: Impossibilium nulla obligatio est.—D. 50, 17, 185.[2]

Ulp.: Generaliter novimus, turpes stipulationes nullius esse momenti.—l. 26, D. de V. O. 45, 1.[3]

Multifarious as may be the possible subject-matter of a legal transaction, the following ingredients admit of distinction:—

1. 'Essentialia negotii,' essential or necessary elements inherent in the idea of a particular transaction, and conditioning its existence, *e.g.*, settlement of the price in purchase and hire.[c]

[c] Cf. § 159.

2. 'Naturalia negotii,' natural or normal elements, which, while governed by positive law, result as of course from the nature of the particular transaction, and therefore in the absence of any different arrangement are taken to have been tacitly intended:[d] such are contemporaneous performance in a purchase,[e] transfer of risk and enjoyment to the purchaser upon the conclusion of the contract.[f]

[d] Cf. § 4.

[e] § 122.

[f] § 124.

Ulp.: In primis sciendum est, in hoc iudicio[g] . . . id praestari, quod inter contrahentes

[g] Sc. empti.

---

1 What is actually transacted avails before what is ostensibly expressed.

2 No obligation can exist in respect of things impossible.

3 It is matter of common knowledge with us that disgraceful stipulations are of no force.

actum est; quodsi nihil convenit, tunc ea praestabuntur, quae naturaliter insunt huius iudicii potestate.—l. 11, § 1, D. de A. E. V. 19, 1.[1]

3. 'Accidentalia,' casual or extraordinary elements, *i.e.*, those dependent on mere private caprice, and not to be assumed without special declaration of will. These are—

(*a*) accessory provisions in the wider sense, such as all variations of the 'naturalia;'

(*β*) supplementary contracts modifying, strengthening, or curtailing the principal contract, such as conventional penalty, security, proviso avoiding a contract;

(*γ*) accessory provisions in the narrower sense, which limit the effect of the declaration of will itself, or self-imposed limitations, such as 'condicio' in the restricted sense,[a] 'dies,' 'modus.' A transaction free from these is called a 'purum negotium.'

[a] In the wider sense 'condicio' is every express arrangement in a legal transaction.

Papin.: Actus legitimi . . . veluti (e)mancipatio acceptilatio, hereditatis aditio, servi optio, datio tutoris, in totum vitiantur per temporis vel condicionis adiectionem.—l. 77, D. de R. J.[2]

Next of CONDITIONS, and first of their nature and varieties.

A 'condicio' is the accessory provision which makes the operation of a declaration arbitrarily depend upon the occurrence or non-occurrence of a future, uncertain event, and as such is either 'affirmative' or 'negative.'

---

[1] One must know before all that in this action is carried out what has been arranged by the parties; but if nothing have been arrived at, such things will have to be carried out as naturally are comprehended in the operation of this action.

[2] Legal acts . . . such as [e]mancipation, an acquittance, the taking up an inheritance, the selection of a slave, the nomination of a guardian, become entirely invalid by the addition of a limitation as to time or of a condition.

According as it determines the beginning or the end of the operation of the transaction, it is a 'suspensive' or a 'resolutory' condition. 'Conditiones iuris' (s. 'quae tacite insunt'), *i.e.*, the actual prerequisites of its operation which already lie in the nature of the transaction[a] are not true conditions; just as little the conditions imposed upon an event present, or past, or of necessary occurrence.

[a] § 171.

Sub condicione stipulatio fit, cum in aliquem casum differtur obligatio, ut, si aliquid factum fuerit aut non fuerit, stipulatio committatur, veluti: 'si Titius consul factus fuerit, quinque aureos dare spondes?'—§ 4, I. de V. O. 3, 15.[1]

Ulp.:—si quidem hoc actum est, ut meliore allata condicione ab emptione discedatur, erit pura emptio, quae **sub condicione resolvitur**; sin autem hoc actum est, ut perficiatur emptio nisi melior condicio offeratur, erit emptio condicionalis.—D. 18, 2, 2 pr.[2]

Id.: Stipulationem, quae propter causam dotis fiat, constat habere in se condicionem hanc: si nuptiae fuerint secutae.—l. 21, D. de J. D. 23, 3.[3]

Inst. iii. 15, 6: Condiciones, quae ad praeteritum vel praesens tempus referuntur, aut statim infirmant obligationem aut omnino non differunt, veluti: 'si Titius consul fuerit,' vel, 'si Maevius

---

[1] A stipulation is made conditionally when the obligation is postponed until some event, so that the stipulation takes effect if something come to pass or does not come to pass: for instance, 'Do you undertake to give me five *aurei*, if Titius become consul?'

[2] . . . if this have been done so as to admit of a withdrawal of the purchase if a better bid follow, it will be an unconditional purchase, which is performed conditionally; but if it have been done so that the purchase shall be completed unless a better bid be forthcoming, the purchase will be conditional.

[3] It is well-established law that a stipulation which arises in consideration of dowry contains this condition: if the marriage shall have followed.

Book I. Chapter I.

vivit, dare spondes?' nam si ea ita non sunt, nihil valet stipulatio; sin autem ita se habent, statim valet. Quae enim per rerum naturam certa sunt, non morantur obligationem, licet apud nos incerta sint.[1]

Ulp.: Qui sub condicione stipulatur, quae omnimodo exstitura est, pure videtur stipulari.—D. 46, 2, 9, 1.[2]

Furthermore, distinction is made between conditions that are 'potestative' and 'casual' and between those that are 'possible,' 'impossible,' and 'illegal' (turpes condiciones).

Imp. Iustinian.: Sin autem aliquid sub condicione relinquatur vel **casuali** vel **potestativa,** vel **mixta,** quarum eventus ex fortuna, vel ex honoratae personae voluntate, vel ex utroque pendeat . . . C. 6, 51, l. un. § 7.[3]

Papin.: Si ita stipulatus fuero: 'si in Capitolium non ascenderis,' vel 'Alexandriam non ieris, centum dari spondes?' non statim committetur stipulatio, . . . sed cum certum esse coeperit, te Capitolium ascendere vel Alexandriam ire non posse.—D. 45, 1, 115.[4]

---

[1] Conditions which relate to past or present time either at once invalidate the obligation, or do not at all postpone it, for instance: 'Do you undertake to give so and so, if Titius has been consul?' or, 'if Maevius is alive?' For if these be not facts, the stipulation is void; if they are facts, it is at once binding. For such things as are actually certain do not suspend the obligation, although uncertain as regards our knowledge of them.

[2] He that stipulates under a condition which certainly will happen is regarded as stipulating unconditionally.

[3] But if anything have been left by testament under a condition subject to the caprice of the legatee, or mixed, the result of which is dependent upon hazard or upon the will of the person provided for, or upon both . . .

[4] If I shall have stipulated thus: 'Do you undertake that a hundred be given, if you should not go up to the Capitol, or should not go to Alexandria?' the stipulation will not take effect at once . . . but when it shall begin to be certain that you cannot go up to the Capitol or go to Alexandria.

Book I. Chapter I.

Paul. iii. 4[b], § 1: Condicionum duo sunt genera, aut enim **possibilis** est aut **impossibilis**; possibilis est, quae per rerum naturam admitti potest, impossibilis, quae non potest.[1]

Gai. iii. 98: Si quis sub ea condicione stipuletur, quae existere non potest, veluti: 'si digito coelum tetigerit,' inutilis est stipulatio. Sed legatum sub impossibili condicione relictum nostri praeceptores proinde deberi putant, ac si sine condicione relictum esset; diversae scholae auctores non minus legatum inutile existimant, quam stipulationem; et sane vix idonea diversitatis ratio reddi potest.[a] [2]

Ulp.: Obtinuit, impossibiles condiciones testamento adscriptas pro nullis habendas.—l 3, D. de C. et D. 35, 1.[3]

Iul.: Stipulatio hoc modo concepta: 'si heredem me non feceris, tantum dare spondes?' inutilis est, quia **contra bonos mores** est haec stipulatio.—D. 45, 1, 61.[4]

Paul.: Condiciones, quae contra bonos mores inseruntur[b] remittendae sunt, veluti 'si parentibus suis alimenta non praestiterit.'—D. 28, 7, 9.[5]

[a] Cf. Brown, s. 'conditions, impossible.'

[b] Sc. testamento.

---

[1] Conditions are of two kinds, for they are either possible or impossible; a possible condition being that which in the nature of things can be entertained, an impossible, that which cannot.

[2] If a man stipulate under a condition which cannot come to pass, as for instance, if he shall touch the sky with his finger, the stipulation is null. But a legacy left subject to an impossible condition, our teachers think, is just as valid as though it had been left unconditionally; authorities of the opposite school consider that the legacy is no less void than the stipulation; and indeed it is scarcely possible to give a satisfactory reason for the difference.

[3] He maintained that if impossible conditions had been attached to a will, they were to be regarded as null.

[4] A stipulation couched in this fashion: Do you undertake, if you shall not make me heir, to give so much? is void, because this stipulation is contrary to sound morals.

[5] Conditions that are inserted contrary to sound morals must

BOOK I. Chapter I.

We come now to the effect of conditions. So long as the suspensive condition is pending ('cond. pendet'), the transaction continues to be inoperative; the right to be set up by it does not yet exist, but the possibility of its commencement receives certain juridical consideration, and a personal link exists between the parties.

Inst. iii. 15, 4: Ex condicionali stipulatione tantum spes est debitum iri, eamque ipsam transmittimus[a] si priusquam condicio existat, mors nobis contigerit.[1]

[a] Sc. ad heredem.

Ulp.: In iure civili receptum est, quotiens per eum, cuius interest condicionem non impleri, fiat quominus impleatur, perinde haberi ac si impleta condicio fuisset.—D. 50, 17, 161.[2]

The occurrence as well as the lapse of the condition ('cond. existit, deficit') puts an end to the uncertainty which attends the operation of the transaction: the lapse, because as regards the commencement of the right it terminates the operation of the transaction as from the first; the occurrence, because imparting operation to it, so that now the relation in question is treated as one created by the conditional declaration of will, the obligation as one already established at the moment when the will was declared (although still suspended in its operation), and the real legal relation as being one indeed now for the first time, but arising in a direct manner.[b]

[b] Cf. also §§ 37, 183. For what is called 'retroaction,' cf. §§ 36, 53, 88.

Gai.:—cum semel condicio **exstitit**, perinde habetur, ac si illo tempore, quo stipulatio inter-

---

be given up, as, for instance, if a man shall not afford his parents sustenance.

[1] A conditional stipulation gives rise to the mere hope that it will become a debt, and we transmit this hope [to our heirs] if death shall overtake us before the condition is fulfilled.

[2] It has been accepted in the *i. c.* that whenever a person whose interest it is that a condition should not be fulfilled procures its non-fulfilment, it is to be regarded just as though the condition had been fulfilled.

posita est, sine condicione facta esset.—D. 20, 4, 11, 1.[1]

Paul.: . . . si sub condicione stipuletur, . . . **ex praesenti** vires accipit stipulatio, quamvis petitio ex ea suspensa sit.—D. 45, 3, 26.[2]

Id.: Si filiusfamilias sub condicione stipulatus emancipatus fuerit, deinde exstiterit condicio, patri actio competit, quia in stipulationibus id tempus spectatur, quo contrahimus.—D. 45, 1, 78 pr.[3]

Id.: Si sub condicione emptio facta sit, pendente condicione emptor usu non capit.—D. 41, 4, 2, 2.[4]

Id.: Quodsi sub condicione res venierit, si quidem **defecerit** condicio, nulla est emptio sicuti nec stipulatio. . . . Quodsi pendente condicione emptor vel venditor decesserit, constat, si extiterit condicio, heredes quoque obligatos esse, quasi iam contracta emptione in praeteritum. . . . Stipulationes et legata condicionalia perimuntur, si pendente condicione res extincta fuerit.—D. 18, 6, 8 pr.[5]

---

1 . . . when once a condition is fulfilled, the stipulation is regarded just as if at that time when it was introduced it had been made unconditionally.

2 . . . if he have stipulated under a condition, . . . the stipulation obtains legal force immediately, although the action arising out of it be suspended.

3 If a *filius-familias* who has stipulated under a condition has been freed from power, and the condition has been fulfilled, the action belongs to the father, because in a stipulation regard is had to the time when we concluded the contract.

4 If a purchase have been made conditionally, time does not run in favour of the buyer as long as the condition is pending.

5 But if a thing have been sold under a condition and this have lapsed, the purchase is void, just like a stipulation. . . . But if, while the condition is pending, the purchaser or vendor die, it is settled the heirs also are under an obligation, should the condition be fulfilled, as though the purchase had been already concluded for the past. . . . Stipulations and conditional legacies are extinguished if the thing be destroyed while the condition is pending.

Book I. Chapter I.

Reversely, a transaction concluded under a resolutory condition has full operation at once, and has retrospective effect upon the occurrence of the condition.[a]

[a] See the passage cited above from Ulp. in D. 18, 2, 2 pr.

Thirdly, the TERM (or day, 'dies'), an addition to the declaration of will, which arbitrarily limits the legal relation established by it in respect of time.

(1) The initial term and the final term.

Paul.: Circa diem duplex inspectio est, nam vel **ex die** incipit obligatio, aut confertur **in diem**; ex die veluti: 'kalendis Martiis dare spondes?' cuius natura haec est, ut ante diem non exigatur; ad diem autem: 'usque ad kalendas dare spondes?' Placet autem ad tempus obligationem constitui non posse,—nam quod alicui deberi coepit, certis modis desinit deberi: plane post tempus stipulator vel pacti conventi vel doli mali exceptione summoveri poterit.—D. 44, 7, 44, 1.[1]

Inst. iii. 15, 3: Si ita stipuleris: 'decem aureos annuos quoad vivam dare spondes?' et pure facta obligatio intelligitur et perpetuatur, quia ad tempus deberi non potest: sed heres petendo pacti exceptione summovebitur.[2]

---

[1] With regard to the *dies* there is a twofold consideration, for either the obligation begins with a *dies*, or it is postponed until a certain *dies*. From a *dies*, as: 'Do you undertake to give so-and-so on the 1st of March?' Its nature is such that no claim can be made before the *dies*. But until a *dies*: 'Do you undertake to give so-and-so until the first day of next month?' But it is considered that an obligation cannot be fixed for a certain length of time . . . for what has begun to be owing to any one can only cease to be owing in a certain manner, but naturally the contracting party can after a time be defeated by the plea of the contractual agreement or of fraud.

[2] If you stipulate thus: 'Do you undertake to give me yearly as long as I live ten gold-pieces?' the obligation is regarded as absolute and perpetual, because a debt cannot be due for a time; but the heir on suing will be defeated by the plea of an agreement.

(2) Dies certus *an*, certus *quando*; certus *an*, incertus *quando*; incertus *an*, certus *quando*; incertus *an*, incertus *quando*. The last avails always, the last but one usually as a condition.

> Papin.: 'Heres meus, cum morietur Titius, centum ei dato:' purum legatum est, quia non condicione sed mora suspenditur; non potest enim condicio non existere.—D. 35, 1, 79 pr.[1]
>
> Ulp.: Si 'cum heres morietur' legetur, condicionale legatum est: denique vivo herede defunctus legatarius ad heredem non transfert.—D. 36, 2, 4 pr.[2]
>
> Pomp.: Si Titio, 'cum is annorum quattuordecim esset factus' legatum fuerit, . . . non solum diem sed et condicionem hoc legatum in se continet 'si effectus esset annorum quattuordecim.'—l. 22 pr. eod.[3]

(3) The 'dies' does but suspend the operation of the declaration of will without placing it in uncertainty. The obligation in question is therefore established forthwith, only that it cannot be made available or be exercised before the occurrence of the 'dies;' or the particular real right, which is certain as to its commencement, substantially exists upon the occurrence of the 'dies.'

> Id autem quod in diem stipulamur, statim quidem debetur, sed peti prius quam dies veniat non potest.—§ 2, I. de V. O.[4]

---

[1] 'My heir when Titius dies shall give to him a hundred' . . . this is an absolute legacy, because it depends not upon a condition but upon delay, for the condition cannot but be fulfilled.

[2] If a legacy be given 'upon the death of the heir,' it is conditional; nor can it during the lifetime of the heir pass from a dead legatee to his heir.

[3] If a legacy have been given to Titius 'upon his having become fourteen years of age' . . . this legacy comprehends *condicio* no less than *dies*: 'if he should have reached the age of fourteen.'

[4] That which we stipulate for with reference to date is indeed

Book I. Chapter I.

Cels.: Quod certa die promissum est, vel statim dari potest: totum enim medium tempus ad solvendum promissori liberum relinqui intelligitur —D. 46, 3, 70.[1]

Paul.: In diem debitor adeo debitor est, ut ante diem solutum repetere non possit.—D. 12, 6, 10.[2]

Ulp.: **Cedere** diem significat, incipere deberi pecuniam; **venire** diem significat, eum diem venisse, quo pecunia peti possit. Ubi **pure** quis stipulatus fuerit, et cessit et venit dies; ubi **in diem**, cessit dies, sed nondum venit; ubi **sub condicione**, neque cessit neque venit dies **pendente** adhuc condicione.—D. 50, 16, 213 pr.[3]

Finally, as to 'Modus,' or limitation of the purpose, incumbered appropriation, which is the accessory provision in the onerous application of property, imposing on the recipient the obligation to appropriate what is received in some particular way, to carry something out, to perform some collateral act or observe some line of conduct, without, however, making the operation of the user dependent upon that, or postponing it.

Gai.: Quodsi cui in hoc legatum sit, ut ex eo aliquid faceret, veluti monumentum testatori vel opus aut epulum municipibus, vel ex eo ut partem

---

an immediate debt, but it cannot be demanded until the day arrives.

[1] That which has been promised for a certain day can be given even at once, for it is supposed that the whole intervening time is left open for the promisor to pay.

[2] A debtor for a limited time is so much a debtor that he cannot before the time reclaim what he has paid.

[a] See Bell, s. vv.

[3] By *cedere diem*[a] is meant that the money is already due, by *venire diem*[a] that the date has arrived when the money can be sued for. Where a person shall have entered into an absolute contract, time both runs and has elapsed; where the stipulation is *in diem*, time runs, but has not yet run out; where *sub condicione*, time neither runs nor has elapsed while the condition is still pending.

alii restitueret: sub modo legatum videtur.—D. 35, 1, 17, 4.[1]

Scaev.:—nec enim parem dicemus eum, cui ita datum sit: **si** monumentum fecerit, et eum cui datum est: **ut** monumentum faciat.—l. 80 eod.[2]

Pomp.: In testamentis quaedam scribuntur, quae ad auctoritatem dumtaxat scribentis referuntur nec obligationem pariunt.—Et in omnibus, ubi auctoritas sola testatoris est, neque omnimodo spernenda neque omnimodo observanda est; sed interventu iudicis haec omnia debent, si non ad turpem causam feruntur, ad effectum perduci.—D. 33, 1, 7.[3]

§ 20. Representation.[a]

[a] See Markby, ss. 247-253.

Under Representation in its wider sense is understood that relation between two persons by virtue of which the legal result of the declaration of the will of one in general takes the place of the other. Representation in its narrower sense exists when some one declares his own will instead of and for another, with legal effect for the latter. From the 'procurator' or representative, we must distinguish the 'nuntius,' or messenger, who is but the communicator of another's will.

---

[1] But if a bequest have been made to a person in order to effect something by it, as a monument to the testator, or a building, or a banquet for the municipalities, or to deliver half thereof to another, the bequest is regarded as conditional.

[2] . . . for we cannot treat as on the same footing the man to whom a gift is made, 'if he shall have erected a monument,' and him to whom a gift is made, 'that he may erect a monument.'

[3] In testaments some things are written which concern only the authority of the writer and create no obligation. And in all where the authority is alone that of the testator, it is neither entirely to be disregarded nor is to be observed entirely, but all such things require the intervention of a *iudex* to be carried out, provided they are not conceived with an evil purpose.

Book I. Chapter I.

Labeo ait, convenire . . . vel per **epistulam** vel per **nuntium** inter absentes quoque posse.—D. 2, 14, 2 pr.[1]

The Roman Law in this proceeds from the following principles:—

1. Persons in domestic subjection (personae alieno iuri subiectae) and slaves always acquire of necessity for their master.[a]

[a] Cf. §§ 50, 112, 149, sq.

Gai. ii. § 86: Adquiritur autem nobis non solum per nosmet ipsos, sed etiam per eos, quos in potestate manu mancipiove habemus.[2]

Id.: Etiam invitis nobis per servos adquiritur paene ex omnibus causis.—D. 41, 1, 32.[3]

2. For persons with capacity to act, a further rule operates, that they can establish a legal relation only by their own expressions of will or personal co-operation, not by that of free third-persons. A representation is only possible indirectly; that is, the representative establishes the legal relation first for himself, and then transfers it to the one he represents.[b]

[b] Cf. §§ 144, 197.

Gai. ii. 95: Ex his apparet, per liberos homines, quos neque iuri nostro subiectos habemus, neque bona fide possidemus, . . . nulla ex causa nobis adquiri posse; et hoc est quod vulgo dicitur, **per extraneam personam nobis adquiri non posse.**[4]

---

[1] Labeo says that an agreement may also be made between parties separated from one another . . . either by means of a letter or by messenger.

[2] Now property is acquired for us not only by ourselves but also by those whom we have under power, marital control, or *mancipium*.

[3] Even without our will acquisition is made for us by slaves in almost all cases.

[4] Whereby it appears that we cannot in any case acquire through freemen that we neither have under power nor possess *bona fide* . . . and this is what is meant by the common saying, that nothing can be acquired for us through a stranger.

It was only in respect of the acquisition of possession and of those rights (as of ownership) which depend upon it, that direct representation was gradually allowed.[a]

[a] Cf. § 88.

Paul. v. 2, § 2: Per liberas personas quae in potestate nostra non sunt, adquiri nobis nihil potest; sed per procuratorem adquiri nobis possessionem posse, utilitatis causa receptum est.[1]

Pomp.: Ea quae civiliter adquiruntur, per eos, qui in potestate nostra sunt, adquirimus, veluti stipulationem; quod naturaliter adquiritur, sicuti est possessio, per quemlibet volentibus nobis possidere adquirimus.—l. 53, D. de A. R. D.[2]

Representation depends—

1. Upon a commission or authority to give the declaration of will in question; succeeding 'ratihabitio' or confirmation is equivalent to a commission, and by it the legal transaction concluded by the representative becomes operative for, or rather binding upon, the representative retrospectively.[b]

[b] 'Ratihabitio mandato comparatur': cf. §§ 89, 139.

2. Upon an office: thus a representative (tutor, curator) is appointed for free persons without capacity to act, and he, supplying the deficiency of their will, acts for them.[c]

[c] See §§ 58, sq.

For many acts in the Law (*e.g.*, making a testament, taking up an inheritance, adoption) even indirect representation is not admitted.

§ 21. Invalid Acts in the Law.

An act in the Law is invalid, when it is legally inadmissible,[d] or lacks an essential requisite of the inten-

[d] Cf. § 4.

---

[1] Nothing can be acquired for us by free persons that are not under our power, but our ability to acquire possession by a representative has been admitted for convenience' sake.

[2] Those things that are acquired by *ius civile*, such as a stipulation, we acquire through those who are under our power; that which is acquired in a natural way, as possession, we acquire, if willing, through any one whatever.

Book I. Chapter I.

tion or declaration of the will, as regards character, form, or substance.[a]

[a] See § 19.

> Impp. Theodos. et Valent.: Non dubium est, in legem committere eum, qui verba legis amplexus contra legis nititur voluntatem. . . . Nullum enim pactum, nullam conventionem, nullum contractum inter eos videri volumus subsecutum, qui contrahunt lege contrahere prohibente.—C. 1, 14, 5.[1]
>
> Inst. iii. 19, §§ 1, 2: Si quis rem, quae in rerum natura non est aut esse non potest, dari stipulatus fuerit, veluti Stichum qui mortuus sit, quem vivere credebat, aut hippocentaurum, qui esse non possit, inutilis erit stipulatio. Idem iuris est, si rem sacram aut religiosam, . . . vel publicam . . . ut forum vel theatrum, vel liberum hominem . . . dari quis stipuletur.[2]

The invalidity can be absolute, *i.e.*, already exist intrinsically, so that there is only the outward semblance of a legal transaction—Nullity; or it may be relative, so that the transaction in itself (ipso iure) is valid, and first becomes ineffectual by controversy, *i.e.*, judicial demonstration of a ground of invalidity (actio, exceptio, rest. in integr.) as affecting him by whom it is claimed—Controvertibility, Revocability.[b]

[b] § 18.

The ground of invalidity can be either present from the first, or arise later on.[c]

[c] See § 161.

---

[1] There is no doubt that he offends against the *lex* who adheres to its words, but struggles against its object. We ordain that no bargain, no agreement, no contract shall be upheld between those who contract notwithstanding a *lex* that prohibits it.

[2] If any one shall have stipulated that a chattel be given which in reality does not or cannot exist, as for instance Stichus, who is dead, whom he believed to be alive, or a hippocentaur, which cannot exist, the stipulation will be void. The same law applies if any one stipulate that a sacred or religious thing, . . . or a public one . . . as a market-place or theatre, or a freeman, be given.

The invalidity can be either total or partial.

Total invalidity occurs constantly when the transaction is invalid in its essential contents.

> Paul.: Cum principalis causa non consistat, plerumque ne ea quidem, quae sequuntur locum habent.—D. 50, 17, 178.[1]

Partial invalidity can relate either to matter not essential to the transaction,[a] or to the scope of its object.[b]

[a] *E.g.*, § 19: *dies*; § 102: *lex commissoria*.

[b] 'utile per inutile non vitiatur.'

> Pomp.: Si vir uxori vel contra quid vendiderit vero pretio et donationis causa paciscantur, ne quid venditor ob eam rem praestet, . . . verius est, pactum dumtaxat irritum esse.—D. 24, 1, 31, 4.[2]

> Marcian.: Placuit, sive supra statutum modum quis usuras stipulatus fuerit, sive usurarum usuras, quod illicite adiectum est pro non adiecto haberi et licitas peti posse.—D. 22, 1, 29.[3]

> Ulp.: Non solent, quae abundant, vitiare scripturas.—l. 94, D. de R. J.[4]

In bilateral transactions, again, it may relate merely to one of the contracting parties personally; which are so-called 'halting' transactions (negotium claudicans).

> Ulp.: Si quis a pupillo sine tutoris auctoritate emerit, ex uno latere constat contractus; nam qui emit, obligatus est pupillo, pupillum sibi non obligat.—D. 19, 1, 13, 29.[5]

---

[1] When the chief subject does not exist, as a rule the things which go with it have no recognition also.

[2] If a man have sold something to his wife, or the converse, for an actual sum, and they should [then] agree to treat it as a present, that the vendor should not perform aught on that account . . . the better opinion is that only the agreement is void.

[3] It has been settled if any one have stipulated for interest beyond the legal rate or for compound interest, that what has been added irregularly shall be considered as not added, and the legitimate interest can be sued for.

[4] That which is superfluous in documents does not usually mar their effect.

[4] If anybody have purchased from a ward without the autho-

§ 22. Legal Signification of Time.[a]

[a] See Markby, ss. 280-290.

Time comes into consideration repeatedly as influencing the operation of juristic acts, and as being an essential factor in the commencement and termination of rights. In this, it is generally a question of the space of time or term within which something must happen, or during which a definite course of action or inaction must continue, or a state of things must exist.

The fixing of such spaces of time depends upon the Calendar, *i.e.*, the civil division of time into years, months, days, and hours, which rests upon astronomical principles. The year[b] of the Romans was originally, in accordance with the Calendar of Numa, of twelve months and 355 days, with twenty-two or twenty-three days[c] intercalated every two years after February 23,[d] which with the five last days of February together formed a special month 'mens intercalaris,' '*Mercedonius*.' In certain cases, especially involving terminal payments, the so-called year of Romulus, of ten months and 304 days, was the basis of the calculation: it was formed from $\frac{10}{12}$ of the solar year containing 365 days.[e] But the Julian Calendar fixed the year at 365 days with one day intercalated every four years, between February 23 and 24,[f] which, however, forms juristically but one day—called 'bissextum'—with that last mentioned. Thus—

[b] Th. Mommsen, die Röm. Chronologie, 2. Aufl. 1859, especially pp. 8-54, 279, *sq.*

[c] According to Mommsen, regularly twenty-two.

[d] Mommsen thinks this was sometimes after Feb. 23, at other times after the 24th day.

[e] Cf. §§106, 147.

[f] According to Mommsen, between the 24th and the 25th.

23 Feb.	d. vii. Kal. Martias (Terminalia).	
24	d. vi. poster. Kal. Mart. (dies intercal.)	bissextum s. dies bissextilis.
25 (24)	d. vi. prior Kal. Mart. (Regifugium)	
26 (25)	d. v. Kal. Mart.	

(The days 24 and 25 (24) are bracketed together on the left, and their two descriptions are joined on the right to "bissextum s. dies bissextilis.")

According to Mommsen, the 24th is d. vi. prior, the 25th d. vi. post (interc.).

rity of his guardian, it is well-established law that there is a contract affecting the one party; for the purchaser is under obligation to the pupil, the pupil does not bind himself.

Book I. Chapter I.

Cels.: Cum bissextum kalendas est, nihil refert utrum priore an posteriore die quis natus sit, et deinceps sextum kalendas eius natalis dies est, nam **id biduum pro uno die habetur**; sed posterior dies intercalatur non prior: ideo quo anno intercalatum non est sexto kalendas natus, cum bissextum kalendas est, priorem diem natalem habet. § 1. Cato putat, mensem intercalarem additicium esse, omnesque eius dies pro momento temporis observat, extremoque diei mensis Februarii attribuit Quintus Mucius. § 2. Mensis autem intercalaris constat ex diebus viginti octo. —D. 50, 16, 98.[1]

The divisions of time occurring in legal dealings are essentially similar to those contained in the Calendar, but have not, like them, fixed but movable points of commencement and termination. Thus the movable month and day is a period of thirty days and twenty-four hours respectively, without restrictions as to the point of commencement;[a] whilst the Calendar months, *i.e.*, those parts of the year with definite designations, are of unequal length, and the Calendar day, or 'dies civilis,' constantly runs from midnight to midnight.

[a] *E.g.*, 5.15 P.M. on June 4th to 5.15 P.M. on June 5th.

Paul.: More Romano dies a media nocte incipit et sequentis noctis media parte finitur; itaque quidquid in his viginti quattuor horis i.e. duabus dimidiatis noctibus, et luce media actum est,

[1] When there is the double sixth day before the first day [of March], it matters not whether a person was born on the first or on the second day, and afterwards the sixth day before the first [of March] is his birthday; for those two days are regarded as one, but the second day is intercalated, not the first. And so he that was born on the sixth day before the first [of March] in a year in which there is no intercalation has the first day as his birthday in a leap year. Cato is of opinion that the intercalated month is an additional one, and he takes all its days for a moment of time, and Quintus Mucius assigns it to the last day of the month of February. But the intercalated month consists of twenty-eight days.

Book I. Chapter I.

perinde est, quasi quavis hora lucis actum esset. —D. 2, 12, 8.[1]

In the calculation of a period of time a distinction is made between 'natural' and 'civil' computation. By the first is meant exact, mathematical reckoning, 'a momento ad momentum;'[a] by the latter that which is usual in common life, the Day being treated as the smallest division of time. In civil computation the calculation is made according to whole (calendar) days; and indeed the day—without regard to the hour —on which the period of time begins, is constantly reckoned in as a complete one. The point of termination admits of a twofold reckoning, because sometimes the last day, that has begun, of the period of time[b] is reckoned in, sometimes only that which is fully run out. Thus, according to the shorter civil computation, the year beginning January 1st, 1885, runs out at midnight of December 30–31; but according to the longer at midnight of Dec. 31st, 1885–Jan. 1st, 1886.

[a] *E.g.*, the year beginning on Jan. 1st, 1885, at 2 P.M. runs out on Jan. 1st, 1886, at 2 P.M.

[b] 'Dies ultimus coeptus pro completo habetur.'

The Romans employ the shorter civil computation when it is a question of the commencement of a right by lapse of time, and so for the acquisition of a right by continuance of a positive condition during a definite period, or for the acquisition of juristic capacity by the attainment of a certain age.

> Paul.: Anniculus non statim ut natus est, sed trecentesimo sexagesimo quinto die dicitur, incipiente plane non exacto die, quia annum civiliter non ad momenta temporum, sed ad dies numeramus.—D. 50, 16, 134.[2]
>
> Ulp.: A qua aetate testamentum vel masculi

---

[1] According to Roman custom the day begins from midnight, and ends with the following midnight; so that all that is done in these four and twenty hours, *i.e.*, two half nights and the intermediate day, is just as though it were done by day.

[2] A child is called a year old, not immediately it is born, but on the 365th day, indeed at the very beginning, not at the finish, of the day, because we reckon the year for civil purposes, not by single moments of time, but by days.

Book I. Chapter I.

vel feminae facere possunt, videamus. Verius est, in masculis quidem quartum decimum annum spectandum, in feminis vero duodecim completum. Utrum autem excessisse debeat quis quartum decimum annum, ut testamentum facere possit, an sufficit complesse? Propone aliquem kalendis Ianuariis natum testamentum ipso natali suo fecisse, an valeat testamentum? Dico valere; plus arbitror, etiam si pridie kalendarum fecerit post sextam horam noctis, valere testamentum: iam enim complesse videtur annum quartum decimum, ut Marciano videtur.—D. 28, 1, 5.[1]

Id.: In usucapionibus non a momento ad momentum, sed totum postremum diem computamus;—ideoque qui hora sexta diei kalendarum Januarium possidere coepit, hora sexta noctis pridie kalendas Ianuarias implet usucapionem.—D. 41, 3, §§ 6, 7.[2]

The longer is used when the termination of a right by lapse of time, and accordingly inaction or delay during a definite period (*e.g.*, limitation of actions, time in the steps of an action), comes into consideration.

Paul.: In omnibus temporalibus actionibus nisi novissimus totus dies compleatur, non finit obligationem.—D. 44, 7, 6.[3]

---

[1] Let us now inquire what age is required in persons of the male or of the female sex for the making of a testament. It is more correct in the case of males to take the 14th, in the case of females the completed 12th year. But in order to be able to make a testament, must one already have passed the 14th year, or is it enough if one have just completed it? We may suppose the case of some one born on January 1st who has made his testament on his birthday—does it hold good? I affirm that it does. Moreover, I consider that it is good even if he have made it the day before January 1st, after midnight, for one supposes, according to the opinion of Marcianus, that he has at the time already completed the 14th year.

[2] In prescriptions we do not reckon from moment to moment, but the last day as a whole one; he, therefore, who has begun to possess at midnight of January 1st, completes the prescription at midnight of the last day of December.

[3] In no action limited by time does the obligation cease before the completion of the last day.

Book I. Chapter I.

Ulp.: Quod dicimus intra dies centum bonorum possessionem peti posse, ita intelligendum est, ut et ipso die centesimo bonorum possessio peti possit.—D. 38, 9, 1, 9.[1]

Paul.: Ubi lex duorum mensium fecit mentionem et qui sexagesimo primo die venerit, audiendus est.—D. 50, 17, 101.[2]

The natural computation is used exceptionally in the reckoning of majority as ground of exclusion in the 'restitutio in integrum.'[a]

[a] Cf. § 49.

Ulp.: Minorem autem vigintiquinque annis natu, videndum, an etiam die natalis sui adhuc dicimus ante horam qua natus est, ut si captus sit restituatur? Et cum nondum compleverit, ita erit dicendum, ut a momento in momentum tempus spectetur.—D. 4, 4, 3, 3.[3]

A period of time in which all the days are counted as unbroken is called 'continuum tempus;' if only those are counted in upon which a certain act could be undertaken—regularly without reference to the knowledge of the beginning of the lapse of time[b]—and those accordingly left out upon which the act in question is hindered by a physical or juristic obstacle (which must be excusable and transitory), then 'utile temp.' is spoken of. This reckoning happens, however, only in cases determined by Law, in which, by the omission of a proceeding that should be taken before a magistrate within the space of a year or less, a right is lost.

[b] Cf. § 63.

Ulp.: Utile tempus est bonorum possessionem

[1] When we say that the succession may be claimed within 100 days, this is to be understood as allowing of its being still demanded on the 100th day.

[2] Where a *lex* has mentioned two months, he also is to be heard who came on the 61st day.

[3] But there is a question whether we should call a person on his birthday before the hour of his birth under 25 years of age, so that if he should have been captured he might be reinstated in his former position. And when he has not yet attained, it will have to be said that the time must be reckoned from moment to moment.

admittendarum. Ita autem utile tempus est, ut **singuli dies in eo utiles** sint, scilicet ut per singulos dies **et scierit et potuerit** admittere; ceterum quacumque die nescierit aut non potuerit, nulla dubitatio est, quin dies ei non cedat. —D. 38, 15, 2 pr.[1]

Id.: Quia tractatus de utilibus diebus frequens est, videamus, quid sit **experiundi potestatem habere.** Et quidem in primis exigendum est, ut sit facultas agendi; neque sufficit reum experiundi secum facere potestatem . . . nisi actor quoque nulla idonea causa impediatur experiri. Proinde sive apud hostes sit, sive reipublicae causa absit, sive in vinculis sit, aut si tempestate in loco aliquo vel in regione detineatur, . . . experiundi potestatem non habet. . . . Illud utique neminem fugit, experiundi potestatem non habere eum, qui praetoris copiam non habuit; proinde hi dies cedunt, quibus ius praetor reddit. —D. 44, 3, 1.[2]

---

[1] *Utile tempus* is the time within which to be admitted to succession. But *utile tempus* is such that every single day thereof serves for legal steps, that is, in such way that a man has known of the succession and could have received it during the several days; every other day, however, that he has not known of it nor could have received it, there is no doubt that he does not lose the day.

[2] Since very often question is raised as to the days appropriated to legal steps, let us consider what is meant by the ability to take legal proceedings. And first of all the chief requisite is, the ability to proceed; and it is not enough for the defendant to afford the possibility of a contest with him unless also the plaintiff is hindered in taking steps by no sufficient cause. If he therefore be in the hands of the enemy, or absent upon public business, or in confinement, or detained in some place or country by stress of weather, he is unable to maintain an action. . . . It moreover need not be mentioned that he to whom it has been impossible to resort to the praetor has not the ability to maintain an action; those days accordingly are alone reckoned upon which the praetor administers Law.

CHAPTER II.

EXERCISE AND PROTECTION OF RIGHTS.

§ 23. NATURE AND SPECIES OF PROTECTION OF RIGHTS.

BOOK I. Chapter II.

A RIGHT without *de facto* validity, *i.e.*, a right which could not be available, would be unreal. The exercise of a right must not be dependent upon the free consent of those in relation with the person entitled: it must admit of operation even against their will. Inasmuch as restriction upon the exercise, or actual non-recognition, of a right shows itself to be the violation of such right, it belongs to the nature of a right that its recognition should be enforceable. Nevertheless, in a politically organized community the individual may not enforce his right independently, at his own discretion, upon his own responsibility, by his own power to make such right available. SELF-HELP, as an expression of individual caprice which in its effect is unreliable and indefinite, and based upon a merely subjective idea of Law, is contrary to the nature of legal order.[a]

[a] For 'Redress by act of parties,' allowed by Engl. Law, see Steph. iii. pp. 240, *sqq.*; cf. Maine, Early Hist. of Institt., ch. ix., Holl. pp. 239, *sqq.*

Paul.: Non est singulis concedendum, quod per magistrum publice possit fieri, ne occasio sit maioris tumultus faciendi.—D. 50, 17, 176 pr.[1]

Callistrat.: Exstat **decretum D. Marci** in haec verba: 'Optimum est, ut si quas putas te habere petitiones, actionibus experiaris; [interim ille in possessione debet morari, tu petitor es].' Cum Marcianus diceret: 'vim nullam feci,' Caesar dixit: 'Tu vim putas esse solum, si homines vulnerentur?' Vis est et tunc, quotiens quis id quod deberi sibi putat, non per iudicem reposcit. Quisquis igitur probatus mihi fuerit, rem ullam

[1] That which can come about publicly through the magistrate must not be committed to individuals, that opportunity may not be afforded of making greater disturbance.

debitoris vel pecuniam debitam, non ab ipso sibi sponte datam, sine ullo iudice temere possidere vel accepisse isque sibi ius in eam rem dixisse, ius crediti non habebit.—D. 4, 2, 13 & 48, 7, 7.[1]

Self-help is only legally admissible as self-defence in extreme necessity, *i.e.*, the immediate repulse of an attack upon our person or our property, which is already in form illegal and prejudicial to one's very personality.

Paul.: —vim vi defendere omnes leges omniaque iura permittunt.—D. 9, 2, 45, 4.[2]

Ulp.: Vim vi repellere licere Cassius scribit, idque ius natura comparatur.—D. 43, 16, 1, 27.[3]

Moreover, since every attack upon the sphere of the private law of the individual clashes at the same time with the positive law that recognises this, it is the function of the State, as the power which puts Law in force, and by instruments appointed for the purpose, to protect the right of the individual upon his appeal to it, and to compel the actual recognition of that right: the place of Self-help is taken by Procedure, to make good before a court the right which has been violated, by investigation and establishment of what is in dispute, and by judicial relief.

---

[1] There is a decree of the late Emperor Marcus which runs thus:—'It is best for you if you seek to give effect by action to those claims which you conceive you have; [in the meanwhile that man must remain in possession and you are but plaintiff].' When Marcianus declared, 'I have employed no force,' the Emperor said, 'Do you consider that force is merely when men are wounded?' There is force also whenever any one does not through the *iudex* demand what he deems due to him. Every one, accordingly, respecting whom proof shall be given me that anything belonging to his debtor or a sum owing to him, without his having received it from the debtor through free will, shall be possessed by him groundlessly without judicial assistance, or if he have received it and thereupon shall have himself laid down the law concerning it, he shall forfeit his right to demand it.

[2] All statutes and all laws allow of our meeting force with force.

[3] Cass. writes that to repel force by force is allowable, and Nature provides that right.

BOOK I. Chapter II.

Regular and ordinary protection of a right consists in judicial recognition of an actually existing right, which is vindicated against some violation that has already occurred.[a] But there are also cases in which from the point of view of 'aequitas' an actual right is extinguished, or one already extinguished is revived.[b] There are further means of protecting rights designed to secure them against future or threatening violations, or against legal claims which are still in abeyance.[c]

[a] §§ 24-29.

[b] 'restitutio in integrum' (§ 30).

[c] *cautiones, missiones* (§ 31).

The description of the legal precepts that apply to the protection of rights and the whole judicial procedure, or steps taken by the parties by way of judicial action, falls under the special doctrine of Civil Procedure.[d] In what follows, only the general principles relating to the several means of protecting a right, and to the modifications which every right undergoes by its being judicially vindicated, have to be discussed.

[d] See Bk. IV.

§ 24. Ordinary Means of Protecting a Right. Nature and Varieties of *Actiones*.[e]

[e] Cf. § 201.

'Actio' in the formal sense (the act of proceeding) is the judicial prosecution of a right; whilst 'actio' in the material sense (right of proceeding, right of action) is the power inherent in every perfect right to operate, that is, the privilege by bringing an action of imposing upon the opponent legal contention as to the right in question and submission to a judicial sentence upon its existence and recognition.[f] 'Actio' is also synonymous with an actionable legal claim, or with 'obligatio.'

[f] This may perhaps be called a right to the institution of a *iudicium*.

> Cels.: Nihil aliud est **actio** quam ius quod sibi debeatur iudicio persequendi.—l. 51, D. h. t. (=de O. et A. 44, 7).[g] [1]

[g] Cf. Inst. IV. 6 pr.

In the widest sense, 'actio' designates every means of legal redress.

> Ulp.: **Actionis** verbo continetur in rem in personam, directa utilis, praeiudicium, . . . stipu-

[1] *Actio* is nothing else than the right to sue in court for that which is due to one.

lationes etiam, quae praetoriae sunt, . . . interdicta quoque actiones verbo continentur.—l. 37 pr. eod.[1]

Id.: Agere etiam is videtur, qui exceptione utitur, nam reus in exceptione actor est.—D. 44, 1, 1.[2]

In the narrower and strict sense, it means only that which initiates a suit whereby a right is prosecuted contentiously against some one, regularly so as to obtain judgment against him.

Paul.: **Actionis** verbo non continetur exceptio. —D. 50, 16, 8, 1.[3]

In the narrowest sense, it means the action to which an obligation gives rise.

Ulp.: Actionis verbum et speciale est et generale: nam omnis actio dicitur, sive in personam sive in rem sit petitio. Sed plerumque **actiones** personales solemus dicere; **petitionis** autem verbo in rem actiones significari videntur; **persecutionis** verbo extraordinarias persecutiones puto contineri, ut puta fideicommissorum, et si quae aliae sunt, quae non habent iuris ordinarii exsecutionem.—l. 178, § 2 eod.[4]

The plaintiff is called 'actor,' 'petitor;' the defendant is spoken of as 'reus,' 'is cum quo agitur.'

---

[1] Under an *actio* is understood one real or personal, immediate or resting upon analogy, or relating to *status* . . . even praetorian stipulations . . . interdicts also are comprised under *actio*.

[2] He also is regarded as maintaining an action who makes use of an *exceptio*, for the defendant is in the *exceptio* plaintiff.

[3] An *exceptio* does not fall under the designation *actio*.

[4] The word *actio* is something both particular and general; for every action is so-called, be the claim *in personam* or *in rem*. But generally by *actiones* we are accustomed to speak of those that are personal; by the word *petitio*, however, real actions seem to be meant. I am of opinion that under *persecutio* are comprehended extraordinary proceedings, *e.g.*, *fidei-commissa* and other such as are not accomplished by ordinary legal process.

Book I. Chapter II.

According to their subject-matter, or the GROUND of action, *actiones* are divided into—

'Act. in rem '[a] s. 'vindicationes' (real actions) and 'in personam '[a] s. 'condictiones' in the widest sense (personal actions). Those 'in personam' are the actions arising out of obligations, actions directed originally only against a certain, the obliged, person; those 'in rem' are such as arise out of all other legal relations, by which a right of the person entitled is vindicated against every third person, and in which the person of the defendant is first determined through the violation of the right.[b]

[a] Stephen, iii. 371; Digby, 'Histy. of Law of Real Propy.,' p. 69, note; Roscoe, 'Court of Admiralty,' pp. 101, 102; Brown, s. vv.; Markby, s. 129; Williams, 'Law of Real Property,' p. 15 (15th edn.).

[b] Cf. § 6.

Omnium actionum . . . summa divisio in duo genera deducitur: aut enim **in rem** sunt, aut **in personam**.—§ 1, I. h. t. (=de act. 4, 6).[1]

Gai. iv. 2, 3: **In personam** actio est, qua agimus cum aliquo, qui nobis vel ex contractu vel ex delicto obligatus est i.e. cum intendimus: DARE, FACERE, PRAESTARE OPORTERE. § **In rem** actio est, cum aut corporalem REM intendimus NOSTRAM ESSE, aut ius aliquod nobis competere velut utendi fruendi.[2]

Ulp.: **In rem** actio . . . semper adversus eum est, qui rem possidet; **in personam** actio . . . semper adversus eundem locum habet.—l. 25 pr. D. h. t.[3]

Quaedam actiones **mixtam causam** obtinere videntur, tam in rem quam in personam; qualis est familiae erciscundae actio . . . communi

---

[1] The principal division of all actions is into two kinds: they are either *in rem* or *in personam*.

[2] An action *in personam* is that by which we proceed against some one who has become liable to us either by contract or by tort, that is, when we allege in our claim that he ought to give, to do, to perform something. The action is *in rem* when we allege in the claim either that a corporeal thing is ours, or that some right belongs to us; for instance, of *usus*, of usufruct.

[3] An action *in rem* is always directed against the possessor of the thing; an action *in personam* always obtains against the same person.

dividundo . . . finium regundorum, . . . in quibus tribus iudiciis permittitur iudici, rem alicui ex ligatoribus ex bono et aequo adiudicare et . . . eum invicem certa pecunia alteri condemnare.—§ 20, I. h. t.[1]

Actiones are further divided into those 'rei persecutoriae' (preservative or recuperatory actions), 'poenales' and 'mixtae.'[a]

[a] § 130.

Sequens illa divisio est, quod quaedam actiones **rei persequendae** gratia comparatae sunt, quaedam **poenae persequendae,** quaedam **mixtae** sunt. § Rei persequendae causa comparatae sunt omnes in rem actiones; earum vero actionum, quae in personam sunt, hae quidem quae ex contractu nascuntur, fere omnes rei persequendae causa comparatae videntur. § Ex maleficiis vero proditae actiones aliae tantum poenae persequendae causa comparatae sunt, aliae tam poenae quam rei persequendae et ob id mixtae sunt.—§§ 16–18, I. h. t.[2]

Paul.: Illae autem rei persecutionem continent, quibus persequimur, quod ex patrimonio nobis abest.—l. 35 pr. D. h. t.[3]

---

[1] Some actions appear to have a mixed character, as well *in rem* as *in personam:* such is the action for the division of an inheritance . . . for the partition of property held in common . . . for the settlement of boundaries . . . in these three actions the *iudex* is empowered to award an article to one of the contending parties according to what is just and right and . . . to order him in turn to pay a certain sum to the other.

[2] The next division is that some actions are provided for the purpose of our suing for a particular thing; others, that we may recover a penalty; others are mixed. § All actions *in rem* are intended for the recovery of a particular thing. Of actions *in personam,* those that arise out of contract seem nearly all intended for obtaining a particular thing. § But of actions that arise out of torts, a portion only are directed to the recovery of a penalty, others to the recovery of a penalty and a thing, and are therefore mixed.

[3] Those embrace legal recovery of a particular thing by means of which we lay claim to anything that is missing from our estate.

Book I. Chapter II.

Gai. iv. 9: Rem vero et poenam persequimur velut ex his causis ex quibus adversus infitiantem in duplum agimus; quod accidit per actionem iudicati, depensi, damni iniuriae e lege Aquilia, aut legatorum nomine, quae per damnationem certa relicta sunt.[1]

According to the functions performed by the parties, a distinction is made between 'iudicia simplicia,' in which the one is plaintiff, the other defendant, and 'iud. duplicia' s. 'act. mixtae,' in which each assumes at the same time the forensic position of plaintiff and defendant (actions for partition).[a]

[a] See above, and comp. § 29.

Iul.: Iudicium communi dividundo, familiae erciscundae, finium regundorum tale est, ut in eo singulae personae **duplex ius** habeant **agentis et eius quocum agitur.**—D. 10, 1, 10.[2]

Ulp.: Mixtae sunt actiones, in quibus uterque actor est.—l. 37, § 1, D. h. t.[3]

According to their relation to the sources of Law, actions are divided into—

(1) act. 'civiles' and 'honorariae' (praetoriae-aediliciae),[b] and

[b] §§ 4. 7, 194.

(2) act. 'directae' and 'utiles.'

The former are the actions prescribed by the particular law-source strictly for the special legal relation; whilst the latter are those devised after the analogy of

---

[1] But we sue for a particular thing and penalty in those cases, for example, in which we proceed for double the amount against a person that denies his liability; as occurs in the action of judgment-debt, of money deposited by a surety, of wrongful damage under the *lex Aquilia*, or for the recovery of specific legacies left by *damnatio*.

[2] The action for partition of property held in common, that for division of an inheritance, and that for settlement of boundaries are such that in them every individual assumes a twofold legal relation, as well that of plaintiff as that of defendant.

[3] Mixed actions are those in which both parties are plaintiff.

such for a similar legal relation or for other persons.[a] The 'utiles actiones' often appear in the form of FICTITIOUS actions.[b]

[a] Cf. § 5.
[b] § 200.

According to the position of the judge towards the case he has to decide, and according to his duties, is the division made into—

'Stricti iuris actiones' (iudicia) and
'bonae fidei act.' (arbitria).

1. In actions 'stricti iuris' the judge has to investigate the particular claim according to the principles of absolute Law, because he must here confine himself strictly to the tenor of the assigned formula (intentio and demonstratio). In actions 'bonae fidei' he assumes a more elastic position: he has to deliver his judgment according to equitable sentiment (ex aequo et bono) and with regard to all special circumstances, not expressed in the formula, of the actual case and of the whole relationship of the parties, and only to give judgment against the defendant for what he is under obligation to perform by the light of integrity and good faith.[c] These spring only out of definite obligations that are constantly directed to an 'incertum.'[d]

[c] § 4.
[d] § 111.

Actionum autem quaedam **bonae fidei** sunt quaedam **stricti iuris**.—§ 28, I. h. t.[1]

In bonae fidei autem iudiciis libera potestas videtur iudici ex bono et aequo aestimandi, quantum actori restitui debeat; in quo et illud continetur, ut si quid invicem actorem praestare oporteat, eo compensato in reliquum is cum quo actum est condemnari debeat; [liberum est tamen iudici nullam omnino invicem compensationis rationem habere nec enim aperte formulae verbis praecipitur, sed quia id bonae fidei conveniens videtur, ideo officio eius contineri creditur: Gai. iv. 63].—§ 30, *ibid.*[2]

---

[1] Now some actions are *bonae fidei*, some *stricti iuris*.

[2] In actions '*bonae fidei*' unlimited power seems given to the

BOOK I.
Chapter II.

Cic. pro Rosc. Com. 4 : aliud est **iudicium** aliud est **arbitrium**. Iudicium est pecuniae certae, arbitrium pecuniae incertae; ad iudicium hoc modo venimus, ut totam litem aut obtineamus aut amittamus; ad arbitrium hoc modo adimus ut neque nihil neque tantum, quantum postulavimus, consequamur; eius rei ipsa verba formulae testimonio sunt. . . . Quid est in iudicio? directum, asperum, simplex: 'SI PARET HS IↃↃↃ DARI.'[a] Hic nisi plenum facit HS IↃↃↃ ad libellam sibi deberi, causam perdit. Quid est in arbitrio? mite, moderatum: 'QVANTVM AEQVIVS MELIVS SIT ID DARI.'[1]

[a] See Smith, Dict. of Antiqq., s. *Sestertius*; Roby, School Lat. Gr. p. 67.

Id. de Off. iii. 17, : Q. Scaevola pont. max. summam vim esse dicebat in omnibus iis arbitriis in quibus adderetur EX FIDE BONA, fideique bonae nomen existimabat manare latissime idque versari in tutelis, societatibus, fiduciis, mandatis, rebus emptis venditis, conductis locatis, quibus vitae societas contineretur: in iis magni esse iudicis

---

iudex of estimating fairly and equitably what is the right amount to be paid to the plaintiff; which comprises that of estimating what the plaintiff ought in turn to pay, so that, allowing such rebate, the *iudex* should make an order upon the defendant for the balance. [The *iudex*, however, is free to take no account whatever of such set-off, for it is not even plainly enjoined by the words of the formula, but is considered to be part of his duty, because it would seem to comport with a *bonae fidei* action.]

[1] . . . *iudicium* and *arbitrium* differ from one another. *Iudicium* is a matter of a liquidated sum, *arbitrium*, of one unascertained. We arrive at a *iudicium* in this way, that we either carry or lose the whole suit; we come to an *arbitrium* thus—that neither do we obtain nothing, nor just so much as we have claimed, as witnessed by the very words of the formula. . . . . What characterises the *iudicium?* It is summary, rigid, simple: 'If it appear that 50,000 sesterces should be given.' Unless he make out that exactly 50,000 sesterces are due to him, he loses the cause. But what characterises the *arbitrium?* It is mild and moderate. 'Let that be given which may be the fairer and better.'

statuere, quid quemque cuique praestare oporteret.[1]

Bonae fidei sunt hae : ex empto vendito, locato conducto, negotiorum gestorum, mandati, depositi [fiduciae], pro socio, tutelae, commodati, pigneraticiae, familiae erciscundae, communi dividundo, praescriptis verbis, quae de aestimato proponitur, et ea quae ex permutatione competit, et . . . rei uxoriae actio.—§§ 28–29, I. h. t. Cf. Gai. iv. 62.[2]

2. 'Arbitrariae actiones.' These are the actions (especially 'in rem') in which the judge, in accordance with the direction contained in the formula NISI ARBITRATV TVO RESTITVAT, before he gives judgment against the defendant, has to enjoin upon him that he should conciliate the plaintiff in the manner 'ex aequo et bono' prescribed by such judge.

Praeterea quasdam actiones **arbitrarias**, i.e. ex arbitrio iudicis pendentes appellamus, in quibus nisi arbitrio iudicis is cum quo agitur actori satisfaciat, veluti rem restituat vel exhibeat vel solvat vel ex noxali causa servum dedat condemnari debeat. Sed istae actiones tam in rem quam in personam inveniuntur. . . . In his enim actionibus . . . permittitur iudici ex bono et aequo

---

[1] Q. Scaevola the *pont. max.* used to say that the greatest virtue resided in all those actions in which was added 'ex fide bona,' and he thought that the designation *bonae fidei* was of the widest extent, and was employed in guardianships, partnerships, pledges, gratuitous agencies, buying and selling, letting and hiring, in which daily intercourse was concerned; that in them it was the part of a great *iudex* to decide what each man ought to give to some one else.

[2] *Bonae fidei* are the following: actions of buying and selling, letting and hiring, management of business, gratuitous agency, deposit [fiduciary agreement to restore], partnership, guardianship, loan, pledge, division of an inheritance, partition of common property, the action *praescriptis verbis*, the action arising out of a commission-sale, the action which arises out of an exchange and . . the action to recover a wife's property.

Book I. Chapter II.

secundum cuiusque rei de qua actum est naturam aestimare, quemadmodum actori satisfieri oporteat. —§ 31, I. h. t.[a] [1]

[a] Cf. D. 4, 2, 14, 4.

'Actiones populares' are such actions as, conceived in the interest of public order, belong to everybody.[b]

[b] The like in English Law (Brown, s. 'p. a.').

1. In the strict sense, honorary penal actions, in which with the public can be associated a private interest of the plaintiff, although not a pecuniary one.[c]

[c] Cf. § 136.

Paul.: Eam popularem actionem dicimus, quae [suum] ius populi tenetur.—l. 1, D. h. t. (de pop. act. 47, 23).[2]

Id.: In popularibus actionibus . . . quis quasi unus ex populo agit.—l. 43, § 2, D. de proc. 3, 3.[3]

Id.: Si plures simul agant populari actione, praetor eligat idoneiorem.—l. 2, D. h. t.—Ulp.: is cuius interest praefertur.—l. 3, § 1, eod.[4]

Ulp.: Omnes populares actiones neque in heredes dantur, neque supra annum extenduntur. —l. 8 eod.[5]

Paul.: Item qui habet has actiones, non intelligitur esse locupletior.—l. 7, § 1 eod.—Ulp.: Si ex populari causa (debeatur), ante litis contes-

---

1 Moreover, certain actions are called capricious, *i.e.*, dependent upon the caprice of the *iudex*, in which the defendant, unless in the opinion of the *iudex* he offers satisfaction to the plaintiff, *e.g.*, restores or produces or pays for a thing or gives up a slave because of injury done by him, must be condemned. Such actions occur both *in rem* and *in personam*. . . . In these actions . . . the *iudex* is allowed to decide according to right and equity in relation to the nature of the matter subject of the action, in what way satisfaction should be rendered to the plaintiff.

2 By a popular action we mean that which upholds the right of the people.

3 In popular actions . . . anybody acts as one of the people.

4 If several at one time bring a popular action, the praetor shall select the fittest . . . the person interested is preferred.

5 No popular actions are given against the heirs, or are extended beyond a year.

tationem recte dicetur creditoris loco non esse, postea esse.—D. 50, 16, 12 pr.[1]

Paul.: Is qui eam (actionem) movet, procuratorem dare non potest.—l. 5 h. t.[2]

Id.: Qui ita de publico agant, ut et privatum commodum defendant, causa cognita permittuntur procuratorem dare.—l. 45, § 1, D. de proc.[3]

2. Those legal, criminal suits for public order by which the State, or the Community, empowers every citizen to take up, in a representative character, such public interest as has been violated, and in which the penalty inflicted goes to the State, a part, however, frequently being given to the plaintiff as a reward.

Lex Iulia mun. c. 23 (24, 27): QVEI . . . ADVERSVS EA FECERIT IS HS IƆƆƆ POPVLO DARE DAMNAS ESTO EIVSQVE QVEI VOLET PETITIO ESTO.[4]

§ 25. Commencement and Termination of Actions; and of Prescription in Particular.

The right of action, as authority for summary prosecution, arises (actio nascitur) or can be exercised in real rights upon their infringement; in obligations, as soon as the creditor can demand the fulfilment of the obligation, and the debtor neglects it. The action once begun remains on foot so long as the right to be protected by it, or rather its violation, continues.

---

1 Likewise he does not appear the wealthier who has this action. If (a debt be owing) in consequence of a popular action, it will be rightly said that before the *litis contestatio* he is not in the position of a creditor, but is afterwards.

2 He who brings that action cannot appoint a representative.

3 They who proceed because of some public matter, that they may also protect their private interest, are allowed upon investigation of the case to appoint a representative.

4 He . . . that shall have transgressed this, let him be sentenced to give 50,000 sesterces to the People, and let such money be claimed by whomsoever it pleases.

Book I. Chapter II.

Thus in particular does the action regularly not determine by the death of a party, with the exception

First, of 'act. populares,' the so-called 'vindictam spirantes,' and certain 'actiones rei persequendae gratia' not having the character of pure Property Law (*e.g.*, act. rei uxoriae,[a] querela inofficiosi[b]) which are extinguished by the death of the party entitled.

[a] § 147.
[b] § 169.

Ulp.: **Iniuriarum actio** neque heredi neque in heredem datur.—D. 47, 10, 13 pr.[1]

Paul.: Magis enim **vindictae** quam pecuniae habet persecutionem.—D. 37, 6, 2, 4.[2]

Secondly, of the 'act. poenales,' which are extinguished by the death of the party entitled.

Non omnes autem actiones, quae in aliquem aut ipso iure competunt aut a praetore dantur, et in heredem aeque competunt aut dari solent. Est enim certissima iuris regula, ex maleficiis **poenales** actiones in heredem non competere, veluti furti, vi bonorum raptorum, iniuriarum, damni iniuriae. Sed heredibus huius modi actiones competunt nec denegantur, excepta iniuriarum actione et si qua alia similis inveniatur.—§ 1, I. h. t. (de perp. et temp. act. 4, 12) = Gai. iv. 112.[3]

'Litis contestatio,' however, makes all actions transmissible as well actively as passively.

Paul.: **Post litem contestatam** heredi quoque

---

[1] The action for injuries is neither given to the heir nor against him.

[2] He has more the pursuit of revenge than of money.

[3] But not all actions that either attach against any one *ipso iure*, or are granted by the Praetor, equally attach against the heir or are wont to be granted. For there is a clearly established rule of law, that venal actions arising out of torts[c] do not lie against the heir; *e.g.*, those of theft, of violent robbery, of injuries, of wrongful damage. But actions of this kind are available for heirs and are not denied them, except the action of injury and other like actions, if such are to be found.

[c] For the Roman conception of Tort, see Maine, 'Anct. Law,' chap. x.

prospicitur et heres tenetur ex omnibus causis.—D. 50, 17, 87.[1]

An exception from the rule, according to which the action exists as long as the right which grounds it, is made by the limitation of actions, *i.e.*, the extinction of the right of action by non-exercise during a certain time: this obtains for the greater certainty and stability of Law.

In the Classical Law, the absence of such restriction as to civil actions (act. perpetuae) was the rule; the actions depending upon prescription (act. temporales) formed the exception. To the latter belonged especially 'actiones honorariae,' 'praetoriae' (especially poenales), the prescription to which was limited generally to an 'annus utilis' (annales), and 'aediliciae,' in which the prescription was limited to a still shorter time. There was, besides, for actions in respect of ownership a prescription of from ten to twenty years ('longi temporis praescriptio') under special conditions.[a] —The prescription was made operative in the form of a plea to the action (exceptio).

[a] Cf. § 81.

> Gai. iv. 110: Quo loco admonendi sumus, eas quidem actiones quae ex lege senatusve consultis profiscuntur, perpetuo solere praetorem accommodare, eas vero, quae ex propria ipsius, iurisdictione pendent, plerumque intra annum dare.—(= pr. Inst. h. t.)[2]
>
> Paul.: In honorariis actionibus sic esse definiendum Cassius ait, ut quae rei persecutionem habeant, hae etiam post annum darentur, ceterae intra annum.—D. 44, 7, 35 pr.[3]

---

1 After *litis contestatio* regard is had also to the heirs, and he is held accountable in all causes.

2 And we must not forget that the Praetor regularly vouchsafes at any time actions arising from a *lex* or *senatus-consulta*, but it is within the year that he generally grants those which rest upon his own jurisdiction.

3 In *actiones honorariae*, Cassius says, it must be laid down

Book I. Chapter II.

Gai. iv. 111: Furti manifesti actio, quamvis ex ipsius praetoris iurisdictione proficiscatur, perpetuo datur; et merito, cum pro capitali poena pecuniaria constituta sit.[1]

By a constitution of Theodosius II. (A.D. 424), the 'perpetuae actiones' were made subject to a thirty years' prescription; for certain actions later on, the time of prescription was extended to forty years. 'Perpetuae actiones' were by this time the actions falling under prescription in thirty years or more; 'temporales,' those falling under prescription in a shorter time.

The prescription begins with the 'actio nata,' without reference to knowledge of the right of action; it is interrupted by the commencement of a suit, not by private remonstrance.

The effect of prescription consists in the indirect extinguishment of the right of action, but not—at least in real rights—of the right that underlies it.[a]

[a] Cf. §§ 81, 114.

EFFECT OF ACTS OF PROCEDURE UPON THE RIGHT ENFORCED.

§ 26. Litis Contestatio.[b]

[b] Bell, Dict. s. vv.; Phillimore, 'Ecclesiastical Law,' vol. ii. p. 1255.

'Litis contestatio' was in the Classical Law the termination of pleadings 'in iure' by the assignment of a formula;[c] in later Law, a statement by the defendant contradicting the averment of the plaintiff.[d] By it, the original legal relation between the parties underwent formal transformation. Whereas the parties made their claims depend upon the proceedings that had been initiated ('rem in iudicium deducere,' 'iudicium accipere') and submitted beforehand to the arbi-

[c] Cf. § 187.

[d] § 194.

that those which embrace a suit for a specific thing are given even after a year, the rest only within the year.

[1] The action for manifest theft, although it springs from the Praetor's own jurisdiction, is given at all times; and justly so, since the pecuniary has been imposed instead of the capital penalty.

tration of the *iudex*, they entered into a new, a quasi-contractual relation which absorbed their previous relation, having become subject of dispute. The following results accordingly ensued from the L.C.

'Actio consumitur': the right of action is once for all extinguished—*ipso iure*, or by means of the 'exceptio rei in iudicium deductae;'[a] that is, the plaintiff can henceforth no more prosecute the same claim against the defendant.[b]

[a] After delivery of the judgment, this was replaced by the *exc. rei iudicatae.*

[b] 'Consumption' of the action, 'bis de eadem re ne sit actio.' Cf. §§ 188, 199, 202.

Gai. iv. §§ 106, sq.: Et si quidem imperio continenti iudicio actum fuerit, sive in rem sive in personam, sive ea formula quae in factum concepta est, sive ea quae in ius habet intentionem, postea nihilominus ipso iure de eadem re agi potest; et ideo necessaria est **exceptio rei iudicatae vel in iudicium** deductae. § At si legitimo iudicio in personam actum sit ea formula quae iuris civilis habet intentionem, postea ipso iure de eadem re agi non potest, et ob id exceptio supervacua est; si vero vel in rem vel in factum actum fuerit, ipso iure nihilominus postea agi potest, et ob id exceptio necessaria est rei iudicatae vel in iudicium deductae.[1]

In place of the extinguished right of action, there arose for the plaintiff a claim to judgment against the defendant under the special conditions and terms set up in the formula, to which was opposed the claim

[1] Now if proceedings have been taken by an action covered by the authority of the magistrate, whether they were *in rem* or *in personam*, whether the formula was one formed upon the facts or containing a civil law claim, another action may nevertheless *ipso iure* be subsequently brought about the same matter; and therefore a plea of *res iudicata* or of a pending action is necessary.—But if proceedings *in personam* have been taken by *legitimum iudicium*, with a formula having a civil law claim, there cannot *ipso iure* be a subsequent action about the same matter, and therefore the plea is superfluous. But if the proceedings taken be *in rem* or based on the facts, a subsequent action can be brought *ipso iure*, and therefore the plea of *res iudicata* or of a pending action is necessary.

Book I. Chapter II.

of the defendant to acquittal under reverse conditions.

Gai. iii. §§ 180, sq.: Tollitur adhuc obligatio litis contestatione, si modo legitimo iudicio fuerit actum: nam tunc obligatio quidem principalis dissolvitur, incipit autem teneri reus litis contestatione; sed si condemnatus sit, sublata litis contestatione, incipit ex causa iudicati teneri. Et hoc est quod apud veteres scriptum est: **ante litem contestatam dare debitorem oportere, post litem contestatam condemnari oportere, post condemnationem iudicatum facere oportere.** § Unde fit, ut si legitimo iudicio debitum petiero, postea de eo ipso iure agere non possim, quia inutiliter intendo 'dari mihi oportere': quia litis contestatione dari oportere desiit.[1]

By it at the same time is determined the material effect of the L.C., the subject of judgment being the legal relation as existing at the moment of the L.C.; the time of the L.C. is accordingly decisive as regards the conditions of condemnation (existence of the plaintiff's claim)[a] as well as its subject and scope.[b]

[a] Vat. fgm. 12.
[b] §§ 73, 90.

Gai. iv. 114: Superest ut dispiciamus, si ante rem iudicatam is cum quo agitur, post acceptum iudicium satisfaciat actori, quid officio iudicis conveniat, utrum absolvere, an ideo potius damnare, quia iudicii accipiendi tempore in ea causa fuerit,

---

[1] Moreover, an obligation is dissolved by joinder of issue, provided steps are taken by a statutable action. For then the original obligation is dissolved, and the defendant begins to incur an obligation by issue joined; but if judgment go against him, the issue joined falls through and he begins to be bound by the judgment. And this is the meaning of what is said by ancient writers, that 'before joinder of issue the defendant ought to pay, after joinder of issue he ought to be condemned, after condemnation he ought to satisfy the judgment.' Hence it follows that if I have sued for a debt by *legitimum iudicium*,[c] I cannot later on sue in respect of it *ipso iure*, because I fruitlessly state my claim to be 'that it ought to be given to me;' for by joinder of issue the duty to give has ceased.

[c] § 188.

ut damnari debeat; nostri praeceptores absolvere eum debere existimant, nec interesse cuius generis sit iudicium: et hoc est quod vulgo dicitur, Sabino et Cassio placere omnia iudicia esse absolutoria.[1]

Ulp.: In hac actione sicut in ceteris **bonae fidei iudiciis . . . rei iudicandae** tempus quanti res sit observatur, quamvis in **stricti iuris litis contestatae** tempus spectetur.—D. 13, 6, 3, 2.[2]

Paul.: Cum fundus vel homo petitus esset, puto hoc nos iure uti, ut post acceptum iudicium **causa omnis** restituenda sit, i.e. omne quod habiturus esset actor, si litis contestandae tempore solutus fuisset.—D. 12, 1, 31 pr.[3]

§ 27. Judgment, and that which represents it.

The suit is ended by the 'sententia,' judgment or decision; *i.e.*, the sentence of the judge regularly containing a condemnation or absolution of the defendant.[a] The signification of the judgment is such that it definitely decides the legal relation in issue, and

[a] § 202.

---

[1] It remains for us to consider what is the duty of the *iudex* when the defendant, having submitted to arbitration, but before award, makes satisfaction to the plaintiff. Ought he to acquit or rather to condemn, because at the time of submission to arbitration the defendant was in such a position that he ought to be condemned? The leaders of our school hold that he ought to acquit, and that it matters not what kind of action it was. And this is what is meant by the common saying that Sabinus and Cassius judged that all actions allow of acquittal.

[2] In this action as in the other actions *bonae fidei* . . . regard is had to the time when the matter is decided in determining the value, although in [actions] under the strict Law the time of joining issue is looked to.

[3] When land or a man had been claimed, I am of opinion . . . the law followed by us would be that after submission to arbitration, the whole legal estate should be given up, that is, all that the plaintiff would have had if it had been offered at the time issue was joined.

BOOK I. Chapter II.

[a] Cf. Pollock, 'Essays in Jurisprudence,' pp. 237-260, and Clark, 'Pract. Jurisprudence,' pp. 214, *sqq.* The article in Holtzendorff's 'Rechts-Lexicon,' referred to by Prof. Clark (p. 224), is neither exact nor complete; better information would be found in that on the *Reichsgericht.*

[b] Cited by Coke on Littleton, 103 a.

[c] § 26.

accordingly, even if it be materially wrong, yet possesses formal truth, *i.e.*, passes as right unconditionally and irreversibly: it has the force of Law, is 'res iudicata.' [a]

Mod.: **Res iudicata** dicitur quae finem controversiarum pronuntiatione iudicis accipit, quod vel condemnatione vel absolutione contingit.—l. 1, D. de re iud. 42, 1.[1]

Ulp.: Res iudicata pro veritate accipitur.—D. 50, 17, 207.[2] [b]

The negative operation of the 'res iudicata' consists in the consumption of the right of action, the 'exceptio r. i.' (instead of and besides the exc. r. in iud. deductae), which is here based upon the mere actual existence of the judgment. Its positive operation is

(1) The grounding of a new obligatory relation of the parties in lieu of that created by the L.C., the subject of which is the 'iudicatum facere oportere' [c] —the 'obligatio, actio iudicati.'

Ulp.:—sicut stipulatione contrahitur, ita iudicio contrahi; proinde non originem iudicii spectandam, sed ipsam **iudicati** velut **obligationem.**—D. 15, 1, 3, 11.[3]

Id.: **Iudicati actio** perpetua est et rei persecutionem continet; item heredi et in heredem competit.—l. 6, § 3, D. de re iud.[4]

(2) The conclusively binding decision which grounds judgment against the defendant, or his absolution, upon the actual right in issue (especially with actiones

[1] A *res iudicata* is so called in which the suit is concluded by the sentence of the *iudex*. This happens either by a judgment against the defendant or by his absolution.

[2] A *res iudicata* is regarded as founded in truth.

[3] That just as a contract is entered into by stipulation, such likewise arises from his being involved in an action; therefore one must not look to the commencement of the suit, but, as it were, to the obligation arising out of the decision.

[4] The action arising out of a judgment is continuous, and carries with it the claim of the thing. It is available both by the heir and against him.

Book I. Chapter II.

in rem), which is upheld in its positive or material function[a] against subsequent infringements also, by means of the 'exc. (or even repl.) rei iudicatae.'[b] The 'exc. rei iudicatae' attaches as soon as the same question of law is raised between the same parties[c] as subject of a new action.

[a] Based upon the contents of the judgment.

[b] See § 90.

[c] 'Res iudicata ius facit inter partes.'

Macer.: Saepe constitutum est, res inter alios iudicatas aliis non praeiudicare.—l. 63, D. de re iud.[1]

Ulp.: Ita definiri potest, totiens **eandem rem** agi, quotiens apud iudicium posteriorem id quaeritur, quod apud priorem quaesitum est.—Et generaliter ut Iulianus definit, exceptio rei iudicatae obstat, quotiens inter **easdem personas eadem quaestio** revocatur, vel alio genere iudicii.—Ceterum cum quis actionum mutat et experitur, dummodo de eadem re experitur, etsi diverso genere actionis, quam instituit, videtur 'de ea re' agere.—D. 44, 2, l. 7, §§ 1, 4, and l. 5.[2]

Paul.: Actiones in personam ab actionibus in rem hoc differunt, quod cum eadem res ab eodem mihi debeatur, singulas obligationes singulae causae sequuntur nec ulla earum alterius petitione vitiatur; at cum in rem ago non expressa causa, ex qua rem meam esse dico, omnes causae una petitione adprehenduntur: neque enim amplius quam semel res mea esse potest, saepius autem deberi potest.—l. 14, § 2 eod.[3]

---

[1] In numerous constitutions it is stated that as between other parties judgments do no detriment to any one.

[2] One can here lay down as a rule that the same thing is claimed whenever the same question comes before the later *iudex* as the earlier one.—And in general one may say with Jul. that the plea of a *res iudicata* avails whenever the same question is dealt with between the same persons although in another set of proceedings. When, moreover, any one changes an action and then goes on suing, provided that it concerns the same object, although in a different sort of action from that which he had begun, he appears to sue for the same object.

[3] Actions *in personam* are distinguished from those *in rem*

Book I. Chapter II.

Gai. iv. 55: Item palam est, si quis aliud pro alio intenderit, nihil eum periclitari eumque ex integro agere posse, quia nihil ante videtur egisse: veluti si is qui hominem Stichum petere deberet, Erotem petierit, aut si quis ex testamento dari sibi oportere intenderit, cui ex stipulatu debebatur.[1]

Ulp.: Cum iudicatur rem meam esse, simul iudicatur illius[a] non esse.—D. 3, 3, 40, 2.[2]

[a] Sc. possessoris.

A suit can also be definitely concluded, as by a legally binding judgment, without a 'iudicium' or delivery of a 'sententia.'

1. When the defendant confesses the plaintiff's claim before the magistrate having jurisdiction (confessio in iure). If the claim and the 'confessio' do not go to a definite sum of money (certa pecunia) there is need further of a judicial 'arbitrium,' to take a valuation of the matter of complaint that has been confessed.[b]

[b] § 194. Cf. § 24.

Confessus pro iudicato est, qui quodammodo sua sententia damnatur.—**Certum** confessus pro iudicato erit, incertum non erit.—D. 42, 2, 1 (Paul.) and 6 pr. (Ulp.).[3]

---

herein, that if any one is indebted to me in respect of the same thing, the several grounds of action remain connected respectively with the several obligations, and none of such is prejudiced by the claim set up by the other; but if I bring a real action without expressly mentioning the ground upon which I maintain it to be mine, all grounds of action are included in the claim, for a thing cannot be mine oftener than once, but may be owing to me repeatedly.

[1] Again, it is clear that if a person claim one thing instead of another, it is not at his peril, and he can bring a fresh action because he seems to have taken no steps previously; for example, when a man who ought to sue for the slave Stichus sues for Eros, or when a man to whom a debt was incurred upon a stipulation alleges in his claim that it is due to him under a will.

[2] When it is decided that the thing is mine, it is at the same time decided that it belongs not to so and so.

[3] One who makes confession is on a par with him that is

Book I. Chapter II.

Paul.: Si is cum quo lege Aquilia agitur, confessus est servum occidisse, licet non occiderit, si tamen occisus sit homo, ex confesso tenetur.—l. 4 eod.[1]

Ulp.: Notandum, quod in hac actione, quae adversus confitentem datur, iudex non rei iudicandae sed **aestimandae** datur, nam nullae partes sunt iudicandi in confitentes.—D. 9, 2, 25, 2.[2]

2. When the defendant or plaintiff makes oath before the magistrate—tendered by or upon reference[a] of the opponent—as to the existence of the right in issue (ius iurandum in iure) there arises the 'exceptio' and 'actio'—in factum—'iuris iurandi,' in place of the 'exc. rei iud.' and the 'actio iud.'

[a] Comp. the *reference to oath* in Scottish Law; see Paterson, 'Compendium,' s. 481.

Gai.: Maximum remedium experiendarum litium in usum venit iurisiurandi religio, qua vel **ex pactione** ipsorum litigatorum vel **ex auctoritate iudicis** deciduntur controversiae.—l. 1, D. de iurej. 12, 2.[3]

Ulp.: **Iusiurandum** vicem rei iudicatae obtinet non immerito, cum ipse quis iudicem adversarium suum de causa sua fecerit, deferendo ei iusiurandum.—D. 44, 5, 1.[4]

---

condemned, since in a measure he is condemned by his own sentence.—He who makes an unmistakable confession will pass as condemned, but not he that makes an uncertain one.

1 If any person defendant under the *lex Aquilia* confesses that he has slain the slave, he is bound by his confession though he may not have slain him.

2 We must observe that in this action which is granted against a person making confession, the *iudex* is not appointed to decide upon the matter but to appraise it, for against a confessor the *iudex* has nothing further to decide.

3 As the most effectual means of arranging actions, the sacredness of an oath has come into use, by which disputes are decided, either in consequence of the agreement of the litigants themselves, or by direction of the *iudex*.

4 The oath takes the place of the *res iudicata*, and rightly, because a man makes the opponent judge in his own matter by tendering the oath.

Book I. Chapter II.

Paul.: Manifestae turpitudinis et **confessionis** est, nolle nec iurare nec iusiurandum referre.—l. 38, D. de iurej.[1]

Ulp.: Iureiurando dato . . . reus quidem adquirit exceptionem . . . , actor vero actionem adquirit, in qua hoc solum quaeritur, an iuraverit **dari sibi oportere.**—§ Si petitor iuravit, possessore deferente, **rem suam esse,** actori, dabitur actio;—sed si possessori fuerit iusiurandum delatum iuraveritque **rem petitoris non esse,** quamdiu quidem possidet, adversus eum qui detulit iusiurandum, si petat, exceptione iusiurandi utetur;—si cum possideret, deferente petitore **rem suam** iuravit, consequenter dicemus, amissa quoque possessione si is qui detulit iusiurandum, nactus sit possessionem, actionem in factum ei dandam.—l. 9, § 1, 7; l. 11 pr., § 1 eod.[2]

[a] Cf. § 198.

§ 28. *Exceptiones* and *Replicationes*.[a]

'Exceptio' (plea) is to be distinguished from simple denial of the ground of action, or negation of the plaintiff's 'intentio;' in other words, from the contention that the right set up by the plaintiff has never existed at all or is already extinct, *i.e.*, has been

[1] It is a mark of plain dishonour and of confession neither to make oath nor to be willing to answer the oath.

[2] After the oath is taken the defendant certainly acquires a plea, but the plaintiff gets an action, in which the only inquiry is if he has sworn that the thing must be given to him.—If the plaintiff, when the defendant tenders the oath, has sworn that the thing is his, then an action will be granted to the plaintiff.—But if the oath should be tendered to the person in possession and he have sworn that the thing does not belong to the plaintiff, he will use the plea of the oath against him who tendered it, if he should claim [the thing], so long, indeed, as he possesses it. If when he possessed he swore, upon tender by the plaintiff, that the thing is his, we shall then say that an action must be granted him for what has happened even after the possession is lost, if he who tendered the oath shall have acquired possession.

annulled by the superinduction of a fact positively extinguishing it according to the law in force (ius civile). It is that means of defence which consists in the appeal to some circumstance—either a right contrary to that of the plaintiff and limiting it, or a fact[a] —which according to Praetorian or Civil Law,[b] and often from grounds of 'aequitas,' avails to release the defendant from an adverse judgment, in spite of the 'intentio,' which is *ipso iure* well founded in law, and consequently, without directly annulling the claim of the plaintiff.—'Exceptio' in the material sense designates the right of a person to that appeal, the possibility of meeting the 'actio' with an 'exceptio.'

[a] *E.g.*, in § 90.

[b] §§ 120, 129, 145.

Paul.: Nihil interest **ipso iure** quis actionem non habeat, an **per exceptionem** infirmetur.—D. 50, 17, 112.[1]

Gai. iv. §§ 116, sq.: Comparatae sunt autem exceptiones defendendorum eorum gratia, cum quibus agitur. Saepe enim accidit, ut quis iure civili teneatur, sed **iniquum** sit eum iudicio condemnari: veluti si stipulatus sim a te pecuniam tamquam credendi causa numeraturus, nec numeraverim; nam eam pecuniam a te peti posse certum est, 'dare' enim te 'oportet,' cum ex stipulatu teneris: sed quia iniquum est te eo nomine condemnari, placet, per exceptionem doli mali te defendi debere. Item si pactus fuero tecum, ne id quod mihi debeas a te petam, nihilo minus [id ipsum] a te petere possum DARE MIHI OPORTERE, quia obligatio pacto convento non tollitur; sed placet, debere me petentem per exceptionem pacti conventi repelli. § In his quoque actionibus, quae non in personam sunt, exceptiones locum habent, veluti si metu me coegeris aut dolo induxeris, ut tibi rem aliquam mancipio dem: nam si eam rem a me petas, datur mihi exceptio,

---

1 There is no difference whether a man have not an action *ipso iure* or it be subverted by a plea.

per quam si metus causa te fecisse aut dolo malo arguero, repelleris.[1]

Paul.: Exceptio est condicio, quae modo eximit reum damnatione, modo minuit damnationem.—l. 22 pr., D. h. t. (=de except. 44, 1).[2]

The ground and contents of an 'exceptio' may be very different; of quite general nature is the 'exc. doli (generalis)'—concurrent with the usually special pleas, and subsidiary—which is always well founded, when the plaintiff, from the point of view of equity, suffers already a material wrong by the action being brought.

Paul.: Ideo autem hanc exceptionem (doli) praetor proposuit, ne cui dolus suus per occasionem iuris civilis contra naturalem aequitatem prosit.—D. 44, 4, 1, 1.[3]

---

[1] Now *exceptiones* have been provided with the object of protecting defendants; for it often happens that a person is liable according to the *i. c.*, but it would be unreasonable that judgment should be given against him in the action, as, for instance, if I have stipulated for money from you which I was about to hand over to you by way of loan, and have not handed it over. For it is certain that such money can be sued for by you, because it is your duty to pay, as you are liable on the stipulation. But as it is unfair that you should be condemned on that account, it is held that you should be protected by the plea of fraud. So also if I have agreed with you that I will not demand what you owe me, I can nevertheless claim [that very thing] from you by the formula 'that you ought to pay me,' because the obligation is not dissolved by the agreement we came to, but it is held that I ought, if I sue, to be defeated by the plea of agreement made. *Exceptiones* are also admissible in actions that are not *in personam*, as for instance, if you have coerced me by intimidation or induced me by fraud to grant you something by formal conveyance, because, if you sue me for that thing, a plea is allowed me by which you will be defeated if I show that you acted with intent to intimidate, or fraudulently.

[2] A plea is a condition which sometimes releases a defendant from condemnation, sometimes reduces the condemnation.

[3] The Praetor has accordingly established this plea, that no one's fraud may serve him so as to make the *i. c.* available against natural equity.

Ulp.: —dolo facere eum qui contra pactum petat, negari non potest.—l. 2, § 4 eod.[1]

Et generaliter sciendum est, ex omnibus in factum exceptionibus **doli** oriri **exceptionem,** quia dolo facit, quicumque id, quod quaque exceptione elidi potest, petit: nam et si inter initia nihil dolo malo fecit, attamen nunc petendo facit dolose, nisi si talis ignorantia sit in eo, ut dolo careat.—l. 2, § 5 eod.[2]

Paul.: Dolo facit, qui petit, quod redditurus est.—l. 8 pr. eod.[3]

Exceptiones are divided—

(1) According to their operation, into 'peremptoriae (perpetuae)' and 'dilatoriae (temporales).' The 'perpetuae' at all times bar the action, and constantly render the right of action entirely inoperative, (destructive pleas); whilst the 'temporales' bar the action only for a while, and thus suspend the validity of the plaintiff's claim (dilatory pleas). The effect of both kinds of 'exceptio' is, however, the same in the case of successful demurrer.

Gai.: **Perpetuae** atque **peremptoriae** sunt, quae semper locum habent, nec evitari possunt, qualis est doli mali, et rei iudicatae, et si quid contra leges senatusve consultum factum esse dicetur, item pacti conventi perpetui, i.e. ne omnino pecunia petatur.—**Temporales** atque **dilatoriae** sunt, quae non semper locum habent sed evitari possunt qualis est pacti conventi temporalis, i.e.

---

1 It cannot be denied that he acts fraudulently who makes a claim in spite of a bargain.

2 And it in general is to be observed that the plea of fraud springs out of all pleas as to matter of fact, because every one acts fraudulently who claims that which can be avoided by some plea; for, although originally he did not act fraudulently, he does now so act by making a claim, unless his ignorance be so great that he is free from fraud.

3 He acts fraudulently who claims what he will have again to give up.

ne forte intra quinquennium ageretur.—l. 3, D. h. t.[1]

Ulp.: —**dilatoria** est exceptio, quae differt actionem.—l. 2, § 4 eod.[2]

Gai. iv. 123: Observandum est autem ei, cui dilatoria obiicitur exceptio, ut differat actionem; alioquin si obiecta exceptione egerit, rem perdit: nec enim post illud tempus, quo integra re eam evitare poterat, adhuc ei potestas agendi superest, re in iudicium deducta et per exceptionem perempta.[3]

(2.) According to their subjective relation, into 'exc. in rem' and 'in personam' (passively real and personal), according as they can be opposed to any, or only a certain, person as plaintiff; and into 'exc. rei' and 'personae cohaerentes' (actively real and personal), according as they belong to any, or only to a particular, person as defendant.

Ulp.: Et quidem illud adnotandum est, quod specialiter exprimendum est, de cuius dolo quis queratur, non in rem: SI IN EA RE NIHIL DOLO MALO FACTVM EST, sed sic: SI IN EA RE NIHIL DOLO MALO ACTORIS FACTVM EST. Docere igitur debet is qui obiicit exceptionem, dolo malo actoris

---

[1] Perpetual and peremptory are those which are always admissible and cannot be avoided, as for example, those of fraud and *res iudicata*, and if it is alleged that aught has been done in contravention of statutes or a *senatus-consultum*; likewise those of a continuous contractual agreement, *i.e.*, that a sum of money shall certainly not be demanded. Temporal and dilatory are those which are not always admissible, but can be avoided, *e.g.*, those of a temporal contractual agreement, *i.e.*, that, it may be, proceedings shall not be taken within five years.

[2] A dilatory plea is that which postpones the action.

[3] Now he against whom a dilatory plea is submitted should see that he postpones his action, otherwise if he continues proceedings after the plea has been submitted, he loses the cause. For not even after the time when he could have avoided it, and the cause was intact, does a right of action survive to him, the matter having been laid before the court and disposed of by the plea.

factum, nec sufficiet ei ostendere in re esse dolum. § Plane ex persona eius, qui exceptionem obiicit, **in rem** opponitur exceptio: neque enim quaeritur, adversus quem commissus sit dolus, sed an in ea re dolo malo factum sit a parte actoris.—D. 44, 4, 2, §§ 1, 2.[1]

Id.: Exceptio doli personam complectitur eius, qui doli fecit enimvero metus causa exceptio **in rem** scripta est: SI IN EA RE NIHIL METVS CAVSA FACTVM EST, ut non inspiciamus, an is qui agit metus causa fecit aliquid, sed an omnino metus causa factum est in hac re a quocumque, non tantum ab eo qui agit.—l. 4, § 33 eod.[2]

Paul.: Exceptiones, quae **personae** cuiusque **cohaerent,** non transeunt ad alios. § **Rei** autem **cohaerentes** exceptiones etiam fideiiussoribus competunt, ut rei iudicatae, doli mali, iurisiurandi, quod metus causa factum est. Igitur et si reus pactus sit in rem, omnimodo competit exceptio fideiussori.—l. 7 pr., § 1, D. h. t.[3]

---

[1] And a point to be observed is, that it must be expressly said for whose fraud any one brings an action; not *in rem:* 'If nothing have been done in the matter through fraud,' but thus: 'If in such matter nothing have been done through fraud of the plaintiff.' Accordingly, as to him who puts forward the plea that something has been done by fraud of the plaintiff, it will not be enough for him to show that fraud lies in the thing itself. —With regard to the person of him who puts forward the plea, it obtains a 'real' character; for it is not a question against whom fraud has been committed, but whether in such matter fraud has taken place on the part of the plaintiff.

[2] The plea of fraud affects the person of him who has acted fraudulently, but the plea 'because of intimidation' has a 'real' relation: 'If in such matter nothing has been done through intimidation,' so that we do not consider whether the plaintiff has done anything in order to intimidate, but whether generally in this matter it have been done by any one whomsoever to intimidate, and not merely by the plaintiff.

[3] Pleas which appertain to a certain person do not pass to others.—§ The pleas which go with the matter belong also to the sureties, as of *res iudicata*, of fraud, of a declaration, on

Book I. Chapter II.

[a] 'Quasi exceptionis exceptio.'

[b] *E.g.*, in §§ 90, 102, 129.

In like manner as the 'actio' by an 'exceptio,' can the latter be met by a 'replicatio,'[a] and this again by a 'duplicatio,' and so on.[b]

Ulp.: **Replicationes** nihil aliud sunt, quam exceptiones, et a parte actoris veniunt; quae quidem ideo necessariae sunt, ut exceptiones excludant.—l. 2, § 1, D. h. t.[1]

Gai. iv. §§ 126–129: Interdum evenit, ut exceptio quae prima facie iusta videatur, inique noceat actori; quod cum accidit alia adiectione opus est adiuvandi actoris gratia: quae adiectio **replicatio** vocatur, quia per eam replicatur atque resolvitur vis exceptionis.—§ Interdum autem evenit, ut rursus replicatio, quae prima facie iusta sit, inique reo noceat; quod cum accidit, adiectione opus est adiuvandi rei gratia, quae **duplicatio** vocatur. § Et si rursus ea prima facie iusta videatur, sed propter aliquam causam inique actori noceat, rursus adiectione opus est, qua actor adiuvetur, quae dicitur **triplicatio**. § Quarum omnium adiectionum usum interdum etiam ulterius quam diximus varietas negotiarum introduxit.—(= pr. §§ 1–3, I. de replicat. 4, 14.)[2]

oath, and of what has been done through intimidation. Accordingly, if the defendant have entered into a contract *in rem*, a plea is at all times available by the surety.

[1] *Replicationes* are nothing else than pleas, and proceed from the plaintiff; and these are necessary in order to restrain pleas.

[2] It sometimes happens that a plea, which *prima facie* seems just, unfairly prejudices the plaintiff. When this occurs, another addition is necessary to aid the plaintiff, and this addition is called a *replicatio*, because by means of it the force of the plea is rebutted and destroyed. § But sometimes it happens that a *replicatio* in its turn, which *prima facie* is just, unfairly prejudices the defendant; and when this occurs there is need of an addition for the purpose of relieving the defendant, which is called a *duplicatio*. § And if again this appear *prima facie* fair, but for some reason unjustly prejudices the plaintiff, another addition is needed in relief of the plaintiff, which is called a *triplicatio*. The variety of transactions has brought about the employment of all these additions even beyond what we have specified.

§ 29. Interdicts.[a]

For certain cases, especially in view of the protection of possession or of other actual condition of things, as well as of public order and the arrangements of intercourse, against arbitrary infringement, injunctions of the praetor, in standing formulae attached to definite presumptions, were put forward in the Edict. These were 'interdicta' in the wider sense, sometimes commands, or 'decreta,' at other times prohibitions, or 'interdicta' in the narrower sense, which the magistrate by virtue of his *imperium* issued in the particular case to those alleged to act in an objectionable way (or even to both parties) upon the application of the one who believed himself injured, and without further investigation in the presence of the parties of the actual circumstances. —The non-observance of the praetor's injunction ('interdictum redditum') led to a further judicial proceeding, in which the existence of the actual presumptions raised by that injunction in the particular case, and accordingly of an actual disobedience to it,[b] was judicially settled, and the case was decided.

[a] Cf. § 202. Represented in English Law by 'injunction' and 'mandamus,' as to which see Stephen, iii. 118, &c., and Brown, s. vv.

[b] 'Adversus edictum praetoris.'

> Gai. iv. §§ 139, sq.: Certis igitur ex causis praetor aut proconsul principaliter auctoritatem suam finiendis controversiis interponit, quod tum maxime facit, cum de possessione aut quasi possessione inter aliquos contenditur; et in summa aut iubet aliquid fieri aut fieri prohibet; formulae autem et verborum conceptiones, quibus in ea re utitur, interdicta decretave vocantur. § Vocantur autem **decreta,** cum fieri aliquid iubet, veluti cum praecipit, ut aliquid exhibeatur aut restituatur; **interdicta** vero, cum prohibet fieri, veluti cum praecipit, ne sine vitio possidenti vis fiat, neve in loco sacro aliquid fiat: unde omnia interdicta aut **restitutoria** aut **exhibitoria** aut **prohibitoria** vocantur.[1]

[1] In certain cases, then, the praetor or proconsul interposes his authority at the outset to put an end to disputes; and this

Book I. Chapter II.

In the later Law the application for and issue of the interdict was omitted, so that an action could be maintained directly upon the ground of the interdict.

Inst. iv. 15, § 8: De ordine et veteri exitu interdictorum supervacuum est hodie dicere: nam quotiens extra ordinem ius dicitur, qualia sunt hodie omnia iudicia, non est necesse reddi interdictum, sed perinde iudicatur sine interdictis, atque si utilis actio ex causa interdicti reddita fuisset.[1]

The 'interdicta' (apart from the division into restit., exhib., prohib.) are divided into—

(1) 'Petitory' (quae proprietatis causam continent) and 'possessory' (quae possessionis caus. cont.).

Gai. iv. 143: Sequens in eo est divisio quod vel adipiscendae **possessionis** causa comparatae sunt vel **retinendae** vel **recuperandae**.[2]

[a] See §§ 91, 98.

(2) 'Simplicia' and 'duplicia.'[a]

Gai. iv. §§ 156–158, 160: Tertia divisio

---

he does particularly when there is a dispute between persons about possession or quasi-possession; and in general he orders something to be done, or forbids its being done. Now the formulae and forms of words which he uses in such matter are called interdicts or decrees. § They are called decrees, when he orders something to be done, as for instance, when he makes an order that something shall be produced or given up; but interdicts, when he forbids a thing being done, as when he orders that no violence shall be done to a person in innocent possession, or that something shall not be done on sacred ground. Hence all interdicts are called either restitutory, or exhibitory, or prohibitory.

[1] Of the system and former result of interdicts it is at the present day superfluous to speak. For whenever the law is administered *extra ordinem*, as now all tribunals, it is unnecessary to grant an interdict, but the trial is conducted without interdicts, just as if a *utilis actio* grounded upon the interdict had been granted.

[2] The next division lies in this, that they are either provided for the purpose of acquiring possession, or of retaining it, or of recovering it.

interdictorum in hoc est, quod aut simplicia sunt aut duplicia. § **Simplicia** sunt, velut in quibus alter actor alter reus est, qualia sunt omnia restitutoria aut exhibitoria: namque actor est, qui desiderat aut exhiberi aut restitui, reus est, a quo desideratur, ut exhibeat aut restituat. § Prohibitoriorum autem interdictorum alia duplicia alia simplicia sunt.—§ **Duplicia** sunt velut VTI POSSIDETIS interdictum et VTRVBI: ideo autem duplicia vocantur, quod par utriusque litigatoris in his condicio est, nec quisquam praecipue reus vel actor intelligitur, sed unusquisque tam rei quam actoris partes sustinet.[1]

§ 30. THE EXTRAORDINARY MEANS OF PROTECTION OF RIGHTS BY *IN INTEGRUM RESTITUTIO*.

Whilst ordinary legal means protect subsisting rights against infringement, and cancel the actual conditions which fetter them, the object of the extraordinary means of 'in integr. rest.'[a] is to remove the disadvantages which attend any one affected by the very determinations of Law; and so, to change a given state of Law, *i.e.*, to terminate a right resting upon the rigour of positive law, and to reinstate what has been lost in its stead. Its intrinsic ground and purpose is the assimilation with 'aequitas' of the rigid and formal, uniformly applied law, which in particular cases readily conceals within it a material wrong. Conformably with the

[a] Restitution to the previous state.

---

[1] A third division of interdicts lies in this, that they are either simple or double. § There are simple, *e.g.*, in which one party is plaintiff and the other defendant—such are all restitutory or exhibitory interdicts. For the plaintiff is he who asks that the thing be produced or given up, the defendant is he of whom the production or delivery up is asked. § Now of prohibitory interdicts there are such as *Uti possidetis* and *Utrubi*: they are called 'double' from the fact that the position of each litigant in these is equal, and neither of them is considered as being specially defendant or plaintiff, but each sustains the part as well of defendant as of plaintiff.

Book I. Chapter II.

idea of justice, it has to remove an injury which has arisen by means of the law itself (*e.g.*, by declaration of will, or any other juristic event), and which is none the less a legal one, but alien to the rational nature and purpose of legal order, and though not an injustice in form, is one in substance. The relief, accordingly, which the *i. i. r.* affords against the consequences of the law, where it would lead to an 'iniquitas,' is affected in such way that the magistrate who administers the law rescinds upon some special ground the injurious legal effect of the juristic fact—the legal alteration which has taken place—and thus treats it as though it had not happened. The *i. i. r.* derives its extraordinary character at the same time from what has been before spoken of.[a]

[a] Cf. also § 4.

Paul. Sent. 1, 7, § 1: Integri restitutio est redintegrandae rei vel causae actio.[1]

Ulp.: Utilitas huius tituli non eget commendatione, ipsa enim se ostendit. Nam sub hoc titulo plurifariam praetor hominibus vel lapsis vel circumscriptis subvenit—. l. 1, de I. I. R. 4, 1.[2]

Marc.: D. Antoninus . . . rescripsit: Etsi nihil facile mutandum est ex solemnibus, tamen ubi aequitas evidens poscit, subveniendum est—. l. 7 pr. eod.[3]

Ulp.: In causae cognitione etiam hoc versabitur, num forte alia actio possit competere citra in integrum restitutionem; nam **si communi auxilio et mero iure** munitus sit, non debet ei

---

[1] *Integri restitutio* is the action for restoration of a thing or a cause.

[2] The usefulness of this title requires no recommendation, because it is self-manifest. For under this title the praetor in manifold ways relieves persons that have been mistaken or have been imposed upon.

[3] The late Emperor Antoninus responded: Although nothing should readily be changed of formalities, nevertheless where manifest equity demands it, relief must be given.

tribui **extraordinarium auxilium.**—D. 4, 4, 16 pr.[1]

Callistr.: Scio illud a quibusdam observatum, ne propter satis minimam rem vel summam, si maiori rei vel summae praeiudicetur, audiatur is qui in integrum restitui postulat.—l. 4, D. de I. I. R.[2]

The following are the presumptions of the *i. i. r.*—

(1) Injury suffered by the petitioner, *i.e.*, a disadvantage entailed by the juristic event in question, neither fortuitous nor self-incurred, as some rule relating to the Law of Property, not entirely without importance.[a] [a] § 107.

Ulp.: Item non restituetur, qui sobrie rem suam administrans occasione damni, non inconsulte accidentis sed fato, velit restitui; nec enim eventus damni restitutionem indulget, sed inconsulta facilitas. . . . Unde Marcellus apud Iulianum notat, si minor sibi servum necessarium comparaverit, mox is decesserit, non debere eum restitui; neque enim captus est emendo sibi rem pernecessariam, licet mortalem.—l. 11, § 4, D. de minor. 4, 4.[3]

---

[1] In the investigation of a cause this will also come into consideration, whether besides the *i. i. r.* another action possibly can be entertained. For if a person is protected by a general remedy and clear law, an extraordinary remedy ought not to be vouchsafed to him.

[2] I am aware that some have remarked that he ought not to be heard who asks to be reinstated in his former position because of a thing or sum very small, if the injury be in respect of a greater thing or sum.

[3] Likewise he will not be reinstated who, administering his property with circumspection, asks to be reinstated upon occasion of an injury that happens by no thoughtless action, but by chance; for it is not the result of the injury itself which conduces to restitution, but unadvised carelessness. . . . Hence Marc. remarks in Jul. if a minor has acquired a necessary slave but the latter have soon died, he is not to be placed in the former position; for neither has he been imposed upon in buying himself a very necessary thing, though it be mortal.

Book I. Chapter II.

Id.: Et placet in delictis minoribus non subveniri.—l. 9, § 2 eod.[1]

Paul.: Non negligentibus subvenitur, sed necessitate rerum impeditis.—D. 4, 6, 16.[2]

(2) The existence of a 'iusta causa,' *i.e.*, of some actual circumstance standing in a casual relation to the injury which has occurred, upon the part of the petitioner or of the person in relation with him, which justifies the extraordinary relief in the particular case. This is the ground of restitution.

Paul.: Is qui reipublicae causa abest, in aliqua re laesus non restituitur, in qua, etiam si reipublicae causa non abfuisset, damnum erat passurus. —D. 4, 6, 44.[3]

Ulp.: Si locupleti heres (minor) exstitit et subito hereditas lapsa sit, puta praedia fuerunt quae chasmate perierunt, insulae exustae sunt, servi fugerunt aut decesserunt, Iulianus quidem sic loquitur, quasi possit minor in integrum restitui; Marcellus autem notat, cessare in integrum restitutionem; neque enim aetatis lubrico captus est adeundo locupletem hereditatem, et quod fato contingit, cuivis patrifamilias quamvis diligentissimo possit contingere. Sed haec res adferre potest restitutionem minori, si adiit hereditatem in qua res erant multae mortales vel praedia urbana, aes autem alienum grave: quod non prospexit posse evenire, ut demoriantur mancipia, praedia ruant, vel quod non cito distraxerit haec quae multis casibus obnoxia sunt.—l. 11, § 5, D. de minor.[4]

---

[1] And the opinion is that in minor offences no relief should be given.

[2] Relief is not given to the careless, but to those clogged by the force of circumstances.

[3] He that is absent on State business, when he has suffered loss in respect of any object, is not reinstated with regard to what he would have suffered loss in, had he not been absent on State affairs.

[4] If [a minor] have succeeded a man of wealth, and the in-

(3) A petition at the proper time for reinstatement to be brought, according to the earlier Law within one 'annus utilis,' according to that of Justinian within a 'quadriennium continuum.'

As grounds of restitution, there are recognised in the Praetor's Edict—

1. Minority. The lex Plaetoria de circumscriptione adulescentium c. 550 U.C. had introduced a public accusation in respect of crafty overreaching of minors; so also 'exc. l. Plaet.' against the action to which the particular transaction gives rise; by general restitution these legal remedies became unnecessary.[a] [a] Cf § 60.

Ulp.: Hoc edictum praetor **naturalem aequitatem** secutus proposuit, quo tutelam minorum suscepit; nam cum constat inter omnes, fragile esse et infirmum huiusmodi aetatum consilium et multis captionibus suppositum, auxilium eis praetor hoc edicto pollicitus est et adversus captiones opitulationem. § Praetor edicit: QVOD CVM MINORE QVAM VIGINTI QVINQVE ANNIS NATV GESTVM ESSE DICETVR, VTI QVAEQVE RES ERIT, ANIMADVERTAM.—D. 4, 4, 1 pr., § 1.[1]

---

heritance has suddenly fallen through, *e.g.*, if there were estates which have disappeared through a landslip, the buildings have been burnt, the slaves have fled or died, J. expresses himself as if the minor can still be reinstated; but M.'s annotation is that the reinstatement is lost; for upon his entering upon a wealthy inheritance he has not been imposed upon through any imprudence attaching to his age, and what happens by fate may happen to even the most circumspect head of a family. But the following circumstance can carry reinstatement: if he have entered upon an inheritance upon which were many beings subject to death, or urban estates, but a heavy debt; because he did not foresee that it could come about that slaves should die, estates be destroyed, or because he has not speedily parted with such things liable to many mishaps.

[1] This edict in which he has undertaken the protection of minors, the praetor has put forth with regard to natural equity; for since every one knows that decision in people of this age is

Book I. Chapter II.

Paul.: Non semper autem ea, quae cum minoribus geruntur, rescindenda sunt, sed ad **bonum et aequum** redigenda sunt, ne magno incommodo huius aetatis homines afficiantur nemine cum his contrahente, et quodammodo commercio eis interdicatur; itaque nisi aut manifesta circumscriptio sit, aut tam negligenter in ea causa versati sunt, praetor interponere se non debet.—l. 24, § 1 eod.[1]

Ulp.: Non omnia, quae minores annis viginti quinque gerunt, irrita sunt, sed ea tantum, quae causa cognita eiusmodi deprehensa sunt, ut vel ab aliis circumventi vel sua facilitate decepti aut quod habuerunt amiserint, aut quod adquirere emolumentum potuerunt omiserint, aut se oneri quod non suscipere licuit obligaverint.—l. 44 eod.[2]

2. Metus, dolus.[a] Concurrent with the i. i. r. is the act. 'quod metus causa' and the act. 'de dolo.'[b]

[a] See § 18. For Mistake, §§ 202, 205.

[b] § 137.

---

easily shaken, and inconstant, and exposed to much deception, the praetor has in this edict promised them help and relief against deception. § The praetor's proclamation is: 'If anything be alleged as transacted with one under 25 years of age, according to the circumstances of each case will I give attention to it.'

[1] Now those dealings which are had with minors are not always to be declared invalid, but they are only to be varied according to justice and equity, so that persons of this age be not greatly inconvenienced by the fact that no one contracts with them, and they be debarred in a manner from business dealings; and so the praetor ought not to intervene unless there be clear overreaching, or the minor have dealt quite imprudently in such matter.

[2] Not everything that persons less than 25 years of age transact is invalid, but that only which, upon investigation of the matter, is shown to be of such character that, whether as imposed upon by others or deceived by their credibility, they have either lost what they had, or have disregarded the benefit they could obtain, or have incumbered themselves with an obligation which they ought not to have incurred.

Ulp.: Ait praetor: QVOD METVS CAVSA GESTVM ERIT, RATVM NON HABEBO.—D. 4, 2, 1.[1]

Marc.: —deceptis sine culpa sua, maxime si fraus ab adversario intervenerit, succurri oportebit, cum etiam de dolo malo actio competere soleat; et boni praetoris est, potius restituere litem, ut et ratio et aequitas postulabit, quam actionem famosam constituere.—l. 7, § 1, D. de I. I. R.[2]

3. Capitis diminutio (minima) of the debtor.[a]

[a] § 56.

Ulp.: Ait praetor: QVI QVAEVE, POSTEAQVAM QVID CVM HIS ACTVM CONTRACTVMVE SIT, CAPITE DEMINVTI DEMINVTAEVE ESSE DICENTVR, IN EOS EASVE, PERINDE QVASI ID FACTVM NON SIT, IVDICIVM BABO.—D. 4, 5, 2, 1.[3]

4. Absence of a party, or otherwise justifiable obstacles, as ground of the non-exercise of a right, by which it is lost: the so-called 'clausula generalis.'

Ulp.: ITEM, inquit praetor, SI QVA ALIA MIHI IVSTA CAVSA ESSE VIDEBITVR, IN INTEGRVM RESTITVAM. Haec clausula edicto inserta est necessario: . . . ut quotiens aequitas restitutionem suggerit, ad hanc clausulam erit descendendum. . . . Et generaliter quotienscumque quis ex necessitate, non ex voluntate abfuit, dici oportet ei subveniendum. Nec non et si quis de causa probabili abfuerit, deliberare debet praetor, an ei subveniri debeat.—D. 4, 6, l. 26, § 9, l. 28 pr.[4]

---

[1] See § 18 (p. 90).

[2] . . . relief will have to be given to those deceived by no fault of their own, especially if the deceit have proceeded from the opponent, since also an action for fraud is generally available; and it is the mark of a good praetor rather to reinstate the suit, according to the requirements of reason and equity, than to create an action in ill repute.

[3] The praetor says: 'Whatever person, male or female, after anything have been done or contracted with them, shall be declared to have experienced a change of status, against them will I grant an action just as if that had not come about.'

[4] 'Likewise,' says the praetor, 'I will grant reinstatement if

Book I. Chapter II.

The *i. i. r.* in the particular case was granted by the Praetor (or other superior magistrate) after the preliminary 'causae cognitio' by a 'decretum iudicium rescindens.'

> Mod.: Omnes in integrum restitutiones causa cognita a praetore promittuntur, scilicet ut iustitiam earum causarum examinet, an verae sint, quarum nomine singulis subvenit.—l. 3, D. de I. I. R.[1]

This grant itself can take place in two ways, according to the nature of the injury: either so that the decree at once re-establishes the former condition, and immediately cancels the prejudice that has accrued to some proprietary right, because, *e.g.*, it enjoins upon the defendant compensation for it; or so that it orders a iudicium (restitutorium, rescissorium) in which the plaintiff shall be able to sue for the right claimed by him, but lost by the particular event, as though this had not happened (actio utilis—ficticia).

> Paul.: Restitutio autem ita facienda est, ut unusquisque integrum ius suum recipiat. Itaque si in vendendo fundo circumscriptus restituetur, iubeat praetor emptorem fundum cum fructibus reddere et pretium recipere.—D. 4, 4, 24, 4.[2]

---

any other cause shall appear to me as lawful.' This clause has been necessarily subjoined to the Edict . . . as whenever equity makes reinstatement advisable, one will have to resort to this passage. . . . And in general it must be said that whenever a person is absent from bare necessity, not of his own accord, relief must be given him. Ay, and if some one should have been absent for an excusable cause, the praetor will have to consider whether relief should be afforded him.

[1] All reinstatements are promised by the praetor after investigation of the matter, that is, his examination of the legality of those cases, whether they are true, in respect of which he relieves individuals.

[2] But the reinstatement is effected in such way that every one recovers his normal position. If, accordingly, a person is to be reinstated who was deceived in the sale of landed estate, the praetor must order the purchaser to restore the estate with its produce and to take back the price.

Ulp.: Interdum autem restitutio et **in rem** datur minori, i.e. adversus rei eius possessorem, licet cum eo non sit contractum; utputa rem a minore emisti et alii vendidisti: potest desiderare interdum adversus possessorem restitui; ne rem suam perdat vel re sua careat, et hoc vel cognitione praetoria vel, rescissa alienatione, dato in rem iudicio.—l. 13, § 1 eod.[1]

Gai.: Si minor annis vigintiquinque sine causa debitori acceptum tulerit, non solum in ipsum, sed et in fideiussores . . . actio restitui debet.—l. 27, § 2 eod.[2]

Paul.: Si coactus hereditatem repudiem, duplici via praetor mihi succurrit, aut utiles actiones quasi heredi dando, aut actionem metus causa praestando.—D. 4, 2, 21, 6.[3]

The performance and execution of the *i. i. r.* consists in the most complete replacement attainable of the earlier condition.

Imp. Sever.: Qui restituitur in integrum sicut in damno morari non debet, ita nec in lucro: et ideo quidquid ad eum pervenit vel ex emptione vel ex venditione vel ex alio contractu, hoc debet restituere.—C. 2, 47 (48), l. un. pr.[4]

---

[1] But sometimes reinstatement even *in rem* is given to a minor, *i.e.*, against the possessor of such thing, although he have not contracted with the same; *e.g.*, you have bought something of a minor and sold it to another person: sometimes he can claim reinstatement as against the possessor, that he may not lose his thing or be deprived of his own property, and this either by a decision of the praetor or, after the cancelling of the conveyance, by a real action being given.

[2] If any one who is not yet 25 years of age shall groundlessly have given his debtor a discharge, not only against himself, but also the sureties . . . an action ought to be given for reinstatement.

[3] If under pressure I refuse an inheritance, the praetor relieves me in two ways, either by giving me equitable actions as though I were heir, or by giving an action *metus causa*.

[4] He who is reinstated must not make a delay in respect of gain any more than of loss; and therefore he must restore

Book I.
Chapter II.

§ 31. Means of Assuring Rights.

In certain cases assurance of a right or of a future claim can be enforced by contract (cautio); such 'cautiones s. stipulationes necessariae' are to be distinguished from the 'voluntariae s. conventionales,' *i.e.*, those which rest upon voluntary agreement. The prescription and imposition of such cautiones was vested only in the higher magistrates, especially the Praetor (praetoriae stipulationes), whose Edict contained standing formulae for them.

> Ulp.: **Praetoriarum** stipulationum tres esse videntur species: iudiciales, cautionales, communes.—§ **Cautionales** sunt autem quae instar actionis habent et, ut sit nova actio, intercedunt, ut de legatis stipulationes et de tutela . . . et damni infecti.—§ Et sciendum est, omnes stipulationes natura sui cautionales esse, hoc enim agitur in stipulationibus, ut quis cautior sit et securior interposita stipulatione.—D. 46, 5, 1. 1 pr., §§ 2, 4.[1]

The giving of security is effected either by 'nuda repromissio,' *i.e.*, a promise in the form of stipulatio (verbal cautio), or by appointment of sureties (satisdatio) or pledges (real cautio).

> Paul.: **Cautum** intelligitur, sive personis sive rebus cautum sit.—D. 50, 16, 188, 1.[2]

---

whatever has come to his hands, whether by purchase, or by sale, or by any other contract.

[1] There seem to be three kinds of praetorian stipulations: judicial, those by way of security, and common stipulations.—§ Now those by way of security are either such as have the force of an action and come in that there may be a fresh action, as stipulations about legacies, about guardianship, . . . and as to threatened injury. § And it must be known that all stipulations are essentially by way of security; for the intention in a stipulation is that a person may by the stipulation introduced be more secure and more settled.

[2] By security being given, is understood that which is given either with persons or with things.

The confirmation also, and further the realising (execution) of legal claims, is contemplated by the 'missiones in bona s. possessionem;' these are such installations in the possession of the whole property or specific things belonging to another as have resulted from magisterial decree—especially as a compulsory remedy against 'contumaces.' The person installed (missus) acquires by securing possession bare, yet legally protected, detention[a] with the view of caretaking and supervision, and a right of pledge.[b]

[a] § 74.

[b] See § 101 and comp. § 204.

> Ulp.: Tres fere causae sunt, ex quibus in possessionem mitti solet: rei servandae causa, item legatorum servandorum gratia, et ventris nomine; damni enim infecti nomine, si non caveatur, non universorum nomine fit missio, sed rei tantum de qua damnum timetur.—D. 42, 4, 1.[1]
>
> Pomp.: Cum bona possidere praetor permittit, . . . non possidemus, sed magis custodiam rerum et observationem nobis concedit.—l. 12 eod.[2]

---

[1] There are generally three reasons for which instalment in possession is wont to be given: for the preservation of a thing, for the preservation of legacies, and on account of pregnancy; for if security be not given on account of the threatened injury, such instalment affects not the whole but only the property in respect of which injury is apprehended.

[2] When the praetor allows possession to be taken . . . we do not possess, but he rather grants us the custody and oversight of the property.

BOOK II.

LAW OF PERSONS ('PERSONAE').[a]

[a] Cf. Savigny, 'System,' vol. ii. by Rattigan; Maine, 'Anct. Law,' ch. v.; Markby, ss. 131 *sqq*.

PART I.—NATURAL PERSONS.

CHAPTER I.

CAPACITY FOR RIGHTS.

§ 32. NOTION OF PERSONALITY; BEGINNING AND END OF NATURAL CAPACITY FOR RIGHTS.

BOOK II. Part I.

EVERY right relates to a subject, who is its bearer: there are no rights without subjects. Man considered as a possible subject of rights is called a PERSON.[b] Personality, otherwise spoken of as capacity for rights or subjectivity of the will, is, accordingly, the capacity recognised by Law which resides in somebody to be the subject of rights; in other words, the potential capacity[c] of having a legal will for oneself. By nature every man is at the same time a Person, which is NATURAL capacity for rights: it is otherwise according to Roman Law, which annexes capacity for rights to special presumptions, called CIVIL capacity, and acknowledges men who are not Persons.[d] The counterpart of Person, subject of rights or of will, is formed by THING, object of rights or of will; but within the sphere of Persons there are different degrees and gradations of capacity for rights, and one person can be more or less subject to the will of another without thereby losing his character as subject of rights. On the other hand, the conception of personality has been extended beyond the range of natural Persons, so that there are subjects of rights called JURISTIC Persons, which are not individual men;

[b] Cf. note in § 17. The strict definition offered by Savigny in the passage from the 'System' cited by Holland (p. 71) is: the 'subject of a *legal relation*' (comprehending relative duties).

§ 58.

[d] *I.e.*, slaves.

but here also the right concerns men indirectly, so that essentially, and in respect of its purpose, it does but serve human interests.[a]

[a] §§ 68, *sq.*

Hermog.: Cum **hominum causa omne ius constitutum** sit, primo de personarum statu . . . dicemus.—D. 1, 5, 2.[1]

Inst. i. 2, 2: servitutes . . . sunt iuri naturali contrariae; iure enim naturali ab initio omnes homines liberi nascebantur.[2]

Natural capacity for rights begins with the birth of men, *i.e.*, the complete separation of a living human being from the mother.

Ulp.: Partus antequam edatur, mulieris portio est vel viscerum.—D. 25, 4, 1, 1.[3]

This is without regard to vitality. There are, indeed, cases where it is a question of rights that belong to the child at birth, in which the Law already bestows consideration in many ways upon the embryo in the mother's womb.[b]

[b] 'Nasciturus pro iam nato habetur.'

Paul.: Qui in utero est, perinde ac si in rebus humanis esset, custoditur, quotiens de commodis ipsius partus quaeritur, quamquam alii, antequam nascatur, nequaquam prosit.—D. 1, 5, 7.[4]

Id.: Quod dicimus eum, qui nasci speratur, pro superstite esse, tunc verum est, cum de ipsius iure quaeritur.—D. 50, 16, 231.[5]

---

1 Since it has been on behalf of men that the whole Law has been established, we will first speak of personal status.

2 Slavery . . . is contrary to the Law of Nature; for according to the Law of Nature all men from the first were born free.

3 The fruit of the body before it is born is part of the mother or the womb.

4 Attention is bestowed upon that which is in the womb, just the same as if it had come to life, whenever a question arises as to the embryo's own privileges, although in no way benefiting another before it is born.

5 Our speaking of him whose birth is anticipated as though he were in existence, is correct when the question is as to his own right.

Book II. Part I.

Id.: Antiqui libero ventri ita prospexerunt, ut in tempus nascendi omnia ei iura integra reservarent, sicut apparet in iure hereditatum.—D. 5, 4, 3.[a] [1]

[a] See Markby, s. 132.

ROMAN CAPACITY FOR RIGHTS.

§ 33. In General.

Man as such is not by Roman Law at the same time a Person; personality, rather, supposes freedom. A distinction thus arises between freemen and slaves. Not all freemen, however, enjoy like capacity for rights. Roman capacity for rights is conditional upon the possession of the right of citizenship (civitas) and by that belonging to a Roman 'familia,' which is inseparably connected with it. This embraces two constituents: 'commercium,'[b] or capacity for all proprietary rights iure civili and for dealings governed by the Civil Law, and 'conubium,' or capacity for a marriage iur civ., and accordingly, for Roman family relationships. But neither is Roman capacity for rights uniform; for according to the position he obtains in the 'familia,' every Roman citizen is either a person independent in a family (free from Power) or a person that is under control in such family (a domestic dependant), respectively described as 'persona sui iuris'[c] and 'persona alieno iuri subiecta.' Only the first-mentioned has full capacity for rights.

[b] Cf. § 79 ad init.

[c] See Brown, s. vv.

Thus, with respect to their capacity for rights, men are divided into—

(1) 'liberi' and 'servi.'

(2) The 'liberi,' again, were on the one hand divided into free-born or 'ingenui,' and the enfranchised or 'libertini,' subject to the right of the Patron; on the other, into 'cives,' 'Latini' (who only possess the commercium, not the conubium of the Romans),

---

[1] The ancients paid regard to the child in the womb in such way that they maintained all rights in its favour intact until the time of birth, as may be seen in the Law of Inheritance.

Book II. Part I.

and 'peregrini' (persons without either conub. or commerc.).

(3) The cives, either 'personae sui iuris' or 'personae alieni iuris.'

Paul.: Tria sunt quae habemus: libertatem, civitatem, familiam.—D. 4, 5, 11.[1]

Ulp. v. 3, 4: Conubium est uxoris iure ducendae facultas. Conubium habent cives Romani cum civibus Romanis; cum Latinis autem et peregrinis ita si concessum sit.—xix. 5: Commercium est emendi vendendique invicem ius.[2]

The condition ('status' in the wider sense, or 'condicio')[a] of the individual is his position in the State, governing his capacity for rights; consequently, the belonging to one of the classes mentioned, which finds expression in Freedom, Citizenship, 'Latinitas,' 'Peregrinitas.' It is determined by birth.

[a] See Austin, lectt. xl.-xlii.; Markby, ss. 176-180.

(1) The child begotten in a marriage according to the ius civile[b] follows the condition of the Father; the child begotten in a marriage not recognised by the ius civile, and also that born out of wedlock, takes the condition of the Mother.

[b] § 44.

Ulp. v. 8, 9: Conubio interveniente liberi semper patrem sequuntur: non interveniente conubio matris condicioni accedunt, excepto eo, qui ex peregrino et cive Romana nascitur: nam is peregrinus nascitur, quoniam lex Minicia ex alterutro peregrino natum deterioris parentis condicionem sequi iubet.—Ex cive Romano et Latina Latinus nascitur, et ex libero et ancilla servus; quoniam, cum his casibus conubia non sint, partus sequitur matrem.[3]

---

[1] We have three things: Freedom, Citizenship, and the Family.

[2] *Conubium* is the capacity for marrying a wife according to Law. Roman citizens have *conubium* with Roman citizens, but with Latins and foreigners it exists only if there have been a special grant.—*Commercium* is the reciprocal right of purchase and sale.

[3] If *conubium* exist between the parties, the children always

BOOK II. Part I.

Gai. i. § 82: Illud quoque his consequens est, quod ex . . . libera et servo liber nascatur.[1]

Ulp.: Lex naturae haec est, ut qui nascitur sine legitimo matrimonio, matrem sequatur, nisi lex specialis aliud inducit.—l. 24, D. h. t. (=de statu hom. 1, 5).[2]

(2) In the former case the time of conception, in the latter that of the birth, is regularly decisive.[a]

[a] For the Engl. Law, see Brown, s. 'Legitimation.'

Gai. i. § 89:—hi qui illegitime concipiuntur, statum sumunt ex eo tempore, quo nascuntur; . . . at hi qui legitime concipiuntur, ex conceptionis tempore statum sumunt.[3]

Marcian.: Ingenui sunt, qui ex matre libera nati sunt; sufficit enim liberam fuisse eo tempore, quo nascitur, licet ancilla concepit; et e contrario si libera conceperit, deinde ancilla pariat, placuit eum, qui nascitur, liberum nasci. Nec interest, iustis nuptiis concepit an vulgo, quia non debet calamitas matris nocere ei, qui in ventre est. § Ex hoc quaesitum est: si ancilla praegnans manumissa sit, deinde ancilla postea facta . . . peperit, liberum an servum pariat? Et tamen rectius probatum est liberum nasci et sufficere ei qui in ventre est, liberam matrem vel medio tem-

---

follow the father: if there be no *conubium*, they approximate to the condition of the mother, save one who is born of a foreigner and a Roman woman, for he is born a foreigner, since the *lex Minicia* ordains that one born of a foreigner on either side shall follow the status of the inferior parent. The child of a Roman citizen and a Latin woman is a Latin, and that of a freeman and a slavewoman, a slave; because, as there is no *conubium* in these cases, the offspring follows the mother.

[1] In keeping with this also is it that the child of a freewoman and a slave is born free.

[2] The Law of Nature is this, that he who is not born of a legal marriage follows the mother, unless a special law prescribes something different.

[3] They that are conceived illegitimately take their status from the moment of their birth; . . . but those that are conceived legitimately take their status from the time of conception.

pore habuisse.—l. 5, §§ 2, 3, D. h. t. (=pr. I. de ingen. 1, 4).[1] Book II. Part I.

FREEDOM AND CITIZENSHIP.

§ 34. *Liberi* and *Ingenui* in particular.

'Ingenui' are as a rule, and according to the older Law, only those free by birth or by conception, *i.e.*, of a free mother, who might be either free-born or enfranchised.[a] [a] D. 1, 5, 2, 3.

Gai. i. §§ 10, 11 : Rursus liberorum hominum alii ingenui sunt, alii libertini.—**Ingenui** sunt, qui liberi nati sunt: **libertini** sunt qui ex iusta servitute manumissi sunt.[2]

Iust. i. 4 pr. : Ingenuus is est, qui statim ut natus est liber est, sive ex duobus ingenuis matrimonio editus, sive ex libertinis, sive ex altero libertino altero ingenuo. Sed et si quis ex matre libera nascatur patre servo, ingenuus nihilominus nascitur : quemadmodum qui ex matre libera et incerto patre natus est, quoniam vulgo conceptus est.[3]

---

[1] *Ingenui* are such as have been born of a free mother; for it is enough that she was free at the time of the birth, although she conceived as a slave; and reversely, if she conceived as a free woman, and afterwards bare the child as a slave, the received opinion is that the child is free-born. And it is all the same whether she conceived in lawful matrimony or in common intercourse, because the misfortune of the mother must not prejudice the child in her womb. Hence a question has arisen: if a woman in servitude with child is manumitted, and after having subsequently been enslaved, has brought forth, does she bear a freeman or a slave? It is nevertheless more justly thought that it is born free, and that it suffices the embryo to have had a free mother in the intervening time alone.

[2] Of free persons, again, some are *ingenui*, others *libertini*. The *ingenui* are such as have been born free; the *libertini*, those that have been liberated from lawful slavery.

[3] An *ingenuus* is he that is free from the moment of his birth, whether the issue of a marriage of two free-born persons, or from persons manumitted, or from one manumitted person, the

BOOK II. Part I.

Hence it is said, 'natalibus non officit manumissio.'

Cum autem ingenuus aliquis natus sit, non officit illi in servitute fuisse et postea manumissum esse : saepissime enim constitutum est, **natalibus non officere manumissionem.**—§ 1 eod.[1]

The 'libertini' can *beneficio principis* acquire the standing of 'ingenui,' and that—

(1) With reservation of the rights of the patron, which imposed certain restraint upon them, by grant of the 'ius aureorum anulorum.'

Vat. fgm. 266 : **Ius anulorum ingenuitatis imaginem** praestat, salvo iure patronorum patronique liberorum.—(Pap.)[2]

Ulp. : Libertinus **si ius anulorum** impetraverit, quamvis iura ingenuitatis salvo iure patroni nactus sit, tamen ingenuus intelligitur.—D. 40, 10, 6.[3]

Id. : Si ius anulorum consecutus sit libertus a principe, . . . **vivit quasi ingenuus, moritur quasi libertus.**—D. 38, 2, 3 pr.[4]

(2) Without those rights ; by grant of the 'natalium restitutio.'

Marcian. : Interdum et servi nati ex postfacto

---

other free-born. But even if a man have been born of a free mother but a slave father, he is nevertheless born free ; in the same way as one that has been born of a free mother and a doubtful father, because he was conceived in common intercourse.

[1] When any one has been born free, he is not prejudiced by the fact that he has been born in servitude and afterwards has been manumitted; for it has been very often laid down that manumission does not prejudice the condition by birth.

[2] The right of wearing rings affords the semblance of *ingenuitas*, with a reservation of the rights of the patrons and the patron's children.

[3] If a freedman have applied for the *ius anulorum*, although he has acquired rights of *ingenuitas*, without disturbing the patron's rights, he is nevertheless regarded as free-born.

[4] If a freedman have obtained the *ius anulorum* from the *princeps* . . . he lives as free-born, he dies as a freedman.

iuris interventu ingenui fiunt: ut ecce si libertinus a principe **natalibus** suis **restitutus** fuerit; illis enim utique natalibus restituitur, in quibus initio omnes homines fuerunt, non in quibus ipse nascitur, cum servus natus esset. Hic enim, quantum ad totum ius pertinet, perinde habetur, atque si ingenuus natus esset; nec patronus eius potest ad successionem venire. Ideoque imperatores non facile solent quemquam natalibus restituere, nisi consentiente patrono.—D. 40, 11, 2.[1]

SERVI.

§ 35. Nature of *Servitus*.

'Servitus' (slavery)[a] is the situation of a human being completely deprived of rights, grounded upon the ius gentium, but in contravention of human nature,[b] *i.e.*, in itself irrational. Such an one is called 'servus,' 'homo,' 'mancipium,'[c] 'ancilla;' and by virtue of this condition is object of the control of another recognised by Private Law.

[a] See Maine, 'Anct. Law,' pp. 162-166.

[b] Cf. Inst. i. 2, 2.

[c] It is not only 'in the non-legal Roman authors' (Brown, s.v.) that slaves are so spoken of: see D. 1, 12, 1, 8 *inf.* and cf. Hunter, p. 228.

Florent.: Servitus est constitutio iuris gentium, qua quis dominio alieno contra naturam subiicitur. —D. 1, 5, 4, 1 (=§ 2, I. de iure pers. i. 3).[2]

Tryph.: —libertas naturali iure continetur et dominatio ex gentium iure introducta est.—D. 12, 6, 64.[3]

---

[1] Sometimes also those that are slaves by birth in consequence of a subsequent event, by the help of Law become *ingenui;* as for instance, if a freedman has been restored by the Emperor to his condition by birth. For he is in that case restored to the condition by birth in which all men have been at the beginning, not in that in which he himself is born, as he was born a slave. Such an one is looked upon, as regards the whole Law, as if born free, and his patron cannot come in for the succession. And therefore the Emperors are not wont readily to restore any one to his condition by birth unless the patron consent.

[2] Slavery is an institution of the *i. g.*, by which one man is against nature placed under the authority of another.

[3] Freedom is inherent in the Law of Nature, and lordship [over slaves] has been let in by the *i. g.*

Book II. Part I.

The slave, as well by the 'ius gentium' as by 'ius civile,' is not a subject capable of rights, is not a Person, and therefore is capable of no legal control,—is a chattel; and it is immaterial whether he is owned by any one, or is for the time being without a master.[a]

[a] § 36, *servus poenae*; § 37, *dominium ex iure Quiritium*.

Ulp. xix. 1: Mancipi res sunt . . . servi et quadrupedes.[1]

Inst. i. 16, 4: Servus . . . nullum caput habet.[2]

Paul.: Servile caput nullum ius habet. (l. 3, § 1, D. eod. 4, 5).—Ulp.: Servitutem mortalitati fere comparamus.—D. 50, 17, 209.[3]

Ulp.: Servus . . . iuris civilis communionem non habet in totum.—D. 28, 1, 20, 7.[4]

In servorum condicione nulla differentia est.—§ 5, I. de iure pers.[5]

Nevertheless as a man he remained a being endued with reason and will, and with capacity to act, and so even the Romans do not treat him in all particulars as a mere chattel, but recognise a personality of the slave according to ius naturale.[b] The possibility is within his reach of becoming a subject of rights by acquisition of freedom; in view of this, accordingly, relationships of slaves are recognised, *e.g.*, obstacles to their marriage;[c] thus also the slave possesses the capacity of undertaking acts with juristic effect, both for his master and himself; so that, in view of the state of manumission, he becomes entitled and bound by legal transactions 'naturaliter,'[d] and is rendered responsible by delicts 'civiliter.'[e]

[b] § 4.

[c] Cf. Ulp. xii. 2, 3.

[d] § 114.

[e] § 113. See further § 149.

Ulp.: Quod attinet ad ius civile, servi pro nullis habentur, non tamen et iure naturali: quia,

---

1 *Res mancipi* are . . . slaves and quadrupeds.

2 A slave never has *caput*.

3 A slave is possessed of no right.—We generally compare slavery to death.

4 A slave . . . has no participation whatever in the *i. c.*

5 There is no difference in the condition of slaves.

quod ad ius naturale attinet, omnes homines aequales sunt.—l. 32, D. de R. J.[1]

Id.: Locum, in quo servus sepultus est, religiosum esse Aristo ait.—D. 11, 7, 2 pr.[2]

Inst. i. 10, 10: Illud certum est, **serviles** quoque **cognationes** impedimento esse nuptiis, si forte pater et filia, aut frater et soror manumissi fuerint.[3]

Ulp.: Nec servus quidquam debere potest, nec servo potest deberi. Sed cum eo verbo abutimur, factum magis demonstramus, quam ad ius civile referimus obligationem.—D. 15, 1, 41.[4]

Id.: Servi ex delictis quidem obligantur et si manumittantur, obligati remanent; ex contractibus autem civiliter quidem non obligantur, sed naturaliter et obligantur et obligant: denique si servo, qui mihi mutuam pecuniam dederat, manumisso solvam, liberor.—D. 44, 7, 14.[5]

Gai.: Cum servo nulla actio est.—l. 107, D. de R. J.[6]

The 'servi publici' (state-slaves)[a] had an especially favourable position.

[a] See Ulp. x 16.

The notion of the slave being a chattel, and at the

---

[1] As far as concerns the *i. c.*, slaves count for nothing, not, however, according to the Law of Nature likewise; because, as regards the Law of Nature, all men are equal.

[2] The place in which a slave has been buried, Aristo says, is sacred.

[3] It is certain that the relationships also of slaves obstruct their marriage, if, for example, father and daughter, or brother and sister, have been manumitted.

[4] Neither can a slave be indebted, nor can a debt be incurred to a slave. But when we make wrong use of that word, we rather describe the fact than connect the obligation with the *i. c.*

[5] Slaves certainly incur an obligation by crimes, and remain liable if they are manumitted. Now, they are not rendered liable by contracts *iure civili*, but they incur and create obligation alone *iure naturali*. And if I make payment to a slave who after having advanced me money was manumitted, I am discharged.

[6] There is no action against a slave.

Book II. Part I.

same time a rational being, makes itself felt also in the relation of the slave to his master, whose right is composed of 'dominium' over the slave as a mere object of ownership, and 'potestas' over the slave as passive member of a familia.

As a result of the 'potestas,' the slave shares to a certain extent the personality and 'commercium' of the master;[a] as his representative, he can undertake all juristic acts, whether under the ius gent. or the ius civ., relating to the acquisition of rights.[b]

[a] Cf. D. 45, 3, 36.

[b] Cf. §§ 20, 75.

Theophil. ad Inst. iii. 17 pr.: οἱ οἰκέται ἀπρόσωποι ὄντες, ἐκ τῶν προσώπων των οἰκείων δεσποτων χαρακτηρίζονται.[1]

Gai. i. § 52: In **potestate** itaque sunt servi dominorum. Quae quidem potestas iuris gentium est; nam apud omnes peraeque gentes animadvertere possumus, dominus in servos vitae necisque potestatem esse, et quodcumque per servum adquiritur, id domino adquiri.[2]

Ulp.: Verbum **potestatis** non solum ad liberos trahimus verum etiam ad servos.—D. 24, 1, 3, 3.[3]

To the master belongs as 'dominus' every possible disposition over the slave, as over other objects of ownership; but this right[c] was limited in imperial times from considerations of humanity and good custom, and to the slave was even accorded a right of complaint for harsh and unworthy treatment.

[c] As also the 'ius vitae necisque,' which flowed from 'potestas,' and the domestic power of correction.

Gai. i. § 53: Sed hoc tempore neque civibus Romanis nec ullis aliis hominibus, qui sub imperio

---

[1] As domestic servants have no personality, they are endued with the personality of their own masters.

[2] Slaves, accordingly, are in the *potestas* of their masters, and this *potestas* is derived from the Law of Nations; for we can observe that amongst all nations uniformly, masters have power of life and death over their slaves, and that whatever is acquired by means of the slave is acquired for the master.

[3] The word *potestas* we apply not merely to children, but also to slaves.

populi Romani sunt, licet supra modum et sine causa in servos suos saevire: nam ex constitutione sacratissimi imperatoris Antonini qui sine causa servum suum occiderit, non minus teneri iubetur, quam qui alienum servum occiderit. Sed et maior quoque asperitas dominorum per eiusdem principis constitutionem coercetur: nam . . . praecepit, ut si intolerabilis videatur dominorum saevitia, cogantur servos vendere. Et utrumque recte fit: **male enim nostro iure uti non debemus.**[1]

Ulp.: Quod autem dictum est, ut servos de dominis querentes praefectus audiat, sic accipiemus: . . . si saevitiam, si duritiam, si famem, qua eos premant, si obscoenitatem, in qua eos compulerint vel compellant, apud praefectum urbi exponant. Hoc quoque officium praefecto urbi a D. Severo datum est, ut mancipia tueatur, ne prostituantur.—D. 1, 12, 1, § 8.[2]

Legally free, and merely as a matter of fact more or less restricted in their freedom, were—

(1) The 'addictus' (nexus, iudicatus).[a]

[a] See § 192, besides §§ 116, 131.

---

[1] But at the present time neither Roman citizens nor any other persons under the dominion of the Roman people are allowed to afflict excessive and groundless severity upon their slaves; for by a constitution also of the most sacred emperor Antoninus, he that kills his own slave without cause is to be no less liable than he that kills the slave of another. But the excessive harshness of masters is restrained, besides, by a constitution of the same emperor. For . . . he directed that if the severity of masters should seem to have been unbearable, they should be compelled to sell the slaves. And both these rules are just, for we must not misuse our right.

[2] But when it was said that a prefect is to listen to slaves that complain of their masters, we understand: . . . if they lay before the city-prefect cruelty, harshness, hunger, with which they are tormented, or lewdness that has been, or is, forced upon them. The following duty also has been assigned to the city-prefect by the late emperor Severus—that he protect slaves from unchaste abuse.

Book II. Part I.

Quintil. v. 10, 60: Aliud est servum esse, aliud servire. . . . Qui servus est si manumittatur, fit libertinus, non itidem addictus.—vii. 3, 26: Ad servum nulla lex pertinet, addictus legem habet.[1]

[a] Gell. xi. 18, 13.
[b] § 36, ad init.

(2) The 'auctoratus'[a] and the 'ab hostibus redemptus.'[b]

Porph. in Hor. sat. ii. 7, 58, 59: Gladiatores ita se vendunt et cautiones faciunt: 'uri flammis, virgis secari, ferro necari.'—Qui se vendunt ludo, auctorati dicuntur.[2]

[c] From the fourth century.

On the other hand, a middle position between freemen and slaves is taken by a class of serfs attached to the soil (coloni), which first obtained recognition in the later imperial legislation;[c] they, together with their descendants, were inseparable from the particular estate, and, placed under the control of the proprietor (dominus patronus), were under obligation to render a yearly *canon* or customary rent for the use of the plots assigned to them.

[d] Sc. coloni.

Imp. Theod.: Ipsi[d] originario iure teneantur, et licet **condicione** videantur **ingenui**, **servi** tamen **terrae ipsius** cui nati sunt aestimantur, nec recedendi quo velint aut permutandi loco habeant facultatem, sed possessor eorum iure utatur et patroni sollicitudine et domini potestate.—C. 11, 52 (51), l. un.[3]

---

[e] The bondman recovered his *ingenuitas*.

[1] It is one thing to be a slave, another to serve. He that is a slave becomes a freedman, if he is manumitted; not in like manner the bondman.[e] There is no *lex* pertaining to a slave: a bondman has *lex*.

[2] Gladiators sell themselves and give security thus: 'to be burned with fire, to be torn with rods, to be killed with the sword.' They that sell themselves for sport are called *auctorati*.

[3] They shall be bound by hereditary law, and although in their status they seem to be free-born, they are nevertheless regarded as slaves of the very soil on which they are born, and have not the right to go whither they will, nor to change their abode, but their proprietor shall by Law exercise both the attention of patron and the power of master.

§ 36. Commencement of *Servitus*.

The condition of slaves comes either of birth[a] or by the following events resulting in the loss of freedom. [a] § 33.

(1) According to the *ius gentium*, through capture by the enemy.

> Inst. i. 3, 4: Servi autem aut nascuntur aut fiunt: nascuntur ex ancillis nostris; fiunt aut iure gentium, i.e. **ex captivitate**, aut iure civili.[1]
>
> Ulp.: **Hostes** sunt, quibus bellum publice populus Romanus decrevit vel ipsi populo Romano: ceteri latrunculi vel praedones appelluntur. Et ideo qui a latronibus captus est, servus latronum non est, nec postliminium illi necessarium est: ab hostibus autem captus et servus est hostium et postliminio statum pristinum recuperat.—l. 24, D. de captiv. 49, 15.[2]
>
> Tryph.: —in pace qui pervenerunt ad exteros, si bellum subito exarsisset, eorum servi efficiuntur, apud quos iam hostes suo(s) facto(s) deprehenduntur.—l. 12 pr. eod.[3]
>
> Pomp.: Si, cum legati apud nos essent gentis alicuius, bellum eis indictum sit, responsum est liberos eos manere.—D. 50, 7, 18 (17).[4]

---

1 Now slaves are either born or become such: they are so born of our female slaves; they become such either by the *i. g.*, *i.e.*, by captivity, or by the *i. c.*

2 Enemies are those against whom the Roman people for State reasons, or who have themselves against the Roman people, declared war; the rest are called highwaymen or robbers. And so he that has been taken by robbers is not the robbers' slave, and has no need of *postliminium;* but he that has been captured by the enemy is slave of the enemy, and by *postliminium* recovers his former condition.

3 They that during peace have come to others, if a war should have suddenly broken out, are rendered slaves of those amongst whom, as already made their enemies, they are seized upon.

4 If, when envoys of another nation were with us, war was declared against them, the opinion was that they remained freemen.

BOOK II. Part I.

Id.: In pace quoque postliminium datum est: nam si cum gente aliqua neque amicitiam neque hospitium neque foedus habemus, hi hostes quidem non sunt, quod autem ex nostro ad eos pervenit illorum fit, et liber homo noster ab eis captus servus fit eorum.—l. 5, § 2, D. de captiv.[1]

But he that returns from captivity enters again upon his status and his former rights 'iure postliminui '[a] as his own act.

[a] The personal as distinct from the real aspects of *postliminium*, for which latter see § 83 *res hostiles*; for its active and passive effect § 47 ad init., § 53.

Id.: **Postliminii** ius competit aut in bello, aut in pace. § In bello cum hi qui nobis hostes sunt aliquem ex nostris ceperunt et intra praesidia sua duxerunt: nam si is reversus fuerit, postliminium habet, i.e. perinde omnia restituuntur ei iura, ac si captus ab hostibus non esset.—pr. § 1, ibid.[2]

Ulp.: Retro creditur in civitate fuisse qui ab hostibus advenit.—l. 16 eod.[3]

Flor.: Nihil interest, quomodo captivus reversus est, utrum dimissus an vi vel fallacia potestatem hostium evaserit, ita tamen, si ea mente venerit, ut non illo reverteretur: nec enim satis est corpore domum quem rediisse, si mente alienus est. Sed et qui victis hostibus recuperantur, postliminio rediisse existimantur.—l. 26 eod.[4]

---

[1] In peace also has *postliminium* been given; for if we have with some nation concluded neither friendship nor right of hospitality nor league, they are not indeed our enemies, but that of ours which has come into their hands becomes their property, and a freeman of ours that has been captured by them becomes their slave.

[2] The right of *postliminium* attaches either in war or in peace. § In war when they that are enemies have captured and led any of us into their camp. For if such has returned from the war, he has the right of *postliminium*, *i.e.*, he is restored to all his rights just as if he had not been captured by the enemy.

[3] He that returns from the enemy is considered to have been in the State in the back period.

[4] It matters not how the captive has returned, whether he have been released or have made his escape from the power of the enemy by force or artifice, if so be, nevertheless, that he has

Pomp.: —in Atilio Regulo, quem Carthaginienses Romam miserunt, responsum est, non esse eum postliminio reversum, quia iuraverat Carthaginem reversurum et non habuerat animum Romae remanendi.—l. 5, § 3 eod.[1]

Paul.: Postliminio carent, qui armis victi hostibus se dederunt.—(Indutiarum) tempore non est postliminium.—Transfugae nullum postliminium est.—l. 17, l. 19, §§ 1, 4 eod.[2]

Pomp.: Cum duae species postliminii sint, ut aut nos revertamur aut aliquid recipiamus: cum filius revertatur, duplicem in eo causam esse oportet postliminii, et quod pater eum reciperet et ipse ius suum.—l. 14 pr. eod.[3]

Pap.: Si emptor, priusquam per usum sibi adquireret, ab hostibus captus sit, placet interruptam possessionem postliminio non restitui, quia . . . possessio plurimum facti habet, causa vero facti non continetur postliminio.—D. 4, 6, 19.[a] [4]

[a] Cf. D. 41, 2, 23, 1.

---

determined not to return thither; for it is not enough that any one should have bodily returned home, if he is mentally elsewhere. But those also who, after victory over the enemy, are recaptured are regarded as having returned by *postliminium.*

[1] In respect of Atilius Regulus, whom the Carthaginians sent to Rome, the opinion was that he had not returned by *postliminium,* because he had sworn to return to Carthage, and had not had the intention to remain behind in Rome.

[2] They are deprived of *postliminium* who, overcome, sword in hand, have surrendered to the enemy.—During the time (of an armistice) there is no *postliminium.*—There is no *postliminium* for the deserter.

[3] Since there are two kinds of *postliminium,* that either we return or we recover something: when the son returns, he must have a double reason for *postliminium,* both because the father recovers him, and he himself his own right.

[4] If the purchaser, before he acquired by user, was captured by the enemy, the opinion is that the interrupted possession is not restored by virtue of *postliminium,* because possession for the most part consists of a fact; but a matter of fact finds no place in *postliminium.*

Si quis capiatur ab hostibus, hi, quos in potestate habuit in incerto sunt, utrum sui iuris facti an adhuc pro filiis familiarum computentur: nam defuncto illo apud hostes, ex quo captus est patres familiarum, reverso numquam non in potestate eius fuisse credentur.—l. 12, § 1, D. de capt. iv.[1]

He that dies in captivity is juridically treated as having died in the position of freedom, as a Roman citizen at the very moment of capture (ficti legis Corneliae).

Iul.: **Lege Cornelia** testamenta eorum, qui in hostium potestate decesserint, perinde confirmantur, ac si hi qui ea fecissent in hostium potestatem non pervenissent.—D. 28, 1, 12.[2]

Ulp.: In omnibus partibus iuris is qui reversus non est ab hostibus, quasi tunc decessisse videtur, cum captus est.—l. 18, D. de captiv.[3]

Iul.: Apparet ergo eadem omnia pertinere ad heredem eius, quae ipse, qui hostium potitus est, habiturus esset, si postliminio revertis set.—l. 22, § 1 eod.[4]

The person who has paid down the redemption-money for the 'ab hostibus redemp.' has a right to retain him until repaid for it; by which right indeed the enjoyment of the earlier legal position and the rights

---

[1] If a man is captured by the enemy, they that he had under his *potestas* are in uncertainty whether they have become *sui iuris* or are hitherto regarded as *filii-familiarum;* for if he die with the enemy, they are regarded as *patres-familiarum* from the time of his capture; if he return, they will be regarded as having never been out of his *potestas.*

[2] By the *l. Cornelia,* the wills of those that die in the power of the enemy obtain the same force as if the testators had not come under the enemy's power.

[3] In all branches of the Law, he that has not returned from the enemy is regarded as dead, as it were, from the time when he was captured.

[4] It is therefore clear that all such things belong to his heir as he that has been captured by the enemy would have had if he had returned by *postliminium.*

of 'ingenuitas' remain for a time suspended; though not the freedom.

Pomp.: Redemptio facultatem redeundi praebet, non ius postliminii mutat.—l. 20, § 2, D. de capt.[1]

Ulp.: Potestatis verbum . . . referendum est etiam ad eum, quem redemit ab hostibus: quamvis placeat hunc servum non esse, sed vinculo quodam retineri donec pretium solvat.—D. 28, 1, 20, 1.[2]

Imp. Diocletian.: Liber captus ab hostibus et commercio redemptus tunc demum cum pretium solverit, vel hoc ei qualicumque remittatur indicio, statum pristinum recipit.—C. 8, 50 (51), 17.[3]

2. According to *ius civile:*

(*a*) Sale abroad (trans Tiberim) to which by the older Law he was subject that avoided either the census or military service, and the debtor that was adjudicated to the creditor;[a] besides delivery over to the enemy.

[a] § 116. Cf. also § 50, *ius vendendi*.

Cic. pro Caec. 34, 99: Populus cum eum vendit, qui miles factus non est, . . . iudicat, non esse eum liberum, qui ut liber sit, adire periculum noluit; cum autem **incensum** vendit, hoc iudicat . . . eum, qui cum liber esset, censeri noluerit, ipsum sibi libertatem abiudicavisse.[4]

---

[1] Redemption affords the privilege of returning; it does not alter the *ius postliminii*.

[2] The word *potestas* is applicable also to such person as he redeemed from the enemy; although it is held that this man is not a slave, but is only kept in a certain relation of dependence until he liquidate the ransom-money.

[3] A freeman who has been captured by the enemy, and redeemed in the course of business, first recovers his former standing when he pays back the ransom-money, or is released from this by some kind of token.

[4] When the People sells him that has not become a soldier . . . it decides that he is not a freeman who, though he be free, has refrained from incurring danger; but when it sells him that has not been enrolled, their judgment is this, that . . . as

Qui ad delectum olim non respondebant, ut proditores libertatis in servitutem redigebantur; . . . sed mutato statu militiae recessum a capitis poena est.—D. 49, 16, 4, 10.[1]

Pomp.: Eum qui legatum pulsasset, Q. Mucius dedi hostibus, quorum erant legati, solitus est respondere; quem hostes si non recepissent, quaesitum est, an civis Romanus maneret, quibusdam existimantibus manere, aliis contra, quia quem semel populus iussisset dedi, ex civitate expulsisse videretur sicut faceret, cum aqua et igni interdiceret; in qua sententia videtur P. Mucius fuisse.—D. 50, 7, 18 (17).[2]

Mod.: An qui hostibus deditus reversus nec a vobis receptus civis Romanus sit, inter Brutum et Scaevolam varie tractatum est: et consequens est, ut civitatem non adipiscatur.—D. 49, 15, 4.[3]

Cic. de orat. 1, 40, 181:—memoria traditum, quem pater suus aut populus vendidisset, aut pater patratus dedidisset, ei nullum esse postliminium.[4]

---

to him who, though he were free, would not be enrolled, he has by his own act declared he has forfeited liberty.

[1] They that formerly did not present themselves for enrolment were consigned to slavery as traitors to freedom; but, with a change in the status of soldiers, a departure has been made from death-punishment.

[2] Q. Mucius was wont to give as his opinion that a man who had struck an ambassador should be given up to the enemy whose embassy it was. The question has arisen, if the enemy should not have accepted him, whether he remained a Roman citizen; and some have considered that he did; others the contrary, because the Roman People, by having once ordered the delivery up of a man, would seem to have exiled him from the State just as much as by putting him under the ban of water and fire. This appears to have been the opinion of P. Mucius.

[3] Whether he that has been delivered up to the enemy, and on his return has not been accepted by us, is a Roman citizen, has been differently dealt with by Brutus and Scaevola; and the conclusion is that he does not acquire *civitas*.

[4] It has been handed down that a man sold by his own father or the People, or given up by the *p. p.*, has no *postliminium*.

(β) Condemnation to capital punishment (to death, or to work in the mines), which made the person affected by it a 'servus poenae.'

Gai.: Hi vero, qui ad ferrum aut ad bestias aut in metallum damnantur, libertatem perdunt bonaque eorum publicantur.—D. 28, 1, 8, 4.[1]

Iust. i. 12, 3: Servi autem poenae efficiuntur, qui in metallum damnantur et qui bestiis subiiciuntur.[2]

(γ) Fraudulent sale of himself by a man over twenty years of age.

Callistr.: Conventio privata neque servum quemquam, neque libertum alicuius facere potest. —D. 40, 12, 37.[3]

Inst. i. 3, 4: Servi . . . fiunt . . . iure civili: cum homo liber maior xx annis ad pretium participandum sese venumdari passus est.[4]

Ulp.: Maiores xx annis ita demum ad libertatem proclamare non possunt, si pretium ad ipsum, qui veniit, pervenerit.—D. 40, 13, 1 pr.[5]

Modest.: Homo liber qui se vendidit, manumissus non ad suum statum revertitur, quo se abdicavit, sed efficitur libertinae condicionis.—D. 1, 5, 21.[6]

(δ) According to the SC. Claudianum, 'contuber-

[1] But they that are condemned to combat with gladiators, or to fight with beasts, or to work in the mines, lose their liberty, and their property is confiscated.

[2] Now they become slaves to punishment who are condemned to work in the mines, and such as are exposed to wild beasts.

[3] A private agreement can make no one either a slave or anybody's freedman.

[4] They become slaves . . . by the *i. c.*: when a freeman who is more than twenty years of age has suffered himself to be sold in order to share the purchase-money.

[5] Those who are more than twenty years old can then only make no claim to freedom, when the purchase-money has passed to him who was sold.

[6] A free person that has sold himself, when manumitted, does not return to his earlier status which he renounced, but he acquires the condition of a freedman.

Book II. Part I.

nium' of a free woman with a foreign slave against the will of the master.

Paul. ii. 21ª, § 1 : Si mulier ingenua civisque Romana vel Latina alieno se servo coniunxerit, si quidem invito et denuntiante domino in eodem contubernio perseveraverit, efficitur ancilla.[1]

Inst. iii. 12, 1 :—libera mulier servili amore bacchata ipsam libertatem per senatusconsultum amittebat et cum libertate substantiam : quod indignum nostris temporibus esse existimantes et a nostra civitate deleri et non inseri nostris Digestis concessimus.[2]

(ε) 'Revocatio in servitutem,' which could befall a freedman from ingratitude towards his patron.[a]

[a] Cf. § 38 ad init.

Imp. Constant. : Si manumissus ingratus circa patronum suum exstiterit, . . . a patrono rursus sub imperio dicioneque mittatur, si in iudicio . . . patroni querela exserta ingratum eum ostendat; filiis etiam qui postea nati fuerint servituris.—C. 6, 7, 2.[3]

TERMINATION OF *SERVITUS*.

§ 37. In General.

The slave regularly acquires freedom and personality by Enfranchisement (manumissio)[b] on the part of the

[b] For villenage in copyhold and the manumission of villeins, see Blackstone, ii. 92-96 (Steph. i. 215-218); Williams' 'Real Property,' pp. 403, *sqq.*; Maine, 'Early Law and Custom,' ch. ix.; Goodeve, 'Real Property' (1st edn.), pp. 26, *sqq.*; Pollock, 'Land Laws,' pp. 196, *sqq.*

1 If a free-born woman and Roman citizen, or a Latin, have united herself to an alien slave, and in spite of the master, and notwithstanding his expressed wishes, have persisted in such connection, she is rendered a slave.

2 A free woman that indulged in attachment to a slave lost her very freedom by a *senatus-consultum*, and with freedom her property: this we have considered unworthy of our time, and have directed that it should be abolished in our realm and excluded from our Digest.

3 Should a freedman have shown himself ungrateful to his manumittor, . . . he shall be consigned again to the control and authority of the Patron, if the complaint of the Patron made public in court represent him to have been ungrateful; the children, besides, born subsequently fall into servitude.

master, and with it that legal capacity which the master had.

Ulp.: Manumissiones quoque iuris gentium sunt. Est autem manumissio de manu missio i.e. datio libertatis: nam quamdiu quis in servitute est, manui et potestati suppositus est, manumissus liberatur potestate.—D. 1, 1, 4.[1]

Thus, he receives citizenship only if his master possess it. But even if the master was a Roman citizen, manumission had not according to older Law everywhere the like result: the freedman became at one time a civis Romanus, at another, did not; while, again, the enfranchisement had only a *de facto* state of freedom as its result,[a] according as the legal requirements all were present in a fully operative enfranchisement, or were more or less lacking to it. [a] § 39.

Ulp. i. 5: Libertorum genera sunt tria: cives Romani, Latini Iuniani, dediticiorum numero.[2]

The following are the requirements of a fully operative manumission, which secures citizenship to the 'libertus.'

The manumittor must have 'dominium ex iure Quiritium' in the slave, *i.e.*, full Roman ownership,[b] and that both as exclusive and unlimited, and must possess him at the same time 'in bonis.' [b] Cf. Ulp. i. 16.

Ulp. i. 18–19: **Communem** servum unus ex dominis manumittendo partem suam amittit eaque adcrescit socio; maxime si eo modo manumiserit, quo si proprium haberet, civem Romanum facturus esset: nam si inter amicos eum manumiserit, plerisque placet nihil eum egisse.—Servus, in quo alterius est ususfructus alterius

---

1 Manumissions also belong to the *ius gentium*. Now *manumissio* is from 'manu missio,' *i.e.*, the conferment of liberty; because so long as a man is in servitude, he is placed under *manus* and *potestas*; the freedman is liberated from *potestas*.

2 There are three classes of freedmen: Roman citizens, *Latini Iuniani*, [and those] in the rank of *dediticii*.

proprietas, a **proprietatis domino** manumissus liber non fit, sed servus sine domino est.[1]

Paul.: Servus pignori datus, etiamsi debitor locuples sit, manumitti non potest.—l. 3, D. de manum. 40, 1.[2]

The enfranchisement must be effected in appropriate form (iusta ac legitima manumissio). There were three of such forms in the older Law.

(1) Manumissio *vindicta*: originally the solemn enfranchisement by 'legis actio' before the magistrate, which took place in the form of a suit concerning freedom, with the master of him that was to be enfranchised as defendant,[a] upon whose 'confessio'[b] the magistrate adjudged freedom to the slave; but later on it was by a mere declaration of the master before the competent authority.

[a] § 40 ad init.

[b] For *confessio in iure*, see § 27.

Ulp. i. 7: **Vindicta** manumittuntur apud magistratum populi, velut consulem praetoremve vel proconsulem.[3]

Gai.: Non est omnino necesse pro tribunali manumittere; itaque plerumque **in transitu** servi manumitti solent, cum aut lavandi aut gestandi aut ludorum gratia prodierit praetor aut proconsul legatusve Caesaris.—l. 7, D. de manum. vind. 40, 2.[4]

---

[1] If one of the owners enfranchise a common slave, he loses his share, and it accrues to the partner; particularly if he have enfranchised him in a form which would have made him a Roman citizen if he had been the sole proprietor. For if he enfranchise him *inter amicos*,[c] the general opinion is that his act is null.—A slave, the usufruct of whom belongs to one man, the ownership to another, when enfranchised by him who has the ownership does not become free, but is a slave without an owner.

[c] See below.

[2] A slave given in pledge, even if the debtor be rich, cannot be enfranchised.

[3] *Manumissio vindicta* is effected before a magistrate of the Roman people, as a consul, proconsul, or praetor.

[4] It is in no way necessary to enfranchise before the court; therefore slaves are generally by custom enfranchised in passing, when the praetor, or proconsul, or imperial legate has gone out either to bathe, or to take exercise, or to the theatre.

Hermog.: Manumissio **per lictores** hodie domino tacente expediri solet et verba solemnia, licet non dicantur, ut dicta accipiuntur.—l. 23 eod.[1]

Ulp.: Ego cum in villa cum praetore fuissem, passus sum apud eum manumitti; etsi lictoris praesentia non esset.—l. 8 eod.[2]

(2) *Censu, i.e.*, enfranchisement by entry on the census-roll.

Ulp. i. 8: **Censu** manumittebantur olim, qui lustrali censu Romae iussu dominorum inter cives Romanos censum profitebantur.[3]

Dos. 17[a] [19, 20]: —est autem **lustrum** quinquennale tempus, quo Roma lustratur. Magna autem dissensio est inter prudentes, quae in censu aguntur, utrum eo tempore vires accipiant omnia, quo census agitur, an eo tempore, quo lustrum conditur.[a] [4]

[a] Cf. Cic. de Orat. i. 40, cited by Poste, 'Elements of Roman Law,' p. 51 (2nd edn.).

(3) *Testamento, i.e.*, enfranchisement by testamentary disposition, which can consist either in the immediate grant of freedom (directa libertas, libertus orcinus) or in a charge addressed to the heir, which is enforceable, to enfranchise the slave (fideicommissaria libertas). If the direct grant of freedom is accompanied by a condition or temporal limitation, the freedman then remains in the meantime a slave,

---

1 Enfranchisement at the present day, if the master is silent, is generally accomplished through the lictors, and the formal words, although not uttered, are taken as uttered.

2 When in the company of the praetor at a country-house, I have allowed enfranchisement to take place before him, though no lictor were present.

3 Those used of old to be enfranchised by *census* who, at the quinquennial census at Rome, by order of their masters, made their return for assessment amongst Roman citizens.

4 Now the *lustrum* is a period of five years in which a census is taken of Rome. But there is great difference of opinion amongst those learned in the Law as to what is done in the census, whether everything acquires force at the time at which the census is going on, or at the time when the *lustrum* is closed.

Book II. Part I.

but with an expectancy of freedom independent of his master, and is called 'statuliber.'

Marcian.: **Testamento** manumissus ita demum fit liber, si testamentum valeat et ex eo adita sit hereditas.—D. 40, 4, 23 pr.[1]

Gai. ii. 267: —nec alius ullus directo ex testamento libertatem habere potest, quam qui utroque tempore testatoris ex iure Quiritium fuerit, et quo faceret testamentum et quo moreretur.[2]

Ulp. ii. 7–8: Libertas et **directo** potest dari hoc modo: LIBER ESTO, LIBER SIT, LIBERVM ESSE IVBEO, et per **fideicommissum**, utputa: ROGO, FIDEI COMMITTO HEREDIS MEI, VT STICHVM SERVVM MANVMITTAT.—Is qui directo liber esse iussus est, testatoris vel **orcinus** fit libertus; is autem cui per fideicommissum data est libertas, non testatoris sed manumissoris fit libertus.[3]

Paul.: Libertas ad tempus dari non potest.—D. 40, 4, 33.[4]

Id.: **Statuliber** est, qui statutam et destinatam in tempus vel condicionen libertatem habet.—l. 1 pr., D. de statulib. 40, 7.[5]

Ulp. ii. 2, 3: Statuliber, quamdiu pendet condicio, servus heredis est.—Statuliber seu aliene-

---

[1] A slave enfranchised in a testament only becomes free when the testament is valid, and, in consequence thereof, entrance has been made upon the inheritance.

[2] And no other can have freedom directly by virtue of a testament than such as belonged to the testator by Quiritarian title at each time, both when he made his testament and at the time of his death.

[3] Freedom may be given both summarily, thus: 'Be free,' 'Let him be free,' 'I bid him be free,' and by *fidei-commissum*, as for example: 'I request,' 'I entrust to my heir's good faith his enfranchisement of the slave Stichus.' He that has been summarily ordered freedom becomes a *libertus orcinus*, but he to whom freedom is given by *fidei-commissum* is a freedman not of the testator, but of the manumittor.

[4] Freedom cannot be granted for a time.

[5] A *statuliber* is he that possesses liberty prescribed and appointed for a time or on condition.

tur ab herede seu usucapiatur ab aliquo, libertatis condicionem secum trahit.[1]

Id.: Statuliberum medio tempore servum heredis esse, nemo est qui ignorare debeat: eapropter noxae dedi poterit, sed deditus sperare adhuc libertatem poterit.—l. 9 pr., D. de statulib.[2]

Id.: Statulibera quidquid peperit, hoc servum heredis est.—l. 16 eod.[3]

Pomp.: Statuliberi a ceteris servis nostris nihilo paene differunt; et ideo quod ad actiones vel ex delicto venientes vel ex . . . contractu pertinet, eiusdem condicionis sunt statuliberi, cuius ceteri, et ideo in publicis quoque iudiciis easdem poenas patiuntur, quas ceteri servi.—l. 29 pr. eod.[4]

Maec.: Libertate sub condicione data huc iam decursum est, ut si per statuliberum non stet, quominus condicioni pareat . . . ad libertatem perveniat.—l. 55 pr., D. de mm. test.[5]

Ulp. ii. 4: Sub ac condicione liber esse iussus: 'si decem milia heredi dederit,' etsi ab herede abalienatus sit, emptori dando pecuniam ab libertatem perveniet: idque lex xii tab. iubet.—Pomp.: lex xii tab. emptionis verbo omnem

---

[1] A *statuliber* is slave of the heir as long as the condition is pending.—Whether the *statuliber* be alienated by the heir or acquired by any one through usucapion, he carries with him his conditional liberty.

[2] That a *statuliber* in the intermediate period is the heir's slave, none should fail to know. He can accordingly be given in compensation, but if he have been so given, he will always still be able to indulge the hope of freedom.

[3] A child born of a woman *statuliber* is the heir's slave.

[4] *Statuliberi* differ scarcely at all from the rest of our slaves; and so as regards actions either arising out of delict or out of contract, *statuliberi* are in the same position as others; and therefore in public proceedings also they suffer the same punishments as other slaves.

[5] With regard to freedom granted conditionally, the idea has already been carried so far as that, unless it rest with the *statuliber* not to comply with the condition, he attains to freedom.

Book II. Part I.

alienationem complexa videretur.—l. 29, § 1, D. de statulib.[1]

Pap.: Statuliberorum iura per heredem fieri non possunt duriora.—l. 33 eod.[2]

To these forms of enfranchisement was added in Christian imperial times the 'manumissio in ecclesia.'

Imp. Constant.: Qui religiosa mente in **ecclesiae** gremio servulis suis meritam concesserint libertatem, eandem eodem iure donasse videantur, quo civitas Romana solemnitatibus decursis dari consuevit. Sed hoc dumtaxat eis, qui sub adspectu antistitum dederint, placuit relaxari.—l. un. pr. Cod. Th. de manum. in eccl. 4, 7.[3]

Informal enfranchisement (inter amicos) had in the most ancient Law no legal effect whatever, in the later Law only a limited one;[a] but Justinian accorded it legal effect under certain presumptions.

[a] § 39.

Imp. Iust.: Sancimus, si quis **per epistulam** servum suum in libertatem perducere maluerit, licere ei hoc facere quinque testibus adhibitis, qui . . . suas litteras supponentes fidem perpetuam possint chartulae praebere.—Sed et si quis **inter amicos** libertatem dare suo servo maluerit, licebit ei, quinque similiter testibus adhibitis, suam explanare voluntatem.—Sed et qui domini funus **pileati** antecedunt, si hoc ex voluntate fiat testa-

[1] If ordered to be free on condition that he give 10,000 sesterces to the heir, though he have been alienated by the heir, he will attain to freedom on giving the money to the purchaser; and this is ordained by a law of the Twelve Tables.—A law of the Twelve Tables, under the word *emptio*, would appear to have embraced every alienation.

[2] The rights of *statuliberi* cannot be curtailed by the heir.

[3] They that of religious sentiment, in the bosom of the church, shall grant just liberty to their slaves shall be regarded as having granted it by the same law as Roman citizenship was wont to be granted with elaborate ceremonies. This, however, it was determined should alone be remitted in favour of those whose grant shall have been made in the presence of the chief priests.

toris vel heredis, fiant ilico cives Romani.—l. un. §§ 1, 2, 5, C. de Lat. lib. 7, 6.[1]

There must be no legal impediment hindering the enfranchisement. Such impediments and limitations were to restrain frivolous and immoderate enfranchisements.

(*a*) Those introduced by the very comprehensive lex Aelia Sentia (A.U. 757).

Gai. §§ 18–20: Quod autem **de aetate servi** requiritur, lege **Aelia Sentia** introductum est: nam ea lex minores xxx annorum servos non aliter voluit manumissos cives Romanos fieri, quam si **vindicta**, apud consilium iusta causa manumissionis adprobata, liberati fuerint. § Iusta autem causa manumissionis est; veluti si quis filium filiamve aut fratrem sororemve naturalem, aut alumnum, aut paedagogum . . . aut ancillam matrimonii causa apud consilium manumittat. § **Consilium** autem adhibetur in urbe Roma quidem quinque senatorum et quinque equitum Romanorum puberum; in provinciis autem viginti recuperatorum civium Romanorum.[2]

---

[1] We ordain that if any one shall choose to bring his slave into liberty by means of a letter, he shall be allowed to do so if he have taken to him five witnesses who, by subscribing their names, may afford permanent credit to the document.—But if any one choose to grant freedom privately to his slave, he shall be allowed, in the presence likewise of five witnesses, to declare his will.—But such also as, clad in fur caps,[a] walk before the corpse of their master, if it be done by desire of the testator or the heir, shall there and then become Roman citizens.

[a] See Smith, Dicty. of Antiqq., s. *Funus.*

[2] Now the requisite as to the age of the slave was introduced by the *l. Aelia Sentia*, for that law prohibited slaves enfranchised under thirty years of age from becoming Roman citizens, save as they were enfranchised by *vindicta* for a legitimate reason approved by the council. There is such legitimate reason, for instance, when a man enfranchises before the council a natural son or daughter, brother or sister, or foster-child, or his children's instructor, . . . or a female slave, in order to marry her. Now the council consists in Rome of five senators and five Roman knights of the age of puberty; in the provinces, of twenty *recuperatores*,[b] Roman citizens.

[b] Cf. § 189.

Book II.
Part I.

Id. i. 38: Item eadem lege minori xx annorum **domino** non aliter manumittere permittitur, quam vindicta, si apud consilium iusta causa manumissionis adprobata fuerit.[1]

Iust. i. 6 pr., § 3: Non tamen cuicumque volenti manumittere licet: nam is qui **in fraudem creditorum** [vel in fraudem **patroni**] manumittit, nihil agit, quia lex Aelia Sentia impedit libertatem.—In fraudem autem creditorum manumittere videtur, qui vel iam eo tempore quo manumittit solvendo non est, vel qui datis libertatibus desiturus est solvendo esse. Praevaluisse tamen videtur, nisi animum quoque fraudandi manumissor habuit, non impediri libertatem, quamvis bona eius creditoribus non sufficiant; saepe enim de facultatibus suis amplius quam in his est sperant homines.—Cf. Gai. i. 37.[2]

Ulp. i. 14: Ab eo domino, **qui solvendo non est**, servus testamento liber esse iussus et heres institutus, etsi minor sit xxx annorum, . . . civis Romanus et heres fit, si tamen alius ex eo testamento nemo heres sit; quod si duo pluresve liberi heredesque esse iussi sint, primo loco scriptus liber et heres fit: quod et ipsum lex Aelia Sentia facit.[3]

---

[1] Also, by the same law, a master under twenty years of age is not allowed to enfranchise, save by *vindicta*, if an adequate reason for manumission have been approved by the council.

[2] It is not, however, allowed every one at pleasure to enfranchise; for he that enfranchises to deceive his creditors [or to deceive his patron] effects nothing, because the *l. Aelia Sentia* bars the freedom.—Now he is considered to enfranchise with the intention of deceiving his creditors, who either already at the time of enfranchisement is insolvent, or by the grant of freedom will cease to be solvent. But the opinion appears to have gained most acceptance that freedom should not be barred unless the manumittor had also the intent to deceive, although he have not property to satisfy his creditors; for men often expect property to be greater than it actually is.

[3] A slave ordered to be free and instituted heir in a testament

(β) By the l. Fufia Caninia (A.U. 761).

Ulp. i. 24–25: **Lex Fufia Caninia** iubet testamento ex tribus servis non plures quam duos manumitti; et usque ad x dimidiam partem manumittere concedit; a x usque ad xxx tertiam partem, ut tamen adhuc v manumittere liceat, aeque ut ex priori numero; a xxx usque ad C quartam partem, aeque ut x ex superiori numero liberari possint; a C usque ad D partem quintam, similiter ut ex antecedenti numero xxv possint fieri liberi: et denique praecipit, ne plures omnino quam C ex cuiusquam testamento liberi fiant.—Eadem lex cavet, ut libertates servis testamento **nominatim** dentur.[1]

—quam (legem) quasi libertatibus impedientem . . . tollendam esse censuimus, cum satis fuerat inhumanum, vivos quidem licentiam habere totam suam familiam libertate donare, nisa alia causa impediat libertati, morientibus autem huiusmodi licentiam adimere.—Tit. J. 1, 7.[2]

In certain cases freedom is bestowed on the slave

by his insolvent master, although he be under thirty years of age . . . becomes a Roman citizen and heir, provided only no one else is heir under such testament. But if two or more are ordered to be free and heirs, the one first mentioned becomes free and heir; and this too the *l. Aelia Sentia* enacts.

[1] The *l. Fufia Caninia* directs that of three slaves not more than two shall be enfranchised by testament, and up to ten allows the enfranchisement of one half the number; from ten to thirty a third, so that at least five may be enfranchised, just as from the previous number; from thirty to a hundred a fourth, just as ten may be enfranchised from a lower number; from a hundred to five hundred a fifth, that those enfranchised be at the like rate of twenty-five from the antecedent number. And finally it ordains that not more than one hundred altogether shall become free under a testament. The same *lex* provides that testamentary gifts of freedom shall be conferred on slaves by name.

[2] This as obstructing freedom . . . we have considered must be repealed, as it was quite inhuman that living persons should be able to confer freedom upon all their household, if no other reason stand in the way of freedom, but to take away such power from those on their deathbed.

Book II. Part I.

when enfranchisement by the master is unnecessary. This happens:

(1) For the punishment of the master.

Modest.: Servo, quem pro derelicto dominus ob gravem infirmitatem habuit, ex edicto D. Claudii competit libertas.—D. 40, 8, 2.[1]

Imp. Iustinian.: Sed scimus etiam hoc esse in antiqua Latinitate ex edicto D. Claudii introductum, quod si quis servum suum aegritudine periclitantem sua domo publice eiecerit, . . . huiusmodi servus in libertate Latina antea morabatur.—C. 7, 6, l. un. § 3.[2]

(2) As a reward to the slave.

Marcian.: Qui ob necem detectam domini praemium libertatis consequitur, fit orcinus libertus.—l. 5 qui si man.[3]

(3) From other causes, especially if the master does not fulfil an obligation incumbent upon him to enfranchise.[a]

[a] See above, *manumissio testamento.*

Paul.: Si servus venditus est, ut intra certum tempus manumitteretur, etiamsi sine herede decessissent et venditor et emptor, servo libertas competit; et hoc D. Marcus rescripsit.—l. 1 eod.[4]

Ulp.: Is qui suis nummis emitur epistula Divorum Fratrum in eam condicionem redigitur,

---

[1] By virtue of an edict of the late emperor Claudius, freedom belongs to a slave whom his master has abandoned because of severe disease.

[2] But we are aware that, according to an edict of the late emperor Claudius, in the old *Latinitas* a provision had been admitted that if a man have publicly cast out of his house his slave who has succumbed to disease . . . such slave found himself in Latin liberty.

[3] He that obtains the reward of liberty for having discovered the murder of his master becomes a *libertus orcinus.*

[4] If a slave has been sold, in order that he may within a certain time be enfranchised, freedom belongs to the slave, even if both vendor and purchaser have died without heirs; and this was subject of a rescript of the late emperor Marcus.

Book II. Part I.

ut libertatem adipiscatur. § Et primo quidem nummis suis non proprie videtur emptus dici, cum suos nummos servus habere non possit; verum coniventibus oculis credendum est suis nummis eum redemptum, cum non nummis eius, qui eum redemit comparatur. § —ab initio hoc agi debet, ut imaginaria fierit emptio et per fidem contractus inter emptorem et servum agatur. § Sive igitur non hoc ab initio esset actum, ut suis nummis redimeretur, sive hoc acto nummos servus non dedit, cessabit libertas.—D. 40, 1, l. 4 pr. §§ 1–3.[1]

Mod.: Divus Vespasianus decrevit, ut, si qua hac lege venierit, ne prostitueretur, et si prostituta esset, ut esset libera, si postea ab emptore alii sine ea condicione veniit, ex lege venditionis liberam esse et libertam prioris venditoris.—D. 37, 14, 7 pr.[2]

§ 38. The Law of Patronage.

The freedman enters into a peculiar relationship of

---

[1] He that is purchased with his own money, according to an *epistula* of the late imperial Brothers, is placed in such position that he acquires freedom. And he appears at first improperly called purchased who is so with his own money, since a slave cannot possess money of his own; but if we overlook it,[a] we must believe that a slave has been purchased with his own money if he have not been acquired with the money of his purchaser. From the outset the intention must be that a fictitious purchase take place, and that there should be a contract by promise between the purchaser and the slave. If, accordingly, either it were not intended from the beginning that he should be redeemed with his own money, or the slave, though it were intended, did not give his own money, the freedom will fall through.

[a] Strictly, 'shut the eyes.'

[2] The late emperor Vespasian decreed that if a slave were sold under the condition that she should not be prostituted, and was prostituted, that she should be free; if afterwards she were sold by her purchaser to another without that condition, she was free from the contract of sale and was freedwoman of the earlier vendor.

BOOK II. Part I.

Family Law to the manumittor, founded upon dutifulness and gratitude, in many respects similar to that between parents and children. This is 'patronatus'; the parties being spoken of as 'patronus' and 'libertus.'

Of the patron's rights, the following are of chief importance.

(1) The 'libertus' is under obligations to the patron and his children of homage, fidelity and ready service (officia obsequii et reverentiae).[a]

[a] Cf. D. 2, 4, 4, 1.

Ulp.: Liberto et filio semper honesta et sancta persona patris ac patroni videri debet.—l. 9, D. de obsequ. 37, 15.[1]

Paul.: . . . **Ingratus** libertus est, qui patrono **obsequium** non praestat, vel res eius filiorumve tutelam administrare detrectat.—l. 19, D. de iure patr. 37, 14.[2]

Ulp.: Patronorum querelas adversus libertos praesides audire et non translaticie exsequi debent. . . . Sed si quidem **inofficiosus** patrono patronae liberisve eorum sit, tantummodo castigari eum . . . et dimitti oportet. Enimvero si contumeliam fecit aut convicium eis dixit, etiam in exilium temporale dari debebit. Quodsi manus intulit, in metallum dandus erit.—l. 1 eod.[3]

Id.: Sed nec **famosae actiones** adversus eos[b] dantur, nec hae quidem, quae doli vel fraudis habet mentionem.—Nec exceptiones doli patiun-

[b] Sc. patronos, patronas, liberosve aut parentes patroni.

---

[1] The person of the father and patron must always be honourable and sacred in the eyes of the freedman and his son.

[2] He is an ungrateful freedman who does not render homage to his patron, or hesitates to undertake the administration of his property or the guardianship of his children.

[3] The complaints of patrons against their freedmen the presidents must attend to and not deal with lightly. . . . But if a freedman be undutiful to his patron or patroness or their children, he must only be chastised . . . and let go. If, however, he have done an injury or reviled them, he will have to be put in temporary banishment. But if he have laid hands on them, he must be consigned to work in the mines.

tur vel vis metusve causa vel interdictum 'unde vi.'—l. 5, § 1, l. 7, § 2, D. de obseq.[1]

(2) The 'libertus' has to perform certain services of attachment (operae officiales), but an action (operarum actio) for their performance, and of 'operae fabriles s. artificiales' of pecuniary value, is only given to the patron when the libertus is under this obligation, in accordance with a contract (by stipulatio) after enfranchisement, or in op. offic. when he has bound himself by oath (iurata promissio); and the libertus is absolved from even this obligation in particular cases.

Ulp.: Ut Servius scribit, antea soliti fuerunt[a] a libertis durissimas res exigere, scilicet ad remunerandum tam grande beneficium, quod in libertos confertur, cum ex servitute ad civitatem Romanam perducuntur. § Et quidem primus praetor Rutilius edixit se amplius non daturum patrono quam operarum et societatis actionem, videlicet si hoc pepigisset, ut nisi obsequium ei praestaret libertus, in societatem admitteretur patronus. § Posteriores praetores certae partis bonorum possessionem[b] pollicebantur.—D. 38, 2, 1 pr., §§ 1, 2.[2]

[a] Sc. patroni.

[b] For *bonorum possessio*, see § 154.

[1] But neither are actions of infamy granted against them [*i.e.*, patrons, patronesses, or the children or parents of a patron], nor those indeed which allege fraud or deceit. Neither are pleas of fraud allowed, nor that something was done from duress or from fear, nor the interdict 'unde vi.'

[2] As Servius writes, they [*i.e.*, patrons] were previously accustomed to require the hardest things from their freedmen, as recompense, that is, for the benefit so great which accrues to freedmen as promoted from slavery to Roman citizenship. The praetor Rutilius was indeed the first to announce that he would grant nothing further to the patron than the action for services and the partnership action, that is, if the patron had stipulated that, unless the freedman rendered him honourable submission, he should be allowed a share of the property. The later praetors used to promise the possession of a certain part of the succession.

BOOK II. Part I.

Paul.: Tales patrono **operae** dantur, quales ex aetate dignitate valetudine necessitate proposito ceterisque eius generis in utraque persona aestimari debent.—l. 16, § 1, D. de op. lib. 38, 1.[1]

Ulp.: Sed **officiales** quidem nec cuiquam alii deberi possunt quam patrono, cum proprietas earum et in edentis persona et in eius cui eduntur consistit; **fabriles** autem aliaeve eius generis sunt, ut a quocumque cuicumque solvi possint: sane enim si in artificio sint, iubente patrono et alii edi possunt.—l. 9, § 1, D. de op lib.[2]

Id.: **Fabriles** operae ceteraeque, quae quasi in pecuniae praestatione consistunt, ad heredem transeunt; **officiales** vero non transeunt.—l. 6 eod.[3]

Id.: Ut **iurisiurandi obligatio** contrahatur, libertum esse oportet qui iuret, et libertatis causa iurare.—Iurare autem debet, operas donum munus se praestiturum, operas qualescumque, quae modo probe iure licito imponuntur.—l. 7 pr., § 3 eod.[4]

Ulp.: Quae **onerandae libertatis** causa stipulatus sum, a liberto exigere non possum; one-

---

[1] Such services are rendered to the patron as must be reckoned for in respect of age, rank, health, necessity, the purpose and other considerations of that kind affecting both persons.

[2] But domestic services cannot be owed to any one other than the patron, because ownership therein lies only in respect as well of the person rendering them as of him to whom they are rendered; but industrial and other services are of such sort that they can be rendered by any one to any one. For if they consist of artistic work, they can be rendered to another also at the order of the patron.

[3] Industrial services, and all others that are equivalent to a money-payment, pass to the heirs; but domestic services do not so pass.

[4] That an obligation upon oath be contracted, it is necessary that the person making oath be a freedman, and that his oath be by reason of freedom.—Now he must swear that he will render services, a gift, or a present; in respect of services, it matters not of what kind they are, provided they are imposed rightly, lawfully, and as allowed.

randae autem libertatis causa facta bellissime ita definiuntur : quae ita imponuntur, ut si patronum libertus offenderit, petantur ab eo semperque sit metu exactionis ei subiectus, propter quem metum quodvis sustineat patrono praecipiente.—D. 44, 5, 1, 5.[1] Book II. Part I.

QVI LIBERTINVS DVOS PLVRESVE A SE GENITOS NATASVE IN SVA POTESTATE HABEBIT . . . NE QVIS EORVM OPERAS DONI MVNERIS ALIVDVE QVIDQVAM LIBERTATIS CAVSA PATRONO PATRONAE LIBERISVE EORVM, DE QVIBVS IVRAVERIT VEL PROMISERIT OBLIGATVSVE ERIT, DARE FACERE PRAESTARE DEBETO.—l. 37 pr., D. de op. lib. (ex l. Iulia et Papia).[2]

Hermog. : Patronus . . . qui libertae nuptiis consensit, operarum exactionem amittit : nam haec, cuius matrimonio consensit, in officio mariti esse debet.—l. 48 pr. eod.[3]

The patron, his children and parents have claim to aliment.

The patron has a right of inheritance in relation to the freedman.[a] [a] §§ 162, 164, 168.

---

1 What I have stipulated with the view of encumbering freedom I cannot exact from the freedman. That anything has been done to clog freedom is most correctly stated thus : Everything that has been imposed in such way that, if the freedman have injured the manumittor, it can be required by him, and the freedman is placed ever under his control from apprehension that he will make good his demand, by reason of which fear the freedman will put up with anything at the behest of the patron.

2 'The freedman that shall have in his power two or several sons or daughters begotten by him . . . none of them shall be obliged to give, to do, or to perform to the patron or the patroness or their children services of gift, of present, or anything else, in consideration of freedom, concerning which he shall have taken an oath, or shall only have made a verbal promise, or shall be bound.'

3 The patron . . . who has consented to the marriage of a freedwoman, loses his claim to her services ; for if consent have been given to her marriage, she must be in the domestic service of her husband.

Book II. Part I.

The right of 'patronatus' is transmissible to the children of the patron,[a] but he can also, according to a SC. Ostorianum, transfer it to one or more of them (adsignatio liberti); on the other hand, it does not extend to the children of the 'libertus.'

[a] § 162; D. 38, 1, 29.

Ulp.: Adsignare autem quis potest quibuscumque verbis, vel nutu vel testamento vel codicillis vel vivus.—D. 38, 4, 1, 3.[1]

Scaev.: Adsignare et pure et sub condicione et per epistulam vel testationem vel chirographum possumus: quia adsignatio liberti neque quasi legatum neque quasi fideicommissum percipitur. —l. 7 eod.[2]

Gai.: Cum libertus promiserit patrono operas se daturum, neque adiecerit liberisque eius, constat liberis eius ita demum deberi, si patri heredes exstiterint.—l. 22, § 1, D. de op. lib.[3]

The patron loses his right—

(1) By abuse of the 'ius patronatus.'

Paul.: Qui contra legem Aeliam Sentiam ad iurandum libertum adegit[b] nihil iuris habet nec ipse nec liberi eius.—D. 37, 14, 15.[4]

[b] Sc. ne liberos tollat, vel libertam, ne nubat.

(2) By violation of the duties incumbent upon him as patron towards the 'libertus.'

Ulp.: Qui cum maior natu esset quam xxv annis, libertum **capitis accusaverit** aut in **servitu-**

---

[1] Any one can assign by such words as he likes, with a gesture, or by a testament, or codicil, or while yet alive.

[2] We can assign absolutely and conditionally, and by a letter or declaration before witnesses, or a manuscript; because the assignment of a freedman is understood neither as a bequest nor as a *fideicommissum*.

[3] When a freedman has promised that he will render services to his patron without adding 'and to his children,' it is settled that such are due to his children only if they have become the father's heirs.

[4] He that in violation of the *l. Aelia Sentia* has compelled a freedman to take an oath [not to beget children, or a freedwoman not to marry] has no right, either himself or his children.

tem petierit, removetur a contra tabulas bonorum possessione.[a]—D. 38, 2, 14 pr.[1]

Marcian.: Imperatoris nostri rescripto cavetur, ut si patronus libertum suum non aluerit, ius patroni perdat.—l. 5, § 1, D. de iure patr.[2]

(3) By 'natalium restitutio.'[b]

[a] § 168.

[b] D. 40, 11, 2.

§ 39. Cives, Latini, Peregrini.[c]

[c] For the British Law on Subjects and Aliens, see Steph. iii. pp. 409, *sqq.*, and for conflict of laws on such subject, Westlake, 'Private International Law,' ch. xv. See also Brown, s. 'Domicile.'

Citizenship is acquired by birth,[d] by fully valid manumission,[e] and by grant (statute).

Gai. i. § 17: Nam in cuius persona tria haec concurrunt, ut maior sit annorum triginta, et ex iure Quiritium domini, et iusta ac legitima manumissione liberetur i.e. vindicta aut censu aut testamento, is civis Romanus fit: sin vero aliquid eorum deerit, Latinus erit.[3]

[d] § 33.

[e] § 37.

It is lost—

(1) By acceptance of the right of citizenship in a foreign colony (colonia Latina).

Gai. iii. § 56: —cives Romani ingenui . . . ex urbe Roma in Latinas colonias deducti, Latini coloniarii esse coeperunt.[4]

(2) By the punishment of exile (aquae et ignis interdictio) and deportation.

Iust. i. 16, 2: Minor sive media est capitis deminutio, cum civitas quidem amittitur, libertas vero retinetur: quod accidit ei, cui aqua et igni

---

1 He that when of more than twenty-five years of age has charged his freedman with a capital crime, or has recalled him into slavery, is refused the *b. p. c. t.*

2 By a rescript of our Emperor it is laid down that, if a patron do not supply his freedman with nourishment, he loses his rights of patron.

3 He becomes a Roman citizen in whose person these three points unite: that he is more than thirty years old, that he belongs to his master upon Quiritarian title, and is liberated by a legal and statutory manumission, *i.e.*, by *vindicta*, census or testament; but if any of these fail, he will be a Latin.

4 Free-born Roman citizens . . . despatched from the city to Latin colonies became *Lat. coloniarii.*

Book II. Part I.

interdictum fuerit, vel ei, qui in insulam deportatus est.[1]

Ulp. x. 3: Peregrinus fit is cui aqua et igni interdictum est.[2]

(3) By desertion to the enemy.

Paul.: Qui deficiunt, capite minuuntur (deficere autem dicuntur, qui ab his quorum sub imperio sunt, desistunt et in hostium numerum se conferunt), sed et hi, quos senatus hostes iudicavit vel lege lata: utique usque eo, ut civitatem amittant.—D. 4, 5, 5, 1.[3]

Midway between the 'cives Romani' and 'Peregrini' came the *Latini*, who had not the Roman 'conubium.' These were especially the members of a community participating in the rights of Latins (Latini coloniarii). 'Latinitas' had originally a national character, and was introduced within narrow local limits: the 'Latini' were the inhabitants of ancient Latium.[a] From them the 'Latinitas' was consequently transferred to the Latin colonies planted from Rome. After that citizenship, in consequence of the war of the Allies, was conferred upon the whole of Latium and the Latin colonies in Italy by the l. Iulia (A.U. 664), 'Latinitas' lost its original meaning, but lasted still for a long time through transfer, *i.e.*, by conferment of the 'ius Latii' upon the several cities and whole provinces, until at last by a constitution of Caracalla, who conferred citizenship upon all free inhabitants of the

[a] 'Nomen Latinum.'

---

[1] The lesser or middle *cap. dem.* is when citizenship only is lost, but freedom remains. This happens in the case of him to whom fire and water shall be forbidden or in the case of one deported[b] to an island.

[2] He becomes a *peregrinus* who has been forbidden fire and water.

[3] Traitors suffer loss of status (now, the expression 'to turn traitor' is applied to such as fall away from those under whose dominion they are, and betake themselves to the ranks of the enemy), but those likewise who have been adjudged enemies by the Senate or by the passing of a *lex;* at any rate in so far that they lose citizenship.

[b] *I.e.*, conveyed away. See Smith, Dicty. of Antiqq. s. *Exsilium*.

Roman empire then living,[a] the communal 'Latinitas' was repealed, and with it disappeared the class of 'Latini coloniarii.'[b]

Ulp.: In orbe Romano qui sunt, ex constitutione imperatoris Antonini cives Romani effecti sunt.—D. 1, 5, 17.[1]

Gai. i. §§ 95, sq.—Alia causa est eorum, qui **Latii iure** cum liberis suis ad civitatem Romanam perveniunt; nam horum in potestate fiunt liberi. § Quod ius quibusdam peregrinis civitatibus datum est vel a populo Romano vel a senatu vel a Caesare. —aut **maius** est Latium aut **minus**: maius est Latium, cum et hi qui decuriones leguntur, et ei, qui honorem aliquem aut magistratum gerunt, civitatem Romanam consequuntur; minus Latium est, cum hi tantum, qui vel magistratum vel honorem gerunt, ad civitatem Romanam perveniunt.[2]

Latinitas, as a personal individual quality, was moreover possessed by the imperfect freedmen,[c] from the time of the l. Iunia Norbana (A.U. 772). They had previously been in no more than a condition of *de facto* freedom which was protected by the Praetor; but the l. Iulia—from which they were called *Lat. Iuniani*—put them upon an equal footing with the 'Latini coloniarii,' without, however, assuring them full capacity for testaments—in particular, the right of

[a] With the exception of exiles and *deportati* (*sup.*), certain freedmen governed by the l. Aelia Sentia (*inf.*), and indeed the class whose rights were determined by the l. Iunia Norbana (*inf.*).

[b] From the *ius Latii* we must distinguish the *ius Italicum*, which in imperial times was granted to particular municipal communities in the provinces, and assured the privileges of Latin soil (see § 71) for the provincial community affected, as well as of Italian communal citizens for the members of such class.

[c] Gai. i. 17, above.

---

[1] All persons to be found within the sphere of the Roman empire received Roman citizenship by a constitution of the emperor Antonine.

[2] The case is different with those who, with their children, attain Roman citizenship by right of *Latinitas*; for their children became subject to their *potestas*. This right has been granted to some foreign States either by the Roman people, the Senate, or the Emperor.—*Latinitas* is either the greater or the lesser. There is the greater *Latinitas*, when those who are elected *decuriones*,[d] and such as fill some high office or magistracy, acquire Roman citizenship; the lesser, when they who fill a magistracy or high office attain Roman citizenship.

[d] See Smith, Dicty. of Antiqq. s. *Colonia*.

BOOK II. Part I.

making a testament for themselves—and with express confirmation of the existing right of the manumittor in respect of succession to the freedman. The children of freedmen of the 'Latini Iuniani' were themselves, again, ordinary Latins.

Ulp. i. 16: Qui tantum in bonis, non etiam ex iure Quiritium servum habet, manumittendo Latinum facit.[1]

Dos. 14 (16): Is qui manumittitur inter amicos, quotcumque est annorum, Latinus fit.[2]

Gai. iii. § 56: —admonendi sumus, . . . eos qui nunc Latini Iuniani dicuntur, olim ex iure Quiritium servos fuisse, sed auxilio praetoris in libertatis forma servari solitos, unde etiam res eorum peculii iure ad patronos pertinere solita est; postea vero per legem Iuniam eos omnes, quos praetor in libertate tuebatur, liberos esse coepisse et appellatos esse Latinos Iunianos: Latinos ideo, quia lex eos liberos proinde esse voluit atque [si essent cives Romani ingenui] qui ex urbe Roma in Latinas colonias deducti Latini coloniarii esse coeperunt; Iunianos ideo, quia per legem Iuniam liberi facti sunt, etiamsi non essent cives Romani. Legis itaque Iuniae lator cum intelligeret futurum, ut ea fictione res Latinorum defunctorum ad patronos pertinere desinerent,—quia scilicet neque ut servi decederent, ut possent iure peculii res eorum ad patronos pertinere, neque liberti Latini hominis bona possent manumissionis iure ad patronos pertinere,—necessarium existimavit, ne beneficium istis datum in iniuriam patronorum converteretur, cavere, ut bona eorum proinde ad manumissores pertinerent, ac si lex lata non esset: itaque iure

---

[1] He that holds a slave in Bonitarian ownership alone, and not also in Quiritarian right, by manumitting him makes him a Latin.

[2] He that is manumitted *inter amicos*, of whatever age he is becomes a Latin.

quodammodo peculii ad manumissores ea lege pertinent.[1] BOOK II. Part I.

Id. i. § 23: Non tamen illis permittit lex Iunia vel ipsis testamentum facere, vel ex testamento alieno capere, vel tutores testamento dari.[2]

Various courses were laid open to the Latins whereby they could obtain the *civitas*; we may particularise—

(1) The 'iteratio (sc. manumissionis).'

Ulp. iii. 1, 4: Latini ius Quiritium consequuntur his modis: beneficio principali, liberis, iteratione, militia, nave, aedificio, pistrino, praeterea ex senatusconsulto (mulier) quae sit ter enixa.—Iteratione fit civis Romanus, qui post Latinitatem quam acceperat maior xxx annorum iterum iuste

---

[1] We must bear in mind . . . that those who are now called *Latini Iuniani* were formerly slaves by Quiritarian law, but, by the aid of the praetor, used to be secured a show of freedom; consequently their property also used to belong to the patrons by the title of *peculium*; but that later on, through the *l. Iunia*, all those whose freedom the praetor protected began to be freemen and to be called *Lat. Iuniani*: Latins, because it was the intention of the statute that they should be freemen just as [if they were free-born Roman citizens] who, having been despatched from the city to Latin settlements, became *Lat. coloniarii*; *Iuniani*, because through the *l. Iunia* they became free, although they were not Roman citizens. And so, when he who carried the *l. Iunia* saw that by such fiction the estates of deceased Latins would cease to belong to the patron (because as they died not in the condition of slaves, their effects could not belong to the patrons by right of *peculium*, neither could the estate of a Latin freedman belong to his patron by right of manumission), he considered it necessary in order to prevent the advantage conferred on these persons from proving an injury to the patrons, to provide that their estates should belong to the manumittors just as if the statute had not been passed; and by virtue of that statute, the effects of Latins belong to their manumittors, in a manner, *iure peculii*.

[2] The *l. Iunia* does not, however, allow them either to make a testament for themselves, or to take under the testament of another, or to be appointed testamentary guardians.

manumissus est ab eo, cuius ex iure Quiritium servus fuit.[1]

Dos. 14: Is autem qui manumittitur inter amicos, quotcumque est annorum, Latinus fit et tantum hoc ei prodest manumissio, ut postea iterum possit vindicta vel testamento manumitti et civis Romanus fieri.[2]

(2) The 'anniculi causae probatio ex l. Aelia Sentia.'

Gai. I. §§ 29–31: Ex lege Aelia Sentia minores XXX annorum manumissi et Latini facti si uxores duxerint vel cives Romanas vel Latinas coloniarias vel eiusdem condicionis cuius et ipsi essent, idque testati fuerint adhibitis non minus quam septem testibus civibus Romanis puberibus, et filium procreaverint, cum is filius anniculus esse coeperit, datur eis potestas per eam legem adire praetorem vel in provinciis praesidem provinciae et adprobare, se ex lege Aelia Sentia uxorem duxisse et ex ea filium anniculum habere: et si is, apud quem causa probata est, id ita esse pronuntiaverit, tunc et ipse Latinus et uxor eius, si et ipsa eiusdem condicionis sit, cives Romani esse iubentur. § Ideo autem in ipsorum filio adiecimus 'si et ipse eiusdem condicionis sit,' quia si uxor civis Romana est, qui ex ea nascitur, ex novo senatusconsulto quod auctore D. Hadriano

---

[1] Latins acquire the *ius Quiritium* in the following ways: by imperial grant, by children, by repetition, by service in the night-watch, by maritime trade, by house-building, by the occupation of a bakery; and further by virtue of a *senatus-consultum*, in being a woman that has thrice borne children.—He becomes a Roman citizen by repetition who, after having received *Latinitas* when more than thirty years of age, has been afresh manumitted in due form by the person whose slave he was upon Quiritarian title.

[2] Now he that is manumitted *inter amicos*, of whatever age he is, becomes a Latin, and the manumission is of advantage to him so far that he can afterwards again be manumitted by rod, or by testament, and become a Roman citizen.

factum est, civis Romanus nascitur [cf. i. § 80: —fuerunt qui putaverunt, ex lege Aelia Sentia contracto matrimonio Latinum nasci, quia videtur eo casu per legem Aeliam Sentiam conubium inter eos dari, et semper conubium efficit, ut qui nascitur patris condicioni accedat.—] § Hoc tamen ius adipiscendae civitatis . . . postea senatusconsulto, quod Pegaso et Pusione coss. factum est, etiam maioribus xxx annorum mamussis Latinis factis concessum est.[1]

(3) The 'erroris causae probatio,' which was also applicable to peregrini.

Gai. 1, §§ 67, 68: Item si civis Romanus Latinam aut peregrinam uxorem duxerit per ignorantiam, cum eam civem Romanam esse crederet, et filium procreaverit, . . . ex senatusconsulto permit-

---

[1] By the *l. Aelia Sentia* those that have been manumitted under thirty years of age and have become Latins, if they have married wives who are either Roman citizens or Latin colonists, or of the same condition as themselves, and have made attestation of this before not less than seven witnesses of Roman citizens of the age of puberty called for the purpose, and have begotten a son, on such son's completing his first year are allowed, by virtue of that statute, to go before the praetor, or in the provinces before the governor, and prove that they have married according to the terms of the *l. Aelia Sentia*, and have by such wife a son a year old; and if he before whom cause has been shown shall pronounce that it is so, then both the Latin himself and his wife, if she be of the same condition, are declared to be Roman citizens. Therefore we add with respect to their son 'if also he be of the same condition,' because if the wife of the Latin be a Roman citizen, her offspring is a Roman citizen by birth according to a recent *sc.* of which the late emperor Hadrian was the author. [Some have thought that if the marriage were contracted in accordance with the *l. Aelia Sentia*, the issue would be a Latin, because it is considered that the right of intermarriage is granted them in such a case, and *conubium* always has the effect of the issue following the condition of the father].—This right of Roman citizenship was afterwards by the *SC.* passed in the consulship of Pegasus and Pusio, conferred upon those also who were manumitted and made Latins when more than thirty years of age.

Book II. Part I.

titur causam erroris probare, et ita uxor quoque et filius ad civitatem Romanam perveniunt, et ex eo tempore incipit filius in potestate patris esse.—§ Item si civis Romana per errorem nupta sit peregrino tamquam civi Romano, permittitur ei causam erroris probare, et ita filius quoque et maritus ad civitatem Romanam perveniunt, et aeque simul incipit filius in potestate patris esse; idem iuris est, si peregrino tamquam Latino ex lege Aelia Sentia nupta sit.—§ 70: Idem constitutum est, si Latinus per errorem peregrinam quasi Latinam aut civem Romanam e lege Aelia Sentia uxorem duxerit.[1]

To the Peregrini, who possessed neither 'connubium' nor 'commercium,' and to whom the ius gentium—or their own country's Law—was alone available, belonged—[a]

[a] Apart from the subjects of foreign States allied with Rome (§ 4).

(1) Persons of foreign nationality received into political connection with Rome, and so especially the inhabitants of the subject provinces and communities incorporated in the Roman State, without grant of 'civitas' or 'Latinitas.' The 'peregrini dediticii' took politically a peculiar, more unfavourable position, and were deprived of a national Law of their own.[b]

[b] Cf. § 156, *testamenti factio.*

[1] Likewise if a Roman citizen through ignorance have taken to wife a Latin or a foreign woman, believing her to be a Roman citizen, and have begotten a son, . . . by a *SC.* he is allowed to prove a case of error, and so both wife and son attain to Roman citizenship, and from that time the son begins to be under the *potestas* of his father.—Likewise if a woman who is a Roman citizen has by mistake married a foreigner as though he were a Roman citizen, she is allowed to prove a case of error, and thus both the son and the husband attain to Roman citizenship, and at the self-same time the son begins to be under his father's *potestas.* The law is the same if, in accordance with the *l. Aelia Sentia,* she have married a foreigner, presumably a Latin.—The same is the rule if a Latin have by mistake married a foreign woman in accordance with the *l. Aelia Sentia,* supposing her to be a Latin or a Roman citizen.

Paul.: Quos nos **hostes** appellamus, eos veteres **perduelles** appellabant.—D. 50, 16, 234 pr.[1]

Cic. de off. 1, 12, 37: **Hostis** enim apud maiores nostros is dicebatur, quem nunc **peregrinum** dicimus; indicant xii tabulae, ut: STATVS[a] DIES CVM HOSTE itemque: ADVERSVS HOSTEM AETERNA AVCTORITAS.[2]

[a] Commonly, *statuta*, or (as in Fest. cited by Wordsw. 'Early Latin,' p. 517) *constituta*.

Gai. i. § 14: Vocantur autem **peregrini dediticii** hi, qui quondam adversus populum Romanum armis susceptis pugnaverunt, deinde victi se dediderunt.[3]

(2) Exiles and 'deportati.'

Marcian.: Item quidam ἀπόλιδες sunt h. e. sine civitate, ut sunt in opus publicum perpetuo dati et in insulam deportati, ut ea quidem quae iuris civilis sunt non habeant, quae vero iuris gentium sunt habeant.—D. 48, 19, 17, 1.[b] [4]

[b] Cf. D. 28, 1, 8, 1; de leg. iii. 32, 1, 2.

Moreover, to the class of 'peregrini dediticii' belonged certain freedmen in virtue of the l. Aelia Sentia.

Gai. i. §§ 13, 27: Lege itaque Aelia Sentia cavetur ut qui servi a dominis poenae nomine vincti sint, quibusve stigmata inscripta sint, deve quibus ob noxam quaestio tormentis habita sit et in ea noxa fuisse convicti sint, quive ut ferro aut cum bestiis depugnarent traditi sint, inve ludum custodiamve coniecti fuerint, et postea vel ab eodem domine vel ab alio manumissi, eiusdem condicionis liberi fiant, cuius condicionis sunt peregrini

---

[1] Those called by us *hostes* the ancients called *perduelles*.[c]

[c] See Clark, 'Early Roman Law,' § 16.

[2] For amongst our ancestors he used to be called 'enemy' whom we now call 'foreigner:' this is shown by the Twelve Tables, as 'a fixed day with the *hostis*,' and likewise, 'There is an indefeasible title against a *hostis*.'

[3] Now those are called *p. d.* who aforetime have taken up arms and fought against the Roman people, and then when conquered surrendered.

[4] Likewise there are those who are called ἀπόλιδες, that is, who have no citizenship, as those condemned to perpetual public penal labour and conveyed away to an island, so that they do not participate in matters pertaining to the *i. c.*, but they do participate in such as pertain to *i. g.*

Book II. Part I.

dediticii.—§ Quin etiam in urbe Roma vel intra centesimum urbis Romae miliarium morari prohibentur; et si contra fecerint, ipsi bonaque eorum publice venire iubentur ea condicione, ut ne in urbe Roma vel intra centesimum urbis miliarium serviant neve umquam manumittantur; et si manumissi fuerint, servi populi Romani esse iubentur.[1]

These last were excluded from the acquisition of 'civitas.'

Gai. i. § 26: Pessima itaque libertas eorum est, qui dediticiorum numero sunt; nec ulla lege aut senatusconsulto aut constitutione principali aditus illis ad civitatem Romanam datur.[2]

[a] § 4.

[b] Save as to legal relations grounded upon the Family system.

With the assimilation of the ius civile and ius gentium,[a] the difference between *cives* and *peregrini* (who indeed constituted the preponderating part of the population) gradually lost its practical importance,[b] until the constitution of Caracalla virtually set the latter aside. But the institution of 'Latini Iuniani,' and 'peregrinitas dediticia' were definitely set aside by Justinian when they had been already long obso-

[1] By the *l. Aelia Sentia* it is provided that such slaves as have been put in chains by their masters by way of punishment and have been branded or have been subjected to examination by torture on account of an offence, and have been convicted of such offence, or have been given up to fight with the sword or with beasts, and have been committed to a gladiatorial school or to prison, and subsequently have been manumitted either by the same or another owner, shall as freemen be of the same condition as are the *p. d.*—And further, they are forbidden to dwell in Rome or within a hundred miles of the city; and if they transgress, a public sale is ordered of themselves and their goods, subject to the condition that they shall not serve as slaves in Rome or within a hundred miles thereof, and be never manumitted; and if they should be, they are to become slaves of the Roman people.

The freedom of those who are in the category of *dediticii* is of the worst order, nor is admission to Roman citizenship granted them by any *lex*, *senatus-consultum*, or imperial constitution.

lete; so that in the last stage of the Law all free Roman subjects were at the same time 'cives,' whilst private legal capacity in general was no longer in any way dependent upon 'civitas.'

§ 40. Legal Remedies for the Protection of Freedom and Citizenship.

If the condition of any person which determined his legal capacity was doubtful or contested, an inquiry could be made into it (status quaestio); sometimes in the immediate interest of the State, at other times in his private interest. The former happened when the status was subject of discussion as presupposed by circumstances of Public Law; the latter, when it was a question of capacity for private rights determined by status, and of the claims under Private Law of or against a person which are governed by it.

Here the 'status quaestio' is subject of a suit between two parties: either that it merely arises incidentally in establishing a claim which itself depends upon the respective status of plaintiff or defendant, or that it forms the immediate and exclusive subject of special proceedings, the purpose of which is only the judicial determination of the question whether the status that is claimed belongs to the plaintiff or defendant. (So-called actions of status.[a]) We have here only to deal with the latter.

The suit concerning freedom and slavery (liberalis causa, liberale iudicium), as maintained in the ancient time, took the form of a 'vindicatio in servitutem' by the alleged owner, and 'contravindicatio in libertatem' by the 'adsertor in lib. (vindex)' as representative of him concerning whose freedom the dispute was—or in the reverse case, of a 'vindicatio in libertatem' and 'contravindicatio in servitutem'—and by means of 'legis actio sacramento.'[b] During the continuance of the proceedings, the person whose freedom was impeached was, in the meantime, in accordance with the direction of the XII Tables, treated as a freeman.[c]

[a] Cf. §§ 51, 54.

[b] Cf. Gai. iv. 16.

[c] 'Praetor vindicias secundum libertatem dicebat.' See Liv. iii. 44-48, for the case of Verginia, and comp. Dig. 1, 2, 2, 24.

Book II. Part I.

Later on, this suit was conducted in the form of a 'praeiudicium.'[a]

[a] Gai. iv. 44.

> Inst. iv. 6, § 13: **Praeiudiciales actiones** in rem esse videntur, quales sunt per quas quaeritur, an aliquis liber vel an libertus sit, vel de partu agnoscendo; ex quibus fere una illa legitimam causam habet, per quam quaeritur, an aliquis liber sit: ceterae ex ipsius praetoris iurisdictione substantiam capiunt.[1]

In this the functions of the parties, and the burden of proof governed by such, were regulated by the settlement of whether he whose freedom was in question had been in possession of freedom thitherto or had been in the condition of *de facto* servitude.

> Ulp.: Si quis ex servitute **in libertatem proclamat**, petitoris partes sustinet; si vero ex libertate in servitutem petatur, is partes actoris sustinet, qui servum suum dicet. Igitur cum de hoc incertum est, . . . hoc ante apud eum, qui de libertate cogniturus est, disceptatur, utrum ex libertate in servitutem aut contra agatur. Et si forte apparuerit eum, qui de statu suo litigat, in libertate sine dolo malo fuisse, is qui se dominum dicit, actoris partes sustinebit et necesse habebit servum suum probare.—D. 40, 12, 7, 5.[2]

---

1 Pre-judicial actions are accounted *in rem*, for instance, those by which inquiry is made whether some one is a freeman or a freedman, or those concerning the acknowledgment of issue. Of such in general only that is grounded upon statute by which the inquiry is whether some one is a freeman; the rest derive their origin from the jurisdiction of the praetor.

2 Whosoever from slavery makes claim to freedom undertakes the functions of plaintiff; but if the claim be made as from freedom to slavery, he assumes the functions of plaintiff who alleges that [the other] is his slave. When, therefore, uncertainty prevail concerning it . . . this is discussed previously before him who shall decide concerning the freedom, whether proceedings are taken as from freedom into slavery, or conversely. And if so be it should appear that he who maintains a suit

Book II. Part I.

Id.: Quod autem diximus 'in libertate fuisse,' sic est accipiendium, non ut se liberum doceat is qui liberale iudicium patitur, sed in possessione libertatis sine dolo malo fuisse.—l. 10 eod.[1]

Here also, after 'litis contestatio,' provisional possession of freedom was accorded such person until the decision of the case.

Paul.: Ordinata liberali causa liberi loco habetur is qui de statu suo litigat.—l. 24 pr. eod.[2]

The necessity of the party concerned having a 'vindex' was only done away with by Justinian.

The suit concerning 'ingenuitas' or 'libertinitas' was also decided in a *praeiudicium* between the alleged patron and libertus.

Ulp.: Quotiens de hoc contenditur, an quis libertus sit, sive operae petantur, sive obsequium desideretur, sive etiam famosa actio intendatur, sive in ius vocetur qui se patronum dicit, sive nulla causa interveniat, redditur praeiudicium. —D. 40, 14, 6.[3]

Venulei.: Qui se ex libertinitate ingenuitati

---

concerning his status has been in liberty without fraud, the one who alleges that he is the master will take upon him the functions of plaintiff, and will of necessity have to prove that [the other] is his slave.

[1] But if we have spoken of 'having been in liberty,' this is to be understood not as that the one who is involved in a suit concerning freedom demonstrates that he is free, but that he has been in possession of freedom without fraud.

[2] If a suit concerning freedom have been commenced, the one who takes proceedings concerning his legal condition is regarded as a freeman.

[3] Whenever a suit is maintained as to whether any one is a freedman, be it that services are claimed or obedience desired, or even an action brought involving infamy, or he is summoned who alleges that he is patron, or if no special cause occur, a *praeiudicium* is granted.

adserant, non ultra quinquennium, quam manumissi fuissent, audientur.—l. 2, § 1 eod.[1]

As regards the distribution of functions between the parties and the burden of proof, the case is precisely the same as that of the Action concerning Freedom.

Ulp.: Circa eum, qui se ex libertinitate ingenuum dicat, referendum est, quis actoris partibus fungatur. Et si quidem in possessione libertinitatis fuit, sine dubio ipsum oportebit ingenuitatis causam agere docereque se ingenuum esse; sin vero in possessione ingenuitatis sit et libertinus esse dicatur, scilicet eius qui ei controversiam movet, hoc probare debet, qui eum dicit libertum suum.—D. 22, 3, 14.[2]

The *SC. de collusione detegenda* related to both suits as to status, and sought to obviate ready abuse, if the proceedings should be only brought as a pretext, and by collusion between the master or patron and the slave or libertus, to procure for the latter the status of 'ingenuitas.'

Gai.: Ne quorundam dominorum erga servos nimia indulgentia inquinaret amplissimum ordinem, eo quod paterentur servos suos in ingenuitatem proclamare liberosque iudicari, senatusconsultum factum est Domitiani temporibus, quo cautum est, ut si quis probasset, per collusionem quidquam

---

[1] They that from the condition of freedmen claim free birth shall not be heard after five years from their manumission.

[2] In respect of him who alleges that he is not in the condition of a freedman, but is freeborn, we have to consider who takes the part of plaintiff. And if he have been in possession of the condition of a freedman, he will without doubt himself have to take proceedings as for free birth and prove that he is freeborn; but if he be in possession of free birth, and it be alleged that he is a freedman, that is of him who brings the action against him, the one must prove this who alleges that such person is his freedman.

factum, si iste homo servus sit, fieret eius servus, qui detexisset collusionem.—D. 40, 16, 1.[1]

Ulp.: Si libertinus per collusionem fuerit pronuntiatus ingenuus, collusione detecta in quibusdam causis quasi libertinus incipit esse.—l. 4 eod.[2]

A decision upon 'civitas,' 'Latinitas,' or 'Peregrinitas' (apart from cases where it came in question incidentally in a private suit) was obtained not by way of iudicium, but summarily through the magistrate.

RELATIONS OF POWER IN THE FAMILY (SO-CALLED *STATUS FAMILIAE*).

§ 41. Family Relations in General: Nature of the Roman Family, and Subject-matter of the Roman Family Law.[a]

[a] Cf. Maine, 'Anct. Law,' pp. 128, *sqq*.

'Familia' as used by the Romans means something essentially different from the Family looked at from the natural point of view, which was not fully recognised amongst them until a late period, but is now that which alone prevails. By 'Family' is now understood that connection of men recognised by Law which rests upon a natural basis (procreation and birth [b]), and is maintained by the moral bond of family affection. It consists of domestic fellowship and relations of protection and control founded upon it, a connection which as a legal relation is alone exhibited externally, *i.e.*, in

[b] For *ius naturale*, see Inst. i. 2 pr.

[1] Lest the too great kindness of certain masters towards their slaves should corrupt the right honourable Senate, by their suffering their slaves to claim free birth and to be adjudged freemen, a *SCtum* was passed in the times of Domitian by which it was provided that, if any one should have proved aught to have been done by secret agreement, that man, if a slave, should become the slave of the person that had discovered the secret agreement.

[2] If by secret agreement a freedman shall have been declared freeborn, after the secret agreement has been discovered, in certain cases he begins to pass as a freedman.

Book II. Part I.

so far as it is one recognised and protected by Law, and as it exercises an influence upon proprietary rights; whilst intrinsically it expresses a merely natural and moral relation. But in the Roman sense it is a purely legal conception, and designates a strict, civil relation of power and dependence.

'Familia' is fundamentally the totality of all that is subject to the Power, by Private Law, of a civis Rom.; hence, his whole domestic surroundings, and, at the same time, that sphere of Power which is created by Private Law. Both things and human beings, free or in bondage, can be objects of such power, or constituents of the 'familia'; and thus, objects of ownership (familia pecuniaque) and Persons. As a group of Persons, the 'familia' is the aggregate of all connected by common descent—or a juristic act legally equivalent to it—who themselves, or those under whose Power they are, were or had been subject to the same Family Power.[a]

[a] Cf. Mommsen, 'History of Rome,' by Dickson, vol. i. pp. 59, *sqq.*

Ulp.: **Familiae** appellatio qualiter accipiatur, videamus; et quidem varie accepta est, nam et in res et in personas deducitur; in **res** utputa in lege xii tabularum his verbis 'ADGNATVS PROXIMVS FAMILIAM HABETO,'[b] ad **personas** autem refertur, . . . cum de patrono et liberto loquitur lex 'EX EA FAMILIA IN EAM FAMILIAM,' et hic de singularibus personis legem loqui constat. § **Familiae** appellatio refertur et ad corporis cuiusdam significationem, quod aut iure proprio ipsorum aut communi universae cognationis continetur. **Iure proprio** familiam dicimus plures personas quae sunt sub unius potestate aut natura aut iure subiectae, ut puta **patremfamilias, matremfamilias, filiumfamilias, filiamfamilias.** . . . **Pater** autem **familias** appellatur, qui in domo dominium habet, recteque hoc nomino appellatur; quamvis filium non habeat; non enim solam personam eius, sed et ius demonstramus: denique et pupillum patremfamilias appellamus. Et cum paterfamilias moritur, quotquot capita ei subiecta fuerint, singulas

[b] Comp. its usage in *actio familiae erciscundae* (§ 174).

familias incipiunt habere, singuli enim patrumfamiliarum nomen subeunt; idemque eveniet et in eo qui emancipatus est, nam et hic sui iuris effectus propriam familiam habet. **Communi iure** familiam dicimus omnium **adgnatorum**; nam etsi patrefamilias mortuo singuli singulas familias habent, tamen omnes, qui sub unius potestate fuerunt, recte eiusdem familiae appellabuntur, quia ex eadem domo et gente proditi sunt. § **Servitutum** quoque solemus appellare **familias**, ut . . . interdicto VNDE VI familiae appellatio omnes servos comprehendit. § Item appellatur **familia** plurium personarum, quae ab eiusdem ultimi genitoris sanguine proficiscuntur, sicuti dicimus familiam Iuliam. § **Mulier** autem familiae suae et caput et finis est.—D. 50, 16, 195, §§ 1–5.[1]

---

[1] Let us see in what way the designation *familia* is used. It has indeed been used in different ways, for it is applied both to things and to persons. To things, for example, in the Law of the Twelve Tables as follows: 'the next agnate shall have the inheritance'; but it relates to persons, when the *lex* speaks of the patron and the freedman: 'from that family into this family'; and it is known that the *lex* here speaks of individual persons. The denomination 'familia' is also used for the designation of any community which either has its special rights, or is comprehended in the common rights of the whole relationship. By a *familia* with special rights, we speak of several persons who are under the power of one person, to whom they are subject either by nature or by Law; for example, the father of a family, the mother of a family, the son of a family, the daughter of a family. Now he is called 'pat. fam.' who has authority in the house, and he is rightly called by this name, although he have no son; for we designate not merely the person, but also the legal relation thereof; accordingly, we call a pupil also 'pat. fam.' And when the *pat. fam.* dies, as many heads as were subject to him begin to have just so many single families, for every individual takes the name 'pat. fam.,' and the same will occur also in the case of one who has been emancipated, for he also has a family of his own, having become *sui iuris*. By a *familia* with common rights, we speak of those composing all the agnates;[a] for although upon the death of

[a] See § 43.

*

Book II. Part I.

Gai.: **Familiae** appellatione et ipse princeps familiae continetur. § **Feminarum** liberos in familia earum non esse palam est, quia qui nascuntur, patris familiam sequuntur.—l. 196 eod.[1]

A person that is subject to no Family Power is free from control, or independent of Family, that is, constitutes the head of a *familia*, or even himself represents a Family, is 'persona sui iuris': 'paterfamilias' (possessed of full Roman capacity for private rights, and himself capable of Family Power) and 'materfamilias.'[a]

[a] Cf. Cic. Top. 3, 14.

Ulp. iv. 1: **Sui iuris** sunt familiarum suarum principes, i.e. paterfamiliae itemque materfamiliae.[2] Id.: Patresfamiliarum sunt, qui sunt **suae potestatis**, sive puberes sive impuberes; simili modo matresfamiliarum.—D. 1, 6, 4.[3]

Free persons subject to the Family control of another, and whose legal capacity is governed by his right under whose power they are, are 'personae alieno iuri subiectae,' persons in subservience to a Family or under domestic dependence. We have here three classes:

---

the *pat. fam.*, every individual has a separate family, yet all that were under the power of the one person will rightly be spoken of as belonging to the same family, because they have sprung from the same house and stock. § We are also accustomed to call a whole body of slaves a 'familia,' as . . . in the interdict '*unde vi*' the designation *familia* takes in all the slaves. . . . Likewise, a *familia* is so called of several persons who are sprung from the blood of the same first ancestor, as when we speak of 'the Julian family.' § But a woman is both the beginning and the end of her family.

[1] Under the designation of 'familia,' the head himself also of a family is included. That women's children are not in their family is plain, because the issue follows the family of the father.

[2] Those are *sui iuris* who are heads of their own families, that is, the *pat. fam.* and the *mat. fam.*

[3] They are *patresfam.* who are in possession of their own right, whether or not they have reached the age of puberty;[b] the like with *matresfam.*

[b] See § 60.

Book II. Part I.

(α) personae *in potestate*, or filius familias, filia familias.

(β) uxor *in manu*.

(δ) personae *in mancipio*.[a]

[a] For *servi*, see § 35.

Gai. i. §§ 48, sq.: Quaedam personae sui iuris sunt, quaedam alieno iuri subiectae.—Sed rursum earum personarum, quae alieno iuri subiectae sunt, aliae **in potestate**, aliae **in manu**, aliae **in mancipio**.[1]

The Roman Family Law, which is to be treated of in the following pages, comprehends accordingly the doctrine of 'patria potestas,' of 'manus,' of 'mancipium'; but since marriage is presupposed as well by Patria Potestas as by Manus, and in general by the Family, it will be well to explain this in the first place.

THE FAMILY AS A GROUP OF PERSONS. KINSHIP.

§ 42. The Natural Family; Blood-relationship, and Affinity by Marriage.[b]

[b] Cf. Roby, 'School Latin Grammar,' App. C; Maine, 'Anc. Law,' pp. 146 *sqq.*

(1) COGNATION.

The Family in the natural sense, or according to *ius gent.*, is the aggregate of persons connected by demonstrable blood-relationship (cognatio), *i.e.*, by common descent. Blood-relationship arises by conception or birth.

Blood-relations (cognati) are the persons that are related to one another in a direct line of descent, or are descended from the same third person. The first are spoken of as kinsmen in an ascending and descending line (linea recta; superior, inferior) or ancestors and descendants, *e.g.*, parentes, avus, proavus, liberi, nepos, pronepos; the latter are called collaterals (linea transversa, a latere), *e.g.*, brothers and sisters, uncle and aunt (upon the paternal side: patruus and amita,

[1] Some persons are *sui iuris*, some are subject to the control of another. But again, of those persons subject to the control of another, some are in *potestas*, others in *manus*, others in *mancipium*.

Book II. Part I.

upon the maternal: avunculus and matertera), children of brothers and sisters, or cousins (patrueles and consobrini), grandchildren of brothers and sisters (sobrini). A diagram[a] will exhibit such relationships.

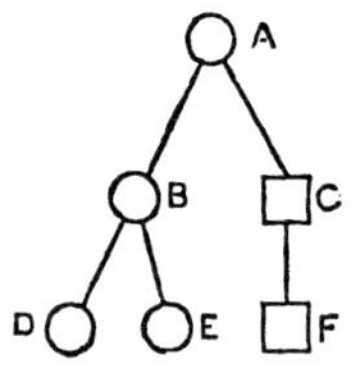

B (filius), C (filia), D, E (nepotes), and F (neptis) are descendants of A;
D and E of B; F of C.—
B and C, D, E and F, B and F, C, D and E are collaterals.

According as the collaterals had paternal and maternal ancestors in common, or only the one or the other, was the distinction made between kinsmen of the whole blood and of the half-blood, especially brothers and sisters (germani, consanguinei, uterini),[b] as will appear from the following diagram.

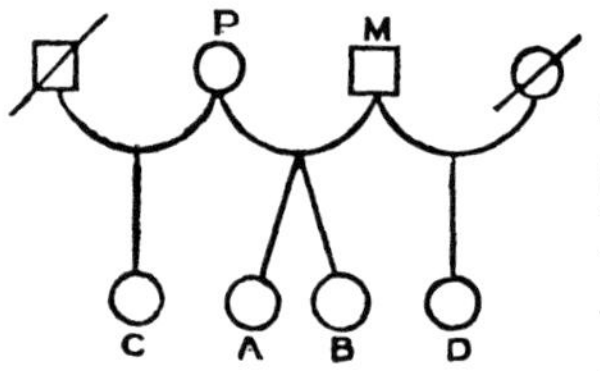

A and B are brother and sister of the full blood (germani); A, B and C or D of the half-blood; whilst A, B and C are consanguinei, A, B and D uterini.

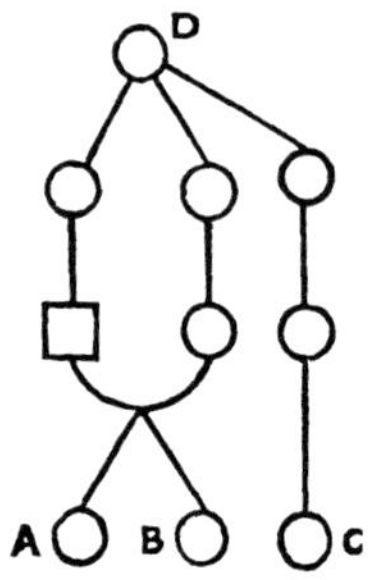

In contrast with simple kinship, various is that which rests upon several grounds. It arises, for instance,

(*a*) by descent from parents related *inter se*, as in the annexed diagram;

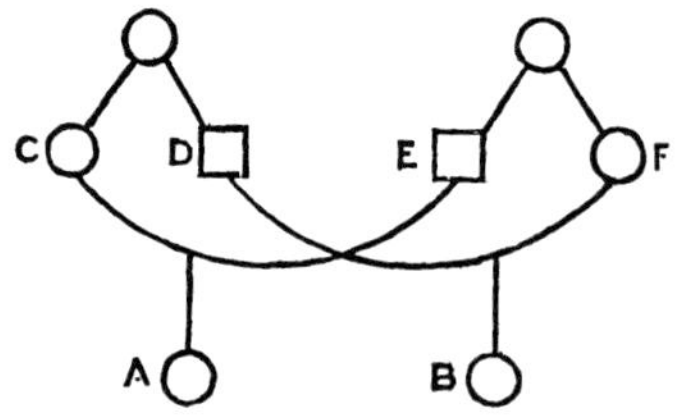

(β) by descent from marriage of several persons related *inter se* with others so related, as shown opposite.

[a] See below.

[b] Cf. § 43.—In the scheme of kinship ○ represents a male, □ a female; the connection of the two by a curved line, marriage; a vertical line, descent; a stroke through the first-mentioned marks, the subtraction of a person.

The nearness of the relationship is reckoned by degrees, *i.e.*, according to the greater or less distance of kinsmen from one another; in other words, the distance on both sides from the common ancestor. Each procreation counts as a degree: just so many are the procreations required to establish the kinship between the persons in question, are there degrees of kinship between them.[a]

[a] 'Quot generationes tot gradus.'

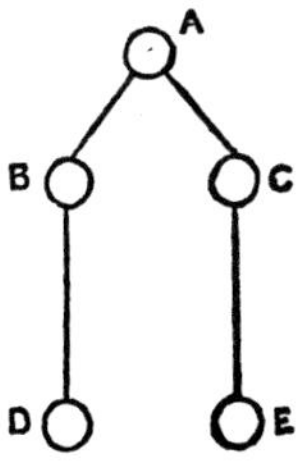

A is related in the first degree to B and C, in the second degree to D and E; B to C in the second; B to E, C to D in the third; D to E in the fourth.

Kinship by marriage alone enjoyed full legal recognition. Only the children begotten in legitimate marriage[b] had juristically a father and paternal relations. On the other hand, as regards the mother and the maternal relations, the Law made no difference between their children begotten in wedlock and out of wedlock (vulgo quaesiti, spurii, liberi naturales in the wider sense).

[b] § 51 ad init.

> Gai. i. § 64: —quos mater **vulgo concepit**, . . . hi patrem habere non intelliguntur, cum is etiam incertus sit; unde solent **spurii** filii appellari, vel a Graeca voce quasi σποράδην concepta, vel quasi 'Sine Patre' filii.[1]
>
> Modest.: **Vulgo concepti** dicuntur, qui patrem demonstrare non possunt, vel qui possunt quidem, sed eum habent, quem habere non licet.—D. 1, 5, 23.[2]

---

[1] —those whom a mother has conceived in promiscuous intercourse, for these are not regarded as having a father, his identity also being uncertain; hence they are commonly called 'spurious' children, either from a Greek word, being, as it were, conceived σποράδην (at random), or because they are children, so to speak, without a father.

[2] They are said to be conceived in common intercourse that cannot show who is their father, or who can do so, but have as a father one whom they should not.

Book II. Part I.

Ulp.: —et si **vulgo quaesitus** sit filius, matrem in ius non vocabit, quia semper certa est, etiamsi vulgo conceperit;—Paul.: **pater vero is est quem nuptiae demonstrant.**[a]—D. 2, 4, l. 4, § 3 and l. 5.[1],

a Blackstone, i. p. 446.

Paul.: Nec vulgo quaesitam filiam **pater naturalis** potest uxorem ducere, quoniam in contrahendis matrimoniis naturale ius et pudor inspiciendus est.—l. 14, § 2, D. de R. N. 23, 2.[2]

(2) A relationship in the wider sense is also contained in AFFINITY. Whilst cognation depends upon conception and birth, 'adfinitas' (step-relationship and connection by marriage) is based upon the marriage with which it begins and ends, whilst it nevertheless operates further as an obstacle to marriage.[b] 'Adfines' are one of the two married persons and the cognates of the other in a direct and a side-line; nevertheless, there is taken to be an affinity between the married persons themselves, and between parties betrothed.

b Gai. i. 63.

Mod.: **Adfines** sunt viri et uxoris cognati; dicti ab eo quod duae cognationes, quae diversae inter se sunt, per nuptias copulantur et altera ad alterius finem accedit; namque coniungendae adfinitatis causa fit ex nuptius.—§ Nomina vero eorum haec sunt: socer socrus, gener nurus, noverca vitricus, privignus privigna § **Gradus** autem adfinitatis nulli sunt.—D. 38, 10, 4, §§ 3–5.[3]

---

1 —and if the son have been acquired by common intercourse, his mother he shall not summon, because she is always certain, although she have conceived from common intercourse. But the father is he that is indicated by marriage.

2 And a natural father cannot marry his daughter born out of wedlock, since in the contracting of a marriage regard must be had to the Law of Nature and modesty.

3 Parties connected by marriage are the relations of the husband and wife, and are called 'adfines' from the fact that two relationships which have a distinct existence as between one another are united by marriage, and the one relationship reaches

Book II. Part I.

Thus:

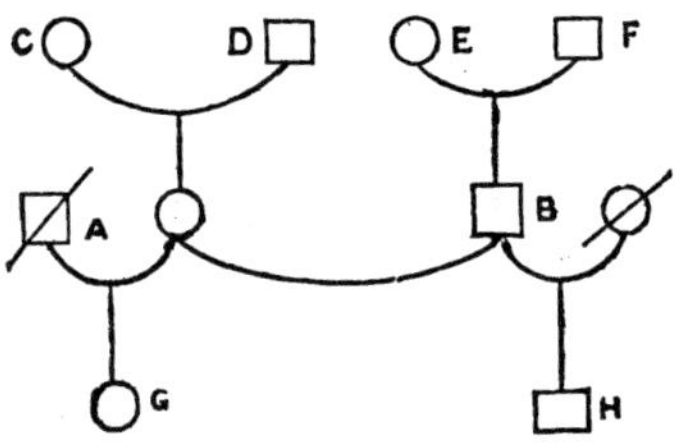

A is gener of E (socer) and F (socrus); B is nurus of C (socer) and D (socrus).—A is vitricus of H (privigna); B noverca of G (privignus); G and H are comprivigni.

§ 43. The *Familia* of the *Jus Civile*—*Agnati*[a] and *Gentiles*.[b]

[a] Maine, *ubi sup.*; Coulanges, 'La Cité Antique,' pp. 58-62 (11th ed.). See also the chapter on 'Descent' in Stephen, vol. i. pp. 388, *sqq.*

[b] Maine, 'Early Law and Custom,' pp. 283, *sqq.*

The familia according to ius civile is founded upon the Power of the Father, and in its narrower meaning comprises persons connected by the bond of the same patria potestas; in its wider meaning, all persons who would be placed under the same Power if the common holder of Power (ancestor) were still alive, who accordingly themselves, or their paterfamilias and his familia, would have been placed under the same Power. The members of a Roman familia in the wider sense are called 'agnati.'[c]

[c] D. 50, 16, 195, 2.

Agnation can only be brought about through the male stem; women can nevertheless quite well be agnates.[d]

[d] 'Ancient Law,' pp. 148, 152.—For relics of this principle in English Law, compare common forms of settlement and entail. As to the exclusion, previous to the Inheritance Act, of brothers of the half blood from succession to each other's real estate, see Digby, pp. 378, *sq.*

> Ulp. xi. 4: **Adgnati** sunt a patre cognati . . . per virilem sexum descendentes eiusdem familiae.[1]
>
> Gai. iii. § 10: Vocantur autem adgnati qui **legitima** cognatione iuncti sunt.[2]
>
> Mod.: Cognationis substantia bifariam apud

---

the limit of the other; for the cause of joining arises from marriage.—Now the following are the designations of such persons: father-in-law, mother-in-law, son-in-law, daughter-in-law, step-mother, step-father, step-son, step-daughter. But there are no degrees of affinity.

[1] Agnates are relatives connected on the father's side . . . tracing their descent through the male sex, and of the same family.

[2] Now those are called 'agnates' who are allied by statutory kinship.

Romanos intelligitur: nam quaedam cognationes iure civili, quaedam naturali connectuntur; nonnumquam utroque iure concurrente, et naturali et civili, copulatur cognatio. . . . Sed **naturalis** quidem cognatio hoc ipso nomine appellatur, **civilis** autem cognatio . . . proprie **adgnatio** vocatur, videlicet quae per mares contingit.—l. 4, § 2, D. de grad. 38, 10.[1]

Agnation arises not merely by procreation in a Roman marriage, but also by adoption and 'in manum conventio,' by which the wife becomes 'filiaefamilias loco.'

Paul. Sent. iv. 8 (Coll. xvi. 3), § 15: Consanguinei sunt eodem patre nati, licet diversis matribus, qui in potestate (sunt), adoptivus quoque frater.[2]

As far as Agnation extends there exists also Cognation, but not conversely.[a]

[a] Cf. § 52.

Ulp.: Inter adgnatos igitur et cognatos hoc interest, quod inter genus et speciem; nam qui est adgnatus, et cognatus est, non utique autem qui cognatus est, et adgnatus est; alterum enim civile, alterum naturale nomen est.—l. 10, § 4, D. de gradib.[3]

Mod.: Verbi gratia patris frater, i.e. patruus

---

[1] The essence of relationship bears a double signification amongst the Romans: for some links of relationship are by the *i. c.*, some by the Law of Nature, sometimes the link of relationship is by a concurrence of both laws, the natural and civil. . . . But *naturalis cognatio* is called by this very name, whilst civil relationship is strictly called *adgnatio*, as being that which arises through males.

[2] Those are *consanguinei* that are born of the same father, although by different mothers, who are under Power; an adoptive brother too.

[3] Between agnates and cognates there is, accordingly, the same difference as between genus and species; for the agnate is always also a cognate, but the cognate is not always an agnate also; the one is a designation pertaining to *i. c.*, the other is a natural designation.

Book II. Part I.

et adgnatus est et cognatus; matris autem frater, i.e. avunculus cognatus est, adgnatus non est.—D. 38, 7, 5 pr.[1]

'Gentiles' are Roman citizens belonging to one of the old Patrician gentes (also called 'familiae'): thus, agnates who—without being able to prove the degree of their relationship—through their like stem-name (nomen gentilicium) exhibit their descent from a common ancestor, and form an exclusive group of persons in the Roman State, held together by common 'sacra.' Already at the beginning of the Empire 'gentilitas' lost all importance in Private Law.

Paul. ex Festo: **Gentilis** dicitur et ex eodem genere ortus et is qui simili nomine appellatur.—(p. 94, M.)[2]

Cic. Top. 6, 29: 'Gentiles sunt inter se, qui eodem nomine sunt:' non est satis. 'Qui ab ingenuis oriundi sunt': ne id quidem satis est. 'Quorum maiorum nemo servitutem servivit': abest etiamnunc. 'Qui capite non sunt deminuti': hoc fortasse satis est; nihil enim video Scaevolam pontificem ad hanc definitionem addidisse.[3]

MARRIAGE.[a]

§ 44. Nature and Forms. Celibacy.

Marriage according to the Roman idea, which

[a] Cf. 'Anct. Law,' pp. 154, *sqq.* For British marriages, see Stephen, vol. ii. ch. ii.; Ld. Mackenzie, 'Roman Law,' pp. 115-118; Eversley, 'Law of the Domestic Relations,' pp. 55, *sqq.*; cf. Westlake, ch. iv.

---

[1] For example, the father's brother, *i.e.*, the paternal uncle, is both an agnate and a cognate; but the mother's brother, *i.e.*, the maternal uncle, is a cognate, not an agnate.

[2] He is called 'Gentilis,' whether as derived from the same genus or as one who is called by a like name.

[3] '*Gentiles* are as between themselves those who bear the same name': it is not enough. 'Who have sprung from free-born persons': not even is that enough. 'None of whose ancestors served in bondage': it still goes not far enough. 'Who have not suffered loss of *caput*': this perhaps is enough; for I do not see that the pont. Scaev. added to this definition.

Book II. Part I.

emphasizes its moral character, is that permanent union of man and wife which contemplates community of all relations in life;[a] 'maritalis affectio' alone distinguishes it from other sexual relations.

[a] D. 25, 2, 1, 2.

Inst. i. 9, 1: **Nuptiae** sive **matrimonium** est viri et mulieris coniunctio, individuam consuetudinem vitae continens.[1]

Modest.: Nuptiae sunt coniunctio maris et feminae et consortium omnis vitae, divini et humani iuris communicatio.—D. 23, 2, 1.[2]

The Romans distinguish—

(1) Marriage according to *ius civile*, only available to a Roman citizen, which supposes 'conubium'[b] on both sides, and is called 'legitimum, iustum matrimonium,' 'iustae nuptiae;' and marriage according to *ius gentium*, from which 'conubium' is absent.

[b] Ulp. v. 3, 4.

Inst. i. 10 pr.: **Iustas nuptias** inter se cives Romani contrahunt.[3]

Ulp. v. 2: Iustum matrimonium est, si inter eos, qui nuptias contrahunt, conubium sit.[4]

(2) The old Roman marriage, in which the wife is placed in the 'manus'[c] of the husband (so-called strict marriage), and that without manus (so-called free marriage). The first was in early time the form of 'iustum matrimonium;' with the introduction and legal recognition of the latter,[d] it became ever less frequent, and at last passed entirely out of use.

[c] See § 48.

[d] Perhaps from the time of the Twelve Tables.

Cic. Top. 3, 14: Genus est uxor; eius duae

---

[1] Marriage, or matrimony, is the union of a man and woman involving indivisible manner of life.

[2] Marriage is the union of a male and female, and fellowship for the whole life, sharing right divine and human.

[3] Lawful marriages are what Roman citizens contract between themselves.

[4] It is a lawful marriage if there be right of intermarriage between the contracting parties.

formae: una **matrumfamilias**, eae sunt, quae in manum convenerunt; altera earum, quae tantummodo uxores habentur.[1] Book II. Part I.

As sexual relations out of wedlock there were—

(α) CONCUBINAGE, amongst the Romans recognised and regulated by Law (especially that between a liberta and patronus[a]), which was a lasting, merely *de facto*, union without 'affectio maritalis.' The issue thereof were named especially 'liberi naturales.'

[a] Cf. §§ 45, 47.

Paul.: **Concubinam** ex sola animi destinatione aestimari oportet.—D. 25, 7, 4.[2]

Marcian.: Quia concubinatus per leges nomen assumpsit, extra legis[b] poenam est.—l. 3, § 1 eod.[3]

[b] Sc. Iuliae de adulteriis.

Ulp.: Cum Atilicino sentio et puto solas eas in concubinatu haberi posse sine metu criminis, in quas stuprum non committitur.—l. 1, § 1 eod.[4]

Paul. ii. 20: Eo tempore, quo quis uxorem habet, concubinam habere non potest.[5]

(β) 'Contubernium,' marriage of slaves.[c]

[c] Cf. § 35.

Id. ii. 19, § 6: Inter servos et liberos matrimonium contrahi non potest, **contubernium** potest.[6]

---

[1] *Uxor* is the genus. It has two forms: one, of the *matres-fam.*, such as have passed under *manus*: the other, of those who merely pass as *uxores*.

[2] Judgment must be formed as to a woman's being a concubine by the determination of the will alone.[d]

[d] Cf. Mommsen, *l. c.* p. 60.

[3] Inasmuch as concubinage has acquired its significance by virtue of *leges*, it is beyond the punishment of a *lex*.

[4] I agree with Atilicinus, and consider that they alone can be had in concubinage, without fear of committing a crime, with whom no *stuprum*[e] is committed.

[e] *Infra.*

[5] For such time as a man has a wife, he cannot have a concubine.

[6] Between slaves and freemen a marriage cannot be contracted, concubinage can.

BOOK II. Part I.

(γ) The marriages forbidden by Law, especially 'adulterium' and 'incestus.'[a]

[a] Gai. i. 59-62.

Gai. i. § 64: Ergo si quis **nefarias** atque **incestas** nuptias contraxerit, neque uxorem videtur habere, neque liberos.[1]

Modest.: Inter **stuprum** et **adulterium** hoc interesse quidam putant, quod adulterium in nuptam, stuprum in viduam[b] committitur.—D. 50, 16, 101 pr.[2]

[b] *I.e.*, non nuptam.

From the beginning of the Empire an endeavour was made through legislation in the public interest to meet constantly prevailing celibacy and childlessness, by annexing important advantages to these under Private Law (especially with regard to inheritance), and again, affording many legal advantages to persons married with children,—'ius (iii vel iv) liberorum.' This was done by the leges Iulia and Papia Poppaea (757 and 762 U.C.)—amongst the most comprehensive of Roman special statutes—which at the same time sought, by prohibition of marriages not in keeping with persons' rank, to raise decrepit and corrupted Roman families, and to purge them of impure elements.[c] Next, the disadvantages of celibacy and childlessness were repealed by Constantine, and the whole 'ius liberorum' by Justinian.

[c] Cf. § 8, s. *leges*.—In Christian imperial times the exactly opposite endeavour, to promote celibacy, made itself felt.

Ulp. xiv.: Feminis lex Iulia a morte anni tribuit **vacationem**, a divortio sex mensium; lex autem Papia a morte viri biennii, a repudio anni et sex mensium.[3]

---

1 If, therefore, a man has contracted a wicked and incestuous marriage, he is considered to have neither wife nor children.

2 Some consider that between *stuprum* and *adulterium* there is this difference, that *adulterium* is committed with a married woman, *stuprum* with an unmarried woman.

3 The *l. Iulia* allows women a respite of one year from the death of their husband, and of six months after a divorce; but the *l. Papia*, of two years from the husband's death, of one year and six months from a divorce.

Ib. xvi. 1, 3, 4: —vir et uxor, . . . si . . . nondum eius aetatis sint, a qua lex liberos exigit, i.e. si vir minor annorum XXV sit, aut uxor annorum XX minor, item si . . . lege Papia finitos annos in matrimonio excesserint, i.e. vir LX annos, uxor L.—Qui intra sexagesimum vel quae intra quinquagesimum annum neutri legi paruerit, licet ipsis legibus post hanc aetatem liberatus esset, perpetuis tamen poenis tenebitur ex senatusconsulto Persiciano.—Sed Claudiano senatusconsulto maior sexagenario si minorem quinquagenaria duxerit, perinde habebitur, ac si minor LX annorum duxisset uxorem. Quodsi maior quinquagenaria minori sexagenario nupserit, id impar matrimonum appellatur.[1]

§ 45. Possibility of, or Impediments to, Marriage.

Entrance upon the married state supposes the legal possibility of the marriage and personal capacity for it between two persons ('conubium' in the wider sense). The reasons that exclude such possibility are called 'impediments to marriage': they are partly absolute, *i.e.*, make a marriage altogether impossible for any one; partly relative, *i.e.*, exclude marriage only between certain persons.

Absolutely incapable to enter into marriage are—

(*a*) the insane;

(*β*) those under the age of puberty;[a]

[a] § 60, ad init.

[1] — a husband and wife, . . . when they are not of the age at which the statute requires issue, *i.e.*, if the husband be under 25 or the wife under 20 years of age; the like when they, while married, have passed the ages limited by the *l. Papia*, *i.e.*, the husband 60, the wife 50.—A man who within his sixtieth year, or a woman within her fiftieth, has complied with neither *lex*, although by the *leges* themselves exempt after such age, yet will be liable to their standing penalties by reason of the *SC. Persicianum*.—But by the *SC. Claudianum* a man over 60 who marries a woman under 50 shall be regarded as having married under 60. But if a woman over 50 have married a man under 60, such marriage is called 'unequal.'

Book II. Part I.

(γ) 'castrati,' but not naturally impotent (spadones);
(δ) those already living in matrimony.

Relative hindrances are—

(1) Close blood-relationship or affinity.

Gai. i. §§ 58–62: A quarundam nuptiis abstinere debemus. Inter eas enim personas, quae **parentum liberorumve** locum inter se obtinent, nuptiae contrahi non possunt nec inter eas conubium est, velut inter patrem et filiam vel inter matrem et filium vel inter avum et neptem; et si tales personae inter se coierint, nefarias atque incestas nuptias contraxisse dicuntur. Et haec adeo ita sunt, ut quamvis **per adoptionem parentum liberorumve** loco sibi esse coeperint, non possint inter se matrimonio coniungi, in tantum, ut etiam dissoluta adoptione idem iuris maneat, itaque eam quae mihi per adoptionem filiae aut neptis loco esse coeperit, non potero uxorem ducere, quamvis eam emancipaverim. § Inter eas quoque personas, quae **ex transverso gradu** cognatione iunguntur, est quaedam similis observatio, sed non tanta.—§ Sane enim inter **fratrem et sororem** prohibitae sunt nuptiae, sive eodem patre eademque matre nati fuerint, sive alterutro eorum: sed si qua **per adoptionem soror** mihi esse coeperit, quamdiu quidem constat adoptio, sane inter me et eam nuptiae non possunt consistere; cum vero per emancipationem adoptio dissoluta sit, potero eam uxorem ducere; sed et si ego emancipatus fuero, nihil impedimento erit nuptiis. § **Fratris filiam** uxorem ducere licet: idque primum in usum venit, cum D. Claudius Agrippinam, fratris sui filiam, uxorem duxisset; **sororis** vero **filiam** uxorem ducere non licet: et haec ita principalibus constitutionibus significantur. Item amitam et materteram uxorem ducere non licet.—§§ 1–2, I. de nupt. 1, 10.[1]

---

[1] From marriage with certain persons we are bound to refrain. Thus, between such persons as stand to each other in the rela-

Fratris vel sorores filiam uxorem ducere non licet; sed nec neptem fratris vel sororis ducere quis potest, quamvis quarto gradu sit—. § Duorum autem **fratrum** vel **sororum liberi** vel fratris et sororis iungi possunt.—§§ 3, 4, I. eod.[1]

Gai. i. § 63: Item eam, quae mihi quondam **socrus** aut **nurus** aut **privigna** aut **noverca** fuit (ducere non licet); ideo autem diximus 'quondam,' quia si adhuc constant eae nuptiae, per quas talis adfinitas quaesita est, alia ratione mihi nupta esse non potest: quia neque eadem duobus nupta esse potest, neque idem duas uxores habere.[2]

---

tion of parents and children, marriage cannot be contracted, neither is there *conubium* between them,—as between father and daughter, or between mother and son, or between grandfather and granddaughter; and if such persons cohabit, they are said to have contracted a wicked and incestuous marriage. And this goes so far, that although the relation in which they stand as parent and child began by way of adoption, they cannot be united in marriage; so that even if the adoption has been dissolved, the same rule stands.—Therefore I cannot take her to wife who has come to be in the position of daughter or granddaughter to me by adoption, although I may have emancipated her. § Again, as between such persons as are connected collaterally, the same remark applies, yet not to the same extent. Marriage is, of course, prohibited between a brother and sister, whether issue of the same father and same mother, or of one or other of them. But if a woman become my sister by adoption, so long as the adoption subsists, marriage cannot obtain between us; yet when the adoption has been destroyed by her emancipation, I may take her to wife; while, if I also be emancipated, there will be no bar to the marriage. § It is lawful to marry one's brother's daughter; and such marriage first came into use when the emperor Claudius had taken to wife his brother's daughter Agrippina; but marriage with a sister's daughter is not allowed. And these things are so laid down in imperial constitutions. It is likewise unlawful to marry a father's or a mother's sister.

[1] A man is not allowed to marry the daughter of his brother or sister; but the granddaughter, too, of his brother or sister he cannot marry, although she is in the fourth degree.—Now the children of two brothers or sisters, or the children of one brother and one sister, can marry one another.

[2] Likewise (it is not lawful to marry) such woman as has for-

Book II. Part I.

Mariti tamen filius ex alia uxore et uxoris filia ex alio marito vel contra matrimonium recte contrahunt, licet habeant fratrem sororemve ex matrimonio postea contracto natos.—§ 8, I. de nupt.[1]

(2) Certain differences of rank in virtue of the leges Iulia et Papia Poppaea, according to which, nevertheless, the marriage itself was valid and only carried with it the penalties upon celibacy; but later on marriages of this kind—in the senatorian rank—were treated as null, until at last Justinian repealed this whole prohibition of marriage.

Ulp. xiii. 1, 2: Lege Iulia prohibentur uxores ducere **senatores** quidem liberique eorum libertinas et quae ipsae quarumve pater materve artem ludicram fecerit.—Ceteri autem ingenui prohibentur ducere palam corpore quaestum facientem et lenam et a leno lenave manumissam et in adulterio deprehensam et iudicio publico damnatam et quae artem ludicram fecerit.[2]

Paul.: Oratione D. Marci cavetur, ut si senatoris filia libertino nupsisset, nec nuptiae essent:

---

merly been my mother-in-law or step-mother, or daughter-in-law or step-daughter. Now we have said 'formerly,' because if the marriage by which such affinity was brought about still exist, she cannot be married to me for another reason—that neither can the same woman be married to two husbands, nor can the same man have two wives.

[1] The husband's son, however, by another wife and the wife's daughter by another husband, or reversely, can contract a legal marriage, although they have a brother or a sister issue of the marriage contracted subsequently.

[2] By the *l. Iulia* senators and their children are forbidden to marry their freedwomen, or women who themselves, or whose father or mother, have followed the theatrical profession. Now, other freeborn persons are forbidden to marry a common prostitute, a procuress, a woman manumitted by a procurer or procuress, a woman taken in adultery, one convicted in a public prosecution, and that has been an actress.

quam et senatusconsultum secutum est.—D. 23, 2, 16 pr.[1]

Ulp.: —honestius (est) patrono libertam concubinam, quam matremfamilias habere.—D. 25, 7, 1 pr.[2]

(3) Official position of the husband. Thus especially was the marriage between a Roman provincial officer and a provincial female disallowed, as also that between a guardian, or his descendant, and the ward.

Paul.: Si quis officium in aliqua provincia administrat, inde oriundam vel ibi domicilium, quamvis sponsare non prohibeatur.[3]

Id.: Senatusconsulto, quo cautum est, ne tutor pupillam vel filio suo vel sibi nuptum collocet, etiam nepos significatur.—l. 59 eod.[4]

Callist.: —ideo prohibuerit eiusmodi nuptias, ne pupillae in re familiari circumscribantur ab his, qui rationes eis gestae tutelae reddere compelluntur. § Tutor autem pupilli non prohibetur filiam suam collocare pupillo suo in matrimonium. —l. 64, §§ 1, 2 eod.[5]

Paul.: Non est matrimonium, si tutor vel curator pupillam suam intra vicesimum et sextum annum, non desponsam a patre nec testamento

---

1 By a speech of the late emperor Marcus it was provided, that if the daughter of a senator had married a freedman, there was no marriage, and this speech was followed by a *Sctum*.

2 It is more reputable for a patron to have his freedwoman as concubine than as *mat. fam.*

3 If anybody exercises an office in any province, he cannot take to wife a native woman, or one having her residence there, although he is not precluded from betrothal.

4 In the *Sctum* by which it is provided that a guardian shall not marry his ward to his son, or take her in marriage himself, the grandson also is meant.

5 —so the senate prohibited a marriage of such kind, lest the property of wards should be curtailed by those who are obliged to render an account to them of the administration of the guardianship. But the guardian of a male ward is not restrained from giving his daughter in marriage to the ward.

Book II. Part I.

destinatam, ducat uxorem vel eam filio suo iungat; quo facto uterque infamatur.—l. 66 pr. eod.[1]

(4) The crime of adultery and elopement, as regards the marriage between adulterer and adulteress, or the abducting and abducted parties.

§ 46. Conclusion of a Marriage. Betrothal.

In the early period, when manus was still constantly connected with Marriage, the solemn formalities of 'in manum conventio' served at the same time as forms for the conclusion of a marriage.[a]

In the classical and later Law, actual cohabitation with mutual intention to complete the marriage[b] was enough, subject to the approval of those under whose Power the contracting parties were.[c]

Paul.: Nuptiae consistere non possunt, nisi consentiant omnes, i.e. qui coeunt quorumque in potestate sunt.—D. 23, 2, 2.[2]

Ulp.: Is, cuius pater ab hostibus captus est si non intra triennium revertatur, uxorem ducere potest.—l. 9, § 1 eod.[3]

There was no need of any form for this: the religious ceremonies in use and marriage customs had no meaning juristically; in particular, the 'deductio in domum mariti' comes into consideration only as the avowal of the actual 'consensus' and of the 'maritalis affectio.'

Pomp.: Mulierem absenti per litteras eius vel per nuntium posse nubere placet, si in domum

[a] *Infra*, § 49 (p. 244).

[b] 'Consensus facit nuptias.'—Marriage is a consensual contract in Scotch Law. But as to the marriage tie, see the treatise of Mr. Fraser; cf. Poste on Gaius, pp. 71-3, and Holland, p. 184.

[c] Cf. §§ 18, 146.

[1] There is no marriage if, before her twenty-sixth year, the tutor or curator take his ward in marriage when not betrothed to him by the father nor designed for him in the testament; or shall affiance her to his son: if this have happened, both parties incur infamy.

[2] A marriage cannot obtain unless all consent, that is, those who unite and those under whose Power they are.

[3] He whose father has been captured by the enemy can take a wife if his father do not return within three years.

eius deduceretur; eam vero quae abesset, ex litteris vel nuntio suo duci a marito non posse: deductione enim opus esse in mariti—non in uxoris—domum, quasi in domicilium matrimonii. —l. 5 eod.[1]

The marriage would often be preceded by BETROTHAL (sponsalia), *i.e.*, mutual promise of marriage. Originally the betrothal was effected in the form of regular mutual stipulation between the bridegroom and the bride's father, from which according to old Latin, and indeed the older Roman Law, could an action be had for fulfilment, and in case of non-fulfilment, condemnation in damages.

Ulp.: Sponsalia autem dicta sunt a **spondendo;** nam moris fuit veteribus stipulari et spondere sibi uxores futuras:—unde et **sponsi sponsaeque** appellatio nata est.—l. 2, 3, D. de spons. 23, 1.[2]

Gellius iv. 4: Sponsalia in ea parte Italiae, quae Latium appellatur, hoc more atque iure solita fieri, scripsit Servius Sulpicius in libro quem inscripsit 'de dotibus.' Qui uxorem, inquit, ducturus erat, ab eo unde ducenda erat stipulabatur eam in matrimonium datum iri; qui daturus erat, id eidem spondebat; item qui uxorem daturus erat, ab eo cui eam daturus erat, stipulabatur eam in matrimonium ductum iri; qui ducturus erat id eidem spondebat. Is contractus stipulationum sponsionumque dicebatur 'sponsalia.' Tum quae promissa erat, 'sponsa' appellabatur, qui spo-

---

[1] It is held that a woman can marry a man in his absence through his letter or by messenger, if she be taken into his house; but that a woman who should be absent cannot be married by a husband by letter or his messenger; for that it is necessary she should be taken into the husband's, not the wife's, house, as it were into the marriage-dwelling.

[2] Now, Betrothal is so named from 'spondere;' for with the ancients it was usual to stipulate for future wives, and to betroth them; and therefore also have arisen the designations 'sponsi' and 'sponsae.'

Book II. Part I.

ponderat ducturum, 'sponsus.' Sed si post eas stipulationes uxor non dabatur aut non ducebatur, is qui stipulatur ex sponsu agebat; iudices cognoscesbant. Iudex, quamobrem data acceptave non esset uxor, quaerebat. Si nihil iustae causae videbatur, litem pecunia aestimabat: quantique interfuerat eam uxorem accipi aut dari, eum qui spoponderat, ei qui stipulatus erat condemnabat.—Hoc ius sponsaliorum observatum dicit Servius ad id tempus, quo civitas universo Latio lege Iulia data est.—Haec eadem Neratius scripsit in libro quem de nuptiis composuit.[1]

Later on, an informal contract between the bridal pair or their fathers sufficed, and the betrothal created only a 'spes matrimonii' not actionable, but protected by Law.

Ulp.: Sufficit **nudus consensus** ad constituenda sponsalia.—Denique constat, et absentem

---

[1] Serv. Sulp. wrote in his work 'de dotibus' that in that part of Italy which is called Latium *sponsalia* used to be effected by the following custom and law. The man that was about to marry a wife, he says, used to make the person from whom she had to be taken engage that she should be so given to him; he that was about to give her away would contract such engagement to the same; likewise he that should give her as wife used to make the person to whom he was about to give her engage that she should be taken in marriage; he that was about to take her used to make such promise to the person in question. That contract of engagements and promises was called 'sponsalia.' Then she that was promised was called 'sponsa,' he that had promised he would take her, 'sponsus.' But if after those engagements, the woman was not given or not taken, the stipulator took proceedings upon the promise; the arbitrators tried the matter. The arbitrator inquired, on what account the woman was not given or received? If no just reason was forthcoming, he valued the pecuniary damages; and he adjudged that the promisor should pay to the promisee the amount of his interest in having the woman given or received. Serv. says that this law of *sponsalia* was retained to the time when citizenship was given to all Latium by the *l Iulia*. Nerat. wrote the like in his work 'de nuptiis.'

absenti desponderi posse et hoc quottidie fieri.—l. 4, D. de spons.[1]

Paul.: —inhonestum visum est, vinculo poenae matrimonia obstringi, sive futura sive iam contracta.—D. 45, 1, 134 pr.[2]

Infamia notatur . . . qui bina sponsalia binasve nuptias in eodem tempore constitutas habuerit.—D. 3, 2, 1.[3]

Ulp.: Divi Severus et Antoninus rescripserunt, etiam in sponsa hoc idem[a] vindicandum, quia neque matrimonium qualecumque, nec spem matrimonii violare permittitur.—D. 48, 5, 13, 3.[4]

[a] Sc. adulterium.

Betrothal required a certain age for the persons to be betrothed, and their consent, as well as that of their patresfamilias.

Mod.: In sponsalibus contrahendis **aetas contrahentium** definita non est, ut in matrimoniis; quapropter et a primordio aetatis sponsalia effici possunt, si modo id fieri ab utraque persona intelligatur, i.e. si non sint minores quam septem annis.—l. 14, D. de spons.[5]

Paul.: In sponsalibus etiam **consensus** eorum exigendus est, quorum in nuptiis desideratur; intelligi tamen semper filiae patrem consentire nisi evidenter dissentiat, Iulianus scribit.—Ulp.:

---

[1] Bare consent is enough for the conclusion of a betrothal. It is well known that in pursuance thereof the absent parties can be betrothed, and that this is of daily occurrence.

[2] It appeared disreputable that marriage, whether future or already contracted, should be fettered by the chain of a penalty.

[3] He is branded with infamy . . . who shall have contracted two betrothals or two marriages at the same time.

[4] The late emperors Sev. and Anton. issued a rescript that this also (*i.e.*, adultery) is to be upheld even in the case of a woman betrothed, because neither matrimony of whatever kind, nor the expectation of matrimony, can be violated.

[5] In respect of the contract of betrothal, the age of the contracting parties is not fixed as in marriages, and therefore can a betrothal be effected from the earliest age, provided that it is understood by both persons that this happens, that is, if they are not less than seven years of age.

BOOK II. Part I.

Tunc autem solum dissentiendi a patre licentia filiae conceditur, si indignum moribus vel turpem sponsum ei pater eligat.—Paul.: Filiofamilias dissentiente sponsalia nomine eius fieri non possunt.—l. 7, § 1, l. 12, § 1, l. 13 eod.[1]

Betrothal was cancelled by an *ex parte* declaration.[a]

[a] As to *arra sponsalicia* (gifts between bride and bridegroom), see § 148.

Gai.: In sponsalibus quoque discutiendis placuit **renuntiationem** intervenire oportere, in qua re haec verba probata sunt: 'condicione tua non utor.'—D. 24, 2, 2, 2.[2]

Ulp.: In potestate manente filia pater sponso nuntium remittere potest et sponsalia dissolvere. —l. 10, D. de spons.[3]

§ 47. DISSOLUTION OF A MARRIAGE. SECOND MARRIAGE.[b]

[b] Cf. Steph. ii. 278-84 (Engl.); Ld. Mackenzie, 128-9 (Scotl.); Eversley, 72-5 (Ireland); Westlake, 70-83.

The grounds of termination of a marriage are in part voluntary, and in part necessary. To the latter belongs also the case of a husband lapsing into slavery, especially into captivity.[c]

[c] Cf. D. 1, 5, 26.

Paul.: Dirimitur matrimonium divortio morte captivitate vel alia contingente servitute utrius eorum.—l. 1, D. h. t. (=de divort. 24, 2).[4]

---

[1] In a betrothal also the consent of those is required whose consent is wanted in a marriage. Jul., however, writes that it is always supposed that the daughter's father consents unless he plainly objects.—But then alone is freedom granted to a daughter of gainsaying her father, if the father choose for her as betrothed a morally unworthy or disreputable man.—If a *fil. fam.* do not concur, a betrothal in his name cannot come about.

[2] It has been held that in the breaking off of betrothal a renunciation must occur, in which the following words have become established: 'I renounce the match with you.'

[3] If the daughter remain under his Power, the father can send back a messenger to her betrothed and dissolve the betrothal.

[4] Marriage is dissolved by divorce, death, captivity, or if servitude befall either of them.

Book II. Part I.

Tryph.: Sed captivi uxor, tametsi maxime velit et in domo eius sit, non tamen in matrimonio est.—D. 49, 15, 12, 4.[1]

Pomp.: Non ut pater filium, ita uxorem maritus iure postliminii recipit, sed consensu redintegratur matrimonium.—l. 14, § 1 eod.[2]

Iul.: Uxores eorum, qui in hostium potestatem pervenerunt, possunt videri nuptarum locum retinere eo solo, quod alii temere nubere non possunt. . . . Sin autem in incerto est, an vivus apud hostes teneatur vel morte praeventus sit, tunc si quinquennium a tempore captivitatis excesserit, licentiam habet mulier ad alias migrare nuptias. (Just.?)[a]—l. 6, D. h. t.[3]

Ulp.: Quodsi deportata sit (uxor), Marcellus ait, non utique deportatione dissolvi matrimonium: nam cum libera mulier remaneat, nihil prohibet et virum mariti affectionem et mulierem uxoris animum retinere.—D. 48, 20, 5, 1.[4]

[a] This, as elsewhere, is intended to denote that the compilators probably conformed the passage to the later Law.

Marriage is dissolved voluntarily by divorce, or actual ending of the conjugal cohabitation with the intention of rescinding the marriage. This can come about sometimes by agreement of both of the married couple, which is 'divortium' in the narrower sense; at other times, by a declaration on the part of one,

1 But the wife of a captive, although she entirely wish it and is in his house, does not, however, live in matrimony.

2 A husband does not receive back his wife *iure postliminii* in the same way as a father his son, but the marriage is renewed by consent.

3 The wives of those who have come into the power of the enemy can be regarded as still married alone because of their inability to marry another easily. . . . But if it is uncertain, whether he is kept alive among the enemy or has come by his death, then, if five years shall have elapsed since the time of the capture, the wife has liberty to embark in another marriage.

4 But if she (*i.e.*, the wife) have been deported, Marc. says, the marriage is not entirely dissolved by the deportation; for since the woman remains free, nothing prevents the husband's retaining the affection of a husband, and the woman's retaining the sentiment of a wife.

Book II. Part I.

which is 'repudium.' As a marriage was contracted solely by consensus of the married pair, freedom of divorce was in the older Roman Law quite without restriction, and divorce itself—apart from a marriage contracted by confarreatio[a]—limited to no form.

[a] § 49.—The first divorce alleged was that of Sp. Carvilius Ruga A.U. 520; see Gell. iv. 3.

> Impp. Diocl. et Max.: Neque ab initio matrimonium contrahere, neque dissociatum reconciliare quisquam cogi potest. Unde intelligis, liberam facultatem contrahendi atque distrahendi matrimonii transferri ad necessitatem non oportere.—C. 5, 4, 14.[1]

> Imp. Alex.: Libera matrimonia esse antiquitus placuit. Ideoque pacta, ne liceret divertere, non valere, et stipulationes, quibus poenae irrogarentur ei qui divortium fecisset, ratas non haberi constat.—C. 8, 38 (39), 2.[2]

It was only by custom and corresponding 'notae censoriae' that frivolous divorces were repressed. An exception was alone made in respect of the marriage of a freedwoman with her patron, who after the l. Iulia et Papia could not divorce herself from him by a unilateral act.

> Ulp.: Quod ait lex: DIVORTII FACIENDI POTESTAS LIBERTAE, QVAE NVPTA EST PATRONO, NE ESTO, non infectum videtur effecisse divortium, quod iure civili dissolvere solet matrimonium; quare constare matrimonium dicere non possumus, cum sit separatum. . . . Merito igitur, quamdiu patronus eius eam uxorem suam esse vult, cum nullo alio conubium ei est; nam quia intellexit legislator facto libertae quasi diremptum matrimonium, detraxit ei cum alio conubium: quare

---

[1] No one can be obliged to contract a marriage at the outset, nor to renew one that has been dissolved. Therefore, you understand that, free right of contracting and of breaking up a marriage ought not to be subjected to compulsion.

[2] It has been held from of old that marriages are voluntary. And so it is established law that agreements impeding divorce are invalid, and that stipulations in which penalties are imposed upon him who had made a divorce are not upheld.

cuicumque nupserit, pro non nupta habebitur. Iulianus quidem amplius putat, neo in concubinatu eam alterius patroni esse posse § Ait lex: QVAMDIV PATRONVS EAM VXOREM ESSE VOLET.—l. 11 pr., § 1, D. h. t.[1]

For the 'repudium' an express declaration before seven special witnesses was prescribed by the l. Iulia de adulteriis, which could be made both orally and by document (repudii libellus, or letter of divorce).[a]

[a] § 163 ad fin.

Paul.: Nullum divortium ratum est, nisi septem civibus Romanis puberibus adhibitis praeter libertum eius, qui divortium faciet.[a]—l. 9 eod.[2]

Gai.: In repudiis autem [i.e. renuntiatione] comprobata sunt haec verba: 'tuas res tibi habeto,' item haec: 'tuas res tibi agito.'—l. 2, § 1 eod.[3]

Ulp.: —si divortium quidem secutum sit, verumtamen iure durat matrimonium, haec successio[b] locum non habet. Hoc autem in huiusmodi speciebus procedit: liberta ab invito patrono divortit,—lex Iulia de maritandis ordinibus retinet istam in matrimonio, dum eam

[b] Sc. 'unde vir et uxor.'

---

[1] When the statute says: 'The freedwoman who has been married to her patron shall not have the power of making a divorce,' it does not seem to have rendered null the divorce which by *i. c.* usually dissolves marriage; and therefore we cannot say that the marriage subsists, since it is severed. . . . Justly therefore, as long as her patron wishes to have her for his wife, has she no right to intermarry with another; for since the legislator has considered that by the act of the freedwoman the marriage, as it were, has been dissolved, it has taken away from her the right to intermarry with another. If, therefore, she have married whom she pleased, she shall be regarded as not married. Jul. indeed carries his opinion further: that she cannot even live in concubinage with another patron. § The statute says: 'As long as the patron wishes her to be his wife.'

[2] No divorce is valid unless seven Roman citizens of the age of puberty have been called in, besides the freedman of him who shall make the divorce.

[3] But in renunciations the following words have become established: 'You may keep your property to yourself;' the following likewise: 'You may take your property with you.'

Book II. Part I.

prohibet alii nubere invito patrono; item Iulia de adulteriis, nisi certo modo divortium factum sit, pro infecto habet.—D. 38, 11, l. un. § 1.[1]

The consensus of the paterfamilias was requisite for the conclusion of the marriage; he could also at his own discretion dissolve the marriage of the filiusfamilias, but according to the later Law the consent of the latter was needed;[a] on the other hand, the approval of the paterfamilias was not necessary for the dissolution of the marriage, at least according to ante-Justinian Law.[b]

[a] § 54.

[b] Ibid.

Imp. Dioclet.: Dissentientis patris, qui initio consensit matrimonio cum marito concordante uxore filiafamilias, ratam non haberi voluntatem D. Marcus pater noster religiosissimus imperator constituit, nisi magna et iusta causa interveniente hoc pater fecerit.—Invitam autem ad maritum redire nulla iuris praecepit constitutio.—C. 5, 17, 5.[2]

Marriage continued in the Law of Justinian to be dissolved by informal private divorce, without any judicial or ecclesiastical concurrence being required; but legislation from the time of Constantine was directed to the restraint of capricious divorce by the imposition of heavy proprietary penalties for divorces that were frivo-

---

[1] If indeed a divorce have followed, but the marriage by Law continue, this succession does not obtain. But the following case belongs to this category: a freedwoman divorces herself from her patron against his will; the *l. Iulia de marit. ordin.* keeps her back in the marriage, whilst it forbids her marrying another against the will of the patron; likewise the *l. Iulia de adult.* holds a divorce as null unless it be effected in a certain manner.

[2] Our late father Marcus, a most pious emperor, directed that if a daughter under paternal power live in harmony with her husband, the desire of her father as opposed, who at first agreed to the marriage, shall be held of no effect, unless he have acted from a weighty and just cause.—But that a wife return to her husband against her will, no constitution of the Law has enjoined.

lous or unjustifiable, as well as by the creation of certain grounds of divorce which alone exclude those penalties.

No restraint was in the earlier period placed upon a SECOND marriage;[a] only the widow, who married within the year of mourning (the Romulean of ten months) after the death of her husband, as well as the paterfamilias of such widow, her husband and his paterfamilias, became liable to the punishment of infamy.[b] Instead of the duty of mourning, regard for the avoidance of uncertainty as to children[c] gradually acquired recognition as a ground of the prohibition of second marriage, whereby such prohibition had to extend also to the marriage dissolved by divorce; the delay was later on extended from ten to twelve months.—Legislation of the Christian emperors, nevertheless, restricted the second marriage of each of the pair, by annexing to it important proprietary advantages in the interest of existing children of the former marriage.

[a] Ulp. xiv.

[b] § 57.

[c] 'Turbatio sanguinis'; 'ne quis de prole dubitet.'

> Paul.: Uxores viri lugere non compelluntur.—D. 3, 2, 9 pr.[1]
>
> Ulp.: Etsi talis sit maritus, quem more maiorum lugeri non oportet, non posse eam nuptam intra legitimum tempus collocari; praetor enim ad id tempus se retulit, quo vir elugeretur qui solet elugeri, propter turbationem sanguinis. § Pomponius eam, quae intra legitimum tempus partum ediderit, putat statim posse nuptiis se collocare; quod verum puto.—l. 11, §§ 1, 2 eod.[2]

---

[1] Husbands are not obliged to mourn for their wives.

[2] Even if he should be such a husband as by the custom of our ancestors ought not to be mourned for, she cannot be married within the statutory period; for the praetor has referred to the time during which the husband would be mourned for who by custom is mourned for, by reason of the confusion of blood. § Pomp. is of opinion that the woman who has given birth to issue within the statutory period can immediately be married; and this I think correct.

Book II. Part I.

MANUS.

§ 48. Nature of *Manus*; its Subject-Matter.

[a] For the *mat. fam.* see Cic. Top. 3, 14.

'Manus' is the control of the husband as paterfamilias over his wife.[a] It was originally the attribute of every 'iustum matrimonium,' and the act of contracting a marriage was at the same time an act to establish manus; later on it became an independent and unessential addition to Marriage, which had to be created by a special act of Law. With this severance from Marriage, manus was at the same time applicable and in use in artificial extension also outside of it, so that a woman, even not 'matrimonii causa' but for other objects, could for the time being place herself in the manus of a third party. It was in the latter form that manus lasted longest throughout the period of the Classical Law, whilst in the first form it appears as an isolated exception already at the beginning of the imperial times.

The legal signification of manus is as follows.

(1) The wife leaves her family for that of the husband (or the third person); to him she stands in the relation of a daughter in domestic subjection, so that in relation to the husband she is 'quasi filiafamilias,' 'filiae loco' (or in relation to his paterfamilias, 'neptis loco'), and in relation to the children under his potestas, she is 'sororis loco;' but she retains freedom of divorce.

Gai. i. 115*b*: —si omnino qualibet ex causa uxor in manu viri sit, placuit eam filiae iura nancisci.[1]

Ibid. i. § 136:—(mulieres, quae in manum conveiunt) potestate parentis liberantur; nec interest, an in viri sui manu sint an extranei, quamvis

[1] If in any case, for whatever reason, a woman is in the *manus* of her husband, it has been decided that she acquires the rights of a daughter.

hae solae loco filiarum habeantur, quae in viri manu sunt.[1] Book II. Part I.

Gell. xviii. 6, § 9: —matremfamilias appellatam esse solam, quae in mariti manu mancipioque aut in eius, in cuius maritus, manu mancipioque esset, quoniam non in matrimonium tantum, sed in familiam quoque mariti et in sui heredis locum venisset.[2]

Gai. i. § 137: Sed filia quidem nulla modo patrem potest cogere,[a] etiamsi adoptiva sit; haec[b] autem virum repudio misso proinde compellere potest, atque si ei numquam nupta fuisset.[3]

[a] Sc. ut emancipetur.
[b] Sc. quae in manu est.

(2) The whole of her property falls by universal succession[c] to the husband; likewise all her future acquisitions; the husband is responsible for the contractual debts she has brought to him to the extent of the property that has devolved upon him.

[c] § 77.

Cic. Top. 4, 23: Cum mulier viro in manum convenit, omnia quae mulieris fuerunt, viri fiunt dotis nomine.[4]

Gai. iii. §§ 83–84: Cum paterfamilias se in adoptionem dedit mulierve in manum convenit, omnes eius res incorporales et corporales quaeque

---

[1] (women who fall into *manus*) are freed from their parents' *potestas*, and it does not matter whether they are in the *manus* of their own husband, or of a stranger; although such only are accounted in the position of daughters as are in the *manus* of a husband.

[2] That she alone was called *mat. fam.* who was in the *manus* and *mancipium* of her husband, or in that of him in whose *manus* and *mancipium* her husband was; since she had entered not merely into wedlock, but into the *familia* also of her husband, and into the place of a *suus heres*.[d]

[d] See § 162.

[3] But a daughter, even though she be one adopted, can in no way compel her father (*i.e.*, to emancipate her), the other (*i.e.*, who is in *manus*), however, who has had a letter of divorce sent to her, can compel her husband,[e] just as if she had never been married to him.

[e] *I.e.*, to release her from *manus*.

[4] When a woman enters into *manus* to a husband, all things that have belonged to the woman become property of the husband under the name of *dos*.

ei debitae sunt, patri adoptivo coemptionatorive adquiruntur, exceptis his quae per capitis deminutionem pereunt.—Ex diverso quod is debuit, qui se in adoptionem dedit quaeque in manum convenit, non transit ad coemptionatorem aut ad patrem adoptivum nisi si hereditarium aes alienum fuerit: tunc enim, quia ipse pater adoptivus aut coemptionator heres fit, directo tenetur iure; is vero qui se adoptandum dedit quaeve in manum convenit, desinit esse heres.[1]

Ibid. ii. § 90: Per eas vero personas quas in manu mancipiove habemus, proprietas adquiritur nobis ex omnibus causis, sicut per eos, qui in potestate nostra sunt.[2]

Ibid. iv. § 80: Quod vero ad eas personas quae in manu mancipiove sunt, ita ius dicitur, ut cum ex contractu earum agatur, nisi ab eo, cuius iuri subiectae sint, in solidum defendantur, bona quae earum futura forent, si eius iuri subiectae non essent, veneant.[3]

Ibid. iii. § 104: Servus et qui in mancipio est

---

[1] When the *pat. fam.* has given himself in adoption, or a woman has entered into *manus*, all their property, incorporeal and corporeal, and all that has been owing to them, is acquired by the adopting father or by the purchaser through coemption,[a] save such things as perish by the loss of *caput*.—On the other hand, a debt owing by one who has given himself in adoption, or by her who enters into *manus*, does not pass to the *coemptionator*, or to the adopting father, unless it were a debt of the inheritance; for in that case, as the adopting father himself or the *coemptionator* becomes heir, he is directly liable; but he who has given himself in adoption, or she who has entered into *manus*, ceases to be heir.

[a] See § 49.

[2] Through such persons as we hold in *manus* or *mancipium* property is acquired for us upon any title, just as through those who are under our *potestas*.

[3] But as regards those persons who are in *manus* or *mancipium*, the law is stated thus: that when proceedings are taken upon their contract, unless they are defended to the full amount by him to whose authority they are subject, all the property which would have been theirs, if they had not been subject to his authority, will be sold.

Book II. Part I.

et filiafamilias et quae in manu est non solum ipsi, cuius iuri subiecti subiectaeve sunt, obligari non possunt, sed ne alii quidem ulli.[a] [1]

[a] Cf. extracts from Gaius in § 56.

§ 49. Origin and Termination of *Manus*.

Manus is created by 'confarreatio,' 'coemptio,' and 'usus.'

'Confarreatio' is the old Roman (patrician) sacral act of concluding a marriage, to the essence of which certain religious ceremonies belong. The marriage by it, though with diminished effect, was retained as prerequisite of capacity for certain priestly offices along with such to a late period.

Gai. i. § 112: Farreo in manum conveniunt per quoddam genus sacrificii quod Iovi Farreo fit, in quo farreus panis adhibetur, unde etiam 'confarreatio' dicitur; complura praeterea huius iuris ordinandi gratia cum certis et solemnibus verbis praesentibus decem testibus aguntur et fiunt. Quod ius etiam nostris temporibus in usu est; nam flamines maiores i.e. Diales, Martiales, Quirinales, item reges sacrorum, nisi qui ex farreatis nati sunt, non leguntur, ac ne ipsi quidem sine confarreatione sacerdotium habere possunt.[2]

Ibid. § 136: —(de flaminica Diali ex auctoritate) Maximi et Tuberonis cautum est, ut haec

[1] A slave, a person *in mancipio*, a *fil. fam.* and a woman *in manu* are not only incapable of becoming liable to those under whose authority they are, but they cannot be liable to any one else.

[2] They come into *manus* by *farreum*, by a certain kind of sacrifice rendered to Jupiter Farreus, in which a cake of fine flour is employed, whence also the expression 'confarreatio;' there are besides many things performed and done for the purpose of ratifying the ceremony, with fixed and solemn words, and with ten witnesses present. And this rite is in use even to our day; for none are elected to the office of superior *flamens*, *i.e.*, of Jupiter, Mars and Quirinus, nor to be a *rex sacrorum*, unless they are born from a marriage by *confarreatio*, nor can they themselves hold the priestly office unless their own marriage be by *confarreatio*.

Book II. Part I.

quod ad sacra tantum videatur in manu esse, quod vero ad ceteras causas proinde habeatur, atque si in manum non convenisset.[1]

[a] A. 24, p. Chr.

Tac. Annal. iv. 16: —lata lex[a] qua flaminica Dialis sacrorum causa in potestate viri, cetera promiscuo feminarum iure ageret.[2]

'Coemptio' is the creation of manus by a formal, simulative sale (mancipatio) which was concluded between man and wife with the concurrence (auctoritas) of the paterfamilias or of their guardians; and by it the wife sold herself into the power of the husband (coemptionator).—At first there was only one coemptio for the purpose of marriage (matrimonii causa); it was itself a form for the conclusion of a marriage.[b] Mancipation was here preceded by an agreement for marriage clothed in colloquy.

[b] *Contra*, Coulanges, 'La Cité Antique,' p. 369, but see below.

Gai. i. § 113: **Coemptione** in manum conveniunt per mancipationem i.e. per quandam imaginariam venditionem: nam adhibitis non minus quam v testibus civibus Romanis puberibus, item libripende, emit eam mulierem is, cuius in manum convenit.[3]

Boeth. in Cic. Top. c. 3, 4: Coemptio vero certis sollemnitatibus peragebatur et sese in coemendo invicem interrogabant. Vir ita: 'an sibi mulier materfamilias esse vellet?' illa respondebat: 'velle.' Item mulier interrogabat:

---

[1] (respecting the wife of a priest of Jupiter, at the instance) of Maximus and Tubero it was provided that she is to be considered in *manus* only as concerns matters of ritual, but for other purposes is to be regarded as though she had not passed under *manus*.

[2] A statute was passed by which a priestess of Jupiter should in matters of ritual be under the control of her husband, but should perform other matters by the common law of women.

[3] They come into *manus* through a mancipation, that is, by a kind of fictitious sale; for, in the presence of not less than five Roman citizens of the age of puberty, brought together as witnesses, as also of a balance-holder, the woman is purchased by him into whose *manus* she comes.

'an vir sibi paterfamilias esse vellet?' ille respondebat: 'velle.' Quam solemnitatem in suis institutis Ulpianus exponit.[1]

Later on the coemptio was applied also to other purposes (fiduciae causa); it was here concluded with an 'extraneus'—or even the husband—under the express condition of remancipation to a prescribed third person in view of manumission (pactum fiduciae), and occurred only as a simulative transaction (dicis causa), *i.e.*, as a mere legal form.[a] Special cases of this coemptio are the 'coemptio tutelae evitandae causa,'[b] and the 'coemptio testamenti faciendi causa;'[c] on the other hand, the 'coemptio sacrorum interimendorum causa' established a marriage with legal formality which was in fact only a simulative marriage.

[a] Gai. i. 136.
[b] § 66.
[c] § 156.

Gai. i. §§ 114–5: Potest autem coemptionem facere mulier non solum cum marito suo, sed etiam cum extraneo, unde aut **matrimonii causa** facta coemptio dicitur, aut **fiduciae causa**: quae enim cum marito suo facit coemptionem, ut apud eum filiae loco sit dicitur matrimonii causa fecisse coemptionem; quae vero alterius rei causa facit coemptionem cum viro suo aut cum extraneo, veluti **tutelae evitandae causa,** dicitur fiduciae causa fecisse coemptionem. § Quod est tale: si qua velit quos habet tutores deponere et alium nancisci, illis auctoribus coemptionem facit; deinde a coemptionatore remancipata ei cui ipsa velit, et ab eo vindicta manumissa incipit eum habere tutorem, a quo manumissa est; qui tutor **fiduciarius** dicitur, sicut inferius apparebit.[2]

---

[1] Now *coemptio* was performed with certain ceremonies, and the parties when contracting it put questions to one another. The man as follows: 'Was the woman willing to be his *mat. fam.?*' She would reply, 'She was.' The woman likewise asked: 'Was the man willing to be her *pat. fam.?*' He would reply, 'He was.' And this is the ceremony which Ulpian describes in his Institutes.

[2] Now a woman can perform a coemption not only with her

Book II. Part I.

Cicero p. Mur. 12, 27: Mulieres omnes propter infirmitatem consilii maiores in tutorum potestate esse voluerunt: hi[a] invenerunt genera tutorum, quae potestate mulierum continerentur. Sacra interire illi noluerunt: horum ingenio senes ad coemptiones faciendas **interimendorum sacrorum causa** reperti sunt.[1]

[a] Sc. iurecon-sulti.

'Usus' gave rise to manus when the wife had continued for a year in her husband's house; the usus was interrupted by absence during three successive nights (trinoctium usurpandi causa).[b]

[b] Cf. § 22.

Gai. i. § 111: **Usu** in manum conveniebat, quae anno continuo nupta perseverabat; quae enim velut annua possessione usucapiebatur, in familiam viri transibat filiaeque locum obtinebat. Itaque lege duodecim tabularum cautum est, ut si qua nollet eo modo in manum mariti convenire, ea quotannis trinoctio abesset atque eo modo usum cuiusque anni interrumperet. Sed hoc totum ius

---

husband, but also with a stranger, and hence it is said that the coemption is performed either for a matrimonial or for a fiduciary purpose; for the woman who performs a coemption with her husband in order that she may stand related to him as daughter is said to have performed it for a matrimonial purpose; but she who performs the coemption with her husband or with a stranger for another purpose, as for example, to rid herself of a guardian, is said to have performed it for a fiduciary purpose. And this is as follows: if a woman desire to set aside her existing guardian and to obtain another, she performs a coemption with the concurrence of those guardians; then being remancipated by the *coemptionator* to such person as she pleases, and mancipated *vindicta* by the latter, she begins to have as guardian him by whom she was manumitted; and he is called 'fiduciary guardian,' as will appear below.[c]

[c] See § 64.

[1] It was the will of our ancestors that all women should be under the control of guardians by reason of weakness of judgment: these men (*i.e.*, lawyers) devised kinds of guardians that should be subject to female dictation. The former were averse to the extinction of *sacra*; by the ingenuity of the latter, old men were found for the performance of coemptions, for the purpose of abolishing *sacra*.

partim legibus sublatum est, partim ipsa desuetudine oblitteratum est.[1]

Gell. iii. 2, § 12, Macrob. Sat. 1, 3: Q. quoque Mucium iureconsultum dicere solitum legi, lege non isse usurpatum, quae cum kalendis Ianuariis apud virum matrimonii causa esse coepisset, ante diem IV kalendas Ianuarias sequentes usurpatum isset: non enim posse impleri trinoctium, quod abesse a viro usurpandi causa ex duodecim tabulis deberet, quoniam tertiae noctis posteriores sex horae alterius anni essent, qui inciperet ex kalendis.[2]

Manus comes to an end with the marriage, by death or divorce;[a] and further, by loss of citizenship, and by remancipation of the wife.

[a] By *diffareatio* when the marriage was by *confarreatio*.

Paul. ex Festo (p. 74, M.): **Diffareatio** genus erat sacrificii, quo inter virum et mulierem fiebat dissolutio; dicta diffareatio, quia fiebat farreo libo adhibito.[3]

---

[1] A woman used to pass into *manus* by usage, who remained married for a year continuously; for she was acquired by usucapion, as it were, through possession for a year, passed into the husband's family, and gained the position of a daughter. Therefore it was provided by the Law of the Twelve Tables, that if a wife was unwilling in such way to pass into the *manus* of her husband, she should every year absent herself for three nights, and in that way interrupt the usage of each year. But the regulation as to all this is obsolete, being in part repealed by statute, in part abolished by very disuse.

[2] I have read that Q. M., too, the jurisconsult, was accustomed to say that by the statute the woman had not broken the *usus*[b] who, having begun to be with a husband *matrimonii causa*[c] on the 1st of January, had broken the *usus* on the 29th of December following; for that the three nights which she was bound by the Twelve Tables to be absent from her husband to effect interruption could not be completed, since the last six hours of the third night belonged to the next year, which would begin from the kalends.

[b] Lit. 'had not gone to usurp.'

[c] *I.e.*, to live with him as his wife.

[3] *Diffareatio* was an order of sacrifice by which a divorce took place between husband and wife; called 'diffareatio,' because it was effected by the employment of meal-cake.

BOOK II. Part I.

§ 50. THE POWER OF THE FATHER: ITS NATURE AND SCOPE.[a]

[a] Maine, 'Anct. Law,' pp. 135, sqq.; 'Early History of Institutions,' pp. 218 and 221, sqq.; Blackstone, i. 452-3 (Steph. ii. 295-8).

[b] Arndts, 'Lehrbuch der Pandekten,' § 436 (15th ed., pp. 812-3).

The Power of the Father (patria potestas) is likewise a strict, civil and national Roman institution, although preserved down to the Law of Justinian, and even to modern Law,[b] in much reduced form.

> Gai. i. § 55: Item in potestate nostra sunt liberi nostri, quos iustis nuptiis procreavimus. Quod ius proprium civium Romanorum est: fere enim nulli alii sunt homines, qui talem in filios suos habent potestatem, qualem nos habemus.[1]

> Ulp. x. 3: Neque peregrinus civem Romanum neque civis Romanus peregrinum in potestate habere potest.[2]

The right of 'patria potestas' of the Roman citizen in his children is very comprehensive, approaches absolute right of dominion, as over slaves, and seems almost entirely to absorb the capacity for rights of the children subject to it. The patria potestas, however, is not identical with the 'dominica potestas.' The filius familias is fully acknowledged as free, and as a Roman citizen; he is not as the slave, a passive, but an active member of the family; he possesses capacity for private rights, according to ius civile (commercium and conubium), but it is controlled by the power of the paterfamilias—naturally of limited duration—after the lapse of whom (especially by death) he freely attains independent exercise of all proprietary and family rights, which were hitherto under the restraint of patria potestas.[c] This restraint upon capacity for private rights shows itself in the fact that all rights arising from the commercium and conubium of the filiusfamilias, so long as he is under potestas, devolve

[c] D. 23, 2, 11; 50, 16, 195, 2; Ulp. x. 2.

[1] Likewise under our *potestas* are our children whom we have begotten in a lawful marriage. And this right is peculiar to Roman citizens; for there are scarcely any other men possessing such power over their sons as we have.

[2] Neither can a foreigner have a Roman citizen, nor a Roman citizen a foreigner, under his *potestas*.

upon the paterfamilias: thus the filius familias himself is incapable also of an actual patria potestas, and his children are under the potestas of his paterfamilias until the patria potestas by which he is governed is extinguished.[a]

[a] Perhaps alone indirectly; cf. Inst. 1, 2, 11; D. 1, 7, 40; ibid. 28.—As to family property in the hands of the *pat. fam.*, see § 167.

> Ulp.: —in sua potestate non videtur habere, qui non est suae potestatis.—D. 48, 5, 21.[1]
>
> Id.: Nam qui ex me et uxore mea nascitur, in mea potestate est; item qui ex filio meo et uxore eius nascitur i.e. nepos meus et neptis aeque in mea sunt potestate, et pronepos et proneptis et deinceps ceteri.—D. 1, 6, 4.[2]

In the Public Law, on the other hand, the filiusfamilias takes the same position as the paterfamilias.

> Pomp.: Filiusfamilias in publicis causis loco patrisfamilias habetur, veluti ut magistratum gerat, ut tutor detur.—l. 9 eod.[3]

As regards the person of the filiusfamilias, the paterfamilias has

(1) the 'ius vitae ac necis,' which was originally unlimited by Law; especially in exercise of the very extensive domestic jurisdiction belonging from of old to the paterfamilias; but this in course of time was converted into a merely domestic right of correction.

> Coll. iv. 8: Cum patri lex regia dederit in filium vitae necisque potestatem—.[4]
>
> Imp. Constant.: Libertati a maioribus tantum impensum est, ut patribus, quibus ius vitae in liberos necisque potestas olim erat permissa,

---

[1] He that is not his own master is not regarded as having any under his *potestas*.

[2] For the issue of myself and wife is under my *potestas*; likewise the issue of my son and his wife, *i.e.*, my grandson and granddaughter, are equally under my *potestas*, and great grandson and great granddaughter and further descendants.

[3] A *fil. fam.* in public concerns is deemed a *pat. fam.*, as for example, that he hold an office, or be appointed a guardian.

[4] Since the *lex regia* gave to the father power of life and death over his son . . .

Book II. Part I.

eripere libertatem non liceret.—l. 10, C. de patr. pot. 8, 46 (47).[1]

Marcian.: D. Hadrianus fertur, cum in venatione filium suum quidam necaverat, qui novercam adulterabat, in insulam eum deportasse, quod latronis magis quam patris iure eum interfecit.—D. 48, 9, 5.[2]

Inauditum filium pater occidere non potest, sed accusare eum apud praefectum praesidemve provinciae debet.—D. 48, 8, 2.[3]

Imp. Alex.: —(filium) si pietatem patri debitam non agnoscit, castigare iure patriae potestatis non prohiberis, artiore remedio usurus, si in pari contumacia perseveraverit, eumque praesidi provinciae oblaturus dicturo sententiam, quam tu quoque dici volueris.—l. 3, C. de patr. pot.[4]

(2) the 'ius vendendi,' whether to a foreigner (trans Tiberim) into slavery,[a] or in the form of mancipation to a Roman citizen, which was later on limited to fictitious sale[b] and sale from necessity.

[a] § 36.

[b] Cf. §§ 52, *sq.*

Gai. i. §§ 117–8: Omnes igitur liberorum personae sive masculini sive feminini sexus, quae in potestate parentis sunt, mancipari ab hoc eodem modo possunt, quo etiam servi mancipari possunt.

---

[1] So great a value was set upon freedom by our ancestors, that fathers, to whom the right of life and power of death over their children had been granted of old, were not allowed to deprive them of freedom.

[2] It is related that when a certain man in hunting had slain a son who committed adultery with the step-mother, the late Emperor Hadrian deported him to an island, because he slew him more by the right of a highwayman than by his right as father.

[3] A father is not competent to kill a disobedient son, but must accuse him before the prefect or president of the province.

[4] If thy son do not acknowledge the filial regard owing to thee his father, thou art not precluded from chastising him by virtue of *patria potestas*, and mayst employ harsher measures if he shall persist in like disobedience, and shalt hand him over to the president of the province to pass such sentence upon him as thou shalt desire.

§ Idem iuris est in earum personis, quae in manu sunt.—§ Sed plerumque solum et a parentibus et a coemptionatoribus mancipantur, cum velint parentes coemptionatoresque e suo iure eas personas dimittere.[1]

Book II. Part I.

Paul. rec. sent. v. 1, § 1: Qui contemplatione extremae necessitatis aut alimentorum gratia filios suos vendiderint, statui ingenuitatis eorum non praeiudicant: homo enim liber nullo pretio aestimatur. Iidem nec pignori ab his aut fiduciae dari possunt; operae tamen eorum locari possunt.[a][2]

[a] Cf. sup. C. 8, 46, 10.

Imp. Dioclet.: Liberos a parentibus neque venditionis neque donationis titulo, neque pignoris iure, aut alio quolibet modo . . . in alium transferri posse, manifesti iuris est.—C. 4, 43, 1.[3]

Imp. Constant.: Si quis propter nimiam paupertatem egestatemque victus causa filium filiamve sanguinolentos [a] vendiderit, venditione in hoc tantummodo casu valente, emptor obtinendi eius servitii habeat facultatem. Liceat autem ipsi qui vendidit vel qui alienatus est, aut cuilibet alii ad ingenuitatem eum propriam repetere, modo sit aut pretium offerat aut mancipium pro huiusmodi praestet.—l. 2 eod.[4]

[a] *I.e.*, modo natos.

---

[1] All children, accordingly, whether male or female, that are under their father's *potestas* can be mancipated by him in the same way as slaves also are mancipated. The like rule obtains in respect of persons *in manu*.—But generally mancipation, as well by parents as by fictitious purchasers, alone takes place when the parents or fictitious purchasers wish to release such persons from their authority.

[2] They that from consideration of dire need, or for the sake of maintenance, have sold their children, do not adversely affect their status of free birth; for a freeman is valued at no price. Neither can the same be given by them in pledge, or as a *fiducia*; but their services can be let.

[3] It is settled law that children cannot be transferred to another by their parents either by virtue of sale or gift, or by pledge-right, or by any other mode.

[4] If any one through dire poverty and need of sustenance have sold a new-born son or daughter, the sale shall be good merely

Book II. Part I.

[a] Cf. §§ 56, 113, and Holmes, 'Common Law,' pp. 8-15.—As to Mr. Roby's criticism of the form here ('Int. to Dig.' p. 132), it may be remarked that 'noxae *dare*' is quite as common as, perhaps more frequent than, *dedere*; on the other hand, 'noxae *deditio*' is certainly the more usual.

(3) the 'ius noxae dandi;'[a] but this disappeared from the Law in its developed form.

Gai. iv. § 75: Ex maleficiis filiorumfamilias servorumque, veluti si furtum fecerint aut iniuriam commiserint, noxales actiones proditae sunt, uti liceret patri dominove, aut litis aestimationem sufferre aut noxae dedere: erat enim iniquum, nequitiam eorum ultra ipsorum corpora parentibus dominisve damnosam esse.[1]

Sed veteres quidem haec et in filiisfamilias masculis et feminis admiserunt. Nova autem hominum conversatio huiusmodi asperitatem recte respuendam esse existimavit: quis enim patitur filium suum et maxime filiam in noxam alii dare, . . . cum in filiabus etiam pudicitiae favor hoc bene excludit?—§ 7, I. de nox. act. 4, 8.[2]

With regard to 'commercium,' the child in patria potestas is—

[b] Cf. §§ 149, 150, and D. 3, 3, 35 pr.

[c] § 20 and Gai. ii. 96.

(1) incapable of having property of his own,[b] but possesses full capacity to acquire for the paterfamilias.[c]

Gai. ii. § 87: Igitur quod liberi nostri, quos in potestate habemus, item quod servi nostri mancipio accipiunt vel ex traditione nanciscuntur,

---

in this case, and the purchaser shall be entitled to acquire such services. But the one who hath sold him or he that was alienated, or any other, shall be empowered to restore him to his personal freedom, provided he either tender the price or supply another slave in his stead.

[1] The wrongful acts of sons under power or of slaves, as for instance, if they have committed theft or outrage, have given rise to noxal actions, whereby the father or owner shall have the option either of bearing pecuniary damages or of surrendering the wrong-doer by way of reparation; for it was unfair that their offence should involve the parents or masters in loss beyond the value of their persons.

[2] But the ancients allowed this even in the case of sons and daughters of the family. The modern manner of life, however, has rightly deemed it necessary to eschew severity of this kind; for who consents to give up by way of reparation to any one his son and, above all, his daughter, . . . whilst in respect of his daughters even regard for decency justly forbids this?

sive quid stipulentur vel ex aliqualibet causa adquirant, id nobis adquiritur: ipse enim qui in potestate nostra est, nihil suum habere potest.[1]

Book II. Part I.

Pomp. ad Sab.: Filiusfamilias suo nomine nullam actionem habet, nisi iniuriarum et quod vi aut clam; et depositi et commodati, ut Iulianus putat.—D. 44, 7, 9.[2]

Ulp.: Iuliano placet, si filiusfamilias legationis vel studiorum gratia aberit et vel furtum vel damnum iniuria passus sit posse eum utili iudicio agere. . . . Unde ego semper probavi ut, si res non ex maleficio veniat sed ex contractu, debeat filius agere utili iudicio, forte depositum repetens vel mandati agens vel pecuniam quam credidit petens: si forte pater in provincia sit, ipse autem forte Romae . . . agat.—l. 18, § 1, D. de ind. 5, 1.[3]

Id.: In factum actiones etiam filiifamiliarum possunt exercere.—l. 13, D. de O. et A.[4]

(2) can validly bind himself.[a]

[a] But see Gai. iii. 104, and D. 50, 12, 2 pr.

Gai.: Filiusfamilias ex omnibus causis tamquam paterfamilias obligatur, et ob id agi cum eo tamquam cum patrefamilias potest.—l. 39 eod.[5]

[1] Therefore, that which our children whom we have under our *potestas*, also that which our slaves receive by mancipation, or obtain by delivery, or stipulate for, or acquire in what way soever, is acquired for us; for he who is under our *potestas* can have nothing of his own.

[2] No action belongs to a *fil. fam.* in his own name, except that for outrage, and that for violent or clandestine dispossessions and those in respect of a deposit or loan, as Iul. thinks.

[3] Julian is of opinion that if a *fil. fam.* is absent by reason of an embassage, or of his studies, and has suffered either a theft or damage with injury, he can take equitable proceedings. . . . I have therefore always supported the view, that if the matter do not proceed from a delict but from a contract, the son ought to sue by *utile iudicium*, when, it may be, he reclaims some deposit, or sues upon a commission, or claims money lent by him; if so be the father is in the province, but he himself happen to sojourn at Rome.

[4] *Filii fam.* also can bring actions for matters of fact.

[5] A *fil. fam.* incurs obligation in all cases like a *pat. fam.*, and can therefore be sued just as a *pat. fam.*

BOOK II. Part I.

Ulp.: Tam ex contractibus quam ex delictis in filiumfamilias competit actio.—l. 57, D. de iud.[1]

§ 51. ORIGINATION OF THE *PATRIA POTESTAS*. THE NATURAL GROUND THEREOF LAID IN PROCREATION. LEGITIMATION.

1. The patria potestas regularly arises—immediately and of itself—by procreation in a 'legitimum matrimonium' [a]; according to later Law, in a marriage of general legal validity: it is immaterial whether the birth of the child takes place during marriage or after dissolution thereof.[b] Only children begotten in wedlock have a father, and indeed, since the fact of procreation never can be discovered, the husband, by virtue of legal presumption, is regularly regarded as father of the child; *i.e.*, he with whom the mother lived in legal matrimony during the time of conception.[c] The time of conception is taken to be the space from 182 to 300 days before the birth. If the paternity is contested, a 'praeiudicium' [d] is needful for its discovery: the child and its mother has the 'actio de partu' against the father for recognition as begotten in wedlock; and special measures were provided by the SC. Plancianum and the Praetorian Edict (edictum de iuspiciendo ventre custodiendoque partu) for the prevention of delay or of embezzlement of a child.

[a] § 44.
[b] D. 49, 15, 25.
[c] § 42.
[d] Inst. iv. 6, 13.

Ulp.: Filium eum definimus, qui ex viro et uxore eius nascitur. Sed si fingamus abfuisse maritum verbi gratia per decennium, reversum anniculum invenisse in domo sua, placet nobis Iuliani sententia, hunc non esse mariti filium. Non tamen ferendum Iulianus ait eum, qui cum uxore sua adsidue moratus nolit filium agnoscere quasi non suum.—D. 1, 6, 6.[2]

---

[1] An action lies against a *fil. fam.* as well upon contracts as upon delicts.

[2] As son we designate him who is born of a man and his wife. But if, for example, we suppose a husband to have been absent ten years, and upon his return to have found a child one year

Book II. Part I.

Paul.: Septimo mense nasci perfectum partum, iam receptum est propter auctoritatem doctissimi viri Hippocratis; et ideo credendum, eum qui ex iustis nuptiis septimo mense natus est, iustum filium esse.—D. 1, 5, 12.[1]

Ulp.: Post decem menses mortis natus non admittetur ad legitimam hereditatem.—De eo autem, qui centesimo octogesimo secundo die natus est, Hippocrates scripsit et D. Pius pontificibus rescripsit, iusto tempore videri natum.—D. 38, 16, 3, §§ 11–12.[2]

Children begotten in a 'non legitimum matrimonium' were free from patria potestas, but became subject to it contemporaneously with the attainment of citizenship, by means of 'anniculi caus. prob. ex l. Aelia Sentia' and the 'erroris caus. prob.'[a]

[a] Gai. i. 29-31, 67-8, 70, 95-6.

Gai. i. §§ 93, 94: Si peregrinus sibi liberisque suis civitatem Romanam petierit, non aliter filii in potestate eius fient, quam si imperator eos in potestatem redegerit, quod ita demum is facit, si causa cognita aestimaverit, hoc filiis expedire. . . . § Item si quis cum uxore praegnante civitate Romana donatus sit, quamvis is qui nascitur civis Romanus sit, tamen in potestate patris non fit, idque subscriptione D. Hadriani significatur.[3]

---

old in his house, we take the view of Julian that this is not a son of the husband. We are not, however, says Julian, to tolerate him who, having lived along with his wife continuously, refuses to recognise [her] son as his own.

1 That a child is perfectly developed when born in the seventh month has already obtained acceptance upon the authority of the learned Hippocrates; and therefore we must suppose that the child born in lawful marriage in the seventh month is a legitimate son.

2 The child born after ten months from the death shall not be admitted to the statutory inheritance.—But as to the child born on the 182nd day, Hippocrates has written, and the late emperor Pius has stated by a rescript, that it must be regarded as born at the right time.

3 If a foreigner applies for Roman citizenship for himself and

BOOK II. Part I.

Neither can children begotten out of wedlock be placed under the potestas of the person that begot them, since he is not juristically accounted their father. But legislation of the Christian imperial, and especially later, times in different ways enabled natural fathers to obtain legal recognition, as though begotten in wedlock, of their 'liberi naturales,' or children by concubinage. This is LEGITIMATION. It can occur

(α) per subsequens matrimonium;

(β) per rescriptum principis;

(γ) per testamentum; and

(δ) per curiae oblationem.—The legitimated children rank fully with those begotten in wedlock.[a]

[a] Cf. Steph. ii. pp. 285-290; Ld. Mackenzie, pp. 133-4; Westlake, pp. 83-87.

Inst. i. 10, § ult.: Aliquando autem evenit, ut liberi qui statim ut nati sunt in potestate parentum non fiant, postea tamen redigantur in potestatem. Qualis est is, qui dum naturalis fuerat, postea curiae datus potestati patris subiicitur. Nec non is, qui a muliere libera procreatus, cuius matrimonium minime legibus interdictum fuerat, sed ad quam pater consuetudinem habuerat, postea ex nostra constitutione dotalibus instrumentis compositis in potestate patris efficitur: quod et aliis, si ex eodem matrimonio fuerint procreati, similiter nostra constitutio praebuit.—[Imp. Iustinian.: si quis mulierem quam in contubernio suo habuerat, praegnantem fecerit, postea autem adhuc gravida muliere constituta dotalia fecerit instrumenta et puer vel puella editus vel edita sit, iusta patri suboles nascatur et in potestate efficiatur.—C. 5, 27, 11, 3.][1]

his children, the children shall not be under his *potestas* unless the Emperor have brought them into it, and this he does only if, upon investigation of the case, he consider it advantageous to the children. . . . Likewise, if Roman citizenship be bestowed upon any man and his pregnant wife, although the child when born is a Roman citizen, yet he is not under the *potestas* of the father; and this is declared in a rescript[b] of the late Emperor Hadrian.

[b] As to *subscriptio*, see above, p. 43.

[1] Sometimes it happens that children who are not under the

Book II. Part I.

§ 52. Artificial Creation by an Act in the Law: Adoption.[a]

Not merely over one's own children, but also over strangers, can the patria potestas be acquired. The legal transaction by which any one is at discretion subjected to the patria potestas of another—with whom he enters into the relation of a child or grandchild—is called ADOPTION in the wider sense. Two kinds of adoption are distinguished: adoption in the narrower sense, and arrogation.

[a] Cf. Maine, 'Anct. Law,' pp. 130-132. Upon legal Fictions in general, ibid. ch. ii.; Savigny, 'Syst.' i. 295; Austin, pp. 629-631; Long's Cicero, vol. i. pp. 181-2; Brown, s.v. For other instances of fiction, see § 36, 53, 56, 90, 154, 194, 200, 204.

Ulp. viii. 1: Non tantum naturales liberi in potestate parentum sunt, sed etiam adoptivi.[1]

Paul.: Adoptare quis nepotis loco potest, etiam si filium non habet.—l. 37 pr., D. h. t. (=de adopt. 1, 7).[2]

Mod.: Quod **adoptionis** nomen est quidem generale; in duas autem species dividitur, quarum altera **adoptio** similiter dicitur, altera **adrogatio**. Adoptantur filiifamilias, adrogantur qui sui iuris sunt.—l. 1, § 1 eod.[3]

---

power of their parents at the moment of their birth, nevertheless come under their power later on. Thus, for example, a natural son who has been afterwards offered to the municipal senate[b] is made subject to the power of the father. Likewise one begotten of a free woman with whom marriage had in no way been forbidden by the law, but with whom the father had cohabited, afterwards, by virtue of our constitution, is brought under the power of the father upon deeds settling a dowry being drawn up. And this is granted by our constitution to others likewise if they have been begotten from the same marriage.—If any one have made a woman pregnant with whom he had cohabited, but subsequently, while the woman is still pregnant, has executed deeds settling a dowry, and a son or daughter is born, such child shall be by birth the lawful offspring of the father, and be rendered subject to his *potestas*.

[b] Cf. Moyle ad loc.; Poste on Gaius, p. 92; Hunter, p. 202.

[1] Not only are natural children under the *potestas* of their parents, but adoptive children as well.

[2] A man can adopt in place of a grandson, even if he have no son.

[3] The expression 'adoption' is indeed a general one, but it is divided into two kinds, of which one is also called 'adoption,'

Book II. Part I.

The following are the requisites of adoption in general.

(1) On the part of the one adopting, capacity for patria potestas and for marriage, as well as being older than the adoptive child.

Feminae adoptare non possunt, quia nec naturales liberos in potestate sua habent: sed ex indulgentia principis ad solatium liberorum amissorum adoptare possunt.—§ 10, I. h. t. (= de adopt. 1, 11).[1]

—et hi qui generare non possunt, quales sunt **spadones**, adoptare possunt, **castrati** autem non possunt.—l. 9, I. eod.[2]

Paul.: Et qui uxores non habent, filios adoptare possunt.—l. 30, D. h. t.[3]

Minorem natu non posse maiorem adoptare placet: adoptio enim naturam imitatur. . . . Debet itaque is, qui sibi per adrogationem vel adoptionem filium facit, **plena pubertate**, i.e. **decem et octo** annis praecedere.—§ 4, I. h. t.[4]

[a] Cf. *infra*, Gai. i. 134; C. 8, 47. l. fi.

(2) Consent of the person interested.[a]

Cels.: In adoptionibus eorum dumtaxat, qui suae potestatis sunt, voluntas exploratur; sin autem **a** patre dantur in adoptionem, in his utriusque arbitrium spectandum est, vel consentiendo vel non contradicendo (Iust.).—l. 5, D. h. t.[5]

---

the other 'arrogation.' *Filiifam.* are adopted, those that are *sui iuris* are arrogated.

[1] Women cannot adopt, because they have not their actual children under their power; but by favour of the Emperor they may adopt as a consolation for the loss of children.

[2] And those who cannot procreate, such as are born impotent, may adopt; but persons made impotent cannot.

[3] And unmarried men can take adoptive sons.

[4] It is held that a younger person cannot adopt an older; for adoption follows the analogy of nature. Therefore he that makes any one his son by arrogation or adoption ought to be the older by the full term of puberty, that is, by eighteen years.

[5] The will is ascertained in adoptions alone of those who are

Paul.: Cum nepos adoptatur quasi ex filio natus, consensus filii exigitur, idque etiam Iulianus scribit.—l. 6 eod.[1] Book II. Part I.

Sed ex contrario si avus ex filio nepotem dat in adoptionem, non est necesse filium consentire. —§ 7, I. h. t.[2]

(3) Absence of positive restrictions.

Paul.: Eum quem quis adoptavit, emancipatum vel in adoptionem datum iterum non potest adoptare.—l. 37, § 1, D. h. t.[3]

The result of adoption consists in the adopted person's entrance into the familia and agnatic relationship of the adoptive father.[a] [a] § 43.

In plurimis autem causis adsimilatur is, qui adoptatus vel adrogatus est, ei qui ex legitimo matrimonio natus est.—§ 8, I. h. t.[4]

Paul.: Qui in adoptionem datur, his, quibus adgnascitur, et cognatus fit, quibus vero non adgnascitur, nec cognatus fit: adoptio enim non ius sanguinis, sed ius adgnationis adfert.—l. 23, D. h. t.[5]

Mod.: In adoptionem datus aut emancipatus

---

their own masters; but if any be given by their father in adoption, the will of each of such must be looked to, either as consenting or not refusing.

[1] When any one is adopted as a grandson, as though born from a son, the consent of the son is required. So also writes Julian.

[2] But if, on the other hand, a grandfather gives in adoption a grandson (born) from his son, it is unnecessary for the son to give his consent.

[3] A person adopted by any one, and emancipated or given in adoption [by him], he cannot again adopt.

[4] Now, in most cases, a person that has been adopted or arrogated is put on the same footing as one sprung from a lawful marriage.

[5] He that is given in adoption becomes the cognate also of those to whom he accrues by adoption,[b] but he does not become the cognate of those to whom he does not accrue by adoption; for adoption transfers no right of blood, but (only) an agnatic right.

[b] As Lewis and Short, 'Latin Dicty.' s. *Agnascor.*

Book II. Part I.

quascumque cognationes adfinitatesque habuit, retinet, adgnationes perdit; sed in ea familia, ad quam per adoptionem venit, nemo est illi cognatus praeter patrem eosve, quibus adgnascitur; adfinis autem ei omnino in ea familia nemo est.—D. 38, 10, 4, 10.[1]

Arrogation, according to ancient Law, was effected in the comitia curiata with the co-operation of the pontifices—who had at the same time to examine the 'causa adrogationis'—and it took the form of an ordinary statute (populi auctoritate); according to later Law, it takes place by imperial rescript (principis auctoritate).

Ulp. viii. 2: Illa adoptio quae **per populum** fit, specialiter adrogatio dicitur.[2]

Gai. i. § 99: **Populi auctoritate** adoptamus eos qui sui iuris sunt; quae species adoptionis dicitur adrogatio, quia et is, qui adoptat, rogatur (i.e. interrogatur), an velit eum, quem adoptaturus sit, iustum sibi filium esse, et is, qui adoptatur, rogatur, an id fieri patiatur, et populus rogatur, an id fieri iubeat.[3]

Gell. v. 19, §§ 4–6: Adrogantur hi, qui cum sui iuris sunt, in alienam sese potestatem tradunt

---

[1] He that has been given in adoption or emancipated retains the relationships and connections he has had, agnatic relationships he loses; but in the family into which he passes by adoption no one is his cognate save his father or those to whom he accrues by adoption; whilst in such family no one at all is related to him by affinity.

[2] That adoption which is effected by the intervention of the *populus* is specially called arrogation.

[3] By the authority of the *populus* we adopt those persons who are *sui iuris*, and this species of adoption is called 'arrogation,' because both he who is adopting is rogated (that is, is interrogated) whether he wishes that the one whom he is about to adopt should be his lawful son, and he who is being adopted is rogated whether he submits to such act, and the *populus* is rogated whether they order the performance thereof.

eiusque rei ipsi auctores fiunt. Sed adrogationes non temere nec inexplorate committuntur: nam comitia, arbitris pontificibus, praebentur, quae '**curiata**' appellantur, aetasque eius qui adrogare vult, an liberis potius gignundis idonea sit, bonaque eius qui adrogatur, ne insidiose adpetita sint, consideratur; iusqueiurandum a Q. Mucio pontifice maximo conceptum dicitur, quod in adrogando iuraretur.—§§ 8–9: 'Adrogatio' autem dicta, quia genus hoc in alienam familiam transitus per populi rogationem fit.—Eius rogationis verba haec sunt: VELITIS IVBEATIS, VTI L. VALERIVS L. TITIO TAM IVRE LEGEQVE FILIVS SIET, QVAM SI EX EO PATRE MATREQVE FAMILIAS EIVS NATVS ESSET, VTIQVE EI VITAE NECISQVE IN EVM POTESTAS SIET, VTI PATRI ENDO FILIO EST. HAEC ITA VTI DIXI, ITA VOS QVIRITES ROGO.[1]

Ulp.: In adrogationibus cognitio vertitur, num forte minor sexaginta annis sit qui adrogat, quia magis liberorum creationi studere debeat: nisi forte morbus aut valetudo in causa sit aut alia iusta causa adrogandi, veluti si coniunctam sibi personam velit adoptare.—l. 15, § 2, h. t.[2]

---

[1] Such persons are arrogated as, being *sui iuris*, subject themselves to the power of another and themselves initiate such transaction. But arrogations are not performed at random or without examination; for *comitia curiata* so-called are convened in the presence of the *pontifices*, and inquiry is made whether the age of the arrogator admits rather of his procreation of children, and lest the property of the 'arrogatus' be fraudulently sought after, and an oath, said to have been framed by Q. M. the *pont. max.*, has to be sworn by the arrogator.—Now, 'adrogatio' is so-called because this description of transit into a strange family comes about by the rogation of the People. The following are the words of such rogation: 'Do you will and command that L. V. shall be son of L. T. by law and statute, just as if he had been his son by such *pat. fam.* and *mat. fam.*, and that L. T. shall have power of life and death over him, as a father has in the case of his son? These things, as I have said, so I ask you, Quirites.'

[2] In arrogations the inquiry is directed to whether the arro-

BOOK II. Part I.

From arrogation were excluded by ancient Law—

(1) Women.

Gell. l. c. § 10: Neque pupillus autem neque mulier, quae in parentis potestate est, adrogari possunt: quoniam et cum feminis nulla comitiorum communio est, et tutoribus in pupillos tantam esse auctoritatem potestatemque fas non est, ut caput liberum fidei suae commissum alienae condicioni subiiciant.[1]

Gai.: —et feminiae ex rescripto principis adrogari possunt.—l. 21, D. h. t.[2]

(2) The 'impubes.' From the time of Antoninus Pius, however, the arrogation of an impubes was allowed in special cases after a preliminary causae cognitio, and with the guarantee of the proprietary interests of the person arrogated and of his heir by certain cautiones. (Quarta D. Pii.)

Gai. i. § 102: Item impuberem apud populum adoptari aliquando prohibitum est, aliquando permissum est; nunc ex epistula optimi imperatoris Antonini, quam scripsit pontificibus, si iusta causa adoptionis esse videbitur, cum quibusdam condicionibus permissum est.[3]

---

gator is not under sixty years of age, because (then) he ought the rather to address himself to the begetting of children, unless, it may be, disease or sickness afford reason, or there be other just cause for arrogating; as for example, if he desire to adopt a person nearly related to him.

[1] But neither can a ward nor a woman who is under parental power be arrogated; since on the one hand women do not participate in the public assemblies, on the other, it is not lawful for guardians to have such authority and power as to subordinate to the status of a stranger an independent person entrusted to their charge.

[2] Women also can be arrogated by virtue of the Emperor's rescript.

[3] Likewise the adoption of a person under the age of puberty before the *populus* has sometimes been forbidden, at other times has been allowed; at the present time, according to an epistle of our excellent Emperor Antonine, which he addressed to the *pontifices*, if an adequate cause for the adoption shall be shown to exist, it is allowed under certain conditions.

Cum autem impubes per principale rescriptum adrogatur, causa cognita adrogatio permittitur: et exquiritur causa adrogationis, an honesta sit expediatque pupillo, et cum quibusdam condicionibus adrogatio fit, i.e. ut caveat adrogator personae publicae hoc est tabulario, si intra pubertatem pupillus decesserit, restiturum se bona illis, qui, si adoptio facta non esset, ad successionem eius venturi essent. Item non alias emancipare eos potest adrogator, nisi causa cognita digni emancipatione fuerint et tunc sua bona eis reddat. Sed et si decedens pater eum exheredaverit vel vivus sine iusta causa eum emancipaverit, iubetur quartam partem ei suorum bonorum relinquere, videlicet praeter bona, quae ad patrem adoptivum transtulit et quorum commodum ei adquisivit postea.—§ 3, I. h. t.[1]

Arrogation has the following results.

(1) Children in the potestas of the person arrogated pass *ipso facto* into the familia of the arrogator.

Mod.: Adrogato patrefamilias liberi, qui in eius erant potestate, nepotes apud adrogatorem efficiuntur simulque cum suo patre in eius recidunt potestatem; quod non similiter in adoptione con-

---

[1] When an *impubes* is arrogated by rescript of the Emperor, the arrogation is allowed after inquiry into the matter; the ground of the arrogation is tested, whether it is honourable and to the advantage of the ward; and the arrogation takes effect under certain conditions, that is, that the arrogator give security to a public personage, to wit, a notary, that if the ward shall die before reaching the age of puberty, he will restore the property to those who would have been the next heirs if the adoption had not taken place. Likewise, the arrogator can emancipate them only if, after inquiry into the matter, they shall merit emancipation, and then he must restore their property to them. But further, if the father at his death disinherit him (the adoptive child) or in his lifetime without sufficient reason emancipate him, he is enjoined to bequeath him a fourth part of his property, apart of course from the property which he brought to the adoptive father, and that of which he procured him the benefit subsequently.

BOOK II. Part I.

tingit, nam nepotes ex eo in avi naturalis retinentur potestate.—l. 40 pr., D. h. t.[1]

(2) The property of him that is arrogated passes by universal succession to the arrogator.[a]

[a] Gai. iii. 83-84.

Ulp.: Si paterfamilias adoptatus sit, omnia, quae eius fuerunt et adquiri possunt, tacito iure ad eum transeunt, qui adoptavit.—l. 15 pr. eod.[2]

Id.: In adrogatorem de peculio actionem dandam quidam recte putant, quamvis Sabinus et Cassius ex ante gesto de peculio actionem non esse dandam existimant.—D. 15, 1, 42.[3]

Inst. iii. 10, 2: Nunc autem nos eandem adquisitionem, quae per adrogationem fiebat, coartavimus ad similitudinem naturalium parentum: nihil etenim aliud nisi tantummodo ususfructus tam naturalibus patribus quam adoptivis per filiosfamilias adquiritur in his rebus, quae extrinsecus filiis obveniunt, dominio eis integro servato.[4]

Adoption in the narrower sense takes place 'imperio magistratus.'

(1) Since there was no jural form for the transfer of patria potestas, which was in itself inalienable, and as, consequently, extinction of the existing and

---

[1] If a *pat. fam.* be arrogated, the children that were under his *potestas* are rendered grandsons in respect of the arrogator, and at the same time with their father lapse into his *potestas*; which does not so happen in an adoption, for the grandsons of such remain under the *potestas* of the natural grandfather.

[2] If a *pat. fam.* have been adopted, everything that has belonged to him, and can be acquired, tacitly passes to the person that has adopted him.

[3] Some are correct in supposing that an action with reference to separate property can be given to an arrogator, although Sab. and Cass. consider that an action with reference to separate property arising out of a previous matter cannot be given.

[4] But the acquisition which came about by arrogation we have now limited, like as in respect of natural fathers; for usufruct alone acquired by natural as by adoptive fathers through *filiifam.*, in such things as devolve upon children from outside, whilst they retain the ownership intact.

origination of a new *potestas* was needed, in the adoption of a son there was required by ancient Law three mancipations of him by the father, two corresponding manumissions, and 'vindicatio in potestatem' on the part of the person adopting; with daughters and grandchildren, one mancipation merely, and the 'vindicatio in potestatem'; but the consent of the adoptive child was not needed.[a]

[a] V. *supra*, and next section (Emancipation).

Gai. i. § 134: Et in filio quidem si in adoptionem datur, tres mancipationes et duae intercedentes manumissiones proinde fiunt, ac fieri solent, cum ita eum pater de potestate dimittit, ut sui iuris efficiatur; deinde aut patri remancipatur et ab eo is, qui adoptat, vindicat apud praetorem FILIVM SVVM ESSE et illo contra non vindicante a praetore vindicanti filius addicitur, aut non remancipatur patri, sed ab eo vindicat is qui adoptat, apud quem in tertia mancipatione est: sed sane commodius est patri remancipari. In ceteris vero liberorum personis, seu masculini seu feminini sexus, una scilicet mancipatio sufficit, et aut remancipantur parenti aut non remancipantur. Eadem et in provinciis apud praesidem provinciae solent fieri.[1]

(2) According to later Law, the adoption is effected by declaration upon record before the com-

[1] And in the case of a son when given in adoption, three mancipations and two intermediate manumissions take place, just as are usual when a father releases him from *potestas*, in order that he may become *sui iuris*. Next, he is either remancipated to the father and claimed from him by the adopter before the praetor as being his son, and upon the father's making no counter claim, the son is adjudged by the praetor to the claimant; or he is not remancipated to the father, but he who is adopting claims him from the person in whose control he is upon the third sale; but it is certainly more convenient for the son to be remancipated to the father. But in respect of other children, be they of the male or female sex, one mancipation is enough, and they are either remancipated to the ancestor or are not. The same process is commonly accomplished in the provinces before the president.

petent magistrate, in the presence and with the acquiescence of the persons concerned.

Imp. Iust.: Veteres circuitus in adoptionibus, quae per tres emancipationes et duas manumissiones in filiis aut per unam emancipationem in ceteris liberis fieri solebant, corrigentes sive tollentes censemus, licere parenti, qui liberos in potestate sua constitutos in adoptionem dare desiderat, sine vetere observatione emancipationum et manumissionum hoc ipsum actis intervenientibus apud competentem iudicem manifestare, praesente eo qui adoptatur et non contradicente, nec non eo qui eum adoptat.—C. 8, 47 (48), l. fi.[1]

(3) Adoption in the Law of Justinian has full effect only when it comes about through an ascendant (adoptio plena); whilst adoption by an 'extraneus' (adoptio minus plena) does not terminate the existing patria potestas.

Sed hodie ex nostra constitutione, cum filiusfamilias a patre naturali extraneae personae in adoptionem datur, iura potestatis naturalis patris minime dissolvuntur nec quidquam ad patrem adoptivum transit nec in potestate eius est, licet ab intestato iura successionis ei ab nobis tributa sunt. Si vero pater naturalis non extraneo, sed avo filii sui materno, vel, si ipse pater naturalis fuerit emancipatus, etiam paterno, vel proavo simili modo paterno vel materno filium suum dederit in adoptionem: in hoc casu, quia in unam personam concurrant et naturalia et adoptionis

---

[1] Now that we are improving or doing away with the ancient circumlocutions in respect of adoptions, which used to be accomplished by three emancipations and two manumissions in the case of sons, or by one mancipation in the case of other children, it is our will that the ancestor who wishes to give in adoption children placed under his *potestas* shall be free to make a declaration of this by means of proceedings before the competent judge, in the presence and with the consent of the person adopted and the adopter, without the observance of the old formality of emancipations and manumissions.

iura, manet stabile ius patris adoptivi, et naturali vinculo copulatum et legitimo adoptionis modo constrictum, ut et in familia et in potestate huiusmodi patris adoptivi sit.—§ 2, I. h. t.[1]

The 'adoptio per testamentum' mentioned in non-juristic authors is not adoption, but institution of an heir with the onus or condition of taking the name of the testator; whilst the 'adoptio regia' (in the first half of the imperial period, the usual nomination of successor to the throne) was indeed in its origin actual adoption, but afterwards a bare inoperative form under Private Law; as was the case also with the frequent designation of the successor in a testament.

Finally must be distinguished from adoption the institution of foster children, which possesses no juristic character.

§ 53. Termination of *Patria Potestas*.

According to its natural continuance, patria potestas remains in full scope and in complete operation so long as the pat. fam. lives and is legally capable of it; it is in particular quite independent of whatever age the child attains. Even the married daughter remains under the potestas of her father, unless she passes into

---

[1] But at the present day by virtue of our constitution, when a *fil. fam.* is given in adoption by his natural father to a stranger, the rights of power possessed by the natural father are not at all destroyed, neither does anything pass to the adoptive father, nor is the *f. f.* under his power, although we have given him the intestate succession. But if the natural father have not given his son to a stranger but to the child's maternal grandfather, or if he the natural father himself is emancipated, and has given him in adoption to the paternal grandfather, or to the paternal or maternal great-grandfather,—in such case the right of the adoptive father, created by a natural bond and cemented by the legal manner of adoption, remains intact; because the natural rights and the rights of adoption meet in one person, so that he (*i.e.*, the son) is both in the family and in the power of such adoptive father.

BOOK II. Part I.

the manus of the husband.—The potestas can either be determined independently of the will of the pat. fam., or by his will; a distinction is accordingly made between necessary and voluntary grounds of termination.

Necessary grounds of termination are—

(1) Death of the pat. fam.; but the children of the filiusfamilias now fall under his potestas.[a]

[a] D. 50, 16, 195, 2.

Ulp. x. 2: Morte patris filius et filia sui iuris fiunt: morte autem avi nepotes ita demum sui iuris fiunt, si post mortem avi in potestate patris futuri non sunt, velut si moriente avo pater eorum aut iam decessit aut de potestate dimissus est: nam si mortis avi tempore pater eorum in potestate eius sit, mortuo avo in patris sui potestate fiunt.[1]

(2) Loss of freedom or citizenship by the pat. fam. or the child.[b]

[b] *Ius postliminii*, D. 49, 15, 14 pr., and l. 12, § 1.

Poenae servus effectus filios in potestate habere desinit.—§ 3, I. h. t. (= qu. mod. i. pot. 1, 12).[2]

Gai. i. § 129: Quodsi ab hostibus captus fuerit parens, quamvis servus hostium fiat, tamen pendet ius liberorum propter ius postliminii, quia hi qui ab hostibus capti sunt si reversi fuerint, omnia pristina iura recipiunt, itaque reversus habebit liberos in potestate: si vero illic mortuus sit, erunt quidem liberi sui iuris, sed utrum ex hoc tempore quo mortuus est apud hostes parens, an ex illo quo ab hostibus captus est, dubitari potest.

---

[1] A son and daughter become *sui iuris* by the death of their father; grandsons, however, become *sui iuris* by the death of their grandfather only when after such death they will not be under the *potestas* of their father, for instance, if upon the death of their grandfather their father either is already dead or released from *potestas;* for if at the time of the grandfather's death, their father is under his *potestas*, by the death of the grandfather they become subject to the *potestas* of their own father.

[2] He that has become a penal slave ceases to have his children under his *potestas*.

Ipse quoque filius neposve si ab hostibus captus fuerit, similiter dicemus, propter ius postliminii potestatum quoque parentis in suspenso esse.[1]

Iul.: Quodsi filius eius qui in hostium potestate est,[a] accipit aut stipulatur, id patre priusquam postliminio rediret mortuo ipsi adquisitum intelligitur, et si vivo patre decesserit, ad heredem patris (non) pertinebit: nam status hominum, quorum patres in hostium potestate sunt, in pendenti est, et reverso quidem patre existimatur numquam suae potestatis fuisse, mortuo tunc paterfamilias fuisse, cum pater eius in hostium potestatem perveniret.—D. 49, 15, 22, 2.[2]

[a] [mancipio?]

Ulp. x. 3: Si patri vel filio aqua etigni interdictum sit, patria potestas tollitur, quia peregrinus fit.[3]

(3) Certain dignities or offices of the child: by ancient Law, the priestly office of 'flamen Dialis'

---

[1] But if the ancestor should be taken prisoner by the enemy, although he becomes a slave of the enemy, yet his right over his child is suspended on account of the *ius postliminii*, because if those that have been taken prisoners by the enemy return, they recover all their original rights; and therefore if he returns, he will have his children under his *potestas;* but if he die there, his children will be *sui iuris;* but whether from the time when their ancestor died amongst the enemy, or from the time when he was taken prisoner by the enemy, admits of doubt. Again, if a son or grandson be taken prisoner by the enemy, we shall say likewise that, by reason of the *ius postliminii*, the *potestas* also of the ancestor is held in suspense.

[2] But if the son of him who is in the power of the enemy acquires or stipulates, it is taken to have been acquired for himself if the father died before returning by *postliminium*, and if he died during the father's lifetime, it will (not) belong to the father's heir, for the status of persons whose fathers are in the power of the enemy is in suspense; and if the father have returned, the son is looked upon as having never been his own master; but if he have died, then the son is regarded as having been a *pat. fam.* from the time that the father fell into the power of the enemy.

[3] If the father or son be interdicted fire and water, the *patr. pot.* is extinguished, because he becomes a foreigner.

and of 'virgo Vestalis'; by Justinianean Law, especially the patriciate and the episcopal dignity.

Gai. i. § 130: Praeterea exeunt liberi virilis sexus de patris potestate, si flamines Diales inaugurentur, et feminini sexus, si virgines Vestales capiantur.[1]

Gell. i. 12, §§ 9, 13: Virgo autem Vestalis simul est capta atque in atrium Vestae deducta et pontificibus tradita est, eo statim tempore sine emancipatione ac sine capitis minutione e patris potestate exit et ius testamenti faciendi adipiscitur. —'Capi' autem virgo propterea dici videtur, quia pontificis maximi manu prensa ab eo parente, in cuius potestate est, veluti bello capta abducitur.[2]

Filiusfamilias si militaverit, vel si senator vel consul fuerit factus, manet in patris potestate: militia enim vel consularis dignitas patris potestate filium non liberat; sed ex constitutione nostra summa patriciatus dignitas ilico ab imperialibus codicillis praestitis a patria potestate liberat.— § 4, I. h. t.[3]

(4) Finally, by later imperial Law, forfeiture of the patria potestas by way of punishment, *e.g.*, in pandering of daughters, exposure of a child, and the like.

---

[1] Furthermore, children of the male sex pass out of the ancestor's *potestas* when consecrated to the office of *flamens* of Jupiter, and those of the female sex when taken as Vestal virgins.

[2] Now a Vestal virgin, as soon as she is taken into the enclosure of Vesta and handed over to the *pontifices*, at that very moment passes from under the power of her father without emancipation and without loss of *caput*, and acquires the right of making a testament. But a virgin is said 'capi' because, seized by the hand of the *pont. max.*, she is led away from the parent under whose power she is, as though taken captive in war.

[3] If the *fil. fam.* have rendered military service, or if he have been appointed senator or consul, (still) he remains under the father's power; for military service or the consular dignity does not release the son from paternal power. But by virtue of our constitution, the highest dignity of the patriciate does release from the *patr. pot.* immediately after the imperial nomination.

The patria potestas is voluntarily extinguished by discharge therefrom, or EMANCIPATION.[a]

(1) By Classical Law, this required the mancipation of the child and his manumission by the person to whom he was mancipated;[b] according to the later Law (ex lege Anastasia), it takes place by imperial rescript, by the Law of Justinian, also through a declaration in Court.

Book II Part I.

[a] Likewise by *datio in adoptionem* and *in manum conventio*.—Cf. Bell, s.v.

[b] Gai. i. 134.

> Gai. i. § 132: Praeterea emancipatione desinunt liberi in potestate parentum esse. Sed filius quidem tribus mancipationibus, ceteri vero liberi, sive masculini sexus sive feminini, una mancipatione exeunt de parentum potestate: lex enim XII tabularum tantum in persona filii de tribus mancipationibus loquitur his verbis: SI PATER FILIVM TER VENVMDVIT, A PATRE FILIVS LIBER ESTO. Eaque res ita agitur: mancipat pater filium alicui; is eum vindicta manumittit; eo facto revertitur in potestatem patris; is eum iterum mancipat vel eidem vel alii (sed in usu est eidem mancipari) isque eum postea similiter vindicta manumittit, quo facto cum rursus in potestatem patris fuerit reversus, tertio pater eum mancipat vel eidem vel alii (sed hoc in usu est, ut eidem mancipetur) eaque mancipatione desinit in potestate patris esse, etiamsi nondum manumissus sit, sed adhuc in causa mancipii.[1]

---

[1] Moreover, children cease by emancipation to be under parental power. A son, indeed, after three mancipations, but other children, whether male or female, pass out of parental power by one mancipation; for the Law of the Twelve Tables alone in the case of the son speaks of three mancipations, in the following words: 'If a father have thrice sold his son, let the son be free from his father.' And this transaction is performed as follows: the father mancipates his son to some one; the latter manumits him by *vindicta*; this done, he falls again under his father's *potestas*; the father again mancipates him, either to the same person or to another (but the custom is to mancipate him to the same), and such person afterwards mancipates him by *vindicta* in like manner; which being done, when the

Gai. epit. i. 6, § 3: Tamen cum tertio mancipatus fuerit filius a patre naturali fiduciario patri, hoc agere debet naturalis pater, ut ei a fiduciario patre remancipetur et a naturali patre manumittatur, ut si filius mortuus fuerit, ei in hereditate naturalis pater, non fiduciarius succedat.[1]

Nostra autem providentia et hoc in melius per constitutionem reformavit, ut fictione pristina explosa recta via apud competentes iudices vel magistratus intrent et filios suos vel filias vel nepotes ac deinceps sua manu dimitterent.—§ 6, I. h. t.[2]

(2) Emancipation lies entirely in the discretion of the pat. fam.; compulsion employed against him occurs only exceptionally, *e.g.*, in the case of the 'impubes adrogatus'; on the other hand, the consent of the person's own child is already necessary for emancipation in the later Classical Law.

Gai.: Liberum arbitrium est ei, qui filium et ex eo nepotem in potestate habebit, filium quidem potestate dimittere, nepotem vero in potestate retinere: vel ex diverso filium quidem in potestate retinere, nepotem vero manumittere: vel omnes sui iuris efficere.—D. 1, 7, 28.[3]

---

son is again brought under his father's *potestas*, the latter a third time mancipates him, either to the same person or to another (but the practice is to mancipate him to the same), and by such mancipation he ceases to be under his father's *potestas*, although he has not yet been manumitted, but is so far in the state of *mancipium*.

[1] When, however, a son shall be mancipated a third time by a natural to a fiduciary father, the natural father ought to secure that the son be remancipated to him by the fiduciary father, and be manumitted by the natural father, so that, in the event of the son's death, the natural, not the fiduciary, father succeeds to his inheritance.

[2] But our forethought has remedied this also by a constitution, so that since the abolition of the old fiction, fathers go directly before the competent judges or magistrates, and release their sons, or daughters, or grandsons and so on, from their power.

[3] He that shall have a son, and by him a grandson, under his

Marcian.: Non potest filius, qui est in potestate patris, ullo modo compellere eum, ne sit in potestate, sive naturalis sive adoptivus.—l. 31 eod.[1]

Papin.: Nonnumquam autem impubes, qui adoptatus est, audiendus erit, si pubes factus emancipari desideret; idque causa cognita per iudicem statuendum erit.—l. 32 pr. eod.[2]

Paul. ii. 25, § 5: Filiusfamilias emancipari invitus non cogitur.[3]

Imp. Anast.: —infantes[a] et sine consensu hoc modo sui iuris efficiuntur.—C. 8, 48 (49), l. 5.[4]

[a] See § 60.

Imp. Dioclet.: Adoptatum emancipatione sollemni separare a familia sua pater adoptivus minime prohibetur.—C. 8, 47 (48), 9.[5]

The person emancipated—not his already existing descendants—leaves the familia of the pat. fam.;[b] who, as manumittor, retains a quasi-patronatus over him.

[b] D. 38, 10, 4, 10.

Gai. i. § 135: Qui ex filio semel iterumve mancipato conceptus est, licet post tertiam mancipationem patris sui nascatur, tamen in avi potestate est, et ideo ab eo et emancipari et in adoptionem dari potest. At is qui ex eo filio conceptus est, qui in tertia mancipatione est, non

---

power, shall be at liberty to discharge the son from power, but to retain the grandson under power; or conversely, to retain the son under power, and to release the grandson therefrom, or to make both of them *sui iuris*.

[1] A son that is under his father's power can by no means compel such to terminate his subjection, whether he be a natural or an adoptive son.

[2] But sometimes an *impubes* who has been adopted ought to be heard if, having reached the age of puberty, he desire to be emancipated; and this must be determined by the judge after a preliminary inquiry.

[3] A *fil. fam.* is not compelled to be emancipated against his will.

[4] Children under seven years, even without their consent, are rendered *sui iuris* in this manner.

[5] An adoptive father is not at all restrained from detaching an adoptive son from his family by a solemn release.

Book II. Part I.

nascitur in avi potestate; sed eum Labeo quidem existimat in eiusdem mancipio esse, cuius et pater sit: utimur autem hoc iure, ut quamdiu pater eius in mancipio est, pendeat ius eius; et si quidem pater eius ex mancipatione manumissus erit, cadat in eius potestatem; si vero is dum in mancipio sit decesserit, sui iuris fiat.[1]

Illud scire oportet, quod, si nurus tuus ex filio tuo conceperit et filium postea emancipaveris vel in adoptionem dederis praegnante nuru tua, nihilo minus quod ex ea nascitur, in potestate tua nascitur.—§ 9, I. h. t.[2]

—ex edicto praetoris in huius filii . . . bonis, qui a parente manumissus fuerit, eadem iura praestantur parenti, quae tribuuntur patrono in bonis liberti; et praeterea si impubes sit filius . . . , ipse parens ex manumissione tutelam eius nanciscitur.—§ 6, I. eod.[3]

---

[1] A child conceived from a son after his first or second mancipation, although not born until after the third mancipation of his father, is nevertheless under the power of his grandfather, and so can both be sold and given in adoption by him. But a child conceived from such son the third time in *mancipium* is not born under his grandfather's power; but Labeo considers that he is in the *mancipium* of the same person as his father; we, however, adopt the rule that so long as his father is in *mancipium*, the child's rights are in suspense; and if indeed his father be manumitted from the *mancipium*, he will lapse under the latter's power; but if such die in *mancipium*, the child becomes *sui iuris*.

[2] It is to be observed that if thy daughter-in-law have conceived from thy son, and thou hast afterwards during the pregnancy of thy daughter-in-law emancipated thy son, or hast given him in adoption, none the less is that which is born of her under thy power.

[3] By an edict of the praetor the same rights are given to the father over the property of the son manumitted by such father as are accorded to a patron over the property of the freedman; and moreover, if his son be an *impubes*, the father himself acquires guardianship of the latter consequent upon the manumission.

§ 54. Protection of *Patria Potestas*.

The patria potestas is enforced against any third person who detains the child from the pat. fam.—

(1) By 'vindicatio in potestatem.' The ordinary 'rei vindicatio'[a] is inadmissible, since the child is not in the ownership of the pat. fam.

[a] Gai. iv. 16; ibid. §§ 2, 3; *infra*, § 90, ad init.

Ulp.: Per hanc autem actionem[b] liberae personae, quae sunt iuris nostri, ut puta liberi qui sunt in potestate, non petuntur. Petuntur igitur aut praeiudiciis aut interdictis aut cognitione praetoria; et ita Pomponius . . . : nisi forte, inquit, adiecta causa quis vindicet. Si quis ita petit FILIVM SVVM, vel IN POTESTATE EX IVRE ROMANO, videtur mihi et Pomponius consentire recte eum egisse: ait enim adiecta causa ex lege Quiritium vindicare posse.—D. 6, 1, 1, 2.[1]

[b] Sc. rei vindicationem.

(2) By the interdictum 'de liberis exhibendis,' and the interdictum (prohibitorium) 'de liberis ducendis.'

Id.: Ait praetor: QVI QVAEVE IN POTESTATE LVCII TITII EST, SI IS EAVE APVD TE EST, DOLOVE MALO TVO FACTVM EST, QVO MINVS APVD TE ESSET, ITA EVM EAMVE EXHIBEAS. § Hoc interdictum proponitur adversus eum, quem quis exhibere desiderat eum, quem in potestate sua esse dicit.— § Si quis filiam suam, quae mihi nupta est, velit abducere vel exhiberi sibi desideret, an adversus interdictum exceptio danda sit: si forte pater concordans matrimonium, forte et liberis subnixum velit dissolvere? Et certo iure utimur, ne bene

---

[1] Now free persons that are under our control, as children who are under power, cannot be sued by this action. Accordingly, they are sued either by means of *praeiudicia*, or by interdicts, or by investigation on the part of the praetor. So also Pomp.: 'unless, it may be, a person make the claim upon an additional ground.' If any one so make a claim against 'his son,' or as that 'he is under power according to Roman Law,' it seems to me that Pomp. also agrees that he has acted rightly; for he says that the Quiritarian Law admits of such claim if there be an additional cause.

Book II. Part I.

concordantia matrimonia iure patriae potestatis perturbentur; quod tamen sic erit adhibendum, ut patri persuadeatur, ne acerbe patriam potestatem exerceat.—D. 43, 30, 1 pr., §§ 1, 5.[1]

Id.: Deinde ait praetor: SI LVCIVS TITIVS IN POTESTATE LVCII TITII EST, QVO MINVS EVM LVCIO DVCERE LICEAT, VIM FIERI VETO.—l. 3 pr. eod.[2]

(3) By 'praeiudicium,' when the question is, whether the patria potestas exists or not.[a]

[a] Cf. § 51, and first extract above.

As against the child himself, notice is taken of the patria potestas by 'extraordinaria cognitio,' in respect of which direct compulsion is used where necessary.

Hoc autem interdictum competit non adversus ipsum filium, quem quis ducere velit, sed utique debet esse is, qui eum interdicto defendat. Ceterum cessat interdictum, et succedere poterit notio praetoris, ut apud eum disceptetur, utrum quis in potestate sit, an non sit.—l. 3, § 3 eod.[3]

---

[1] The praetor says: 'As to the man or the woman who is under the power of L. T., if he or she be within thy control, or it have happened by thy fraud that he or she was not within thy control, thou must produce him or her.' § This interdict is set forth against the person from whom any one claims the production of such person as he alleges is under his power.—§ If any one desire to withdraw his daughter who has been married to me, or claims her production, will a plea have to be granted against the interdict, if perchance the father wishes to break up a marriage that is harmonious, and perhaps cemented by children? It is a positive maxim of our Law that essentially harmonious marriages cannot be disturbed by the right of *patr. pot.*; this, nevertheless, must be so applied that an endeavour be made to induce the father to make no harsh use of his *patr. pot.*

[2] Afterwards the praetor says: 'If L. T. is under the power of L. T., that L. T. be not allowed to take him away, I forbid his exerting force.'

[3] But this interdict does not attach against the son himself that a man desires to take away, but of course there must be a person to defend him against the interdict. But the interdict is determined, and the inquiry by the praetor can then ensue, so that before him the discussion is as to whether a person is under power or not.

Paul.: Si filius in potestate patris esse se neget, praetor cognoscit ita, ut prior doceat filius, quia . . . se liberum esse quodammodo contendit. —D. 22, 3, 8.[1]

§ 55. Mancipium.

'Mancipium' is that servile relation of a Roman citizen[a] in a strange familia which, without assuring him rights in it, makes him a dependent member of it, like the slave in relation to Property Law.[b] According to the later juridical view of the Roman jurists, the 'persona in mancipio' retains 'conubium' and the rights arising from it, and in this respect stands to his master as an 'extranea persona,' but he is himself not 'suae potestatis,' and is incapable of exercising domestic rights of power, which are therefore suspended for the time being.[c] As regards commercium, the 'persona mancipio' takes a position towards the master similar to that of the 'adrogatus.'[d]

[a] Or perhaps a *Latinus*.

[b] *Servilis condicio*: cf. Gai. iii. 104.

[c] Ibid. i. 135.

[d] Ibid. ii. 90 iv. 80.

Liv. 41, 8: Lex sociis nominis Latini, qui stirpem ex sese domi relinquerent, dabat, ut cives Romani fierent. Ea lege male utendo alii sociis, alii populo Romano iniuriam faciebant: nam ne stirpem domi relinquerent, liberos suos quibusquibus Romanis in eam condicionem, ut manumitterentur, mancipio dabant, libertinique cives essent.[2]

Gai. i. § 123: —a parentibus vel a coemptionatoribus mancipati mancipataeve servorum

---

[1] If a son say that he is not under *patr. pot.*, the praetor upon inquiry rules that the son first show this, because . . . he maintains that he is in some way or other independent.

[2] The statute granted to allies of the Latin name, who left at home their own offspring, that they should become Roman citizens. By misuse of that *lex* some did harm to the allies, others to the Roman people; for lest they should leave their offspring at home, they gave their children as slaves to any Roman whatever, upon condition that they were manumitted and became citizens that were *libertini*.

BOOK II. Part I.

loco constituuntur, adeo quidem ut ab eo, cuius in mancipio sunt, neque hereditatem neque legata aliter capere possint, quam si simul eodem testamento liberi esse iubeantur, sicuti iuris est in persona servorum.[1]

Ibid. § 141: In summa admonendi sumus, adversus eos quos in mancipio habemus, nihil nobis contumeliose facere licere: alioquin iniuriarum actione tenebimur.[2]

'Mancipium' arises by exercise of the right of sale which belongs to the pat. fam. of some person, and so by mancipatio of the 'persona subiecta' to a third person. At first indeed the 'mancipii causa' was always originated as a real and continuous relation of Power, through the sale of the child by the pat. fam. into foreign servitude, partly for the sake of personal gain, partly for the maintenance of such child.[a] In later Law mancipatio occurs—

(1) for the most part merely 'dicis gratia,'[b] in view of creating or of dissolving a domestic relation of Power,[c] so that the 'mancipii causa' is only a momentary relation.

Gai. ibid.: Ac ne diu quidem in eo iure detinentur homines, sed plerumque hoc fit dicis gratia uno momento; nisi scilicet ex noxali causa mancipentur.[3]

(2) Mancipatio, however, may occur exceptionally of set purpose, as in the 'noxae deditio;'[d] the man-

[a] Gai. i. 118: Paul. Sent. v. 1, 1.

[b] *Cum pacto fiduciae.*

[c] Adoption, Emancipation, termination of *manus*: see Gai. i. 134, ibid. § 132 and §§ 114-5.

[d] Gai. iv. 75; Inst. iv. 8, 7.—As to the form, see note on § 50.

[1] Persons of either sex mancipated by ancestors or by *coemptionatores* are set in the position of slaves to such an extent that not even can they take either an inheritance or legacies from him in whose *mancipium* they are, unless by the same testament they are bidden to be free, as the rule is in the case of slaves.

[2] We must finally observe that we are not allowed to treat with indignity those whom we hold *in mancipio*; otherwise we shall be liable to an action for injuries.

[3] Indeed, men are not kept in this condition long, but in general it happens for form's sake, for a moment, unless, that is, they are mancipated because of their tortious act.

cipium is consequently originated as a permanent condition.

Gai. iv. § 79: Cum autem filiusfamilias ex noxali causa mancipio datur, diversae scholae auctores putant, ter eum mancipio dari debere, quia lege XII tabularum cautum sit, ne filius de postestate patris aliter exeat, quam si ter fuerit mancipatus: Sabinus et Cassius ceterique nostrae scholae auctores, sufficere unam mancipationem crediderunt, et illas tres legis XII tabularum ad voluntarias mancipationes pertinere.[1]

'Mancipium' is terminated by remancipation and by release, but not by the death of the master.

Gai. i. §§ 138–140: Ii qui in causa mancipii sunt, quia servorum loco habentur, vindicta censu testamento manumissi sui iuris fiunt. § Nec tamen in hoc casu lex Aelia Sentia locum habet. —§ Quin etiam invito quoque eo cuius in mancipio sunt, censu libertatem consequi possunt, excepto eo quem pater ea lege mancipio dedit, ut sibi remancipetur; nam quodammodo tunc pater potestatem propriam reservare sibi videtur eo ipso quod mancipio recipit. Ac ne is quidem dicitur invito eo, cuius in mancipio est, censu libertatem consequi, quem pater ex noxali causa mancipio dedit, veluti quod furti eius nomine damnatus est et eum mancipio actori dedit: nam hunc actor pro pecunia habet.[2]

---

[1] But when a *fil. fam.* is given up by mancipation, on the ground of a wrongful act, the leaders of the opposite school consider that he ought thrice to be given by mancipation, because by a law of the Twelve Tables it has been provided that, unless a son be thrice mancipated, he shall not pass out of paternal power. Sab. and Cass. and the other leaders of our school supposed that one mancipation is enough, and that the three mancipations derived from the Twelve Tables relate to such as are voluntary.

[2] Inasmuch as those in the condition of *mancipia* are regarded as in the position of slaves, they become *sui iuris* when manu-

Book II. Part I.

Coll. ii. 3: Per hominem liberum noxae deditum si tantum adquisitum sit, quantum damni dedit, manumittere cogendus est a praetore qui noxae deditum accepit.—(Papin.)[1]

§ 56. Capitis diminutio.

The legal personality, *i.e.*, in general the civil existence, of the civis Romanus, especially the personality of the individual under Private Law as bearer of a concrete aggregate of rights, is designated by the expression 'caput.' The caput of the individual is annexed to his status,[a] that is, conditioned and determined by three prerequisites: Freedom, Citizenship, Family position.[b] Every change in one of these three relations personally experienced by the civis Romanus also operates destructively upon his existing aggregate of rights, and, as the destruction of his existing personality, is called 'capitis di- [or de] minutio.' According as the freedom or the citizenship of which that is the condition, or the family position which is conditioned by the citizenship, alone as prerequisite of the legal position is lost, a distinction is made between 'capitis

[a] § 33.

[b] *I.e.*, belonging to a certain *familia* as 'persona sui iuris,' or 'alieno iuri subiecta.'

mitted by *vindicta*, census or testament. Nor does the *l. Aelia Sentia* apply to their case; nay more, they may obtain freedom by the *census* even against the will of the person who holds them *in mancipio*, except him whom the father has given by *mancipium* upon condition that he is remancipated; for in such a case the father is considered in some way to reserve his own power from the very fact that he receives him back from *mancipium*; and it is said, too, that he cannot obtain freedom by the census against the will of the person holding him *in mancipio*, whose father gave him by mancipation upon the ground of a wrongful act; for instance, when the father has on his account been condemned in an action of theft, and has surrendered him to the plaintiff, for the plaintiff holds him in lieu of money.

[1] If any one have obtained through a freeman surrendered for an injury as much as the injury that was done amounted to, the praetor who received the man so surrendered must require such person to emancipate him.

diminutio maxima (s. magna),'[a] 'media (s. minor),'[b] and 'minima.'

[a] § 36.
[b] § 39, ad init.

Paul.: **Capitis deminutionis** tria genera sunt: maxima, media, minima; tria enim sunt, quae habemus: libertatem, civitatem, familiam. Igitur cum omnia haec amittimus, hoc est libertatem et civitatem et familiam, **maximam** esse capitis deminutionem; cum vero amittimus civitatem, libertatem retinemus, **mediam** esse capitis deminutionem, cum et libertas et civitas retinetur, familia tantum mutatur, **minimam** esse capitis deminutionem constat.—l. 11, D. h. t. (=de cap. min. 4, 5).[1]

Gai. i. §§ 159–60: Est autem capitis diminutio prioris status permutatio; eaque tribus modis accidit.—Maxima est capitis deminutio, cum aliquis simul et civitatem et libertatem amittit.[2]

Whilst the capitis diminutio 'maxima' and 'media' plainly destroy the caput of a Roman citizen (and so personality or legal capacity in general, or only that according to ius civile), the 'minima' capitis diminutio is the mere destruction of the existing caput, the place of which is taken by another, so that he who is affected by it is acounted by Civil Law as a new private Person. A 'minima' capitis diminutio is experienced by such as without loss of citizenship (by an event affecting himself) exchanges his status for a new one, and loses his position in the existing familia;

---

[1] There are three orders of loss of status, greatest, intermediate, and least; for we have three things: liberty, citizenship, and family rights. When accordingly we lose all three, that is *libertas*, *civitas*, and *familia*, it is the greatest loss of status; when we lose citizenship, [but] retain freedom, there is the intermediate loss of status; but if freedom and citizenship are retained and family rights alone lost, that is the least loss of status.

[2] Now *capitis diminutio* is a change of one's former status, and this happens in three ways.—There is the greatest *cap. dem.* when a person at the same time loses both citizenship and liberty.

Book II. Part I.

and it is immaterial whether his legal position is thereby actually improved or impaired. This happens when a 'persona sui iuris' is subjected to some one's patria potestas;[a] or if a person subject to Power becomes sui iuris by an act of Civil Law, and so forms for himself a new familia;[b] or if a person subject to Power passes into the Family Power of another.[c]

[a] Arrogation, *in manum conventio* of the woman free from Power.

[b] Emancipation, *manumissio ex mancipio*: cf. Gell. 1, 12, 9 and 13 (§ 53).

[c] Adoption, arrogation in respect of the children of the one arrogated, *mancipatio*, in *manum conventio* of the *filiafamilias*: cf. § 49.

Gai. i. § 162: Minima capitis diminutio est, cum et civitas et libertas retinetur, sed status hominis commutatur; quod accidit in his qui adoptantur, item in his quae coemptionem faciunt, et in his qui mancipio dantur, quique ex mancipatione manumittuntur: adeo quidem ut quotiens quisque mancipetur aut manumittatur, totiens capite diminuatur.[1]

Liberos qui adrogatum parentem sequuntur, placet minui caput, cum in aliena potestate sint et cum familiam mutaverint. § Emancipato filio et ceteris personis capitis minutio manifesto accidit, cum emancipari nemo possit, nisi in imaginariam servilem causam deductus; aliter atque cum servus manumittitur, quia servile caput nullum ius habet ideoque nec minui potest:—hodie enim incipit statum habere.—l. 3 (Paul.), l. 4 (Mod.), D. h. t.[2]

---

[1] There is the least abatement of status when both citizenship and liberty are retained, but the status of the individual is changed, which happens in the case of those who are adopted, likewise in the case of those who perform a coemption, and in the case of those who are given by *mancipium*, and those that are manumitted after mancipation; so that indeed as often as a man is mancipated or is manumitted, so often does he suffer an abatement of status.

[2] It is held that children who follow their arrogated parent experience an abatement of status, since they are under the power of another, and have changed their family. An abatement of status plainly befalls an emancipated son and other persons, since no one can be emancipated save as he is ostensibly led away into servitude. It is otherwise when a slave is

Book II. Part I.

Gai. iii. § 153: —civili ratione capitis diminutio morti coaequatur.[1]

Next, as to the effect of capitis diminutio.

(1) In general: the 'maxima' and 'media' destroy all legal relations dependent upon freedom or citizenship, whilst by capitis diminutio 'minima' only such relations are terminated as, arising out of Civil Law, depend upon the earlier family status.

Ulp.: Servitutem mortalitati fere comparamus. —D. 50, 17, 209.[2]

Id.: —deportatos mortuorum loco habendos. D. 37, 4, 1, 8.[3]

Inst. i. 16, 6: Si maxima capitis deminutio incurrat, ius quoque cognationis perit. . . . Sed et si in insulam deportatus quis sit, cognatio solvitur.[4]

Ulp.: Capitis minutio[a] privata hominis et familiae eius iura, non civitatis amittit.—l. 6, D. h. t.[5]

[a] Sc. minima.

Paul.: Si libertate adempta capitis deminutio subsecuta sit, nulli restitutioni adversus servum locus est, quia nec praetoris iurisdictione ita servus obligatur, ut cum eo actio sit. Sed utilis actio adversus dominum danda est, ut Iulianus scribit, et nisi in solidum defendatur, permittendum mihi est in bona quae habuit mitti.—l. 7, § 2 eod.[6]

---

manumitted, because a slave has no right, consequently can suffer no abatement of status—for on the day [of the manumission] he begins to have a status.

[1] By the doctrine of the *ius civile*, loss of status is tantamount to death.

[2] See p. 168.

[3] Persons deported must be regarded as dead.

[4] If the highest degree of abatement of status take place, cognatic rights also are destroyed. Indeed, if a man have been deported to an island, cognatic relationship is extinguished.

[5] The [*i.e.*, lowest] abatement of status works the loss of a man's private and family rights, not that of citizenship.

[6] If an abatement of status have ensued from deprivation of

Book II. Part I.

(2) Particular effects of the minima capitis diminutio are: the destruction of the existing agnatic relationship, although without attainment of rights of agnation in the new familia;[a] the extinction of certain rights[b] and the destruction of claims ex iure civili[c] against the 'capite minutus'; but in the latter respect the Praetorian Edict aided by renewed grant of actions against the person, and by the grant of real execution against his property, although he had ceased to be a personal debtor.[d]

[a] Gai. i. 136, § 55.
[b] Gai. iii. 114.
[c] But not claims *ex delicto*.
[d] D. 4, 5, 2, 1; Gai. iii. 83. Cf. also D. 15, 1, 42, 4, 5, 2, 2.

Gai. i. § 158: Sed adgnationis quidem ius capitis diminutione perimitur, cognationis vero ius eo modo non commutatur: quia civilis ratio civilia quidem iura corrumpere potest, naturalia vero non potest.[1]

Ibid. § 83: —per capitis diminutionem pereunt (quales sunt) ususfructus, operarum obligatio libertorum, quae per iusiurandum contracta est, et lites contestatae [constituto?] legitimo iudicio.[2]

Ibid. § 84: —de eo vero quod proprio nomine eae personae debuerint, licet neque pater adoptivus teneatur, neque coemptionator, neque ipse quidem qui se in adoptionem dedit quaeve in manum convenit, maneat obligatus obligatave, quia scilicet per capitis diminutionem liberetur, tamen in eum eamve utilis actio datur rescissa capitis diminutione, et si adversus hanc actionem non defen-

---

freedom, restitution does not obtain against a slave, because not even by the praetor's jurisdiction is a slave under obligation, for an action to lie against him. But, as Jul. writes, an equitable[e] action should be given against the master, and unless he is defended in respect of the whole, I must be allowed to assume possession of the effects that belonged to him.

[e] Or 'analogous': cf. Abdy and Walker on Inst. ii. 1, 34

[1] But while the right of agnation is destroyed by *cap. dim.*, the right of cognation is not so changed; for though a doctrine of *ius civile* can impair civil, it cannot destroy natural rights.

[2] —things that perish through *cap. dim.* (such as) usufruct, an undertaking for services of freedmen which has been contracted by oath, and the joinder of issues by (the obtaining of) a *legitimum iudicium*.

dantur, quae bona eorum futura fuissent, si se alieno iuri non subiecissent, universa vendere creditoribus praetor permittit.[1]

Id. iv. § 38: Praeterea aliquando fingimus, adversarium nostrum capite diminutum non esse; nam si ex contractu nobis obligatus obligatave sit et capite diminutus diminutave fuerit, veluti mulier per coemptionem masculus per adrogationem, desinit iure civili debere nobis, nec directo intendi potest, 'sibi dare eum eamve oportere': sed ne in potestate eius sit ius nostrum corrumpere, introducta est contra eum eamve actio utilis rescissa capitis diminutione, i.e. in qua fingitur capite diminutus diminutave non esse.[2]

§ 57. Civic Reputation. *Infamia.*

Civic Reputation is the public appreciation and recognition of his dignity, to which every man has claim as a Person and a member of the State. The basis of full civic reputation, as of full capacity for rights, in Roman Law is Citizenship. Loss of citizenship, coupled with

---

[1] But with regard to debts which such persons owed on their own account, although neither the adoptive father nor the *coemptionator* is liable, and neither the man who has given himself in adoption nor the woman who has come under *manus* remain liable, as being relieved by the *cap. dim.*, yet an analogous action is granted against him or her, the *cap. dim.* being cancelled; and if no defence is put in for them against this action, the praetor allows the crediters to sell all the effects that would have been theirs if they had not subjected themselves to another's authority.

[2] Moreover, we sometimes employ the fiction that our opponent has not experienced *cap. dim.*; for if any man or woman be bound to us on a contract, and suffer *cap. dim.*, as a woman by coemption, or a man by arrogation, the person is no longer under liability to us by the *i. c.*, nor can it be directly maintained 'that he or she ought to give'; but to prevent either of them impairing our right, a *utilis actio* has been invented as against him or her, their *cap. dim.* being cancelled; *i.e.*, one in which there is a fiction that he or she has not experienced *cap. dim.*

BOOK II. Part I.

capital punishment, carries with it also the loss of Roman honour. But, besides, any man's civic reputation can be merely diminished, so that he retains citizenship, though it is curtailed as to some rights: this abatement of reputation, which arises by virtue of a legal precept, is INFAMY. The legal conception of 'infamia' rests essentially upon habit and custom, the recognition and operation of which were especially procured by the censors by means of their official power,[a] as well as by the other magistrates in the conduct of elections and the decision appertaining to that upon qualification to vote, and in legal sentences; it attained full development in the Praetorian Edict.[b]

[a] *Nota censoria, tribu movere,*—limited in operation to the period of the censor's service.

[b] And in the l. Iulia municip. (§ 7).

From 'infamia' must be distinguished the mere *de facto* abatement of honour, which consists in reproachable conduct or ill-repute of a person (turpitudo, ignominia, turpis persona). This is not a legal conception, and comes into question jurally alone when the judge or magistrate, in some decision or ordinance, has to take into account the moral character of such person.

> Callistr.: **Existimatio** est dignitatis illaesae status legibus ac moribus comprobatus, qui ex delicto nostro auctoritate legum aut minuitur aut consumitur. § **Minuitur** existimatio, quotiens manente libertate circa statum dignitatis poena plectimur, sicuti cum relegatur quis . . . vel cum in eam causam quis incidit, quae edicto perpetuo infamiae causa enumeratur. § **Consumitur** vero, quotiens magna capitis deminutio intervenit, veluti cum aqua et igni interdicitur.—D. 50, 13, 5, §§ 1–3.[1]

[1] Reputation is the condition of unimpaired dignity, established by laws and customs, which, by virtue of the laws, is either lessened or destroyed by our fault. § Reputation is lessened whenever, while retaining our freedom, we suffer penal punishment in respect of the status appertaining to our dignity; as when a man is banished . . . or when any one lapses into that condition which, in the perpetual edict, is assigned as a cause of infamy. § But it is destroyed whenever great abatement of status occurs, as when a person is interdicted fire and water.

Gell. xv. 13, § 11: Item ex XII tabulis id est: QVI SE SIERIT TESTARIER LIBRIPENSVE FVERIT, NI TESTIMONIVM FARIATVR, INPROBVS INTESTABILISQVE ESTO.[1]

Gai.: Cum lege quis intestabilis iubetur esse, eo pertinet, ne eius testimonium recipiatur, et eo amplius, ut quidam putant, neve ipsi dicatur testimonium.—D. 28, 1, 26.[2]

The ground of 'infamia' is always conduct dishonourable according to Roman sentiment. As regards particular cases of infamy, it sometimes appears as the immediate result of certain notorious, dishonourable acts or conditions;[a] at other times, as the effect of a judicial sentence (actiones famosae) or magisterial decree.

[a] Ulp. xiii. 1, 2.

Ulp.: **Probrum et opprobrium** idem est; probra quaedam natura turpia sunt, quaedam civiliter et quasi more civitatis: ut puta furtum, adulterium natura turpe est; enimvero tutelae damnari, hoc non natura probrum est, sed more civitatis: nec enim natura probrum est quod potest etiam in hominem idoneum incidere.—D. 50, 16, 42.[3]

Praetoris verba dicunt: INFAMIA NOTATVR

---

[1] And so it is according to the Twelve Tables: 'He that shall allow himself to be summoned as a witness or shall be balance-holder, in default of his vouching as witness, shall be a marked man and incapable of acting as a witness.

[2] When a man is by statute declared to be incapable of testation, that comprehends the non-reception of his testimony, and more than that, as some are of opinion that testimony neither should be given in his own favour.

[3] *Probrum* and *opprobrium* are the same. Some outrageous acts are by Nature disgraceful, some according to the *ius civile*, and, as it were, by the custom of the State; *e.g.*, theft and adultery are by Nature disgraceful, but to be condemned in the action of guardianship is not by Nature outrageous, but is according to the custom of the State; for indeed that is not by Nature outrageous which can even befall an upright man.

Book II. Part I.

(1) QVI AB EXERCITV IGNOMINIAE CAVSA AB IMPERATORE EOVE, CVI DE EA RE STATVENDI POTESTAS FVERIT, DIMISSVS ERIT; (2) QVI AR TIS LVDICRAE PRONVNTIANDIVE CAVSA IN SCAENAM PRODIERIT: QVI LENOCINIVM FECERIT; (3) QVI IN IVDICIO PVBLICO CALVMNIAE PRAE VARICATIONISVE CAVSA QVID FECISSE IVDICATVS ERIT; (4) QVI FVRTI, VI BONORVM RAPTORVM, INIVRIARVM, DE DOLO MALO ET FRAVDE SVO NOMINE DAMNATVS PACTVSVE ERIT; QVI PRO SOCIO, [FIDVCIAE,] TVTELAE, MANDATI, DEPOSITI SVO NOMINE NON CONTRARIO IVDICIO DAMNATVS ERIT; (5) QVI EAM, QVAE IN POTESTATE EIVS ESSET, GENERO MORTVO, CVM EVM MORTVVM ESSE SCIRET, INTRA ID TEMPVS, QVO ELVGERE VIRVM MORIS EST, ANTEQVAM VIRVM ELVGERET IN MATRIMONIVM COLLOCAVERIT; EAMVE SCIENS QVIS VXOREM DVXERIT NON IVSSV EIVS IN CVIVS POTESTATE EST; ET QVI EVM, QVEM IN POTESTATE HABERET, EAM DE QVA SVPRA COMPREHENSVM EST, VXOREM DVCERE PASSVS FVERIT; [QVAEVE CVM IN PARENTIS SVI POTESTATE NON ESSET, VIRO MORTVO, CVM EVM MORTVVM ESSE SCIRET, INTRA ID TEMPVS, QVO ELVGERE VIRVM MORIS EST, NVPSERIT;] (6) QVIVE SVO NOMINE, NON IVSSV EIVS IN CVIVS POTESTATE ESSET, EIVSVE NOMINE QVEM QVAMVE IN POTESTATE HABERET, BINA SPONSALIA BINASVE NVPTIAS IN EODEM TEMPORE CONSTITVTAS HABVERIT.—D. 3, 2, 1 (cf. Vat. Fgm. § 320).[1]

[1] The words of the Praetor run: 'He is marked with the brand of infamy (1) who shall be dismissed from the army because of disgrace, by the general, or by such person as shall have power to deal with such matter; (2) who shall take to the stage for pantomimes or declamation; who shall carry on the business of a procurer; (3) who in a public trial shall be condemned for having done something for the sake of chicanery and collusion; (4) who hath been or shall be condemned in his own name, or as having entered into an agreement upon the ground of theft, of robbery, offences against personal reputation, fraud and deceit; who in his own name, and not by the

—QVEIVE LEGE PLAETORIA OB EAMVE REM, QVOD ADVERSVS EAM LEGEM FECIT FECERIT, CONDEMNATVS EST ERIT; . . . QVOIVSVE BONA EX EDICTO . . . POSSESSA PROSCRIPTAVE SVNT ERVNT. —Lex Iulia municip. c. 25.[1]

The effect of infamy was especially and essentially one of Public Law; the 'infamis' was divested of citizenship in its political significance, *i.e.*, he lost the 'ius suffragii et honorum,' and indeed eligibility not only for offices of the State and commonwealth, but also for the senate and decurionatus. With respect to Private Law, infamy limited the right to the 'postulare.'

Ulp.: **Postulare** autem est, desiderium suum vel amici sui in iure apud eum qui iurisdictioni praeest; exponere vel alterius desiderio contradicere.—Hoc edicto continentur etiam omnes, qui edicto praetoris ut infames notantur; qui

counter-claim, shall be condemned upon a contract of partnership [of pledge], of guardianship, of commission, of deposit; (5) he that shall marry a woman who was under his power after the death of his son-in-law, upon knowing of his death, within the period in which the custom is to mourn for the husband, and before her lamentation for the husband has taken place; or he who shall marry her while knowing that it is not by the direction of him under whose power she is; and he that shall suffer such person as he had under power to marry a woman included in the above provision; [or the woman that, while not under the power of her parent, and her husband being dead, when she knew that he was dead, shall marry within that period in which the custom is to mourn for the husband]; (6) or he that in his own name, not by the direction of the person in whose power he was, or in the name of him or her whom he had in power, has contracted two betrothals or two marriages at the same time.

[1] 'Or he that has been or shall be condemned by the *l. Praetoria*, or because he has done or shall do what is contrary to that *lex* . . . or whosesoever goods are or shall be possessed or proscribed according to the Edict.

Book II. Part I.

omnes nisi pro se et certis personis ne postulent. —D. 3, 1, l. 1, §§ 2, 8.[1]

Paul. i. 2, 1: Omnes infames, qui postulare prohibentur, cognitores fieri non possunt, etiam volentibus adversariis.[2]

Infamy operated also as a relative obstacle to marriage;[a] but in the Justinianean Law it lost for the most part all practical application.[b]

[a] § 45.

[b] For the application given by the Modern Law to the Roman doctrines as to the capacity for rights of natural Persons, see Arndts, 'Lehrbuch der Pandekten,' § 32.

CHAPTER II.

CAPACITY TO ACT.

§ 58. In General.

Capacity to act, in contrast with capacity for rights,[c] is that capacity recognised by Law of a person to undertake acts with juristic effect; and so, himself to declare the legal will that belongs to him as a Person. The general prerequisite of capacity to act is the natural faculty of will of the person (natural capacity to act); but juristic capacity to act requires besides as special element a comprehension, inherent in the person, of the meaning and purpose of the legal act to be undertaken. According as the one or the other is wanting, we speak of full or of limited capacity to act. In both cases the person needs a representative who

[c] *Supra*, § 32.

---

[1] Now *postulare* is, for a man to make his claim or that of his client, or to gainsay the claim of the other party, before the court and in the presence of him who administers the Law.—In this edict all persons, besides, are included who are branded as *infames* by the Praetorian Edict; none of whom shall make any claim save for themselves and certain persons.

[2] All persons under infamy, who are forbidden to make claims, are unable to become representatives, even if the opponent consent.

supplements his will, but the species of representation is variable; whilst in the first case the representative constantly makes known his will instead of the one incapable to act, in the latter case it is the person represented who himself undertakes the act, and the business of the representative is limited to a concurrence which supplements the imperfect declaration of will and affords it legal operation.

GROUNDS OF IMPERFECT CAPACITY TO ACT.

§ 59. Sex.

Equal private capacity to act of the male and female sex forms the rule in Roman Law.[a]

> Ulp.: Verbum hoc '**si quis**' tam masculos quam feminas complectitur.—D. 50, 16, 1.[1]

[a] But see Cic. Top. 4, 18; Gai. i. 115, and ii. 274; Paul. iv. 8, 22; Inst. i. 11, 10, § 63, ad init.

But women, with respect to the 'pudicitia sexui congruens' and the 'sexus fragilitas,' in some jural relations are disregarded, as on the other hand favoured.

> Papin.: In multis iuris nostri articulis deterior est condicio feminarum quam masculorum.—D. 1, 5, 9.[2]
>
> Ulp.: Feminae ab omnibus officiis civilibus vel publicis remotae sunt; et ideo nec iudices esse possunt, nec magistratum gerere, nec postulare, nec pro alio intervenire, nec procuratores existere.—D. 50, 17, l. 2 pr.[3]
>
> Liv. 34, 2, 11: Maiores nostri nullam, ne privatam quidem rem agere feminas sine tutore

[1] This expression 'si quis' embraces both males and females.

[2] In many parts of our Law the position of women is less advantageous than that of men.

[3] Women are entirely excluded from the rendering of civil or public services; and thus can neither be *iudices* nor exercise a magisterial office, nor make judicial applications nor appear for another, nor hold the position of *procuratores*.

Book II. Part I.

auctore voluerunt, in manu esse parentum, fratrum, virorum.[1]

§ 60. Age.[a]

[a] See Brown, s.v.; Westlake, pp. 43-46.

In Roman Law the following degrees of age are of importance with respect to capacity to act:—

'Pubertas' (qualified majority), introducing full capacity to act.[b]

[b] See Bell, s.v.

(1) Accounted as 'Puberes' (mulieres viripotentes)—in contrast with 'impuberes,' 'pupilli'—are persons of the male sex who have completed their fourteenth year, and of the female sex who have completed their twelfth year. There originally existed in respect of the male sex no fixed limit of age for the commencement of puberty: this was determined by the assumption of the 'toga virilis,' which was subject to the discretion of the family of the minor; it commonly took place upon his entering on natural puberty,—in the course of the fifteenth year (vesticeps).[c] When, with the decline of this custom, practical necessity required in lieu of such capricious act other regulation of the limits of minority, there arose a controversy upon it between the Schools—especially with regard to the termination of guardianship—which was only disposed of by Justinian.

[c] Cf. Gell. v. 19, 7.

> Ulp. xi. 28: Puberem autem Cassiani quidem eum esse dicunt, qui habitu corporis pubes apparet, i.e. qui generare possit; Proculeiani autem eum, qui quattuordecim annos explevit; verum Prisco visum, eum puberem esse, in quem utrumque concurrit, et habitus corporis et numerus annorum.[2]

---

[1] Our ancestors willed that women should transact no matter, not even a private one, without the concurrence of a guardian, [and] should be in the *manus* of their parents, brothers, husbands.

[2] Now the Cassians state that he has reached puberty who appears to have done so from his bodily condition, *i.e.*, who is

Book II. Part I.

Inst. i. 22 pr.: Nostra autem maiestas dignum esse castitate temporum nostrorum bene putavit, quod in feminis et antiquis impudicum esse visum est, i.e. inspectionem habitudinis corporis, hoc etiam in masculos extendere: et ideo sancta constitutione promulgata pubertatem in masculis post quartum decimum annum completum ilico initium accipere disposuimus, antiquitatis normam in feminis personis bene positam suo ordine relinquentes, ut post duodecimum annum completum viripotentes esse credantur.[1]

(2) 'Impuberes' are divided into

(α) 'infantes,' children under seven years, and

(β) 'infantia maiores.'

The former are altogether incapable to act, the latter act in their own person with the concurrence (auctoritas) of the guardian, and are moreover capable of acquiring rights by independent legal acts, but cannot alienate, neither can they bind themselves.[a]

Paul.: In negotiis contrahendis alia causa habita est furiosorum, alia eorum qui fari possunt, quamvis actum rei non intelligerent: nam furiosus nullum negotium contrahere potest, pupillus omnia tutore auctore agere potest.—l. 5, D. de R. J. 50, 17.[2]

[a] D. 19, 1, 13, 29; 46, 3, 148; 46, 6, 6; Gai. ii. 82; Ulp. xx. 12-3; *infra*, § 151.

---

able to beget children; the Proculians, however, say that he has done so who has completed his fourteenth year; but Priscus considered that he only is of puberty in whom both these points combine, bodily condition, and number of years.

[1] We have in our imperial character considered it in keeping with the decorum of our times, that what already our ancestors regarded as immodest in the case of women, *i.e.*, the examination of their person, we extend to males also; and therefore, by the promulgation of a sacred constitution, we have settled that puberty in the case of males begin immediately after the completion of the fourteenth year, allowing the old rule to stand with regard to females as well founded, so that they should be regarded as marriageable after completion of their twelfth year.

[2] In business contracts the relation of lunatics is regarded as different from that of those who are already able to speak,

Gai. iii. §§ 107, 109: Pupillus . . . alium sibi obligare etiam sine tutoris auctoritate potest. —infans et qui infanti proximus est, non multum a furioso differt, quia huius aetatis pupilli nullum intellectum habent.[1]

Id.: Pupillus licet ex quo fari coeperit, recte stipulari potest, tamen si in parentis potestate est, ne auctore quidem patre obligatur.—l. 141, § 2, D. de V. O. 45, 1.[2]

Gai. ii. §§ 83, 84: —pupillis . . . meliorem condicionem suam facere etiam sine tutoris auctoritate concessum est. § Itaque si debitor pecuniam pupillo solvat, facit quidem pecuniam pupilli, sed ipse non liberatur, quia nullam obligationem pupillus sine tutoris auctoritate dissolvere potest . . . , sed tamen si ex ea pecunia locupletior factus sit et adhuc petat, per exceptionem doli summoveri potest.[3]

(3) No fixed limit of age underlies the distinction of 'infantiae proximi' and 'pubertati prox.' ('doli capaces') with respect to the capacity for delict of 'infantia maiores.'

Gai.: Pupillum, qui proximus pubertati sit,

---

although they do not yet understand the transaction of the matter; for a lunatic can enter into no business engagement, whilst a ward can transact anything under the authorisation of his guardian.

[1] A ward . . . can bind another towards himself even without the concurrence of his guardian. . . . An infant and a child bordering on infancy do not differ much from a lunatic, because wards of this age lack understanding.

[2] Although a ward can legally stipulate from the time that he has begun to speak, yet if he be under parental power, he does not incur liability even with the sanction of the father.

[3] Wards are allowed to improve their condition even without their guardian's concurrence. Therefore, if a debtor pay money to a ward, he makes the money the ward's, but he is not himself released, because a ward can dissolve no obligation without his guardian's concurrence . . . but if he have become richer by such money, and yet sue for it, he can be met by a plea of fraud.

capacem esse et furandi et iniuriae faciendae.—l. 111 pr., D. de R. J.[1]

Ulp.: Iulianus saepissime scripsit, doli pupillos, qui prope pubertatem sunt, capaces esse.—D. 44, 4, 4, 26.[2]

'Maior aetas' (majority), beginning with the completion of the twenty-fifth year; according to which, *puberes* are divided into 'maiores' and 'minores XXV annis,' or those of full age and minors. This limit of age only acquired juristic importance after the l. Plaetoria (aetas legitima).[a] The capacity to act of 'puberes' is limited alone in respect of the maintenance of actions (litis curator) and also, in case they have a curator, in respect of alienatory transactions; on the other hand, they can always validly bind themselves,[b] since entry into obligations does not at all suppose the possession of property,[c] much less independent right of disposition.[d] Moreover, a minor can obtain the legal standing of a full-aged person by imperial grant (venia aetatis).

[a] § 30. For the *curatela* of minors which connected itself with this, see § 67.

[b] Perhaps merely by *ius civile.*

[c] Cf. § 50, ad fin.

[d] See also § 114.

Inst. i. 23 pr.: Masculi puberes et feminae viripotentes usque ad vicesimum quintum annum completum, . . . licet puberes sint, adhuc tamen huius aetatis sunt, ut negotia sua tueri non possint.[3]

Ulp.: Et ideo hodie in hanc usque aetatem adulescentes curatorum auxilio reguntur, nec ante rei suae administratio eis committi debebit, quamvis bene rem suam gerentibus.—D. 4, 4, 1, 3.[4]

---

[1] That a ward who borders upon puberty is capable both of theft and of inflicting insult.

[2] Jul. has very frequently written that wards who are near to puberty are capable of fraud.

[3] *Puberes* of the male sex and marriageable females, until they have completed their twenty-fifth year, . . . although they are of puberty, are still of such an age that they cannot look after their own concerns.

[4] And so nowadays young people are up to this age regulated by the help of curators, nor ought the administration of

BOOK II. Part I.

Mod.: Puberes sine curatoribus suis possunt ex stipulatu obligari.—l. 101, D. de V. O.[1]

Paul.: Obligari potest paterfamilias suae potestatis: pubes compos mentis.—D. 44, 7, 43.[2]

[a] Cf. *supra*.

Gai.: —[a] pubes vero qui in potestate est, proinde ac si paterfamilias, obligari solet.—l. 141, § 2, de V. O.[3]

§ 61. Infirmity. Prodigality.

[b] § 45. As to *castrat*, see Inst. i. 11, 9.

[c] D. 45, 1, 1, and Ulp. xx. 13.

Physical condition has in general no influence upon capacity to act, but the undertaking of a juristic act can for a time be hindered by infirmity (morbus sonticus). Corporal defects incapacitate for such jural acts as suppose integrity of the body; and so for instance, impotence for marriage,[b] or blindness, deafness and dumbness, for legal transactions which require seeing, hearing and speaking.[c]

Mod.: Verum est, **morbum** esse temporalem corporis imbecillitatem, **vitium** vero perpetuum corporis impedimentum.—D. 50, 16, 101, 2.[4]

Iul.: **Sonticus** autem existimandus est, cui cuiusque rei agendae impedimento est.—D. 42, 1, 60.[5]

[d] See Brown, s. 'Lunatic;' Paterson, p. 265; Westlake, pp. 47-48.

[e] D. 9, 2, 5, 2.

Those suffering from mental disease, or the insane and imbeciles [d] (furiosi, dementes, fatui), are absolutely unable to act, and are therefore also incapable of delict.[e]

---

their own estate to be entrusted to them earlier, although they otherwise manage their affairs well.

[1] *Puberes* can be made liable upon a stipulation even independently of their curators.

[2] A *pat. fam.*, being his own master, can become liable, who is of the age of puberty and in possession of his reason.

[3] Now a *pubes* who is under power is wont to become liable just as a *pat. fam.*

[4] It is true that sickness is a temporary weakness of the body but crime a perpetual obstruction to the body.

[5] Now every sickness is to be regarded as severe which is an obstacle to the performance of any matter.

Pomp.: Furiosi . . . nulla voluntas est.—D. 50, 17, 40.[1]

Gai. iii. § 106: Furiosus nullum negotium gerere potest, quia non intelligit quid agat.[2]

Ulp.: Qui furere coepit, et statum et dignitatem, in qua fuit, et potestatem videtur retinere, sicut rei suae dominium retinet.—D. 1, 5, 20.[3]

But this does not apply to so-called lucid intervals (dilucida intervalla).

Imp. Iustinian.: Sancimus, . . . per intervalla, quae perfectissima sunt, nihil curatorem agere, sed ipsum posse furiosum, dum sapit, et hereditatem adire et omnia alia facere, quae sanis hominibus competunt.—C. 5, 70, 6.[4]

Imp. Diocl.: Intermissionis tempore furiosos . . . venditiones et alios quoslibet contractus posse facere, non ambigitur.—C. 4, 38, 2.[5]

Prodigality, or dissipation, likewise is treated as a kind of mental infirmity or immaturity. A 'prodigus' is one deprived by magisterial decree of the management of his property because of dissipation.

Ulp.: Lege XII tabularum prodigo interdicitur bonorum suorum administratio; quod moribus quidem ab initio introductum est.—D. 27, 10, 1 pr.[6]

---

[1] A lunatic possesses no will.

[2] A lunatic can transact no business, because he does not understand what he is doing.

[3] He that becomes insane retains both his personal condition and the dignity with which he was invested, and is considered to retain his *potestas*, just as he retains the ownership of his property.

[4] We enact that . . . during the intervals which are most perfect, the curator shall not act, but that the lunatic himself can, so long as he has his reason, both enter upon an inheritance and do all things else that are competent to men of sound mind.

[5] There is no doubt that during the interval lunatics can effect sales and all other contracts they please.

[6] By the Law of the Twelve Tables the spendthrift is for-

Book II. Part I.

Paul. iii. 4[a], § 7: Moribus per praetorem bonis interdicitur hoc modo: QVANDO TIBI (?) BONA PATERNA AVITAQVE NEQVITIA TVA DISPERDIS, LIBEROSQVE TVOS AD EGESTATEM PERDVCIS, OB EAM REM TIBI EA RE COMMERCIOQVE INTERDICO.[1]

Gai. i. § 53: —male enim nostro iure uti non debemus: qua ratione et prodigis interdicitur bonorum suorum administratio.[2]

With respect to the capacity to act, he is in all respects on the same footing as the 'impubes infantia maior,'[a] apart from the auctoritas of the guardian, which is impossible in his case.[b]

[a] § 60.

[b] Cf. § 67.

Ulp.: Is cui bonis interdictum est, stipulando sibi adquirit; tradere vero non potest, vel promittendo obligari.—D. 45, 1, 6.[3]

Id.: Iulianus scribit, eos quibus per Praetorem bonis interdictum est, nihil transferre posse ad aliquem, quia in bonis non habeant, cum eis deminutio sit interdicta.—D. 27, 10, 10.[4]

AID SUPPLIED BY GUARDIANSHIP TO DEFECTIVE CAPACITY TO ACT.

§ 62. Nature and Species of Guardianship.[c]

[c] See 'Anct. Law,' pp. 160-162; Steph. ii. 304-316; Bell, s. 'Tutor' and 'Curatory;' Westlake, *ubi sup.*

Guardianship is the right of protection, subject to

bidden the administration of his property; and this was originally introduced by custom.

[1] An interdict is attached to a right course of conduct by the Praetor thus: 'Since you by vice waste property derived from your father and grandfather, and are bringing your children to penury, I do therefore forbid your engaging in that transaction and in business.'

[2] —for we must not make a bad use of our right; and upon this principle also are spendthrifts forbidden the management of their property.

[3] He who has been forbidden the control of his property, acquires by stipulation; but he cannot alienate, or be rendered liable by promise.

[4] Jul. writes that they who are by the Praetor forbidden the control of their property can make over nothing to anybody, because they have nothing in ownership, since they have been forbidden the diminution thereof.

public authority, by a private person of 'personae sui iuris' entirely or partially incapable to act, for the purpose of supplementing their defective capacity, and for the maintenance of their property. It was originally a relation of Power—analogous to patria potestas—certainly based upon 'fides,' and to be exercised in the interest of the ward; and was therefore a private (family) right;[a] but in time it was converted into a public office (manus publicum), to undertake which was a duty (onus).

[a] Cf. § 64, *legitima tutela;* also § 66, and D. 26, 7, 27.

Gai. i. § 189: Sed impuberes quidem in tutela esse, omnium civitatum iure contingit: quia id naturali rationi conveniens est, ut is, qui perfectae aetatis non sit, alterius tutela regatur.[1]

Paul.: Tutela est, ut Servius definit, vis ac potestas in capite libero ad tuendum eum, qui propter aetatem sua sponte se defendere nequit, iure civili data ac permissa.—l. 1 pr., D. de tut. 26, 1.[2]

Gell. v. 13: —constabat, ex moribus populi Romani primum iuxta parentes locum tenere pupillos debere, fidei tutelaeque nostrae creditos.[3]

—et tutelam et curam placuit publicum munus esse.—pr. I. de excus. 1, 25.[4]

—plerumque ubi successionis est emolumentum, ibi et tutelae onus esse debet.—tit. I. de leg. patron. 1, 17.[5]

---

[1] But that those under the age of puberty should be in tutelage, happens to be the law of all communities, because it accords with natural reason that he who is not of full age should be controlled by the tutelage of another.

[2] Tutelage is, according to the definition of Servius, a power and control over a free person, given and allowed by the *i. c.*, for the charge of one who by reason of age cannot independently protect himself.

[3] It was settled that, according to the customs of the Roman people, wards ought to have the first place alongside of parents, as confided to our trust and tutelage.

[4] It has been decided that[b] both *tutela* and *cura* are public offices.

[b] *Infra.*

[5] In most cases where there is an advantage in succession there should also be the burden of guardianship.

Book II. Part I.

Guardianship is divided into *TUTELA* of impuberes and mulieres, and *CURA* of puberes; only the first was in the ancient time endued with that character under Private Law of which we have spoken.

The most important differences between Tutela and Cura are the following—

The Tutor, for the purposes of Property Law, always represents the whole personality of his ward; a Curator can be appointed also for a particular act in the Law, as well as a particular proprietary relation. Upon the Tutor devolves especially the supplementing of the ward's defective capacity to act; the essential function of the Curator is alone the management of the property (gestio). Further, concurrence in the entry into legal transactions consists for the Tutor in the 'auctoritatis interpositio'; for the Curator it is limited to mere 'consensus.'[a]

[a] § 151, *tutoris auctoritas.*

Ulp. xi. 1: Tutores constituuntur tam masculis quam feminis; sed masculis quidem impuberibus dumtaxat propter aetatis infirmitatem; feminis autem tam impuberibus quam puberibus et propter sexus infirmitatem et propter forensium rerum ignorantiam.[1]

Inst. i. 14, 4: Certae autem rei vel causae tutor dari non potest, quia **personae non causae vel rei** datur.—Ibid. i. 25, 17: Datus autem tutor ad universum patrimonium datus esse creditur.[2]

Ibid. i. 23, 2: Curator et ad certam causam dari potest.[3]

---

[1] Tutors are appointed to both males and females; but to males only while under the age of puberty on account of their infirmity of age; to females, however, both as *puberes* and *impuberes*, as well on account of their infirmity of sex as on account of their ignorance of forensic matters.

[2] But a tutor cannot be given for a determinate thing or matter, because he is given to the person, not to the matter or thing. Now the instituted tutor is regarded as instituted for the whole property.

[3] A curator can be given also for a determinate case.

TUTELA IMPUBERUM.

§ 63. Capacity for Guardianship. *Excusationes.*

As regards the capacity to undertake guardianship, the only requisites in ancient time, as long as guardianship was still a private right of the guardian, were possession of citizenship and belonging to the male sex; in case of individual incapacity to exercise guardianship (because of immature age, bodily defects, mental infirmity), the person appointed could decline it, and another guardian was appointed in his stead.

Imp. Diocletian.: In servili condicione constitutum tutorem vel curatorem dari non posse, nullam habet iuris dubitationem.—C. 5, 34, 7.[1]

Inst. i. 14 pr., § 1: Dari autem potest tutor non solum paterfamilias sed etiam filiusfamilias. —Sed et servus proprius testamento cum libertate recte tutor dari potest.[2]

Gai.: Tutela virile officium est.—l. 16 pr., D. de tut. 26, 1.[3]

Nerat.: Feminae tutores dari non possunt, quia id munus masculorum est, nisi a principe filiorum tutelam specialiter postulent.—l. 18 eod.[4]

Nov. 118, c. 5: Mulieres etiam nos tutelae munus subire prohibemus, nisi mater vel avia

---

[1] That a man placed in the condition of a slave cannot be appointed a tutor or curator admits of no doubt in Law.

[2] As tutor can be appointed, not only a *pat. fam.*, but a *fil. fam.* also.—But one's own slave can be legally appointed tutor in the testament, with freedom.

[3] *Tutela* is a service rendered by a male.

[4] Women cannot be appointed tutors, because this is an office for males, save as they specially petition the Emperor for the *tutela* of their children.

sit. His enim solis secundum hereditatis ordinem etiam tutelam subire permittimus, si apud acta et secundis nuptiis et beneficio. SC. Velleiani renuntiaverint.[1]

Paul.: Complura senatusconsulta facta sunt, ut in locum furiosi et muti et surdi tutoris alii tutores dentur.—l. 17, D. de tut.[2]

According to later and Justinianean Law, the following persons are absolutely incapable—

(α) impuberes and minores,

(β) muti, surdi, furiosi,

(γ) soldiers, bishops and monks;

while incapable relatively were—

creditors and debtors of the ward.

Minores autem XXV annis olim quidem excusabantur: a nostra autem constitutione prohibentur ad tutelam vel curam adspirare, adeo ut nec excusatione opus fiat; qua constitutione cavetur, ut nec pupillus ad legitimam tutelam vocetur nec adultus, cum erat incivile eos, qui alieno auxilio in rebus suis administrandis egere noscuntur et sub aliis reguntur, aliorum tutelam vel curam subire.—§ 13, I. de excus. 1, 25.[3]

---

[1] Women also we prohibit from undertaking the office of *tutela*, with the exception of the mother or grandmother. For it is these alone we allow, according to the order of succession, to undertake *tutela*, if in the course of the proceedings they shall renounce both a second marriage and the benefit of the *SC. Velleianum*.

[2] Many *Sca.* have resulted from the purpose to appoint other tutors in the place of an insane, and dumb, and deaf tutor.

[3] Those who were under 25 years of age were formerly able to decline; but since our constitution they are forbidden to aspire to a *tutela* or *curatela*, so that neither is the right to decline of any use. By this constitution it is provided that neither a ward nor a minor shall be called to a legal *tutela*, since it was subversive of law for persons who are known to need the 'help of another' in the conduct of their own affairs, and are under the control of others, to undertake *tutela* or *curatela* of others.

A person capable of guardianship can decline it only upon grounds fixed by statute.[a] These are the 'excusationes tutorum,' which either absolve from the duty of undertaking a guardianship, or from one already taken: *e.g.*, illness and blemishes, great age, official position or a certain vocation, administration of three guardianships, having had 3–5 children of one's own.[b] The concurrence of several imperfect grounds of 'excusatio' as a rule affords no discharge.

[a] Except, perhaps, testamentary tutors in the Classical Law: Ulp. xi. 17.

[b] See Inst. i. 25, 1.

> Vat. Fgm. 245: Qui complura allegant, quae singula non sint firma, interdum excusari solent.—(Paul.)[1]
>
> Imp. Sever.: Sed imperfectae diversae species vacationis, licet permixtae, ad excusationem non proficiunt. Scire igitur debes, eum qui duos filios habet et duas tutelas administrat, excusationem non mereri.—C. 5, 69 l. un.[2]

The 'excusatio' must be made good by petition at the right time, and allowed, otherwise the guardian is responsible for any delay in undertaking the office.

> Qui excusare se volunt, . . . intra dies L continuos, ex quo cognoverunt, excusare se debent, . . . si intra centesimum lapidem sunt ab eo loco, ubi tutores dati sunt: si vero ultra centesimum habitant, dinumeratione facta XX milium diurnorum et amplius XXX dierum; quod tamen, ut Scaevola dicebat, sic debet computari, ne minus sint quam quinquaginta dies.—§ 16, I. de excusat.[3]

---

1 They that set up several things which taken separately are inadequate can sometimes be excused.

2 But incomplete various grounds of release, although connected with one another, do not avail for excuse. You must therefore know that he who has two sons and exercises two guardianships has no claim for excuse.

3 Those desiring to decline . . . must decline during the period of fifty days, from the day when it came to their knowledge, . . . if they are within one hundred miles of the place where they were appointed tutors; but if they reside further off than one

Book II. Part I.

Ulp.: Tutor vel curator, cuius . . . excusatio recepta non sit, ex quo accedere ad administrationem debuit, erit obligatus.—D. 26, 7, 20.[1]

Earlier on the tutor nominated by the magistrate could be liberated also by 'potioris nominatio,' *i.e.*, proof that some person was more closely related or was better fitted for the exercise of the guardianship; but this potioris nominatio—with, moreover, very lengthy procedure—disappeared in the later Law, after it had been materially circumscribed by Septimus Severus.

Paul. ii. 28, 1: Non recte potiorem videtur nominare, qui causam nominati potioris non expresserit.[2]

Vat. fgm. 157: Tunc demum excusandus est, qui prius datus fuerat, si is, quem nominaverit, et potior necessitudine et idoneus re fideque nec absens deprehendatur.[3]

158: Pars orationis imperatoris Severi: 'Promiscua facultas potioris nominandi nisi intra certes fines cohibeatur, ipso tractu temporis pupilles fortunis suis privabit: cui rei obviam ibitur, patres conscripti, si censueritis, ut collegae patris vel pupilli in decuria vel corpore, item cognati vel adfines utriusque necessitudinis, qui lege Iulia et Papia excepti sunt, potiorem non nominent; ceteri cognati vel adfines amicive atque municipes eos tantummodo nominent, quos supra complexus

---

hundred miles, twenty miles are reckoned for a day, and thirty days are added; this, however, as Scaevola used to say, must be so reckoned that there be not less than fifty days.

[1] A tutor or curator whose . . . excuse has not been acknowledged, will be liable from the time when he ought to enter upon the administration.

[2] He is not considered rightly to nominate one under a preferential obligation, who has not declared the ground for such preferential obligation.

[3] Then only is he to be excused who had been appointed before, if the person he has named is found to be preferable, both by reason of relationship and as suitable in means and in credit, and not absent.

sum; vicinitatis autem iure nemo potior existimetur.'[1]

Book II. Part I.

216: Excipiuntur autem lege quidem Iulia cognatorum sex gradus et ex septimo sobrino sobrinave natus, sed et nata per interpretationem.—218: Lege autem Papia hi abfines excipiuntur: qui vir et uxor, et gener et nurus, et socer et socrus umquam fuerunt; item vitricus noverca, privignus privigna.[2]

§ 64. Nomination of Tutor. Assumption of the Guardianship.

There are three grounds of the 'delatio' of Tutela, *i.e.*, species and forms of the appointment of a tutor: Testament, Statute, Magisterial disposition.

'Testamentaria tutela.'—

(1) A paterfamilias can by testament nominate a guardian (tutor testamentarius, dativus) for the children, being impuberes, placed under his potestas.[a]

Ulp. xi. 14: Testamento nominatim tutores

[a] For the *testamenti factio*, see § 156, and comp. D. 26, 2, 9.

[1] Part of a speech of the Emperor Severus: 'The indiscriminate right of naming a preferential person, unless confined within certain limits, will, by very lapse of time, deprive wards of their fortunes, which will be met, conscript fathers, if you shall decide that the joint guardians of the father or ward, by ten or in a body, cognates too, or near kinsmen of either relationship, who are excluded by the *l. Iul. et Pap.*, shall not name a preferential person; other cognates, or next of kin, or friends and burghers, may nominate those only whom we have included above; but let no one be thought preferential by virtue of being neighbours.

[2] Now six degrees of cognates are excepted by the *l. Iulia*, and a son of a cousin-german from the seventh, but a daughter also by interpretation of the statute. By the *l. Papia* the following next of kin are excepted: those that have ever been husband or wife, son-in-law, daughter-in-law, father-in-law, mother-in-law, likewise a step-father, step-mother, step-son, step-daughter.

Book II. Part I.

dati confirmantur lege XII tabularum his verbis: VTI LEGASSIT SVPER PECVNIA TVTELAVE SVAE REI, ITA IVS ESTO: qui tutores **dativi** appellantur.[1]

Q. Mucius: Nemo potest tutorem dare cuiquam, nisi ei, quem **in suis heredibus**[a] cum moritur habuit habiturusve esset, si vixisset.—l. 73, § 1, D. de R. J. 50, 17.[2]

[a] For *sui heredes*, see § 62.

Gai. i. § 146: Nepotibus neptibusque ita demum possumus testamento tutores dare, si post mortem nostram in patris sui potestatem iure recasuri non sint.[3]

§ 149: Rectissime autem tutor sic dari potest: LVCIVM TITIVM LIBERIS MEIS TVTOREM DO LEGO aut DO; sed et si ita scriptum sit: LIBERIS MEIS vel VXORI MEAE TITIVS TVTOR ESTO, recte datus intelligitur.[4]

Inst. i. 14, 3: Ad certum tempus vel ex certo tempore vel sub condicione posse dari tutorem non dubitatur.[5]

(2) In case of defective nomination, magis-

---

[1] Tutors appointed by name in a testament are also confirmed by the Law of the Twelve Tables in the following words: 'As a man shall have made a *lex* concerning his property or the tutelage of his property, so let it be regarded as *ius* (*i.e.*, valid)'; and these tutors are called 'dative.'

[2] No one can appoint a tutor to another than him whom at the time of his death he had amongst his own heirs, or would have had if he had lived.

[3] To our grandsons and granddaughters we can appoint tutors by testament only when they will not, upon our death, fall by Law under the power of their father.

[4] Now the most regular way in which a tutor can be appointed is: 'I give and bequeath' (or, 'give') 'L. T. as a tutor to my children'; but even if it be thus written: 'T. shall be tutor to my children,' or 'to my wife,' the appointment is considered to be regular.

[5] It is beyond doubt that a tutor can be appointed for a certain time, or from a certain point of time, or under a certain condition.

terial confirmation (confirmatio) of the guardian ensues.

Inst. i. 13, 5: Sed si **emancipato** filio tutor a patre testamentato datus fuerit, confirmandus est ex sententia praesidis omnimodo.[1]

Iul.: Qui a patre tutor scriptus est aut **non iusto testamento,** aut non ut lege praecipiebatur, confirmandus est ad tutelam gerendam perinde, ac si ex testamento tutor esset.—D. 26, 3, 3.[2]

Ner.: **Mulier** liberis non recte testamento tutorem dat; sed si dederit, decreto praetoris vel proconsulis ex inquisitione confirmabitur.—l. 2 pr. eod.[3]

'Legitima tutela.'—In the absence of a testamentary guardian,[a] the guardians appointed by statute are admitted as of course.

[a] *Infra.*

Ulp.: Legitimae tutelae lege XII tabularum adgnatis delatae sunt et consanguineis, item patronis, i.e. his qui ad legitimam hereditatem admitti possint; hoc summa providentia, ut qui sperarent hanc successionem, iidem tuerentur bona, ne dilapidarentur.—l. 1 pr., D. de leg. tut. 26, 4.[4]

---

[1] But if a tutor has been appointed to an emancipated son by his father in a testament, he must in every case be confirmed after the sentence of the president.

[2] A tutor that was appointed by a father either in an invalid testament or not according to legal precept, must be confirmed for the exercise of the tutelage, just as if he were tutor by the testament.

[3] The appointment by a woman of a tutor to her children is invalid; but if she have made an appointment, the tutor shall be confirmed by a decree of the praetor or proconsul, or after inquiry.

[4] Statutory guardianships were by the Law of the Twelve Tables assigned to the agnates and those who are brothers by the same father, to patrons likewise, *i.e.*, to those capable of

Q. Mucius: Eo tutela redit, quo et hereditas pervenit, nisi cum feminae heredes intercedunt. —l. 73 pr., D. de R. J.[1]

Statutory guardianship attaches to—

(1) the nearest agnates of the pupil.

Gai. i. § 155: Quibus testamento quidem tutor datus non sit, eis ex lege XII tabularum adgnati sunt tutores, qui vocantur **legitimi.**[2]

Gai.: Si plures sunt adgnati, proximus tutelam nanciscitur, si eodem gradu plures sint, omnes tutelam nansiscuntur.—l. 9, D. de leg. tut.[3]

(2) The Patron and his children over the freedman.

Gai. i. § 165: Ex eadem lege XII tabularum libertarum et impuberum libertorum tutela ad patronos liberosque eorum pertinet, quae et ipsa tutela legitimo vocatur: non quia nominatim ea lege de hac tutela cavetur, sed quia perinde accepta est per interpretationem, atque si verbis legis introducta esset. Eo enim ipso quod hereditates libertcrum libertarumque, si intestati decessissent, iusserat lex ad patronos liberosve eorum pertinere crediderunt veteres voluisse legem etiam tutelas ad eos pertinere, quia et adgnatos, quos ad hereditatem vocavit, eosdem et tutores esse iusserat.—[= Tit. I. de leg. patron. tut. 1, 17.][4]

---

being admitted to the legal inheritance. This was by the greatest forethought, because they that had expectation of the inheritance would guard the property from waste.

[1] And the tutelage falls to him upon whom also the inheritance devolves, except when females come in as heirs.

[2] Those to whom a tutor has not been appointed by testament have their agnates as tutors by a law of the Twelve Tables; and they are called 'tutors at law.'

[3] If several agnates exist, the nearest acquires the tutelage; if there are several in the same degree of relationship, all acquire it.

[4] According to the same law of the Twelve Tables, the tutelage of freedwomen and of freedmen under the age of puberty

Ulp. xi. 19: Lex Iunia tutorem fieri iubet Latinae vel Latini impuberis eum, cuius ea isve ante manumissionem ex iure Quiritium fuit.[a] [1]

[a] Cf. Ulp. i. 16. (§ 75.)

(3) The 'parens manumissor,' in respect of the emancipated child.

Ulp.: Si parens filium vel filiam vel nepotem vel neptem vel deinceps impuberes, quos in potestate habeat, emancipet, vicem legitimi tutoris sustinet.—l. 3, § 10, D. de leg. tut.[2]

(4) The 'extraneus manumissor,' in respect of one released from mancipium, and the sons of the 'parens manumissor,' in respect of the emancipatus, as 'fiduciarii tutores.'[b]

[b] § 53.

Mod.: —quo defuncto si liberi perfectae aetatis [virilis sexus] extant, **fiduciarii** tutores (filiorum suorum) fratris vel sororis (et ceterorum) efficiuntur.—l. 4 eod.=I. de fiduc. tut. 1, 19.[3]

Ulp. xi. 5: Qui liberum caput, mancipatum

---

belongs to the patrons and their children; this also is called a tutelage 'at law'; not because express provision is made in such law as to this tutelage, but because it has been adopted by way of interpretation just as if it had been introduced by the language of the statute. For from the very fact that the statute had directed that the inheritances of freedmen and freedwomen dying intestate should belong to their patrons, or to their children, the ancients supposed that the law intended the tutelages also to belong to them, because it had directed that the same agnates whom it called to the inheritance should be tutors as well.

[1] The *l. Iunia* directs that a female Latin or a male Latin under puberty shall have the person as tutor to whom he or she belonged by Quiritarian law previous to their manumission.

[2] If an ancestor emancipates a son, or daughter, or grandson, or granddaughter, or further descendants under the age of puberty, held by him under power, he is invested with the functions of a statutory tutor.

[3] If he die, and there exist children of full age [of the male sex], they become the fiduciary tutors of (their own sons) brother, or sister (and the rest).

sibi vel a parente vel a coemptionatore, manumisit, per similitudinem patroni tutor efficitur, qui **fiduciarius** tutor appellatur.[1]

(5) According to the latest Justinianean Law, in general the next successors by intestacy of the pupil.[a]

[a] Cf. tit. of Inst. i. 17.

Nov. 118, c. 5: Sancimus, ut unusquisque eo gradu et ordine, quo ad hereditatem vel solus vel cum aliis vocatur, etiam munus tutelae suscipiat, neque ulla differentia ex iure adgnationis aut cognationis introducatur, sed omnes similiter ad tutelam vocentur, tam ii, qui per masculos, quam ii, qui per feminas impuberibus iunguntur.[2]

Magisterial guardianship (Tutor a magistratu vel ex lege datus s. dativus). This occurs for a permanency, as a rule only when neither a testamentary nor a statutory guardian at all exists,[b] as well as in the case of incapacity, 'excusatio,' or the removal of the testamentary or statutory guardian.[c]

[b] 'Tutorem habenti tutor dari non potest.'

[c] § 63, ad init.

Ulp.: Et si semel ad testamentarium devoluta fuerit tutela, deinde excusatus sit tutor testamentarius, adhuc dicimus in locum excusati dandum, non ad legitimum tutorem redire tutelam.—Idem dicimus, et si fuerit remotus; nam et hic idcirco abit, ut alius detur.—Quodsi tutor testamento datus decesserit, ad legitimum tutela redit.—D. 26, 2, 11, §§ 1–3.[3]

[1] He that has manumitted a free person, mancipated to him either by an ancestor or by a *coemptionator*, becomes tutor through similarity to a patron, and is called a 'fiduciary' tutor.

[2] We enact that every one shall also undertake the office of tutelage in that degree of relationship and order in which he is called to the inheritance, either alone or with others, and that no difference shall by virtue of Law obtain in respect of agnatic or cognatic right, but all shall be called alike to the tutelage, those of kin with the *impuberes*, whether through males or through females.

[3] And when once the tutelage shall have devolved upon the

A tutor can also be appointed for the passing moment by the magistrate in an exceptional way, or for particular juristic acts, on behalf of one who already has a tutor.[a]

[a] Cf. § 60, ad fin.

—sciendum est, quamdiu testamentaria tutela speratur, legitimam cessare.—l. 11 pr. eod.[1]

Gai. i. §§ 186, sq.: Si cui testamento tutor **sub condicione** aut **ex die certo** datus sit, quamdiu condicio aut dies pendet, tutor dari potest; item si pure datus fuerit, quamdiu nemo heres existat, tamdiu ex his legibus[b] tutor petendus est: qui desinit tutor esse, posteaquam aliquis ex testamento tutor esse coeperit. § **Ab hostibus** quoque **tutore capto,** ex his legibus tutor peti debet, qui desinit tutor esse, si is qui captus est, in civitatem reversus fuerit: nam reversus recipit tutelam iure postliminii.[2]

[b] Ibid. § 185 (*inf.*).

Id. § 184: Olim cum legis actiones[c] in usu erant, etiam ex illa causa tutor dabatur, si inter tutorem et mulierem pupillumve lege agendum erat; nam quia ipse tutor in re sua auctor esse

[c] § 192.

---

testamentary tutor, and he has then renounced, we still affirm that a tutor must be appointed in the place of the one refusing to act, not that the tutelage lapses to the tutor-at-law.—We say the like even when he is removed, for this also results in the appointment of another.—But if the tutor appointed by testament die, the tutelage lapses to the tutor-at-law.

[1] Let it be understood that so long as the testamentary tutelage is matter of expectation, the statutory one is in abeyance.

[2] If a tutor have been appointed to any one by a testament, under a condition or as from a certain time, so long as the condition or the term await accomplishment, a tutor can be appointed. Again, let him have been appointed unconditionally: as long as no heir is forthcoming by these statutes must a tutor be applied for, who ceases to be a tutor after that any one has become tutor under the testament. When, besides, a tutor has been taken captive by the enemy, by these statutes a tutor ought to be applied for, who ceases to be tutor if the captive tutor shall return into the state, for on his return he recovers the tutelage *iure postliminii*.

non poterat, alius dabatur, quo auctore legis actio perageretur: qui dicebatur **praetorius** tutor, quia a praetore urbano dabatur. Sed post sublatas legis actiones quidam putant hanc speciem dandi tutoris in usu esse desiisse, aliis autem placet adhuc in usu esse, si legitimo iudicio agatur.[1]

Inst. i. 21, 3: —non praetorius ut olim constituitur, sed curator in locum eius datur, quo interveniente iudicium peragitur et eo peracto curator esse desinit.[2]

Legislation varied with respect to competence for the nomination of a tutor.

Ulp.: Tutoris datio neque imperii est neque iurisdictionis, sed ei soli competit, cui nominatim hoc dedit vel lex vel senatusconsultum vel princeps.—D. 26, 1, 6, 2.[3]

Gai. i. § 185: Si cui nullus omnino tutor sit, ei datur in urbe Roma ex lege **Atilia** a praetore urbano et maiore parte tribunorum plebis, qui **Atilianus** tutor vocatur: in provinciis vero a praesidibus provinciarum ex lege **Iulia et Titia.**[4]

---

[1] Formerly when *legis actiones* were employed, a tutor used also to be appointed when proceedings had to be taken between a tutor and a woman or a ward; for since a tutor could not be *auctor* in any matter of his own, another used to be appointed, under whose authorisation the *l. a.* was prosecuted; and he was called a 'Praetorian' tutor, because he was appointed by the Urban Praetor. But some are of opinion that after the abolition of *legis actiones* this species of appointment of tutor was discontinued, whilst others hold that it is still available in proceedings by *legitimum iudicium.*

[2] A Praetorian tutor is not appointed as formerly, but a curator is nominated in his place, under whose guidance the suit is prosecuted, and upon the conclusion of such suit he ceases to be curator.

[3] The appointment of tutor is the function neither of official power nor of administration of the Law, but it appertains to him alone to whom either a statute, or a decree of the senate, or the Emperor has granted it.

[4] If a person have no tutor at all, one is given him, in the

Inst. i. 20, §§ 3–4 : Sed ex his legibus pupillis tutores desierunt dari, postquam primo consules pupillis utriusque sexus tutores ex inquisitione dare coeperunt, deinde praetores ex constitutionibus.—Sed hoc iure utimur, ut Romae quidem praefectus urbis vel praetor secundum suam iurisdictionem, in provinciis autem praesides ex inquisitione tutores crearent, vel magistratus iussu praesidum, si non sint magnae pupilli facultates.[1]

The mother of the ward and—by the latest Law—all his eventual successors, were under obligation to apply for, and specify, a guardian.

Mod.: Divus Severus Cuspio Rufino : 'Omnem me rationem adhibere subveniendis pupillis, cum ad curam publicam pertineat, liquere omnibus volo ; et ideo quae mater vel non petierit tutores idoneos filiis suis, vel prioribus excusatis reiectisve non confestim aliorum nomina dederit, ius non habeat vindicandorum sibi bonorum intestatorum filiorum.'—D. 26, 6, 2, 2.[2]

---

city of Rome under the *l. Atilia* by the Urban Praetor and the majority of the plebeian tribunes, who is called an 'Atilian' tutor; but in the provinces, by the governor thereof, under the *l. Iulia et Titia.*

[1] But, by virtue of these statutes, the appointment of tutors to wards ceased after that the consuls in the first instance had begun to give guardians to wards of either sex after inquiry, and subsequently the praetors, as a result of constitutions.—But now the law in force is that at Rome the prefect of the city or the praetor, according to his jurisdiction, in the provinces the governors, appoint the guardians after inquiry, or the magistrates do so upon the order of the governors, if the ward's property be inconsiderable.

[2] The divine Sever. to Cusp. Ruf.: 'I would have all men understand that I apply my whole wisdom to the assistance of wards, since this is subject of state supervision, and accordingly, every mother that shall not have applied for suitable guardians for her children, or have immediately proposed others if the earlier ones shall have declined or have been discarded, shall have no

BOOK II. Part I.

[a] Stipulatio 'rem pupilli salvam fore.'

[b] § 31.—Cf. Inst. i. 24, 1, and for English Law, Brown, s. *satisdatio.*

Upon assumption of the guardianship, the guardian has to make an inventory, and the 'legitimus tutor' to give, besides, a cautio[a] by way of security.[b]

Gai. i. §§ 199, 200: Ne tamen pupillorum et eorum, qui in curatione sunt, negotia a tutoribus curatoribusque consumantur aut deminuantur, curat praetor, ut et tutores et curatores eo nomine satisdent. § Sed hoc non est perpetuum: nam et tutores testamento dati satisdare non coguntur, quia fides eorum et diligentia ab ipso testatore probata est; et curatores ad quos non e lege curatio pertinet, sed qui vel a consule vel a praetore vel a praeside provinciae dantur, plerumque non coguntur satisdare, scilicet quia satis honesti electi sunt.—(Inst. i. 24, pr.: —ex inquisitione tutores vel curatores dati satisdatione non onerantur, quia idonei electi sunt.)[1]

Gai.: Servum pupilli stipulari ita necesse est, si pupillus abest aut fari non potest: nam si praesens sit et fari potest, etiamsi eius aetatis erit, ut non intelligat quid agat, tamen propter utilitatem receptum est, recte eum stipulari.—D. 46, 6, 6.[2]

---

right to make a title to the goods of such children as shall die intestate.

[1] That, however, the property of pupils and of those persons who are under curators be not wasted or reduced, the praetor takes care that both tutors and curators find security on such behalf. § But this is not universal; for tutors appointed by testament are not required to find security, because their integrity and carefulness have been accredited by the testator himself; and curators to whom the curatorship does not come by virtue of a statute, but who are appointed either by a consul or by a praetor, or by the governor of the province, are in general not required to find security, because sufficiently trustworthy persons have been chosen (—tutors or curators appointed after inquiry are not burdened with the finding of security, because it was as suitable persons that they were chosen).

[2] A slave of the pupil must stipulate when the pupil is absent, or cannot yet speak; for if he is present and can speak, even if he be of such age as not to understand what he is doing,

Pomp.: Quod in tutelae iudicium venit, hoc et ea stipulatione continetur.—l. 9 eod.[1]

§ 65. End of Guardianship.

Guardianship ends in general by death and every capitis diminutio of the pupil, as well as by attainment of puberty.

> Ulp.: Si adrogati sunt adhuc impuberes vel deportati sint pupilli, tutores habere desinunt.—Item si in servitutem pupillus redigatur, utique finitur tutela.—D. 26, 1, 14, §§ 1, 2.[2]

It ends as regards the person of him who has been hitherto guardian, by entrance upon the final term of the testamentary *tutela;* by 'magna' (in legitima tutela also by 'minima') capitis diminutio, by 'excusatio' (in testamentary *tutela* of ante-Justinianean Law, 'abdicatio' also) of the tutor; and finally, by his removal on account of conduct in violation of his duty, preceded by a complaint which may be laid by any one (accusatio suspecti).

> Sed et capitis deminutione tutoris, per quam libertas vel civitas eius amittitur, omnis tutela perit.—§ 4, I. h. t. 1, 22.[3]

> Paul.: Tutelas non amittit capitis minutio, exceptis his quae in iure alieno personis positis deferuntur. Igitur ex testamento dati vel ex lege vel ex senatusconsulto erunt nihilo minus tutores: sed legitimae tutelae ex duodecim tabulis intervertuntur eadem ratione, qua et

---

yet for convenience' sake the opinion is that he makes a lawful stipulation.

[1] That which enters into the action of guardianship is contained also in such stipulation.

[2] If those who are still under the age of puberty have been arrogated, or pupils have been deported, they cease to be under tutors. Also if a ward be reduced to slavery, doubtless there is an end to guardianship.

[3] But every tutelage ceases also by the *cap. dem.* of the tutor, by which his freedom or citizenship is lost.

Book II. Part I.

hereditates exinde legitimae, quia adgnatis deferuntur, qui desinunt esse familia mutati.—D. 4, 5, 7 pr.[1]

Ulp. xi. 17 : —tutor testamento datus . . . si abdicaverit se tutela, desinit esse tutor: **abdicare** autem est dicere nolle se tutorem esse : . . . legitimus . . . abdicare se non potest.[2]

Inst. i. 26 pr. : Sciendum est **suspecti** crimen e lege XII tabularum descendere.—§ 1, Datum est autem ius removendi suspectos tutores Romae praetori et in provinciis praesidibus earum et legato proconsulis.—§ 3, Consequens est ut videamus, qui possint suspectos postulare ; et sciendum est quasi publicam esse hanc actionem h. e. omnibus patere.—§ 6, Suspectus autem remotus, si quidem ob dolum, famosus est ; si ob culpam, non aeque.[3]

[a] See 'Anct. Law,' pp. 152-154.

§ 66. Tutela Mulierum.[a]

From of old all women free from Power were placed

[1] *Cap. dim.* does not determine guardianships, except those which devolve upon agnates placed under the authority of another. Those, therefore, who have been appointed by virtue of a testament, or statute, or decree of the senate, will be none the less tutors; but statutory guardianships according to the Twelve Tables are invalid for the same reason as statutory inheritances also, because they devolve upon agnates who no longer pass as such upon a change of family.

[2] If the guardian appointed in a testament resign, he ceases to be guardian : now *abdicare* is, to state that he declines to be tutor . . . a statutory guardian cannot resign.

[3] It should be noted that the accusation against a person under suspicion is derived from a law of the Twelve Tables.—The right to remove suspected guardians has been given, at Rome to the praetor, and in the provinces to the governors thereof and the proconsular legate.—Next we must see who can proceed against suspected persons, and have to note that this action is, as it were, a public one, *i.e.*, the action lies open to all.—Now he that has been removed as under suspicion, is dishonoured if it has been because of deceit; but not if it has happened from carelessness.

under life-long guardianship. Although later on the custom was to regard the ground of this sexual guardianship as furnished by the women's own interest, and to trace it back to 'sexus fragilitas' (infirmitas consilii, animi levitas) and 'forensium rerum ignorantia,' yet we must look for its actual cause in the subordinate position of the female sex under Private Law,[a] and in the interest, exalted into a right, which the members of a family had in preserving a woman's property for the familia.[b] The work of the guardian is here confined—apart from the pupillae—simply to giving 'auctoritas' for certain transactions.[c] From the time, however, that such auctoritas could in certain cases either be enforced, or could be legally avoided, and after the principal instance of the guardianship of women, that of agnates, was abolished by statute, this too continually lost importance: it had already in the second century seemed alien to people of the time, and quite disappeared towards the end of the third century.

[a] § 59.

[b] § 62, ad init.

[c] *Infra:* Gai. ii. 47; Vat. fgm. 1; Gai. iii. 104.

> Gai. i. §§ 144–5: Veteres voluerunt feminas, etiamsi perfectae aetatis sint, propter animi levitatem in tutela esse.—Tantum ex lege Iulia et Papia Poppaea iure liberorum tutela liberantur feminae; loquimur autem exceptis virginibus Vestalibus, quas etiam veteres in honorem sacerdotii liberas esse voluerunt: itaque etiam lege XII tabularum cautum est.[1]
>
> Ulp. xi. 25: Pupillorum pupillarumque tutores et negotia gerunt et auctoritatem interponunt; mulierum autem tutores auctoritatem dumtaxat

---

[1] The ancients thought it right for women, even if of full age, to be under tutelage, because of weakness of intellect. By the *l. Iulia et Pap. Popp.* it is only by the privilege they possess as having borne children that women are freed from tutelage. In saying so, however, we make an exception of the vestal virgins, whom also the ancients, in honour of their office, wished to be free; and therefore it was so provided by a law of the Twelve Tables.

BOOK II. Part I.

interponunt.—27: Tutoris auctoritas necessaria est mulieribus quidem in his rebus: si lege aut legitimo iudicio agant, si se obligent, si civile negotium gerant, si libertae suae permittant in contubernio alieni servi morari, si rem mancipi alienent.[1]

Gai. ii. §§ 80, 81: Nunc admonendi sumus, neque feminam neque pupillum sine tutoris auctoritate **rem mancipi** alienare posse; **nec mancipi** vero feminam quidem posse, pupillum non posse.—§ Ideoque si quando mulier mutuam pecuniam alicui sine tutoris auctoritate dederit, quia facit eam accipientis, cum scilicet pecunia res nec mancipi sit, contrahit obligationem.—§ 85: Mulieri etiam sine tutoris auctoritate recte solvi potest; . . . at si non accipiat,[a] sed . . . per acceptilationem velit debitorem sine tutoris auctoritate liberare, non potest.[2]

[a] Sc. pecuniam.

Cicero, p. Flacco 34, 84: 'In manum convenerat.' . . . Nihil potest de tutela legitima nisi omnium tutorum auctoritate deminui.[3]

---

[1] The tutors of pupils male and female both transact their business and furnish authorisation, but the tutors of women do but furnish authorisation. The sanction of their tutor is necessary for women in the following matters: if they sue by *legis actio* or a *legitimum iudicium*, if they undertake an obligation, if they transact any matter of Civil Law, if they give leave to their freedwoman to cohabit with another person's slave, if they alienate a mancipable thing.[b]

[b] § 74.

[2] We must now observe that neither a woman nor a ward can, without the sanction of the guardian, alienate a *res mancipi;* but that a woman indeed can alienate a *res nec mancipi*, that a pupil cannot. § And therefore, whenever a woman shall make a loan to any one without the sanction of her guardian, she contracts an obligation, because she makes it the property of the borrower, since of course money is a *res nec mancipi.*—§ To a woman, too, payment can rightly be made without her guardian's authority . . . yet if she does not receive it, but desires to give the debtor a discharge without the sanction of the guardian, she cannot do so.

[3] 'She had passed into *manus.*' . . . As regards *tut. legit.*,

Gai. i. §§ 190–1: Feminas vero perfectae aetatis in tutela esse, fere nulla pretiosa ratio suas isse videtur: nam quae vulgo creditur, quia levitate animi plerumque decipiuntur et aequum erat, eas tutorum auctoritate regi, magis speciosa videtur quam vera; mulieres enim, quae perfectae aetatis sunt, ipsae sibi negotia tractant, et in quibusdum causis dicis gratia tutor interponit auctoritatem suam; saepe etiam invitus auctor fieri a praetore cogitur. § Unde cum tutore nullum ex tutela iudicium mulieri datur.[1]

The grounds of devolution in respect of the 'tutela mulierum' are the same as in the case of 'tutela impuberum.'

(1) The pat. fam. can by testament nominate a tutor for the daughters under his potestas, as well as for the 'uxor in manu.' For the latter there is a peculiar kind of appointment, the 'tutoris optio,' the object of which was as far as possible to free the wife from onerous guardianship through the choice of a tutor acceptable to her.

Gai. i. § 148: Uxori quae in manu est, proinde ac filiae, item nurui quae in filii manu est, proinde ac nepti tutor dari potest.—§§ 150–4: In persona tamen uxoris, quae in manu est, recepta est etiam **tutoris optio,** i.e. ut liceat ei permittere, quem velit ipsa tutorem sibi optare, hoc modo: TITIAE

---

nothing can be curtailed save by the sanction of all the guardians.

[1] But there seems to have been scarcely any appreciable reason afforded for women of full age being under tutelage: the reason which is commonly received, that owing to their fickleness of mind they are generally imposed upon, and that it is right they should be guided by the authority of guardians, appears more plausible than true. For women who are of full age conduct their business for themselves, and in certain matters the guardian furnishes his authority for form's sake; he is also frequently compelled by the praetor to concur against his will. § Hence no action is given to a woman against her guardian as arising from the tutelage.

Book II. Part I.

VXORI MEAE TVTORIS OPTIONEM DO; quo casu licet uxori (tutorem optare) vel in omnes res vel in unam forte aut duas. § Ceterum aut **plena** optio datur aut **angusta.** § Plena ita dari solet, ut proxime supra diximus; angusta ita dari solet: TITIAE VXORI MEAE TVTORIS OPTIONEM DVMTAXAT SEMEL DO, aut DVMTAXAT BIS DO. § Quae optiones plurimum inter se differunt: nam quae plenam optionem habet, potest et semel et bis et ter et saepius tutorem optare: quae vero angustam habet optionem, si dumtaxat semel data est optio, amplius quam semel optare non potest; si tantum bis, amplius quam bis optandi facultatem non habet. § Vocantur autem hi qui . . . ex optione sumuntur, **optivi.**[1]

(2) The legitima mulierum tutela—

(*a*) is transferred to the same persons as tutela impuberum;[a] but the tutela of agnates was abolished by Claudius.

[a] § 64.

Gai. i. § 157: Sed olim quidem, quantum ad legem XII tabularum attinet, etiam feminae **adgnatos** habebant tutores; sed postea lex Claudia lata est, quae quod ad feminas attinet,

---

[1] A tutor can be appointed to a wife *in manu* precisely as to a daughter, likewise to a daughter-in-law in the *manus* of our son, precisely as to a granddaughter. § In respect, however, of a wife *in manu*, the choice of a tutor is also allowed, *i.e.*, she may be permitted to choose for herself a tutor as she pleases, in this form: 'I give to Titia my wife the choice of a tutor,' in which case the wife is at liberty (to choose a tutor) either for all matters or, it may be, for one or two. § Moreover, she is given a choice either unlimited or restricted. § The grant of unlimited choice is usually as just mentioned above; but the limited power is commonly given thus: 'To Titia my wife I give only a single choice of tutor,' or 'only twice.' § These modes of selection differ considerably from one another; for she who has an unlimited choice, can select her tutor once, twice, thrice, or oftener; whilst she that has a limited choice, if it have been given only for once, cannot choose more than once; if only twice, she has no power of choosing more than twice. § Now those tutors who are taken in virtue of a selection are called *optivi.*

Book II. Part I.

tutelas illas sustulit: itaque masculus quidem impubes fratrem puberem aut patruum habet tutorem, femina vero talem habere tutorem non potest.[1]

Ulp. xi. 8: Feminarum legitimas tutelas lex Claudia sustulit, excepta tutela patronorum.[2]

(β) It is marked by the following peculiarities:

First, the regular non-enforceable character of the tutelae auctoritas; as was certainly always recognised in the case of 'patroni et parentes,' but with agnates scarcely indeed until the time of Claudius.[a] But as against the 'alterius generis tutores,' the auctoritas could ever be obtained peremptorily, first of all in respect of 'in manum conventio,' and later on in other cases also.

[a] Except in the case of *fiduciarii tutores* (Gai. i. 114, *sq.*), who, as also the *optivi*, always gave their authority only as a matter of form (*dicis causa*).

Gai. i. § 192: Sane **patronorum et parentum** legitimae tutelae vim aliquam habere intelliguntur eo, quod hi neque ad testamentum faciendum, neque ad res mancipi alienandas, neque ad obligationes suscipiendas auctores fieri coguntur, praeterquam si magna causa alienandarum rerum mancipi obligationisve suscipiendae interveniat: eaque omnia ipsorum causa constituta sunt, ut quia ad eos intestatarum mortuarum hereditates pertinent, neque per testamentum excludantur ab hereditate, neque alienatis pretiosioribus rebus susceptoque aere alieno minus locuples ad eos hereditas perveniat.[3]

---

[1] But formerly indeed, so far as concerns the Law of the Twelve Tables, women also had their agnates as tutors; but the *l. Claudia* was afterwards passed, which, in relation to women, abolished those guardianships; accordingly, while a male under puberty has as his guardian a brother of the age of puberty or paternal uncle, a woman cannot have a guardian of that kind.

[2] The *l. Claudia* abolished the statutory guardianships of women, with the exception of those held by patrons.

[3] The statutory guardianships of patrons and ancestors are certainly seen to have some force from the fact that these persons are not compelled to sanction either the execution of a testament, or the conveyance of a *res mancipi*, or the undertaking

Book II. Part I.

Secondly, the possibility of 'in iure cessio tutelae' by the guardian to a third party.

Gai. i. §§ 168–170: Adgnatis et patronis et liberorum capitum manumissoribus permissum est feminarum tutelam alii in iure cedere; pupillorum autem tutelam non est permissum cedere, quia non videtur onerosa, cum tempore pubertatis finiatur. § Is autem cui ceditur tutela **cessicius** tutor vocatur. § Quo mortuo aut capite diminuto revertitur ad eum tutorem tutela, qui cessit; ipse quoque qui cessit si mortuus aut capite diminutus sit, a cessicio tutela discedit et revertitur ad eum qui post eum, qui cesserat, secundum gradum in ea tutela habuerit.[1]

(3) A guardian is appointed to a woman by the magistrate, either for a permanency, in the event of her otherwise having no tutor,[a] or for a particular legal act, if her tutor is prevented from giving auctoritas. This occurs especially—

[a] *Supra*, p. 310.

(*a*) in case of absence.

Gai. i. § 173: Senatusconsulto mulieribus permissum est, in absentis tutoris locum alium

---

of obligations, unless a weighty reason present itself for the conveyance of *res mancipi* or the undertaking of obligations. And all such things have been settled on behalf of the tutors themselves, inasmuch as the inheritances of women dying intestate pass to them, and they are not excluded from the inheritance by a testament, nor does the inheritance come to them depreciated by alienation of the more valuable things, or by its being charged with a debt.

[1] Agnates and patrons and those who have manumitted free persons are allowed to transfer the tutelage of women to a third person by surrender in court; but not the tutelage of male pupils, because it is not regarded as burdensome, since it comes to an end at the time of puberty. § Now he to whom the tutelage is transferred is called 'tutor cessicius.' § Upon his death, or loss of status, the tutelage reverts to the tutor who transferred it. And if the transferor himself dies, or experiences loss of status, the tutelage passes from the 'tutor cessicius' and reverts to the person who in respect of such tutelage shall stand next in succession to the transferor.

petere: quo petito prior desinit, nec interest, quam longe aberit is tutor.[1]

Ulp. xi. 22: Item ex senatusconsulto tutor datur mulieri ei cuius tutor abest, praeterquam si patronus sit, qui abest: nam in locum patroni absentis aliter peti non potest, nisi ad hereditatem adeundam et nuptias contrahendas.[2]

(β) In the case of minority or insanity of the tutor.

Ulp. xi. 20: Ex lege Iulia de maritandis ordinibus tutor datur a praetore urbis ei mulieri virginive, quam ex hac ipsa lege nubere oportet, ad dotem dandam dicendam promittendamve, si legitimum tutorem pupillum habeat.[3]

Gai. i. §§ 180, sq.: Item si qua in tutela legitima furiosi aut muti sit, permittitur ei senatusconsulto dotis constituendae gratia tutorem petere. —Quibus casibus salvam manere tutelam patrono patronique filio manifestum est.[4]

As to the termination of tutela mulierum, the same rule holds as in respect of tutela impuberum. The

[1] By a decree of the senate women are allowed to apply for a new tutor in the place of one that is absent; and the former ceases to be tutor upon this application being entertained, neither does it matter how far distant such tutor shall be.

[2] Likewise, by a decree of the senate, a tutor is appointed to a woman whose tutor is absent, unless he that is absent is her patron; for no application can be made for a tutor in place of an absent patron, except for the purpose of taking up an inheritance and contracting a marriage.

[3] By the *l. Iulia de maritandis ordinibus* a tutor is appointed by the Urban Praetor to such woman or virgin as is required to marry by this very statute, in order that he may give, specify or promise her dowry, if she have a pupil as her guardian-at-law.

[4] Likewise if a woman be under the statutory guardianship of a lunatic or a dumb person, she is allowed by the decree of the senate to apply for a guardian for the purpose of settling her dowry. In these cases it is clear that the guardianship remains undisturbed for the patron and the son of the patron.

Book II. Part I.

[a] Cf. Gai. i. 114.

'coemptio tutelae evitandae causa'[a] is a peculiar kind of release, which, however, originally was applied only to testamentary and magisterial guardianship, and not until a later period to that of agnates; as it saved the difficulty of enforcing auctoritas in the particular case, it in general, according to its practical result, as good as relieved women from the bondage of guardianship, oppressive and contrary as it was to the spirit of the time.

Gai. i. § 196[a]: Item si sit a masculo manumissa, et auctore eo coemptionem fecerit, deinde remancipata et manumissa sit, patronum quidem habere tutorem desinit, incipit autem habere eum tutorem, a quo manumissa est, qui fiduciarius dicitur.[1]

§ 67. Cura.

Curators were appointed either by Law or by the magistrate.

Ulp. xii. 1: Curatores aut **legitimi** sunt, i.e. qui ex lege XII tabularum dantur, aut **honorarii,** i.e. qui a praetore constituuntur.[2]

Dantur autem curatores ab eisdem magistratibus, a quibus et tutores; sed curator testamento non datur, sed datus confirmatur decreto praetoris vel praesidis.—§ 1, I. h. t (1, 23).[3]

The following are the chief cases of 'curatela.'

[b] § 61.

(1) The 'cura furiosi' and 'cura prodigi,'[b] accord-

---

[1] Likewise if she has been manumitted by a male, and with his sanction has made a coemption, and then has been remancipated and manumitted, she ceases to be under the guardianship of her patron, but begins to have him as guardian by whom she was manumitted, who is called a 'fiduciary' guardian.

[2] Curators are either *legitimi, i.e.*, who are assigned by virtue of a law of the Twelve Tables, or are *honorarii, i.e.*, are appointed by the praetor.

[3] Curators are appointed by the same officers as are tutors. But the curator is not appointed by testament, though when so appointed he is confirmed by a decree of the praetor or the governor.

ing to the Twelve Tables devolving upon the agnates, which, however, in default of agnates, and later on quite universally,[a] were imposed by the competent magistrate.[b]

[a] In the extended application by the Praetor.

[b] For the English 'committee of lunatic,' see Steph. ii. 514; and for conflict of laws, Westl. pp. 48, *sqq.*

Cic. de inv. ii. 50, 148: Lex: SI FVRIOSVS ESCIT, ADGNATVM GENTILIVMQVE IN EO PECVNIAQVE EIVS POTESTAS ESTO.[1]

Ulp.: —lex XII tabularum ita accepta est, ut ad pupillos vel pupillas non pertineat.—D. 26, 1, 3 pr.[2]

Ulp. xii. 2, 3: Lex XII tabularum furiosum itemque prodigum, cui bonis interdictum est, in curatione iubet esse adgnatorum.—A praetore constituitur curator, quem ipse praetor voluerit, libertinis prodigis, itemque ingenuis qui ex testamento parentis heredes facti male dissipant bona: his enim ex lege curator dari non poterat, cum ingenuus quidem non ab intestato, sed ex testamento heres factus sit patri, libertinus autem nullo modo patri heres fieri possit, qui nec patrem habuisse videtur, cum servilis cognatio nulla sit.[3]

Id.: Sed solent hodie praetores vel praesides, si talem hominem invenerint, qui neque tempus

---

[1] The statute runs: 'If he be a madman, his agnates and relations of the same *gens* shall have control over him and his property.'

[2] The law of the Twelve Tables has been understood not to refer to pupils male or female.

[3] A law of the Twelve Tables directs that a lunatic, as also a spendthrift who has been interdicted the administration of his property, shall be under the charge of his agnates. By the praetor is appointed a curator, at his discretion, to free-born spendthrifts, and to freedmen likewise who, being testamentary heirs of their ancestor, are squandering their estate; for to such a curator could not be appointed by statute, since the man of free-birth was made heir by his father not *ab intestato*, but by testament, and the freedman because he could not be heir to his father in any way; and he is not regarded as having a father, since servile cognation does not exist.

Book II. Part I.

neque finem expensarum habet, sed bona sua dilacerando et dissipando profundit, curatorem ei dare exemplo furiosi.—D. 27, 10, 1 pr.[1]

[a] § 60. See Westlake, *ubi sup.*

(2) The cura minorum.[a] It came into use as a permanent guardianship from the time of Marcus Aurelius; but a curator was given to minors by the magistrate only upon their petition; the acceptance of this was down to the latest times made compulsory alone indirectly for particular legal acts, but this compulsion proved sufficiently operative to cause every minor to apply for a standing guardian.

Capitol. Marc. Ant. Phil. 10: De curatoribus vero, cum ante non nisi ex lege Plaetoria vel propter lasciviam vel propter dementiam darentur, ita statuit, ut omnes adulti curatores acciperent non redditis causis.[2]

Item inviti adulescentes curatores non accipiunt praeterquam in litem.—§ 2, I. h. t.[3]

Ulp.: Sed et si ei pecunia a debitore paterno soluta sit vel proprio, et hanc perdidit, dicendum est, ei subveniri. Et ideo si minor conveniat debitorem, adhibere debet curatores, ut ei solvatur pecunia; ceterum non ei compellitur solvere. Sed hodie solet pecunia in aedem deponi . . . aut curatoribus solvi, si sunt. Permittitur etiam ex constitutione principum debitori, compellere adulescentem ad petendos sibi curatores.—D. 4, 4, 7, 2.[4]

---

[1] But at the present day it is usual for the praetors or governors, if they find such a man as regards neither time nor limit in his outlay, but lavishly and wastefully squanders his property, to appoint a curator, as is done in the case of a lunatic.

[2] But as concerning curators, whereas previously they were only according to the *lex Praetoria* assigned either because of profligacy or because of insanity, he ordained that all adults should receive curators without reasons being given.

[3] Likewise, young people do not receive curators against their will, save for a suit.

[4] But even if he have been paid money by a debtor of his father or his own, and have lost this, we must state that relief

PART II.—JURISTIC PERSONS.[a]

[a] Cf. Markby, ss. 136-145; Holl. ch. xiv.

§ 68. Nature of Juristic Persons.

A Juristic (moral, imaginary) Person, that is, one existing only for juristic purposes, is a subject of rights who is first created by the Law itself. As such occurs sometimes an organised association of persons with particular property (universitas, sc. personarum, corpus, CORPORATION);[b] at other times, a collection of goods devoted to a definite permanent purpose (FOUNDATION, universitas bonorum) to which personality and legal capacity of its own is attributed by the State for the sphere of Property Law. The supposition and recognition of a special juristic personality besides that natural to individuals is based upon the fact that the object pursued by such association of persons, or, it may be, for which such collection of goods is designed, could not be realised if the former were treated as a mere plurality of individual subjects of rights existing for themselves in a relation of Property Law, or if the latter were made subject to the control, under Property Law, of a natural Person.

[b] Blackst. i. 467-85 (Steph. ii. pp. 2, *sqq.*).

The capacity for rights possessed by Juristic Persons is limited to the Law of Property, and is of different scope in respect of individual Juristic Persons. The subject of all rights in respect of foundations is the purpose itself, clothed with personality, for which the

---

is given to such person. And so if a minor sue a debtor, he ought to have recourse to curators, that the money may be paid to him; otherwise, the debtor need not pay it to him. But at the present day it is usual for the money to be deposited in a temple . . . or to be paid to curators, if there are any. The debtor is also permitted by an imperial constitution to oblige the young person to apply for curators.

Book II. Part II.

property is designed; in the universitas, the personified[a] totality of the members for the time being as such, in contrast with individuals as subjects of rights upon their own footing.

[a] *I.e.*, as *one* subject not appearing as a mere plurality of persons.

Marcian.: Universitatis sunt, non singulorum, veluti quae in civitatibus sunt theatra et stadia et similia, et si qua alia sunt communia civitatum; ideoque nec servus communis civitatis singulorum pro parte intelligitur, sed universitatis.—D. 1, 8, 6, 1.[1]

Ulp.: —Idemque in ceteris servis corporum dicendum est: nec enim plurium servus videtur, sed corporis.—D. 48, 18, 1, 7.[2]

Id.: Si quid universitati debetur, singulis non debetur, nec quod debet universitas, singuli debent. —l. 7, § 1, D. h. t. (=qu. cuiusq. univ. 3, 4).[3]

Id.: Si municipes vel aliqua universitas ad agendum det actorem, non erit dicendum, quasi a pluribus datum sic haberi; hic enim pro republica vel universitate intervenit, non pro singulis.—l. 2 eod.[4]

Every Juristic Person requires independent property and special representation, *i.e.*, an organ by which it

---

[1] As belonging to a community, and not to individuals, are such things as are to be found in cities—theatres and race-courses and the like, and whatever else belongs to the cities as common property; and so, a common slave does not also belong to individuals in a city, but is regarded as belonging to the community.

[2] The same holds of the rest of slaves that belong to a corporation; for a slave is not considered to belong to several persons, but to the corporation.

[3] If anything be owing to a community, it is not owed to individuals, and individuals do not owe that which is chargeable to the community.

[4] If a municipal corporation or any community appoint a representative to maintain an action, we shall not have to state that he is regarded as though appointed by several; for he appears for the state or community, not for individuals.

manifestly acts. The inner relations of the corporation (rights and duties of the members, administration and application of the property, decision upon a course of action) are regulated by their constitution (statutes), which fixes their purpose and organization, the method of carrying out the collective will, and the juristic representation of the universitas, in relation to third parties as well as to members.

> Gai.: Quibus autem permissum est corpus habere (collegii, societatis, sive cuiusque alterius eorum nomine) proprium est ad exemplum rei publicae habere **res communes, arcam communem et actorem** sive **syndicum,** per quem tamquam in republica, quod communiter agi fierique oporteat, agatur fiat.—l. 1, § 1, h. t.[1]
>
> Ulp.: Refertur ad universos, quod publice fit per maiorem partem.—D. 50, 17, 160, 1.[2]

For the origin of a Juristic Person there is requisite—

(1) the existence of its natural or actual substratum, and so, in the universitas, an organised association of persons invested with particular property; in foundations—the creation of such by the appointment and appropriation of a mass of goods to an independent permanent purpose.

(2) It being recognised by the State as a subject of rights: whether by a general legal maxim, which establishes juristic personality for a certain category of associations, foundations, institutions; or by a 'constitutio personalis,' *i.e.*, special conferment of

---

1 For those who are allowed to have a corporation (under the name of a guild, a partnership or any other of the kind) it is proper, after the type of a republic, to have things shared in common, a common exchequer, and a representative or syndic, by whom, as in a state, that which ought to be done and take place in common may be so done and so take place.

2 That which takes place publicly through the greater part is referred to the whole number.

Book II. Part II.

[a] In Roman Law, by special approval of the association as such on the part of the legislative power.

juristic personality, or, it may be, of the rights of a corporation.[a]

Gai.: Neque societas neque collegium neque huiusmodi corpus passim omnibus haberi conceditur, nam et legibus et senatusconsultis et principalibus constitutionibus ea res coercetur.—l. 1 pr., h. t.[1]

With the cessation of the one or other, the Juristic Person comes to an end; by change of the individual members, however, the universitas is not itself affected.

Ulp.: In . . . universitatibus nihil refert, utrum omnes iidem maneant an pars maneat, vel omnes immutati sint; sed et si universitas ad unum redit, magis admittitur posse eum convenire et conveniri, cum ius omnium in unum reciderit et stet nomen universitatis.—l. 7, § 2 eod.[2]

The ultimate appropriation by Law of property belonging to a corporation is upon dissolution determined alone by its purpose and its constitution, whilst the property of foundations falls to the State.

Just as the State must necessarily co-operate in the origin of a Juristic Person, it is placed also always under the more or less comprehensive superintendence of the State, which takes account of the interest of the community as contrasted with that of individuals, and is concerned for the fulfilment of the will of the founder, and of the purpose of the foundation or association, through its administrators or members for the time being.

---

[1] All alike are not allowed to have a partnership or guild or a corporation of this kind, for this is limited by statutes, by decrees of the senate and imperial constitutions.

[2] In . . . *universitates* it is immaterial whether all remain as they are, or a part remain, or all are changed. But if the *universitas* be reduced to one person, it is allowed that he can sue and be sued, because the right of all has devolved upon the one, and the name of a universitas is kept up.

§ 69. The Several Kinds of Juristic Persons.

There are universitates to which every man of necessity belongs. Those which take a special position amongst Juristic Persons are—

(1) the State as subject of private legal relations; the State property, and at the same time the personality, under Property Law, of the State itself is called 'Fiscus' (aerarium). Hence the 'privilegia fisci.'

(2) Urban and rural communities, whether civitates, rei publicae, or municipa, whose representatives are the 'curia s. decuriones.' The State and communities whose personality was from of old recognised in Roman Law afford the type for the rest of Juristic Persons, which is ever fixed in their constitution.[a]

[a] D. 3, 4, 1, 1 (*supra*).

Other universitates are voluntary combinations, as collegia, corpora (corporations in the narrow sense). To these in particular belonged amongst the Romans—

the standing unions or guilds of those associated officially and professionally, *e.g.*, Priestly colleges, 'decuriae scriliarum,' the ancient companies of artisans, and industrial societies with a corporate organization, as 'societates publicanorum' and the like.

> Paucis admodum in causis concessa sunt huiusmodi corpora, ut ecce vectigalium publicorum sociis permissum est corpus habere, vel aurifodinarum vel argentifodinarum vel sabinarum. Item collegia Romae certa sunt, quorum corpus senatusconsultis atque principalibus constitutionibus confirmatum est, veluti pistorum et quorundam aliorum, et naviculariorum qui et in provinciis sunt.—l. 1 pr., h. t.[1]

---

[1] Only in very few cases have corporations of such kind been allowed, as for instance, partners in the farming of public revenues, or in gold mines, or silver mines and salt-works, to form a corporation. There are likewise certain guilds at Rome,

Book II. Part II.

Associations with manifold other objects, 'sodalitates s. collegia sodalicia,' as social and political clubs—under especially rigorous State-control, and restricted in many ways by police-regulations—and benefit societies, *e.g.*, Burial Clubs (coll. funeraticia).[a]

[a] Cf. § 8, ad fin.

> Marcian.: Mandatis principalibus praecipitur praesidibus provinciarum, ne patiantur esse collegia sodalicia . . . ; sed permittitur tenuioribus stipem menstruam conferre, dum tamen semel in mense coeant.—Collegia si qua fuerint illicita, mandatis et constitutionibus et senatusconsultis dissolvuntur, sed permittitur eis, cum dissolvuntur; pecunias communes, si quas habent, dividere pecuniamque inter se partiri.—D. 47, 22, l. 1 pr., l. 3 pr.[1]

The second class of Juristic Persons, the totality of goods devoted to an independent purpose, only acquired further development in Christian imperial times; the recognition of juristic personality, moreover, was limited to churches and so-called pious or benign foundations (piae causae).

---

whose corporation has been confirmed by decrees of the senate and imperial constitutions, as of bakers and certain others, and of ship-captains who are also in the provinces.

[1] It is laid down in imperial mandates to governors of provinces not to allow companies and unions . . . ; but the support of poorer persons with one month's pay is allowed, so long as they only meet once a month.—Guilds that are prohibited are dissolved by mandates and constitutions and decrees of the senate, but upon dissolution they are allowed to divide moneys shared in common, if they have any, and to distribute the money amongst themselves.

BOOK III.

LAW OF PROPERTY ('RES').[a]

[a] Cf. Holland, pp. 76, 77; Moyle, pp. 68, 69.

PART I.—PURE OR SIMPLE LAW OF PROPERTY.

CHAPTER I.

LAW OF Things.

Title I.—NOTION AND DIVISION OF THINGS.

§ 70. Notion of Thing.[b] *Res Corporalis—incorporalis; in Commercio—extra Commercium.*

[b] See Markby, ss. 125-130.

Thing in the juristic sense is, strictly, every portion of external nature which, limited in space, and subject to the control of the Person, has a money value—'res corporalis.'[c] According to the idea of the Romans, it was everything existing in space, not possessed of Personality. They accordingly speak besides of 'res incorporales,' amongst which—in contrast with objects of ownership—they understand all incorporeal objects of a right (but existing merely in thought) which can belong to Property; as for instance, usufruct, obligations. It is more correct to speak of such as the other proprietary rights in contrast with the right of Ownership, which is often identified with its object.[d]

[c] Cf. § 32.

[d] Cf. Austin, ii. 707, 708; Williams, 'Law of Real Property '(15th ed.) pp. 12, note, and 14, note; Markby, s. 322; Digby, 'Histy. of Law of Real Propy.' (3rd ed.), p. 262.

> Gai.: Quaedam praeterea res corporales sunt, quaedam incorporales. **Corporales** hae sunt, quae tangi possunt, veluti fundus homo vestis aurum argentum et denique aliae res innumera-

BOOK III. Pt. I. Ch. I.

biles: **incorporales** sunt, quae tangi non possunt, qualia sunt ea quae in iure consistunt, sicut hereditas ususfructus obligationes quoque modo contractae. Nec ad eam rem pertinet, quod in hereditate res corporales continentur (nam) et fructus, qui ex fundo percipiuntur, corporales sunt, et id quod ex aliqua obligatione nobis debetur plerumque corporale est, veluti fundus homo pecunia: nam ipsum ius successionis et ipsum ius utendi fruendi et ipsum ius obligationis incorporale est. Eodem numero sunt et iura praediorum urbanorum et rusticorum, quae etiam servitutes vocantur.—l. 1, § 1, D. h. t. (=de R. D. 1, 8).[1]

Cic. Top. 5, 29: Esse ea dico, quae cerni tangive possunt, ut fundum aedes parietem stillicidium mancipium pecudem suppellectilem penus, cetera;—non esse rursus ea dico, quae tangi demonstrarive non possunt, cerni tamen animo atque intelligi possunt,—quarum rerum nullum subest quasi corpus.[2]

---

[1] Moreover, some things are corporeal, and some incorporeal. Corporeal are such as can be touched, as a farm, a slave, a garment, gold, silver, and innumerable other things; incorporeal are those that cannot be touched, as those things which consist in a right, such as an inheritance, a usufruct, and all obligations contracted in whatever way. And it does not affect the matter that corporeal things are included in the inheritance, for fruits also obtained from an estate are corporeal, and that which is owing to us upon an obligation is generally corporeal, for instance, a farm, a slave, money; for the right itself of inheritance, the right itself of usufruct, and the right itself of obligation is incorporeal. To the same list belong also rights of civic and provincial estates, which also are called servitudes.

[2] I say that such things exist as can be seen or touched, as a farm, a house, a wall, a gutter, a slave, an ox, furniture, provisions, and so on;—again I say that such things do not exist as are not susceptible of touch or proof, but can be seen and mentally apprehended, of which things no body, as it were, subsists.

Ulp.: **Rei** appellatione et causae et iura continentur.—D. 50, 16, 23.[1]

Book III. Pt. I. Ch. I.

Most things, in agreement with their natural purpose, are subject to individual control. But there are also things which do not fall under individual ownership, and cannot consequently be objects of private proprietary right. To such is given the name of 'res extra commercium.'

> Videamus de rebus; quae vel **in nostro patrimonio** sunt, vel **extra nostrum patrimonium** habentur: quaedam enim naturali iure communia sunt omnium, quaedam publica, quaedam universitatis, quaedam nullius, pleraque singulorum.—pr. I. h. t. (=de R. D. 2, 1).[2]
>
> Gai.: Summa rerum divisio in duos articulos deducitur: nam aliae sunt divini iuris, aliae humani. . . . Quod autem divini iuris est, id nullius in bonis est. . . . Hae autem res, quae humani iuris sunt, aut publicae sunt aut privatae; quae publicae sunt, nullius in bonis esse creduntur, ipsius enim universitatis esse creduntur; privatae autem sunt, quae singulorum sunt.—l. 1 pr., D. h. t.[3]

This is because they

(1) are either by nature the common property of

---

[1] Under the designation 'thing' are comprised both appurtenances and rights.

[2] Let us now consider the things which are either in our ownership or are regarded as outside of it. For some things are by the Law of Nature common to all, others are public, others, again, belong to a community, some to no one, most to individuals.

[3] The principal division of things falls into two classes, for some appertain to divine, others to human law. . . . But that which is of divine right belongs to no one. Now those things which are of human right are either public or private; the public are considered to belong to no one, for they are regarded as belonging to the community. But private are those which belong to individuals.

Book III. Pt. I. Ch. I.

all, and thus called 'res communes,' or are designed for public use—'res publicae,' in a twofold sense.[a]

[a] D. 1, 8, 6, 1.

Et quidem naturali iure **communia** sunt **omnium** haec: aer et aqua profluens et mare et per hoc litora maris.—Est autem litus maris, quatenus hibernus fluctus maxime excurrit.—§§ 1, 3, I. h. t.[1]

Scaev.: In litore iure gentium aedificare licere, nisi usus publicus impediretur.—D. 43, 8, 4.[2]

Marcian.: —in tantum, ut et soli domini constituantur, qui ibi aedificant, sed quamdiu aedificium manet.—l. 6 pr., D. h. t.[3]

(2) Or because they are devoted to religious purposes, or have been consecrated by a religious act,—'res divini iuris,' whether 'sacrae,' 'sanctae,' or 'religiosae.'[b]

[b] See Maine, 'Early Law and Custom,' ch. iii.

Gai. ii. §§ 4–5: **Sacrae** sunt, quae Diis superis consecratae sunt; **religiosae**, quae Diis Manibus relictae sunt.—Sed sacrum quidem hoc solum existimatur, quod ex auctoritate populi Romani consecratum est, veluti lege de ea re lata aut senatusconsulto facto.[4]

Sacra sunt, quae rite et per pontifices deo consecrata sunt, veluti aedes sacrae et dona, quae rite ad ministerium dei dedicata sunt.—§ 8, I. h. t.[5]

---

1 Now by the Law of Nature the following things are common to every one: the air, flowing water, and the sea, and consequently the shores of the sea.—The sea-shore extends as far as the highest winter-tide goes out.

2 By the *i. g.* one is allowed to build upon the shore, unless the use by the public be thereby prevented.

3 —so that even those building there become sole owners, but only so long as the structure remains.

4 Things sacred are those which have been consecrated to the gods above; things religious those which have been given up to departed spirits. But that alone is accounted sacred which has been consecrated by authority of the Roman people, as if a statute have been passed, or by a decree of the senate, concerning such matter.

Now sanctuaries are such things as solemnly and by the

Gai. ii. § 6: **Religiosum** vero nostra voluntate facimus, mortuum inferentes in locum nostrum, si modo eius mortui funus ad nos pertineat.[1] Book III. Pt. I. Ch. I.

Ibid. § 8: **Sanctae** quoque res, velut muri et portae, quodammodo divini iuris sunt.[2]

Marcian.: Sanctum est, quod ab iniuria hominum defensum atque munitum est.—l. 8 pr., D. h. t.[3]

Ulp.: **Purus** locus dicitur, qui neque sacer neque sanctus est neque religiosus.—D. 11, 7, 2, 4.[4]

These 'res extra commercium' can in no wise be object of private rights and of private dispositions, so long as they are not restored to private commerce by a special legal act.

Ulp.: Bona civitatis abusive **publica** dicta sunt, sola enim publica sunt, quae populi Romani sunt.—D. 50, 16, 15.[5]

Flumina [paene] omnia et portus **publica** sunt: ideoque ius piscandi omnibus commune est in portu fluminibusque.—§ 2, I. h. t. Cf. Marcian. in l. 4, § 1, D. h. t.[6]

Gai.: Riparum **usus publicus** est iure gentium

---

pontifices have been set apart to God; *e.g.*, sacred houses, and presents which have been solemnly designed for the service of God.

[1] But we can of our own will make a place belonging to us religious by conveying a corpse into it, provided the interment of such corpse devolves upon us.

[2] Hallowed places also, such as walls and gates, in a manner appertain to divine law.

[3] That is hallowed which has been secured and protected against illegal acts of men.

[4] Such a place is called 'pure' as is neither sacred, nor hallowed, nor religious.

[5] Improperly has property of a city been called 'public,' for things are alone public that belong to the Roman people.

[6] [Almost] all rivers and harbours are public; therefore the right of fishing in harbours and rivers is common to all persons.

Book III. Pt. I. Ch. I.

sicut ipsius fluminis. . . . Sed proprietas illorum est, quorum praediis haerent.—l. 5 pr., D. h. t.[1]

Ulp.: Loca publica utique privatorum usibus deserviunt, iure scilicet civitatis non quasi propria cuiusque.—D. 43, 8, 2, 2.[2]

Papin.: Si res non **in usu publico** sed **in patrimonio fisci** erit, venditio eius valebit.—D. 18, 1, 72, 1.[3]

Pomp.: Celsus ait, hominem librum scientem te emere non posse, nec cuiuscumque rei, si scias alienationem (non) esse,[a] ut sacra et religiosa loca aut quorum commercium non sit, ut publica, quae non **in pecunia populi** sed **in publico usu** habeantur, ut est campus Martius.—l. 6 pr. eod.[4]

[a] =quamcumque rem, si scias eius etc. *v. add.:* emptionem esse.

§ 71. Res Mobiles—Immobiles.

'Res mobiles' are all movables, inclusive of things which are readily set in motion.

Cels.: **Moventium** item **mobilium** appellatione idem significamus, nisi tamen apparet defunctum animalia dumtaxat, quia se ipsa moverent, moventia vocasse.—l. 93, de V. S. 50, 16.[5]

---

[1] The use of river-banks is public according to the *i. g.*, as of the river itself.—But the ownership therein belongs to them with whose lands it is in contact.

[2] The public places serve also for private use, that is, by virtue of the right of the State, not as though belonging properly to any one.

[3] If a thing be not public, but the property of the treasury, the sale thereof will be valid.

[4] Cel. says you cannot knowingly purchase a freeman, nor anything whatever if you know it to be unsaleable; as sacred and religious places, or those which do not admit of being traded with, as public places which do not belong to the public purse but are regarded as put to public use, such as the Campus Martius.

[5] And further, by the designation *moventia* and *mobilia* we denote the same thing unless, however, it appear that the deceased spoke only of animals as moving by reason of their setting themselves in motion.

'Res immobiles' are ground and soil, and whatever is attached thereto. (Solum et res soli, i.e. solo cohaerentes.) Book III. Pt. I. Ch. I.

(1) Special parts of the soil are: 'fundus' (praedium); 'ager' and 'area'; 'villa' and 'aedes.'

Iavol.: **Fundus** est omne quidquid solo tenetur; **ager** est, si species fundi ad usum hominis comparatur.—l. 115 eod.[1]

Ulp.: **Locus** est non fundus, sed portio aliqua fundi, **fundus** autem integrum aliquid est; et plerumque sine villa 'locum' accipimus. . . . Non magnitudo 'locum' a 'fundo' separat, sed nostra affectio: et quaelibet portio fundi poterit fundus dici, si iam hoc constituerimus; nec non et fundus 'locus' constitui potest: nam si eum alii adiunxerimus fundo, locus fundi efficietur.—§ Sed fundus quidem suos habet fines; locus vero latere potest, quatenus determinetur et definiatur.—l. 60 pr., § 2 eod.[2]

Flor.: **Fundi** appellatione omne aedificium et omnis ager continetur; sed in usu urbana aedificia **aedes,** rustica **villae** dicuntur. Locus vero sine aedificio in urbe **area,** rure autem **ager** appellatur. Idemque ager cum aedificio fundus dicitur.—l. 211 eod.[3]

---

[1] *Fundus* is everything whatsoever that is comprised [a] by ground. An *ager* exists if some kind of *fundus* be adapted to human use.

[a] Dirksen, s. v.

[2] *Locus* is not a *fundus,* but a certain part of a *fundus;* whilst a *fundus* is some whole; and generally we understand by it a place without a country house.[b] . . . It is not the great size which distinguishes a 'locus' from a 'fundus,' but our disposition; and every part of a *fundus* can be called a *fundus,* if we have so already determined. Indeed, one can also make a *fundus* into a *locus,* for if we shall have added it to another *fundus,* a 'place' of the *fundus* will be created.—But whilst a *fundus* has its boundaries, the scope of the limitation and marking out of a *locus* may be beyond discovery.

[b] *Infra.*

[3] Under the designation *fundus* is included every building and field; but by habit we call town-buildings *aedes,* country-buildings *villae.* But a place without a building is in the town called

(2) Estates are divided, according to their agricultural purpose, into 'praedia rustica' and 'praedia urbana.'

Ulp.: **Urbana praedia** omnia aedificia accipimus, non solum ea quae sunt in oppidis, sed et si forte stabula sunt vel alia meritoria in villis, . . . vel praetoria voluptati tantum deservientia, quia urbanum praedium non locus facit, sed materia. Proinde hortos quoque, si qui sunt in aedificiis constitui, dicendum est urbanorum appellatione contineri; plane si plurimum horti in reditu sunt, vinearii forte vel etiam olitorii, magis haec non sunt urbana.—l. 198 eod.[1]

(3) Of special importance in the older Roman Law is the division of 'solum Italicum' and 'solum provinciale' (praedia stipendaria, tributaria), the latter of which was conceived of as property of the State, and to it the legal relations of the ius civile were not applicable.

Gai. ii. § 7: In **provinciali** solo . . . dominium populi Romani est vel Caesaris, nos autem possessionem tantum et usumfructum habere videmur.[2]

Ibid. ii. § 21: —**provincialia** praedia, quorum alia stipendiaria, alia tributaria vocamus: **stipendiaria** sunt ea, quae in his provinciis sunt, quae

an *area*, but in the country an *ager*. And again, an *ager* with a building is called a *fundus*.

[1] By town-houses we understand all buildings, not only those that are in towns, but it may be also stables or other quarters amongst homesteads, . . . or stately buildings serving alone for pleasure, because it is not the place, but the character, that makes an estate urban. Wherefore, if any gardens also are situated amongst buildings, we must state that they are comprised under the designation of things urban; certainly if gardens are for the most part in produce, vineyards it may be, or even kitchen gardens, these are rather not urban.

[2] On provincial soil, the ownership belongs to the Roman people or to the Emperor, whilst we are considered to have only the possession and the enjoyment.

propriae populi Romani esse intelliguntur; **tributaria** sunt ea, quae in his provinciis sunt, quae propriae Caesaris esse creduntur.[1]

Inst. ii. 1, 40: Vocantur autem stipendaria et tributaria praedia, quae in provinciis sunt; inter quae nec non Italica praedia ex nostra constitutione nulla differentia est.[2]

In respect of juristic treatment, no difference as a rule finds place in Roman Law between movables and immovables.

§ 72. Species and Genus. Things Representable and Consumable.

'Species' (certum corpus) is the thing marked off as individual; 'genus,' the thing as classified.[a]

[a] Cf. § 105.

(1) Things which in commerce regularly come into consideration only as a genus, *i.e.*, according to quantity and quality, are called 'representable' things, 'fungibles' and 'quantities.'

Paul.: Mutui datio consistit in his rebus, quae **pondere numero mensura** consistunt [qualis est pecunia numerata vinum oleum frumentum aes argentum aurum], quoniam eorum datione possumus in creditum ire, quia in genere suo functionem recipiunt per solutionem, quam specie.—l. 2, § 1, D. de R. C. 12, 1, cf. Gai. iii. § 90.[3]

---

[1] —provincial lands, some of which we call stipendiary, others tributary: stipendiary are those which are in such provinces as are understood to belong specially to the Roman people; tributary are those which are in such provinces as are considered to belong specially to the Emperor.

[2] Now those lands are called stipendiary and tributary which are in the provinces; between these and Italian estates there is by our constitution no difference.

[3] The grant of a loan lies in such things as are reckoned by weight, number, measure [such as coin, wine, oil, corn, copper, silver, gold], since by the grant of such things we can originate a loan, because they admit of discharge by payment in their genus rather than by species.

BOOK III. Pt. I. Ch. I.

Ulp.: Si legetur pecunia quae in arca est, vel vinum quod in apothecis est, . . . species legatur. —l. 30, § 6, D. de leg. i. 30.[1]

(2) To such belongs especially Money, as the general measure of value recognised and guaranteed by the State,[a] and general medium of exchange or payment, as alone designed for this purpose.[b] There was in Rome originally no coined money (pecunia signata forma publica populi Romani) but only marked bars of copper (aes rude, aes signatum), which first obtained in each individual case the character of money by its being publicly weighed under the guarantee of the State.[c]

[a] D. 50, 16, 222.
[b] Cf. § 122, ad init.
[c] § 79, ad init.

Paul.: Origo emendi vendendique a permutationibus coepit; olim enim non ita erat nummus, neque aliud merx aliud pretium vocabatur, sed unusquisque secundum necessitatem temporum ac rerum utilibus inutilia permutabat: quando plerumque evenit, ut quod alteri superest, alteri desit. Sed quia non semper nec facile concurrebat, ut, cum tu haberes quod ego desiderarem, invicem haberem quod tu accipere velles, electa materia est, cuius publica ac perpetua aestimatio difficultatibus permutationum aequalitate quantitatis subveniret: eaque materia forma publica percussa usum dominumque non tam ex substantia praebet, quam ex quantitate, nec ultra merx utrumque, sed alterum pretium vocatur.—D. 18, 1, 1 pr.[2]

[1] If money have been bequeathed which is in a chest, or wine which is in a cellar, it is a specific bequest.

[2] The origin of buying and selling began with exchange; for there was formerly no coin, neither was one thing called merchandise, another price, but every one, according to the requirement of the times and of circumstances, exchanged things without use for those that had a use; since it generally happens that what one has in superfluity another lacks. But since it did not always nor readily happen that, when you had what I wanted, I on the other hand possessed what you

Gai. i. § 122: —olim aereis tantum nummis utebantur; et erant asses, dupondii, semisses, quadrantes, nec ullus aureus vel argenteus nummus in usu erat, sicut ex lege XII tabularum intelligere possumus; eorumque nummorum vis ac potestas non in numero erat, sed in pondere nummorum; . . . (itaque) qui dabat . . . pecuniam, non numerabat eam, sed adpendebat.[1]

'Consumables' is the name given to those things the purpose and use of which consist precisely in their being used up immediately, *i.e.*, according to their individuality, either as in general perishable (things naturally consumable) or as use is to be made of them (juristically consumable things, *e.g.*, money).

Ulp. xxiv. 27: —si earum rerum, quae **in abusu continentur,** utputa vini olei tritici, ususfructus legatus sit.[2]

Inst. ii. 4, 2: —(res) quae **ipso usu consumuntur** . . . quo numero sunt vinum, oleum frumentum vestimenta (?); quibus proxima est pecunia numerata: namque in ipso usu adsidua permutatione quodammodo extinguitur.[3]

---

desired to acquire, a material was chosen, the general and unchangeable value of which should obviate the difficulties of exchange by equality of quantity; and this material, imprinted with a public stamp, furnishes us with the use and right of ownership not so much by substance as by quantity, and thenceforth both are not called merchandise, but one of them price.

[1] Formerly copper coins were alone used; and they were the *as*, the double *as*, half *as*, and quarter *as*; and no gold or silver coins were employed, as we may see from a law of the Twelve Tables. The force and power of such money did not consist in the number, but in the weight thereof; . . . (therefore) he who paid over . . . the money, did not count it, but weighed it.

[2] —if the usufruct have been bequeathed of such things as derive their character from consumption, for example, wine, oil, wheat.

[3] —things which are consumed by very use . . . in which category are wine, oil, fruit, clothing; next to which is coined

Book III. Pt. I. Ch. I.

§ 73. Things Divisible and Indivisible; Simple and Compound; Principal and Accessory.

A distinction is made in Law between things that are physical or corporeal (real) and such as are juristic or ideal.

The division into 'physical' or 'corporeal' consists in the breaking up of a thing into several independent wholes, 'real' parts (partes pro diviso, certae partes). Whilst by Nature all movable things are interminably divisible, in Law only such things are regarded as corporally divisible (res dividuae) as can be divided without destruction of their essence [a] or essential diminution of their money-value; on the other hand, the ground and soil, which are naturally indivisible, are in Law treated as divisible (by boundaries, without extinction of physical cohesion); whereby in general estates are at first formed, and things going with them.

[a] Cf. § 72, ad init.

> Paul.:—Quintus Mucius ait, **partis** appellatione rem **pro indiviso** significari: nam quod **pro diviso** nostrum sit, id non partem sed totum esse: Servius non ineleganter, partis appellatione utrumque significari.—D. 50, 16, 25, 1.[1]
>
> Pomp.: In his tamen rebus partem dare heres conceditur, quae **sine damno** dividi possunt; sin autem vel **naturaliter indivisae** sint, vel sine damno divisio earum fieri non potest, aestimatio ab herede praestanda est.—l. 26, § 2, D. de leg. i. 30.[2]

---

money, for it is in a manner destroyed in use by constant exchange.

[1] Q. Mucius says that by the designation 'part' a thing is denoted which is divided only in thought, for if anything belong to us which is actually divided, that is not a part, but a whole. Servius says, not inappropriately, that the designation a 'part' denotes both.

[2] In such things, however, as can be divided without damage, the heir is allowed to pay a part; but if they are either by nature indivisible, or a division thereof cannot be effected without damage, the heir must discharge the estimated amount.

Ulp.: Plane si divisit fundum **regionibus** et sic partem tradidit **pro diviso,** . . . non est pars fundi, sed fundus. Quod et in aedibus potest dici, si dominus pariete medio aedificato unam domum in duas diviserit, ut plerique faciunt: nam et hic pro duabus domibus accipi debet.—D. 8, 4, 6, 1.[1]

Paul.: (Res morbilis) numquam pro diviso possideri potest.—D. 6, 1, 8.[2]

The 'juristic' or 'ideal' division consists in the division of a thing, or, more precisely, of the right in the whole and undivided thing, according to fractional parts (quotas), *i.e.*, 'intellectual' parts, merely existing in thought (partes pro indiviso).[a]

[a] Cf. § 75, ad init.

Ulp.: Servus communis sic omnium est, non quasi singulorum totus, sed pro partibus utique **indivisis,** ut **intellectu** magis partes habeant, quam corpore.—D. 45, 3, 5.[3]

Papin.: Plures in uno fundo dominium iuris intellectu, non divisione corporis obtinent.—l. 66, § 2, D. de leg. ii. 31.[4]

In agreement with the doctrine of the Stoics, the Roman jurists make the following distinctions.

(1) The individual thing (una, singularis res) can be either one, that is 'simple,' consisting of one piece, or one mechanically 'compounded' of several constituents; this so-called 'universitas rerum co-

---

[1] If a man have clearly divided an estate according to pieces and then have given up a part as a divided whole . . . it is not a part of an estate, but an estate. This can also be said of buildings if the owner has divided a house into two by building an intermediate wall, as many do; for here also we must consider there are two houses.

[2] (Of a movable thing) there cannot be divided possession.

[3] A slave owned in common belongs to all his masters in such a way that as individuals they do not possess him wholly, but only in undivided shares, so that they possess portions rather in idea than substantially.

[4] Several persons together hold the ownership of one estate by legal acceptation, not by division of the material thing.

Book III. Pt. I. Ch. I.

haerentium' is treated as an independent whole in relation to its constituents, and is juristically always regarded as ONE thing.[a]

[a] § 76.

Pomp.: Tria autem genera sunt corporum: unum quod continetur uno spiritu et graece ἡνωμένον vocatur, ut homo tignum lapis, et similia; alterum quod ex contingentibus h. e. pluribus inter se cohaerentibus constat, quod συνημμένον vocatur, ut aedificium navis armarium; tertium quod ex distantibus constat, ut corpora plura soluta, sed uni nomini subiecta, veluti . . . grex.—D. 43, 3, 30 pr.[1]

Iavol.: —separatis corporibus, ex quibus aedes constant, universitas aedium intelligi non poterit. —l. 23 pr. eod.[2]

Alf.: Navem, si adeo saepe refecta esset, ut nulla tabula eadem permaneret, quae non nova fuisset, nihilominus eandem navem existimari. . . . Quapropter cuius rei **species eadem** consisteret, **rem** quoque **eandem** esse existimari.—D. 5, 1, 76.[3]

(2) Besides individual things, there come into consideration in commerce the so-called 'totalities of things'—'universitates rerum (distantium),' collective, ideal-wholes—*i.e.*, several independent things of like kind, which are conjoined as a unity simply

---

[1] Now there are three kinds of bodies: first, those which consist of a whole, and in Greek called ἡνωμένον (simple), as a man, a beam, a stone and the like; the second, such as consist of compounds, *i.e.*, things connected, called συνημμένον (compound), as a house, a ship, a closet; thirdly, such as consist of diverse things, as several bodies independent, but comprised under one name, for example, a flock.

[2] If the objects of which the house consists are divided from one another, the totality of the house will be inconceivable.

[3] That a ship, if it were so often repaired that no plank remained the same which had not been renewed, none the less was considered the same ship . . . Therefore, if the form of a thing remained the same, the thing also is considered to be the same.

by virtue of their common purpose. These in legal treatment regularly appear as a mere plurality of individual things: only those collective wholes to the essence of which intrinsically belongs a natural interchange and complement of their constituent parts (as a herd) are in some relations conceived as unities of things, without an essentially practical meaning attaching to this idea.[a]

Inst. ii. 20, 18: Grege legato etiam eas noves, quae post testamentum factum gregi adiiciuntur, legato cedere Iulianus ait: esse enim gregis unum corpus ex distantibus capitibus, sicuti aedium unum corpus est ex cohaerentibus lapidibus.[1]

Pomp.: Si grege legato aliqua pecora vivo testatore mortua essent, in eorumque locum aliqua essent substituta, eundem gregem videri.—l. 22, D. eod. i. 30.[2]

[a] D. 6, 1, 1, 3, 20, 1, 13 pr. Cf. I. ii. 5, 21, and see Bell, s. 'universitas.'

Mutual relations of things in Law.

1. In the connection of one thing with another the question may arise, which of the two is the 'principal' thing (res principalis) and which is the 'accessory' (accessio). In general we can designate as principal thing that which forms the prerequisite and substratum of the other, or which as compared with the other appears to be the essential one (and giving it its name), on account of which, accordingly, the other exists. But the idea of principal and accessory thing is largely relative; in the particular case, therefore, the question must be decided by the importance which the prevailing ideas of commerce, or even individual custom,

---

[1] Jul. says that if a flock have been bequeathed, those fresh sheep which are added to the flock after the making of the testament also appertain to the bequest; for that the flock is a whole which consists of different members, just as a house is a whole formed from stones united together.

[2] That if a flock be bequeathed, and some sheep should die in the lifetime of the testator, and some be substituted in their place, it is considered to be the same flock.

Book III. Pt. I. Ch. I.

attribute to the one or the other thing. However this be, 'accessio cedit principali.' [a]

[a] § 84.

In Roman Law the following are regarded as accessory things.

(1) vincta fixaque.

Ulp.: Aedibus distractis vel legatis ea esse aedium solemus dicere, quae **quasi pars aedium** vel **propter aedes** habentur.—Fundi nihil est, nisi quod terra se tenet.—D. 19, 1, l. 13, § 31, and l. 17 pr.[1]

(2) appurtenances—also with movables, *e.g.*, ships—that is, independent things which are alone intended and used for another thing,—'quae perpetui usus (fundi, aedium) causa comparata sunt.'

Aedium autem multa esse, quae aedibus adfixa non sunt, ignorari non oportet, utputa seras claves claustra.—Labeo generaliter scribit, ea quae **perpetui usus causa** in aedificiis sunt, aedificii esse; quae vero ad praesens, non esse aedificii.—Pali qui vineae causa parati sunt, antequam collocentur, fundi non sunt.—l. 17 pr., §§ 7, 11, cit.[2]

'Ruta caesa' [b] are not accounted accessory things.

[b] See Brown, s. vv.

—ea placuit esse **ruta**, quae eruta sunt, ut arena creta et similia; **caesa** ea esse, ut arbores caesas carbones et his similia.—Ib. § 6.[3]

---

[1] If a house have been sold or bequeathed, we commonly speak of those things as belonging to the house which, as it were, form a part of the house or exist because of it.—Nothing belongs to an estate save what is attached to the earth.

[2] But to a building belong many things which have not been fixed in it, as for example, locks, keys, bolts.—Labeo writes that in general that which exists for perpetual use in buildings belongs to the building, but that which is there only for the moment, does not belong to the building. Stakes that have been provided for a vine do not belong to the estate until they are driven in.

[3] It has been held that those things are *ruta* which have been dug up, as sand, chalk, and the like; *caesa*, trees that have been cut, charcoal, and such like things.

Pomp.: —ruta caesa ea sunt, quae neque aedium neque fundi sunt.—D. 18, 1, 66, 2.[1]

2. 'Fructus.'

(1) By 'fruits' are comprehended in general all natural and regular organic products of a thing, especially such as are derived from it in agreement with its purpose, as well fruits and other products of the soil as the young of animals, but not children of slaves.[a]

[a] D. 7, 1, 68.

Paul.: **Frugem** pro reditu appellari non solum quod frumentis aut leguminibus, verum et quod ex vino, silvis caeduis, cretifodinis, lapidicinis capitur.—D. 50, 16, 77.[2]

Gai.: In pecudum fructu etiam foetus est, sicut lac et pilus et lana.—**Partus** vero **ancillae** in fructu non est; absurdum enim videbatur, hominem in fructu esse, cum omnes fructus rerum natura hominum gratia comparaverit.—l. 28 pr., § 1, D. de usur. 22, 1.[3]

Ulp.: Ancillarum partus . . . fructus esse non existimantur, quia non temere ancillae eius rei causa comparantur, ut pariant.—D. 5, 3, 27 pr.[4]

(2) Important is the distinction of 'fructus pendentes,' 'separati' and 'percepti.' The fruit first becomes an independent object of rights (a thing for itself) by separation from the thing pro-

---

[1] —*ruta caesa* are such things as belong neither to a building nor to an estate.

[2] That the expression *frux* is taken of produce, and not merely of crops or vegetables but also of that derived from wine, coppices, chalk pits, quarries.

[3] To the fruit of animals belong also their young, as well as their milk, hair and wool.—But the issue of a slave-woman does not form part of fruits; for it seemed nonsensical that a human being should be (reckoned) amongst fruits, since nature provided all fruits for the sake of men.

[4] The issue of slave-women are not regarded as fruits, because slave-women are not lightly procured for such a purpose as that of bearing children.

Book III. Pt. I. Ch. I.

ducing it, to which it hitherto belonged as a mere part.[a]

[a] § 85.

Gai.: Fructus **pendentes** pars fundi videntur. —D. 6, 1, 44.[1]

Paul.: Labeo ait . . fructum **percipi** spica aut foeno caeso, aut uva adempta, aut excussa olea, quamvis nondum tritum frumentum, aut oleum factum, vel vindemia coacta sit. Sed ut verum est, quod de olea excussa scripsit, ita aliter observandum de ea olea, quae per se deciderit. Iulianus ait, fructuarii fructus tunc fieri, cum eos perceperit, bonae fidei autem possessoris, mox quam a solo separati sint.—D. 7, 4, 13.[2]

Regarded as Fructus in the wider sense are, 'fructus civiles,' *i.e.*, all other products of a thing or revenues from it, especially—

(*a*) Rents.

Ulp.: Praediorum urbanorum **pensiones** pro fructibus accipiuntur.—l. 36, D. de usur.[3]

Id.: **Mercedes** plane a colonis acceptae loco sunt fructuum; **operae** quoque servorum in eadem erunt causa, qua sunt pensiones; item **vecturae** navium et iumentorum.—D. 5, 3, 29.[4]

(*β*) Interest.

Id.: **Usurae** vicem fructuum obtinent, et

---

[1] Hanging fruits are regarded as part of an estate.

[2] Labeo says that . . . the fruit is gathered when the ears or hay are cut, or the grapes plucked, or the olives shaken out, although the corn is not yet thrashed, or the oil made, or vintage pressed. But although it is correct what he wrote of the olive shaken out, yet the remark does not hold with respect to the olive that has fallen of its own accord. Jul. says that the fruits become the property of the usufructuary when he has gathered them, but belong to the *bonae fidei* possessor[b] as soon as they have been detached from the ground.

[b] See § 85.

[3] The rents of urban estates are regarded as fruits.

[4] The farm-rents received from cultivators clearly take the place of fruits; also the services of slaves will stand in the same relation as rents, likewise the freights of ships and hire of beasts of draught.

merito non debent a fructibus separari.—l. 34, D. de usur.[1]

Pomp.: Usura pecuniae, quam percipimus, in fructu non est, quia non ex ipso corpore, sed ex alia causa est, i.e. nova obligatione.—D. 50, 16, 121.[2]

Natural and civil fruits are at the same time comprised in the expression 'omnis causa rei,' which designates everything belonging juristically to an object of rights to which claim is made, constituting the augmentation thereof which likewise has to be accounted for.

§ 74. Res Mancipi—Nec Mancipi.

A distinction peculiar to the Roman people is that of 'res mancipi' and 'res nec mancipi.' [a]

[a] 'Anct. Law,' pp. 273, *sqq.*; 'Early Law and Custom,' pp. 249-251.

Ulp. xix. 1: **Mancipi** res sunt praedia in Italico solo tam rustica, qualis est fundus, quam urbana, qualis domus; item iura praediorum rusticorum, velut via iter actus aquaeductus; item servi et quadrupedes, quae dorso collove domantur, velut boves muli aequi asini. Ceterae res **nec mancipi** sunt; elefanti et cameli, quamvis collo dorsove domentur, nec mancipi sunt, quoniam bestiarum numero sunt. (—nam ne nomen quidem eorum animalium illo tempore notum fuit, quo constituebatur quasdem res mancipi esse quasdam nec mancipi. Gai. ii. § 16.)[3]

---

1 Interest represents fruits, and rightly ought not to be separated from them.

2 The interest of money drawn by us is not amongst fruits, because it does not arise from the thing itself but from another cause, that is, a new obligation.

3 *Res mancipi* are *praedia* on Italian soil, both rural, as a field, and urban, as a house; likewise rights belonging to rural *praedia*, as *via*, *ita*, *actus*, *aquaeductus*, besides slaves and quadrupeds which are tamed by yoke or saddle, such as oxen, mules, horses, asses. The rest of things are *nec mancipi;* elephants and camels, although they are tamed by yoke and

BOOK III. Pt. I. Ch. I.

Gai. ii. § 15: —(nostri quidem praeceptores) statim ut nata sunt, mancipi esse putant: Nerva vero et Proculus et ceteri diversae scholae auctores non aliter ea mancipi esse putant, quam si domita sunt; et si propter nimiam feritatem domari non possunt, tunc videri mancipi esse incipere, cum ad eam aetatem pervenerint, qua domari solent.[1]

The practical significance of this distinction consists in the fact that, in respect of res mancipi amongst Roman citizens, full Roman ownership can only be transferred by a civil act of acquisition, as especially the formal transaction of 'mancipatio' and 'in iure cessio.'[a]

[a] § 79.

Gai. ii. § 18: Magna autem differentia est inter mancipi res et nec mancipi.—§ 19: Nam res nec mancipi ipsa traditione pleno iure alterius fiunt.—§ 22: Mancipi vero res sunt, quae per mancipationem ad alium transferuntur; unde etiam mancipi res sunt dictae; quod autem valet mancipatio, idem valet et in iure cessio.[2]

Comprehensive as is this distinction between res mancipi and nec mancipi, which in later time disappeared, and was literally abolished by Justinian, the

---

saddle, are *nec mancipi*, being reckoned amongst wild beasts (—for not even was the name of such animals known at that time when it was settled that some things should be *mancipi*, some *nec mancipio*).

1 —(the leaders of our school) consider that these animals are *mancipi* immediately they are born; but Nerva and Proculus and other leaders of the opposite school think they become so only when broken in; and if on account of their extreme ferocity they cannot be broken in, then they are considered first to be *mancipi* when they reach the age at which such animals are commonly broken in.

2 Now there is a great difference between things *mancipi* and *nec mancipi*.—§ For *res nec mancipi* become the property of another in full ownership by mere delivery.—§ But things are *mancipi* which are conveyed to another by mancipation, whence also their name of *r. m.* Now the effect of a mancipation is that also of a surrender in court.

reason for it has been subject of much dispute. 'Mancipi res' are supposed to have been those objects of ownership which by virtue of their nature, according to the old national idea, stood in close relationship to the Roman family life (familia and heredium), of which they constituted the basis and most important ingredient. That at the same time explains their relation to agriculture.

Title II.—OWNERSHIP AND POSSESSION.[a]

[a] See 'Anct. Law,' pp. 290, *sqq.*

§ 75. Nature, Forms, and History of Roman Ownership.

Ownership[b] is the total and exclusive legal control over a corporeal thing. The positive element characteristic of the owner consists in the legal power to operate upon the thing in every direction; the negative, in excluding every other person from the thing. It comprises the following features.

[b] Cf. Austin, lect. 47; Markby, ch. viii.; Holland, pp. 139-140, 149, *sqq.* For the English conception, see Brown, s. v.

A 'dominium plurium in solidum' is inconceivable; and further, if the same thing is the property of several persons, the co-owners are only entitled 'pro partibus indivisis,'[c] so that the one proprietary right in the thing belongs to several together, and each possesses the aggregate of proprietary rights in respect of a quota of the thing.[d]

[c] D. 45, 3, 5.

[d] D. § 135.

> Ulp.: (Celsus) ait, duorum quidem in solidum dominium vel possessionem esse non posse, nec quemquam partis corporis dominum esse, sed totius corporis pro indiviso pro parte dominium habere.—D. 13, 6, 5, 15.[1]
>
> Papin.: Sabinus, in re communi neminem dominorum iure facere quidquam invito altero posse. Unde manifestum est, prohibendi ius

[1] (Cels.) says, There cannot be ownership or possession of two persons for the entirety, and no one is owner of a part of a material thing, but each has the ownership of the whole *corpus* as undivided for a portion.

Book III. Pt. I. Ch. I.

esse; in re enim pari potiorem causam esse prohibentis constat.—D. 10, 3, 28.[1]

On the other hand, particular rights inherent in ownership can be specifically restricted or can be extinguished, without any resulting encroachment upon the idea of ownership, as of full control, which apprehends the thing not in this or that particular relation, but in the whole significance attached to it by Private Law.

These limitations can obtain—

(1) through private disposition,—'iura in re aliena.'[a]

[a] § 92.

Paul.: Recte dicimus eum fundum **totum** nostrum esse, etiam cum ususfructus alienus est, quia ususfructus non dominii pars . . . sit; nec falso dici totum meum esse, cuius non potest ulla pars dici alterius esse.—D. 50, 16, 25 pr.[2]

(2) Through prescription by the Law in the public interest, as especially takes place in landed estates. (So-called legal servitudes.)

Ulp.: Si quis sepulcrum habeat, **viam** autem **ad sepulcrum** non habeat, et a vicino iure prohibeatur, . . . praeses compellere debet, iusto pretio iter ei praestari.—D. 11, 7, 12 pr.[3]

Pliny, hist. nat. xvi. 5 (6), 15: —Cautum est lege XII tabularum, ut **glandem** in alienum fun-

---

[1] Sab. (says), In respect of common property no one of the proprietors can legally do anything against the will of the other. Therefore it is clear that he possesses a right of forbiddal; for it is a recognised rule of law that in equal circumstances the position prevails of the one that forbids.

[2] We are right in saying that the estate belongs to us entirely even when another has the usufruct, because the usufruct is no part of the ownership; and that it is not erroneous to allege that to be entirely mine, of which it is impossible to affirm that any part belongs to another.

[3] If any one possess a tomb, but have no way to the tomb, and is prevented by his neighbour from going thither, . . . the president must insist upon access being granted to such person for a reasonable sum.

dum procidentem colligere liceret.—Ulp.: Glandis nomine omnes fructus continentur.—D. 43, 28, l. un. § 1.[1]

We have first to distinguish between Roman and non-Roman ownership. The latter, the ownership of Peregrini and possessors of provincial estates,[a] was protected by Law, like other legal relations of the Peregrini.[b]

[a] § 71, ad fin.

[b] § 4.

As regards the right of Roman ownership, there was originally only a single form of it, the 'dominium ex iure Quiritium,' of which the requisite, besides the commercium (civitas or Latinitas) of the subject entitled, and the passive commercium of the thing,[c] was some recognised kind of acquisition. All else is entirely uncertain. Thus it is supposed ownership was established not merely by the grounds of acquisition appertaining to the 'ius civile propr. Rom.,'[d] but also in certain cases of so-called 'adquisitiones naturales': as certainly, from the first, by the occupation of things originally without owners and 'res hostiles'[e] (but scarcely of 'res derelictae' of Roman citizens), and in the cases where actual ownership was naturally extended to a new thing, as in the acquisition of fruits.[f] There was otherwise in fact need originally, without distinction between 'res mancipi' and 'nec mancipi,' of a completion of the acquisition by 'usucapio'; so especially in derivative acquisition by 'traditio' on the part of a civis Romanus, whilst the traditio of a Peregrinus always transferred ownership. Later on, however, the need of a civil act of acquisition was still only maintained for res mancipi, so that full Quiritarian ownership in res nec mancipi was always brought about by traditio in particular.

[c] § 70.

[d] §§ 73-80.

[e] § 83.

[f] § 85.

Besides Quiritarian ownership, a 'Bonitarian' owner-

[1] It was provided by a law of the Twelve Tables that if an acorn fall into the land of another, it would be lawful to gather it.—All fruits are comprised by the expression *glans*.

BOOK III. Pt. I. Ch. I.

ship (rem in bonis habere, esse) of Roman citizens, resulting from the increased influence of the ius gentium, obtained recognition by means of the Praetor's jurisdiction. This was supposed when any one had acquired a res mancipi from a Roman citizen by mere tradition, or some other non-civil act of acquisition; or even when the acquisition of the thing (without distinction between res mancipi and nec mancipi) was only originated in the Praetorian Law, as with the Praetorian heir (bonorum possessor).[a]

[a] See § 154, and comp. Gai. iii. 80.

Gai. ii. §§ 40–41: Sequitur ut admoneamus, apud peregrinos quidem unum esse dominium: nam aut dominus quisque est, aut dominus non intelligitur. Quo iure etiam populus Romanus olim utebatur: aut enim ex iure Quiritium unusquisque dominus erat, aut non intelligebatur dominus. Sed postea divisionem accepit dominium, ut alius possit esse ex iure Quiritium dominus, alius in bonis habere.—Nam si tibi rem mancipi neque mancipavero neque in iure cessero, sed tantum tradidero, in bonis quidem tuis ea res efficitur, ex iure Quiritium vero mea permanebit, donec tu eam possidendo usucapias: semel enim impleta usucapione, proinde pleno iure incipit, i.e. in bonis et ex iure Quiritium tua res esse, ac si ea mancipata vel in iure cessa esset.[1]

---

[1] We have next to observe that amongst foreigners there is but a single ownership, for every one is either regarded as owner or non-owner. This law was also formerly in use by the Roman people; for by the law of the Quirites a man was either owner or was not regarded as owner. But afterwards ownership became subject to division, so that one man could be owner upon Quiritarian title, another was Bonitary owner. For if I have neither mancipated to you a *res mancipi* nor have conveyed it to you by surrender in court, but have merely delivered it, the thing is made part of your goods, but it will remain mine *ex iure Quiritium* until you acquire it by usucapion-possession; because once the usucapion is completed, it straightway begins to fall under plenary ownership, *i.e.*, to be your property both *in*

Book III. Pt. I. Ch. I.

Thus a 'duplex dominium' of two persons could meet even in the same thing: Quiritarian ownership of the one, and Bonitarian of the other. In this case, the former availed in nearly all juristic relations as one merely nominal (nudum ius Quiritium), the latter as the real ownership,[a] which, as generally, so also against the Quiritarian owner, was protected by the Praetor with fictitious actions (*e.g.*, act. Publiciana) and pleas (exceptio and replicatio doli, rei venditae et traditae).[b]

[a] But comp. Ulp. xi. 19.—See further Digby, 'Real Property,' p. 272; Markby, s. 336.

[b] D. 21, 3, 1 pr.; and § 505, *Publiciana actio.*

Gai. i. § 54: Ceterum cum apud cives Romanos duplex sit dominium (nam vel in bonis vel ex iure Quiritium vel ex utroque iure cuiusque servus esse intelligitur), ita demum servum in potestate domini esse dicemus, si in bonis eius sit, etiamsi simul ex iure Quiritium eiusdem non sit: nam qui nudum ius Quiritium in servo habet, is potestatem habere non intelligitur.[1]

Ulp. xix. 20: Si servus alterius in bonis, alterius ex iure Quiritium sit, ex omnibus causis adquirit ei, cuius in bonis est.—Gai. iii. 166: Placet, ex nulla causa ei[c] adquiri posse: adeo ut etsi nominatim ei dari stipulatus fuerit servus mancipiove nomine eius acceperit, quidam existiment, nihil ei adquiri.[2]

[c] Sc. qui nudum ius Quiritium in servo habet.

---

bonis and *ex iure Quiritium*, as if it had been mancipated to you or surrendered in court.

1 But since amongst Roman citizens there is a twofold ownership,—for a man's slave is regarded as belonging to him either upon Bonitarian or Quiritarian title, or by both—we shall speak of a slave as being under the *potestas* of his master, if his *in bonis*, although not at the same time belonging to him upon Quiritarian title; for he that has the bare Quiritarian right is not regarded as having *potestas* in respect of a slave.

2 If a slave be *in bonis* of one man, another's *ex iure Quiritium*, it is in every case for his Quiritarian owner that he makes acquisitions.—It is held that in no case can there be acquisition for him;[d] to such an extent that, although the slave have stipulated expressly for the grant to him, or have taken in his name a conveyance by mancipation, some think that he acquires nothing.

[d] (*i.e.* who has a bare Quiritarian title to the slave.)

BOOK III. Pt. I. Ch. I.

Ulp. i. 16: Qui tantum in bonis, non etiam ex iure Quiritium servum habet, nanumittendo Latinum facit.[1]

Mod.: Rem in bonis nostris habere intelligimur, quotiens possidentes exceptionem, aut amittentes ad recuperandam eam actionem habemus.—D. 41, 1, 52.[2]

In the course of time, ownership 'ex iure Quiritium' ever increasingly lost practical importance, until at last Justinian abolished the whole distinction of Quiritarian ownership, on the one hand, and Bonitarian and Peregrinarian on the other, even in name; so that there henceforth remains only one ownership, equally available to all persons, without distinction between a civil and a natural act of acquisition.[a]

[a] § 74, ad fin.

§ 76. Nature and Kinds of Possession.[b]

[b] Cf. Savigny, on Possn. by Perry; Markby, ch. ix.; Holl, pp. 141-9; Holmes, Lect. vi.

Possessio is the total and exclusive *de facto* control over a thing, which by law is protected as such against actual disturbance on the part of every third person (even the owner), unless it has been acquired from the latter in an illegal manner;[c] and though possession in itself is not a legal relation, yet it is protected by law for its own sake, as giving effect to the possessor's personality and his will as recognised by law.[d] Possession, accordingly, exhibits itself as the *de facto* side of Ownership, as the actual, material exercise thereof,[e] which nevertheless has legal importance also as separated from it, and precisely in this separation affords juristic interest. From the right of possession we have indeed to distinguish the right to possess,[f] which is based upon ownership in the thing, or a privilege granted by the owner, or again, in certain circum-

[c] Cf. § 83, ad init.—For Trover and Trespass, see Dicey, 'Parties to an Action,' pp. 331-366; Williams, 'Persl. Propy.' ch. ii. (Apparent possn., p. 67). For Larceny, see Stephen, 'Dig. of Crim. Law,' pp. 210-214.

[d] Holmes, pp. 206-8.

[e] § 75.

[f] Cf. Dicey, p. 345 note.

---

[1] He that only holds a slave *in bonis*, and not also *ex iure Quiritium*, by manumission makes him a Latin.

[2] A thing is regarded as belonging to our property while, if it is in our possession, a plea is available to us, or an action to recover the thing if we lose it.

stances, upon a legal acquisition of the thing.[a] In the doctrine upon this topic, Possession as such, apart from its legal basis, always is the subject of consideration.

[a] § 90.

Paul.: Iusta an iniusta adversus ceteros possessio sit, in hoc interdicto nihil refert; qualiscumque enim possessor hoc ipso, quod possessor est, plus iuris habet, quam ille, qui non possidet. —(l. 2, D. uti poss. 43, 17.) Id.: In pari causa possessor potior haberi debet (50, 17, 128 pr.).[1]

Ulp.: Nihil commune habet proprietas cum possessione.—l. 12, § 1, D. h. t. (= de A. v. A. P. 41, 2).—Id.: Separata esse debet possessio a proprietate: fieri enim potest, ut alter possessor sit, dominus non sit, alter dominus quidem sit, possessor vero non sit; fieri potest, ut et possessor idem et dominus sit.—D. 43, 17, 1, 2.[2]

Possession consists of two elements, one *de facto* (res facti), the actual relation of control over the thing, *i.e.*, the potentiality of discretionary and exclusive corporal operation upon the thing (corpus); and the other mental (res iuris), *i.e.*, the will actually to have command of the thing exclusively—though not continuously—like the owner. This latter is spoken of as the 'animus possidendi'; it is not to be confounded with the 'opinio dominii,' and is to be distinguished likewise from the will of ownership, that is, the intention to exercise proprietary right.[b]

[b] The author had added: 'and from the will to appropriate, which possibly may be absent, as, for instance, in the case of the finder whose intention it is to return the thing to the unknown loser,' but he now regards this as very doubtful.

---

[1] In this interdict it does not depend upon whether the possession against others is lawful or unlawful; every possessor, by the fact that he possesses, has more right than he who possesses not.—In a position of equality we must consider the preference attaches to the possessor.

[2] Ownership has nothing in common with possession.—Possession must be kept distinct from ownership; for the case can arise of one being possessor and not owner, another indeed owner, but not possessor; it may be that the same person is both possessor and owner.

Book III. Pt. I. Ch. I.

Pap.: Possessio non tantum **corporis**, sed et **iuris** est.—l. 49, § 1. D. h. t.[1]

Nemo ambigit, possessionis duplicem esse rationem, aliam quae iure consistit, aliam quae corpore.—C. 7, 32, 10.[2]

From the idea of Possession results, accordingly, that a 'possessio plurium in solidum' is impossible.

Paul.: Plures eandem rem in solidum possidere non possunt; contra naturam quippe est, ut cum ego aliquid teneam, tu quoque id tenere videaris. Sabinus tamen scribit, eum qui precario dederit et ipsum possidere, et eum qui precario acceperit; idem Trebatius probabat existimans posse alium iuste, alium iniuste possidere . . .; quem Labeo reprehendit, quoniam in summa possessionis non multum interest, iuste quis an iniuste possideat. Quod est verius: non magis enim eadem possessio apud duos esse potest, quam ut tu stare videaris in eodem loco in quo ego sto, vel in quo ego sedeo tu sedere videaris.—l. 3, § 5, D. h. t.[3]

On the other hand, the will of the holder can be directed to the possession of the thing not for himself, but for some other definite person—'alieno nomine'—

---

[1] Possession not only is something material, but is a matter of right.

[2] It is beyond all doubt that possession embraces a twofold relation, one that lies in *ius*, another in *corpus*.

[3] Several persons cannot possess the same thing in its entirety, because it is contrary to nature that, if I detain a thing, you can also be regarded as detaining it. Sab. nevertheless writes that he who has delivered anything as a *precarium* himself possesses no less than he who received it as a *precarium*. Trebatius supported the same opinion, because he considers that the one possesses lawfully, the other unlawfully . . ; Lab. criticizes him, on the ground that where possession comes in general into account, it does not much matter whether one possess lawfully or unlawfully. And that is the better opinion; for the same possession can no more be with two persons than that you should be regarded as standing where I do, or as sitting in the same place as I.

who himself has the will to possess, so that the latter appears juristically as the possessor, who exercises possession through the *de facto* occupier, a mere Detentor. Such are a lessee and hirer, bailee, usufructuary, whose will is also only directed to the control of the thing in a definite direction or in particular relations.[a]

[a] As to occupation by a servant, see Dicey, *l. c.*, pp. 335, 358; and for the difference between occupation and possession, ibid. pp. 336-7.

Gai.: Generaliter quisquis omnino nostro nomine sit **in possessione**, veluti procurator hospes amicus, nos possidere videmur.—l. 9 eod.[1]

Cels.: —nec idem est **possidere** et **alieno nomine possidere**; nam possidet, cuius nomine possidetur, procurator alienae possessioni praestat ministerium.—l. 18 pr. eod.[2]

Imp. Alex.: Qui ex conducto possidet, quamvis corporaliter teneat, non tamen sibi, sed domino rei creditur possidere.—C. 7, 30, 1.[3]

But there are cases in which the 'alieno nomine possidens' is regarded as the Juristic possessor with 'animus possidendi,' although without 'animus domini s. rem sibi habendi' (so-called DERIVATIVE possession), because he exercises the other's right of possession transferred to him; *e.g.*, the sequestrator,[b] the pledgee, the possessor upon sufferance.

[b] See Brown, s. *sequestre*.

Flor.: Rei depositae proprietas apud deponentem manet, sed et possessio, nisi apud sequestrem deposita est: nam tum demum sequester possidet.—D. 16, 3, 17, 1.[4]

---

[1] It is a general rule that whoever at all is in possession in our name as an agent, a guest, a friend, it is we who are regarded as possessing.

[2] And it is not the same thing to possess, and to possess on behalf of another; for he possesses on whose behalf the possession is had, whilst an agent affords exercise to possession vested in another.

[3] He that possesses on the ground of letting, although he detain the thing physically, is considered nevertheless to possess not for himself, but for the owner thereof.

[4] The ownership of a thing deposited remains with the depositor, but the possession likewise, unless it has been

BOOK III. Pt. I. Ch. I.

Iavol.: Qui pignori dedit, ad usucapionem tantum possidet; quod ad reliquas omnes causas pertinet, qui accepit, possidet.—D. 41, 3, 16.[1]

In the person of the possessor, possession supposes capacity for possession, *i.e.*, will recognised by law for possession. Of Juristic possession in general, or in their own person, the following, accordingly, are incapable.

[a] D. 4, 6, 19.

(1) Slaves.[a]

Ulp.: Qui in servitute est, usucapere non potest; nam cum possideatur, possidere non videtur.—l. 118, D. de R. J.[2]

Iavol.: —qui in hostium potestatem pervenerunt, . . . possessionem amittunt, neque enim possunt videri aliquid possidere, cum ipsi ab alio possideantur; sequitur ergo, ut reversis his nova possessione opus sit, etiamsi nemo medio tempore res eorum possederit.—l. 23, § 1, D. h. t.[3]

(2) Persons in domestic dependence, who indeed can possess for their master or paterfamilias, but not for themselves, in consequence of their having no capacity for rights, or their incapacity for property.[b]

[b] Cf. § 89, ad fin.

Pap.: Qui in aliena potestate sunt rem peculiarem tenere possunt, habere possidere non possunt.—l. 49, § 1 eod.[4]

---

deposited with a sequestrator, for then only does the sequestrator possess.

[1] The pledgor possesses only until *usucapio;* but in every other relation the receiver is possessor.

[2] He that is in slavery cannot acquire by prescription; for since he is possessed, he is regarded as unable to possess.

[3] They that have fallen under the power of the enemy . . . lose possession, for they cannot be supposed to possess anything, since they themselves are possessed by another; it follows therefore that upon their return they need a new possession, even if in the meantime no one has possessed their property.

[4] They who are in the power of another can detain a thing as their own property; hold and possess it they cannot.

Gai. ii. §§ 89–90: Non solum autem proprietas per eos quos in potestate habemus adquiritur nobis, sed etiam possessio; cuius enim rei possessionem adepti fuerint, id nos possidere videmur: unde etiam per eos usucapio procedit. § Per eas vero personas quas in manu mancipiove habemus, . . . an possessio adquiratur, quaeri solet, quia ipsas non possidemus.[1]

Possession is only possible in corporeal things, single or compound, not in so-called 'universitates' of things.[a]

[a] § 73.

Paul.: Possideri autem possunt, quae sunt corporalia;—nec possideri intelligitur ius incorporale.—l. 3, pr., D. h. t., and l. 4, § 27, D. usurp. 41, 3.[2]

Iavol.: Qui aedes mercatus est, non puto aliud, quam ipsas aedes possidere. Nam si singulas res possidere intelligetur, ipsas aedes non possidebit: separatis enim corporibus, ex quibus aedes constant, universitas aedium intelligi non poterit.—l. 23 pr. eod.[3]

Pomp.: —non tamen universi gregis ulla est usucapio, sed singulorum animalium sicuti possessio, ita et usucapio.—l. 30, § 2 eod.[4]

---

[1] Now it is not only ownership which is acquired for us by those we have under power, but also possession; for we are considered to possess that of which they have acquired possession; wherefore *usucapio* enures through them also. But it is a question whether possession is acquired through such persons as we hold *in manu* or *in mancipio*, because they themselves are not possessed by us.

[2] All can be possessed that is corporeal;—not even is the possession of an incorporeal right supposed.

[3] He that has bought a house in my opinion possesses nothing but the house itself. For if one would suppose he possesses the single things, he will not possess the house itself; for if the single things of which the house is composed be separated from one another, the idea of the universality of the house will not be possible.

[4] There is, however, no usucapion to the whole herd, but just as the single animals are possessed, so also are they acquired by usucapion.

Book III. Pt. I. Ch. I.

But the notion of Juristic possession is transferred analogically to those real rights in which also, as with Ownership, a mere *de facto* exercise of their subject-matter is possible, and appears to need protection, as in particular with servitudes: 'iuris quasi possessio.'[a]

[a] §§ 96, 98.

Iavol.: Ego puto usum eius iuris pro traditione possessionis accipiendum esse; ideoque et interdicta veluti possessoria constituta sunt.—D. 8, 1, 20.[b][1]

[b] Cf. ib. § 96.

The Roman Law distinguishes the following kinds of Possession.

(1) 'Naturalis (corporalis) possessio,' or DETENTION, that is, the bare actual control over a thing without 'animus possidendi' (tenere, in possessione esse), which affords no claim to protection by Law.[c]

[c] *Supra.*

Ulp.: Aliud est **possidere** longe aliud **in possessione esse**; denique rei servandae causa, legatorum, damni infecti non possident, sed sunt in possessione custodiae causa.—l. 10, § 1, D. h. t.[2]

Id.: Fructuarius et colonus et inquilinus sunt in praedio et tamen non possident.—D. 43, 26, 6, 2.[3]

Id.: **Naturaliter** videtur possidere is qui usumfructum habet.—l. 12 pr., D. h. t.[4]

(2) JURISTIC or Interdict-possession, that is, possession with 'animus possidendi' (possessio in the narrower sense), by Law protected through Interdicts. The prerequisite of protection by Interdicts (with

---

[1] I am of opinion that the exercise of that right is to be taken as the delivery of possession: on which account also interdicts, as those that are possessory, have been established.

[2] It is one thing to possess, quite another thing to be in possession; thus people do not possess in order to preserve a thing, or on account of legacies, or because of injury apprehended, but are in possession for caretaking.

[3] The usufructuary, the tenant-farmer and the lodger are on the estate, and yet do not possess.

[4] He that has the usufruct is regarded as having natural possession.

the exception of the interdictum unde vi) against the disturber of the possession is, that the possessor have acquired the possession of the thing from the adverse party neither with violence, nor clandestinely, nor by entreaty (vitiosa possessio).[a]

[a] *Supra.*

Paul.: Si inter virum et uxorem donatio facta sit, cessat usucapio. . . . **Possidere** autem uxorem rem a viro donatam Iulianus putat. (D. 41, 6, 1, 2);—licet illa **iure civili possidere** non intelligatur (24, 1, 26 pr.).[1]

Id.: Si vir uxori cedat possessione, . . . plerique putant possidere eam: quoniam res facti infirmari iure civili non potest.—l. 1, § 4, h. t.[2]

Ulp.: Deiicitur is qui possidet, sive **civiliter** sive **naturaliter** possideat, nam et naturalis possessio ad hoc interdictum pertinet.—Denique et si maritus uxori donavit, eaque deiecta sit, poterit interdicto uti: non tamen si colonus.—D. 43, 16, 1, §§ 9–10.[3]

Id.: Perpetuo autem hinc interdicto[b] insunt haec: quod **nec vi nec clam nec precario ab illo**[c] possides.—D. 43, 17, 1, 5.[4]

[b] Sc. 'uti possidetis.'

[c] Sc. adversario.

A special kind of Juristic possession is that 'bona fide' and rightful possession (resting upon a 'iusta

---

1 If a gift have been made between husband and wife, usucapion is suspended. . . . Julian is of opinion that the wife possesses the thing given her by the husband;—although by the civil Law she is supposed not to possess.

2 If the husband give up possession to the wife, most are of opinion that she possesses; because a matter of fact cannot be impeached by the civil Law.

3 The possessor is ejected whether his possession be by civil Law or be natural, for this interdict has to do with natural possession also. The wife besides will be able to make use of this interdict whose husband has made her a present, and who has been ejected; but not the tenant-farmer.

4 Now inherent in this interdict are the following points: that your possession is neither by force, nor clandestine, nor upon sufferance by him (*i.e.*, the opponent).

Book III. Pt. I. Ch. I.

[a] § 80.

causa') which affords the possibility of usucapion,[a] and is exhibited as 'incipient ownership'—Usucapion Possession. This is 'civilis possessio' in a special sense; in other words, Possession in the legal sense, or that which rests upon a recognised ground of Law.

[b] § 91 (D. 6, 1, 24); Gai. iv. 16.

The origin of the theory of Juristic possession is indeed to be sought in the distribution of the party-functions in proceedings taken by 'vindicatio' (Proprietary Action).[b]

Gai. iv. § 148: Retinendae possessionis causa solet interdictum reddi, cum ab utraque parte de proprietate alicuius rei controversia est et ante quaeritur, uter ex ligatoribus possidere et uter petere debeat.[1]

Iust. iv. 15, 4: Namque nisi ante exploratum fuerit, utrius eorum possessio sit, non potest petitoria actio institui, quia et civilis et naturalis ratio facit, ut alius possideat alius a possidente petat. Et quia longe commodius est possidere potius quam petere, ideo plerumque et fere semper ingens existit contentio de ipsa possessione. Commodum autem possidendi in eo est, quod, etiamsi eius res non sit qui possidet, si modo actor non potuerit suam esse probare, remanet suo loco: propter quam causam, cum obscura sint utriusque iura, contra petitorem iudicari solet.[2]

---

[1] The interdict for retaining possession is commonly granted when there is a dispute between two parties upon the ownership of a thing, and there is a preliminary question which of the litigants ought to be looked upon as in possession, and which should be plaintiff.

[2] For unless it have been previously ascertained to which of them the possession belongs, a proprietary action cannot be brought, because grounds as well of civil as of natural Law require that one must possess, the other must make his claim against the possessor. And in that it is much more convenient to possess than to make a claim, there arises for the most part, and nearly always, a great contest for the possession itself. The advantage of possession consists in this, that even if the

ACQUISITION AND LOSS OF OWNERSHIP.[a]

§ 77. Outline.

The several grounds of acquisition admit of being variously classified.

(α) Adquisitiones 'rerum singularum' and 'per universitatem;'[b] the principal case of which is succession by inheritance. In the following account we have to do only with those first mentioned.

(β) 'Original' and 'derivative' grounds of acquisition.[c]

(γ) Adquisitiones 'civiles' and 'naturales,' *i.e.*, grounds of acquisition according to *ius civile* and according to *ius gentium*.

(δ) Such species of acquisition as are necessary, that is, conditioned by already existing ownership in a thing, and ensuing without the knowledge and will of the acquirer (*e.g.*, acquisition of fruits); and such as are voluntary, *i.e.*, resting upon one-sided will or contract (*e.g.*, Usucapion, Tradition).

> Gai. ii. §§ 97–8: Videamus . . . , quibus modis per universitatem res nobis adquirantur.—Si cui heredes facti sumus, sive cuius bonorum possessionem petierimus, sive cuius bona emerimus, sive quem adoptaverimus, sive quam in manum ut uxorem receperimus, eius res ad nos transeunt.[1]

We meet in the Roman jurists with catalogues of the species of acquisition.

[a] Cf. Markby, ch. xii.; Holland, pp. 156, *sqq.*

[b] § 17.

[c] Ibid.

---

thing do not belong to the possessor, yet if the plaintiff cannot prove that it belongs to him, the possession remains unchanged; therefore also if the rights of both parties are uncertain, judgment commonly goes against the plaintiff.

[1] Let us see how things are acquired by us in a mass. If we have become any one's heirs, or have applied for possession of some one's estate, or have bought a bankrupt's estate, or have adopted any one, or have received some woman into *manus* as our wife, such person's fortunes[d] pass to us.

[d] The liabilities as well as the assets.

Book III. Pt. I. Ch. I.

Ulp. xix. 2: Singularum rerum dominium nobis adquiritur mancipatione, traditione, in iure cessione, usucapione, adiudicatione, lege.[1]

Varro de re rust. ii. 10, § 4: Dominium legitimum sex fere res perficiunt: si hereditatem iustam adiit, si ut debuit mancipio ab eo accepit, a quo iure civili potuit, aut si in iure cessit qui potuit cedere et id uti oportuit, aut si usucepit, aut si e praeda sub corona emit, tumve cum in bonis sectioneve cuius publice venit.[2]

THE SEVERAL SPECIES OF ACQUISITION AND LOSS. *ADQUISITIONES CIVILES.*

§ 78. Adjudication by the State and the like.

Assignment by the competent magistrate of State-ownership to a private person.

(1) Through 'addictio' (adjudication) by the quaestor to the highest bidder, which took place at a public auction (auctio, venditio sub hasta) of military booty and captives of war—whether in separate lots or in the lump; as well as of property (bona publicata) which fell to the State by confiscation in respect of sentences, proscription, nonfulfilment of an obligation existing towards the State, and when there was no heir;[a] the proceeds going to the 'aerarium.' In the last-mentioned case a wholesale 'venditio' of the goods took place (sectio bonorum), originating a universal succession

[a] Cf. D. 48, 19, 17, 1.

[1] We acquire the ownership of single things by mancipation, by delivery, by surrender in court, by usucapion, by adjudication, by law.

[2] Six things in general produce legal ownership: if a man have entered upon a lawful inheritance, if he have taken a conveyance according to the requirements of mancipation from such a person as he could by *ius civile*, or if a person have made a surrender in court who could do so, and that in manner required, or if he have acquired a thing by usucapion, or if he have bought it from booty by auction *s.c.*, or when it is publicly sold amongst the goods or in the distribution of any one's estate.

for the purchaser (sector) whose concern it was to sell such goods retail.[a] Book III. Pt. I. Ch. I.

Gell. vi. (vii.) 4: Caelius Sabinus: . . . antiquitus mancipia iure belli capta coronis induta venibant et idcirco dicebantur 'sub corona' venire.[1]

[a] § 204.

Ps. Ascon. in Cic. Verr. ii. 1, § 52: **Sectorem** dicit aestimatorem redemptoremque bonorum damnati atque proscripti, qui . . . bona omnia auctione (redempta) vendit, et semel infert pecuniam aerario.[2]

Gai. iv. § 146: Sectores vocantur qui publice bona mercantur.[3]

Further, by allotment of State-lands (ager publicus)[b] by means of 'assignatio' or sale by the Quaestor.

[b] Brown, s. vv.

Sicul. Flacc. p. 152, Lachm.: **Quaestorii** dicuntur agri, quos ex hoste captos pop. Rom. per quaestores vendidit.[4]

(2) Award (adiudicatio) by the judge in proceedings for partition, but only in the 'legitimum iudicium.'[c]

[c] I. iv. 6, 20. Cf. § 188.

(3) Immediate acquisition as the result of a legal precept.[d]

[d] Cf. § 37, requisites of manumission; § 83, *thesaurus*; and § 175.

Ulp. xix. 17: Lege nobis adquiritur, veluti **caducum** vel **ereptorium** ex lege Papia Poppaea, item **legatum** ex lege XII tabularum, sive mancipi res sint sive nec mancipi.[5]

---

1 C. S.:—From of old slaves captured by right of war were sold encircled with garlands, and therefore were spoken of as sold *s. c.*

2 The term *sector* he applies to the appraiser and contractor for the goods of a person condemned and proscribed, who . . . sells all the goods (contracted for) by action and once for all pays the money into the treasury.

3 They are called *sectores* who purchase property sold on behalf of the State.

4 Lands are called 'quaestorian' which the Roman people took from the enemy and sold through the quaestors.

5 We acquire by operation of law, as a testamentary gift lapsed or forfeited, by virtue of the l. Pap. Popp. and a legacy

Book III. Pt. I. Ch. I.

§ 79. Transfer *Jure Civili* by the Existing Owner.

There are two forms of the transfer under Civil Law of ownership, the significance and efficacy of which rest upon the public character peculiar to them.

(1) The *mancipatio*, belonging to the category of 'nexum' in the wider sense,[a] was originally an actual sale for Roman public money;[b] afterwards, when the payment of the price had been severed from the act of mancipation (which itself, accordingly, from being a material, was converted into a formal act), the mancipatio became a nominal sale (nummo uno) in solemn form (emptio per aes et libram), with the co-operation of five witnesses, who, we may perhaps say, represented the Roman people classified according to the Census. As such it was a universal form of ownership and legal transfer, without reference to the causa that underlay the conveyance, *i.e.*, its legal ground and material object, which indeed did not hinder its subsequent operation as a real act of sale.[c] It was only applicable to res mancipi.[d]

[a] § 116.
[b] D. 18, 1, 1, pr.; Gai. i. 122.
[c] D. 21, 2, 53, 1.
[d] § 74.

As a mere legal form (dicis gratia) the mancipatio occurs also in the origination and dissolution of relations of power and dependence in Family Law,[e] as well as in the execution of a testament.[f]

[e] §§ 50, 52-3, 55-6.
[f] § 157.

> Ulp. xix. 3, 4: Mancipatio propria species alienationis est rerum mancipi, eaque fit certis verbis, libripende et quinque testibus praesentibus. Mancipatio, locum habet inter cives Romanos et Latinos eosque peregrinos, quibus commercium datum est.[1]

---

by the Law of the Twelve Tables, whether the things be *mancipi* or *nec mancipi*.

[1] Mancipation is a mode of conveyance peculiar to *res mancipi* and is made by prescribed words in the presence of a balance-holder and five witnesses. It obtains between Roman citizens and Latins, and those foreigners that have had a grant of *commercium*.

Gai. i. § 119: Est autem mancipatio imaginaria quaedam venditio: quod et ipsum ius proprium civium Romanorum est; eaque res ita agitur: adhibitis non minus quam quinque testibus civibus Romanis puberibus et praeterea alio eiusdem condicione is qui libram aeneam teneat, qui appellatur libripens, is qui mancipio accipit, aes tenens ita dicit: HVNC EGO HOMINEM EX IVRE QVIRITIVM MEVM ESSE AIO ISQVE MIHI EMPTVS ESTO HOC AERE AENEAQVE LIBRA; deinde aere percutit libram idque aes dat ei, a quo mancipio accipit, quasi pretii loco.—§ 121: In eo solo praediorum mancipatio a ceterorum mancipatione differt, quod personae serviles et liberae, item animalia quae mancipi sunt, nisi in praesentia sint, mancipari non possunt; adeo quidem, ut eum qui mancipio accipit, adprehendere id ipsum, quod ei mancipio datur, necesse sit: unde etiam mancipatio dicitur, quia manu res capitur; praedia vero absentia solent mancipari.[1]

From the act of mancipation itself, by which the ownership is transferred, we have indeed to distinguish the agreements which accompany it, governing the special rights and obligations of the donor and donee,

[1] Now mancipation, as we above stated, is a kind of imaginary sale, and the right itself is peculiar to Roman citizens. It is performed thus: five Roman citizens of the age of puberty are called together as witnesses, and another person of the same status holds copper scales, and is called *libripens*, and the person that takes *mancipio* having hold of the copper speaks as follows: 'I say that this slave is mine by Quiritarian right and my purchase he shall be by this coin and the copper scales'; and then with the coin he strikes the scales and gives the coin to the mancipator, as if by way of price.—Mancipation of estates differs from other mancipations in this particular only, that slaves and free persons, and likewise animals that are *mancipi*, cannot be mancipated unless they are present, to such an extent that it is necessary for him who takes *mancipio* to lay hold of the very thing which is transferred to him in *mancipium*—whence also it is called *mancipatio*, because the thing is taken with the hand; but estates are commonly mancipated at a distance.

BOOK III. Pt. I. Ch. I.

and the unilateral stipulations of the former (nuncupationes, leges mancipii).[a] To these belongs in particular the 'pactum fiduciae,' or the informal collateral agreement, to be made good by an actio fiduciae, upon the remancipation of the thing in general, or under certain conditions by which the mancipatio received application extending to the most multifarious legal transactions.[b]

[a] Cf. §§ 96, 122, fin.

[b] Cf. §§ 100, 121.

Fest. v. nuncupata p. 173 Müll.: (XII tab.:) CVM NEXVM FACIET MANCIPIVMQVE, VTI LINGVA NVNCVPASSIT . . . ITA IVS ESTO.[1]

Boeth. in Cic. Top. 10: **Fiduciam** vero accepit, cuicumque res aliqua mancipatur, ut eam mancipanti remancipet; velut si quis tempus dubium timens amico potentiori fundum mancipet, ut ei, cum tempus quod suspectum est praeterierit, reddat: haec mancipatio **fiduciaria** nominatur idcirco, quod restituendi fides interponitur.[2]

(2) That by way of *IN IURE CESSIO*[c] was a solemn legal transfer in the form of a nominal vindicatio by means of legis actio[d] before the magistrate having jurisdiction (praetor or praeses provinciae), in which he adjudged (addictio) the thing to the 'vindicans,' which corresponded to the will to alienate of the owner expressing itself in the confessio.[e] Applicable as well to res mancipi as to nec mancipi, and in respect of the former indeed especially meant for those cases in which the mancipatio could not take place in its original form (as actual purchase or acquisition for money weighed

[c] See 'Anct. Law,' p. 289. For the former Fines and Recoveries of English Law, see Blackstone, ii. 348-364 (Steph. i. 563, *sqq.*).

[d] Gai. iv. 16, §§ 27, 37, and Gai. i. 134.

[e] Cf. § 97.

---

[1] Let the oral declaration upon the occasion of making a bond and a conveyance be regarded as *ius*.

[2] Now he has accepted a *fiducia* to whom some thing is mancipated, with the intention that he reconvey it to the mancipator; as when any one apprehensive of a critical time mancipates an estate to a more powerful friend, with the intention that he should return it when the anxious time has passed: this mancipation is called fiduciary, because of the introduction of the trust for reconveyance.

out), its application continued as a rule only in the case of transfer of res nec mancipi. Moreover, it served as a legal form for manumission and for the origination and dissolution of relations of power under Family Law. Pacta fiduciae were in respect of it used in the same way as with mancipatio.

Ulp. xix. 9–11: In iure cessio quoque communis alienatio est et mancipi rerum et nec mancipi; quae fit per tres personas, in iure cedentis, vindicantis, addicentis: —in iure cedit dominus, vindicat is cui ceditur, addicit praetor. —In iure cedi etiam res incorporales possunt, velut ususfructus, et hereditas et tutela legitima libertae.[1]

Gai. ii. § 24: In iure cessio autem hoc modo fit: apud magistratum populi Romani veluti praetorem, is cui res in iure ceditur, rem tenens, ita dicit. HVNC EGO HOMINEM EX IVRE QVIRITIVM MEVM ESSE AIO; deinde postquam hic vindicaverit, praetor interrogat eum qui cedit, an contra vindicet: quo negante aut tacente tunc ei, qui vindicaverit, eam rem addicit; idque legis actio vocatur; hoc fieri potest etiam in provinciis apud praesides earum.[2]

Ibid. § 96: In summa sciendum est, his,

---

[1] Surrender in court also is a form of conveyance common both to *res mancipi* and *res nec mancipi;* and this is performed by means of three persons, the surrenderor, the claimant, and the adjudicant; the owner surrenders, the transferee is claimant, the praetor adjudicates. Even incorporeal things can be surrendered in court; as for example, a usufruct, an inheritance, the guardianship at law of a freedwoman.

[2] Now surrender in court is accomplished thus: in the presence of a Roman magistrate, as a praetor, the person to whom the thing is being surrendered having hold of it, says, 'I say that this slave is mine by Quiritarian right;' then, after his claim has been put in, the praetor asks the surrenderor, if he makes a counter-claim: on his replying 'No,' or remaining silent, the praetor adjudges the thing to the claimant, and this is called a *legis actio.*[a] It can be employed even in the provinces before governors thereof.

[a] § 192.

BOOK III. Pt. I. Ch. I.

qui in potestate manu mancipiove sunt, nihil in iure cedi posse; cum enim istarum personam nihil suum esse possit, conveniens est scilicet, ut nihil SVVM ESSE in iure vindicare possint.[1]

'Mancipatio' and 'in iure cessio' did not outlast the classical Law; the latter in concurrence with mancipatio was already earlier in little favour, and passed entirely out of use as a form of transfer of res nec mancipi, since mere tradition assured Quiritarian ownership in them, whilst it remained in use somewhat longer for res incorporales.

Gai. ii. § 25: Plerumque tamen et fere semper mancipationibus utimur: quod enim ipsi per nos praesentibus amicis agere possumus, hoc non est necesse cum maiore difficultate apud praetorem aut apud praesidem provinciae agere.[2]

PRESCRIPTION.[a]

§ 80. OLDER LAW: *USUCAPIO.*

PRESCRIPTION (usucapio in the wider sense) is acquisition of the ownership by continued possession of a thing.[b]

Modest.: Usucapio est adiectio dominii per continuationem possessionis temporis lege definiti. —l. 3, D. h. t. (=de usucap. 41, 3).[3]

It rests upon the consideration that length of time affords legal security to relations of fact; its object is

[a] See 'Anct. Law,' pp. 248, *sqq.*; Markby, ch. xiii. The Roman Law was discussed by Lord Blackburn in Dalton *v.* Angus (6 App. Ca. pp. 818, *sqq.*).

[b] Holland, p. 157. For 'extinctive' prescription, see below, § 97.

[1] Finally, we must understand that there can be no surrender in court to those under *potestas*, *manus*, or *mancipium*, for as none of them can have aught of their own, it follows of course that there is nothing which they can claim in court as theirs.

[2] In general, however, and almost always, we make use of mancipations; for as we can effect the transaction ourselves in the presence of friends, it is needless to employ more troublesome procedure before the praetor or provincial governor.

[3] Usucapion is the addition of ownership through continued possession according to the rule of a fixed period.

to establish legal certainty as to the ownership of a thing by supplementing an ownership acquired defectively, or merely so as to be supported by insufficient evidence.[a]

[a] Cf. § 25.

Gai.: Bono publico usucapio introducta est, ne scilicet quarundam rerum diu et fere semper incerta dominia essent, cum sufficeret dominis ad inquirendas res suas statuti temporis spatium. —l. I eod.[1]

In the Roman Law have to be distinguished two kinds of prescription, amalgamated by Justinian: the older, strictly civil, usucapio (in the narrower sense) which yielded Quiritarian ownership,[b] and the later 'longi temporis possessio' derived from the *ius gentium*, with which extraordinary prescription connects itself, as a particular species of prescription.

[b] Gai. ii. 40, *sq.*

The following are the requisites of usucapio (usus auctoritas).

(I) The period of usucapion extends in movables to one year, in immovables to two years.

Gai. ii. § 54: Lex XII tabularum soli quidem res biennio usucapi iussit, ceteras vero anno.[2]

Cic. p. Caec. 19, 54: Lex usum et auctoritatem fundi iubet esse biennium; at utimur eodem iure in aedibus, quae in lege non appellantur.[3]

(2) During this time the thing must be possessed continuously; by every loss of possession the usucapion is also interrupted (usurpatio), and must begin

---

[1] *Usucapio* was introduced for the general good; that is, that the ownership of certain things should not be uncertain for a long time and almost for ever, whilst the length of the fixed time should suffice owners for searching after their property.

[2] The law of the Twelve Tables directed that landed property should be acquired by *usucapio* in two years, other things in one year.

[3] The statute directs that the enjoyment of and control over a farm shall be for two years; but we employ the same law in respect of a house, which is not named in the statute.

Book III. Pt. I. Ch. I.

[a] D. 49, 15, 12, 1; 41, 2, 23, 1.

[b] Gai. iv. 151.

afresh.[a] Nevertheless, successio 'in usucapionem defuncti,' *i.e.*, continuation of the prescription of the predecessor, takes place; in contrast with which, addition of the time of possession by the 'auctor' (accessio possessionis) was originally excluded in singular succession.[b]

Paul.: **Usurpatio** est usucapionis interruptio.—l. 2, D. h. t.[1]

Ib.: Si rem alienam emero, et cum usucaperem, eandem rem dominus a me petierit, non interpellari usucapionem meam litis contestatione.—l. 2, 21, D. pro empt. 41, 4.[2]

Vat. fgm. 12:—usucapio frustra complebitur anticipata lite.—(Pap.)[3]

Iavol.: Possessio testatoris ita heredi procedit, si medio tempore res a nullo possessa est.—l. 20, D. h. t.[4]

Nerat.: Coeptam usucapionem a defuncto posse et ante aditam hereditatem impleri, constitutum est.—l. 40 eod.[5]

Pap.: Heres eius, qui bona fide rem emit, usu non capiet sciens alienum, si modo ipsi possessio tradita sit: continuatio vero non impedietur heredis scientia.—l. 43 eod.[6]

Inter venditorem quoque et emptorem coniungi

---

1 *Usurpatio* is the interruption of *usucapio*.

2 If I have bought a thing belonging to another, and whilst I was acquiring it by *usucapio*, the owner has made a claim upon me for the same, my prescription is not interrupted by the commencement of the suit.

3 *Usucapio* will fail of completion if forestalled by a suit.

4 The possession of a testator runs for the heir, if in the meantime the property has been possessed by no one.

5 It has been settled that possession commenced by a testator can even be completed before entry upon the inheritance.

6 The heir of him who has bought a thing in good faith will not acquire it by *usus* when aware that it belongs to another, if the possession has been only delivered to himself; but the continuation [of the testator's possession] will not be barred by the cognizance of the heir.

tempora divus Severus et Antoninus rescripserunt. —§ 13, I. eod. 2, 6.[1]

(3) The 'usucapiens' must have acquired the possession of the thing 'bona fide' and 'iusto titulo,' *i.e.*, not merely 'animo rem sibi habendi s. domina,' but in the honest conviction, based upon a ground of acquisition conformable to Law, that he might treat the thing as his own; *i.e.*, that he had become mostly—yet not always—owner, even if it were only as Bonitarian. This is the 'opinio domini.' Such usucapion titles are, *e.g.*, 'pro emptore,' 'pro legato,' 'pro dote.'—The maxim here comes in: 'Mala fides superveniens non nocet.'

The non-transfer of Quiritarian ownership notwithstanding the iustus titulus can in the particular case be occasioned either by the ownership of the auctor being defective—or generally by his not being entitled to the transfer of the ownership, or again by a defective form of transfer (traditio rerum mancipi).

Gai. ii. § 43: Ceterum etiam earum rerum usucapio nobis competit, quae non a domino nobis traditae fuerint, sive mancipi sint eae res sive nec mancipi, si modo eas bona fide acceperimus, cum crederemus eum qui traderet, dominum esse.[2]

Mod.: Bonae fidei emptor esse videtur, qui ignoravit eam rem alienam esse, aut putavit eum qui vendidit ius vendendi habere, puta procuratorem aut tutorem esse.—D. 50, 16, 109.[3]

---

1 The Emperors Severus and Antoninus ordained that as between vendor and purchaser also the periods should be united.

2 Moreover, things also admit of our prescription which were delivered to us by a non-owner, whether they are *mancipi* or *nec mancipi*, if so be we have taken them in good faith, with the belief that the person who delivered them was the owner.

3 A possessor in good faith seems to be one who did not know that the thing belonged to another, or supposed that the vendor had a power of sale, *e.g.*, that he was an agent or guardian.

Book III. Pt. I. Ch. I.

Paul.: —si eo tempore, quo mihi res traditur, putem vendentis esse, deinde cognovero alienam esse, perseverat usucapio.—D. 41, 1, 48, 1.[1]

Id.: —si sciens stipuler rem alienam, usucapiam, si cum traditur mihi existimen illius esse: at in emptione et illud tempus inspicitur quo contrahitur; igitur et bona fide emisse debet et possessionem bona fide adeptus esse.—l. 2 pr., D. pro empt.[2]

Ulp.: Si aliena res bona fide empta sit, . . . utrum emptionis initium ut bonam fidem habeat, exigimus, an [a] traditionis? et obtinuit Sabini et Cassii sententia traditionis initium spectandum. —l. 10 pr., h. t.[3]

[a] et?

(4) A merely putative title, *i.e.*, a ground of acquisition based upon an erroneous supposition—as well as ignorantia iuris [b]—as a rule has in itself no meaning; only in the case when the possession was acquired in the conviction—justified by circumstances, and resting upon an excusable mistake of fact—of the legal origination of the acquisition (iustus titulus) does bona fides alone suffice exceptionally for prescription; especially where an outwardly legal ground of acquisition exists.[c]

[b] D. 22, 6, 7.

[c] In respect of regular putative titles see § 155, ad fin. *pro herede*, and § 83 (*pro derelicto*, to some extent).

Ulp.: Celsus errare eos ait, qui existimarent, cuius rei quisque bona fide adeptus sit posses-

---

[1] —if I suppose it belongs to the vendor at the time when the thing is delivered to me, and afterwards learn that it is the property of another, *usucapio* continues to run.

[2] If I stipulate for what I know to be property of another, I shall acquire it by *usucapio*, if, when it is delivered to me, I think it to be his. But in a purchase the time also is considered when the contract is made; therefore one must both have concluded the contract in good faith and have acquired possession in good faith.

[3] If property of another has been purchased in good faith . . . the question is whether we require that good faith should be present at the beginning of the purchase, or at that of delivery? The opinion of both Sab. and Cass. has prevailed, that regard should be had to the beginning of delivery.

sionem, 'pro suo' usucapere eum posse, nihil referre, emerit necne, donatum sit necne, si modo emptum vel donatum sibi existimaverit: quia neque quo legato neque pro donato neque pro dote usucapio valeat, si nulla donatio nulla dos nullum legatum sit.—l. 27, D. eod.[1]

Afr.: Quod vulgo traditum est eum, qui existimat se quid emisse nec emerit, non posse 'pro emptore' usucapere, hactenus verum esse ait,[a] si nullam iustam causam eius erroris emptor habeat.—l. 11, D. pro empt.[2]

[a] Sc. Iulian.

Paul.: Si a pupillo emero sine tutoris auctoritate quem puberem esse putem, dicimus usucapionem sequi, ut hic plus quam in re sit in existimatione; quodsi scias pupillum esse, putes tamen pupillis licere res suas sine tutoris auctoritate administrare, non capies usu, quia iuris error nulli prodest.—Si a furioso, quem putem sanae mentis, emero, constitit usucapere utilitatis causa me posse, quamvis nulla esset emptio; et ideo neque de evictione actio nascitur mihi, nec competit accessio possessionis.—l. 2, §§ 15, 16 eod.[3]

---

[1] Cels. says that they were mistaken who thought that every one could by *usucapio* acquire as his own a thing of which he acquired possession in good faith; that it does not matter whether he bought it or not, or whether it was given to him or not, provided that he believe that the one or the other happened; because the *usucapio* avails neither as bequest, nor as gift, nor as dowry, if there have been no gift, no dowry, no bequest.

[2] The general rule, that he who thinks he has bought something, and has not bought it, cannot as purchaser acquire by *usucapio*, he says is so far correct if the purchaser has no legal ground of excuse for his mistake.

[3] If, without the sanction of his guardian, I have made a purchase from a ward, whom I supposed to be of the age of puberty, we say that *usucapio* follows, so that here more importance attaches to opinion than to fact; but if you are aware that he is a ward, but suppose that wards are allowed the administration of their property without the authorisation of their guardians, you do not acquire by *usucapio*, because a mistake in law avails no one. If I have purchased of a lunatic under the

Book III. Pt. I. Ch. I.

Pomp: Iuris ignorantia in usucapione negatur prodesse.—D. 22, 6, 4.[1]

Paul.: Id quod pro derelicto habitum est et haberi putamus, usucapere possumus, etiamsi ignoramus, a quo derelictum sit.—Nemo potest pro derelicto usucapere, qui falso existimaverit rem pro derelicto habitam esse.—D. 41, 7, 4, 6.[2]

The whole requisite of the bona fides and the iustus titulus disappeared in the older Law: in respect of usucapio ex Rutiliana constitutione,[a] of usucapio pro herede,[b] of usureceptio ex praediatura,[c] and of usureceptio of the thing mancipated fiduciae causa.[d]

[a] Cf. extract from Gai. ii. 80, *sqq.*, in § 66 *supr.*
[b] § 155.
[c] § 118, ad fin.
[d] Gai. ii. 59, 60.

Gai. ii. § 61: Item si rem obligatam sibi populus vendiderit, eamque dominus possederit, concessa est **usureceptio**; sed hoc casu praedium biennio usurecipitur; et hoc est quod vulgo dicitur ex 'praediatura possessionem usurecipi': nam qui mercatur a populo, praediator appellatur.[3]

Ibid. § 47: Mulieris, quae in adgnatorum tutela erat, res mancipi usucapi non poterant, praeterquam si ab ipsa tutore auctore traditae essent: idque ita lege XII tab. cautum erat.[4]

---

supposition that he was of sound mind, it is well known that I can acquire by *usucapio* for enjoyment, although there was no purchase; and on that account neither does an action for ejectment fall to me, nor is accrual of possession available.

[1] It is maintained that ignorance of law is of no avail in *usucapio*.

[2] That which has been regarded as abandoned, and we suppose to be so regarded, we can acquire by *usucapio*, even if we know not by whom it has been abandoned.—No one can by *usucapio* acquire a thing as abandoned, who erroneously believed that the thing was so regarded.

[3] Likewise, if the People have sold property of his mortgaged to them, and the owner have taken possession thereof, resumption by use has been allowed; but in this case the *praedium* is recovered in two years; and this is what is commonly called the recovery of possession from a *praediatura*, because the purchaser from the People is called *praediator*.

[4] The *res mancipi* of a woman in agnatic tutelage could not be acquired by use unless they had been delivered by the woman

Vat. fgm. 1: Qui a muliere sine tutoris auctoritate sciens rem mancipi emit . . . non videtur bona fide emisse: itaque et veteres putant et Sabinus et Cassius scribunt. Labeo quidem putabat, nec pro emptore eum possidere sed pro possessore; Proculus et Celsus, pro emptore: quod est verius, nam et fructus suos facit, quia scilicet voluntate dominae percipit, et mulier sine tutoris auctoritate possessionem alienare potest; Iulianus propter **Rutilianam constitutionem** eum, qui pretium mulieri dedisset, etiam usucapere; et si ante usucapionem offerat mulier pecuniam, desinere eum usucapere.—(Paul.)[1]

Furthermore, usucapio supposes—

(1) 'commercium' of the subject.

Gai. ii. § 65: —usucapionis ius proprium est civium Romanorum.[2]

Cic. de off. 1, 12, § 37: —XII tabulae: . . . ADVERSVS HOSTEM AETERNA AVCTORITAS.[3]

(2) Possibility of Quiritarian ownership in the thing.

Gai. ii. § 46: Item provincialia praedia usucapionem non recipiunt.—§ 48: Item liberos

---

herself with her guardian's sanction; and that was so provided by a law of the Twelve Tables.

[1] He that knowingly purchases a *res mancipi* from a woman without the sanction of her guardian is regarded as not having purchased in good faith, and so write both the older jurists and Sabinus and Cassius as well. Labeo indeed was of opinion that he did not possess as purchaser, but as possessor; Proculus and Celsus, that it was as purchaser, and this is the better opinion, for not only does he make the fruits his own, inasmuch as he gathers them by the will of her the owner, but the woman can alienate the possession without the concurrence of her guardians; Julian, that by virtue of the Rutilian constitution, the person also acquires it by *usucapio* who had given the price to the woman, and that if the woman tenders the money before usucapion is perfect, his usucapion comes to an end.

[2] The right of *usucapio* is peculiar to Roman citizens.

[3] *Supra*, § 39 (p. 205).

Book III. Pt. I. Ch. I.

homines et res sacras et religiosas usucapi non posse manifestum est.[1]

Id.: Usucapionem recipiunt maxime res corporales, exceptis rebus sacris sanctis publicis populi Romani et civitatum.—l. 9, D. h. t.[2]

(3) Susceptibility of the thing for usucapion: not susceptible of usucapio are—besides res extra commercium—stolen things, according to the Twelve Tables and the l. Atinia (which may date from A.U. 577), and 'fundi vi possessi' according to the l. Iulia et Plautia (the date of which may perhaps be put at A.U. 664).[a]

[a] Cf. § 131.

Gai. ii. § 45: Sed aliquando etiamsi maxime quis bona fide alienam rem possideat, non tamen illi usucapio procedit, velut si quis rem furtivam aut vi possessam possideat: nam furtivam lex XII tabularum usucapi prohibet, vi possessam lex Iulia et Plautia.—§§ 49–51: Quod ergo vulgo dicitur furtivarum rerum et vi possessarum usucapionem per legem XII tabularum prohibitam esse, non eo pertinet, ut ne ipse fur quive per vim possidet usucapere possit (nam huic alia ratione usucapio non competit, quia scilicet mala fide possidet): sed nec ullus alius, quamquam ab eo bona fide emerit, usucapiendi ius habeat. § Unde in rebus mobilibus non facile procedit, ut bonae fidei possessori usucapio competat, quia qui alienam rem vendidit et tradidit, furtum committit, idemque accidit etiam si ex alia causa tradatur. Sed tamen hoc aliquando aliter se habet: nam si heres rem defuncto commodatam aut locatam vel apud eum depositam existimans eam esse hereditariam, vendiderit aut donaverit, furtum non committit, item

[1] Likewise provincial lands are not susceptible of *usucapio*. And further, it is clear that freemen and things sacred and religious cannot be acquired by use.

[2] Especially susceptible of *usucapio* are *res corporales*, with the exception of things sacred, consecrated and public of the Roman people and of townships.

si is ad quem ancillae ususfructus pertinet, partum suum esse credens vendiderit furtum non committit. . . . § Fundi quoque alieni potest aliquis sine vi possessionem nancisci, quae vel ex neglegentia domini vacet, vel quia dominus sine successore decesserit vel longo tempore afuerit: quam si ad alium bona fide accipientem transtulerit, poterit usucapere possessor.[1]

Gell. xvii. 7, 1: Legis veteris Atiniae verba sunt: QVOD SVBRVPTVM ERIT, EIVS REI AETERNA AVCTORITAS ESTO.[2]

Paul: —dicit lex Atinia, ut res furtiva non

---

[1] But sometimes even though a man possess in perfect good faith, usucapion does not run in his favour, as when a man possesses a thing stolen or taken by violence; for a law of the Twelve Tables prohibits usucapion of stolen goods, the *l. Iulia et Plautia* of what is taken by violence. The common saying, that by a law of the Twelve Tables usucapion is forbidden of things stolen or taken by violence, does not concern incapacity for usucapion of the thief himself or person forcibly taking possession (for then usucapion is not available for another reason, that of course he possesses in bad faith), but the fact that no other person has the right of usucapion, although he have purchased from him in good faith. Wherefore in respect of movables it does not readily happen that usucapion attaches to a *bonae fidei possessor*, because he who has sold and delivered property of another commits a theft, and the like happens if the delivery have been upon some other ground. Sometimes, however, it is different; for if an heir sell or present a thing that has been lent or let to, or deposited with the deceased, thinking it to belong to the inheritance, he commits no theft; the like, if the usufructuary of a female slave sell her offspring in the belief that it is his own, for no theft is committed. . . . It is possible also for a man without violence to acquire possession of another's estate; which is void either through neglect of the owner, or because the owner has died without a successor, or has been absent for a long time; and if he transfer it to another who takes it in good faith, the possessor will be able to acquire by *usus*.

[2] The words of the ancient *lex Atinia* are: 'Of such things as shall have been stolen let the title [of the owner] be perpetual.'

usucapiatur, **nisi in potestatem eius, cui subrepta est, revertatur.**—l. 4, § 6, D. h. t.[1]

Id.: In lege Atinia in potestatem domini rem furtivam venisse videri, et si eius vindicandae potestatem habuerit, Sabinus et Cassius aiunt.—D. 50, 16, 215.[2]

Id.: Si tu me vi expuleris de fundi possessione nec apprehenderis possessionem, sed Titius in vacuam possessionem intraverit, potest longo tempore capi res;—(Iul.) quia lex Plautia et Iulia ea demum vetuit longa possessione capi, quae vi possessa fuissent, non etiam, ex quibus vi quis deiectus fuisset.—l. 4, § 22, l. 33, § 2, h. t.[3]

Imp. Dioclet.: Servum **fugitivum** sui furtum facere et ideo non habere locum nec usucapionem nec longi temporis praescriptionem manifestum est.—C. 6, 1, 1.[4]

The effect of Usucapion consists in the conversion of the (bonae fidei) possessio or of Bonitarian ownership into that which was Quiritarian.

---

1 The *lex Atinia* states that a stolen thing is not acquired by *usus* unless it return under the control of him from whom it was stolen.

2 Sab. and Cass. say that in the *lex Atinia* stolen property is regarded as coming under the control of the owner if he have had so much as the power to claim it.

3 If you have driven me by violence out of the possession of an estate, and have not taken possession, but Titius has entered upon the void possession, the property admits of usucapion after lapse of long time;—because the *l. Plaut. et Iul.* forbade only usucapion of those things which had been possessed by violence, not also [usucapion] of things from which some one had been forcibly ejected.

4 It is clear that an escaped slave commits the theft of himself, and that therefore neither usucapion nor *longi temp. praesc.* obtains.

§ 81. Later Law (*Longi Temporis Possessio*).

Already in the earlier Classical Law there originated a means of security for the possession of provincial estates continued for ten years 'inter praesentes,' for twenty years 'inter absentes,' and acquired with 'iustum initium,' which for the possession of Peregrini supplied the place of usucapion, in their case not applicable: this was the 'longi temporis praescriptio s. exceptio' against the *rei vindicatio* of the owner, which in course of time was converted into a true prescription of ownership (longi temporis possessio), applicable also to Italian estates and for Roman citizens.

Modest.: Longae possessionis praescriptionem tam in praediis quam in mancipiis locum habere manifestum est.—D. 44, 3, 3.[1]

Imp. Iust.: Si quis emptionis vel donationis vel alterius cuiuscumque contractus titulo rem aliquam bona fide per decem vel viginti annos possederit et longi temporis exceptionem contra dominos eius sibi adquisierit, posteaque fortuito casu possessionem eius rei perdiderit: posse eum etiam actionem ad vindicandam eandem rem habere sancimus. Hoc enim et veteres leges, si quis eas recte inspexerit, sanciebant.—C. 7, 39, 8 pr.[2]

This 'longi temporis possessio' was by Justinian amalgamated with the civil usucapio in such way that thenceforth only the former should obtain in all Immovables (without distinction between Italian and

[1] It is manifest that the plea of long possession obtains in relation as well to estates as to slaves.

[2] Whosoever by virtue of the legal title of sale, or gift, or any other contract, has possessed a thing during ten or twenty years, and has acquired against its owners the plea of limitation, and afterwards by chance has lost the possession of such thing, we enact that he can have also the action for proprietary restitution of the same. For this was enacted by the old statutes also, if they have been correctly examined.

BOOK III. Pt. I. Ch. I.

provincial estates), but for Movables always a prescription of three years, by this time exclusively called *Usucapio*, should be introduced; both subject to the retention of the other requisites of usucapion, with full allowance, however, of the accessio possessionis.[a]

[a] But this seems to be due to interpolations in the sources.

[b] C. 7, 31, l. un.

—constitutionem[b] promulgavimus qua cautum est, ut res quidem mobiles per triennium usucapiantur, immobiles vero per longi temporis possessionem, i.e. inter praesentes decennio, inter absentes viginti annis usucapiantur, et his modis non solum in Italia, sed in omni terra, quae nostro imperio gubernatur, dominium rerum iusta causa possessionis praecedente adquiratur.—pr. I. h. t. 2, 6.[1]

Alongside of this, the limitation of the action of ownership as an extraordinary kind of prescription, longissimi temporis[c] possessio, which existed from the time of Constantine, was still recognised by Justinian, without distinction between movables and immovables, and without reference to the capacity of the thing for usucapion; its requisite was alone bona fides on the part of the possessor, which, however, merely obtains against persons subject to Limitation of Actions.

[c] Sc. XXX vel XL annor.

Quodsi quis eam rem desierit possidere, cuius dominus exceptione XXX vel XL annorum expulsus est, praedictum auxilium[d] non indiscrete, sed cum moderata divisione ei praestare censemus, ut, si quidem bona fide ab initio rem tenuit, simili possit uti praesidio, sin vero mala fide eam

[d] Sc. rei vindicationem.

---

[1] We have put forth a constitution with the provision that movables should be acquired by *usus* in the space of three years, but immovables by *longi temp. poss.*, *i.e.*, ten years as between parties residing in the same locality, twenty years as between parties locally separated from each other, and that ownership of things in this way should be acquired not only in Italy, but in every country subject to our sovereignty, if a legal ground exist for possession.

adeptus est, indignus eo videatur.—l. 8, § 1, C. cit.[1]

ADQUISITIONES NATURALES.

§ 82. Traditio.[a]

[a] 'Anct. Law,' p. 279.

Traditio (delivery) is the yielding up of possession, that is, the grant to some one of the actual control over a thing with the agreed purpose—in pursuit of a definite, legally admissible, object of some legal transaction (iusta causa traditionis)—to transfer and to secure ownership to him.[b] And further, taking possession with the consent of the owner falls under the notion of Tradition in the wider sense.[c]—It is not requisite that the taker acquire or retain possession which is also protected by Law.

[b] Inst. iv. 1, 41, and § 148, ad init.

[c] § 89.

Gai.: Hae quoque res, quae traditione nostrae fiunt, iure gentium nobis adquiruntur: nihil enim tam conveniens est naturali aequitati, quam voluntatem domini, volentis rem suam in alium transferre, ratam haberi.—l. 9, § 3, D. h. t. (=de A. R. D. 41, 1).[2]

Paul.: Numquam nuda traditio transfert dominium, sed ita, si venditio aut aliqua iusta causa praecesserit, propter quam traditio sequeretur.—l. 31 pr. eod.[3]

---

[1] But if a person have ceased to possess such thing, the owner of which has been defeated by a plea of 30 or 40 years, we deem that the aforesaid aid shall be afforded him not indiscriminately, but with some difference, so that if indeed he have held the thing from the beginning, he can avail himself of like defence, but if he have acquired it in bad faith, he shall be considered as having no claim upon it.

[2] Moreover, those things are acquired by us through the *i. g.* which become ours by delivery, for nothing is so conformable to natural equity as to uphold the will of the owner who desires to transfer his property to another.

[3] Bare delivery never passes ownership, but only if sale or some lawful cause has preceded, by reason of which delivery followed.

Book III. Pt. I. Ch. I.

Ulp.: Si procurator meus vel tutor rem suam, quasi meam vel pupilli, alii tradiderint, non recessit ab eis dominium et nulla est alienatio, quia nemo errans rem suam amittit.—l. 35 eod.[1]

Iul.: Cum in corpus quidem, quod traditur, consentiamus, in causis vero dissentiamus, non animadverto, cur inefficax sit traditio; veluti si ego credam, me ex testamento tibi obligatum esse, ut fundum tradam, tu existimes ex stipulatu tibi eum deberi: nam et si pecuniam numeratam tibi tradam donandi gratia, tu eam quasi creditam accipias, constat proprietatem ad te transire.—l. 36 eod.[a] [2]

[a] Cf. Pollock, 'Contract,' p. 420.

Whilst according to Classical Law traditio was meant especially for res nec mancipi,[b] it became in the Law of Justinian the general and unique form for the transfer of ownership.

[b] § 75.

Ulp. xix. 7: Traditio propria est alienatio rerum nec mancipi.[3]

Cuiuscumque generis sit corporalis res, tradi potest et a domino tradita alienatur.—§ 40, I. h. t. (=de D. R. 2, 1).[4]

Imp. Diocl.: Traditionibus et usucapionibus

---

[1] If my agent or the guardian of a pupil have delivered to another his property as if it were mine or that of the pupil, the ownership does not pass from them, and there is no transfer, because no one loses his property by a mistake.

[2] When we agree as to the object of delivery, but are disagreed as to the cause thereof, I do not see why the delivery should be inoperative. For instance, if I believe I am bound under a testament to deliver to you a field, and you think that it is due to you upon the ground of a stipulation. For so also if I deliver to you coined money with the intention of presenting it to you, and you accept it as a loan, it is settled that the ownership passes to you.[c]

[c] But see the opinion of Ulpian in D. 12, 1, 18 pr., and Dr. Walker's note on the passage in text (Selected Titt. from the Digest, pt. ii.).

[3] *Traditio* is a mode of transfer appropriate to *res nec mancipi*.

[4] Every corporeal thing of whatever kind can be object of delivery, and is alienated by the owner's delivery.

dominia rerum, non nudis pactis[a] transferuntur. —C. 2, 3, 20.[1]

[a] See § 115 and note there.

In the person of the transferor, traditio requires capacity for the transfer of ownership, and so:

(1) Ownership, or title to alienate in the name of the owner as representative, or by one's own right.

Ulp.: Traditio nihil amplius transferre potest ad eum qui accipit, quam est apud eum qui tradit. Si igitur quis dominium in fundo habuit, id tradendo transfert: si non habuit, ad eum, qui accipit, nihil transfert.—Quotiens autem dominium transfertur, ad eum qui accipit, tale transfertur, quale fuit apud eum qui tradit.—l. 20 pr., § 1, D. h. t.[2]

Gai.: Nihil autem interest, utrum ipse dominus per se tradit alicui rem, an voluntate eius aliquis: qua ratione, si cui libera negotiorum administratio ab eo qui peregre proficiscitur permissa fuerit, et is ex negotiis rem vendiderit et tradiderit, facit eam accipientis.—l. 9, § 4 eod.[3]

Id. ii. § 64: Ex diverso adgnatus furiosi curator rem furiosi alienare potest ex lege XII tabularum; . . . item creditor pignus ex pactione, quamvis eius ea res non sit.[4]

---

[1] Property in things is transferred by delivery and prescription, not by mere bargains.

[2] Delivery cannot make over to the taker more than the deliverer possesses. If, accordingly, any one has had the ownership of an estate, he transfers it by delivery; if he has not had it, he transfers nothing to the taker.—But whenever ownership is transferred, it is transferred to the taker such as it was in the hands of the deliverer.

[3] Now it matters not whether the owner himself deliver his property to some one, or some one by his desire. And by this principle, if any one have had the absolute management of business committed to him by a person going abroad, and he sells and delivers an article from the business, he conveys it to the taker.

[4] Contrariwise, the agnatic curator of a lunatic is by the

Book III. Pt. I. Ch. I.

(2) Capacity to act and power of alienation on the part of the owner.

Ibid. § 62: Accidit aliquando, ut qui dominus sit, alienandae rei potestatem non habeat.[1]

A special kind of traditio is that 'in incertam personam collocata,' as in the so-called 'iactus missilium.'

Gai.: Hoc amplius interdum et in incertam personam collocata voluntas domini transfert rei proprietatem: ut ecce qui missilia iactat in vulgus; ignorat enim quid eorum quisque excepturus sit, et tamen, quia vult, quod quisque exceperit, eius esse, statim eum dominum efficit.—l. 9, § 7, h. t.[2]

Pomp.: Id quod pro derelicto habuerit, continuo meum fit, sicuti cum quis aes sparserit.—D. 41, 7, 5, 1.[3]

[a] See 'Anct. Law,' pp. 245, *sqq.*; Blackstone, ii. pp. 1-9 (Steph. i. 151-9).

§ 83. Occupatio.[a]

'Occupatio' is the acquisition of ownership in a thing which is without an owner by taking possession with intent to appropriate.

Gai.: Quod enim nullius est id ratione naturali occupanti conceditur.—l. 3 pr., D. h. t. (=de A. R. D. 41, 1).[4]

Twelve Tables able to alienate the property of such . . . likewise a creditor by agreement may alienate a pledge, although the thing does not belong to him.

[1] It sometimes happens that he who is owner has not power of alienation.

[2] Yet more, sometimes the will of the owner passes the ownership of a thing when directed towards an uncertain person; as for example, he that scatters bounty among the mob, for he does not know what each person among them will catch up, and yet because he intends that what each catches up shall belong to him, he makes him at once owner thereof.

[3] That which any one has regarded as abandoned straightway becomes mine, as when some one has scattered money.

[4] For that which belongs to no one is by natural reason allowed to the person who first assumes it.

To things without an owner belong the following. Book III. Pt. I. Ch. I.

(1) Such things as have hitherto not been in any one's ownership.

Paul.: Dominium rerum ex naturali possessione coepisse Nerva filius ait eiusque rei vestigium remanere in his, quae **terra mari coeloque capiuntur**: nam haec protinus eorum fiunt, qui primi possessionem eorum adprehenderint.—l. 1, § 1, D. de A. P. 41, 2.[1]

(α) Lifeless things.[a] [a] § 70.

Lapilli, gemmae et cetera, quae in litore inveniuntur, iure naturali statim inventoris fiunt.—§ 18, I. h. t. (=de R. D. 2, 1).[2]

Gai.: Insula, quae in mari nascitur, occupantis fit: nullius enim esse creditur.—l. 7, § 3, D. h. t.[b][3] [b] Cf. Inst. *l. c.* § 22.

Pomp.: Aristo ait, sicut id quod in mare aedificatum sit, fieret privatum, ita quod mari occupatum sit, fieri publicum.—D. 1, 8, 10.[4]

(β) Wild animals, in the state of natural freedom, which, however, remain in the possession of the occupant just so long as they are subject to his control.

Gai. ii. § 67: Itaque si feram bestiam aut piscem ceperimus [simul atque captum hoc animal fuerit, statim nostrum fit] et eo usque nostrum esse intelligitur, donec nostra custodia coerceatur; cum vero custodiam nostram evaserit et in naturalem libertatem se receperit, rursus occupantis

---

[1] Nerva the younger asserts that the ownership of things begins with natural possession, and that a trace of this still exists in those things which are caught on the earth, in the sea or air; for these at once become the property of those who first take possession of them.

[2] Precious stones, jewels, and whatever else is found on the sea-shore, according to natural Law at once become the property of the finder.

[3] An island rising up in the sea becomes the property of him who takes possession of it, for it is considered to belong to no one.

[4] Aristo asserts, that just as a house built in the sea becomes private, so what the sea has occupied becomes public property.

fit, quia nostrum esse desinit: naturalem autem libertatem recipere videtur, cum aut oculos nostros evaserit, aut licet in conspectu sit nostro, difficilis tamen eius persecutio sit.[1]

Id.: Nec interest, quod ad feras bestias et volucres, utrum in suo fundo quisque capiat, an in alieno. Plane qui in alienum fundum ingreditur venandi aucipandive gratia, potest a domino, si is providerit, iure prohiberi, ne ingrederetur.—l. 3, § 1, D. h. t.[2]

Id.: Illud quaesitum est, an fera bestia quae ita vulnerata sit, ut capi possit, statim nostra esse intelligitur; Trebatio placuit statim nostram esse et eo usque nostram videri, donec eam persequamur, quodsi desierimus persequi, desinere nostram esse et rursus fieri occupantis; . . . plerique non aliter putaverunt eam nostram esse, quam si eam ceperimus, quia multa accidere possunt, ut eam non capiamus: quod verius est.—l. 5, § 1 eod.[3]

---

[1] Therefore if we have caught a wild beast, or a bird, or fish [the moment this animal has been caught it becomes ours], and it is regarded as ours so long as it is under the restraint of our safe keeping, but when it has escaped from our keeping and regained its natural liberty, it becomes the property of the first taker, because it ceases to be ours. Now it is considered to regain its natural liberty when either it has escaped out of our sight, or, though still in our sight, the pursuit is difficult.

[2] And it matters not, as regards wild beasts and birds, whether a man captures them on his own land, or on another's. It is clear that he who enters upon the land of another in order to hunt or catch birds may lawfully be forbidden (by the owner) to enter if perceived by him.

[3] The question has been raised whether a wild beast which is so wounded that it can be captured is to be regarded as our immediate property. Trebat. concluded that it was ours at once, and that it would seem to be ours as long as we pursue it, but that if we desist from its pursuit, it ceases to be ours and again becomes the property of the first taker. . . . The opinion of most has been that it is not ours unless we have captured it, because much may happen to prevent our capturing it; which is the better opinion.

Ownership in tame animals lasts as long as their custom is to return home.[a]

[a] Cf. Blackstone, ii. 392 (Steph. ii. pp. 5-6).

> Gai. ii. § 68: In his autem animalibus, quae ex consuetudine abire et redire solent, veluti columbis et apibus, item cervis qui in silvis ire et redire solent, talem habemus regulam traditam ut si revertendi animum habere desierint, etiam nostra esse desinant et fiant occupantium: revertendi autem animum videntur desinere habere, cum revertendi consuetudinem deseruerint.[1]

Occupatio is entirely excluded in respect of domestic animals that have escaped from the custody of the owner.

> Gai.: Gallinarum et anserum non est fera natura: palam est enim alias esse feras gallinas et alios feros anseres. Itaque si quolibet modo anseres mei et gallinae meae turbati turbataeve adeo longius evolaverint, ut ignoremus ubi sint, tamen nihilominus in nostro dominio tenentur.—l. 5, § 6, D. h. t.[2]

(2) 'Res derelictae,' *i.e.*, things the possession of which the owner has given up, intending to renounce ownership in them.—According to the Proculian opinion, merely Bonitarian ownership is originated by occupatio of such things when res mancipi.

> Pro derelicto habetur, quod dominus ea mente

---

[1] But in respect of such animals as are in the habit of going and returning, as pigeons and bees, and deer, which are accustomed to go into the woods and come again, we have this traditional rule, that if they cease to have the intention of returning, they also cease to be ours and become the property of the first taker; now they appear to cease to have the *anim. revert.* when they have discontinued their habit of returning.

[2] Fowls and geese are not by nature wild, for it is manifest that wild fowls are different and wild geese are different. Therefore if my geese and fowls being in anywise frightened have flown away so far that one does not know where they are, they remain nevertheless in our ownership.

Book III. Pt. I. Ch. I.

abiecerit, ut id rerum suarum esse nollet.—§ 47, I. h. t.[1]

Ulp.: Si res pro derelicto habita sit, statim nostra esse desinit et occupantis statim fit.—Paul.: Sed Proculus non desinere eam rem domini esse, nisi ab alio possessa fuerit; Iulianus, desinere quidem omittentis esse, non fieri autem alterius, nisi possessa fuerit: et recte.—D. 41, 7, l. 1, and l. 2, § 1.[2]

Ulp.: —cum placeat Sabini et Cassii sententia existimantium, statim nostram esse desinere rem, quam derelinquimus.—D. 47, 2, 43, 5.[3]

Iavol.: Quod servus stipulatus est, quem dominus pro derelicto habebat, nullius est momenti.—D. 45, 3, 36.[4]

From the above have indeed to be distinguished on the one hand lost things, on the other, things the possession of which the owner has not given up 'animo derelinquendi,' as for instance, Jettison.[a]

[a] See Brown, s. v.

Gai.: Alia causa est earum rerum, quae in tempestate maris levandae navis causa eiiciuntur; hae enim dominorum permanent, quia non eo animo eiiciuntur, quod quis eas habere non vult, sed quo magis cum ipsa nave periculum maris effugiat: qua de causa si quis eas fluctibus

---

[1] That passes for abandoned which the owner has thrown away with the intention of having it no more as part of his property.

[2] If a thing have passed for abandoned, it ceases at once to be ours and straightway becomes the property of the first taker. —But Proculus (says) that such a thing does not cease to belong to its owner until it has been possessed by another; Jul., that it at any rate ceases to belong to him who abandons it, but will not belong to another until it has been taken in possession; and he is right.

[3] —because the opinion of Sab. and Cass. has been accepted, who think that a thing at once ceases to be ours which we abandon.

[4] That is of no effect for which the slave has stipulated whom the master treated as abandoned.

expulsas vel etiam in ipso mari nanctus lucrandi animo abstulerit, furtum committit.—l. 9, § 8, D. h. t.[1] Book III. Pt. I. Ch. I.

Nec longe discedere videntur ab his, quae de rheda currente non intelligentibus dominis cadunt.—§ 48, I. h. t.[2]

Iavol.: Quod ex naufragio expulsum est, usucapi non potest, quoniam non est in derelicto sed in deperdito.—D. 41, 2, 21, 1.[3]

(3) 'Res hostiles.'[a]

(*a*) Such things as, belonging to the other side, upon the outbreak of war on hostile territory are subject to occupatio.[b]

Gai.: Item quae ex hostibus capiuntur, iure gentium statim capientium fiunt.—l. 5, § 7, D. h. t.[4]

Cels.: —quae res hostiles sunt apud nos, sunt non publicae sed occupantium fiunt.—l. 51, § 1 eod.[5]

(*β*) On the other hand booty falls to the State as owner.[c] Under booty are generally comprised also such things as have been taken from the enemy, which earlier on were in the ownership of domestic subjects.

[a] Cf. Gai. iv. 16, ad fin.

[b] D. 49, 15, ll. 5 and 26.

[c] Gell. vi. 4.

---

[1] The case is different with such things as in a storm at sea are thrown overboard so as to lighten the ship; for these continue to belong to their owners, inasmuch as they are not thrown overboard because a person does not desire to possess them, but rather that he may escape with the ship itself from the peril of the sea. Wherefore if any one lay hands upon them when thrown out by the waves or even in the sea itself, and remove them with the intent of gain, he commits a theft.

[2] And these seem not to differ much from such things as fall from a running waggon unobserved by the owners.

[3] That which has been cast on the shore after a shipwreck cannot be acquired by *usus*, since it has not been abandoned, but lost.

[4] Again, things taken from the enemy do by the *i. g.* immediately become the property of the captors.

[5] Property of the enemy found amongst us is not public, but belongs to the first possessors.

Book III. Pt. I. Ch. I.

Lab.: Si quid bello captum est, in praeda est, non postliminio redit.—l. 28, D. de capt. 49, 15.[1]

(γ) A return, however, to the earlier relation of ownership arises by 'ius postliminii'; in the first case exceptionally, but in the second only in respect of certain things.[a]

[a] § 36. For modern rights of *postl.*, see Hall, 'International Law,' pp. 446, *sqq.*; cf. 'Anct. Law,' pp. 246, *sqq.*

Paul.: Postliminium est ius amissae rei recipiendae ab extraneo et in statum pristinum restituendae, inter nos ac liberos populos regesque moribus legibus constitutum: nam quod bello amisimus aut etiam citra bellum, hoc si rursus recipiamus, dicimur postliminio recipere.—l. 19 pr. eod.[2]

Pomp.: Verum est, expulsis hostibus ex agris, quos ceperint, dominia eorum ad priores dominos redire, nec aut publicari aut praedae loco cedere; publicatur enim ille ager, qui ex hostibus captus sit.—l. 20, § 1 eod.[3]

Cic. Top. 8, 36: Postliminio redeunt haec: homo navis mulus clitellarius equus equa quae frenos recipere solet.[4]

Tryph.: Si quis servum captum ab hostibus redemerit, protinus est redimentis, quamvis scientis alienum fuisse; sed oblato ei pretio quod dedit,

---

[1] If aught have been taken in war, it forms part of the booty, it does not return by *postliminium*.

[2] *Postliminium* is the right to recover from a stranger a lost thing, and to restore it to its former condition, by custom and laws established between us and free kings and peoples. For what we have lost by war, or even without war, if we recover it, we say that we recover by *postliminium*.

[3] It is true that if the enemy have been driven from lands of which they had taken possession, the ownership in these reverts to the earlier proprietors, and they are neither confiscated nor can they be treated as booty; for only such land is confiscated as has been taken from the enemy.

[4] The following revert by *postliminium*: a man, a ship, a pack-saddle mule, a horse, a mare accustomed to take the bit.

postliminio redisse aut receptus esse servus credetur.—D. 49, 15, 12, 7.[1]

(4) Ownership in the thing found (thesaurus) is acquired also by the finder by means of occupatio; but here special legal rules find place.[a]

[a] Cf. Blackstone, i. pp. 295, *sqq.* (Steph. ii. pp. 549, *sqq.*).—Upon the application of ownership to 'Trover,' see Dicey, 'Parties to an Action,' pp. 347-352; and for property in stolen goods, Steph. 'Dig. of Criminal Law,' p. 210.

Paul.: Thesaurus est vetus quaedam depositio pecuniae, cuius non exstat memoria, ut iam dominium non habeat: sic enim fit eius qui invenerit, quod non alterius sit; alioquin si quis aliquid vel lucri causa vel metus vel custodiae condiderit sub terra, non est thesaurus.—l. 31, § 1, D. h. t.[2]

Thesauros, quos quis in suo loco invenerit, D. Hadrianus naturalem aequitatem secutus ei concessit, qui invenerit; idemque statuit, si quis in sacro aut in religioso loco fortuitu casu invenerit; at si quis in alieno loco non data ad hoc opera, sed fortuitu invenerit, dimidium domino soli concessit.—§ 39, I. h. t.[3]

Callistr.: Si in locis fiscalibus vel publicis religiosisve aut in monumentis thesauri reperti fuerint, Divi Fratres constituerunt, ut dimidia

---

[1] If any one have redeemed a slave that was captured by the enemy, he becomes at once the property of the redeemer, although the latter be aware that he was the property of another; but if the price he paid be offered to him, the slave is considered to have returned by *postliminium* or to have been received back.

[2] Treasure is money deposited as long ago as memory does not avail, so that it has no longer an owner, for it becomes property of the finder because belonging to no one else. Otherwise, if a man have hidden anything under ground for the sake of gain, or by reason of fear, or for safe keeping, it is not treasure.

[3] Treasure which any one has found at a place belonging to him, the late Emp. Hadrian allowed to the finder in pursuance of natural equity. And he directed the same, if one chance to find something in a sacred or religious spot. But if a man have by chance found something on ground belonging to another, without having laboured for it, he adjudged a moiety to the owner of the ground.

Book III. Pt. I. Ch. I.

pars ex his fisco vindicaretur; item si in Caesaris possessione repertus fuerit, dimidiam aeque partem fisco vindicari.—D. 49, 14, 3, § 10.[1]

§ 84. Combination and Intermixture (*Accessio, Commixtio, Confusio.*)

The following species of acquisition obtain prominence by the fact that they require no special act of acquisition for the acquisition of the ownership; the new ownership, rather brought about by one already existing of the acquirer, naturally devolves upon him. They all rest upon changes experienced by a thing already subject to ownership, so that, if a strict view be taken, no new right of ownership arises.

Acquisition of ownership by 'accessio,' that is, increase to a thing or combination with it, whether in respect of immovables or movables.[a]

[a] Cf. Blackstone, ii. 404 (Steph. ii. 21-22).

The owner of an estate naturally acquires the ownership

(1) of the natural enlargement of it by 'alluvio' (gradual and unobserved deposit of earth), 'avulsio,' 'insula in flumine nata,' and 'alvei mutatio' (alteration in the bed of the river).

Gai.: Praeterea quod per **alluvionem** agro nostro flumen adiicit, iure gentium nobis adquiritur; per alluvionem autem id videtur adiici, quod ita paulatim adiicitur, ut intelligere non possumus, quantum quoque momento temporis adiiciatur.—Quodsi vis fluminis partem aliquam ex tuo praedio detraxerit et meo praedio attulerit, palam est eam tuam manere; plane si longiore

[1] The imperial brothers ordained that, if treasure have been found at places belonging to the treasury, or at public places, or in burying grounds, a moiety thereof should be claimed for the treasury; and likewise if such have been found upon property of the Emperor, a moiety should all the same be claimed for the treasury.

tempore fundo meo haeserit arboresque, quas secum traxerit, in meum fundum radices egerint, ex eo tempore videtur meo fundo adquisita esse.—l. 7, §§ 1, 2, D. h. t. (=A. R. D. 41, 1).[1]

Flor.: In agris limitatis ius alluvionis locum non habere constat.—l. 16 eod.[2]

Insula in flumine nata . . . . si quidem mediam partem fluminis tenet, communis est eorum, qui ab utraque parte fluminis prope ripam praedia possident, pro modo latitudinis cuiusque praedii, quae latitudo prope ripam sit; quodsi alteri parti proximior sit, eorum est tantum, qui ab ea parte prope ripam praedia possident.—l. 7, § 3 eod.[3]

Quodsi toto naturali **alveo relicto** flumen alias fluere coeperit, prior quidem alveus eorum est, qui prope ripam praedia possident, pro modo scilicet latitudinis cuiusque praedii, quae latitudo prope ripam sit; novus autem alveus eius iuris esse incipit, cuius et ipse flumen, id est publicus iure gentium.—Ibid. § 5.[4]

---

[1] Moreover, what a river adds to our field by alluvion is according to the *i. g.* acquired by us. Now by alluvion that appears to be added which is added so gradually that we cannot perceive the extent of the increase at any instant of time. But if the force of the river has torn away some portion from your estate and has carried it to mine, that manifestly remains yours. If for a considerable time it be attached to my field, and trees which it has carried with it have spread their roots into my land, from that time it is considered to be appurtenant to my land.

[2] It is settled law that the right of alluvion does not obtain in lands with allotted boundaries.

[3] An island that has arisen in a river, if it occupies the middle thereof, is the common property of those who possess lands along the bank on either side of the river, in proportion to the breadth of each piece of land along the bank; but if it be nearer to one side than the other, it belongs to them alone that possess lands along the bank on that side.

[4] If a river have entirely left its natural bed and begun to

Book III. Pt. I. Ch. I.

(2) All that through tillage (as long as the tillage exists), planting or sowing becomes (for ever) an integral part of the ground and soil.[a]

[a] Cf. D. 19, 2, 22, 2; 18, 1, 20.

Gai. ii. §§ 73–75: Praeterea id quod in solo nostro ab aliquo aedificatum est, quamvis illo suo nomine aedificaverit, iure naturali nostrum est, quia **superficies solo cedit.** § Multoque magis id accidit et in planta, quam quis in solo nostro posuerit, si modo radicibus terram complexa fuerit. § Idem contingit et in frumento, quod in solo nostro ab aliquo satum fuerit.[1]

Paul.: Item si quis ex alienis caementis in solo suo aedificaverit, domum quidem vindicare poterit, caementa autem resoluta prior dominus vindicabit.—D. 6, 1, 23, 7.[2]

Ulp.: Redemptores, qui suis caementis aedificant, statim caementa faciunt eorum, in quorum solo aedificant.—l. 39 pr. eod.[3]

Paul.: Arbor radicitus eruta et in alio posita . . . ubi coaluit, agro cedit, et si rursus eruta sit, non ad priorem dominum revertitur.—l. 26, § 2, D. h. t.[4]

---

take another course, the earlier bed belongs to those who possess lands along the bank, and that according to the proportion of the breadth of the land of each along the bank; but the new bed begins to be of the same character as the river itself, that is, to be public according to the *i. g.*

[1] Moreover, that which has been built on our land by any one, although he may have built it on his own account, by natural Law becomes ours, because the superstructure goes with the soil. § Much more does this apply in respect of a plant which a man has placed in our ground, provided only it has laid hold of the earth with its roots. § The same happens with corn sown in our ground by any one.

[2] Similarly, he that has built with another's stone on his own ground will be able to claim the house by *vindicatio*,[b] but the former owner of the stone will have a claim by *vindicatio* for it if it has been broken up.

[b] § 90.

[3] Contractors who build with their own stone forthwith make the stone the property of those on whose land they build.

[4] A tree plucked up by the roots and transplanted elsewhere,

The acquisition of ownership by accession in the narrower sense obtains when with one's own thing another's is mechanically united—not in consequence of a contract—so as to be inseparable (*i.e.*, indivisible, without prejudice to the integrity of the combined thing) in such way that the latter by the combination perpetually loses its independent character and appears as a mere portion of the former. Ownership of the former (the material whole, PRINCIPAL thing) carries with it ownership of that to which it is united (part, ACCESSORY thing), which ownership is continuous, yet temporary in respect of a combination that is separable.[a]

[a] Cf. § 73.

Paul.: Gemma inclusa auro alieno vel sigillum candelabro vindicari non potest, sed ut excludatur, ad exhibendum agi potest.—D. 10, 4, 6.[1]

Iul.: Habitator in aliena aedificia fenestras et ostia imposuit, eadem post annum dominus aedificiorum dempsit. . . . Respondit . . . quae alienis aedificiis connexa essent, ea quamdiu iuncta manerent, eorundem aedificiorum esse, simul atque inde dempta essent, continuo in pristinam causam reverti.—D. 6, 1, 59.[2]

Paul.: Si quis rei suae alienam rem ita adiecerit, ut pars eius fieret, veluti si quis statuae suae brachium aut pedem alienum adiecerit, aut . . . mensae pedem, dominum eius totius rei effici vereque statuam **suam** dicturum . . .

---

when it has taken root goes with the soil, and if it be again uprooted, does not return to the former owner.

[1] A jewel enclosed in a gold ornament belonging to another, or a medallion in a bracelet, cannot be claimed by *vindicatio*, but proceedings can be taken for its delivery, that it may be detached.

[2] The occupier has put windows and doors into buildings owned by another, and the proprietor of the buildings has after the space of a year taken them away. . . . The answer is that things attached to buildings owned by others belong to the same while they continue so united, but as soon as they have been detached, they revert at once to their former condition.

Book III. Pt. I. Ch. I.

plerique recte dicunt.—Si statuae meae brachium alienae statuae addideris, non posse dici brachium tuum esse, quia tota statua uno spiritu continetur. —l. 23, §§ 2, 5 eod.[1]

Id.: Proculus indicat hoc iure nosuti, quod Servio et Labeoni placuisset: in quibus propria qualitas rei spectaretur, si quid additum erit, toti cedit, ut statuae pes aut manus, scypho fundus aut ansa, lecto fulcrum, navi tabula, aedificio caementum: tota enim eius sunt, cuius ante fuerant.—l. 26, § 1, D. h. t.[2]

As particular cases of indivisible combination there are—

(1) Embroidery and the like.

Si alienam purpuram quis intexuit suo vestimento, licet pretiosior est purpura, accessionis vice cedit vestimento.—§ 26, I. h. t. (= de R. D. 2, 1).[3]

(2) 'Ferruminatio,' *i.e.*, every combination effecting cohesion whereby a simple thing[a] comes into existence.

[a] § 73.

Item quaecumque aliis iuncta sive adiecta accessionis loco cedunt, ea quamdiu cohaerent,

---

[1] If a man have united a thing belonging to another with his own in such a way that it has become a part thereof, for instance, an arm or foot belonging to another with his own statue or . . . a foot with a table, very many are right in saying that he becomes owner of the whole thing, and can rightly call the statue his own.—If you add to my statue the arm of another, it cannot be said that the arm is yours, because the statue constitutes a single whole.

[2] Proc. says that our Law is what Serv. and Lab. supposed, that in respect of things in which regard would be had to the peculiar character of the object, if the thing have been united to something else, it follows the whole, as a foot or hand with a statue, a stand or handle with a goblet, a support with a bed, a plank with a ship, building-stone with a building; for the whole continues to belong to him whose it was before.

[3] If a man have woven into his own garment purple owned by another, although the purple be more valuable as an accessory to the garment.

dominus vindicare non potest; sed ad exhibendum agere potest, ut separentur et tunc vindicentur: scilicet excepto eo, quod Cassius de ferruminatione scribit. Dicit enim, si statuae suae ferruminatione iunctum brachium sit, unitate maioris partis consumi, et quod semel alienum factum sit, etiam si inde abruptum sit, redire ad priorem dominum non posse. Non idem in eo quod adplumbatum sit, quia ferruminatio per eandem materiam facit confusionem, plumbatura non idem efficit.—Cit. l. 23, § 5.[1]

(3) Writing upon another's material.

Sed et id quod in charta mea scribitur aut in tabula pingitur statim meum fit, licet de pictura quidam contra senserint propter pretium picturae: sed necesse est ei rei cedere id, quod sine illa esse non potest.—Ibid. § 3.[2]

(4) Painting on another's table or canvas; but this case, upon which there was controversy amongst the Roman jurists, is better treated under the aspect of specification.[a]

[a] § 86. Cf. §§ 90, 137.

Si quis in aliena tabula pinxerit, quidam putant tabulam picturae cedere, aliis videtur

[1] Whatever is united with something else, or is added as an appurtenance to it, the owner cannot reclaim as his property so long as it is annexed to it, but he can take proceedings for delivery, that a separation be made and the thing then reclaimed; of course with the exception of what Cass. writes as to welding. For he says, if an arm have by welding been fixed to a statue, it is extinguished by union with the larger part, and that what has once become the property of another, even if again broken off from it, cannot be restored to its original owner. That it is not the same in respect of what has been soldered with lead, because soldering with the same material effects a combination, but that lead-soldering does not have the same effect.

[2] That too which is written on my paper or painted upon my tablet straightway becomes mine, although some have thought the contrary in respect of painting because of its value; but it is necessary that it should follow the thing, because it cannot exist without it.

Book III. Pt. I. Ch. I.

picturam, qualiscumque sit, tabulae cedere: sed nobis videtur melius esse, tabulam picturae cedere: ridiculum est enim, picturam Apellis vel Parrhasii in accessionem vilissimae tabulae cedere.—§ 34, I. h. t.[1]

A claim for damage is possessed by the person deprived of his property only when the combination has been effected by a third person, or in case it have been effected by himself, yet by mistake. This is made available in different ways, according as the loser or the gainer is in possession of the thing. If the gainer have undertaken the combination mala fide, there is ground also for an 'actio furti.'[a]

[a] Cf. §§ 90, 137.

In omnibus igitur istis, in quibus mea res per praevalentiam alienam rem trahit meamque efficit, si eam rem vindicem, per exceptionem doli mali cogar pretium eius quod accesserit dare.—In omnibus his casibus, in quibus neque ad exhibendum neque in rem locum habet, in factum actio necessaria est.—Cit. l. 23, §§ 4–5.[2]

Lex XII tabularum neque solvere permittit **tignum** furtivum aedibus vel vineis **iunctum** neque vindicare; quod providenter lex effecit, ne vel aedificia sub hoc praetextu diruantur, vel vinearum cultura turbetur. Sed in eum qui convictus est iunxisse, in duplum dat actionem.—Tigni autem appellatione continetur omnis materia, ex

---

[1] If any one have painted upon a tablet owned by another, some think that the tablet belongs to the painting, others consider that the painting, be it what it may, belongs to the tablet; but the better view in our judgment is that the tablet belongs to the painting, for it is ridiculous that a painting of Apelles or Parrhasius should belong as accessory to the commonest tablet.

[2] In all those cases, however, in which my article by overweight carries with it an article owned by another, and renders it my property, if I claim such thing as my property, I am by a plea of fraud obliged to pay over the accrued value.—In all cases in which neither proceedings *ad exhibendum*[b] nor those *in rem*[c] are to be had, an action *in factum*[d] is necessary.

[b] § 137.
[c] § 24.
[d] § 200.

qua aedificium constet, vineaeque necessaria.—D. 47, 3, 1 pr., § 1.[1]

'Confusio' and 'commixtio.'

(1) By casual, indivisible and substantial intermixture of quantities of the same or a different kind or class, and belonging to different owners, there arises a joint ownership of the whole.[a]

[a] Cf. Blackstone, ii. p. 405 (Steph. ii. 23).

Si duorum materiae ex voluntate dominorum confusae sint, totum id corpus, quod ex confusione fit, utriusque commune est, veluti si qui vina sua confuderint aut massas argenti vel auri conflaverint; . . . quodsi fortuitu et non voluntate dominorum confusae fuerint vel diversae materiae vel quae eiusdem generis sunt, idem iuris esse placuit. § Quodsi frumentum Titii tuo frumento mixtum fuerit, si quidem ex voluntate vestra, commune erit, quia singula corpora i.e. grana, quae cuiusque propria fuerunt, ex consensu vestro communicata sunt; quodsi casu id mixtum fuerit, vel Titius id miscuerit sine voluntate tua, non videtur commune esse, quia singula corpora in sua substantia durant.—§§ 27–8, I. h. t.[2]

---

[1] The Law of the Twelve Tables neither allows the detaching of a beam that has been stolen and built into a house or a vineyard-trellis, nor a claim thereto by proprietary action. The statute did so advisedly, in order that neither should buildings be demolished under this pretext nor the cultivation of vines be destroyed.—But against him who has been convicted of building such in, it gives an action for double the amount.—Now under the designation 'beam' is included all timber of which a building may consist, and necessary to a vineyard.

[2] If materials belonging to two persons have been mixed together by the owners, the whole body that comes of the mixture is common property of both; for example, if two persons have mixed their wines or have melted together masses of silver or gold; . . . but if the materials—whether of like kind or diverse—have been mixed by accident and not by the intention of the owners, the like rule has obtained acceptance. § But if Titius' corn have been mingled with yours, it is your common property, if it have happened by your intention;

Ulp.: Pomponius scribit, si quid quod eiusdem naturae est, ita confusum est atque commixtum, ut diduci et separari non possit, non totum sed pro parte esse vindicandum; . . . pro rata ponderis quod in massa habemus.—D. 6, 1, 3, 2.[1]

Id.: Idem Pomponius scribit: si frumentum duorum non voluntate eorum confusum sit, competit singulis in rem actio in 'quantum paret in illo acervo suum cuiusque esse.'—l. 5 pr. eod.[2]

(2) It is otherwise with money belonging to others: this, in case it is not distinguishable, passes into the ownership of him who has mixed it with his own, whilst a right of claim against him arises in favour of the loser for the sum represented by it.

Iavol.: Si alieni nummi inscio vel invito domino soluti sunt, manent eius, cuius fuerunt; si mixti essent, ita ut discerni non possent, eius fieri, qui accepit, in libris Gaii scriptum est.—D. 46, 3, 78.[3]

§ 85. Acquisition of Fruits.

[a] § 73.

The natural fruits of a thing,[a] without regard to the

---

because the individual bodies, that is the single grains, which had belonged to each of you, have been united by your consent. If the mixture have happened by chance, or Titius have made the mixture not by your intention, it is not considered common property, because the bodies continue distinct in their substance.

[1] Pomp. writes: If anything of the same material have been so melted and mixed together that it cannot be severed and divided, we cannot reclaim it in the bulk, but only by way of shares; . . . according to the proportion of weight which we possess in the mass.

[2] The same Pomp. writes: If the corn of two persons have been mingled not by their intention, a real action is available to each for as much of that heap as appears to belong to each.

[3] If money belonging to another have been paid without the privity or consent of the owner, it remains his to whom it belonged; we find written in the books of Gaius that if it were mixed so as not to admit of distinction, it becomes the property of him who received it.

person by whom they may be raised, are acquired not merely by the owner of the thing (so that the right in the fruit-bearing thing naturally extends to the fruit, as to a customary material part which by the separation has become an independent object of right), but also by the 'bonae fidei possessor,' and him that has an independent right to the thing in respect of its produce; so that the ownership of the produce, as of a new, hitherto non-existing thing, rest upon special grounds of Law. Nevertheless, with such things acquisition obtains in different ways.

Through SEPARATION, by whomsoever it may have been effected, the fruits are acquired—

(1) by the owner.

Inst. ii. 1, 19: Item ea, quae ex animalibus dominio tuo subiectis nata sunt, eodem iure[a] tibi adquiruntur.[1]

[a] Sc. naturali.

Ulp.: (Pomponius) scribit, si equam meam equus tuus praegnantem fecerit, non esse tuum, sed meum quod natum est.—D. 6, 1, 5, 2.[2]

Iul.: Qui scit fundum sibi cum alio communem esse, fructus quos ex eo perceperit invito vel ignorante socio, non maiore ex parte suos facit, quam ex qua dominus praedii est. Nec refert ipse an socius an uterque eos severit, quia **omnis fructus non iure seminis sed iure soli percipitur.**—D. 22, 1, 25 pr.[3]

(2) By the bonae fidei possessor,[b] who however has to restore to the owner, as defending his right to

[b] Cf. § 83, and D. 7, 1, 12, 5.

[1] Likewise, that which is born to you from animals in your ownership you acquire by the same right.

[2] (Pomp.) writes that if your stallion have made my mare pregnant, the foal is not yours but mine.

[3] He that is aware he owns a field in common with another, makes the fruits which he shall have gathered from it without the consent or knowledge of the partner in no greater share his own than that by which he is owner of the field. Nor does it matter whether he himself, or the partner, or both of them, have sown them, because all fruit is gathered, not by right of the seed, but by right of the ground.

the principal thing (and to that perhaps alone), the 'fructus exstantes' along with such principal thing, whilst for 'fructus consumpti'—used up and alienated—he has not generally to offer any compensation.

In alieno fundo, quem Titius bona fide mercatus fuerat, frumentum sevi; an Titius bonae fidei emptor perceptos fructus suos faciat? . . . Respondi . . . in fructibus magis **corporis ius, ex quo percipiuntur, quam seminis, ex quo oriuntur,** adspicitur; et ideo nemo umquam dubitavit, quin, si in meo fundo frumentum tuum severim, segetes et quod ex messibus collectum fuerit meum fieret. Porro bonae fidei possessor in percipiendis fructibus id iuris habet, quod dominis praediorum tributum est: . . . cum fructuarii quidem non fiant, antequam ab eo percipiantur, ad bonae fidei autem possessorem pertineant, quoque modo a solo separati fuerint; sicut eius, qui vectigalem fundum habet, fructus fiunt, simul atque solo separati sunt.—Ibid. § 1.[1]

Paul.: Bonae fidei emptor non dubie percipiendo fructus etiam ex aliena re suos **interim** facit: non tantum eos, qui diligentia et opera eius pervenerunt, sed omnes, quia quod ad fructus

---

[1] I have sown a crop in a field owned by another, which Tit. had purchased in good faith: does Tit. the *bon. fid.* purchaser make the fruit when gathered his own? The opinion I gave was: . . . in respect of fruits, regard must be had rather to the right of the body from which they are gathered than to the seed from which they spring; and therefore no one has ever doubted that if I have sown your crop in my field, the crop, and whatever should be gathered by the harvest, was mine. Moreover a *bon. fid.* possessor has the same title to the gathering of fruits as has been accorded to owners of estates . . . since they do not become the property of the fructuary until they are gathered by him, but belong to the *bon. fid.* possessor in whatever way they have been separated from the ground; like as fruits become the property of him who possesses a stipendiary estate, as soon as they have been separated from the ground.

attinet, loco domini paene est. Denique etiam priusquam percipiat, statim ubi a solo separati sunt, bonae fidei emptoris fiunt. Nec interest, ea res, quam bona fide emi longo tempore capi possit necne.—In contrarium quaeritur, si eo tempore quo mihi res traditur putem vendentis esse, deinde cognovero alienam esse, quia perseverat per longum tempus capio, an fructus meos faciam? Pomponius, verendum, ne non sit bonae fidei possessor, quamvis capiat.—D. 41, 1, 48 pr., § 1.[1]

Afr.: —simul haec fere cedere, ut quo casu **fructus** praediorum **consumptos suos faciat** bona fide possessor, eodem per servum ex opera et ex re ipsius ei adquiratur.—l. 40 eod.[2]

Certum est, malae fidei possessores omnes fructus solere cum ipsa re praestare; bonae fidei vero exstantes, post litis autem contestationem universos.—C. 3, 32, 22.[3]

---

[1] A *bon. fid.* purchaser, by gathering the fruits even of property belonging to another, makes them his own for the meantime, not merely those which have accrued from his industry and toil, but all, because as concerns the fruits he is almost in the position of the owner. Accordingly, even before he gather them, immediately upon their separation from the ground they become the property of the *bon. fid.* purchaser. And it is immaterial whether the article which I have purchased in good faith can be acquired through length of time or not.—On the other hand, if at the time when the thing is delivered to me I believe that it is the property of the vendor, and afterwards learn that it belongs to another, the question arises whether I make the fruits my own, because usucapion is assured by lapse of time. Pompon. thinks that we must hesitate as to his being a *bon. fid.* possessor, though his usucapion attach.

[2] —that these cases are almost identical, in that whenever the *bon. fid.* possessor makes himself owner of the consumed fruits of land, he also acquires through the slave by his services and his own substance.

[3] It is certain that possessors in bad faith generally offer all the fruits with the thing itself; but those in good faith only the existing fruits, but after *lit. cont.* the whole.

Book III. Pt. I. Ch. I.

(3) By the 'Emphyteuta.'[a]

[a] § 99.

[b] §§ 73, 131.

The fruits are acquired by the usufructuary and the lessee[b] through PERCEPTION (taking possession), upon the ground of the independent right to the thing which belongs to him, or of the privilege in respect of the produce assured to him by the owner—by a sort of delivery.

> Is ad quem ususfructus fundi pertinet non aliter fructuum dominus efficitur, quam si eos perceperit; et ideo licet maturis fructibus, nondum tamen perceptis decesserit, ad heredem eius non pertinent, sed domino proprietatis adquiruntur. Eadem fere et de colono dicuntur.—§ 36, I. de R. D.[1]
>
> Afric.: —colonum, quia voluntate domini eos percipere videatur, suos fructus facere.—D. 47, 2, 61, 8.[2]

§ 86. Specification.

By so-called Specification, that is, work done or recast upon another's material, by which a new object of property (nova species) or artificial production is created, ownership (according to the intermediate view of the Roman Jurists, approved by Justinian), is acquired in such work by its maker, provided that the material so worked up cannot again be restored to its original form, and that the maker have done it 'suo nomine,' *i.e.*, for himself, and 'bona fide,' *i.e.*, not fraudulently.[c] Otherwise, the new thing devolves upon the owner of the material.

[c] But this last is questionable.—As to compensation in such cases, see § 84.

---

[1] He that possesses the usufruct of an estate is only made owner of the fruits if he has gathered them in; and therefore should he have died whilst the fruits indeed are ripe, but not gathered, they do not belong to his heir, but are appropriated by the ground owner. The like is generally affirmed of the tenant-farmer.[d]

[2] —that the tenant-farmer makes the fruits his own, because he is considered to gather them with the consent of the owner.

[d] For English law as to Emblements, see Blackst. ii. 122-3, 146, 403-4 (Steph. ii. 258-9, 288-9).

Gai.: Cum quis ex aliena materia speciem aliquam suo nomine fecerit, Nerva et Proculus putant hunc dominum esse, qui fecerit: quia **quod factum est, ante nullius fuerat**; Sabinus et Cassius magis naturalem rationem efficere putant, ut qui materiae dominus fuerit, idem eius quoque, quod ex eadem materia factum sit, dominus esset; quia **sine materia nulla species** effici potest; veluti si ex auro vel argento tuo vel aere vas aliquod fecero, vel ex tabulis tuis navem aut armarium aut subsellia fecero, vel ex lana tua vestimentum, vel ex vino et melle tuo mulsum, vel ex medicamentis tuis emplastrum aut collyrium, vel ex uvis aut olivis aut spicis tuis vinum vel oleum aut frumentum. Est tamen etiam [Et post multas Sabinianorum et Proculianorum ambiguitates placuit.—§ 25, I. de R. D. 2, 1] media sententia recte existimantium, **si species ad materiam reverti possit,** verius esse quod Sabinus et Cassius senserunt; si non possit reverti, verius esse quod Nervae et Proculo placuit: ut ecce vas conflatum ad rudem massam auri vel argenti vel aeris reverti potest, vinum vero vel oleum vel frumentum ad uvas et olivas et spicas reverti non potest, ac ne mulsum quidem ad mel et vinum, vel emplastrum aut collyria ad medicamenta reverti possunt. Videntur tamen mihi recte quidam dixisse non debere dubitari, quin alienis spicis excussum frumentum eius sit, cuius et spicae fuerunt: cum enim grana, quae spicis continentur, perfectam habeant suam speciem, qui excussit spicas, non novam speciem, facit, sed eam quae est detegit.—l. 7, § 7, D. de A. R. D. 41, 1.[1]

[1] If a man have converted material belonging to another into a new species on his own account, Nerva and Procul. are of

Quodsi partim ex sua materia partim ex aliena speciem aliquam fecerit, . . . dubitandum non est hoc casu eum esse dominum qui fecerit: cum non solum operam suam dedit, sed et partem eiusdem materiae praestavit.—§ 25, I. cit.[1]

Call.: —propter consensum domini tota res eius fit, cuius nomine facta est.—l. 25, D. de A. R. D.[2]

Paul.: Si quis ex uvis meis mustum fecerit, vel ex olivis oleum vel ex lana vestimenta, cum sciret haec aliena esse, utriusque nomine

---

opinion that the manufacturer is owner, because that which has been made belonged previously to no one. But Sab. and Cass. are of opinion that natural principle rather dictates that he who was owner of the material should also be of that which has been made from it, because nothing could be made without existing material; for example, if from your gold, or silver, or copper I have made a vessel, or from boards belonging to you a ship, or a closet, or benches, or from your wool a garment, or mead from your wine and honey, or from your drugs a plaister or a salve, or from your grapes, olives or ears, wine, oil or corn. There is, however, also [and after many controversies of the Sabinians and Proculians, it has prevailed] an intermediate opinion of those who are right in supposing that if the new species can again be reconverted into its material, the opinion of Sab. and Cass. is the more correct, but if not, that of Nerva and Proculus; thus, for instance, if a molten vessel can again be converted into the raw material of gold, or silver, or copper; but wine, oil or corn cannot again become grapes, olives or ears, and not even mead can be converted into honey and wine, or a plaister or salve into drugs. I think, however, some were right who have stated that there can be no doubt but that corn thrashed out of ears owned by another belongs to the owner of the ears, for since the grains contained in the ears have their perfect form, he that thrashes out the ears makes no new species, but he discloses the existing species.

[1] But if a man have made a new species partly from material of his own and partly from that belonging to another, . . . we cannot doubt that in this case the manufacturer is the owner; since he has devoted to it not only his labour, but also a portion of the same material.

[2] —by reason of the owner's consent the article becomes entirely the property of him on whose behalf it was made.

ad exhibendum actione tenebitur: quia quod ex re nostra fit, nostrum esse verius est.—D. 10, 4, 12, 3.[1]

Gai. ii. § 79: —nec minus adversus eundem condictionem competere, quia extinctae res, licet vindicari non possint, condici tamen furibus et quibusdam aliis possessoribus possunt.[2]

Paul.: Si ex lana furtiva vestimentum feceris, verius est, ut substantiam spectemus: et ideo vestis furtiva erit.—D. 41, 3, 4, 20.[3]

§ 87. Loss of Ownership from Special Causes.

Apart from the physical or juristic[a] destruction of the object, from the loss or surrender of possession in respect of wild animals and res derelictae,[b] and from the grounds of termination of ownership corresponding to those of its acquisition, loss of ownership in a thing occurs—

[a] § 70.
[b] § 83.

(1) in the case of prohibited private redress.[c]

[c] § 23.

Imp. Valent.: Si quis in tantam furoris pervenerit audaciam, ut possessionem rerum . . . violenter invaserit, dominus quidem constitutus possessionem, quam abstulit, restituat possessori et dominium eiusdem rei amittat.—Cod. 8, 4, 7.[4]

---

[1] If a man have made must from my grapes, or oil from my olives, or garments from wool of mine, and knew that they were the property of another, he will be liable in respect of both by an action *ad exhibendum*, because that which has been made from a thing owned by us is ours, according to the better opinion.

[2] —and he has a personal action[d] also against the same person, because although things which have been destroyed cannot be recovered by *vindicatio*, they can nevertheless be claimed by a personal action as against thieves and certain other possessors.

[d] See § 24.

[3] If you have made a garment from stolen wool, the better opinion is that we must look to the substance, and so the garment will be one stolen.

[4] When a man shall have gone such lengths of frenzied arrogance as to have taken violent possession of things . . . if he

Book III. Pt. I. Ch. I.

(2) In respect of a fraud on the Revenue.

Ulp.: —quod commissum est, statim desinit eius esse, qui crimen contraxit, dominiumque rei vectigali adquiritur.—D. 39, 4, 14.[1]

(3) Upon desertion of a landed estate.

Imp. Valent.: Qui agros domino cessante desertos . . . ad privatum pariter publicumque compendium excolere festinat, . . . si biennii fuerit tempus emensum, omni possessionis et dominii carebit iure qui siluit.—Cod. 11, 59, (58), 8.[2]

(4) Upon alienation by the Treasury or the Princeps of property owned by another.[a]

[a] Inst. 2, 6. § ult.

§ 88. Acquisition through others.

Those that are 'alieno iure subiecti' always acquire for him under whose power they are.[b] But also through 'extraneae personae'—free representatives—was the acquisition of ownership allowed by the Classical Law in cases where it is brought about by possession; official representatives, *e.g.*, tutors, likewise here acquire ownership for the person they represent.

[b] §§ 20, 149, 150.

Ulp.: —placet, per liberam personam omnium rerum possessionem quaeri posse et per hanc dominium.—D. 41, 1, 20, 2.[3]

Ner.: Si procurator rem mihi emerit ex mandato meo, eique sit tradita meo nomine, dominium

---

be the owner, he shall restore the possession abstracted by him to the possessor and forfeit his ownership of such property.

[1] That which has been confiscated at once ceases to belong to the delinquent, and the ownership of the property falls to the Revenue.

[2] When a man sets about cultivating lands left desolate by their owner, and that as well for the public as for his own advantage . . . the person that has remained inactive for the space of two years shall forfeit his whole right of ownership and possession.

[3] —it is held that through a free person possession can be acquired of anything, and ownership thereby.

. . . mihi adquiritur etiam ignoranti.[a]—Et tutor pupilli pupillae, similiter ut procurator, emendo nomine pupilli pupillae, proprietatem illis adquirit etiam ignorantibus.—l. 13 eod.[1]

[a] See note by Walker, ad loc.

The usufructuary of a slave, and the bonae fidei possessor[b] of another's slave or of a freeman acquire by him ownership and claims only so far as the acquisition is made from their own property, or is brought about through the labour put forth by such person.

[b] § 85.

Gai. ii. §§ 91–2: De his autem servis, in quibus tantum usumfructum habemus, ita placuit, ut quidquid **ex re nostra vel ex operis suis** adquirunt, id nobis adquiratur; quod vero extra eas causas, id ad dominium proprietatis pertineat: itaque si iste servus heres institutus sit legatumve quod ei datum [aut donatum] fuerit, non mihi sed domino proprietatis adquiritur.—Idem placet de eo, qui a nobis bona fide possidetur, sive liber sit sive alienus servus: . . . itaque quod extra duas istas causas adquiritur, id vel ad ipsum pertinet, si liber est, vel ad dominium, si servus est.[2]

Ulp.: Tamdiu autem adquirit, quamdiu bona

---

[1] If an agent has by my commission purchased a thing for me, and it has been delivered to him on my account, the ownership is acquired for me, even if unaware of it.—And the guardian of a pupil male or female, in like manner as an agent, by purchase of a thing in the name of the pupil male or female, acquires for them the ownership, even without their cognizance.

[2] Now as regards those slaves in whom we have only a usufruct, it has been held that whatever they acquire from our substance or by their own labour is acquired for us, but whatever from other causes than these belongs to their owner. Therefore, if such slave be appointed heir, or anything is bequeathed to him, it is acquired not for me but for the proprietor. The same rule holds in respect of him whom we possess in good faith, whether he be a freeman or the slave of another. . . . Therefore, whatever is acquired from sources other than these two belongs either to the man himself, if he is a freeman, or to his master, if he is a slave.

fide servit: ceterum si coeperit scire, esse eum alienum vel liberum, videamus, an ei adquirat. Quaestio in eo est, utrum initium spectamus an singula momenta? et magis est, ut singula momenta spectemus.—D. 41, 1, 23, 1.[1]

Id.: Interdum tamen in pendenti est, cui adquirat iste fructuarius servus, ut puta si servum emit et per traditionem accepit necdum pretium numeravit, sed tantummodo pro eo fecit satis. . . . Et Iulianus . . . scripsit in pendenti esse dominium eius et numerationem pretii declaraturam, cuius sit.—D. 7, 1, 25, 1.[2]

The slave that is owned in common regularly acquires for each of his masters according to their share in the ownership.

Gai. iii. § 167: Communem servum **pro dominica** parte dominis adquirere certum est, excepto eo, quod uni **nominatim** stipulando aut mancipio accipiendo illi soli adquirit, velut cum ita stipuletur: TITIO DOMINO MEO DARI SPONDES? aut cum ita mancipio accipiat: HANC REM EX IVRE QVIRITIVM LVCII TITII DOMINI MEI ESSE AIO, EAQVE EI EMPTA ESTO HOC AERE AENEAQVE LIBRA.[3]

---

[1] Now his acquisitions avail so long as he serves in good faith; if, however, he once learn that he is the slave of another, or a freeman, we have to consider whether he acquires for him. The question goes to whether we should look to the beginning or to the separate moments; and it is the rather to be supposed that we should look to the separate moments.

[2] Sometimes, however, it is in suspense for whom such a usufructuary slave acquires, as for instance, if a man have bought a slave who has been delivered to him, but he has not yet paid the price, having only given security for it. And Julian has written . . . that the ownership of such slave is in suspense, and the payment of the price will determine to whom he belongs.

[3] It is beyond doubt that a slave held in common acquires for his masters according to their proprietary shares, except that when stipulating, or when taking a conveyance for one of them in particular, he acquires for that one alone, as for

Ibid. § 167a: Illud quaeritur, an quod domini nomen adiectum efficit, idem faciat unius ex dominis **iussum** intercedens. Nostri praeceptores, perinde ei qui iusserit soli adquiri existimant, atque si nominatim ei soli stipulatus esset servus mancipiove accepisset; diversae scholae auctores proinde utrique adquiri putant, ac si nullius iussum intervenisset.[1]

Pomp.: Ofilius recte dicebat, et per traditionem accipiendo vel deponendo commodandoque posse soli ei adquiri, qui iussit.—l. 6, D. de stip. serv. 45, 3.[2]

Ulp.: Hoc iure utimur, ut soli ei adquirat cuius iussu stipulatus est.—l. 5 eod.[3]

Iul.: —quod **ex re alterius domini** servus communis adquisierit, ad utrumque dominum pertinebit.—l. 37, § 2, de A. R. D.[4]

Id.: Persona servi communis eius condicionis est, ut in eo, quod alter ex dominis potest adquirere alter non potest, perinde habeatur,

---

example, when he stipulates thus: 'Do you undertake that it shall be given to my master Titius?' or when he takes a conveyance thus: 'I declare this thing to belong to my master Luc. Tit. by Quiritarian Law, and let it be now purchased for him with this piece of copper and this copper balance.'

1 It is matter of dispute whether an order of one master intervening has the same effect as the addition of the name of the master. Our authorities think that it is acquired for him alone who gave the order, just as if the slave had stipulated or had taken a conveyance expressly for him alone. The leaders of the opposite school are of opinion, that it is just as much acquired for both masters as if no one's order had intervened.

2 Ofil. was right in saying that, even upon acceptance of delivery, or in respect of a deposit and loan, he only can acquire who gave the order.

3 We adopt this rule, that he acquires alone for the one by whose order he stipulated.

4 —what a slave owned in common shall acquire by property belonging to one of two masters will belong to both masters.

Book III. Pt. I. Ch. I.

ac si eius solius esset, cui adquirendi facultatem habeat.—l. 1, § 4, de stip. serv.[1]

§ 89. Acquisition and Loss of Possession.

[a] § 76.

Possession is acquired 'corpore et animo (sc. possidendi),'[a] *i.e.*, by apprehension of the thing with the will to possess for oneself.

As apprehension is accounted not merely the corporal seizure of the thing, but every act by which the thing is subjected to the *de facto* control of a person, *i.e.*, is grounded upon the possibility of direct and exclusive operation upon the thing.

Paul.: Et adipiscimur possessionem corpore et animo, neque per se animo aut per se corpore. Quod autem diximus, et corpore et animo adquirere nos debere possessionem, non utique ita accipiendum est, ut qui fundum possidere velit, omnes glebas circumambulet: sed sufficit quamlibet partem eius fundi introire, dum mente et cogitatione hac sit, uti totum fundum usque ad terminum velit possidere.—l. 3, § 1, D. h. t. (= de A. P. 41, 2).[2]

Cels.: Si venditorem, quod emerim, deponere in mea domo iusserim, possidere me certum est, quamquam id nemo dum attigerit.—l. 18, § 2 eod.[3]

---

[1] The functions of a common slave are of such a character that in respect of what one of the two masters can acquire, but the other cannot, it is treated just as though it belonged only to the one for whom he is in the position to acquire it.

[2] And we acquire possession by physical control and intention, not by *animus* alone, nor by *corpus* alone. But as to our having said that we must acquire possession by both physical control and intention, this must not merely be understood as that he who desires to possess a field must walk round every clod; but it is sufficient for him to enter upon any part of such field, if only he have the intention and idea of possessing the whole field to its boundary.

[3] If I have directed a vendor to deposit in my house what I

Book III. Pt. I. Ch. I.

Paul.: —non est enim corpore et actu necesse adprehendere possessionem, sed etiam oculis et affectu; et argumento esse eas res, quae propter magnitudinem ponderis moveri non possunt, ut columnas: nam pro traditis eas haberi, si in re praesenti consenserint; et vina tradita videri, cum claves cellae vinariae emptori traditae fuerint.—l. 1, § 21 eod.[1]

If the thing be already under such *de facto* control, there is no need on the part of the so-called Detentor of new apprehension to acquire possession, but the mere animus possidendi[a] suffices; not, however, invariably.

[a] *Brevi manu traditio.* Cf. D. 41, 3, 33, 1.

Neratius et Proculus (scribunt) **solo animo** non posse nos adquirere possessionem, si non antecedat naturalis possessio.—l. 3, § 3 eod.[2]

Gai.: Interdum etiam sine traditione **nuda voluntas** domini sufficit ad rem transferendam, veluti si rem, quam commodavi aut locavi tibi aut apud te deposui, vendidero tibi: licet enim ex ea causa tibi non tradiderim, eo tamen, quod patior eam ex causa emptionis apud te esse, tuam efficio.—D. 41, 1, 9, 5.[3]

Ulp.: Si quis rem apud se depositam vel sibi commodatam vel pignori sibi datam emerit, pro

---

have purchased, it is clear that I have possession, although no one has yet touched it.

[1] —for that it is not necessary to seize the thing by a physical act, but it can be seized even by the sight and the will; and it is proved by those things which cannot be moved from their great weight, as pillars, for these are regarded as delivered if the parties have agreed in sight of the thing; and wine[b] is regarded as delivered when the keys of the wine-cellar have been handed to the purchaser.

[b] Prof. Holland, citing this passage, by a *lapsus calami*, speaks of 'wheat' (p. 142).

[2] Nerat. and Procul. (write) that we cannot acquire possession by mere intention, unless natural custody already exists.

[3] Sometimes also the mere desire of the owner without delivery suffices for the transfer of the property, for example, if I sell to you a thing which I have lent or let out to you or have deposited with you; for although I did not deliver it to you upon that ground, nevertheless in that I allow it to be in your hands on the ground of purchase, I make it yours.

Book III. Pt. I. Ch. I.

tradita erit accipienda, si post emptionem apud eum remansit.—D. 6, 2, 9, 1.[1]

Illud quoque a veteribus praeceptum est, **neminem sibi ipsum causam possessionis mutare posse.**—l. 3, § 19, D. h. t.[a] [2]

[a] See Poste on Gaius, p. 191; Brown, s. 'Adverse Possession'; Walker, *in loc.*

Iul.: Quod vulgo respondetur 'ipsum sibi causam possessionis mutare non posse' totiens verum est, quotiens quis sciret se bona fide non possidere et lucri faciendi causa inciperet possidere. —D. 41, 3, 33, 1.[3]

Id.: Quod vulgo respondetur causam possessionis neminem sibi mutare posse, sic accipiendum est, ut possessio non solum civilis sed etiam naturalis intelligatur. Et propterea responsum est, neque colonum, neque eum apud quem res deposita aut cui commodata est, lucri faciendi causa pro herede usucapere posse.—D. 41, 5, 2, 1.[4]

As regards the animus possidendi—

(1) persons naturally incapable of will, as furiosi and infantes, cannot acquire juristic possession by their own act alone.

Paul.: Furiosus, et pupillus sine tutoris auctoritate, non potest incipere possidere, quia affectionem tenendi non habent, licet maxime corpore suo rem contingant; sicuti si quis dormienti aliquid in manu ponat. . . . Ofilius quidem et

---

[1] If a man purchase property deposited with him or lent or pledged to him, there will be constructive delivery if it remain with him after the purchase.

[2] It has also been laid down by the old writers[b] that no one can for himself vary his possessory title.

[b] See p. 37.

[3] The common dictum, that no one can of himself change the ground of his possession, is always true when a person knows that he does not possess in good faith, and his possession begins to be directed to the obtaining of an advantage.

[4] The common dictum, that no one can of himself change his title to possession, must be understood as that not only civil possession, but natural is meant. And therefore the opinion has also been given, that neither the tenant nor depositary nor borrower can as quasi-heir make a title by usucapion, with intent to benefit.

Nerva filius, etiam sine tutoris auctoritate possidere incipere posse pupillum aiunt: eam enim rem facti non iuris esse; quae sententia recipi potest, si eius aetatis sint, ut intellectum capiant. —l. 1, § 3, D. h. t.[1]

(2) In the acquisition of possession by representatives,[a] the animus possidendi must always be present on the part of him who is to acquire the possession; except the case of the acquisition of possession 'ex peculiari causa' by slaves and filiifamilias (*i.e.*, in things falling to the peculium)[b] for the master or paterfamil., and the possession of the tutor and curator for the ward.

[a] §§ 20, 76. Cf. D. 41, 1, 13.

[b] See § 149.

Paul. v. 2, § 1: Possessionem adquirimus et animo et corpore, animo utique nostro, corpore vel nostro vel alieno.[2]

Id.: Procurator, si quidem mandante domino rem emerit, protinus illi adquirit possessionem, quodsi sponte emerit, non nisi ratam habuerit dominus emptionem.—l. 42, § 1 eod.[3]

Imp. Sever.: Per liberam personam ignoranti quoque adquiri possessionem et, postquam scientia intervenerit, usucapionis condicionem inchoari posse, tam ratione utilitatis quam iuris pridem receptum est.—C. 7, 32, 1.[4]

---

[1] A madman, and a ward without the authorisation of his guardian, cannot begin to possess, because they have not the disposition to detain, although they even physically touch the object; just as if a man place anything in the hand of one asleep. . . . Ofil., however, and Nerva the younger assert that a ward can begin to possess even without the sanction of his guardian; for that possession is matter of fact, not of law; which view may be entertained if they are of such an age as to be capable of discretion.

[2] We obtain possession by both *animus* and *corpus*; *animus* only our own, *corpus* either our own or that of another person.

[3] An agent, if he purchase a thing by the commission of the principal, from that moment acquires possession for him, but if he make the purchase of his own free will, he does not, unless the principal confirms the purchase.

[4] That possession can also be acquired through a freeman for

BOOK III. Pt. I. Ch. I.

Item adquirimus possessionem per servum aut filium qui in potestate est; et quidem earum rerum, quas peculiariter tenent, etiam ignorantes, sicut Sabino et Cassio et Iuliano placuit: quia nostra voluntate intelliguntur possidere, qui eis peculium habere permiserimus. Igitur ex causa peculiari et infans et furiosus adquirunt possessionem et usucapiunt.—l. 1, § 5, D. h. t.[1]

Pap.: Quaesitum est, cur ex peculii causa per servum ignorantibus possessio quaereretur. Dixi, utilitatis causa iure singulari receptum, ne cogerentur domini per momenta species et causas peculiorum inquirere.—l. 44, § 1 eod.[2]

(3) He that possesses anything 'suo nomine' can make another person possessor thereof without the necessity of apprehension on the part of the latter, by the fact that, with his knowledge and will—upon the ground of a contract containing an obligation for detention—the possessor exercises the actual control henceforth in the name of such person.[a]

[a] *Constitutum possessorium.* Cf. D. 17, 2, 1, 1.

Cels.: Quod meo nomine possideo, possum alieno nomine possidere; nec enim muto mihi causam possessionis, sed desino possidere et alium

---

a person not cognizant of it, and that after notice thereof his usucapion may commence, has been accepted upon principles as well of utility as of law.

[1] Moreover, we acquire possession by a slave or a son that is under our power; and indeed of those things which they possess as their separate property, even without our privity, as was the opinion of Sabin. and Cass. and Jul.; because they are considered to possess by our consent, for we have allowed them to have separate property. Accordingly, both an infant and a madman acquire possession and make a title by usucapion in respect of *peculium.*

[2] The question was raised, why possession should be acquired for us without our privity by a slave in respect of his *peculium.* I replied, that it was allowed for the sake of convenience, by virtue of privileged right, that masters should not be obliged constantly to investigate the composition and titles of *peculia.*

possessorem ministerio meo facio.—l. 1, § 18 pr., D. h. t.[a] [1]

Ulp.: Quaedam mulier fundum non marito donavit per epistulam et eundem fundum ab eo conduxit; posse defendi in rem ei competere, quasi per ipsam adquisierit possessionem, veluti per colonam.—D. 6, 1, 77.[2]

[a] Cf. context in § 76, *supra*.

Possession is LOST 'aut corpore aut animo,' *i.e.*, it endures as long as either the *de facto* element or that of the will—by the coalescence of which it arises and exists—is not positively extinguished.

Paul.: Quemadmodum nulla possessio adquiri nisi animo et corpore potest, ita nulla amittitur, nisi in qua utrumque in **contrarium** actum est. —l. 8, D. h. t.[3]

Possession is lost 'corpore'—except in respect of slaves[b]—if an event occur which renders impossible the re-establishment at will of the corporal relation to the thing of the previous possessor, the relation by virtue of which he can exercise exclusive operation upon it. This may happen—

[b] § 76.

(1) when another has taken possession—not mere detention[c]—of the thing. This must not, indeed, be in respect of only temporary removal of the owner from the thing, especially from the estate.[d]

[c] Ibid.

[d] 'Animo retinetur possessio.'

Gai.: Rem quae nobis surrepta est perinde in-

[1] That which I possess on my own account, I can also possess on behalf of another, for I do not change for myself my possessory title, but I can cease to possess, and by my instrumentality make another the possessor.

[2] A certain woman by letter presented an estate to another person not her husband, and took a lease from him of the same estate; (the law is) that he commands the real action in support of his title as though he acquired the possession by her—by a female tenant, for example.

[3] Just as possession cannot be acquired save by intention with physical control, so none is lost except when the opposite has occurred in respect of one or other.[e]

[e] For the force of *uterque* here, cf. D. 38, 10, 10, 13, cited by Savigny, 'Possession,' *ad loc.* (Perry, p. 250). See also Poste on Gaius, p. 646.

Book III. Pt. I. Ch. I.

telligimur desinere possidere, atque eam quae vi nobit erepta est.—l. 15, D. h. t.[1]

Paul.: Si rem apud te depositam furti faciendi causa contrectaveris, desino possidere.—l. 3, § 18 eod.[2]

Afr.: Si forte colonus, per quem dominus possideret decessisset, propter utilitatem receptum est, ut per colonum possessio et retineretur et continuaretur: quo mortuo non statim dicendum eam interpellari, sed tunc demum, cum dominus possessionem adipisci neglexerit.—l. 40, 1 eod.[3]

Papin.: Cum de amittenda possessione quaeratur, multum interesse dicam, per nosmet ipsos an per alios possideremus: nam eius quidem, quod corpore nostro teneremus, possessionem amitti vel animo vel etiam corpore,[a] si modo eo animo inde digressi fuissemus ne possideremus; eius vero, quod servi vel etiam coloni corpore possidetur, non aliter amitti possessionem, quam si eam alius ingressus fuisset, eamque amitti nobis quoque ignorantibus. Illa quoque possessionis amittendae separatio est: nam saltus hibernos et aestivos, quorum possessio retinetur animo—licet neque servum neque colonum ibi habeamus—quamvis saltus proposito possidendi fuerit alius ingressus, tamdiu priorem possidere dictum est, quamdiu possessionem ab alio occupatam ignoraret.—l. 44 § 2—l. 46, D. eod.[4]

[a] *Supra.*

---

[1] We are regarded as ceasing to possess a thing that has been stolen from us, just as a thing which has been taken from us by violence.

[2] If, with the intention of stealing, you meddle with a thing deposited with you, I cease to possess.

[3] If the tenant through whom the owner possesses have died, it has for convenience' sake been allowed that the possession is maintained and continued by the tenant, upon the death of whom it is not at once to be described as interrupted, but only when the owner has neglected to acquire possession.

[4] When it is a question of the loss of possession, I will say that it makes a great difference whether we possess of ourselves,

(2) The thing may otherwise have passed out of the custody of the possessor—*i.e.*, be lost—not merely mislaid or allowed to remain abroad—or have become inaccessible.[a]

[a] § 83.

Paul.: Nerva filius res mobiles, excepto homine, quatenus sub custodia nostra sint, hactenus possideri, i.e. quatenus, si velimus, naturalem possessionem nancisci possimus: nam pecus simul atque aberraverit, aut vas ita exciderit, ut non inveniatur, protinus desinere a nobis possideri, licet a nullo possideatur; dissimiliter atque si sub custodia mea sit nec inveniatur, quia praesentia eius sit et tantum cessat diligens inquisitio eius.—l. 3, § 13, D. h. t.[1]

Gai.: —Et haec ratio est, quare videamur servum fugitivum possidere, quod is, quemadmodum aliarum rerum possessionem [b] intervertere non potest, ita ne suam quidem potest.—l. 15 eod.[c] [2]

[b] Sc. domino.

[c] Cf. D. 41, 2, 1, 14; 40, 12, 25, 2.

---

or through others; for possession of that which we should have in our physical custody is lost either by *animus* or *corpus* also, provided we abandoned the thing with the intention no longer to possess; but of that which is possessed by the physical custody of a slave, or even a tenant, possession is not lost save as another has entered upon it and it is lost without our knowledge. There is also the following difference in respect of loss of possession: for winter and summer pastures, of which the possession is retained by *animus*—although we have there neither slave nor tenant—notwithstanding that some stranger has entered upon them with the intention to possess, it is said that the former possessor still possesses, so long as he is unaware that possession has been taken by another.

[1] Nerva the younger [says] that movables, with the exception of a slave, are possessed by us so long as they are in our custody, that is, so long as we, if we will, can obtain the natural possession. For that as soon as an animal has strayed, or a vessel is so lost that it cannot be found, at that moment does it cease to be possessed by us, although it may be possessed by no one else; it is otherwise when I have it in my custody and simply cannot find it, because there is the fact of its presence, and all that is wanting is a diligent search for it.

[2] And this is the reason why we are treated as possessing a

BOOK III. Pt. I. Ch. I.

Possession of a thing is lost 'animo,' not indeed in the case of mere absence—whether continuous or temporary—of the animus possidendi (*e.g.*, with the furiosus and him whose mind is not set on the thing), but only when the possessor gives up the intention to possess, and so declares a positive 'animus *non* possidendi,' which supposes such person has capacity to act.[a]

[a] Cf. D. 41, 2, 18 pr.; 6, 1, 77, *supra*.

In amittenda quoque possessione affectio eius, qui possidet, intuenda est. Itaque si in fundo sis, et tamen nolis eum possidere, protinus amittes possessionem. Igitur amitti et animo solo potest, quamvis adquiri non potest.—l. 3, § 6 eod.[1]

Proc.: Furiosus non potest desinere animo possidere.—l. 27 eod.[2]

Ulp.: Possessionem pupillum sine tutoris auctoritate amittere posse constat, non ut animo, sed ut corpore desinat possidere. Alia causa est, si forte animo possessionem velit amittere: hoc enim non potest.—l. 29 eod.[3]

LEGAL PROTECTION OF OWNERSHIP AND POSSESSION.

§ 90. PROPRIETARY ACTIONS.[b]

[b] Called 'Petitory' in Scottish Law.

The legal means appointed for the protection of ownership are the 'rei vindicatio,' the 'actio negatoria,' the 'actio Publiciana'; and further, under the same

runaway slave, because, as he cannot defraud his master of the possession of other things, not even can he of himself.

[1] As to loss of possession besides, the inclination of the possessor must be looked to; therefore, if you are on the land, and yet do not wish to possess it, you will at once lose possession. Thus, although it cannot be acquired, possession can be lost even by *animus* alone.

[2] A madman cannot cease to possess by his intent.

[3] It is settled that a pupil can lose possession without his guardian's concurrence, not that he cease to possess by *animus*, but by *corpus*. The case is different if he happen to wish to lose possession by his will; for this he cannot do.

aspect may be treated the 'actio finium regundorum,' which is indeed a special, and not Real, action.

The *rei vindicatio* (s. specialis in rem actio) is the action with which the proprietor (originally alone the Quiritarian) of a thing makes good his ownership against every one that withholds the possession of it against his will.

The following are the requisites of the action.

(1) In the person of the plaintiff, ownership, proof of which is incumbent upon him.[a]

[a] Inst. 4, 15, 4.

Paul.: In rem actio competit ei, qui aut iure gentium aut iure civili dominium adquisivit.—l. 23 pr., D. h. t. (= de R. V. 6, 1).[1]

(2) In the person of the defendant, Juristic or Natural possession.[b] In the light of a possessor (fictus possessor) is accounted 'is qui liti se obtulit' (alleged possessor) as well as 'qui dolo desiit possidere' (he that has fraudulently divested himself of possession); false repudiation of possession, as a generally defective defensio[c] on the part of the defendant, results in its transfer to the plaintiff.

[b] D. 44, 7, 25.

[c] § 195.

Ulp.: Officium autem iudicis in hac actione in hoc erit, ut iudex inspiciat, an reus possideat; nec ad rem pertinebit, ex qua causa possideat: ubi rem probavi rem meam esse, necesse habebit possessor restituere, qui non obiecit aliquam exceptionem. Quidam tamen, ut Pegasus, eam solam possessionem putaverunt hanc actionem complecti, quae locum habet in interdicto 'uti possidetis' vel 'utrubi': denique ait ab eo, apud quem deposita est vel commodata vel qui conduxerit, . . . quia hi omnes non possident, vindicari non posse. Puto autem ab omnibus, qui tenent et habent restituendi facultatem, peti posse.—l. 9, h. t.[2]

---

[1] A real action belongs to him who has acquired ownership either by the *i. g.* or by the *i. c.*

[2] Now the duty of the *iudex* in this action consists in his

Book III. Pt. I. Ch. I.

Ei vero qui possidet non est actio prodita, per quam neget rem actoris esse: sane **uno casu** qui possidet nihilominus actoris partem obtinet.—§ 2, I. de act. 4, 6.[1]

Paul.: Sin autem, cum a Titio petere vellem, aliquis dixerit se possidere et ideo liti se obtulit, et hoc ipsum in re agenda testatione probavero, omnimodo condemnandus est.—Sed et is qui ante litem contestatam dolo desiit rem possidere, tenetur in rem actione.—l. 27 pr., § 3 eod.[2]

Ulp. inst. fgm. iv. (vi.): —tam adipiscendae quam reciperandae possessionis . . . sunt interdicta QVEM FVNDVM et QVAM HEREDITATEM; nam si fundum vel hereditatem ab aliquo petam, nec lis defendatur, cogitur ad me transferre possessionem, sive numquam possedi sive ante possedi deinde amisi possessionem.[3]

---

ascertaining whether the defendant is in possession. The matter will not be affected by the title upon which he possesses: when I have proved that the thing belongs to me, the possessor will have to give it up, if he has not defended by way of plea. Some, however, as Pegasus, have supposed that this action merely concerns such possession as obtains in the interdict 'uti possidetis' or 'utrubi.'[a] Thus he says, the proprietary action cannot be brought against him who is a depositary, or a borrower, or hirer, . . . because none of them possess. But I am of opinion that a claim can be made against all who have the custody and have the means of restitution.

[a] As to which interdicts, see § 91.

[1] But to him that is in possession no action is given whereby he can deny that the thing belongs to the plaintiff; only in one case does the possessor none the less perform the part of plaintiff.

[2] But if when I desire to bring an action against Tit., any one has stated he is possessor, and so has voluntarily intermeddled with the suit, and I in the course of the proceedings prove this very point by witnesses, he must at any rate be condemned.—But he also who before joinder of issue has craftily ceased to have possession of the property is liable to an action *in rem*.

[3] There are, as well for the origination as for the restoration of possession, the interdicts *Q.f.* and *Q.h.* For if I sue a person for land or a heritage, and he does not defend the suit, he is obliged to transfer the possession to me, whether I never have

Fur. Anth.: In rem actionem pati non compellimur, quia licet alicui dicere se non possidere: ita ut, si possit adversarius convincere, rem ab adversario possideri, transferat ad se possessionem per iudicem, licet suam esse non adprobaverit.—l. ult. D. h. t.[1]

Book III. Pt. I. Ch. I.

(3) The subject of the action is as a rule an individual corporeal thing, alone exceptionally a so-called 'universitas' of things.[a]

[a] Cf. § 73.

Ulp.: Per hanc autem actionem non solum singulae res vindicabuntur, sed posse etiam gregem vindicari Pomponius scribit. . . . Sed enim gregem sufficiet ipsum nostrum esse, licet singula capita nostra non sint.—l. 1, § 3, h. t.[2]

(4) If the thing by union with another have temporarily forfeited its independent character, the action can only lie after severance, to be enforced by 'actio ad exhibendum.'[b]

[b] §§ 84, 137.

The action is well founded if the plaintiff prove his ownership; but pleas are at the command of the defendant, by which he can avert the condemnation. These rest in general upon a right attaching to the defendant to possess or to detain the thing (*e.g.*, right of pignus, ususfructus, hire). To such belongs especially the 'exceptio doli.'

(1) In respect of the obligation of the plaintiff to transfer the ownership (exceptio rei venditae et traditae).[c]

[c] Cf. § 75.

Ulp.: Marcellus scribit, si alienum fundum

---

had possession, or previously had possession and afterwards lost it.

[1] We are not obliged to put up with a real action, because a man can declare that he is not possessor; so that if one opponent can prove that the thing is possessed by the other, he by means of judicial relief procures the possession, although he have not proved that the thing belongs to him.

[2] Now by this action there will be claimed not only individual things, but Pomp. writes that a flock even can be claimed. . . . But it will suffice if the flock itself is ours, although the separate heads of cattle are not ours.

Book III. Pt. I. Ch. I.

vendideris et tuum postea factum petas, hac exceptione recte te repellendum.—Sed et si dominus fundi heres venditori existat, idem erit dicendum.—D. 21, 3, 1, 1 pr.[1]

(2) Because of the lien of the defendant for outlay upon the thing which he has incurred, to be recouped by the plaintiff.[a] These are impensae *necessariae* which are in all cases refunded, and *utiles* disbursed by the bonae fidei possessor. Impensae *voluptariae* are never refunded.

[a] Connected with these are the analagous cases in § 84 (*s. accessio*). As to lien for meliorations, see Story's Equity, § 1239 (Grigsby, p. 862).

Paul.: Impensae **necessariae** sunt, quae si factae non sint, res aut peritura aut deterior futura sit. — **Voluptariae** sunt, quae speciem dumtaxat ornant, non etiam fructum augent, ut sunt viridaria et aquae salientes . . . picturae.—D. 50, 16, 79 pr., § 2.[2]

Ulp. vi. 16: **Utiles** sunt, quibus non factis quidem deterior (res) non fuerit, factis autem fructuosior effecta est, veluti si vineta et oliveta fecerit.[3]

Pap.: Sumptus in praedium, quod alienum esse apparuit, a bona fide possessore facti neque ab eo qui praedium donavit neque a domino peti possunt, verum exceptione doli posita per officium iudicis aequitatis ratione servantur, scilicet si fructuum ante litem contestatam perceptorum

---

[1] Marc. writes, if you have sold an estate belonging to another, and should claim it as having subsequently become yours, you are to be rightly defeated by this plea. But the same will have to be said even if the owner of the estate should become heir of the vendor.

[2] Necessary outlays are those by the omission of which the property would either be ruined or dilapidated.—Ornamental outlays are such as only embellish the exterior of the property, and do not add to its productivity, such as pleasure-gardens and fountains, . . . paintings.

[3] Useful outlays are those by the omission of which (the property) indeed will not suffer, but when they have been incurred, it has been rendered more profitable; as if the man have made vineyards and olive-gardens.

summam excedant: etenim admissa compensatione superfluum sumptum meliore praedio facto dominus restituere cogitur.—l. 48, h. t.[1]

Gai. ii. § 76: Sed si ab eo petamus fundum vel aedificium et impensas in aedificium vel in seminaria vel in sementem factas ei solvere nolimus, poterit nos per exc. doli mali repellere, utique si bonae fidei possessor fuerit.[2]

Cels.: —(dominus) reddat impensam, ut fundum recipiat, usque eo dumtaxat, quo pretiosior factus est.—l. 38, D. h. t.[3]

The aim of the action is to obtain an acknowledgment of the ownership and restoration of the thing 'cum omni causa post litem contestatam'[a]—to which the 'arbitrium iudicis'[b] is directed; and in default of this, condemnation in the value of the property, which, in case of dolus or contumacia of the defendant, is established by the unqualified estimate upon oath of the plaintiff (ius iurandum in litem). As regards the fruits taken before litis contestatio, the bonae fidei possessor is only accountable for the 'exstantes';[c] the malae fidei possessor both for 'consumpti' and 'percipiendi' (*i.e.*, those left ungathered by negligentia).

[a] D. 12, 1, 31 pr.
[b] Inst. 4, 6, 31.
[c] § 85.

Gai.: Nec sufficit corpus ipsum restitui, sed opus est, ut et causa rei restituatur, id est ut omne habeat petitor, quod habiturus foret, si eo

---

[1] Expenses incurred by a *bon. fid.* possessor upon an estate which has turned out to belong to another person cannot be claimed, either from the donor of the estate or from the owner, but upon equitable principle are recovered through the judicial authority by the counter-claim of *exceptio doli;* that is, if they exceed the amount of the fruits gathered before joinder of issue; for the owner must refund the surplus of expense by which the estate has been improved, according to the set-off allowed.

[2] But if we claim from him the land or a building, and refuse to pay him the outlay he has incurred over the building, or the planting, or sowing, he will be able to defeat us by the plea of fraud, at any rate if he has been a possessor in good faith.

[3] In order to get back the estate, (the owner) must refund the outlay so far at least as it has been benefited.

tempore, quo iudicium accipiebatur, restitutus ille homo fuisset.—l. 20, h. t.[1]

Ulp.: Si vero non potest restituere, si quidem dolo fecit, quominus possit, is, quantum adversarius in litem sine ulla taxatione in infinitum iuraverit, damnandus est. Si vero nec potest restituere nec dolo fecit, quominus possit, non pluris quam quanti res est, . . . condemnandus est.—l. 68 eod.[2]

The actio NEGATORIA is directed against every one who, without deprivation of possession by actual encroachments, disturbs the plaintiff in the exercise of his proprietary right: frequently by usurpation of a right (especially of a servitude) limiting the ownership of the plaintiff—in its positive, it may be, certainly in its negative element. It goes to the acknowledgment of the freedom of ownership from such limitation—which freedom has not to be proved by the plaintiff—and to the removal of the means of disturbance, to compensation for injury that may already have arisen from such disturbance, and to the giving of cautiones for abstention from further disturbances (cautio de non amplius turbando).

Contra quoque de usufructu et de servitutibus praediorum . . . invicem proditae sunt actiones, ut quis intendat, ius non esse adversario utendi fruendi, eundi agendi aquamve ducendi, item altius tollendi prospiciendi proiiciendi

[1] And it is not enough that the bulk itself be restored, but it is necessary that restitution be made of the appurtenances to the property, that is, that the claimant may have all that he would have had, if that slave had been restored to him at the time when he engaged in the action.

[2] But should he be unable to make restitution, if it was by fraud he acted so as to be unable, he shall be condemned in such unlimited damages as the opponent shall assess upon oath, without any rebate. But if he neither can make restitution nor has acted fraudulently, so as to be unable, he must not be condemned for more than the thing is worth.

immittendi: istae quoque actiones in rem sunt, sed negativae.—§ 2, I. de act. 4, 6.[1] Book III. Pt. I. Ch. I.

Ulp.: Quodsi forte qui agit, dominus proprietatis non sit, quamvis fructuarius ius utendi non habet, vincet tamen iure quo possessores sunt potiores, licet nullum ius habeant.—D. 7, 6, 5 pr.[2]

The *publiciana* actio is the praetorian action shaped according to the analogy of the 'rei vindicatio.'

Ulp.: In Publiciana actione omnia eadem erunt, quae in rei vindicatione diximus.—l. 7, § 8, D. h. t. (de Publ. act. 6, 2).[3]

Publiciana actio ad instar proprietatis, non ad instar possessionis respicit.—Ibid. § 6.[4]

It is based upon the fiction of completed usucapion which—originally designed also for the protection of Bonitary ownership[a]—belongs to the previous bonae fidei possessor (according to the verba edicti, primarily alone on the ground of tradition) who has lost possession of the thing before usucapion was complete, against every possessor, for delivery up of the property.

Ait praetor: SI QVIS ID QVOD TRADITVR EX IVSTA CAVSA NON A DOMINO ET NONDVM VSVCAPTVM PETET, IVDICIVM DABO.—l. 1 pr. eod.[5]

[a] § 75.

---

[1] On the other hand also, in respect of usufruct and praedial servitudes,[b] actions have been given of a different character, as when a man's statement of claim is that his opponent has no right to use and enjoyment, to passage, to the leading of cattle or drawing of water, or again, to raising his house, to having a prospect, to projecting his house, to having a beam in the adjoining wall: those actions also are *in rem*, but negative.

[b] § 94.

[2] But if he who takes proceedings happen not to be the ground owner, although the fructuary has not right of user, he will succeed, however, by the rule of possessors having preference, in spite of their having no claim.

[3] In respect of the *Public. actio*, entirely the same things will hold as we have spoken of with regard to the *rei vindic.*

[4] The *Public. actio* contemplates the analogy of[c] ownership, not of possession.

[c] Or, 'approximates to.'

[5] The Praetor says: 'If a man shall claim that which upon

BOOK III. Pt. I. Ch. I.

Namque si cui ex iusta causa res aliqua tradita fuerit, veluti ex causa emptionis aut donationis aut dotis aut legatorum, necdum eius rei dominus effectus est, si eius rei casu possessionem amiserit, nullam habet directam in rem actionem ad eam rem persequendam; . . . sed quia sane durum erat eo casu deficere actionem, inventa est a praetore actio, . . . quae actio Publiciana appellatur, quoniam primum a Publicio praetore in edicto proposita est.—§ 4, I. de act.[1]

Gai. iv. § 36: —quia non potest eam 'ex iure Quiritium suam esse' intendere, fingitur rem usucepisse, et ita quasi ex iure Quiritium dominus factus esset, intendit velut hoc modo: IVDEX ESTO. SI QVEM HOMINEM AVLVS AGERIVS EMIT ET SI EI TRADITVS EST, ANNO POSSEDISSET, TVM SI EVM HOMINEM, DE QVO AGITVR, EX IVRE QVIRITIVM EIVS ESSE OPORTERET, et reliqua.[2]

Id.: Quaecumque sunt iustae causae adquirendarum rerum, si ex his causis nacti res amiserimus, dabitur nobis earum rerum persequendarum gratia haec actio.—l. 13 pr., D. h. t.[3]

---

a lawful ground was delivered to him by a non-owner, and has not yet been acquired by *usus*, I will grant an action.'

[1] For if a thing have been delivered to a man for a lawful consideration, for example, upon the ground of purchase, or donation, or dowry, or bequest, and he has not yet become owner thereof, if he by accident lose possession of such thing, he has no direct action *in rem* for its recovery; . . . but inasmuch as it was certainly hard that in such case no action should be available, one was devised by the Praetor . . . this is called the 'act. Publ.,' because it was first put forth in his edict by the praetor Publicius.

[2] —inasmuch as he cannot allege that the thing belongs to him by Quiritarian Law, he feigns to have acquired it by *usus*, and so, as if he had become owner by Quiritarian Law, he states his claim, for example, thus:—'Let so and so be *iudex*. If A. A. have possessed for one year a slave that he bought and who was delivered to him, then if that slave as to whom proceedings are taken ought to belong to him by Quiritarian Law,' &c.

[3] If we have lost things which we obtained by virtue of any

Ulp.: Haec actio in his, quae usucapi non possunt, puta furtivis, locum non habet.—l. 9, § 5 eod.[1]

If the defendant be owner of the thing, the 'exceptio iusti dominii' is granted to him as against the action (causa cognita).

Ner.: Publiciana actio non ideo comparata est, ut res a domino auferatur; eiusque rei argumento est primo aequitas, deinde exceptio '**si ea res possessoris non sit.**'—l. 17 eod.[2]

The plaintiff may under certain circumstances meet this with a 'replicatio doli' in particular: as especially in respect of an 'exceptio rei venditae et traditae'[a] with the 'replicatio r. v. e. t.'

[a] *Supra.*

Ulp.: Si a Titio fundum emeris, qui Sempronii erat, isque tibi traditus fuerit pretio soluto, deinde Titius Sempronio heres exstiterit, . . . si ipse Titius fundum a te peteret, exceptione in factum comparata vel doli mali summoveretur, et si ipse eum possideret et Publiciana peteres, adversus excipientem 'si non suus esset' replicatione utereris.—D. 44, 4, 4, 32.[3]

Iul.: Si quis rem a non domino emerit, mox petente domino absolutus sit, deinde possessionem amiserit et a domino petierit, adversus excipientem

---

lawful grounds of acquisition, this action will be granted to us for their recovery.

[1] This action is not available in respect of things which are not susceptible of usucapion, stolen things, for instance.

[2] The *act. Publ.* has not been introduced to deprive the owner of his property, and the proof thereof is equity first of all, and next the plea: 'if such things do not belong to the possessor.'

[3] If from Tit. you have bought an estate belonging to Semp., and it has been delivered to you upon payment of the purchase-money, but Tit. has afterwards become heir of Semp.; . . . should Tit. himself claim the field from you, he would be defeated by a plea framed *in factum* or of fraud, and if he himself should possess it, and you bring the *act. Publ.* against him as urging the plea: 'if it was not his property,' you could avail yourself of a *replicatio*.

Book III. Pt. I. Ch. I.

'si non eius sit res' replicatione hac adiuvabitur 'at si res iudicata non sit.'—D. 44, 2, 24.[1]

To the owner also this action is advantageous because of the proof of ownership not being necessary. Moreover, the Publiciana is also as 'recissoria actio' (*i.e.*, abandoning the fiction of usucapio) given to the past owner, whose property another has acquired by usucapion, in a case where he has claim to 'in integrum restitutio' as against the usucapion.[a]

[a] § 30, ad fin.

Rursus ex diverso, si quis cum reipublicae causa abesset vel in hostium potestate esset, rem eius qui in civitate esset usuceperit, permittitur domino si possessor reipublicae causa abesse desierit, tunc intra annum rescissa usucapione eam petere, ut dicat possessorem usu non cepisse et ob id suam esse rem.—§ 5, I. de act.[2]

The actio *FINIVM REGVNDORVM*, or suit for the defining of boundaries—an 'actio mixta'[b]—is that which is intended to terminate the community in a part subject of dispute, which obtained between the possessors of contiguous rural estates through a confusion of, or mistake as to, boundaries; and thus to regulate the same. According to the Twelve Tables, in controversies as to boundaries 'intra quinque pedes' (the dividing line), three arbitri or skilled land-

[b] Inst. 4, 6, 20.

---

1 If a man have purchased a thing from a non-owner, and presently upon the owner's bringing an action against him has been acquitted, but afterwards has lost the possession, and then again has sued the owner, relief will be given him against the plea, 'if the thing be not his,' by the replication, 'but if the matter have not been adjudicated.'

2 If again, on the other hand, a man who was absent on the public service, or in the power of the enemy, has by *usus* acquired a thing belonging to another resident within the State, the owner is allowed, if the possessor is no longer away upon public business, within one year to annul the usucapion and sue for the property, that is, to sue for it in such way as to maintain that the possessor has not acquired by *usus*, and that therefore the property belongs to himself.

surveyors, (agri) mensores—after the l. Manilia replaced by one—had to determine the boundary according to the rules of their profession (controversia de fine); whilst in disputes as to boundaries 'extra quinque pedes' the iudex decided according to the principles of the Civil Law (controversia de loco). After legislation hereon had fluctuated much, Justinian abolished that distinction, and allowed always thenceforth only of the surveyors as experts.

> Paul.: Finium regundorum actio in personam est, licet pro vindicatione rei est.—D. 10, 1, 1.[1]
>
> Id.: Hoc iudicium locum habet in confinio praediorum rusticorum: nam in confinio praediorum urbanorum displicuit, neque enim confines hi, sed magis vicini dicuntur, et ea communibus parietibus plerumque disterminantur. Et ideo et si in agris aedificia iuncta sint, locus huic actioni non erit: et in urbe hortorum latitudo contingere potest, ut etiam finium regundorum agi possit.—l. 4, § 10 eod.[2]
>
> Ulp.: Iudici finium regundorum permittitur, ut ubi non possit dirimere fines, adiudicatione controversiam dirimat.—l. 2, § 1 eod.[3]

§ 91. Legal Means of protecting Possession. Possessory Interdicts.

Possession is protected by the Possessory Interdicts,

---

[1] The action for the adjustment of boundaries is one *in personam*, although it is in lieu of the *rei vindicatio*.

[2] This action obtains in respect of the boundary of rural estates, for it was not in favour as regards the boundary of urban estates, because the latter are not said to bound upon, but to be contiguous to, one another, and are also generally divided by party-walls: if therefore buildings exist joined to one another amongst fields, this action will not be employed. Within the town also gardens can extend so in breadth that proceedings can be taken for regulation of boundaries.

[3] The *iudex* for adjustment of boundaries is allowed to settle a dispute by his decision, where it is impossible to determine the boundaries.

Book III. Pt. I. Ch. I.

which are divided into two classes; 'interdicta *retinendae* possessionis,' which are granted in respect of disturbance of possession, and 'interdicta *recuperandae* possessionis,' which are granted in respect of deprivation of possession.

Interdicta *retinendae* possessionis are—

(1) the interdictum *VTI POSSIDETIS* (a duplex interdictum, for the protection of possession of Immovables, in which he succeeds whose possession at the time of the issue of the interdict was free from faults as against the opponent.

Ulp.: Ait praetor: VTI EAS AEDES, QVIBVS DE AGITVR, NEC VI NEC CLAM NEC PRECARIO ALTER AB ALTERO POSSIDETIS, QVO MINVS ITA POSSIDEATIS, VIM FIERI VETO.—Hoc interdictum de soli possessore scriptum est; et est prohibitorium ad retinendam possessionem:—nam huius rei causa redditur, ne vis fiat ei qui possidet.—l. 1 pr., §§ 1, 4, D. uti poss. 43, 17.[1]

Quod ait praetor in interdicto 'nec vi nec clam . . .' hoc eo pertinet, ut si quis possidet vi aut clam aut precario, si quidem ab alio, prosit ei possessio: si vero ab adversario suo, non debet eum propter hoc, quod ab eo possidet, vincere.—Ibid. § 9.[2]

Gai.: Is qui destinavit rem petere, animadvertere debet, an aliquo interdicto possit nancisci possessionem, quia longe commodius est ipsum

---

[1] The Praetor says: 'As you possess that house subject of the action, neither by violence, nor secretly, nor by sufferance[a] one against the other, that you should not so possess it, I forbid all violence.' This interdict has been composed with reference to the occupier of the ground, and it is prohibitive for the maintenance of possession:—for the reason assigned of this is, that violence be not done to the possessor.

[a] See Abdy and Walker's note on Gai. iv. 150.

[2] The words of the Praetor in this interdict, 'neither violently nor secretly . . .' mean, that although a man possess by violence, or secretly, or upon sufferance against another, the possession shall accrue to his benefit; but if against his opponent, he ought not to win by reason of his possession being adverse to such person.

possidere et adversarium ad onus petitoris compellere, quam alio possidente petere.—D. 6, 1, 24.[1]

(2) The interdictum *utrubi* (also duplex) for the protection of possession of Movables; the one here succeeds who, as against the opponent, has possessed 'sine vitio,' the greatest part of the preceding year, and that including the possession of the auctor. In the Justinianean Law the interdictum 'utrubi' was placed on the same footing as the 'uti possidetis.'

Praetor ait: VTRVBI HIC HOMO, QVO DE AGITVR, MAIORE PARTE HVIVSCE ANNI FVIT, QVO MINVS IS EVM DVCAT, VIM FIERI VETO.—Hoc interdictum de possessione rerum mobilium locum habet.—l. un D. utrubi, 43, 31.[2]

Gai. iv. § 152: Annus autem retrorsus numeratur: itaque si tu verbi gratia VIII mensibus possederis prioribus et ego VII posterioribus, ego potior ero, quod trium priorum mensium possessio nihil tibi in hoc interdicto prodest, quia alterius anni possessio est.[3]

Lic. Ruf.: 'Maiore parte anni' possedisse quis intelligitur, etiamsi duobus mensibus possederit, si modo adversarius eius paucioribus diebus possederit.—D. 50, 16, 156.[4]

---

1 He that has determined to claim property ought to consider whether he can acquire possession by any interdict, because it is far more convenient himself to possess, and to oblige his opponent to the trouble of undertaking the functions of claimant, than to bring the action whilst another is in possession.

2 The Praetor says: 'with whichever party this slave in question was for the greater part of this year, to prevent his abduction by so and so, I prohibit the use of violence.—This interdict obtains in respect of the possession of movable things.

3 Now the year is reckoned backwards; therefore, if you, for example, have been in possession for the first eight months previously, and I for the last seven, I shall have the better claim; because possession for the three earlier months is of no service to you in respect of this interdict, inasmuch as the possession belongs to another year.

4 That any one has possessed for the greater part of the year means, even if he has been in possession for two months, pro-

Gai. iv. § 151: In '**utrubi**' interdicto non solum sua cuique possessio prodest, sed etiam alterius, quam iustum est ei accedere, velut eius cui heres exstiterit; eiusque a quo emerit vel ex donatione aut dotis nomine acceperit; . . . sed si vitiosam habeat possessionem, i.e. aut vi aut clam aut precario ab adversario adquisitam, non datur accessio: nam ei (possessio) sua nihil prodest.[1]

Iust. iv. 15, 4[a]: Hodie tamen aliter observatur: nam utriusque interdicti potestas, quantum ad possessionem pertinet, exaequata est, ut ille vincat et in re soli et in re mobili, qui possessionem nec vi nec clam nec precario ab adversario litis contestationis tempore detinet.[2]

Both interdicts have at the same time a recuperatory effect, that is, in consequence of their twofold character, and the so-called 'exceptio vitiosae possessionis,' they can serve for the recovery of possession already lost.

Interdicta *recuperandae* possessionis.

(1) The interdictum UNDE VI[a] belongs to the past possessor of an estate against its occupier, who has ousted the former from possession by the employment of direct force (vis atrox), or in the case of

[a] For the Assize of Novel Disseisin, see Scrutton, 'Influence of the Roman Law on the Law of England,' pp. 112-115.

vided his opponent's possession has been for a less number of days.

[1] In the interdict 'utrubi' not only is a man's own possession of service to him, but also that of any other person which rightfully accrues to him; as for example, of him whose heir he has become, and of one from whom he has purchased, or from whom he has received it by way of gift or dower; . . . but if the possession he has is tainted, that is, acquired from his adversary either by violence, or clandestinely, or upon sufferance, the accession is not allowed, for his own possession is of no avail to him.

[2] At the present day, however, the usage is different; for the operation of both interdicts as far as concerns possession has been assimilated, so that both in respect of an immovable and a movable thing, he wins who at the time when the proceedings begin has detention neither by force, nor secretly, nor upon sufferance as against his opponent.

clandestine occupation, by obstructing his return,[a] whilst by older Law the first already alone grounded the 'interdictum de *clandestina* possessione,' which at a later period ceased to be indispensable. It goes 'intra annum utilem' to restitution 'cum omni causa' and full compensation for damage—is an actio in factum. In the earlier Law there were two special interdicts, in respect of ejection by armed violence (vis armata)[b] and by simple force (vis quottidiana); in the latter case the 'deiiciens' could appeal to the fact that he had illegally ('vi clam precario') lost the possession through the disseisee himself. This distinction was done away with in the Law of Justinian, and 'vitiosa possessio' of the 'deiectus' as against the 'deiiciens' always irreversibly avails in the interdictum unde vi.

[a] Cf. D. 41, 2, 44, 2, and l. 46. 41, 3, 4, 22, and l. 33, § 2.

[b] See Cicero's oration Pro Caecina, and Long's notes on same.

Ulp.: Praetor ait: VNDE TV ILLVM VI DEIECISTI AVT FAMILIA TVA DEIECIT [EO RESTITVAS, . . .] DE EO QVAEQVE ILLE TVNC IBI HABVIT TANTVMMODO INTRA ANNVM, POST ANNVM DE EO, QVOD AD EVM QVI VI DEIECIT PERVENERIT, IVDICIVM DABO.—Ad solam autem atrocem vim pertinet hoc interdictum, et ad eos tantum, qui de solo deiiciuntur, ut puta de fundo sive aedificio; ad alium autem non pertinet.—l. 1 pr., § 3, D. de vi 43, 16.[1]

Id.: Qui ad nundinas profectus neminem reliquerit et, dum ille a nundinis redit, aliquis occupaverit possessionem, videri eum clam possidere Labeo scribit (retinet ergo possessionem is qui ad nundinas abiit): verum si revertentem

[1] The Praetor says: 'In the place whence thou hast violently ejected so and so, or thy servants have ejected him, [in that place reinstate him]; in respect of whatever he possessed there at that time, I will give an action, but only within the space of a year, after the expiration of a year in respect of what came to the hands of the violent dispossessor.'—But this interdict relates merely to violence coupled with outrage, and to those only who are ejected from the ground, as for example, from an estate or building; others it does not concern.

Book III. Pt. I. Ch. I.

dominum non admiserit, vi magis intelligi possidere, non clam.—D. 41, 2, 6, 1.[1]

Id.: Si clam dicatur possidere . . . de clandestina possessione competere interdictum (Iulianus) inquit.—D. 10, 3, 7, 5.[2]

Id.: Ex interdicto **unde vi** etiam is, qui non possidet restituere cogetur.—l. 1, § 42, de vi.[3]

Qui vi deiectus est, quidquid damni senserit ob hoc, quod deiectus est, recuperare debet: pristina enim causa restitui debet, quam habiturus erat, si non fuisset deiectus.—Quod autem ait praetor '**quaeque ibi habuit**' sic accipimus, ut omnes res contineantur, non solum quae propriae ipsius fuerunt, verum etiam si quae apud eum depositae vel ei commodatae vel pigneratae vel . . . locatae sunt.—Ibid. §§ 31, 33.[4]

Ex causa huius interdicti in heredem . . . in factum actio competit in id quod ad eos pervenit. —Ibid. § 48.[5]

Id.: non solum resistere est permissum, ne

---

[1] When a man has set out for the market without leaving any one behind, and whilst he returns from market, some one assumes possession, Labeo writes that such person is considered to have clandestine possession (he accordingly retains possession who went to market), but that if he refuse admittance to the owner upon his return, his possession is the rather to be taken as violent, not clandestine.

[2] If it be alleged that he possesses secretly. . . . (Jul.) says the interdict concerning clandestine possession is available.

[3] And he that does not possess is obliged to deliver up by virtue of the interdict 'unde vi.'

[4] He that has been dispossessed by violence ought to recover whatever loss he has sustained by reason of his having been ousted; for the former state of things must be restored in which he would have been if he had not been ejected.—The words of the Praetor, 'what he at that time held,' must be so understood that all things are included in them, not only property that was his own, but whatever was deposited with him, lent or pledged, . . . or let out to him.

[5] Upon the ground of this interdict an action *in factum* lies against the heir, . . . for that which has come to their hands.

deiiciatur, sed et si deiectus quis fuerit, eundem deiicere non ex intervallo, sed ex continenti.—l. 3, § 9 eod.[1]

(2) The interdictum *DE PRECARIO* is given against a person who does not upon the request of the 'precario dans' restore to him the thing—movable or immovable—the possession of which has been allowed him 'precario,' that is, with power of revocation.

Ulp.: Precarium est, quod precibus petendi utendum conceditur tamdiu, quamdiu is, qui concessit, patitur.—D. 43, 26, 1 pr.[2]

Ait praetor: QVOD PRECARIO AB ILLO HABES AVT DOLO MALO FECISTI VT DESINERES HABERE, QVA DE RE AGITVR, ID ILLI RESTITVAS.—l. 2 pr. eod.[3]

Ulp.: Meminisse autem nos oportet, eum qui precario habet etiam possidere.—l. 4, § 1 eod.[4]

Id.: —receptum est rei suae precarium non esse.—Quaesitum est, si quis rem suam pignori mihi dederit et precario rogaverit, an hoc interdictum locum habeat, . . . mihi videtur verius precarium consistere in pignore.—l. 4, § 3, l. 6, § 4 eod.[5]

---

[1] A man is allowed not only to offer resistance to ejectment, but even if he have been ejected, to oust the disseisor, not after a respite, but there and then.

[2] A precatory possession is that which is granted upon the request of the applicant, to be used so long as the grantor suffers.

[3] The Praetor says: 'That which you hold by sufferance of so and so, or of which you have fraudulently managed to terminate your possession, that concerning which proceedings are taken, do you make over again to so and so.'

[4] But we must remember that he who holds anything upon sufferance also has possession.

[5] —it has been supposed that no *precarium* obtains of one's own property.—The question has been raised, if a man has given me his property in pledge, and has applied for it as a *precarium*, whether this interdict is available. . . . I rather think that a *precarium* can exist in a pledge.

Book III. Pt. I. Ch. I.

Id.: Illud adnotatur, quod culpam non praestat is qui precario rogavit, sed solum dolum; . . . culpam tamen dolo proximam contineri quis merito dixerit.[a]—l. 8, § 3 eod.[1]

[a] Cf. D. 41, 2, 3, 5; 16, 3, 17, 1; 41, 3, 16; 43, 26, 2, 2; Gai. 59-60, and § 121, *infra*.

[b] Cf. Austin, lect. 52.

Tit. III.—IURA IN RE ALIENA.[b]

§ 92. General View.

The essence of the 'iura in re sc. aliena' (real rights in a thing owned by another) consists in this, that the non-owner of a thing possesses an independent privilege, contained in the ownership, immediately to operate upon such thing in a definite direction, and to treat it as subservient to a definite proprietary interest of his own. The thing itself is thereby partially subjected to his control, and a limit is imposed upon the control of the owner, whether on its positive or negative side. All iura in re aliena are called forth by requirements of human society and intercourse; in particular, they contemplate the full economic exercise and realisation of ownership, in the interest of the particular owner, as well as of the community, which would be impeded if the Law should only recognise unlimited ownership.

The several kinds of rights in things owned by others are—

1. Servitudes, as the oldest kind of what by the Romans are simply called iure in re.
2. Superficies.
3. Emphyteusis.
4. Right of Pledge (pignus, hypotheca).

---

[1] It is remarked that he who has applied for it as a *precarium* commits no offence, but only sharp practice; . . . but that an offence closely related to sharp practice is contained in it might be justly maintained.

§ 93. Nature of Servitudes,[a] and the Rules of Law in general applicable to them.

Servitudes are real rights of user in property owned by another inseparable from the subject entitled, *i.e.*, transferable to no other subject, by which such thing becomes subservient to a person who is not its owner (res serviens; servitus—libertas rei). The servitude can either belong to an individual person, or to a particular estate, that is, to the owner of it as such—Personal and Praedial servitudes. According to their fundamental principle, Praedial servitudes rest upon the reciprocal operation, called forth by vicinity of estates (urban or rural) and the necessity of an adjustment of their mutually permanent requirements; whilst Personal servitudes—which, moreover, for the most part are grounded upon an act of pure liberality—have as their object the vesting in a definite person that use or enjoyment of a thing which is perpetual and independent (*i.e.*, of the person owner for the time being), and so resting on a more assured basis.

[a] Represented in English Law by Easements and Profits a prendre. See, generally, Markby, ss. 404, *sqq.*; and Holland, pp. 163, *sqq.* Cf. Austin, lectt. 48-50.

> Ulp.: —ius suum deminuit, alterius auxit, hoc est servitutem aedibus suis imposuit.—D. 39, 1, 5, 9.[1]
>
> Marc.: Servitutes aut personarum sunt, ut usus et ususfructus,[b] aut rerum, ut servitutes rusticorum praediorum et urbanorum.[c]—l. 1, D. de serv. 8, 1.[2]

[b] § 95.

[c] § 94.

Diverse as are personal and praedial servitudes, according to their intrinsic principle and object, so also is their special legal form. But some general legal principles exist for both kinds.

(1) All servitudes relate either to the positive or to the negative element of ownership: in the

---

[1] —he abridged his own right, enlarged that of another man, that is, burdened his house with a servitude.

[2] Servitudes either belong to persons, as use and enjoyment, or to things, as the servitudes of rural and urban estates.

Book III. Pt. I. Ch. I.

first case they consist of a forbearance of the owner of the servient thing (servitutes 'quae in *non faciendo* sc. domini consistunt'—NEGATIVE servitudes); in the latter, a suffering by him (servitudes 'quae in *patiendo* consistunt'—AFFIRMATIVE servitudes). On the other hand, there cannot be a servitus 'quae in *faciendo* consistit,' *i.e.*, one that consists of a positive action on the part of the owner of the servient property, for this would not be a real limitation of the ownership, but a personal (obligatory) Duty of the owner, since there is no forbearance in respect of the thing belonging to him to which, by virtue of his proprietary right, the owner as such would be entitled.[a]

> Pompon.: Servitutum non ea natura est, ut aliquid faciat quis, veluti viridia tollat, aut amoeniorem prospectum praestet, aut in hoc ut in suo pingat, sed ut aliquid patiatur aut non faciat. —D. 8, 1, 15, 1.[1]

> Ulp.: Etiam de servitute, quae **oneris ferendi**[b] causa imposita erit, actio nobis competit, ut et onera ferat et aedificia reficiat. . . . Et Gallus putat non posse ita servitutem imponi, ut quis facere aliquid cogeretur, sed ne me facere prohiberet: nam in omnibus servitutibus refectio ad eum pertinet, qui sibi servitutem adserit, non ad eum cuius res servit. Sed evaluit Servii sententia in proposita specie, ut possit quis defendere, ius sibi esse cogere adversarium reficere parietem ad onera sua sustinenda; Labeo autem hanc servitutem **non hominem debere, sed rem**:[c] denique licere domino rem derelinquere scribit.—D. 8, 5, 6, 2.[2]

[a] § 92.

[b] See Dalton *v.* Angus (6 App. Ca. pp. 773-4), remarks of Lord Selborne.

[c] See Holmes, pp. 383, *sqq.*

---

[1] The essence of servitudes consists not in somebody's doing anything, for example, the removal of plantations, or the affording of a more pleasant view, or that a man exhibit pictures on his own ground, but that he suffer or forbear from the doing of something.

Again, in respect of the servitude which has been imposed

(2) No one can have a servitude in his own property.[a]

Nulli res sua servit.—D. 8, 2, 26. Nullum praedium ipsum sibi servire potest.—l. 33, § 1, D. de S. P. R. 8, 3.[1]

[a] §§ 97, 98.

(3) In one servitude there cannot be yet another.

Paul.: Nec usus nec ususfructus itineris actus viae aquaeductus[b] legari potest, quia servitus servitutis esse non potest.—D. 33, 2, 1.[2]

[b] § 94.

(4) Every servitude must satisfy some one Real interest, *i.e.*, carry some advantage to the person entitled, or to the dominant estate.

Pomp.: Quotiens nec hominum nec praediorum servitutes sunt, quia nihil vicinorum interest, non valet: veluti ne per fundum tuum eas aut ibi consistas.—l. 15 pr., D. de serv.[3]

(5) Servitudes are inalienable, cannot be separated from the person, or it may be the property, for which they have been originated.[c]

[c] Cf. § 95.

---

for the support of a weight,[d] an action lies in our favour for the support of the weight and the repair of buildings . . . and Gall. is of opinion that a servitude cannot be imposed in such way, that a man should be obliged to do anything, but that he should not hinder my doing it; for in all servitudes repairs devolve upon him who claims the servitude for himself, not upon the owner of the servient property. But in respect of this question the opinion of Serv. prevailed, that any one can claim his right to oblige the opponent to repair the wall that the burdens may be sustained; but Labeo writes that this servitude is not obligatory upon the individual but on the property; accordingly, that the former is at liberty to abandon the property.

[d] *I.e.*, support of a building.

[1] No one has a servitude in his own property.—No estate can be servient to itself.

[2] There can be a bequest neither of use nor enjoyment of a footway, of driving cattle, of a carriage-way, of a watercourse, because there cannot be a servitude of a servitude.

[3] Whenever a servitude accrues to neither men nor estates, inasmuch as neighbours are in no way benefited, it is of no use; for example, that you must not go through your field, or tarry there.

Book III. Pt. I. Ch. I.

Paul.: (ususfructus) a personis discedere sine interitu sui (non) potest.—D. 10, 2, 15.[1]

Id.: Cum fundus fundo servit,[a] vendito quoque fundo servitutes sequuntur.—l. 12, D. comm. praed. 8, 4.[2]

[a] Holmes, *ubi supra.*

(6) Servitudes—with the exception of usufruct—are indivisible.

Pomp. fgm.: Et servitutes dividi non possunt: nam earum usus ita connexus est, ut qui eum partiatur naturam eius corrumpat.[3]

Ulp.: Per partes servitus imponi non potest.—l. 6, § 1, comm. praed.[4]

Paul.: Si unus ex sociis stipuletur iter ad communem fundum, inutilis est stipulatio, quia nec dari ei potest: sed si omnes stipulentur sive communis servus, singuli ex sociis 'sibi dari oportere' petere possunt.—l. 19, D. de S. P. R.[5]

Pap.: Unus ex sociis fundi communis permittendo 'ius esse ire agere' nihil agit.—l. 34 pr. eod.[6]

Paul.: Si praedium tuum mihi serviat, sive ego partis praedii tui dominus esse coepero sive tu mei, **per partes servitus retinetur,** licet ab initio **per partes adquiri non poterat.**—l. 8, § 1, D. de serv.[7]

---

1 —for it cannot be separated from the persons (entitled) save as they die.

2 When one estate is servient to another, even if it have been sold, the servitudes go with it.

3 And servitudes cannot be divided; for their enjoyment is of so close a character that he who breaks it up perverts its essence.

4 A servitude cannot be imposed by parts.

5 If one of the co-owners stipulates that he shall have a footway to a field owned in common, the stipulation is useless, because it cannot be granted; but if all stipulate, or a slave owned in common, the individual co-owners can claim that 'it ought to be granted to them.'

6 One of several co-owners of a common field does an invalid act if he grant the right to passage on foot or for driving cattle.

7 If your estate be servient to mine, whether I become owner

§ 94. Praedial Servitudes.[a]

Praedial servitudes (servitutes, iura praediorum) are those servitudes which belong to the owner at any time of an estate as such, in an estate owned by another, to the advantage of the former, so that ownership itself of the first experiences enlargement, but that of the latter, a limitation.[b] The praedial servitude appears, accordingly, as a juristic, and at the same time economical, quality appertaining to both estates, which consists in the legal dependence of the one (praedium serviens s. quod servitutem debet, servient estate) upon the other (praedium dominans s. cui servitus debetur, dominant estate).

[a] Bell, s. Servitude.

[b] D. 39, 1, 5, 9.

> Ideo autem hae servitutes praediorum appellantur, quoniam sine praediis constitui non possunt; nemo enim potest servitutem adquirere urbani vel rustici praedii, nisi qui habet praedium nec quisquam debere, nisi qui habet praedium. —§ 3, I. de serv. 2, 3 (= Ulp. in D. 8, 4, 1, 1).[1]
>
> Cels.: Quid aliud sunt iura praediorum, quam praedia qualiter se habentia, ut bonitas salubritas amplitudo?—D. 50, 16, 86.[2]

The praedial servitude must through the servient estate satisfy a permanent requirement (perpetua causa) [c] of the dominant one. The following considerations underly this.

(1) The servitude must directly benefit the estate

[c] As to which, see Gale, 'Law of Easements' (5th ed.), p. 18.

---

of part of yours or you of part of mine, the servitude is kept up divided by shares, though originally it could not be acquired by shares.

[1] These servitudes are therefore called servitudes of estates, because they cannot exist without them; for no one can acquire or owe a servitude of an urban or rural estate, unless he possess an estate.

[2] What else are the rights of lands than the qualities possessed by such lands, as excellence of the soil, healthy situation, spaciousness?

Book III. Pt. I. Ch. I.

itself, must indeed augment its intrinsic value (fundo utilis).

Paul.: Ut pomum decerpere liceat et ut spatiari et ut coenare in alieno possimus, servitus imponi non potest.—D. 8, 1, 8 pr.[1]

Pap.: Pecoris pascendi servitus, . . . si praedii fructus maxime in pecore consistat, praedii magis quam personae videtur.—l. 4, D. de S. P. R. 8, 3.[2]

(Neratius) dicit, ut maxime calcis coquendae et cretae eximendae servitus constitui possit, non ultra posse, quam quatenus ad eum ipsum fundum opus sit: —veluti si figlinas haberet, in quibus ea vasa fierent, quibus fructus eius fundi exportarentur; . . . sed si, ut vasa venirent, figlinae exercerentur, ususfructus erit.—l. 5, 1 (Ulp.), and l. 6 pr. (Paul.) eod.[3]

(2) The servient estate, by virtue of an abiding property or natural characteristic, must be in a condition to afford this service continually (perpetua causa in special sense).

Paul.: Omnes autem servitutes praediorum perpetuas causas habere debent, et ideo neque ex lacu neque ex stagno concedi aquaeductus potest. Stillicidii quoque immittendi naturalis et perpetua causa esse debet.—l. 28, D. de S. P. U. 8, 2.[a][4]

[a] Cf. Markby, s. 410.

[1] A servitude cannot be imposed to enable us to pluck an apple, to walk about, and to sup upon ground belonging to another.

[2] The servitude of pasturing cattle, . . . if the enjoyment of land consist especially in (the grazing of) cattle, appears to appertain to the land rather than to the person.

[3] (Ner.) says, although in particular the servitude can be created of burning lime and extracting chalk,[b] it cannot go beyond the requirements of such estate itself;—for example, if it should have potteries in which those vessels should be made wherein to convey away the products of such estate . . . but if the potteries should be employed for the sale of vessels, there will be a usufruct.

[b] Or 'clay.'

[4] Now, all praedial servitudes must have permanent causes,

(3) The position of the estates to each other must admit of the one benefiting the other (praedia vicina).

Neratius ait, nec haustum nec pecoris appulsum nec cretae eximendae calcisque coquendae ius posse in alieno esse, nisi fundum vicinum habeat.—l. 5, § 1, de S. P. R.[1]

Paul.: In rusticis autem praediis impedit servitutem medium praedium quod non servit.—l. 7, § 1 eod.[2]

Id.: Si intercedat solum publicum vel via publica, neque itineris actusve neque altius tollendi servitutes impedit.—l. 1 pr., de S. P. U.[3]

According to the character of the dominant estate,[a] upon which also depends the want to be satisfied, servitudes are divided into servitutes praediorum *rusticorum* and *urbanorum*. Amongst the first named, the rights of way and of water call for special mention: via, iter, actus,[b] aquaeductus,—the oldest Roman iura praediorum.[c]

[a] D. 50, 16, 198.

[b] Bell, s. v. As to this division, see also Gale, p. 26.

[c] § 74.

Ulp.: Servitutes rusticorum praediorum sunt hae: iter actus via aquaeductus. **Iter** est ius eundi ambulandi homini, non etiam iumenti agendi. **Actus** est ius agendi vel iumentum vel vehiculum: itaque qui iter habet, actum non habet; qui actum habet, et iter habet etiam sine iumento. **Via** est ius eundi et agendi et ambulandi: nam et iter et

---

and therefore a right of leading water cannot be granted either out of a lake or a pond. A water-drip, again, ought to have a natural and permanent cause.

[1] Ner. says that one cannot have the drawing of water or leading of cattle or the right to extract chalk and burn lime in land owned by another, unless one possesses adjoining land.

[2] Now in rural estates an intermediate estate which is not servient hinders a servitude.

[3] If public land or a public way intervene, it does not hinder servitudes of footway or of driving cattle or of raising a house higher.

Book III. Pt. I. Ch. I.

[a] Cf. Gale, pp. 340-2, citing Co. Litt. 56[a].

actum in se via continet.[a] **Aquaeductus** est ius aquam ducendi per fundum alienum.—In rusticis computanda sunt: aquae haustus, pecoris ad aquam appulsus, ius pascendi, calcis coquendae, arenae fodiendae.—l. 1 pr., § 1, de S. P. R.[1]

Gai.: **Viae** latitudo ex lege XII tabularum in porrectum octo pedes habet, in anfractum, i.e. ubi flexum est, sedecim.—l. 8 eod.[2]

Iust. ii. 3, § 1: Praediorum urbanorum sunt servitutes, quae aedificiis inhaerent; . . . sunt hae: ut vicinus onera vicini sustineat; ut in parietem eius liceat vicino tignum immittere; ut stillicidium vel flumen recipiat quis in aedes suas vel in aream, vel non recipiat; et ne altius tollat quis aedes suas, ne luminibus vicini officiatur.[3]

§ 95. Personal Servitudes.

Personal servitudes are those servitudes which belong to a determinate individual person, and serve his requirements.

---

[1] The following are the servitudes of rural estates: right of footway, of driving cattle, of carriage-way, of leading water. *Iter* is the right for a man to pass upon foot, not to lead cattle as well. *Actus* is the right of driving either a beast or a carriage: therefore, he that hath *iter* hath not *actus*; he that hath *actus*, hath *iter* also without beasts. *Via* is the right of passage both of driving and walking; for *via* includes both *iter* and *actus*. *Aquaeductus* is the right of leading water over the land of another. Amongst rural servitudes are to be reckoned: drawing of water, driving cattle to water, the right of pasture, of burning lime, of digging sand.

[2] The breadth of the carriage-way, according to a law of the Twelve Tables, amounts to 8 feet in a straight line, and at an angle, that is, where it turns, 16 feet.

[3] The servitudes of urban estates are those which incumber buildings; . . . they are the following: that a neighbour support the weight of an adjoining house; that he must allow his neighbour to insert a beam in his wall; that he receive dropping water or running water into his house or his court-yard, or do not receive such; and that he may not carry his house higher so as to interfere with his neighbour's lights.

The most comprehensive personal servitude is that of 'ususfructus,'[a] which occurs with both movables and immovables.

(1) As to the rights of the usufructuary—

(a) He has the complete and exclusive enjoyment of a thing owned by another—which is in the detention of the former[b]—without prejudice to its substance, *i.e.*, he is entitled both to the use of it (usus) and to the appropriation of all products and revenues (fructus) derived from the thing, conformably to its purpose,[c] and irrespectively of his own requirements. In relation to the right of the usufructuary, that of the owner of the property (dominus proprietatis) appears as 'nuda proprietas.'

a Digby, 'Real Property,' p. 273. Markby, s. 336.—On the difference between *ususfructus* and our Life Estate, see Campbell, note to Austin, pp. 856-8 (abridged in Student's edn. p. 400).

b § 76.

c §§ 73, 85, 88.

Paul.: Ususfructus est ius alienis rebus utendi fruendi salva rerum substantia.—l. 1, D. h. t. (de usufr. 7, 1).[1]

Gai.: Consistit autem ususfructus non tantum in fundo et aedibus, verum etiam in servis et iumentis ceterisque rebus.—l. 3, § 1 eod.[2]

Ulp.: Vetus fuit quaestio, an partus[d] ad fructuarium pertineret; sed Bruti sententia obtinuit, fructuarium in eo locum non habere: neque enim in fructu hominis homo esse potest; hac ratione nec usumfructum in eo fructuarius habebit.—l. 68 pr. eod. [—partus ancillae sitne in fructu habendus, (disseritur) inter principes civitatis P. Scaevolam Maniumque Manilium ab hisque M. Brutus (dissentit).—Cic. de fin. 1, 4, 12.][3]

d Sc. ancillae.

---

1 Usufruct is the right of using and enjoying things of another whilst the substance of the things remains unimpaired.

2 Usufruct obtains not only in respect of land and houses, but also in respect of slaves, cattle, and other things.

3 It was an old question whether the issue (of a woman slave) would belong to the fructuary, but the opinion of Brut. prevailed, that the fructuary had no share in it, for man cannot be regarded as for the enjoyment of man; by this principle the fructuary will not have a usufruct in it. [—whether the offspring of a woman slave is to be regarded as *fructus* is discussed

BOOK III. Pt. I. Ch. I.

Pap.: Ususfructus et ab initio pro parte indivisa vel divisa constitui, et . . . similiter amitti . . . potest.—l. 5, D. h. t.[1]

(β) The usufruct is intransmissible and itself inalienable, but the usufructuary can make over to another the exercise of it.[a]

[a] Prof. Holland says 'a usufruct in Roman Law was a life-interest' (p. 168). But it could also be granted for a less period: see C. 3, 33, 5.

Ulp.: Usufructuarius vel ipse frui ea re, vel alii fruendam concedere, vel locare vel vendere potest: nam et qui locat, utitur, et qui vendit, utitur. Sed et si alii precario concedat vel donet, puto eum uti.—l. 12, § 2 eod.[b] [2]

[b] Cf. D. 18, 6, 8, 2.

(2) As to obligations.—He has to make such use of the thing as is well regulated (boni viri arbitratu), to which also belongs the preservation of the thing (keeping up the buildings, suitable cultivation of agricultural property, maintenance of slaves and animals and the like) to which, as well as to the restoration of the thing after the termination of the usufruct, the security that has to be given to the owner has reference; and it is this which first founds a personal obligation of the usufructuary.[c]

[c] For the *cautio usufructuaria* of Scottish Law, see Bell, s. Usufruct.

Ulp.: Fructuarius causam proprietatis deteriorem facere non debet.—l. 13, § 4 eod.[3]

Id.: Cassius scribit, . . . fructuarium per arbitrum cogi reficere,[d] quemadmodum adserere cogitur arbores.—Celsus scribit, . . . cogi eum posse recte colere.—l. 7, § 3, and l. 9, § pr. eod.[4]

[d] Sc. aedes.

---

between the leading men of the state, P. Scaevola and Man. Manilius, and from these M. Brutus dissents.]

[1] A usufruct can both from the outset be created in undivided or divided parts, and can be lost in like manner.

[2] A usufructuary can either himself have the enjoyment of such thing, or allow or lease or sell to another the enjoyment thereof; for both the lessor and vendor make use of it. But if he allow or give it to another as a *precarium*, in my opinion, he makes use of it.

[3] The fructuary must not deteriorate the condition of the property.

[4] Cass. writes, that . . . a fructuary can through a referee be

Ulp.: Plane si gregis vel armenti sit ususfructus legatus, debebit ex adgnatis gregem supplere, i.e. in locum defunctorum—vel inutilium alia summittere; . . . et sicut substituta statim domini fiunt, ita priora quoque ex natura fructus desinunt eius esse.—l. 68, § 2, and l. 69 pr. eod.[1]

Ulp.: Si cuius rei ususfructus legatus sit, aequissimum praetori visum est, de utroque legatarium cavere: et usurum se boni viri arbitratu, et cum ususfructus ad eum pertinere desinet, restiturum quod inde exstabit (D. 7, 9, 1 pr.).—Haec autem ad omnem usumfructum pertinere Iulianus probat (l. 13 pr., h. t.).[2]

(3) According to the very idea of it, usufruct is inconceivable in respect of things consumable;[a] but the Roman Law for such admitted a quasi-usufructus, in which (by means of the cautio) a right of use[b] is given, certainly in respect of its juristic nature entirely different from actual usufruct, but similar to it as regards external, economic result—*i.e.*, its subject-matter, origination and termination.

[a] § 72.

[b] Cf. § 120.

Ulp.: Senatus censuit, ut omnium rerum quas in cuiusque patrimonio esse constaret, ususfructus legari possit: quo senatusconsulto inductum

---

compelled to repair [the house], in the same way as he is compelled to plant trees.[c]—Cels. writes, that he can be compelled to cultivate properly.

[c] See Roby, in loc.

[1] If a bequest have been made of the usufruct in a flock or plough-beasts, he will clearly have to fill up the flock from those born to the flock, *i.e.*, in the place of those that have died, or in place of useless animals to rear others . . . and just as those substituted at once become the property of the owner, so the earlier ones also, according to the nature of *fructus*, cease to belong to him.

[2] If the usufruct in anything have been bequeathed, the Praetor has considered it most fair that the legatee should give security for both things: both to use it as a good man would think right, and upon the termination of his usufruct to restore what shall exist of it.—Now Julian agrees that this attaches to every usufruct.

Book III. Pt. I. Ch. I.

videtur, ut earum rerum, quae usu tolluntur vel minuuntur, possit ususfructus legari.—D. 7, 5, 1.[1]

Gai.: Quo senatusconsulto non id effectum est, ut ususfructus proprie esset (nec enim naturalis ratio auctoritate senatus commutari potuit), sed remedio introducto coepit **quasi** ususfructus haberi.—l. 2, § 1 eod.[2]

Id.: Si vini olei frumenti ususfructus legatus erit, proprietas ad legatarium transferri debet et ab eo cautio desideranda est, ut, quandoque is mortuus aut capite deminutus sit, eiusdem qualitatis res restituatur, aut aestimatis rebus certae pecuniae nomine cavendum est, quod et commodius est. Idem scilicet de ceteris quoque rebus, quae abusu continentur, intelligemus.—l. 7 eod.[3]

[a] Markby, *ubi supr.*

[b] Cf. Tenant at will.

Usus[a] is the bare right of use or enjoyment of a thing owned by another, the subject-matter of which is alone determined by the individual requirements of the person entitled (usuarius),[b] the exercise of which is therefore untransferable. The 'usuarius' may, besides, in certain circumstances, claim the natural produce of the thing, and especially if the usefulness of the thing consists alone in its produce; but always

[1] The Senate has decreed that a usufruct can be bequeathed of all things which any one should have in his property; this decree of the Senate seems to have originated the possibility of bequeathing a usufruct of such things as are by use destroyed or diminished.

[2] The result of this *SCtum* was, not that there could strictly be a usufruct (for natural principle could not be altered by the authority of the Senate), but quasi-usufruct came into use by the relief afforded.

[3] If the usufruct of wine, oil or corn be bequeathed, the ownership must be made over to the legatee, and security must be sought from him that, after his death or upon loss of his status, the thing be restored of the same quality, or the things must be appraised, and then security given for a fixed sum, which is even more convenient. We shall of course also understand the same of other things that are characterised by consumption.

only in particular for the satisfaction of his personal and immediate domestic requirements.

Ulp.: Cui usus relictus est, uti potest, frui non potest.—D. 7, 8, 2 pr.[1]

Gai.: —nec ulli alii ius quod habet aut vendere aut locare aut gratis concedere potest.—l. 11 eod.[2]

Iust.: Item is qui aedium usum habet, hactenus iuris habere intelligitur, ut ipse tantum habitet, nec hoc ius ad alium transferre potest: et vix receptum videtur, ut hospitem ei recipere liceat, et cum uxore sua liberisque suis, item libertis nec non aliis personis, quibus non minus quam servis utitur habitandi ius habeat.—§ 2, I. eod. 2, 5.[3]

Ulp.: Praeter habitationem, quam habet, cui usus [a] datus est, deambulandi quoque et gestandi ius habebit. Sabinus et Cassius, et lignis ad usum quottidianum et horto et pomis et oleribus et floribus et aqua usurum, non usque ad compendium, sed ad usum, scilicet non usque ad abusum: idem Nerva, et adiicit, stramentis etiam usurum, sed neque foliis neque oleo neque frumento neque frugibus usurum. Sed Sabinus et Cassius et Labeo et Proculus hoc amplius etiam ex his quae in fundo nascuntur, quod ad victum sibi suisque sufficiat, sumpturum . . . ; Iuventius, etiam cum convivis et hospitibus posse uti: quae sententia mihi vera videtur.—§ Sed si pecoris ei usus relictus est, puta gregis ovilis, ad stercorandum usurum

[a] Sc. fundi vel villae.

---

[1] The person to whom the use has been bequeathed can have the use, but not the enjoyment.

[2] And he cannot sell, or lease, or make a gratuitous grant to another of the right he has.

[3] Likewise the right of a person that has the use of a house is taken to extend so far only, that he himself can inhabit it, and he cannot transfer this right to another; indeed it seems scarcely to have been admitted that he may receive a guest in it; and he has the right of dwelling with his wife and children, and with freedmen besides and other persons in his service on a footing no better than slaves.

dumtaxat Labeo ait, sed neque lana neque agnis neque lacte usurum: haec enim magis in fructu esse. Hoc amplius etiam modico lacte usurum puto.—§ Sed si bovum armenti usus relinquatur, omnem usum habebit et ad arandum et ad cetera, ad quae boves apti sunt.—l. 12, §§ 1–3, D. eod.[1]

'Habitatio' and 'operae servi' are two special varieties of usus which have arisen in the course of time, by way of 'voluntatis interpretatio' in testamentary provisions: of more limited content than usus, and more of a *de facto* and alimentary character, by which the rules of law that obtain in that here undergo some modifications.

Sed si cui habitatio legata sive aliquo modo constituta sit, neque usus videtur neque ususfructus, sed quasi proprium aliquod ius. Quam habitationem habentibus propter rerum utilitatem . . . permisimus non solum in eo degere, sed etiam aliis locare.—§ 5, I. eod.[2]

---

[1] Besides habitation to which the person is entitled to whom the use [of a field or homestead] has been granted, he will have also the right of walking about and riding. Sab. and Cass. say, he can also use wood for daily need, and the garden, fruit, vegetables, flowers and water, not to make profit from them, but for use, that is, not for abuse. Nerva says the same, and adds, he can also use the straw, but not leaves, or oil, or corn, or fruit. But Sab., Cass., Lab. and Procul. say he can besides also take what suffices for the maintenance of himself and his family, of all that grows upon the estate. . . . Juvent. says, he can also make use of them with his guests and friends under his roof; and this opinion I regard as correct.—§ But if the use of cattle have been bequeathed to him, for example, of a flock of sheep, Sab. says the use only extends to manuring; wool, lambs and milk are excluded from it, for that these rather appertain to the enjoyment. Moreover, I think that he can also make reasonable use of the milk.—§ But if the use of draught-oxen has been bequeathed, he will have the full use both for ploughing and for other purposes for which oxen are useful.

[2] If a man have had bequeathed the right of habitation, or it have been created in his favour in any other way, it is not

Ulp.: (Habitatio) nec non utendo amittitur nec capitis deminutione.—l. 10 pr., D. eod.[1]

Paul.: Sed operis servi legatis, neque usus neque ususfructus in eo legato esse videtur.—D. 35, 2, 1, 9.[2]

Pap.: Hominis operae legatae capitis deminutione vel non utendo non amittuntur; et quoniam ex operis mercedem percipere legatarius potest, etiam operas eius ipse locare poterit.—D. 33, 2, 2.[3]

§ 96. Origin of Servitudes.

As in Ownership, so also in Servitudes, we meet in Roman Law with two different forms, resting upon the distinction of 'ius civile' and 'ius gentium': CIVIL and PRAETORIAN servitudes. The former (servitutes iure constitutae)—such servitudes as at the beginning were alone recognised in Roman Law—suppose Quiritarian ownership in the servient property with commercium of the subject, and Quiritarian ownership in the 'praedium dominans'; whilst they are originated by a civil act of acquisition. The latter (servitutes quae tuitione praetoris consistunt, *i.e.*, resting alone upon Praetorian jurisdiction) arise through a natural act of acquisition. They were originally meant for Provincial estates, and persons not enjoying Roman commercium, but came continually more into use in respect also of estates and persons susceptible or capable of Civil

---

regarded either as *usus* or as *ususfructus*, but a sort of special right. Those who possess this right of habitation we have from grounds of convenience permitted not only to dwell in the house, but also to let it out to others.

[1] Occupation is not forfeited either by non-user or by loss of status.

[2] But if a bequest be made of the services of a slave, it is considered that neither the use nor the usufruct is contained in such legacy.

[3] The services of a slave that have been bequeathed are not forfeited by loss of status or by non-user; and since a legatee can reap profit from services, he will be able also to let out his services.

Book III. Pt. I. Ch. I.

servitudes, because of the more convenient form of constitution.[a]

[a] Cf. D. 8, 1, 16; 6, 2, 11, 1.

Civil servitudes arose—

(1) by direct testamentary provision; wherein they must be distinguished from the obligation created for the heir to constitute a servitude.[b]

[b] Paul. 3, 6, 17.

Ususfructus a proprietate separationem recipit idque pluribus modis accidit; ut ecce si quis alicui usumfructum legaverit: nam heres habet nudam proprietatem, legatarius usumfructum; et contra si fundum legaverit deducto usufructu, legatarius nudam habet proprietatem, heres vero usumfructum; item alii usumfructum, alii deducto eo fundo legare potest.—§ 1, I. de usufr. 2, 4.[1]

Gai.: Potest etiam in testamento heredem suum quis damnare, ne altius eades suas tollat, ne luminibus aedium vicinarum officiat, vel ut patiatur eum tignum in parietem immittere vel stillicidia adversus eum habere, vel ut patiatur vicinum per fundum suum vel heredis ire agere aquamve ex eo ducere.—l. 16, D. comm. praed. 8, 4.[2]

(2) By contract ex iure civili.—The common form of constitution for all servitudes was that 'in iure cessio'[c]: the 'mancipatio' was only admissible

[c] Ulp. xix. 11.

[1] The usufruct undergoes severance from the ownership, and that occurs in several ways. When, for example, a man has bequeathed the usufruct to another; for the heir has then only the bare ownership, the legatee has the use and enjoyment; and conversely, if any one has bequeathed an estate, reserving the usufruct, the legatee has the bare ownership, the heir the usufruct; moreover, it is possible to bequeath to one person the usufruct, to another the estate, reserving the usufruct.

[2] A man can also charge his heir in the testament not to raise his house higher, not to interfere with the lights of the neighbouring house, or that he suffer the neighbour to insert a beam in the wall, or have as against him a right of drip, or that he suffer the neighbour to pass, to drive cattle over his or the heir's land, or to lead water thence.

in respect of the four old 'iura praediorum rusticorum'[a]; and further, the owner that transferred to another the thing itself by mancipatio or in iure cessio could by means of 'deductio' and 'exceptio' —*i.e.*, abatement or reserve—originate a personal or praedial servitude in it for himself—or by informal charge upon his own land in favour of that transferred.[b]

[a] § 74.

[b] 'Lex rei dicta'; see Fest. v. *nuncupata*.

Gai. ii. §§ 29–30: Sed **iura praediorum urbanorum** in iure cedi tantum possunt; **rusticorum** vero etiam mancipari possunt. § **Ususfructus** in iure cessionem tantum recipit: nam dominus proprietatis alii usufructum in iure cedere potest, ut ille usumfructum habeat et ipse nudam proprietatem retineat.—§ 33: Quod autem diximus usumfructum in iure cessionem tantum recipere, non est temere dictum, quamvis etiam per mancipationem constitui possit eo, quod in mancipanda proprietate detrahi potest: non enim ipse ususfructus mancipatur, sed cum in mancipanda proprietate deducatur, eo fit, ut apud alium ususfructus, apud alium proprietas sit.[1]

Vat. fgm. 50: In mancipatione vel in iure cessione an deduci possit vel extempore vel ad tempus vel ex condicione vel ad condicionem, dubium est: quemadmodum si is cui in iure

---

[1] But rights appertaining to urban estates can only be conveyed by surrender in court; those, however, which appertain to rural estates can be mancipated also. § Usufruct admits alone of surrender in court, for the ground-owner can make a surrender in court of the usufruct to another, so that the latter can have the usufruct, and he himself retain the bare ownership.—§ But when we said that usufruct admits alone of surrender in court, our statement was no rash one, although the usufruct may be created by mancipation also, inasmuch as it can be excepted in a mancipation of the property; for it is not the usufruct itself which is mancipated, but when it is reserved in the mancipation of the property, the result is that the usufruct is with one person, the ownership with another.

Book III. Pt. I. Ch. I.

ceditur dicit AIO HVNC FVNDVM MEVM ESSE DEDVCTO VSVFRVCTV EX KAL. IAN. vel DEDVCTO VSVFRVCTV VSQVE AD KAL. IAN. DECIMAS, vel AIO HVNC FVNDVM MEVM ESSE DEDVCTO VSVFRVCTV, SI NAVIS EX ASIA VENERIT; item in mancipatione: EMPTVS MIHI ESTO (PRETIO . . .) DEDVCTO VSVFRVCTV EX KAL. ILLIS VEL VSQVE AD KAL. ILLAS; et eadem sunt in condicione. Pomponius igitur putat non posse ad certum tempus deduci nec per in iure cessionem nec per mancipationem. Ego didici et deduci ad tempus posse quia et mancipatione[a] et in iure cessionem[b] lex XII tab. confirmat. Numquid ergo et ex tempore et condicione deduci possit?—(Paul.)[1]

[a] ? mancipationum.

[b] ? cessionum leges.

Vat. fgm. 47: In re nec mancipi per traditionem deduci ususfructus non potest; civili enim actione constitui potest, non traditione quae iuris gentium est.—(Id.)[2]

Gai.: Duorum praediorum dominus si alterum ea lege tibi dederit, ut id praedium quod datur serviat ei quod ipse retinet vel contra, iure

---

[1] It is doubtful in respect of a mancipation or a surrender in court whether it can be reserved from some time or until such time, or from the happening of a condition or until its happening: as if he who takes the surrender in court says, 'I affirm that this land is mine, subject to a usufruct from Jan. 1,' or 'subject to a usufruct until Jan. 10,' or 'I affirm that this land is mine, subject to a usufruct if a ship shall arrive from Asia.' The like in respect of a mancipation: 'It shall be my purchase . . . subject to a usufruct from the first of such month,' or 'until the first of such month;' and the same words are used in a condition. Pomp. accordingly is of the opinion that it cannot be reserved for a fixed time, neither by surrender in court nor by mancipation. I have taught that it can also be reserved *ad tempus*, because the Law of the Twelve Tables confirms both a mancipation and a surrender in court. Can it therefore be reserved both from a time and upon a condition?'

[2] In respect of a *res n. m.* the usufruct cannot be reserved by *traditio*, for it can be constituted by a civil action, not by *traditio*, which appertains to *i. g.*

Book III. Pt. I. Ch. I.

imposita servitus videtur.—l. 3, D. comm. praed.[1]

(3) By adjudication in an action for partition.

Gai.: Constituitur adhuc ususfructus in iudicio familiae erciscundae et communi dividundo, si iudex alii proprietatem adiudicaverit, alii usumfructum.—l. 6, § 1, D. de usufr. 7, 1. [—fam. erc. vel comm. div. iudicio legitimo.—Vat. fgm. 47.][2]

Ulp.: Sed etiam cum adiudicat, poterit imponere aliquam servitutem, ut alium[a] alii servum faciat ex his, quos adiudicat.—D. 10, 2, 22, 3.[3]

[a] Sc. fundum.

(4) In the ancient time usucapion was here also recognised, but only indeed in praedial servitudes; it was however excluded by a lex Scribonia; but it may be doubted whether those servitutes praediorum urbanorum, which by some external work or arrangement on the praedium dominans or serviens had a visible appearance, fell under that lex.[b]

[b] Cf. Paul. i. 17.

Paul.: —eam usucapionem sustulit lex Scribonia, quae servitutem constituebat, non etiam eam, quae libertatem praestat sublata servitute.—D. 41, 3, 4, 29.[4]

Ulp.: Hoc iure utimur ut servitutes per se nusquam longo tempore [c]capi possint, cum aedificiis possint.—l. 10, § 1 eod.[5]

[c] ? usu.

[1] If the owner of two estates grant one to you upon the condition that the estate which is granted be servient to the one which he himself retains, or the reverse, the servitude is considered as lawfully imposed.

[2] Moreover, a usufruct can be created in the suit for the division of an inheritance and for the partition of common property; if the *iudex* adjudge to one person the ownership, to another the usufruct. [—by the statutory action for division of an inheritance or of partition of common property.]

[3] But even when he adjudicates, he will be at liberty to impose some servitude, so as to make one [field] servient to another from those which he adjudicates upon.

[4] —the *l. Scrib.* did away with such usucapion as founded a servitude, but not also that which re-establishes freedom by removal of the servitude.

[5] The Law with us is that servitudes by themselves alone

Book III. Pt. I. Ch. I.

Paul.: Servitutes praediorum rusticorum, etiamsi corporibus accedunt, incorporales tamen sunt, et ideo usu non capiuntur; vel ideo, quia tales sunt servitutes, ut non habeant certam continuamque possessionem: nemo enim tam perpetuo, tam continenter ire potest, ut nullo momento possessio eius interpellari videatur. Idem et in servitutibus praediorum urbanorum observatur.—l. 14 pr., D. de serv. 8, 1.[1]

The Praetorian servitudes arise—

(1) by informal contract of appointment (pactio)[a] with which a stipulation relating to allowance of the exercise of servitudes (stipulatio 'uti frui,' 'ire agere licere'[b]) used to be connected, without the necessity of tradition, *i.e.*, *de facto* grant of the servitude, or allowance of its exercise. The like by reservation or imposition of the servitude in the traditio of the property.[c]

[a] To be distinguished from the contract that grounds the obligation to create a servitude.

[b] Different from the stipulatio 'usumfructum,' 'viam dari.'

[c] Cf. Vat. fgm. 47; D. 8, 4, 3.

Gai. ii. § 31: Alioquin in provincialibus praediis sive quis usumfructum, sive ius eundi agendi aquamve ducendi, vel altius tollendi aedes aut non tollendi, ne luminibus vicini officiatur, ceteraque similia iura constituere velit, pactionibus et stipulationibus id efficere potest: quia ne ipsa quidem praedia mancipationem aut in iure cessionem recipiunt.[2]

---

never can be acquired through *usus* during a long period, they can in connection with buildings.

[1] Servitudes that appertain to rural estates, although adhering to material substances, are yet incorporeal, and so are not taken by *usus*; or for the reason that they are servitudes of such kind as to make no definite uninterrupted possession possible; for no one can go so uninterruptedly and continuously that his possession is regarded as at no moment interrupted. The same remark applies in respect of servitudes appertaining to urban estates.

[2] On the other hand, in provincial estates, whether a man wish to create a usufruct, or a right of passage for driving cattle, or of watercourse, or of raising buildings higher, or not

Iavol.: Quotiens via aut aliquod ius fundi emeretur, cavendum putat esse Labeo, 'per te non fieri quominus eo iure uti possit': quia nulla eiusmodi iuris vacua traditio esset.—l. 20, D. de serv.[a] [1]

[a] Cf. ibid. § 76, supr.

Pomp.: Si quis aedes vel . . . fundum tradit, excipere potest id quod personae, non praedii est, velut usum et usumfructum.—l. 32, D. de usufr.[2]

Ulp.: Si quis duas aedes habeat et alteras tradat, potest legem traditioni dicere, ut vel istae, quae non traduntur, servae sint his quae traduntur, vel contra ut traditae retentis aedibus serviant. . . . Duas autem aedes simul tradendo non potest efficere alteras alteri servas, quia neque adquirere alienis aedibus servitutem neque imponere potest.—l. 6, pr. D. comm. praed.[3]

(2) By prescription—longa (iuris quasi) possessio—that is, uninterrupted exercise, continued for ten years 'inter praesentes,' twenty years 'inter absentes' (nec vi nec clam nec precario), of the privilege forming the subject of the servitude, without regard to 'bona fides' and 'iustus titulus.'[b]

[b] D. 43, 19, 9.

Ulp.: Si quis diuturno usu et longa quasi

---

raising them to prevent obstruction of the neighbour's lights, and other like rights, he can carry it out by agreements and stipulations; because not even do the lands themselves allow of mancipation or of surrender in court.

[1] Whenever a carriage-way or any right in land should be sold, Labeo thinks there should be a proviso 'that nothing shall take place through you to hinder the exercise of such right,' because there can be no bare delivery of a right of that kind.

[2] If a man deliver a house or field, he can reserve what is personal, not what is praedial; for example, the use and usufruct.

[3] If a man have two buildings and deliver one of them, he can set a condition upon the delivery, either that the one which is retained be servient to that which is delivered, or, on the other hand, that the one delivered be servile to that which is retained. . . . But by the delivery at one time of two buildings, he cannot make one servient to the other, because he can neither acquire nor impose a servitude over buildings owned by another.

possessione ius aquae ducendae nactus sit, non est ei necesse docere de iure quo aqua constituta est, veluti ex legato (vel alio modo), sed utilem habet actionem, ut ostendat, per annos forte tot usum se non vi non clam non precario possedisse.—D. 8, 5, 10 pr.[1]

Paul.: Servitute usus non videtur, nisi qui suo iure uti se credidit; ideoque si quis pro via publica vel pro alterius servitute usus sit, nec interdictum nec actio utiliter competit.—D. 8, 6, 25.[2]

In the Law of Justinian the distinction between Civil and Praetorian servitudes disappeared. The servitudes originated by an informal contract, which altogether took the place of the in iure cessio and mancipatio, and those by prescription are always 'iure constitutae.'

Si quis velit vicino aliquod ius [alii usumfructum] constituere, pactionibus atque stipulationibus id efficere debet.—§ 4, I. de serv., together with § 1, I. de usufr.[3]

§ 97. Termination of Servitudes.

Servitudes are extinguished—

(1) by natural or juristic destruction:

---

1 If a man by long-standing use and long-continued quasi-possession has acquired a right of leading water, it is not necessary for him to show the right by virtue of which the water-course has been constituted, as for example, in consequence of a legacy or in any other way, but he has an analogous action that he may show that he has perhaps through so many years possessed the use, not by violence, nor secretly, nor upon sufferance.

2 A man is not regarded as having made use of a servitude unless he has supposed he exercised it as a right of his own; if, therefore, any one have used it in the belief that it was a public road, or a servitude belonging to another person, neither an interdict nor analogous action is available.

3 If a man desire to create in favour of his neighbour a right [in favour of another, a usufruct], he must do so by agreements and stipulations.

(a) of the servient property; the personal servitudes already by material change in the form of the latter.

Ulp.: Rei mutatione interire usumfructum placet; veluti ususfructus mihi aedium legatus est, aedes corruerunt vel exustae sunt: sine dubio extinguitur. An et areae? Certissimum est, exustis aedibus nec areae nec cementorum usumfructum deberi; et ita et Iulianus.—D. 7, 4, 5, 2.[1]

(β) By such destruction of the dominant estate (but not indeed by demolition of the buildings); in respect of usus and ususfructus, by death or capitis diminutio[a] of the person entitled.

Paul. iii. 6, § 29: Capitis minutione amittitur, si . . . statum ex adrogatione vel adoptione mutaverit.[2]

Inst. ii. 4, § 3: Finitur ususfructus morte fructuarii et duabus capitis deminutionibus, maxima et media.[3]

(2) By coincidence in the same person of the title to the servitude (in respect of praedial servitudes, of the ownership in the dominant estate) and the ownership in the servient property. (Confusio—consolidatio.[b])

Ib. § 3: Item finitur ususfructus . . . si fructuarius proprietatem rei adquisierit, quae res consolidatio appellatur.[4]

[a] Gai. iii. 83.

[b] See Brown, s. v. Cf. D. 8, 2, 26; 8, 3, 33, 1; 8, 5, 8, 1.

---

[1] It is held that a usufruct is extinguished by the change of a thing; for example, a usufruct has been bequeathed to me of buildings, but these have collapsed or have been burnt: it without doubt is extinguished. Is that of the site also? It is quite certain that, if buildings have been burnt, a right of usufruct exists neither in the site nor in the masonry; so also Julian too.

[2] Loss is experienced of *caput* if a man have changed his status by arrogation or adoption.

[3] Usufruct is determined by the death of the fructuary and by two kinds of *cap. dem.*, the greatest and intermediate.

[4] The usufruct is also determined . . . if the fructuary have

Book III. Pt. I. Ch. I.

Gai.: Servitutes praediorum confunduntur, si idem utriusque praedii dominus esse coeperit.—D. 8, 6, 1.[1]

Paul.: Si quis aedes, quae suis aedibus servirent, cum emisset, traditas sibi accepit, confusa sublataque servitus est; et si rursus vendere vult, nominatim imponenda servitus est, alioquin liberae veniunt.—Si partem praedii nactus sim, quod mihi aut cui ego serviam, non confundi servitutem placet, quia pro parte servitus retinetur.—l. 30 pr., § 1, D. de S. P. U. 8, 2.[2]

(3) By surrender of the servitude on the part of the person entitled. In the older Law it was by in iure cessio to the owner.

Gai. ii. § 30: Ipse usufructuarius in iure cedendo domino proprietatis usumfructum, efficit, ut a se discedat et convertatur in proprietatem; alii vero in iure cedendo nihilo minus ius suum retinet: creditur enim ea cessione nihil agi.[3]

Pomp.: Diximus usumfructum a fructuario cedi non posse nisi domino proprietatis, et si extraneo cedatur . . . . nihil ad eum transire,

---

acquired the ownership of the thing; this is called Consolidation.

[1] Praedial servitudes are merged if the same person once be owner of both estates.

[2] If a man had purchased and received delivery of a building which was servient to his own, the servitude was thereby united and extinguished, and if again he desire to sell it, the servitude must be expressly imposed afresh, otherwise such building is sold unincumbered.—If I have acquired a portion of an estate, which is servient to me, or I to it, it is held that no merger of the servitude takes place, because the servitude is kept up in part.

[3] The usufructuary personally making a judicial surrender of the usufruct to the groundowner causes it to shift from him and to merge in the ownership. But if he make a surrender of it to a third party, he nevertheless retains his right, for it is considered that nothing results from such a surrender.

sed ad dominum proprietatis reversurum usumfructum.—D. 23, 3, 66.[1]

Paul.: Si per tuum fundum via mihi debeatur, et permisero tibi in eo loco, per quem via mihi debeatur, aliquid facere, amitto ius viae.—D. 8, 6, 8 pr.[2]

(4) By Limitation.

(*a*) The servitutes praediorum rusticorum, as well as usufructus and usus, are destroyed by non-exercise (non usus), according to the older Law, the first in two years, the latter in one or two years as the case may be.

Paul. i. 17: Viam iter actum aquaeductum, qui biennio usus non est, amisisse videtur.—Servitus hauriendae aquae vel ducendae biennio omissa intercidit, et biennio usurpata recipitur.[3]

Id. iii. 6, § 30: Non utendo amittitur usus-fructus, si possessione **fundi** biennio fructuarius non utatur, vel **rei mobilis** anno.[4]

(*β*) In servitutes praediorum urbanorum, for the non-exercise there must further be added 'usucapio libertatis'[a] on the part of the owner of the servient estate, which consists in two years' uninterrupted possession of it as of one actually free from servitudes, and requires a consequent arrangement or

[a] D. 41, 3, 4, 29.

---

[1] We have said that the usufruct cannot be surrendered by the fructuary except to the ground owner, and that if it be surrendered to a stranger . . . nothing passes to him, but the usufruct will revert to the ground owner.

[2] If a right of carriage-way over your field belongs to me, and I permit you to do anything in that place over which my carriage-way is, I lose such right.

[3] It would appear that a right of way, of passage, of leading cattle, and of watercourse is lost when not used for two years.—A servitude of drawing or leading water lapses upon forbearance for two years, and is acknowledged when exercised for two years.

[4] A usufruct is forfeited by non-user if the usufructuary do not avail himself of possession of land for two years, or of a movable thing for one year.

BOOK III. Pt. I. Ch. I.

change upon the land which makes the exercise of the servitude impossible—nec vi nec clam nec precario.

Gai.: Haec autem iura similiter, ut rusticorum quoque praediorum, certo tempore non utendo pereunt: nisi quod haec dissimilitudo est, quod non omnino pereunt non utendo, sed ita si vicinus simul libertatem usucapiat. Veluti si aedes tuae aedibus meis serviant, ne altius tollantur, ne luminibus mearum aedium officiatur, et ego per statutum tempus fenestras meas praefixas habuero vel obstruxero, ita demum ius meum amitto, si tu per hoc tempus aedes tuas altius sublatas habueris. . . . Item si tigni immissi aedes tuae servitutem debent, et ego exemero tignum, ita demum amitto ius meum, si tu foramen, unde exemptum est tignum, obturaveris et per constitutum tempus ita habueris: alioquin si nihil novi feceris, integrum ius meum permanet.—l. 6, D. de S. P. U.[1]

Iul.: Libertas servitutis usucapitur, si aedes possideantur: quare si is qui altius aedificatum habebat, ante statutum tempus aedes possidere desiit, interpellata usucapio est; is autem, qui postea easdem aedes possidere coeperit, integro

[1] Now these rights, in like manner as those also appertaining to rural estates, are extinguished by non-user throughout a certain period, only that this difference obtains, that by non-user they are not extinguished absolutely, but only if the neighbour at the same time acquires his independence by *usus*. Thus, for instance, if your house is so far servient to mine that it may not be raised higher, in order not to interfere with the lights of my house, and I throughout the statutory period have had my windows closed or blocked up, I only lose my right if you have had your house raised higher throughout this period. Likewise if your building owes the servitude of an inserted beam, and I have removed the beam, I lose the right if you have stopped up the hole out of which the beam was taken, and have so had it during the fixed period; if you, on the other hand, have done nothing fresh, my right remains intact.

statuto tempore libertatem usucapiet.—l. 32, § 1 eod.[1]

(γ) Justinian extended the period of limitation to ten years 'inter presentes' and twenty years 'inter absentes.'

§ 98. Legal Protection of Servitudes.

The person entitled to the servitude has at his command, so as to make his right available, even though he is in possession, the following petitory actions.[a]

(1) The actio confessoria s. servitutis vindicatio[b] —petitio ususfructus—supposes a legally valid creation of the servitude, to be proved by the plaintiff, and in praedial servitudes, furthermore, ownership of the plaintiff in the dominant estate. It goes (not merely, although for the most part, against the owner of the servient property, but in general) against every one who actually disturbs the person entitled to the servitude in the exercise of his right, or raises a claim against him; its object is the recognition by Law of the servitude, restoration of the state of things before the molestation, compensation for damage, and the giving of security for forbearance from future molestation.

Inst. iv. 6, § 2: Aeque si agat '**ius sibi esse**' fundo forte vel aedibus utendi fruendi, vel per fundum vicini eundi agendi, vel ex fundo vicini aquam ducendi in rem actio est; eiusdem generis est actio de iure praediorum urbanorum, veluti si agat ius sibi esse altius aedes tollendi prospici-

[a] See Bell, s. 'Action.'

[b] § 90.

[1] Freedom from a servitude is acquired by *usus* if the buildings are occupied; wherefore, if he that had a house built higher have ceased to occupy it before the statutory time, usucapion is destroyed; but a person that afterwards begins to occupy the same building will acquire independence upon the perfecting of the statutory period.

Book III. Pt. I. Ch. I.

endive, vel proiiciendi aliquid vel immittendi in vicini aedes.[1]

Ulp.: 'Uti frui ius sibi esse,' solus potest intendere, qui habet usumfructum; dominus autem fundi non potest, quia qui habet proprietatem, utendi fruendi ius separatum non habet: nec enim potest ei suus fundus servire.—l. 5 pr., D. si ususfr. 7, 6.[2]

Id.: Haec autem in rem actio confessoria nulli alii quam domino fundi competit: servitutem enim nemo vindicare potest quam is qui dominium in fundo vicino habet, cui servitutem dicit haberi.—D. 8, 5, 2, 1.[3]

Id.: Si quis mihi itineris vel actus vel viae controversiam non faciat, sed reficere sternere non patiatur, Pomponius scribit confessoria actione mihi utendum; nam et si arborem impendentem habeat vicinus, qua viam vel iter invium vel inhabile faciat, Marcellus notat iter petendum vel viam vindicandam.—l. 4, § 5 eod.[4]

---

[1] The like if a man by action claim that he has a right to the use and enjoyment over land it may be, or a house, or of footway or carriage-way over his neighbour's land, or of leading water from his neighbour's land, there is an action *in rem*. Of the same class is the action relating to urban servitudes; for example, if a man by action claim that he has a right of raising his house higher, or a right of view, or of making some building overhanging the boundary, or of inserting a beam in his neighbour's house.

[2] He alone can claim to have a right of use and enjoyment who has the usufruct; the owner of the estate cannot, because the person who has the ownership has no separate right of use and enjoyment; for his own estate cannot be servient to him.

[3] Now this real *actio confessoria* belongs to none other than the owner of an estate; for a servitude can be claimed by no one but him that has the ownership of adjacent land, maintaining that a servitude belongs to it.

[4] If a man do not dispute my right of footway, of driving cattle or of carriage-way, but will not permit me to repair it, or to pave it, Pomp. writes, that I must avail myself of the *act. conf.*, for even if my neighbour have an overhanging

Book III. Pt. I. Ch. I.

Id.: Agi autem hac actione poterit non tantum cum eo, in cuius agro aqua oritur vel per cuius fundum ducitur, verum etiam cum omnibus, quicumque aquam nos ducere impediunt, exemplo ceterarum servitutum.—l. 10, § 1 eod.[1]

(2) As 'utilis,' the actio confessoria is given for the protection of Praetorian servitudes;[a] and further, to the Pledgee, Emphyteuta and Superficiary. [a] § 96.

Iul.: Ei qui pignori fundum accepit, non est iniquum, utilem petitionem servitutis dari; . . . idem servari convenit et in eo, ad quem vectigalis fundus[b] pertinet.—D. 8, 1, 16.[2] [b] § 99.

(3) As 'Publiciana,' the actio confessoria belongs to every one who has by traditio acquired the servitude bona fide and ex iusta causa—although from the non-owner of the servient land[c]—and has not yet acquired the right by prescription.[d] [c] D. 8, 1, 20. [d] § 90.

Ulp.: Si de usufructu agatur tradito, Publiciana datur; itemque servitutibus urbanorum praediorum per traditionem constitutis vel per patientiam (forte si per domum quis suam passus est aquaeductum transduci), item rusticorum: nam et hic traditionem et patientiam tuendam constat.—D. 6, 2, 11, 1.[3]

---

tree, by which he makes the carriage-way or footway impassable or encumbers it, Marc. remarks that the footway must be subject of a suit, or the carriage-way of a claim.

[1] Now this action can be brought not only against him in whose field the water springs up, or through whose land it is led, but also against each and all that obstruct our leading the water, after the manner of the other servitudes.

[2] He that has received land in pledge is not unfairly allowed an analogous action in respect of the servitude. . . . The same holds in respect of a person in whom is vested a stipendiary estate.

[3] If proceedings be taken about usufruct by delivery, the *Publiciana* is given; and no less if servitudes in buildings have been constituted by delivery, or by acquiescence (for example, if a man have allowed a watercourse to be carried through his

BOOK III. Pt. I. Ch. I.

The holder of the servitude is, moreover, protected by possessory remedies.

(1) The one prerequisite for this is quasi possessio, *i.e.*, *de facto* exercise, 'nec vi nec clam nec precario,' of the servitude as of one's own right, irrespective of bona fides.[a]

[a] D. 8, 5, 10 pr.; 8, 6, 25.

Cels.: Si per fundum tuum nec vi nec clam nec precario commeavit aliquis, non tamen tamquam id suo iure faceret, sed si prohiberetur non facturus, inutile ei est interdictum: nam ut interdictum competat, ius fundi possedisse oportet.—l. 7, D. de itin. 43, 19.[1]

(2) The interdicta retinendae and recuperandae possessionis,[b] as employed analogically, serve for the protection of the quasi-possession of the personal servitudes, and affirmative servitutes praediorum urbanorum.

[b] § 91.

Ulp.: In summa puto dicendum, et inter fructuarios hoc interdictum[c] reddendum, et si alter usumfructum, alter possessionem sibi defendat.—D. 43, 17, 4.[2]

[c] Sc. 'uti possidetis' utile.

Id.: —ex aedibus meis in aedes tuas proiectum habeo, . . . quo facilius possim retinere possessionem eius proiectionis, interdicto tecum sic 'uti nunc possidetis eas aedes, ex quibus proiectum est.'—l. 3, § 6 eod.[3]

---

house), like as of rustic estates; for even in respect of such it is settled that delivery and acquiescence are to be protected.

[1] If a man neither by violence, nor covertly, nor upon sufferance have traversed your land, not, however, under the impression that he did so by virtue of a right of his, but would have forborne, if forbidden, an interdict is of no avail to him; for that an interdict attach, it is necessary that he should have possessed a right in the land.

[2] I am of opinion we can in general say that this interdict can also be granted between fructuaries, even if one upholds his usufruct, the other his possession.

[3] If I have built into your house any part of mine, that I may the more easily retain possession of the projection, I can avail

Id.: Interdictum necessarium fuisse fructuario apparet 'si prohibeatur uti frui usufructu fundi.' —Uti frui autem prohibuisse is videtur, qui vi deiecit utentem et fruentem, aut non admisit, cum ex fundo exiisset. . . . Ceterum si ab initio volentem incipere uti frui prohibuit, . . . debet fructuarius usumfructum vindicare.—Qui ususfructus nomine qualiterqualiter fuit quasi in possessione, utetur hoc interdicto.—D. 43, 16, 3, §§ 13, 14, 17.[1]

(3) The Edict puts forward special interdicts for the servitutes praediorum rusticorum, as for example, the interdictum 'de itinere actuque privato,' 'de aqua quottidiana et aestiva.'

Praetor ait: QVO ITINERE ACTVQVE PRIVATO, QVO DE AGITVR, HOC ANNO NEC VI NEC CLAM NEC PRECARIO AB ILLO VSVS ES, QVO MINVS ITA VTARIS, VIM FIERI VETO.—l. 1 pr., D. de itin.[2]

Ulp.: Ait praetor: VTI HOC ANNO AQVAM, QVA DE AGITVR, NON VI NON CLAM NON PRECARIO AB ILLO DVXISTI, QVO MINVS ITA DVCAS, VIM FIERI VETO.—Aristo putat eum demum interdictum hoc habere, qui se putat suo iure uti, non eum, qui

---

myself of the interdict against you 'as you now possess the building from which the projection proceeds.'

[1] The interdict would seem to have been necessary to the fructuary 'if he be hindered in the use and enjoyment of an estate.'—Now he seems to have obstructed the usufruct who has violently dispossessed the fructuary, or has not again granted him admittance after having left the land. . . . If, however, a man from the outset obstructed him who wished to enter upon his usufruct, . . . the fructuary must pursue his remedy by *vindicatio*.—He that by the title of usufruct has been in quasi-possession, in whatever way he came by it, will be able to avail himself of this interdict.

[2] The Praetor says: 'Whatever be the private way or the carriage-way in question which you have used against so-and-so during this year, neither by violence, nor secretly, nor upon sufferance, to prevent your so using it, I prohibit violence.'

scit se nullum ius habere et utitur.—D. 43, 20, l. 1, pr. 1, § 19.[1]

§ 99. Superficies and Emphyteusis (Ager Vectigalis).

Superficies is the real right originated by the Praetorian Law of use and disposition, transmissible and alienable, in a building (superficies, -um) or even parts of such building (*e.g.*, stories), erected upon ground (solum) owned by another, or possibly in an already existing building; which has been granted for ever by the ground owner to the person entitled (superficiarius), or indeed for a very long time by way of hire, or purchase perhaps, in consideration of a ground-rent (solarium, pensio)—or gratuitously for a nominal rent.

Gai.: Superficiarias aedes appellamus, quae in conducto solo positae sint: quarum proprietas et civili et naturali iure eius est, cuius et solum.—l. 2, D. h. t. (de superfic. 43, 18).[2]

Ulp.: Si quis nemine prohibente in publico aedificaverit, . . . si obstet id aedificium publico usui, utique is, qui operibus publicis procurat, debebit id deponere, aut si non obstet, solarium ei imponere: vectigal enim hoc solarium appellatur ex eo, quod pro solo pendatur.—D. 43, 8, l. 2, § 17.[3]

---

[1] The Praetor says: 'As you during this year have not led the water in question by violence, secretly, or upon sufferance, to prevent your leading it, I forbid violence.'—Aristo thinks he alone has this interdict who supposes he uses it by his own right, not the person who is aware that he has no right, and yet makes use of it.

[2] We call buildings 'superficiary' which are situated upon ground hired out, the ownership of which both by civil and natural Law is his to whom also the ground belongs.

[3] If a man, without opposition, builds in a public place . . . but such building interferes with public communication, he that looks after the public works must in any case pull it down, or if it be not an obstruction, must charge a ground-rent upon it;

Id.: Qui superficiem in alieno solo habet, civili actione subnixus est: nam si conduxit superficium, ex conducto, si emit ex empto agere cum domino soli potest; . . . sed longe utile visum est, quia et incertum erat, an locati existeret, et quia melius est possidere potius quam in personam experiri, hoc interdictum proponere et quasi in rem actionem polliceri.—l. 1, § 1, h. t.[1]

The ground owner remains also owner of the building,[a] but the right of the superficiary in the building ostensibly approaches very nearly to ownership.

[a] § 84, ad init.

Sed et tradi posse[b] intelligendum est, ut et legari et donari possit.—Servitutes quoque praetorio iure constituentur.—Ib. §§ 7, 9.[2]

[b] Sc. superficiem.

The superficiary is also protected—even against the ground owner—by a special (quasi-possessory) interdictum 'de superficie' and an 'in rem actio (utilis rei vindicatio)' conceived 'in factum.'

Ait praetor: VTI EX LEGE LOCATIONIS SIVE CONDVCTIONIS[c] SVPERFICIE, QVA DE AGITVR, NEC VI NEC CLAM NEC PRECARIO ALTER AB ALTERO FRVIMINI, QVO MINVS FRVAMINI, VIM FIERI VETO; SI QVA ALIA ACTIO DE SVPERFICIE POSTVLABITUR, CAVSA COGNITA DABO.—Ib. pr.[3]

[c] VENDITIONIS?

---

this impost being called a ground-rent, because it is paid for the ground.

[1] He that has a lease of ground belonging to another is protected by a civil action, for he can take proceedings against the ground owner, if he has hired the tenement, upon the ground of the hire; if he has purchased it, upon the ground of the purchase. But, as it was even uncertain whether a lease existed, and as it is better to be in possession than to bring a personal action, it seemed highly advantageous to offer this interdict, and to promise a real action, so to speak.

[2] It [that is, the tenement] must also be understood to admit of being delivered, bequeathed and given.—Moreover, servitudes may also be created according to Praetorian Law.

[3] The Praetor says: 'As you by virtue of the contract of lease or hiring have the enjoyment of the tenement in question,

Book III. Pt. I. Ch. I.

Superficiario—*i.e.* qui in alieno solo superficiem ita habet, ut certam pensionem praestet—praetor causa cognita in rem actionem pollicetur. —D. 6, 1, 73, 1.—l. 75 (Paul., Ulp.).[1]

Is autem, in cuius solo superficies est, utique non indiget utili actione, sed habet in rem, qualem habet de solo; plane si adversus superficiarium velit vindicare, dicendum est exceptione utendum in factum data.—l. 1, § 4, h. t.[2]

A Lease is in itself only an obligatory relation, but the lessees of public lands (agri vectigales) had by Praetorian Law a 'real' right of use, which was transmissible, in the lands let to them, which upon due discharge of the ground-rent (vectigal) was protected by interdicts,[a] and by an in rem actio against third persons as well as the lessor. The right of the agri vectigalis was next, in the later imperial Law, blended with the right of Emphyteusis,[b] which from the third century came up and was customary in the eastern part of the Empire, and was an hereditary or long lease of uncultivated imperial and fiscal lands, intended to promote their cultivation. The name Emphyteusis was transferred to all grants of civic, municipal, ecclesiastical and private lands; and the contract of hereditary lease was declared by an ordinance of Zeno to be a peculiar contract, alike different from Lease

[a] *Interdictum de loco publico fruendo?*

[b] See 'Anct. Law,' pp. 299, *sqq.*

---

neither by violence, nor covertly, nor upon sufferance the one from the other, to hinder such enjoyment, I forbid violence; if any other action shall be asked for concerning a tenement, I will grant it after inquiry into the matter.'

[1] To the superficiary, *i.e.*, the person who possesses a tenement upon ground belonging to another in such way as to pay a fixed sum for it, the Praetor promises a real action upon investigation of the matter.

[2] Now the person upon whose ground the tenement is does not at all need an analogous action, but he has the same real action as in respect of the ground. Certainly if he desire to bring the proprietary action against the lessee, we must state that the latter will have to employ a plea granted *in factum*.

and Purchase, which point earlier on had been subject of dispute.

The Emphyteuta has juristic possession of the land and can dispose of it as owner, only that he may not deteriorate it, has to pay the taxes charged upon it, and is in particular obliged to pay the owner an hereditary rent (canon, pensio), in default of payment of which for three years, the owner can dispossess the Emphyteuta (right of ejectment). If the Emphyteuta alienates his right, the owner has a right of pre-emption.

> Agri civitatum vectigales vocantur, qui in perpetuum locantur id est hac lege, ut quamdiu pro his vectigal pendatur, tamdiu neque ipsis, qui conduxerint, neque his, qui in locum eorum successerunt, auferri eos liceat.—§ Qui in perpetuum fruendum conduxerunt a municipibus, quamvis non efficiantur domini, tamen placuit competere eis in rem actionem adversus . . . ipsos municipes :—ita tamen, si vectigal solvant. —D. 6, 3, l. 1 (Paul.), l. 2 (Ulp.).[1]
>
> Gai. iii. § 145 : —in quibusdam causis quaeri (solet), utrum emptio et venditio contrahatur, an locatio et conductio: veluti si qua res in perpetuum locata sit, quod evenit in praediis municipum, quae ea lege locantur, ut quamdiu id vectigal praestetur, neque ipsi conductori neque heredi eius praedium auferatur; sed magis placuit locationem conductionemque esse.[2]

---

[1] The lands of civic communities are called stipendiary which are leased in perpetuity, *i.e.*, upon the condition that as long as a tax is paid for them, so long neither they themselves who have taken such lease nor their successors shall be deprived of them.—§ They that have taken a lease of the perpetual enjoyment of estates from a corporation, although not becoming owners, it is held possess the real action against the corporation itself, yet only if they discharge the rent.

[2] In some cases it is a matter of doubt whether a contract of buying and selling or of letting and hiring is made. For example, if any property has been leased in perpetuity, as happens

Book III. Pt. I. Ch. I.

Iust. iii. 24, § 3: —lex Zenoniana lata est, quae emphyteuseos contractui propriam statuit naturam neque ad locationem neque ad venditionem inclinantem, sed suis pactionibus fulciendam.[1]

LAW OF PLEDGE.[a]

[a] Markby, ss. 437-465, 481; Holland, pp. 170, *sqq.*; Scrutton, p. 157.

§ 100. Nature and History of the Pledge-right.

The *ius pignoris* is that right in a thing owned by another which belongs to a creditor, providing security for his claim, by virtue of which he can upon non-performance sell such thing, and can reimburse himself out of the purchase-money. It is essentially distinguished from the other iura in re aliena by the fact that (1) it assures to the person entitled a merely transitory, partial control over the thing without right of user—or the privilege of transferring the ownership by sale of the thing—with the full exercise of which it is itself extinguished; that (2) by the latter step it destroys the proprietary right itself; and that (3) it is an accessory right, *i.e.*, one existing on account of the claim.[b]

[b] But cf. § 103

The institution of real security of claims by an object of ownership (pledge-right, pignus in the wider sense) mortgaged to the creditor as an eventual means of satisfaction, was by the Roman Law developed in three different stages and forms: interim ownership, juristic possession, ius in re.

The oldest form of security is the *FIDVCIA*,[d] *i.e.*, the

[c] Boeth. in Cic. Top. 10.

in the case of estates of corporations which are leased upon the condition that as long as such rent is paid, the estate shall not be taken away from he lessee himself nor his heir. But the prevailing view is that this is a letting and hiring.

[1] —the *l. Zenoniana* was passed, which settled that the contract of *emphyteusis* had a special character, and did not approximate either to Hiring or to Sale, but should rest on its own agreements.

transfer to the creditor of the ownership[a] of the thing as giving him security, by mancipatio (or in iure cessio), subject to a proviso for remancipatio upon due payment of the debt; whereby the debtor by agreement with the creditor (precarium, hire) could retain possession of the thing. Upon fulfilment of the 'pactum fiduciae,' the debtor had the 'actio fiduciae,' which entailed infamia. In respect of this the 'lex commissoria' was also in use, *i.e.*, the agreement that upon non-payment of the debt the thing, which until then had still formed part of the property of the debtor, should definitely remain in the hands of the creditor as his own.—We have already adverted to the 'usureceptio fiduciae.'[b]

[a] Comp. the English mortgage: see Williams, 'Real Property,' pt. iv. ch. ii.; 'Personal Property,' p. 62.

[b] § 80.

Gai. ii. §§ 59–60: Adhuc etiam ex aliis causis sciens quisque rem alienam usucapit; nam qui rem alicui fiduciae causa mancipio dederit vel in iure cesserit, si eandem ipse possederit, potest usucapere, anno scilicet etiam soli si sit: quae species usucapionis dicitur **usureceptio**, quia id quod aliquando habuimus recipimus per usucapionem. § Sed cum fiducia contrahatur aut cum creditore pignoris iure, aut cum amico quo tutius nostrae res apud eum sint, si quidem cum amico contracta sit fiducia, sane omni modo competit usureceptio; si vero cum creditore, soluta quidem pecunia omnimodo competit, nondum vero soluta ita demum competit, si neque conduxerit eam rem a creditore debitor, neque precario rogaverit, ut eam rem possidere liceret: quo casu lucrativa usucapio competit.[1]

[1] A man by *usus* consciously acquires the property of another by yet other grounds; for he who has transferred a thing to another by mancipation or by surrender in court for a fiduciary purpose, if he himself get possession of the same, can acquire it by *usus*, and that in one year even if it belong to the soil. This kind of usucapion is called 'retaking by use,' because we take back by usucapion that which we once possessed. § But since a fiduciary contract is made either with a creditor in respect of

Book III. Pt. I. Ch. I.

Paul. ii. 13, §§ 2–3: Quidquid creditor per fiduciarium servum quaesivit, sortem debiti minuit. Debitor creditori vendere fiduciam non potest; sed aliis si velit vendere potest, ita ut ex pretio eiusdem pecuniam offerat creditori, atque ita remancipatam sibi rem emptori praestet.—§ 5: Si inter creditorem et debitorem convenerit ut fiduciam sibi vendere non liceat, non solvente debitore creditor denuntiare ei sollemniter potest et distrahere: nec enim ex tali conventione fiduciae actio nasci potest.[1]

The second form of security is the PIGNUS (pawn), which arises by transfer of the possession of the thing to the creditor under a condition for its re-transfer upon satisfaction of the debt (rem pignori obligare), by which also the creditor originally obtained a merely *de facto* security. The original of this pledge-right is to be found in the old 'pignoris capio' (magisterial or private pledge).[a]

[a] Cf. § 192, and *sup.* § 31.

The right of sale in case of default in performance used in ancient time to be granted to the creditor only as derived from special agreement (so that otherwise

---

a pledge, or with a friend in order that our property in his hands should be the better secured; if the fiduciary contract be made with a friend, *usureceptio* is indeed allowable in any case; but if with a creditor, then, upon payment of the money, it is always allowable; but if the money has not been paid, it only attaches if the debtor has neither hired such property from the creditor, nor asked for possession thereof from him upon sufferance: in such cases lucrative usucapion is allowable.

[1] Whatever the creditor has acquired through a fiduciary bondman reduces the state of the debt. The debtor cannot sell the pawn to the creditor; but if he so desire, he can sell it to others, in such way as from the purchase-money to tender the amount to the creditor, and so as to have the property reconveyed to himself for conveyance to the purchaser.—If there have been an agreement between the creditor and debtor, that the creditor is to have no power to sell the pawn, then, upon the debtor's default, the creditor can give him formal notice and foreclose; for an action of *fiducia* cannot arise from such an agreement.

the pledge served for nothing more than an indirect means of pressure upon the debtor, not as a mode of satisfaction for the creditor); later on it was admitted even in the absence of such agreement, and indeed where there was an agreement to the contrary, as especial requisite of the contract of Pledge.[a]—The pledgor is protected in his possession by the possessory interdicts.[b]

[a] *Sup.*, Paul. ii. 13, 5.

[b] D. 16, 3, 17, 1; 41, 3, 16.

Isid. orig. v. 25, § 22: **Pignus** est quod propter rem creditam obligatur, cuius rei possessionem solam ad tempus consequitur creditor, dominium penes debitorem est.[1]

Iavol.: Si is qui pignori rem accepit, cum de vendendo pignore nihil convenisset, vendidit, . . . furti se obligat.—D. 47, 2, 74 (73).[2]

Gai. ii. § 64: —voluntate debitoris intelligitur pignus alienari, qui olim pactus est, ut liceret creditori pignus vendere, si pecunia non solvatur.[3]

Ulp.: Sed et si non convenerit de distrahendo pignore, hoc tamen iure utimur, ut liceat distrahere, si modo non convenit, ne liceat; ubi vero convenit ne distraheretur, creditor si distraxerit, furti obligatur (debitori) nisi ei ter fuerit denuntiatum, ut solvat, et cessaverit.—D. 13, 7, 4.[4]

---

1 A pawn is an obligation entered into by reason of property consigned, the possession alone of which is for a time obtained by the creditor; the ownership is with the debtor.

2 If he that took property in pledge has sold it, when no agreement had been made for the sale of the pledge, . . . he makes himself liable for a theft.

3 —the pledge is considered as alienated by the consent of the debtor, who afore agreed that the creditor might sell the pledge if the money were not paid.

4 But even if no agreement has been made concerning the sale of the pledge, yet the rule that we employ is, that there may be a sale, provided there has been no agreement to preclude it; but where it has been agreed that it should not be sold, if the creditor sell, he makes himself liable (to the debtor) for a theft, unless notice to pay have been thrice given to the debtor, and he has delayed.

Book III. Pt. I. Ch. I.

The increased requirements of commerce led finally to the development of the legal institution of *HYPOTHECA*, *i.e.*, a ius pignoris originated by a merely informal contract, without transfer of possession, and protected by a Praetorian in rem actio.

Gai.: Contrahitur hypotheca per factum conventum, cum quis paciscatur, ut res eius propter aliquam obligationem sint hypothecae nomine obligatae; nec ad rem pertinet, quibus fit verbis. —l. 4, D. de pign. 20, 1, 4.[1]

Ulp.: Proprie dicimus . . . hypothecam, cum non transit nec possessio ad creditorem.—D. 13, 7, 9, 2.[2]

This was at first recognised and accorded legal protection by the Praetor in the mortgage of the inventory (invecta et illata)[a] of the lessee of agricultural land to the lessor, where the employment of the fiducia or of the pignus appeared impossible or impracticable (interdictum Salvianum; later on, the in rem actio Serviana).

[a] See Paterson, s. 409, and Bell, s. vv.

Cato de re rust. c. 146: '—Donicum solutum erit aut ita satisdatum erit, quae in fundo illata erunt, pignori sunto. Ne quid eorum de fundo deportato; si quid deportaverit domini esto.'—c. 149:—'Donicum pecuniam satisfecerit, pecus et familia, quae illic erit, pignori sunto.'[3]

Gai. iv. § 147: Interdictum quod appellatur Salvianum adipiscendae possessionis causa comparatum est, eoque utitur dominus fundi de rebus

---

[1] A mortgage is contracted by compact, when a man engages that his property shall by reason of some obligation be liable by way of mortgage; and it matters not in what words it is done.

[2] We rightly speak of a mortgage when not even possession passes to the creditor.

[3] 'Until discharge or security given, let such things as have been placed on the farm be in pledge. He shall remove none of them from the farm; if he remove aught, it shall belong to the owner.'—'Until he shall have discharged the amount, the cattle and household that may be there shall be in pledge.'

coloni, quas is pro mercedibus fundi pignori futuras pepegisset.[1]

But it was therefore progressively extended to all remaining cases of the merely contractual as well as tacit pledge (actio quasi Serviana s. hypothecaria). The same real action which was meant for the protection of the 'hypotheca' was then also allowed to the pledgee, since an hypothecary contract is contained in every pawn; and accordingly Pignus and Hypotheca were placed on the same footing.

Inst. iv. 6, § 7: Item Serviana et quasi Serviana, quae etiam hypothecaria vocatur, ex ipsius praetoris iurisdictione substantiam capit. Serviana autem experitur quis de rebus coloni, quae pignoris iure pro mercedibus ei tenentur; quasi Serviana autem (qua) creditores pignora hypothecasve persequuntur. Inter pignus autem et hypothecam quantum ad actionem hypothecarium nihil interest; nam de qua re inter creditorem et debitorem convenerit, ut sit pro debito obligata, utraque hac appellatione continetur.[2]

Marcian.: Inter pignus et hypothecam tantum nominis sonus differt.—l. 5, § 1, D. de pign.[3]

Whilst therefore the development of the hypotheca

---

[1] The so-called *interdictum Salvianum* has been provided for the obtaining of possession, and it is employed by the owner of a farm in respect of the property of the tenant which the latter has engaged should be security for the rent of the farm.

[2] The Servian and quasi-Servian (also called the hypothecarian) actions likewise derive their origin from the Praetor's own jurisdiction. Now a person avails himself of the Servian action in respect of property of a tenant which by pledge-right is held by him as security for rent; whilst the quasi-Servian action is that whereby creditors sue for things pledged or mortgaged. There is no difference between a pledge and a mortgage, so far as the hypothecarian action is concerned; for the property which by agreement between creditor and debtor has to answer for the debt is in either case designated by this term.

[3] Between Pledge and Hypothec there is no other difference than that of the name.

Book III. Pt. I. Ch. I.

raised the ius pignoris in things in general to a jus in re aliena, it on the other hand made this right, as a non-real one, also applicable to incorporeal portions of property (*e.g.*, claims), with which hitherto real security could not be given.

§ 101. Pre-requisites and Origin of the Pledge-right.

a § 114.

Every pledge-right supposes a claim—although one merely natural [a]—of the person entitled to the pledge (the pledge creditor) whose *accessorium* it is; but another can also on behalf of the debtor mortgage his property to the creditor of such.

Marcian.: Res hypothecae dari posse sciendum est pro quacumque obligatione, sive mutua pecunia datur sive dos sive emptio vel venditio contrahatur vel etiam locatio et conductio vel mandatum, et sive pura est obligatio vel in diem vel sub condicione, et sive in praesenti contractu sive etiam praecedat; sed et futurae obligationis nomine dari possunt, . . . et vel pro civili obligatione vel honoraria vel tantum naturali. Dare autem quis hypothecam potest sive pro sua obligatione sive pro aliena.—l. 5 pr., § 2, D. h. t. (= de pign. 20, 1).[1]

As object of the pledge, or pledge-right, can be—

(1) corporeal things:

Gai.: Et quae nondum sunt, futura tamen sunt, hypothecae dari possunt, ut fructus pen-

---

[1] It should be known that property can be given by mortgage for whatever obligation, whether a loan be given, or a dowry, or a purchase and sale contracted, or a letting and hiring, or a commission, and whether the obligation be absolute, or temporal, or conditional; and whether as embodied in the contract, or as preceding it; but mortgages can also be given for future obligations . . . and even for a civil, or a magisterial, or only a natural obligation. Now a man can give a mortgage either for his own obligation, or for another man's.

dentes, partus ancillae, fetus pecorum.—l. 15 pr. eod.[1]

(2) Not only such, but in general, all alienable proprietary rights, transferable, that is at least as regards exercise, *e.g.*, usufruct, claims; since also in respect of these a right of sale obtains in favour of the creditor.

Id.: Quod emptionem venditionemque recipit, etiam pignerationem recipere potest.—l. 9, § 1 eod.[2]

Marcian.: Ususfructus an possit pignori hypothecaeve dari, quaesitum est, sive dominus proprietatis convenerit, sive ille qui solum usumfructum habet. Et scribit Papinianus tuendum creditorem, et si velit cum creditore proprietarius agere '**non esse ei ius uti frui invito se**,' tali exceptione eum praetor tuebitur '**si non inter creditorem et eum, ad quem ususfructus pertinet, convenerit, ut ususfructus pignori sit**'; nam et cum emptorem ususfructus tuetur praetor, cur non et creditorem tuebitur? Eadem ratione et debitori obiicietur exceptio.—l. 11, § 2 eod.[3]

Paul.: Si convenerit, ut nomen debitoris mei pignori tibi sit, tuenda est a praetore haec con-

---

[1] And things can be mortgaged which do not exist, but will do so, as hanging fruits, the children of a woman-slave, the offspring of cattle.

[2] That which admits of being purchased and sold can also be the object of a pledge.

[3] Whether a usufruct can be pledged or mortgaged has been matter of doubt, no matter whether agreement have been made by the ground owner or by him who has the mere usufruct. Pap. writes that the creditor should be protected, and if the ground owner wish by action against him to assert 'that such person has no right to the usufruct against his will,' the Praetor shall protect him by the plea, 'unless an agreement has been made between the creditor and him to whom the usufruct belongs, that the usufruct shall be pledged.' For if the Praetor protect the purchaser of the usufruct, why shall he not also protect the creditor? Upon the same ground will the plea be urged against the debtor also.

ventio, ut et te in exigenda pecunia et debitorem adversus me, si cum eo experiar, tueatur. Ergo si id nomen pecuniarium fuit, exactam pecuniam tecum pensabis: si vero corporis alicuius, id quod acceperis erit tibi pignoris loco.—l. 18 pr., D. de pign. act. 13, 7.[1]

And (3), not merely single things for themselves (special pledge), but also a definite mass of things, as, *e.g.*, movables, stock in trade, household inventory (collective pledge), as well as, finally, a whole property itself, present and future (general mortgage).

Ulp.: Obligatione generali rerum, quas quis habuit habiturusve sit, ea non continebitur, quae verisimile est quemquam specialiter obligaturum non fuisse, ut puta supellex, item vestis.—l. 6, D. h. t.[2]

Scaev.: Cum tabernam debitor creditori pignori dederit, . . . ea, quae mortis tempore debitoris in taberna inventa sunt, pignori obligata esse videntur.—l. 34 pr. eod.[3]

Marcian.: Grege pignori obligato, quae postea nascuntur, tenentur; sed et si prioribus capitibus decedentibus totus grex fuerit renovatus, pignori tenebitur.—l. 13 pr. eod.[4]

---

[1] If it have been agreed that the claim against my debtor shall serve as a pledge to you, this agreement has to be protected by the Praetor, so that he both protects you when claiming the money, and the debtor against me, if I proceed against him. Accordingly, if that was a money debt, you will set off against your claim the money demanded; but if it were a claim of some material substance, that which you will have received will be for you instead of the pledge.

[2] Under a general mortgage of his property which a man possesses, or shall possess, such things are not included as probably no one would have wished expressly to mortgage, *e.g.*, furniture and clothing.

[3] When a debtor pledges a shop to his creditor, . . . the things found in the shop at the death of the debtor are regarded as bound by the pledge.

[4] If a flock have been pledged, the security extends to young born subsequently; even if all the former cattle have died off,

The pledge-right is originated—

(1) by private disposition (pignus voluntarium), either by formal contract between the creditor and pledgor (pignus conventionale)[a] or by testamentary provision.

[a] D. 20, 1, 4. Cf. Brown, s. 'Hypothèque.'

Lucius Titius libertis suis cibaria et vestiaria annua certorum nummorum reliquit et posteriore parte testamenti ita cavit: 'obligatos eis (esse volo) ob causam fidei commissi fundos meos . . . illum et illum . . . , ut ex reditu eorum alimenta supra scripta percipiant.'—D. 34, 1, 12.[1]

(2) By magisterial disposition: (α) praetorium pignus,[b] (β) pignus in causa iudicati captum.[c]

[b] § 31.

[c] § 204, ad fin. Brown, *ubi sup.*

Ulp.: Non est mirum, si ex quacumque causa magistratus in possessionem aliquem miserit, pignus constitui.—Sciendum est, ubi iussu magistratus pignus constituitur, non alias constitui, nisi ventum fuerit in possessionem.—l. 26, D. de pign. act.[2]

Imp. Anton.: Res ob causam iudicati eius iussu, cui ius iubendi fuit pignoris iure teneri ac distrahi posse saepe rescriptum est: nam in vicem iustae obligationis succedit ex causa contractus auctoritas iubentis.—C. 8, 22 (23), 1.[3]

---

and the whole shall have become a new herd, it will be held as security.

[1] L. T. bequeathed to his freedmen pensions of food and raiment in a definite sum of money, and in the latter part of his testament provided (as follows): 'It is my will that such and such of my lands be chargeable to them for the purposes of the trust, so that from the produce thereof they may derive the above written sustenance.'

[2] It is not surprising that if the magistrate should for some reason have installed a man in possession, a pledge is originated.—It should be known that where a pledge is originated by order of the magistrate, it is not originated otherwise than upon one's having entered into possession.

[3] It has often been stated in rescripts that property can according to the Law of Pledge be retained and sold because of a judgment-debt, upon the order of him who had authority to

Book III. Pt. I. Ch. I.

(3) Directly consequent upon a legal precept in respect of certain claims: statutory, legal, tacit ius pignoris (pignus legale, tacitum);[a] to which belongs, *e.g.*,

[a] Brown, ibid.

(*a*) the pledge-right possessed by the landlord in the invecta and illata of the tenant.[b]

[b] Cf. right of distress in English Law: Blackst. iii. pp. 6, *sqq.* (Steph. iii. 247, *sqq.*).

> Ner.: Eo iure utimur, ut quae in praedia urbana inducta illata sunt, pignori esse credantur, quasi id tacite convenerit; in rusticis praediis contra observatur.—D. 20, 2, 4 pr.[1]

(β) The right of the lessor to the fruits of the land.

> Pomp.: In praediis rusticis fructus, qui ibi nascuntur, tacite intelliguntur pignori esse domino fundi locati, etiamsi nominatim id non convenerit. —l. 7 pr. eod.[2]

(γ) The pledge-right possessed by the Treasury, by a ward, and a married woman, in the whole property of the public debtor, or of the guardian and the husband in respect of claims for guardianship and dos.

> Imp. Anton.: Certum est eius, qui cum fisco contrahit, bona veluti pignoris titulo obligari, quamvis specialiter id non exprimitur.—C. 8, 14 (15), 2.[3]

---

issue such order. For the authority of the person issuing the order takes the place of a legal pledge upon a contractual title.

[1] Our rule is, that what has been brought upon urban estates is supposed to be pledged as if there was an implied agreement; in rural[c] estates the opposite is the rule.

[c] Mr. Hunter, citing D. 20, 2, 7, 1, and 20, 1, 32, by an oversight speaks of 'urban hypothec' only by special agreement: p. 444.

[2] In respect of rural estates, the fruits there raised are treated as by implication pledged to the owner of the land leased, even if there have been no such express agreement.

[3] The effects of a person who contracts with the Treasury are certainly liable under the title of Pledge, so to speak, although that be not expressly stated.

§ 102. Rights of the Pledge-creditor; Concurrence of *iura pignoris*, and Protection of such Rights.

The essential subject-matter of the right belonging to the pawnee is the privilege of selling the pledge (ius distrahendi) in case the claim when due is not fully discharged, and of satisfying himself out of the purchase-money.[a]

The sale is undertaken by the pawnee as representative of the pawnor or owner, although by virtue of his own right and in his own interest,[b] for which also certain formalities are prescribed. It transfers to the purchaser the ownership as possessed by the pawnor at the time when the pledge-right came into existence (condicio usucapiendi), without right of redemption, and destroys the vendor's rights, as those of other creditors.

[a] Cf. § 100, and D. 13, 7, 18 pr.

[b] § 82.

> Imp. Iust.: Sancimus si quis rem creditori suo pigneraverit, si quidem in pactione cautum est, quemadmodum debeat pignus distrahi, . . . ea observari, de quibus inter creditorem et debitorem conventum est. Sin autem nulla pactio intercesserit, licentia dabitur foeneratori ex denuntiatione vel ex sententia iudiciali post biennium . . . eam vendere.—C. 8, 33 (34), l. 3, § 1.[c] [1]
>
> Imp. Alex.: Creditor hypothecas sive pignus cum proscribit, notum debitori facere, si bona fide rem gerit, et quando licet testato dicere debet.—C. 8, 27 (28), 4.[2]

[c] Cf. Story, *l. c.*

---

[1] Be it enacted that, if any one have pledged property to his creditor, in case provision has by agreement been made as to the way in which the pledge should be sold, . . . such things shall be observed as have been agreed upon between the creditor and debtor. But if no agreement have existed, the lender shall have power given him after two years to sell the same in pursuance of a notice or judicial sentence.

[2] When a creditor offers for sale by auction property in mortgage or pledge, if he go to work in good faith, he ought to

BOOK III. Pt. I. Ch. I.

Ulp.: Non est novum ut qui dominium non habeat, alii dominium praebeat: nam et creditor pignus vendendo causam dominii praestat, quam ipse non habuit.—D. 41, 1, 46.[a] [1]

[a] See Walker, *in loc.*

Imp. Alex.: Si vendidit is qui ante pignus accepit, persecutio tibi hypothecaria superesse non potest.—C. 8, 19 (20), 1.[2]

Mod.: Cum posterior creditor a priore pignus emit, non tam adquirendi dominii, quam servandi pignoris sui causa intelligitur pecuniam dedisse.—l. 6, D. de distr. pign. 20, 5.[3]

As regards the excess of the purchase-money over the amount of the claim (superfluum s. hyperocha), the creditor is held responsible to the pawnor by the 'actio pigneraticia.'[b]

[b] § 121, ad fin.

Pap.: Creditor iudicio quod de pignore dato proponitur, ut superfluum pretii cum usuris restituat, iure cogitur.—D. 13, 7, 42.[4]

The earlier, very usual, agreement that, in case of non-satisfaction by the debtor, the thing pledged should itself lapse to the creditor (lex commissoria) was disallowed in the later Law.[c]

[c] Cf. § 100, and Scrutton, p. 157.

Vat. fgm. 9: Creditor a debitore pignus recte emit, sive in exordio contractus ita convenit sive postea. Nec incerti pretii venditio videbitur, si convenerit, ut pecunia foenoris non soluta creditor iure empti dominium retineat, cum sortis et

---

apprise the debtor thereof, and when practicable, to inform him before witnesses.

[1] It is nothing new for a man who has not had the ownership to confer it upon a third party, for even a creditor by selling a pledge furnishes a proprietary title which he himself had not.

[2] If a man who previously received a pledge has sold it, no further hypothecary proceedings can be available to you.

[3] When the second creditor has purchased the pledge from the first, he is regarded as having paid over the money, not so much to acquire the ownership, as to retain his security.

[4] The creditor, by the action afforded in respect of what has been pledged, is lawfully compelled to account for excess of purchase-money with interest.

usurarum quantitas ad diem solvendae pecuniae praestitutam certa sit.—(Pap.)[1]

Imp. Const.: Quoniam inter alias captiones praecipue commissoriae pignorum legis crescit asperitas, placet infirmari eam et in posterum omnem eius memoriam aboleri.—C. 8, 34 (35), 3.[2]

Marcian.: Potest ita fieri pignoris datio, ut si intra certum tempus non sit soluta pecunia, iure emptoris possideat rem iusto pretio tunc aestimandum.—D. 20, 1, 16, 9.[3]

A right of user in the property pawned is possessed by the pawnee only when such has been specially accorded to him in lieu of interest (antichresis).

Id.: Si ἀντίχρησις facta sit, . . . eo usque retinet[a] possessionem pignoris loco, donec illi pecunia solvatur, cum in usuras fructus percipiat aut locando aut ipse percipiendo habitandoque.—l. 11, § 1 eod.[4]

[a] Sc. creditor.

Special legal relations arise in respect of the concurrent rights of several pawnees.

---

[1] The creditor rightly purchases the pledge from the debtor, whether in keeping with the agreement at the outset, or as arranged subsequently. The sale too shall not be regarded as for value not ascertained, if it have been agreed that, upon the sum for interest not being discharged, the creditor is to retain the ownership by right of purchase, since the amount of principal and interest is ascertained up to the day appointed for the payment of the money.

[2] Since amongst other hazardous contracts the hardship increases in particular of the condition as to the default of pledgors, we consider it meet to extinguish the same, and entirely to abolish for the future the remembrance thereof.

[3] A pledge can be given upon the condition that, if the debt be not discharged within a certain time, the creditor shall by the title of purchaser possess the property, to be thereupon appraised according to its true value.

[4] If a contract have been made of *antichresis*, the creditor retains possession in lieu of the pledge until his money is repaid, whilst he takes the fruits as interest, either by way of lease or by his own harvesting and occupation.

Book III. Pt. I. Ch. I.

The same thing can, that is, be pledged to several creditors, either to each to the extent of a definite part (pro partibus), or to each as a whole (in solidum), and then again as between themselves at one time collaterally, at another by postponement. In the latter case an order of precedence exists between the several iura pignoris, so that the property in pledge is security primarily for the claim of the earlier pawnee,[a] and not until he is satisfied is it available as such for the claim of the second, third and so on following (posterior creditor); these latter, upon a sale of that which is in pawn, can alone look to the 'superfluum' over and above the earlier claim.

[a] 'Prior creditor potior in pignore.'

> Ulp.: Si debitor res suas duobus simul pignori obligaverit ita, ut utrique **in solidum** obligatae essent, singuli in solidum adversus extraneos Serviana utentur, inter ipsos autem si quaestio moveatur, possidentis meliorem esse condicionem; dabitur enim possidenti haec exceptio: **'si non convenit ut eadem res mihi quoquo pignori esset.'** Si autem id factum fuerit, ut **pro partibus** res obligarentur, utilem actionem competere et inter ipsos et adversus extraneos per quam partis possessionem adprehendant singuli. —D. 20, 1, 10.[1]

> Papinianus respondit . . . posse priorem[b] vendere, ut . . . quod superfluum ex anteriore

[b] Sc. creditorem.

---

[1] If a debtor has pledged his property to two persons at one time, in such way that it shall be pledged to both for the whole, they can individually avail themselves of the Servian action against strangers for the whole, but if a dispute arise between themselves, the possessor has the advantage, for the following plea will be given to him: 'Unless it have been settled that the same thing should be pledged also to me.' But if it has been settled that the property should be pledged by parts, an analogous action is available, both as between themselves and against strangers, in consequence of which each takes half the possession.

credito accepit, hoc secundo restituat.—l. 12, § 5, D. qui potior. 20, 4.[1]

The rank of the several iura pignoris is as a rule determined by the time when they were originated (conditioned by the existence of the claim, of the object pledged, and by the creative act). This is termed Priority.[a] The 'privileged' iura pignoris, however, form an exception to this: they take precedence over all iura pignoris in the same property, which arose either contemporaneously or previously. To such belong, *e.g.*, his pledge-right who has advanced money to procure or preserve the object of pledge; the pledge-right of the Treasury; the pledge-right of the married woman on account of her claim for dowry; the pledge-right of the ward against the guardian.

[a] 'Prior tempore potior iure.'

Gai.: Potior est in pignore, qui prior credidit pecuniam et accepit hypothecam, quamvis cum alio ante convenerat, ut, si ab eo pecuniam acceperit, sit res obligata, licet ab hoc postea accepit.—Videamus an idem dicendum sit, si sub condicione stipulatione facta hypotheca data sit, qua pendente alius credidit pure et accepit eandem hypothecam, tunc deinde prioris stipulationis existat condicio: ut potior sit qui postea credidisset. Sed vereor, num hic aliud sit dicendum. —l. 11 pr., § 1 eod.[b] [2]

[b] Cf. ibid. § 19 (*supr.*).

[1] Papinian answers, that the earlier creditor can sell, so that he account to the second creditor for what he receives over and above the earlier loan.

[2] He has a preferential claim in respect of security who was the first to advance his money and took a mortgage, even if an agreement had been before made with a third party, that if the debtor received money from such party, the property should be pledged to him, and notwithstanding that he did afterwards receive money from the latter.—Let us see whether the same is to be said if a mortgage has been created upon entering into a conditional stipulation, and whilst it is pending a third party has made an unconditional advance and taken the same mortgage-security, and thereupon the condition of the earlier stipulation is fulfilled, so that the subsequent creditor have a preferential claim. I fear we must in this case affirm the contrary.

Book III. Pt. I. Ch. I.

Imp. Ant.: Si decreto praetoris . . . in possessionem fundi . . . prius inducti estis, quam adversarius vester in causa iudicati eiusdem fundi pignus occupavit, . . . tempore potiores estis. Nam cum de pignore utraque pars contendat, praevalet iure, qui praevenit tempore.—l. 2, C. eod. 8, 17 (18).[1]

Marcian.: Si idem bis, i.e., ante secundum et post eum crediderit, in priore pecunia potior est secundo, in posteriore tertius est.—l. 12, § 3, D. eod.[2]

Ulp.: Interdum posterior potior est priore, ut puta si in rem istam conservandam impensum est quod sequens credidit, veluti si navis fuit obligata et ad armandam eam vel reficiendam ego credidero:—huius enim pecunia salvam fecit totius pignoris causam.—ll. 5 and 6, pr. eod.[3]

Imp. Diocl.: Licet . . . priores habeantur potiores, tamen eum, cuius pecunia praedium comparatum probatur; quod ei pignori esse specialiter statim convenit, omnibus anteferri iuris auctoritate declaratur.—l. 7, C. eod.[4]

The *posterior* creditor has towards the *prior* the 'ius

---

[1] If by a decree of the Praetor you have been installed in possession of a farm before your opponent, upon the ground of a judgment, has taken possession of the same farm as a pledge, you have a preferential claim according to time. For when both parties dispute about a pledge, he by law prevails who has been the first in point of time.

[2] If the same creditor has made two advances, *i.e.*, before and after a second creditor, he has precedence of the second creditor in respect of the first claim; he is third in respect of the other.

[3] Sometimes the later creditor has precedence of the earlier; for example, if the later advance has been laid out upon the preservation of the property: thus, if a ship had been pledged, and I have made an advance for the equipment or repair thereof; for the money of such a creditor has served for the maintenance of the whole security.

[4] Although earlier creditors are treated as preferential, it is nevertheless settled by legal authority that he with whose money the estate was demonstrably purchased, which it has been agreed at once should be a special security for it, has precedence of all.

offerendi,' *i.e.*, the right by settlement with such preceding creditor, or by effectual offer of such settlement, to take his place in respect of claim and pledge-right.[a]

[a] Cf. Story, § 635 (Grigsby, p. 415).

Marcian.: Cum secundus creditor oblata priori pecunia in locum eius successerit, venditionem ob pecuniam solutam et creditam recte facit.—l. 5 pr., D. de distr. pign.[1]

Imp. Sever.: Qui pignus secundo loco accepit, ita ius suum confirmare potest, si priori creditori debitam pecuniam solverit aut, cum obtulisset isque accipere noluisset, eam obsignavit et deposuit.—l. 1, C. qui potior.[2]

Si paratus est posterior creditor priori creditori solvere quod ei debetur, . . . nolente priore creditore pecuniam accipere, . . . dicimus priori creditori inutilem esse actionem, cum per eum fiat, ne ei pecunia solvatur.—l. 11, § 4, D. eod.[3]

The action supposes mortgage of the thing by him to whose property it appertained (owner, Publician possessor) to the plaintiff for a valid claim, the maturity of this (apart from pawn), and non-satisfaction of such claim.[b]

[b] D. 20, 4, 11, 4, *supra.*

Imp. Diocl.: Serviana actio declarat evidenter, iure pignoris teneri non posse, nisi quae obligantis in bonis fuerint; et per alium rem alienam invito

[1] When a second creditor through settlement with the first has succeeded to his position, he can lawfully proceed to the sale (of the pledge) for money paid and advanced.

[2] He that has taken a second pledge, can make his right available by paying the first creditor the amount owing, or, when he had offered it and the latter had refused to accept it, has sealed it up and deposited it.

[3] If the latter is ready to pay the earlier creditor the amount of his debt . . . and the earlier creditor declines to receive it, . . . we maintain that the action is of no avail to the first creditor, because it is the result of his own act that his money is not paid.

domino pignori obligari non posse, certissimum est.—C. 8, 15 (16), 6.[1]

Gai.: Quod dicitur creditorem probare debere, cum conveniebat, rem in bonis debitoris fuisse, ad eam conventionem pertinet, quae specialiter facta est, non ad illam ut . . . cetera etiam bona teneantur debitoris quae nunc habet et quae postea adquisierit.—l. 15, § 1, D. de pign.[2]

Paul.: Si ab eo, qui Publiciana uti potuit, quia dominium non habuit, pignori accepi, sic tuetur me per Servianam praetor, quemadmodum debitorem per Publicianam.—l. 18 eod.[3]

Marcian.: Si paciscatur creditor, ne intra annum pecuniam petat, intelligitur de hypotheca quoque idem pactus esse.—D. 20, 6, 5, 1.[4]

Its object is, restitution of the thing, and eventual condemnation of the defendant for the ‘litis aestimatio’; but the defendant can by settlement with the plaintiff avoid restitution, and then acquires, as legal possessor —and especially as owner—his claim and right under the pledge.

Id.: In vindicatione pignoris quaeritur, an rem de qua actum est possideat is cum quo actum est:

---

[1] The Servian action manifestly declares that nothing can be held by way of pledge but what has appertained to the property of the pledgor; and it is quite settled that an article belonging to another cannot be pledged by a third party without the consent of the owner.

[2] When it is said that the creditor must prove that the article was part of the debtor's property at the time the agreement was made, this concerns an agreement which was specially made, not such as would give (the creditor) control also of the rest of the goods of the debtor, (both) as in possession and as subsequently acquired by him.

[3] If I have taken aught as security from a person who could avail himself of the Publician action, as not having the ownership, the praetor protects me by the Servian action, in the same way as the debtor by the Publician.

[4] If a creditor by contract engage not to demand his money within one year, his engagement is understood to extend to the mortgage also.

> nam si non possideat nec dolo fecerit, quominus possideat, absolvi debet; si vero possideat, et aut pecuniam solvat aut rem restituat, aeque absolvendus est; si vero neutrum horum faciat, condemnatio sequetur.—l. 16, § 3, de pign.[1]
>
> Ulp.: Si res pignerata non restituatur, lis adversus possessorem erit aestimanda, sed utique aliter adversus ipsum debitorem, aliter adversus quemvis possessorem: nam adversus debitorem non pluris, quam quanti debet, quia non pluris interest; adversus ceteros possessores etiam pluris, et quod amplius debito consecutus creditor fuerit, restituere debet debitori pigneraticia actione.—l. 21, § 3 eod.[2]

If the defendant have a better or an equal pledge-right in the thing, he possesses an exceptio[a] against the actio hypothecaria, as on the other hand the cause of the preceding pawnee always prevails against the one following him when in possession.

[a] D. 20, 1, 10.

> Marcian.: Creditor, qui prior hypothecam accepit, sive possideat eam et alius vindicet hypothecaria actione, exceptio priori utilis est: **'si non mihi ante pignori hypothecaeve nomine sit res obligata,'** sive alio possidente prior creditor vindicet hypothecaria actione et

[1] In claiming a pledge, the question arises whether the defendant possesses the thing which has been pledged or not; for if he does not possess it, and has not fraudulently divested himself of the possession, he must be exonerated; but if he does possess it, and either pays the money or restores the thing, he must be exonerated all the same; if, however, he do neither of these, condemnation will ensue.

[2] If the security be not restored, damages must be assessed against the possessor, but there is of course a difference according as the claim is against the debtor himself or against any other possessor; for, as against the debtor, it is a matter of no greater amount than what he owes, because the damages cannot exceed that; against other possessors it goes somewhat further, and the creditor has by the action of Pledge to account to the debtor for what has come to his hands over and above the debt.

ille excipiat: **'si non convenit ut sibi res sit obligata,'** hic in modum supra relatum replicabit; sed si cum alio possessore creditor secundus agat, recte aget et adiudicari ei poterit hypotheca, ut tamen prior cum eo agendo auferat ei rem.—l. 12 pr., D. qui potior.[1]

§ 103. Termination of the Pledge-right.

The pledge-right is extinguished—

(1) by destruction of the object pledged.

Marcian.: Sicut re corporali extincta, ita et usufructu extincto pignus hypothecave perit.—l. 8, pr. D. h. t. (gb. mod. pign. 20, 6).[2]

Paul.: Si quis caverit, ut silva sibi pignori esset, navem ex ea materia factam non esse pignori Cassius ait, quia aliud sit materia aliud navis.—l. 18, § 3, D. de pign. act. 13, 7.[3]

Id.: Domus pignori data exusta est eamque aream emit L. Titius et exstruxit: quaesitum est de iure pignoris. Paulus respondit, pignoris persecutionem perseverare et ideo ius soli super-

---

[1] If the creditor that was the first to take a mortgage be in possession thereof, and another brings the hypothecary action, a plea is available to the former: 'If the property have not previously been pledged or mortgaged to me'; or if, another being in possession, the first creditor brings the hypothecary action, and the latter employs a plea, 'If there was not an agreement that the property should also be pledged to him,' the first creditor will put in a replication in the manner above mentioned; but if the second creditor proceed against another possessor, his proceedings are in order, and the property in mortgage will be adjudicated to him, so that nevertheless the first creditor, by an action against him, recovers the property from him.

[2] Just as a pledge or mortgage is destroyed by the extinction of a corporeal thing, so also is it by the extinction of a usufruct.

[3] If a man should provide for a forest being his security, Cass. says that a ship made from such wood is not subject to the pledge, because the wood is one thing, the ship another.

ficiem secutam videri, i.e. cum iure pignoris: sed bona fide possessores non aliter cogendos creditoribus aedificium restituere, quam (si) sumptus in exstructione erogatos, quatenus pretiosior res facta est, reciperent.—l. 29, § 2, D. de pign. 20, 1.[1]

(2) By 'confusio,'[a] *i.e.*, coalescence in the same person of the pledge-right and the ownership; but under certain circumstances the owner can make the pledge available by way of action and exceptio, where the pledge-right gives him better security as regards the thing than the proprietary right; as for instance, in relation to other pawnees; in which case also a pledge-right is possible without a claim.[b]

[a] Merger.

[b] Cf. § 102.

Iul.: Si rem alienam bona fide emeris et mihi pignori dederis, . . . deinde me dominus heredem instituerit, desinit pignus esse.—D. 13, 7, 29.[2]

Imp. Alex.: Si potiores creditores pecunia tua dimissi sunt, quibus obligata fuit possessio, quam emisse te[c] dicis, ita ut pretium perveniret ad eosdem priores creditores, in ius eorum successisti et contra eos, qui infirmiores illis fuerunt, iusta defensione te tueri potes.—C. 8, 18 (19), 3.[3]

[c] Sc. a debitore.

---

[1] A house given as security was burnt down, and L. T. bought the site, and built thereon: a question arose con-concerning the pledge-right. Paul. gave as his opinion that the pledge could still be followed, and that therefore what was built upon the ground was considered to pass with it, that is, with the pledge-right; that possessors in good faith can, however, be obliged to restore the building to creditors only upon condition that they recover their outlay upon the structure, to the extent of the increase effected in the value.

[2] If in good faith you have purchased a thing belonging to another, and have pledged it to me, . . . and afterwards the owner institutes me as heir, the pledge ceases to exist.

[3] If the previous creditors have been paid with your money, to whom a possession was pledged which you allege you have purchased, so that the purchase-money came to the hands of the same earlier creditors, you have succeeded to their place, and can protect yourself with a legal defence against such as were in a weaker position than they.

Book III. Pt. I. Ch. I.

[a] Cf. D. 46, 3, 49.

(3) By the complete cancelling of the mortgage-debt, whether by payment (solutio), or by other satisfaction of the creditor (satisfactio).[a]

Ulp.: Item liberatur pignus, sive solutum est debitum sive eo nomine satisfactum est.—l. 6 pr., D. h. t.[1]

Id.: Omnis pecunia exsoluta esse debet aut eo nomine satisfactum esse, ut nascatur pigneraticia actio. Satisfactum autem accipimus, quemadmodum voluit creditor, licet non sit solutum, . . . sive reo dato, sive pretio aliquo vel nuda conventione.—l. 9, § 3, D. de pign. act.[2]

Id.: Qui pignori plures res accepit, non cogitur unam liberare, nisi accepto universo, quantum debetur.—l. 19, D. de pign.[3]

(4) By contract of release (remissio pignoris), which may even be tacit.

Id.: Si in venditione pignoris consenserit creditor, vel ut debitor hanc rem permutet vel donet vel in dotem det, dicendum erit pignus liberari, nisi salva causa pignoris sui consensit vel venditioni vel ceteris.—l. 4, § 1, D. h. t.[4]

Et generaliter dicendum est, quotiens recedere

---

[1] Moreover the pledge is extinguished if the debt have been paid, or security given in that behalf.

[2] The whole claim must have been cleared off, or security given in that behalf, for the action of Pledge to arise. Now by security given we understand, in the way desired by the creditor, although payment may not have been made . . . whether by surety found, or by some purchase-money, or by bare agreement.

[3] He that has taken several things in pledge cannot be made to release a single one, save as he has received the whole of his debt.

[4] If the creditor has agreed to the sale of the pledge, or that the debtor should change the property so pledged, present it, or give it as a dowry, the pledge must be said to be discharged, unless he has consented either to the sale thereof, or the like, without prejudice to his pledge-right.

voluit creditor a pignore, videri ei satisfactum.—cit. l. 9, § 3.[1]

(5) By sale on the part of the pawnee entitled.[a]

(6) By Limitation.

(α) If the owner or usucapion possessor of the thing pledged has had the continued possession of such thing ten years 'inter praesentes,' twenty years 'inter absentes,' without knowing of the ius pignoris, this is extinguished (usucapio libertatis).

Pap.: Persecutio pignoris . . . usucapione rei non perimitur.—D. 41, 3, 44, 5.[2]

Imp. Gord.: Diuturnum silentium longi temporis praescriptione corroboratum creditoribus pignus persequentibus inefficacem actionem constituit, praeterquam si debitores vel qui in iura eorum successerunt, oblagatae rei possessioni incumbant.—C. 7, 36, 1.[3]

(β) The actio hypothecaria falls under prescription against the debtor and subsequent pledge-creditors in forty, against other possessors of the pledge in thirty, years; on the other hand, prescription of the claim under the pledge leaves the pledge-right intact.[b]

Id.: Intelligere debes vincula pignoris durare personali actione summota.—C. 8, 30 (31), 2.[4]

[a] § 102, ad init.

[b] § 114.

---

[1] And in general it must be stated that, whenever the creditor has cared to relax his hold upon the pledge, satisfaction would seem to have been rendered to him.

[2] The following of the pledge is not destroyed by usucapion of the property.

[3] Long-standing silence, supported by regular limitation, renders nugatory the action for creditors taking proceedings for their pledge, unless the debtors, or those who have entered into their rights, command possession of the security.

[4] Be it known that, although the personal action is extinguished, the obligations of the pledge still subsist.

CHAPTER II.

LAW OF Obligations.

Tit. I.—NATURE OF OBLIGATIONS.

§ 104. Essence of *Obligatio*.

Book III. Pt. I. Ch. II.

Obligatio is that legal relation between two persons by virtue of which the one, called 'debitor s. reus debendi,' is bound to the other, or 'creditor s. reus credendi,' for a definite PERFORMANCE of something bearing a pecuniary value, whereby the 'creditor' has, accordingly, a right to an act (facere, or non-facere) [b] by the 'debitor,' has a CLAIM (actio, also called obligatio) to it.[c]

[a] Best, but imperfectly, expressed in the language of Engl. Law by 'promisor' and 'promisee:' cf. Holl. p. 196

[b] Forbearance.

[c] Inst. iii. 13 pr.—Cf. 'Anct. Law,' pp. 323-4.

Paul.: Obligationum substantia non in eo consistit, ut aliquod corpus **nostrum** aut servitutem nostram **faciat**, sed ut alium nobis **obstringat** ad dandum aliquid vel faciendum vel praestandum.[d] —l. 3 pr. D. de O. et A. 44, 7.[1]

[d] Cf. § 105, and Holl. p. 181.

Gai.: **Creditorum** appellatione non hi tantum accipiuntur, qui pecuniam crediderunt, sed omnes, quibus ex qualibet causa debetur:—ut si cui ex empto vel ex locato vel ex alio ullo contractu debetur; sed et si ex delicto debeatur, mihi videtur posse creditoris loco accipi.—D. 50, 16, l. 11 (Gai.), and l. 12 (Ulp.)[2]

Mod.: **Debitor** intelligitur is, a quo invito exigi pecunia potest.—l. 108 eod.[3]

---

[1] The essence of an obligation does not consist in its making any material object our property, or a servitude ours, but in its binding another person to grant something, or to do or make good something in our favour.[e]

[e] Cf. Macleod, 'Theory and Practice of Banking,' p. 81.

[2] Under the designation 'creditors' are understood not only those who have lent money, but all to whom a debt is owing from whatever cause:—for example, if a debt be owing to any man from a purchase, or from a hiring, or upon the ground of any other contract; but even if it be owing upon a delict, it appears to me he can be regarded as a creditor.

[3] By 'debtor' is understood a person from whom money can be exacted against his will.

Octavenus: . . . ea in obligatione consistere, quae pecunia lui praestarique possunt.—D. 40, 7, 9, 2.[1]

As regards the declaration of will contained in the acceptance of an obligatio, and besides, the object of performance, reference must be made to the universal principles of law which avail for legal transactions in general.[a]

[a] §§ 18, 19.

Every obligatio is annexed to two definite subjects, from which it cannot be severed, since the object of the obligatio is an act that springs from individual determination.[b]

[b] § 144

OBJECT OF OBLIGATIONS.

§ 105. General View.

The performance constituting the object of obligation can either lie in 'dare,' *i.e.*, transfer of property, or origination of a servitude;[b] or in 'facere,'[c] that is, in other action or forbearance (obligationes dandi—faciendi). The 'praestare'[d] which is mentioned besides in the sources—of questionable meaning, perhaps merely pleonastic—falls under the category of 'facere,' and comprehends responsibility for those modifications which the original content of the obligation experiences from acts of the debtor or outward influences; for instance, the obligation to pay damages, and in general, any obligation for satisfaction, even in respect of 'obligationes ex delicto.'

[c] Cf. Sav. 'System,' v. p. 516, and note on p. 589.

[d] Ibid. p. 589.

[e] Ibid. iv. 101, note; v. 599.

Paul.: Stipulationum quaedam in **dando**, quaedam in **faciendo** consistunt.—l. 2 pr., de V. O. 45, 1.[2]

Non solum **res** in stipulatum deduci possunt,

---

[1] Octav. (used to say) . . . that the object of an obligation is that which can be redeemed and replaced by money.

[2] Some stipulations consist of giving, some of doing.

sed etiam **facta**: ut si stipulemur fieri aliquid vel non fieri.—§ 7, I. eod. 3, 15.[1]

Ulp.: Haec stipulatio: **fundum Tusculanum dari?** ostendit se certi esse continetque, ut dominium omnimodo efficiatur stipulatoris quoquo modo.—l. 75, § 10, D. eod.[2]

Id.: —Nemo rem suam utiliter stipulatur; . . . sane rem meam mihi restitui recte stipulari videor. —l. 82 pr. eod.[3]

Id.: —si quis faciendum aliquid stipulatus sit, ut puta fundum tradi vel fossam fodiri vel insulam fabricari, vel operas, vel quid his simile. —l. 72 pr. eod.[4]

Pomp.: **Faciendi** verbo reddendi etiam causa continetur.—D. 50, 16, 175.[5]

Paul.: **Facere oportere** et hanc significationem habet, ut abstineat quis ab eo facto, quod contra conventionem fierit, et curet ne fiat.—l. 189 eod.[6]

According as the object of the performance is one in all respects definite from the very first (certum) or

---

[1] Not only things, but also acts, can be made the object of a stipulation; as, if we stipulate for something to be done or not to be done.

[2] This stipulation: 'to give the Tusculan estate' proves that it belongs to those that are definite, and comprehends the complete vesting of the ownership in every way in the stipulator.

[3] No one makes a valid stipulation for his own property; . . . it certainly appears to me that I lawfully stipulate for the return to me of my property.

[4] If a man have stipulated for anything to be done, for example, for the delivery of an estate, or the digging of a ditch, or the construction of a house, or services, or aught like these things.

[5] Under the word 'do' is included also the case of 'giving up.'

[6] 'To have to do' has indeed the meaning, that a man refrain from such act as would be contrary to the agreement, and, that one take care it does not happen.

Book III. Pt. I. Ch. II.

one devoid of such certainty as to its pecuniary value, which has first to be ascertained (incertum), obligations are divided into those 'certi' (ae)—condictio certi,[a] and those 'incerti' (ae)—actio ex stipulatu (condictio incerti).[b] The 'faciendi obligatio' always contemplates an incertum; whilst the object of the 'dandi obligatio' can be either a certum or an incertum. Special examples of the incertum are generic performance—by which the object of obligation is not determined specifically, but merely according to genus—and, as a rule, that of which the determination admits of an alternative, *i.e.*, a voluntary one.

[a] 'Si paret dare oportere.'

[b] 'Quidquid paret dare facere oportere' (§ 198).

Gai.: Stipulationum quaedam certae sunt quaedam incertae: **certum** est, quod ex pronuntiatione apparet, quid quale quantumque sit, ut ecce aurei decem, fundus Tusculanus, homo Stichus, tritici Africi optimi modii centum, vini Campani optimi amphorae centum.—D. 45, 1, 74.[1]

Id.: —Ubi autem non apparet, quid quale quantumque est in stipulatione, **incertam** esse stipulationem dicendum est. § Ergo si qui fundum sine propria appellatione vel hominem generaliter sine proprio nomine, aut vinum frumentumve sine qualitate dari sibi stipulatur, incertum deducit in obligationem. . . . § Fundi certi si quis usumfructum stipulatus fuerit, incertum intelligitur in obligationem deduxisse: hoc enim magis iure utimur. . . . § Qui id, quod in faciendo vel non faciendo consistit, stipulatur, incertum stipulari videtur. . . . § Qui illud aut illud stipulatur veluti 'decem vel hominem Stichum,' utrum certum an incertum in obligationem deducat, non

[1] Of stipulations, some are determinate, others indeterminate: a determinate one is that which itself appears from the language, what it is, of what kind, and of what quantity; as, for instance, 10 gold-pieces, the Tusculan farm, the slave Stichus, 100 measures of the best African wheat, 100 jars of the best Campanian wine.

immerito quaeritur: nam et res certae designantur, et utra earum potius praestanda sit, in incerto est. Sed utcumque is qui sibi electionem constituit adiectis his verbis 'utrum ego velim,' potest videri certum stipulatus, cum ei liceat vel '**hominem**' tantum vel '**decem**' tantum intendere '**sibi dari oportere**': qui vero sibi electionem non constituit, incertum stipulatur.—l. 75 pr., §§ 1, 3, 7, 8 eod.[1]

Id.: —Si quis certum stipulatus fuerit, **ex stipulatu** actionem non habet, sed illa condicticia actione id persequi debet, per quam certum petimus.—D. 12, 1, 24.[2]

---

1 But where it is not clear what a thing is, of what kind, and of what quantity the object of the stipulation is, we must speak of it as an indeterminate stipulation. § If, therefore, a man stipulate for the conveyance to him of an estate without a particular designation, or of a slave in general without his proper name, or of wine or corn without (a specification of) the quality, he contracts an indeterminate obligation. . . . § If a man have stipulated for the usufruct of a definite parcel of land, he is taken to have contracted an indeterminate obligation; for this is the better rule, adopted by us. § He that makes a stipulation consisting of an act or forbearance is considered to make an indefinite stipulation. . . . § He that stipulates this or that, as, for example, 'ten [*aurei*] or the slave Stichus,' in respect of such the question not unjustly arises, whether he contracts a determinate or an indeterminate obligation; for although definite things be designated, yet it remains uncertain which of the two shall the rather be rendered. But at any rate one can suppose of him who has made his choice, by the addition of these words: 'Whichever of the two I like,' that he stipulates for something certain, since he is at liberty to apply 'that which must be given him' to the 'slave' only, or to the 'ten' only; but he that does not make his choice makes an uncertain stipulation.

2 If a man should have made a determinate stipulation, he has no action upon the stipulation, but he must take proceedings by that *actio condicticia* by which we sue for what is certain.

§ 106. Principal and Accessory Object. Interest.[a]

[a] Cf. Smith, 'Dicty. of Antiqq.' s. *Fenus*.

Besides the original and principal object of performance, the obligation may also comprise the increase thereof—natural or juristic products[b]—as accessory object. In particular, the debtor, if the obligation relates to a sum of money (or a quantity of other fungibles), has besides this, which is called Capital (sors, caput), often still to pay Interest (usurae, foenus) as an equivalent, represented by a percentage upon such capital, for the use of it allowed to the debtor or withdrawn from the creditor. The obligation to pay interest is always an addition to the principal obligation, with the discharge of which it is—at any rate for the future—*ipso facto* extinguished.[c] It rests either upon contract (usurae conventionales) or upon statutory provision and judicial disposition (usurae legales, iudiciales, i.e. quae officio iudicis praestantur), *e.g.*, interest charged in respect of delay. The latter occurs only in bonae fidei obligationes: the former both in these and in a stricti iuris obligatio, but in different forms. To ground an obligation to pay interest in a bonae fidei obligatio, there is need only of an informal collateral agreement, and it then constitutes (just as that which rests upon a legal precept) a mere extension of the principal obligation, but can also be made independently available by the action that arises upon it; whilst the principal contract can only be enforced in conjunction with it. On the other hand, in stricti iuris obligationes (*e.g.*, loan) an obligation to pay interest is originated only by an independent stipulatio, and it then forms the subject of a special—although accessory—obligation besides the principal obligation relating to the capital; and naturally, with the same result, a stipulatio for interest can be also contracted in respect of a bonae fidei obligatio.

[b] § 73.

[c] D. 46, 2, 18.

Imp. Gord.: Si deposita pecunia is qui eam suscepit usus est, non dubium est etiam usuras debere praestare. Sed si, cum deposita actione expertus es, tantummodo sortis facta condemnatio est, ultra non potes propter usuras experiri. Non enim duae sunt actiones, alia sortis alia usurarum, sed una, ex qua condemnatione facta, iterata actio rei iudicatae exceptione repellitur.—C. 4, 34, 4.[1]

Hermog.: Pretii sorte licet post moram soluta, usurae peti non possunt, cum hae non sint in obligatione, sed officio iudicis praestentur.—D. 19, 1, 49, § 1.[2]

Ulp.: Qui sortem stipulatur et usuras quascumque, certum et incertum stipulatus videtur; et tot stipulationes sunt, quot res sunt.—D. 45, 1, 75, 9.[3]

The rate of interest (modus usurarum) is the fractional relation between the interest and the capital lent, reckoned for a definite space of time (ordinarily a year). In the most ancient time interest amongst the Romans was reckoned according to the uncial system. Thus:

Unciarium foenus is 1 uncia for 1 as (= 12 unciae) pro anno, equal to $8\frac{1}{3}$ per cent. for the year of ten months, or 10 per cent. for that of twelve months.[a]

Semiunciarium foenus = 5 per cent.[b]

[a] § 22.

[b] § 147.

Later on the calculation was made according to monthly percentages—(Kalendaria, instrumentum Kal-

---

[1] If he that has received money upon deposit has made use of it, there is no doubt he must also find interest. But if, when you have taken proceedings by the action of deposit, condemnation has alone followed for the capital, you cannot proceed further on account of the interest. For there are not two actions, one for capital, the other for interest, but a single action; and if condemnation have resulted from this, a repeated action is met by the plea of *res iudicata*.

[2] If the principal have been paid, although after a delay, interest cannot be sued for, since this is not contained in the obligation, but is given[c] by the judicial authority.

[c] *I.e.*, if at all.

[3] He that stipulates for principal and any interest, is considered to stipulate for something definite and indefinite; and there are as many stipulations as there are objects.

-endarii) in which the centesimae usurae, *i.e.*, 1 per cent. per month, formed the unit of interest. Thus:

centesimae usurae was equal to 12 per cent.
semisses (sc. centesimae) = 6 per cent.
besses . . . . 8 . . . . .
trientes . . . . 4 . . . . . yearly.

In Christian imperial times the last-mentioned percentages were equal to $12\frac{1}{2}$, $6\frac{1}{4}$, $8\frac{1}{3}$, since from the solidus, which contained 24 siliquae, for the sake of convenience 3 siliquae were taken as centesimae usurae.

The legitimate maximum interest (usurae legitimae, maximae) was according to the Twelve Tables the unciarium foenus; later on it was centesimae usurae, and remained so even after many fluctuations down to the time of Justinian, who reduced it (subject to many exceptions) to semisses usurae.

The taking of interest was moreover checked by the prohibition of compound interest (anatocismus), and by the provision that arrears of interest should never increase and run on 'ultra duplum' (*i.e.*, beyond the amount of the capital lent).[a]

[a] D. 22, 1, 29.

Interest was often reserved in the form of a penal stipulation.

—'si die supra scripta summa P. Maevio . . . soluta non erit, tunc eo amplius, quo post solvam, poenae nomine in dies triginta inque denarios centenos denarios singulos dari stipulatus est P. Maevius, spopondi ego L. Titius.'—D. 12, 1, 40.[1]

Mod.: Poenam pro usuris stipulari nemo supra modum usurarum licitum potest.—D. 22, 1, 44.[2]

---

[1] If upon the above-written day the amount shall not have been paid by P. M. . . . then P. M. has stipulated, and I, Luc. Tit., have undertaken, that so much more shall be given as I shall pay later on, as punishment for thirty days, and for every hundred denarii one denarius.

[2] No one can, in lieu of interest, stipulate for a penal sum above the amount of interest permitted.

BOOK III. Pt. I. Ch. II.

§ 107. COMPENSATION FOR INJURY, AND DAMAGES.

DAMNUM is every detriment to property suffered by any one through some event. If this proceed from mere accident (casus), the person affected has, as a rule, no claim to compensation for the damage (casus a nullo praestantur; casum sentit dominus); still less if he himself is author of it. The legal ground of responsibility to make compensation for damage (damni praestatio) is either Contract or Tort. That is to say, a claim to compensation for damage exists—

(1) if a third party is under obligation to make reparation for harm done to property (praestatio periculi) by accident (or the act of another) as a result of special agreement (*e.g.*, in commodatum, or independent agreement by way of security) or positive rule of law.[a]

(2) If the harmful event can be referred to the illegal will of a third party.

In the first case, the compensation for damage can come into consideration as the original and sole object of the obligation; in the latter, it always does when the harmful act of the third party is one in itself illegal or disallowed (delictum). But it can also consist in violation of the special duty imposed upon him by an existing obligation (dolus, culpa, mora of the debtor, refusal to perform the obligation); and accordingly, the compensation for damage forms the consequential and immediate object of the obligation, because it either replaces the original object of performance, or is added to it, extending the principal performance of the debtor as a collateral object.

Since in Roman Law there is only a pecuniaria condemnatio,[b] and directly to compel performance of an obligation is not permitted, every obligation (not relating to a definite sum of money), whatever may be its original object, is, as a result of vicarious non-fulfilment and of judicial condemnation, converted into a claim to compensation for damage to property caused

[a] § 136, *actio de recepto.*

[b] § 197.

by the debtor, *i.e.*, to the extent of the pecuniary value of the performance originally owing (litis aestimatio).

> Pomp.: Quod quis ex culpa sua damnum sentit, non intelligitur damnum sentire.—D. 50, 17, 203.[1]
>
> Paul.: Nemo damnum facit, nisi qui id fecit, quod facere ius non habet.—l. 151 eod.[2]

The damage that a person suffers may—

(1) either diminish the already existing property in some constituent part,—Positive damage (damnum emergens), or preclude augmentation of the property, —Negative damage, intercepted augmentation (lucrum cessans).

> Paul.: —amisisse dicimur quod aut consequi potuimus aut erogare cogimur.—l. 33 pr., D. ad l. Aq. 9, 2.[3]
>
> Id.: Et sive quid amiserit vel lucratus non sit, restitutio facienda est, etiamsi non ex bonis quid amissum sit.—D. 4, 6, 27.[4]

(2) In both cases the damage may either be the direct result of the harmful event, or that which comes about through special individual circumstances (damnum directum—indirectum).

> Id.: Proinde si servum occidisti, quem sub poena tradendum promisi, utilitas venit in hoc iudicium.—Item causae corpori cohaerentes aestimantur, si quis ex comoedis, aut symphoniacis, aut gemellis, aut quadriga, aut ex pari mularum unum vel unam occiderit: non solum enim per-

---

1 When any man suffers damage in consequence of his own fault, he is not considered to suffer damage.

2 No one does damage save a person who did that which he has no right to do.

3 We are said to have lost what we either could have obtained or are obliged to expend.

4 And whether it be that a man has lost something or has not gained an advantage, restitution must be made, even if nothing has been lost from the property itself.

L L

Book III. Pt. I. Ch. II.

empti corporis aestimatio facienda est, sed et eius ratio haberi debet, quo cetera corpora depretiata sunt.—l. 22, D. ad l. Aq.[1]

Ulp.: Inde Neratius scribit, si servus heres institutus occisus sit, etiam hereditatis aestimationem venire.—l. 23 pr. eod.[2]

GROUNDS OF COMPENSATION FOR DAMAGE.

§ 108. *Dolus* and *Culpa*.

The obligation to atone for damage by reason of the tort supposes blame for the latter as attaching to the wrongdoer (culpa in the wider sense): the harmful result of the act or forbearance must admit of being altogether imputed to the author.[a] This culpability may consist either—

[a] D. 9, 2, 5, 1; Gai. iii. 211.

(1) in a positive intention directly contemplating the tort (dolus, deceit), or,

(2) in negative conduct, as regards the tort, which in violation of such person's duty leaves out of sight the possibility, foreseen or which could be foreseen, or probability of the illegal result of his act or forbearance (culpa in the narrower sense). Under the notion of Culpa falls both the lack of dutiful care and attention on the part of a person who has altogether failed to consider the illegal result of his act or forbearance, although this could have been foreseen (unconscious negligence, remiss-

[1] If, accordingly, you have killed a slave whom I, under a penalty, have promised to deliver, his usefulness comes into account in respect of this action.—Likewise bodily properties are at the same time appraised, *e.g.*, if any one has killed an actor, or a singing-boy, or a twin, or a horse from a team of four, or one of a pair of mules. For not merely must we put a value upon the body slain, but account must be taken of how much the rest have lost in value.

[2] Ner. therefore writes that if a slave has been killed who was instituted an heir, the value of the inheritance also comes into account.

ness, thoughtlessness)[a] and wantonness and levity (luxuria, lascivia) of him who incurs the blame of the act, in spite of his having foreseen the possible illegal result of it (conscious culpa).[b]

Paul.: Si putator ex arbore ramum cum deiiceret, hominem praetereuntem occidit, ita tenetur, si is in publicum decidat nec ille proclamarit, ut casus eius evitari possit. Sed Mucius etiam dixit, si in privato idem accidisset, posse de culpa agi: **culpam** autem esse, quod cum a **diligente providere potuerit, non esset provisum,** aut tum denuntiatum esset, cum periculum evitari non possit. . . . Quodsi nullum iter erit, dolum dumtaxat praestare debet, ne immittat in eum, quem viderit transeuntem: nam culpa ab eo exigenda non est, cum divinare non potuerit, an per eum locum aliquis transiturus sit.—D. 9, 2, 31.[1]

For torts induced by Dolus a person is always responsible.

Culpa, as ground of the obligation to make amends for damage, comes into account only—

(1) in respect of indirect damage to property by the wrongdoer, which engenders an independent obligatio ex delicto (damnum iniuria datum ex l. Aquilia)[c]—the so-called 'Aquilian culpa.' It here consists in illegal positive action (culpa in faciendo),

[a] See Campbell, 'Law of Negligence' (2nd ed.), pp. 2-3.

[b] See generally Austin, i. 441-3 (Stud's ed. pp. 211-12); Markby, ss. 679-685.

[c] § 133.

---

[1] If a wood-cutter by throwing down a branch from a tree kills a passer-by, he is only liable if the branch fall upon the public road and he has not called out, that its fall might be avoided. But Muc. says, besides, that proceedings could be taken for the negligence even if the same thing had happened on private ground, for that negligence consists in the non-exercise of precaution when such could have been taken by a careful person, or if notice was given when the danger could not be avoided. . . . But if there shall be no road there, compensation ought to be given for bad intention alone, so that the man do not cast the branch on one he sees passing by; for negligence does not attach to him, since he could not foresee whether any one was about to pass through such place.

Book III. Pt. I. Ch. II.

which already exhibits itself as the violation of the general duty of citizens 'alterum non laedere.'

(2) In obligatory relations, in which some one violates the special positive duty incumbent upon him to take some course of action on behalf of another, or to avert damage (diligentia, custodia). Here the Culpa may consist not merely in positive action, but also in forbearance (culpa in non faciendo, so-called 'extra-Aquilian culpa').[a]

[a] But see § 117.

Id.: Illud nulla pactione effici potest, ne dolus praestetur.—Pacta quae turpem causam continent, non sunt observanda: veluti si paciscar, ne furti agam vel iniuriarum, si feceris; . . . sed post admissa haec pacisci possumus.—D. 2, 14, 27, §§ 3–4.[1]

Ulp.: —ait Iulianus, tutores nisi bonam fidem in administratione praestiterint, damnari debere, quamvis testamento comprehensum sit, ut anec-logisti essent.—D. 26, 7, 5, 7.[2]

Marcian.: Si servus vetitus est a testatore rationes reddere, non hoc consequitur, ut ne quod apud eum sit reddat et lucri faciat, sed ne scrupulosa inquisitio fiat, hoc est ut neglegentiae ratio non habeatur, sed tantum fraudum.—l. 119, D. de leg. i. 30.[3]

---

1 It is impossible to contract oneself out of making compensation for *dolus*. . . . No heed is to be given to agreements which contain a disgraceful reason; for example, if I engage not to take proceedings upon a theft or for insults inflicted, if you shall commit such; . . . but after the commission thereof, we can enter into such engagements.

2 Jul. says that guardians must be condemned if they do not evince good faith in their management, although a provision be contained in the testament that they should not be accountable.

3 If a slave has by a testator been directed to render no account, the effect of this is, not that he should not account for and should profit by what is in his hands, but that no strict investigation be made, that is, that account be not taken of remissness, but only of fraud.

The so-called 'Aquilian culpa'—just as dolus and casus—admits of no gradation.

Ulp.: In lege Aquilia et levissima culpa venit.[a]—l. 43 pr., D. ad l. Aq.[1]

[a] Cf. Campbell, p. 23.

In contractual culpa, however, are distinguished two degrees, answering to the greater or less *diligentia* to be put forth: 'culpa lata'[b] and 'culpa levis.' Since 'culpa lata' in respect of responsibility is generally placed on the same footing as dolus,[b] it is ordinarily comprehended under this, so that culpa in juxtaposition, and in contrast, with dolus denotes 'culpa levis' (omnis culpa).

[b] Campbell, *ubi supra*; cf. Brown, s. 'Negligence.'

Paul.: Magna negligentia culpa est, magna culpa dolus est.—l. 226, D. de V. S. 50, 16.[c][2]

Ulp.: Culpa dolo proxima dolum repraesentat.—D. 47, 4, 1, 2.[3]

[c] Cf. D. 44, 7, 1, 5?

The standard by which the degree of culpa is determined is—

(1) an abstract, absolute, objective culpa. According to it, he is in culpa *lata* whose conduct is not marked by 'diligentia cuiusvis hominis,' and he in culpa *levi* who fails in 'diligentia boni ac diligentis patrisfamilias."

Ulp.: Lata culpa est nimia negligentia, id est non intelligere, quod omnes intelligunt.—l. 213, § 2, D. de V. S.[4]

Alf.: Si vendita insula combusta esset, cum incendium sine culpa fieri non possit, quid iuris sit? Respondit . . . si venditor eam diligentiam adhibuisset in insula custodienda, quam debent homines frugi et diligentes praestare, si quid

---

[1] In the *l. Aquilia* the very slightest negligence comes into account.

[2] Great neglect is *culpa*; great *culpa* is *dolus*.

[3] The negligence that comes nearest to *dolus* represents *dolus*.

[4] Gross *culpa* is excessive negligence—that is, not to know what all people know.

Book III. Pt. I. Ch. II.

accidisset, nihil ad eum pertinebit.—D. 18, 6, 12 (11).[1]

Gai.: —culpa autem abest, si omnia facta sunt, quae diligentissimus quisque observaturus fuisset.—D. 19, 2, 25, 7.[2]

Id.: In rebus commodatis talis diligentia praestanda est, qualem quisque diligentissimus paterfamilias suis rebus adhibet, ita ut tantum eos casus non praestet, quibus resisti non possit. —D. 13, 6, 18 pr.[3]

(2) But in certain obligatory relations, in the assumption of which special regard is had to the individuality of the other contracting party,[a] or into which any one gets without his own concurrence, the standard may also be a concrete, relative, subjective one (culpa in concreto). As such appears 'diligentia qualem suis rebus adhibere solet (s. diligentia quam suis),' *i.e.*, the care which the person concerned is wont to observe in his own affairs. By application of this concrete standard, the responsibility of the person may be curtailed, so that what would be culpa (levis) according to the abstract standard, here appears as conduct grounding no responsibility, and analogous to that of 'casus.' On the other hand, where in general responsibility is set up for culpa lata, the conduct of the debtor in his own affairs remains entirely without consideration, so that neither an otherwise culpa lata is here

[a] But cf. Cic. p. Rosc. Am. 38, 111.

---

[1] If a house that has been purchased should be burnt down, when a fire could not happen without negligence, what is the law? He replies . . . if the vendor has applied to the safekeeping of the house such care as upright and careful men ought to exercise, he will not be answerable for any accident.

[2] But *culpa* is absent if everything have been done which any thoroughly careful person would have attended to.

[3] In respect of things lent, such care has to be shown as any thoroughly careful head of a family applies to his affairs, so that he is not answerable for such mistakes as it is impossible to obviate.

treated in the concrete as lata,[a] nor could even the responsibility for lata culpa in the particular case be excluded by appeal to the 'nimia diligentia in suis.'[b]

[a] This is the opinion of the present writer, not according with that generally entertained.

[b] Cf. D. 23, 3, 17 pr.; 26, 7, 33 pr.

Paul.: Non tantum dolum sed et culpam in re hereditaria praestare debet coheres; . . . non tamen diligentiam praestare debet qualem diligens paterfamilias; . . . talem igitur diligentiam praestare debet, qualem in suis rebus.—D. 10, 2, 25, 16.[1]

Gai.: Socius socio etiam culpae nomine tenetur, id est desidiae atque negligentiae. Culpa autem non ad exactissimam diligentiam dirigenda est; sufficit etenim talem diligentiam communibus rebus adhibere, qualem suis rebus adhibere solet: quia qui parum diligentem sibi socium adquirit, de se queri debet.—D. 17, 2, 72. Cf. Inst. iii. 2, 5, 9.[2]

Cels.: Quod Nerva diceret latiorem culpam dolum esse, Proculo displicebat, mihi verissimum videtur. Nam et si quis non ad eum modum, quem hominum natura desiderat, diligens est, nisi tamen ad suum modum curam in deposito praestat, fraude non caret: nec enim salva fide minorem is, quam suis rebus diligentiam praestabit.—D. 16, 3, 32.[c] [3]

[c] Cf. D. 44, 7, 1, 5.

[1] A co-heir has to answer not only for *dolus*, but also for *culpa*, in respect of matters affecting the inheritance; . . . but he is not responsible for such care as that of the solicitous head of a family; . . . he must therefore be responsible for such diligence as he observes in his own affairs.

[2] One partner is liable to another for *culpa* also; that is, inattention and carelessness. But the *culpa* is not to be extended so as to mean the strictest carefulness; for it is enough that a partner use in partnership matters such care as he generally uses in his own affairs; because he that procures a partner not sufficiently careful has only himself to blame.

[3] What N. said, as to the more gross negligence being bad intention, was disapproved by P., (but) to me seems to be very true. For even if a man has not been diligent to the degree required

Book III. Pt. I. Ch. II.

The degree of culpa to be made good depends upon the nature of the particular obligations. The following rule is not without exceptions.

[a] Afr. probably refers to a sentence of Julian.

[b] Sc. creditoris.

> Afric.[a]: In contractibus fidei bonae servatur, ut si quidem utriusque contrahentis commodum versetur, etiam culpa: sin unius solius[b] dolus malus tantummodo praesetur.—l. 108, § 12, D. de leg. i. 30.[1]

§ 109. Mora.

[c] Bell, s. v. The 'laches' of English Law. —Cf. Aust. vol. i. pp. 490, *sq.* (Stud's ed. 1 p. 233, *sq.*).

Mora[c] is illegal, unjustified and inexcusable delay in the performance of an obligation, which may occur as well on the part of the debtor (mora solvendi—per debitorem stat, quominus solvat) as of the creditor (refusal of acceptance, mora accipiendi—per creditorem stat, quominus accipiat, si solvatur). 'Mora solvendi'—apart from actionability and maturity of performance—presupposes suitable reminder (interpellatio) of the debtor by the creditor;[d] 'mora accipiendi,' an appropriate offer (oblatio) of performance conformable to the obligation.

[d] Cf. D. 45, 1, 33.

> Marcian.: Mora fieri intelligitur non ex re sed ex persona, id est, si interpellatus opportuno loco non solverit.—l. 32 pr., D. de usur. 22, 1.[2]
>
> Scaev.: Nulla intelligitur mora ibi fieri, ubi nulla petitio est.—D. 50, 17, 88.[3]

---

by human nature, he is not innocent of fraud, unless at least he uses care in respect of the deposit up to his own standard; for without prejudice to good faith he will exhibit not less diligence than in his own affairs.

[1] In respect of contracts of good faith it is maintained that, where the benefit of both contracting parties is in question, so is *culpa* likewise; but if the benefit appertain to one alone, compensation is only given for fraud.

[2] Delay is regarded as arising not from the matter, but from the person, that is, if, upon being reminded at a seasonable place, he has not paid.

[3] No delay is considered to arise, where there is no claim.

The effect—

(1) of the mora in general is, responsibility to make full reparation for the injury (payment of the special value to the person).[a]

[a] § 110.

Ulp.: Si fundum certa die praestari stipuler et per promissorem steterit, quominus ea die praestetur, consecuturum me quanti mea intersit, moram factam non esse.—l. 114, D. de V. O. 45, 1.[1]

Marc.: In bonae fidei contractibus ex mora usurae debentur.—l. 32, § 2, D. de usur.[2]

Cels.: Si per emptorem steterit, quominus ei mancipium traderetur, pro cibariis per arbitrium indemnitatem posse servari Sextus Aelius, Drusus dixerunt.—D. 19, 1, 38, 1.[3]

Pomp.: Si per venditorem vini mora fuerit, quominus traderet, condemnari eum oportet, utro tempore pluris vinum fuit, vel quo venit vel quo . . . agatur.—l. 3, § 3 eod.[4]

(2) Of the mora *solvendi* in particular: the perpetuation of the obligation, *i.e.*, liability of the debtor for the casual destruction of the object of debt.

Paul.: —veteres constituerunt, quotiens culpa intervenit debitoris, perpetuari obligationem.—Effectus huius constitutionis ille est, ut adhuc homo peti possit, sed et acceptum ei posse ferri

---

[1] If I stipulate for the conveyance to me of land on a certain day, and it shall be the fault of the promisor that it is not conveyed on such day, I shall obtain as much as the amount of my interest in the nonoccurrence of delay.

[2] In contracts of good faith, interest is due upon the ground of delay.

[3] If delay in the delivery of a slave has been owing to the purchaser, S. A. and Drus. have stated that an indemnity for his maintenance can be assured by an award.

[4] If it have been through the seller of wine that the delivery thereof has been delayed, he must be condemned for it, at whichever time the wine was of the more value, whether when sold, or upon proceedings being taken.

BOOK III. Pt. I. Ch. II.

[a] Cf. Paul. v. 7, 4.

creditur et fideiussorem accipi eius obligationis nomine.—l. 91, §§ 3, 6, D. de V. O.[a] [1]

Ulp.: Si post moram promissoris homo decesserit, tenetur nihilominus proinde, ac si viveret.—l. 82, § 1 eod.[2]

(3) Of the mora *accipiendi:* release of the debtor by the casual destruction of the object of debt, if he hitherto had to bear the risk, and diminution of his liability for dolus and culpa lata.

Marc.: Qui decem debet, si ea obtulerit creditori et ille sine iusta causa ea accipere recusavit, deinde debitor ea sine sua culpa perdiderit, doli mali exceptione potest se tueri: . . . etenim non est aequum teneri pecunia amissa, quia non teneretur, si creditor accipere voluisset. Quare pro soluto id, in quo creditor accipiendo moram fecit, oportet esse.—D. 46, 3, 72.[3]

The mora is cured (purgatur) by appropriate offer (oblatio) of the performance owing, or by declaration of readiness to accept it. (Posterior mora nocet.)

Celsus adulescens scribit eum, qui moram fecit in solvendo Sticho quem promiserat, posse emendare eam moram postea offerendo.—cit. l. 91, § 3.[4]

---

[1] The older jurists have ruled that, whenever negligence intervenes on the part of the debtor, the obligation is perpetuated.—The effect of this rule is such that the slave can still be claimed, but it is held that an acquittance can be given to such person, and a surety be accepted for this obligation.

[2] Should the slave have died subsequent to the delay of the promisor, he is held liable no less than if such were alive.

[3] If he that owes ten *aurei* shall have offered them to the creditor, and he without just cause has declined to accept, and then the debtor by no fault of his has lost them, he can protect himself by the plea of bad intention; for it is not fair that he should be liable after the loss of the money, inasmuch as he would not have been liable if the creditor had been willing to receive it. Therefore that must pass for paid in respect of the acceptance of which the creditor has caused delay.

[4] Cels. the younger writes that a man who has caused delay

Imp. Diocl.: Sed ita demum oblatio debiti liberationem parit, si eo loco, que debetur solutio, fuerit celebrata.—C. 8, 42 (43), 9.[1]

Pomp.: Sed videndum est, ne posterior mora ei damnosa sit. Quid enim si interpellavero venditorem et non dederit id quod emeram, deinde postea offerente illo ego non acceperim? sane hoc casu nocere mihi deberet. Sed si per emptorem mora fuisset, deinde cum omnia in integro essent, venditor moram adhibuerit, cum possit se exsolvere, aequum est posteriorem moram venditori nocere.—D. 18, 6, 18 (17).[2]

§ 110. Estimate of the Compensation to be Rendered for Injury. Personal Interest.

Compensation for injury is afforded by the render of an amount by the which the property of the party injured would be greater if the harmful act or event had not occurred, or the obligation had been duly fulfilled.[a] This is Personal Interest (id quod interest: 'quidquid dare facere oportet'; 'quanti ea res est')[b] in the wider sense; at one time an original, at another consequential, at a third time collateral, object of the obligation.

[a] § 107.

[b] See formula in § 198.

Underlying the estimate, according to the difference of cases are—

---

in the release of Stichus, promised by him, can amend such delay by a subsequent tender.

[1] But the tender of the debt only operates a release if perfected at the place where payment is due.

[2] But it requires consideration whether subsequent delay be not prejudicial to him. For how if I have warned the vendor, and he has not made over what I had purchased, and, upon subsequent tender by him, I have not accepted it? In this case I would of course have to bear the loss. But if the delay have proceeded from the purchaser, and afterwards, when all was unimpaired, the purchaser has incurred delay, whilst he was in the position to fulfil his obligation, it is fair that his subsequent delay should cast the loss upon the vendor.

Book III. Pt. I. Ch. II.

(1) the general, material or market value of the object withdrawn or to be performed (vera rei aestimatio, verum rei pretium).

[a] Sc. in actione furti.

Ulp.: Haec verba:[a] QVANTI EAM REM PARET ESSE non ad id quod interest, sed ad rei aestimationem referuntur.—D. 50, 16, 193.[1]

(2) Or, as a rule, the special pecuniary value which it bears for the person injured (creditor): the Personal Interest, 'id quod interest' in the narrower sense, omnis utilatas; so that the reparation to be afforded comprehends both positive and negative, direct and indirect damage, provided that it stands in a casual connection with the harmful act or event, or non-fulfilment of the obligation.

Id.: Si res vendita non tradatur, in id quod interest agitur, hoc est quod rem habere interest emptoris; hoc autem interdum pretium egreditur, si pluris interest, quam res valet vel empta est.—D. 19, 1, 1 pr.[2]

Paul.: Cum per venditorem steterit, quominus rem tradat, omnis utilitas emptoris in aestimationem venit, quae modo circa ipsam rem consistit; neque enim, si potuit ex vino puta negotiari et lucrum facere, id aestimandum est.—l. 21, § 3 eod.[3]

(3) On the other hand, the so-called *pretium affectionis*, which is purely personal and not pecuniary, does not come into account.

---

[1] These words, 'As much as it appears is the value of such thing,' are not referable to the personal, but to the material value.

[2] If a thing that has been sold is not delivered, proceedings are taken for the value to the individual, that is, the value of its possession to the purchaser; now this sometimes exceeds the selling price, if more value is put upon it than the thing is worth or the purchase-money.

[3] When it shall be owing to the vendor that he does not deliver the thing, the whole advantage to the purchaser enters into the estimate, which only turns on the thing itself; for if he could trade and make gain with wine, for instance, that is not to be estimated.

Id.: Si servum meum occidisti, non affectiones aestimandas esse puto (veluti si filium tuum naturalem quis occiderit, quem tu magno emptum velles), sed quantum omnibus valeret. Sextus quoque Pedius ait, **pretia rerum non ex affectione . . . singulorum, sed communiter fungi**: itaque eum, qui filium naturalem possidet, non eo locupletiorem esse, quod eum plurimo, si alius possideret, redempturus fuit.—D. 9, 2, 33 pr.[1]

The personal interest is ascertained by evidence and judicial assessment, under certain conditions also by 'iuramentum in litem' (sworn assessment).[a]

[a] D. 6, 1, 68, and *infra*, § 137.

Marcian.: In actionibus in rem et in ad exhibendum et in bonae fidei iudiciis in litem iuratur.—Sed iudex potest praefinire certam summam, usque ad quam iuretur.—D. 12, 3, l. 5 pr., § 1.[2]

Paul.: Interdum quod intersit agentis solum aestimatur, veluti cum culpa non restituentis aut non exhibentis punitur; cum vero dolus aut contumacia non restituentis vel non exhibentis, quanti in litem iuraverit actor.—l. 2, § 1 eod.[3]

---

[1] If you have slain my slave, in my opinion no estimate is to be made of personal attachment (as, for instance, if any one has slain your natural son, whom you would have purchased for a high price), but only of such value as he possessed for anybody. S. P. also says that the value of things is estimated not according to the affection of individuals, but according to their general use; that, accordingly, a person who possesses a natural son is not better off by the fact that, if another possessed him, he would purchase him at a high price for himself.

[2] In real actions, and in those for production, and in actions of good faith, an oath of assessment is sworn. But the arbitrator can prescribe a certain sum to which the oath is directed.

[3] Sometimes merely the interest of the plaintiff is assessed, as when a fault of the person who does not make restitution or does not produce is punished, but if the bad intention, or the disobedience of him who does not make restitution, or does not produce (is punished, the assessment is made for as much) as the plaintiff shall have estimated it upon oath.

§ 111. Subjects of Obligation, in General.

Every obligation is a legal relation between two persons[a] who stand in the relation to one another of Debtor and Creditor.[b] But their standing towards each other can be diverse.

[a] See note on § 32, ad init.
[b] See note on § 104, ad init.

(1) One person can be Creditor alone, the other merely Debtor, which is a UNILATERAL obligation. Such are all obligationes *ex delicto*, and such obligations arising from legal transactions as are *stricti iuris* (*e.g.*, Loan, stipulatio).

(2) Each person can be at the same time Creditor and Debtor, which is a BILATERAL obligation. Such are all *bonae fidei* obligationes.[c]

[c] § 24.

Again, the bilateral relation is diverse.

(*a*) It finds its grounds in the essence of the obligation in question, which is a necessary, essentially bilateral, or mutual obligation, *ultro citroque* obligatio—so that each of the two subjects is always and necessarily Creditor and Debtor, and the claims and duties on both sides, or performance and counter-performance, cross one another and condition each other. Examples of this are afforded by Sale and Partnership.

(β) Or it rests upon casual circumstances, so that one is originally and essentially the Creditor, the other is Debtor, but the latter can have casual and secondary counter-claims upon the former, which do not touch the essence of the obligation. These relate to indemnification (*e.g.*, for outlay), and necessarily are made available by an actio contraria (cross action) flowing out of the contract: imperfect, bilateral, or unilateral obligations with an actio contraria (*e.g.*, mandate, commodatum).

In most cases there is on one side a single debtor, and on the other a single creditor; but there can also be a plurality of subjects, upon the active or the passive side. And herein we have to distinguish the following cases.

Each of several creditors or debtors has to require, or to perform, a share of the object that is owing and is juristically divisible; which is an 'obligatio plurium pro parte s. rata.' Here are, accordingly, as many separate obligations as creditors or debtors (*e.g.*, several heirs).[a]

[a] § 174, ad fin.

Each of several creditors or debtors has besides the other to require, or to perform, the same whole object (or its aestimatio), which is an 'obligatio in solidum' in the wider sense (*e.g.*, in the obligation to pay a penalty arising from delict, and further, if the same whole thing has been bequeathed to several).[b] Here also there are as many independent individual obligations as there are creditors or debtors.

[b] § 134, and Ulp. xxiv. 12.

> Tryph.: Si tutores rem pupilli furati sunt, videamus, an . . . singuli in solidum teneantur et, quamvis unus duplum praestiterit, nihilominus etiam alii teneantur: nam in aliis furibus eiusdem rei pluribus non est propterea poenae deprecatio, quod ab uno iam exacta est.—D. 26, 7, 55, 1.[1]

Each of several debtors has to perform the same object, but by performance on the part of one the obligation of the others is cancelled, which is 'obligatio in solidum' in the narrower sense, a bare SOLIDARY obligation. An example of this is the responsibility of several to make compensation arising out of a common delict or quasi-delict, or out of the breach of a contract entered into in common. Here in fact likewise occur several independent obligations, which are only linked together through the identity of the object owing.

> Ulp.: Si plures in eodem coenaculo habitent,

---

[1] If the guardians have purloined the property of the wards, we must see whether all are liable for the whole, and whether, although one has performed the double, the others notwithstanding are liable also; for in respect of several other thieves of the same thing, a penalty is not to be averted because it has already been exacted from one.

unde deiectum est, in quemvis haec actio dabitur, —et quidem in solidum. Sed si cum uno fuerit actum, ceteri liberabuntur—**perceptione**, non litis contestatione.—D. 9, 3, l. 1, § 10, l. 3 (Ulp.) and l. 4 (Paul.).[1]

Ulp. : Si apud duos sit deposita res, adversus unum quemque eorum agi poterit; nec liberabitur alter, si cum altero agatur: non enim electione sed **solutione** liberantur. Proinde si . . . alter quod interest praestiterit, alter non convenietur exemplo duorum tutorum.—D. 16, 3, 1, 43.[2]

But finally, an obligation may relate wholly and inseparably to several subjects, so that there is but a single performance in obligatione, and each of the several creditors or debtors stands related to the common debtor or creditor just as if he were the only creditor or debtor; and so one speaks of CORREAL obligation, whether active or passive, the subjects of which are described as duo (s. plures) rei *credendi* (s. stipulandi) *debendi* (s. promittendi) or *correi*. Correal obligations necessarily presuppose a single originative act, and always depend upon a legal transaction, either a contract (especially stipulatio) or testamentary provision. They are essentially distinguished from the purely solidary obligations by the fact, that the claim or obligation of the rest is discharged not merely by a single performance of the object owing, but already by litis contestatio with the one creditor or debtor.

---

[1] If several persons live in the same loft, from which something has been thrown out, this action will lie against all,—and that for the whole. But if proceedings have been taken against one, the rest shall be discharged—by satisfaction, not by the joinder of issue.

[2] If a thing shall have been deposited with two persons, proceedings will be available against each of them; and the one will not be released if the proceedings be taken against the other, for they are not released by (such) choice, but by performance. Accordingly, if one shall have made good the damages, the other will not be sued, by the analogy of two guardians.

Iavol.: Cum duo eamdem pecuniam aut promiserint aut stipulati sint, ipso iure et singulis in solidum debetur et singuli debent; ideoque petitione, acceptilatione unius tota solvitur obligatio.—l. 2, D. h. t. (de duob. r. 45, 2).[1]

Venulei.: Si duo rei stipulandi sint, . . . convenit et uni recte solvi et unum iudicium petentem totam rem in litem deducere, item unius acceptilatione perimi utrisque obligationem: ex quibus colligitur unumquemque perinde sibi adquisiisse, ac si solus stipulatus esset, excepto eo, quod etiam facto eius, cum quo commune ius stipulantis est, amittere debitorem potest.—D. 46, 2, 31, 1.[2]

Ulp.: Ubi duo rei facti sunt, potest vel ab uno eorum solidum peti; . . . et partes autem a singulis peti posse nequaquam dubium est.—l. 3, § 1, D. h. t.[3]

Pomp.: Cum duo eandem pecuniam debent, si unus capitis deminutione exemptus est obligatione, alter non liberatur; multum enim interest, utrum res ipsa solvatur an persona liberetur: cum persona liberatur manente obligatione, alter durat obligatus.—l. 19 eod.[4]

---

[1] When two persons have either promised or stipulated for one and the same sum, each individual is both entitled to and liable for the whole by the very operation of law; and so the whole obligation is discharged by the demand or the acquittance of one.

[2] If there are two correal creditors . . . it is settled that payment can be rightly made to one, and that one, if he claim an action, makes the whole matter actionable; and likewise by the acquittance of one the claim of both is destroyed. From which we gather, that each has also acquired for himself as if he alone had stipulated, with the exception that the promisee can forfeit the debtor by the act also of him with whom he has a right in common.

[3] Where two debtors have been constituted, the whole can be claimed even from one of them; . . . now there is no doubt whatever that parts also can be claimed from the individual debtors.

[4] When two owe the same sum, if one has been released from

Book III. Pt. I. Ch. II.

Et stipulandi et promittendi duo pluresve rei fieri possunt; **stipulandi** ita, si post omnium interrogationem promissor respondeat 'spondeo': ut puta cum duobus separatim stipulantibus ita promissor respondeat 'utrique vestrum dare spondeo'; nam si prius Titio spoponderit, deinde alio interrogante spondeat, alia atque alia erit obligatio nec creduntur duo rei stipulandi esse. Duo pluresve rei **promittendi** ita fiunt [veluti si ita interrogati]: 'Maevi, quinque aureos dare spondes? Sei, eosdem quinque aureos dare spondes?' respondeant singuli 'spondeo.'—pr. I. eod. 3, 16.[1]

Pap.: —fiunt duo rei promittendi . . . testamento: ut puta si pluribus heredibus institutis testator dixit 'Titius aut Maevius Sempronio decem dato.'—l. 9 pr., D. h. t.[2]

Cels.: Si 'Titio aut Seio utri heres vellet,' legatum relictum est, heres alteri dando ab utroque liberatur; si neutri dat, uterque perinde petere potest, atque si ipsi soli legatum foret: nam ut

---

the obligation by a loss of status, the other is not released; for it makes a great difference whether the debt itself is extinguished, or whether the person is released. When [one] person is released, but the obligation is kept up, the other remains liable.

[1] Two or more persons can take part in the act of stipulation and promise. In stipulation, in such way that the promisor to the question of all makes answer, 'I do engage';[a] for example, if the promisor answers two persons stipulating independently of one another: 'I engage to convey to each of you.' For if he has first given the undertaking to Titius, and afterwards upon the inquiry of another, to him also, the obligations will be different; and it is not considered that two persons take part in the stipulation. Two or several persons can participate in the act of promise as follows: 'Do you, Maevius, engage to give five gold-pieces?' 'Do you, Seius, also engage to give five gold-pieces?' Each must answer, 'I do engage.'

[a] Or 'vow': see § 117, ad init.

[2] Two persons become liable by the promise . . . in a testament; for instance, if the testator after instituting several heirs, has said: 'Titius or Maevius shall pay ten [gold-pieces] to Sempronius.'

stipulando duo rei constitui possunt, ita et testamento potest id fieri.—l. 16, D. de leg. ii. 31.[1]

Book III. Pt. I. Ch. II.

BEARING OF OBLIGATIONS UPON THIRD PARTIES.

§ 112. Rights and Liabilities from Contracts of Third Parties.[a]

[a] Cf. Pollock, 'Cont.,' p. 186. —Upon Representation, see Savigny, 'Obligationenrecht,' §§ 54-59.

In keeping with the essence of the obligation, as an individual relation between two definite subjects, the Roman Law imposes the following rules.

(1) Representation[b] is not allowed in the contracting of obligations. Every obligation is operative alone as between the persons who have created it, so that by it a third person can become neither creditor nor debtor.

[b] § 20.

Paul.: Quaecumque gerimus, cum ex nostro contractu originem trahunt, nisi ex nostra persona obligationis initium sumant, inanem actum nostrum efficiunt; et ideo neque stipulari neque emere vendere contrahere, ut alter suo nomine recte agat, possumus.—D. 44, 7, 11.[2]

If the performance be placed directly to the name of the third party, the obligation itself is invalid.

Ulp.: Alteri stipulari nemo potest, praeterquam si servus domino, filius patri stipuletur: inventae sunt enim huiusmodi obligationes ad hoc, ut unusquisque sibi adquirat quod sua interest; ceterum ut alii detur, nihil interest

[1] If a legacy has been left to 'Titius or Seius, at the discretion of the heir,' the heir by payment to one is discharged by both; if he pay neither, both can sue just as if the bequest had been made to himself alone; for just as there can be two joint creditors constituted by a stipulation, so too this can happen by a testament.

[2] Whatever we undertake, if it arise from our contract, makes our act of none effect unless the obligation originate from us personally; and thus we can neither make a stipulation, purchase, sale, contract, so that another lawfully sue thereon in his own name.

Book III. Pt. I. Ch. II.

mea. Plane si velim hoc facere, poenam stipulari conveniet, ut, si ita factum non sit, ut comprehensum est, committatur stipulatio.—l. 38, § 17, D. de V. O. 45.[1]

Gai. iii. § 103: Quaesitum est, si quis sibi et ei, cuius iuri subiectus non est, dari stipuletur, in quantum valeat stipulatio? Nostri praeceptores putant in universum valere et proinde ei soli, qui stipulatus sit, solidum deberi atque si extranei nomen non adiecisset: sed diversae scholae auctores dimidium ei deberi existimant, pro altera vero parte inutilem esse stipulationem.[2]

Si quis alium daturum facturumve quis spoponderit, non obligabitur, veluti si spondeat 'Titium quinque aureos daturum.'—§ 3, I. de inut. stip. 3, 19.[3]

At si quis velit factum alienum promittere, poenam potest promittere.—l. 38, cit. § 2.[4]

But the right can already by the contract be accorded to the debtor of performance to a definite

---

[1] No one can stipulate for another, except it be a slave that stipulates for his master, a son for his father; for obligations of this kind have been invented for the purpose of every one acquiring what concerns his own advantage; but that it be given to another is of no advantage to me. Clearly if I wish to effect this, it will be meet for me to stipulate for a penalty, so that, if the thing be not done as was intended, the stipulation shall take effect.

[2] The question has arisen, how far is the stipulation valid, if a person stipulate for a sum to be paid over to himself and to one to whose power he is not subjected? Our teachers consider that it is good for the whole amount, and, accordingly, that the whole is due to the promisee alone, just as if he had not added the name of a stranger. But the authorities of the opposite school think that a moiety is due to him, that as far as the other half is concerned, however, the stipulation is void.

[3] If a man have engaged that another shall do or give anything, he will be under no obligation; for example, if he have engaged that Tit. shall give five *aurei*.

[4] But if a man would promise an act done by another, he can promise a penalty.

third person instead of to the creditor (solutionis causa adiectus), who, however, himself has no right of claim.

Si quis alii, quam cuius iuri subiectus sit, stipuletur, nihil agit; plane solutio etiam in extranei personam conferri potest (veluti si quis ita stipuletur 'mihi aut Seio dare spondes?'), ut obligatio quidem stipulatori adquiratur, solvi tamen Seio etiam invito eo recte possit, ut liberatio ipso iure contingat, sed illo adversus Seium habeat mandati actionem.—§ 4, I. de inut. stip.[1]

If the operation of an obligatory agreement is to affect a third party, it can only extend to such party indirectly through transfer of the claim or obligation that has arisen, by way of cession[a] or delegation.[b]

(2) By the obligations of slaves and persons under domestic dependence, the patresfamilias are directly and necessarily entitled, yet not bound.[c]

Inst. iii. 17, § 1: Sive autem domino suo sive sibi sive conservo sive impersonaliter servus stipuletur, domino adquirit. Idem iuris est in liberis, qui in potestate patris sunt.[2]

Iul.: Servus vetante domino si pecuniam ab aliquo stipulatus sit, nihilominus obligat domino promissorem.—l. 62, D. de V. O.[3]

[a] § 144.

[b] § 142.

[c] §§ 50, 88.

---

[1] If a man stipulate for another than him to whose authority he is subjected, his act is void. It is clear that provision can be made for payment to a stranger (*e.g.*, if a man stipulate thus: 'Do you undertake to make payment to me or Seius?'), so that the benefit of the obligation indeed is acquired for the stipulator; to Seius, however, payment can lawfully be made even against the will of the stipulator, so that a release attaches by virtue of law, but the stipulator has against Seius the action of agency.[d]

[d] § 125.

[2] Now whether a slave stipulate for his master, or for himself, or a fellow-slave, or without designation of a person, he acquires for his master. The same holds also of children that are under the power of their father.

[3] If a slave has stipulated for money from another against

Book III. Pt. I. Ch. II.

Gai.: Melior condicio nostra per servos fieri potest, deterior fieri non potest.—D. 50, 17, 133.[1]

From this rule there arose in course of time many exceptions, especially with regard to liability through others.

In cases where the representation is derived from a public office (*e.g.*, guardianship) even without formal transfer, actions were upon termination of the office given, as utiles actiones, alone to and against the representative, upon the obligations entered into by him.[a]

[a] § 205, ad init.

Imp. Iust.: Invenimus generaliter definitum, post officium depositum omnes actiones, quas tutor vel curator ex necessitate officii subierit, in quondam pupillum vel adultum transferri.—C. 5, 37, 26, 3.[2]

Imp. Alex.: Etsi tutores tui, cum pecuniam pupillarem crederent, ipsi stipulati sunt, utilis actio tibi datur.—C. 5, 39, 2.[3]

It was accessorily that the paterfamilias (or the person represented) was under certain presumptions rendered liable by the contractual obligations of slaves and persons subject to power; in one case also a free representative. The Praetorian Edict gave against him the common actions arising out of the obligation entered into by a persona subiecta (or the representative) with an addition in the formula,[b] as collateral actions. The

[b] § 201.

---

the command of his master, he nevertheless binds the promisor to the master.

[1] Our position can be made better by slaves, but cannot be made worse.

[2] We find as a general rule that, upon laying down his office, all actions which the guardian or curator undertook by the requirements of the office pass to the former ward or minor.

[3] Even if thy guardians, upon lending out the ward's money, contracted a stipulation in their own name, an analogous action will be granted to thee.

following are the several cases of these so-called 'actiones adiectitiae qualitatis.'

(1) As an actio *quod iussu* is the action given against the paterfam., if any one has concluded the contract with the slave or filiusfam. by virtue of special authorisation or behest of such paterfam.

Gai. iv. § 70: In primis itaque si iussu patris dominive negotium gestum erit, in solidum praetor actionem in patrem dominumve comparavit: et recte, quia qui ita negotium gerit, magis patris dominive quam filii servive fidem sequitur.[1]

Ulp.: 'Iussum' autem accipiendum est, sive testato quis sive per epistulam sive verbis aut per nuntium, sive specialiter in uno contractu iusserit sive generaliter.—D. 15, 4, 1, 1.[2]

(2) As an actio *de peculio*, the action upon the contracts of the person under domestic dependence who possesses a peculium[a] lies against the paterfam. or master, so far as the peculium extends to such person after withdrawal of the claims of the paterfam.[b]

[a] § 149.

[b] D. 15, 1, 42.

Iust. iv. 6, § 36: Sunt praeterea quaedam actiones, quibus non solidum quod debetur nobis persequimur, sed modo solidum consequimur, modo minus: ut ecce si in peculium filii servive agamus. Nam si non minus in peculio sit, quam persequimur in solidum pater dominusve condemnatur; si vero minus inveniatur, eatenus condemnat iudex, quatenus in peculio sit.[3]

---

[1] In the first place, then, if any business has been transacted by the order of the father or master, the Praetor has provided an action against the father or master for the full amount; and rightly, because he that so contracts relies rather upon the credit of the father or master than upon that of the son or slave.

[2] Now 'ordered' must be taken to be, if a man by a testament, or by a letter, or by words, or a messenger, or especially in an individual contract, has made some direction, or in general.

[3] Moreover, there are some actions by which we do not recover the whole that is owing to us, but at one time we obtain the whole, at another less; as for instance, if we sue for the separate

Gai.: Etiam si prohibuerit contrahi cum servo dominus, erit in eum de peculio actio.—l. 29, § 1, D. de pec. 15, 1.[1]

Cum autem quaeritur, quantum in peculio sit, ante deducitur, quidquid servus domino, quive in potestate eius sit, debet, et quod superest id solum peculium intelligitur.—§ 4[c], I. h. t. (qu. c. eo. 4, 7).[2]

Ulp.: Si quis cum filiofamilias contraxerit, duos habet debitores: filium in solidum et patrem dumtaxat de peculio.—l. 44, de pec.[3]

Id: Quamdiu servus vel filius in potestate est, de peculio actio perpetua est; post mortem autem eius, vel postquam emancipatus manumissus alienatusve fuerit, temporaria esse incipit, i.e. annalis. —D. 15, 2, 1, 1.[4]

(3) With the actio *de in rem verso* the paterfam. is responsible to the creditor of the persona subiecta, and so far as the property of the former has been enriched by the creditor's performance to such person, *i.e.*, has been immediately increased, or a diminution of it has been prevented.

In rem autem domini versum intelligitur,

---

property of a son or slave. For if the separate property does not amount to less than we claim, the father or master is condemned for the whole, but if it is found to be less, the judge condemns to the extent of the separate property.

1 Even if the master has forbidden contracting with his slave, an action will lie against him in respect of the separate property.

2 But when it is a question of the amount of the separate property, all is first subtracted which the slave owes to his master or the person under his power, and only the residue is considered separate property.

3 If any one have contracted with a *fil. fam.*, he has two debtors, the son for the whole, and the father at least as regards the *peculium*.

4 As long as a slave or a son is under power, the action concerning separate property is perpetual, but after his death or after his emancipation, manumission or sale, it begins to be temporary, that is, annual.

quidquid necessario in rem eius impenderit servus: veluti si mutuatus pecuniam creditoribus eius solverit, aut aedificia ruentia fulserit, aut familiae frumentum emerit, vel etiam fundum, aut quamlibet aliam rem necessariam mercatus erit.—Itaque si ex decem utputa aureis, quos servus tuus a Titio mutuos accepit, creditori tuo quinque aureos solverit, reliquos vero quinque quolibet modo consumpserit, pro quinque quidem in solidum damnari debes, pro ceteris vero quinque eatenus, quatenus in peculio sit: ex quo scilicet apparet, si toti decem aurei in rem tuam versi fuerint, totos decem aureos Titium consequi posse; licet enim una est actio, qua de peculio deque eo quod in rem domini versum sit agitur, tamen duas habet condemnationes.—§§ 4^a, 4^b, I. h. t.[1]

Gai. iv. § 74: Eadem formula et de peculio et de in rem verso agitur.[2]

(4) Creditors of a person under domestic dependence who carries on commercial transactions with his own property, with the foreknowledge (patientia) of the paterfam., have the 'actio tributoria' against the paterfam. for division of the trade-property pro rata of their claims and those

---

[1] Now everything is regarded as having turned to the master's profit which the slave has necessarily laid out over his property; as for instance, if the slave has borrowed money and paid his master's creditors, or propped up his dilapidated buildings, or has purchased corn for his household, or even land, or has purchased some other necessary thing.—Therefore if out of say, ten *aurei*, which your slave borrowed from Tit., he has paid five to your creditor, but has expended the rest in some way, you ought to be condemned in respect of the five *aurei* for the payment of the whole, in respect of the other five to the extent of the separate property. Hence of course it appears that, if the whole of the ten *aurei* have turned to your profit, Tit. can recover them all; for although there is but one action wherewith to sue for the separate property and the amount that has turned to the master's profit, yet it commands two condemnations.

[2] It is by one and the same formula that one sues *de peculio* and *de in rem verso*.

of the pat. fam.; the latter are in this case not previously subtracted.

Introduxit et aliam actionem praetor, quae tributoria vocatur. Namque si servus in peculiari merce sciente domino negotietur et quid cum eo eius rei causa contractum erit, ita praetor ius dicit, ut quidquid in mercibus erit quodque inde receptum erit, id inter dominum, si quid ei debebitur, et ceteros creditores pro rata portione distribuatur; et quia ipsi domino distributionem permittit, si quis ex creditoribus queratur, quasi minus ei tributum sit quam oportuerit, hanc ei actionem accommodat.—Is quoque, cui tributoria actio competit, aeque de peculio et in rem verso agere potest; sed sane huic modo tributoria expedit agere, modo de peculio et in rem verso. Tributoria ideo expedit agere, quia in ea domini condicio praecipua non est, i.e. quod domino debetur non deducitur, sed eiusdem iuris est dominus, cuius et ceteri creditores; . . . rursus de peculio ideo expedit agere, quod in hac actione totius peculii ratio habetur, at in tributoria eius tantum, quod negotiatur, et potest quisque tertia forte parte peculii aut quarta vel etiam minima negotiari, maiorem autem partem in praediis aut mancipiis aut foenebri pecunia habere.—§§ 3, 5, I. h. t.[1]

[1] The Praetor has introduced yet another action, which is called the 'tributorian.' For if a slave with the privity of his master trade with his own wares, and a contract has been made with him in relation to such property, the Praetor decides that the whole stock of such wares and what has been derived from them shall be divided between the master, if aught shall be owing to him, and the rest of the creditors in the proportion of their shares; and inasmuch as he allows the master himself to make the distribution, if any creditor complain that less has been assigned to him than ought to be, the Praetor provides this action for him.—And he to whom the *actio tributoria* is available can in like manner sue concerning his separate property and what has turned to the profit of the master; but it is certainly of advantage for him to sue sometimes by the tributorian action,

(5) As 'exercitoria' and 'institoria' actio is given the action upon contracts which anyone has concluded with a magister navis (ship's representative, captain) or institor (factor, *i.e.*, appointed for a certain business transaction), within the limits of their authority; and the same whether he be a person under dependence or free; and this is given against the exercitor (shipowner) or dominus (principal) by whom they have been appointed.

Gai. iv. § 71: Tunc autem **exercitoria** locum habet, cum pater dominusve filium servumve magistrum navis praeposuerit, et quod cum eo eius rei gratia, cui praepositus fuit, negotium gestum erit; . . . quin etiam licet extraneum quis quemcumque magistrum navis praeposuerit, sive servum sive librum, tamen ea praetoria actio in eum redditur; ideo autem exercitoria actio appellatur, quia exercitor vocatur is, ad quem quottidianus navis quaestus pervenit. **Institoria** vero formula tum locum habet, cum quis tabernae aut cuilibet negotiationi filium servumve aut quemlibet extraneum, sive servum sive liberum, praeposuerit, et quid cum eo eius rei gratia, cui praepositus est, contractum fuerit; ideo autem institoria vocatur, quia qui tabernae praeponitur, institor appellatur.[1]

---

sometimes by that *de peculio et in rem verso.* To such the *tributoria* is advantageous, because the master in this has no preferential position, that is, there is no deduction of what is owing to him, but he and the other creditors stand on the same footing. Again, it is advantageous to sue by the action concerning separate property, because in this action account is taken of the whole separate property; but in the tributorian only of what is traded with, and any one can trade with, it may be, the third part of his separate property, or the fourth part, or even a very small part, whilst he has the greater part in lands, or slaves, or in money at interest.

[1] Now the exercitorian action obtains when the father or master has appointed a son or slave as captain of a vessel, and a transaction has been entered into with him relating to

Ulp.: Magistrum navis accipere debemus, cui totius navis cura mandata est.—D. 14, 1, 1, 1.[1]

Est autem nobis electio, utrum exercitorem an magistrum convenire velimus (Ibid. § 17)—hoc enim edicto non transfertur actio, sed adiicitur.—l. 5, § 1 eod.[2]

§ 113. Liability from Delicts of Third Parties. (Noxal Actions.)[a]

[a] Cf. Holmes, 'Common Law,' pp. 8-15.

As arising from the delicts of slaves and filii-familias, the injured party can employ the given action, as noxalis actio, against the master as paterfam. (or even possessor of the slave), who—in case he at all undertake the defence—has to pay the litis aestimatio (compensation for the damage or penal sum), but is freed from responsibility by 'noxae deditio' of the offender to such party.[b] It is possible that originally the pat. fam. or master was principally and directly under the obligation of noxae deditio; from which he could free himself by means of payment of the litis aestimatio.[c] The condemnation, accordingly, admitted of an alternative. But whether the Intentio did actually, as is supposed, contemplate the pat. fam. or master (which is the rather

[b] Gai. i. 140; iv. 75, 79; Inst. iv. 8, 7; Coll. ii. 3.

[c] Cf. Holl. p. 116, note.

---

the business he was appointed to manage; . . . and further, although a person has appointed some stranger as captain of the vessel, whether slave or free, still the praetorian action is given against him. And the action is called 'exercitorian,' because he is called 'exercitor' to whom the daily earnings of a ship accrue. The institorian formula obtains, however, when a person has appointed his son, or slave, or any stranger he pleased, whether slave or free, to the management of a ship or business of any kind, and a contract has been made with him relating to such matter as he has been appointed to manage. The action is called 'institorian,' because he that is appointed manager of a shop is called an 'institor.'

[1] By the captain of a ship we must understand the person to whom the charge of the whole ship has been deputed.

[2] Now we have our choice whether we will sue the owner or the captain—since, by this Edict, there is no transfer, but addition, of an action.

to be acknowledged in the case of slaves) remains questionable. On the other hand, Dig. 44, 7, 14[a] demands consideration, as well as the effect of consumption of Litis Contestatio and Judgment.[b]

[a] *Supra*, p. 169.

[b] Cf. D. 9, 4, 22, 4.

Iust. iv. 8, § 1 : **Noxa** est corpus quod nocuit, i.e. servus, **noxia** ipsum maleficium.—Serv. in Verg. Aen. 1, 41 : Noxia culpa est, i.e. peccatum, noxa autem poena.[1]

Fest. h. v.: —Noxia (damnum significat); . . . noxa peccatum aut pro peccato poenam; . . . cum lex iubet noxae dedere, pro peccato dedi iubet.—(p. 174, M.)[2]

Gai.: (Noxalium) actionum vis et potestas haec est, ut si damnati fuerimus, liceat nobis deditione ipsius corporis quod deliquerit, evitare litis aestimationem.—l. 1 pr., D. h. t. (de nox. act. 9, 4).[3]

Id.: Non solum adversus bona fide possessorem, sed etiam adversus eos, qui mala fide possident, noxalis actio datur.—l. 13 eod.[4]

Call.: Is qui in aliena potestate est si noxam commisisse dicatur, si non defendatur, ducitur; et si praesens est dominus, tradere eum et de dolo malo promittere debet (l. 32 eod.). Gai.: —sed huic necesse est ius suum ad actorem transferre, perinde ac si damnatus esset (l. 29 eod.).—Pomp.: Noxali iudicio invitus nemo cogitur alium defendere, sed carere debet eo, quem non defendit,

---

[1] *Noxa* is the body which has caused the injury, that is, the slave; *noxia* is the tort itself.—*Noxia* is the fault, that is, offence, whilst *noxa* is the punishment.

[2] *Noxia* (denotes injury); . . . *noxa*, an offence or punishment for an offence; . . . when the statute enjoins *noxae dedere*, it enjoins delivery up for an offence.

[3] The force and power of noxal actions is this, that if we have been condemned, we are allowed, by surrender of the actual person of the wrongdoer, to avoid an assessment of the damages.

[4] A noxal action is given not only against the possessor in good faith, but against those who possess in bad faith.

si servus est: quod si liber est qui in potestate sit, ipsi sui defensio danda est.—l. 33, D. eod.[1]

Iust. iv. 17, § 1: —noxali iudicio . . . si condemnandus videbitur dominus, ita debeat condemnare: 'Publium Maevium Lucio Titio decem aureis condemno aut noxam dedere.'[2]

Ulp.: 'Decem aut noxae dedere' condemnatus iudicati in decem tenetur: facultatem enim noxae dedendae ex lege accipit. . . . Iudicium solius noxae deditionis nullum est, sed pecuniariam condemnationem sequitur; et ideo iudicati decem agitur, his enim solis condemnatur; noxae deditio in solutione est, quae e lege tribuitur.—D. 42, 1, 6, 1.[3]

Next, 'Noxa caput sequitur.'

Paul.: Actionum ex delicto venientium obligationes cum capite ambulant.—D. 4, 5, 7, 1.[4]

Gai. iv. §§ 76–78: Constitutae sunt autem noxales actiones aut legibus aut edicto praetoris:

---

[1] If he who is under the power of another be alleged to have committed an injury, and is not defended, he is led away [by the plaintiff]; and if the master be present, he must deliver him up and undertake to answer for his bad intention.—But the latter has to transfer his right to the plaintiff, just as if he had been condemned.—No one can be compelled against his will to defend another in a noxal action, but if the one whom he does not defend is a slave, the master must renounce him; but if he is a freeman under power, he must be allowed to defend himself.

[2] If in a noxal action he shall consider the master ought to be condemned, he must give judgment thus: 'I condemn P. M. (to pay) ten *aurei* to L. T., or to surrender the wrongdoer.'

[3] He that has been condemned to pay 'ten [*aurei*] or to surrender for punishment' is liable for ten, &c.; for by virtue of the statute he is empowered to surrender for punishment . . . There is no judgment of mere surrender for punishment. but it follows the pecuniary condemnation; and therefore the action is directed to a judgment for ten, &c., for in such alone is he condemned. The surrender for punishment lies in the payment, which is given by the statute.

[4] Obligations appertaining to actions arising from delict shift with the person.

legibus, velut furti lege XII tabularum, damni iniuriae lege Aquilia; edicto praetoris velut iniuriarum et vi bonorum raptorum. § Omnes autem noxales actiones caput sequuntur: nam si filius tuus servusve noxam commiserit, quamdiu in tua potestate est, tecum est actio; si in alterius potestatem pervenerit, cum illo incipit actio esse; si sui iuris coeperit esse, directa actio cum ipso est et noxae deditio extinguitur. Ex diverso quoque directa actio noxalis esse incipit: nam si paterfamilias noxam commiserit et is se in adrogationem tibi dederit, . . . incipit tecum noxalis actio esse. § Sed si filius patri aut servus domino noxam commiserit, nulla actio nascitur; nulla enim omnino inter me et eum, qui in potestate mea est, obligatio nasci potest; ideoque et si in alienam potestatem pervenerit aut sui iuris esse coeperit, neque cum ipso neque cum eo, cuius nunc in potestate est, agi potest. Unde quaeritur, si alienus servus filiusve noxam commiserit mihi et is postea in mea esse coeperit potestate, utrum intercidat actio an quiescat? Nostri praeceptores intercidere putant, quia in eum casum deducta sit, in quo actio consistere non potuerit, ideoque licet exierit de mea potestate, agere me non posse: diversae scholae auctores, quamdiu in mea potestate sit, quiescere actionem putant (quia ipse mecum agere non possum) cum vero exierit de mea potestate, tunc eam resuscitari.[1]

---

[1] Now noxal actions have been created either by *leges* or the Praetor's Edict: by *leges*, for instance, in respect of theft according to a law of the Twelve Tables, and of wrongful damage according to the *l. Aquilia*; by the Praetor's Edict, for example, in respect of insults and goods taken with violence. § All noxal actions follow the person, for if your son or slave has committed an offence, so long as he is in your power, an action lies against you; if he has come under the power of another, an action arises against that other; if he is once independent, a direct action lies against him and noxal surrender is at an end. On the other hand, the direct action also becomes noxal, for if the *pat. fam.* has

If the delict have been committed with the knowledge and by the will (scientia) of the master or paterfam., the action lies against him with the omission of the noxae deditio.

> Ulp.: Si servus sciente domino occidit, in solidum dominum obligat, . . . si autem iusciente, noxalis est.—Is qui non prohibuit, sive dominus manet sive desiit esse dominus, hac actione tenetur.—l. 2 pr., § 1, h. t.[1]
>
> Id.: Scientia . . . domini sic accipienda est, si, cum prohibere posset, non prohibuit.—l. 3 eod.[2]

§ 114. Effect of Obligations with regard to Legal Enforcement. *Naturalis Obligatio.*[a]

[a] See Bell, s. vv.

To the legal and complete efficacy of an obligation belongs its actionable character, *i.e.*, the power of the

---

committed a wrong, and then have given himself to you in arrogation . . . the action becomes noxal against you. § But if a son has committed a wrongful act against his father, or a slave against his master, no action arises; for there can be no obligation at all between me and a person who is under my power; and therefore, although he may have passed under the power of a third party, or has become independent, no action can be brought against either the man himself or the person under whose power he now is. Hence arises the question, whether if another's slave or son has committed an injury against me, and he afterwards has become subject to my power, the right of action is gone, or is only in abeyance. The authorities of our school think it is gone, because matters have fallen into such a plight, that no action can arise, and therefore, although he should pass out of my power, I cannot sue. The authorities of the opposite school are of opinion that, as he is under my power, the action is in abeyance (since I cannot proceed against myself); but that it is revived when he passes out of my power.

[1] If the slave with the privity of the master have committed a murder, he renders his master liable for the whole . . . but if without such privity, it is noxal. To this action he is liable who did not forbid the act, whether he remain master or have ceased to be master.

[2] By knowledge of the master we must understand: if he did not forbid it when he could.

creditor to give effect by actio to the claim which belongs to him.[a]

(1) According as the protection afforded by Law to the obligation is that derived from ius civile or from ius praetorium, we have the distinction of obligationes 'civiles' and 'praetoriae' (honorariae); on the other hand, to 'civiles' obligationes, as those rooted in the ius proprium civium Romanorum,[b] are opposed the 'naturales' obligationes,[c] as those obligations which are already grounded in the ius gentium, but recognised in the Roman Civil Law.[d]

Inst. iii. 13, § 1.: Omnium autem obligationum summa divisio in duo genera deducitur, namque aut civiles sunt, aut praetoriae: **civiles** sunt, quae aut legibus constitutae aut certe iure civili comprobatae sunt; **praetoriae** sunt, quas praetor ex sua iurisdictione constituit, quae etiam **honorariae** vocantur.[1]

(2) As a rule, however, the distinction between obligationes civiles and naturales relates to the efficacy of the obligations, so that civilis obligatio is every one that has to be made good by an actio, is actionable or perfect; whilst obligatio (tantum) naturalis is an imperfect obligation deprived of an actio, but otherwise in various ways juristically operative: in contrast with obligations fully inoperative, whether 'ipso iure' or 'ope exceptionis.'[e]

Iul.: **Naturales** obligationes non eo solo aestimantur, si actio aliqua earum nomine competit, verum etiam cum soluta pecunia repeti non potest: nam licet minus proprie debere dicantur **naturales debitores**, per abusionem intelligi

[a] D. 50, 16, 108.

[b] § 116: Gai. iii. 92-93; § 119, ad init.

[c] See Poste, 'Gaius,' p. 359; Brown, s. 'Moral Obligations,' and s. vv.

[d] Inst. i. 2, 2; D. 2, 14, 7.

[e] § 128, ad init.

---

[1] Now the chief division of all actions is reduced to two classes; for they are either Civil or Praetorian. Civil are such as either are founded upon statutes, or at least are recognised by the Civil Law. Praetorian are such as the Praetor has created by virtue of his jurisdiction; they are also called Magisterial.

Book III. Pt. I. Ch. II.

possunt debitores et, qui ab his pecuniam recipiunt, debitum sibi recepisse.—l. 16, § 4, D. de fidej. 46, 1.[a] [1]

[a] *Infra*, D. 50, 17, 84, 1.

Ulp.: **Creditores** accipiendos esse constat eos, quibus debetur ex quacumque actione vel persecutione, vel iure civili sine ulla exceptionis perpetuae remotione vel honorario; . . . quodsi natura debeatur, non sunt loco creditorum.—D. 50, 16, 10.[2]

The several cases of naturales obligationes are either—

(1) obligations originated in the ius gentium,[b] but which have not acquired full recognition in the Roman Civil Law, and always arise just as unactionable obligations, *e.g.*, obligations of slaves,[c] obligations between the pat. fam. and the persona subiecta, which however (apart from a peculium allowed to the latter)[d] have not effective expression until the extinction of the potestas; engagement by nudum pactum.[e]

[b] 'Anct. Law,' p. 308.

[c] D. 15, 1, 41; 44. 7, 14.

[d] D. 2, 14, 7, 6.

[e] § 115.

Paul.: Is natura debet, quem iure gentium dare oportet, cuius fidem secuti sumus.—D. 50, 17, 84, 1.[3]

Id.: Naturaliter etiam servus obligatur: et ideo

[1] Natural obligations are not judged of alone by the contingency of some action available by reason thereof, but even of the impossibility of recovering money paid; for although it is short of accuracy to say that there are debtors indebted by Natural Law, they can loosely be regarded as debtors, and those who receive money from such, as having received what was due to them.

[2] It is well known that by 'creditors' are to be understood those to whom anything is owing upon whatever action or process, whether according to Civil Law without any rebutter by a perpetual plea, or by Praetorian Law; . . . but if it is owing naturally, they are not regarded as creditors.

[3] He is indebted by nature who has to give something according to the *ius gentium*, and upon whose integrity we have relied.

si quis nomine eius solverit vel ipse manumissus . . . repeti non poterit; et ob id fideiussor pro servo acceptus tenetur et pignus pro eo datum tenebitur.—l. 13 pr., D. de cond. ind. 12, 6.[1]

Tryph.: Si quod dominus servo debuit, manumisso solvit, quamvis existimans ei aliqua teneri actione, tamen repetere non poterit, quia naturale adgnovit debitum.—l. 64 eod.[2]

Afr.: Si pater quod filio debuisset, eidem emancipato solverit, non repetet; nam hic quoque manere naturalem obligationem . . . probatur. —l. 38, § 2 eod.[3]

Imp. Sever.: Quamvis usurae foenebris pecuniae citra vinculum stipulationis peti non possunt, tamen ex pacti conventione solutae neque ut indebitae repetuntur, neque in sortem accepto ferendae sunt.—C. 4, 32, 3.[4]

(2) Or obligations which have been intrinsically originated in the ius civile also, but which have for some reason from the beginning been denied full operation, or their originally actionable character has been taken away by some succeeding circumstance only operative iure civili; *e.g.*, loan contra SC.

---

[1] It is by Natural Law that a slave incurs liability; and therefore, if any one should make a payment in his name, or he himself when manumitted . . . it cannot be recovered; and because of it a person accepted as surety for a slave is held liable, and liability will attach to a pledge given on his behalf.

[2] If a master pay to his slave when manumitted what he has owed him, then, although he supposed he was liable to him by some action, yet he will be unable to recover, because he recognised its being a debt by Natural Law.

[3] If a father shall have paid his son what he had owed him, he will not recover; for here also it is proved that the natural obligation remains.

[4] Although no interest upon a loan can be recovered without an obligatory stipulation, yet if it have been paid in pursuance of a contractual agreement, neither does it admit of recovery as not owing, nor is it to be regarded as received in discharge for capital.

Book III. Pt. I. Ch. II.

Macedonianum,[a] liability of the ward without tutoris auctoritas,[b] or claims destroyed by capitis diminutio,[c] Litis Contestatio,[d] Limitation of actions.[e]

[a] § 120.
[b] § 151; D. 46, 2, 1, 1; Gai. iii. 176, 179.
[c] § 56, ad fin.
[d] §§ 199, 202.
[e] § 103, ad fin.

Marcian.: Ubi in odium eius, cui debetur, exceptio datur, perperam solutum non repetitur: veluti si filiusfamilias contra Macedonianum mutuam pecuniam acceperit et paterfamilias factus solverit, non repetit.—l. 40 pr., D. de cond. ind.[1]

Ulp.: Hi qui capite minuuntur, ex his causis, quae capitis deminutionem praecesserunt, manent obligati naturaliter.—D. 4, 5, 2, 2.[2]

Id.: Et post litem contestatam fideiussor accipi potest, quia et civilis et naturalis subest obligatio.—l. 8, § 3, D. de fidej.[3]

The effects of naturales obligationes, which however by no means everywhere occur uniformly, consist—

(*a*) in the operation of the performance, which avails not as a gift, but as a payment of a debt, whence no recovery (soluti retentio);[f]

(β) in the allowance of security[g] and pledge[h] for the debitum naturale;

(γ) in the possibility of the novation[i] of a naturalis obligatio;

(δ) in the possibility of making good the natural demand by way of set-off.[j]

[f] § 135.
[g] § 118.
[h] § 101.
[i] § 142.
[j] § 140.

Ulp.: Si quis servo pecuniam crediderit, de-

---

[1] Where a plea is given in censure of the creditor, that which has been wrongly paid is not recovered; for example, if a *fil. fam.* has taken a loan contrary to the '*SCtum Macedonianum*,' and shall have paid it after becoming a *pat. fam.*, he does not recover.

[2] Those who suffer loss of status remain liable by Natural Law in respect of such matters as preceded the loss of status.

[3] A surety can be accepted even after joinder of issue, because both a civil and a natural obligation subsists.

inde is liber factus eam expromiserit, non erit donatio, sed debiti solutio.—D. 39, 5, 19, 4.[1]

Tit. II.—ORIGIN OF OBLIGATIONS.

§ 115. Survey of the Grounds of Initiation. *Contractus* and *Pacta*. Unilateral Promise.[a]

[a] See 'Anct. Law,' p. 323; Pollock, 'Contract,' pp. 134 *sqq.*; Markby, ss. 603, *sqq.*

All obligations arise either from legal transactions, or torts, or from other juristic facts (variae causarum figurae) which the Roman jurists are accustomed to annex to the one or other analogically.

Gai.: Obligationes aut ex contractu nascuntur, aut ex maleficio, aut proprio quodam iure ex variis causarum figuris.—D. 44, 7, 1 pr.[2]

Iust. iii. 13, 2: (Obligationum) divisio in quattuor species deducitur: aut enim ex contractu sunt, aut quasi ex contractu, aut ex maleficio, aut quasi ex maleficio.[3]

Obligations arising from legal transactions always presuppose an agreement.[b] But it is not every agreement that has the effect of producing an actionable obligation between the contracting parties. The rather, in older Roman Civil Law this effect was acknowledged only in some special agreements (contractus), distinguished by their form or their subject-matter (causa); and furthermore, all obligatory operation was denied to other agreements (nuda pacta).[c] A number of 'pacta' were, however, later on by gradual development placed on the same footing as 'contractus' by the

[b] § 18.

[c] See Pollock, p. 135.

---

[1] If a man shall have lent money to a slave, and then the latter upon becoming free shall have promised [to pay it], it shall not be a donation, but the payment of a debt.

[2] Obligations arise either from contract, or from tort, or some special rule of law as the result of various kinds of cases.

[3] A division of obligations is made into four kinds; for they arise either from contract, or what is analogous to contract, or from tort, or what is analogous to tort.

Book III. Pt. I. Ch. II.

ius civile and praetorium, so that in them also resides the power of engendering an obligation (so-called pacta vestita: adiecta, legitima, praetoria).

Ulp.: **Conventionis** verbum generale est ad omnia pertinens, de quibus negotii contrahendi transigendique causa consentiunt, qui inter se agunt. . . . Adeo autem conventionis nomen generale est, ut eleganter dicat Pedius nullum esse contractum, nullam obligationem, quae non habeat in se conventionem, sive re sive verbis fiat.—D. 2, 14, 13.[1]

Id.: Iuris gentium conventiones quaedam actiones pariunt, quaedam exceptiones.—Quae pariunt actiones, in suo nomine non stant, sed transeunt in proprium nomen contractus, et emptio venditio, locatio conductio, societas, commodatum depositum et ceteri similes contractus.—Igitur nuda pactio obligationem non parit, sed parit exceptionem.—l. 7 pr., §§ 1, 4 eod.[2]

Paul. ii. 14, § 1: Ex nudo pacto inter cives Romanos actio non nascitur.[3]

Without agreement, consequently by one-sided (non-accepted) promise,[a] an obligation arises only in case of pollicitatio to a community, and of the votum under sacral Law, by which an obligation is created towards the Deity.

[a] An 'offer': See Poll. p. 6.

---

[1] *Conventio* is a general expression, and relates to all things concerning which persons who have dealings with one another agree for the purpose of entering into a business contract and transaction. . . . But the expression *conventio* is so general, that Ped. neatly says, there is no contract, no obligation, which does not include a convention, whether it be in substance or in words.

[2] Some conventions of the *i. g.* produce actions; some, pleas. Those that produce actions do not retain their name, but pass under the special designation of the contract; for instance, Purchase and Sale, Letting and Hire, Partnership, Contract of Loan, Deposit and other like contracts.—Therefore a bare agreement engenders no obligation, but engenders a plea.

[3] Amongst Roman citizens no action arises from a bare bargain.[b]

[b] Steph. ii. 258, note; Pollock, p. 676.

Ulp.: Pactum est duorum consensus atque conventio: pollicitatio vero offerentis solius promissum. Et ideo illud est constitutum, ut si ob honorem pollicitatio fuerit facta, quasi debitum exigatur; sed et coeptum opus, licet non ob honorem promissum, perficere promissor cogetur. —D. 50, 12, 3 pr.[1]

Id.: Si quis rem aliquam voverit, voto obligatur; quae res personam voventis, non rem quae vovetur, obligat.—Voto autem patresfamiliarum obligantur puberes sui iuris: filius enim familias vel servus sine patris dominive auctoritate voto non obligantur.—l. 2 pr., § 1 eod.[2]

The ground of the binding force of contracts according to Civil Law consisted originally—by the *ius civile* proprium Romanorum—alone in a definite (oral or written) form of engagement. The Formal Contracts were 'nexum,' VERBAL contracts (stipulatio, dotis dictio), and the LITERAL contract.[a] An actionable character was, accordingly, in the older Roman Law (in the sixth or seventh century U.C.) attributed to certain informal contracts. These were the Material Contracts, determined by the auctoritas prudentium and Praetorian Edict, as based solely upon 'fides' (keeping one's word, reliance upon performance of what was promised, integrity in dealings) and ranged under the *ius gentium*. The element upon which the action was based was in

[a] 'Anct. Law,' p. 325.

---

[1] A bargain is the agreement and convention of two persons; whilst a proposal is the promise alone of the person making the offer. And so it has been ordained that an offer can be enforced as though a debt, if it have been made for the sake of office; but even work begun the promisor must complete, although it were not promised for the sake of office.

[2] If a man has vowed something, he is bound by his vow, and he that makes the vow is personally bound by this, and not the thing vowed.—Now by a vow *patresfam.* are bound that are of the age of puberty and independent, for a *fil. fam.* or slave, apart from the authority of the father or master, is not bound by a vow.

BOOK III. Pt. I. Ch. II.

the case of some of them the parting with, and the receipt of, a thing under agreement for restitution. Such were the REAL Contracts:[a] 'mutuum,' 'fiducia,'[b] 'depositum,' 'commodatum,' 'pignus.' In four very important and frequent contracts, however, the mere agreement of the contracting parties (nudus consensus) was already, on account of their subject-matter, recognised as a legally valid causa. These were the CONSENSUAL Contracts: Purchase and Sale, Letting for hire, Partnership and Mandate, which, with the single exception of the last mentioned, always engendered reciprocal obligations. With these were ranged later on the so-called INNOMINATE Contracts.[c]

[a] Ibid.

[b] Which is doubtful.

[c] § 126.

Cic. de off. 1, 8, 23: Fundamentum autem est iustitiae **fides**, i.e. dictorum conventorumque constantia et veritas; . . . credamusque, quia fiat quod dictum est, appellatam fidem.[1]

Gell. xx. 1, 39–40: Omnium (virtutum) maxime atque praecipue fidem (populus Romanus) coluit sanctamque habuit tam privatim quam publice. . . . Hanc autem fidem maiores nostri non modo in officiorum vicibus, sed in negotiorum contractibus sanxerunt.[2]

Gai. iii. § 89: Et prius videamus de his quae ex contractu nascuntur; harum quattuor genera sunt: aut enim **re** contrahitur obligatio aut **verbis** aut **litteris** aut **consensu.**[3]

Ibid. §§ 135–137: Consensu fiunt obligationes

---

[1] Now the basis of all justice is *fides*, *i.e.*, adhesion to, and truth of, things said and agreed; . . . and let us suppose that it is called 'fides' because what has been said is done.

[2] Of all (virtues, the Roman people) primarily and chiefly cultivated *fides*, and regarded it as sacred both in private and in public. . . . Now our ancestors have put a sacred character on this *fides*, not merely in respect of mutual obligations, but in contracts of business.

[3] And first let us consider those which arise from contract. Of these there are four classes; for an obligation is contracted either by the thing done, or by words, or by writing, or by consent.

in emptionibus venditionibus, locationibus conductionibus, societatibus, mandatis.—Ideo autem istis modis consensu dicimus obligationem contrahi, quia neque verborum neque scripturae ulla proprietas desideratur [ac ne dari quidem quidquam necesse est, ut substantiam capiat obligatio], sed sufficit eos qui negotium gerunt consensisse. —Item in his contractibus alter alteri obligatur de eo, quod alterum alteri ex bono et aequo praestare oportet, cum alioquin in verborum obligationibus alius stipuletur, alius promittat.—Cf. Inst. iii. 22, § 1.[1]

I. OBLIGATIONES *EX CONTRACTU*.[a]

[a] Holl. pp. 191, *sqq.*

THE SYSTEM OF CONTRACTS *IURE CIVILI*.

§ 116. First, *Nexum*.[b]

[b] 'Anct. Law,' pp. 314, *sqq.*

'Nexum' in the wider sense is every legal transaction 'per aes et libram';[c] in the narrower sense, such as relates to the creation of a pecuniary claim. It was the oldest loan, the antique national money-transaction, and was entered into by the weighing of Roman money in balances, in the form of 'mancipatio,' accomplished by a solemn harangue, which enunciated the purpose of such weighing. The form employed was perhaps as follows: 'Quod ego tibi mille asses (s. libras aeris) hoc aere aeneaque libra nexos dedi, eos tu mihi post annum cum foenore unciario dare damnas

[c] § 79.

---

[1] Obligations arise from consent in buying and selling, letting and hiring, partnerships and mandates. We therefore say that in these forms obligations are created by consent, because there is no speciality either of words or writing required [and it is not even necessary that anything should be given, for the obligation to acquire binding force], but it is enough that those who are contracting the business have come to a common understanding. Likewise, in these contracts, the one is bound to the other for all that the one ought in fairness and equity to do for the other, whereas in verbal obligations, one party stipulates and the other promises.

BOOK III. Pt. I. Ch. II.

[a] So Huschke.

[b] Thus at the same time a Real and a Formal contract.

[c] D. 21, 2, 53, 1.

[d] Ulp. 24, 4, 8.

esto.'[a] Originally the form of the actual loan;[b] the nexum could also occur as a symbolic or fictitious loan, after that the practice of weighing the money was entirely discontinued, and also the money-payment separated from the legal act itself; and in this shape, —being an abstract form of obligation—it was applicable to most of the obligatory agreements for the formal creation and change of pecuniary claims arising therefrom. Moreover, a 'nexi obligatio' arose in purchase per mancipationem in respect of the purchase-money to be repaid by the vendor upon eviction of the thing,[c] and in a legacy by damnatio.[d]

Fest. h. v.: **Nexum** est, ut ait Gallus Aelius, quodcumque per aes et libram geritur; idque necti dicitur; quo in genere sunt haec: testamenti factio, nexi datio, nexi liberatio. **Nexum** aes apud antiquos dicebatur pecunia, quae per nexum obligatur (p. 165, M.).[1]

Varro de LI. VII. § 105 (Müll.): Nexum Manilius scribit, omne quod per aes et libram geritur, in quo sint mancipia. Mucius, quae per aes et libram fiant ut obligentur, praeter quae mancipio dentur.[2]

The significance of the nexum lay in the notoriety of the sanctiori, and in the strict, public nature of the obligation entered into. After the lapse of the term for payment, the claims could be at once realised; the debtor was situated exactly like the 'iudicatus' or 'in iure confessus'; he him-

---

[1] A *nexum*, as says G. A., is any transaction by copper and balance, and that is said to be bound; in which category are the following—the making of a testament, the giving of a bond, discharge from a bond. Property made liable *per nexum* was spoken of amongst the ancients as *nexum aes*.

[2] Man. by *nexum* describes every transaction by copper and scales, amongst which are *mancipia*. Muc.: whatever comes about by copper and scales, so as to be binding, besides things granted by *mancipium*.

self became 'nexus' and was subject, as they, to the 'manus iniectio,' to being led away into slavery for debt, and besides to sale by the creditor.[a] However, after this right of private incarceration by the creditor was curtailed by some lex that is uncertain, but perhaps the l. Valeria, and was abolished by a lex Poetelia (variously put at 440 and 429 A.U.C.), the nexum also passed out of use, and very soon disappeared.

[a] For the *vindex poena dupli* of the person guilty of falsehood, see § 192.

Varro l. c.: Liber qui suas operas in servitutem pro pecunia, quam debebat, dat, dum solveret, **nexus** vocatur, ut ab aere **obaeratus**.[1]

Liv. VIII. § 28: Eo anno plebei Romanae velut aliud initium libertatis factum est, quod necti desierunt.—Victum eo die . . . ingens vinculum diei; iussique consules ferre ad populum, ne quis, nisi qui noxam meruisset donec poenam lueret, in compedibus aut in nervo teneretur; pecuniae creditae bona debitoris, non corpus obnoxium esset: ita nexi soluti cautumque in posterum, ne necterentur.[2]

Secondly, *Verborum* Obligationes.

§ 117. In General. *Stipulatio* and *Dotis Dictio*.

The most important and most frequent case of 'verborum obligationes' in Roman legal dealings is the 'Stipulatio.'[b]

[b] See 'Anct. Law,' pp. 326-330.

---

[1] A freeman that gives his labour for slavery, in consideration of the money he owed, until he should discharge the debt, is called *nexus*, as enslaved for debt.

[2] In that year another beginning, so to speak, of liberty was made for the Roman Plebs., for they ceased to be bound.—A great bond of credit was gained on that day; and the consuls were ordered to propose to the people that no one should be detained in stocks or in fetters, save him that had deserved punishment, until he had satisfied the penalty; that the goods of a debtor, not his body, should be liable for money owing: thus *nexi* were released, and it was provided for the future that they should not be bound.

Book III. Pt. I. Ch. II.

It is an obligatory agreement clothed in an oral interrogatory of the creditor (stipulator s. reus stipulandi—stipulari) and corresponding answer of the debtor (promissor s. reus promittendi) engendering a unilateral, stringent claim,[a] which probably was derived from the old promissory oath—sponsio ad aram (maximam)—and so is of sacral origin.[b]

[a] § 111 and Gai. iii. 137.

[b] Cf. authorities cited by Pollock, 'Cont.' p. 134; and for a criticism of different theories, Hunter, 'Roman Law,' pp. 536, *sqq.*

Fest. h. v.: **Stipem** esse nummum signatum, testimonio est et id quod datur stipendium militi, et cum spondetur pecunia, quod stipulari dicitur (p. 297, M.)[1]

Id. h. v.: **Spondere** Verrius putat dictum, quod sporte sua, i.e. voluntate promittatur; deinde oblitus inferiore capite sponsum et sponsam ex Graeco dictum ait, quod ii σπονδὰς interpositis rebus divinis faciant.—P. 329, M.[2]

(Stipulatio) hoc nomine inde utitur, quia stipulum apud veteres firmum appellatur, forte a stipite descendens.—pr., I. h. t. (de V. O. 3, 15).[3]

Pomp.: Stipulatio autem est verborum conceptio, quibus is qui interrogatur, daturum facturumve se, quod interrogatus est, responderit.—l. 5, § 1, D. h. t. (de V. O. 45, 1).[4]

Ulp.: Stipulatio non potest confici nisi utroque loquente; et ideo neque mutus neque surdus neque infans stipulationem contrahere possunt,

---

[1] That a *stips* is a stamped coin is evidenced also by that payment which is made to a soldier, and when money is promised, which is called *stipulari*.

[2] V. supposes that the expression *spondeo* is used because the promise is made *sua sponte, i.e.*, voluntarily; then, forgetfully, he speaks in a later chapter of the expression *sponsus* and *sponsa* being taken from Greek, because they make σπονδαὶ (treaties) through the medium of religious matters.

[3] It has this name of stipulation, because *stipulum* among the ancients means something firm, and is perhaps derived from *stipes* (trunk of a tree).

[4] Now *stipulatio* is a framing of words by which he who is interrogated answers that he will give or do that which has been asked.

> nec absens quidem, quoniam exaudire invicem debent.—l. I pr. eod.[1]

Having grown out of national Roman custom, and having been at first connected with prescribed formulae, the stipulatio, in course of time, acquired an evermore elastic form, inasmuch as it also made its way into dealings with the peregrini; and finally, a congruity between question and answer, which was no longer formal but merely substantial, was held sufficient.

> Gai. iii. §§ 92–93: Verbis obligatio fit ex interrogatione et responsione: velut DARI SPONDES? SPONDEO;—DABIS? DABO;—PROMITTIS? PROMITTO;—FACIES? FACIAM. § Sed haec quidem verborum obligatio DARI SPONDES? SPONDEO propria civium Romanorum est; ceterae vero iuris gentium sunt, itaque inter omnes homines, sive cives Romanos sive peregrinos, valent.[2]
>
> Adhuc inutilis est stipulatio, si quis ad id quod interrogatus erit non responderit, veluti si sestertia X a te dari stipuler, et tu sestertia V promittas. (Ibid. § 102.)—Ulp.: Si stipulanti mihi X tu XX respondeas, non contractam stipulationem nisi in X constat; ex contrario si me XX interrogante tu X respondeas, obligatio nisi in X non erit contracta. —(l. I, § 4, h. t.)[3]

---

[1] A stipulation cannot be effected unless both persons speak; and so neither a dumb nor a deaf person, nor an infant, can contract a stipulation, not even an absent person, since they must hear one another.

[2] A verbal obligation results from a question and answer: as for instance, 'Do you undertake that it shall be given?' 'I do undertake.' 'Will you give?' 'I will give.' 'Do you promise?' 'I do promise.' 'Will you do?' 'I will do.' § But this form of verbal obligation, 'Do you undertake that it shall be given?' 'I do undertake,' is peculiar to Roman citizens; whilst the other forms belong to the *ius gentium*, and so are valid amongst all men, whether Roman citizens or aliens.

[3] Moreover, a stipulation is void if a man do not reply to the question he is asked; for example, if I stipulate for ten thousand sesterces to be given by you, and you promise five thousand

Book III. Pt. I. Ch. II.

Eadem an alia lingua respondeatur nihil interest: proinde si quis Latine interrogaverit, respondeatur ei Graece, dummodo congruenter respondeatur, obligatio constituta est.—l. 1, § 6, h. t.[1]

[a] ? interrogetur.

Si quis ita interroget [a] 'dabis?' responderit 'quidni?' et is in ea causa est, ut obligetur; contra si sine verbis adnuisset.—ib. § 2.[2]

Imp. Leo: Omnes stipulationes, etiam si non solemnibus vel directis, sed quibuscumque verbis pro consensu contrahentium compositae sint, . . . suam habeant firmitatem.—C. 8, 37 (38), l. 10.[3]

The debtor by stipulatio was—apart from dolus—responsible only for 'culpa in faciendo.' Frequently therefore responsibility for dolus was expressly included in the stipulatio itself (doli clausula),[b] in order to obviate a too narrow interpretation of the debtor's responsibility from the words of the stipulatio as they ran.[c]

[b] D. 4, 3, 7, 3.

[c] Cf. § 28.

Paul. v. 7, § 4: Cum facto promissoris res in stipulatum deducta intercidit, perinde agi ex stipulatu potest, ac si ea res exstaret.[4]

---

sesterces.—If, when I stipulate for ten, you answer twenty, it is settled that a stipulation has been contracted only for ten; conversely, if when my question is as to twenty, and you answer ten, there will also be an obligation for ten only.

[1] It matters not whether the answer is made in the same or another language: accordingly, if a man has put the question in Latin, and he is answered in Greek, an obligation has been created, provided only that the answer is conformable.

[2] If a man ask thus: 'Will you give?' and receives answer, 'Why not?' even such enters into an obligatory relation; the reverse, if he nodded without speaking.

[3] All obligations, even if they have been cast, not in formal or direct, but language of whatever kind, for the consent of the contracting parties, . . . have a legal effect of their own.

[4] When by the act of the promisor a matter that had been made subject of engagement falls through, proceedings can be taken upon the engagement just as if such matter subsisted.

Id.: —Si servum stipulatus fuero et nulla mora intercedente servus decesserit, . . . sin negligat infirmum, an teneri debeat promissor? . . . an culpa, quod ad stipulationem attinet, in faciendo accipienda sit, non in non faciendo? Quod magis probandum est.—l. 91 pr., h. t.[1]

Iul.: Stipulationes commodissimum est ita componere, ut quaecumque specialiter comprehendi possint, contineantur, doli autem clausula ad ea pertineat, quae in praesentia occurrere non possint et ad incertos casus.—l. 53 eod.[2]

Pap.: Ex ea parte cautionis 'dolumque malum huic rei promissionique abesse abfuturumque esse stipulatus est ille spopondit ille' incerti agetur. —l. 121 pr. eod.[3]

Moreover—especially in the case of the 'stipulatio incerti'[a]—it was usual to provide for a penal sum in default of performance. This, which was fixed, or adequate to the damages a creditor could claim ('quanti ea res est'), was intended to secure performance. It was called *poenae stipulatio*, or 'conventional penalty.'[b]

[a] § 105.

[b] Cf. D. 12, 1, 40; 22, 1, 44; 45, 1, 38. §§ 17.

Ulp.: Cum quid ut fiat, stipulemur poenam sic recte concipiemus 'si ita factum non erit'; cum quid ne fiat, sic 'si adversus id factum sit.' —l. 71 eod.[4]

---

1 If I shall have stipulated for a slave, and, without any delay occurring, the slave has died, . . . if the promisor neglect him in sickness, ought he to be liable? . . . or is negligence as regards a stipulation, to be taken account of in an act, not in a forbearance? We must the rather take the latter view.

2 It is most convenient to frame stipulations in such a way that they contain whatever can be specially included, but the clause as to *dolus* must concern such things as cannot immediately happen, and uncertain events.

3 Upon that part of a deed, 'So-and-so has stipulated, and so-and-so has undertaken,' proceedings will be taken for what is uncertain.

4 When, to provide for the performance of something, we

Book III. Pt. I. Ch. II.

[a] Sc. faciendi.

In huiusmodi[a] stipulationibus optimum erit poenam subiicere, ne quantitas stipulationis in incerto sit ac necesse sit actori probare, quid eius intersit.—§ 7, I. h. t.[1]

Paul.: Si ita stipulatus sim 'si fundum non dederis, centum dare spondes?' sola centum in stipulatione sunt, in exsolutione fundus.—D. 44, 7, 44, 5.[2]

For the purposes of proof, it was customary to draw up a written document (cautio) as to the stipulation verbally concluded, in which the formula of stipulation itself was appended to the contract as a final clause; and this recommended itself especially when the agreement which formed the subject-matter of the stipulation was one very comprehensive and complex.

Ulp.: —fere novissima parte pactorum ita solet inseri: 'rogavit Titius, spopondit Maevius.'—D. 2, 14, 7, 12.[3]

Paul.: Duo societatem coierunt, ut grammaticam docerent et quod ex eo artificio quaestus fecissent, commune eorum esset; de ea re quae voluerunt fieri, in pacto convento societatis proscripserunt, deinde inter se his verbis stipulati sunt: 'haec quae supra scripta sunt, ea ita dari fieri, neque adversus ea fieri: si ea ita data facta

---

stipulate for a penalty, we shall be right in framing the stipulation thus: 'in case it should not happen,' and when our purpose is to prevent its performance, thus: 'if it have happened contrariwise.'

[1] In respect of stipulations of this kind it will be best to subjoin a penalty, that the amount of the stipulation be not uncertain, and that it be not necessary for the plaintiff to prove the extent of his interest.

[2] If I have stipulated thus: 'if you shall not give the estate, do you undertake to give a hundred, &c.,' the hundred &c. are alone the object of the stipulation, but the estate serves for its discharge.

[3] In the last part of contracts it is usual to insert, 'Tit. has put the question, Maev. has undertaken.'

non erunt, tum viginti milia dari.'—D. 17, 2, 71 pr.[1]

This gradually led to importance being no longer attached to the verbal promise of the contracting parties, when there was such written evidence of the employment of the formula of stipulatio, and supposing that they were personally present.

Paul. v. 7, § 2: Quodsi scriptum fuerit instrumento, promisisse aliquem, perinde habetur, atque si interrogatione praecedente responsum sit.[2]

Id.: Cum Septicius litteris suis praestiturum se caverit pecuniam, . . . si inter praesentes actum est, intelligendum etiam a parte Lucii Titii praecessisse verba stipulationis.—l. 134, § 2, D. h. t.[3]

Indeed, finally, an actual presumption obtained of the presence of the contracting parties.

Inst. iii. 19, § 12: Item verborum obligatio inter absentes concepta inutilis est. Sed cum hoc materiam litium contentiosis hominibus praestabat, . . . ideo nostra constitutio . . . introducta est, per quam disposuimus, tales scripturas, quae praesto esse partes indicant, omnimodo esse

---

[1] Two persons have entered into partnership, to give instruction in grammar, and to share such profit as they should derive from that pursuit; their wishes as to the performance of such transaction they have in writing set forth in a partnership agreement, and they have then made a mutual stipulation in the following terms: 'that which is above written shall be so done and performed, and nothing shall be done in contravention of it; if such things shall not be given and done, then twenty thousand &c. shall be given.'

[2] But if it shall have been written in a document that any one has made a promise, it is regarded just as if a question precede and answer be given.

[3] When Sept. in writing bound himself to pay the principal sum, . . . if the transaction took place between the parties in each other's presence, it is to be supposed a stipulative inquiry also proceeded from L. T.

BOOK III. Pt. I. Ch. II.

credendas, nisi ipse, qui talibus utitur improbis allegationibus, manifestissimis probationibus, vel per scripturam vel per testes idoneos, approbaverit, in ipso toto die, quo conficiebatur instrumentum, sese vel adversarium suum in aliis locis esse.[1]

In its very nature, the stipulatio was an extremely subservient, and therefore much favoured, form of contract, to which every juristically possible subject-matter of a contract could be adapted. Actionability, and the character of a stringently binding obligation, was accordingly imparted to every obligatory agreement by its being clothed in a stipulatio, or by appending the formula of stipulation;[a] by which at the same time is explained how the Romans in the discussion of the general doctrines of the Law of Obligation (especially the principles that govern the entering into contracts) give the primary place to STIPULATIO, as the chief and normal case of obligations.

[a] D. 2, 14, 7, 12.

Pomp.: Conventionales[b] sunt quae ex conventione reorum fiunt; quarum totidem genera sunt, quot paene dixerim, rerum contrahendarum: nam et ob ipsam verborum obligationem fiunt et pendent ex negotio contracto.—l. 5 pr., D. h. t.[2]

[b] Sc. stipulationes.

---

[1] Likewise, a verbal obligation entered into between persons absent (from each other) is invalid. But as this afforded occasion for suits by litigious persons, . . . our constitution . . . has been introduced, by which we have enacted that those documents which prove the presence of the parties should be credited in all cases, unless he who avails himself of such disreputable assertions, by the clearest proofs, whether by means of a written document or by credible witnesses, has established that during the whole day on which the document was prepared, he himself or his opponent was at another place.

[2] Conventional (stipulations) are such as arise from the agreement of the contracting parties; of which there are just as many classes as, I might almost say, matters to contract about; for they arise by reason of the verbal obligation itself, and depend upon the business contracted.

Paul. v. 7, § 1: Obligationum firmandarum gratia stipulationes inductae sunt.[1]

Id. ii. 22, § 2: Omnibus pactis stipulatio subiici debet, ut ex stipulatu actio nasci possit.[2]

A second case of the verborum obligationes is 'dotis dictio,' *i.e.*, a promise made to the intending husband, and by him informally accepted, of a definite dos, but which bound only certain persons.[a] [a] § 146.

Ulp. vi. 2: Dotem dicere potest mulier, quae nuptura est, et debitor mulieris, si iussu eius dicat; item parens mulieris virilis sexus per virilem sexum cognatione iunctus, veluti pater, avus paternus.[3]

Terent. Andr. v. 4, 47: Ch. Dos, Pamphile, est decem talenta.—P. Accipio.—Donat. ad h. l.: Ille nisi dixisset 'accipio,' dos non esset; datio enim ab acceptione confirmatur.[4]

The 'iurata operarum promissio' of the libertus has already been dealt with.[b] [b] § 38.

§ 118. *Adstipulatio* and *Adpromissio*. Suretyship.

Both upon the active and the passive side of the verborum obligatio can other persons also come in besides the original contracting parties, as accessory creditor or debtor for the same performance.[c] [c] § 111.

---

[1] Stipulations have been introduced in order to strengthen obligations.

[2] A stipulation ought to be added to all bargains, so that an action can arise from the stipulation.

[3] A woman about to marry can specify a dowry, and a woman's debtor, if he do so by her direction; likewise a male ascendant of the woman related to her through males, as her father, or paternal grandfather.

[4] The dowry, Pamphilus, is ten talents.—Agreed! Unless he had said, 'Agreed,' there would not have been a dowry; for a gift is confirmed by acceptance.

BOOK III. Pt. I. Ch. II.

The form for this was 'adstipulatio' and 'adpromissio.'

Gai. iii. § 113: Item minus adstipulari potest, plus non potest . . . non solum autem in quantitate, sed etiam in tempore minus et plus intelligitur.—§ 126: In eo iure quoque par condicio est omnium, sponsorum fidepromissorum fideiussorum, quod ita obligari non possunt, ut plus debeant, quam debet is pro quo obligantur: at ex diverso, ut minus debeant, obligari possunt, sicut in adstipulatoris persona diximus: nam ut adstipulatoris ita et horum obligatio accessio est principalis obligationis, nec plus in accessione esse potest, quam in principali re.[1]

The 'Adstipulator' is the third party whose participation is procured by the principal stipulator, and who obtains a promise from the debtor of the same performance to himself.[a]

[a] Idem mihi dare spondes?

Correality exists between him and the principal creditor; but he is responsible to the latter to make over the payment rendered to him by the debtor (for which at first indeed a stipulation of restitution was necessary) with the 'actio mandati,' as well as for the fraudulent destruction of the obligation effected by him, with the 'actio legis Aquiliae'[b]—since the 'actio doli'[c] was not introduced until a later period.

[b] D. 9, 2, 27, 5.

[c] Or mandati?

Gai. iii. §§ 110–111: Possumus ad id quod stipulamur, alium adhibere qui idem stipuletur,

[1] He can likewise adstipulate for less, but cannot for more. . . . But the more and the less are to be understood with reference not only to quantity but also to time.—In one point of law the position of all, sponsors, fidepromissors and fidejussors, is alike, that they cannot be so made liable as to owe more than he owes for whom they are bound. But, on the other hand, they can be so bound as to owe less, as we have stated in the case of the adstipulator; for, like the adstipulator, their obligation is accessory to the principal one, and there cannot be more in the accessory than in the principal thing.

quem vulgo adstipulatorem vocamus.—Et huic proinde actio competit proindeque ei recte solvitur ac nobis; sed quidquid consecutus erit, mandati iudicio nobis restituere cogetur.[1]

Ib. § 215: Capite secundo [a] in adstipulatorem, qui pecuniam in fraudem stipulatoris acceptam fecerit, quanti ea res est, tanti actio constituitur.[2]

[a] Sc. legis Aquiliae.

The adstipulatio was indeed originally intended to effect the judicial enforcement by another of the claim when the appointment of a representative was still disallowed or much restricted; later on its employment was confined to the 'stipulatio post mortem,' with the recognition of which it naturally sank into obscurity.[b]

[b] Cf. Inst. 3, 19, 4.

Ib. § 117: Adstipulatorem vero fere tunc solum adhibemus, cum ita stipulamur, ut aliquid post mortem nostram detur, [quod cum] stipulando nihil agimus, adhibetur adstipulator, ut is post mortem nostram agat: qui si quid fuerit consecutus, de restituendo eo mandati iudicio heredi nostro tenetur.[3]

Inst. iii. 19, § 13: Post mortem suam dari sibi nemo stipulari poterat, non magis quam post eius mortem, a quo stipulabatur. . . . Sed cum ex consensu contrahentium stipulationes valent, pla-

---

[1] We can, however, join another to stipulate for the same as that for which we stipulate, whom we commonly call an 'adstipulator.' And an action is equally available to him, and payment can as well be made to him as to us. But whatever he has recovered he may be compelled to restore to us by an action of mandate.

[2] By the second chapter, an action for such an amount as the value of the thing is established against the adstipulator, who in fraud of the stipulator has given an acquittance.

[3] But we generally employ an adstipulator alone when we are stipulating for something to be given after our death; for since we accomplish nothing by such a stipulation, an adstipulator is added, that he may take proceedings after our death; and if he recover anything, he is liable by the action of mandate to make it over to our heir.

Book III. Pt. I. Ch. II.

cuit nobis etiam in hunc iuris articulum necessariam inducere emendationem, ut sive post mortem, sive pridie quam morietur stipulator sive promissor concepta est, valeat stipulatio.[1]

From this object of the adstipulatio, the special legal rules which obtain in respect of it also find their explanation.

Gai. iii. § 114: In hoc autem iure quaedam singularia observantur: nam adstipulatoris heres non habet actionem; item servus adstipulando nihil agit, qui ex ceteris omnibus causis stipulatione domino adquirit; idem de eo qui in mancipio est magis placuit, nam et is servi loco est; is autem qui in potestate patris est, agit aliquid, sed parenti non adquirit, quamvis ex omnibus ceteris causis stipulando ei adquirat, ac ne ipsi quidem aliter actio competit, quam si sine capitis diminutione exierit de potestate parentis.[2]

What the adstipulatio is on the active, adpromissio is on the passive side of the obligation.

[a] Gai. iii. 92-93.

There are three kinds of adpromissio: 'sponsio,'[a]

---

[1] No one used to be able to stipulate for anything to be given to him after his death, any more than after the death of the person from whom he took the stipulation. . . . But since stipulations are binding through the agreement of the contracting parties, we have decided to introduce a necessary improvement in this part of the Law also, so that the stipulation is valid, whether it be worded 'after the death,' or 'a day before the death of the stipulator or the promisor.'

[2] Now in this branch of law some peculiar rules are observed. For the heir of the adstipulator has no action; likewise a slave who in all other cases acquires for his master by a stipulation, effects nothing by an adstipulation. The better opinion has been the same in respect of one who is *in mancipio*, for he, too, is in the position of a slave; but one who is under paternal power does a valid act, but does not acquire for an ancestor, although in all other cases he acquires for him by stipulation; and he has no action available to himself unless he has passed from parental power without loss of status.

'fidepromissio,' 'fideiussio,' the common object of which in particular is to safeguard the claim of the creditor. This is SURETYSHIP.[a]

[a] §§ 125, 128.

> Gai. iii. §§ 115–117: Pro eo quoque qui promittit solent alii obligari, quorum alios sponsores, alios fidepromissores, alios fideiussores appellamus. § Sponsor ita interrogatur: 'idem dari spondes?' fidepromissor: 'idem fide promittis?' fideiussor: 'idem fide tua esse iubes?' —Sponsores quidem et fidepromissores et fideiussores saepe solemus accipere, dum curamus, ut diligentius nobis cautum sit.[1]

According to their legal importance, these three forms of suretyship are distinguished in various particulars, especially by the sponsio and fidepromissio being only admissible in verborum obligationes, whilst the fideiussio is allowed in all obligations.

> Ib. §§ 118–119: Sponsoris vero et fidepromissoris similis condicio est, fideiussoris valde dissimilis. § Nam **illi** quidem **nullis obligationibus** accedere possunt **nisi verborum**, quamvis interdum ipse, qui promiserit, non fuerit obligatus: velut si mulier aut pupillus sine tutoris auctoritate aut quilibet post mortem suam dari promiserit.—**Fideiussor** vero **omnibus** obligationibus, i.e. sive re sive verbis sive litteris sive consensu contractae fuerint obligationes, adiici potest; ac ne illud quidem interest, utrum civilis an naturalis obligatio sit, cui adiiciatur: adeo quidem, ut pro servo quoque obligetur, sive extraneus sit, qui a servo fide-

[1] For the promisor also others are commonly made liable, some of whom we call sponsors, others fidepromissors, others fidejussors. A sponsor is interrogated thus: 'Do you undertake that the same thing shall be given?' A fidepromissor, 'Do you promise the same on your honour?' A fidejussor, 'Do you authorise the same on your honour?' We are accustomed often to take sponsors, fidepromissors and fidejussors when we are anxious to be more carefully secured.

Book III. Pt. I. Ch. II.

iussorem accipiat, sive dominus in id quod sibi debeatur.[1]

Ib. § 120: Praeterea sponsoris et fidepromissoris **heres** non tenetur, . . . fideiussoris autem etiam heres tenetur.[2]

Ib. § 121: Item sponsor et fidepromissor **lege Furia** biennio liberantur, et quotquot erunt numero eo tempore quo pecunia peti potest, in tot partes diducitur inter eos obligatio et (a) singuli(s) viriles partes debentur. Fideiussores vero perpetuo tenentur, et quotquot erunt numero, singuli in solidum obligantur; itaque liberum est creditori a quo velit solidum petere: sed nunc **ex epistula D. Hadriani** compellitur creditor a singulis, qui modo solvendo sint, partes petere [ideoque si quis ex fideiussoribus eo tempore solvendo non sit, hoc ceteros onerat.—§ 4, I. de fidej. 3, 20]. Sed cum lex Furia tantum in Italia locum habeat, evenit, ut in ceteris provinciis sponsores quoque et fidepromissores proinde ac fideiussores in perpetuum teneantur et singuli in solidum obligentur—.[3]

---

[1] The positions of a sponsor and a fidepromissor are of like character, but that of a fidejussor is widely different. § For the former can be accessory to none but verbal obligations, although sometimes he who has so promised is not bound; for example, if a woman or a ward have made a promise without the tutor's sanction, or if any one have promised that something shall be given after his death.—But a fidejussor can be joined in any obligations, that is, whether the obligations have been contracted by the thing done, or by words, or by writing, or by consent; and it does not even matter whether the obligation to which he is added be civil or natural, to the extent that he can even be liable for a slave, whether it be a stranger that takes the surety from the slave, or the master for what may be due to him.

[2] Moreover, the heir of a sponsor and fidepromissor is not liable, . . . but the heir also of a fidejussor is bound.

[3] Again, a sponsor and fidepromissor are by the *l. Furia* discharged after two years; and whatever be their number at the time when a suit is maintained for the money, the obligation is

Book III. Pt. I. Ch. II.

Ib. § 122: Praeterea inter sponsores et fidepromissores **lex Apuleia** quandam societatem introduxit: nam si quis horum plus sua portione solverit, de eo quod amplius dederit, adversus ceteros actiones constituit. Quae lex ante legem Furiam lata est, quo tempore in solidum obligabantur: unde quaeritur, an post legem Furiam adhuc legis Apuleiae beneficium supersit; et utique extra Italiam superest—.[1]

Ib. § 123: Praeterea lege **Cicereia** cautum est, ut is qui sponsores aut fidepromissores accipiat, praedicat palam et declaret, et de qua re satis accipiat et quot sponsores aut fidepromissores in eam obligationem accepturus sit; et nisi praedixerit, permittitur sponsoribus et fidepromissoribus, intra diem trigesimum praeiudicium postulare, quo quaeratur an ex ea lege praedictum sit; et si iudicatum fuerit, praedictum non esse, liberantur. Qua lege fideiussorum mentio nulla fit; sed in usu est, etiam si fideiussores accipiamus, praedicere.[2]

---

divided amongst them into so many shares, and each is liable for his individual share. But fidejussors are liable for ever, and whatever be their number, each is bound for the whole amount. And so the creditor is at liberty to demand the whole from whichever of them he likes. But now, in pursuance of an epistle of the late Emperor Hadrian, the creditor is compelled to sue each for their shares, provided they are solvent [and so, if any one of the sureties be insolvent at that time, the rest bear the burden of it]. But inasmuch as the *l. Furia* obtains in Italy alone, it follows that in the provinces sponsors and fidepromissors also, just as fidejussors, are liable for ever, and each for the full amount.

[1] Moreover, the *l. Apuleia* introduced a sort of partnership amongst sponsors and fidepromissors; for if any one of them has paid more than his share, it allows an action against the rest for that which he has given in excess. This statute was passed before the *l. Furia*, at which time they were bound for the full amount; hence the question arises whether since the *l. Furia* the benefit of the *l. Apuleia* survives. And outside of Italy it certainly does survive.

[2] Further, it was provided by the *l. Cicereia* that a person

BOOK III. Pt. I. Ch. II.

Common to them is—

(1) that sureties of each kind have the 'beneficium legis Corneliae.'

Ib. §§ 124–125: **Sed beneficium legis Corneliae** omnibus commune est: qua lege idem pro eodem apud eundem eodem anno vetatur in ampliorem summam obligari creditae pecuniae quam in XX milia.—Ex quibusdam tamen causis permittit ea lex in infinitum satis accipere: veluti si dotis nomine, vel eius quod ex testamento tibi debeatur, aut iussu iudicis satis accipiatur.[1]

(2) That the surety who pays can take steps for repayment [a] against the chief debtor (actio depensi [b] mandati).

[a] In Engl. Law, 'recoupment': see Brown, s. *fideiussor*.

[b] Probus de notis iur. § 4.

Ib. § 127: In eo quoque par omnium causa est, quod si quid pro reo solverint, eius reciperandae causa habent cum eo mandati iudicium; et hoc amplius sponsores **ex lege Publilia** propriam habent actionem in duplum, quae appellatur depensi.[2]

---

accepting sponsors or fidepromissors shall make a previous public statement, and declare both in respect of what matter he is taking security, and how many sponsors or fidepromissors he is about to take in respect of that obligation; and in default of his making such previous declaration, the sponsors and fidepromissors are allowed within thirty days to demand a preliminary investigation, in which the matter of inquiry is, whether previous declaration was made according to such statute; and if the judgment be that the declaration was not made, they are discharged. In this statute no mention is made of fidejussors, but the practice is to make a previous declaration, even if we be accepting fidejussors.

[1] But the benefit of the *l. Cornelia* is common to all sureties. By this statute the same person is forbidden on behalf of the same person, and to the same, and in the same year, to become liable for a greater sum of borrowed money than twenty thousand sesterces.—In certain cases, however, that statute allows us to take security for an unlimited amount; for example, if security be taken in respect of a dowry, or for a debt owing under a testament, or by the order of a *iudex*.

[2] In this respect also the position of all of them is the same,

It must be observed that in consequence of the correal relation existing between surety and principal debtor, by litis contestatio with the one the other was already liberated: an attempt was made to obviate this result by the form of the so-called 'suretyship of indemnity,' but it was entirely removed by Justinian.

Paul. ii. 17, § 16: Electo reo principali fideiussor vel heres eius liberatur.[1]

Cels.: Si ego decem stipulatus a Titio, deinceps stipuler a Seio, quanto minus a Titio consequi possim, si decem petiero a Titio, non liberatur Seius, . . . at si iudicatum fecerit Titius, nihil ultra Seius tenebitur.—D. 12, 1, 42 pr.[2]

Imp. Iust.: —generali lege sancimus nullo modo electione unius ex fideiussoribus vel ipsius rei alterum liberari, vel ipsum reum fideiussoribus vel uno ex his electo liberationem mereri, . . . sed manere ius integrum, donec in solidum ei pecuniae persolvantur.—C. 8, 40 (41), l. 28.[3]

In the Justinianean Law there remains—

(1) only the suretyship by 'fideiussio,' which had already become rather informal in the later Classical Law,[a] like stipulatio in general.[b]

[a] Cf. § 128; and for forms of suretyship according to the modern Law, see Arndts, 'Pandekten,' § 353.

[b] § 117.

---

because if they have paid anything for the principal debtor, they have an action of mandate against him for the purpose of recovering it; and sponsors by the *l. Publilia* have yet further a special action for double the amount, which is called the *actio depensi*.

[1] When the choice has fallen upon the principal debtor, the surety or his heir is released.

[2] If I have stipulated for ten, &c., from Tit. and afterwards stipulate for them from S., S. is not released in respect of the deficiency in what I am able to recover from T. . . . but if T. should satisfy the judgment, S. will be liable no further.

[3] —we by a general *lex* enact that, by the selection of one of the sureties or of the debtor himself, the other is in no way released, neither does the debtor himself obtain a release if the sureties or one of them have been selected, . . . but the creditor's right remains intact until his claim is wholly satisfied.

Ulp.: Sciendum est generaliter, quod si quis se scripserit fideiussisse, videri omnia sollemniter acta.—D. 45, 1, 30.[1]

Iul.: Fideiussor accipi potest, quotiens est aliqua obligatio civilis vel naturalis cui applicetur. —D. 46, 1, 16, 3.[2]

Ulp.: Stipulatus sum a reo nec accepi fideiussorem; postea volo adiicere fideiussorem; si adiecero, fideiussor obligatur.—Adhiberi autem fideiussor tam futurae quam praecedenti obligationi potest.—l. 6 pr., § 2 eod.[3]

(2) Besides the 'beneficium divisionis ex epistula D. Hadriani,' the sureties further have the 'beneficium cedendarum actionum' and the 'beneficium excussionis s. ordinis'[a] (the principal debtor being sued before the surety).

[a] For the English Law, see Brown, s. 'Suretyship'; for the Scottish, Bell, s. vv., or Paterson, s. 626.

Iul.: Fideiussoribus succurri solet, ut stipulator compellatur ei, qui solidum solvere paratus est, vendere ceterorum nomina.—l. 17 eod.[4]

Nov. 4, c. i.: Si quis crediderit et fideiussorem . . . acceperit, non statim ab initio fideiussorem . . . conveniat neque debitore neglecto intercessoribus molestus sit, sed primo eum, qui pecuniam accepit et debitum contraxit, conveniat.[5]

---

[1] It should in general be understood that, if a man has in writing stated that he has become surety, all formalities are supposed to have been observed.

[2] A surety can be taken as often as there is any civil or natural obligation to which he may be joined.

[3] I have taken a stipulation from a debtor and have not taken a surety; afterwards I wish to join a surety: if I shall join him, the surety is made liable.—Now a surety can be joined both to a prospective and to an already existing obligation.

[4] It is customary to exonerate sureties by stipulators being compelled to sell the claims against the rest to him who is prepared to discharge the full amount.

[5] If a man have made an advance and taken a surety, let him not at once from the outset sue the fidejussor, nor neglecting the debtor press the sureties, but let him first sue the person who took the money and contracted the debt.

A peculiar form of suretyship with the characteristics of Public Law is the 'praedis obligatio' (praedibus praediisque cavere praedes dare praediaque subsignare), common in the older Law in respect of contracts by the state and communities (especially in respect of locationes)[a] and strictly administrative. In these the surety with his whole property (familia pecuniaque)—originally with his person also—was bound by way of pledge particularly in respect of the lands made over, so that, in case of the claim falling due, all was forthwith made subject to sale (praedes praediaque vendere) by auction, without judicial intervention[b] (praediatura; praediatores; ius praediatorium).[c]

[a] § 123, ad fin.

[b] The universal succession of the purchaser is questionable.

[c] Cf. Gai. ii. 61, and iv. 13, 16.

Varro de li. lat. vi. 74: 'Praes' qui a magistratu interrogatus, in publicum ut praestet,[d] (a quo et) quom respondet, dicit: 'praes.'[1]

[d] ? praes siet.

Id. v. 40: 'Praedia' dicta, item ut 'praedes' a praestando, quod ea pignore data publice mancupis fidem praestent.[2]

Lex Mal. c. 63: QVASQVE LOCATIONES FECERIT[e] QVASQVE LEGES DIXERIT, . . . ET QVI PRAEDES ACCEPTI SINT QVAEQVE PRAEDIA SVBDITA SVBSIGNATA OBLIGATAVE SINT QVIQVE PRAEDIORVM COGNITORES ACCEPTI SINT, IN TABVLAS COMMVNES MVNICIPVM EIVS MVNICIPI REFERANTVR FACITO ET PROPOSITA HABETO.[3]

[e] Sc. II VIR.

Ib. c. 64: QVICVMQVE . . . IN COMMVNE MVNICIPVM PRAEDES FACTI SVNT ERVNT QVAEQVE PRAEDIA

---

1 A 'praes,' asked by the magistrate to afford public security, when he answers says, 'Praes.'

2 'Praedia' are so called, like as 'praedes' from *praestare*, because, being given in pledge, they publicly afford the guarantee of a surety.[f]

[f] Or 'afford security to sales.'

3 'And the leases that he [*i.e.*, the duumvir] shall make, all the laws that he shall promulgate, . . . and the sureties that may be accepted, and the lands which are made subject to mortgage, scheduled and bound, and the recognizances which are accepted for such lands he shall cause to be registered in common tables belonging to the citizens of that corporation, and the same shall exhibit.'

Book III. Pt. I. Ch. II.

ACCEPTA SVNT ERVNT, . . . II OMNES ET QVAE CVIVSQVE EORVM TVM EVERVNT, CVM PRAES FACTVS ERIT, QVAEQVE POSTEA ESSE, CVM OBLIGATI ESSE COEPERVNT, COEPERINT . . . EOSQVE PRAEDES EAQVE PRAEDIA . . . , QVI QVAVE SOLVTI LIBERATI SOLVTA LIBERATAQVE NON SVNT NON ERVNT, . . . II VIRIS . . . VENDERE LEGEMQVE HIS VENDVNDIS DICERE IVS POTESTASQVE ESTO: DVM EAM LEGEM IS REBVS VENDVNDIS DICANT, QVAM LEGEM EOS, QVI ROMAE AERARIO PRAEERVNT, E LEGE PRAEDIATORIA PRAEDIBVS PRAEDISQVE VENDVNDIS DICERE OPORTERET; AVT SI EMPTOREM NON INVENIET, QVAM LEGEM IN VACVOM VENDENDIS DICERE OPORTERET; ET DVM ITA LEGEM DICANT, VTI PECVNIA IN PVBLICVM MVNICIPI REFERATVR.[1]

Ib. § 65: QVOS PRAEDES QVAEQVE PRAEDIA . . . HAC LEGE VENDIDERINT, DE IIS . . . ITA IVS DICITO IVDICIAQVE DATO, VT EI QVI EOS PRAEDES EA PRAEDIA MERCATI ERVNT . . . DE IS REBVS AGERE EASQVE RES PETERE PERSEQVI RECTE POSSINT.[2]

---

[1] 'Whatever bondsmen have been or shall be constituted for the common benefit of the citizens, and whatever lands have been or shall be taken in mortgage, . . . all these and all that belonged then to each of them when the bondsmen shall be constituted, and whatever hath afterwards begun to belong to them when they began to be bound . . . and those bondsmen and those lands which respectively have not been or shall not be discharged or released . . . the Duumviri shall have title and power to impose a condition upon the sale of these, provided they impose such condition on the sale of such things, which condition they that superintend the treasury at Rome ought to impose, according to the *l. Praediatoria*, upon the sale of the bondsmen and lands; or if he shall not meet with a purchaser, such conditions as he ought to impose on sales where there is no purchaser; and provided they impose a condition that the money be deposited in the public receptacle of the municipality.'

[2] 'Such bondsmen and lands . . . as they have sold by this statute, concerning them let him so lay down the law and give judgments, that they who have bought such bondsmen and lands may be able properly to sue for such things, and to claim and maintain such.'

§ 119. Thirdly, *Litterarum Obligatio*

A mere written acknowledgment of debt (chirographum), while it serves as evidence for an existing claim, can never engender a claim. On the other hand, a strictly unilateral claim, in the form of a written composition, was already created in the LITERAL contract.[a]

[a] See 'Anct. Law,' pp. 330, *sq.*

This is closely connected with the Roman custom of keeping exact cash-books—'codices s. tabulae accepti et expensi'—in which all mere receipts and outgoings (especially money-transactions) were entered, as taken out of the 'adversaria' after certain intervals (commonly, every month), according to chronological order, and under the headings Acceptum and Expensum.

> Ps. Ascon. in Cic. or. in Verr. ii. 1, § 60: Moris fuit, unumquemque domesticam rationem sibi totius vitae suae per dies singulos scribere, quo appareret, quid quisque de reditibus suis, quid de arte foenore lucrove seposuisset et quo die, et quid item sumtus damnive fecisset.[1]

A 'litterarum obligatio' arose by the creditor's entering in his ledger (expensum alicui ferre), with the debtor's consent, the sum owing to him upon some lawful ground as if received by the debtor, and his again paying, *i.e.*, crediting himself (transcriptio a re in personam) or another (transcriptio a persona in personam); to this act corresponded the converse process in the debtor's ledger, which, however, was not necessary. A claim that had so arisen was called '*nomen transcripticium*.'[b]

[b] Cf. § 142, and see Brown, s. '*Expensilatio*.'

> Gai. iii. §§ 128–130: Litteris obligatio fit veluti nominibus transcripticiis; fit autem nomen transcripticium duplici modo, vel a re in personam, vel a persona in personam.—A re

[1] There was a custom for every one to keep a household account day by day of all his doings, that it might appear what each had laid by from his returns, from his calling, gains or profit, and on what day, and what also he had incurred of expenditure or of loss.

in personam transcriptio fit, veluti si id quod tu ex emptionis causa aut conductionis aut societatis mihi debeas, id expensum tibi tulero.—A persona in personam transcriptio fit, veluti id quod mihi Titius debet, tibi id expensum tulero, id est si Titius te delegaverit mihi.[1]

Ib. § 133: Transcripticiis vero nominibus an obligentur peregrini, merito quaeritur, quia quodammodo iuris civilis est talis obligatio: quod Nervae placuit; Sabino autem et Cassio visum est, si a re in personam fiat nomen transcripticium, etiam peregrinos obligari, si vero a persona in personam, non obligari.[2]

The entry of a merely guaranteed loan (nomen arcarium), on the other hand, did not give rise to a litterarum obligatio, but left the claim upon loan untouched.

Ib. § 131: Alia causa est eorum nominum quae arcaria vocantur: in his enim rei non litterarum obligatio consistit, quippe non aliter valeat, quam si numerata sit pecunia, numeratio autem pecuniae rei facit obligationem: qua de causa recte dicemus arcaria nomina nullam facere obligationem, sed obligationis factae testimonium praebere.[3]

---

[1] An obligation by writing arises,—for example, in the transfer of accounts. Now this transfer of accounts may occur in two ways, either from matter to person, or from one person to another.—The transfer of an entry from matter to person occurs, for example, if I debit you with what you owe me by reason of a sale, a letting, or partnership. A transfer from person to person occurs, for example, if I debit you with what Tit. owes to me, that is, if Tit. make you his substitute to me.

[2] But whether aliens are bound by transferred entries is justly questioned, because such an obligation in a manner appertains to the Civil Law; and such was the opinion of Nerva. But Sab. and Cass. considered that if the entry were from thing to person, even aliens were bound, but if from person to person, they were not bound.

[3] The case is different with those entries which are called *nomina arcaria*. For in these the obligation is real, not in

Of Greek origin, and only appertaining to the Law of Peregrini, is the obligation by 'chirographa' and 'syngrapha' (informal bonds).

> Ib. § 134: Praeterea litterarum obligatio fieri videtur chirographis et syngraphis, id est si quis debere se aut daturum se scribat, ita scilicet, ut eo nomine stipulatio non fiat: quod genus obligationis proprium peregrinorum est.[1]

The Literal Contract disappeared with the 'codices accepti et expensi,' and in Justinian's time had been long obsolete. The theory introduced instead of it by Justinian, of a new litterarum obligatio, which is based upon the conclusive evidence of the bond—acknowledgment of the receipt of a loan—after the lapse of two years from the giving of it, has nothing to do with the old Roman Literal Contract.

> Inst. iii. 21: Olim scriptura fiebat obligatio, quae nominibus fieri dicebatur; quae nomina hodie non sunt in usu. Plane si quis debere se scripserit, quod numeratum ei non est, de pecunia minime numerata post multum temporis exceptionem opponere non potest: . . . sic fit ut et hodie, dum queri non potest, scriptura obligetur; et ex ea nascitur condictio, cessante scilicet verborum obligatione. Multum autum tempus in hac exceptione . . . per constitutionem nostram coartatum est, ut ultra biennii metas huiusmodi exceptio minime extendatur.[2]

writing, inasmuch as they have no effect unless the money be paid; but the paying down of money creates a real obligation; therefore we shall be right in saying that cash entries create no obligation, but afford evidence of one having been made.

[1] Moreover, an obligation in writing is considered to arise from *chirographa* and *syngraphae*, *i.e.*, if a man states in writing that he owes, or will give something, in such way of course as that no stipulation is made regarding such matter. This class of obligation is peculiar to aliens.

[2] Formerly an obligation was created by writing, which was said to be made by entries, but these entries are not now in use.

Book III. Pt. I. Ch. II.

[a] 'Anct. Law,' pp. 331, *sq.*

Fourthly, OBLIGATIONES *QUAE RE CONTRAHUNTUR* (REAL CONTRACTS).[a]

§ 120. Loan for Consumption.

[b] At first a friendly, unactionable loan.

[c] D. 50, 16, 11.

[d] § 72.

[e] 'All commercial loans are *mutua*': Macleod, 'T. and P. of Banking,' p. 95. The mutuum of Scottish Law is the English 'exchange.'

[f] D. 46, 3, 78.

Loan for consumption (mutuum,[b] pecunia credita), a special kind of Creditum,[c] consists in the transfer of a quantity of fungible things,[d] especially of a sum of money,[e] into the ownership—or, in general, the property[f]—of another for consumption, under the obligation to give back a like quantity of the same genus in the same quality—after a time expressly limited or even left undetermined—and engenders a strictly unilateral obligation (condictio certi, triticaria).

Ulp.: —ut Celsus ait, **credendi** generalis appellatio est; . . . nam cuicumque rei assentiamur alienam fidem secuti, mox recepturi quid ex hoc contractu, credere dicimus.—l. 1, D. h. t. (de R. C. 12, 1).[1]

Gai. iii. § 124: Pecuniam creditam dicimus non solum eam quam credendi causa damus, sed omnem quam tum, cum contrahitur obligatio, certum est debitum iri, i.e. quae sine ulla condicione deducitur in obligationem.[2]

Clearly if a man have stated in writing that he owes what has not been paid to him, after a long space of time he can no more set up the plea of non-payment. It thus happens that even at the present day, as he has no remedy, he is bound by the writing, and from this arises a personal action, that is, in the absence of a verbal obligation. But the long space of time in this plea . . . has been shortened by our constitution, so that this plea is not operative beyond the limit of two years.

1 —as Cels. says, the expression *credere* is a general one; . . . for when we agree to anything in reliance upon the honour of another, in order presently to receive back something by this contract, we are said to give credit.

2 By borrowed money we speak not only of that given by us for the purpose of creating a loan, but all that which, at the time of contracting the obligation, it is certain will become a debt, that is, which is made a matter of obligation without any condition.

Paul.: Creditum ergo a mutuo differt, qua genus a specie: nam creditum consistit extra eas res, quae pondere numero mensura continentur, sicut si eandem recepturi sumus, creditum est.—l. 2, § 3, D. h. t.[1]

Gai.: Mutui autem datio consistit in his rebus, quae pondere numero mensurave constant, . . . quas res in hoc damus, ut fiant accipientis, postea alias recepturi eiusdem generis et qualitatis.—D. 44, 7, 1, 2.[2]

Mutuum damus recepturi non eandem speciem (alioquin commodatum erit aut depositum), sed idem genus.—Appellata est autem mutui datio ab eo, quod de **meo tuum** fit; et ideo si non fiat tuum, non nascitur obligatio.—In mutui datione oportet dominum esse dantem.—l. 2 pr., §§ 2, 4, D. h. t.[3]

Afr.: Si pecuniam apud te depositam convenerit ut creditam habeas, credita (fiet): quia tunc nummi, qui mei erant, tui fiunt.—D. 17, 1, 34 pr.[a][4]

[a] Cf. D. 14, 6, 3, 3, *inf.*

Ulp.: —cum ex causa mandati pecuniam

[1] A credit consequently differs from a loan as genus from species; for a credit consists also in other than things which are contained by weight, number, measure; as, if we are about to receive back the same, it is a credit.

[2] The grant of a *mutuum* consists in such things as are weighed, numbered, or measured, which things we grant with the object of their becoming the property of the receiver, and with the intention of afterwards receiving others of the same kind and character.

[3] We grant a *mutuum* not in order to receive back in the future the same specific thing as we have given (otherwise it will be a commodatum, or deposit), but the same genus. Now it has been called *mutui datio*, because from being mine it becomes yours; and so, if it do not become yours, an obligation does not arise.—In the grant of a *mutuum*, the grantor must be the owner.

[4] If it has been agreed that money deposited with you shall become a loan, a loan (will be created); because then money which was mine becomes yours.

BOOK III.
Pt. I. Ch. II.

[a] Cf. ibid. *inf.*

[b] Sc. mutuam pecuniam dederit.

mihi debeas et convenerit, ut crediti nomine eam retineas, (videtur) mihi data pecunia et a me ad te profecta.—l. 15, D. h. t.[a] [1]

Gai. ii. § 82: Si pupillus idem fecerit,[b] quia pecuniam non facit accipientis, nullam contrahit obligationem; unde pupillus vindicare quidem nummos suos potest.[2]

Iul.: Si pupillus sine tutoris auctoritate crediderit, . . . consumpta pecunia condictionem habet non alia ratione, quam quod facto eius intelligitur ad eum qui acceperit pervenisse. . . . Nam omnino qui alienam pecuniam credendi causa dat, consumpta ea habet obligatum eum qui acceperit.—l. 19, § 1, D. h. t.[3]

Ulp.: Si tibi dedero decem sic, ut novem debeas, Proculus ait, et recte, non amplius te ipso iure debere quam novem: sed si dedero, ut undecim debeas, putat Proculus amplius quam decem condici non posse.—l. 11, § 1 eod.[4]

Paul.: Re enim non potest obligatio con-

---

[1] —when you owe me money by reason of a commission, and it has been agreed that you keep it as a loan, the money (appears) to have been given by me and to have passed from me to you.

[2] If a ward have done the same (*i.e.*, made an advance), he contracts no obligation, because he does not make the money the property of the receiver: hence the ward can recover his money by *vindicatio*.

[3] If a ward has lent money without the sanction of his guardian, . . . after the money is used up he has the personal action, for no other reason than that the money is regarded as having come to the hands of the receiver by an act of his. . . . For he who pays over money belonging to another with the purpose of making a loan, after it is used up, has always made him who received it liable.

[4] If I have given you ten, that you may owe me nine, Proc. says, and rightly, that you by operation of law owe me no more than nine. But if I should have made such gift to you, that you may owe me eleven, Proc. thinks that no more than ten can be sued for by a personal action.

trahi, nisi quatenus datum sit.—D. 2, 14, 17 pr.[1]

Ulp.: Si ego pecuniam tibi quasi donaturus dedero, tu quasi mutuam accipias, Iulianus scribit donationem non esse; . . . et puto nec mutuam esse.—Si ego quasi deponens tibi dedero, tu quasi mutuam accipias, nec depositum nec mutuum est.—l. 18 pr., § 1, h. t.[a] [2]

[a] Cf. ibid. *supr.* § 82.

A stipulatio is frequently associated with the loan.

Paul.: Quotiens pecuniam mutuam dantes eandem stipulamur, non duae obligationes nascuntur, sed una verborum.—D. 45, 1, 126, 2.[3]

Pomp.: —magis implendae stipulationis gratia numeratio intelligenda est fieri.—D. 46, 2, 7.[4]

Of stipulation for interest—'foenus,' 'foenebris pecunia,' in contrast with 'gratuita pecunia,' loan by a friend 'pecuniam utendam dare'[b]—we have already spoken.[c]

[b] Cf. D. 13, 6, 1 pr. § 1.

[c] § 106.—Cf. D. 13, 6, 1, 1.

Since the foundation of an obligation by loan is derived from the enlargement of the receiver's property, to the extent of the quantity made over from property belonging to another, agency was by later legal opinion recognised in the obligation by loan, in such way that a claim by loan arises directly against the receiver in favour of the third party in whose name and to whose account, with his consent, such delivery takes place; and further, it makes no difference whether the payment

---

[1] For by a thing an obligation can be contracted only so far as the extent of the gift.

[2] If I shall have given you money as though I would make a present of it, but you accept it as a loan, Jul. writes that there is no donation; . . . and I think it is not a loan either.—If I shall have given money as though I deposited it, but you accept it as a loan, it is neither a deposit nor a loan.

[3] Whenever upon making the grant of a loan of money we stipulate for the same, two obligations do not arise, but one verbal obligation.

[4] Payment is to be understood as made rather in order to fulfil the stipulation.

Book III. Pt. I. Ch. II.

of the loan is made immediately to the receiver thereof, or to a third party, upon his instructions, or with his approval.

Ulp.: Iulianus scribit . . . nec dubitari, quin, si meam pecuniam tuo nomine voluntate tua dedero, tibi adquiratur obligatio, cum quottidie credituri pecuniam mutuam ab alio poscamus, ut nostro nomine creditor numeret futuro debitori nostro.—l. 9, § 8, h. t.[1]

Id.: Singularia quaedam recepta sunt circa pecuniam creditam: nam si tibi debitorem meum iussero dare pecuniam, obligaris mihi, quamvis meos nummos non acceperis.—l. 15 eod.[a] [2]

[a] Cf. D. 50, 17, 18; 46, 3, 64.

An appropriate limitation was put upon the contract of mutuum by the SC. Macedonianum (under Vespasian), which forbids money loans to filiifamilias; upon the ground of which the action of loan against the fil. fam. is met by an exceptio.

Ulp.: Verba SC[ti] Macedoniani haec sunt: 'Cum inter ceteras sceleris causas Macedo, quas illi natura administrabat, etiam aes alienum adhibuisset, et saepe materiam peccandi malis moribus praestaret qui pecuniam, ne quid amplius diceretur, incertis nominibus crederet: **placere, ne cui, qui filiofamilias pecuniam dedisset, etiam post mortem parentis eius, cuius in potestate fuisset, actio petitioque daretur,** ut scirent qui pessimo exemplo foenerarent, nullius

---

[1] Jul. writes, . . . that there is no doubt that if I shall have paid over my money in your name, by your desire, the benefit of an obligation is acquired by you, since with the intention of lending money we are daily accustomed to request another in our name to make a disbursement as creditor to our future debtor.

[2] Certain peculiarities have obtained acceptance in respect of borrowed money; for if I shall have instructed my debtor to pay over money to you, you become liable to me, although you shall not have received my money.

posse filiifamilias bonum nomen exspectata patris morte fieri.'—D. 14, 6, 1 pr.[1]

In filiofamilias nihil dignitas facit, quominus SC^tum Macedonianum locum habeat: nam etiamsi consul sit vel cuiusvis dignitatis, SC^to locus est.—Ib. § 3.[2]

Id.: Hoc SC^tum ad filias quoque familiarum pertinet.—l. 9, § 2 eod.[3]

Id.: Is autem solus SC^tum offendit, qui mutuam pecuniam filiofamilias dedit, non qui alias contraxit, puta vendidit locavit vel alio modo contraxit: . . . et ideo etsi in creditum abii filiofamilias vel ex causa emptionis vel ex alio contractu, . . . et si stipulatus sim (licet coeperit esse mutua pecunia), tamen quia pecuniae numeratio non concurrit, cessat SC^tum. Quod ita demum erit dicendum, si non fraus SC^to sit cogitata, ut qui credere non potuit, magis ei venderet, ut ille rei pretium haberet in mutui vicem.—l. 3, § 3 eod.[4]

---

1 The following are the words of the *SC^tum Macedonianum*, 'Whereas Macedo, amongst other sources of vice fostered by his disposition, had incurred debt also, and material for crime was frequently afforded to his debauchery by a person who, to avoid any further remark, made advances to him upon unlimited accounts, it was decreed that to no one who had advanced money to a *fil. fam.* should an action and claim be given even after the death of the ancestor under whose power he had been, so that those who set an evil example by usury might know that the debt of no *fil. fam.* could be made good by the anticipated death of the father.'

2 In respect of a *fil. fam.*, no rank hinders the application of the *SC^tum Maced.*, for even if he be a consul, or of whatever rank, the *SC^tum* is applicable.

3 This *SC^tum* concerns also *filiae fam.*

4 It is he who advances money to a *fil. fam.* that alone transgresses the *SC^tum*, not such a person as contracts with him in any other way, *e.g.*, has sold or let to him, or concluded any other contract with him; . . . and therefore, although I have entered upon a credit transaction with a *fil. fam.* by reason of a purchase, or some other contract, . . . and if I have taken a

Book III. Pt. I. Ch. II.

Pomp.: Iulianus scribit exceptionem SC[ti] Macedoniani nulli obstare, nisi qui sciret aut scire potuisset filiumfamilias esse eum cui credebat.—l. 19 eod.[a][1]

[a] See further, l. 40 pr.

§ 121. Depositum, Commodatum, Pignus.

A common feature of these three contracts is that the entrusted thing, whether it belong to the giver or not, does not pass into the ownership, nor indeed—with the exception of the pignus[b]—into the juristic possession of the debtor, and must be restored by him in specie;[c] and further they give rise to a unilateral bonae fidei obligatio with actio contraria.[d] In the earlier period they were also initiated by *fiducia*.[e]

[b] D. 16, 3, 17, 1.

[c] Cf. Macleod, pp. 90-91.

[d] § 111, ad init.

[e] Boeth. in Ci. Top. 10, and *supr.* § 100.

Iul.: Qui **rem suam** deponi apud se patitur vel utendam rogat, nec depositi nec commodati actione tenetur.—D. 16, 3, 15.[2]

Ulp.: Neque pignus neque depositum neque precarium neque emptio neque locatio rei suae consistere potest.—D. 50, 17, 45.[3]

Depositum is the contract by which some person

---

stipulation (although it began to be a loan), yet inasmuch as it is accompanied by no disbursement of money, the *SC[tum]* is dormant. This, however, can be stated only in so far as no evasion of the *SC[tum]* has been contemplated by the creditor's rather making a sale to him, so as to have the purchase-money of the property as a loan, in lieu of making a loan because he could not make such advance.

[1] Jul. writes, the plea of the *SC[tum] Maced.* stands in the way of no one but a person who knew or could have known that the person to whom he was making the advance was a *fil. fam.*

[2] He that suffers his own property to be deposited with him, or asks for the use of it, is liable neither to the *actio depositi* nor to the *actio commodati*.

[3] Neither a pledge, nor a deposit, nor a revocable grant, nor a purchase, nor a hire can exist in respect of a thing (if it be) one's own.

(depositor) entrusts to another (depositarius) a movable thing for gratuitous custody.[a]

Id.: Si vestimenta servanda balneatori data perierunt, si quidem nullam mercedem servandorum accepit, depositi eum teneri et dolum dumtaxat praestare debere puto; quodsi accepit, ex conducto. —l. 1, § 8, D. h. t. (depos. 16, 3).[1]

[a] D. 16, 3, 17, 1.

Si praedo vel fur deposuerint, et hos Marcellus putat recte depositi acturos.—Ibid. § 39.[2]

The depositary is merely under obligation to take charge of the thing—not for positive custodia—and to restore it when desired; in which he is responsible only for dolus and culpa lata.

Gai.: Is . . . apud quem rem aliquam deponimus, etiamsi negligenter rem custoditam amiserit, securus est; quia enim non sua gratia accipit, sed eius, a quo accipit, in eo solo tenetur, si quid dolo perierit: negligentiae vero nomine ideo non tenetur, quia qui negligenti amico rem custodiendam committit, de se queri debet; magnam tamen negligentiam placuit in doli crimen cadere.—D. 44, 7, 1, 5.[b][3]

[b] D. 16, 3, 32.

For treatment of the thing in violation of the con-

[1] If garments have perished that were given into the charge of the bath-keeper, even if he has received no remuneration for keeping them, I am of opinion that he is liable to the action of deposit, and that he must at least answer for *dolus;* but if he did receive remuneration he is liable upon the hiring contract.

[2] If a robber or thief have deposited anything, they too, in the opinion of Marcellus, would be right in suing upon the deposit.

[3] The person with whom we deposit anything, even if he has been careless in looking after it and has lost it, is protected; for inasmuch as he received it not on his own account, but on behalf of him from whom he got it, he is liable only in the event of its having perished through *dolus;* but on the score of negligence he is not responsible for it, because a person who entrusts a thing to the charge of a careless friend, has himself to blame. Gross negligence, however, it has been held falls under the offence of *dolus.*

Book III. Pt. I. Ch. II.

[a] Gai. iv. 47. Cf. *inf.* § 131.

tract (*e.g.*, use), and for culpable non-restitution, the depositor has against the depositary the 'actio depositi' leading to infamy[a]—originally perhaps an action of delict for breach of faith (actio poenalis).

Si quis tabulas testamenti apud se depositas pluribus praesentibus legit, ait Labeo depositi actione recte de tabulis agi posse.—l. 1, § 38, D. h. t.[1]

Coll. x. 7, 11: Ex causa depositi lege XII tabularum in duplum actio datur, edicto praetoris in simplum.—(Paul.)[2]

Inst. iv. 6, 17: Plane si depositi agetur eo nomine, quod tumultus incendii ruinae naufragii causa depositum sit, in duplum actionem praetor reddit, si modo cum ipso, apud quem depositum sit, aut cum herede eius ex dolo ipsius agitur; quo casu mixta est actio.[3]

The depositary has the 'actio depositi contraria.'

Coll. x. 25: Actione depositi servi conventus cibariorum nomine apud eundem iudicem utiliter experitur.—(Mod.)[4]

Imp. Iust.: Si quis vel pecunias vel res quasdam per depositionis accepit titulum, eas volenti ei qui deposuerit reddere illico compellatur,

---

[1] If a man in the presence of several persons have read testamentary writings deposited with him, Labeo says proceedings can be rightly taken for the writings by the *actio depositi*.

[2] Upon the ground of a deposit, an action is given by the Law of the Twelve Tables for double the amount, by the Praetor's Edict for the actual amount.

[3] Clearly where the action of deposit is brought upon the ground that an article has been deposited because of an uproar, fire, fall of buildings, shipwreck, the praetor gives an action for double the amount, provided the proceedings are taken against the person himself with whom the thing has been deposited, or against his heir on account of *dolus* on his part: in this case the action is mixed.

[4] When sued in respect of the slave's food, he takes equitable proceedings by the *act. dep.* before the same *iudex*.

nullamque compensationem vel deductionem vel doli exceptionem opponat, quasi et ipse quasdam contra eum, qui deposuit, actiones personales vel in rem praetendens.—C. 4, 34, 11.[1]

Commodatum (Loan for use[a])—to be distinguished from precarium[b]—consists in the entrusting of a thing (chiefly a movable) for gratuitous use, which is of determinate character and compass, and for a period fixed beforehand, or resulting from the object of the loan.

[a] See Bell s. 'Commodate.'
[b] § 91, ad fut.

Ulp.: Ait praetor: QVOD QVIS COMMODASSE DICETVR, DE EO IVDICIVM DABO.—Huius edicti interpretatio non est difficilis; unum solummodo notandum, quod qui edictum concepit commodati fecit mentionem, cum Pacuvius utendi dati fecit mentionem. Inter commodatum autem et **utendum datum** Labeo ait tantum interesse, quantum inter genus et speciem: commodari enim rem mobilem non etiam soli, utendam dari etiam soli; sed, ut apparet, proprie commodata res dicitur, et quae soli est: idque et Cassius existimat.—D. 13, 6, 1 pr.[2]

Paul.: Sicut autem voluntatis magis et officii,

---

[1] If a man has received either money or certain things by the title of deposit, he must, when the depositor desires it, restore them to him there and then, and can raise no counterclaim for compensation, or plea of fraud, on the pretext of himself having certain actions, personal or real, against the depositor.

[2] The Praetor says: 'If the allegation be that a man has lent something, I will allow an action for it.'—The interpretation of this Edict is not difficult: one thing alone calls for remark, that he who framed the Edict has spoken of what is lent, whilst Pac. has spoken of what is given for use. Now between that which is lent and what is given for use Labeo says there is as great a difference as between genus and species; for a movable thing is lent, but not also a part of the ground; a part of the ground also is given for use; but, as it appears, that which belongs to the ground is also properly spoken of as lent. And that is the opinion of Cassius also.

Book III. Pt. I. Ch. II.

quam necessitatis est commodare, ita modum commodati finemque praescribere eius est, qui beneficium tribuit. Cum autem id fecit, i.e. postquam commodavit, tunc finem praescribere et retro agere atque intempestive usum commodatae rei auferre, non officium tantum impedit, sed et suscepta obligatio inter dantem accipientemque. . . . Igitur non . . . recte facies importune repetendo. . . . Idemque est, si ad fulciendam insulam tigna commodasti, deinde protraxisti aut etiam sciens vitiosa commodaveris: adiuvari quippe nos, non decipi beneficio oportet. Ex quibus causis etiam contrarium iudicium utile esse dicendum est.—l. 17, § 3 eod.[1]

The 'commodatarius,' or borrower, has to safeguard the thing, to treat it conformably to its nature and to the contract,[a] to restore it to the 'commodator,' or lender, when use has been made of it, as received; and is in this responsible for omnis culpa,[b] in respect of which the 'actio commodati directa' lies against him.

[a] § 131.

[b] D. 13, 6, 18 pr.

Ulp.: Commodatum plerumque solam utilitatem continet eius cui commodatur: et ideo verior est Quinti Mucii sententia existimantis, et culpam praestandam et diligentiam.—l. 5, § 2 eod.[2]

---

[1] But just as it is more a matter of the will and of duty, than of necessity, to make a loan, so it is the concern of him who confers the benefit to prescribe the measure and the purpose of the loan. But when he has done so, that is, after he has made the loan, not only duty, but also the obligation entered into between giver and receiver, hinders his then prescribing such purpose, retracing his action, and inopportunely withdrawing the use of the thing lent. . . . Therefore you will not act rightly by reclaiming it at an inconvenient time. . . . And so again, if you have lent me planks to prop up a house, and afterwards have taken them away, or should have advisedly lent me what is faulty; for by a benefit we must be aided, not deceived. Upon these grounds also we must state is a *iudic. contr.* available.

[2] The (contract of) loan generally contemplates the advan-

Pomp.: Si commodavero tibi equum, quo uteris usque ad certum locum, si nulla culpa tua interveniente in ipso itinere deterior equus factus sit, non teneris commodati.—l. ult. eod.[1]

Gai.: Si cui ideo argentum commodaverim, quod is amicos ad coenam invitaturum se diceret, et id peregre secum portaverit, sine ulla dubitatione etiam piratarum et latronum et naufragii casum praestare debet.—l. 18 pr. eod.[2]

On the other hand, he has the 'actio commodati contraria' for return of the outlay he has incurred, and compensation for damage.

Possunt iustae causae intervenire, ex quibus cum eo, qui commodavit, agi deberet, veluti de impensis in valetudinem servi factis, . . . nam cibariorum impensae naturali scilicet ratione ad eum pertinent qui utendum accepisset.—Item qui sciens vasa vitiosa commodavit, et ibi infusum vinum vel oleum corruptum effusumve sit, condemnandus eo nomine est.—Quod autem contrario iudicio consequi quisque potest, id etiam recto iudicio, quo cum eo agitur, potest salvum habere iure pensationis.—Ib. §§ 2–4.[a] [3]

Contraria commodati actio etiam sine princi-

[a] Cf. the case of Blakemore v. Bristol and Exeter Railway Company, 8 E. and B. 1035: 'it cannot but be part of our law' (Coleridge, J. citing § 3).

---

tage merely of him to whom the loan is made, and therefore the opinion of Q. M. is the more correct, who supposes that one must answer for both negligence and diligence.

[1] If I have lent you a horse, to be used by you as far as a certain place, you are not liable upon the loan, if, without any neglect occurring on your part, the horse has been injured upon that very journey.

[2] If I have lent a man silver because he said that he meant to invite friends to supper, and he has taken it with him abroad, he must without any doubt be answerable also for mishap through pirates and highwaymen and shipwreck.

[3] Just grounds can intervene upon which proceedings ought to be taken against the lender; for example, for expenses incurred in respect of the sickness of a slave, . . . for the cost of food, of course by natural reason, attaches to the person who had received him for use.—Again, a man who has advisedly lent faulty vessels, if the wine or oil poured in has been spoilt

Book III. Pt. I. Ch. II.

pali moveri potest, sicut et ceterae quae dicuntur contrariae.—l. 17, § 1 eod.[1]

Pignus is the contract which is concluded between the pawnor or pledge-debtor, as creditor, and the pawnee or pledge-creditor, as debtor, by the delivery of a thing for pledge, or acquisition of the possession of the thing pledged.

> Gai.: Creditor quoque qui pignus accepit, re tenetur; qui et ipse de ea ipsa re, quam accepit, restituenda tenetur.—D. 44, 7, 1, 6.[2]

The debtor has to bear omnis culpa, and is responsible to the pledgor for treatment of the thing in keeping with the contract, for restitution thereof after extinction of the pledge-debt, as well as for the handing over of the 'superfluum,' enforced by 'actio pigneraticia.'

> Paul.: Ea quae diligens paterfamilias in suis rebus praestare solet, a creditore exiguntur.—D. 13, 7, 14.[3]
>
> Ulp.: In pigneraticio iudicio venit, et si res pignori datas male tractavit creditor vel servos debilitavit.—l. 24, § 3 eod.[4]

The same action is as 'contraria' given against the pledgor.

---

or has run out, is to be condemned on that account. But what every one can obtain by the *iudic. contr.* he can also secure in the direct action brought against him, by right of counter-claim.

[1] The *act. contr.* upon a loan can also be brought independently of the principal action, just as the rest of so-called contrary actions.

[2] The creditor also that has taken a pledge is liable in respect of the property; and is himself liable too for the return of the very thing pledged.

[3] Those things are required of the creditor for which a diligent *pat. fam.* is commonly answerable in respect of his own property.

[4] It comes into account also in the action of pledge if the creditor has misused things given as security, or has disabled slaves.

Pomp.: Si necessarias impensas fecerim in servum aut in fundum, quem pignoris causa acceperim, non tantum retentionem, sed etiam contrariam pigneraticiam actionem habebo: finge enim medicis, cum aegrotaret servus, dedisse me pecuniam et eum decessisse.—l. 8 pr. eod.[1]

Ulp.: Si rem alienam mihi debitor pignori dederit aut malitiose in pignore versatus sit, dicendum est, locum habere contrarium iudicium.—l. 9 pr. eod.[2]

Fifthly, OBLIGATIONES *QUAE CONSENSU CONTRAHUNTUR*, OR CONSENSUAL (MUTUAL) CONTRACTS.[a]

[a] 'Anct. Law,' pp. 332, *sqq.*

§ 122. Purchase and Sale.[b]

[b] See Benjamin, 'Law of Sale of Personal Property,' pp. 355-364 (3rd ed.).

Purchase and Sale is the informal Contract for the irrevocable transfer of a specific chattel (merx) in consideration of the payment of a certain sum of money (pretium).[c]—It was originally the parting with, and appropriation of, a thing in consideration of the price paid; so that the real and the obligatory element coalesced.[d]

[c] D. 18, 1, 1 pr.

[d] § 79, ad init.

Paul.: Sed an sine nummis venditio dici hodieque possit, dubitatur, veluti si ego togam dedi, ut tunicam acciperem. Sabinus et Cassius esse emptionem et venditionem putant; Nerva et Proculus permutationem, non emptionem hoc esse. . . . Sed verior est Nervae et Proculi sententia: nam ut aliud est vendere aliud emere alius emptor alius venditor, sic aliud est premium aliud merx; quod in permutatione discerni non potest, uter emptor uter venditor sit.—l. 1, § 1, D. de C. E. 18, 1.[3]

---

1 If I have incurred necessary expenses over a slave or an estate which I took as a pledge, I shall have not only a lien, but also the contrary action of pledge; for suppose I had paid money to the doctors when the slave was ill, and he had died.

2 If the debtor has given me in pledge a thing owned by another, or should have gone to work dishonestly in respect of the security, we must state that the contrary action obtains.

3 But whether a sale without money can be spoken of at the

Book III. Pt. I. Ch. II.

Gai. iii. § 141: Pretium in numerata pecunia consistere debet: nam in ceteris rebus an pretium esse possit, veluti homo aut toga aut fundus alterius rei pretium esse possit, valde quaeritur. Nostri praeceptores putant etiam in alia re posse consistere pretium: unde illud est, quod vulgo putant, per permutationem rerum emptionem et venditionem contrahi. . . . Diversae scholae auctores dissentiunt aliudque esse existimant permutationem rerum, aliud emptionem et venditionem: alioquin non posse rem expediri permutatis rebus, quae videatur res venisse et quae pretii nomine data esse. . . . Sed ait Sabinus, si rem tibi venalem habenti veluti fundum accesserim et pretii nomine hominem forte dederim, fundum quidem videri venisse, hominem autem pretii nomine datum esse, ut fundus acciperetur.[1]

The contract is concluded, or complete, the moment the agreement of the will (consensus) upon object and

present day also, is matter of doubt; for example, if I have given a toga, that I might receive a tunic. Sab. and Cass. are of opinion that it is a purchase and sale; Nerva and Procul. that this is barter, not a purchase and sale. But the view of Nerva and Procul. is the more correct; for just as sale is different from purchase, and the purchaser from the vendor, so price is different from merchandise; because in respect of barter, one cannot distinguish which is purchaser and which vendor.

[1] The price must consist of coined money. For whether the price can consist of other things, as a slave, or a toga, or a field, is rightly matter of question. Our teachers think that the price may consist of some other thing; and hence the common notion, that by the exchange of things a purchase and sale is contracted. . . . The authorities of the other school are of a different opinion, and think that an exchange of things is different from buying and selling, otherwise it would be impossible to ascertain upon an exchange of things which may be considered sold, and which given by way of price. . . . But, says Sabinus, if I come to you who have something for sale, land for example, and give a slave, say, for the price, the land is to be considered sold, and the slave given by way of price, in order that the land may be received.

price is declared, whereupon the risk and use of the article sold passes to the purchaser: it is regarded as already forming part of his substance, although until traditio is still in the ownership of the vendor.[a]

[a] D. 47, 2, 14, pr. For the 'property,' in English Law, see Anson, 'Cont.' p. 64 (3rd ed.); and below, as to payment of the price.

Gai. iii. § 139: Emptio et venditio contrahitur, cum de pretio convenerit, quamvis nondum pretium numeratum sit, ac ne **arra** quidem data fuerit; nam quod arrae nomine datur, argumentum est emptionis et venditionis contractae.[1]

Callistr.: Si ager ex emptionis causa ad aliquem pertineat, non recte hac actione[b] agi poterit, antequam traditus sit ager tuncque possessio amissa sit.—D. 6, 1, 50.[2]

[b] Sc. rei vindicatione.

Paul: Perfecta emptione periculum ad emptorem respiciet;[c] et si id quod venierit appareat, quid quale quantum sit, sit et pretium, et pure veniit, perfecta est emptio.—D. 18, 6, 8 pr.[3]

[c] Expressed in English Law by the maxim, 'Res perit domino.'

Cum autem emptio et venditio contracta sit, . . . periculum rei venditae statim ad emptorem pertinet, tametsi adhuc ea res emptori tradita non sit. Itaque si homo mortuus sit vel aliqua parte corporis laesus fuerit, aut aedes totae aut aliqua ex parte incendio consumptae fuerint, aut fundus vi fluminis totus vel aliqua ex parte ablatus sit, sive etiam inundatione aquae aut arboribus turbine deiectis longe minor aut deterior esse coeperit: emptoris damnum est, cui necesse est, licet rem non fuerit nactus, pretium solvere; quidquid

---

[1] A contract of purchase and sale is complete when the price is agreed upon, even though the price may not yet have been paid, nor even earnest given; for what is given by way of earnest is only evidence that a contract of purchase and sale has been effected.

[2] If a field belong to any one upon the title of purchase, he will not by Law be able to sue by this [*i.e.* real] action before delivery of the field and subsequent loss of possession.

[3] Upon completion of the purchase, the risk will pass to the purchaser; and if the quality, quantity and price of the thing sold be ascertained, and it is sold unconditionally, the purchase has been completed.

Book III. Pt. I. Ch. II.

enim sine dolo et culpa venditoris accidit, in eo venditor securus est. Sed et si post emptionem fundo aliquid per alluvionem accessit, ad emptoris commodum pertinet: nam et commodum eius esse debet, cuius periculum est.—§ 3, I. h. t. 3, 23.[1]

In the contract of Purchase there are very often conditions and collateral agreements,[a] *e.g.*,

(1) sale upon approval.[b]

Ibid. § 4: Emptio tam sub condicione quam pure contrahi potest; sub condicione, veluti: 'si Stichus intra certum diem tibi placuerit, erit tibi emptus aureis tot.'[2]

(2) in diem addictio.

Paul.: In diem addictio ita fit: 'ille fundus centum esto tibi emptus, nisi si quis intra Kalendas Ianuarias proximas meliorem condicionem fecerit, quo res a domino abeat.'—D. 18, 2, 1.[3]

[a] Cf. § 127.

[b] For the so-called *pactum displicentiae*, see Savigny, v. 301.

[1] Now when the contract of purchase and sale has been made, . . . risk attending the article sold falls at once upon the purchaser, although the article have not yet been delivered to the purchaser. If therefore a slave has died, or has suffered injury in some part of his body, or if a house has been wholly or partially burnt down, or land has wholly or in part been washed away by the force of a stream, or has become much less or worse even by an overflow of water, or by trees having been rooted up by a hurricane, the damage is the purchaser's, who is obliged to pay the price, although he have not acquired the property. For the vendor is protected in respect of whatever happens without fraud and neglect on his part. But even if after the purchase some addition is made to the land by alluvion, it appertains to the gain of the purchaser, for the gain must accrue to him whose is the danger.

[2] A contract of purchase can be entered into either as conditional or as unconditional; conditional, as: 'if Stich. within a certain time give you satisfaction, he shall be your purchase for so many *aurei*.'

[3] The reserve of the better bid occurs thus: 'that land shall be your purchase for a hundred, &c., unless some one by the 1st of January next make a better bid, by which the property shall pass from the owner.'

(3) lex commissoria.

Pomp.: Cum venditor fundi in lege ita caverit: 'si ad diem pecunia soluta non sit, ut fundus inemptus sit,' ita accipitur inemptus, si venditor inemptum eum esse velit.—D. 18, 3, 2.[1]

Requisites. Every alienable object of a right[a] can be object of sale, both corporeal things—even res futurae v. speratae[b]—and rights.

[a] D. 18, 1, 6 pr.

[b] Not to be confounded with the *emptio spei*.

Paul.: Omnium rerum, quas quis habere vel possidere vel persequi potest, venditio recte fit; quas vero natura vel gentium ius vel mores civitatis commercio exuerunt, earum nulla venditio est.—l. 34, § 1, D. de C. E.[2]

Pomp.: Nec emptio nec venditio sine re, quae veneat, potest intelligi; et tamen fructus et partus futuri recte ementur, ut cum editus esset partus, iam tunc, cum contractum esset negotium, venditio facta intelligitur.—Aliquando tamen et sine re venditio intelligitur, veluti cum quasi alea emitur; quod fit, cum captus piscium vel avium emitur: emptio enim contrahitur, etiamsi nihil inciderit, quia spei emptio est.—l. 8 eod.[3]

---

[1] When the vendor of land in the conditions of sale has provided 'that the land shall not be purchased, if by the time appointed payment of the money has not been made,' the land is not to be regarded as purchased if it be the will of the vendor that it should not be purchased.

[2] It is lawful to sell any things which a man can appropriate, or possess, or recover by action; but a sale is void of those things which the law of Nature, or the *i. g.*, or the customs of the State have withdrawn from commerce.

[3] Neither a purchase nor sale is conceivable without an article which is sold; both fruits and future issue may, however, be lawfully purchased, so that when the young should be born, the sale is regarded as having taken place at that time when the transaction was contracted.—Sometimes, however, even without a thing is a sale conceived of, as if a man purchase a venture, so to speak; this is the case if a catch of fish or fowl is purchased; for a purchase is contracted, even if nothing have come of it, because there is the purchase of an expectation.

Book III. Pt. I. Ch. II.

Paul. : Cum usumfructum mihi vendis, interest, utrum ius utendi fruendi quod solum tuum est, vendas, an vero in ipsum corpus, quod tuum sit usumfructum mihi vendas: nam priore casu, etiamsi statim morieris, nihil mihi heres tuus debebit, heredi autem meo debebitur, si tu vivis; posteriore casu heredi meo nihil debebitur, heres tuus debebit.—D. 18, 6, 8, 2.[1]

Ulp.: Nomina eorum, qui sub condicione vel in diem debent, et emere et vendere solemus: ea enim res est, quae emi et venire potest.—D. 18, 4, 17.[2]

The pretium must be 'certum,' and also, according to later Law (from Diocletian), 'iustum,' *i.e.*, it may not fall short of half of the actual value of the thing (laesio enormis, i.e. ultra dimidium), for in such case the purchase can be disputed by the vendor.[a]

[a] Cf. D. 4, 4, 16, 4.

Gai. iii. § 140 : Pretium autem certum esse debet: nam alioquin si ita inter nos convenerit, ut 'quanti Titius rem aestimaverit,' tanti sit empta, Labeo negavit ullam vim hoc negotium habere, cuius opinionem Cassius probat: Ofilius et eam emptionem esse putat et venditionem, cuius opinionem Proculus secutus est.[3]

---

[1] When you sell me the usufruct, it is of importance whether you sell me the right of use and enjoyment which alone is yours, or usufruct in the object itself which is your property; for in the former case, even if you die at once, your heir will owe me nothing, but he will be indebted to my heir if you go on living; in the latter case he will be in nothing indebted to my heir, it will be your heir who is indebted.

[2] We are accustomed both to buy and sell claims against those who are indebted under a condition or for a definite time.

[3] The price, however, must be definite; for otherwise, if we have agreed that the purchase is for as much 'as T. shall value the thing at,' Sab. has said that this transaction has no effect, and his opinion is approved by Cass.; Ofil. thinks that there is both a purchase and a sale, whose opinion was followed by Proculus.

Sed nostra decisio ita hoc constituit, ut quotiens sic composita sit venditio 'quanti ille aestimaverit,' sub hac condicione staret contractus, ut, si quidem qui nominatus est pretium definierit, . . . venditio ad effectum perducatur . . . sin autem ille vel noluerit vel non potuerit pretium definire, tunc pro nihilo esse venditionem quasi nullo pretio statuto ; quod ius . . . non est absurdum et in locationibus et conductionibus trahere. —§ 1, I. h. t.[1]

Paul. : —in emendo et vendendo naturaliter concessum est, quod pluris sit minoris emere, quod minoris sit pluris vendere, et ita invicem se circumscribere.—D. 19, 2, 22, 3.[2]

The Contract of Purchase gives rise to a mutual obligation with the following claims and liabilities, to which the purchaser has to give effect by the 'actio empti,' the vendor by the 'actio venditi.'

The performance and counter-performance, unless otherwise provided, must be contemporaneous, *i.e.*, come about reciprocally. The vendor has to take all care of the object of purchase.[a]

[a] D. 18, 6, 12 (11).

Ulp. : Offerri pretium ab emptore debet, cum ex empto agitur ; et ideo et si pretii partem offerat, nondum est ex empto actio : venditor enim quasi pignus retinere potest eam rem,

---

[1] But our decision has settled it thus, that when a sale has been arranged 'for the price so and so shall assess,' the contract shall stand good on this condition, that if the nominee fix the price, . . . the sale is carried out ; . . . but if so and so has either been unwilling or unable to fix the price, then the sale is void, on the ground that no price has been fixed ; and there is no absurdity in applying this rule to contracts of letting and hiring.

[2] By natural Law, in buying and selling one is permitted to purchase for a smaller price that which is more valuable, and for a higher price that which is less valuable, and that so the parties mutually overreach themselves.

Book III. Pt. I. Ch. II.

[a] Cf. Story, 'Equity,' §§ 1221-2 (Grigsby, pp. 850-1).

quam vendidit.—l. 13, § 8, D. de A. E. V. 19, 1.[a] [1]

The purchaser has to make the vendor owner of the purchase-money.

Id.: Emptor nummos venditoris facere cogitur.—l. 11, § 2 eod.[2]

Veniunt in hoc iudicium in primis pretium . . . item usurae pretii post diem traditionis.—l. 13, § 20 eod.[3]

The vendor is responsible—

(1) for the delivery (vacuae possessionis traditio) of the thing,—grant of the juristic possession—but not for the transfer of the ownership (mancipatio).

Ulp.: Qui vendidit, necesse non habet fundum emptoris facere, ut cogitur, qui fundum stipulanti spopondit.—l. 25, § 1, D. de C. E.[4]

Lab.: Nemo potest videri eam rem vendidisse, de cuius dominio id agitur, ne ad emptorem transeat, sed hoc aut locatio est aut aliud genus contractus.—l. 80, § 3 eod.[5]

Paul.: Vacua possessio emptori tradita non intelligitur, si alius . . . in possessione est.—l. 2, § 1, D. de A. E. V.[6]

---

[1] The purchase-money must be tendered by the purchaser when he sues upon the purchase, and accordingly, even if he tender a part of the price, there is not yet an action upon the purchase; for the vendor can retain the thing purchased as a pledge.

[2] The purchaser is obliged to make the money the property of the vendor.

[3] In this action come into account especially the purchase-money . . . likewise interest upon the purchase-money since the day of delivery.

[4] It is not necessary that the vendor should make the land the property of the purchaser, as he is obliged to do so who promised the land to the stipulator.

[5] No one can be regarded as the vendor of a thing the ownership of which it is intended should not pass to the purchaser, but this is a letting, or another class of contract.

[6] The vacant possession is not regarded as delivered to the purchaser if another is in possession.

Ulp.: Et in primis ipsam rem praestare venditorem oportet, id est tradere: quae res, si quidem dominus fuit venditor, facit et emptorem dominum, . . . si modo pretium est numeratum aut eo nomine satisfactum.—Iulianus probat nec videri traditum, si superior in possessione[a] emptor futurus non sit.—l. 11, §§ 2, 13 eod.[1]

[a] I.e., in lite de poss.

Inst. ii. 1, 41: Venditae vero et traditae (res) non aliter emptori adquiruntur, quam si is venditori pretium solverit vel alio modo ei satisfecerit, veluti expromissore aut pignore dato: quod cavetur quidem etiam lege XII tabularum, tamen recte dicitur et iure gentium id effici. Sed si is, qui vendidit, fidem emptoris secutus fuerit, dicendum est statim rem emptoris fieri.[b][2]

[b] Cf. Story, § 1220 (Grigsby, p. 850).

(2) For the warranty of 'habere licere,' *i.e.*, of the quiet enjoyment of the object sold; if the thing be recovered by some one from the purchaser, *i.e.*, obtained by litigation (evincere, evictio), the vendor is liable to pay damages,[c] but the purchaser must, as a rule, by 'litis denuntiatio,' afford his 'auctor' (warrantor) opportunity of supporting him in the suit. In Roman trade it was customary for the purchaser to obtain a promise from the vendor of, as a rule, double the amount of purchase-money, to provide for the chance of evictio. This 'duplae stipulatio' can itself be

[c] § 110.

---

[1] And before all, the vendor must assure the thing itself, that is, make delivery; and this, if the vendor was, in fact, owner, makes the purchaser also owner . . . provided the purchase-money has been paid, or security given for it. Julian approves of their being no constructive delivery if the purchaser shall not prevail in possession.

[2] But goods sold and delivered are only acquired by the purchaser if he has paid the price to the vendor, or satisfied him in another way; for example, by finding guarantee or security. This is also provided by a law of the Twelve Tables; but the statement is correct that it takes place also by the *ius gent.* If the vendor have given credit to the purchaser, we must say the thing forthwith becomes the property of the purchaser.

BOOK III. Pt. I. Ch. II.

enforced by the actio empti. In the evictio of the thing assigned 'venditionis causa' the action (auctoritatis actio) was always for double the amount, even without special stipulation.[a]

[a] § 116.

Ulp.: Stipulatio ista: 'habere licere spondes?' hoc continet, ut liceat habere, nec per quemquam omnino fieri, quominus nobis habere liceat.—D. 45, 1, 38 pr.[1]

Pomp.: **Duplae stipulatio** committi dicitur tunc, cum res restituta est petitori, vel damnatus est litis aestimatione, vel possessor ab emptore conventus absolutus est.—l. 16, § 1, D. de evict. 21, 2.[2]

Ulp.: Sive tota res evincatur sive pars, habet regressum emptor in venditorem.—l. 1 eod.[3]

Gai.: Si ab emptore ususfructus petatur, proinde is venditori denuntiare debet, atque is a quo pars petitur.—l. 49 eod.[4]

Cels.: Cum venderes fundum non dixisti 'ita ut optimus maximusque'; verum est, quod Q. Mucio placebat, non liberum, sed qualis esset, fundum praestari oportere.—l. 59, 3, de C. E.[5]

Pomp.: Duplae stipulatio evictionem non

---

1 The stipulation, 'Do you promise the undisturbed possession?' includes the assurance of quiet possession, and that absolutely nothing shall be done to prevent our quiet possession.

2 It is said that the stipulation for double the amount becomes due when the thing has been restored to the claimant or (the purchaser) has been condemned in damages assessed, or the possessor when sued by the purchaser has been acquitted.

3 Whether it be the whole property or a part that is recovered, the purchaser has his remedy against the vendor.

4 If the usufruct should be claimed from the purchaser, he must cite the vendor just as does the person from whom a part is claimed.

5 When selling the land you did not say, 'so that it be free from all incumbrances'[b]: the opinion of Q. M. is correct that the land ought to be delivered, not unincumbered, but in such condition as it was.

[b] Servitudes, as explained by Brisson, s. vv.

unam eam continet, si quis dominium rei petierit et evincerit, sed et si Serviana actio experiatur.—l. 34, § 2, D. de evict.[1]

Paul.: Evicta re ex empto actio non ad pretium dumtaxat recipiendum, sed ad id quod interest competit; ergo et si minoris esse coepit, damnum emptoris erit.—l. 70 eod.[2]

Ulp.: Emptori duplam promitti a venditore oportet, nisi aliud convenit.—l. 37 pr. eod.[3]

Afric.: Si sciens alienam rem ignoranti mihi vendideris, etiam prius quam evincatur, utiliter me ex empto acturum putavit in id, quanti mea intersit meam esse factam.—l. 30, § 1, D. de A. E. V.[4]

Paul.: Si vendideris servum mihi Titii, deinde Titius heredem me reliquerit, Sabinus ait amissam actionem pro evictione, quoniam servus non potest evinci: sed in ex empto actionem decurrendum est.—l. 9, D. de evict.[5]

Id.: Si cum possit emptor auctori denuntiare, non denuntiasset idemque victus fuisset, quoniam parum instructus esset, hoc ipso videtur dolo

---

[1] The stipulation for double the amount extends not merely to that single recovery when a man claims and recovers the ownership of property, but also when the Servian action is brought.

[2] When property has been recovered, the action upon the purchase avails not only for the recovery of the purchase-money, but for the value to the person; therefore even if it has diminished in value, the loss is the purchaser's.

[3] Double the amount must be promised to the purchaser by the vendor, unless another amount be agreed upon.

[4] If you have advisedly sold to me, without my knowledge, property of another man, he[a] was of opinion that even before recovery I can bring an equitable action upon the purchase for the amount of my interest in the thing being made mine.

[a] Africanus.

[5] If you have sold to me Titius's slave, and Tit. has afterwards made me his heir, Sabin. says the action for recovery is gone, since the slave cannot be recovered; but I must have recourse to an action upon the purchase.

Book III. Pt. I. Ch. II.

fecisse et ex stipulatu agere non potest.—l. 53, § 1 eod.[1]

Imp. Alex.: Emptor fundi, nisi auctori denuntiaverit, evicto praedio neque ex stipulatu neque ex empto actionem contra venditorem habet.—l. 8, C. eod. 8, 44 (45).[2]

Paul. ii. 17, 3: Res empta, mancipatione et traditione perfecta, si evincatur, auctoritatis venditor duplotenus obligatur.[3]

The vendor has always to warrant the qualities of the thing of which assurance is given (dicta promissa). For the more considerable latent defects of a thing, which were not disclosed, he was according to ius civile only responsible in the case of fraudulent silence, but by the Aedilian Edict he is liable absolutely. The purchaser has by this edict the option of the 'actio redhibitoria'[a] for rescission of the purchase, or the 'actio aestimatoria' (quanti minoris) for proportionate reduction of the purchase-money. Here also 'duplae stipulatio' was usual.

[a] See Paterson, 'Comp. of Engl. and Scott. Law,' s. 454.

Cic. de off. iii. 16, 65: Cum ex XII tabulis satis esset ea praestari, quae essent lingua nuncupata, quae qui infitiatus esset dupli poenam subiret, a iurisconsultis etiam reticentiae poena est constituta.[4]

---

[1] If the purchaser, when in a position to cite his warrantor, had not cited him, and had been worsted, since he was little prepared (for the defence), in this very point does his act appear to have been colourable, and he cannot sue upon the stipulation.

[2] Unless the purchaser of land, upon the recovery of the estate, has cited the warrantor, he has against the vendor neither an action upon the stipulation nor one upon the purchase.

[3] If a thing is recovered, the purchase of which has been made perfect by mancipation and delivery, the vendor of the title is made liable in double the amount.

[4] Whilst by the Twelve Tables it was enough that compensation should be given for such points as had been expressly mentioned, and that he who had misrepresented them should be liable for double damages, a like penalty was imposed by the jurists on silence.

Ulp.: Quod venditor ut commendet dicit, sic habendum, quasi neque dictum neque promissum est.—D. 4, 3, 37.[1]

Paul. ii. 17, § 4: Distracto fundo si quis de modo mentiatur, in duplum eius, quod mentitus est, officio iudicis aestimatione facta convenitur.[2]

Aiunt aediles: QVI MANCIPIA VENDVNT, CERTIORES FACIANT EMPTORES, QVID MORBI VITIIVE CVIQVE SIT, QVIS FVGITIVVS ERROVE SIT NOXAVE SOLVTVS NON SIT, EAQVE OMNIA, CVM EA MANCIPIA VENIBVNT, PALAM RECTE PRONVNCIANTO: QVODSI MANCIPIVM ADVERSVS EA VENISSET, SIVE ADVERSVS QVOD DICTVM PROMISSVMVE FVERIT CVM VENIRET, QVOD EIVS PRAESTARI OPORTERE DICITVR, EMPTORI OMNIBVSQVE AD QVOS EA RES PERTINET IVDICIVM DABIMVS, VT ID MANCIPIVM REDHIBEATVR.—D. 21, 1, 1, 1.[3]

Aediles aiunt: QVI IVMENTA VENDVNT PALAM RECTE DICVNTO, QVID IN QVOQVE EORVM MORBI VITIIQVE SIT: . . . SI QVID ITA FACTVM NON ERIT, . . . MORBI VITIIVE CAVSA INEMPTIS FACIENDIS IN SEX MENSIBVS, VEL QVO MINORIS CVM VENIRENT FVERINT, IN ANNO IVDICIVM DABIMVS.—l. 38, pr. eod.[4]

---

[1] That which a vendor alleges in order to recommend his wares is to be regarded as though neither alleged nor promised.

[2] If a person make a false representation as to the measure of a field subject to distraint, he is sued for double the amount that he has misrepresented, after due valuation made by the *iudex*.

[3] The aediles say: 'Let them that sell slaves apprise the purchasers of disease or flaw affecting each that is a fugitive, or vagrant, or not discharged from punishment for a tort, and let them openly and correctly declare all such things when those slaves shall be sold. But if a slave should have been sold contrary to these rules, or contrary to that which shall have been stated or promised when he was sold, for so much of it as it is said ought to be made good, we will give an action to the purchaser and to all whom this concerns, that such slave may be taken back.'

[4] The aediles say: 'Let those who sell beasts of draught

Book III. Pt. I. Ch. II.

Ulp.: Causa huius edicti proponendi est, ut occurratur fallaciis vendentium et emptoribus succurratur: . . . dummodo sciamus venditorem, etiamsi ignoravit ea quae aediles praestari iubent, tamen teneri debere. Nec hoc est iniquum: potuit enim ea nota habere; neque enim interest emptoris, cur fallatur, ignorantia venditoris an calliditate.—l. 1, § 2 eod.[1]

Labeo scribit edictum aedilium curulium de venditionibus rerum esse tam earum quae soli sunt, quam earum quae mobiles aut se moventes.—Ibid. pr.[2]

§ 123. Hiring or Letting.

[a] See Bell, s. 'Location.'

[b] D. 19, 5, 5, 2; and § 122, ad init.

[c] § 122, and D. 19, 5, 22.

Hiring or Letting (locatio et conductio[a]) is the contract by which is promised either the transfer of the use of a thing (locatio conductio rei), or the performance of certain services (locatio conductio operarum, or operis) for a certain time, in consideration of an equivalent in money (merces, pensio, vectura);[b] exceptionally also in natural produce of a fruit-bearing thing (colonus partiarius). The same holds good with regard to the merces[c] and the completion of the contract as with purchase. The contract of Hiring or

---

openly and correctly declare what disease or flaw any one of them may have . . . if anything shall not have so been done, we will give an action within six months for a rescission of the purchase, upon the ground of disease or flaw, or within one year for as much as they were depreciated when sold.'

[1] The reason for setting forth this edict is, to check the devices of vendors, and that relief may be afforded to purchasers . . . only that we ought to know that a vendor, although he was not aware of what the aediles command to be done, must nevertheless be held liable. And this is not unfair; for the vendor could have known it, for it makes no difference to the purchaser why he is deceived, whether by the ignorance or the craft of the vendor.

[2] Labeo writes that the edict of the curule aediles treats of purchases as well of those things which appertain to the soil, as of those which are movable or set themselves in motion.

Letting creates a mutual obligation, to be enforced by the 'actio locati conducti'; but performance by the lessor must precede that of the hirer. The contracting parties are answerable to one another for omnis culpa.

> Sicut vulgo quaerebatur, an permutatis rebus emptio et venditio contrahitur, ita quaeri solebat de locatione et conductione, si forte rem aliquam tibi utendam sive fruendam quis dederit et invicem a te aliam utendam sive fruendam acceperit: et placuit non esse locationem et conductionem, sed proprium genus esse contractus. Veluti si, cum unum quis bovem haberet et vicinus eius unum, placuerit inter eos, ut per denos dies invicem boves commodarent, ut opus facerent, et apud alterum bos periit: neque locati vel conducti neque commodati competit actio, quia non fuit gratuitum commodatum, verum praescriptis verbis agendum est.—§ 2, I. h. t. (de loc. 3, 24).[1]

First, of the hiring of a thing (locatio conductio rerum). The hirer, called conductor (colonus, inquilinus), acquires the mere detention of the thing,[a] which he has to treat conformably to the contract; upon the termination of which he has to return it to the lessor in the same condition as he received it, and to discharge the amount of the hire.

[a] C. 7, 30.

> Conductor omnia secundum legem conductionis facere debet, et si quid in lege praetermissum

[1] Just as it used to be a moot point whether a contract of purchase results from an exchange of commodities, so too was a question commonly raised concerning letting and hiring, if a man gave you anything to be used or enjoyed, and in turn received from you something else to be used or enjoyed; and it has been settled that this is not a letting and hiring, but a special class of contract. For example, if when a man should have an ox, and his neighbour one, and they have mutually decided to lend one another the oxen for ten days at a time to do some work, and an ox has died in the hands of one party, an action lies neither upon hiring or letting, nor upon loan, because it was not a gratuitous loan, but proceedings must be taken by an action on the case.[b]

[b] § 200.

> fuerit, id ex bono et aequo debet praestare; qui pro usu aut vestimentorum aut argenti aut iumenti mercedem aut dedit aut promisit, ab eo custodia talis desideratur, qualem diligentissimus paterfamilias suis rebus adhibet: quam si praestiterit et aliquo casu rem amiserit, de restituenda ea non tenebitur.—§ 5, I. eod.[1]
>
> Gai.: —ante omnia colonus curare debet, ut opera rustica suo quoque tempore faciat, ne intempestiva cultura deteriorem fundum faceret; praeterea villarum curam agere debet, ut eas incorruptas habeat.—l. 25, § 3, D. h. t. (loc. 19, 2).[2]
>
> Imp. Alex.: Nemo prohibetur rem, quam conduxit fruendam, alii locare, si nihil aliud convenit. —l. 6, C. eod. 4, 65.[3]

Upon the lessor (locator) is incumbent the granting of the 'uti frui licere'; he is liable, moreover, for injury that has arisen to the hirer from undisclosed defects of the thing, as well as for the refunding of 'impensae necessariae.'

> Ulp.: Ex conducto actio conductori datur.—Competit autem ex his causis fere: ut puta si re quam conduxit frui ei non liceat (forte quia possessio ei aut totius agri aut partis non praestatur, aut villa non reficitur vel stabulum vel ubi greges

---

[1] The hirer must do all in accordance with the terms of the hiring, and if he shall have omitted any point in the terms, he must make it good according to what is fair and equitable. When a man has given or promised a sum for the hire either of clothes, or silver, or a beast of draught, such safe-keeping is required of him as a most attentive head of a household exercises in his own affairs: if he has exhibited such, and yet by some mishap has lost the thing, he will not be liable to restore it.

[2] The agricultural tenant must above all take care to do all work in the field at its proper time, so as not to deteriorate the land by unseasonable cultivation; moreover, he must give an eye to the buildings so as to avoid dilapidation.

[3] No one is prevented from letting out to another for enjoyment property which he has hired, if no agreement have been made to the contrary.

eius stare oporteat), vel si quid in lege conductionis convenit, si hoc non praestatur, ex conducto agetur.—l. 15 pr., § 1, D. h. t.[1]

Id.: Si quis dolia vitiosa ignarus locaverit, deinde vinum effluxerit, tenebitur in id quod interest, nec ignorantia eius erit excusata.—l. 19, § 1 eod.[2]

The contract of hiring is discharged by lapse of the stipulated time; but in agricultural estates, in the absence of any declaration, a tacit further hiring is assumed; not, however, by alienation of the thing,[a] nor by the death of one of the contracting parties.

[a] Expressed in the modern Law by the dictum, 'Purchase cancels hire,' as to which see Arndts, 'Pandekten,' § 313. —Cf. D. 19, 1, 13, 30.

Id.: Qui impleto tempore conductionis remansit in conductione, . . . reconduxisse videbitur. . . . Quod autem diximus taciturnitate utriusque partis colonum reconduxisse videri, ita accipiendum est, ut in ipso anno, quo tacuerunt, videantur locationem renovasse, etsi lustrum forte ab initio fuerat praestitutum; sed et si secundo quoque anno post finitum lustrum nihil fuerit contrarium actum, eandem videri locationem in illo anno permansisse: hoc enim ipso, quod tacuerunt, consensisse videntur; et hoc deinceps in uno quoque anno observandum est. In urbanis autem praediis alio iure utimur, ut pro ut quisque habitaverit, ita et obligetur: nisi in scriptis certum tempus conductioni comprehensum est.—l. 13, § 11 eod.[3]

---

[1] The action upon the hiring is given to the hirer.—Now it is generally available upon the following grounds: if, for example, he is not allowed to enjoy the property he has hired (it may be because the possession either of the whole or a fixed part thereof is not accorded to him, or a homestead is not repaired, or a stable, or such place as his cattle must stand in), or if there be any default of performance in contravention of the terms of hiring, he can sue upon the hiring.

[2] If any one, without knowing it, has let out leaky jars, and then wine has run out, he will be liable for the personal interest, and his ignorance will not be condoned.

[3] If a man after completion of the period of hire remains on the farm, . . . he will be regarded as having renewed the tenancy.

Book III. Pt. I. Ch. II.

Qui fundum fruendum vel habitationem alicui locavit, si aliqua ex causa fundum vel aedes vendat, curare debet, ut apud emptorem quoque eadem pactione et colono frui et inquilino habitare liceat; alioquin prohibitus is aget cum eo ex conducto.—l. 25, § 1 eod.[1]

Mortuo conductore intra tempora conductionis heres eius eodem iure in conductionem succedit. —§ ult. I. h. t.[2]

The following passage bears upon the limits of contract between Purchase and Hire.[a]

[a] *Infra*, ad fin., and see Gai. iii. 145.

Gai. iii. 146: Item si gladiatores ea lege tibi tradiderim, ut in singulos, qui integri exierint, pro sudore denarii XX mihi darentur, in eos vero singulos, qui occisi aut debilitati fuerint, denarii mille, quaeritur, utrum emptio et venditio an locatio et conductio contrahatur: et magis placuit eorum, qui integri exierint, locationem et conductionem contractam videri, at eorum, qui occisi aut debilitati sint, emptionem et venditionem esse;

But when we said that by the silence of both parties it is presumed the tenant has renewed the hiring, it must be understood that they are regarded as having renewed the tenancy for the year itself in which they were silent, even if originally provision had been made for a five years' tenancy. But even if in the second year again after the completion of the *lustrum* nothing shall have been done to the contrary, the tenancy is regarded as continuous for that year; for the consent is gathered from their very silence, and this is to be observed thenceforth in every year. But in respect of urban estates our rule is different, that every man's liability is according to what his occupation has been, unless the writings contain a definite period of hiring.

[1] If a man, who has let out to any one the enjoyment or occupation of an estate, for any reason sells land or house, he must take care that both the cultivator be allowed the enjoyment of the same hiring, and the tenant the occupation, at the hands of the purchaser; otherwise the lessee, if obstructed, can sue him upon the hiring.

[2] On the death of the hirer during the hiring term, his heir succeeds to the hiring with the same rights.

idque ex accidentibus apparet, tamquam sub condicione facta cuiusque venditione an locatione.[1]

Secondly, of the hiring of services. This can take place in two ways: either several services as such (but only operae locari solitae), or the performance of certain work and the general result (opus, universitas consummationis), can form the object of the services hired. In the 'locatio operarum,' the one that renders the services is the lessor (locator); in the 'locatio operis' (contract work), conversely, he that procures the performance of work by another is the locator (hirer), whilst he that provides his labour for remuneration is the conductor sc. operis (redemptor, contractor). In some cases it may be doubtful whether the actual hiring of service is more of one kind than of the other.[a]

[a] Cf. D. 19, 3, 1 pr.

Paul.: **Opere locato conducto** his verbis Labeo significari ait id opus, quod Graeci ἀποτέλεσμα vocant (non ἔργον) id est ex opere facto corpus aliquod perfectum.—D. 50, 16, 5, 1.[2]

Frequently also the boundary line is doubtful between 'locatio conductor operis,' on the one hand, and hiring of a thing or purchase, on the other.

Id.: —si tota navis locata sit, qui conduxit ex conducto . . . agere potest: si vero res perferen-

---

[1] Again, if I have delivered gladiators to you upon the condition that for each one that comes out unhurt 20 *denarii* should be given to me for his exertions, but for each one that is killed or disabled, 1000 *denarii*, it is debated whether the contract is one of buying and selling, or of letting and hiring; and the better opinion is that, as to those who come out unhurt, there seems to be a contract of letting and hiring, but that, as to those who are killed or disabled, it is a buying and selling; and this is seen from the event, the sale or hire of each one being, as it were, made subject to a condition.

[2] If work be given and taken in hire, Labeo says that by these terms is denoted such work as the Greeks call ἀποτέλεσμα (not ἔργον), that is, a material thing completed by the performance of work.

das nauta conduxit, ex locato convenietur.—D. 4, 9, 3, 1.[1]

Gai. iii. 147: Item quaeritur, si cum aurifice mihi convenerit, ut is ex auro suo certi ponderis certaeque formae anulos mihi faceret, et acciperet verbi gratia denarios CC, utrum emptio et venditio, an locatio et conductio contrahatur. Cassius ait materiae quidem emptionem venditionem contrahi, operarum autem locationem et conductionem; sed plerisque placuit emptionem et venditionem contrahi: atqui si meum aurum ei dedero, mercede pro opera constituta, convenit locationem conductionem contrahi.[2]

Paul.: Cum insulam aedificandam loco, ut sua impensa conductor omnia faciat, proprietatem quidem eorum ad me transfert, et tamen locatio est: locat enim artifex operam suam, id est faciendi necessitatem.—l. 22, § 2, D. h. t.[3]

Pomp.: Sabinus respondit . . . nec posse ullam locationem esse, ubi corpus ipsum non datur ab eo, cui id fieret: aliter atque si aream darem, ubi insulam aedificaret, quoniam tunc a me substantia proficiscitur.—D. 18, 1, 20.[4]

---

1 —if a whole ship has been let out, the hirer can sue *ex conducto*; but if the skipper has undertaken the conveyance of things, he will be sued *ex locato*.

2 Likewise the question comes up, if when I have agreed with a goldsmith that he should make rings for me out of his own gold, of a certain weight and of a certain form, and receive, say, 200 *denarii*, is a buying and selling, or a letting and hiring contracted? Cass. says that there is a contract of buying and selling of the material, but of letting and hiring of the labour; but the view taken by most is that the contract is one of buying and selling; though, if I shall give him my gold, a price being appointed for the work, it is agreed that the contract is of letting and hiring.

3 When I let out the building of a house, so that the contractor shall do all at his own cost, he makes over to me the ownership thereof, and yet there is a letting; for the builder lets out his services, *i.e.*, the necessity of the process.

4 Sab. answers that . . . there cannot be any letting where

In both cases of hiring of services, the responsibility of him that lets his services is increased to the extent of making good 'imperitia.'[a]

[a] Cf. § 133.

Tryph.: Celsus etiam imperitiam culpae adnumerandam[b] scripsit: si quis vitulos pascendos, vel sarciendum quid poliendumve conduxit, culpam eum praestare debere, et quod imperitia peccavit culpam esse, quippe ut artifex, inquit, conduxit.—l. 9, § 5, D. h. t.[1]

[b] Cf. Inst. iv. 3, 7, and Blackst. iii. 122 (Steph. iii. 386).

Ulp.: Adversus **mensorem** agrorum praetor in factum actionem proposuit, a quo falli nos non oportet: nam interest nostra, ne fallamur in modi renuntiatione, si forte vel de finibus contentio sit, vel emtor scire velit vel venditor, cuius modi ager veneat. Ideo autem hanc actionem proposuit, quia non crediderunt veteres inter talem personam locationem et conductionem esse, sed magis operam beneficii loco praeberi et id quod datur ei, ad remunerandum dari et inde honorarium appellari; si autem ex locato conducto fuerit actum, dicendum erit nec tenere intentionem.—Haec actio dolum malum dumtaxat exigit; . . . proinde si imperite versatus est, sibi imputare debet qui eum adhibuit; sed et si negligenter, aeque mensor securus erit; lata culpa plane dolo comparabitur.—D. 11, 6, 1 pr., § 1.[2]

---

the object itself is not given by him for whom that would be made; but it is otherwise if I should give a piece of land unbuilt on, where he should build a house, since then the material issues from me.

[1] Cels. has written that unskilfulness is also to be counted as a fault: if a man have undertaken the pasturing of calves, or to mend or clean something, he must make good his fault, and his error through unskilfulness is a fault because, (Cels.) says, it was as a skilled workman that he undertook it.

[2] Against a land-surveyor the Praetor has created an action *in factum*, by which we must not be deceived: for it concerns us not to be deceived in a report as to the dimensions, if so be either there is a dispute as to the boundaries, or the

Book III. Pt. I. Ch. II.

As still requiring special mention, there are the public farmings (locationes, venditiones) of the State-revenues (vectigalia),—which generally extended to a 'lustrum'—customary with the Romans, especially of the taxes, the use of mines and the like; and further, the leasing of public works, structures and purveyance (ultro tributa) to particular contractors (publicani, mancipes), as a rule to societies of capitalists (societates publicanorum)[a] as agent of whom the manceps concluded the contract with the State, to which other 'socii' were made parties as praedes.[b]

[a] D. 3, 4, 1 pr.

[b] Cf. § 118, ad fin., and see further, § 192.

Festus: **Venditiones** olim dicebantur censorum locationes, quod velut fructus publicorum locorum venibant.—s. h. v. (p. 376, M.).[1]

Gai.: Eum, qui vectigal populi Romani conductum habet, **publicanum** appellamus.—D. 50, 16, 16.[2]

Paul. ex Festo: **Manceps** dicitur, qui quid a populo emit conducitve, quia manu sublata significat se auctorem emptionis esse.—h. v. (p. 151, M.).[3]

---

purchaser or vendor wishes to know the measure of the land which is sold. Now he created this action because the old jurists supposed there is no letting and hiring with such a person, but rather that the labour is given as a kindness, and that what is given to him is given as a fee, and so is called an 'honorarium'; but that if proceedings have been taken upon the letting and hiring, one must say the claim is not entertained. This action only excludes fraud; . . . if accordingly he has gone to work unskilfully, one must blame the person that employed him; but even if he have been negligent, the surveyor will be protected all the same. Gross negligence will clearly be equivalent to fraud.

[1] *Venditiones* was the name formerly given to leases granted by the censors because, as it were, the fruits of public places were sold.

[2] We call a person *publicanus* who farms the taxes of the Roman people.

[3] He is called *manceps* who purchases or hires anything from the people, because by raising the hand he signifies that he initiates a purchase.

§ 124. Contract of Partnership.[a]

The Contract of PARTNERSHIP (societas) is that agreement concluded between two or several persons (socii) as to any association relating to property, ordinarily—but not always[b]—to promote a common, permissible, chiefly pecuniary purpose. This association can relate to the whole present and future property (societas omnium bonorum, and in the earlier time especially in the form of consortium of a family, who by inheritance from their parents retained an undivided property), or to a single thing, *e.g.*, parcel of land, slave, team (societas unius rei)—indeed the two oldest forms of partnership; or to the future individual acquisitions of partnerships (societas quaestus, lucri, compendii); or finally, to acquisitions from a joint and permanent undertaking, or a single business jointly undertaken (societas quaestus, negotiationis).[c]

[a] For analogies between the Roman and our Common Law, see Story on Partnership; several set out by Scrutton, pp. 159-161. For Equity, see Story on that topic, § 682 (Grigsby, p. 449).

[b] Cf. D. 38, 2, 1, 1.

[c] Cf. D. 17, 2, 71 pr.

> Ulp.: Societates autem contrahuntur sive universorum bonorum, sive negotiationis alicuius, sive vectigalis, sive etiam rei unius.—l. 5 pr., D. h. t. (pro soc. 17, 2).[1]
>
> Paul.: In societate omnium bonorum omnes res, quae coeuntium sunt, continuo communicantur.—l. 1, § 1 eod.[2]
>
> Ulp.: Coire societatem et simpliciter licet et, si non fuerit distinctum, videtur coita esse universorum, quae ex quaestu veniunt, hoc est si quod lucrum ex emptione, venditione, locatione, conductione descendit.—l. 7 eod.[3]

---

[1] Now partnerships are contracted either in respect of the whole property, or in respect of some transaction, or the revenue, or in respect of a single matter.

[2] In respect of partnership in the whole property, all things which belong to those who join are uninterruptedly held in common.

[3] One can enter into a partnership even for an undefined purpose, and if nothing have been determined, it is regarded as

Book III. Pt. I. Ch. II.

The duration also of the partnership can be variously settled.

Societas coiri potest vel in perpetuum, i.e. dum vivunt, vel ad tempus, vel sub condicione.—l. 1 pr. eod.[1]

[a] Cf. D. 38, 1, 2.

As regards the contributions[a] of the partners, these can be dissimilar, indeed, of a different kind (res, operae).

Societas autem coiri potest et valet etiam inter eos, qui non sunt aequis facultatibus, cum plerumque pauperior opera suppleat, quantum ei per comparationem patrimonii deest.—l. 5, § 1 eod.[2]

Gai. iii. § 149: Nam et ita posse coiri societatem constat, ut unus pecuniam conferat, alter non conferat, et tamen lucrum inter eos commune sit: saepe enim opera alicuius pro pecunia valet.[3]

Ulp.: Donationis causa societas recte non contrahitur.—l. 5, § 2, D. h. t.[4]

The shares of profit and loss may likewise be different.

Quodsi expressae partes fuerint, hae servari debent: nec enim umquam dubium fuit, quin valeat conventio, si duo inter se pacti sunt, ut ad unum quidem duae partes et damni et lucri per-

---

entered into in respect of all that accrues from receipts, that is, whatever profit come of a purchase, a sale, a letting, a hiring.

[1] A partnership can be entered into either for a permanency, that is, while the parties live, or temporarily, or conditionally.

[2] But a partnership can also be entered into and is valid between persons who do not possess the same means, since commonly the poorer party supplies by his labour what he lacks by comparison of his estate.

[3] For it is well known that a partnership can be entered into upon such terms that one shall contribute capital, the other shall not, and yet the profit shall be common between them; for often the services of one have the value of money.

[4] A partnership is not properly contracted upon the ground of a gift.

tineant, ad alium tertia.—§ 1, I. h. t. (=de societ. 3, 25).[1]

Gai. iii. § 149: Magna autem quaestio fuit, an ita coiri possit societas, ut quis maiorem partem lucretur, minorem damni praestet: quod Quintus Mucius etiam [contra naturam societatis esse existimavit; sed Servius Sulpicius, cuius] praevaluit sententia, adeo ita coiri posse societatem existimavit, ut dixerit illo quoque modo coiri posse, ut quis nihil omnino damni praestet, sed lucri partem capiat.—(=§ 2, I. h. t.)[2]

Paul.: Mucius scribit non posse sociatatem coiri, ut aliam damni aliam lucri partem socius ferat; Servius in notatis Mucii ait nec posse societatem ita contrahi, neque enim lucrum intelligitur nisi omni damno deducto, neque damnum nisi omni lucro deducto: sed potest coiri societas ita, ut eius lucri, quod reliquum in societate sit omni damno deducto, pars alia feratur, et eius damni, quod similiter relinquatur, pars alia capiatur.—l. 30, D. h. t. [quod ita intelligi oportet, ut si in aliqua re lucrum in aliqua damnum allatum sit, compensatione facta solum quod superest intelligatur lucri esse.—§ 2, I. h. t.][3]

---

[1] But if the shares have been specified, these must be adhered to; for it has never been doubted that an agreement is binding if two persons have together arranged that two-thirds of the profit and loss shall belong to one, one-third to the other.

[2] But there has been much controversy whether a partnership can be so entered into, for one partner to take the bulk of the profit, but bear the smaller part of the loss. This Q. M. [thought to be contrary to the very nature of a partnership, but S. S., whose] opinion has prevailed, went so far to think that such a partnership could be entered into, that he has said that it could be entered into so that one partner bear no loss whatever, but take a share of the profit.

[3] Muc. writes that a partnership cannot be contracted for a partner to have one share of profit, another share of loss. Serv. says, in his comments upon Muc., such a partnership cannot be entered into, for profit is to be taken as existing only

BOOK III. Pt. I. Ch. II.

Ulp.: Aristo refert Cassium respondisse, societatem talem coiri non posse, ut alter lucrum tantum, alter damnum sentiret, et hanc societatem, 'leoninam' solitam appellari; et nos consentimus talem societatem nullam esse.—l. 29, § 2, D. h. t.[1]

If no more particular arrangement has been made, the partners have absolutely equal shares; in case only the share of profit of the several partners has been fixed, the same distribution obtains also in respect of the loss.

Gai. iii. § 150: Et illud certum est, si de partibus lucri et damni nihil inter eos convenerit, aequis ex partibus commodum et incommodum inter eos commune esse; sed si in altero partes expressae fuerint, velut in lucro, in altero vero omissae, in eo quoque quod omissum est, similes partes erunt.[2]

The partners are responsible to one another for 'diligentia quam suis rebus.'[a] For the enforcement of his claims under the partnership agree-

[a] D. 17, 2, 72.

---

after deduction of all loss, and loss only after deduction of all profit. But a partnership can be contracted upon the terms that, of such profit as remains after deduction of the whole loss of the partnership, one share should fall (to one), and of such loss remaining over in like manner another share shall be taken. [—and this must be understood so that, if profit has been derived in one matter, loss in another, only what remains over after striking a balance is to be regarded as profit.]

[1] Aristo tells of an opinion given by Cassius, that such a partnership—where one should enjoy the profit alone, the other suffer the loss—cannot be contracted, and that such a partnership is generally called 'leonine.' We too agree that such a partnership is void.

[2] And this is certain, that, if there have been no agreement between them as to the share of profit and loss, yet the profit and loss must be shared between them equally; but if the shares have been specified with regard to one particular, for example, in respect of profit, but not mentioned as to the other, the shares will correspond in respect of that of which no mention is made.

ment, every socius has at his command the 'actio pro socio,' entailing infamy.[a]

Paul.: Si tecum societas mihi sit et res ex societate communes, quam impensam in eas fecero, quosve fructus ex his rebus ceperis, vel pro socio vel communi dividundo me consecuturum, et altera actione alteram tolli Proculus ait.—l. 38, § 1, h. t.[1]

Id.: Si quis societatem contraxerit, quod emit, ipsius fit, non commune: sed societatis iudicio cogitur rem communicare.—l. 74 eod.[2]

The societas is dissolved—

(1) by agreement (dissensus),[b] or one-sided withdrawal (renuntiatio).

Paul.: Nulla societatis in aeternum coitio est. —Si conveniat ne omnino divisio fiat, huiusmodi pactum nullas vires habere manifestissimum est. —l. 70, h. t., and l. 14, § 2, D. comm. div. 10, 3.[3]

Paul.: Diximus dissensu solvi societatem; hoc ita est, si omnes dissentiunt: quid ergo si unus renuntiet? Cassius scripsit eum, qui renuntiaverit societati, a se quidem liberare socios suos, se autem ab illis non liberare. Quod utique observandum est, si dolo malo renuntiatio facta sit, veluti si, cum omnium bonorum societatem inissemus, deinde cum obvenisset uni hereditas, propter hoc renuntiavit: ideoque si quidem damnum attulerit hereditas, hoc ad eum qui renun-

[a] § 135.

[b] *I.e.*, 'consensus contrarius.' Cf. § 141.

---

[1] If I am in partnership with you, and have joint property in virtue of the partnership, Proc. says that I shall recover what I spend on it, or the revenue that you have derived from it, either by the partnership action or by that for the partition of joint property, and that the one action is excluded by the other.

[2] If a man has contracted a partnership, that which he purchases becomes his own, not joint property; but by the partnership action he is compelled to make it joint property.

[3] There is no such thing as entering into partnership for ever. —It is very clear that such an agreement as that no division whatever shall take place is of no force.

Book III. Pt. I. Ch. II.

tiavit pertinebit, commodum autem communicare cogetur actione pro socio.—Labeo autem scripsit, si renuntiaverit societati unus ex sociis eo tempore, quo interfuit socii non dirimi societatem, committere eum in pro socio actionem: nam si emimus mancipia inita societate, deinde renunties mihi eo tempore, quo vendere mancipia non expedit, . . . teneri te pro socio iudicio.—l. 65, §§ 3, 5, D. h. t.[1]

(2) By death.

Solvitur adhuc societas etiam morte socii, quia qui societatem contrahit, certam personam sibi elegit; sed et si consensu plurium societas coita sit, morte unius solvitur, etsi plures supersint: nisi si in coeunda societate aliter convenerit.—§ 5, I. h. t.[2]

Ulp.: In heredem quoque socii pro socio actio

---

[1] We have said that partnership is dissolved by agreement; that is, if all are agreed. What, then, if one renounce? Cass. writes that he who has renounced the partnership discharges his colleagues from obligation towards himself, but is not himself discharged by them. And this is always to be noted, if the renunciation has been made fraudulently, for example, if when we had entered into partnership of all property, afterwards, upon an inheritance devolving upon one, he renounced because of it. And accordingly, if the inheritance have in fact brought loss, this will attach to him that has renounced, but by the partnership action he will be compelled to make a gain partnership property.—Now Labeo has written, if one of the partners has renounced the partnership at a time when it was to their advantage that his partnership should not be determined, he is liable to the partnership action; for if we have bought slaves upon entering into partnership, and you afterwards renounce the partnership with me at a time when it is not of advantage to sell slaves, you are liable to the partnership action.

[2] A partnership is, further, dissolved by the death also of a partner, because he that contracts a partnership selects a particular person as his partner; but even if the partnership has been created by the consent of several, it is dissolved by the death of a single partner, although several survive, unless there was an agreement to the contrary upon the creation of the partnership.

competit, quamvis heres socius non sit.—l. 63, § 8, D. h. t.[1]

Paul.: —quod ex re communi postea quaesitum est, item dolus et culpa in eo, quod ex ante gesto pendet, tam ab herede quam heredi praestandum est.—l. 65, § 9 eod.[2]

(3) Or capitis diminutio (maxima and media).

Societas quemadmodum ad heredes socii non transit, ita nec adrogatorem, ne alioquin invitus quis socius efficiatur, cui non vult; ipse autem adrogatus socius permanet: nam et si filiusfamilias emancipatus fuerit, permanebit socius.—Ibid. § 11.[3]

(4) By bankruptcy of a socius.

Item bonis a creditoribus venditis unius socii distrahi societatem Labeo ait.—Ibid. § 1.[4]

Since partnership as an obligatory relation only concerns the partners—in contrast with a corporation[a] —it has no influence whatever upon the position under Private Law of the individual partner towards third parties, so that the legal effect of transactions concluded for the partnership operates directly in favour of the individual partner; and there is no jural distinction made between partnership and private claims or debts of the individual partners upon or to third parties.[b]

[a] § 68.

[b] Cf. Hunter, p. 521.

---

[1] The partnership action is available against the heir also of a partner, although the heir is not a partner.

[2] —that which has been subsequently acquired from joint property, and fraud and negligence in respect of that which depends upon a previous transaction, must be made good as well by the heir as for him.

[3] Just as a partnership does not pass to the heirs of the partner, so also neither to an arrogator, lest a man against his will be made a partner of one not wishing it; but the person arrogated himself remains partner; for even if a *fil. fam.* shall be emancipated, he remains partner.

[4] Likewise Labeo says that if the property of one partner has been sold by the creditors, the partnership is dissolved.

Book III. Pt. I. Ch. II.

§ 125. Mandate.[a]

[a] Bell, s. v.

Mandatum is the contract by which some one (Mandatory, procurator) undertakes a commission for the gratuitous management of a lawful business—whether the performance of work or service, administration, or legal transaction.[b]

[b] See the leading case of Coggs v. Bernard.

Paul.: Mandatum, nisi gratuitum, nullum est, nam originem ex officio atque amicitia trahit, contrarium ergo est officio merces: interveniente enim pecunia res ad locationem et conductionem potius respicit.—Si remunerandi gratia honor intervenit, erit mandati actio.—l. 1, § 4, l. 6 pr., D. h. t. (mand. 17, 1).[1]

Quibus casibus sine mercede suscepto officio mandati aut depositi contrahitur negotium, his casibus interveniente mercede locatio et conductio contrahi intelligitur: et ideo si fulloni polienda curandave vestimenta dederis aut sarcinatori sarcienda nulla mercede constituta neque promissa, mandati competit actio.—§ ult. I. h. t. 3, 26.[2]

Gai.: Mandatum inter nos contrahitur, sive mea tantum gratia tibi mandem, sive aliena tantum, sive mea et aliena, sive mea et tua, sive tua et aliena. § Mea tantum gratia intervenit mandatum, veluti si tibi mandem, ut negotia mea geras, vel ut fundum mihi emeres, vel ut pro me fideiubeas. § Aliena

---

[1] A mandate is nothing save as gratuitous, for it originates in kindness and friendship: a reward is, accordingly, inconsistent with kindness, for when money comes in, the transaction contemplates rather a letting and hiring.—If an honorarium obtains by way of reward, an action of mandate will lie.

[2] In all cases in which upon a service being undertaken without reward a contract exists of commission or deposit, in such cases, when remuneration does obtain, the contract is understood to be of letting and hiring. If therefore one have given to a fuller clothes to clean or look after, or to a tailor to repair, without fixing or promising remuneration, an action of mandate is available.

tantum, veluti si tibi mandem, ut Titii negotia gereres, vel ut fundum ei emeres, vel ut pro eo fideiubeas.—§ Tua autem gratia intervenit mandatum, veluti si mandem tibi, ut pecunias tuas potius in emptiones praediorum colloces quam foeneres, vel ex diverso . . . : cuius generis mandatum magis consilium est quam mandatum et ob id non est obligatorium, quia nemo ex consilio obligatur.—l. 2 pr., §§ 1, 2, 6, D. h. t.[1]

A special kind of mandate is the so-called 'mandatum credendi s. qualificatum,' containing a guaranty;[a] that is, the commission to give credit to another. [a] § 118.

Tua et aliena, veluti si tibi mandem, ut Titio sub usuris crederes: quodsi, ut sine usuris crederes, aliena tantum gratia intervenit mandatum. —Ib. § 5.[2]

Ulp.: Si, ut expectares nec urgeres debitorem ad solutionem, mandavero tibi, ut ei des intervallum, periculoque meo pecuniam fore dicam, verum puto omne nominis periculum debere ad mandatorem pertinere.—l. 12, § 14 eod.[3]

---

[1] A mandate is contracted between us, whether I give you a commission on my behalf merely, or on that of a stranger alone, or on my own and a stranger's, or on my own and yours, or on yours and a stranger's. . . . § A mandate is alone on my behalf when, for example, I commission you to conduct my business, or to buy land for me, or to be surety for me. § It is only on behalf of a stranger when, for example, I commission you to conduct the business of Tit., or to buy land for him, or to be his surety.—But it is on your behalf when, for example, I commission you to invest your money in the purchase of land rather than to lend it at interest, or conversely . . . : a commission of this kind is rather advice than a commission, and therefore creates no obligation, because no one is responsible for advice.

[2] It is on your behalf and a stranger when, for example, I commission you to lend to Tit. at interest; but if it be to lend without interest, the commission is on your behalf alone.

[3] If I have commissioned you to wait and not press the debtor for payment, so as to give him a respite, and I state that the money shall be at my risk, I am of opinion that it is correct that the risk of the money should fall to me as *mandator*.

Book III. Pt. I. Ch. II.

Iul.: Si mandatu meo Titio decem credideris et mecum mandati egeris, non liberabitur Titius; . . . item si cum Titio egeris, ego non liberabor. —D. 46, 1, 13.[1]

If the commission comprehends representation of the 'Mandant' for proprietary matters in general, or for a single legal act, we speak of authorisation. The Mandant is called the 'dominus,' the other party, the '*procurator* omnium rerum, vel unius rei.' [a]

[a] § 20.

Id.: Procurator est, qui aliena negotia mandatu domini administrat.—Procurator autem vel omnium rerum vel unius rei esse potest.—l. 1 pr., § 1, D. de proc. 3, 3.[2]

From the mandatum arise the following claims and liabilities, which are made operative by the 'actio mandati,' involving infamia.

(1) The mandatory is under obligation to execute the business he has undertaken, in doing so to keep strictly within the limits of the commission, and to put forth omnis diligentia, as well as to render an account and hand over to the mandant all that comes to his hands in consequence of the commission: for this there lies the 'actio mandati directa.'

Paul.: Voluntatis est enim suscipere mandatum, necessitatis consummare (D. 13, 6, 17, 3). —Gai.: Qui mandatum suscepit, si potest id explere, deserere promissum officium non debet: alioquin, quanti mandatoris interest, damnabitur. —l. 27, §2, D. h. t.[3]

---

[1] If you upon my commission have lent Titius ten [*aurei*], and shall have sued me by the action of mandate, Tit. will not be discharged; . . . and so if you shall sue Tit., I shall not be discharged.

[2] A *procurator* is one that manages the affairs of another upon the commission of the principal.—Now there can be a *procurator* either of all one's affairs or of a single matter.

[3] For it is a matter of good-will to undertake a mandate, and of necessity to carry it out.—A person that has undertaken a

Cicero p. Rosc. Am. 38, iii. : Si qui rem mandatam non modo malitiosius gessisset sui quaestus aut commodi causa, verum etiam negligentius, eum maiores summum admisisse dedecus existimabant; itaque mandati constitutum est iudicium non minus turpe quam furti, credo propterea, quod quibus in rebus ipsi interesse non possumus, in eis operae nostrae vicaria fides amicorum supponitur.[1]

Gai. iii. § 161 : Cum autem is, cui recte mandaverim, egressus fuerit mandatum, ego quidem eatenus cum eo habeo mandati actionem, quatenus mea interest, implesse eum mandatum, si modo implere potuerit: at ille mecum agere non potest. Itaque si mandaverim tibi, ut verbi gratia fundum mihi sestertiis C emeres, tu sestertiis CL emeris, non habebis mecum mandati actionem, etiamsi tanti velis mihi dare fundum, quanti emendum tibi mandassem—[namque iniquum est non esse mihi cum illo actionem, si nolit, illi vero, si velit, mecum esse.—Paul. l. 3, § 2, D. h. t.]—idque maxime Sabino et Cassio placuit—[diversae scholae auctores recte te usque ad C acturum existimant, quae sententia sane benignior est.—§ 8, I. h. t.]—; quodsi minoris emeris, habebis mecum scilicet actionem, quia qui mandat, ut C emeretur, is utique mandare intelligitur, uti minoris si posset emeretur.[2]

---

mandate, if able to fulfil it, ought not to abandon his promised service; otherwise, he will be mulcted in the amount of the personal interest of the *mandator*.

[1] Whosoever had conducted a matter entrusted to him, not only fraudulently for his own gain or advantage, but also carelessly, was by our ancestors considered to have incurred supreme dishonour; accordingly, the action for breach of trust has been established, not less disgraceful than that in respect of theft, I suppose because in matters in which we ourselves cannot take part, the fidelity of friends is substituted for our services.

[2] When a person whom I have duly commissioned has trans-

Id.: Procurator ex bona fide rationem reddere debet.—l. 46, § 4, D. de proc.[1]

Paul.: Ex mandato apud eum, qui mandatum suscepit, nihil remanere oportet.—l. 20 pr., D. h. t.[2]

Ulp.: Proinde si tibi mandavi, ut hominem emeres, tuque emisti, teneberis mihi ut restituas. —l. 8, § 10 eod.[3]

(2) The mandant is by the 'actio mandati contraria' responsible to the mandatory to indemnify him.

Id.: Si mihi mandaveris, ut rem tibi aliquam emam, egoque emero meo pretio, habebo mandati actionem de pretio recuperando.—l. 12, § 9 eod.[4]

---

gressed the terms of the mandate, I have an action of mandate against him for the amount of my interest in his performance of the mandate, provided it was possible for him to have performed it; but he cannot sue me. If therefore I have charged you with the purchase for me of land for, say, a hundred thousand sesterces, and you have purchased it for a hundred and fifty thousand, you will not have an action of mandate against me, even though you should be willing to make over the estate to me for the price which I commissioned you to give [for it is inequitable that I should not have an action against so and so if he be unwilling, but that he should have one against me if he be willing].—And this was decided by the opinion of Sab. and Cass. [the authorities of the opposite school are of opinion that you can effectually sue for the hundred *aurei*, and this is certainly the better opinion]. But if you have purchased it for less, you will doubtless have an action against me, because he that commissions a person to purchase for a hundred thousand sesterces is certainly considered to give a commission to purchase it for less if possible.

[1] A *procurator* must render an account according to good faith.

[2] Nothing ought to be kept back by the mandatory of what is in his hands by virtue of the mandate.

[3] Accordingly, if I have commissioned you to purchase a slave, and you have made the purchase, you will be responsible to me for his delivery.

[4] If you have given a commission to me to buy something for you, and I purchase it with my own money, I shall have an action of mandate for the recovery of the price.

Gai.: Impendia mandati exsequendi gratia facta, si bona fide facta sunt, restitui omnimodo debent; nec ad rem pertinet, quod is qui mandasset, potuisset, si ipse negotium gereret, minus impendere.—l. 27, § 4 eod.[1]

The mandate is put an end to—

(1) by the death of the mandant or mandatory.

Gai. iii. § 160: Si adhuc integro mandato mors alterutrius interveniat, i.e. vel eius qui mandaverit, vel eius qui mandatum susceperit, solvitur mandatum; sed utilitatis causa receptum est, ut si mortuo eo, qui mihi mandaverit, ignorans eum decessisse exsecutus fuero mandatum, posse me agere mandati actione.[2]

(2) By revocation 're integra' on the part of the mandant.

Paul.: Si mandassem tibi, ut fundum emeres, postea scripsissem, ne emeres, tu, antequam scias me vetuisse, emisses: mandati tibi obligatus ero. —l. 15, D. h. t.[3]

(3) By renunciation at the proper time on the part of the mandatory.

Id.: Sicut autem liberum est mandatum non suscipere, ita susceptum consummari oportet, nisi renuntiatum sit. Renuntiari autem ita potest, ut

---

[1] Expenses incurred in the execution of the mandate, if incurred in good faith, must in all cases be refunded; and it is immaterial that the *mandator*, if he had transacted the business in person, could have spent less.

[2] If the death of either party occur before the execution of the mandate, that is, either the death of him who gave the mandate, or of him who undertook it, the mandate is cancelled. But for convenience' sake the rule has been adopted, that if after the death of the *mandator* I, being ignorant that he is dead, execute the mandate, I can sue by the action of mandate.

[3] If I had commissioned you to purchase land, and afterwards wrote that you were not to make the purchase, but you purchased before you knew of my countermand, I shall be liable to you in an action of mandate.

BOOK III. Pt. I. Ch. II.

integrum ius mandatori reservetur, vel per se vel per alium eandem rem commode explicandi.—l. 22, § 11 eod.[1]

§ 126. Extension of the System of Civil Contracts by the so-called Innominate Contracts.

The circle of obligatory agreements operative by Civil Law was from the beginning of imperial times extended, by actionability being gradually accorded to all informal agreements (nova negotia) relating to performance in consideration of corresponding counter-performance, which did not fall under the conception of one of the already established typical contracts[a] (perhaps under the aspect of the lex [dationi] rei dicta), where performance had already been rendered on one side. These were the innominate, or nameless, real contracts.

[a] Those 'characterised by individuality.' Cf. § 115.

Gai.: In traditionibus rerum quodcumque pactum sit id valere manifestissimum est.—l. 48, D. de pact. 2, 14.[2]

Ulp.: Labeo definit . . . 'contractum' **ultro citroque obligationem,** quod Graeci *συνάλλαγμα* vocant, veluti emptionem venditionem, locationem conductionem, societatem.—D. 50, 16, 19.[3]

Id.: Sed etsi in alium contractum res non transeat, subsit tamen causa, eleganter Aristo Celso respondit esse obligationem, ut puta dedi

---

Now just as one is at liberty not to undertake a mandate, so when undertaken it ought to be carried out, unless it have been renounced. But it can be renounced (only) in such way that power is reserved without prejudice to the *mandator* of either himself or through another conveniently accomplishing the transaction.

[2] It is quite certain that validity attaches to whatever agreement has been made upon the occasion of the delivery of things.

[3] Labeo defines a contract as a reciprocal obligation, which the Greeks call *συνάλλαγμα*; for example, a purchase and sale, a letting and hiring, a partnership.

tibi rem, ut mihi aliam dares, dedi ut aliquid facias : hoc συνάλλαγμα esse et hinc nasci civilem obligationem.—l. 7, § 2, D. de pact.[1]

Paul. : Emptio ac venditio nuda consentientium voluntate contrahitur; **permutatio** autem ex re tradita initium obligationi praebet: alioquin si res nondum tradita sit, nudo consensu constitui obligationem dicemus, quod in his dumtaxat receptum est, quae nomen suum habent, ut in emptione venditione, conductione, mandato.—D. 19, 4, 1, 2.[2]

The action by which the fulfilment of the contract, *i.e.*, counter-performance, was exacted was the '(civilis) actio praescriptis verbis,' conceived 'in factum,'[a] which operated altogether as an auxiliary action, when the legal nature of the contract was doubtful, because of the absence of the special characteristic marks belong-iug to the juristic essence of one of the established particular contracts.[b]

[a] § 203.

[b] § 123; D. 19, 5, 6.

Pap. : Domino mercium in magistrum navis, si sit incertum, utrum navem conduxerit an merces vehendas locaverit, civilem actionem in factum esse dandam Labeo scribit.—Item si quis pretii explorandi gratia rem tradat, neque depositum neque commodatum erit, sed non exhibita fide in factum civilis subiicitur actio,—(Cels. : nam cum

[1] But although while the transaction does not pass into another contract, *causa* (material consideration) is present. Aristo judiciously replies to Celsus, that there is an obligation; for example, I have given a thing to you that you might give another to me, I have made a gift (to you) that you might do something; that this is a συνάλλαγμα (contract), and a civil obligation arises therefrom.

[2] A purchase and sale is contracted by the mere will of the consenting parties ; but an exchange originates an obligation from the time of the delivery of the thing; otherwise, if the thing has not yet been delivered, we shall say that the obligation is created by bare consent, which, however, only occurs in respects of those contracts that have a definite name, as with purchase and sale, hiring, mandate.

Book III. Pt. I. Ch. II.

deficiant vulgaria atque usitata actionum nomina, praescriptis verbis agendum est)—Iul.: in quam necesse est confugere, quotiens contractus existunt, quorum appellationes nullae iure civili proditae sunt;—Ulp.: natura enim rerum conditum est, ut plura sint negotia, quam vocabula.—l. 1, § 1, 2, and ll. 2–4, D. h. t. (de praescr. verb. 19, 5.)[1]

Id.: Actio de **aestimato** proponitur tollendae dubitationis gratia: fuit enim dubitatum, cum res aestimata vendenda datur, utrum ex vendito sit actio propter aestimationem, an ex locato, quasi rem vendendam locasse videor, an ex conducto, quasi operas conduxissem, an mandati. Melius itaque visum est hanc actionem proponi; quotiens enim de nomine contractus alicuius ambigeretur, conveniret tamen aliquam actionem dari, dandam aestimatoriam praescriptis verbis actionem: est enim negotium civile gestum et quidem bona fide. —D. 19, 3, 1 pr.[2]

---

[1] Labeo writes that a civil action upon the case must be given to the owner of the merchandise against the captain of the ship, if there be uncertainty as to whether he chartered the ship or procured the conveyance of the merchandise. Likewise if a man make delivery of a thing to ascertain its value, there will be neither a deposit nor a loan, but if good (faith) have not been shown, a civil action is afforded on the case—(for when the common and usual names of actions fail, proceedings must be taken by fixed words)—to which, therefore, recourse must be had whenever contracts exist for which the civil law has no designations; for it lies in the nature of things that there are more transactions than names.

[2] The action upon a *contractus aestimatorius* is proposed to remove doubts; for it has been doubted, when a thing is appraised and given for sale, whether there is an action upon the purchase for the assessed price, or upon the letting of it, as if I am considered to have let out the sale of the thing, or upon the hire, as if I had hired the services, or upon the commission. It seemed better therefore that this action should be proposed, for whenever there should be doubt as to the designation of any contract, but the grant of an action should be appropriate, the *actio aestimatoria* should be given by fixed words: for there has been the performance of a civil transaction, and that in good faith.

Id.: Si tibi rem vendendam certo pretio dedissem, ut quo pluris vendidisses tibi haberes, placet neque mandati neque pro socio esse actionem, . . . quia et mandata gratuita esse debent, et societas non videtur contracta in[a] eo, qui te non admisit socium distractionis, sed sibi certum pretium excepit.—l. 13 pr., h. t.[1]

[a] ? cum.

Gai.: Si tibi polienda sarciendave vestimenta dederim, si quidem gratis hanc operam te suscipiente, mandati est obligatio: si vero mercede data aut constituta, locationis conductionisque negotium geritur: quodsi neque gratis hanc operam susceperis neque protinus aut data aut constituta sit merces, sed eo animo negotium gestum fuerit, ut postea tantum mercedis nomine daretur, quantum inter nos statutum sit, placet quasi de novo negotio in factum dandum esse iudicium i.e. praescriptis verbis.—l. 22, D. h. t.[2]

Ulp.: Cum quid **precario** rogatum est, non solum interdicto uti possumus, sed etiam praescriptis verbis actione, quae ex bona fide oritur.—D. 43, 26, 2, 2.[3]

---

[1] If I should have given you a thing for sale at a certain price, for you to retain to your use whatever more you should have sold it for, it is held that there is no action either of mandate or partnership, . . . because mandates must be gratuitous, and there seems to be no contract of partnership in respect of him who has not taken you as a partner in the sale, but has reserved for himself a certain price.

[2] If I have given you clothes to clean or repair, and you undertake this service without remuneration, the obligation is one of mandate; but if remuneration has been given or arranged for, a transaction is entered into of letting and hiring. But if you have undertaken this business neither for remuneration, nor have at once given or arranged for remuneration, but the transaction has been entered into with the intention that afterwards so much should be given for remuneration as we should agree upon, it is held that an action must be given upon the case as for a new transaction, *i.e.*, by fixed words.

[3] If anything has been asked for *precario*, we can avail ourselves not only of the interdict, but the action *praescr. verbis*, which arises in equity.

Book III. Pt. I. Ch. II.

The performance already rendered could, however, be recalled at discretion, until fulfilment by the other side of the contract, by means of 'condictio'[a]; but upon indemnifying the receiver (prepared for performance) for loss sustained in consequence of the contract, and especially if by no fault of his the counter-performance had become impossible (ius poenitendi).

[a] § 135.

Id.: Sed si tibi dedero (pecuniam), ut Stichum manumittas: si non facis, possum condicere, aut si me poeniteat, condicere possum.—D. 12, 4, 3, 2.[1]

Id.: Si pecuniam ideo acceperis, ut Capuam eas, deinde parato tibi ad proficiscendum condicio temporis vel valetudinis impedimento fuerit, quominus proficiscereris, an condici possit videndum. Et cum per te non steterit, potest dici repetitionem cessare; sed cum liceat poenitere ei qui dedit, procul dubio repetetur id quod datum est, nisi forte tua intersit non accepisse te ob hanc causam pecuniam. Nam si ita res se habeat, . . . ut ita rem composueris, ut necesse habeas proficisci, vel sumptus, qui necessarii fuerunt ad profectionem, iam fecisti, ut manifestum sit te plus forte quam accepisti erogasse, condictio cessabit; sed si minus erogatum sit, condictio locum habebit, ita tamen, ut indemnitas tibi praestetur eius quod expendisti.—l. 5 pr. eod.[2]

---

[1] But if I have given you (money) to enfranchise Stichus, and you fail to do it, or if I change my mind, I can bring a personal action.

[2] If therefore you should have received money to go to Capua, but afterwards, when you were ready to make the journey, circumstances of time and health should have hindered your setting out, we must see whether (the money) can be recovered by a personal action. And as it has not been your fault, one may say that the recovery falls through; but since he who gave it is allowed to change his mind, it is beyond doubt that what was given can be recovered, unless perhaps it be to your advantage not to have received the money for this reason. For if the matter should stand so . . . that you have so arranged that you

The innominate contracts are classified by the Romans according to categories.

(1) *do ut des.*

Paul.: Et si quidem pecuniam dem, ut rem accipiam, emptio et venditio est: sin autem rem do ut rem accipiam, quia non placet **permutationem** rerum emptionem esse, dubium non est nasci civilem obligationem, in qua actione id veniet, non ut reddas quod acceperis, sed ut damneris mihi, quanti interest mea illud, de quo convenit, accipere; vel si meum recipere velim, repetatur quod datum est, quasi ob rem datum re non secuta.—l. 5, § 1, D. h. t.[1]

(2) *do ut facias.*

At cum do ut facias, si tale sit factum, quod locari solet, puta ut tabulam pingas, pecunia data locatio erit: si rem do, non erit locatio, sed nascetur vel civilis actio in hoc quod mea interest, vel ad repetendum condictio: quodsi tale est factum, quod locari non possit, puta ut servum manumittas, . . . condici ei potest vel praescriptis verbis agi.—§ 2, ib.[2]

---

must needs make the journey, or you have already incurred the expense which was necessary for the journey, so that it is plain you have laid out more perhaps than you have received, the personal action will fall through; but if less have been spent, the *condictio* will obtain, so nevertheless that an indemnity be rendered to you for that which you have disbursed.

[1] If I make a payment to receive a thing, it is a purchase and sale; but if I make over a thing to receive a thing, inasmuch as an exchange of things is held to be not a purchase, there is no doubt a civil obligation is begotten; in which action the result will be, not that you return what you received, but that I get judgment against you for damages for the loss sustained by me in not receiving the object of the agreement, or if I wish to get back my own property, that which was conveyed shall be recovered, which was made over presumably for a consideration that has failed.

[2] But when I make a conveyance in consideration of a performance by you, and the act is of such a character as is commonly done by letting, for example, that you paint a

Book III. Pt. I. Ch. II.

(3) *facio ut des.*—This form was doubted by some Roman jurists.[a]

[a] D. 19, 5, 22.

Quodsi faciam ut des, et postea quam feci, cessas dare, nulla erit civilis actio et ideo de dolo dabitur.—§ 3, ib.[1]

[b] Cf. D. 19, 5, 6.

(4) *facio ut facias.*[b]

Si pacti sumus, ut tu a meo debitore Carthagine exigas, ego a tuo Romae, vel ut tu in meo, ego in tuo solo aedificem et tu cessas, . . . tutius erit . . . praescriptis verbis dari actionem, quae actio similis erit mandati actioni, quemadmodum in superioribus casibus locationi et emptioni.—l. 5, § 4, h. t.[2]

ACTIONABLE *PACTA*.

§ 127. Pacta Adiecta.

[c] § 19

'Pacta adiecta' are the subordinate clauses[c] added to an agreement immediately upon the conclusion thereof (in continenti), qualifying its subject-matter; which, if the principal agreement is a *bonae fidei* contractus, can be enforced by the action that arises upon it.

Ulp.: Ait praetor: PACTA CONVENTA, QVAE

---

picture, the letting will follow payment of the money; if I convey a thing, it will not be a letting, but there arises either an action for my damages, or a personal action for recovery; but if such a thing has been done which cannot be done by letting, for example, that you enfranchise a slave, . . . a *condictio* can be brought against him, or proceedings *praescr. verbis*.

[1] But if I shall do something in consideration of a conveyance by you, and after performance by me you forbear to make the conveyance, there will be no civil action, and therefore an action will be given for fraud.

[2] If we have agreed that you are to recover from my debtor at Carthage, I from yours at Rome, or that you are to build on my ground, I on yours, and you forbear, . . . it will be safer . . . for an action to be given *praescr. verbis*, which action will be analogous to that of mandate, as in the above cases to letting and purchase.

NEQVE DOLO MALO, NEQVE ADVERSVS LEGES PLEBISCITA SENATVSCONSVLTA EDICTA PRINCIPVM, NEQVE QVO FRAVS CVI EORVM FIAT, FACTA ERVNT, SERVABO. —D. 2, 14, 7, 7.[1]

Quin imo interdum (nuda pactio) format ipsam actionem: solemus enim dicere pacta conventa inesse bonae fidei iudiciis. Sed hoc sic accipiendum est, ut si quidem ex continenti pacta subsecuta sunt, etiam ex parte actoris insint; ex intervallo, non inerunt nec valebunt, si agat, ne ex pacto actio nascatur: . . . ea enim pacta insunt, quae legem contractui dant i.e. quae in ingressu contractus facta sunt.—§ 5, ib.[2]

These subordinate agreements can be of unlimited variety.

Id.: Si venditor habitationem exceperit, ut inquilino liceat habitare, vel colono ut perfrui liceat ad certum tempus, magis esse Servius putabat ex vendito esse actionem.—l. 13, § 30, D. de A. E. V. 19, 1.[3]

Nerat.: Insulam hoc modo, ut aliam insulam reficeres, vendidi. Respondit nullam esse vendi-

---

[1] The Praetor says: 'Agreements that shall have been made neither by fraud, nor against statutes, decrees of the People, of the Senate, imperial edicts, nor so that any one of them is evaded, I will uphold.'

[2] Nay rather, sometimes, (a mere agreement) shapes the action itself; for we are accustomed to speak of agreements as inherent in *bon. fid.* actions. But this must be taken to mean that, if the agreements are immediately annexed (to the contract), they also form part of the plaintiff's case; if they followed some time afterwards, they are not an integral part of it, and will be of no effect if he take proceedings, that no action may arise upon a (mere) agreement, . . . for those agreements are operative which annex a condition to a contract, *i.e.*, which were made upon the conclusion of the contract.

[3] If the vendor has reserved the occupation, to allow of his lodger's occupation, or of his tenant's enjoyment for a term, Serv. was of opinion that the action is rather upon the sale.

Book III. Pt. I. Ch. II.

tionem, sed civili intentione incerti agendum.—D. 19, 5, 6.[1]

Pomp.: Si vendidi tibi insulam certa pecunia et ut etiam insulam meam reficeres, agam ex vendito, ut reficias: si autem hoc solum, ut refi-ceres eam, convenisset, non intelligitur emptio et venditio facta.—l. 6, § 1, de A. E. V.[2]

Hermog.: Qui fundum vendidit, ut eum certa mercede conductum ipse habeat, vel si ven-dat, non alii sed sibi distrahat, vel simile aliquid paciscatur, ad complendum id quod pepigerunt, ex vendito agere poterit.—D. 18, 1, 75.[a] [3]

[a] § 122. Cf. Gai. iv. 46.

§ 128. Pacta Praetoria.

Certain informal agreements were furnished by the Praetors with an action. To these belong—

(1) the 'constitutum s. pecunia constituta' (promise of payment),[b] *i.e.*, the agreement by which any one promises the fulfilment of an existing civil or natural obligation (especially a money debt), one's own or another's, commonly, and at first regularly, accom-panied by the appointment of a definite term for payment (constitutum debiti proprii—alieni).[c]

[b] Cf. English account stated and guaranty (Pollock, 'Contract,' p. 149).

[c] See Bell, s. 'Constitution, decree of.'

Ulp.: Debitum autem ex quacumque causa potest constitui, id est ex quocumque contractu.

---

[1] I have sold a house subject to this condition, that you repair another house. His answer is, there is no sale, but proceedings must be taken by a civil claim *incerti*.

[2] If I have sold you a house for a certain sum, and in consideration also of your repairing a house of mine, I shall sue upon the sale for your repairs; but if the agreement had been alone that you should repair it, it is not considered that a purchase and sale has been concluded.

[3] He that has sold land under the condition that he himself is to have the hire of it at a certain rent, or that if (the purchaser) sell it, he shall dispose of it to none other but himself, or shall make any like bargain, he will be able to sue *ex vendito* for performance of their agreement.

—Debitum autem vel natura sufficit.—l. 1, §§ 6, 7, D. h. t. (de pec. const. 13, 5).[1]

Id.: Si quis autem constituerit quod iure civili debebat, iure praetorio non debebat, id est per exceptionem, . . . Pomponius scribit eum non teneri, quia debita iuribus non est pecunia, quae constituta est.—l. 3, § 1 eod.[2]

Paul.: Si is qui . . . debebat, in diem sit obligatus,—Labeo ait teneri;[a] . . . et adiicit, vel propter has potissimum pecunias, quae nondum peti possunt, constituta inducta.—Sed et si citeriore die constituat se soluturum, similiter tenetur. —§ 2, ib., l. 4 eod.[3]

[a] Sc. constituendo.

Ulp.: Constituere et praesentes et absentes possumus.—l. 14, § 3 eod.[4]

Id.: Quod exigimus, ut sit debitum quod constituitur, in rem exactum est, non utique ut is, cui constituitur, creditor sit: nam et quod ego debeo tu constituendo teneberis, et quod tibi debetur, si mihi constituatur, debetur.—l. 5, § 2 eod.[5]

Scaev.: Quidam ad creditorem litteras eiusmodi

---

[1] Now an undertaking can be given to pay by whatever title, *i.e.*, by virtue of whatever contract.—But a debt even by Natural Law is sufficient.

[2] Now if a man has undertaken to pay what he owed by Civil Law, but did not owe by Praetorian Law, *i.e.*, by a plea, . . . Pomp. writes that he is not liable, because money the payment of which has been undertaken is not owing by the laws.

[3] If the debtor have bound himself to pay at a fixed date, Labeo says he is liable; . . . and he adds that *constituta* have been introduced even because of these claims in particular which cannot yet be enforced,—but even if he should undertake to pay at an earlier date, he is likewise liable.

[4] We can undertake payment either as present or absent.

[5] When we claim that it is a debt the payment of which is undertaken, the claim has been made *in rem*, not of course that he to whom the undertaking is given is creditor, for both what I owe you will by your undertaking be liable for, and what is owing to you, if an undertaking is given to me, is a debt [to me].

BOOK III. Pt. I. Ch. II.

fecit: 'Decem, quae Lucius Titius ex arca tua mutua acceperat, salva ratione usurarum habes penes me.' Respondit actione de constituta pecunia eum teneri.—l. 26 eod.[1]

The action that arises from this is the 'actio de pecunia constituta.'[a] From the formal[b] acknowledgment of debt by bankers (receptum argentarii), a special, and indeed civil, 'actio recepticia' obtained; and this could be applied to every subject, whilst the constitutum originally was confined to money and other quantities; but Justinian abolished the actio recepticia, and at the same time every restriction upon the constitutum.—The constitutum leaves the original claim untouched, and always engenders only an accessory obligation, so that thus the 'constitutum debiti alieni' exhibits itself as an informal suretyship.

[a] § 206.

[b] With Bruns, Ztschr. f. R. G. vol. i. pp. 84-86. For the opposite view, see vol. xv. pp. 67-69 (Lenel).

Gai.: Ubi quis pro alio constituit se soluturum, adhuc is, pro quo constituit, obligatus manet.—l. 28, D. h. t.[2]

Titius Seio epistulam emisit in haec verba: 'Remanserunt apud me L ex credito tuo ex contractu pupillorum meorum, quos tibi reddere debebo Idibus Maiis probos; quodsi ad diem suprascriptum non dedero, tunc dare debebo usuras tot.' Quaero an Titius in locum pupillorum hac cautione reus successerit? Marcellus respondit, si intercessisset stipulatio, successisse.—l. 24 eod.[3]

---

[1] A certain person drew up a letter to a creditor in these terms: 'The ten [*aurei*] which L. T. had received as a loan from your chest, you have as in my possession, the account for interest being kept up.' He answers, that such person was liable to the action *de constituta pecunia*.

[2] When any one has become surety for another, the person for whom he has become surety still remains liable.

[3] Tit. sent a letter to Sejus in these terms: 'There have remained in my hands fifty [*aurei*] of your claim [which belonged to you] by virtue of a contract with my wards, which I shall have to return to you in good coin on the 15th of May; but if I shall not have paid it over by the above-written day, then I

Ulp.: Vetus fuit dubitatio, an qui hac actione egerit, sortis obligationem consumat. Et tutius est dicere, solutione potius ex hac actione facta liberationem contingere, non litis contestatione, quoniam solutio ad utramque obligationem proficit. —l. 18, § 3 eod.[1]

(2) The 'receptum arbitrii.'

(a) If any one as umpire (arbiter ex compromisso) have undertaken the decision of the suit between them assigned to him by regular 'compromissum' (pecunia compromissa) of the parties, he is by coercive measures of the Praetor required to deliver the award.

Paul.: Compromissum ad similitudinem iudiciorum redigitur et ad finiendas lites pertinet.—D. 4, 8, 1.[a][2]

[a] But see Moyle, p. 619.

Ulp.: Recepisse autem arbitrium videtur, ut Pedius dicit, qui iudicis partes suscepit finemque se sua sententia controversiis impositurum pollicetur.—l. 13, § 2 eod.[3]

Id.: Arbitrum autem cogendum non esse sententiam dicere, nisi compromissum intervenerit. —Item Iulianus scribit non cogendum arbitrum, si alter promiserit alter non.—l. 11, §§ 1, 4.[4]

---

shall have to pay such and such interest.' I ask, whether L. T. by this engagement has taken the place of the wards as debtor? Marc. answers, that he has taken their place, if a stipulation had intervened.

[1] There was an ancient doubt whether he who has sued by this action extinguishes the obligation as to the capital.[b] And it is safer to say that it is rather by payment which has been made in consequence of this action that the release comes about, not by joinder of issue, since payment avails for both obligations.

[b] *I.e.*, the obligation of the principal debtor.

[2] A reference is put on the same footing as actions, and concerns the termination of suits.

[3] But, as Ped. says, he is to be regarded as having taken upon himself the decision of the suit who has undertaken the functions of *iudex*, and promises by his award to put an end to the disputes.

[4] But the arbitrator is under no compulsion to deliver his award, unless a reference has intervened (to that effect).—Like-

Book III. Pt. I. Ch. II.

(β) On the other hand, the award itself is not of direct enforcement. Operation is only indirectly assured to it by stipulations (especially stipulatio poenae), by which the parties, already upon the appointment of the tribunal of arbitration, must mutually engage to obey the award.

Id.: Ex compromisso placet exceptionem non nasci, sed poenae petitionem.—l. 2 eod.[1]

Id.: Sed si poena non fuisset adiecta compromisso sed simpliciter sententia stari quis promiserit, incerti adversus eum foret actio.—l. 27, § 7 eod.[2]

Imp. Anton.: Ex sententia arbitri ex compromisso . . . nec iudicati actio praestari potest, et ob hoc invicem poena promittitur, ut metu eius a placitis non recedatur.—C. 2, 55, 1.[3]

[a] § 136, ad fin.

(3) The 'receptum nautarum, etc.'[a]

§ 129. Pacta Legitima; *Donatio* in Particular.

Of the informal agreements to which by enactment or customary Law (pacta legitima) actionability was in the later period accorded, without thus being ranged in the closed circle of civil contractus, the most important is the contract of DONATION.[b]

[b] Cf. C. 5, 11, 6.

Paul.: Legitima conventio est, quae lege aliqua confirmatur; et ideo interdum ex pacto actio

---

wise Jul. writes that the arbitrator is under no compulsion if one party has pledged himself, the other not.

[1] It is held that no plea arises out of a reference, but the claim of a penalty.

[2] But if no penalty should have been attached to the reference, but a man should have given the simple promise that he would abide by the award, there would be an action against him *incerti*.

[3] From the award of an arbitrator upon a reference, . . . the action for execution cannot be given, and on that account a penalty is mutually promised, that by fear of it there may be no departure from the contract.

nascitur vel tollitur, quotiens lege vel senatusconsulto adiuvatur.—D. 2, 14, 6.[1]

'Donatio' in the wider sense comprises every grant from pure liberality of a proprietary advantage, though it may be only a temporary one.

Pap.: Donari videtur, quod nullo iure cogente conceditur.—D. 50, 17, 82.[2]

Pomp.: In aedibus alienis habitare gratis donatio videtur; id enim ipsum capere videtur qui habitat, quod mercedem pro habitatione non solvit. Potest enim et citra corporis donationem valere donatio, veluti si donationis causa cum debitore meo paciscar, ne ante certum tempus ab eo petam.—l. 9 pr., D. h. t. (do donat. 39, 5).[3]

Donatio in the strict sense is only that voluntary and gratuitous alienation of an object of property which diminishes the property of the donor (donator), permanently augments that of the donee, and is done with the intention of enrichment (animus donandi)

Iul.: Dat aliquis ea mente, ut statim velit accipientis fieri nec ullo casu ad se reverti, et propter nullam aliam causam facit, quam ut liberalitatem et munificentiam exerceat: haec proprie donatio appellatur.—l. 1 pr. eod.[4]

---

[1] A statutory convention is that which is confirmed by some statute; and accordingly sometimes an action arises or is extinguished by a bargain, whenever it is assisted by a statute or a decree of the Senate.

[2] That appears to be presented which is granted under the compulsion of no right.

[3] The occupation of another's house without payment is considered a donation; for there seems to be an acquisition by him in the very fact that he pays no hire for the occupation. For a donation can avail even without the present of a material thing, for example, if I for the sake of a present engage with my debtor that I will make no claim upon him before a time certain.

[4] Some one gives with the intention that the donee should at once become owner, and that (the thing) in no case should

[a] Sc. inter virum et uxorem.

Ulp.: —de finirisolet eam demum donationem impediri solere,[a] quae et donantem pauperiorem et accipientem facit locupletiorem.—Si maritus heres institutus repudiet hereditatem donationis causa, Iulianus scripsit donationem valere: neque enim pauperior fit qui non adquirat, sed qui de patrimonio suo deposuit; repudiatio autem mariti mulieri prodest, si vel substituta sit mulier vel etiam ab intestato heres futura.—Simili modo et si legatum repudiet, placet nobis valere donationem, si mulier substituta sit in legato vel etiam si proponas eam heredem institutam.—Ubicumque igitur non deminuit de facultatibus suis qui donavit, vel etiamsi deminuat, locupletior tamen non fit qui accepit, donatio valet.—D. 24, 1, 5, §§ 8, 13, 14, 16.[1]

Cic. Top. 8, 37: —neque donationem sine acceptione intelligi posse.[2]

Ulp.: Non potest liberalitas nolenti adquiri.—l. 19, § 2, D. h. t.[3]

Every kind of property can be subject of donatio

---

revert to himself, and he does it for no other reason than to exercise liberality and generosity: this is called a donation in the strict sense.

[1] It is customary to fix the rule that only such a donation is commonly prohibited [that between husband and wife] as makes the donor poorer, the donee richer.—If a husband instituted heir renounce the inheritance for the sake of a present, Jul. has written that the donation is valid; for he certainly does not become poorer who does not acquire something, but he that of his own property has given something away; but the renunciation on the part of the husband benefits the wife, if the wife has either been substituted, or become heiress by intestacy.—In like manner we suppose that the donation also holds good if he should renounce a legacy, if the wife has been substituted in the legacy, or even, if you imagine the case that she has been instituted heiress.—When, therefore, the donor has made no diminution in his property, or even if he diminish it, but the donee does not become richer, the gift is good.

[2] —and that a donation without acceptance is inconceivable.

[3] A present cannot be acquired by a person against his will.

and, according to its nature, the gift can be effected by the most various legal transactions—dare, obligare, liberare—as, for instance, by transfer of ownership, grant or surrender of a servitude, creation of a claim (*e.g.*, by cessio), or release of the debtor from a liability.

Gai.: Iuliano placet, licet solvendo non sit debitor, cui acceptum latum sit, videri ei donatum.—Per acceptilationem egens debitor liberatus totam eam pecuniam, qua liberatus est, cepisse videtur.—D. 39, 6, l. 31, §§ 1, 4.[1]

Iul.: Cum ego Titio pecuniam donaturus te, qui mihi tantundem donare volebas, iussero Titio promittere, inter omnes personas donatio perfecta est.—l. 2, § 2, D. h. t.[2]

If the donation consist in an obligation of the donor for some performance, and so, in the creation of a claim of the donee upon the donor, we speak of the contract or promise of donation. By Justinianean Law such a contract required no further form,[a] whilst by older Law it had to be clothed in a stipulatio.

[a] *Secus* in English Law (Brown, s. v.)

Vat. fgm. 263: Eam quae bona sua filiis per epistulam citra stipulationem donavit si neque possessionem rerum singularum tradidit, neque per mancipationem praediorum dominium transtulit, nec interpositis delegationibus aut inchoatis litibus actiones novavit, nihil egisse placuit.—(Pap.)[3]

---

1 Jul. holds that, although the debtor to whom a claim has been released is unable to pay, a present would seem to have been made to him.—An indigent debtor released by acquittance is considered to have acquired the whole of that claim from which he has been discharged.

2 When I, with the intention of presenting money to Tit., have directed you, who wished to present me with just so much, to promise it to Tit., a donation has been completed between all the parties.

3 It was decided that the act of a woman was void who gave her property to her sons by letter without a stipulation, if she neither delivered possession of the several things, nor made over

Book III. Pt. I. Ch. II.

Perficiuntur autem (donationes) cum donator suam voluntatem scriptis aut sine scriptis manifestaverit: et ad exemplum venditionis nostra constitutio eas etiam in se habere necessitatem traditionis voluit, ut, et si non tradantur, habeant plenissimum et perfectum robur et traditionis necessitas incumbat donatori.—§ 2, I. h. t. (de don. 2, 7).[1]

The donation can obtain both between living persons (donatio inter vivos) and in the event of death (donatio mortis causa).[a]

[a] For the latter, cf. § 186.

Ibid. pr. § 1: Donationum autem duo genera sunt: mortis causa et non mortis causa.—Mortis causa donatio est, quae propter mortis fit suspicionem, cum quis ita donat, ut si quid humanitus ei contigisset, haberet is qui accepit: sin autem supervixisset qui donavit, reciperet, vel si eum donationis poenituisset aut prior decesserit is cui donatum sit.[2]

Donations, both as regards the donee personally and their extent, were made subject to several restrictions.

Gifts between spouses are entirely precluded.[b]

[b] § 148.

The l. Cincia de donis et muneribus (A.U. 550),[c] which was in full force at the time of the classical jurists, but became obsolete by desuetudo, allowed

[c] A lex imperfecta: cf. Ulp. fgm. I.

---

the ownership of lands by mancipation, and did not take fresh proceedings by interposing assignments or commencing suits.

[1] Donations are completed when the donor has made known his intention with or without writing; and, as with a sale, our constitution has directed that they shall involve the necessity of delivery, so that, even if the things are not delivered, the present shall have entire and complete effect, and impose upon the vendor the necessity of delivery.

[2] There are two classes of donations: in view of death, and not in view of death.—A donation *mortis causa* is one made through the apprehension of death, when a man making the gift upon the condition that, if any fatality should befall him, the donee shall hold it, but that if the donor should survive, or if he should regret the donation, or the person should first die to whom it was made, the donor shall get it back.

until the death of the donor the revocation of every gift exceeding a certain—unknown—limit (donatio immodica), by means of an actio or exceptio (or replicatio) in case they were not—

(1) already effected completely juristically and materially (donatio perfecta).[a]

[a] According to another opinion, of every *donatio immodica* and of every *donatio non perfecta*.

Vat. fgm. 259: Mulier sine tutoris auctoritate praedium stipendiarium instructum non mortis causa Latino donaverat: perfectam in praedio ceterisque rebus nec mancipi donationem esse apparuit, servos autem et pecora, quae collo vel dorso domarentur, usu non capta. Si tamen voluntatem mulier non mutasset, Latino quoque doli profuturam duplicationem respondi—non enim mortis causa capitur quod aliter donatum est—: quoniam morte Cincia removetur.—(Papin.)[b] [1]

[b] Cf. Gai. ii. §§ 80, *sqq.*; ib. § 47, Vat. fgm. 1.

Ib. §§ 310–311: Perficitur donatio in exceptis personis sola mancipatione vel promissione, quoniam neque Cinciae legis exceptio obstat neque in factum: '**si non donationis causa mancipavi vel promisi me daturum.**'—Sed in persona non excepta sola mancipatio vel promissio non perficit donationem; in rebus mobilibus, etiamsi traditae sint, exigitur, ut et interdicto **utrubi** superior sit is cui res donata est, sive mancipi mancipata sit, sive nec mancipi tradita.—(Paul.)[2]

---

[1] A woman, without the consent of her guardian, had given to a Latin, subject to a ground-rent, an estate with every convenience, but not *mortis causa*: it appeared that the gift was complete in respect of the estate and other things *nec mancipi*, but that the slaves and cattle which are tamed by collar or saddle were not acquired by use. But the opinion I gave was that, if the woman did not alter her intention, the twofold evasion of the law would also benefit the Latin—for a thing is not acquired *mortis causa* which has otherwise been presented—since the Cincian law is defeated by death.

[2] In respect of persons excepted, a gift is made perfect by mere mancipation, or by promise; since neither does the plea of the *l. Cincia* hinder even as against the fact: 'If I did not

Ib. § 266: Si quis contra legem Cinciam obligatus non excepto solverit, debuit dici repetere eum posse: nam semper exceptione Cinciae uti potuit, nec solum ipse, verum, ut Proculeiani contra Sabinianos putant, etiam quivis, quasi popularis sit haec exceptio; sed ut heres eius, nisi forte durante voluntate decessit donator: tunc enim doli replicationem locum habere, imperator noster rescripsit.—(Ulp.)[1]

Iavol.: Fideiussori eius, qui donationis causa pecuniam supra modum legis promisit, exceptio dari debebit etiam invito reo.—l. 24, h. t.[2]

Cels.: Sed si debitorem meum tibi donationis immodicae causa promittere iussi, an summoveris donationis exceptione necne, tractabitur. Et meus quidem debitor exceptione te agentem repellere non potest, quia perinde sum, quasi exactam a debitore meo summam tibi donaverim et tu illam ei credideris. Sed ego, si quidem pecuniae a debitore meo nondum solutae sint, habeo adversus debitorem meum rescissoriam in id, quod supra legis modum tibi promisit, ita ut in reliquum tantummodo tibi maneat obligatus: sin autem pecunias a debitore

---

mancipate so as to make a gift, or promise that I would give it.' But in respect of a person not excepted, mere mancipation or promise does not make the gift perfect. In movables, even if they have passed by delivery, it is required that also by the interdict *utrubi* he be in a better position to whom the gift has been made, whether the delivery have been of a thing *mancipi* or *nec mancipi*.

[1] If any one have in violation of the l. Cincia bound himself, and paid money to a person not excepted from such statute, it ought to be stated that he can reclaim it; for he could always employ the Cincian plea, not himself only, but also, as the Proculeians suppose against the Sabinians, any one, as if this plea were a 'popular' one; but his heir also, unless perhaps the grantor died while his intention remained; for our Emperor's rescript was that the *replicatio* of fraud then attaches.

[2] To the surety of him who, for the sake of a present, has promised money beyond the limits of the statute, a plea will have to be allowed even against the will of the debtor.

meo exegisti, in hoc, quod modum legis excedit, habeo contra te condictionem.—l. 21, § 1, D. h. t.[1]

(2) Or was not made to certain persons nearly related (personae exceptae).

l. c. § 299: Quinque gradus[a] pleni excepti sunt et ex sexto una persona, sobrinus et sobrina. § 300: Excipiuntur et ii, qui in potestate eorum vel manu mancipiove, item quorum in potestate manu mancipiove erunt. § 304: Excipiuntur et adfinium personae, ut privignus privigna, noverca vitricus, socer socrus, gener nurus, vir et uxor, sponsus sponsa. § 304: Excipit tutorem, qui tutelam gerit, si dare volet: nam quia tutores quasi parentes proprii pupillorum sunt, permisit eis in infinitum donare. § 307: Item excipit: 'si quis a servis suis . . . accipit.' His verbis . . . liberti continentur, ut patronis dare possint. § 309: Contra an item liberti a patronis excepti sunt? Et hoc iure utimur, ne[b] excepti videantur. —(Paul.)[2]

[a] Sc. cognatorum.

[b] ? ut.

[1] But if I have directed my debtor to make a promise to you, for the sake of a present, of an excessive amount, the question will be, whether you can be defeated by the plea of the donation. My debtor indeed cannot by the plea rebut you if you sue, because I am to be regarded just as if I presented to you the sum enforced by my debtor, and you credited him with it. But if the money have not yet been paid by my debtor, I have an action for revocation against my debtor for that which he promised to you beyond the limit of the statute; so that he remains liable to you only for the residue; but if you have recovered the money from my debtor, I have a *condictio* against you for that which exceeds the limit of the statute.

[2] Five degrees (*i.e.*, of representatives) are excepted in full, and one person from a sixth degree, a cousin-german of either sex.—They too are excepted who are under the *potestas*, or *manus*, or in the *mancipium* of such; likewise those under whose *potestas* and *manus* or in whose *mancipium* they shall be.—Excepted also are some persons among the next-of-kin, as a step-son, step-daughter, step-mother, step-father, father-in-law, mother-in-law, son-in-law, daughter-in-law, husband and wife,

Book III. Pt. I. Ch. II.

Excepted are certain kinds of gifts.

Ib. § 305: Item excipit: 'si quis mulieri virginive cognatus dotem conferre volet'; igitur quocumque gradu cognatus dotis nomine donare potest.[1]

Paul. v. 11, § 6: Ei, qui aliquem a latrunculis vel hostibus eripuit, in infinitum donare non prohibetur (si tamen donatio et non merces eximii laboris appellanda est): quia contemplationem salutis certo modo aestimari non placuit.[2]

[a] Cf. Moyle on Inst. i. 11, 12.

The form of judicial 'insinuatio'[a] (declaration made in court, professio apud acta) was prescribed for gifts to non exceptae personae, and by Constantine for all gifts; but after many fluctuations of legislation, this form continued to be requisite in the latest Law (a constitution of Justinian of 531) alone for gifts above 500 solidi, with some exceptions. Omission of the insinuatio leads to the invalidity of the gift, so far as it exceeds the amount named.

In the older Law, the patron could at discretion revoke the gift he had made to his libertus; later on, only in certain cases; but according to the Law of

---

betrothed persons of either sex.—It excepts the guardian, who exercises a *tutela*, if he desire to make such gift; for, inasmuch as guardians are strictly like parents of the wards, it permitted them to make gifts without limit.—A further exception is: 'whoever accepts from his slave.' Freedmen are comprised in these words, that they can give to their patrons. On the other hand, can freedmen be excluded likewise by the patrons? This law also we employ lest they may be regarded as excluded.

[1] It contains also the following exception: 'Whatever cognate desires to bestow a gift on a woman or a maiden'; and so a cognate in any degree can make a gift under the name of *dos*.

[2] No restriction is placed upon a perpetual gift to him who has delivered any one from highwaymen or enemies (though it have to be called a *donatio*, and not a reward for extraordinary service); because it has not been thought well to put a fixed valuation upon regard for safety.

Justinian every gift is revocable for base ingratitude of the donee, except such gifts as are mentioned in Paul. v. 11, § 6, *supra*.

§ 130. Obligationes *ex Delicto* in General.[a]

Delicta privata—in contrast with *publica, i.e.*, crimina[b]—are illicit and illegal acts, which ground independent obligations. The object of the obligation is either compensation for the injury done, or payment of a pecuniary penalty (poena sc. privata) to the party injured, or, as a rule, both at the same time: actiones rei persecutoriae, poenales, mixtae.[c] The wrongdoer is, as a rule, only responsible for dolus, sometimes indeed for culpa. Finally, all obligationes ex delicto agree in being passively untransmissible.[d]—In the course of time the delicts committed by dolus admitted also of criminal prosecution, so that the party injured had the choice of public or private redress.

[a] See 'Anct. Law,' pp. 367-372; Mkby. s. 600, also ch. xvi.

[b] See 'Anct. Law,' pp. 372, *sqq.*, and Stephen, 'History of the Crim. Law of England,' vol. i. ch. ii.

[c] Inst. iv. 6. §§ 16-18.

[d] § 25.

§ 131. Furtum.

Furtum is the corporal dealing with a movable thing, done with intent to obtain an illegal advantage by its appropriation (dolus, animus furandi), by which dealing some one, violating property of another, illegally usurps the thing itself, if it be another's; or the use of it, if it be entrusted to him;[e] or the possession of it, if, while it is his own, it is in the disposition of another.[f]

> Paul.: Furtum est **contrectatio** rei fraudulosa lucri faciendi gratia: vel **rei** ipsius, vel etiam **usus** eius **possessionisve**.—l. 1, § 3, D. h. t. (de furt. 47, 2).[1]
>
> Cels.: Infitiando depositum nemo facit furtum; nec enim furtum est ipsa infitiatio, licet prope

[e] Cf. Stephen, *l. c.* pp. 30, *sqq.*

[f] Cf. Gai. ii. §§ 45, *sqq.*; D. 41, 1, 9, 8; 47, 2, 74 (73).

[1] Theft is the fraudulent meddling with a thing in order to make profit, either with the thing itself or even the use or possession of it.

BOOK III. Pt. I. Ch. II.

furtum sit: sed si possessionem eius adipiscatur intervertendi causa, facit furtum.—l. 68 pr. eod.[1]

Paul.: Si locatum tibi servum subripias, utrumque iudicium adversus te est exercendum, locati et furti.—D. 19, 2, 42.[2]

Id.: Si tibi centum dedero, ut ea Titio dares, tuque non dederis sed consumpseris, furti teneri te Proculus ait.—D. 17, 1, 22, 7.[3]

Scaev.: Furtum fit, cum quis indebitos nummos sciens acceperit.—D. 13, 1, 18.[4]

Sabinus ap. Gell. xi. 18, § 21: Qui alienum [quid] iacens lucri faciendi causa sustulit, furti obstringitur, sive scit, cuius sit, sive nescit.—(= l.—43, § 4, h. t.)[5]

Paul.: Rei hereditariae furtum non fit, sicut nec eius, quae sine domino est, et nihil mutat existimatio subripientis.—D. 47, 19, 6.—Gai. iii. § 201: Interdum alienas res occupare concessum est nec creditur furtum fieri, velut res hereditarias, quarum heres non est nactus possessionem, nisi necessarius heres extet.[a][6]

[a] §§ 153, ad fin, 155.

---

[1] By denying a deposit no one commits a theft; for the theft is not the denial itself, although it borders upon it; but if he acquires possession of it for embezzlement, he does commit a theft.

[2] If you steal a slave let out to you, both actions should be employed against you—of letting and theft.

[3] If I have given you 100 [*aurei*] for you to give them to Tit., and you have not given them, but have spent them, Proc. says you are liable for theft.

[4] A theft is committed when a man advisedly accepts money not owing to him.

[5] He that with avaricious intent has taken property of another lying before him is liable for theft, whether he knows to whom it belongs or does not.

[6] No theft occurs of hereditary property, as little as of that without an owner, and the belief of the thief makes no difference. —We are sometimes allowed to take possession of another's property and acquire a title to it by use, and no theft is held to have been committed; as, for instance, in the case of things

Labeo: si quis cum sciret quid sibi subripi, non prohibuit, non potest furti agere. Paulus: immo contra; nam si quis scit sibi rapi et, quia non potest prohibere, quievit, furti agere potest; at si potuit prohibere nec prohibuit, nihilominus furti aget.—l. 92, h. t.[1]

Gai. iii. § 198: Sed et si credat aliquis, invito domino se rem contrectare, domino autem volente id fiat, dicitur furtum non fieri. Unde illud quaesitum est: cum Titius servum meum sollicitaverit, ut quasdam res mihi subriperet et ad eum perferret, servus id ad me pertulit; ego dum volo Titium in ipso delicto deprehendere, permisi servo quasdam res ad eum perferre—.[2]

Ib. iii. § 197: Furtum sine dolo malo [affectu furandi] non committitur.—§ 7, I. h. t. 4, 1.[3]

Sabin. ap. Gell. l. c. § 20: Qui alienam rem adtrectavit, cum id se invito domino facere iudicare deberet, furti tenetur.[4]

Ulp.: Sed si non fuit derelictum, putavit

---

belonging to an inheritance, of which the heir has not yet obtained possession, unless there be a necessary heir.

[1] Lab.: if a man, when he knew something was being stolen from his person, did not forbid it, he cannot sue for a theft. Paul.: nay, on the contrary, for if a man knows that (something) is snatched from him and, from his not being able to forbid it, has kept his peace, he can sue for a theft; but if he was able to forbid it and did not, he will none the less sue for a theft.

[2] But even if a person believe he is meddling with a thing against the will of the owner, yet if the owner consent to such act, it is said that no theft is committed. Whence arises this question: when Tit. has worked upon my slave to steal certain things from me, and carry them to him, and the slave has brought me information of it, I, wishing to detect Tit. in the very act, allowed the slave to carry some things to him—.

[3] Theft is not committed without unlawful intention [the intention of stealing].

[4] He that has appropriated property of another, when he ought to have accounted that he did it against the will of the owner, is liable for theft.

BOOK III. Pt. I. Ch. II.

tamen derelictum, furti non tenetur.—l. 43, § 6, h. t.[a] [1]

[a] Cf. ib. l. 4, supr.

Gai.: Species lucri est, ex alieno largiri et beneficii debitorem sibi adquirere: unde et is furti tenetur qui ideo rem amovet, ut eam alii donet.—l. 55, § 1 eod.[2]

[b] Sc. Sabini, libro de furtis.

Gell. l. c. § 13: In quo[b] id quoque scriptum est, quod vulgo inopinatum est, non hominum tantum neque rerum moventium, quae auferri occulte et subripi possunt, sed fundi quoque et aedium fieri furtum: condemnatum quoque colonum, qui fundo, quem conduxerat, vendito possessione eius dominum intervertisset.[3]

Gai.: Abolita est quorundam veterum sententia existimantium etiam fundi locive furtum fieri.—D. 41, 3, 38.[4]

Gai. iii. § 199: Interdum autem etiam liberorum hominum furtum fit, velut si quis liberorum nostrorum, qui in potestate nostra sint, sive etiam uxor, quae in manu nostra sit, sive etiam iudicatus vel auctoratus meus subreptus fuerit.[5]

Ib. §§ 195–197: Furtum autem fit non

---

[1] But if it was not abandoned, but he thought it was, he is not liable for theft.

[2] It is a kind of gain, to make a liberal use of property of another and acquire for oneself a debtor of the munificence; whence also he is liable for theft who removes a thing to bestow it upon another.

[3] Wherein [*i.e.*, the work of Sab. upon thefts] also is found written what is commonly unexpected, that not only can a theft take place of slaves and of movables which can privily be removed and stolen, but also of a farm and house; that a tenant also is guilty who, having sold a farm that he had hired, had defrauded the owner of the possession thereof.

[4] The opinion has been long rejected of certain old jurists, who thought that there could be a theft even of a field or a place.

[5] But sometimes a theft will be committed of free persons, as, for instance, if any one of our children under our power, or even a wife in our *manus*, or even my judgment-debtor, or my hired gladiator has been kidnapped.

solum, cum quis intercipiendi causa rem alienam amovet, sed generaliter cum quis rem alienam invito domino contrectat. § Itaque si quis re, quae apud cum deposita sit, utatur, furtum committet; et si quis utendam rem acceperit, eamque in alium usum transtulerit, furti obligatur, veluti si quis . . . equum gestandi gratia commodatum longius aliquo duxerit: quod veteres scripserunt de eo, qui in aciem perduxisset. § Placuit tamen eos, qui rebus commodatis aliter uterentur, quam utendas accepissent, ita furtum committere, si intelligant id se invito domino facere, eumque, si intellexisset, non permissurum.[1]

Q. Mucius Scaev. ap. Gell. vi. (vii.) 15: Quod cui servandum datum est, si id usus est, sive quod utendum accepit, ad aliam rem atque accepit usus est, furti se obligavit.[2]

Gai.: Si pignore creditor utatur, furti tenetur. —Eum, qui quod utendum accepit ipse alii commodaverit, furti obligari responsum est.—l. 55 pr., § 1, h. t.[3]

---

[1] A theft takes place not only when a person removes the property of another with intent to deprive him of it, but generally when any one meddles with the property of another against the owner's will. § Therefore, if a person make use of a thing which has been deposited with him, he commits a theft, and if he who has been accorded some use of a thing converts it to another use, he is liable for a theft; as, for instance, if a person has taken to a distance a horse for the purpose of a ride; as the old jurists wrote of him who had taken one into battle. § It has, however, been decided that they who make use of things otherwise than they received them for, only commit theft if they know that they are doing so against the will of the owner, and that he, if aware of it, would not allow it.

[2] If a man have made use of a thing which was given him to keep, or have taken a thing to use and have put it to some purpose other than that for which he received it, he has made himself liable for theft.

[3] If the creditor use the pledge, he is liable for theft. The answer was, that he is liable for theft who himself has lent to another that which he received for use.

Book III. Pt. I. Ch. II.

Id. iii. § 200: Aliquando etiam suae rei quisque furtum committit, veluti si debitor rem, quam creditori pignori dedit, subtraxerit vel si bonae fidei possessori rem meam possidenti subripuerim.[1]

Paul.: Dominus qui rem subripuit, in qua ususfructus alienus est, furti usufructuario tenetur.—l. 15, § 1, D. h. t.[2]

Important is the difference between furtum 'manifestum' and 'nec manifestum.' The former occurs when the thief is caught in the very act—with the stolen thing; the latter, in all other cases.

Gell. xi. 18, § 11: Manifestum furtum est, ut ait Masurius, quod deprehenditur, dum fit; faciendi finis est, cum perlatum est, quo ferri coeperat.[3]

Gai. iii. § 134: Manifestum quidam id esse dixerunt, quod dum fit, deprehenditur; alii vero ulterius, quod eo loco deprehenditur, ubi fit, velut si in . . . domo furtum factum sit, quamdiu in ea domo fur sit; alii adhuc ulterius eousque manifestum furtum dixerunt, donec perferret eo, quo perferre fur destinasset; alii adhuc ulterius, quandoque eam rem fur tenens visus fuerit: quae sententia non obtinuit; sed et illorum sententia, qui existimaverunt, donec perferret eo quo fur destinasset, deprehensum furtum manifestum esse . . . non videtur probari . . .; ex duabus itaque superioribus opinionibus alterutra adpro-

---

[1] Sometimes also a man commits a theft of his own property, for example, when a debtor by stealth takes away a thing which he has given to his creditor as a pledge, or I have secretly taken away my property from a person possessing it in good faith.

[2] An owner that has secretly withdrawn a thing, the usufruct of which belongs to another, is liable to the usufructuary for a theft.

[3] A manifest theft, according to M., is that which is detected whilst it is being committed; there is an end of the performance when it has been carried whither it had begun to be carried.

batur; magis tamen plerique posteriorem probant.[1]

Ulp.: Magis est, . . . esse furem manifestum, si cum re furtiva fuerit apprehensus, priusquam eo loci rem pertulerit, quo destinaverat. Celsus deprehensioni hoc adiicit, si cum vidisses eum subripientem et ad comprehendendum eum accurrisses, abiecto furto effugit, furem manifestum esse.—l. 3, § 2, l. 7, § 2, D. h. t.[2]

The penal actio (actio furti)[a] belongs to the person that has suffered the theft, who may be not merely nor always the owner, but every one that has an interest in the thing stolen; hence also the person responsible for the custodia thereof. [a] § 201.

Gai. iii. §§ 203–206: Furti autem actio ei competit, **cuius interest rem salvam esse**, licet dominus non sit: itaque nec domino aliter competit, quam si eius intersit rem non perire. § Unde constat creditorem de pignore subrepto furti agere posse.—§ Item si fullo polienda curandave aut sarcinator sarcienda vestimenta certa

---

[1] Some have stated that a manifest theft is that which is detected whilst it is being committed. But others have gone further,—that it is detected in the place where it is committed; for example, if a theft have been committed . . . in a house, as long as the thief is in such house. Others have gone yet further, so far as to say that a theft is manifest until the thief should carry the thing to the place to which he purposed carrying it. Others still further: whenever the thief is seen having hold of the thing; this opinion has not naturally acceptance. But the opinion of those also who have thought the theft was manifest if detected before the thief has carried it to the place he intended, does not seem to be in favour. . . . Therefore one or other of the two former opinions is adopted; but most incline rather to the latter view.

[2] It is more the fact . . . that he is a manifest thief if he has been caught with the stolen property before he reached the place of his destination.—Celsus adds this to detection: if when you had seen him stealing it, and had run to arrest him, he threw away the object of theft and took to flight, he was a manifest thief.

mercede acceperit, eaque furto amiserit, ipse furti habet actionem, non dominus; . . . si solvendo non est, tunc quia ab eo dominus suum consequi non potest, ipsi furti actio competit, quia hoc casu ipsius interest rem salvam esse. § Quae de fullone aut sarcinatore diximus, eadem transferemus et ad eum cui rem commodavimus: nam hic . . . similiter necesse habet custodiam praestare.[1]

Ulp.: Eum qui emit, si non tradita est ei res, furti actionem non habere, sed adhuc venditoris esse hanc actionem Celsus scripsit, mandare eum plane oportebit emptori furti actionem et condictionem et vindicationem.—l. 14 pr., h. t.[2]

Iul.: Neque is, cuiuscumque interierit rem non perire, habet furti actionem, sed qui ob eam rem tenetur, quod ea res culpa eius perierit.—Ib. § 10.[3]

This lies against not only the fur, but his accomplices also.

---

[1] Now an action for theft is open to him who has an interest in the safety of the thing, although he is not the owner; and therefore it is only open to the owner when it is to his interest that the property should not perish. § Hence it is settled that a creditor can bring an action for theft in respect of a stolen pledge— . . . § Likewise if a fuller has received clothes to be cleaned or looked after, or a tailor to repair for fixed remuneration, and have lost them by theft, it is he that has the action of theft, not the owner; . . . if he be insolvent, then, as the owner cannot recover his property from such person, he himself possesses the action for theft, because in this case he is himself interested in the safety of the property. § What we have said in respect of the fuller or the tailor we may apply also to him to whom we have lent a thing; for he . . . has likewise to answer for its safekeeping.

[2] Cels. has written that a purchaser has no action of theft if the article has not been delivered to him, but the action still belongs to the vendor; he will clearly have to make over to the purchaser the action of theft, as well as the personal action and the proprietary action.

[3] And the action of theft does not appertain to any person whatever interested in the article not perishing, but to him who is liable because of its perishing by his fault.

Gai. iii. § 202: Interdum furti tenetur qui ipse furtum non fecerit, qualis est, cuius ope consilio furtum factum est.[1]

Ulp.: Consilium autem dare videtur, qui persuadet et impellit atque instruit consilio ad furtum faciendum; opem fert qui ministerium et adiutorium ad subripiendas res praebet.—l. 50, § 3, D. h. t.[2]

Ope consilio eius quoque furtum admitti videtur, qui scalas forte fenestris supponit aut ipsas fenestras vel ostium effringit, ut alius furtum faceret, quive ferramenta ad effringendum aut scalas, ut fenestris supponerentur, commodaverit, sciens cuius gratia commodaverit. Certe qui nullam operam ad furtum faciendum adhibuit, sed tantum consilium dedit atque hortatus est ad furtum faciendum, non tenetur furti.—§ 11, I. h. t. (=de obl. qu. ex del. 4, 1).[3]

In furtum manifestum the action was, by the Twelve Tables, for the addictio of the thief to the person that suffered the theft, in case they could not agree as to the penal sum to be paid (pro fure damnum decidere);[a] but by the Praetorian Edict, it was for four times the value of the object stolen.

[a] Cf. D. 2, 14, 27. §§ 3, 4.

Gai.: Lex XII tabularum furem noctu depre-

---

[1] Sometimes a man is chargeable with theft who did not himself commit it; of such sort is he by whose aid and advice the theft was committed.

[2] Now he is considered to give advice who by advice induces, and urges and gives instruction in the accomplishment of a theft; a person co-operates who affords his service and a helping hand in the covert removal of things.

[3] A theft also is held to be committed by the aid and counsel of him that, it may be, places a ladder against windows, or breaks the very windows or door, in order that another might commit a theft, or who lends iron tools to break in, or a ladder to be placed against the windows, if he knew the purpose of the loan. Of course he that has afforded no aid in the theft, but has only given advice and encouragement to accomplish it, is not liable to the action of theft.

hensum occidere permittit, ut tamen id ipsum cum clamore testificetur, interdiu autem deprehensum ita permittit occidere, si is se telo defendat, ut tamen aeque cum clamore testificetur.—l. 4, 1, D. ad leg. Aq. 9, 2.—Id.: Teli autem appellatione et ferrum et fustis et lapis et denique omne, quod nocendi causa habetur, significatur.—l. 55, § 2, D. h. t.[1]

Gai. iii. § 189: Poena manifesti furti ex lege XII tabularum capitalis erat: nam liber verberatus addicebatur ei cui furtum fecerat: utrum autem servus efficeretur ex addictione, an adiudicati loco constitueretur, veteres quaerebant. Sed postea improbata est asperitas poenae et . . . quadrupli actio praetoris edicto constituta est.[2]

Ulp.: Si pro fure damnum decisum sit, . . . furti actio, non autem condictio tollitur.—l. 7, pr. D. de cond. furt. 13, 1.[3]

In furtum nec manifestum it was for double thereof.

Gai. iii. § 190: Nec manifesti furti poena per legem XII tabularum dupli irrogatur, eamque etiam praetor conservat.[a] [4]

[a] Cf. D. 50, 16, 193; 'Anct. Law,' p. 379.

[1] A law of the Twelve Tables allows one to kill a thief caught by night, but so that he notifies it by a loud shout; but it allows killing him when caught in the day-time upon condition that he defends himself with a weapon, but so also that he make this known by a loud shout.—By weapon is meant both a sword and club and stone, and in fine, anything in one's hands to work mischief.

[2] The punishment of manifest theft, according to a law of the Twelve Tables, affected a man's *caput*.[b] For a freeman was scourged, and adjudged to him whose property he had stolen; but whether he was rendered a slave by virtue of the adjudication, or was in the position of judgment-debtor, was a moot point with the old jurists. But afterwards the severity of the punishment met with disapproval and . . . an action for fourfold the value was created by the Praetor's edict.

[b] Dirksen, s. v.; and see above, § 56.

[3] If terms have been arranged on behalf of a thief as to the damage, . . . an action of theft, but not a personal action, is taken away.

[4] A penalty for non-manifest theft of double the value is

The actiones 'furti concepti, oblati, prohibiti' disappeared in the later Law, along with the formal search of the house (of ante-Roman origin) upon which they were grounded.

Gai. iii. §§ 186–188: **Conceptum** furtum dicitur, cum apud aliquem testibus praesentibus furtiva res quaesita et inventa est: nam in eum propria actio constituta est, quamvis fur non sit, quae appellatur concepti. § **Oblatum** furtum dicitur, cum res furtiva tibi ab aliquo oblata sit eaque apud te concepta sit; utique si ea mente data tibi fuerit, ut apud te potius, quam apud eum qui dederit, conciperetur: nam tibi, apud quem concepta est, propria adversus eum qui obtulit, quamvis fur non sit, constituta est actio, quae appellatur oblati. Est etiam **prohibiti** furti adversus eum, qui furtum quaerere volentem prohibuerit. —§§ 191–2: Concepti et oblati poena ex lege XII tabularum tripli est, eaque similiter a praetore servatur. § Prohibiti actio quadrupli est ex edicto praetoris introducta: lex autem eo nomine nullam poenam constituit; hoc solum praecepit, ut qui quaerere velit, nudus quaerat, licio cinctus, lancem habens; qui si quid invenerit iubet id lex furtum manifestum esse.[1]

---

imposed by a law of the Twelve Tables, and this the Praetor also keeps up.

[1] It is said to be *furtum* when the stolen thing has been searched for, and discovered in the presence of witnesses, in some one's possession; for a special action has been appointed against him, although he be not the thief, which is called the *actio concepti.* § It is said to be *furtum oblatum* when the stolen thing has been brought to you by some one, and has been discovered in your possession; at least if it has been given you with the view of its being discovered in your possession rather than in that of the donor. For there is a special action appointed for you in whose possession it has been discovered against him who placed it in your possession, although he be not the thief, which is called the *actio oblati.* There is also an *actio prohibiti furti* against one who impedes a person in his

Book III. Pt. I. Ch. II.

Sed hae actiones . . . in desuetudinem abierunt. Cum enim requisitio rei furtivae hodie secundum veterem observationem non fit, merito ex consequentia etiam praefatae actiones ab usu communi recesserunt: cum manifestissimum est, quod omnes, qui scientes rem furtivam susceperint et celaverint, furti nec manifesti obnoxii sunt.—§ 4, I. h. t.[1]

Besides the actio furti, the owner that has suffered the theft has still the 'condictio furtiva'—grounded upon an obligatio quasi ex contractu—against the thief and his heirs for restitution (dare) of the stolen thing.[a] In respect of this duty of restitution, the thief is regarded as constantly 'in mora.'[b]

[a] *Supra*. D. 13, 1, 7 pr.
[b] § 109.

Gai. iv. § 4: —certum est non posse nos rem nostram ab alio ita petere SI PARET EVM DARE OPORTERE; nec enim quod nostrum est, nobis dari potest, cum scilicet id dari nobis intelligatur, quod ita datur, ut nostrum fiat: nec res quae est nostra, nostra amplius fieri potest. Plane odio furum, quo magis pluribus actionibus teneantur, receptum est, ut extra poenam dupli

---

desire to search for stolen property. § The penalty for stolen property, discovered or introduced, according to a law of the Twelve Tables was threefold the value, and this the Praetor likewise retains. § The *actio furti prohibiti* was for fourfold the value, and was introduced by the edict of the Praetor. But the law of the Twelve Tables had provided no penalty on that behalf; it only directed that he who wishes to search should do so naked, girt with a 'linteum' (linen cloth) and carrying a plate; and if he shall have discovered anything, the statute directs that the theft shall be regarded as manifest.

[1] But these actions . . . have fallen into disuse. For since the search for stolen property is not made at the present day according to the ancient practice, the actions just mentioned have also in consequence appropriately passed out of common use, since it is quite clear that all who have advisedly received and concealed stolen property are chargeable with non-manifest theft.

aut quadrupli rei recipiendae nomine fures ex hac actione etiam teneantur: SI PARET EOS DARE OPORTERE, quamvis sit etiam adversus eos haec actio, qua 'rem nostram esse' petimus.[1]

Furti actio poenam petit legitimam, condictio rem ipsam.—Condictio rei furtivae, quia rei habet persecutionem, heredem quoque furis obligat, nec tantum si vivat servus furtivus, sed etiam si decesserit.—l. 7, §§ 1–2, D. de cond. furt.[2]

In furtiva re soli domino condictio competit. —l. 1 eod.[3]

§ 132. Vi bona Rapta.[a]

[a] Stephen, *l. c.* pp. 38, *sq.*

The acts of violence that prevailed during the civil wars occasioned the grant in the Praetorian Edict (edictum Luculli)[b] of an action for the cases of outrage (plunder and injury to things) perpetrated by armed mobs. The ground was thereby laid for the development of the special delict of Robbery (rapina), as an appropriation of something belonging to another combined with application of personal violence; in which

[b] Cf. D. 41, 3, 4, 22; l. 33, § 2; and § 91.

---

1 —it is certain we cannot claim our own property from another thus: 'If it appear that he ought to give'; for that which is our own cannot be given to us, since of course that is regarded as given to us which is given so that it may become ours; and a thing which is ours cannot become more so. It is manifestly from detestation of thieves, and that they might be made liable to a greater number of actions, that it has been received as law, that besides the penalty of double or fourfold the amount, thieves may, with the view of recovering the thing, be made liable under such action: 'If it appear that they ought to give,' although there also lies against them the action in which we claim a thing as ours.

2 The action of theft claims the statutory penalty, the *condictio* the thing itself. The *condictio* of the stolen property, inasmuch as it comprises the recovery of the property, binds also the heir of the thief, and that not only if the stolen slave should live, but also if he has died.

3 In respect of stolen property, the *condictio* is open to the owner alone.

Book III. Pt. I. Ch. II.

essentially the same principles obtain as in Furtum. This was the 'actio vi bonorum raptorum.'

Praetor ait: SI CVI DOLO MALO [VI] HOMINIBVS COACTIS [ARMATISVE] DAMNI QVID FACTVM ESSE DICETVR, SIVE CVIVS BONA RAPTA ESSE DICENTVR, IN EVM, QVI ID FECISSE DICETVR [INTRA ANNVM, QVO PRIMVM DE EA RE EXPERIVNDI POTESTAS FVERIT, IN QVADRVPLVM, POST ANNVM IN SIMPLVM], IVDICIVM DABO.—l. 2 pr., D. h. t. = vi bon. rapt. 47, 8.[1]

Ulp.: Item si proponas **solum** damnum dedisse, non puto deficere verba; hoc enim quod ait 'hominibus coactis' sic accipere debemus: **etiam** hominibus coactis, vel armatis vel inermibus, ut, sive solus vim fecerit sive etiam hominibus coactis, hoc edicto teneantur.—Ib. § 7.[2]

Gai. iii. § 209: Qui res alienas rapit, tenetur etiam furti: quis enim magis alienam rem invito domino contrectat, quam qui vi rapit? Itaque recte dictum est eum improbum furem esse; sed propriam actionem eius delicti nomine praetor introduxit, quae appellatur vi bonorum raptorum: . . . quae actio utilis est, et si quis unam rem, licet minimam, rapuerit.[3]

---

[1] The Praetor says: 'If it is alleged that an injury has been craftily [and by force] done to any one by bands of persons [or armed men], or that any one's property has been robbed, against such person as shall be alleged to have done this I will give an action [within a year from the time when it was first possible to sue for it, for the fourfold, but after a year for the simple amount].

[2] Likewise, if you suppose a single person has inflicted the damage, I do not think the words fail of application; for the phrase 'by bands of men' we must take to mean: Even bands of men, either armed or unarmed, so that, whether it be a single person has done the violence, or even bands of men, they shall be liable by this edict.

[3] He that takes by violence the property of another is also liable for theft; for who meddles with another's property more against the owner's will than one who takes it by violence?

Ulp.: Et generaliter dicendum est, ex quibus causis furti mihi actio competit in re clam facta, ex iisdem causis habere me hanc actionem.—l. 2, § 23, h. t.[1]

Quadruplum autem non totum poena est, et extra poenam rei persecutio, . . . sed in quadruplo inest et rei persecutio, ut poena tripli sit. —pr. I. h. t., 4, 2.[2]

§ 133. Damnum Iniuria Datum.[a]

Damage to property by illegal, culpable destruction of, or injury to, a thing belonging to another (damnum iniuria[b] datum) was within the scope of the lex Aquilia, a plebiscite of uncertain date,[c] in three chapters.[d]

Ulp.: Lex Aquilia omnibus legibus, quae ante se de damno iniuriae locutae sunt, derogavit, sive XII tabulis, sive alia quae fuit: quas leges nunc referre non est necesse. Quae lex Aquilia plebiscitum est cum eam Aquilius tribunus plebis a plebe rogaverit.—l. 1, D. h. t. (ad l. Aq. 9, 2).[3]

This lex, by virtue of the development it received from interpretation by the jurists, gave the owner of the thing a penal action for reparation against the

[a] Cf. Holmes, 'Common Law,' Lect. i., and notes to Vicars *v.* Willcocks (Smith, Leading Cases, vol. ii. pp. 556, *sqq.*).

[b] § 2; D. 50, 17, 151.

[c] ? 467 U.C.

[d] Upon the second, see Gai. iii. 215 (*supra*, § 118).

Therefore it is rightly said that he is an abandoned thief. But the Praetor has introduced a special action in respect of such wrong, which is called the action for robbery with violence . . . and this action is available even if a man has taken by violence a single thing, although the most trifling.

[1] And we must say in general that in all the cases where the action of theft belongs to me in respect of a matter done clandestinely, upon the same grounds have I this action.

[2] The fourfold value, however, is not altogether a penalty, and a recovery of the article besides the penalty . . . but the recovery of the article is included also in the fourfold value, so that the penalty is threefold.

[3] The *l. Aquilia* altered all earlier statutes which treated of wrongful damage as well the law of the Twelve Tables as all others: an enumeration of these statutes is now unnecessary. The Aquilian statute is a decree of the *plebs*, since the plebeian tribune Aquilius carried it upon inquiry of the *plebs*.

Book III. Pt. I. Ch. II.

wrong-doer, which, according to the nature of the thing injured, is directed to the highest value such thing had within the last year or month.

Gai.: Lege Aquilia capite primo cavetur: SI QVIS SERVVM SERVAMVE ALIENVM ALIENAMVE QVADRVPEDEMVE PECVDEM INIVRIA OCCIDERIT, QVANTI ID IN EO ANNO PLVRIMI FVIT, TANTVM AES DARE DOMINO DAMNAS ESTO.—Et infra deinde cavetur ut adversus infitiantem in duplum actio esset.—l. 2 pr., § 1 eod.[1]

Ulp.: Huius legis secundum quidem capitulum in desuetudinem abiit.—Tertio autem capite ait eadem lex Aquilia: CETERARVM RERVM PRAETER HOMINEM ET PECVDEM OCCISOS SI QVIS ALTERI DAMNVM FAXIT VSSERIT FREGERIT RVPERIT INIVRIA, QVANTI EA RES FVIT IN DIEBVS TRIGINTA PROXIMIS, TANTVM AES DOMINO DARE DAMNAS ESTO.—l. 27, §§ 4, 5 eod.[2]

Quod autem non praecise de quadrupede, sed de ea tantum quae pecudum numero est cavetur, eo pertinet, ut neque de feris bestiis neque de canibus cautum esse intelligamus, sed de his tantum, quae proprie pasci dicuntur: quales sunt equi muli asini boves oves caprae; de suibus quoque idem placuit.—§ 1, I. h. t. (de l. Aq. 4, 3).[3]

---

[1] By the first chapter in the *l. Aquilia* it is provided, 'He that hath illegally slain another man's slave or slave-woman, or a quadruped of his cattle, shall be condemned to pay to the owner in money as much as the amount of its highest value in such year.' And then lower down it is provided that against a disclaimant there shall be an action for twofold the value.

[2] The second chapter, as it is, of this statute has fallen into disuse. But in the third chapter, the *l. Aquilia* speaks as follows: 'If a man have caused injury to another in other things besides a slave and cattle slain, he shall be condemned to make good to the owner in money what he hath illegally injured, burnt, broken, or spoiled, according to the value which the thing had in the thirty days next (preceding).'

[3] But that provision is made, not for four-footed animals exactly, but for four-footed animals only comprised under cattle,

Ulp.: Iniuriam autem hic accipere nos oportet . . . quod non iure factum est,[a] hoc est contra ius, i.e. si culpa quis occiderit; . . . igitur iniuriam hic damnum accipiemus culpa datum etiam ab eo, qui nocere noluit.—Et ideo, si furiosus damnum dederit, . . . cessabit Aquiliae actio, quemadmodum, si quadrupes damnum dederit, Aquilia cessat aut si tegula ceciderit; sed et si infans damnum dederit, idem erit dicendum.—l. 5, §§ 1, 2, D. h. t.[1]

Book III. Pt. I. Ch. II.

[a] See Markby, p. 327 note.

Gai. iii. § 211: Impunitus est, qui sine culpa et dolo malo casu quodam damnum committit.[2]

Inquit lex 'ruperit'; rupisse verbum fere omnes veteres sic intellexerunt 'corruperit.'—Rupisse eum utique accipiemus qui vulneravit vel virgis cecidit,[b] . . . sed ita demum, si **damnum** iniuria datum est; ceterum si nullo servum pretio viliorem deterioremve fecerit, Aquilia cessat iniuriarumque erit agendum:—Si quis frumentum meum effuderit in flumen, sufficit Aquiliae actio.—Si olivam immaturam decerpserit vel segetem desecuerit immaturam vel vineas crudas; Aquilia tenebitur; quodsi iam maturas, cessat Aquilia: nulla enim iniuria est.—l. 27, §§ 13,

[b] Sc. servum.

---

concerns our not understanding the provision of wild animals, nor of dogs, but only of animals which are properly said to pasture, for instance, of horses, mules, asses, oxen, sheep, goats. The same holds also of swine.

1 Now by *iniuria* we must understand, what has been done unlawfully, that is, against the Law, *i.e.*, if a man has killed (another) by negligence: . . . here, accordingly, we shall consider as an injury damage inflicted by negligence, although by one who did not wish to do harm.—And therefore, if a madman has inflicted damage, . . . the Aquilian action will be suspended in the same way as the *l. Aquilia* is suspended when a quadruped has inflicted damage, or a brick has fallen from the roof; and the same will have to be said if an infant has inflicted damage.

2 He is unpunished who by some accident commits damage without negligence or wrongful intention.

BOOK III. Pt. I. Ch. II.

[a] Sc. rupti.

[b] Cf. *infra*, l. 27, §§ 14, 20, D. h. t.

17, 19, 25, D. h. t.—Et effusa et quoquo modo perempta atque deteriora facta hoc verbo [a] continentur: denique responsum est, si quis in alienum vinum aut oleum id immiserit, quo naturalis bonitas vini vel olei corrumperetur, ex hac parte legis eum teneri.[b]—§ 13, I. h. t.[1]

Ulp.: Haec verba: 'quanti in triginta diebus proximis fuit,' etsi non habent 'plurimi,' sic tamen esse accipienda constat.—l. 29, § 8, D. h. t.[2]

His autem verbis legis: 'quanti etc.' illa sententia exprimitur, ut si quis hominem tuum, qui hodie claudus aut luscus aut mancus erit, occiderit, qui in eo anno integer aut pretiosus fuerit, non tanti teneatur, quanti is hodie erit, sed, quanti in eo anno plurimi fuerit.—§ 9, I, h. t.[3]

---

[1] The statute says 'ruperit' (has destroyed); almost all the old jurists understood this word as 'corruperit' (has spoiled).—We shall say at least that he has spoiled who has caused wounds or has smitten [*i.e*., a slave] with rods . . . but only if damage has been tortiously inflicted; but if he has rendered the slave no less valuable or worse, the Aquilian action is inapplicable, and the action for injuries will have to be brought. If any man has cast my corn into the river, the Aquilian action meets the case. If he has plucked my olive before it was ripe, or has cut my corn before it was ripe, or sour grapes, he will be liable by the Aquilian action; but if they were already ripe, the Aquilian does not apply, for there is no wrongful act.—And things spilled and in any way destroyed and made worse are comprised in this word [*i.e.*, 'broken']; finally, the opinion was given, if any one has mixed with another's vine or oil that by which the natural goodness of the vine or oil is marred, he is liable under this portion of the statute.

[2] These words 'as much as was the value in the next (preceding) thirty days,' although they do not include 'the highest,' yet it is settled they are to be so understood.

[3] Now the sense conveyed by these words of the statute: 'of the highest value in that year,' is that if any man have killed your slave who is at the time being lame, or one-eyed, or maimed, but shall have been in the course of such year sound or valuable, he is liable not for such amount as the slave's value at the present time, but for his highest value in such year.

Ulp.: Quodsi mortifere fuerit vulneratus et postea post longum intervallum mortuus sit, inde annum numerabimus secundum Iulianum ex quo vulneratus est, licet Celsus contra scribit.—l. 20, § 1, D. h. t.[1]

Id.: In heredem vel ceteros haec actio non dabitur, cum sit poenalis, nisi forte ex damno locupletior heres factus sit.—l. 23, § 8 eod.[2]

This, moreover, comprehends not merely the 'verum rei pretium,' but the full damages of the party injured, damage as well direct as indirect, positive as negative.[a]

Id.: Sed utrum corpus eius solum aestimamus, quanti fuerit cum occideretur, an potius quanti interfuit nostra non esse occisum? Et hoc iure utimur, ut eius quod interest fiat aestimatio.—l. 21, § 2 eod.[3]

Against the disclaiming wrong-doer the action lies for double the amount,[b] whilst the 'confessus' has to pay the simple value, ascertained by 'arbitrium rei aestimandae.'[c]

[a] § 107; D. 9, 2, l. 33 pr.

[b] Gai. iv. 9.

[c] § 27.

The party causing the injury is likewise responsible for dolus, as for all culpa, which, in the particular case, where claims could be made to a certain measure of material knowledge, physical power and skill, comprises also 'imperitia' and 'infirmitas.'[d]

Gai.: Mulionem, si per imperitiam impetum mularum retinere non potuerit, si eae alienum hominem obtriverint, vulgo dicitur culpae nomine

[d] D. 9, 2, 43 pr.; cf. 19, 2, 9, 5.

---

[1] But if the wound have proved mortal, but the death has occurred subsequently after a long interval, with Jul. we reckon the year from the time when the wound was inflicted, although Cels. writes to the contrary.

[2] This action will not be given against the heir or others, since it is a penal action, unless perhaps the heir has been enriched by the damage.

[3] But are we to assess his body only according to his value when he was killed, or rather according to our interest in his not having been killed? Our rule is, that the assessment must be according to the personal interest.

Book III. Pt. I. Ch. II.

teneri; idem dicitur et si propter infirmitatem sustinere mularum impetum non potuerit: nec videtur iniquum, si infirmitas culpae adnumeratur, cum affectare quisque non debeat, in quo vel intelligit vel intelligere debet infirmitatem suam alii periculosam futuram. Idem iuris est in personam eius, qui impetum equi, quo vehebatur, propter imperitiam vel infirmitatem retinere non potuerit.—l. 8, § 1, D. h. t.[1]

Proculus ait, si medicus servum imperite secuerit, vel ex locato vel ex lege Aquilia competere actionem.—Idem iuris est si medicamento perperam usus fuerit; sed et qui bene secuerit et dereliquit curationem, . . . culpae reus intelligitur.—l. 7, § 8, l. 8 pr. eod.[2]

The lex Aquilia was limited to cases of immediate injury to a thing induced by physical influence or destruction (damnum corpore corpori datum); but later on the actio legis Aquiliae was given in analogous cases of injury to property,[a] as utilis or in factum actio.

[a] § 200; D. 9, 1, l. 1 pr. §§ 3, 4. 7, 10, 12.

Gai. iii. § 219: Et placuit ita demum ex ista lege actionem esse, si quis corpore suo damnum dederit; ideoque alio modo damno dato, utiles actiones dantur: veluti si quis alienum hominem aut pecudem incluserit; et fame necaverit, aut

---

[1] It is commonly said that the mule-driver who through want of skill has been unable to hold in the mules, if they have overrun the slave of another man, is liable on the score of negligence. The same is said also if he has been unable to manage the pace of the mules from lack of strength. And it does not appear unfair, if weakness is accounted a fault, for one ought not to engage where he either perceives or ought to perceive that his weakness will endanger another. The same holds in respect of him who from unskilfulness or weakness has been unable to hold in a horse upon which he was riding.

[2] Proc. says, if a surgeon has unskilfully bled a slave, an act is available either upon the hire or as grounded upon the *l. Aquilia*.—The same holds, if he has badly applied his drugs; but even he who has bled well, and has omitted further treatment, . . . is held guilty of negligence.

iumentum tam vehementer egerit, ut rumperetur.[1]

Ulp.: Celsus multum interesse dicit, occiderit an mortis causam praestiterit, ut, qui mortis causam praestitit non Aquilia, sed in factum actione teneatur; unde adfert eum, qui venenum pro medicamento dedit, et ait causam mortis praestitisse.—l. 7, § 6, h. t.[2]

Id.: Celsus quaerit, si lolium aut avenam in segetem alienam inieceris, . . . in factum agendum . . .: nam alia quaedam species damni est ipsum quid corrumpere et mutare, ut lex Aquilia locum habeat, alia nulla ipsius mutatione applicare aliud, cuius molesta separatio sit.—Item si quis frumento arenam vel aliud quid immiscuit, ut difficilis separatio sit, quasi de corrupto agi poterit. —l. 27, §§ 14, 20 eod.[3]

Sed si non corpore damnum fuerit datum, neque corpus laesum fuerit, sed alio modo damnum alicui contigit, . . . placuit eum, qui obnoxius

---

[1] And it was decided that the action grounded upon that statute only lies if a man has done damage by his own body; and so, if the damage was inflicted in any other way, equitable actions are given; as for instance, if a person has shut up another's slave or cattle and caused it to die of starvation, or has driven a beast of burden so violently as to have brought it down.

[2] Cels. says it makes a great difference whether one has killed a man or has caused his death, because he who has caused death is not liable by the Aquilian action but by that on the case. Whence he gives as example a man who has given poison for medicine, and says he has caused death.

[3] Cels. says, if you have cast darnel or wild oats among the crop of another man, . . . proceedings must be taken on the case . . .; for that which comes of anything being itself spoilt and changed so that the *l. Aquilia* is applicable is one kind of damage, whilst the addition, without change of the thing, of something else, separation of which is difficult, is another kind. —Likewise if a man has mixed sand or something else with wheat so that the separation is difficult, proceedings can be taken as for corruption.

Book III. Pt. I. Ch. II.

fuerit, in factum actione teneri: veluti si quis misericordia ductus alienum servum compeditum solverit, ut fugeret.—§ ult. I. h. t.[1]

Paul.: Si quis alienum vinum vel frumentum consumpserit, non videtur damnum iniuria dare ideoque utilis danda est actio.—l. 30, § 2, D. h. t.[2]

Id.: In damnis, quae lege Aquilia non tenentur, in factum datur actio—l. 33, § 1 eod.[3]

§ 134. Iniuria.[a]

[a] Cf. Holmes, *ubi sup.*; Stephen, *l. c.* pp. 39-41.

[b] Cf. D. 47, 10, 1 pr.

[c] Animus iniurandi.

[d] Cf. § 57.

Iniuria in the narrower sense[b] is every intentional[c] and illegal violation of honour, *i.e.*, the whole personality of another.[d]

Generaliter iniuria dicitur omne quod non iure fit: specialiter alias contumelia, quae a contemnendo dicta est, . . . alias culpa, . . . sicut lege Aquilia damnum iniuria accipitur, alias iniquitas vel iniustitia.—pr. I. h. t. (de iniur. 4, 4).[4]

Ulp.: —iniuria ex affectu facientis consistit. —Itaque pati quis iniuriam, etiamsi non sentiat, potest; facere nemo, nisi qui scit se iniuriam facere, etiamsi nesciat, cui faciat.—l. 3, §§ 1, 2, D. h. t. (de iniur. 47, 10).[5]

---

[1] But if no damage has been inflicted, nor a body injured by a physical act, but the damage happens in some other way . . . it has been held that he who has been in fault is liable to an action upon the case; for example, if a man moved by sympathy has released another man's slave from his fetters, so that he might make his escape.

[2] If a man has consumed wine or corn belonging to another, he is not regarded as doing wrongful damage, and so an analogous action is to be given.

[3] In respect of damage not comprised by the *l. Aquilia* an action is given upon the case.

[4] In general everything is called *iniuria* which happens wrongfully; in a special sense, sometimes contumely, insult, which is derived from *contemnere* . . . at other times culpability . . . as in the *l. Aquilia* damage is taken as *iniuria*, at other times iniquity and injustice.

[5] —*Iniuria* lies in the will of the agent. Therefore any

This may be committed by insulting oral or written words or signs (so-called verbal and symbolic injuries), by deeds (so-called real injuries), by slander, and speeches and acts which cast suspicion upon, or are prejudicial to, the social or pecuniary position of any one, or other acts interfering with the right of personality.

Id.: Iniuriam autem fieri Labeo ait aut re aut verbis; re, quotiens manus inferuntur; verbis autem, quotiens non manus inferuntur, sed convicium fit.—l. 1, § 1 eod.[1]

Gai. iii. § 220: Iniuria autem committitur non solum cum quis pugno puta aut fuste percussus vel etiam verberatus erit, sed et si cui convicium factum fuerit sive quis bona alicuius quasi debitoris, sciens eum nihil sibi debere, proscripserit, sive quis ad infamiam alicuius libellum aut carmen scripserit, sive matremfamilias aut praetextatum adsectatus fuerit, et denique aliis pluribus modis.[2]

Ulp.: Si quis virgines appellasset, . . . iniuriarum tenetur.—Aliud est appellare aliud adsectari: appellat enim, qui sermone pudicitiam adtemptat, adsectatur, qui tacitus frequenter sequitur; adsidua enim frequentia quasi praebet nonnullam infamiam.—l. 15, §§ 15, 22, D. h. t.[3]

---

one can suffer an *iniuria*, even if he feel it not; no one can commit an *iniuria* without knowing that he commits it, even if he know not against whom he commits it.

[1] Now Labeo says that *iniuria* happens either by act or by words; by act, when hands are applied; but by words, when hands are not applied, but insult is committed.

[2] Now an outrage is committed not only when a man shall be struck with the fist, say, or with a club, or even flogged, but also if abusive language has been used to one, or when a person knowing that some one, who he pretends is his debtor, owes him nothing has advertised his goods for sale, or when any one shall write a libel or a song defamatory of another or shall follow about a married woman or a lad, and, in short, in many other ways.

[3] If a man should have addressed virgins, . . . he is liable for outrage.—It is one thing to address, another to follow about;

Gai.: Si creditor meus, cui paratus sum solvere, in iniuriam meam fideiussores meos interpellaverit, iniuriarum tenetur.—l. 19 eod.[1]

Ulp.: Si quis me prohibeat in mare piscari, . . . sunt qui putent iniuriarum me posse agere; et plerique esse huic similem eum, qui in publicum lavare, vel in cavea publica sedere, vel in quo alio loco agere sedere conversari non patiatur, aut si quis re mea uti me non permittat: nam et hic iniuriarum conveniri potest.—l. 13, § 7 eod.[2]

It may have been done to the injured party directly or indirectly, *i.e.*, in the person of those 'qui vel potestati eius vel affectui subiecti sunt.'

Gai. iii. §§ 221–222: Pati autem iniuriam videmur non solum per nosmet ipsos, sed etiam per liberos nostros quos in potestate habemus, item per uxores nostras, quamvis in manu nostra non sint: itaque si filiae meae, quae Titio nupta est, iniuriam feceris, non solum filiae nomine tecum agi iniuriarum potest, verum etiam meo quoque et Titii nomine.—Servo autem ipsi quidem nulla iniuria intelligitur fieri, sed domino per eum fieri videtur: non tamen iisdem modis, quibus etiam per liberos nostros vel uxores iniuriam pati videmur, sed ita cum quid atrocius commissum fuerit, quod aperte in contumeliam domini fieri videtur, veluti si quis alienum servum verberaverit.[3]

---

for he addresses who by speech tempts modesty: he follows about who continually follows without speaking; for a constant following also works a kind of outrage.

[1] If my creditor whom I am prepared to pay, has resorted to my sureties, in order to wrong me, he is liable for injuries.

[2] If a man prevents my fishing in the sea, some are of opinion that I can take proceedings for injuries; . . . and most that he is like the man who does not allow one to wash in public, or sit in a public seat in a theatre, or to loiter, sit and pass one's life in any other place, or if a man does not allow us to use our own property: for he also can be sued for injuries.

[3] We are looked upon as suffering injury not merely in our

The punishment for iniuriae was—

(1) by the Twelve Tables, according to the nature of the case, sometimes capital punishment, sometimes 'talio,'[a] at other times a definite private, pecuniary penalty.

[a] Upon retaliation, see Markby, ss. 128-9.

Cic. de Rep. iv. 10, 12:[b] Nostrae XII tabulae cum perpaucas res capite sanxissent, in his hanc quoque sanciendam putaverunt, 'si quis occentavisset sive carmen condidisset, quod infamiam faceret flagitiumve alteri.[1]

[b] Cf. August. de civ. dei. ii. 9.

Festus h. v. p. 363, M.: **Talionis** mentionem fieri in XII ait Verrius hoc modo: SI MEMBRVM RVPSIT, NI CVM EO PACIT, TALIO ESTO. Neque id quid significet indicat, puta quia notum est: permittit enim lex parem vindictam.[2]

Gell. xx. 1, §§ 37–38: Nolo hoc ignores, hanc quoque ipsam talionem ad aestimationem iudicis redigi necessario solitam. Nam si reus qui depacisci noluerat, iudici talionem imperanti non

---

own persons, but also in the persons of our children whom we have under power, and in the persons of our wives, although they may not be under *manus*.—If therefore you do an injury to my daughter who is married to Tit., not only can proceedings be taken against you for injury in the name of my daughter, but also in my name and in that of Tit. But to a slave himself it is considered no injury can be done, but it is regarded as done to his master through him. We are not however looked upon as suffering an injury through him in the same way as through our children or wives, but only when some gross act is done, which is plainly seen to be meant for the insult of the master; for example, when a person has flogged another's slave.

[1] Whereas our Twelve Tables enacted punishment affecting *caput* for very few things, they contemplated amongst such also the enactment, 'whosoever should have sung a satirical song, or invented a rhyme to bring disrepute or outrage upon another.'

[2] V. states that *talio* is spoken of in the Twelve Tables thus: 'If he have maimed a limb, unless a compromise shall be made with such person, there shall be retaliation.' Nor does he show what this means, perhaps because it is known: for the *lex* allows equal compensation.

Book III. Pt. I. Ch. II.

parebat, aestimata lite iudex hominem pecuniae damnabat, atque ita si res et pactio gravis et acerba talio visa fuerat, severitas legis ad pecuniae multam redibat.[1]

[a] Coll. II, 5, § 5; Gell. *l. c.* § 12.

L. XII tab.:[a] MANV FVSTIVE SI OS FREGIT LIBERO CCC, SI SERVO CL POENAM SVBITO—SI INIVRIAM ALTERI FAXIT, VIGINTI QVINQVE POENAE SVNTO.[2]

Gai. iii. § 223: Poena autem iniuriarum ex lege XII tabularum propter membrum quidem ruptum talio erat; propter os vero fractum aut collisum trecentorum assium poena erat, si libero os fractum erat, at si servo CL; propter ceteras vero iniurias XXV assium poena erat constituta: et videbantur illis temporibus in magna paupertate satis idoneae istae pecuniariae poenae.[3]

According to the Praetorian Edict, it is always an arbitrary, private, pecuniary penalty, to be pursued by the 'actio iniuriarum (aestimatoria),' conceived 'in bonum et aequum,' but involving infamy; the maximum amount of which, first of all to be estimated by the plaintiff himself, but in grave injuries by the Praetor (and equal to the summa vadimonii),[b] is always settled by the iudex according to the character of the

[b] § 191

---

[1] I would not have you ignorant that also this very recompense used of necessity to be diminished according to the assessment by the *iudex*. For if the defendant who had declined to enter into an agreement, disobeyed the order of the *iudex* to make recompense, the damages having been assessed, the *iudex* used to inflict a pecuniary penalty on the man, and so if a bargain had seemed onerous and the recompense harsh to the defendant, the severity of the statute was reduced to a pecuniary fine.

[2] 'If with fist or club he have struck the face of a freeman, let him suffer a fine of 300 *asses*, if of a slave 150.'—'If he have wronged another, the penalty shall be 25 *asses*.'

[3] Now the penalty for injuries, according to the Twelve Tables, was retaliation for a limb destroyed; but for a bone broken or dislocated the penalty was 300 *asses*, if a freeman's bone was broken, but 150 if a slave's; whilst for other injuries the penalty was fixed at 25 *asses*, and those money-penalties seemed to be enough in those times of great poverty.

iniuria (atrox or levis), and with regard to the special circumstances of the particular case.

Labeo ap. Gell. l. c. § 13: L. Veratius . . . pro delectamento habebat, os hominis liberi manus suae palma verberare. Eum servus sequebatur, ferens crumenam plenam assium; ut quemque depalmaverat, numerari statim secundum XII tabulas quinque et viginti asses iubebat. Propterea praetores postea hanc [legem] abolescere et relinqui censuerunt iniuriisque aestimandis recuperatores se daturos edixerunt.[1]

Gai. iii. § 224: Sed nunc alio iure utimur: permittitur enim nobis a praetore ipsis iniuriam aestimare, et iudex vel tanti condemnat, quanti nos aestimaverimus, vel minoris prout ei visum fuerit; sed cum atrocem iniuriam praetor aestimare soleat, si simul constituerit, quantae pecuniae nomine fieri debeat vadimonium, hac ipsa quantitate taxamus formulam, et iudex quamvis possit vel minoris damnare, plerumque tamen propter ipsius praetoris auctoritatem non audet minuere condemnationem.[2]

Ait Praetor: 'QVI ADVERSVS BONOS MORES CONVICIVM CVI FECISSE CVIVSVE OPERA FACTVM ESSE

---

[1] L. V. used to regard it as an amusement with the palm of his hand to strike the face of a freeman. He used to be followed by a slave carrying a purse full of *asses*: when he had smitten any one, he ordered twenty-five to be at once counted, according to the Twelve Tables; wherefore the Praetors afterwards considered this law to be effete and abandoned, and announced that they would appoint *recuperatores* to assess the damages.

[2] But now we follow another rule; for we are allowed by the Praetors to make the assessment for ourselves; and the *iudex* gives judgment for as much as our assessment, or for less, according as he thinks of it. But as the Praetor commonly accounts an injury gross, if he have at the same time settled in respect of what amount security should be given, we limit the formula to this very amount, and although the *iudex* can give judgment for even a smaller amount, yet generally, by reason of the authority of the Praetor himself, he does not dare to diminish the amount of the condemnation.

Book III. Pt. I. Ch. II.

DICETVR, QVO ADVERSVS BONOS MORES CONVICIVM FIERET: IN EVM IVDICIVM DABO.'—Ait praetor: 'NE QVID INFAMANDI CAVSA FIAT; SI QVIS ADVERSVS EA FECERIT, PROVT QVAEQVE RES ERIT, ANIMADVERTAM.—l. 15, §§ 2, 25, h. t.[1]

Coll. ii. 6, §§ 1, 4, 5: QVI INIVRIARVM AGIT, CERTVM DICAT, QVID INIVRIAE FACTVM SIT ET TAXATIONEM PONAT NON MAIOREM, QVAM QVANTI VADIMONIVM FVERIT.—Certum non dicit, qui dicit pulsatum se vel verberatum; sed et partem corporis demonstret, et quem in modum, pugno puta an fuste an lapide, sicut formula proposita est: QVOD AVLO AGERIO A NVMERIO NEGIDIO PVGNO MALA PERCVSSA EST.—Item si dicat infamatum esse, debet adiicere, quemadmodum infamatus sit. Sic enim et formula concepta est: QVOD NVMERIVS NEGIDIVS SIBILVM IMMISIT AVLO AGERIO INFAMANDI CAVSA.—(Paul.)[2]

Secundum gradum dignitatis vitaeque honestatem crescit aut minuitur aestimatio iniuriae.[a]—§ 7, I. h. t.[3]

Gai. iii. § 225: Atrox autem iniuria aesti-

[a] Cf. *aestimatio capitis* in early English Law (Brown, s. vv.)

[1] The Praetor says: 'He that is alleged to have done an outrage to some one against good manners, or by whose instrumentality it shall be alleged to have happened that an outrage has been done to some one against good manners, against him will I give an action.'—The Praetor says: 'Let nothing be done to defame: if any man have acted contrariwise, according to the circumstances of the case, I will consider it.'

[2] 'Let him that sues for injuries declare what injury has been done, and let him precisely put the valuation at no more than security was given for.' He does not make a precise statement who says that he was beaten or scourged; but let him set forth the part of the body, and in what manner, whether, for example, with the fist, or club, or stone, as the formula has been published: 'Whereas A. A. was struck on the cheek with the fist by N. N.'—Likewise if he allege that he has been defamed, he ought to add how he has been defamed. For so the formula is framed: 'Whereas N. N. hissed at A. A. with a view to defamation.'

[3] The estimate of injury increases or is reduced according to rank and reputation.

matur vel ex facto, velut si quis ab aliquo vulneratus aut verberatus fustibusve caesus fuerit; vel ex loco, veluti si cui in theatro aut in foro iniuria facta sit; vel ex persona velut si magistratus iniuriam passus fuerit, vel senatoribus ab humili persona facta sit iniuria [aut parenti patronoque fiat a liberis vel libertis.—§ 9, I. h. t.].[1]

Ulp.: Iniuriarum actio ex bono et aequo est et dissimulatione aboletur: si quis enim iniuriam dereliquerit, hoc est statim passus ad animum suum non revocaverit, postea ex poenitentia remissam iniuriam non potest recolere; . . . proinde et si pactum de iniuria intercessit, et si transactum est . . . actio iniuriarum non tenebit. —l. 11, § 1, D. h. t.[2]

In the cases of so-called real injury, of house-breaking and of libels under the lex Cornelia (A.U. 673), and the interpretation thereof, the choice lies, for the party injured, between a criminal action and a civil actio iniuriarum.[a]

[a] *Supra.* § 25 ad init.

Id.: Lex Cornelia de iniuriis competit ei, qui iniuriarum agere volet ob eam rem, quod se 'pulsatum verberatumve domumve suam vi introitam' esse dicat. . . . Apparet igitur omnem iniuriam, quae manu fiat, lege Cornelia contineri. —l. 5 pr. eod.[3]

---

[1] Now an injury is accounted gross, either from the nature of the act, as when a man is wounded or flogged or beaten with clubs by some one; or by reason of the place, as when an injury is done to a man in a theatre or in the forum; or by reason of the person, as when a magistrate has suffered injury, or an injury has been done to senators by a person of low rank [or to a parent or patron by children or freedmen].

[2] The action for injuries comes of what is right and fair, and falls to the ground through pretence; for if a man has left an injury behind, *i.e.*, immediately when he suffered it, called it not to mind, he cannot afterwards through regret rekindle the injury he passed over; . . . accordingly, even if an agreement concerning the injury has intervened, or a compromise has been effected, the action for injuries will not obtain.

[3] The *l. Cornelia* concerning injuries is open to him who

Book III. Pt. I. Ch. II.

Marcian.: Etiam ex lege Cornelia iniuriarum actio civiliter moveri potest condemnatione aestimatione iudicis facienda.—l. 37, § 1 eod.[1]

Hermog.: De iniuria nunc extra ordinem ex causa et persona statui solet.—l. ult. eod.[2]

OBLIGATIONES *EX VARIIS CAUSARUM FIGURIS.*

§ 135. Obligationes quasi ex Contractu.

'Obligationes quasi ex contractu' are obligations similar in their subject-matter to contractual obligations, which arise from permissible one-sided acts (legal transactions), the immediate primary object of which is not the creation of an obligation. To these belong the following, in themselves quite different cases.

Negotiorum gestio is the conduct of business for another (dominus) which is voluntary, *i.e.*, undertaken without a commission, and gratuitous.

Ulp.: Ait praetor: SI QVIS NEGOTIA ALTERIVS, SIVE QVIS NEGOTIA, QVAE CVIVSQUE CVM IS MORITVR FVERINT, GESSERIT, IVDICIVM EO NOMINE DABO.—'Negotia' sic accipe: sive unum sive plura.—l. 3 pr., § 2, D. h. t. (de N. G. 3, 5).[3]

Id.: Hoc edictum necessarium est, quoniam

---

desires to sue for injury because he alleges that he has been 'beaten, struck, or that his house has been entered by force.' . . . It appears therefore that every injury occasioned by the hand is included in the *l. Cornelia*.

[1] A civil action for injuries can also be brought by virtue of the *l. Cornelia*, in which the condemnation has to be arrived at by the assessment of the *iudex*.

[2] At present it is usual for a decision to be given concerning injury by extraordinary procedure, according to the case and the party.

[3] The Praetor says: 'If a man shall have conducted affairs of another, or what shall have been the affairs of some one at the time of his death, I will give an action on that behalf.—'Affairs' understand as one or several.

magna utilitas absentium versatur, ne indefensi rerum possessionem aut venditionem patiantur vel pignoris distractionem vel poenae committendae actionem, vel iniuria rem suam amittant. —l. 1 eod.[1]

Gai.: Si quis absentis negotia gesserit . . . sine mandatu, placuit quidem sane eos invicem obligari, eoque nomine proditae sunt actiones, quas appellamus negotiorum gestorum; quibus invicem experiri possunt de eo, quod ex bona fide alterum alteri praestare oportet. Sed neque ex contractu neque ex maleficio actiones nascuntur; neque enim is qui gessit cum absente creditur ante contraxisse, neque ullum maleficium est sine mandatu suscipere negotiorum administrationem . . . sed utilitatis causa receptum est invicem eos obligari.—D. 44, 7, l. 5 pr.[2]

Ulp.: Si quis negotia mea gessit non mei contemplatione, sed sui lucri causa, Labeo scripsit suum eum potius, quam meum negotium gessisse. . . . Sed nihilo minus, immo magis et is tenebitur negotiorum gestorum actione.—l. 5 (6), § 5 (3), D. h. t.[3]

---

[1] This edict is necessary, because in it lies considerable advantage for absent persons, that they do not, without defence, suffer dispossession or sale of their property, or the sale of a pledge, or an action to attach a penalty, or by some wrong lose their property.

[2] If a person have conducted the affairs of one in his absence . . . without a commission, it has as a matter of fact been held that they are certainly under mutual liability, and actions have been provided in that behalf, which we call actions appertaining to the transaction of business. By these they can mutually take proceedings concerning that which it behoves the one to render the other according to good faith. But it is neither from contract nor from tort that the actions arise; for it is not supposed that he who conducted the business previously contracted with the absent party, and it is no tort to undertake the management of affairs without a commission . . . but for convenience' sake it has been accepted that they are under mutual liability.

[3] But also if a person has conducted my business not with

Book III. Pt. I. Ch. II.

That the claims on both sides which arise herefrom may be made available, the 'actio negotiorum gestorum directa,' on the one hand, appertains to the dominus.

—is qui gesserit negotia . . . tenetur, ut administrationis rationem reddat: quo casu ad exactissimam quisque diligentiam compellitur rationem reddere, nec sufficit talem diligentiam adhibere, qualem suis rebus adhibere soleret.—§ 1, I. h. t. (de obl. qu. ex. contr. 3, 27).[1]

The 'negotiorum gestor,' on the other hand, provided that he has managed the business 'utiliter,' that is, in the well-understood interest of the principal and not against prohibition, possesses the 'actio negotiorum gestorum contraria,' which is intended for essentially the same object as the actio mandati.[a]

[a] § 115.

Gai.: Si quis absentis negotia gesserit, licet ignorantis, tamen quidquid utiliter in rem eius impenderit, vel etiam ipse se in rem absentis alicui obligaverit, habet eo nomine actionem.—l. 2, D. h. t.[2]

Lab.: Cum pecuniam eius nomine solveres, qui tibi nihil mandaverat, negotiorum gestorum actio tibi competit, cum ea solutione debitor a creditore liberatus sit: nisi si quid debitoris

---

reference to me, but for his own gain, Labeo has written that he has conducted his own business rather than mine. . . . But none the less, nay rather, will he be liable by the action of business transacted.

[1] —he that has conducted another's business . . . is liable to render an account of his management. In this case every one is made to render an account for the most perfect care, and it is not enough to use such care as a man would generally use over his own affairs.

[2] If any one has managed a man's business in his absence, although without his knowledge, yet for whatever he has expended over such man's business to his advantage, or even the personal liability incurred to any one over the property of the absent party, he has an action in that behalf.

interfuit eam pecuniam non solvi.—l. 42 (43) eod.[1]

Ulp.: Is autem qui negotiorum gestorum agit, non solum si effectum habuit negotium quod gessit, actione ista utetur, sed sufficit si utiliter gessit, etsi effectum non habuit negotium; et ideo si insulam fulsit vel servum aegrum curavit, etiamsi insula exusta est vel servus obiit, aget negotiorum gestorum. . . . Ego quaero: quid si putavit se utiliter facere, sed patrifamilias non expediebat? dico hunc non habiturum negotiorum gestorum actionem: ut enim eventum non spectamus, debet utiliter esse coeptum.—l. 9 (10), § 1 eod.[2]

Mod.: Titium, si pietatis respectu sororis aluit filiam, actionem hoc nomine contra eam non habere respondi.—l. 26 (27), § 1 eod.[3]

—Ipse tamen si circa res meas aliquid impenderit, non in id quod ei abest, quia improbe ad negotia mea accessit, sed in quod ego locupletior

---

[1] Since you paid money in his name, who had given you no commission, the action for the management of business is open to you, because by that payment the debtor has been discharged by the creditor; unless it have been to the interest of the debtor that such money be not paid.

[2] But he who brings the action of the management of business will not merely be able to employ that action, if the business which he has conducted has had result, but it is enough if he has conducted it with advantage, although the business has had no result; and therefore he may bring the action of the management of business if he propped up a house or cured a sick slave, although the house has been burnt or the slave has died. . . . I ask: How if he thought he was doing it with advantage, but it was not serviceable to the *pat. fam.*? Such a man, I maintain, will not have the action of the management of business; for, as we look not to the result, it must have been to advantage that it was begun.

[3] I gave the opinion, that Tit., if he maintained his sister's daughter from affection, has no action against her on this account.

Book III. Pt. I. Ch. II.

factus sum habet contra me actionem.—l. 5, § 5 eod.[a] [1]

[a] *Supra*, ibid.

Imp. Iust.: —sancimus, si contradixerit dominus et eum res suas administrare prohibuerit, . . . nullam esse adversus eum contrariam actionem, . . . licet res bene ab eo gestae sint.—l. ult. C. eod. 2, 19.[2]

The conduct of guardianship engenders obligations between guardian and ward.[b]

[b] § 152.

From 'communio'—*i.e.*, the community of property, in respect of things or real rights, whether contractual (cum societate),[c] or casual (communio incidens)—arises an obligation between the partners (socii), by virtue of which each can take proceedings upon dissolution of the partnership and separation. This action,[d] with which at the same time the personal claims on both sides created by the common interest (praestationes personales)[e] are made available, is, in community of several objects of property, the actio COMMVNI DIVIDVNDO; in the community of inherited property, which has arisen by succession, the 'actio FAMILIAE ERCISCVNDAE.'[f]

[c] § 124.

[d] §§ 24, 198.

[e] D. 10, 2, 25, 16. Cf. 10, 3, 23.

[f] § 174, ad fin.; cf. § 90, ad fin.

Paul.: Communi dividundo iudicium ideo necessarium fuit, quod pro socio actio magis ad personales invicem praestationes pertinet, quam ad communium rerum divisionem. Denique cessat communi dividundo iudicium, si res communis non sit.—l. 1, D. h. t. (comm. div. 10, 3).[3]

---

[1] But he himself, if he should have spent anything over my affairs, has the action against me, not for what he is out of pocket, because he went to work at my affairs dishonourably, but in so far as I have been enriched.

[2] —we enact that, if the owner countermanded it, and forbade him to manage his affairs, . . . there is no contrary action against such person, . . . although the business have been well managed by him.

[3] The action for the partition of property owned in common is necessary, because the action upon the partnership contract

Gai.: Nihil autem interest, cum societate an sine societate res inter aliquos communis sit: nam utroque casu locus est communi dividundo iudicio.—l. 2 pr. eod.[1]

Ulp.: Communiter autem res agi potest etiam citra societatem, ut puta cum non affectione societatis incidimus in communionem ut evenit in re duobus legata, item si a duobus simul empta res sit, aut si hereditas vel donatio communiter nobis obvenit.—D. 17, 2, 31.[2]

Id.: In communi dividundo iudicio nihil pervenit ultra divisionem rerum ipsarum quae communes sint, et si quid in his damni datum factumve est, sive quid eo nomine aut abest alicui sociorum aut ad eum pervenit ex re communi.—l. 3 pr., h. t.[3]

Furthermore, to these belongs the obligation, arising by entry upon the inheritance, between the heir and legatee for discharge of the bequest.[a]

[a] § 183.

Heres quoque qui legatum debet, neque ex contractu neque ex maleficio obligatus esse intelligitur: nam neque cum defuncto neque cum herede contraxisse quidquam legatarius intelli-

relates more to reciprocal personal performances than to the division of things owned in common.

[1] Now it makes no difference whether it is with or without partnership that a thing is common property between several people; for in both cases the action obtains for division of common property.

[2] But a matter can be transacted in community even without a partnership, for example, when without intending partnership we lapse into community, as happens when a thing is bequeathed to two persons, and if a thing has at the same time been bought by two, or if an inheritance or a donation devolves upon us in common.

[3] In the action for the division of common property nothing comes into account besides the division of things themselves which are common, even if an injury has been inflicted or done to them, or anything is in this respect lacking to one of the co-owners, or has come to him from common property.

BOOK III. Pt. I. Ch. II.

gitur ; maleficium autem nullum in ea re esse plus quam manifestum est.—D. 44, 7, 5, 2.[1]

Finally, there is a series of cases in which from the performance rendered by some one, without agreement between giver and receiver, an obligatio,[a] grounded upon aequitas, arises for restitution of the thing received, the general ground of which is illegal command of a thing (unjustifiable enrichment): 'condictiones sine causa,' in the wider sense.[b]

[a] re contracta?

[b] Cf. D. 12, 6. 65, 2.

Pomp. ad Q. Muc.: Damus aut **ob causam** aut **ob rem**: ob causam praeteritam, veluti cum ideo do, quod aliquid a te consecutus sum vel quia aliquid a te factum est, ut etiamsi falsa causa sit, repetitio eius pecuniae non sit; ob rem vero datur, ut aliquid sequatur, quo non sequente repetitio competit.—l. 52, D. de cond. indeb. 12, 6.[2]

Ulp.: Perpetuo Sabinus probavit veterum opinionem existimantium, id quod ex iniusta causa apud aliquem sit posse condici.—D. 12, 5, 6.[3]

Pap.: Haec condictio ex bono et aequo introducta, quod alterius apud alterum sine causa deprehenditur, revocare consuevit.—l. 66, de cond. ind.[4]

---

1 An heir also who has to discharge a legacy is considered to be liable neither upon contract, nor tort, for the legatee is not deemed to have made any contract, either with the deceased or with the heir; but that there is no tort in this is more than clear.

2 We make a grant either because of a consideration or because of a thing: for a past consideration, as when I make a grant because I have obtained something from you, or because something has been done by you, so that even if it be a false consideration there is no recovery of such money; but because of a thing, in order that something should follow, and if it does not follow, recovery is available.

3 Sab. has constantly approved the opinion of the old jurists, who thought that what was in some one's hands upon an unlawful title could be sued for by a personal action.

4 This *condictio*, introduced by reference to what is right and fair, has usually served for the recovery of property of one person found in the hands of another not entitled to it.

Pomp.: Iure naturae aequum est, neminem cum alterius detrimento et iniuria fieri locupletiorem.—D. 50, 17, 206.[1]

He that in the mistaken acceptance of a legal liability renders a performance not even naturally due[a] has the 'condictio indebiti'[b] against the receiver, for restitution of the thing received.

[a] § 114.

[b] See Bell, s. VV.

Gai. iii. § 91: Is quoque qui non debitum accepit ab eo, qui per errorem solvit, re obligatur: nam proinde ei condici potest 'SI PARET EVM DARE OPORTERE,' ac si mutuum accepisset. . . . Sed haec species non videtur ex contractu consistere, quia is, qui solvendi animo dat, magis distrahere vult negotium quam contrahere.[2]

Paul.: Indebitum est non tantum, quod omnino non debetur, sed et quod alii debetur si alii solvatur, aut si id quod alius debebat, alius quasi ipse debeat solvat.—D. 12, 6, 65, 9.[3]

Pomp.: —si heredem se . . . falso existimans creditori hereditario solverit, . . . neque verus heres liberatus et is quod dedit repetere poterit. —l. 19, § 1 eod.[4]

Paul.: Cuius per errorem dati repetitio est, eius consulto dati donatio est.—D. 50, 17, 53.[5]

---

1 According to the Law of Nature, it is fair that no one become richer with loss to another, and by wrong.

2 He also who receives what is not due to him from one paying in mistake is bound by the thing. For he can be sued by the personal action: 'If it appear that he ought to give,' just as if he had received a loan. . . . But this sort of obligation does not appear to arise from contract, since he who gives with the thought of making payment, wishes rather to dissolve a contract than to enter into one.

3 *Indebitum* is not only what is altogether not owing, but also a debt to another if that other is paid, or if what one person owed is paid by another as if he himself were the debtor.

4 —if he, falsely supposing himself to be heir, shall pay a creditor of the inheritance, . . . the real heir is not discharged, and the former will be able to recover what he paid.

5 In the case in which there would be recovery of a thing given in error a donation exists, if it has been given advisedly.

BOOK III. Pt. I. Ch. II.

Imp. Diocl.: Ea, quae per infitiationem in lite crescunt, ab ignorante etiam indebita soluta repeti non posse certissimi iuris est.—C. 4, 5, 4.[1]

The performance which is rendered in expectation of a counter-performance[a] or other 'causa futura' (*i.e.*, in the supposition of a future circumstance that forms the legal ground of performance), if this do not come about, can be recalled by the 'condictio ob causam datorum s. causa data non secuta.'[b]

[a] § 126.

[b] D. 12, 6, 52, *supra*.

Paul.: Ob rem honestam datum ita repeti potest, si res propter quam datum est, secuta non est.—D. 12, 5, 1, 1.[2]

Quod ob rem datur, ex bono et aequo habet repetitionem, veluti si tibi dem, ut aliquid facias, nec feceris.—l. 65, cit. § 4.[3]

Iul.: Fundus dotis nomine traditus, si nuptiae insecutae non fuerint, condictione repeti potest.—D. 12, 4, 7, 1.[4]

Ulp.: Sed etsi ob causam promisit, causa tamen secuta non est, dicendum est condictionem locum habere.—D. 12, 7, 1, 1.[5]

Imp. Alex.: Si quasi accepturi mutuam pecuniam adversario cavistis, quae numerata non est, per condictionem obligationem repetere . . . potestis.—C. 4, 30, 7.[6]

---

1 That sums which accumulate in a suit through disclaimer, and though not owing, have been paid out of ignorance, cannot be recovered, is incontestable law.

2 That which was given in consideration of an honourable thing can be recovered, provided the thing on account of which it was given has not followed.

3 That which was given because of a thing admits of recovery by virtue of what is right and fair, as, if I make a conveyance to you in consideration of a performance by you, and you shall be in default.

4 An estate delivered by way of dowry can be recovered by a personal action, if the marriage shall not have followed.

5 But although he made the promise because of a consideration, but the consideration has not followed, we must say that a personal action obtains.

6 If you as about to receive a loan have given security to your

If the legal ground (legal purpose) of the performance is for the receiver (and indeed for him alone) an immoral one, the 'condictio ob turpem causam' obtains.

> Quodsi turpis causa accipientis fuerit, etiamsi res secuta sit, repeti potest.—Ut puta dedi tibi, ne sacrilegium facias, ne furtum, ne hominem occidas. Item si tibi dedero, ut rem mihi reddas depositam apud te,—si tibi dedero, ne mihi iniuriam facias.—D. 12, 5, 1, 2 (Paul.), l. 2 pr., §§ 1, 2 (Ulp.).[1]
>
> Paul.: Ubi autem et dantis et accipientis turpitudo versatur, non posse repeti dicimus, veluti si pecunia datur, ut male iudicetur.—l. 3 eod.[2]
>
> Pap.: Dixi, cum ob turpem causam dantis et accipientis pecunia numeretur, cessare condictionem et in delicto pari potiorem esse possessorem.—D. 12, 7, 5 pr.[3]

§ 136. Obligationes quasi ex delicto.[a]

[a] See Ortolan, 'Instituts,' ii. pp. 449, *sqq.*

'Obligationes quasi ex delicto' are such obligations directed to compensation for, or punishment of, injury,

---

opponent, and the money has not been paid over, you can recall the obligation by a *condictio*.

1 But if the consideration on the part of the receiver shall be immoral, even if the thing has followed, it can be recalled. For example, I have made a grant to you, in consideration of your committing no sacrilege, no theft, killing no man. . . . The like if I have made a grant to you in consideration of your rendering to me a thing deposited with you,—if I shall make a grant to you in consideration of your doing me no injury.

2 But where infamous conduct occurs on the part of both giver and receiver, we maintain that there is no possible recovery; for example, if money is paid in consideration of a bad judgment being given.

3 I have said that since the money was paid because of a consideration disgraceful for both giver and receiver, the *condictio* falls through, and in an equal wrong the possessor is the more favoured.

Book III. Pt. I. Ch. II.

[a] §§ 130-134.
[b] Cf. Inst. iv. 9, 1.

which arising out of disallowed, illegal acts or forbearance, do not fall under delicta proper.[a] The most important cases[b] are the following.

(1) The 'in factum actio' against the *iudex qui litem suam fecerit,* i.e., the judge that by remissness in performance of his duty, or by neglect, has prejudiced either party.

Gai.: Si iudex litem suam fecerit, non proprie ex maleficio obligatus videtur; sed quia neque ex contractu obligatus est et utique peccasse aliquid intelligitur, licet per imprudentiam, ideo videtur quasi ex maleficio teneri in factum actione, et in quantum de ea re aequum religioni iudicantis visum fuerit, poenam sustinebit.—D. 50, 13, 6.[1]

(2) The actio *de effusis et deiectis* against the occupier of the place from which something is thrown or poured out on a thoroughfare, in case this has caused damage.

Item is, ex cuius coenaculo vel proprio ipsius vel conducto vel in quo gratis habitabat deiectum effusumve aliquid est, ita ut alicui noceretur, quasi ex maleficio obligatus intelligitur; ideo autem non proprie ex maleficio obligatus intelligitur, quia plerumque ob alterius culpam tenetur, aut servi aut liberi. . . . De eo vero, quod deiectum effusumve est, dupli quanti damnum datum sit, constituta est actio.—I. h. t. (de obl. q. qua. ex del. 4, 5).[2]

---

[c] Lit. 'made a suit his own.'

[1] If a *iudex* has given a partial decision,[c] he is not strictly to be regarded as liable upon a tort; but since he is not liable either by any contract, and yet is certainly regarded as having erred, although through inadvertence, he is therefore considered liable, upon the ground of a quasi delict, to an action on the case, and must bear such penalty as shall seem fair to the conscience of the person who adjudicates upon the case.

[2] Likewise he from whose chamber (whether his own or hired, or one in which he was dwelling rent-free) anything has been thrown or poured out in such wise as to injure some per-

Ulp.: Parvi autem interesse debet, utrum publicus locus sit, an vero privatus, dummodo per eum vulgo iter fiat.—l. 1, § 2, D. h. t. (de his qui eff. 9, 3).[1]

Sed cum homo liber periit, damni aestimatio non fit in duplum (quia in homine libero nulla corporis aestimatio fieri potest), sed quinquaginta aureorum condemnatio fit.—Ibid. § 5.[2]

Gai.: Cum liberi hominis corpus ex eo, quod deiectum effusumve quid erit, laesum fuerit, iudex computat mercedes medicis praestitas ceteraque impendia, quae in curatione facta sunt, praeterea operarum, quibus caruit aut cariturus est ob id, quod inutilis factus est.—l. 7 eod.[3]

Ulp.: Haec actio, quae competit de effusis et deiectis, perpetua est et heredi competit, in heredem vero non datur. Quae autem de eo competit, quod liber periisse dicetur, intra annum dumtaxat competit, neque in heredem datur neque heredi: nam est poenalis et popularis; dummodo sciamus ex pluribus desiderantibus hanc actionem ei potissimum dari debere, cuius

---

son, is considered to be liable for a quasi delict; for he is not strictly considered liable for delict, because in general he is responsible for the fault of some one else, either slave or free. . . . But in respect of that which has fallen or been poured out, an action has been provided for double the amount of the damage done.

[1] But it ought to matter little whether it is a public or private place, so long as there is a public thoroughfare over it.

[2] But when a freeman has perished no estimate is made of damage for double the amount (because there can be no valuation of the body in respect of a freeman), but condemnation ensues for fifty *aurei*.

[3] When the body of a freeman shall be injured by anything thrown or poured out, the *iudex* estimates the doctors' fees that have been paid and other expenses which have been incurred in respect of the cure, and further, the work which such person has been or will be deprived of by reason of his having been incapacitated.

interest vel qui adfinitate cognationeve defunctum contingat.—l. 5, § 5 eod.[1]

(3) The actio popularis *de posito et suspenso* against him that has set or hung up anything in a public place in a manner to endanger, or leaves it there.[a]

[a] § 24, ad fin

Cui similis est is qui ex parte, qua vulgo iter fieri solet, id positum aut suspensum habet, quod potest, si ceciderit, alicui nocere: quo casu poena decem aureorum constituta est.—§ 1, I. h. t.[2]

Ulp.: 'Positum habere' etiam is recte videtur, qui ipse quidem non posuit, verum ab alio positum patitur.—D. 9, 3, 5, 10.[3]

(4) It is upon an obligatio quasi ex delicto that the liability rests of *nautae, caupones, stabularii* for thefts of, and injuries to, effects of travellers received by them, who have against such persons actiones in factum, namely:

(*a*) a penal actio in duplum.

Item exercitor navis aut cauponae aut stabuli de damno aut furto, quod in nave aut caupona aut stabulo factum sit, quasi ex maleficio teneri

---

[1] This action, which lies for things thrown out and poured out, is perpetual, and is available to an heir, but is not given against an heir. But that which lies in respect of a freeman being alleged to have perished is available only within a year, and is given neither against an heir nor to an heir; for it is a penal and popular action. We have only to notice that, of several persons desiring this action, it ought especially to be given to him that is interested therein, or is connected with the deceased person by affinity or relationship.

[2] In like position is a person who has placed or hung up in a part where the public are wont to pass that which, if it fall, may do injury to some one: in this case a penalty has been appointed of ten *aurei*.

[3] A person also is rightly considered to have placed a thing who did not place it himself indeed, but allowed it to be placed by another.

videtur, si modo ipsius nullum est maleficium, sed alicuius eorum, quorum opera navem aut cauponam aut stabulum exerceret; cum enim neque ex contractu sit adversus eum constituta haec actio et aliquatenus culpae reus est, quod opera malorum hominum uteretur, ideo quasi ex maleficio teneri videtur. In his autem casibus in factum actio competit, quae heredi quidem datur, adversus heredem autem non competit. (§ 3, I. h. t.)—Ulp.: Haec actio in factum in duplum est.—D. 4, 9, 7, 1.[1]

(β) An actio de recepto,[a] purely 'rei persequendae causa.'

[a] Cf. § 107.

Id.: Ait praetor: NAVTAE CAVPONES STABVLARII QVOD CVIVSQVE SALVVM FORE RECEPERINT, NISI RESTITVENT, IN EOS IVDICIVM DABO.—l. 1 pr. eod.[2]

Id.: Ex hoc edicto in factum actio proficiscitur . . . Pomponius miratur, cur honoraria actio sit inducta, cum sint civiles: nisi forte, inquit, ideo,—quia in locato conducto culpa, in deposito dolus dumtaxat praestatur, ut hoc edicto omnimodo qui receperit tenetur, etiamsi sine culpa eius res periit vel damnum datum est, nisi si quid damno fatali contingit.—Haec autem[b] rei persecutionem

[b] Sc. actio.

---

[1] Likewise the master of a ship, or an innkeeper, or a stableman, is considered liable for a quasi-delict in respect of loss or theft committed in the ship, or inn, or stable, provided there is no wrongful act on his own part, but on the part of one of those employed by him in working the ship, or in the inn or stable. For since this action has not been brought against him as grounded in contract, and yet he is to some extent liable for negligence in employing worthless persons, therefore he is considered liable for a quasi-delict. Now in these cases an action lies on the case, and it is given to the heir, but it does not lie against the heir.

[2] The Praetor says: 'Unless sea-captains, innkeepers, stablemen restore whatever they have received of any man's property for safe keeping, I will give an action against them.'

Book III. Pt. I. Ch. II.

continet, ut Pomponius ait, et ideo et in heredem et perpetuo datur.—l. 3, §§ 1, 4 eod.[1]

[a] Holland, p. 183, note.

§ 137. Obligations from Mere Circumstances.[a]

Already the mere fact that some one is owner or possessor of a thing, or that he has been enriched at the expense of a third party, by reason of another's illegal act, may in certain cases engender an obligation between him and another.

(1) For the injury which a domestic animal has committed by no one's fault, its owner for the time being is responsible by the noxal 'actio de pauperie.'[b]

[b] Cf. § 113.

Ulp.: 'Si quadrupes pauperiem fecisse dicetur,' actio ex lege XII tabularum descendit; quae lex voluit aut dari id quod nocuit, i.e. animal quod noxiam commisit, aut aestimationem noxiae offerri. § Pauperies est damnum sine iniuria facientis datum.—§ Itaque (ut Servius scribit) tunc haec actio locum habet, cum commota feritate nocuit quadrupes, puta si equus calcitrosus calce percusserit, aut bos cornu petere solitus petierit. § Et generaliter haec actio locum habet, quotiens contra naturam fera mota pauperiem dedit: ideoque si equus dolore concitatus calce petierit, cessare istam actionem, sed eum qui equum percusserit aut vulneraverit, in factum magis quam lege Aquilia teneri, utique ideo, quia non ipse suo corpore damnum dedit. § In bestiis autem

---

[1] From this edict proceeds an action on the case. . . . Pomp. expresses his surprise why a magisterial action has been introduced, where there are civil actions existing, unless perhaps, he says, because *culpa* is made good alone in a hiring contract, *dolus* in a deposit, whilst by this edict the receiver is in every way liable, even if the article perish or damage has been inflicted by no fault of his, unless anything arise by fortuitous loss.—Now this (action) goes to the recovery of the thing, as Pomp. says, and so is given not only against the heir, but perpetually.

propter naturalem feritatem haec actio locum non habet. § Et cum etiam in quadrupedibus noxa caput sequitur, adversus dominum haec actio datur, non cuius fuerit quadrupes cum noceret, sed cuius nunc est.—l. 1 pr., §§ 3, 4, 7, 10, 12, D. si quadrup. 9, 1.[a] [1]

[a] Cf. Holmes, p. 9.

Ceterum sciendum est aedilicio edicto prohiberi nos canem verrem aprum ursum leonem ibi habere, qua vulgo iter fit: et si adversus ea factum erit et nocitum homini libero esse dicetur, quod bonum et aequum iudici videtur, tanti dominus condemnetur, ceterarum rerum, quanti damnum datum sit, dupli.—§ 1, I. eod. 4, 9.[2]

(2) Against the possessor of a movable chattel,

---

[1] 'If a quadruped shall be alleged to have caused damage,' an action for it originates from a law of the Twelve Tables. This law required that either that which did the harm, that is, the animal which inflicted the damage, be delivered, or compensation rendered for the damage. § *Pauperies* is damage inflicted without a wrongful act on the part of the agent. . . . § Therefore (as Serv. writes), this action obtains when a quadruped has done harm by the excitement of its wild nature; for example, if a horse apt to kick has struck with its hoof, or a bullock accustomed to thrust has thrusted. § And in general this action is employed whenever a beast, stirred against nature, has inflicted damage. And so, if a horse under pressure of pain has smitten with its hoof, that action falls through, but he that struck the horse, or wounded it, is liable rather by an action on the case than by the *l. Aquilia*, namely, because he did not himself immediately inflict the damage with his body. § But this action does not obtain in respect of animals because of their innate fierceness. § And since even in respect of quadrupeds damage attaches to the person, this action is given against the owner,—not the person to whom the quadruped belonged when it did the harm, but him to whom it now belongs.

[2] Moreover we must notice that in the Aedilian edict we are forbidden to have a dog, a boar tame or wild, a bear or a lion where there is a thoroughfare; and if this be disobeyed and injury shall be alleged to have been done to a freeman, the owner may be condemned for as much as appears right and fair to the *iudex*; in other cases, for double the amount of damage done.

BOOK III. Pt. I. Ch. II.

the person who has a demonstrable legal interest in it has the 'actio ad exhibendum' for production thereof, as for separation of a composite thing, permission to enter, to take away. This interest must be founded on a claim vested in him, and forthwith to be enforced in respect of the thing itself (principal action, iudicium directum), giving rise to a real (especially rei vindicatio) or noxal action. The action is sometimes preparatory to the principal action, sometimes of direct operation as an action of tort.[a]

[a] D. 10, 4, 6; 6, 1, 23, 5; § 84, ad fin. D. 10, 4, 12, 3; § 90.

Paul.: Exhibere est facere in publico potestatem, ut ei qui agat experiundi sit potestas.—l. 2, D. h. t. (ad exhib. 10, 4).[1]

Ulp.: Haec actio perquam necessaria est et vis eius in usu quottidiano est et maxime propter vindicationes inducta est.—Qui ad exhibendum agit, non utique dominum se dicit nec debet ostendere, cum multae sint causae ad exhibendum agendi.—Est autem personalis actio et ei competit, qui in rem acturus est qualicumque in rem actione, etiam pigneraticia Serviana.—Item si optare velim servum vel quam aliam rem, cuius optio mihi relicta est, ad exhibendum me agere posse constat, ut exhibitis possim vindicare.—l. 1, l. 3, §§ 1, 3, 6 eod.[2]

Sciendum est autem . . . competere ad ex-

---

[1] To produce is to afford an opportunity in public, that the plaintiff may have opportunity of taking proceedings.

[2] This action is very necessary; and as used is in daily operation, and has been introduced especially for proprietary actions.—He that sues for production does not absolutely maintain that he is owner, nor must he give proof of it, because there are many grounds of a suit for production.—This is a personal action, and is open to him who intends to sue by a real action of whatever kind, even by the Servian action of pledge. It is likewise settled that, if I wish to select a slave or any other thing the selection of which has been bequeathed to me, I can sue for production, in order that I may be able by *vindicatio* to claim one of the objects produced.

hibendum actionem ei, cuius interest exhiberi; iudex igitur summatim debebit cognoscere, an eius intersit, non an eius res sit.—Eleganter definit Neratius, iudicem ad exhibendum hactenus cognoscere, an iustam et probabilem causam habeat actionis, propter quam exhiberi sibi desideret.—Ibid. §§ 9, 11.[1]

Id.: Glans ex arbore tua in fundum meum decidit, eam ego immisso pecore depasco. . . . Pomponius scribit competere actionem ad exhibendum, si dolo pecus immisi: nam et si glans exstaret nec patieris me tollere, ad exhibendum teneberis, quemadmodum si materiam meam delatam in agrum suum quis auferre non pateretur. —l. 9, § 1 eod.[2]

Paul.: —nec (tigni iuncti) nomine ad exhibendum agi nisi adversus eum, qui sciens alienum iunxit aedibus.—D. 6, 1, 23, 6.[3]

(3) To such obligations in some measure attach the actio metus and actio doli for liability extending to the person of the wrong-doer.

(*a*) The arbitraria[a] actio quod metus causa[b]—'formula Octaviana'—lies as actio in rem scripta

[a] D. 4, 6, 31.
[b] D. 4, 2, 1.

---

[1] But it is to be noticed that the action for production is open to him who had an interest in the production; the *iudex* must therefore summarily ascertain whether he has an interest in it; not whether the thing belongs to him.—Nerat. shrewdly says: the *iudex* in a suit for production directs his inquiry to this, whether (the plaintiff) has a lawful and demonstrable ground of action, on account of which he desires production of the thing to him.

[2] Fruit falls from your tree into my field; I turn my cattle in and make them eat it. . . . Pomp. writes, that an action lies for production, if I turned the cattle in with wrongful intention; for even if the fruit existed, and you will not suffer me to pick it, you will be liable for production, in the same way as if a man should not suffer me to remove my timber that had been washed into his field.

[3] —and proceedings cannot be taken in respect of a plank built in, save against him who has built it into his house while aware of its belonging to another man.

Book III. Pt. I. Ch. II.

against every third person, who by dint of coercion has control over a part of the property of the person coerced, for the restitution thereof.

Ulp.: In hac actione non quaeritur, utrum is qui convenitur, an alius metum fecit; sufficit enim hoc docere, metum sibi illatum vel vim et ex hac re eum qui convenitur, etsi crimine caret, lucrum tamen sensisse.—Quidam putant, bona fide emptorem ab eo qui vim intulit comparantem non teneri, nec eum qui dono accepit vel cui res legata est; sed rectissime Viviano videtur etiam hos teneri, ne metus quem passus sum mihi captiosus sit. Pedius quoque scribit arbitrium iudicis in restituenda re tale esse, ut eum quidem qui vim admisit iubeat restituere, etiamsi ad alium res pervenit, eum autem ad quem pervenit, etiamsi alius metum fecit.—D. 4, 2, 14, §§ 3, 5.[1]

Paul.: In heredem autem et ceteros in id, quod pervenit ad eos, datur non immerito.—l. 16, § 2 eod., 2.[2]

In the event of non-restitution, if the action be brought intra annum utilem, judgment can be had for the quadruplum, otherwise for the simple amount.[a]

[a] § 18.

Si quis non restituat, in quadruplum in eum

---

[1] In this action it is not asked whether the defendant or another has caused the fear; for it is enough if (the plaintiff) prove that fear was awakened in him or violence put forth, and that the defendant, although free from crime, has derived profit from this circumstance.—Some are of opinion that a *bona fide* purchaser buying of one that has employed violence, is not liable, nor he that has received a donation or a legacy. But Viv. very justly supposes that they too are liable, in order that the fear which I have experienced may not be prejudicial to me. Ped. also writes that the decision of a *iudex* in respect of a thing that has to be restored is such that, as a matter of fact, he enjoins the person who practised the violence to make restitution, even if the thing has come to the hands of another, but also him to whose hands it has come, even if a third person caused fear.

[2] Now it is not without good ground allowed against an heir and others for that which has come to their hands.

iudicium pollicetur; quadruplabitur autem omne quodcumque restitui oportuit.—l. 14, § 1 eod.[1]

(β) The 'arbitraria actio doli' (involving infamy, but which is subsidiary) for fraudulent infliction of injury—not falling under another delict—lies against the author himself for the full damages (to be confirmed by ius iurandum in litem) and against his heir, and the person represented by him in the particular matter, for the enrichment.[a]

[a] D. 4, 3, 1, 2; 44, 4, 2. §§ 1, 2, 4, 1, 7, 1.

Cic. de nat. deor. iii. 30, 74: Everriculum malitiarum omnium, iudicium de dolo malo C. Aquilius protulit, quem dolum tum teneri putat, cum aliud sit simulatum aliud actum.[2]

Verba edicti: QVAE DOLO MALO FACTA ESSE DICENTVR, SI DE HIS REBVS ALIA ACTIO NON ERIT ET IVSTA CAVSA ESSE VIDEBITVR, IVDICIVM DABO.—D. 4, 3, 1, 1.[3]

Ulp.: Praetor ita demum hanc actionem pollicetur, si alia non sit, quoniam famosa actio non temere debuit a praetore decerni.—Pomponius refert Labeonem existimasse etiam si quis in integrum restitui possit, non debere ei hanc actionem competere.—l. 1, §§ 4, 6 eod.[4]

Paul.: Si servum, quem tu mihi promiseras,

---

[1] If a man do not make restitution, he promises judgment against him for the fourfold; but in respect of the reckoning of the fourfold, everything will come into account of which restitution ought to be made.

[2] As a drag-net of all dishonesties, C. Aquil. brought forward the action of fraud; this fraud he considers to be contemplated when one thing is held out, another done.

[3] The words of the Edict: 'In respect of that which shall be alleged to have been done by fraud, if there be no other action for such matters, and the ground shall appear to me to be lawful, I will allow an action.'

[4] The Praetor only promises this action if there be no other, because an action involving infamy ought not lightly to be decreed by the Praetor.—Pomp. relates that Labeo was of opinion that, even if a man could acquire restitution to the former state, this action ought not to be open to him.

Book III. Pt. I. Ch. II.

alius occiderit, de dolo malo actionem in eum dandum plerique recte putant, quia tu a me liberatus sis.—l. 18, § 5 eod.[1]

Gai.: In heredem eatenus daturum se eam actionem pollicetur, quatenus ad eum pervenerit, i.e. quatenus ex ea re locupletior ad eum hereditas pervenerit.—l. 26 eod.[2]

Ulp.: Sed et ex dolo tutoris si factus est locupletior,[a] puto in eum dandam actionem.—Item si quid ex dolo procuratoris ad dominum pervenit, datur in dominum de dolo actio, in quantum ad eum pervenit.—l. 15 pr., § 2 eod.[3]

[a] Sc. pupillus.

EXTINCTION AND TRANSFER OF OBLIGATIONS.

FIRST, OF EXTINCTION OF OBLIGATIONS.

§ 138. Outline.

Every obligation carries with it the purpose of being again extinguished; dissolution of the obligation is the ultimate object and necessary result of the full exercise of that right to which the creditor can lay claim as arising from it. The dissolution (solutio in the wider sense) can first of all ensue by satisfaction being rendered to the claim of the creditor (satisfactio),[b] whether by performance, *i.e.*, discharge of the debtor's liability (solutio in the narrower sense), or by agreement of the parties; or lastly by some other legal

[b] Cf. § 103.

---

[1] If a slave whom you had promised to me has been killed by another, most are right in thinking that an action for fraud is to be allowed against him, because you have been exonerated by me.

[2] Against the heir (the proconsul) promises to allow such action to the extent of his benefit, that is, so far as by reason of such circumstance a richer inheritance has devolved upon him.

[3] But if he has been enriched also by *dolus* of the guardian, I am of opinion that an action should be allowed against him.—The like, if benefit has accrued to a principal from the fraud of his agent, an action *de dolo* is allowed against the principal for the amount of his benefit.

incident which materially involves satisfaction of the creditor.[a] But the obligation can also be destroyed without satisfactio, by an outward event, so that the debtor is released without reference to the will, and without material satisfaction, of the creditor.[b]

[a] § 140.

[b] § 143.

Paul.: Solutionis verbum pertinet ad omnem liberationem quoquo modo factam, magisque ad substantiam obligationis refertur, quam ad nummorum solutionem.—l. 54, D. de solut. 46, 3.[1]

Ulp.: Solutionis verbo satisfactionem quoque omnem accipiendam placet.—D. 50, 16, 176.[2]

Marcian.: Quodsi acceptum latum sit . . . solutionis quidem verbum non proficiet, sed satisfactionis sufficit.—l. 49, D. de solut.[3]

Whilst by the performance of that which is owing every obligation is extinguished conformably to its nature and purpose, in (direct) dissolution of an obligation by agreement between the parties strict conformity between the act of release and act that created the obligation is always requisite, except as to novation.

Pompon.: Prout quidque contractum est ita et solvi debet: ut cum re contraxerimus, re solvi debet; . . . et cum verbis aliquid contraximus, vel re vel verbis obligatio solvi debet; . . . aeque cum emptio vel venditio vel locatio contracta est, quoniam consensu nudo contrahi potest, etiam dissensu contrario dissolvi potest.—l. 80 eod.[4]

---

[1] The word *solutio* (payment) extends to every release in whatever way made, and relates more to the contents of the obligation than to the payment of money.

[2] It is held that by the word 'payment' we must understand also every satisfaction.

[3] But if a discharge has been given . . . the word payment will not avail, but satisfaction is enough.

[4] Everything must also be discharged according as it was contracted; so that, when we have made a contract with a

BOOK III. Pt. I. Ch. II.

Ulp.: Fere quibuscumque modis obligamur, iisdem in contrarium actis liberamur.—D. 50, 17, 153.[1]

According to their effect, the several grounds of extinction are distinguishable by their either destroying the obligation ipso iure (directly and substantially), or as engendering a peremptory exceptio to the claim (actio) of the creditor.[a]

[a] Cf. D. 50, 16, 10; 12, 6, 40 pr.

Marc.: Desinit debitor esse is, qui nactus est exceptionem iustam nec ab aequitate naturali abhorrentem.—l. 66 eod.[2]

§ 139. SOLUTIO.

Every obligation has for its object the 'solutio eius quod debetur' (discharge, performance, payment). It is the natural and normal mode of extinction that substantially destroys every obligation. The following are the requisites of solutio.

(1) The object owing (thing or act) must itself be performed, and that completely; an only partial performance, as part payment, will not usually be accepted by the creditor;[b] 'datio in solutum,' that is, performance of another object in place of payment, can only come about by the consent of the creditor.

[b] Cf. § 103.

Gai. iii. § 168: Tollitur autem obligatio praecipue solutione eius quod debeatur: unde quaeritur, si quis consentiente creditore aliud pro alio sol-

---

thing, it must be discharged with a thing, . . . and when we have contracted anything with words, the obligation must be discharged either with a thing or with words . . . in like manner, if a contract has been made of purchase or sale or hire, since the contract can be made by mere consent, it can be discharged also by agreement to the opposite effect.

[1] As a rule, in whatever ways we become liable, by the same acts to the opposite effect are we released.

[2] He ceases to be a debtor who has acquired a plea that is good in law and not repugnant to natural equity.

verit, utrum ipso iure liberetur, quod nostris praeceptoribus placet, an ipso iure maneat obligatus, sed adversus petentem exceptione doli mali defendi debeat, quod diversae scholae auctoribus visum est.[1]

Modestinus respondit, si non hac lege mutua pecunia data est, uti liceret et particulatim quod acceptum est exsolvere, non retardari totius debiti usurarum praestationem, si cum creditor paratus esset totum suscipere, debitor, qui in exsolutione totius cessabat, solam partem deposuit. —D. 22, 1, 41, 1.[2]

Pomp.: Cassius ait, si cui pecuniam dedi, ut eam creditori meo solveret, si suo nomine dederit, neutrum liberari, me quia non meo nomine data sit, illum quia alienum dederit; ceterum mandati eum teneri. Sed si creditor eos nummos sine dolo malo consumpsisset, is qui suo nomine eos solvisset, liberatur.—l, 17. D. h. t. (de sol. 46, 3).[3]

(2) The performance can be rendered, not merely

---

[1] Now an obligation is extinguished primarily by payment of what is due. Whence arises the question whether, if a man with the consent of his creditor, pays instead of another, he is discharged by operation of law, as our leaders hold, or continues bound in law, but should be defended against a claimant by a plea of fraud, which is the view of the authorities of the opposite school.

[2] Mod. answers, that if the advance has not been made upon the condition that it should be allowable to pay back what has been received by instalments, the payment of interest for the whole debt is not thereby impeded, if the debtor, who was backward with the repayment of the whole when the creditor was prepared to receive the whole, merely deposited a part.

[3] Cass. says, if I have given money to any one to pay to my creditor, neither is discharged, if he gave it in his own name: not I, because it was not paid in my name; not he, because he paid that which belonged to another; that he, moreover, is liable to the action of mandate. But if the creditor had spent such money without bad intention, he that should have paid it in his own name will be discharged.

BOOK III. Pt. I. Ch. II.

[a] Just. iii. 19, 4.

[b] D. 46, 3, 23. For English Law, see Pollock, 'Cont.' pp. 423-4.

to the creditor himself, but also to one designated by him, or else to the person empowered to accept it (*e.g.*, solutionis causa adiectus).[a] As a rule, it matters not who renders it.[b]

Ulp.: Vero procuratori recte solvitur; verum autem accipere debemus eum, cui mandatum est vel specialiter, vel cui omnium negotiorum administratio mandata est.—Sed etsi non vero procuratori solvam, ratum autem habeat dominus quod solutum est, liberatio contingit: rati enim habitio mandato comparatur.—l. 12 pr., § 4, D. eod.[1]

Paul.: Quod iussu alterius solvitur, pro eo est, quasi ipsi solutum esset.—D. 50, 17, 180.[2]

Id.: Cum iussu meo id quod mihi debes solvis creditori meo, et tu a me et ego a creditore meo liberor.—l. 64, h. t.[3]

Gai. iii. § 160: Plerisque placuit, si debitor meus manumisso dispensatori meo per ignorantiam solverit, liberari eum, cum alioquin stricta iuris ratione non posset liberari eo quod alii solvisset, quam cui solvere deberet.[4]

Id.: Solvendo quisque pro alio, licet invito et

---

[1] But to an actual agent payment is rightly made. Now we ought to treat him as an actual one to whom either a special commission has been given, or who has been commissioned to manage the whole of the affairs. But even if I do not pay the actual agent, but the principal should have approved the payment made, a discharge ensues; for the approval is held analogous to the commission.

[2] If any payment has been made by the direction of another, it is regarded as though paid to himself.

[3] If you pay to my creditor that which you owe to me, you will be discharged by me, and I also by you.

[4] Most hold that my creditor is discharged if he has by mistake paid my steward who has been manumitted; whilst otherwise by strict legal principle he could not be discharged from that which he paid to another than him to whom he ought to have made payment.

ignorante, liberat eum.—D. 3, 5, 39. Cf. Inst. iii. 29 pr.[1]

(3) Payment and corresponding acceptance thereof presuppose capacity for alienation.[a]

[a] Gai. ii. 84.

Pupillum sine tutoris auctoritate nec solvere posse palam est.—Pupillo solvi sine tutoris auctoritate non potest; . . . si tamen solverit ei debitor et nummi salvi sint, petentem pupillum doli mali exceptione debitor summovebit.—l. 14, § 8 (Ulp.), l. 15 (Paul.), h. t.[2]

(4) *Delegatio* in effect is fully equivalent to payment. It is the stipulation concluded by assignation (iussus) of the debtor (delegans), between the creditor (delegatarius) and a third party (delegatus)—and indifferently whether 'debitor debitoris' or not—for the object of debt, especially a sum owing.[b]

[b] Cf. § 142, ad init.; D. 39, 5, 21, 1.

Ulp.: Solvit et qui reum delegat.—D. 16, 1, 8, 3.[3]

Iul.: Qui debitorem suum delegat, pecuniam dare intelligitur, quanta ei debetur.—D. 46, 1, 18.[4]

Paul.: —licet is solvendo non fuerit: quia bonum nomen facit creditor, qui admittit debitorem delegatum.—D. 17, 1, 26, 2.[5]

Certain debtors have assured to them the legal

---

1 Everybody by payment for another, although without his consent and knowledge, procures his discharge.

2 It is manifest that a ward cannot make a payment without his guardian's sanction.—A payment cannot be made to a ward without the sanction of his guardian; . . . if, however, a debtor has paid him, and the money is untouched, the debtor will defeat the ward, if he sue, with the plea of bad intention.

3 He too makes payment who delegates a debtor.

4 If a man delegate his debtor, it is treated as though he pays as much money as is owing to him.

5 —although the debtor shall not have been solvent; because the creditor that accepts a delegated debtor treats the debt as a good one.

Book III. Pt. I. Ch. II.

benefit, that they need to pay, not the whole amount of the debt, but only 'id quod facere possunt,' *i.e.*, just so much as they can pay for the time being:[a] 'beneficium competentiae.'[b] This, according to a later legal opinion, was without deprivation of the means of subsistence.

[a] For which alone they can be condemned (§ 197).

[b] § 204. Cf. Bell, s. vv.

> Paul.: In condemnatione personarum, quae in id quod facere possunt damnantur, non totum quod habent extorquendum est, sed et ipsarum ratio habenda est, ne egeant.—D. 50, 17, 173.[1]
>
> Ulp.: Sunt, qui in id quod facere possunt conveniuntur, id est non deducto aere alieno; et quidem sunt hi fere: qui pro socio conveniuntur; item parens, patronus patrona liberique eorum et parentes; item maritus de dote in id quod facere potest convenitur.—D. 42, 1, 16, 17.[2]
>
> Paul.: Is quoque, qui ex causa donationis convenitur, in quantum facere potest condemnatur: et quidem is solus deducto aere alieno.—l. 19, § 1 eod.[3]

§ 140. Compensatio.[c]

[c] Bell, s. v.

'Compensatio' (set-off) is the mutual extinction of the creditor's claim and of the debtor's counter-claim upon the creditor—the subject of both claims being quantities of the same kind—so far as they cover one another in amount.

---

[1] In the condemnation of persons who are condemned for that which they are able to pay, not all that they have is to be taken away, but consideration must be paid also to themselves, that they be not in want.

[2] Some persons are sued for that which they can render, that is, without deduction of debts. And indeed they are in general the following: those sued *pro socio;* a parent likewise, a patron, and patroness, and their children, and ancestors; a husband, again, is sued as to *dos*, for that which he can render.

[3] He too that is sued upon a donation is condemned for as much as he can render, and indeed such person alone after deduction of debts.

Mod.: Compensatio est debiti et crediti inter se contributio.—l. 1, D. h. t. (de comp. 16, 2).[1] Book III. Pt. I. Ch. II.

The compensatio does not arise of itself, *i.e.*, already in consequence of the coexistence of both claims—each claim, the rather, independently remains intact—but always first by effect being given to that co-existence: whether it be that the parties by agreement set both claims against one another (agreement for compensatio, or for settlement of accounts), or that the debtor upon whom the claim is made relies upon his counter-claim.

Pomp.: Ideo compensatio necessaria est, quia interest nostra potius non solvere, quam solutum repetere.—l. 3 eod.[a] [2]

Ulp.: Etiam quod natura debetur, venit in compensationem.—l. 6 eod.[3]

[a] See Haynes, 'Outlines of Equity' (5th ed.), p. 104.

(2) In the older Law such reliance (right of compensatio) of the defendant upon his claim against the plaintiff was admissible only in the *bonae fidei* iudicia—in respect of which the judge already had ex officio to take into account possible counter-claims[b]—and here also it was at first only entertained if the claims made available by way of compensatio had arisen 'ex eadem causa,' that is, from the same obligatory relation. In the *stricti iuris* iudicia, on the other hand, the defendant could indeed make good his counter-claim by means of exceptio doli,[c] but the result was then not compensatio at the outset, but dismissal of the plaintiff's claim in case the judge, upon proof being afforded of the counter-claim, found the exceptio doli established.

[b] Iust. iv. 6. 28, 30. Gai. iv. 63.

[c] § 28.

---

[1] Set-off is the mutual balancing of a debt and a claim.

[2] Therefore set-off is necessary, because it is to our advantage rather not to pay than to reclaim what has been paid.

[3] That also which is owing by Natural Law enters into set-off.

BOOK III. Pt. I. Ch. II.

Iul.: Unusquisque creditorem suum eundemque debitorem petentem summovet, si paratus est compensare.—l. 2 eod.[1]

Besides this, the compensatio was recognised as an independent and peculiar right in the actions of the 'argentarius' and of the 'bonorum emptor,'[a] for which there existed the legal precept of 'cum compensatione—cum deductione agere.'

[a] Gai. iv. 35.

Gai. iv. §§ 64–65: Alia causa est illius actionis qua argentarius experitur: nam is cogitur **cum compensatione agere** et ea compensatio verbis formulae exprimitur, adeo quidem ut ab initio compensatione facta minus intendat sibi dari oportere: ecce enim si sestertium X milia debeat Titio, atque ei XX debeantur, sic intendit: SI PARET TITIVM SIBI X MILIA DARE OPORTERE AMPLIVS QVAM IPSE TITIO DEBET. § Item bonorum emptor **cum deductione** agere iubetur, id est ut in hoc solum adversarius condemnetur, quod superest deducto eo, quod invicem ei bonorum emptor defraudatoris nomine debet. § Inter compensationem autem quae argentario opponitur et deductionem quae obiicitur bonorum emptori, illa differentia est, quod in **compensationem** hoc solum vocatur, quod eiusdem generis et naturae est: veluti pecunia cum pecunia compensatur, triticum cum tritico, vinum cum vino, adeo ut quibusdam placeat, non omnimodo vinum cum vino aut triticum cum tritico compensandum, sed ita si eiusdem naturae qualitatisque; in **deductionem** autem vocatur et quod non est eiusdem generis: itaque si pecuniam petat bonorum emptor et invicem frumentum aut vinum is debeat deducto quanti id erit in reliquum experitur. § 68: Praeterea **compensationis** quidem ratio in intentione ponitur; quo fit, ut si facta compensatione

[1] Every one repels his creditor who is at the same time his debtor, when he sues, if he is prepared to make a counter-claim.

plus nummo uno intendat argentarius, causa cadat et ob id rem perdat: deductio vero ad condemnationem ponitur, quo loco plus petenti periculum non intervenit; utique bonorum emptore agente, qui licet de certa pecunia agat, incerti tamen condemnationem concipit.[1]

In further development, compensatio was allowed also in the stricti iuris iudicia—indeed, at first in the actiones with intentio incerti—in such way that the judge, when a doli exceptio was pleaded, was held em-

---

1 The case is different in respect of that action employed by a banker, for he is obliged to sue *cum compensatione* (*i.e.*, to embrace set-off), and this is expressed by the words of the formula. And so, making the set-off to begin with, the banker alleges in his statement of claim that the reduced sum ought to be paid to him. Thus, suppose he owes Tit. 10,000 sesterces, and Tit. owes him 20,000, he words his claim thus: 'If it appear that Tit. ought to pay him 10,000 sesterces more than he himself owes to Tit.' § Again, the purchaser of a bankrupt's estate ought to sue *cum deductione* (*i.e.*, to take in the rebate), that is, for his opponent to be condemned for such balance as remains after deducting the sum which is in turn due to him (by the plaintiff) on the part of the fraudulent debtor. But between the set-off that is pleaded against a banker and the rebate which is debited to the purchaser of a bankrupt's estate, the difference is such that, in set-off, only what is of the same class and character is taken into account; as, for example, money is set off against money, wheat against wheat, wine against wine, to such an extent that some think wine cannot in all cases be set off against wine, nor wheat against wheat, but only when they are of the same character and quality. But that also may be made matter of deduction which is not of the same class; therefore, if the purchaser of a bankrupt's estate sue for money, and himself in turn owe corn or wine, he sues for the balance after deduction of the value thereof. § Moreover, the amount of a set-off is stated in the claim; the result of which is that, if the banker on making his set-off claim too much by a single sesterce, the case breaks down, and he therefore loses the cause. But a deduction is placed in the *condemnatio*, where no danger attends too great a claim, at least when the plaintiff is the purchaser of a bankrupt's estate, who, although he sues for a liquidated sum, frames his *condemnatio* for an indeterminate one.

Book III. Pt. I. Ch. II.

powered to deduct from the claim sued for the concurrent amount of the counter-claim, and to give judgment against the defendant for the residue.[a] This view was confirmed and made law by a rescript of Marcus Aurelius, since which the right of compensatio was recognised in all claims—even 'ex dispari causa' —as quite universal. By Justinian, compensatio was finally declared to be allowable also in respect of in rem actiones, but on the other hand—so as to prevent delay in procedure—the necessity was imposed of every claim laid to compensatio being made provable.[b]

[a] Cf. D. 44, 1, 22 pr.

[b] But comp. C. 4, 34, 11.

> Sed et in strictis iudiciis ex rescripto D. Marci opposita doli mali exceptione compensatio inducebatur. Sed nostra constitutio eas compensationes, quae iure aperto nituntur, latius introduxit, ut actiones ipso iure minuant sive in rem sive personales sive alias quascumque excepta sola depositi actione.—§ 30, I. de act. 4, 6.[1]

Already in the later classical Law compensatio ipso iure (by virtue of law) constantly occurs; that is,[c] it is not primarily affected by a judicial act (allowance by the Court of compensatio and rebate)—as it, on the other hand, is also entirely independent of the plaintiff's consent—but certainly by legal precept: so that, if the defendant makes good and carries his counterclaim by way of compensatio (in stricti iuris actiones, by means of exceptio doli), the plaintiff's claim must be regarded as extinguished from the very moment of its arising, so far as both cover one another. In the Law of Justinian the 'ipso iure compensari' has the yet further signification, that it requires no other formal exceptio consequent upon the change in judicial

[c] This, it is true, is contested and doubtful.

[1] But even in actions *stricti iuris* set-off was by a rescript of the Emperor Marcus allowed when a plea of fraud was put in. But our constitution has more widely introduced those claims of set-off which rest upon a manifest right, so that they reduce actions, whether real, personal, or of any other kind, by mere operation of law, with the single exception of the action of deposit.

procedure, in order to make good the compensatio; but that, as previously only in the bonae fidei iudicia, so now invariably, if the defendant relies upon it, it has to be taken into consideration already 'officio iudicis.'

Imp. Alex.: Si constat pecuniam invicem deberi, ipso iure pro soluto compensationem haberi oportet ex eo tempore, ex quo ab utraque parte debetur, utique quoad concurrentes quantitates.—C. 4, 31, 4.[1]

Ulp.: Cum alter alteri pecuniam sine usuris, alter usurariam debet, constitutum est a D. Severo, concurrentis apud utrumque quantitatis usuras non esse praestandas.—l. 11, D. eod.[2]

Paul.: Posteaquam placuit inter omnes id quod invicem debetur ipso iure compensari, si procurator absentis conveniatur, non debebit de rato cavere, quia nihil compensat, sed ab initio minus ab eo petitur.—l. 21 eod.[3]

§ 141. The Agreement for Release.

Nexi Liberatio, Acceptilatio; Pactum de non Petendo; Contrarius Dissensus.

The dissolution here ensues, not by performance of the obligation, but by agreement between the two subjects thereof, by which the debtor is absolved from

---

[1] If it is established that there is a debt on both sides, set-off must by operation of law be regarded as in lieu of payment from the time when there was a debt owing by both parties, at least as regards amounts due at the same time.

[2] When one man owes another money without interest, and the other owes money carrying interest, it has been enacted by the late Emperor Severus that interest is not to be paid in respect of the amount due upon both sides at the same time.

[3] After its having been held by all that what is mutually owing is by virtue of law made a set-off, if the agent of an absent party be sued, he will not have to give security for ratification, because he makes no set-off, but his claim is less from the first.

the obligatory nexus. With the exception of 'pactum de non petendo,' these agreements for release operate ipso iure, and are only applicable to such obligations as are created by a binding act answering to the form of such agreements. In 'nexi liberatio' and 'acceptilatio,' the performance of the obligation can concur with the act of release, so that this appears as a solemn verification of the solutio (formal acknowledgment of receipt); which indeed happens as a rule in the older Law.

[a] § 116.

The 'nexi liberatio' is the solemn solutio per aes et libram, corresponding to the nexi obligatio,[a] which was applicable to claims arising from a nexum and iudicatum.

> Gai. iii. §§ 173–175: Est etiam species imaginariae solutionis, per aes et libram, quod et ipsum genus certis in causis receptum est, veluti si quid eo nomine debeatur, quod per aes et libram gestum sit, sive quid ex iudicati causa debeatur. § Eaque res ita agitur: adhibentur non minus quam quinque testes et libripens; deinde is qui liberatur ita oportet loquatur: QVOD EGO TIBI TOT MILIBVS CONDEMNATUS SVM, ME EO NOMINE A TE SOLVO LIBEROQVE HOC AERE AENEAQVE LIBRA HANC TIBI LIBRAM PRIMAM POSTREMAMQVE EXPENDO SECVNDVM LEGEM PVBLICAM; deinde asse percutit libram eamque dat ei, a quo liberatur, veluti solvendi causa. § Similiter legatarius heredem eodem modo liberat de legato quod per damnationem relictum est; . . . de eo tamen tantum potest hoc modo liberari, quod pondere numero constet, et ita si certum sit: quidam et de eo, quod mensura constat, idem existimant.[1]

---

[1] There is also another kind of fictitious payment, that by copper and scale. This form of release has been adopted in certain cases, as for example, when anything is due on the

'Acceptilatio'[a] is the agreement for Release answering to the stipulatio, and only applicable to verborum obligationes; consisting in a formal acknowledgment of receipt, clothed in an oral interrogatory and answer, which later on was written, like the stipulatio,[b] and also curtailed in form.

[a] See Bell, s. 'Acceptilation.'

[b] § 117.

> Mod.: Acceptilatio est liberatio per mutuam interrogationem, qua utriusque contingit ab eodem nexu absolutio.—l. 1, D. h. t. (de accept. 46, 4).[1]
>
> Gai. iii. § 169: Acceptilatio autem est veluti imaginaria solutio; quod enim ex verborum obligatione tibi debeam, id si velis mihi remittere, poterit sic fieri, ut patiaris haec verba me dicere: 'quod ego tibi promisi, habesne acceptum?' et ut respondeas: 'habeo.'[2]
>
> Pomp.: Verborum obligatio aut naturaliter resolvitur aut civiliter: naturaliter veluti solu-

---

score of a transaction by copper and scale, or due by virtue of a judgment. § And such matter is carried out as follows. Not less than five witnesses and a balance holder are procured. Then he who is being released must speak thus: 'Whereas I have been condemned to you in so many thousand sesterces, in respect thereof I release and free myself from you with this copper and these scales: I weigh out to you this the first and last pound, according to the public law.' Then he strikes the scale with the coin, and gives it to him from whose claim he is being released, as though by way of payment. § In like manner a legatee releases the heir from a legacy which has been bequeathed *per damnationem*; . . . but he can be freed in this way only in respect of that which lies in weight or number, and so if it is of definite amount; some think the same of what goes by measure.

1 *Acceptilatio* is discharge by mutual inquiry, which operates release of both persons from the same bond.

2 Now *acceptilatio* is, so to speak, a fictitious payment; for if you are willing to forgive me that which I owe you upon a verbal contract, it can be done by your letting me say these words: 'Have you received that which I promised you?' and by your replying, 'I have.'

BOOK III. Pt. I. Ch. II.

tione; . . . civiliter veluti acceptilatione.—l. 107, D. de solut. 46, 3.[1]

Ulp.: Inter acceptilationem et apocham hoc interest, quod acceptilatione omnimodo liberatio contingit, licet pecunia soluta non sit, apocha non alias, quam si pecunia soluta sit.—l. 19, § 1, h. t.[2]

Id.: Acceptum fieri non potest, nisi quod verbis colligatum est: acceptilatio enim verborum obligationem tollit, quia et ipsa verbis fit.—l. 8, § 3 eod.[3]

Si accepto latum fuerit ei, qui non verbis sed re obligatus est, non liberatur quidem, sed exceptione doli mali vel pacti conventi se tueri potest.—l. 19 pr. eod.[4]

Other obligations, for acceptilatio, must first be converted by novation[a] into a verborum obligatio. The 'Aquiliana stipulatio' contained a formula applicable in general settlement of accounts for complete extinction, by means of acceptilatio, of all claims that had arisen from whatever cause.

[a] § 142.

Gai. iii. § 170: Sed et id, quod ex alia causa debeatur, potest in stipulationem deduci et per acceptilationem dissolvi.[5]

---

[1] A verbal obligation is again dissolved either by natural or by civil Law; by natural, as for instance, by payment; . . . by civil, as by *acceptilatio*.

[2] Between an *acceptilatio* and a receipt there is this difference, that by *acceptilatio* a release avails in all cases, although the money have not been paid: a receipt, not unless the money has been paid.

[3] By *acceptilatio* that alone can be remitted which has been concluded by word; for an *acceptilatio* dissolves a verbal obligation, because it also arises by words.

[4] If a release shall have been given by *acceptilatio* to one who did not become liable by words, but by a thing, he is not in fact released, but he can defend himself by the plea of fraud or by agreement made.

[5] But that also which is due upon some other ground can be made the subject of a stipulation, and dissolved by an *acceptilatio*.

Flor.: Eius rei stipulatio, quam acceptilatio sequatur, a Gallo Aquilio talis exposita est: 'Quidquid te mihi ex quacumque causa dare facere oportet oportebit praesens in diemve, quarumque rerum mihi tecum actio quaeque adversus te petitio vel adversus te persecutio est eritve, quodve tu meum habes tenes possides: quanti quaeque earum rerum res erit, tantam pecuniam dari stipulatus est $A^{s.}$ $A^{s.}$ spopondit $N^{s.}$ $N^{s.}$; quod $N^{s.}$ $N^{s.}$ $A^{o.}$ $A^{o.}$ promisit spopondit, id haberetne a se acceptum $N^{s.}$ $N^{s.}$ $A^{m.}$ $A^{m.}$ rogavit. $A^{s.}$ $A^{s.}$ $N^{o.}$ $N^{o.}$ acceptum fecit.'—l. 18, § 1, D. h. t.[a][1]

[a] Cf. I. 3, 29, 2.

The 'pactum de non petendo' (informal agreement for release) confers upon the debtor, as a rule,[b] only an exceptio to the action.[c]

Paul.: Quaedam actiones per pactum ipso iure tolluntur, ut iniuriarum, item furti.—l. 17, 1, D. de pact. 2, 14.[2]

Pap.: Naturalis obligatio . . . iusto pacto ipso iure tollitur, quod vinculum aequitatis, quo solo sustinebatur, conventionis aequitate dissolvitur.—l. 95, § 4, D. de solut.[3]

A distinction is made between pactum de non petendo *in rem* and *in personam*.

[b] Cf. D. 13, 1, 7 pr. Fest. s. 'Iniuria.' D. 47, 10, 11, 1.

[c] Gai. iv. 116, *sq.*, 119.

[1] A stipulation of the kind that is followed by *acceptilatio* has been drawn up by Gall. Aquil. as follows: 'What you should or will have to give or do to me, now or under a temporal condition, and such matters in respect of which I shall have an action against you, whatever is or shall be my claim against you, or proceedings against you, or what you have, hold, or possess of mine, for so much as each of these things shall be worth, for the payment of so much money has A. A. stipulated and N. N. given his undertaking. What N. N. has promised and undertaken to A. A., N. N. has asked A. A. whether he acknowledged the same; A. A. has acknowledged it.

[2] Some actions are *ipso iure* extinguished by bargain, as those about outrage, and theft likewise.

[3] A natural obligation is extinguished *ipso iure* by a lawful agreement, because the bond of equity by which alone it was maintained is unloosed by the equity of a convention.

Book III. Pt. I. Ch. II.

Ulp.: Pactorum quaedam in rem sunt, quaedam in personam: in rem sunt, quotiens generaliter paciscor, ne petam; in personam, quotiens ne a persona petam, id est ne a Lucio Titio petam. Utrum autem in rem an in personam pactum factum est, minus ex verbis quam ex mente convenientium aestimandum est.—l. 7, § 8, D. de pact.[1]

A further distinction obtains between pactum de non petendo *in certum tempus* (agreement for respite) and *in perpetuum*.[a]

Cf. § 28.

Gai. iv. § 122: Dilatoriae exceptiones sunt, quae ad tempus valent, veluti illius pacti conventi quod factum est verbi gratia, ne intra quinquennium peteretur, finito enim eo tempore non habet locum exceptio.[2]

By an informal agreement (contrarius consensus s. mutuus dissensus), all obligations contracted nudo consensu can be extinguished before they have yet been performed by either party.

Paul.: Emptio et venditio sicut consensu contrahitur, ita contrario consensu resolvitur antequam fuerit res secuta.—l. 3, D. de resc. vend. 18, 5.[3]

Si Titius et Seius inter se consenserunt, ut fundum Tusculanum emptum Seius haberet cen-

---

[1] Some agreements relate to the thing, some to the person. Those are *in rem* whenever I undertake in general not to sue; *in personam*, whenever it is that I will not sue the (particular) person, *i.e.*, that I will not sue L. T. But whether an agreement has been made *in rem* or *in personam* is to be gathered rather from the language than from the intention of the parties thereto.

[2] Dilatory pleas are those which hold good for a time; as for example, that of a covenant that no claim shall be made for, say, five years; for at the end of such time a plea is inadmissible.

[3] A purchase and sale, just as it is contracted by consent, so, before fulfilment, it is again dissolved by an agreement to the opposite effect.

tum aureorum, deinde re nondum secuta (i.e. neque pretio soluto neque fundo tradito) placuerit inter eos, ut discederetur ab emptione et venditione, invicem liberantur; idem est et in conductione et locatione et omnibus contractibus, qui ex consensu descendunt.—§ 4, I. h. t. 3, 29.[1]

Pomp.: —post pretium solutum infectam emptionem facere non possumus.—l. 2, de resc. vend.[2]

Ner.: Ab emptione venditione locatione conductione ceterisque similibus obligationibus quin integris omnibus consensu eorum, qui inter se obligati sint, recedi possit, dubium non est. . . . Nec quidquam interest, utrum integris omnibus, in quae obligati essemus, conveniret, ut ab eo negotio discederetur, an in integrum restitutis his, quae ego tibi praestitissem, consentiremus, ne quid tu mihi eo nomine praestares.—l. 58, de pact.[3]

§ 142. Novatio.[a]

[a] Cf. Pollock, 'Contract,' ch. v. pp. 193, *sq.*; Bell, s. 'Novation.'

Novatio, occupying a middle place between 'solutio' and the agreement for release, is the extinction of an

---

[1] If Tit. and Sejus have agreed together that Sej. should purchase the Tusculan estate for one hundred *aurei*, and then while the matter is still inchoate (*i.e.*, before the price has been paid, or the land delivered) they consent to a withdrawal from this buying and selling, they are mutually released. The same holds in respect of letting and hiring and all contracts which spring from consent.

[2] We cannot undo the purchase after payment made of the purchase-money.

[3] There is no doubt but that by the consent of those who have mutually bound themselves we can withdraw from a purchase and sale, letting and hiring, and all like obligations, if everything remain in the same state. . . . And it makes no matter whether an agreement has been made that we should withdraw from such transaction when all as to which we were bound remained unfulfilled, or whether it was after the return of what I performed for you we agreed that you should do nothing for me in that behalf.

BOOK III. Pt. I. Ch. II.

obligation by entering into a verborum obligatio (stipulatio debiti)—or into a literarum obligatio[a]—which relates to the object of the previous obligation (id quod debetur), and has to take its place; so that, consequently, a new 'causa debendi' is constituted for an already existing debt.[b]

[a] § 119.

[b] This must not be confounded with the cases in D. 41, 1, 9, 5; 6, 2, 9, 1 (§ 89); and D. 17, 1, 34 pr., 12, 1, 15 (§ 120).

Ulp.: Novatio est prioris debiti in aliam obligationem, vel civilem vel naturalem, transfusio atque translatio, hoc est cum ex praecedenti causa ita nova constituatur, ut prior perimatur; novatio enim a **novo** nomen accipit et a **nova** obligatione. —l. 1 pr., D. h. t. (de novat. 46, 2).[1]

The novating, or substituted, obligation (stipulatio) can be created between the same persons, as: 'Quidquid te mihi ex empto dare facere oportet, tantam pecuniam mihi dare spondes?'; or between the previous creditor and a new debtor, which is so-called *expromissio*, as: 'Quod Titius mihi debet, id tu mihi dare spondes?'; or finally, between the previous debtor and a new creditor, to whom the debtor is delegated, or assigned, by the previous creditor, which is *delegatio* in the narrower sense, as: 'Quod Titio debes, id mihi dare spondes?'[c]

[c] Cf. Vat. fgm. 263; D. 39, 5, 21, 1; and *inf.* § 144, ad init.

Gai. iii. § 176: Praeterea novatione tollitur obligatio, veluti si quod tu mihi debeas a Titio dari stipulatus sim: nam interventu novae personae nova nascitur obligatio et prima tollitur translata in posteriorem.[2]

Ulp.: Non tamen si quis stipuletur, quod mihi debetur, aufert mihi actionem, nisi ex voluntate

---

1 *Novatio* is the commutation and transformation of an earlier debt into another obligation, either one of civil or natural Law, that is, if from a pre-existing title a new one is so formed that the earlier one is destroyed. For novation has its name *a novo* (from what is new) and from the new obligation.

2 An obligation is, besides, dissolved by novation; for example, if I stipulate for the payment by Tit. of what you owe to me; for a fresh obligation arises by the introduction of a new person, and the first one is dissolved by being transferred into the later one.

mea stipuletur; liberat autem me is, qui quod debeo promittit, etiamsi nolim.—l. 8, § 5, D. h. t.[a] [1]

Id.: Delegare est vice sua alium reum dare creditori, vel cui iusserit.—l. 11 pr. eod.[2]

[a] Compare extract below (ibid.).

The following are the requisites of Novation.

(1) Every obligation, civil or natural, can be novated.

Ulp.: Illud non interest qualis praecessit obligatio, utrum naturalis an civilis an honoraria, et utrum verbis an re an consensu; qualiscumque igitur obligatio sit, quae praecessit, novari verbis potest: dummodo sequens obligatio aut civiliter teneat aut naturaliter, ut puta si pupillus sine tutoris auctoritate promiserit.—l. 1, § 1, D. h. t.[3]

(2) The pre-existing (praecedens, prior) obligation is only destroyed, if a new (posterior), valid, although inoperative, obligation obtains.

Pomp.: Novatio non potest contingere ea stipulatione, quae non committitur.—l. 24 eod.[4]

Gai. iii. § 176: —prima[b] tollitur translata in posteriorem, adeo ut interdum licet posterior stipulatio inutilis est, tamen prima novationis iure tollatur; veluti si quod mihi debes, a Titio post mortem eius vel a muliere pupillove sine tutoris auctoritate stipulatus fuero: quo casu rem

[b] Sc. obligatio.

---

[1] But he who stipulates for that which is owing to me does not deprive me of an action, unless he stipulate by my consent; but he that promises what I owe, even against my will, releases me.

[2] To delegate is to give in one's own place another debtor to the creditor, or to whom he shall direct.

[3] It makes no difference what obligation has preceded, whether one by natural or civil Law, or a magisterial one, and whether it rested upon words, or a thing, or consent. Of whatever kind, therefore, the obligation was that preceded, it can be novated by words, provided the subsequent obligation binds either by civil or by natural Law; as for example, if a ward has made a promise without his guardian's sanction.

[4] A novation cannot come about by such stipulation as is not enforced.

Book III. Pt. I. Ch. II.

amitto, nam et prior debitor liberatur et posterior obligatio nulla est; non idem iuris est si a servo stipulatus fuero: nam tunc (prior) proinde adhuc obligatus tenetur, ac si postea a nullo stipulatus fuissem.[a] § 179: Servius tamen Sulpicius . . . respondit, si quis id quod sibi Lucius Titius deberet, a servo fuerit stipulatus, novationem fieri et rem perire, quia cum servo agi non potest: sed alio iure utimur; nec magis . . . novatio fit, quam si id quod tu mihi debeas, a peregrino, cum quo sponsus communio non est, SPONDES verbo stipulatus sim.[1]

[a] Cf. ibid. extract above.

For extinction of the subsisting by the new obligation, 'animus novandi' is requisite, and besides, by the latest Law, declaration of the intention of novation; otherwise both obligations continue collateral to one another (accessory stipulation).

Ulp.: Omnes res transire in novationem possunt; quodcumque enim sive verbis contractum est sive non verbis, novari potest et transire in verborum obligationem ex quacumque obligatione: dummodo sciamus novationem ita demum fieri, si hoc agatur, ut novetur obligatio; ceterum si

[1] The original obligation is extinguished by being transferred into the later one, to such an extent that sometimes, although the later stipulation is invalid, yet the original one is extinguished by virtue of the novation; for instance, if I shall have taken a stipulation from Tit. for payment by him after his death of what you owe me, or from a woman or a ward without the guardian's sanction, in this case I lose the thing; for the earlier debtor is discharged, and the later obligation is void. The rule is not the same if I have taken the stipulation from a slave; for then the (earlier debtor) remains bound, just as if I had not afterwards taken a stipulation from any one. § Serv. Sulp., however, . . . gave an opinion that if a person took a stipulation from a slave for that which Luc. Tit. owed (the former), a novation was produced and the thing was lost, proceedings being impossible against a slave. But we observe a different rule; for a novation is no more effected . . . than it would be if I stipulated by means of the word *spondes?* with a foreigner, with whom there is no dealing by suretyship.

non hoc agatur, duae erunt obligationes.—l. 2, D. h. t.[1]

Quod ego debeo si alius promittat, liberare me potest, si novationis causa hoc fiat; si autem non novandi animo hoc intervenit, uterque quidem tenetur, sed altero solvente alter liberatur.—l. 8, § 5 eod.[2]

Inst. iii. 29, § 3[a]: Sed cum hoc quidem inter veteres constabat tunc fieri novationem, cum novandi animo in secundam obligationem itum fuerat, per hoc autem dubium erat, quando novandi animo videretur hoc fieri et quasdam de hoc praesumptiones alii in aliis casibus introducebant: ideo nostra processit constitutio, quae apertissime definivit tunc solum fieri novationem, quotiens hoc ipsum inter contrahentes expressum fuerit, quod propter novationem prioris obligationis convenerunt; alioquin manere et pristinam obligationem et secundam ei accedere, ut maneat ex utraque causa obligatio.[a] [3]

[a] Cf. Brown, s. v.

---

[1] All matters can pass into a novation. For whatever has been contracted, whether by words or not by words, can be novated, and pass from any obligation into a verbal one. Only we must know that a novation is alone produced if it be intended that the obligation should be novated; but if that be not the intention, there will be two obligations.

[2] For if another promises that which I owe, he can release me, if this is done in view of novation; if, however, it has not occurred for the purpose of novation, both indeed are liable; but if payment be made by one, the other is discharged.

[3] But since it was in fact settled amongst the old jurists that a novation took place when the second obligation has been entered into with the purpose of effecting a novation, but it was thereby doubtful when this act should be held to have operated with the purpose to novate, and different presumptions were set up by different persons to suit various cases, our constitution has therefore been published, which has expressly provided that novation shall alone be produced when this particular statement shall be made by the contracting parties, that their agreement was in view of the novation of the former obligation; otherwise the earlier obligation remains in force, and the second

The substituted obligation can always relate only to the object of the earlier obligation (idem debitum), but, as regards modification in the terms of performance, can be distinguished from it in many ways (*e.g.*, as to dies, condicio, locus, payment of interest, conventional penalty, mode of payment, and the like).

Gai. iii. § 177: Si eadem persona sit, a qua postea stipuler, ita demum novatio fit, si quid in posteriore stipulatione novi sit, forte si condicio vel dies vel sponsor adiiciatur aut detrahatur.[1]

Ulp.: Legata vel fideicommissa si in stipulationem fuerint deducta et hoc actum ut novetur, fiet novatio; si quidem pure vel in diem fuerint relicta, statim; si vero sub condicione, non statim, sed ubi condicio exstiterit: nam et alias qui in diem stipulatur, statim novat; . . . at qui sub condicione stipulatur, non novat, nisi condicio exstiterit.—l. 8, § 1, D. h. t.[2]

Gai. iii. § 179: Quod autem diximus, si condicio adiiciatur, novationem fieri, sic intelligi oportet, . . . si condicio exstiterit; alioquin si defecerit, durat prior obligatio: sed videamus num is qui eo nomine agat, doli mali aut pacti conventi exceptione possit summoveri, quia videtur inter eos id actum, ut ita ea res peteretur si posterioris stipulationis exstiterit condicio.

---

is added to it, so that an obligation remains which is grounded upon both transactions.

[1] If it be the same person from whom I afterwards take a stipulation, there is a novation only when there is something new in the later stipulation, as when a condition, or a date, or a surety is added or omitted.

[2] If legacies or bequests in trust have been brought into a stipulation, and this has been done with intent to novate, a novation will be produced: if in fact they have been left unconditionally, or for a term, then at once; but if under a condition, not at once, but when the condition shall come to pass. For even otherwise does he novate at once who stipulates for a term; . . . but he that stipulates conditionally does not novate, save as the condition shall take effect.

Servius tamen Sulpicius existimavit statim et pendente condicione novationem fieri, et si defecerit condicio, ex neutra causa agi posse et eo modo rem perire.[a] [1]

[a] Compare extract above (ibid.).

The effect of novation consists in the substantial destruction, resulting ipso iure, of the previous obligation, together with what has been superadded to it.

Paul.: Novatione legitime facta liberantur hypothecae et pignus, usurae non currunt.—l. 18, D. h. t.[2]

A kind of quasi-novation (novatio necessaria) is involved in 'Litis Contestatio' and Judgment.[b]

[b] Gai. iii. 180, sq.; D. 15, 1, 3, 11; 42, 1, 6, 3; Vat. fgm. 263.

Ulp.: Fit autem delegatio vel per stipulationem, vel per litis contestationem.—l. 11, § 1 eod.[3]

§ 143. Involuntary Grounds of Extinction.

To the reasons that destroy an obligation without co-operation of the persons interested belong—

(1) lapse of one of the subjects:

(α) by the death of the debtor or creditor in actions not hereditary;[c]

(β) by capitis diminutio of the debtor;[d]

(γ) by confusio, that is, merger of claim and debt in the same person, consequent upon inheritance.[e]

[c] § 25.

[d] § 56.

[e] §§ 97, 103.

---

[1] But our having said that, if a condition is added, a novation is operated, must be thus understood . . . if the condition come to pass: otherwise, if it should fail, the original obligation still subsists. But let us see whether he who sues on that account can be met by a plea of fraud or covenant; because it seems to have been agreed that the thing should only be claimed upon fulfilment of the condition of the subsequent obligation. Serv. Sulp., however, considered that novation comes about at once and while the condition is pending; and if the condition have failed, no proceedings can be taken on either ground, and in that way the thing is lost.

[2] If a novation have happened conformably to law, hypothecs and pledge are released, and interest does not run.

[3] Now delegation comes about either by stipulation or by joinder of issue.

BOOK III. Pt. I. Ch. II.

Pap.: Aditio hereditatis nonnumquam iure confundit obligationem, veluti si creditor debitoris, vel contra debitor creditoris adierit hereditatem.—D. 46, 3, 95, 2.[1]

(2) The natural or juristic destruction of the object of debt (impossibility of performance), which supposes that neither has the debtor to bear the periculum, nor that responsibility for culpa or mora exists on his part. Hence it is said: '*Species* perit ei cui debetur; *genus* perire non censetur.'[a]

[a] §§ 108, *sq.*, 117; Inst. iii. 23, 3.

Pomp.: Si Stichus certo die dari promissus ante diem moriatur, non tenetur promissor.—D. 45, 1, 33.[2]

Paul.: Cum quis rem profanam aut Stichum dari promisit, liberatur, si sine facto eius res sacra esse coeperit aut Stichus ad libertatem pervenerit, nec revocantur in obligationem, si rursus lege aliqua et res sacra profana esse coeperit et Stichus ex libero servus effectus est.—l. 83, § 5 eod.[3]

§ 144. SECONDLY, OF TRANSFER OF CLAIMS. CESSION.

Since the obligation is a legal relation between persons marked out individually, a Singular Succession can neither attach to the rights of the creditor nor to

---

[1] Entry upon an inheritance sometimes by law extinguishes an obligation by merger; for example, if the creditor shall have entered upon his debtor's inheritance, or conversely, the debtor upon his creditor's.

[2] If the delivery of Stichus have been promised for a fixed day, but he dies before the day, the promisor is not liable.

[3] When a person has promised to give a profane thing or (the slave) Stichus, he is released if by no act of his the thing has become sacred, or Stichus has attained to freedom; and they cannot be claimed back for the obligation if again by some law the profane thing shall become sacred, and Stichus from being a freeman has become a slave.

the liability of the debtor. An obligation can be transferred only in regard of practical result, and that in two ways.

Book III. Pt. I. Ch. II.

(1) Through Novation, that is, by delegatio of the debtor to the new creditor, or expromissio of the debtor by a third party; by which, however, the subsisting obligation is not transferred: it is rather extinguished, and its place taken by a new obligation, though of like content.

Gai. ii. § 38: Obligationes quoquo modo contractae nihil eorum[a] recipiunt; nam quod mihi ab aliquo debetur, id si velim tibi deberi, nullo eorum modo, quibus res corporales ad alium transferuntur, id efficere possum, sed opus est, ut iubente me tu ab eo stipuleris: quae res efficit, ut a me liberetur et incipiat tibi teneri. Quae dicitur novatio obligationis.[1]

[a] Sc. traditionem, mancipationem, in iure cessionem.

(2) Through CESSION, that is, through transfer of the exercise of a claim by the previous creditor conferring powers (mandare, cedere, praestare, actionem) on another, the 'cessionarius,' as his representative (procurator, cognitor),[b] for the judicial enforcement of the claim in the name of the 'cedens,' but in his own interest and upon his own account (in rem suam), for which the consent of the debtor (debitor cessus)—otherwise than in delegatio—is not required.

[b] §§ 197, 200.

Gai. ii. 39: Sine hac vero novatione non poteris tuo nomine agere, sed debes ex persona mea quasi cognitor aut procurator meus experiri.[2]

---

[1] Obligations, in whatever way they are contracted, admit of none of these transfers. For if I wish that what is owed by some one to me should be owed to you, I cannot accomplish it by any of those modes by which corporeal things are transferred to another person, but you must by my direction take a stipulation from him: the result of which, is, that he is released by me and begins to be liable to you. This is called a novation of the obligation.

[2] But without this novation you will be unable to sue in your

Imp. Alex.: Delegatio debiti, nisi consentiente et stipulatanti promittente debitore, iure perfici non potest: nominis autem venditio et ignorante vel invito eo, adversus quem actiones mandantur, contrahi solet.—l. 1, C. de novat. 8, 41 (42).[1]

The 'cedens' here at first remains creditor, and can also recall the mandatum agendi; he does not lose the general control of the claim until by litis contestatio of the 'cessionarius' with the debtor;[a] though by later Law, notice to the debtor of the cessio having taken place (denuntiatio) operated this. On the other hand, the debtor also retains against the 'cessionarius' all pleas that connect themselves with the 'cedens' personally.

[a] § 142, ad fin.

Mac.: Meminisse oportet, quod procurator lite contestata **dominus litis** efficitur.—D. 49, 1, 4, 5.[2]

Imp. Gord.: Si delegatio non est interposita debitoris tui ac propterea actiones apud te remanserunt, quamvis creditori tuo adversus eum solutionis causa mandaveris actiones, tamen antequam lis contestetur vel aliquid ex debito accipiat vel debitori tuo denuntiaverit, exigere a debitore tuo debitam quantitatem non vetaris et eo modo tui creditoris exactionem contra eum inhibere.—l. 3, C. de novat.[3]

---

own name, but you must take proceedings in my name in the character of my *cognitor* or *procurator*.

[1] The assignment of a debt can be legally perfected alone by consent, and by a promise given to the stipulating creditor by the debtor. But the sale of a claim is, as a rule, contracted without the knowledge, or against the will, of him against whom the actions are transferred.

[2] It must be borne in mind that upon joinder of issue the *procurator* becomes master of the suit.

[3] If an assignment of your debtor has not taken place and, accordingly, the actions have continued at your command, although you have transferred to your creditor the actions against such debtor in lieu of payment, nevertheless, before joinder of issue, or the acceptance by him of any part of the

The 'cedens' is answerable to the 'cessionarius' as a rule only for the existence (verum nomen) of the claim, not for its admitting of realisation, or for the solvency of the debtor (bonum nomen).

> Ulp.: Si nomen sit distractum, Celsus scribit, locupletem esse debitorem non debere praestare, debitorem autem esse praestare: nisi aliud convenit.—D. 18, 4, 4.[1]

Already in the later classical, and further in the yet later Law, the express conferment of a special mandatum agendi was not always requisite for the cessio to take effect; because in some transactions, which doubtless involved the intention of cessio, as for instance, in an 'emtio nominis' or sale of an obligatory claim, the defective mandatum agendi—or even that recalled or otherwise extinguished—was gradually replaced by the grant of utiles actiones, whereby the cessionarius altogether, in relation to the cedens, acquired a more assured and more independent position. Moreover, in certain cases, where a legal liability was existing for the assignment of the claim,[a] the cessio itself was regarded as effected without, indeed against, the will of the previous creditor; and the action belonging to him was, as utilis actio, conferred upon the party entitled (cessio legis).

[a] Cf. § 112.

> Imp. Valer.: Nominibus in dotem datis, quamvis nec delegatio praecesserit nec litiscontestatio subsecuta fuerit, utilem tamen marito actionem ad similitudinem eius, qui nomen emerit, dari oportere saepe rescriptum est.—C. 4, 10, 2.[b] [2]

[b] Cf. Pollock, 'Cont.' p. 207.

claim, or notice given by him to your debtor, you are not prevented from claiming the amount owing from your debtor, and in this way hindering a claim being made upon him by your creditor.

[1] If a debt has been sold, Cels. writes, that (the vendor) has not to answer for the solvency of the debtor, but he has to answer for his being debtor, unless it is otherwise agreed.

[2] If claims to dowry have been made over, it has often been laid down in rescripts that, although neither an assignment have preceded nor joinder of issue followed, an equitable action

BOOK III. Pt. I. Ch. II.

Imp. Diocl.: In solutum nomine dato non aliter nisi mandatis actionibus ex persona sui debitoris adversus eius debitores creditor experiri potest; suo autem nomine utili actione recte utetur.—C. 4, 15, l. ult.[a] [1]

[a] Ibid.

Id.: Ex legato nominis, actionibus ab his qui successerunt non mandatis, directas quidem actiones legatarius habere non potest, utilibus autem suo nomine experietur.—C. 6, 37, 18.[2]

Ulp.: Si procurator vendiderit, . . . dicendum est, utilem ex empto actionem domino competere.—D. 19, 1, 13, 25.[3]

A peculiar limitation of cessio is contained by the *lex Anastasiana*,[b] according to which the purchaser of a claim shall be allowed to exact from the debtor no more than he himself purchased.

[b] C. 4, 35, 22 (a. 506).

§ 145. THIRDLY, OF INTERCESSION. *SENATUSCONSULTUM VELLEIANUM.*

A SC. Velleianum under Claudius[c] enacted that, having regard to their inexperience of law and ignorance of business, as well as to 'sexus imbecillitas,' the INTERCESSION of women was invalid.

[c] Cf. Gai. i. 157. Ulp. xi. 8.

Paul.: Velleiano senatusconsulto plenissime comprehensum est, ne pro ullo feminae intercederent.—l. 1 pr., D. h. t. (ad SC. Vell. 16, 1).[4]

---

must be given to the husband after the analogy of the purchaser of a claim.

[1] If a claim has been made over in lieu of payment, the creditor can take proceedings alone by actions transferred to him in the name of his debtor against the latter's debtors, but he may lawfully avail himself of an equitable action in his own name.

[2] A legatee can in fact have no direct actions upon the bequest of a debt if the actions have not been transferred to him by the heirs; but he may sue by equitable actions in his own name.

[3] If an agent has sold . . . we must say that an equitable action upon the purchase lies for the principal.

[4] By the *SCtum Velleianum* most complete provision has been

Ulp.: Et primo quidem temporibus D. Augusti, mox deinde Claudii edictis eorum erat interdictum, ne feminae pro viris suis intercederent. § Postea factum est senatusconsultum, quo plenissime feminis omnibus subventum est; cuius senatusconsulti verba haec sunt: '**Quod Marcus Silanus et Velleus Tutor consules verba fecerunt de obligationibus feminarum, quae pro aliis reae fierent, quid de ea re fieri oportet, de ea re ita censuere: quod ad fideiussiones et mutui dationes pro aliis, quibus intercesserint feminae, pertinet, tametsi ante videtur ita ius dictum esse, ne eo nomine ab his petitio sit neve in eas actio detur, cum eas virilibus officiis fungi et eius generis obligationibus obstringi non sit aequum, arbitrari senatum, recte atque ordine facturos ad quos de ea re in iure aditum erit, si dederint operam, ut in ea re senatus voluntas servetur.**'—l. 2 pr., § 1 eod.[1]

---

made that women should not make themselves sureties for any one.

[1] And first indeed in the times of the late Emperor Augustus, and soon afterwards of Claudius, by their edicts women were forbidden to become sureties for their husbands. § Afterwards a *Sctum* was passed by which, in the most complete way, relief was given to all women. The following are the words of this edict: 'Whereas Marc. Sil. and Vell. Tut., the consuls, have delivered a discourse upon the obligations of women, who should undertake the debts of others, as to what should be done concerning such matter, the conclusion come to thereon was this: As regards guaranties and debts incurred for others, for whom women shall become sureties, although previously the law seems to have been laid down, that there should be no claim against them in this behalf, and no action should be given against them, it not being fair that they should perform men's functions and be involved in obligations, the Senate is of opinion that the tribunal which shall give audience concerning such matter will act rightly and in order if they shall be at pains to uphold its intention as to such matter.'

BOOK III. Pt. I. Ch. II.

The notion of 'intercessio' was developed by Roman jurisprudence by way of interpretation of this SCtum, to the extent that it comprehends every engagement for the liability of another by which responsibility is undertaken.

Imp. Anton.: Sed si pro aliis, cum obligatae non essent, pecuniam exsolvunt, intercessione cessante repetitio nulla est.—l. 1, C. h. t. 4, 29.[1]

This may be by responsibility collateral to the debtor (so-called 'cumulative' intercessio) by means of fideiussio, mandatum qualificatum, constitutum debiti alieni.

Id.: Si cum ipse mutuam pecuniam acciperes, mater tua contra amplissimi ordinis consultum fidem suam interposuit, exceptione se tueri potest. —l. 3, C. eod.[2]

Or it may be by the undertaking of another's debt by means of expromissio[a] (so-called 'privative' intercessio), or by contracting liability in the place, and in the sole interest, of a third party (so-called intercessio tacita).

[a] § 142.

Imp. Alex.: SCtum locum habet, sive eam obligationem, quae in alterius personam constitit, mulier in se transtulerit vel participaverit, sive cum alius pecuniam acciperet, ipsa se ab initio ream constituit.—l. 4, C. eod.[3]

Ulp.: Si cum essem tibi contracturus, mulier

---

[1] But if they pay money for others, without having contracted any liability, in the absence of *intercessio*, there is no recovery.

[2] If upon your taking a loan, your mother made herself liable against the decree of the august order, she can protect herself by a plea.

[3] The *Sctum* is applicable whether it be that a woman has transferred to herself, or has taken a share in, an obligation which affects another, or when another received money, she at the outset made herself the debtor.

intervenerit, ut cum ipsa potius contraham, videtur intercessisse.—l. 8, § 14, D. h. t.[1]

But the debt for which the engagement is made must be materially, and in its pecuniary relation, always another's.

Gai.: Aliquando licet alienam obligationem suscipiat mulier, non adiuvatur hoc senatusconsulto; quod tum accidit, cum prima facie quidem alienam, re vera autem suam obligationem suscipiat: ut ecce si ancilla ob pactionem libertatis expromissore dato post manumissionem id ipsum suscipiat, quod expromissor debeat, aut si hereditatem emerit et aes alienum hereditarium in se transcribat, aut si pro fideiussore suo intercedat. —l. 13 pr., D. eod.[2]

The female surety has the exceptio SC[i] Vell[i] to the action of the creditor, provided that he knew of the intercessio.

Sed ita demum eis subvenit, si non callide sint versatae; . . . nam deceptis non decipientibus opitulatur.—l. 2, § 3, D. h. t.[3]

Paul.: Si mulier tamquam in usus suos pecuniam acceperit, alii creditura, non est locus senatusconsulto: alioquin nemo cum feminis contrahet,

---

[1] If when I was about to contract with you, a woman shall have intervened, that I might the rather make the contract with her, she would seem to have given a guaranty.

[2] Sometimes, although a woman undertakes the obligation of another person, she is not relieved by this *SCtum*, which occurs when she undertakes, at the first glance indeed another person's, but in fact her own obligation; as, for example, if a slave-woman, when a substitute has been appointed because of an agreement for freedom, after the manumission should undertake just what the substitute may owe, or if a woman should have purchased an inheritance and takes upon herself the debts of the inheritance, or if she answer for her surety.

[3] But relief is afforded them only when they have not gone to work deceitfully; . . . for to those that are deceived, not deceivers, is relief given.

Book III. Pt. I. Ch. II.

quia ignorari potest, quid acturae sint.—Immo tunc locus est senatusconsulto, cum scit creditor eam intercedere.—ll. 11, 12 eod.[1]

And further, she can by condictio indebiti recover what has been paid by mistake.

Marcian.: Si quidem eius causa exceptio datur cum quo agitur, solutum repetere potest, ut accidit in senatusconsulto de intercessionibus.—D. 12, 6, 40 pr.[2]

In favour of the creditor, to meet this the action against the debtor released by the intercessio is revived: the 'actio restitutoria.'

Quotiens pro debitore intercesserit mulier, datur in eum pristina actio, etsi ille prius acceptilatione liberatus sit, quam mulier intercesserit.—l. 8, § 7, D. h. t.[3]

Aequum visum est, ita mulieri succurri, ut in . . . eum, qui pro se constituisset mulierem ream, actio daretur.—l. 1, § 2, h. t.[4]

---

[1] If a woman has received money as though for her own use, with the intention of lending it to another person, the *Sctum* does not attach; otherwise, no one would contract with women, because one cannot tell what they may intend to do.—But the *Sctum* does by all means attach when the creditor is aware that she becomes guarantor.

[2] If in fact the plea is given on behalf of him against whom proceedings are taken, he can reclaim what has been paid, as happens in respect of the *Sctum* upon guaranties.

[3] Whenever a woman shall give guaranty for a debtor, the earlier action is given against him, although he should have been previously released by *acceptilatio* before the woman gave the guaranty.

[4] It has appeared fair that relief should be given to a woman in such way that an action be given against . . . him who had appointed the woman as debtor on his own behalf.

PART II.—LAW OF FAMILY PROPERTY.

CHAPTER I.

Book III. Part II.

INFLUENCE OF MARRIAGE UPON PROPERTY.[a]

§ 146. Nature and Constitution of *Dos*.

Apart from in manum conventio,[b] Marriage in Roman Law leaves the property of the spouses on both sides untouched.[c] But from of old it was usual —even in marriage by manus—for the wife, or another on her behalf, to make over to the husband, or his paterfamilias, some property called *dos* (dowry, marriage-portion)[d] as a contribution to the burdens of maintenance (onera matrimonii) to be borne by him.

> Paul.: Ibi dos esse debet, ubi onera matrimonii sunt.—Post mortem patris statim onera matrimonii filium sequuntur, sicut uxor.—l. 56, §§ 1, 2, D. h. t. (de I. D. 23, 3).[1]

> Pomp.: Dotium causa semper et ubique praecipua est; nam et publice interest dotes mulieribus conservari, cum dotatas esse feminas ad sobolem procreandam replendamque liberis civitatem maxime sit necessarium.—D. 24, 3, 1.[2]

From this custom was developed in course of time quite a legal duty for the wife's parent of providing a marriage-portion.

[a] See Maine, 'Early Histy. of Instns.' ch. xi.—For English Law, Kenny, 'Effects of Marriage on Property,' and Steph. ii. 263-277. For Scotch Law: Ld. Mack. 119-122. For conflict of laws: Westl. 119-122.

[b] § 48.

[c] Notwithstanding what is stated in § 44, ad init.

[d] See Brown, s. v. Cf. Blackstone, ii. 129 (Steph. i. 267).—Glanvil uses *dos* both in the sense of Dowry and of 'dower': Kenny, p. 76.

---

[1] The dowry must be where the burdens of the marriage are. —After the father's death the burdens of the marriage pass forthwith to the son, just as the wife.[e]

[2] The ground of marriage-portions is always and everywhere a special one; for it also concerns the public welfare that marriage-portions be preserved to women, since it is highly necessary for women to be endowed, for the procreation of offspring and the supply of children to the State.

[e] *I.e.*, as she then passes under her own husband's *manus*.

Book III. Part II.

Marcian.: Capite xxxv legis Iuliae qui liberos, quos habent in potestate, iniuria prohibuerint ducere uxores vel nubere, vel qui dotem dare non volunt, ex constitutione divorum Severi et Antonini per proconsules praesidesque provinciarum coguntur in matrimonium collocare et dotare; prohibere autem videtur et qui condicionem non quaerit.—D. 23, 2, 19.[1]

Imp. Diocl.: Mater pro filia dotem dare non cogitur, nisi ex magna vel probabili vel lege specialiter expressa causa.—l. 14, C. h. t. 5, 12.[2]

The rest of the wife's property (bona recepticia, parapherna) remains, even without special reservation, subject to the free disposition and control of the wife.[a] She is likewise capable of independent acquisition during the coverture; but here attaches the so-called praesumptio Muciana.[b]

[a] Whether in marriage with manus the wife could retain a portion of her property by express reservation to herself, as *peculium*, is exceedingly doubtful.

[b] Cf. § 148.

Gell. xvii. 6, § 6: Quando mulier dotem marito dabat, tum quae ex suis bonis retinebat neque ad virum transmittebat, ea 'recipere' dicebatur, sicuti nunc quoque in venditionibus 'recipi' dicuntur, quae excipiuntur neque veneunt.[3]

Imp. Theod.: Hac lege decernimus, ut vir in his rebus quas extra dotem mulier habet, quas Graeci παράφερνα dicunt, nullam uxore prohi-

---

[1] By the thirty-fifth chapter of the *l. Iulia*, those who without lawful cause have restrained children under their power from taking wives or marrying, or those who decline to give a dowry, are, in accordance with the constitution of the late Emperors Sev. and Ant., required by the pro-consuls and provincial presidents to give (their children) in marriage and endow them; and a person also is regarded as using restraint who does not seek a match.

[2] A mother is not required to give a dowry for her daughter unless upon a ground weighty, or reasonable, or by the special terms of a statute.

[3] When a woman made over dowry to her husband, then she was said to 'receive' such things as she kept back of her goods and did not hand over to the man, just as now also in sales such things are said to be 'received' which are reserved and not sold.

bente habeat communionem; . . . nullo modo, muliere prohibente, virum in paraphernis se volumus immiscere.—C. 5, 14, 8.[1]

Pomp.: Quintus Mucius ait, cum in controversiam venit, unde ad mulierem quid pervenerit, et verius et honestius est, quod non demonstratur unde habeat, existimari a viro aut qui in potestate eius esset ad eam pervenisse: evitandi autem turpis quaestus gratia circa uxorem hoc videtur Q. Mucius probasse.—D. 24, 1, 51.[2]

A legally valid marriage is the natural requisite of every dos.[a]

[a] D. 23, 3, 21; Gai. i. 64; D. 50, 16, 101 pr.; 12, 4, 7, 1.

Ulp.: Dotis appellatio non refertur ad ea matrimonia, quae consistere non possunt: neque enim dos sine matrimonio esse potest; ubicumque igitur matrimonii nomen non est, nec dos est.—l. 3, D. h. t.[3]

A distinction is made between dos *profecticia*, that is, the dos which is given by the paternal ancestor, and dos *adventicia*, that is, such as is given by any other; whilst a subordinate species of the latter is the dos *recepticia*.

---

[1] By this law do we decree that a husband without the consent of the wife has no share in such things as she holds over and above the dowry, which the Greeks call παράφερνα; . . . it is our will that a husband in no way meddle with the *parapherna* without the consent of the wife.

[2] Q. M. says: If it become matter of dispute, from what quarter anything has come to the wife, it is both fairer and more honourable that we suppose, as to the source from which the wife holds it, since it is not proven, that it has come to her from her husband or one who was under his power; but Q. M. seems to have approved this view so as to eschew (the suspicion of) a dishonourable acquisition as regards the wife.

[3] The designation 'dowry' is not applied to such marriages as cannot exist; for neither can there be a dowry without a marriage. Wherever, therefore, the word 'marriage' does not obtain, neither does 'dowry.'

Book III. Part II.

Ulp. vi. 3, 5: Dos aut profecticia dicitur, id est quam pater mulieris dedit; aut adventicia, id est ea quae a quovis alio data est.—Adventicia autem dos, . . . si is qui dedit, ut sibi redderetur[a] stipulatus fuerit, . . . specialiter recepticia dicitur.[1]

[a] Sc. mortua in matrimonio muliere.

Id.: Sive igitur parens dedit dotem sive procurator eius sive iussit alium dare, sive cum quis dedisset negotium eius gerens, parens ratum habuerit: profecticia dos est.—Si pater pro filia emancipata dotem dederit, profecticiam nihilominus dotem esse nemini dubium est, quia non ius potestatis, sed parentis nomen dotem profecticiam facit: sed ita demum si ut parens dederit; ceterum si, cum deberet filiae, voluntate eius dedit, adventicia dos est.—l. 5, §§ 1, 11, D. h. t.[2]

The dos is created as soon as the husband's property has been increased 'dotis nomine.' The constitutio of the dos comes about either[b] by 'dare,' that is, immediate transfer of the object of dowry (corporeal thing, ius in re, claim)[c] to the ownership of the husband; or by 'promittere,' that is, by creation of a claim against the party constituting, to which a stipulatio was necessary in the classical Law, but in the

[b] Cf. § 129.

[c] C. 4, 10, 2.

---

[1] A dowry is said to be either 'profectitious,' *i.e.*, one given by the father of the woman; or 'adventitious,' *i.e.*, one given by somebody else.—An adventitious dowry, however, . . . if the donor stipulated for its return to him,[d] is called specifically 'receptitious.'

[d] *I.e.*, upon the death of the woman during coverture.

[2] If, therefore, the father or his agent has given the dowry, or has directed another to give it, or if the father, when any one who conducts his affairs had given it, has confirmed this, the dowry is profectitious.—If a father shall have given a dowry for his daughter when emancipated from his power, no one has a doubt that the dowry is none the less profectitious, because it is not the right of paternal power, but the name of the father, that makes the dowry profectitious; but only when he shall have given (the dowry) as father; if, however, when he was indebted to the daughter, he gave it according to her will, it is an adventitious dowry.

later Law an informal agreement (nuda pollicitatio) suffices; or by 'dicere.'[a]

[a] § 117.

Ulp. vi. 1: Dos aut datur aut dicitur aut promittitur.[1]

Imp. Theod.: Ad exactionem dotis, quam semel praestari placuit, qualiacumque sufficere verba censemus, sive scripta fuerint sive non, etiamsi (dictio vel) stipulatio in pollicitatione rerum dotalium minime fuerit subsecuta.—l. 6, C. de dot. prom. 5, 11 = l. 4, C. Th. eod. 3, 13.[2]

Paul.: Accepti quoque latione dos constituitur, cum debitori marito acceptum feratur dotis constituendae causa.—l. 41, § 2, D. h. t.[3]

The dos passes into the husband's estate, but the wife has a legal expectancy[b] in it, which is grounded in the essence of dos as of property destined for the wife and the purposes of the marriage (res uxoria); and this is realised upon the dissolution of the marriage by virtue of the duty of restitution.

[b] Reversion.

Tryph.: Quamvis in bonis mariti dos sit, mulieris tamen est.—l. 75, D. h. t.[4]

The husband has discretionary disposition over the objects of dowry, with the exception of the 'fundus dotalis.'

Ter.: Possunt res in dotem datae plerumque alienari et pecunia in dotem converti.—l. 61, § 1 eod.[5]

---

[1] A dowry is either given, or specified, or promised.

[2] For the enforcement of a dowry, the constitution of which has once been resolved upon, words of any kind shall suffice, written or verbal, although no (specification or) formal undertaking in respect of the promise of dotal property shall have followed.

[3] A dowry is constituted by *acceptilatio* also, when a discharge is given to the husband, debtor (of the wife), in order to constitute a dowry.

[4] Although the dowry forms part of the goods of the husband, it nevertheless belongs to the wife.

[5] Things given as dowry can generally be alienated, and the purchase-money transmuted into dowry.

Book III. Part II.

Ulp.: Si dotalem quis servum manumisit, ipse patronus habetur et ad legitimam hereditatem admittitur.—D. 38, 16, 3, 2.[1]

Id.: Ob res amotas vel proprias viri vel etiam dotales tam vindicatio quam condictio viro adversus mulierem competit, et in potestate (eius) est, qua velit actione uti.—D. 25, 2, 24.[2]

Gai. ii. §§ 62–3: Accidit aliquando, ut qui dominus sit, alienandae rei potestatem non habeat.—Nam dotale praedium maritus invita muliere per legem Iuliam prohibetur alienare, quamvis ipsius sit vel mancipatum ei dotis causa vel in iure cessum vel usucaptum; quod quidem ius utrum ad Italica tantum praedia, an etiam ad provincialia pertineat, dubitatur.[3]

[a] Sc. Iulia de adulteriis.

Inst. ii. 8 pr.: Cum lex[a] in soli tantummodo rebus locum habebat, quae Italicae fuerant, et alienationes inhibebat, quae invita muliere fiebant, hypothecas autem earum etiam volente: utrisque remedium imposuimus, ut etiam in eas res, quae in provinciali solo positae sunt, interdicta fiat alienatio vel obligatio et neutrum eorum neque consentientibus mulieribus procedat, ne sexus muliebris fragilitas in perniciem substantiae earum converteretur.[4]

---

[1] If a person has enfranchised a dotal slave, he himself is regarded as patron, and is admitted to the legal inheritance.

[2] Because of things purloined, either belonging to the husband or appertaining to the dowry, both a real action and a personal action against the woman are open to the husband, and he has it in his control which action he likes to employ.

[3] It sometimes happens that he who is owner has not the power of alienating a thing.—For by the *l. Iulia* a husband is restrained from alienating an estate appertaining to the dowry, against the wish of his wife, although it is his own, whether as mancipated to him for the purposes of dowry, or surrendered in court, or acquired by *usus*. But whether this rule relates alone to Italian or provincial lands also, is doubtful.

[4] Since the statute applied only to immovables which were Italian, and forbade alienations made without the wife's con-

He also has the benefit of the produce.

Ulp.: Dotis fructum ad maritum pertinere debere aequitas suggerit; cum enim ipse onera matrimonii subeat, aequum est eum etiam fructus percipere.—l. 7 pr., D. h. t.[1]

Pap.: Partum dotalium ancillarum dotis esse portionem convenit.—l. 69, § 9 eod.[2]

Ulp.: —servus dotalis . . . quod ex re mariti quaesiit vel ex operis suis, id ad maritum pertinet.—D. 15, 1, 19, 1.[3]

He is, however, responsible for omnis culpa.[a]

[a] § 108.

Paul.: In rebus dotalibus virum praestare oportet tam dolum quam culpam, quia causa sua dotem accipit; sed etiam diligentiam praestabit quam in suis rebus exhibet.—l. 17 pr., h. t.[4]

Gai.: Res in dotem datae, quae pondere numero mensura constant, mariti periculo sunt, quia in hoc dantur, ut eas maritus ad arbitrium suum distrahat et quandoque soluto matrimonio eiusdem generis et qualitatis alias restituat.—l. 42 eod.[5]

---

sent, and mortgages thereof even with her consent, we have effected a reform in both cases, so that an alienation or a charge is prohibited even of property situated on provincial soil, and neither shall take place, although there be consent of wives, lest the weakness of their sex be turned to the waste of their fortune.

[1] Equity dictates that the revenue of the dowry should belong to the husband; for, since he bears the burdens of the marriage, it is fair that he take the revenues also.

[2] It is agreed that the offspring of slave-women appertaining to the dowry are a part of the dowry.

[3] What a dotal slave has acquired by property of the husband, or by his own labours, belongs to the husband.

[4] In respect of dotal property, a man has to answer for both bad intention and negligence, because he receives the dowry on his own account; but he will also be responsible for such diligence as he displays in his own affairs.

[5] Things given for dowry which pass by weight, number, measure, are at the risk of the husband; because they are given with the intention that he dispose of them at his discretion, and

BOOK III. Part II.

If things have been given for dos at an appraised value, they are accounted as sold in case the aestimatio has not taken place merely 'taxationis causa.'

Imp. Alex.: Quotiens res aestimatae in dotem dantur, maritus dominium consecutus, summae velut pretii debitor efficitur.—C. 5, 12, 5.[1]

Plerumque interest viri res non esse aestimatas idcirco, ne periculum rerum ad eum pertineat. —l. 10 pr. eod.[2]

Pap.: Cum res in dotem aestimatas soluto matrimonio reddi placuit, summa declaratur, non venditio contrahitur.—l. 69, § 7 eod.[3]

§ 147. THE *Dos* AFTER DISSOLUTION OF THE MARRIAGE.

Notwithstanding that the husband becomes owner of the dos, he becomes so only for the purpose and duration of the marriage. After the dissolution thereof, he must as a rule restore the dos. The following principles operate in the classical Law with respect to this restitution.

In the question as to whom the dos falls after dissolution of the marriage, we have to determine whether the marriage has been dissolved by the death of the wife.

Ulp. vi. 4, 5: Mortua in matrimonio muliere dos a patre profecta ad patrem revertitur, quintis in singulos liberos in infinitum relictis penes

at any time upon the dissolution of the marriage he must make over others of the same kind and quality.

[1] Whenever things are valued and given as dowry, the husband acquires the ownership, and becomes only debtor, as it were, for the value of the whole.

[2] In general it is the concern of the husband that the property be not valued, on this account, that the risk thereof may not attach to him.

[3] When it has been settled that property given for dowry which has been valued should be restored upon the dissolution of the marriage, the value is alleged: there is no contract of sale.

virum; quodsi pater non sit, apud maritum remanet.—Adventicia autem dos semper penes maritum remanet.[1] Book III. Part II.

Or whether it occurred by the husband's death, or by divorce.[a] [a] Inf. Ulp. vi. 7.

Ib. § 6: Divortio facto si quidem sui iuris sit mulier, ipsa habet rei uxoriae actionem id est dotis repetitionem; quodsi in potestate patris sit, pater adiuncta filia habet actionem; nec interest adventicia sit dos, an profecticia.[2]

As regards the object of restitution, the dos has to be restored with all accessions, except the fruits. The fruits of the last dotal year are divided between husband and wife in the proportion of the duration of coverture.

Imp. Iust.: Itaque partus dotalium ancillarum, id est quae aestimatae non sunt, vel quae servi dotales ex quacumque causa, nisi ex re mariti vel operis suis adquisierint, ad mulierem pertinere. . . . Foetus autem iumentorum et omnium quae fructuum nomine continentur, ad lucrum mariti pertineant. . . . Sed et novissimi anni, in quo matrimonium solvitur, fructus pro rata temporis portione utrique parti debere adsignari.—C. 5, 13, l. un. § 9.[3]

---

[1] If the woman die while the marriage lasts, a dowry which proceeded from the father reverts to the father, a fifth being left in the husband's hands for each child until exhausted.—An adventitious dowry, however, always remains in the hands of the husband.

[2] When a divorce takes place, the woman herself, if she be *sui iuris*, has the action for the wife's property, that is, recovery of the dowry; but if she be under her father's power, he has the action, the daughter being joined with him; and it is of no consequence whether the dowry is adventitious or profectitious.

[3] Therefore the offspring of dotal slave-women, that is, of those who have not been valued, and that which dotal slaves have acquired upon any legal title whatever, save by the property of the husband or by their labours, shall belong to the woman. . . . But the young of beasts of draught, and all

Book III. Part II.

—in fructibus a viro retinendis neque dies dotis constitutae neque nuptiarum observabitur, sed quo primum dotale praedium constitutum est, i.e. tradita possessione.—Si ante nuptias fundus traditus est, ex die nuptiarum ad eundem diem sequentis anni computandus annus est.—l. 5 (Ulp.), l. 6 (Paul.), D. h. t. (=sol. matr. 24, 3).[1]

The husband, however, is allowed certain deductions from the dos in case the marriage is dissolved by divorce for which the wife is to blame, 'propter liberos'[a] and 'propter mores;' in all other cases only 'propter res donatas, amotas' and 'propter impensas.'[b]

[a] Not to be confounded with those named in Ulp. vi. 4, 5, *supr.*

[b] § 90.

Ulp. vi. 10, 12: Propter liberos retentio fit, si culpa mulieris aut patris, cuius in potestate est, divortium factum sit: tunc enim singulorum liberorum nomine sextae retinentur ex dote, non plures tamen quam tres.—Morum nomine graviorum quidem sexta retinetur, leviorum autem octava; graviores mores sunt adulteria tantum, leviores omnes reliqui.[2]

Inst. iv. 6, § 37: Propter retentionem quoque dotis repetitio minuitur: nam ob impensas in res

---

that has to be reckoned as fruits, shall belong to the husband. . . . But the fruits of the last year in which the marriage is dissolved must be assigned to both parties according to apportionment of time.

[1] —in respect of the fruits to be retained by the husband, regard will not be had either to the day when the dowry was constituted or to that of the wedding, but to that on which the dotal estate was constituted, that is, when there was delivery of possession.—If there was delivery of the estate before the wedding, the year is to be reckoned from the wedding-day to the same day in the following year.

[2] Retention is made on account of children if the divorce have occurred through the fault of the woman, or of her father, under whose power she is; for then a sixth part is retained from the dowry on behalf of the several children.—A sixth is retained on account of gross immorality, an eighth for that of a lighter sort. Adulteries alone constitute gross immorality: all other is the lighter.

dotales factas, marito retentio concessa est, quia ipso iure necessariis sumptibus dos minuitur.[1]

Ulp.: —quod diximus, ipso iure dotem impensis minui, non ad singula corpora, sed ad universitatem erit referendum.—D. 33, 4, 1, 4.[2]

Utiles non quidem minuunt ipso iure dotem, verumtamen habent exactionem.—Utilium nomine ita faciendam deductionem quidam dicunt, si voluntate mulieris factae sint; . . . quod summam habet aequitatis rationem.—D. 25, 1, l. 7, § 1 (Ulp.), l. 8 (Paul.).[3]

In respect of the time for restitution, a difference arises between fungibles and other objects.

Ulp. vi. 8: Dos si pondere numero mensura contineatur, annua bima trima die redditur, nisi ut praesens reddatur, convenerit; reliquae dotes statim redduntur.[4]

Crimes of the husband which have given occasion to the divorce are punished by a curtailment of the time allowed for restitution and by deduction from the fruits that have been taken.[a]

[a] § 106.

Ib. § 13: Mariti mores puniuntur in ea quidem dote, quae annua die reddi debet, ita ut propter maiores mores praesentem dotem reddat, propter minores senum mensium die; in

[1] The recovery of the dowry is also reduced by reason of retention; for a retention is allowed the husband for outlay incurred in respect of the dotal property, because a dowry is *ipso iure* reduced by necessary outlays.

[2] Our statement, that a dowry is reduced by expenses, must not be applied to single bodies, but to the aggregate.

[3] Useful outlays do not in fact by operation of law reduce the dowry, but nevertheless command recovery.—Some say that a rebate must be made on the score of useful outlays, if they were incurred by desire of the wife; . . . and this has the highest reason of equity.

[4] If the dowry consist of things that pass by weight, number or measure, it is restored by instalments at the end of one, two and three years, save as there has been an agreement for its summary restitution. Other dowries are restored forthwith.

Book III. Part II.

ea autem quae praesens reddi solet, tantum ex fructibus iubetur reddere, quantum in illa dote, quae triennio redditur, repraesentatio facit.[1]

A legal liability of the husband in respect of restitution of the dos was not recognised or further developed until the sixth century U.C.—with the upgrowth of capricious and frivolous divorces.[a] The action for demand of restitution of the dos was the intransmissible 'actio rei uxoriae (de dote),' an actio bonae fidei[b] with condemnatio in 'id quod facere potest.'[c] Simultaneous special stipulations as to Dowry (cautiones rei uxoriae) in respect of restitution were also usual, from which, after dissolution of the marriage, the 'actio ex stipulatu' belonged to the wife (or the stipulator) and her heirs; by which also, consequently, after development of the action of Dowry, the right of the wife to recovery was strengthened, and was released from the limitations attaching to it in the 'actio rei uxoriae.' For, apart from the transmissibility of the action, the stipulation contracted was alone decisive in respect of the conditions and mode of the restitution, so that the distinction to which we have first adverted was without importance, and the delay in respect of restitution (partly also the retentiones) was discontinued.

[a] § 47.

[b] 'quantum aequius melius.'

[c] § 139.

Paul. ad Sab.: Dotis causa perpetua est et cum voto eius, qui dat, ita contrahitur, ut semper apud maritum sit.—D. 23, 3, 1.[2]

Gell. iv. 3: Memoria traditum est, quingentis

---

[1] The immorality of a husband is punished, in the case of a dowry which must be repaid by annual instalments, by his having to restore it at once for the greater immorality, in six months for the lighter immorality. In the case of that which it is usual to restore summarily, he is ordered to restore as much out of the profits as represents full payment in respect of a dowry which is returnable in three years.

[2] The appointment of dowry is of a lasting character, and by the wish of the donor it is so constituted as always to be in the hands of the husband.

fere annis post Romam conditam nullas rei uxoriae neque actiones neque cautiones in urbe Roma aut in Latio fuisse : quia profecto nihil desiderabantur, nullis etiamtunc matrimoniis divertentibus. Servius quoque Sulpicius in libro quem composuit de dotibus tum primum cautiones rei uxoriae necessarias esse visas scripsit, cum Sp. Carvilius . . . divortium fecit.—Cf. xvii. 21, 44.[1]

Ulp. vi. 7 : Post divortium defuncta muliere heredi eius actio non aliter datur, quam si moram in dote mulieri reddenda maritus fecerit.[2]

Justinian [a] blended the rei uxoriae actio and the actio ex stipulatu in such manner that thenceforth invariably, even if the restitution of the dos was not specially stipulated for, only the latter action should obtain, but that it should have the character of a bonae fidei actio ; moreover, the wife by reason of her dotal claim acquired a highly privileged legal pledge-right in the husband's property.[b] The 'retentiones ex dote' are no longer permissible.[c] As regards the reversion of the dowry itself—unless there was an express stipulation that it should remain with the husband—it must henceforth be restored to the wife (or to her father, if she is under patria potestas), or in case she have died, to her heirs (or the dos profecticia to the parens) ; except when the marriage has been dissolved by divorce chargeable to the wife.

[a] C. 5, 13, l. un.

[b] § 101, ad fin. ; § 102.

[c] For the *impensae necessariae*, see Inst. iv. 6, 37, *supra*.

---

[1] It has been handed down by memory that for almost five hundred years after the foundation of Rome there were neither actions nor guaranties in respect of property of wives, in the city of Rome or in Latium; because at first there was no desire for them, as not even did divorces then exist. And Serv. Sulp., in the book he composed upon dowries, wrote that guaranties first appeared necessary when Sp. Carv. . . . made his divorce.

[2] If the woman die after the occurrence of a divorce, an action is not given to her heir unless the husband have incurred delay in restoring the dowry to her.

BOOK III. Part II.

Restitution ensues immediately in immovables, after a year in movables.

Inst. iv. 6, 29: Fuerat antea et rei uxoriae actio ex bonae fidei iudiciis: sed cum pleniorem esse ex stipulatu actionem invenientes omne ius, quod res uxoria ante habebat, cum multis divisionibus in ex stipulatu actionem, quae de dotibus exigendis proponitur, transtulimus, merito rei uxoriae actione sublata, ex stipulatu, quae pro ea introducta est, naturam bonae fidei iudicii tantum in exactione dotis meruit, ut bonae fidei sit. Sed et tacitam ei dedimus hypothecam: praeferri autem aliis creditoribus in hypothecis tunc censuimus, cum ipsa mulier de dote sua experiatur, cuius solius providentia hoc induximus.[1]

§ 148. GIFTS BETWEEN SPOUSES. *DONATIO PROPTER NUPTIAS. RES AMOTAE.*

Donations between spouses were from ancient times forbidden, as contravening the moral nature and object of marriage.[a]

[a] D. 39, 5, §§ 299, sqq.; 24, 1, 31, 4.—Cf. Scrutton, pp. 90-91.

Ulp.: Moribus apud nos receptum est, ne inter virum et uxorem donationes valerent; hoc autem receptum est, ne mutuo amore invicem spoliarentur donationibus non temperantes, sed profusa

---

[1] Formerly the action to enforce restitution of the wife's property also belonged to *bonae fidei* actions; but when, finding the action upon a stipulation more comprehensive, we transferred all rules which formerly availed as to a wife's property, with many distinctions, to the action upon a stipulation which is given for the recovery of the dowry, the action for the recovery of the wife's property being very properly abolished, the action upon a stipulation, introduced in its place, acquired the character of a *bon. fid.* action in respect of the recovery of a dowry, only provided that it be *bon. fid.* But we have also given her an implied mortgage; we have, however, decreed that she shall have precedence of other mortgagees only when she herself is suing for her dowry, as it is for her protection alone that we have made this provision.

erga se facilitate:—nec esset eis studium liberos potius educendi. Sextus Caecilius et illam causam adiiciebat, quia saepe futurum esset, ut discuterentur matrimonia, si non donaret is qui posset, atque ea ratione eventurum, ut venalicia essent matrimonia.—l. 1 (Ulp.), l. 2 (Paul.), D. h. t. (de don. int. v. et u. 24, 1).[1]

Ulp.: Haec ratio et oratione imperatoris nostri Antonini Augusti electa est; nam ita ait: 'Maiores nostri inter virum et uxorem donationes prohibuerunt, amorem honestum solum animis aestimantes, famae etiam coniunctorum consulentes, ne concordia pretio conciliari videretur, neve melior in paupertatem incideret, deterior ditior fieret.'—l. 3 pr. eod.[2]

Si corpus sit quod donatur, nec traditio quidquam valet, et si stipulanti promissum sit vel accepto latum, nihil valet: ipso enim iure, quae inter virum et uxorem donationis causa geruntur, nullius momenti sunt.—Ib. § 10.[3]

---

[1] It has been accepted amongst us by custom that gifts between husband and wife should not be valid. But this has been accepted lest they should reciprocally rob themselves through mutual affection, by their not observing moderation in gifts, but through lavish readiness towards one another;—and lest they should not rather have zeal for the training of their children. Sext. Caecil. added this further reason, that it would often happen that marriages would be dissolved, if he who could did not make a gift, and thus the result would be that marriages would be venal.

[2] This reason was also chosen in the oration of our august Emperor Antoninus; for he speaks thus: 'Our ancestors have forbidden gifts between husband and wife, appraising honourable affection by sentiment alone, and because they had a concern for the reputation of the married pair, lest their harmony should seem to be gained by payment, and lest the better spouse should fall into penury, the worse become more affluent.'

[3] If it should be something corporeal which is given, the delivery is of no avail, or if a promise or acquittance has been given to a person stipulating for it, it does not stand; for, by operation of law, transactions between husband and wife in view of a donation are of no force.

BOOK III. Part II.

[a] Cf. ibid. § 18, ad fin.

Ulp.: Hoc inter ceteros; inter virum vero et uxorem donationis causa venditio facta pretio viliore nullius momenti est.—D. 18, 1, 38.[a 1]

Id.: Hactenus revocatur donum ab eo eave cui donatum est, ut, si quidem exstet res, vindicetur, si consumpta sit, condicatur hactenus, quatenus locupletior quis eorum factus est.—l. 5, § 18, h. t.[2]

Excepted from the prohibitions are—

(1) donationes *mortis causa.*

Inter virum et uxorem mortis causa donationes receptae sunt,—quia in hoc tempus excurrit donationis eventus, quo vir et uxor esse desinunt.—l. 9, § 2 (Ulp.); l. 10 (Gai.) h. t.[3]

(2) donationes *divortii causa.*

(Iulianus) ait, si divortii causa facta sit donatio, valere; quae tamen sub ipso divortii tempore, non quae ex cogitatione quandoque futuri divortii fiant.—l. 11, § 11 (Ulp.); l. 12 (Paul.) eod.[4]

(3) donationes *honoris causa.*

Ulp. vii. 1: Hoc amplius principalibus constitutionibus concessum est mulieri in hoc donare viro suo, ut is ab imperatore lato clavo vel equo publico similive honore honoretur.[5]

---

[1] The same between all other persons; but a sale made between husband and wife at a lower price because of a donation is of no force.

[2] A gift is so far recovered from him or from her to whom it was given, that, if the thing in fact still exist, a claim is made by a real action; if it is consumed, a claim is made by a personal action in so far as one of them has been rendered richer.

[3] Gifts between husband and wife in view of death have been allowed,—because the effect of the gift extends to the period when they cease to be husband and wife.

[4] (Jul.) says, if a donation is made because of a divorce, it is valid; but only such an one as is made exactly at the time of the divorce, not one made with the thought of a divorce at some future time.

[5] Moreover, by imperial constitutions, a woman is allowed to make a gift to her husband to ground his promotion by the Emperor to the senatorial or equestrian rank, or like honour.

(4) Moreover, the prohibition was treated by the Roman jurists, in agreement with its intrinsic ground and object, not rigorously, but with a certain flexibility, especially by their very strict interpretation of the necessity of the 'pauperiorem et locupletiorem fieri ex donatione.'[a]

[a] D. 24, 1, 5, 8, etc.

Paul.: Si quas servi viri operas uxori praestiterint vel contra, magis placuit, nullam habendam earum rationem: et sane non amare et tamquam inter infestos ius prohibitae donationis tractandum est, sed ut inter coniunctos maximo affectu et solam inopiam timentes.—l. 28, § 2, D. h. t.[1]

Ulp.: Concessa donatio est sepulturae causa; . . . hoc autem ex eo venit, quod definiri solet eam demum donationem impediri solere, quae et donantem pauperiorem et accipientem faciat locupletiorem: porro hic non videtur fieri locupletior in ea re quam religioni dicavit; nec movit quemquam, quod emeret, nisi a marito accepisset: nam etsi pauperior ea fieret, nisi maritus dedisset, non tamen idcirco fit locupletior, quod non expendit.—l. 5, § 8 eod.[2]

Pomp.: Si vir uxori munus immodicum Kalendis Martiis aut natali die dedisset, donatio est: sed si (fecisset) impensas, quas faceret mulier,

---

[1] If the husband's slaves have rendered any service to the wife, or conversely, no account is to be taken thereof; and, indeed, the rule as to forbidden donation is not to be treated harshly, and as though it obtained between persons in a relation of hostility, but as between persons united by the highest affection, and fearing penury alone.

[2] A donation is allowed for burial; . . . but this comes of the fact that it is common to make a rule that only such a donation is generally forbidden which both makes the donor poorer and the donee richer: now the latter does not seem enriched by such a thing as he has devoted to religion; and no one is misled by a woman's purchasing a place, if she had not received it from her husband; for, although she would be poorer if the husband had not given the place, she is not enriched, by the fact that she has spent nothing.

BOOK III. Part II.

quo honestius se tueretur, contra est.—l. 31, § 8 eod.[1]

(5) And further, by a senatusconsultum (upon an oratio of Caracalla) of 206 A.D., every donation becomes valid[a] if the spouse that is donor dies before—that is, not after—the donee without revoking it.

[a] *Supra*, § D. 24, 1, 3 pr.

> Ulp.: Cum hic status esset donationum inter virum et uxorem, quem ante retulimus, imperator noster Antoninus Augustus ante excessum D. Severi patris sui oratione in senatu habita auctor fuit senatui censendi Fulvio Aemiliano et Nummio Albino consulibus, ut aliquid laxaret ex iuris rigore. § Oratio autem imperatoris nostri de confirmandis donationibus . . . pertinet . . . ad omnes donationes inter virum et uxorem factas. § Ait oratio: 'Fas esse eum quidem qui donavit poenitere; heredem vero eripere forsitan adversus voluntatem supremam eius, qui donaverit, durum et avarum esse.'—l. 32 pr., §§ 1, 2 eod.[2]

Donations between parties betrothed (donatio ante nuptias, sponsalicia largitas, arra sponsalicia)[b] were

[b] Cf. Jointure.

[1] If a husband should have given his wife an immoderate present on the first of March, or on her birthday, it is a donation; but if he should have incurred expenses that the wife would incur in order to maintain herself more honourably, the opposite is the case.

[2] Since the condition of donations between husband and wife was such as we have before described, our august Emperor Antoninus, before the decease of his late father, Severus, under the consuls, Fulv., Aemil., and Numm. Alb., by a speech delivered in the Senate, caused it to decree that some abatement should be made in the stringency of the law. § But the speech of our Emperor upon the confirmation of gifts relates . . . to all gifts made between husband and wife. § The speech says: 'It is right indeed for a donor to change his mind; but that an heir should snatch away the donation, perhaps against the last will of the donor, is hard and covetous.'

subject to the ordinary rules of donation. From the time of Constantine nuptial presents can, however, as a rule be recovered in the event of the marriage not taking place, except (1) when this is due to the fault of the donor himself; (2) when the present was made by the sponsus, 'osculo interveniente,' and the betrothal has been dissolved by the death of one party, in which case a moiety shall remain with the bride or her heirs.

Vat. fgm. 262: Sponsae res simpliciter donatae non insecutis nuptiis non repetuntur; set etsi adfinitatis contrahendae causa donationes factae sunt et nuntium sponsus culpa sua remiserit, aeque non repetuntur.—(Pap.)[1]

In the later imperial period the 'ante nuptias donatio' was developed into the special legal institution of a counter-dos (ἀντίφερνα), *i.e.*, into a counter-gift answering to dos, but remaining under the control of the husband, which gift he made to the wife for the object of marriage. After Justinian's enactment, which allowed it even during the coverture, it henceforth bears the name of '*propter nuptias* donatio.'

Inst. ii. 7, 3: Est et aliud genus inter vivos donationum, quod veteribus quidem prudentibus penitus erat incognitum, postea autem a iunioribus divis principibus introductum est, quod ante nuptias vocabatur et tacitam in se condicionem habebat, cum matrimonium fuerit insecutum: ideoque ante nuptias appellabatur, quod ante matrimonium efficiebatur et nunquam post nuptias celebratas talis donatio procedebat. Sed primus quidem D. Iustinus pater noster, cum augeri dotes et post nuptias fuerat permissum, si quid tale evenit, etiam ante nuptias donationem augere et

---

[1] Things given informally to a bride, if the marriage do not follow, are not recovered; but although the gifts were made in view of contracting relationship, and the bridegroom is to blame for having sent a letter of divorce, they are not recovered all the same.

Book III. Part II.

constante matrimonio permisit: sed nomen tamen inconveniens remanebat. . . . Sed nos . . . constituimus, ut tales donationes non augeantur tantum, sed et constante matrimonio initium accipiant, et non ante nuptias sed propter nuptias vocentur.[1]

Because of thefts committed by one spouse against the other—originally alone by occasion of divorce—the Praetorian edict gives to the party defrauded, after dissolution of the marriage, the actio rerum amotarum, in place of the condictio furtiva, here inadmissible,[a] which it resembled.[b]

[a] § 44.
[b] Cf. D. 25, 2, 24.

> Rerum amotarum iudicium singulare introductum est adversus eam, quae uxor fuit, quia non placuit cum ea furti agere posse: quibusdam existimantibus, ne quidem furtum eam facere ut Nerva, Cassio, quia societas vitae quodammodo dominam eam faceret; aliis, ut Sabino et Proculo, furtum quidem eam facere, sicuti filia patri faciat, sed furti non esse actionem constituto iure, in qua sententia et Iulianus rectissime est: —nam in honorem matrimonii turpis actio adversus uxorem negatur.—D. 25, 2, l. 1 (Paul.), l. 2 (Gai.).[2]

---

[1] There is also another class of gifts, *inter vivos*, which was altogether unknown to the old jurists, but was afterwards introduced by the later emperors, and used to be called *ante nuptias* (before the marriage), and embraced a condition that it should only hold good if the marriage was concluded. And so it was called *ante nuptias*, because it was effected before marriage, and such a gift was never made after its celebration. But as augmentation of the dowry had been allowed even after marriage, the late Emperor Justin, our father, was the first to permit by a constitution that, where anything of this kind happened, the gift *ante nuptias* might also be increased, even during the marriage; but the inappropriate name, nevertheless, was still kept up. But we . . . have enacted that such gifts may not only be increased, but may begin also during marriage, and shall be called, not gifts before marriage, but gifts on account of marriage.

[2] A special action has been introduced in respect of stolen things against her that has been a wife, because it was deemed

Ulp.: Res amotas dicimus non solum eas, quas mulier amovit cum divortii consilium iniisset, sed etiam eas, quas nupta amoverit, si cum discederet eas celaverit.—l. 17, § 1 eod.[1] Book III. Part II.

Gai.: Rerum amotarum actio condictio est.—l. 26 eod.[2]

Marcian.: Rerum amotarum iudicium sic habet locum, si divortii consilio res amotae fuerint et secutum divortium fuerit; sed si in matrimonio uxor marito res subtraxerit, licet cessat rerum amotarum actio, tamen ipsas res maritus condicere potest: nam iure gentium condici puto res ab his, qui non ex iusta causa possident.—l. 25 eod.[3]

LAW OF THE PROPERTY OF *PERSONAE ALIENO IURI SUBIECTAE.*

§ 149. THE OLDER LAW. *PECULIUM PROFECTICIUM AND CASTRENSE.*[a]

[a] Cf. 'Anct. Law,' pp. 135-146.

Filii familias—and the same holds absolutely of

---

not well to be able to proceed against her for theft, as some thought that she does not at all commit a theft, as Nerva and Cass., because community of life would make her in some measure owner; others, as Sab. and Proculus, that she does in fact commit a theft, as the daughter commits it on her father, but that, according to the law in force, the *actio furti* does not apply; and of this opinion is Julian, quite rightly; —for in honour of marriage an action against a wife involving infamy is withheld.

[1] By stolen things we speak of not only those which a woman has stolen, having conceived the resolution of a divorce, but those also which she stole when married, if she concealed them when she was divorced.

[2] The action for things stolen is a *condictio*.

[3] The action for stolen things indeed obtains when things shall be stolen with the purpose of divorce, and a divorce shall have followed; but if the wife shall have taken things away from the husband during the marriage, although the action for stolen things falls through, the husband can sue for them by a personal action; for I suppose that by the *i. g.* he can claim things by *condictio* from those who have not possession thereof upon a legal title.

Book III. Part II.

slaves—have no property of their own; what they acquire they acquire for the paterfam., who, however, as a rule, is not bound by them;[a] between them and the pat. fam., as well as between those subject to the same potestas, no legal transactions can be concluded and no obligation can exist.

[a] §§ 20, 50, 112.

> Gai. iv. 78: Nulla omnino inter me et eum, qui in potestate mea est, obligatio nasci potest.[1]
>
> Ulp.: Inter patrem et filium contrahi emptio non potest.—D. 18, 1, 2 pr.[2]

The principle of the incapacity for ownership of persons under domestic subjection was, however, curtailed increasingly—in particular more *de facto* than *de iure*—by the gradual development of the law of 'peculia.'

Peculium is separate property, *de facto* severed from the property of the paterfam. (or master), and intended for one subject to his potestas, which can be committed to the more or less free control of such.

> Ulp.: '**Peculium**' dictum est quasi pusilla pecunia sive patrimonium pusillum.—l. 5, § 3, D. h. t. (de pec. 15, 1).—Cels.: —Proculus ait . . . audisse se rusticos senes ita dicentes 'pecuniam sine peculio fragilem esse,' peculium appellantes quod praesidii causa seponeretur.—l. 79, § 1, D. de leg. III. 32.[3]
>
> Ulp.: Peculium autem Tubero quidem sic definit, ut Celsus refert: quod servus domini permissu separatum a rationibus dominicis habet

---

[1] No obligation whatever can arise between me and a person under my power.

[2] No sale can be contracted between a father and son.

[3] The word 'peculium' is, as it were, a small sum of money, or a small patrimony.—Proc. says . . . he has heard aged peasants speaking thus: 'Money without *peculium* is not to be depended on,' calling *peculium* that which was set aside for their support in need.

deducto inde, si quid domino debetur.—l. 5, § 4, D. h. t.[1]

Pomp.: Peculii est non id, cuius servus seorsum a domino rationem habuerit, sed quod dominus ipse separaverit, suam a servi rationem discernens. —Ex his apparet, non quid servus ignorante domino habuerit peculii esse, sed quid volente.—l. 4 pr., § 2 eod.[2]

Paul.: Non statim quod dominus voluit ex re sua peculii esse, peculium fecit, sed si tradidit aut, cum apud eum esset, pro tradito habuit: desiderat enim res naturalem dationem; contra autem simul atque noluit peculium servi, desinit peculium esse.—l. 8 eod.[3]

Ulp.: In peculio autem res esse possunt omnes et mobiles et soli: vicarios quoque in peculium potest habere et vicariorum peculium; hoc amplius et nomina debitorum.—l. 7, § 4 eod.[4]

Gai.: Peculii libera administratio specialiter

---

[1] Now, according to Cels., Tubero thus defines *peculium:* what a slave with the approval of his master has set apart from the master's accounts, after deduction of what he owes the master.

[2] No part of the *peculium* is that which the slave may have computed independently of his master, but what the master himself shall have set apart, distinguishing his own account from that of the slave.—From these considerations it appears that not what the slave has had unknown to the master, but what he has had with his consent, appertains to the *peculium.*

[3] That which a master has been willing from his own property to treat as part of separate property he has not straightway made *peculium,* but if he has delivered it, or has regarded it as if delivered in the hands of the slave; for the property requires natural transfer. But, on the other hand, as soon as he is unwilling that a slave should have *peculium,* it ceases to be *peculium.*

[4] But all things can be *peculium,* both movable and immovable; one can also have under-slaves as *peculium,* and the *peculium* of under-slaves; besides also capital sums in the hands of debtors.

BOOK III. Part II.

concedenda est.—Ib. § 1. —verum est quod Iuliano placet, etiamsi maxime quis administrationem peculii habeat concessam, donandi ius eum non habere.—D. 2, 14, 28, 2.[1]

The pater fam. always remains legally master of the peculium and of what is acquired 'ex re peculiari,' that is, subject of all proprietary rights contained in the peculium, so that the several active ingredients of the peculium legally belong to his property; he can reduce it at discretion, indeed entirely put an end to it; upon the death of the holder of the peculium, it reverts naturally to the pat. fam., and upon his death it forms part of his inheritance. But since it forms an independent whole separated from the rest of the family property, and capable of self-augmentation—intrinsically as well as by active acquisition by the holder of it—which whole is entirely and exclusively liable for the obligations of the subjecta persona to his creditors by the 'actio de peculio,'[a] it in fact appears as the holder's own property.

[a] § 112.

Peculium ex eo consistit, quod parsimonia sua quis paravit vel officio meruerit a quolibet sibi donari idque velut proprium patrimonium servum suum habere quis voluerit.—Flor. l. 39, D. h. t. —quasi patrimonium liberi hominis peculium servi intelligitur.—Paul. l. 47, § 6 eod.[2]

Ulp.: —qui cum servo contrahit, peculium eius veluti patrimonium intuetur.—l. 32 pr. eod.[3]

---

[1] The free control of the *peculium* must be granted in particular. —the opinion of Jul. is correct, that even if the quite free control of *peculium* has been granted, the slave has no right of donation.

[2] A *peculium* consists of that which a man has acquired by his thrift, or by render of services has earned as a present, from any one whatever, if somebody has desired that his slave should have it as his own patrimony. —the separate property of a slave is regarded like the patrimony of a freeman.

[3] —he that contracts with a slave has his separate property, his patrimony as it were, in view.

Id.: Quod servo debetur ab extraneis dominus recte petet; quod servus ipse debet, eo nomine in peculium et si quid inde in rem domini versum est, in dominum actio datur.—l. 41 eod.[a][1]

Book III. Part II.

So that even obligations—only natural, it is true—between the pater fam. and the person subject to power are rendered possible by the peculium.[b]

[a] Cf. ibid., *supra* § 35.

[b] § 114.

Id.: Sive autem ex contractu quid domino debeat sive ex rationum reliquiis, deducet dominus; sed et si ex delicto ei debeat, aeque deducetur.—l. 9, § 6 eod.[2]

Id.: Sed et id quod dominus sibi debet in peculium habebit, si forte in domini rationem impendit et dominus ei debitor manere voluit, aut si debitorem eius dominus convenit.—l. 7, § 6 eod.[3]

In the manumission of the slave, or emancipation of the filius fam., the peculium that is not taken back is regarded as presented to him.

Paul.: Si Sticho peculium, cum manumitteretur, ademptum non est, videtur concessum: debitores autem convenire, nisi mandatis sibi actionibus, non potest.—l. 53 eod.[4]

Besides this peculium profecticium s. concessum,

---

[1] A master will be right in claiming from third parties what is owing to his slave; as to the slave's own debt, an action is given against the master in that behalf for the *peculium*, and for what may have therefrom accrued to the master's property.

[2] Now, whether aught be due to a master upon a contract or upon balances of accounts, the master will deduct it; but even if it is due to him upon a delict, it will be deducted all the same.

[3] But that also which the master owes to him he will possess as *peculium*, if so be the debt accrues to the master's benefit, and the master has desired to remain his debtor, or if the master has sued his debtor.

[4] If the *peculium* has not been taken from Stichus upon his enfranchisement, it is considered to have been allowed to him; but he cannot sue debtors save by actions which have been made over to him.

Book III. Part II.

there was introduced at the beginning of the imperial times the *castrense* peculium.

Recognition was given to the legal rule, that the acquisitions of the filius fam. in his character of a miles, including what was given to him upon entering into military service, represented also in Law his own property, capable of independent development, and in this respect he was to be treated as a paterfamilias.

Mac.: Castrense peculium est, quod a parentibus vel cognatis in militia agenti donatum est, vel quod ipse filius familias in militia adquisiit, quod, nisi militaret, adquisiturus non fuisset.—l. 11, D. h. t. (de castr. pec. 49, 17).[1]

Imp. Alex.: Peculio castrensi cedunt res mobiles, quae eunti in militiam a patre vel a matre aliisve propinquis vel amicis donatae sunt, item quae in castris per occasionem militiae quaeruntur; in quibus sunt etiam hereditates eorum, qui non alias noti esse potuerunt, nisi per militiae occasionem, etiamsi res immobiles in his erunt.—empta ex castrensi peculio praedia eius condicionis efficiantur.—C. 12, 36 (37), 1.[2]

Pap.: Servus peculii, quod ad filium spectat, si stipuletur aut per traditionem accipiat, . . . res ad filium pertinebit.—l. 15, § 3, D. h. t.[3]

---

[1] Separate property acquired in the field is what has been given by parents or relations to one spending his life in military service, or what the *fil. fam.* has acquired in military service, which he would not have acquired had he not been a soldier.

[2] To military *peculium* belong movables which have been presented to a *fil. fam.* entering upon military service, by his father, or mother, or by other relations or friends, likewise those that are acquired in the field by reason of military service; amongst which also are the inheritances of those who could not have been famous save by reason of military service, even if immovables shall form part of these.—Lands purchased with military *peculium* are rendered of such character.

[3] If a slave appertaining to the *peculium* of the son stipulates for, or by delivery receives, a thing, . . . it will belong to the son.

Tryph.: Si servus peculii castrensis a quocumque sit heres scriptus, . . . (hereditas) fiet bonorum castrensis peculii.—l. 19, § 1 eod.[1]

Pap.: Si stipulanti filio spondeat (pater), si quidem ex causa peculii castrensis, tenebit stipulatio ; ceterum ex qualibet alia causa non tenebit.—Si pater a filio stipulatur, eadem distinctio servabitur.—l. 15, §§ 1, 2 eod.[2]

Ulp.: In filiofamilias nihil dignitas facit, quominus SC. Macedonianum locum habeat, . . . nisi forte castrense peculium habeat : tunc enim SCtum cessabit—usque ad quantitatem castrensis peculii : cum **filiifamilias in castrensi peculio vice patrumfamiliarum** fungantur.—D. 14, 6, l. 1, § 3, l. 2.[3]

Maec.: Sed nec cogendus est pater propter aes alienum, quod filius peculii nomine, quod in castris adquisiit, fecisse dicetur, de peculio actionem pati.—l. 18, § 5, h. t.[4]

If, however, the fil. fam. died without having made a testamentary disposition of such property, as was generally allowed him from the time of Hadrian,[a] this property also fell to the pater fam. 'pristino, i.e. peculii iure' (that is, as an ordinary peculium).

[a] § 156.

---

[1] But if a slave appertaining to military *peculium* has been instituted heir by any one whomsoever, . . . (the inheritance) will become part of the effects of the military *peculium*.

[2] If the son by stipulation take a promise (from the father), the stipulation will hold good, should it relate to military *peculium ;* but in every other relation it will not stand.—If a father take a stipulation from a son, the same distinction will be observed.

[3] In respect of a *fil. fam.*, no dignity hinders the application of the *SC. Macedon.* . . . unless he possesses military *peculium ;* for then the *SCtum* will fall through—as far as the amount of military *peculium* extends, since *filii fam.* in respect of military *peculium* discharge the functions of *patres fam.*

[4] But neither is a father required to put up with an action *de peculio* in respect of a debt which his son is alleged to have incurred in connection with *peculium* that he has acquired in the field.

3 C 2

Inst. ii. 12 pr.: —militibus, qui in potestate parentum sunt, . . . de eo quod in castris adquisierint permissum est ex constitutionibus principum testamentum facere: quod quidem initio tantum militantibus datum est tam ex auctoritate D. Augusti quam Nervae nec non optimi imperatoris Traiani, postea vero subscriptione D. Hadriani etiam dimissis militia, i.e. veteranis, concessum est.[1]

Ulp.: Si filiusfamilias miles decesserit, si quidem intestatus, bona eius non quasi hereditas, sed quasi peculium patri deferuntur: si autem testamento facto, hic pro hereditate habetur castrense peculium.—l. 2, D. de castr. pec.[2]

§ 150. The Later Law: *Peculium quasi Castrense*; *Bona Adventicia*.

From the time of Constantine a proprietary independence was gradually acquired by filii fam., to an ever wider extent.

Acquisitions by public office (state, court or ecclesiastical service) were placed on the same footing as military acquisitions: Peculium *quasi castrense*.

Inst. ii. 11, § ult.: Sciendum tamen est, quod ad exemplum castrensis peculii tam anteriores leges quam principales constitutiones quibusdam quasi castrensia dederunt peculia, atque eorum

[1] Soldiers that are under parental power . . . have been allowed by imperial constitutions to make a testament concerning such property as they have acquired in the field; and this right was at the outset granted by the late Emperors Augustus and Nerva and the excellent Emperor Trajan only to those engaged in the service, but afterwards it was allowed by a *subscriptio* of the late Emperor Hadrian to soldiers discharged from the service, *i.e.*, to veterans.

[2] If a *fil. fam.* has died as a soldier, and that intestate, his estate devolves upon his father not as inheritance, but as *peculium*; but if a testament has been made, in this case the military *peculium* is treated as an inheritance.

quibusdam permissum erat etiam in potestate degentibus testari: quod nostra constitutio latius extendens permisit omnibus in his tantummodo peculiis testari.[1]

Moreover, a maternal inheritance (bona materna) was in general recognised in every acquisition proceeding from the maternal side (bona materni generis), and finally, inheritance by marriage (lucra nuptialia), as the peculiar property of the fil. fam., in which the pat. fam. should possess only the usufruct for life: bona *adventicia.*[a] In certain cases the father's usufruct even was not allowed, as when the acquisition, especially of an inheritance, was made against the declared will of the pater fam., or if the donor had by stipulation taken away the right of the latter to the user: bona adventicia irregularia.

[a] Cf. Curtesy (Scrutton, pp. 98-99).

Finally, Justinian provided that every non-military acquisition of filii fam., which they had not made from the property of the pater, should be on the same footing as bona materna; so that there was thenceforth—

(1) fully free property of the child (bona castrensia vel quasi);

(2) bona adventicia of the same, and besides,

(3) as in the older Law, still merely one peculium, that is, 'a patre profectum.'

Inst. ii. 9, § 1: Sancitum etenim a nobis est, ut si quid ex re patris ei obveniat, hoc secundum antiquam observationem totum parenti adquirat: . . . quod autem ex alia causa sibi filiusfamilias adquisivit, huius usumfructum quidem patri ad-

[1] We must, however, note that, according to the analogy of military *peculium*, both ancient statutes and imperial constitutions have conferred quasi-military *peculia* on certain persons; and to some of such persons leave has been given to make a testament, even while under paternal power, and our constitution, by wider development of this, has allowed all to make a testament in respect alone of this *peculium*.

Book III. Part II.

quirat, dominium autem apud eum remaneat, ne quod ei suis laboribus vel prospera fortuna accessit, hoc in alium perveniens luctuosum ei procedat.[1]

INFLUENCE OF GUARDIANSHIP UPON PROPERTY.

[a] For English Law, see Steph. ii. 316-7.

§ 151. The Discharge of Guardianship.[a]

Upon the guardian devolves the administration of the property of the ward, representation of him, and concurrence in his legal transactions.[b]

[b] In respect of *tutela mulierum*, see Ulp. xi. 25, 27.

As regards the administration of the property (administratio, gestio) and the whole representation, by Private Law, of pupils, the tutor

[c] D. 26, 1, 1 pr.

(1) in the older Law[c] assumes an entirely unfettered position: he can alienate property of the pupil, has to conclude legal transactions,[d] and to conduct law-suits, but his administration must be to the advantage of the ward under his protection, and he must in general guard his interest in all particulars, and in this is responsible for culpa *in concreto.*[e]

[d] § 112.

[e] § 108.

Paul.: Tutor qui tutelam gerit, quantum ad providentiam pupillarem, domini loco haberi debet.—l. 27, D. h. t. (de adm. tut. 26, 7).[2]

Id.: Tutor ad utilitatem pupilli et novare et rem in iudicium deducere potest: donationes autem ab eo factae pupillo non nocent.—l. 22 eod.[3]

---

[1] For we have ordained that whatever devolves upon him by virtue of his father's property shall, according to the ancient practice, be wholly acquired by him for the father; . . . but whatever the *fil. fam.* has gained for himself upon another title, of this the father shall in fact have the usufruct, whilst the ownership shall remain with him, that what has come into his possession through his own effort or success may not pass into another's hands and cause him trouble.

[2] A guardian that conducts the guardianship must be regarded as owner in so far as concerns solicitude for the ward.

[3] A guardian can for the benefit of the ward undertake nova-

Marc.: Tutoris praecipuum est officium, ne indefensum pupillum relinquat.—l. 30 eod.[1]

Ulp.: Generaliter quotienscumque non fit nomine pupilli quod quivis paterfamilias idoneus facit, non videtur defendi: sive igitur solutionem sive iudicium sive stipulationem detrectat, defendi non videtur.—l. 10 eod.[2]

Callistr.: A tutoribus et curatoribus pupillorum eadem diligentia exigenda est circa administrationem rerum pupillarium, quam paterfamilias rebus suis ex bona fide praebere debet.—l. 33 pr. eod.[3]

The administrative authority of the guardian was first limited by the Oratio D. Severi (195 A.D.), which rendered necessary the issue of a magisterial decree, after preliminary causae cognitio, for alienations of praedia rustica and suburbana. In the succeeding period this prohibition of alienation was transferred also to other property in wardship, to the widest extent, and the independent administration of guardians was thereby circumscribed within very narrow limits.

Ulp.: Imperatoris Severi oratione prohibiti sunt tutores et curatores praedia rustica vel suburbana distrahere. § Quae oratio in senatu recitata est Tertullo et Clemente consulibus Idibus Iuniis, et sunt verba eius huiusmodi: § 'Praeterea, patres conscripti, interdicam tu-

---

tion and carry a cause before the *iudex;* but donations made by him do not prejudice the ward.

1 The main duty of the guardian is, not to leave the ward unprotected.

2 A ward seems in general to be without a protector whenever that is not done in the name of the ward which is done by every capable head of a household; and whether it is the guardian refuses to make a payment, or to institute proceedings, or to give a stipulative undertaking, the ward appears to be without protection.

3 From tutors and curators of wards the same carefulness is required in respect of the management of the ward's affairs as the head of a household ought in good faith to exhibit in his own affairs.

Book III. Part II.

toribus et curatoribus, ne praedia rustica vel suburbana distrahant, nisi ut id fieret, parentes testamento vel codicillis caverint: quodsi forte aes alienum tantum erit, ut ex rebus ceteris non possit exsolvi, tunc praetor urbanus vir clarissimus adeatur, qui pro sua religione aestimet, quae possint alienari obligarive debeant, manente pupillo actione, si postea potuerit probari obreptum esse praetori; si communis res erit et socius ad divisionem provocet, aut si creditor, qui pignori agrum a parente pupilli acceperit, ius exsequetur, nihil novandum censeo.'—D. 27, 9, l. 1 pr., §§ 1, 2.[1]

Imp. Constant.: Iam venditio tutoris nulla sit sine interpositione decreti, exceptis his dumtaxat vestibus, quae detritae usu aut corruptae servando servari non potuerint. Animalia quoque supervacua minorum quin veneant, non vetamus. —C. 5, 37, 22, 6.[2]

---

[a] Or 'agricultural.'

[b] Or 'horticultural.'

[1] By a speech of the Emp. Severus, tutors and curators were forbidden to dispose of rural[a] or suburban[b] estates. § And this speech was read in the senate under the consuls Tertullus and Clemens on the 13th June, and the wording of it is as follows: 'Moreover, conscript fathers, I shall prohibit tutors and curators from disposing of rural or suburban estates, unless the parents should have provided for that being done in the testament or in codicils. But if the debts shall chance to be so great that they cannot be paid out of the rest of the property, then resort shall be had to the Urban Praetor, a most honourable personage, that he may conscientiously determine what lands can be sold or should be mortgaged, so that an action remain for the ward, should he afterwards be able to prove that the Praetor's decree has been obtained covertly. If the thing shall be owned in common, and the joint-owner shall press for partition, or if a creditor who shall have received land in pledge from the ward's father shall enforce his right, I am of opinion that no change should be made (in the pre-existing right).'

[2] There shall now be no sale on the part of a tutor without the issue of a decree, with the exception alone of such garments as, worn out or spoilt by use, cannot be preserved by keeping. And we do not forbid the sale of superfluous cattle belonging to minors.

The 'pupillus infantia maior' can himself undertake legal transactions,[a] and even judicial acts, wherever possible, but the 'auctoritatis interpositio,' that is, the personal co-operation of the tutor which supplements the defective legal capacity of the pupil, is necessary for their operation, if the property of the pupil be directly or indirectly diminished by such transaction.[b]

[a] D. 46, 6, 6, and 9.

[b] Cf. § 60; D. 19, 1, 13, 29; § 114. Gai. ii 82; D. 12, 1, 19, 1; § 139.

Ulp.: Licentia (tutoribus) erit, utrum malint ipsi suscipere iudicium, an pupillum exhibere, ut ipsis auctoribus iudicium suscipiatur, ita tamen ut pro his, qui fari non possunt vel absint, ipsi tutores iudicium suscipiant: pro his autem, qui supra septimum annum aetatis sunt et praesto fuerint, auctoritatem praestent.—l. 1, § 2, D. h. t.[1]

Gai.: Obligari ex omni contractu sine tutoris auctoritate non potest: adquirere autem sibi stipulando et per traditionem accipiendo etiam sine tutoris auctoritate potest; sed credendo sibi obligare non potest, quia sine tutoris auctoritate nihil alienare potest.—l. 9 pr., D. de auct. tut. 26, 8.[2]

Paul.: Furiosus et pupillus, ubi ex re actio venit, obligantur etiam sine curatore vel tutoris auctoritate, veluti si communem fundum habeo cum his et aliquid in eum impendero vel damnum in eo pupillus dederit: nam iudicio communi dividundo obligabuntur.—D. 44, 7, 46.[3]

---

[1] It is left to the discretion of the guardians, whether they will themselves rather undertake an action or produce the ward, that he may with their authorisation undertake the action, but so that for those who cannot yet speak, or are absent, the guardians themselves undertake the action; they can extend their sanction, however, on behalf of those who have passed their seventh year of age, and are present.

[2] A ward cannot be made liable upon any contract without the sanction of the guardian; but he can acquire for himself by stipulation and acceptance through delivery even without the tutor's sanction; but he can contract no obligation for himself by loan, because he can dispose of nothing without the tutor's sanction.

[3] Where an action arises from the thing, a madman and

BOOK III. Part II.

Ulp.: Si tutor mutuam pecuniam pupillo dederit, . . . naturaliter obligabitur in quantum locupletior factus est: nam in pupillum cuivis actionem in quantum locupletior factus est dandam D. Pius rescripsit.—l. 5 pr., D. de auct. tut.[1]

The tutoris auctoritas must follow the conclusion of the legal transaction itself, and unconditionally.

Gai.: Tutor statim in ipso negotio praesens debet auctor fieri, post tempus vero aut per epistulam interposita eius auctoritas nihil agit.—l. 9, § 5 eod.[2]

Ulp.: Etsi condicionalis contractus cum pupillo fiat, tutor debet pure auctor fieri.—l. 8 eod.[3]

In an affair of his own (in rem suam) the tutor can never give his auctoritas.[a]

[a] Gai. i. 184.

Id.: Pupillus obligari tutori eo auctore non potest.—l. 5 pr. eod.[4]

Id.: Quamquam regula sit iuris civilis in rem suam auctorem tutorem fieri non posse, tamen potest tutor proprii sui debitoris hereditatem adeunti pupillo auctoritatem accommodare, quamvis per hoc debitor eius efficiatur: prima enim ratio auctoritatis ea est, ut heres fiat, per

---

ward become liable even without the curator or sanction of the tutor; for example, if I possess land in common with them, and shall have spent something upon it, or the ward has caused some damage on it; for they will be liable by the action for the partition of joint property.

[1] If a guardian shall have made an advance to a ward . . . he will incur a natural obligation for so much as he has been enriched; for the late Emp. Pius by rescript stated that an action must be given to any one soever against a pupil for so much as he has been enriched.

[2] The guardian must at once give his authorisation at the moment of the transaction itself, whilst this authorisation interposed after the time or by letter is of no effect.

[3] Although a conditional contract be made with a pupil, the guardian must give his authorisation unconditionally.

[4] A ward cannot become liable to a guardian by his authorisation.

consequentias contingit, ut debitum subeat.—l. 1 pr. eod.[1]

Transactions entered into by minors are, as a rule, operative even without the co-operation of the curator, but for certain cases 'consensus,' *i.e.*, informal—even supplementary—confirmation thereof is requisite.[a]

[a] § 60, ad fin. § 67, ad fin.

If there be several tutors, sometimes the auctoritas of all is requisite; at other times that of a single tutor suffices for the validity of acts in the Law.

> Ulp. xi. 26: Si plures sint tutores, omnes in omni re debent auctoritatem accommodare, praeter eos qui testamento dati sunt: nam ex his vel unius auctoritas sufficit.[2]

If, however, the administration has been committed to one alone of them (tutor gerens), the rest (tutores honorarii) have merely to take an oversight of it, and the auctoritas of the former alone is operative.

> Inst. 1, 24, 1: Sed et si ex testamento vel inquisitione duo pluresve dati fuerint, potest unus offerre satis de indemnitate pupilli vel adulescentis et contutori vel concuratori praeferri, ut solus administret. . . . Quodsi nemo eorum satis offerat, si quidem adscriptum fuerit a testatore quis gerat, ille gerere debet: quodsi non fuerit adscriptum, quem maior pars elegerit, ipse gerere debet, ut edicto praetoris cavetur; sin autem ipsi tutores dissenserint circa eligendum eum vel eos, qui gerere debent, praetor partes suas interponere debet.[3]

---

[1] Although there is a rule of civil law that no guardian can give his sanction (to his ward) for his own business, yet he can give his sanction to the ward upon taking up the inheritance of his own debtor, although the ward become his debtor thereby; for the first reason of the sanction is that the ward become heir, and in consequence thereof it happens that he incurs the debt.

[2] If there be several guardians, they must all give their sanction in every matter, unless they are testamentary tutors, for of these the authority of one is enough.

[3] But if two or more shall have been nominated by testament

Ulp.: Ceteri igitur tutores non administrabunt, sed erunt hi quos vulgo honorarios appellamus; nec quisquam putet ad hos periculum nullum redundare; . . . dati sunt enim quasi observatores eius [a] et custodes, imputabiturque eis quandoque, cur, si male eum conversari videbant, suspectum eum non fecerunt.—l. 3, § 2, D. h. t.[1]

[a] Sc. qui gerit.

Pomp.: Etsi pluribus datis tutoribus unius auctoritas sufficiat, tamen si tutor auctoretur, cui administratio tutelae concessa non est, id ratum a praetore haberi non debet.—l. 4, D. de auct. tut.[2]

The administration, finally, can be also divided between the several tutors according to special departments, or according to localities; particularly in the case of an extensive tutelary property and management on a large scale; and each tutor then is accounted 'honorarius' in respect of the limits of management by the other.

Ulp.: Item si dividi inter se tutelam velint tutores, audiendi sunt, ut distribuatur inter eos

---

or after inquiry, any one of them can offer security for the indemnification of the ward or youth, and be preferred to his co-tutor or co-curator, so that he may administer alone. . . . But if none of them offer security, if it has been specified by the testator who is to act, that one must act; but if no specific appointment has been made, he must act whom the majority elect, as is provided by the Praetor's Edict. But if the guardians themselves shall have disagreed about the election of the one or those who ought to act, the Praetor must interfere.

[1] The remaining guardians, accordingly, will not administer, but there will be so-called honorary guardians; and let not any one suppose that no risk extends to them; . . . for they were appointed as though to have an oversight and watch over him, and it will at the proper time be fixed upon them to account for their not having treated him with suspicion, if they observed him engaged in malpractices.

[2] Although when several guardians have been appointed the sanction of one is sufficient, yet an act must not be treated by the Praetor as valid if the guardian sanction it from whom the administration of the guardianship has been withheld.

administratio—vel in partes vel in regiones: et si ita fuerit divisa, unusquisque exceptione summovebitur pro ea parte vel regione, quam non administrat.—l. 3, § 9, l. 4, D. h. t.[1]

§ 152. Obligations arising from the Discharge of Guardianship.

From the conduct of the guardian's business, obligations arise between him and the ward which are grounded upon a quasi-contractual relation.[a] [a] § 135.

Gai.: Tutelae quoque iudicio qui tenentur, non proprie ex contractu obligati intelliguntur (nullum enim negotium inter tutorem et pupillum contrahitur): sed quia sane non ex maleficio tenentur, quasi ex contractu teneri videntur. Et hoc autem casu mutuae sunt actiones: non tantum enim pupillus cum tutore, sed et contra tutor cum pupillo habet actionem, si vel impenderit aliquid in rem pupilli, vel pro eo fuerit obligatus, aut rem suam creditori eius obligaverit. —D. 44, 7, 5, 1.[2]

After the termination of the guardianship, the 'actio tutelae,' involving infamy, lies against the tutor for render of accounts, handing over the property adminis-

---

[1] Likewise if the guardians desire that the guardianship be divided amongst them, they must be attended to, that the administration may be distributed amongst them—either in parts, or according to localities; and if the division have been so made, every one will be excluded from a plea in respect of such part or such locality as he does not administer.

[2] Those too who are liable by the action of guardianship are not properly regarded as liable upon a contract (for no transaction is contracted between a guardian and ward); but inasmuch as they are certainly not liable upon a wrongful act, they are considered to be liable upon a quasi-contract. Now in this case also the actions are reciprocal; for not only has the ward an action against the guardian, but, on the other hand, the guardian has one against the ward, if he has either spent anything upon the ward's property, or has become liable for him, or has pledged his own property to his creditor.

tered, and compensation for loss incurred; whilst he himself by the 'actio tutelae contraria' can proceed against the pupil for his own indemnity.

> Paul.: Nisi finita tutela sit, tutelae agi non potest.—(l. 4 pr., D. de tutelae 27, 3.) Ulp.: Finito autem officio hanc[a] actionem competere dicemus tutori; ceterum quamdiu durat, nondum competit.—(D. 27, 4, 1, 3.)[1]

[a] Sc. contrariam tutelae.

The tutor is liable in respect of embezzlements for double the amount, by the 'actio de rationibus distrahendis,' which was derived from the Twelve Tables.

> Paul.: Actione de rationibus distrahendis nemo tenetur, nisi qui in tutela gerenda rem ex bonis pupilli abstulerit.—Haec actio licet in duplum sit, in simplo rei persecutionem continet, non tota dupli poena est.—l. 2 pr., § 2, D. de tutelae.[2]

A utilis actio negotiorum gestorum directa and contraria obtains between the curator and the ward.

> Cum furiosi curatore negotiorum gestorum actio est, quae competit etiam dum negotia gerit.—l. 4, § 3 eod.[3]

Under secondary liability to the pupil are—

(1) the guardian's sureties.[b]

[b] § 64, ad fin.

> Cum 'rem salvam fore' pupillo cavetur, committitur stipulatio, si, quod ex tutela dari fieri oportet, non praestetur—agi ex ea (stipulatione)

1 Only when the guardianship has come to an end can proceedings be taken in respect of the guardianship.—But we shall say that this action lies for the guardian at the end of his office.

2 No one is liable to the action *de rationibus distrahendis* save him that during the conduct of the guardianship shall have made away with some of the ward's goods. Although this action lies for double the amount, yet it embraces recovery of the simple amount of the thing; the penalty does not consist entirely of the double.

3 Against the curator of a madman there is the action of management of business, which also lies whilst he is conducting the business.

tunc potest, cum et tutelae potest.—D. 46, 6, l. 11 (Ner.), l. 1 (Paul.).[1]

(2) His 'adfirmatores' and 'nominatores.'

Ulp.: Fideiussores a tutoribus nominati si praesentes fuerunt et non contradixerunt et nomina sua referri in acta publica passi sunt, aequum est perinde teneri, ac si iure legitimo stipulatio interposita fuisset; eadem causa videtur adfirmatorum, qui scilicet, cum idoneos esse tutores adfirmaverint, fideiussorum vicem sustinent.—D. 27, 7, 4, 3.[2]

(3) The magistratus acting as official superintendent guardian.

Inst. 1, 24, 2: Sciendum autem est non solum tutores vel curatores pupillis et adultis ceterisque personis ex administratione teneri, sed etiam in eos, qui satisdationes accipiunt, subsidiariam actionem esse, quae ultimum eis praesidium possit adferre. Subsidiaria autem actio datur in eos, qui vel omnino a tutoribus vel curatoribus satisdari non curaverint, aut non idonee passi essent caveri.[3]

---

[1] If security be given to the ward that his property shall remain intact, the stipulation takes effect if there is no performance of what ought to be given or done by virtue of the guardianship—proceedings can be taken upon that (stipulation) when they can be taken in respect of the guardianship also.

[2] It is fair that sureties nominated by guardians, if they have been present, and have not declined, and have allowed their names to be inserted on the public records, should be liable just as if a stipulation had intervened according to legal rule. The same relation obtains in respect of *adfirmatores,* who of course, when they have given assurance of the fitness of guardians, represent sureties.

[3] We must, however, note that not only are the tutors or curators liable to wards and youths and other persons for their administration, but an auxiliary action, which can serve as a final means of protection to them, lies also against those who accept the security. Now the auxiliary action is granted against such as either have wholly neglected to take security from the tutors or curators, or have allowed insufficient security to be given.

[a] 'Anct. Law,' ch. vi.; Markby, ch. xviii.

PART III.—LAW OF INHERITANCE.[a]

CHAPTER I.

GENERAL DOCTRINES.

§ 153. NATURE AND SUBJECT-MATTER OF THE LAW OF INHERITANCE.

BOOK III. Part III.

THE Law of INHERITANCE in the wider sense is the sum of legal rules as to the succession of living persons to the property, or heritage, left by a deceased person. If there be only single portions of property upon which the survivor enters, Singular Succession occurs. Such a singular succession can also come into account in the Law of Inheritance in respect of the doctrine of legacies; but in it lies not the essence of inheritance, which is the rather presupposed by it, and in relation to it is seen as something subordinate and immaterial. According to Roman Law, Inheritance or Succession is always UNIVERSAL Succession,[b] that is, the succession of one or several survivors to the property of the deceased as a whole, by which the successor takes the place of the previous subject of ownership, and becomes the one who sustains the control of the property (familia defuncti); in other words, assumes the personality of the deceased under Property Law, and by representation continues it. The totality of the legal precepts that avail as to this succession, as well as the subjective 'ius succedendi,' is the Law of Inheritance in the wider sense, *HEREDITAS*, which word likewise designates the heritage, whilst the successor is called 'heres' (heir).

[b] D. 37, 1, 3 pr., § 17.

Iul.: Hereditas nihil aliud est, quam successio

in universum ius quod defunctus habuerit.—l. 62, D. de R. J. 50, 17.[1]

Ulp.: Heredem eiusdem potestatis iurisque esse, cuius fuit defunctus, constat.—l. 59 eod.[2]

Pap.: Hereditas etiam sine ullo corpore iuris intellectum habet.—D. 5, 3, 50 pr.[3]

Cic. de legib. ii. 48: Nulla est persona, quae ad vicem eius, qui e vita migravit, propius accedat.[a][4]

[a] Sc. quam heres.

The succession is as a rule perfected first by the acquisition of the inheritance (*adquisitio* hereditatis); but the acquisition always supposes the calling to, or devolution of, the inheritance (*delatio* hereditatis), that is, a legal right to assume it.

Ter. Clem.: Delata hereditas intelligitur, quam quis possit adeundo consequi.—l. 151, D. de V. S. 50, 16.[5]

'Delatio' and acquisition of the inheritance are exceptionally concurrent in the case of 'heredes necessarii.'[b]

[b] See § 171, ad init.

In Roman Law there are only two grounds of delatio, viz., Testament and *Law*;[c] and accordingly, a distinction is made between TESTAMENTARY succession (successio heres ex testamento s. secundum tabulas sc. testamenti) and INTESTATE or Legal succession (successio intestati s. ab intestato, legitima hereditas, legitimus heres).

[c] Not Contract: cf. D. 45, 1, 61.

Gai. ii. § 99: (Hereditatum) duplex condicio

---

[1] Inheritance is nothing else than the succession to the whole of the rights which a deceased person shall have possessed.

[2] It is well known that the heir has the same power and the same rights which the deceased possessed.

[3] Hereditas constitutes a legal conception even without any material thing.

[4] There is no person that more nearly (that is, than the heir) approaches representation of him that has departed this life.

[5] An inheritance is regarded as offered which a man can acquire by entry.

Book III. Part III.

> est: nam vel ex testamento, vel ab intestato ad nos pertinent.[1]

The latter, that is, the appointment to the inheritance of certain persons closely related to the deceased, in a certain order of succession, by the law itself, only obtains in the absence of a testament.

> Ulp.: Quamdiu potest ex testamento adiri hereditas, ab intestato non defertur.—D. 29, 2, 39.[2]

Both grounds of delatio simply exclude each other according to Roman civil Law, so that, if the testator has nominated an heir only for the one part of his heritage, the legal heirs are nevertheless not collateral to the latter, or called to the other part, but the former remains sole heir. The ground for this lies, on the one hand, in the principle of the Totality of the inheritance,—because he that nominates his heir by a testament simply makes a disposition of his property as a WHOLE and of the continuance of his absolute control under Property Law— ; on the other hand, in the subsidiary character of the Legal succession, which cannot obtain so long as the testament is effectual.[a]

[a] In t. 2, 18, 6.

> Pomp.: Ius nostrum non patitur eundem in paganis et testato et intestato decessisse, earumque rerum naturaliter inter se pugna est: 'testatus' et 'intestatus.'—l. 7, D. de R. J.[3]

> Cic. de inv. ii. 21, 63: Unius pecuniae plures dissimilibus de causis heredes esse non possunt, nec umquam factum est, ut eiusdem pecuniae alius testamento alius lege heres esset.[4]

---

[1] Inheritances have a twofold character; for they belong to us either upon the ground of a testament, or by an intestacy.

[2] As long as entry can be made upon an inheritance, there is no devolution of it by intestacy.

[3] Our law does not admit amongst civilians of the same person having died both with a testament and intestate, and there is a natural repugnancy between those two relations: 'testate' and 'intestate.'

[4] Several cannot be heirs to one sum of money for different reasons; nor has it ever been effected that one person was heir by a testament, another heir by law to the same sum of money.

Ulp.: Miles pro parte testatus potest decedere, pro parte intestatus.—D. 29, 1, 6.[1]

In certain cases a Legal succession obtains even contrary to the testament: 'successio contra tabulas,' the law of NECESSARY succession.[a]

[a] § 167.

From the death of the testator until acquisition of the inheritance the heritage remains[b] as an independent property, regarded yet as still controlled and kept together by the will of the testator—upon whose continued action, indeed, the very significance and operation of the testament are based.

[b] *Hereditas iacens:* see Brown and Bell, s. vv. Contra, in English Law: 'mortuus saisit vivum' (Paterson, s. 779).

Ulp.: 'Hereditas' iuris nomen est, quod et accessionem et decessionem in se recipit.—l. 178, § 1, de V. S.[2]

Hermog.: Hereditas in multis partibus iuris pro domino habetur adeoque hereditati quoque ut domino per servum hereditarium adquiritur.—D. 41, 1, 61 pr.[3]

Ulp.: Hereditas non heredis personam sed defuncti sustinet.—l. 34 eod.[4]

Iavol.: Heres et hereditas tametsi duas appellationes recipiunt, unius personae tamen vice funguntur.—D. 41, 3, 22.[5]

Gai.: Res hereditariae, antequam aliquis heres existat, nullius in bonis sunt.—D. 1, 8, 1 pr.[6]

Iavol.: Inter hereditarium servum et eum, qui

---

[1] A soldier can die with a testament in respect of part of his property, intestate in respect of (the other) part.

[2] 'Inheritance' is the name of a right which admits both of increase and decrease.

[3] An inheritance in many parts of the Law is regarded in the light of its owner, and so an acquisition is made for the inheritance as owner by a slave appertaining to the inheritance, just as for his owner.

[4] The inheritance represents not the person of the heir, but that of the deceased.

[5] Although heir and inheritance are two different designations, both nevertheless represent one person.

[6] Inheritances belong to no one previous to the coming forward of an heir.

pro derelicto habetur, plurimum interest, quoniam alter hereditatis iure retinetur nec potest relictus videri, qui universo hereditatis iure continetur.—D. 45, 3, 36.[a][1]

[a] Cf. ibid. § 83.

Scaevola ait . . . hereditati furtum non fieri, quia possessionem hereditas non habet, quae facti est et animi.—D. 47, 4, 1, 15.[2]

§ 154. THE PRAETORIAN SUCCESSIONAL SYSTEM OF *BONORUM POSSESSIO.*

Besides the civil successional system of 'hereditas,' which rests essentially on the Twelve Tables, there arose already during the Republic the Praetorian successional system of 'bonorum possessio,'[b] which, as the Praetorian Law in general,[c] taking account of the growing and more elastic conceptions and requirements of Law—'adiuvandi, supplendi, corrigendi iuris civilis gratia'—connected itself with the system of the *ius civile.*

[b] D. 37, 1, 3 pr.

[c] § 7.

Ulp.: **Lege** obvenire hereditatem non improprie quis dixerit et eam, quae ex testamento defertur, quia lege xii tabularum testamentariae hereditates confirmantur.—D. 50, 16, 130.[3]

Paul.: Hereditatis appellatione bonorum quoque possessio continetur.—l. 138 eod.[4]

---

[1] There is much difference between a slave of the inheritance and him that is regarded as abandoned, since the former is retained by the right belonging to the inheritance, and he cannot be regarded as abandoned who is embraced in the aggregate of the rights of the inheritance.

[2] Scaev. says . . . an inheritance cannot be stolen, because the inheritance has not possession, which is a matter of fact and of intention.

[3] One might not improperly say that even such an inheritance devolves by Law which is offered by virtue of a testament, because testamentary inheritances are confirmed by the Law of the Twelve Tables.

[4] Under the designation *hereditas* is also comprised possession of the goods.

Ius bonorum possessionis introductum est a praetore emendandi veteris iuris gratia.—§ Aliquando tamen neque emendandi neque impugnandi veteris iuris, sed magis confirmandi gratia pollicetur bonorum possessionem.—§ Adhuc autem et alios complures gradus praetor fecit in bonorum possessionibus dandis, dum id agebat, **ne quis sine successore moriatur**: nam angustissimis finibus constitutum per legem XII tabularum ius percipiendarum hereditatum praetor ex bono et aequo dilatavit.—pr., §§ 1, 2, I. h. t. (de B. P. 3, 9).[1]

The name 'bonorum possessio' springs from the assignment by the Praetor to certain persons of possession of the heritage, in the event of their making an application to him at the proper time (petere, admittere, adgnoscere bonorum possessio). Originally the Praetor only granted the bonorum possessio to non-civil heirs, after a preliminary causae cognitio for the particular case, by a special decree (bonorum possessio decretalis). But after the Praetorian Edict had gradually developed and set up fixed principles as to what persons should be admitted to bonorum possessio, and after what intervals and in what order of succession [a] they should be admitted, the grant of bonorum possessio was made, as a rule, upon the simple declaration by the applicant of his entry and evidence afforded of his right, without further investigation (de plano). This was 'bonorum possessio edictalis, ordinaria.'

[a] 'Successorium edictum.'

[1] The right to possession of the goods was introduced by the Praetor with the view of amending the ancient law.—Sometimes, however, he promises possession of the goods with no intention either of amending or of impeaching the ancient law, but rather with the view of confirming it.—Now the Praetor has also created several other degrees in the grant of possession of the goods, whilst taking care that no one die without a successor; for, in accordance with what is fair and reasonable, he has extended the right of taking inheritances which, through the Law of the Twelve Tables, had been confined within very narrow limits.

BOOK III.
Part III.

Ulp.: Bonorum possessionem ita recte definiemus: ius persequendi retinendique patrimonii sive rei quae cuiusque, cum moritur, fuit.—Invito autem nemini bonorum possessio adquiritur.—l. 3, §§ 2, 3, D. h. t. (de B. P. 37, 1).[1]

Id. xxviii. 10, 11: Bonorum possessio datur parentibus et liberis intra annum ex quo petere potuerunt; ceteris intra centum dies.—Qui omnes intra id tempus si non petierint bonorum possessionem, sequens gradus admittitur, perinde atque si superiores non essent.[2]

Id.: Successorium edictum idcirco propositum est, **ne bona hereditaria vacua sine domino diutius iacerent** et creditoribus longior mora fieret. E re igitur praetor putavit praestituere tempus his, quibus bonorum possessionem detulit, et dare inter eos successionem, ut maturius possint creditores scire, utrum habeant cum quo congrediantur, an vero bona vacantia fisco sint delata, an potius ad possessionem bonorum procedere debeant, quasi sine successore defuncto.—D. 38, 9, 1 pr.[3]

---

[1] We shall accordingly be right in defining possession of goods as: the right of legally recovering and maintaining property or an inheritance[a] which belonged to some one at the time of his decease.—The possession of goods is acquired for no one against his will.

[a] See Dirksen, s. v. (p. 838).

[2] Possession of the goods is granted to the ascendants and descendants within a year from the time when they were in a position to claim it; to other persons within one hundred days.—When all of these have forborne to claim the *bon. poss.* within such time, the next degree is admitted, just as if those preceding did not exist.

[3] The Edict as to succession has been put forth lest hereditary property should lie longer void without a master, and the creditors suffer longer delay. The Praetor therefore considered it advantageous to prescribe a respite for those to whom he has offered possession of the goods, and to grant the succession amongst them, that the creditors may be sooner able to know whether there is any one against whom they can proceed, or whether the goods as without an owner have devolved upon the

The grounds of delatio in bonorum possessio are the same as in hereditas; it is given by the testament, in the absence of such, and contrary to such :—'si tabulae testamenti exstabunt (bonorum possessio contra tabulas and secundum tabulas); si tabulae testamenti nullae exstabunt (bonorum possessio intestati).'

> Paul.: Bonorum possessionis beneficium multiplex est: nam quaedam bonorum possessiones competunt contra voluntatem, quaedam secundum voluntatem defunctorum, nec non ab intestato habentibus ius legitimum vel non habentibus propter capitis deminutionem.—l. 6, § 1, D. h. t.[1]
>
> Sunt autem bonorum possessiones ex testamento quidem hae: prima, quae . . . vocatur contra tabulas; secunda, quam omnibus iure scriptis heredibus praetor pollicetur ideoque vocatur secundum tabulas; et cum de testamentis prius locutus est, ad intestatos transitum fecit.—§ 3, I. h. t.[2]

As concerns the effect of the grant of bonorum possessio: the bonorum possessor is in the first place not heres, but only 'heredis loco,' and therefore the actions of inheritance also are given to him and against him, as ficticiae actiones;[a] whilst to effect the acquisition of possession of the hereditary property, a peculiar interdict is at his command, the interdictum QUORUM BONORUM.[b]

[a] Cf. Gai. iv. 37; iii. 80.

[b] § 176, ad fin.

Treasury, or whether they should rather proceed to appropriate the property as if the testator had died without successors.

1 The beneficial result of *bon. poss.* is manifold; for some kinds of *bon. poss.* obtain against the will, some in accordance with the will of the deceased persons, and indeed they either belong to those who have a statutory right from intestacy, or to those who have not got it by reason of loss of *status*.

2 Now the species of *bon. poss.* which arise from a testament are in fact the following: first, that . . . which is styled 'against the (contents of) the testament'[c]; secondly, that which the Praetor promises to all legally instituted heirs, and therefore styled 'according to the contents of the testament'; and, having first spoken of testaments, he passes to intestates.

[c] Strictly, 'tablets.'

BOOK III. Part III.

Quos autem praetor solus vocat ad hereditatem, heredes quidem ipso iure non fiunt (nam praetor heredem facere, non potest: per legem enim tantum vel similem iuris constitutionem heredes fiunt, veluti per senatusconsultum et constitutiones principales): sed cum eis praetor dat bonorum possessionem, loco heredum constituuntur et vocantur bonorum possessores.—§ 2, I. h. t.[1]

Ulp.: In omnibus vice heredum bonorum possessores habentur.—l. 2, D. h. t.[2]

Gai. iv. 34: Habemus adhuc alterius generis fictiones in quibusdam formulis, veluti cum is, qui ex edicto bonorum possessionem petit, ficto se herede agit: cum enim praetorio iure, non legitimo succedat in locum defuncti, non habet directas actiones et neque id, quod defuncti fuit, potest intendere SVVM ESSE, neque id, quod ei debebatur, potest intendere DARI SIBI OPORTERE; itaque ficto se herede intendit, velut hoc modo: IVDEX ESTO. SI AVLVS AGERIVS (id est ipse actor) LVCIO TITIO HERES ESSET, TVM SI FVNDVM, DE QVO AGITVR, EX IVRE QVIRITIVM EIVS ESSE OPORTERET; [et si debebatur L. Titio pecunia] praeposita simili fictione intentio ita subiicitur: TVM SI PARET NVMERIVM NEGIDIVM AVLO AGERIO SESTERTIVM X MILIA DARE OPORTERE.[3]

---

[1] But those whom it is the Praetor alone calls to an inheritance do not in fact become heirs-at-law (for the Praetor cannot make an heir, heirs being only created by statute or like appointment by law, for example, by a decree of the senate and imperial constitutions); but when the Praetor grants them possession of the goods, they are placed in the position of heirs, and are called 'possessors of the goods.'

[2] In all things the *bonorum possessores* are regarded as instead of heirs.

[3] We have, moreover, fictions of another kind in certain formulae; as, for instance, when he that seeks *bonorum possessio* on the ground of the Edict sues upon the fiction that he himself is heir; for since he succeeds to the place of the deceased according to Praetorian, not according to Statutory right, he

As regards the civil heir, the bonorum possessio is sometimes 'cum re' (with result), at other times 'sine re' (without result): the former, if the civil heir is called after or together with the Praetorian in the edict for bonorum possessio; the latter, if the civil heir is appointed before him, and thus would himself have been able to acquire the bonorum possessio,—in which case the bonorum possessio is given only provisionally.[a]

Book III. Part III.

Ulp. xxviii. 13: Bonorum possessio aut cum re datur aut sine re: **cum re,** si is qui accepit, cum effectu bona retineat; **sine re,** cum alius iure civili evincere hereditatem possit.[1]

[a] Cf. Gai. ii. 120, and *inf.* § 161.

Gai. iii. 36: Nam si verbi gratia iure facto testamento heres institutus creverit hereditatem, sed bonorum possessionem secundum tabulas testamenti petere noluerit, contentus eo quod iure civili heres sit, nihilominus ii, qui nullo facto testamento ad intestati bona vocantur, possunt petere bonorum possessionem: sed sine re ad eos (bonorum possessio) pertinet, cum testamento scriptus heres evincere hereditatem possit.[2]

---

has no direct actions, and he cannot maintain that to be 'his own' which belonged to the deceased, nor can he maintain that what was owing to the deceased 'ought to be paid to him'; and so, upon the fiction that he is heir, he states his claim, for example, thus: 'Let so and so be *iudex*. If Aul. Ag.' (that is, the plaintiff himself) 'were the heir of Luc. Tit., then should it appear that the estate in question ought to be his by the law of the Quirites'; (and if money was owing to L. T.) a like fiction is prefixed, and the claim is appended thus: 'Then if it appear that Num. Neg. ought to give Aul. Ag. 10,000 sesterces.'

[1] *Bon. poss.* is granted either *cum re* or *sine re*: *cum re* when the recipient can retain the goods effectively; *sine re*, when some one else can by civil law wrest the inheritance from him.

[2] For if, by way of example, the heir instituted in a testament legally executed have declared his acceptance of[b] the inheritance, but have not cared to sue for possession of the goods 'in accordance with the tablets,' content with the fact that he is heir by civil law, those who, in the absence of a testament, are

[b] For *cretio*, see § 171.

Book III. Part III.

Both systems of succession remained independently collateral to one another down to the Justinianean period, although in the course of time some persons acquired a right of civil inheritance who at the first were entitled to merely Praetorian inheritance. Bonorum possessio and hereditas were first essentially blended together through the comprehensive reform by Justinian of the whole Law of Inheritance.

In the history of bonorum possessio much is obscure and largely controverted, as in particular its starting-point, that is, the question, what was its original signification, and further, how the whole Praetorian system of succession in general arose, and in what form, in relation to the Civil Law, it first procured validity. Most probable is the supposition that bonorum possessio was introduced originally 'adiuvandi iuris civilis gratia' for the civil heirs, whether testamentary or intestate, so as to remove possible delay in entering upon an inheritance in the absence of civil intervals for deliberation,[a] and for prevention of the breaking up of the heritage impending in the civil 'pro herede usucapio'[b]; but then (perhaps already simultaneously) it was also given 'supplendi iuris civilis gratia'—in order further to obviate the want of an heir, which readily happened according to Civil Law[c]—in default of civil heirs of other persons;[d] and that, on the contrary, the corrective function of bonorum possessio, given along with, indeed before, the civil heir,[e] was not developed until later on, keeping pace with legal conceptions of the ius gentium, which made their way also into the Law of Inheritance.

[a] *Supra.*

[b] § 155.

[c] *Supra*, and § 162, ad fin.

[d] *Ab intestato*, § 163, ad fin., and *sec. tab.* § 157.

[e] §§ 163, 168; Ulp. xxii. 23.

§ 155. Pro Herede Usucapio.

In the oldest law the hereditas itself, or a fraction thereof, could be acquired through usucapio[f] by every one

[f] § 80.

---

called to the property of the intestate can nevertheless sue for possession of the property; but the *bon. poss.* belongs to them *sine re*, since an heir appointed by the testament can wrest the inheritance from them.

without bona fides and iustus titulus, if there had been continued possession for one year of the hereditary things, which was acquired as against the heir; with restriction, however, to the acquisition of 'corpora hereditaria,' so that such person assumed the position of an heir, particularly in relation to the creditors of an inheritance. But later on,[a] this usucapion of the hereditas itself was converted into a usucapion of the several things composing the inheritance, which gradually began to come in conflict with the general ideas of Law. (Improba, lucrativa usucapio.)

[a] Perhaps already towards the end of the Republic.

> Gai. ii. §§ 52–56: Rursus ex contrario accidit, ut qui sciat alienam rem se possidere, usucapiat, veluti si rem hereditariam, cuius possessionem heres nondum nactus est, aliquis possederit; nam ei concessum est usucapere, si modo ea res est, quae recipit usucapionem: quae species possessionis et usucapionis pro herede vocatur. § Et in tantum haec usucapio concessa est, ut et res quae solo continentur, anno usucapiantur. § Quare autem etiam hoc casu soli rerum annua constituta sit usucapio, illa ratio est, quod olim rerum hereditariarum possessione velut ipsae hereditates usucapi credebantur, scilicet anno: lex enim XII tabularum soli quidem res biennio usucapi iussit, ceteras vero anno; ergo hereditas in ceteris rebus videbatur esse, quia soli non est, quia neque corporalis est. Et quamvis postea creditum sit ipsas hereditates usucapi non posse, tamen in omnibus rebus hereditariis, etiam quae solo tenentur, annua usucapio remansit. § Quare autem omnino tam improba possessio et usucapio concessa sit, illa ratio est, quod voluerunt veteres maturius hereditates adiri, ut essent qui sacra facerent, quorum illis temporibus summa observatio fuit,[b] et ut creditores haberent, a quo suum consequerentur. § Haec autem species possessionis et usucapionis etiam lucrativa vocatur: nam sciens quisque rem alienam lucrifacit.—§ 58: Necessario tamen

[b] Compare next extract. See also Maine, 'Early Law and Custom,' ch. iv., and Hunter, pp. 745, sqq.

Book III, Part III.

herede exstante nihil ipso iure pro herede usucapi potest.[1]

Cic. de legib. ii. 48–49:—ut conserventur semper et perpetua sint sacra. . . . Quaeruntur,[a] qui adstringantur sacris. Heredum causa iustissima est . . . ; deinde qui morte testamentove eius tantumdem capiat quantum omnes heredes . . . ; tertio loco, si nemo sit heres, is qui de bonis, quae eius fuerint cum moritur, usuceperit plurimum possidendo; quarto qui [de] creditoribus eius plu-

[a] Sc. a iurisconsultis.

---

[1] Again, on the other hand, it sometimes happens that he who is aware he possesses a thing belonging to another may yet acquire by *usus*, as for instance, if any one should take possession of an article appertaining to an inheritance which the heir has not yet reduced into possession; for the right of acquiring by *usus* is allowed to him, provided such property is susceptible of usucapion. This kind of possession and usucapion is designated *pro herede* (in the character of heir). § And this acquisition by *usus* has been allowed to such an extent that even things which appertain to the soil may be acquired in one year. § Now the reason why in this case usucapion in one year of immovables has been established is, because it was formerly supposed that the thing appertaining to the inheritance could, like the inheritance itself, be acquired by *usus*, and that in one year; for a law of the Twelve Tables directed that things forming part of the soil may be acquired by *usus* in two years, but the rest of things in one year. Therefore an inheritance seemed to be included among 'the rest of things,' because it is no part of the soil, as not being even a corporeal thing. And although the view has later on been accepted that inheritances themselves cannot be acquired by *usus*, yet in respect of all things appertaining to inheritances, even those which are attached to the soil, usucapion in one year held its ground. § Now the reason why such an unjust possession and usucapion have been allowed at all is, because our ancestors wished inheritances to be entered upon very promptly, so that there might be persons to perform family rites, the observance of which was of chief moment in those times, and that creditors might have some one from whom they could recover their claim. § But this kind of possession and usucapion is also styled 'profitable'; because every one knowingly makes profit of a thing owned by another. § Nevertheless, if there is a necessary heir in existence, there can be no usucapion *pro herede* of anything by operation of law.

rimum servet. . . . Haec nos a Scaevola didicimus; non ita descripta sunt ab antiquis. Nam illi quidem his verbis docebant tribus modis sacris adstringi: hereditate, aut si maiorem partem pecuniae capiat, aut, si maior pars pecuniae legata est, si inde quippiam ceperit.[1]

Seneca de benef. vi. 5: Iurisconsultorum istae ineptiae sunt acutae, qui hereditatem negant usucapi posse, sed ea quae in hereditate sunt: tamquam quidquam aliud sit hereditas, quam ea quae in hereditate sunt.[2]

This lucrativa pro herede usucapio held its ground notwithstanding throughout the classical Law,[a] although it had lost its importance for inheritance and continued to be of practical use only when no heir existed. This was after the Praetor had put forward the interdictum quorum bonorum[b] for the protection of the bonorum possessor against every possessor of hereditary property, and accordingly, a senatus-consultum under Hadrian had declared the pro herede usucapio inoperative

[a] D. 41, 2, 3, 19; 41, 3, 33, 1; 41, 5, 2, 1.

[b] § 176, ad fin.

---

[1] —that family worship may be always kept up and maintained. . . . The question (raised by lawyers) is,[c] who are under obligation to perform the family worship? The case of heirs is most consonant with justice . . .; next he that shall take in the event of death or by bequest just as much as all heirs . . .; thirdly, if there be no heir, he that of the goods belonging to the testator at his death has acquired most by length of possession; fourthly, he that preserves to the creditors of the deceased most of their claims. . . . These points we have learnt from Scaevola; they have not been so put forth by older jurists. For their teaching was to the following effect, that a man was bound to perform family worship in one of three ways: in respect of the inheritance, or if he should take the greater part of the money, or, the greater part of the money having been bequeathed, if he have taken anything of it.

[c] *Quaeruntur* is for *Quaeritur*, by attraction.

[2] Sagacious are the subtleties of lawyers who say that it is not an *hereditas* which can be acquired by usucapion, but such things as are contained in the *hereditas*: just as if an *hereditas* were something different from the things contained in such *hereditas*.

Book III. Part III.

also against the civil heir coming forward with hereditatis petitio.

> Gai. ii. § 57 : Sed hoc tempore iam non est lucrativa : nam ex auctoritate D. Hadriani senatusconsultum factum est, ut tales usucapiones revocarentur ; et ideo potest heres ab eo, qui rem usucepit, hereditatem petendo proinde eam rem consequi, atque si usucapta non esset.[1]

Besides, later on even a special 'crimen expilatae hereditatis,' as representing the actio furti[a] (here inadmissible), was introduced, because of thefts of hereditary property the possession of which had not yet been acquired by the heir.

> Paul. ii. 31, § 11 : Rei hereditariae, antequam ab herede possideatur, furtum fieri non potest.[2]

> Marc.: Si quis alienam hereditatem expilaverit, extra ordinem solet coerceri per accusationem expilatae hereditatis, sicut et oratione D. Marci cavetur.—D. 47, 19, 1.[3]

But furthermore, there still existed (and it is the only one that continues to exist in the Law of Justinian) a usucapio pro herede as ordinary usucapio of hereditary property,[b] on the part of him who erroneously[c] gives himself out as heir, and of the bonorum possessor.[d]

> Paul.: Constat eum, qui testamenti factionem habet, pro herede usucapere posse.—D. 41, 5, 4.[4]

[a] D. 47, 19, 6; Gai. iii. 201; D. 47, 4, 1, 15.

[b] It is doubtful whether this down to Justinian was universally in the space of one year.

[c] For such putative title, see § 80.

[d] Gai. iii. § 80.

---

1 But at the present time it is no longer profitable ; for it was enacted by a decree of the Senate, upon the authority of the late Emp. Hadrian, that such acquisitions by *usus* should be annulled ; and therefore the heir, by suing for the inheritance, can obtain such property from him who has acquired it by *usus*, just as though it had not been so acquired.

2 There cannot be a theft of successional property before possession is had by the heir.

3 He that has pillaged an inheritance belonging to another is generally punished by the extraordinary process, through a charge made of having pillaged the inheritance, as is provided in a speech of the late Emp. Marcus.

4 It is settled that he who has testamentary capacity can as heir make a title by *usus*.

Iul.: Si quis emerit fundum sciens ab eo cuius non erat, possidebit pro possessore; sed . . . si iustam causam habuerit existimandi se heredem vel bonorum possessorem domino exstitisse, fundum pro herede possidebit nec causam possessionis sibi mutare videtur.—D. 41, 3, 33, 1.[a] [1]

Imp. Diocl.: Nihil pro herede posse usucapi **suis** existentibus heredibus obtinuit.—C. 7, 29, 2.[2]

[a] Cf. ibid. § 89.

CHAPTER II.

DELATIO OF THE INHERITANCE.

SUCCESSION *EX TESTAMENTO*: *TESTAMENTARIA HEREDITAS*.[b]

§ 156. Nature of a Testament. Capacity for making one.

Testamentum is the free declaration of the testator by last will, in a solemn form, as to who shall be his heir, and the further disposition of property left by him which is linked to it, though not of necessity.[c]

Ulp. xx. 1: Testamentum est mentis nostrae iusta contestatio, in id sollemniter facta, ut post mortem nostram valeat.[3]

Mod.: Testamentum est voluntatis nostrae iusta sententia de eo,[4] quod quis post mortem suam fieri velit.[e]—l. 1, D. h. t. (qui test. fac. 28, 1).

[b] For the history of testamentary succession, see 'Anct. Law,' chh. vi.-vii. To the Biblical passages adduced by Blackstone (ii. 490-1, cf. Steph. i. 594) add such as Isa. 38, 1 (see Delitzsch, *ad loc.*), where 'set his house in order' is literally 'gave commandment to,' &c.

[c] § 159.

[d] Cited in Steph. i. 592, note.

[e] Cited by Blackstone, ii. 499.

[1] If any one has knowingly purchased an estate from him to whom it did not belong, he will possess it *pro possessore*, but if he has had a legitimate reason for the belief that he became the heir or the *bon. poss.* to the owner he will possess the land *pro herede*, and he is not regarded as changing his possessory title.

[2] The opinion has prevailed, that nothing can be acquired by use *pro herede* if necessary heirs exist.

[3] A testament is the legal voucher of our intention made in solemn form, so as to be operative after our death.

[4] A testament is the legal declaration of our will concerning that which a man wishes should be done after his death.

Book III. Part III.

Pap.: Testamenti factio non privati sed publici iuris est.—l. 3, D. eod.[1]

Lex XII tab. (Ulp. xi. 14): VTI LEGASSIT SVPER (FAMILIA ?) PECVNIA (QVE ?) TVTELAVE SVAE REI, ITA IVS ESTO.[2]

Ulp.: Ambulatoria est voluntas defuncti usque ad vitae supremum exitum.—D. 34, 4, 4.[3]

The requisites of validity of the testament are, observance of the prescribed form, and capacity of the testator for making it. The following are the presumptions of the latter.

[a] D. 28, 1, 5.

Capacity to act,[a] and absence of those defects which exclude the observance of the testamentary forms.

Ulp. xx. 12–13: Impubes, licet sui iuris sit, facere testamentum non potest, quoniam nondum plenum iudicium animi habet.—Mutus surdus furiosus itemque prodigus, cui lege bonis interdictum est, testamentum facere non possunt.[4]

By 'testamenti factio' is to be understood Roman legal capacity (commercium) in relation to testamentary acts in general, that is, the capacity either to make a testament,[b] or to be 'honoratus,' *i.e.*, to be instituted or treated as heir, to be nominated tutor, or to take part in the testamentary act as witness.

[b] D. 28, 1, 12.

Gai. ii. § 114: Igitur si quaeramus, an valeat

---

[1] The making of a testament appertains not to Private but to Public Law.

[2] 'In accordance with the bequest that a man shall have made concerning his household and money, or the tutelage of his property, so let it be law.'

[3] The will of a testator[c] is shifting up to his final departure from life.

[c] Strictly, 'deceased.'

[4] A person not of the age of puberty, although he be independent, cannot make a testament, since he does not yet possess full mental discrimination.—A dumb person, or deaf person, or madman, and also a spendthrift, who is by law forbidden the control of his property, cannot make a testament.

testamentum, imprimis advertere debemus, an is qui fecerit, habuerit testamenti factionem.[1]

Ulp. xxii. 1: Heredes institui possunt, qui testamenti factionem cum testatore habent.[2]

Iust. ii. 10, 6: Testes autem adhiberi possunt ii, cum quibus testamenti factio est.[3]

No 'testamenti factio' is possessed by slaves, peregrini, and those persons from whom it has been penally taken away.[a]

[a] Gell. xv. 13, 11; D. 28, 1, 26.

Iust. ii. 12, 5: Eius qui apud hostes est testamentum quod ibi fecit, non valet, quamvis redierit: sed quod dum in civitate fuerat fecit, sive redierit, valet iure postliminii, sive illic decesserit, valet ex lege Cornelia.[4]

Ulp. xx. 16: Servus publicus populi Romani pro peculii parte dimidia testamenti faciendi habet ius.[5]

Gai.: Si cui aqua et igni interdictum sit, eius nec illud testamentum valet quod ante fecit, nec id quod postea fecerit.—l. 8, § 1, D. h. t.—Ulp.: Hi quibus aqua et igni interdictum est, item deportati . . . nec testamenti faciendi ius habent, cum sint ἀπόλιδες.—l. 1, § 2, D. de leg. III. 32.[6]

---

[1] If then we are inquiring whether a testament be valid, we first ought to ascertain whether he who made it had testamentary capacity.

[2] Those can be instituted heirs who have testamentary capacity in connection with the testator.

[3] Now those persons can be called in as witnesses in connection with whom the testator has testamentary capacity.

[4] The testament of such person as is in the hands of the enemy, made by him there, is invalid even if he return; but that made whilst he was at home is valid, if he return, by the *ius postliminii*, if he have died there, according to the *l. Cornelia.*

[5] A public slave of the Roman people has the right of making a testament of one-half his separate property.

[6] If a man has been forbidden water and fire, neither is such testament valid as he has previously made, nor that which he has made subsequently.—Those who have been interdicted water and fire, *deportati* too, . . . have not the right of testation, since they are without a country.

Ulp. xx. 14: Latinus Junianus, item is qui dediticiorum numero est testamentum facere non potest: Latinus quidem, quoniam nominatim lege Iunia prohibitus est; is autem qui dediticiorum numero est, quoniam nec quasi civis Romanus testari potest, cum sit peregrinus, nec quasi peregrinus, quoniam nullius certae civitatis civis est, ut secundum leges civitatis suae testetur.[1]

Ib. xxii. 2: Dediticiorum numero heres institui non potest, quia peregrinus est, cum quo testamenti factio non est.[2]

Id.: Intestabilis . . . nec testamentum facere poterit, nec ad testamentum adhiberi.—l. 18, § 1, D. h. t.[3]

The incapacity to make a testament does not, however, of itself include the absence of testamenti factio.

Inst. ii. 19, 4: Testamenti autem factionem non solum is habere videtur, qui testamentum facere potest, sed etiam qui ex alieno testamento vel ipse capere potest vel alii adquirere, licet non potest facere testamentum; et ideo et furiosus et mutus (et surdus) et postumus et infans et filiusfamilias et servus alienus testamenti factionem habere dicuntur: licet enim testamentum facere non possunt, attamen ex testamento vel

---

[1] A Junian Latin, likewise such person as is numbered among the *dediticii*, cannot make a testament: the Latin, as he has been expressly forbidden by the *l. Iunia;* he that is numbered among the *dediticii*, because he can neither make a testamentary disposition as a Roman citizen, because he is a foreigner, nor as a foreigner, since he is not a citizen of any particular State, so as to make such a disposition according to the laws of his own State.

[2] One numbered among *dediticii* cannot be instituted heir, because he is a foreigner, with whom there is no relation of testamentary capacity.

[3] An *intestabilis* can neither make a testament nor be employed for a testament.

sibi vel alii adquirere possunt (cf. Pomp. l. 16 pr., D. h. t.).[1]

Unrestricted capacity for property rights; therefore filii fam. cannot make a testament, except with regard to peculium castrense vel quasi.[a]

Ulp. xx. 10: Filiusfamilias testamentum facere non potest, quia nihil suum habet, ut testari de eo possit.[2]

Gai.: Qui in potestate parentis est, testamenti faciendi ius non habet: adeo ut, quamvis pater ei permittat, nihilo magis tamen iure testari possit.—l. 6 pr., D. h. t.[3]

Women were at first[b] purely incapable of testation if they belonged to a family of agnates, and that even from the time of the lex Claudia;[c] and this in the interest of their legitimi heredes, from whom the property should not be taken away. For the purpose of making a will, a woman required to have her previous agnatic connection destroyed by means of coemptio fiduciaria.[d] This, however, was done away with by Hadrian as an empty formality.

Cic. Top. 4, 18: Si ea mulier testamentum fecit, quae se capite numquam deminuit, non

[a] §§ 149, ad fin.; 150, ad init.

[b] Exceptions in Gell. i. 12, and perhaps also Gai. i. 144, *sqq*.

[c] Gai. i. 157; Ulp. xi. 8.

[d] § 49.

---

[1] But not only is he considered to have testamentary capacity who is able to make a testament, but also he who, under the testament of another, can take for himself or acquire for a third person, although he cannot make a testament. And therefore a madman, a dumb person (and deaf person), a posthumous child, an infant, a *fil. fam.* and the slave of another, are said to have testamentary capacity; for although they cannot make a testament, yet they can acquire by testament either for themselves or another.

[2] A *fil. fam.* cannot make a testament, because he has nothing of his own, so as to be able to make a testamentary disposition in respect thereof.

[3] He that is under parental power has no right to make a testament; so far that, even if his father allows him, he can, however, none the more by Law make a testamentary disposition.

BOOK III. Part III.

videtur ex edicto praetoris secundum eas tabulas possessio dari.[1]

Gai. i. § 115[a]: Olim **testamenti faciendi gratia** fiduciaria fiebat coemptio : tunc enim non aliter feminae testamenti faciendi ius habebant, exceptis quibusdam personis, quam si coemptionem fecissent remancipataeque et manumissae fuissent; sed hanc necessitatem coemptionis faciendae ex auctoritate D. Hadriani senatus remisit.[2]

Women, according to ius civile, always required tutoris auctoritas for the making of a will so long as tutela mulierum in general existed, but this had only actual significance in 'legitima tutela parentum ac patronorum,'[a] so that emancipated daughters and libertae were in fact at any rate as good as incapable of testation. The Praetor, however, later on gave the bonorum possessio secundum tabulas also upon a testament made without tutoris auctoritas, but this at the outset—always in the case of those last mentioned—was 'sine re' as regards civil intestate heirs.

[a] Gai. i. 192.

Gai. ii. §§ 118–122 : Observandum praeterea est, ut si mulier quae in tutela est faciat testamentum, tutore auctore facere debeat : alioquin inutiliter iure civili testabitur. § Praetor tamen si septem signis testium signatum sit testamentum, scriptis heredibus secundum tabulas testamenti bonorum possessionem pollicetur, et si nemo sit, ad quem ab intestato iure legitimo pertineat

---

[1] If a testament has been made by such woman as never suffered loss of *caput*, possession according to those tablets does not seem to be given by the Praetor's Edict.

[2] Formerly a fiduciary coemption took place for the purpose of making a testament. For at that time women, with the exception of certain persons, had no right of making a testament, unless they had performed a coemption, and had been remancipated and manumitted. But on the authorisation of the late Emp. Hadrian, the senate dispensed with this necessity of performing the coemption.

hereditas, velut frater eodem patre natus aut patruus aut fratris filius, ita poterunt scripti heredes retinere hereditatem.—§ Sed videamus an etiamsi frater aut patruus exstent, potiores scriptis heredibus habeantur: rescripto enim imperatoris Antonini. . . .—[a] § Quod sane quidem ad masculorum testamenta pertinere certum est; item ad feminarum, quae ideo non utiliter testatae sunt, quod verbi gratia familiam non vendiderint aut nuncupationis verba locutae non sint: an autem et ad ea testamenta feminarum, quae sine tutoris auctoritate fecerint, haec constitutio pertineat, videbimus. § Loquimur autem de his scilicet feminis, quae non in legitima parentum aut patronorum tutela sunt, sed de his quae alterius generis tutores habent, qui etiam inviti coguntur auctores fieri: alioquin parentem et patronum sine auctoritate eius facto testamento non summoveri palam est.[1]

[a] V. *infra*, p. 796.

---

[1] We have, moreover, to observe that, if a woman who is under guardianship makes a testament, she must make it with the concurrence of the guardian; otherwise her testament will be inoperative by civil law. § The Praetor, however, if the testament is sealed with the seals of seven witnesses, promises the *bon. poss.* to the testamentary heirs *secundum tabulas*, and if there is no one to whom the inheritance by intestacy legally belongs, as a brother by the same father, or a paternal uncle, or a brother's son, the testamentary heirs will thus be able to retain the inheritance. § But let us see whether, although a brother or a paternal uncle exist, they will be held to have preference over the testamentary heirs. For it is laid down in a rescript of the Emp. Antonine . . . § That this applies to testaments of males is certain; also to those of females who have made an invalid testament because, for instance, they have not sold their *familia*,[b] or have not recited the words of nuncupation, but whether this constitution also applies to those testaments of females which they have made without the concurrence of their guardian, we shall have to consider. § We speak, however, of course of such females as are not under the statutory guardianship of parents or patrons, but of those who have guardians of another kind, who are compelled to give their sanction even against their will; on the other hand, it is clear

[b] Explained by Gaius in § 102 (*infra*). See, however, Muirhead on § 104.

BOOK III. Part III.

The testator himself must, moreover, have sure knowledge of his legal standing.

De statu suo dubitantes vel errantes testamentum facere non possunt;—nam qui incertus de statu suo est, certam legem testamento dicere non potest.—l. 15 (Ulp.), l. 14 (Paul.), D. h. t.[1]

Finally, the Latini Iuniani had no capacity for testation, notwithstanding that they enjoyed testamenti factio.[a]

[a] See above, Ulp. xx. 14, and § 39.

§ 157. Regular Forms of the Testament.

The oldest forms of testament were the 'testamentum *calatis comitiis*' (in comitia curiata collected for testimony) and the 'testamentum *in procinctu factum*,' that is, in the army divided according to centuries, and in battle array; both of political, sacral character.

Gai. ii. § 101: Testamentorum genera initio duo fuerunt: nam aut calatis comitiis testamenta faciebant, quae comitia bis in anno testamentis faciendis destinata erant; aut in procinctu, i.e. cum belli causa arma sumebant: procinctus est enim expeditus et armatus exercitus. Alterum itaque in pace et in otio faciebant, alterum in proelium exituri.[2]

Gell. xv. 27:—scriptum est . . . 'calata' comitia esse, quae pro collegio pontificum habentur. . . . Iisdem comitiis, quae 'calata' appellari diximus,

---

that a parent and a patron cannot be set aside by a testament made without his concurrence.

[1] Those who are in doubt or in error as to their status cannot make a testament;—for he that is uncertain about his status can declare no definite testamentary regulation.

[2] There were originally two sorts of testaments; for men made them in summoned assemblies, which were held twice a year for the purpose of making testaments; or in battle array, that is, when they took up arms on account of war, for *procinctus* means an army equipped and armed. One, therefore, was made during peace and leisure, the other when they were about to go forth to battle.

et sacrorum detestatio et testamenta fieri solebant.[1]

These two forms, however, were soon displaced by the more convenient 'testamentum per aes et libram,' which was recognised in the Twelve Tables, and consists in a mancipatio of the 'familia pecuniaque' of the testator to the 'familiae emptor'[a] and nuncupatio associated with it.

According to the older form of the mancipatory testament, the familiae emptor was himself heres, and indeed already in the lifetime of the testator, so as entirely to assume the same position in respect of his property as the 'suus.'[b] According to the later form, he acted a merely formal part, and the point of gravity in the act of testation was by this time the nuncupatio, with which the heir was nominated by word of mouth, and other dispositions by last will were enunciated as to the heritage. It soon, however, became usual to make the last will in the form of a written document, and to acknowledge and confirm as one's testament the document exhibited (tabulae testamenti) after previous, by this time only formal, familiae mancipatio with a solemn declaration (nuncupatio); whereupon the sealing of the testament and subscription of their names by the witnesses usually followed.

[a] Compare the fundamental character of an English will of real estate before the Wills Act (7 Will. IV. & 1 Vict. c. 26): Digby, p. 338.

[b] Gai. ii. 157; D. 28, 2, 11; ib. 7, 12.—Cf. § 173, ad init.

Gai. ii. §§ 102–104: Accessit deinde tertium genus testamenti quod per aes et libram agitur; qui enim neque calatis comitiis neque in procinctu testamentum fecerat, is si subita morte urguebatur, amico familiam suam (i.e. patrimonium suum) mancipio dabat eumque rogabat, quid cuique post mortem suam dari vellet: quod testamentum dicitur per aes et libram, scilicet quia per mancipationem peragitur. § Sed illa quidem duo

[1] It is written that the *com. cal.* are such as are held in place of the college of pontiffs. . . . In the same *comitia* which, as we have said, are called *calata*, both family rites used to be renounced and testaments made.

Book III. Part III.

genera testamentorum in desuetudinem abierunt; hoc vero solum, quod per aes et libram fit, in usu retentum est. Sane nunc aliter ordinatur quam olim solebat: namque olim familiae emptor, i.e. qui a testatore familiam accipiebat mancipio, heredis locum obtinebat et ob id ei mandabat testator, quid cuique post mortem suam dari vellet: nunc vero alius heres testamento instituitur, a quo etiam legata relinquuntur, alius dicis gratia propter veteris iuris imitationem familiae emptor adhibetur. § Eaque res ita agitur: qui facit testamentum adhibitis sicut in ceteris mancipationibus, V testibus civibus Romanis puberibus et libripende, postquam tabulas testamenti scripserit, mancipat alicui dicis gratia familiam suam; in qua re his verbis familiae emptor utitur: FAMILIAM PECVNIAMQVE TVAM ENDO [MANDATELA ?] TVTELA CVSTODELAQVE MEA ESSE AIO EAQVE, QVO TV IVRE TESTAMENTVM FACERE POSSIS SECVNDVM LEGEM PVBLICAM, HOC AERE [et ut quidam adiiciunt ?] AENEAQVE LIBRA ESTO MIHI EMPTA; deinde aere percutit libram idque aes dat testatori velut pretii loco; deinde testator tabulas testamenti tenens ita dicit: HAEC ITA VT IN HIS TABVLIS CERISQVE SCRIPTA SVNT, ITA DO ITA LEGO ITA TESTOR, ITAQVE VOS QVIRITES TESTIMONIVM MIHI PERHIBETOTE: et hoc dicitur nuncupatio: nuncupare est enim palam nominare, et sane quae testator specialiter in tabulis testamenti scripserit, ea videtur generali sermone nominare atque confirmare.[1]

---

[1] There was afterwards added a third sort of testament, which is executed by means of copper and balance. For a man who had neither made his testament in the *com. cal.* nor *in proc.*, if he was apprehensive of imminent death, used to make over his *familia* (that is, his patrimony) by mancipation to a friend, and instructed him as to what he wished should be given to each person after his death: this testament is called 'by copper and balance,' of course because it is performed by

Ulp. xx. 9: In testamento quod per aes et libram fit duae res aguntur: familiae mancipatio et nuncupatio testamenti: . . . quae nuncupatio et testatio vocatur.[1]

Id.: Heredes palam, ita ut exaudiri possint, nuncupandi sunt; licebit ergo testanti vel nuncupare heredes vel scribere; sed si nuncupat, palam debet.—l. 21 pr., D. h. t. (qui test. fac. 28, 1).[2]

---

mancipation. § But those two varieties of testament have in fact become obsolete, whilst only that is retained in use which is accomplished by copper and balance. It is now, to be sure, arranged in a different way to that in which it used to be. For formerly the *fam. empt.*, that is, he who received the patrimony from the testator by mancipation, held the place of heir, and therefore the testator charged him with what he wished should be given to each person after his death; but now one person is instituted heir in the testament, and on him the legacies are charged, and another, for form's sake and in imitation of the ancient law, is joined as *fam. empt.* § The transaction is conducted thus: the person who is making the testament, having called together, as in all other mancipations, five witnesses, Roman citizens of the age of puberty, and a balance-holder, after he has written the tablets of his testament, mancipates his patrimony to some one for form's sake; in doing which the *fam. empt.* employs these words: 'I declare your patrimony[a] and money to be in my charge, guardianship and custody, and since you are able duly to make a testament, according to public law, let these things be purchased by me with this copper' (and as some add) 'and with this copper balance.' Then he strikes the balance with the copper, and gives that piece of copper to the testator, as if by way of price. The testator next, holding the testamentary tablets, speaks thus: 'These things, just as they are written in these wax tablets, so I give, so I bequeath, so I dispose of, and do you, Quirites, bear me witness.' And this is called the nuncupation; for *nuncupare* is to declare openly; and what the testator has written in detail upon the tablets of the testament he is regarded as declaring and confirming by such general statement.

[a] *Supra.*

[1] In a testament by copper and balance two acts are performed, the mancipation of the patrimony, and the nuncupation of the testament. . . . This nuncupation is also called attestation.

[2] The names of the heirs must be pronounced clearly, so that they may be thoroughly heard. The testator will therefore

The five witnesses, the familiae emptor and the libripens, besides capacity to act and to see and hear, had further to possess testamenti factio, and might not be connected with the testator by the bond of potestas, no more the witnesses with the familiae emptor (or heir).

Id. xx. 7, 8: Mutus surdus furiosus pupillus femina neque familiae emptor esse, neque testis libripensve fieri potest. — Latinus Iunianus et familiae emptor et testis et libripens fieri potest, quoniam cum eo testamenti factio est.[1]

Ib. § 3: Qui in potestate testatoris est aut familiae emptoris, testis aut libripens adhiberi non potest, quoniam familiae mancipatio inter testatorem et familiae emptorem fit, et ob id domestici testes adhibendi non sunt.[2]

Gai. ii. § 108: Is vero qui in potestate heredis aut legatarii est, cuiusve heres ipse aut legatarius in potestate est, quique in eiusdem potestate est adeo testis et libripens adhiberi potest, ut ipse quoque heres aut legatarius iure adhibeantur; sed tamen quod ad heredem pertinet, quique in eius potestate est, cuiusve is in potestate erit, minime hoc iure uti debemus.[3]

---

be at liberty to appoint heirs by word of mouth or in writing; but if by word of mouth, he must do so clearly.

[1] A dumb person, a deaf person, a madman, a ward, a woman, can neither be *fam. empt.* nor be made a witness or balance-holder.—A Junian Latin can be made either purchaser of the patrimony, balance-holder, or witness, inasmuch as there is a relation of testamentary capacity with him.

[2] He who is under the power of the testator, or of the *fam. empt.*, cannot be employed as a witness or a balance-holder, since the mancipation of the patrimony takes place between the testator and the *fam. empt.*, and on that account members of their households must not be employed as witnesses.

[3] But he who is under the power of the heir or of the legatee, or he under whose power the heir himself or the legatee is and any one who is under the same power, can be present as a witness and as a balance-holder, just as the heir himself or the legatee can legally be; but yet, so far as this extends to the heir, and to any one under his power, or to the person under

Ulp.: Qui testamento heres instituitur, in eodem testamento testis esse non potest.—l. 20 pr., h. t.[1] Book III. Part III.

The Praetorian Edict, however, upon the ground of the written testament duly sealed by seven witnesses—the remaining requisites for the validity of the last will being presumed—gave to the heir nominated the bonorum possessio secundum tabulas, without having regard to whether the civil formalities of the mancipatio and the nuncupatio were observed.

Cic. in Verr. 1, 45, 117: SI DE HEREDITATE AMBIGITVR ET TABVLAE TESTAMENTI OBSIGNATAE NON MINVS MVLTIS SIGNIS QVAM E LEGE OPORTET AD ME PROFERENTVR, SECVNDVM TABVLAS TESTAMENTI POTISSIMVM POSSESSIONEM DABO; hoc translaticium est.[2]

Ulp. xxviii. 6: Etiamsi iure civili non valeat testamentum, forte quod familiae mancipatio vel nuncupatio defuit, si signatum testamentum sit non minus quam septem testium civium Romanorum signis, bonorum possessio datur.[3]

This bonorum possessio, as regards the civil intestate heirs, was originally 'sine re'; [a] not until after Marcus Aurelius [b] was an exceptio doli given to the bonorum possessor against the 'hereditatis petitio' of the latter.[c]

[a] Gai. ii. §§ 118, sqq.

[b] Or perhaps Antoninus Pius.

[c] Cf. D. 28, 3, 2.

---

whose power he shall be, we ought to use such right as little as possible.

[1] He that is instituted heir in the testament cannot be a witness in respect of the same testament.

[2] 'If there be a doubt concerning the inheritance, and the testamentary tablets, having been sealed by a not less number of witnesses than is required by the statute, shall be produced to me, I will grant possession in the main according to it.' This is a standing clause.

[3] Although a testament be invalid by the Civil Law, because perhaps the mancipation of the patrimony or the nuncupation was omitted, possession of the effects is granted if the testament have been sealed with the seals of not less than seven witnesses, Roman citizens.

Book III. Part III.

Gai. ii. § 120: Rescripto imperatoris Antonini significatur eos, qui secundum tabulas testamenti non iure factas bonorum possessionem petierint, posse adversus eos qui ab intestato vindicant hereditatem, defendere se per exceptionem doli mali.[1]

From that time the solemn form of mancipatio passed always more out of use for the written testament, whilst it still for a long while held its ground for the verbal testament, but in the case of the latter also it was completely abolished by Theodosius II.

In the Law of Justinian there are the following forms for the making of a testament.

Private testaments: these can be made

(1) in writing; for this is required a declaration of the testator, before seven witnesses,[a] that the document produced contains his testament, the subscription of the testator and the witnesses, and the addition of seals by the latter.

[a] See above.

Sed cum paulatim tam ex usu hominum, quam ex constitutionum emendationibus coepit in unam consonantiam ius civile et praetorium iungi, constitutum est, ut uno eodemque tempore, quod ius civili quodammodo exigebat, septem testibus adhibitis et subscriptione testium, quod ex constitutionibus inventum est, et ex edicto praetoris signacula testamentis imponerentur. § Sed neque heres scriptus, neque is qui in potestate eius est, neque pater eius qui habet eum in potestate, neque fratres qui in eiusdem patris potestate sunt, testes adhiberi possunt: quia totum hoc negotium quod agitur testamenti ordinandi gratia, creditur hodie inter heredem et testatorem agi. § Legatariis autem et fideicommissariis, quia non iuris successores

[1] By a rescript of the Emp. Antonine it is declared that those who have applied for possession of the effects in accordance with testamentary tablets not legally executed, can defend themselves by a plea of fraud against those who claim the inheritance *ab intestato*.

sunt, . . . testimonium non denegamus.—§§ 3, 10, 11, I. h. t. (de test. ord. 2, 10).[1]

(2) By word of mouth:[a] by a complete declaration of the last will understood by the witnesses, without further formality.[b]

[a] For the nuncupative will under English Law, see Steph. ii. 594, 593.

[b] *Supra*: D. 28, 1, 21 pr.

Si quis autem voluerit sine scriptis ordinare iure civili testamentum, septem testibus adhibitis et sua voluntate coram eis nuncupata, sciat hoc perfectissimum testamentum iure civili firmumque constitutum.—§ ult., I. eod.[2]

(3) In both cases, the making of the testament must, moreover, take place 'uno eodemque actu,' that is, be interrupted by no other (legal) act.

Ulp.: Uno contextu actus testari oportet; est autem 'uno contextu' nullum actum alienum testamento intermiscere: quod si aliquid pertinens ad testamentum faciat, testamentum non vitiatur. —l. 21, § 3, D. qui test. fac.[3]

---

[1] But when gradually, as much by popular custom as by the improvements contained in constitutions, the Civil and Praetorian Law began to be blended into a united whole, it was established that at one and the same time, which was required to some extent by the Civil Law, seven witnesses were procured and the subscription of the witnesses, which was derived from constitutions, and, according to the Praetorian Edict, the seals should be impressed on the testament. § But neither the appointed heir, nor any one under his power, nor his father under whose power he is, nor his brother under the power of the same father, can be employed as witnesses; because this whole business which is transacted in view of executing a testament is at the present day considered as a transaction between the heir and the testator. § But we do not deny to legatees and to beneficiaries under a trust the right to attest because they are not successors to the rights (of the deceased).

[2] Now if a man desire to make an unwritten testament according to the Civil Law, let him know that, by procuring seven witnesses and publicly declaring his will before them, this testament is quite complete and made stable by the Civil Law.

[3] The testamentary disposition must be an uninterrupted act: now it is 'uninterrupted' if no other act foreign to the testa-

Book III. Part III.

Besides PRIVATE, there are still PUBLIC testaments (testamenta publica), which can be made either by declaration upon record before a public magistrate (testamentum apud acta conditum s. iudiciale) or by delivery to the Emperor for safe custody (testamentum principi oblatum) without further solemnity.

§ 158. ANOMALOUS FORMS, ESPECIALLY *TESTAMENTUM MILITIS*.[a]

[a] Cf. Böcking, 'Pandekten,' iii. § 17.

In many cases the solemnities in the making of a testament were in part increased—so as to have a greater guarantee for the authenticity of the last will (*e.g.*, in the testament of the blind, deaf, dumb)—and in part were curtailed (privileged testaments). Amongst the latter, the 'testamentum militis' deserves special mention. According to imperial constitutions,[b] this required no formalities. Whilst this privilege originally appertained to all milites according to their standing, from the time of Justinian it avails only for military testaments made in the field. The testament so made remains in force even for a year after honourable discharge. In respect of its contents also the military testament was variously absolved of legal rules otherwise binding;[c] thus the heritage of the miles is uniformly treated 'not as familia according to ius civile proprium Romanorum, but as bona according to ius gentium.'[d]

[b] Cf. § 149, ad fin.

[c] Cf. §§ 153, 159, ad fin.; 160, 167, ad fin.; 169, ad fin.

[d] Böcking.

> Ulp.: Militibus liberam testamenti factionem primus quidem D. Iulius Caesar concessit, sed ea concessio temporalis erat. Postea vero primus D. Titius dedit, post hoc Domitianus; postea vero D. Nerva plenissimam indulgentiam in milites contulit, eamque et Traianus secutus est et exinde mandatis inseri coepit caput tale: . . . 'Faciant testamenta quo modo volent, faciant quo modo poterint sufficiatque ad bonorum suorum divisio-

ment occur in between. But if he do anything relating to the testament, the testament is not vitiated.

nem faciendam nuda voluntas testatoris.'— D. 29, 1, 1 pr.[1]

Ulp. xxiii. 10: Sed quod testamentum miles contra iuris regulam fecit, ita demum valet, si in castris mortuus sit, vel post missionem intra annum.[2]

Inst. ii. 11 pr.: Supradicta diligens observatio in ordinandis testamentis militibus propter nimiam imperitiam constitutionibus principalibus remissa est: nam quamvis hi neque legitimum numerum testium adhibuerint, neque aliam testamentorum sollemnitatem observaverint, recte nihilominus testantur: videlicet cum in expeditionibus occupati sunt, quod merito nostra constitutio induxit. Quoquo enim modo voluntas eius suprema sive scripta inveniatur, sive sine scriptura, valet testamentum ex voluntate eius. Illis autem temporibus, per quae citra expeditionum necessitatem in aliis locis vel in suis sedibus degunt, minime ad vindicandum tale privilegium adiuvantur.[3]

---

[1] The late Emp. Julius Caesar was the first to grant to soldiers free execution of a testament, but that concession was limited to a certain time. But the late Emperor Titus was the first to grant it to them afterwards; after that Domitian; and subsequently the late Emp. Nerva conferred upon soldiers the fullest indulgence, and his example was followed by Trajan also; and from thenceforth a chapter began to be included in the mandates as follows: '. . . They may make their testament in such manner as they like, they may make them in such way as they can, and the mere will of the testator shall suffice for the distribution of his property.'

[2] But when a soldier has made a testament contrary to a rule of law, it is only valid if he have died in the field, or within a year after his discharge.

[3] By imperial constitutions, the strict observance of what is above mentioned in the framing of testaments has been dispensed with in the case of soldiers, on account of their excessive inexperience. If, accordingly, they do not employ the lawful number of witnesses, nor observe some other usual form in respect of testaments, they nevertheless make valid testaments; that is to say, when they are engaged on active

Book III. Part III.

CONTENTS OF THE TESTAMENT.

§ 159. Institution of Heir.[a]

[a] Compare in English Law the nomination of an executor (Brown, s.v.).

The testament can contain the most various dispositions, but its essential and necessary subject-matter is uniquely and always the nomination of an heir. 'No testament without institution of an heir; no institution of heir without a testament.'[b]

[b] Cf. Arndts, § 483.

Gai. ii. § 229: Testamenta vim ex institutione heredis accipiunt et ob id velut caput et fundamentum intelligitur totius testamenti **heredis institutio.**'[1]

Ulp. xxiv. 15: Ante heredis institutionem legari non potest, quoniam vis et potestas testamenti ab heredis institutione incipit.[2]

Institution requires, according to classical Law, prescribed FORM (verba imperativa).

Gai. ii. § 117: Sollemnis autem institutio haec est: TITIVS HERES ESTO; sed et illa iam comprobata videtur: TITIVM HEREDEM ESSE IVBEO; at illa non est comprobata: TITIVM HEREDEM ESSE VOLO; sed et illae a plerisque improbatae sunt: HEREDEM INSTITVO, item HEREDEM FACIO.[3]

---

service: this has with good reason been introduced by our constitution. For in whatever manner his last intention is discovered, whether as written or without writing, his testament holds good by virtue of his intention. But during those times when they are living exempt from the necessity of service, in other places or at their homes, they are not allowed to claim such a privilege.

[1] Testaments derive their force from the institution of an heir, and on that account the institution of the heir is regarded as the head and foundation of the whole testament.

[2] There can be no bequest of a legacy before the institution of the heir, since the force and power of a testament begins with the institution of an heir.

[3] Now the solemn institution is this: 'Tit., be my heir'; but this also now seems approved: 'I order Tit. to be heir.' This, however, is not approved: 'My will is that Tit. should be heir'; but further, these following are by most disapproved: 'I institute heir,' and 'I make heir.'

By later Law, however, any declaration is sufficient by which the personality of an heir is directly and plainly set forth.

Imp. Constant.: Placuit ademptis his quorum imaginarius usus est, institutioni heredis verborum non esse necessariam observantiam, utrum imperativis et directis verbis fiat, an inflexis; . . . sed quolibet loquendi genere formata institutio valeat, si modo per eam liquebit voluntatis intentio.—C. 6, 23, 15.[1]

Next, as to capacity to inherit[a] of the heir instituted. He is incapable that has no testamenti factio; but one's own slaves can be instituted as heirs 'cum libertate,' and the slaves of others have testamenti factio from and for their master personally.[b]

[a] To be distinguished from capacity to acquire, § 172.

[b] Inst. ii. 19, 4.

Ulp. xxii. 7–9: Servos heredes instituere possumus: nostros cum libertate, alienos sine libertate, communes cum libertate vel sine libertate.—Eum servum, qui tantum in bonis noster est, nec cum libertate heredem instituere possumus, quia Latinitatem consequitur, quod non proficit ad hereditatem capiendam.—Alienos servos heredes instituere possumus eos tantum, quorum cum dominis testamenti factionem habemus.—12: Proprius servus . . . si sine libertate sit institutus, omnino non consistit institutio.[2]

---

[1] It has been decided to do away with those formalities of which only fanciful use is made, and, in respect of the institution of an heir, that the observance of (certain) words is unnecessary, whether the institution be effected by peremptory and direct, or indirect terms; . . . but in whatever manner of speech the institution has been expressed, it shall hold good, so long as the intention of the will shall thereby clearly appear.

[2] We may institute slaves as heirs; accompanied by liberty if they belong to us, without liberty if they are owned by other people; with or without liberty if they are common property.—A slave that is ours alone upon a Bonitary title we cannot institute heir, even as accompanied by liberty, because he attains Latinity, and this is of no avail for taking an inheritance.—

BOOK III. Part III.

Hodie vero etiam sine libertate ex nostra constitutione heredes (servos proprios) instituere permissum est.—pr., I. h. t. (de her. inst. 2, 14).[1]

Flor.: In extraneis heredibus illa observantur, ut sit cum eis testamenti factio, . . . et id duobus temporibus inspicitur, testamenti facti, ut constiterit institutio, et mortis testatoris, ut effectum habeat; hoc amplius et cum adibit hereditatem, esse debet cum eo testamenti factio; . . . medio autem tempore inter factum testamentum et mortem testatoris vel condicionem institutionis existentem mutatio iuris heredi non nocet.—l. 50 (49), § 1, D. h. t. (de her. inst. 28, 5).[2]

After the lex Voconia (A.U. 585), women, other than Vestal virgins, could not be instituted as heirs by citizens enrolled in the first class [a]—a restriction which naturally disappeared in the later period.

[a] Paul. iv. 8, 22. Gai. ii. 226.

Gai. ii. § 274: Item mulier, quae ab eo qui centum milia aeris census est per legem Voconiam heres institui non potest, tamen fidei commisso relictam sibi hereditatem capere potest.[3]

Slaves belonging to other people we can alone institute as heirs with whose masters we have testamentary capacity.—If our own slave have been instituted without the accompaniment of liberty, the institution altogether fails.

[1] But at the present day, according to our constitution, leave is given to institute (one's own slaves) as heirs without the accompaniment of liberty.

[2] The following points are observed in respect of stranger-heirs: that there be with them a relation of testamentary capacity; . . . and that is measured by two periods, according to the time when the testament was made, that the institution should hold good, and according to the time when the testator died, that it should take effect. Moreover, there must be a relation of testamentary capacity with him at the time when he shall enter upon the inheritance. But if a change of status should happen in the interval between the making of the testament and the death of the testator, or until the fulfilment of the condition attached to the institution, it does not prejudice the heir.

[3] Again, a woman who, according to the *l. Voconia*, cannot be instituted heir by any one who is registered as possessing one

Incertae personae have no capacity for inheritance; these are primarily juristic persons, in case capacity for inheritance has not been especially conferred upon them; and further, those persons of whose individuality the testator has no definite idea.[a] To the latter belong also postumi; but those could be instituted who were born '(postumi) sui'[b] after the death of the testator, already according to older civil Law—although not from the beginning—, and those who were born 'sui' in his lifetime, after the making of the will, or had become 'sui' by the lapse of an intermediate person, according to the lex Iunia Velleia and the interpretation thereof. Justinian eventually permitted the institution of all incertae personae, including 'postumi alieni.'

[a] Ulp. xxiv. 18.

[b] Paul. iv. 8, 7.

> Ulp. xxii. 5, 6: Nec municipium nec municipes heredes institui possunt, quoniam incertum corpus est: . . . Senatusconsulto tamen concessum est, ut a libertis suis heredes institui possint.—Deos heredes instituere non possumus praeter eos, quos senatusconsulto constitutionibusve principum instituere concessum est.[1]
>
> Ib. § 4: Incerta persona heres institui non potest, velut hoc modo: QVISQVIS PRIMVS AD FVNVS MEVM VENERIT, HERES ESTO; quoniam certum consilium debet esse testantis.[2]
>
> Gai. ii. § 238: Incerta videtur persona, quam per incertam opinionem animo suo testator subiicit.[3]

---

hundred thousand *asses*, may yet take the inheritance bequeathed to her by way of *fideicommissum*.

[1] Neither a municipality nor the burghers can be instituted heirs, since the body is an uncertain one. . . . A decree of the senate, however, has allowed them to be instituted heirs by their own freedmen.—We cannot institute the gods as heirs, except those whose institution has been allowed by the senate's decree or imperial constitutions.

[2] An uncertain person cannot be instituted heir; for example, thus: 'Whoever shall first come to my funeral, let him be my heir,' since the institution of the testator must be definite.

[3] An uncertain person appears to be one whom the testator brings before his mind without any definite idea (who he is).

Book III. Part III.

Ulp.: Postumos autem dicimus eos dumtaxat, qui post mortem parentis nascuntur; sed et hi qui post testamentum factum in vita nascuntur. —D. 28, 3, 3, 1.[1]

Gai.: Postumorum loco sunt et hi, qui in sui heredis loco succedendo quasi adgnascendo fiunt parentibus sui heredes; ut ecce si filium et ex eo nepotem neptemve in potestate habeam, quia filius gradu praecedit, is solus iura sui heredis habet: . . . sed si filius meus me vivo moriatur aut qualibet ratione exeat de potestate mea, incipit nepos neptisve in eius loco succedere et eo modo iura suorum heredum quasi adgnatione nanciscuntur.—l. 13 eod.[2]

Id. ii. § 242: Ne heres quidem potest institui postumus alienus: est enim incerta persona.— § 241: Est autem alienus postumus, qui natus inter suos heredes testatoris futurus non est; ideoque ex emancipato quoque filio conceptus nepos extraneus postumus est; item qui in utero est eius, quae iure civili non intelligitur uxor, extraneus postumus patris intelligitur.[3]

---

[1] Now we speak alone of those as posthumous who are born after the death of their parent; but such also are those who come into the world after the making of a testament.

[2] In the position of posthumous persons are those also who by stepping into the place of a *suus heres,* as it were by agnation, become *sui heredes* to their parents; as, for instance, if I have a son and by him a grandson or granddaughter under my power; since the son comes before (the grandson) by one degree, he alone has the rights of a *suus heres;* but if my son die during my lifetime, or passes in any way from under my power, the grandson or granddaughter begins to step into his place. And in this way they acquire, as it were by agnation, the rights of *sui heredes.*

[3] A posthumous stranger cannot even be appointed heir; for he is an indeterminate person. Now a posthumous stranger is a person who on birth will not be amongst *sui heredes.* And so a grandson conceived from an emancipated son is a posthumous stranger, likewise the unborn issue of her who is not regarded as wife by civil law is considered a posthumous stranger in respect of the father.

Paul.: Verum est omnem postumum qui moriente testatore in utero fuerit, si natus sit, bonorum possessionem [a] petere posse.—D. 37, 11, 3.[1]

[a] Sc. secundum tabulas.

The testator can nominate any number of heirs he likes.

Et unum hominem et plures in infinitum, quot quis velit, heredes facere licet.—Hereditas plerumque dividitur in duodecim uncias, quae assis appellatione continentur; habent autem et hae partes propria nomina ab uncia usque ad assem, ut puta haec: sextans, quadrans, triens, quincunx, semis, septunx, bes, dodrans, dextans, deunx, as.—§§ 4, 5, I. h. t. (=Ulp. l. 50, § 2, D. h. t. 28, 5).[2]

The institution of heir can also take place subject to the addition of a 'suspensive' condition,[b] but never—except as to the testamentum militis—of a 'resolutory' condition, or of a dies *ex quo* or *ad quem*. (Semel heres, semper heres: PERPETUITY of the inheritance.)

[b] D. 35, 1, 3; 28, 7, 9.

Heres et pure et sub condicione institui potest: ex certo tempore aut ad certum tempus non potest, veluti 'post quinquennium quam moriar' vel 'ex Kalendis illis' aut 'usque ad Kalendas illas heres esto'; diemque adiectum pro supervacuo haberi placet et perinde esse ac si pure heres institutus esset.—§ 9, I. eod.[3]

---

[1] It is well founded that every posthumous person that shall have been in the mother's womb at the death of the testator, when he has been born, can claim the *bon. poss.*

[2] A man may appoint as heir either one person or as many as he pleases, without limitation.—An inheritance is generally divided into twelve *unciae*, which are included under the designation an *as*. Now these portions have special names, from the *uncia* up to the *as*, thus: *sextans, quadrans, triens, quincunx, semis, septunx, bes, dodrans, dextans, deunx, as.*[c]

[c] See Smith, s. As, or Roby, Gr. sect. 189.

[3] An heir may be instituted absolutely or conditionally: he cannot be instituted 'from a certain time,' or 'to a certain time'; for instance, 'after five years from my death,' or 'from such Kalends,' or 'to such Kalends he shall be my heir;' and it is held that the date so added should be treated as superfluous, and that the heir was instituted absolutely.

Book III. Part III.

Ulp.: Miles et ad tempus heredem facere potest et alium post tempus, vel ex condicione, vel in condicionem.—D. 29, 1, 15, 4.[1]

§ 160. Substitutions.

The testator can in the institution of heir create several degrees, so that a second is nominated heir in the event of the first not being his heir—because he would not or could not be—and likewise a third in the place of the second, and so on (substituere,—primo, secundo, tertio gradu heredem scribere—primus, secundus heres). This eventual institution of heir is called SUBSTITUTION, 'substitutio *vulgaris* s. in primum casum.'

Mod.: Heredes aut instituti dicuntur aut substituti: instituti primo gradu, substituti secundo vel tertio.—l. 1 pr., D. h. t. (de vulg. et pup. subst. 28, 6).[2]

Marcian.: Potest quis in testamento plures gradus heredum facere, puta: 'Si ille heres non erit, ille heres esto,' et deinceps plures.—Et vel plures in unius locum possunt substitui vel unus in plurium, vel singulis vel singuli, vel invicem ipsi qui heredes instituti sunt.—l. 36 eod.[3]

Iul.: Si Titius coheredi suo substitutus fuerit, deinde ei Sempronius, verius puto in utramque

---

[1] A soldier can nominate an heir for a time, and another after the lapse of such time, or from (the fulfilment) of a condition, or until the fulfilment of a condition.

[2] Heirs are called either 'instituted' or 'substituted': instituted, if in the first degree; substituted, if in the second or third degree.

[3] A man can create several degrees of heirs in his testament; for example, 'If this one shall not be heir, that one shall be heir'; and several in succession.—And either several can be substituted in the place of one, or one in the place of several, or single heirs for single, or reciprocally those who themselves have been instituted heirs.

partem Sempronium substitutum esse.—l. 27 eod.[1]

If the institutus (primus heres) enters upon the inheritance, the substitution loses all significance. With the substitution it was still in the classical Law customary to connect the provision of the 'cretio'—perfecta or imperfecta—for the primus heres, that is, of a formal entry upon the inheritance within a definite interval.[a]

[a] Gai. ii. 164-6. Ulp. xxii. 30-2.

Gai. ii. § 174: Interdum duos pluresve gradus heredum facimus, hoc modo: LVCIVS TITVS HERES ESTO CERNITOQVE IN DIEBVS CENTVM PROXIMIS, QVIBVS SCIES POTERISQVE. QVODNI ITA CREVERIS, EXHERES ESTO. TVM MAEVIVS HERES ESTO CERNITOQVE IN DIEBVS CENTVM et reliqua; et deinceps in quantum velimus, substituere possumus.—§ 176: Primo itaque gradu scriptus heres hereditatem cernendo fit heres et substitutus excluditur; non cernendo summovetur, etiamsi pro herede gerat, et in locum eius substitutus succedit.[2]

Ulp. xxii. 34: Si sub imperfecta cretione heres institutus sit, id est non adiectis his verbis: SI NON CREVERIS, EXHERES ESTO, sed ita: SI NON CREVERIS, TVNC MAEVIVS HERES ESTO, cernendo quidem superior inferiorem excludit: non cernendo autem, sed pro herede gerendo in partem

---

[1] If Tit. shall have been substituted for his co-heir, and then Sempr. for Tit., I am of opinion that it is more correct that Sempr. is substituted for both parts.

[2] Sometimes we create two or more degrees of heirs, in this way: 'Luc. Tit., be heir, and make your decision within the next hundred days after it comes to your knowledge and you are in a position to act. If you shall not accept, be disinherited. Then Maev., be heir, and decide within a hundred days whether you will act,' and so on; and we can in succession make as many substitutes as we wish. § Thereïore the person nominated heir in the first degree by signifying his acceptance of the inheritance becomes heir, and the substitute is excluded. By not making such declaration, he is set aside, even though he act as heir, and the substitute steps into his place.

Book III. Part III.

admittit substitutum ; sed postea D. Marcus constituit, ut et pro herede gerendo ex asse fiat heres.[1]

Substitutio *in secundum casum*, that is, substitution in the event of the instituted heir dying after the acquisition of the inheritance, is—except as to the testamentum militis — as a rule inadmissible, since it contradicts the nature of Inheritance.[a]

[a] § 159, ad fin.

Gai. ii. § 184 : Extraneo heredi instituto ita substituere non possumus, ut si heres exstiterit et intra aliquod tempus decesserit, alius ei heres sit.[2]

Tryph. : Miles ita heredem scribere potest: 'quoad vivit Titius heres esto, post mortem eius Septicius.'—D. 29, 1, 41.[3]

It is permitted in Roman Law alone in the form of Pupillary substitution. That is, the testator can nominate an heir for the child under age in his potestas, not merely in the event of its not acquiring the inheritance (either by dying before the father, or by reason of abstinence),[b] but also in the event of its dying before the attainment of puberty.[c]

[b] § 171.
[c] Ulp. xi. 14.

Gai. ii. §§ 179-180 : Liberis nostris impuberibus, quos in potestate habemus, non solum ita . . . substituere possumus, ut si heredes non

---

1 If an heir have been substituted under an imperfect *cretio*, that is, without the addition of the following words : 'If you shall not decide, be disinherited,' but thus : 'If you shall not decide, then, Maevius, be heir,' by the very act of deciding the first heir excludes the one postponed to him ; if however he do not decide, but act as heir, the first heir lets in the substituted heir for a part of the inheritance. But the late Emp. Marcus afterwards by a constitution enacted that, even by acting as heir, he (*i.e.*, the heir proper) becomes heir to the whole.

2 When a stranger is instituted heir, we cannot substitute to him in such way, that if he become our heir and die within a certain time, another person shall be heir to him.

3 A soldier can nominate an heir thus : 'So long as Tit. lives, he shall be my heir ; after his death, Sept.'

exstiterint, alius nobis heres sit, sed eo amplius et etiamsi heredes nobis exstiterint et adhuc impuberes mortui fuerint, sit eis aliquis heres, velut hoc modo: TITIVS FILIVS MEVS MIHI HERES ESTO. SI FILIVS MEVS HERES NON ERIT, SIVE HERES ERIT ET PRIVS MORIATVR QVAM IN SVAM TVTELAM VENERIT, TVNC SEIVS HERES ESTO. § Quo casu si quidem non exstiterit heres filius, substitutus patri fit heres: si vero heres exstiterit filius et ante pubertatem decesserit, ipsi filio fit heres substitutus. Quamobrem duo quodammodo sunt testamenta, aliud patris aliud filii, tamquam si ipse filius sibi heredem instituisset; aut certe unum est testamentum duarum hereditatum.[1]

The pupillary substitute is the father's heir in accordance with the original fundamental idea in 'pupillaris substitutio'; according to the later one, he is nominated by the father for the impubes, who can himself be disinherited, so that the pupillary substitute receives nothing whatever of the paternal property, but, on the other hand, he appears as the father's heir always alone indirectly when the child has not been disinherited.

Cicero, de invent. ii. 21, 62: Quidam pupillum heredem fecit; pupillus autem ante mortuus est, quam in suam tutelam venit; de hereditate ea,

[1] We can substitute an heir for our children under the age of puberty, and under our power, not only in such way that, if they shall not become heirs, another person may be our heir; but further that, if they do become our heirs, and yet shall have died under puberty, somebody may be heir to them; for example, thus: 'Tit., my son, be my heir; if my son shall not be my heir, or if he become heir, and die before he is free from guardianship, then, Seius, be heir.' § In which case, if in fact the son shall not become heir, the substitute becomes heir to the father; but if the son become heir, and die before puberty, the substitute becomes heir to the son himself. Wherefore there are in a way two testaments, one of the father, the other of the son, just as if the son himself had instituted his own heir; or at any rate there is one testament in respect of two inheritances.

Book III. Part III.

quae pupillo venit, inter eos, qui patris pupilli heredes secundi sunt, et inter adgnatos pupilli controversia est; possessio heredum secundorum est. Intentio est adgnatorum: 'nostra pecunia est, de qua is cuius adgnati sumus testatus non est.' Depulsio est: 'immo nostra, qui heredes secundi testamento patris sumus.' Quaestio est: utrorum sit? Ratio: 'pater enim et sibi et filio testamentum scripsit, dum is pupillus esset; quare quae filii fuerunt, testamento patris nostra fiant necesse est.' Infirmatio rationis: 'immo pater sibi scripsit et secundum heredem non filio, sed sibi iussit esse; quare, praeterquam quod ipsius fuit, testamento illius vestrum esse non potest.' Iudicatio: 'possitne quisquam de filii pupilli re testari; an heredes secundi ipsius patrisfamilias, non filii quoque eius pupilli heredes sint'?[1]

Ulp.: Moribus introductum est, ut quis liberis impuberibus testamentum facere possit, donec

---

[1] A certain person made his ward his heir, but the ward died before he entered into his tutelage.[a] There is a dispute as to the inheritance which devolved upon the ward, between the secondary heirs of the ward's father and the next of kin of the ward: the possession belongs to the secondary heirs. The statement of claim by the next of kin is: 'The money is ours of which he whose next of kin we are made no disposition.' The rebutter is: 'Nay rather, it is ours who are secondary heirs by the father's testament.' The issue is: To which of the two does it belong? The principle (set up) is: 'The father wrote a testament for himself and his son whilst a ward; wherefore things which belonged to the son must needs become ours by the father's testament.' The demurrer to such principle is: 'Nay rather, the father wrote the will for himself, and directed that the secondary heir should be not his son's, but his own; wherefore, save as to what was the son's own, (the property) cannot be yours by the father's testament.' It is for the judge to say, whether any man can make a testament in respect of property of a son who is a ward, or whether the secondary heirs are heirs of the *pat. fam.* himself, and not also those of his son, being a ward.

[a] Or 'his property *in tutela*.'

masculi ad quattuordecim annos perveniant, feminae ad duodecim.—l. 2 pr., D. h. t.[1]

Gai. ii. § 182 : Non solum autem heredibus institutis impuberibus liberis ita substituere possumus, . . . sed etiam exheredatis : itaque eo casu si quid pupillo ex hereditatibus legatisve aut donationibus propinquorum adquisitum fuerit, id omne ad substitutum pertinet.[2]

Ulp.: Neque enim suis bonis testator substituit, sed impuberis.—l. 10, § 5, D. h. t.[3]

The pupillary substitution can take place as well in the same testament in which the father has instituted his heir—the child or a third party—as in a special one (pupillare testamentum, secundae tabulae) ; but the validity of the latter is always conditioned by that of the former (primae tabulae).

Liberis autem suis testamentum facere nemo potest, nisi et sibi faciat : nam pupillare testamentum pars et sequela est paterni testamenti, adeo ut si patris testamentum non valeat, ne filii quidem valebit.—§ 5, I. de pup. subst. 2, 16.[4]

Gai. ii. § 181 : Ceterum ne post obitum parentis periculo insidiarum subiectus videretur pupillus, . . . substitutionem . . . separatim in

---

[1] By our customs it has come about that a man can make a testament for his children under puberty, and for those of the male sex until their fourteenth year, for those of the female sex until their twelfth year.

[2] Now we can not only substitute to our children under puberty whom we have instituted heirs, . . . but we may also provide a substitute for children disinherited; in such a case therefore, if anything has come to the ward from inheritance, legacies, or gifts of relations, it all belongs to the substitute.

[3] For the testator has not nominated after-heirs for his own property, but for that of the person under puberty.

[4] But no one can make a testament for his children unless he make one also for himself; for the pupillary testament is part and appendage of the paternal testament, and this to such an extent that, if the testament of the father is invalid, the son's also will have no effect.

Book III. Part III.

inferioribus tabulis scribimus easque tabulas proprio lino propriaque cera consignamus, et in prioribus tabulis cavemus, ne inferiores tabulae vivo filio et adhuc impubere aperiantur.[1]

Vulgar and pupillary substitution were by custom mostly blended together (duplex substitutio); but, even when this had not happened, the pupillary was expounded at the same time as the vulgar substitution already in the last period of the Republic.

Cic. de inv. ii. 42, 122: Paterfamilias cum liberorum haberet nihil, uxorem autem haberet, in testamento ita scripsit: 'si mihi filius genitur unus pluresve, is mihi heres esto,' deinde quae adsolent; postea: 'si filius ante moritur, quam in tutelam suam venerit, tum mihi ille heres esto.' Filius natus non est; ambigunt adgnati cum eo, qui est heres, si filius antequam in suam tutelam veniat, mortuus sit.[2]

Id. de orat. 1, 39, 180: Clarissima M' Curii causa Marcique Coponii nuper apud Cviros . . . defensa est. Cum Q. Scaevola . . . negaret, nisi postumus et natus et, antequam in suam tutelam veniret, mortuus esset, heredem eum esse posse, qui esset secundum postumum et natum et mortuum heres institutus: ego[a] autem defenderem eum hac tum mente fuisse qui testamentum

[a] Sc. Crassus.

[1] But lest the ward be exposed to the risk of sharp practice after his parent's death, we write the substitution by itself in the concluding tablets, and seal up these tablets with a cord and seal of their own; and in the earlier tablets we provide that the concluding ones are not to be opened during the life of the son and whilst he is under puberty.

[2] As a *pat. fam.* had no children, but had a wife, he wrote this in his testament: 'If one or more sons be born to me, such shall be my heir,' followed by what is usual; afterwards: 'If my son die before he enter upon his tutelage, then so and so shall be my heir.' A son was not born: the next of kin are at issue with the heir as to whether the son died before entering upon his tutelage.

> fecisset, ut si filius non esset, qui in suam tutelam veniret, M' Curius heres esset.[1]

And from the time of Marcus Aurelius, the vulgar avails at the same time as the pupillary substitution for the impubes under power (in utrumque casum).

> Mod.: Iam hoc iure utimur ex D. Marci et Veri constitutione, ut cum pater impuberi filio in alterum casum substituisset, in utrumque casum substituisse intelligatur, sive filius heres non exstiterit, sive exstiterit et impubes decesserit.—l. 4 pr., D. h. t.[2]

§ 161. Invalidity of the Testament.

The invalidity of the testament is spoken of in different senses. For the testament can

(1) be either ipso iure null, or be merely disputable;

(2) be either invalid from the outset, or be deprived of force by a later event;

(3) the invalidity can be either total or partial, that is, relate merely to single dispositions.

The testament is null (nullum)—and that totally—from the outset, if it lack one of its essential requirements (testamentum non iure factum, iniustum); and so

---

[1] The celebrated case of Man. Cur. and Marc. Cop. was lately defended before the Centumvirs. When Q. Scaev. said that unless a posthumous son not only was born but died before he came into his tutelage, he could not be heir who was instituted heir after a posthumous son had both been born and died, I (Crassus), however, stated for the defence that he who had made the testament was then of this opinion, that if there were no son to come into his tutelage, Man. Cur. would be heir.

[2] With us it is now, according to a constitution of the late Emperors Marcus and Verus, an accepted rule that, when a father shall have created a substitute for his son under the age of puberty, for one of two events, he shall be regarded as having created a substitute for both events, whether the son shall not become heir, or whether he shall become heir and die under the age of puberty.

Book III. Part III.

(1) if the required form is not observed;

(2) if there exist no valid institution of heir;

(3) if the testator had no capacity for making a testament;

(4) in the 'praeteritio' (passing over) of a 'suus heres.'

A testament so as to be legally valid is deprived of force (testamentum infirmatur)—

(1) by the testator's losing testamenti factio or independence of Family (testamentum irritum).

Gai. ii. §§ 145–146: Testamenta iure facta infirmantur, velut cum is qui fecerit testamentum capite diminutus sit.—Hoc autem casu irrita fieri testamenta dicemus.[1]

Ulp.: Exigit praetor, ut is cuius bonorum possessio datur utroque tempore ius testamenti faciendi habuerit, et cum facit testamentum et cum moritur. . . . Sed si quis utroque tempore testamenti factionem habuerit, medio tempore non habuerit, bonorum possessio secundum tabulas peti poterit.—D. 37, 11, 1, 8.[2]

Id. xxiii. 6: Si septem signis testium signatum sit testamentum, licet iure civili ruptum vel irritum factum sit, praetor scriptis heredibus iuxta tabulas bonorum possessionem dat, si testator et civis Romanus et suae potestatis, cum moreretur, fuit: quam bonorum possessionem cum re, i.e. cum effectu habent, si nemo alius iure heres sit.[3]

---

[1] Testaments duly executed are annulled, for example, when the testator shall have suffered loss of status. But in this case we shall say that testaments become untenable.

[2] The Praetor requires that he of whose effects possession is granted must have had testamentary capacity at both times, when making the testament, and when dying. . . . But if a man had testamentary capacity at both times, but had it not in the intermediate period, the *bon. poss. sec. tab.* can be claimed.

[3] If a testament have been sealed with the seals of seven witnesses, though it may have been broken or untenable by civil law, yet the Praetor in accordance with the will grants

(2) By lapse of the instituted heir (testamentum destitutum).

Pomp.: Si nemo hereditatem adierit, nihil valet ex his quae testamento scripta sunt.—D. 26, 2, 9.[1]

(3) By cancellation, for which, according to ius civile, the making of a fresh testament was required (testamentum posteriore testamento ruptum), but according to Praetorian and later Law, it is sufficient that there should be any intentional destruction of the testament, cancelling the institution of heir,[a] injury to the seals and the like, but not informal revocation,—which certainly is doubtful in respect of the Praetorian Law.

[a] Cf. D. 34, 9, 16, 2.

Gai. ii. § 151: Potest ut iure facta testamenta contraria voluntate infirmentur. Apparet autem non posse ex eo solo infirmari testamentum, quod postea testator id noluerit valere, usque adeo, ut si linum eius inciderit, nihilominus iure civili valeat. Quin etiam si deleverit quoque aut obleverit tabulas testamenti, nihilominus non desinent valere quae ibi fuerunt scripta, licet eorum probatio difficilis sit.[2]

Et si quidem [testamentum] concidit testator, denegabuntur actiones; si vero alius invito testatore, non denegabuntur.—Si, ut intestatus moreretur, incidit tabulas et hoc adprobaverint hi qui

---

possession of the effects to the heirs appointed, if the testator was both a Roman citizen and his own master at the time of his decease; and this possession they take *cum re*, that is, effectually, if there be no other person heir-at-law.

[1] If no one enters upon the inheritance, no validity attaches to what has been written in the testament.

[2] Testaments, duly executed, may be invalidated by a contrary intention. But it seems that a testament cannot be rendered nugatory by the mere fact that the testator afterwards did not wish it to be operative; to such an extent that, even though he should cut the thread, it would nevertheless continue good by civil law. Nay more, if he should even have effaced or besmeared the tablets of the testament, what was there written does not immediately cease to be valid, although proof of such may be difficult.

ab intestato venire desiderant, scriptis avocabitur hereditas.—D. 28, 4, l. 1, § 3 (Ulp.), l. 4 (Paul.).[1]

Ulp.: Si heres institutus non habeat voluntatem, vel quia incisae sunt tabulae, vel quia cancellatae, vel quia alia ratione voluntatem testator mutavit voluitque intestato decedere, dicendum est ab intestato rem habituros eos, qui bonorum possessionem acceperunt.—D. 38, 6, 1, 8.[2]

Gai. ii. § 144: Posteriore quoque testamento, quod iure factum est, superius rumpitur; nec interest an exstiterit aliquis ex eo heres an non exstiterit: hoc enim solum spectatur, an existere potuerit; ideoque si quis ex posteriore testamento, quod iure factum est, aut noluerit heres esse, aut vivo testatore aut post mortem eius, antequam hereditatem adiret, decesserit, aut per cretionem exclusus fuerit, aut condicione, sub qua heres institutus est, defectus sit, . . . paterfamilias intestatus moritur: nam et prius testamentum non valet, ruptum a posteriore, et posterius neque nullas vires habet, cum ex eo nemo heres exstiterit.[3]

---

[1] And if it be the testator has cut through the testament, actions will be withheld, but if another did this against the testator's will, actions will not be withheld.—If the testator, in order to die without a testament, cuts the testamentary tablets, and proof has been given of this by the persons who seek entry under intestacy, the inheritance will be taken away from the designated heirs.

[2] If the appointed heir have no desire, either because the tablets have been cut, or have been cancelled, or the testator in some other way has changed his will and wished to die intestate, we must say that the persons that have received possession of the effects will receive the property without a testament.

[3] An earlier testament is revoked also by a later one which has been duly executed; and it is immaterial whether any one becomes heir under the later testament or not; for the only point regarded is, whether there could have been an heir. Therefore if the heir under the later testament, duly executed, either refuses to be heir, or dies in the lifetime of the testator, or after his decease, but before entry upon the inheritance, or

Ulp.: Tunc autem prius testamentum rumpitur, cum posterius rite perfectum est: nisi forte . . . in eo scriptus est, qui ab intestato venire potest.—D. 28, 3, 2.[1]

Iust. ii. 17, 7: Ex eo autem solo non potest infirmari testamentum, quod postea testator id noluit valere.[2]

(4) By 'agnatio postumi' (testamentum ruptum in the narrower sense).[a]

(5) By employment of the 'querela inofficiosi.'[b]

[a] § 167.

[b] § 169.

SUCCESSION *AB INTESTATO*.[c]

[c] See 'Anct. Law,' pp. 195-6, 217-221.

§ 162. According to the Older Civil Law *Legitima Hereditas*.[d]

[d] Ibid. pp. 199-201.

Intestate succession occurs if no valid testament exists, or the inheritance is not entered upon by virtue of such.[e]

[e] D. 29, 2, 39.

Intestatus decedit, qui aut omnino testamentum non fecit, aut non iure fecit, aut id quod fecerat ruptum irritumve factum est, aut nemo ex eo heres exstitit.—pr., I. h. t. (de her. q. ab int. 3, 1).[3]

The members of the testator's family, as the persons standing nearest to him, by the Law[f] are called to the inheritance in a course of orderly succession. In this the principle of Agnation[g] uniquely underlies the old civil Law of intestate inheritance.

[f] Perhaps by supplying his presumable will.

[g] § 42.

---

does not fulfil the condition under which he was instituted heir . . . the *pat. fam.* dies intestate; for the first testament is void, having been revoked by the later one, and the later one is equally of no force, since no one becomes heir under it.

[1] An earlier testament is only revoked when the later one has been completed in proper form, unless perhaps a person has been designated therein who can enter without a testament.

[2] A testament cannot be rendered invalid merely because the testator afterwards wished that it should be inoperative.

[3] A person dies intestate who either has made no testament at all, or has made one not according to law, or when that which he made has been revoked or become inoperative, or when no one has become heir by virtue thereof.

BOOK III. Part III.

Ulp. xxvii. 5: Legitimae hereditatis ius, quod lege XII tabularum descendit, capitis minutione amittitur.[1]

But in the latest Law of Justinian (Nov. 118) exclusive precedence was given to the principle of Cognation;[a] its progressive recognition—which at first gained authority in the bonorum possessio intestati—forms the subject-matter of the history of the Roman Law of intestate inheritance.—The call to the intestate succession always supposes that the person called (delatee) is entitled to inherit at the moment of the devolution of the intestate succession, and further, that he existed—at least as 'nasciturus'[b]—already in the testator's lifetime.

[a] § 43.

[b] § 32.

Cum autem quaeritur an quis suus heres existere potest: eo tempore quaerendum est, quo certum est aliquem sine testamento decessisse.—§ 7, I. h. t.[2]

Paul.: Haec verba: SI INTESTATO MORITVR ad id tempus referuntur, quo testamentum destituitur, non quo moritur.—D. 28, 2, 9, 2.[3]

Inst. iii. 2, 6: Proximus autem,[c] si quidem nullo testamento facto quisque decesserit, per hoc tempus requiritur, quo mortuus est is cuius de hereditate quaeritur; quodsi facto testamento quisquam decesserit, per hoc tempus requiritur, quo certum esse coeperit, nullum ex testamento heredem exstaturum: tum enim proprie quisque intelligitur intestatus decessisse. Quod quidem aliquando longo tempore declaratur: in quo spatio temporis saepe accidit, ut proximiore mortuo proximus esse

[c] Sc. eres.

[1] The right of inheritance-at-law which is derived from the Law of the Twelve Tables is lost by abatement of status.

[2] But when it is questionable whether some man can be *suus heres*, we must look for the time when it is certain the deceased died without a testament.

[3] These words, 'if he die intestate,' are referable to the time when the testament is deprived of force, not to that of his death.

incipiat, qui moriente testatore non erat proximus.[1] Book III. Part III.

Qui post mortem avi sui concipitur, is neque legitimam hereditatem eius tamquam suus heres, neque bonorum possessionem tamquam cognatus accipere potest, quia lex XII tabularum eum vocat ad hereditatem, qui moriente eo de cuius bonis quaeritur in rerum natura fuerit—vel si vivo eo conceptus est, quia conceptus quodammodo in rerum natura esse existimatur.—D. 38, 16, l. 6 (Iul.), l. 7 (Cels.).[2]

Vestal virgins[a] were entirely excluded from intestate succession : neither could they inherit ab intestato nor was such inheritance possible from them.

[a] Gell. I, 12, §§ 9, 13.

Gell. i. 12, § 18 : In commentariis Labeonis, quae ad XII tabulas composuit, ita scriptum est : 'Virgo Vestalis neque heres est cuiquam intestato, neque (ei) intestatae quisquam, sed bona eius in publicum redigi aiunt. Id quo iure fiat, quaeritur.'[3]

---

[1] When any one has died without having made a testament, the next heir is looked for as from the time when the person died whose inheritance is in question. But if a man have died after making a testament, such person is looked for as from the time when it is certain that there will be no heir under the testament; for it is then that a man is strictly understood to have died intestate. And this in fact sometimes is a long time in being evinced; in which interval it often happens that the next heir dies, and some one obtains the next place who was not next at the time of the testator's death.

[2] He that was conceived after the death of his grandfather can neither receive his inheritance-at-law as *suus heres*, nor possession of the effects as cognatic kinsman, because the Law of the Twelve Tables calls such person to the inheritance as was in the world at the death of him whose succession is in question;—or if he was conceived during the lifetime of such person, because he is in a manner regarded as in the world when conceived.

[3] In the commentaries of Labeo, which he wrote upon the Twelve Tables, the following is found written : 'A Vestal virgin is not heir to an intestate, neither is any one heir to her as in-

BOOK III. Part III.

To the inheritance of a free-born person are called by the Law of the Twelve Tables, first of all, the SUI of the deceased, *i.e.*, persons becoming free from power by the death of the testator (or more precisely, members of a family made free from power upon the devolution of the intestate succession)—inclusive of the 'postumi'[a]—in whose case the transfer of the control of the property of the pat. fam. is in the Twelve Tables presumed naturally to take place, so that here one cannot speak of 'becoming an heir' and of the 'acquisition' of inheritance.[b]

[a] D. 28, 3, 3, 1, and l. 13.

[b] Cf. D. 41, 1, 34; §§ 167, 171, 173.

[c] See Coll. xvi. 2, derived from Gaius, the MS. of whose Institutes is here defective. Cf. Muirhead, *in loc.*

Gai. iii. §§ 1–4:[c] Intestatorum hereditates lege XII tabularum primum ad **suos heredes** pertinent. § Sui autem heredes existimantur liberi, qui in potestate morientis fuerunt, veluti filius filiave nepos neptisve ex filio; . . . nec interest, utrum naturales sint liberi an adoptivi. Ita demum tamen nepos neptisve . . . suorum heredum numero sunt, si praecedens persona desierit in potestate parentis esse, sive morte id acciderit, sive alia ratione, veluti emancipatione: nam si per id tempus, quo quis moritur, filius in potestate eius sit, nepos ex eo suus heres esse non potest; item et in ceteris deinceps liberorum personis dictum intelligemus. § Uxor quoque, quae in manu morientis est, si sua heres est, quia filiae loco est; item nurus quae in filii manu est, nam et haec neptis loco est; sed ita demum erit sua heres, si filius cuius in manu fuit, cum pater moritur, in potestate eius non sit. § Postumi quoque, qui si vivo patre nati essent, in potestate eius futuri forent, sui heredes sunt.[1]

---

testate, but it is said such person's effects are converted into public property. It is a question by what law this takes place.'

[1] The inheritances of intestates, by the Law of the Twelve Tables, belong in the first place to their *sui heredes*. § Now those children are accounted *sui heredes* who were under the power of the dying man, as a son or daughter, grandson or granddaughter by a son: . . . and it is immaterial whether

Ib. § 51 : Numquam feminae **suum** heredem habere possunt.[1]

Id. ii. § 157 : Sed **sui** quidem heredes ideo appellantur, quia **domestici** heredes sunt et vivo patre quodammodo domini existimantur.[2]

Paul.: In **suis** heredibus evidentius apparet, continuationem dominii eo rem perducere, ut nulla videatur hereditas fuisse, quasi olim hi domini essent, qui etiam vivo patre quodammodo domini existimantur : unde etiam filiusfamilias appellatur sicut paterfamilias, sola nota hac adiecta, per quam distinguitur genitor ab eo qui genitus sit. Itaque post mortem patris non hereditatem percipere videntur, sed magis liberam bonorum administrationem consequuntur.[a] Hac ex causa, licet non sint heredes instituti, domini sunt ; nec obstat, quod licet eos exheredare, quos et occidere licebat.—D. 28, 2, 11.[3]

[a] Cf. Markby, p. 379, note; Holmes, p. 342.

---

they are actual or adopted children. A grandson and a granddaughter, however, are only numbered amongst *sui heredes* if the person who precedes has ceased to be under the power of his ascendant, whether that has happened by death or by some other means, emancipation, for instance ; for if when a man dies his son is under his power, the grandson by him cannot be a *suus heres*. The like we understand is asserted in respect of other classes of descendants consecutively.—§ A wife also who is under the *manus* of the dying man is *sua heres* to him, because she is in the position of a daughter. Likewise a daughter-in-law, who is under the *manus* of a son, for she again is in the position of a granddaughter, but she will only be *sua heres* if the son under whose *manus* she is when the father dies be not under his father's power. § Posthumous children too, who, if they had been born in the lifetime of the father, would have been under his power, are *sui heredes*.

[1] Women can never have a *suus heres*.

[2] But they are called *sui heredes* because they are heirs of the family, and even in the lifetime of their ascendant are in a manner regarded as owners.

[3] In respect of *sui heredes*, it is very manifestly clear that the continuation of the ownership results in there seeming to have been no inheritance, as if the persons that even during the lifetime of the father are in a manner regarded as owners were in

Book III. Part III.

Id.: Cum ratio naturalis quasi lex quaedam tacita liberis parentum hereditatem addiceret, velut ad debitam successionem eos vocando, propter quod et in iure civili **suorum** heredum nomen eis indictum est ac ne iudicio quidem parentis, nisi meritis de causis, summoveri ab ea successione possunt.—D. 48, 20, 7 pr.[1]

Pap.: Scripto herede deliberante filius exheredatus mortem obiit atque ita scriptus heres omisit hereditatem: nepos ex illo filio susceptus avo suus heres erit.—D. 38, 6, 7 pr.[a][2]

[a] Cf. *sup.* D. 28, 2, 9, 2.

Paul. iv. 8, § 7 (Coll. xvi. 3): Post mortem patris natus, vel ab hostibus reversus, aut ex primo secundove mancipio manumissus, cuiusve erroris causa probata est, licet non fuerint in potestate, sui tamen patri heredes efficiuntur.[3]

The 'sui' inherit without regard to proximity of

---

time past owners; by which is explained also the designation 'son of the family' and 'father of the family,' this mark being alone added to distinguish between the parent and his child. Therefore after the death of the father they are not considered to acquire the inheritance, but they rather obtain the unrestricted control of the effects. Upon this ground, although they are not instituted heirs, they are owners; and no hindrance arises by one's being allowed to disinherit them, for one might indeed also kill them.

[1] Since natural reason, as a sort of tacit law, assigned to children their parents' inheritance, by calling them to the inheritance which, as it were, is due to them, on which account also in the Civil Law the name of *sui heredes* has been given to them, and they themselves cannot even be excluded from such inheritance by the will of the father except upon well-merited grounds.

[2] Whilst the designated heir was considering the matter, the disinherited son died, and thereupon the designated heir declined the inheritance: a grandson by that son acknowledged by the father will be his *suus heres*.

[3] A person born after his ascendant's death, or that has returned from the enemy, or has been emancipated from a first or second *mancipium*, or the reason of whose wandering has been approved, although such have not been under power, yet become *sui heredes* to the ascendant.

degree, and the division is made according to stocks (in stirpes).[a]

[a] Cf. Maine, 'Early Histy. of Instns.,' p. 195.

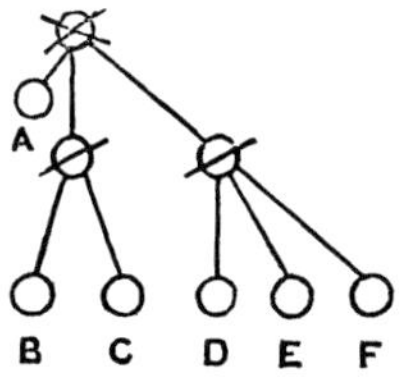

A receives $\frac{1}{3}$; B and C each $\frac{1}{6}$; D, E and F each $\frac{1}{9}$.

Ulp. xxvi. 2: Si defuncti sit filius et ex altero filio iam mortuo nepos unus vel etiam plures, ad omnes hereditas pertinet, non ut in capita dividatur, sed in stirpes, id est ut filius solus mediam partem habeat et nepotes, quotquot sunt, alteram dimidiam: aequum est enim, nepotes in patris sui locum succedere et partem habere, quam pater eorum si viveret, habiturus esset.[1]

If no 'suus' exist, the inheritance falls to the next agnate. The nearer agnate unconditionally excludes those more remote; such as are equally near inherit by heads, that is, in equal shares. Of female agnates, only the 'consanguineae'[b] are entitled to the succession, by virtue of the interpretation put upon the lex Voconia.[c]

[b] Paul. iv. 8.

[c] Gai. ii. 274.

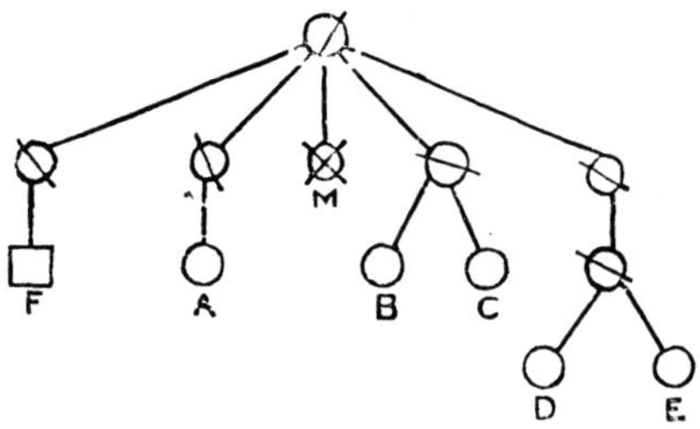

M is testator; A, B, C each inherit $\frac{1}{3}$; D, E, F are dropped.

[1] If there be one son of the deceased and also one grandson (or even more) born of another son already dead, the inheritance belongs to them all, not so as to be divided among them individually, but as branches (of the stem), that is, that the single son has one moiety and the grandsons, however many, have the other moiety; for it is fair that the grandsons should succeed to their father's place, and should have that share which their father would have if alive.

BOOK III. Part III.

Ulp. xxvi. 1 : Cautum est lege XII tabularum : SI INTESTATO MORITVR CVI SVVS HERES NEC ESCIT, ADGNATVS PROXIMVS FAMILIAM HABETO.[1]

Paul. iv. 8, § 22: Feminae ad hereditates legitimas ultra consanguineorum successiones non admittuntur: idque iure civili Voconiana ratione videtur effectum; ceterum lex XII tabularum sine ulla discretione sexus adgnatos admittit.[2]

[a] § 43. Agnates failing, gentiles[a] are called to the inheritance.

Ulp. xxvi. 1[a] (Coll. xvi. 4): Si adgnatus defuncti non sit, eadem lex XII tabularum gentiles ad hereditatem vocat his verbis: SI ADGNATVS NEC ESCIT, GENTILES FAMILIAM HABENTO. Nunc nec gentiles nec gentilicia iura in usu sunt.[3]

The inheritance of a civis Romanus *libertus*, according to the Twelve Tables, was offered to his 'sui'; in default of such, to the patronus and his agnatic descendants,[b] and finally to the gens.

[b] § 36.

Ulp. xxvii. 1–4: Libertorum intestatorum hereditas primum ad suos heredes pertinet; deinde ad eos, quorum liberti sunt, velut patronum patronam liberosve patroni.—Si sit patronus et alterius patroni filius, ad solum patronum hereditas pertinet.—Item patroni filius patroni nepotibus obstat.—Ad liberos patronorum hereditas defuncti pertinet ita, ut in capita, non in stirpes dividatur.[4]

---

[1] So it was provided by a law of the Twelve Tables: 'If any one die intestate, without *suus heres*, the nearest agnate shall have the patrimony.[c]'

[c] Or 'inheritance.'

[2] Women are not admitted to legal inheritances beyond the succession of blood-relations; and that seems to result from the *i. c.* upon the principle of the *l. Voconia*; but a law of the Twelve Tables admits agnates without any discrimination of sex.

[3] If there be no agnate of the deceased, the same law of the Twelve Tables calls the members of the same gens to the inheritance, in the following terms: 'If no agnate exist, let the *gentiles* have the patrimony.' There is now no observance either of *gentiles* or of the rights of *gentiles*.

[4] The inheritance of intestate freedmen belongs first to their *sui heredes*; next to the persons whose freedmen they are, such

> Id. xxix. 2: Si intestata moriatur liberta, semper ad eum[a] hereditas pertinet, quoniam non sunt sui heredes matri, ut obstent patrono.[1]

[a] Sc. patronum.

The manumissor ex mancipio—parens manumissor[b]—takes the place of the patronus in the inheritance of the *emancipatus*.

[b] Cf. Inst. i. 12, 6; §§ 64, 66.

> Inst. iii. 2, § ult.: Ad legitimam successionem vocatur etiam parens, qui contracta fiducia filium vel filiam, nepotem vel neptem ac deinceps emancipat.[2]

The heritage of a Latinus Iunianus, after the manner of a peculium, falls to the patron and his heirs, but the children of the patron that have not been disinherited must, according to a SC. Largianum, precede his 'extranei heredes.'

> Gai. iii. § 58: Civis Romani liberti hereditas ad extraneos heredes patroni nullo modo pertinet; ad filium autem patroni nepotesque ex filio . . . omnimodo pertinet, etiamsi a parente fuerint exheredati: Latinorum autem bona tamquam peculia servorum etiam ad extraneos heredes pertinent, et ad liberos manumissoris exheredatos non pertinent. § 63: Postea Lupo et Largo consulibus senatus censuit, ut bona Latinorum primum ad eum pertinerent, qui eos liberasset; deinde ad liberos eorum non nominatim exheredatos, uti quisque proximus esset; tunc antiquo iure ad heredes eorum qui liberassent.[3]

---

as their patron, patroness, or the patron's children.—If there should be a patron and the son of another patron, the inheritance belongs to the patron alone.—Again, the son of a patron excludes his grandsons. The inheritance of the deceased belongs to the children of the patron in such way that it is divided *in capita*, not *in stirpes*.

[1] If the freedwoman die intestate, the inheritance always belongs to him (*i.e.*, the patron), since there are no *sui heredes* to the mother for the exclusion of the patron.

[2] To the succession-at-law is the ascendant likewise called who under a covenant for redemption emancipates his son or daughter, grandson or granddaughter, and so on.

[3] The inheritance of a Roman citizen that was a freedman in

BOOK III. Part III.

A 'successio ordinum et graduum,' *i.e.*, a successive following of the class next inheriting, if the previous one is discarded, is unknown to the civil Law of intestate inheritance, and similarly—in the class of agnates—a replacement of the lapsed grade that is nearer by the more remote. This very readily resulted in lack of heirs, an impropriety[a] which, in a somewhat rough fashion, might be met by in iure cessio hereditatis[b] and pro herede usucapio,[c] but against which the Praetorian order of succession was the first to furnish effective relief.

[a] 'In legitimis hereditatibus successio non est.'
[b] § 173.
[c] § 155.

ACCORDING TO PRAETORIAN LAW.
BONORUM POSSESSIO INTESTATI.

§ 163. In Respect of the Freeborn.

The Praetorian Edict set up certain classes (ordines) of those entitled to inherit, to whom the bonorum possessio is given upon a petition[d] being presented by them within certain intervals, so that, if no one of the preceding class claims the bonorum possessio, it is offered to that succeeding (successio ordinum). To the bonorum possessio are called both the civil heirs—to them it is merely 'utilis' (interdictum 'quorum bonorum')—and persons not entitled iure civili, to whom it is necessary. In relation to the former, the bonorum possessio granted to the latter was originally *sine re*, but after the principles by which the Praetor was guided in setting up classes for inheritance had taken deep root in general legal opinion (which indeed only adapted the Praetorian Edict to its own prin-

[d] § 154.

no way belongs to the stranger-heirs of the patron; but in every case it belongs to the son of the patron, and to the grandsons by a son, even though they have been disinherited by their ancestor; whilst the property of Latins, like the separate property of a slave, belongs to stranger-heirs, and does not belong to the disinherited descendants of the manumittor. § Later on, in the consulship of Lupus and Largus, the Senate decreed that the property of Latins should in the first place belong to him who had freed them; secondly, to the descendants of such persons, not expressly disinherited, according to their several proximity; then, by the ancient rule, to the heirs of those who had freed them.

ciples), it had naturally to be converted into bonorum possessio *cum re*.[a]

Ulp.: Quibus ex edicto bonorum possessio dari potest, si quis eorum aut dari sibi noluerit aut in diebus statutis non admiserit, tunc ceteris bonorum possessio perinde competit, ac si prior ex eo numero non fuerit.—Sed videndum est, an inter ceteros ipse quoque, qui exclusus est, admittatur. . . . Et hoc iure utimur, ut admittatur: poterit igitur ex sequenti parte[b] succedere ipse sibi.—D. 38, 9, l. 1, §§ 10–11.[1]

[a] § 154.

[b] Sc. edicti.

The following are the several classes for inheritance.

(1) *Unde liberi*, that is, the 'sui' and children severed from the familia by capitis diminutio, and thus in particular emancipati of the testator.

Ulp. xxviii. 8: Liberis bonorum possessio datur tam his, qui in potestate usque in mortis tempus fuerunt, quam emancipatis; item adoptivis, non tamen etiam in adoptionem datis.[2]

Gai. ii. § 137:—si vero emancipati fuerint ab adoptivo patre, tunc incipiunt in ea causa esse, qua futuri essent, si ab ipso naturali patre emancipati fuissent.[3]

Ulp.: Sed adoptivos hactenus admittimus si

---

[1] If any one of those to whom possession of the effects can be granted according to the Edict either has not desired to have it, or has not accepted it during the prescribed interval, the *bon. poss.* belongs to the rest, as if the former had not belonged to that number.—But we have to consider whether he who has been excluded himself also is admitted amongst the rest. . . . And our rule is that he is so admitted; therefore upon the ground of the part (*i.e.*, of the Edict) that follows, he will succeed to himself.

[2] The *bon. poss.* to children is granted both to those who have been under power up to the time of the ascendant's death, and to those who have been emancipated; to adopted children likewise, not however to those given in adoption.

[3] But if they were emancipated by their adoptive father, they then begin to be in the same position in which they would have been if they had been emancipated by their natural father himself.

Book III. Part III

fuerint in potestate; ceterum si sui iuris fuerint, ad bonorum possessionem non invitantur, quia adoptionis iura dissoluta sunt emancipatione.—D. 38, 6, 1, 6.[1]

As in the case of legitima hereditas, they succeed *in stirpes;* in the same stock, the nearer degree excludes the more remote, but the emancipatus, according to the 'nova clausula (Iuliani) de coniungendis cum emancipato liberis eius' added to the Edict under Hadrian, inherits together with his children left behind in the potestas of the grandfather as one stock.

Pomp.: Si quis ex his, quibus bonorum possessionem praetor pollicetur, in potestate parentis de cuius bonis agitur, cum is moritur, non fuerit, ei liberisque, quos in eiusdem familia habebit, si ad eos hereditas suo nomine pertinebit, . . . bonorum possessio eius partis datur, quae ad eum pertineret, si in potestate permansisset, ita ut ex ea parte dimidiam habeat, reliquum liberi eius.—l. 5 pr. eod.[2]

To re-establish a pecuniary equality between those entitled to inherit, the emancipati have to unite in, or bring into, the inheritance in common with the 'sui' that are their co-heirs the acquisitions they have made since emancipation, and the daughters (suae and emancipatae) the dos they have received:—collatio bonorum,[a] dotis.

[a] Cf. Blackstone, ii. 516-517 (Steph. ii. 211-212), and Paterson, 'Compend.,' c. 741.

Ulp. xxviii. 4: Emancipatis liberis ex edicto

[1] But we admit adoptive children only so far as they have been under power; if, on the other hand, they have been independent, they are not invited to the *bon. poss.*, because the rights of adoption have been destroyed by emancipation.

[2] If any one of those to whom the Praetor promises the *bon. poss.* was not at the time of his death under the power of the ancestor whose property is in question, the *bon. poss.* shall be granted to him and the descendants whom he shall have in his family, if the inheritance shall belong to them upon their own behalf, of such part as would appertain to him if he had remained under power, so that of such part he has a moiety, his descendants the residue.

datur bonorum possessio, si parati sint cavere fratribus suis, qui in potestate manserunt, bona quae moriente patre habuerunt se collaturos.[1]

Coll. xvi. 7, 2 (Ulp.): Nam aequissimum putavit,[a] neque eos bonis paternis carere per hoc, quod non sunt in potestate, neque praecipua bona propria habere, cum partem sint ablaturi suis heredibus.[2]

[a] Sc. Praetor.

Ulp.: Emancipatus filius . . . fratribus suis conferet, . . . quia veniendo ad bonorum possessionem illis iniuriam[b] facit.—D. 37, 8, 1, 13.[3]

[b] Sc. iure civili?

(2) *Unde legitimi*, that is, the heirs according to ius civile, and so 'sui,' 'adgnati,' 'gentiles.'

Iul.: Haec verba edicti: 'tum quem ei heredem esse oportet, si intestatus mortuus esset' . . . non ad mortis testatoris tempus referuntur, sed ad id quo bonorum possessio peteretur; et ideo legitimum heredem, si capite deminutus esset, ab hac bonorum possessione summoveri palam est.—D. 38, 7, 1.[4]

Ulp.: Haec autem bonorum possessio omnem vocat, qui ab intestato potuit esse heres, sive lex XII tabularum eum legitimum heredem faciat, sive alia lex senatusve consultum.—l. 2, § 4 eod.[5]

---

1 *Bon. poss.* is granted to emancipated children by virtue of the Edict, if they are prepared to give security to their brothers who have continued under power, that they will bring into division the property they had at their father's death.

2 For he [*i.e.*, the Praetor] thought it most equitable that they should neither forfeit the patrimony by the fact that they are not under power, nor should have special control over their own effects, since they are about to carry off a portion for their *sui heredes*.

3 An emancipated son . . . will collate with his brethren . . . because by acquiring the *bon. poss.* he does what is harmful to them.

4 The following words of the Edict: 'then he who would have to be his heir, if he had died intestate' . . . are not referable to the time of the testator's death, but to that when the *bon. poss.* is claimed; and therefore it is clear that the heir-at-law, if he has suffered loss of status, is excluded from this *bon. poss.*

5 Now this *bon. poss.* calls every one who could be heir under

BOOK III. Part III.

It was matter of dispute whether successio graduum obtained in the case of agnates.

[a] Sc. ut tertio gradu vocetur.

Gai. iii. § 28: Idem iuris est,[a] ut quidam putant, in eius adgnati persona, qui proximo adgnato omittente hereditatem, nihilo magis iure legitimo admittitur; sed sunt qui putant, hunc eodem gradu a praetore vocari, quo etiam per legem adgnatis hereditas datur.[1]

(3) *Unde cognati* (bonorum possessio proximitatis nomine), that is, the blood-relations of the testator, inclusive of liberi and adgnati, according to proximity of degree.

Ulp.: Haec bonorum possessio nudam habet praetoris indulgentiam, neque ex iure civili originem habet: nam eos invitat ad bonorum possessionem, qui iure civili ad successionem admitti non possunt, id est cognatos.—l. 1 pr., D. unde cogn. 38, 8.[2]

Id. xxviii. 9: Proximi cognati bonorum possessionem accipiunt non solum per feminini sexus personas cognati, sed etiam adgnati capite diminuti: nam licet legitimum ius adgnationis capitis minutione amiserint, natura tamen cognati manent.[3]

---

an intestacy, whether the statute of the Twelve Tables, or another statute, or a decree of the Senate, makes him heir-at-law.

[1] The rule is the same (that is, as to be called in the third degree) according to some, in the case of such agnate as, though the nearest agnate declines the inheritance, is not any the more admitted by statute-law; but some are of opinion that such a man is called by the Praetor in the same degree as that in which the inheritance is given by statute to the agnates.

[2] This *bon. poss.* has the mere indulgence of the Praetor, and has no source in the Civil Law; for it invites those persons to the *bon. poss.* who by the Civil Law cannot be admitted to the inheritance—*i.e.*, the cognates.

[3] Not only do the nearest kinsmen receive the *bon. poss.* who are cognates through a female, but also those next of kin who have experienced a *cap. dim.*; for although by the *cap. dim.* they have lost the statutory right of agnation, they nevertheless remain kinsmen by nature.

Book III. Part III.

> Gai. iii. § 29: Feminae certae adgnatae, quae consanguineorum gradum excedunt, tertio gradu vocantur.—§ 31: Liberi quoque qui in adoptiva familia sunt, ad naturalium parentum hereditatem hoc eodem gradu vocantur.[1]

But this was with successio graduum, and with restriction to the sixth (or to the seventh) degree.

> Haec autem bonorum possessio . . . cognatorum gradus sex complectitur, et ex septimo duas personas, sobrino et sobrina natum et natam.—l. 1, § 3, D. unde cogn.[2]

(4) *Unde vir et uxor*, that is, the survivor of spouses.[a]

> Ulp.: Ut bonorum possessio peti possit 'unde vir et uxor,' iustum esse matrimonium oportet. —l. un. pr., D. unde vir. 38, 11.[3]

[a] D. 38, 11, l. un., § 1.

§ 164. In Respect of Freedmen.

The bonorum possessio intestati in the case of inheritance of a freedman is given to the seven following classes.[b]

(1) *Unde liberi*, that is, 'sui'—but here only of the testator's own body—and those who have been 'sui,' as in § 163 (ad init.).[c]

> Gai. iii. § 41: Si vero intestatus moriatur suo herede relicto adoptivo filio vel uxore, quae in manu ipsius esset, vel nuru, quae in manu filii eius fuerit, datur patrono adversus hos suos heredes partis dimidiae bonorum possessio: pro-

[b] § 168.

[c] Ibid.

---

[1] Female agnates who are beyond the degree of consanguinity are undoubtedly called in the third degree. Children also who are in an adoptive family are called in the same degree to the inheritance of their natural parents.

[2] Now the *bon. poss.* embraces six degrees of relationship, and two persons from the seventh, of either sex, born to a cousin of either sex.

[3] In order that *bon. poss.* may be claimed 'unde vir et uxor,' the marriage must be a legal one.

Book III. Part III.

sunt autem liberto ad excludendum patronum naturales liberi, non solum quos in potestate mortis tempore habet, sed etiam emancipati et in adoptionem dati.[1]

[a] See § 162.

(2) *Unde legitimi.*[a] The place of patronus in the case of the emancipated child is here also taken by the parens or extraneus manumissor, but precedence is taken over the latter by ten near blood-relations, which in the Praetorian Edict form the special class 'unde decem personae.'

Coll. xvi. 9, 2 (Ulp.): Quodsi is qui decessit, liber fuit ex mancipatione citra remancipationem manumissus, lex quidem XII tabularum manumissori legitimam hereditatem detulit; sed praetor aequitate motus decem personas cognatorum ei praetulit has: patrem matrem, filium filiam, avum aviam, nepotem neptem, fratrem sororem, ne quis occasione iuris sanguinis necessitudinem vinceret.[2]

(3) *Unde cognati,* that is, the next blood-relations of the freedman, according to proximity of degree.

Ulp.: Pertinet autem haec (bonorum possessio) ad cognationes non serviles; nec enim facile ulla servilis videtur esse cognatio.—D. 38, 8, 1, § 2.[3]

---

[1] But if he die intestate, leaving as his *suus heres* an adoptive son, or a wife under his own *manus*, or a daughter-in-law who has been under the *manus* of his son, the *bon. poss.* is granted to the patron, as against these *sui heredes*, of one half share. But his actual children avail the freedman for the exclusion of the patron; not only those under his power at the time of his death, but also those who have been emancipated or given in adoption.

[2] But if he that died was free by mancipation, being emancipated without remancipation, the Law of the Twelve Tables offered the legal inheritance to the manumittor; but the Praetor, from considerations of equity, gave precedence over him to ten agnatic relations, as follows—the father, mother, son, daughter, grandfather, grandmother, nephew, niece, brother, sister, that no one should by an accident of law defeat blood-relationship.

[3] But this (*bon. poss.*) does not affect relationships of slaves; for the existence of any relationship amongst slaves seems inconceivable.

(4) *Tum quem ex familia patroni*, that is, the agnates of the latter.

(5) *Patronus patrona, item liberi et parentes patroni patronaeve*, if the patron of the libertus in respect of whom the inheritance arises is himself a freedman.

(6) *Unde vir et uxor se libertae libertive.*

(7) *Unde cognati manumissoris* with limitation as in § 163.

§ 165. *Senatusconsultum Tertullianum* and *Orphitianum*.

According to ius civile, the mother had hitherto not been heir at all to her children—in case she had not been in the manus of the husband, so as to be 'consanguineae loco' [a] towards the children—whilst according to Praetorian Law she had been so first in the class *unde cognati*. The SC. Tertullianum (under Hadrian) eventually, in case she had the 'ius liberorum,' gave to her a purely cognatic right of intestate inheritance in the class of the *legitimi*, which had to precede that of all agnates, with the exception of the father (parens manumissor) and of the 'frater consanguineus' of the testator.

[a] Cf. § 48.

> Ulp. xxvi. 8: Intestati filii hereditas ad matrem ex lege XII tabularum non pertinet; sed si ius liberorum habeat, ingenua trium libertina quattuor, legitima heres fit ex SC. Tertulliano, si tamen ei filio neque suus heres sit quive inter suos heredes ad bonorum possessionem a praetore vocatur, neque pater, ad quem lege hereditas bonorumve possessio cum re pertinet, neque frater consanguineus: quodsi soror consanguinea sit, ad utrasque pertinere iubetur hereditas.[1]

[1] The inheritance of an intestate son does not belong to his mother by the Law of the Twelve Tables; but if she has the prerogative of children, three in the case of a free-born woman, four in that of a freedwoman, she becomes statutory heir by the *SCtum Tertullianum*, provided that her son has neither a *suus heres* nor any one who is called by the Praetor to the *bon. poss.*

Inst. iii. 3, § 4: Dedimus ius legitimum plenum matribus sive ingenuis sive libertinis, etsi non ter enixae fuerint vel quater.—§ 7: Licet autem vulgo quaesitus sit filius filiave, potest ad bona eius mater ex Tertulliano senatusconsulto admitti.[1]

Conversely, her children could not be heirs to the mother at all by Civil Law, and by Praetorian Law were so first in the class of *cognati*: the SC. Orphitianum under Marcus Aurelius (178 A.D.) eventually gave to them, in relation to the mother, a (cognatic) right of intestate inheritance before all agnates.

Ulp. xxvi. 7: Ad liberos matris intestatae hereditas sine in manum conventione ex lege XII tabularum non pertinebat, quia feminae suos heredes non habent; sed postea imperatorum Antonini et Commodi oratione in senatu recitata id actum est, ut matrum legitimae hereditates ad filios pertineant, exclusis consanguineis et reliquis adgnatis.[2]

Sciendum est etiam illos liberos, qui vulgo quaesiti sunt, ad matris hereditatem ex hoc senatusconsulto admitti.—§ 3, I. de SC. Orph. 3, 4.[3]

---

amongst the *sui heredes*, nor a father to whom by law the inheritance or the effectual possession of the goods belongs, nor a brother on the father's side; but if he has a sister on the father's side, the inheritance is to belong to both.

[1] We have granted to mothers full statutory right, whether they are freeborn or freed, although they may not have given birth to children three or four times.—But although a son or daughter is born out of wedlock, the mother, by the *SCtum Tertullianum*, can be admitted to the property of such.

[2] The inheritance of an intestate mother, according to the Law of the Twelve Tables, did not belong to her children when there had been no *conventio in manum*, because women have no *sui heredes*; but later on, in pursuance of an oration by the Emperors Antonine and Commodus delivered in the senate, it was enacted that the statutory inheritances of mothers should belong to their sons, to the exclusion of the *consanguinei* and the other next of kin.

[3] It is to be noted that even those children who are born out

Imp. Alex.: Si intestatae mulieris consanguinei existant et mater et filia, ad solam filiam ex SC. Orphitiano hereditas pertinet.—l. 1, C. eod. 6, 57.[1]

§ 166. The Latest Law of Intestate Inheritance, under Justinian.[a]

[a] Cf. the English Statute of Distributions, and remarks in Blackstone, vol. ii. pp. 516, sq.; Stephen, ii. pp. 211, sq.

The tendency of the later, very fruitful, imperial legislation always went in the direction of obtaining increased recognition of the cognatic right of inheritance. But since it nevertheless left the existing principle of succession intact, and did not disturb the old framework of the Civil and Praetorian classes for inheritance, because it was restricted to the mechanical insertion in it of all innovations, as far as was practicable, a condition of Law was developed out of this which was characterised by medley and confusion, as well as by great profusion of controversies and intrinsic contradictions that scarcely admitted of solution. Justinian was the first comprehensively to reshape the Law of intestate inheritance, after he himself by many semi-legislative measures had in vain endeavoured to reform it.[b] This he did by Nov. 118 (543 A.D.)—the rules of which were supplemented by Nov. 127—and, by basing it solely on COGNATION (including adoption), he restored to such Law long-lost inner unity and perspicuity.

[b] See Inst. iii. 1, 3-9.

In the latest Law of intestate inheritance, there are four classes of persons entitled to inherit, with successio ordinum, partly also of graduum, running through them.

The first class: DESCENDANTS of the testator, without reference to the proximity of the degree, but with exclusion of the more remote degree by the nearer in

---

of wedlock are admitted to the inheritance of the mother by this *SCtum*.

[1] If a woman has died intestate, leaving brothers of the whole blood, a mother and a daughter, according to the *SCtum Orphitianum* the inheritance belongs to the daughter alone.

BOOK III. Part III.

the same stock, *e.g.*, of the grandchild by its father. In their case the division *in stirpes* obtains.

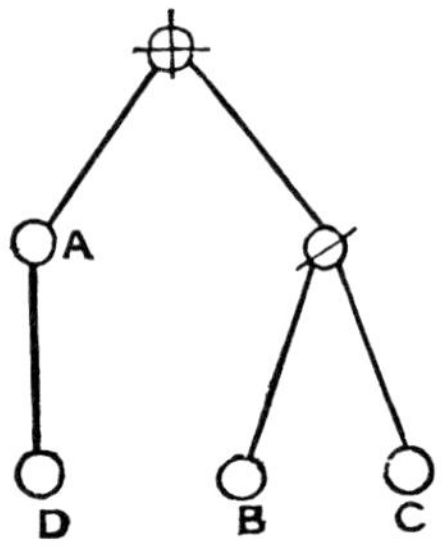

A receives $\frac{1}{2}$
B " $\frac{1}{4}$
C " $\frac{1}{4}$

The second class: ASCENDANTS (according to proximity of degree); brothers and sisters fully related and children of deceased brothers and sisters fully related. Equally near ascendants divide *in lineas*.

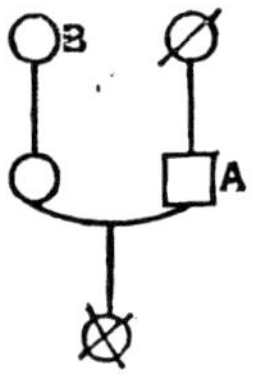

Here A alone inherits.

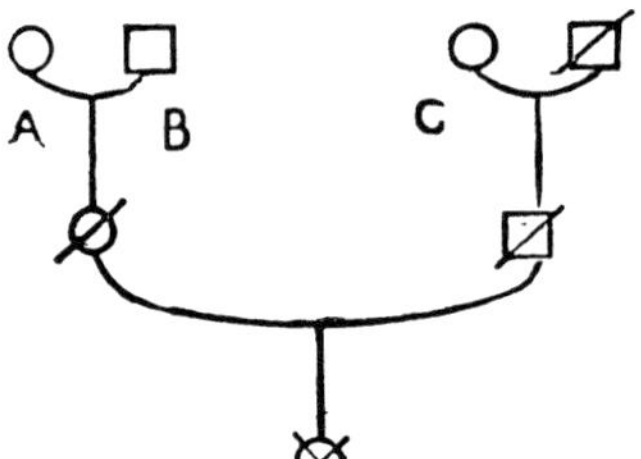

A receives $\frac{1}{4}$
B " $\frac{1}{4}$
C " $\frac{1}{2}$

When ascendants are concurrent with brothers and sisters, division *in capita* comes in.

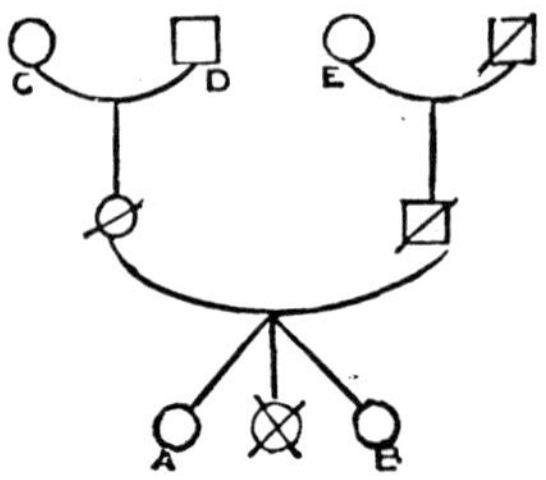

A–E each receive $\frac{1}{5}$

Book III. Part III.

When brothers and sisters are concurrent with children of brothers and sisters, division is made *in stirpes.*

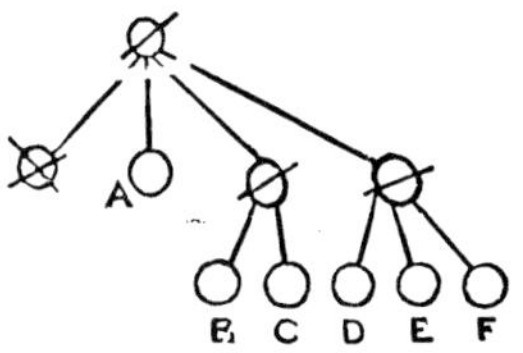

A	receives	$\frac{1}{3}$
B, C	receive	$\frac{1}{6}$
D, E, F	,,	$\frac{1}{9}$

The third class: Brothers and sisters of the half-blood, and children of deceased brothers and sisters of the half-blood.

The fourth class: The remaining collateral relations of the testator, according to proximity of degree, and without restriction to any remote degree; those equally near inherit according to heads. (The uncle always precedes the grand-nephew and cousin, the nephew the uncle.)

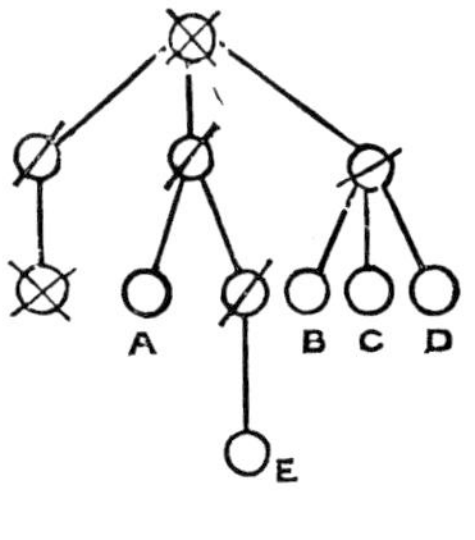

A–D each receive $\frac{1}{4}$
E is dropped.

The Praetorian Law of inheritance of spouses[a] was retained as subsidiary.

Intestate succession to the heritage of a freedman was settled by a constitution of Justinian (A.D. 531): that descendants from freedmen, sprung from their own body, should first be their heirs; in default of such, the patron and his descendants; and finally, the patron's collateral relations to the fifth degree inclusively.[b]—The right of inheritance of the pa-

[a] § 163, ad fin.

[b] Cf. § 168.

BOOK III. Part III.

rens manumissor was completely abolished by Nov. 118.

SUCCESSION CONTRARY TO A TESTAMENT (LAW OF NECESSARY INHERITANCE).

LAW OF *PRAETERITIO* (FORMAL LAW OF NECESSARY INHERITANCE).

§ 167. ACCORDING TO *IUS CIVILE*.

It is doubtful whether freedom of testation in the oldest Law was entirely unlimited, so that no succession against the Testament itself was opened to the next relations who were passed over. Of the original form of the mancipatory testament, to which indeed also the 'uti legassit' of the Twelve Tables[a] relates, it can with certainty alone be shown that in it neither institution nor disinherison of the fil. fam. was possible, and that consequently it was intended for the case where the paterfamilias had not already an heir in the fil. fam., in which event the latter was replaced by the familiae emptor.[b] But since at the moment of the death of the pater fam. the 'sui' enter *ipso iure* into control of the property left behind,[c] it is most improbable that the testament had no validity, if 'sui heredes' existed; and even if the filii fam., in consequence of the familiae mancipatio, had been excluded from expectation of the property already in the lifetime of him in whom resided the potestas, by the familiae emptor standing related to them as master of the familia defuncti, this could have held good always alone in respect of such as were living at the moment of the testator's death, not of those only born later on (postumi).[d]

[a] Ulp. xi. 14.

[b] § 157.

[c] § 162.

[d] *Infra*.

Pomp.: Verbis legis XII tabularum his VTI LEGASSIT SVAE REI ITA IVS ESTO latissima potestas tributa videtur et heredis instituendi et legata et libertates dandi, tutelas quoque constituendi: sed id interpretatione coangustatum est vel legum vel auctoritate iura constituentium.—D. 50, 16, 120.[1]

At any rate, this freedom of testation already very early, and indeed from the first, found its corrective in the legal proposition, 'adgnatione postumi testamentum rumpitur,' which already supplemented the presumed will of the testator.

Ulp. xxii. 18 : Postumi quicumque liberi cuiuscumque sexus omissi, quod valuit testamentum, adgnatione rumpunt.[2]

Id. xxiii. 3 : Adgnascitur suus heres aut adgnascendo aut adoptando aut in manum conveniendo aut in locum sui heredis succedendo, velut nepos mortuo filio aut emancipato, aut manumissione, id est si filius prima secundave mancipatione manumissus reversus sit in patris potestatem.[3]

Finally, a formal limitation also of the freedom of testation was undoubtedly blended with the recasting of the form of the testament. For since now the heir nominated in the testament did not become owner of the property by acquisition of the inheritance until after the testator's death, but the control of the property *ipso iure* fell to the 'sui' immediately upon the death of the pat. fam., it was necessary for the testator, in order to obtain the heritage for him, to remove the 'sui' from the inheritance by express and

---

[1] By these words of a Law of the Twelve Tables, 'As a man shall have bequeathed his property, so let it be regarded as law,' the most comprehensive power seems to be given both of instituting heirs and bequeathing legacies and freedom, besides creating guardianships; but this has been in part curtailed by statutory rules, and in part by the opinion of those who frame the laws.

[2] Any after-born descendants of either sex, left out, by their after-birth upset a testament previously valid.

[3] A *suus heres* accrues either by after-birth or by adoption, or by passing under *manus*, or by stepping into the place of a *suus heres*, as a grandson, if the son have died or been emancipated, or by manumission, that is, if a son who has been manumitted from a first or second mancipation have returned under his father's power.

Book III. Part III.

formal declaration in the testament, that is, to deprive them of the character of heirs (ex-heredes). Thus, then, arose the legal rule, that a testament in which the testator has not thought of his already existing 'suus' (*i e.*, has passed him over) is from the beginning invalid, and the duty arose for the testator either of instituting as heirs his 'sui'—both those already existing, and 'postumi'—or of duly (rite) disinheriting them (exheredare). The persons in respect of which this merely formal duty devolves upon the testator are called 'heirs by necessity' [a]; the legal rules relating to this constitute the Law of 'praeteritio,' or Law of formal necessary inheritance.

[a] Which have indeed to be distinguished from *heredes necessarii*, § 171.

Id. xxii. 14: Sui heredes vel instituendi sunt vel exheredandi.[1]

Gai. ii. § 123: Qui filium in potestate habet, curare debet, ut eum vel heredem instituat vel nominatim exheredet; alioquin si eum silentio praeterierit, inutiliter testabitur: adeo quidem, ut nostri praeceptores existiment, etiamsi vivo patre filius defunctus sit, neminem heredem ex eo testamento existere posse, quia scilicet statim ab initio non constiterit institutio; sed diversae scholae auctores, si quidem filius mortis patris tempore vivat, sane impedimento eum esse scriptis heredibus et suum ab intestato heredem fieri confitentur, si vero ante mortem patris interceptus sit, posse ex testamento hereditatem adiri putant, nullo iam filio impedimento.[2]

---

[1] *Sui heredes* must be either instituted or disinherited.

[2] He who has a son under his power must take care either to institute him heir or expressly to disinherit him; otherwise, if he pass him over in silence, the testament will be void; and this is so far the fact that, as our authorities think, even if the son should have died in the lifetime of his father, there can be no heir under that testament, because of course the institution was void from the very first. But the authorities of the opposite school acknowledge that, if the son in fact should be alive at the time of the death of the father, he certainly is in the way of the appointed heirs, and becomes *suus heres* by intestacy;

Paul.: Si filius qui in potestate est praeteritus sit et vivo patre decedat, testamentum non valet nec superius rumpitur: et eo iure utimur.—D. 28, 2, 7.[1]

Ulp.: Postumus praeteritus vivo testatore natus decessit; licet iuris scrupulositate nimiaque subtilitate testamentum ruptum videatur, attamen si signatum fuerit testamentum, bonorum possessionem secundum tabulas accipere heres scriptus potest remque obtinebit, ut et D. Hadrianus et imperator noster rescripserunt.—l. 12 pr., D. de iniusto, 28, 3.[a][2]

[a] Cf. Fgm. xxiii. 6.

Pap.: Scripto herede deliberante filius exheredatus obiit, . . . et si non sit exheredatus nepos adiri poterit ex testamento hereditas a scripto herede, filio mortuo.—D. 38, 6, 7 pr.[b]—Ulp.: Adgnascendo quidem is rumpit, quem nemo praecedebat mortis tempore; ab intestato vero is succedit, cui [et] ante eum alii non est delata hereditas.—l. 6 pr., de iniusto.[3]

[b] Cf. § 162 (ibid.).

---

but they are of opinion that, if he die before the death of his father, the inheritance can be taken up by virtue of the testament, the son being now no obstacle.

[1] If a son under power have been passed over, and dies in the father's lifetime, the testament is invalid and an earlier one is not revoked; and this is with us an accepted rule of law.

[2] A child born after the making of a testament, who has been passed over in it, was born in the testator's lifetime, and died: although according to the exactitude and over-refinement of the law the testament appears to be upset, nevertheless if it were sealed, the instituted heir can receive the possession of the effects according to the tablets, and will obtain the property, according to rescripts of the late Emp. Hadrian and our Emperor.

[3] Whilst the appointed heir was considering the matter, the disinherited son died, . . . although the grandson have not been disinherited, the inheritance can be taken up by the appointed heir upon the death of the son.—Such person as, being born after its execution, was preceded by no one at the time of the death, upsets a testament. Now the person succeeds under an intestacy in priority to whom the inheritance was offered to none other.

BOOK III. Part III.

Between the filius (natus or postumus) and the remaining 'sui' the difference subsisted, that the former had to be disinherited *nominatim* ('Titius filius meus exheres esto'; 'Quicumque mihi filius genitus fuerit, exheres esto'), the latter could be disinherited also *inter ceteros* ('Ceteri omnes exheredes sunto'); but Justinian in this placed all 'sui' and 'postumi' on the same footing as the filius.

As regards the effect of non-institution of an heir or disinherison, the praeteritio of a filius, whether 'iam natus' or 'postumus,' results in the total, that of another 'suus' in a particular, partial invalidity of the testament. This difference also was done away with by Justinian.—'Postumus sibi locum facit.'

Ulp. xxii. 16, 17: Ex suis heredibus filius quidem neque heres institutus neque nominatim exheredatus non patitur valere testamentum.—Reliquae vero personae liberorum, velut filia nepos neptis, si praeteritae sint, valet testamentum, (et) scriptis heredibus adcrescunt, suis . . . heredibus in partem virilem, extraneis . . . in partem dimidiam.[1]

Pap.: Ventre praeterito . . . quamdiu rumpi testamentum potest, non defertur ex testamento hereditas.—D. 29, 2, 84.[2]

Ulp.: Rumpendo testamentum **sibi locum facere** postumus solet, quamvis filius[a] sequentem gradum, a quo exheredatus est, patiatur valere. Si a primo gradu praeteritus, a secundo

[a] Sc. iam natus praeteritus.

[1] The fact that one of the *sui heredes* being a son is neither instituted heir nor expressly disinherited, precludes the validity of the testament.—But if other descendants, a daughter for example, or a grandson, or a granddaughter, be passed over, the testament is valid, (and) they come in for a share with the appointed heirs; with the *sui heredes* for a proportional part, with outside heirs for a moiety.

[2] Upon the embryo being passed over, the testamentary inheritance is not offered so long as the testament can be avoided.

> exheredatus sit, si . . . nascatur postumus, . . . totum testamentum ruptum est: nam tollendo primum gradum sibi locum facit.—D. 28, 3, 5.[1]

The necessity of formal disinherison is suspended in the case of a testamentum militis.[a]

[a] D. 29, 1, 29, 3.

> Inst. ii. 13, 6: Sed si expeditione occupatus miles testamentum faciat et liberos suos iam natos vel postumos . . . silentio praeterierit, non ignorans an habeat liberos, silentium eius pro exheredatione nominatim facta valere constitutionibus principum cautum est.[2]

§ 168. According to Praetorian Law (*Bonorum Possessio contra Tabulas*).

The Praetorian Edict generally gave 'bonorum possessio contra tabulas' not merely to the 'sui,' but to 'liberi[b] praeteriti' entitled by intestacy, upon the death of the testator, and moreover required express disinherison in the case of all liberi of the male sex.

[b] Ulp. xxviii. 8

> Ulp. xxii. 23: Emancipatos liberos utriusque sexus, quamvis iure civili neque heredes instituere neque exheredare necesse sit, tamen praetor iubet, si non instituantur heredes, exheredari, masculos omnes nominatim, feminas vel inter ceteros:

---

[1] By upsetting the testament an after-born descendant generally procures a position, although the disinherison of a son (already born and passed over) by the nomination of the second degree admits of the validity of the latter. If a posthumous child be born who in respect of the first degree[c] was passed over, in respect of the second[d] disinherited, the whole testament has been avoided; for by displacing the first degree he procures a position.

[c] *I.e.*, institution.

[d] *I.e.*, substitution.

[2] But if a soldier whilst on a march makes a testament and . . . in silence passes over his children already born or posthumous, although not in doubt as to whether he has children, it is provided by imperial constitutions that his silence shall be equivalent to his having expressly disinherited them.

Book III. Part III.

alioquin contra tabulas bonorum possessionem eis pollicetur.[1]

Inst. ii. 13, § ult.: Mater vel avus maternus necesse non habent liberos suos aut heredes instituere aut exheredare, sed possunt eos omittere; . . . sive de iure civili quaeramus sive de edicto praetoris, quo praeteritis liberis contra tabulas bonorum possessionem promittit.[2]

Praeteritio, according to Praetorian Law, does not involve avoidance of the testament and the letting in of intestate succession, but rather—

(1) if no one claims the bonorum possessio contra tabulas, the bonorum possessio secundum tabulas is given to the instituted heirs; and the grant of bonorum possessio contra tabulas only results in the displacement of the testamentary heirs by the praeteritus.

Ulp.: Exspectandi igitur liberi erunt, quamdiu bonorum possessionem petere possunt; quodsi tempus fuerit finitum, aut ante decesserint vel repudiaverint vel ius petendae bonorum possessionis amiserint, tunc revertitur bonorum possessio ad scriptos.—D. 37, 11, 2 pr.[3]

---

[1] Although by the Civil Law it is not necessary either to institute or to disinherit emancipated children of either sex, yet the Praetor orders that, if not instituted, they shall be disinherited, if males all by name, but if females in a general clause; otherwise he promises them possession of the goods in opposition to the testament.

[2] It is unnecessary for either a woman or a maternal grandfather either to institute their children heirs or to disinherit them, but they can omit mention of them; . . . whether we have regard to the Civil Law or the edict of the Praetor, by which he promises to those children who have been passed over possession of the effects in opposition to the testament.

[3] One must therefore wait upon the children as long as they are able to claim the *bon. poss.*; but if the period has elapsed, or they have previously died, or have renounced or lost the right of claiming *bon. poss.*, then the *bon. poss.* reverts to the persons designated.

(2) If, however, liberi (even being *in adoptiva familia*) have been instituted heirs in the testament, upon bonorum possessio contra tabulas being allowed, they can also claim it for the praeteritus.

Id.; Si quis ex liberis heres scriptus est, ad contra tabulas bonorum possessionem vocari non debet: cum enim possit secundum tabulas habere possessionem, quo bonum est ei contra tabulas dari? Plane si alius committat edictum, et ipse ad contra tabulas bonorum possessionem admittitur. —l. 3, § 11, D. h. t. (de B. P. contra tab. 37, 4).[1]

Id.: Non est novum, ut emancipatus praeteritus plus iuris scriptis heredibus fratribus suis tribuat, quam habituri essent, si soli fuissent: quippe si filius qui in potestate patris est ex duodecima parte heres scribatur emancipato praeterito, dimidiam partem beneficio emancipati occupat, qui si emancipatum fratrem non haberet, duodecimam partem habiturus esset.—l. 8, § 14 eod.[2]

In adoptionem datos filios non summoveri praetor voluit, si modo heredes instituti sint: . . . ergo si fuerint heredes scripti, accipient contra tabulas bonorum possessionem; sed ipsi

---

[1] If any one of the children has been designated heir, he must not be called to the possession of the goods as against the testament; for since he can have possession in keeping with the testament, what is the good of its being granted to him in opposition to the testament? If it is clear that another can apply the Edict, he is also himself admitted to the *bon. poss. contra tabulas*.

[2] It is nothing new that an emancipated son who has been pretermitted makes over to his brothers, designated heirs, more rights than they would have had if they had been alone; because a son under paternal power, who is instituted heir to the twelfth part, if an emancipated son has been passed over, by the prerogative of the emancipated brother gains possession of one half part, who but for his having an emancipated brother, would have had a twelfth part.

soli non committent edictum, nisi fuerit alius praeteritus ex liberis, qui solent committere edictum.—Ib. § 11.[1]

'Rite exheredati,' on the other hand, remain always entirely excluded from bonorum possessio.

Id.: Exheredati liberi quemadmodum edictum non committunt, ita nec commisso per alios edicto cum illis venient ad bonorum possessionem.—l. 10, § 5 eod.[2]

Even pupillary substitutions and legacies to certain near kinsmen (exceptae personae) are upheld. Collatio bonorum also obtains here, as in § 163.

Afric.: Etiamsi contra patris tabulas bonorum possessio petita sit, substitutio tamen pupillaris valet, et legata omnimodo praestanda sunt, quae substitutione data sunt.—D. 28, 6, 34, 2.[3]

Ulp.: Hic titulus aequitatem quandam habet naturalem, . . . ut qui iudicium patris rescindunt, ex iudicio eius quibusdam personis legata et fideicommissa praestarent, hoc est liberis et parentibus, uxori nuruique dotis nomine legatum.—l. 1 pr., D. 'de legatis praestandis,' 37, 5.[4]

The Praetor gave to the Patron (or Father) the

[1] Sons given in adoption the Praetor has willed should not be rejected, provided they have been instituted heirs: . . . consequently when they have been designated heirs, they will receive *bon. poss. contra tab.*; but by themselves alone they will not apply the Edict unless another has been passed over of the children who generally give the Edict application.

[2] Just as disinherited children do not give effect to the Edict, neither will they, when the Edict has been put in operation by others, come in with such for *bon. poss.*

[3] Even if *bon. poss.* was claimed in opposition to the father's testament, pupillary substitution nevertheless avails, and in all cases the legacies given by the substitution must be discharged.

[4] This title has a certain natural equity, . . . that those who make the will of their father of no effect should, in pursuance of his will, account to certain persons for the legacies and bequests in trust, that is to say, to the children and the parents, to the wife and daughter-in-law for a legacy in lieu of *dos*.

'partis dimidiae bonorum possessio' against the testament of a libertus (or emancipatus), in which such person had left nothing at all to the Patron (or parens manumissor), or less than the half of his property, and this if in the testament children of the body (in the case of emancipatus, also adoptive children) were not instituted as heirs, or were passed over.[a]

[a] § 164. Cf. D. 38, 1, 2 pr. §§ 1, 2.

Ulp. xxix. 1: Civis Romani liberti hereditatem lex XII tabularum patrono defert, si intestato sine suo herede libertus decesserit: ideoque si testamento facto decedat, licet suus heres ei non sit, . . . lex patrono nihil praestat. Sed ex edicto praetoris, (si) testato libertus moriatur, ut tamen aut nihil aut minus quam partem dimidiam bonorum patrono relinquat, contra tabulas testamenti partis dimidiae bonorum possessio illi datur, nisi libertus aliquem ex naturalibus liberis successorem sibi relinquat.[1]

Id.: Emancipatus a parente in ea causa est, . . . ut parens exemplo patroni ad contra tabulas bonorum possessionem admittatur.—D. 37, 12, 1 pr.[2]

Patri eius, qui in emancipatione ipse manumissor exstitisset, contra tabulas testamenti dandam bonorum possessionem partis debitae placet exceptis his rebus, quas in castris adquisisset, quarum liberam testamenti factionem habet:—nam

---

[1] A law of the Twelve Tables confers the inheritance of a Roman citizen who was a freedman upon the patron, when the freedman has died intestate without a *suus heres;* and therefore if he die after making a testament, although he have no *suus heres,* . . . the law gives nothing to the patron. By virtue of the Praetor's Edict if the freedman die with a testament, but so as to bequeath to the patron either nothing or less than a moiety of his property, *bon. poss. contra tab.* of a moiety is granted to him, unless the freedman leave some one of his actual children as his successor.

[2] A child emancipated by the parent is in this position . . . that the parent by the analogy of a patron is admitted to *bon. poss. contra tab.*

Book III. Part III.

in bona castrensia non esse dandam contra tabulas filiifamilias bonorum possessionem D. Pius Antoninus rescripsit.—D. 29, 1, l. 29, § 3 (Marc.), l. 30 (Paul.).[1]

After that the Law of inheritance in respect of the Patron—especially as regards the liberta[a] and the patrona—had been much modified by the lex Papia Poppaea, and in the course of time had become not a little confused, it was reformed by Justinian, and again brought back to simpler principles.[b]

[a] Ulp. xxix. 2.

[b] § 166, ad fin.

Gai. iii. § 42: Postea lege Papia aucta sunt iura patronorum, quod ad locupletiores libertos pertinet: cautum est enim ea lege, ut ex bonis eius, qui sestertiorum nummorum centum milium plurisve patrimonium reliquerit et pauciores quam tres liberos habebit, sive is testamento facto sive intestato mortuus erit, virilis pars patrono debeatur.[2]

In bonis libertinarum nullam iniuriam antiquo iure patiebantur patroni: cum enim hae in patronorum legitima tutela essent, non aliter scilicet testamentum facere poterant, quam patrono auctore.—Sed postea lex Papia cum quattuor liberorum iure libertinas tutela patronorum liberaret et eo modo concederet eis etiam sine tutoris auctoritate condere testamentum, prospexit, ut

---

[1] To the father of such (soldier) as in respect of emancipation had himself become a patron it is held *bon. poss. contra tab.* must be given for the portion due to him, with the exception of such things as the son had acquired in the field, in respect of which he has unlimited testamentary capacity; for, by a rescript of the late Emp. Antonine, *bon. poss. contra tab.* in regard of a *fil. fam.* is not to be given over military property.

[2] Later on, by the *l. Papia*, the rights of patrons were increased in respect of the more affluent freedmen . . . for it was provided by that statute that a proportionate share shall be due to the patron of the property of him who has left a patrimony of 100,000 sesterces or more, and had fewer than three children, whether he had made a testament or died intestate.

pro numero liberorum quos liberta mortis tempore habuerit, virilis pars patrono debeatur.—Ib. §§ 43–4.[1] Book III. Part III.

Inst. iii. 7, 3: Sed nostra constitutio . . . ita huiusmodi causas definivit, ut si quidem libertus vel liberta minores centenariis sint, i.e. minus centum aureis habeant substantiam, . . . nullum locum habeat patronus in eorum successionem, si tamen testamentum fecerint.—Cum vero maiores centenariis sint, si heredes vel bonorum possessores liberos habeant, sive unum sive plures cuiuscumque sexus vel gradus, ad eos successionem parentum deduximus, omnibus patronis una cum sua progenie semotis . . .; si vero testamentum quidem fecerint, patronos autem vel patronas praeterierint, cum nullos liberos haberent vel habentes exheredaverint, . . . tunc ex nostra constitutione per bonorum possessionem contra tabulas, non dimidiam, ut ante, sed tertiam partem bonorum liberti consequantur: . . . ut tam patroni patronaeque quam liberi eorum nec non qui ex transverso latere veniunt usque ad quintum gradum ad successionem libertorum vocentur.[2]

---

[1] Patrons used to suffer no injustice by the old law in respect of the property of freedwomen; for since they were under the statutory guardianship of their patrons, of course they could not make a testament except with the patron's sanction.—But later on, when the *l. Papia* liberated freedwomen with four children from the guardianship of their patrons, and thereby empowered them to make testaments even without the patron's sanction, it provided that a proportionate share should be due to the patron according to the number of the children that the freedwoman had at the time of her death.

[2] But a constitution of ours . . . has thus determined cases of this kind: that if in fact a freedman or freedwoman be less than *centenarii*, that is, have property of less value than 100 gold-pieces,[a] . . . the patron shall have no title to their inheritance, if they have made a testament.—But when they are more than *centenarii*, and have one or more children of whichever sex or degree, as their heirs or possessors of the

[a] *I.e.*, 100,000 sesterces.

Book III. Part III.

§ 169. Right to the Legitimate Portion (Material Law of Necessary Inheritance).[a]

[a] See 'Anct. Law,' pp. 215, *sqq.*; Bell, Dict. s. 'Legitim.'

The testator has in the testament not merely to remember certain persons (by institution or disinherison), but to bequeath to them a certain part of his property, otherwise the testament can be disputed (set aside) by them. This material Law of necessary inheritance especially gained acceptance by the practice of the Centumviral court, and was further developed and established by Jurisprudence, and later on by Legislation. This was effected by an action for rescission of the testament (querela inofficiosi sc. testamenti) being given to the near kinsman of the testator, whom the latter had allowed to go away empty from mere lack of affection, and by no fault of his own; because of the violation of 'officium pietatis,' under the aspect of such unsound state of the testator's mind as this expressed (color insaniae).[b] The action was not hereditary,[c] and lapsed in five years.

[b] Cf. Blackstone, i. 447-8; ii. 491-3 (Steph. ii. 181-3, 291-2).

[c] § 23.

> Marcian.: Hoc colore de inofficioso testamento agitur, quasi non sanae mentis fuerunt, cum testamentum ordinarent; et hoc dicitur non quasi vere furiosus vel demens testatus sit, sed recte quidem fecit testamentum, sed non ex officio pietatis: nam si vere furiosus esset vel demens, nullum est testamentum.—l. 2, D. h. t. (de inoff. 5, 2).[1]

---

property, we have conferred on them the inheritance of their parents, rejecting all patrons along with their issue. . . . But if they have in fact made a testament, and have passed over patrons or patronesses, while having no descendants, or if they have any, have disinherited them, . . . then by our constitution, the patrons or patronesses obtain by *bon. poss. contra tab.*, not a moiety as previously, but a third part of the freedman's property: . . . so that as well patrons and patronesses, as their descendants and collaterals besides to the fifth degree, are called to the inheritance of freedmen.

[1] Proceedings are takenupon an undutiful testament under the appearance of the testators having been of unsound mind when

Marcell.: Inofficiosum testamentum dicere hoc est: allegare, quare exheredari vel praeteriri non debuerit; quod plerumque accidit, cum falso parentes instimulati liberos suos vel exheredant vel praetereunt.—Huius autem verbi 'de inofficioso' vis illa est: docere, immerentem se et ideo indigne praeteritum vel etiam exheredatione summotum; resque illo colore defenditur apud iudicem, ut videatur ille quasi non sanae mentis fuisse, cum testamentum inique ordinaret.—ll. 3, 5 eod.[1]

Such a claim to consideration, and so the 'querela inofficiosi,' is possessed—

(1) by ascendants and descendants (without reference to agnation and paternal power).

Nam et his, qui non ex masculis descendunt, facultas est agendi, cum et de matris testamento agant et obtinere adsidue soleant.—cit. l. 5.[2]

Pap.: Nam etsi parentibus non debetur filiorum hereditas propter votum parentum et naturalem erga filios caritatem: turbato tamen ordine mor-

---

they made their testament. And this is not said as though the testator was actually mad or void of understanding, but he did in fact duly make the testament, yet not from dictates of affection; for if he was actually mad or void of understanding, the testament is null.

[1] To speak of a testament as undutiful means, to bring forward reasons why one ought not to have been disinherited or passed over; and this generally happens when parents, governed by a wrong reason, disinherit or pass over their children.—Now the force of that phrase 'concerning want of natural affection' is: to prove that one was unworthily, and therefore also without having given occasion, passed over, or even set aside by disinherison; and the matter is contested before the *iudex* under the aspect of his appearing, as it were, to have been of unsound mind when he made an unfair testament.

[2] For those also who are not descended from males have a right of action, since they sue even upon a mother's testament, and are wont frequently to obtain (their rights).

talitatis non minus parentibus quam liberis pie relinqui debet.—l. 15 pr. eod.[1]

(2) By brothers and sisters, from the time of Constantine, alone when the heir who is preferred to them is a 'turpis persona,'[a] and to the exclusion of 'uterini.'—And further, he that would dispute the testament by the querela inofficiosi must at the time be the nearest intestate heir, by Civil or Praetorian Law.

[a] § 57.

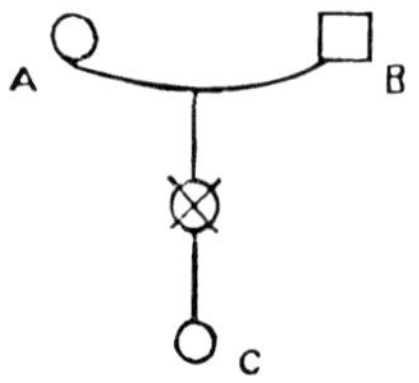

A and B are excluded by C.

Imp. Const.: Fratres vel sorores uterini ab inofficiosi actione contra testamentum fratris vel sororis penitus arceantur; consanguinei autem [adgnatione durante] contra testamentum fratris vel sororis de inofficioso quaestionem movere possunt, si scripti heredes infamiae vel turpitudinis vel levis notae macula adsparguntur.—l. 27, C. eod. 3, 28; cf. l. 1, C. Th. 2, 19.[2]

The testator can prevent the querela inofficiosi by bequeathing a portion of his property (legitimate part, *legitima portio*), which

(1) was originally unlimited, but later on, accord-

---

[1] For although parents have no claim to inherit from their children, because of desire and natural affection for them, yet if the order of mortality be reversed, a bequest ought to be made to parents from filial regard, no less than to children.

[2] Brothers and sisters by the same mother are to be altogether precluded from the suit for want of affection in opposition to a brother's or sister's testament; but those of the same blood can [whilst agnation continues] take proceedings in opposition to a brother's or sister's testament upon want of affection, if the designated heirs are tainted by the blemish of infamy or immorality or minor brand.

ing to the analogy of the lex Falcidia,[a] amounted to one-fourth of the portion under intestacy appertaining to the necessary heir; but Justinian by Nov. 18 raised this to one-third, in the case of four or less portions for intestate inheritance, and to one-half in the case of more than four.

[a] § 182.

Ulp.: Quoniam autem quarta debitae portionis sufficit ad excludendam querelam, videndum erit, an **exheredatus partem faciat,** qui non queritur: ut puta sumus duo filii exheredati. Et utique faciet, ut Papinianus respondit, et si dicam inofficiosum, non totam hereditatem debeo sed dimidiam petere. Proinde si sint ex duobus filiis nepotes, ex uno plures, tres puta, ex uno unus: unicum sescuncia, unum ex illis semuncia querela excludit.—Quarta autem accipietur scilicet deducto aere alieno.—l. 8, §§ 8, 9, D. h. t.[1]

If to the necessary heir there have been bequeathed only something less than the legitimate part, by a constitution of Justinian he can sue alone for the deficiency (actio ad supplendam legitimam s. suppletoria).

Sin vero quantacumque pars hereditatis vel res eis fuerit relicta, de inofficioso querela quiescente id quod eis deest usque ad quartam legitimae partis repletur, licet non fuerit adiectum boni viri arbitratu debere eam repleri.—§ 3, I. h. t. 2, 18.[2]

---

[1] But since a fourth part of the portion due is enough to avert a complaint, we shall have to consider whether a disinherited person is to be included who raises no complaint: for example, we are two brothers disinherited. And at any rate, according to the opinion given by Papinian, he will be included, and if I allege that the testament is undutiful, I must claim not the whole inheritance, but a moiety. If, accordingly, there are grandsons by two sons, by the one several, say three, by the other only one, the receipt of a quarter of the moiety hinders the one, that of a quarter of the sixth part each of those, from raising a complaint. Now by quarter will of course be understood, after deduction of debts.

[2] But if any portion whatsoever of the inheritance or any

The legitimate part need not be left exactly in the form of the institution of heir, but can be in any discretionary form, whilst originally the mere satisfaction with a portion of property, without institution of heir, scarcely sufficed in fact.

> Igitur quartam quis debet habere, ut de inofficioso testamento agere non possit: sive iure hereditario, sive iure legati vel fideicommissi, vel si mortis causa ei quarta donata fuerit.—§ 6, I. eod.[1]

The whole querela inofficiosi is only a subsidiary legal remedy, and is thus, *e.g.*, excluded by the possibility of bonorum possessio contra tabulas.

> —Liberi . . . ita demum de inofficioso testamento agere possunt, si nullo alio iure ad bona defuncti venire possunt: nam qui alio iure veniunt ad totam hereditatem vel partem eius, de inofficioso agere non possunt.—§ 2, I. h. t.[2]
>
> Paul. iv. 5, § 5: Filius ex asse heres institutus inofficiosum dicere non potest: nec interest, exhausta nec ne sit hereditas, cum apud eum quarta aut legis Falcidiae aut senatusconsulti Pegasiani beneficio sit remansura.[3]

---

article has been left to them, the complaint of an undutiful will is in abeyance, and the deficiency is made up to them, so far as the quarter of the legitimate part, although there was nothing added to the effect that it should be made up according to the arbitrament of an honest man.

[1] Therefore, a person must have a fourth part, in order that he should be unable to sue upon an undutiful testament: whether he have this part by inheritance, or legacy, or bequest in trust, or as a gift *mortis causa*.

[2] Children . . . can only sue upon an undutiful testament if they can come at the property of the deceased by no other process; for those who can come at the whole inheritance or a part thereof by other process cannot sue upon an undutiful testament.

[3] A son instituted universal heir cannot allege that the testament is undutiful; neither does it matter whether the inheritance be exhausted or not, since the fourth part will

Its object and its effect is, rescission of the testament and letting in intestate succession.

> Si ex causa de inofficiosi cognoverit iudex et pronuntiaverit contra testamentum nec fuerit provocatum, ipso iure rescissum est; et suus heres erit secundum quem iudicatum est et bonorum possessor, si hoc se contendit, et libertates ipso iure non valent, nec legata debentur.—l. 8, § 16, D. h. t.[1]

But under certain circumstances even merely partial avoidance of the testament can ensue, and inheritance to the testator thus be 'pro parte testatus pro parte intestatus.'

> Paul.: Mater decedens extraneum ex dodrante heredem instituit, filiam unam ex quadrante, alteram praeteriit. . . . Respondi: filia praeterita id vindicare debet, quod intestata matre habitura esset. . . . Sed non est admittendum, ut adversus sororem audiatur agendo de inofficioso. . . . Et ideo ab extraneo semissem vindicandum, . . . quasi semis totus ad hanc pertineat. Secundum quod non in totum testamentum infirmatur, sed pro parte intestata efficitur.—l. 19 eod.[2]

---

remain in his hands by the aid either of the *l. Falcidia* or the *SCtum Pegasianum.*

[1] If a *iudex* in a suit upon want of affection has investigated the matter, and pronounced against the testament, without an appeal having been brought, it is rescinded by force of law; he in whose favour judgment has been given will be both *suus heres* and *bonorum possessor,* if this is the contention; and the manumissions take no effect by force of law, neither are the legacies obligatory.

[2] A dying mother has instituted a stranger heir to three-fourths, one of her daughters to a fourth, and has passed over another daughter. . . . The opinion I gave was: the daughter passed over must claim what she would have had if her mother had been intestate. . . . But it is inadmissible that she should have audience by bringing an action for want of affection against her sister . . . and therefore that one half must be claimed from the stranger . . . a whole moiety, so to speak, belongs to the latter sister. According to this, not the whole testament is invalidated, but the mother becomes intestate for a part.

Ulp.: Circa inofficiosi querelam evenire plerumque adsolet, ut in una atque eadem causa diversae sententiae proferantur. Quid enim si fratre agente heredes scripti diversi iuris fuerunt? Quod si fuerit, pro parte testatus pro parte intestatus decessisse videbitur.—l. 24 eod.[1]

The whole Law of the legitimate part is in abeyance in the case of a testamentum militis.

§ 170. The Law of Necessary Inheritance according to Nov. 115.

By Nov. 115 (542 A.D.) the previous Law of praeteritio and that of the legitimate part were blended as follows.

(1) Ascendants may henceforth neither pass over nor disinherit their descendants (taken as purely cognatic) and reversely—not even with a bequest of the legitimate part—save for certain statutory reasons to be alleged in the testament itself, and to be proved by the heir instituted. Of such grounds for exclusion on account of grave culpability, there are fourteen for disinherison of descendants, eight for that of ascendants.

(2) In the case of praeteritio or groundless disinherison of a necessary heir—and it is immaterial whether anything have been otherwise left to him—the result shall be: avoidance of the testament in respect of the institution of heirs, in case the necessary heir that has suffered injury makes it available (contested, so-called relative nullity), and pure intestate succession; but its other contents (as

[1] In respect of a complaint as to want of affection, it commonly happens that in one and the same case different judgments are put forth. For how if, when a brother sues, the designated heirs have been in opposite legal relations? If this is the case, it will be considered that the testament subsists in part, and in part does not.

provision for legacies and guardianships and the like) are upheld.—The persons disinherited or passed over make good their right by 'hereditatis petitio.'[a]

If the necessary heirs have been instituted, but for an amount less than the legitimate part, they can only require the making good the deficiency by the other testamentary heirs.[b]

In respect of the brothers and sisters of the testator, no change was made in the existing Law.

[a] § 176.

[b] Inst. ii. 18, 3.

CHAPTER III.

ACQUISITION OF INHERITANCE AND PROTECTION OF THE RIGHT OF INHERITANCE.

§ 171. Manner and Form of Acquisition.

Delatio[c] confers only the legal possibility of becoming heir: the delatee first becomes actual heir by acquisition of the inheritance (adquisitio hereditatis). The acquisition is, as a rule, effected by a voluntary act on the part of the person called (heredes voluntarii, extranei).

[c] D. 50, 16, 151. (§ 153, *supra*.)

> Gai. ii. § 152: Heredes autem aut necessarii dicuntur aut sui et necessarii aut extranei.—§ 161: Qui testatoris iuri subiecti non sunt, extranei heredes appellantur: itaque liberi quoque nostri, qui in potestate nostra non sunt, heredes a nobis instituti sicut extranei videntur; qua de causa et qui a matre heredes instituuntur, eodem numero sunt, quia feminae liberos in potestate non habent.[1]

---

[1] Now heirs are said to be *necessarii* or *sui et necessarii* or *extranei*.—Those who are not subject to the power of the testator are called stranger-heirs; therefore our children also who are not under our power, when they are instituted heirs by us, are looked upon as strangers. For which cause also those who are instituted heirs by their mother are in the same category, because women have no children under their power.

Book III. Part III.

In respect, however, of certain persons it obtains *ipso iure*, independently of the cognizance and volition of the person called.

Ib. § 157: —necessarii vero ideo dicuntur, quia omnimodo sive velint sive nolint, tam ab intestato quam ex testamento heredes fiunt.[1]

Hermog.: Verba haec: 'Publius Maevius si volet, heres esto' in necessario condicionem faciunt, ut si nolit, heres non existat: nam in voluntarii heredis persona frustra adduntur, cum, etsi non fuerint addita, invitus non efficitur heres.—D. 28, 7, 12.[2]

These persons (heredes necessarii) are—

[a] Gai. ii. 157: D. 28, 2, 11.

(1) the 'sui' of the testator,[a] to whom, however, the Praetor gives the 'beneficium abstinendi,' which is of importance in the case of an inheritance burdened with debt.

Gai.: Necessariis heredibus non solum impuberibus, sed etiam puberibus abstinendi se ab hereditate proconsul potestatem facit, ut quamvis creditoribus hereditariis iure civili teneantur, tamen in eos actio non detur, si velint derelinquere hereditatem. Sed impuberibus quidem etiamsi se immiscuerint hereditati, praestat abstinendi facultatem, puberibus autem ita, si se non immiscuerint.—l. 57 pr., D. h. t. (de A. v. O. H. 29, 2).[3]

---

[1] But they are called *necessarii*, because in any case, whether they are willing or not, they become heirs, as well under intestacy as by virtue of a testament.

[2] The following words: 'P. M. shall be heir, if he will,' create a condition in respect of a necessary heir, so that if he is unwilling, he does not become heir. For in the case of a voluntary heir their addition is useless, since although the addition were not made, he does not become heir against his will.

[3] To necessary heirs, not only *impuberes* but even *puberes*, the proconsul gives power to renounce an inheritance, so that, although by civil law they are liable to the creditors of the inheritance, yet no action is given against them if they desire to abandon the inheritance. But upon *impuberes* he confers

Ulp.: —non est sine herede,[a] qui suum heredem habet licet abstinentem se.—D. 40, 5, 30, 10.[1]

[a] Sc. iure civili.

Iul.: Praetor permittendo his, qui in potestate fuerint, abstinere se hereditate paterna manifestum facit ius se in persona eorum tribuere, quod futurum esset, si liberum arbitrium adeundae hereditatis habuissent.—l. 89, D. de leg. 1.[2]

(2) Slaves whom the testator has instituted as heirs 'cum libertate.'[b]

[b] §§ 37, 159; Gai. iii. 78.

Gai. ii. §§ 153–155: Necessarius heres est servus cum libertate heres institutus; ideo sic appellatus, quia, sive velit sive nolit, omnimodo post mortem testatoris protinus liber et heres est. § Unde qui facultates suas suspectas habet, solet servum primo aut secundo vel etiam ulteriore gradu liberum et heredem instituere, ut si creditoribus satis non fiat, potius huius heredis quam ipsius testatoris bona veneant, id est ut ignominia, quae accidit ex venditione bonorum, hunc potius heredem quam ipsum testatorem contingat; quamquam apud Fufidium Sabino placeat eximendum eum esse esse ignominia, quia non suo vitio, sed necessitate iuris bonorum venditionem pateretur: sed alio iure utimur. § Pro hoc tamen incommodo illud ei commodum praestatur, ut ea quae post mortem patroni sibi adquisierit, sive ante bonorum venditionem sive postea, ipsi reserventur.[3]

---

this power even if they have intermeddled with the inheritance; upon *puberes*, however, in case they have not intermeddled.

[1] A man is not without an heir who has a *suus heres*, although he renounce.

[2] The Praetor, by allowing those who were under power to renounce their ancestor's inheritance, shows plainly that he confers on them the right that they would have had if they had had free discretion as to entering upon the inheritance.

[3] A necessary heir is a slave instituted heir with a grant of freedom: so called because, whether he will or not, he is in any case and forthwith free and heir upon the death of the testator.

Book III. Part III.

Ulp. xxii. 24: Necessariis tantum heredibus abstinendi potestas non datur.[1]

Gai. ii. § 160: Quin etiam similiter abstinendi potestatem facit praetor etiam ei qui in causa mancipii est, si cum libertate heres institutus sit, quamvis necessarius, non etiam suus heres sit, tamquam servus.[2]

The voluntary heir acquires the inheritance by entry (aditio hereditatis).[a] This comes about either by means of express, yet informal, declaration of the will to be heir, or tacitly by acts expressing, and giving effect to, such will (pro herede gestio).[b]

[a] Brown, s.vv.

[b] Paterson, s. 781; Bell, s. 'Behaviour as heir.'

Ulp.: Pro herede gerere videtur is, qui aliquid facit quasi heres: . . . nam hoc animo esse debet, ut velit esse heres; ceterum si quid pietatis causa fecit, si quid custodiae causa fecit, . . . apparet non videri pro herede gessisse.—l. 20 pr., D. h. t.[3]

Wherefore, a man who is apprehensive of his own insolvency commonly appoints a slave free and heir in the first, second, or even a lower grade, so that if there is not sufficient for the creditors, the goods may be sold rather as those of such heir than of the testator himself; that is, that the disgrace which attaches to the sale of the goods may fall upon this heir rather than upon the testator himself: although Sab., according to Fufid., holds that the slave ought to be exempted from disgrace, because he submits to the sale of the goods not from his own fault, but from legal necessity; but we follow the contrary rule. § In return, however, for this drawback there is allowed to him the advantage that whatever he himself has acquired after the patron's death, whether before the sale of the goods or after, is reserved for his own use.

[1] To heirs alone that are *necessarii* no power is granted of renunciation.

[2] Nay more, in like manner the Praetor gives power of renunciation to a person who is in the condition of bondage, if he has been appointed heir with grant of freedom, since he, although he is a *heres necessarius*, is not also a *suus*, as being a slave.

[3] He is considered to act as heir who performs any act as if heir: . . . for he must be in such a mind as to wish to be heir; but if he has done anything from pious impulse, or any act for

Inst. ii. 19, 7: Pro herede autem gerere videtur, si rebus hereditariis tamquam heres utatur, vel vendendo res hereditarias aut praedia colendo locandove et quoquo modo si voluntatem suam declaret de adeunda hereditate.[1]

In the Classical Law there was also still—for testamentary heirs originally indeed solely—a solemn form of entry which could be prescribed by the testator at the same time with a respite for it: *cretio* (vulgaris—continua; perfecta—imperfecta).[a]

[a] See § 160.

Gai. ii. §§ 164-6: Extraneis heredibus solet cretio dari, id est finis deliberandi, ut intra certum tempus vel adeant hereditatem, vel si non adeant, temporis fine summoveantur: ideo autem cretio appellata est, quia cernere est quasi decernere et constituere. § Cum ergo ita scriptum sit: HERES TITIVS ESTO, adiicere debemus: CERNITOQVE IN CENTVM DIEBVS PROXIMIS, QVIBVS SCIES POTERISQVE. QVOD NI ITA CREVERIS, EXHERES ESTO. § Et qui ita heres institutus est si velit heres esse, debebit intra diem cretionis cernere, i.e. haec verba dicere: QVOD ME PVBLIVS MAEVIVS TESTAMENTO SVO HEREDEM INSTITVIT, EAM HEREDITATEM ADEO CERNOQVE; quodsi ita non creverit, finito tempore cretionis excluditur; nec quidquam proficit, si pro herede gerat.[2]

---

safe-keeping, . . . he seems not to be considered as having acted as heir.

[1] Now a person is considered to act as heir if he use the hereditary property as though he were heir, either by selling them, or by cultivating or letting the lands, and in any other way makes known his intention to take up the inheritance.

[2] Time for announcing their acceptance is commonly given to stranger-heirs, that is, a term for deliberation, so that within a fixed time they may either enter upon the inheritance, or if they do not enter, they are set aside at the expiration of the time. Now it has been called *cretio*, because *cernere* is, as it were, to decide and determine. § When, therefore, it is thus written: 'Titius, be heir,' we ought to add 'and, make your declaration within the next hundred days, after it has come to your know-

Ulp. xxii. §§ 30–2: Cum cretione heres institutus sicut cernendo fit heres, ita non aliter excluditur, quam si intra diem cretionis non creverit: ideoque etiamsi constituerit nolle se heredem esse, tamen si supersint dies cretionis, poenitentia actus cernendo heres fieri potest.—Cretio aut vulgaris dicitur aut continua; **vulgaris,** in qua adiiciuntur haec verba: QVIBVS SCIERIS POTERISQVE; **continua,** in qua non adiiciuntur.—Ei qui vulgarem cretionem habet, dies illi dumtaxat computantur, quibus scivit se heredem institutum et potuit cernere; ei vero qui continuam habet cretionem, etiam illi dies computantur, quibus ignoravit se heredem institutum, aut scivit quidem, sed non potuit cernere.[1]

a Cf. §§ 154, 155.

Without the provision of a 'cretio,' the entry upon the inheritance is confined to no fixed respite;[a] but if

ledge and you are able to act. In default of your so deciding, be disinherited.' § And he that has been thus instituted heir, if he wishes to be heir, will have to make a declaration within the term for deliberation, that is, he must utter the following words: 'Since P. M. has instituted me as heir by testament, I enter upon and declare my acceptance of that inheritance.' But if he has not thus decided, when the time for declaring his acceptance has expired, he is excluded, and it is of no avail for him to act as heir.

[1] But in like manner as a person appointed heir with *cretio* becomes heir by making his declaration, so he is not excluded on any other ground than that of failing to make his declaration within the term for *cretio;* and therefore, although he may have decided that he does not care to be heir, yet if any part of the time for *cretio* remains, urged by repentance, he can still become heir, by making his declaration.—*Cretio* is termed either 'common' or 'continuous': common being the one in which these words are added, 'after it comes to your knowledge and you are able to act'; continuous, where they are not added.—Against him who has the common *cretio* those days only are reckoned during which he is aware that he was instituted heir and was able to decide; but against him who has continuous *cretio* those days also are reckoned during which he was ignorant of his having been appointed heir, or did in fact know it, but could not decide.

creditors of the inheritance[a] by means of interrogatio in iure[b] press for a declaration of the heir that is called, a respite can upon his petition be appointed him by the magistrate (tempus, beneficium deliberandi),[c] which, however, according to Justinian's rule, may not exceed one year.

[a] Or perhaps legatees.
[b] § 194.
[c] Paterson, s. 779.

Gai. ii. § 167: Ei[d] liberum est, quocumque tempore voluerit, adire hereditatem, sed solet praetor postulantibus hereditariis creditoribus tempus constituere, intra quod, si velit, adeat hereditatem, si minus, ut liceat creditoribus bona defuncti vendere.[1]

[d] Sc. qui sine cretione heres institutus est

Qui interrogatur, an heres sit, . . . ad deliberandum tempus impetrare debet:—et quia hoc defunctorum interest, ut habeant successores, interest et viventium, ne praecipitentur, quamdiu iuste deliberant.—D. 11, 1, l. 5 (Gai.), l. 6 pr. (Ulp.).[2]

Ulp.: Ait praetor: SI TEMPVS AD DELIBERANDVM PETET, DABO.—Cum dicit 'tempus' nec adiicit diem, sine dubio ostendit esse in ius dicentis potestate, quem diem praestituat.—Itaque pauciores centum dierum non sunt dandi.—D. 28, 8, l. 1, §§ 1–2 (Ulp.), l. 2 (Paul.).[3]

The lex Iulia et Papia Poppaea introduced a limita-

---

[1] He (*i.e.*, who has been instituted heir without *cretio*) is free to enter upon the inheritance whenever he chooses; but the Praetor usually, on the petition of the creditors of the estate, fixes a period within which he may enter upon the inheritance if he please; but if he does not enter, the creditors are allowed to sell the effects of the deceased.

[2] He to whom the question is put whether he is heir, . . . ought to claim time for deliberation:—and inasmuch as it is of importance to deceased persons that they should have successors, it is of importance to the living not to be hurried, as long as they are within their rights in deliberation.

[3] The Praetor says: 'If he seek time for deliberation, I will grant it.'—When he says 'time,' and does not add the fixed term, he undoubtedly sets forth that it is in the power of the judge, what term to vouchsafe. Accordingly, not less than one hundred days must be given.

BOOK III. Part III.

tion in respect of the period for the acquisition of the inheritance, according to which no acquisition can occur upon the ground of a testament before it is opened.[a]

[a] § 175.

The entrance upon, as well as the renunciation of, the inheritance (repudiatio hereditatis) apart from delatio, supposes—

(1) knowledge of the delatio and the species thereof.

Pomp.: In repudianda hereditate vel legato certus esse debet de suo iure is qui repudiat.—l. 23, h. t.[1]

Ulp.: Sed et si de condicione testatoris incertus sit, paterfamilias an filiusfamilias sit, non poterit adire hereditatem.—l. 32, § 2 eod.[2]

Iul.: Si quis se filiumfamilias existimat, cum sit paterfamilias, poterit adquirere hereditatem.—D. 35, 1, 21.[3]

Paul.: Ut quis pro herede gerendo obstringat se hereditati, scire debet qua ex causa hereditas ad eum pertineat: veluti adgnatus proximus iusto testamento scriptus heres, antequam tabulae proferantur, cum existimaret intestato patremfamilias mortuum, quamvis omnia pro domino fecerit, heres tamen non erit.—l. 22, D. h. t.[4]

Ulp.: Heres institutus idemque legitimus si

---

[1] In the renunciation of an inheritance or a legacy the renouncing party ought to be assured as to his legal position.

[2] But if he be uncertain as to the status of the testator, whether he was a *pat. fam.* or a *fil. fam.*, he cannot enter upon the inheritance.

[3] When any one supposes he is a *fil. fam.*, whilst he is a *pat. fam.*, he will be able to acquire the inheritance.

[4] In order that a man by acting as heir should make himself liable for the inheritance, he ought to know upon what title the inheritance belongs to him: for example, the nearest agnate designated heir by a lawful testament, whilst supposing that the *pat. fam.* died intestate, will not be heir before the tablets are propounded, although he have transacted everything as owner.

quasi institutus repudiaverit, quasi legitimus non amittit hereditatem; sed si quasi legitimus repudiavit, si quidem scit se heredem institutum, credendus est utrumque repudiasse: si ignorat, ad neutrum ei repudiatio nocebit, neque ad testamentariam, quoniam hanc non repudiavit, neque ad legitimam, quoniam nondum ei fuerat delata.—l. 17, § 1 eod.[1]

(2) Capacity for obligation of the person entering.

Id.: More nostrae civitatis neque pupillus neque pupilla sine tutoris auctoritate obligari possunt: hereditas autem quin obliget nos aeri alieno, etiam si non sit solvendo, plus quam manifestum est.—l. 8 pr. eod.[2]

(3) Command of the pater fam. or master, in the case of one subject to power.

Gai. ii. § 87: Ipse qui in potestate nostra est, . . . si heres institutus sit, nisi nostro iussu hereditatem adire non potest; et si iubentibus nobis adierit, hereditas nobis adquiritur proinde atque si nos ipsi heredes instituti essemus.[3]

Ulp.: Iussum eius, qui in potestate habet, praecedere debet.—Sed in bonorum possessione placuit ratam haberi posse eam, quam citra

---

[1] If an instituted, and at the same time legal, heir shall renounce the inheritance as instituted, he does not also forfeit it in the character of legal heir, we must presume that he renounced both. If he does not know of it, the renunciation will in no way harm him, either with regard to the testamentary inheritance, because this he did not renounce, or with regard to the legal, since it has not yet been offered to him.

[2] According to the Customary Law of our state, wards of either sex can incur no liability without the sanction of their guardian; but it is notorious that an inheritance makes us liable for the payment of debts, even if it be in a state of insolvency.

[3] A person that is under our power, if he be instituted heir, cannot enter upon the inheritance, except by our direction; and if he shall enter by our direction, the inheritance is acquired for us, just as if we ourselves were the instituted heirs.

BOOK III. Part III.

voluntatem agnovit is qui potestati subiectus est. —l. 25, § 4, l. 6, § 1, D. h. t.[1]

(4) The inheritance, moreover, must be entered upon, just as it is offered, since partial entry or renunciation is contradictory to the principle of the totality of the inheritance.

Paul.: Qui totam hereditatem adquirere potest, is pro parte eam scindendo adire non potest.—l. 1 eod.[2]

Ulp.: Si ex asse heres destinaverit partem habere hereditatis, videtur in assem pro herede gessisse.—l. 10 eod.[3]

Marc.: Respondit nihil actum esse, cum ex semisse scriptus heres ex quadrante per errorem adiit hereditatem.—l. 75 eod.[4]

Ulp.: Sed etsi quis ex pluribus partibus in eiusdem hereditate institutus sit, non potest quasdam partes repudiare quasdam adgnoscere.—l. 2 eod.[5]

§ 172. CAPACITY FOR ACQUISITION OF THE INHERITANCE.

[a] § 159.

Capacity to inherit[a] is the pre-requisite of a valid delatio, whilst capacity of the person called to acquire an inheritance is the pre-requisite of the acquisition.

---

[1] The order of the *pat. fam.* must precede.—But in respect of *bon. poss.*, it has been held that the act of a son subject to power who has laid claim to the *bon. poss.* against the wish (of the *pat. fam.*) can be confirmed (by him).

[2] A person capable of acquiring the whole inheritance cannot by dividing it enter upon it only for a part.

[3] If a universal successor have purposed to hold a part of the inheritance, he is considered to have acted as heir for the whole inheritance.

[4] His answer is: Nothing was accomplished, because the heir designated for one half entered upon the inheritance by mistake for one fourth.

[5] But although a man have been instituted for several parts in one and the same person's inheritance, he cannot renounce some parts and lay claim to others.

The capacity to acquire a testamentary inheritance, or a legacy, was taken away from the following persons (incapaces). Book III. Part III.

According to the lex Iulia et Papia Poppaea,[a] as *incapaces* in respect of the testaments of all persons not related to them at the least in the sixth (to the seventh) degree, and of the next affines were— [a] § 44, ad fin.

(1) 'caelibes,' entirely.

Gai. ii. § 286: Caelibes . . . per legem Iuliam hereditates legataque capere prohibentur.[1]

Ulp. xvii. 1: Quod quis sibi testamento relictum, ita ut iure civili capere possit, aliqua ex causa non ceperit, **caducum** appellatur, veluti ceciderit ab eo: verbi gratia si caelibi vel Latino Iuniano legatum fuerit, nec intra dies centum vel caelebs legi paruerit, vel Latinus ius Quiritium consecutus sit.[2]

(2) 'orbi,' to the extent of half of that which is left to them.

Gai. ii. § 286[a]: Item orbi per legem Papiam dimidias partes hereditatum legatorumque perdunt.[3]

(3) Childless spouses, as between each other for certain portions; in which, however, many exceptions obtained, especially such as were founded on the 'ius liberorum.'

Ulp. xv. 1: Vir et uxor inter se matrimonii nomine decimam capere possunt; quodsi ex alio matrimonio liberos superstites habeant, praeter

---

[1] Unmarried persons are forbidden by the *l. Iulia* to take inheritances and legacies.

[2] If a man from any cause have forborne to take a testamentary gift, although it was bequeathed to him in such way that he could take it by civil law, it is called a Lapse, as if it had slipped from him; for example, if a legacy be left to an unmarried man, or to a Junian Latin, and either the unmarried man has not within one hundred days complied with the statute, or the Latin has not obtained Roman citizenship.

[3] Childless persons, by the *l. Papia*, lose one half of their inheritances and legacies.

BOOK III. Part III.

decimam, quam matrimonii nomine capiunt, totidem decimas pro numero liberorum accipiunt. —xvi. 1: Aliquando vir et uxor inter se solidum capere possunt, velut si etc.[a] Libera inter eos testamenti factio est, si ius liberorum a principe impetraverint.[1]

[a] Ibid.

According to the l. Iunia, Latini Iuniani were incapaces.[b]

[b] Gai. i. 23; Ulp. xx. 14.

§ 173. In Iure Cessio Transmissio Hereditatis.

The delatio of the inheritance avails only for him personally that is called, so that he alone can enter upon the inheritance; but there are two exceptions to this.

(1) The person, as a rule the proximus adgnatus (the suus and necessarius being excepted), whose right of inheritance was offered to him *ab intestato*, could still in the Classical Law, by means of 'in iure cessio'[c] of such inheritance not yet acquired, transfer it to another person in such way that the cessionary was by the Praetorian addictio acknowledged as the actual heir. The want of an heir,[d] which was apt to arise, was thereby at the same time obviated. The in iure cessio of the inheritance already taken up effected only the transfer of the several things composing such inheritance, and resulted, moreover, in the transfer of its obligations, whilst the in iure cessio of an inheritance first

[c] § 79.

[d] § 162, ad fin.

1 A husband and wife may receive one-tenth of each other's estate, on the strength of their marriage. But if either of them have children by another marriage surviving, they can, besides the tenth on the ground of their marriage, take as many more tenths as is the number of their children.—Sometimes a husband and wife can receive from each other the whole inheritance, for example, if &c.—They have unrestricted testamentary capacity as between themselves if they have obtained from the Emperor the privileges accompanying issue.

offered *ex testamento* was already rebutted by the juristic character of that legal act.[a]

Gai. ii. §§ 34–7 : Hereditas quoque in iure cessionem recipit. § Nam si is ad quem ab intestato legitimo iure hereditas pertinet, in iure eam alii ante aditionem cedat, id est antequam heres exstiterit, proinde fit heres is cui in iure cesserit, ac si ipse per legem ad hereditatem vocatus esset: post obligationem vero si cesserit, nihilominus ipse heres permanet et ob id creditoribus tenebitur, debita vero pereunt eoque modo debitores hereditarii lucrum faciunt; corpora vero eius hereditatis proinde transeunt ad eum cui cessa est hereditas, ac si ei singula in iure cessa fuissent. § Testamento autem scriptus heres ante aditam quidem hereditatem in iure cedendo eam nihil agit; postea vero quam adierit si cedat, ea accidunt quae proxime diximus de eo, ad quem ab intestato legitimo iure pertineat hereditas, si post obligationem in iure cedat. § Idem et de necessariis heredibus diversae scholae auctores existimant, quod nihil videtur interesse, utrum aliquis adeundo hereditatem fiat heres, an invitus existat; . . . sed nostri preceptores putant, nihil agere necessarium heredem, cum in iure cedat hereditatem.[1]

[a] Cf. § 97, ad init.

---

[1] An inheritance also admits of surrender in court. § For if he to whom an inheritance under intestacy belongs by statute-law makes a surrender of it to another before entry, *i.e.*, before he has become heir, the surrenderee becomes heir, just as if he himself had been called by law to the inheritance. But if he have made a surrender of it after incurring liability, he still himself remains heir, and will therefore be liable to the creditors, but the debts are extinguished, and in that way debtors to the inheritance are gainers; the corporeal things, however, belonging to such inheritance pass to him to whom the inheritance has been surrendered, just as if they had been surrendered to him one by one. § But if the heir appointed by testament make a surrender to another before actual entry on the inheritance, he effects nothing; whilst if he surrender it after entry,

BOOK III. Part III.

The delatio is regularly uninheritable.

Imp. Iust.: Hereditatem, nisi fuerit adita, transmitti[a] nec veteres concedebant nec nos patimur.—C. 6, 51, l. un. § 5.[1]

[a] Sc. ad heredes.

But already in the Classical Law extraordinary relief was given in certain cases, where the person called was by no fault of his own—especially by legal obstacles not affecting him personally—temporarily prevented from entering upon the inheritance which had been lawfully offered to him,[b] and had died during this period; and to his heirs by means of a decree of the Praetor.

[b] Cf. D. 29. 2. 84.

Ulp.: Si ea sit mater, de cuius statu dubitatur, utrum materfamilias sit an filiafamilias, ut puta quoniam pater eius ab hostibus captus sit, si certum esse coeperit matremfamilias esse, liberi admittentur;[c] unde tractari potest, an medio tempore dum status pendet, succurri eis a praetore debeat, ne si medio tempore decesserint, nihil ad heredem transmittant: et magis est ut subveniatur, ut in multis casibus placuit.—D. 38, 17, 1, 1.[2]

[c] Sc. ad hereditatem eius ex SC. Orph.

---

the results are the same as those of which we have just spoken in respect of one to whom an inheritance on an intestacy belongs by statute-law, if he make a surrender after incurring liability. § The authorities of the opposite school think the same, as to *heredes necessarii*, from its seeming immaterial whether a man becomes heir by entering upon an inheritance, or becomes heir against his will. . . . But our teachers are of opinion that the *heres necessarius* does a void act when making a surrender of the inheritance.

[1] Save as entry shall have been made upon it, neither did the ancients allow nor do we suffer the transmission of an inheritance.

[2] If she be a mother concerning whose status doubt exists, whether she is a *mat. fam.* or a *filia fam.*, for example, because her father has been captured by the enemy, her children will be admitted (*i.e.*, to her inheritance, by the SC. Orph.) when it is once certain that she is a *mat. fam.* From this the question can arise whether relief must be afforded them by the Praetor in the interval during which the status is in suspense, lest if they die in the meantime, they should transmit nothing to their heir; and the fact is rather that relief is to be given, as has been held in many cases.

Paul.: Si quis eum, qui in utero est, praetermiserit, etiam nondum nato eo alius [a] qui heres institutus est, bonorum possessionem contra tabulas admittere potest.—Sed et si decesserit, antequam peteret bonorum possessionem, non est iniquum praetorem decernere heredibus (eius) salvum fore commodum bonorum possessionis secundum tabulas vel contra tabulas.—D. 37, 4, l. 4, § 3 (Paul.), l. 5 (Iul.).[1]

[a] Sc. e liberis.

In the later Law, the delatio to the heirs of the person called (successio in delationem) was developed for certain cases (so-called cases of transmission) as a regular institute of law; of widest extent is the so-called *transmissio Iustinianea.*

Imp. Iust.: Sancimus: si quis vel ex testamento vel ab intestato vocatus deliberationem meruerit vel hoc quidem non fecerit, non tamen successioni renuntiaverit, . . . praedictum arbitrium in successionen suam transmittat, ita tamen, ut unius anni spatio eadem transmissio fuerit conclusa; et si quidem is, qui sciens hereditatem sibi esse vel ab intestato vel ex testamento delatam, deliberatione minime petita intra annale tempus decesserit, hoc ius ad suam successionem intra annale tempus extendat.—C. 6, 30, 19.[2]

---

[1] If a man has passed over a child in the womb, another person who has been appointed heir, even if the child has not yet been born, can claim *bon. poss.* as against the testament.—But also if the child has died before he claimed *bon. poss.*, it is not unfair for the Praetor to decide that the advantage of the *bon. poss.* shall remain secured to his heirs, as well in agreement with the testament as contrary to it.

[2] We enact that every one who, having been called to the testamentary or the intestate succession, is entitled to deliberation, or has not in fact done so, but has not renounced the inheritance, may transmit to his heirs the above-mentioned legal privilege, in such manner, however, that the same transmission shall be completed within the space of one year. And if he who is aware that an inheritance has devolved upon him, either under intestacy or by virtue of a testament, dies within a year without laying claim to the respite for deliberation, he may transmit this right to his heirs within the period of one year.

BOOK III. Part III.

§ 174. EFFECT OF THE ACQUISITION (*BENEFICIUM INVENTARII, SEPARATIONIS; ACTIO FAMILIAE ERCISCUNDAE*).

By the acquisition of an inheritance the control of the testator's property passes in perpetuity to the heir,[a] and that reckoned from the moment of the death of the former. This is the principle of the CONTINUITY of inheritance.

[a] § 153.

Pomp.: Heres in omne ius mortui, non tantum singularum rerum dominium succedit, cum et ea, quae in nominibus sint, ab hereditatem transeant.—D. 29, 2, 37.[1]

Flor.: Heres quandoque adeundo hereditatem, iam tunc a morte successisse defuncto intelligitur.—l. 54 eod.[2]

Paul.: Omnis hereditas, quamvis postea adeatur, tamen cum tempore mortis continuatur.—D. 50, 17, 138.[3]

Thus he enters also in respect of the ownership, as well as of the claims and debts of the testator, entirely into his place, so that in proprietary relations both count as one person; therefore in respect of inherited actions the intentio is always placed to the name of the heir;[b] and the heir is liable for debts of the testator beyond the extent of the inheritance.[c]

[b] Gai. iv. 34.

[c] D. 29, 2, 8, pr.; 37, 1, 3 pr.

Pomp.: Hereditatis appellatio sine dubio continet etiam damnosam hereditatem: iuris enim nomen est, sicuti bonorum possessio.—D. 50, 16, 119.[4]

---

[1] An heir succeeds to the whole legal position of the deceased, not only to the ownership of the individual objects, since even the liabilities pass to the heir.

[2] At whatever time the heir enters upon the inheritance, he is regarded as having succeeded to the deceased immediately upon his death.

[3] Every inheritance, although the entry be made at a later stage, is nevertheless continued as from the time of the death.

[4] The denomination *haereditas* without doubt comprises also a disadvantageous inheritance; for it is the name of a right, just as *bon. poss.*

Liability for the debts beyond the value of the inheritance, the heir that enters can, from the time of Justinian, avoid by preparation of an inventory of the estate (beneficium inventarii),[a] in certain form and within certain intervals. Soldiers are exceptionally always liable alone to the extent of the property left. On the other hand, the Classical Law already gives to the creditors of the testator—for protection against the risk of the personal insolvency of the heir—the 'beneficium separationis,' by means of which they can effect a severance, through the magistrate, of the property inherited from that which is the heir's own, and exclusive satisfaction from the former in preference to the creditors of the heir.

> Ulp.: Solet autem separatio permitti creditoribus ex his causis: ut puta debitorem quis Seium habuit, hic decessit, heres ei exstitit Titius, hic non est solvendo, patitur venditionem; creditores Seii dicunt bona Seii sufficere sibi, creditores Titii contentos esse debere bonis Titii, et sic quasi duorum fieri bonorum venditionem.—Ex contrario autem creditores Titii non impetrabunt separationem—nam licet alicui adiiciendo sibi creditorem creditoris sui facere deteriorem condicionem.—Illud sciendum est eos demum creditores posse impetrare separationem, qui non novandi animo ab herede stipulati sunt: ceterum . . . amiserunt separationis commodum, quippe cum secuti sunt nomen heredis, nec possunt iam se ab eo separare, qui quodammodo eum elegerunt; sed et si usuras ab eo ea mente quasi eum eligendo exegerunt, idem erit probandum.—Praeterea sciendum est, posteaquam bona hereditaria bonis heredis mixta sunt, non posse impetrari separationem.—De his autem omnibus, an admittenda separatio sit nec ne, praetoris erit praesidis notio.—Item sciendum est vulgo placere creditores quidem heredis, si quis superfuerit ex bonis testatoris, posse habere in suum debitum,

[a] Cf. Blackstone, ii. 510 (Steph. ii. 202); Markby, s. 800; Paterson, ss. 695, 782.—The present law in Scotland rests upon the Conveyancing Act of 1874, sect. 12.

creditores vero testatoris ex bonis heredis nihil.—D. 42, 6, l. 1, §§ 1, 2, 10, 12, 14, 17.[1]

If several heirs (cohaeredes) exist, there arises between them by the entry a *communio*, in respect of the inheritance, to accomplish the destruction of which, by severance and settlement of accounts, there belongs to each the actio *erciscundae*, 'erctum ciere.'[a]

[a] Cf. § 135.

Gai.: Haec actio proficiscitur e lege XII tabularum: namque coheredibus a communione discedere necessarium videbatur aliquam actionem constitui, qua inter eos res hereditariae distribuerentur.—l. 1 pr., D. fam. erc. 10, 2.[2]

Ulp.: Familiae erciscundae iudicium ex duobus

---

[1] Now separation is commonly allowed to creditors from the following causes: *e.g.*, some one has Seius as his debtor; the latter is dead: Tit. becomes his heir; he is insolvent and suffers a sale; the creditors of Seius say his goods meet their claim, the creditors of Tit., accordingly, must be satisfied with the property of Tit., and that thus a sale must take place of two estates, so to speak. But on the other hand, the creditors of Tit. will not claim a separation. For any one is at liberty to place his creditor in a worse position by getting a new creditor.—It is to be noted that only those creditors can claim separation who have taken a stipulation from the heir with no thought of novation; but . . . they have forfeited the advantage of separation, for such persons have once for all followed the indebtedness of the heir, and cannot now detach themselves from him, since they have in a manner made choice of him; the same will hold good even if they have required interest from him with the intention, as it were, of making choice of him.—It is, moreover, to be noted that after the hereditary goods have been mingled with those of the heir, it is impossible to claim separation. . . . Now the praetor or president with regard to all such matters shall determine whether separation is to be allowed or not.—Moreover, it is to be noted that it is commonly held that, if aught remains over from the *bon. poss.* of the testator, the heir's creditors may have it for their claims, but the testator's creditors can have nothing from the goods of the heir.

[2] This action is derived from a law of the Twelve Tables; for it seemed necessary that an action should be created for those heirs who wish to be quit of the community, by virtue of which the hereditary property should be divided amongst them.

constat, id est rebus atque praestationibus, quae sunt personales.—l. 22, § 4 eod.[1]

The claims and debts of the inheritance are divided *ipso iure* in the ratio of shares in the inheritance.

Imp. Gord.: Et quae in nominibus sunt non recipiunt divisionem, cum ipso iure in portiones hereditarias ex lege XII tabularum divisa sunt.—l. 6, C. eod. 3, 36.[2]

Gai.: Plane ad officium iudicis nonnumquam pertinet, ut debita et credita singulis pro solido aliis alia adtribuat, quia saepe et solutio et exactio partium non minima incommoda habet; nec tamen scilicet haec adtributio illud efficit, ut quis solus totum debeat vel totum alicui soli debeatur, sed ut, sive agendum sit, partim suo partim procuratorio nomine agat, sive cum eo agatur, partim suo partim procuratorio nomine conveniatur.—l. 3, D. eod.[3]

§ 175. Right of Accrual. *Caduca. Ereptoria.*

1. *Ius antiquum.* If of several testamentary or intestate heirs one lapse before the acquisition—whether because the condition under which he has been instituted is defective, or that it is not his will to acquire his hereditary portion (repudiation and omission),

---

[1] The action for partition of an inheritance comprises two objects, things and performances, which (latter) are personal.

[2] That which consists of debts does not admit of division, since, according to a Law of the Twelve Tables, it has by operation of law been divided into shares of the inheritance.

[3] It is clearly part of the duty of the *iudex* to assign debts and credits integrally to individual heirs, different ones to different persons, because the payment and getting in of the shares is often attended by great inconvenience. The result of this assignment, however, is not that a single heir undertakes a whole debt, or the whole is owed to any one heir alone, but that, whether it be necessary to bring an action, he shall sue firstly in his own name, partly as agent, or if proceedings be taken against him, he must be sued partly in his own name, partly as agent.[a]

[a] Cf. Hunter, pp. 759, sq.

BOOK III. Part III.

or that he cannot do so (death before entry upon the inheritance, loss of the testamenti factio)—then, in default of substitutions, and except as to cases of transmission, the hereditary portion which lapses is *ipso iure* and of necessity acquired by the joint-heirs, in virtue of the principle of the totality of the inheritance [a]: right of ACCRUAL, or augmentation (ius adcrescendi).[b]

[a] § 153.

[b] For the English doctrine of survivorship in Joint Tenancy, see Blackst. ii. 183-4 (Steph. i. 342-3).

> Gai.: Qui semel aliqua ex parte heres exstitit, deficientium partes etiam invitus excipit, id est tacite ei deficientium partes etiam invito adcrescunt.—D. 29, 2, 53, 1.[1]

> Marc.: Si ex pluribus legitimis heredibus quidam omiserint adire hereditatem, vel morte vel qua alia ratione impediti fuerint, quominus adeant, reliquis qui adierint adcrescit illorum portio, et licet decesserint antequam adcresceret, hoc ius ad heredes eorum pertinet.—D. 38, 16, 9.[2]

If several heirs exist, the hereditary portion which lapses accrues to all in the ratio of their own portions in such inheritance.

> Cels.: Cum quis ex institutis, qui non cum aliquo coniunctim institutus sit, heres non est, pars eius omnibus pro portionibus hereditariis adcrescit.—l. 60 (59), § 3, D. de her. inst. 28, 5.[3]

This is, however, subject to the institution of an heir jointly with the one that has lapsed, to the same hereditary portion, or his inheriting with such in the same

---

[1] He that has once become heir for any share takes, even against his will, the shares of those that fail, *i.e.*, the shares of those that fail come tacitly to him even without his wishing it.

[2] If some of several heirs-at-law have neglected to enter upon the inheritance, whether as hindered from entering by death, or any other cause, their share accrues to the rest who have entered, and though they may have died before such accrual, this right belongs to their heirs.

[3] When one of those nominated, who was not nominated jointly with some one, is not heir, his share accrues to all in the ratio of their shares in the inheritance.

stock, in which case the portion that becomes unappropriated accrues to him alone.

Iavol.: Heredes sine partibus utrum coniunctim an separatim scribantur, hoc interest, quod, si quis ex coniunctis decessit, non ad omnes, sed ad reliquos qui coniuncti erant: sin autem ex separatis, ad omnes, qui testamento eodem scripti sunt heredes, portio eius pertinet.—l. 64 (63) eod.[1]

Cels.: Coniunctim heredes instituti aut coniunctim legari hoc est: totam hereditatem et tota legata singulis data esse, partes autem concursu fieri.—l. 80, D. de leg. III. (32).[2]

Gai.: Si duobus filiis et ex altero filio duobus nepotibus bonorum possessio competat, et alter ex nepotibus non petat, pars eius fratri adcrescit; si vero ex filiis alter non petat, tam fratri quam nepotibus id prodest: namque tunc duo semisses fiunt, ex quibus alterum filius alterum nepotes consequuntur.—D. 37, 4, 12 pr.[3]

2. Into the pre-existing Law the lex Iulia et Papia Poppaea penetrated very deeply with its capricious rules upon escheat. As *caducum*—in contrast with the 'pro non scripto,' *i.e.*, what was from the outset imperfectly bequeathed, in respect of which it remained in the subsisting Law—everything counts that cannot

---

[1] Whether heirs without definite shares are nominated jointly or separately causes this difference, that if one of those jointly nominated should die, his share comes not to all, but only to the rest of those jointly nominated with him. But if one of those separately instituted should die, his share belongs to all who were designated heirs in the same testament.

[2] By joint institution of heirs or a joint bequest is meant, that the whole inheritance and the whole of the legacies have been given to individuals, but that the shares arise by coalescence.

[3] If the *bon. poss.* belongs to two sons and two grandsons by another son, and one of the grandsons makes no claim, his share accrues to his brother; but if one of the sons makes no claim, that benefits as well his brother as the grandsons; for there are then formed two halves, of which the son receives one, and the two grandsons receive the other.

Book III. Part III.

be acquired by a testament,[a] whether on account of incapacity of the person to whom regard is had (part heir or legatee), or by reason of a disposition by last will being impaired or not operating, either after the death of the testator (caducum in the narrower sense) or while he is still alive (in causa caduci). By the lex Papia, no right of accrual obtained in respect of the caducum, but the heirs instituted in the testament, and after them the legatees, who had children (ius patrum) could—down to Caracalla—vindicate it cum suo onere; and in this 'collegatarii coniuncti' had precedence over all others.[b]

[a] § 171.

[b] § 183. ad fin.

> Gai. ii. § 207: Et quamvis prima causa sit in caducis vindicandis heredum liberos habentium, deinde si heredes liberos non habeant, legatariorum liberos habentium, tamen ipsa lege Papia significatur, ut collegatarius coniunctus, si liberos habeat, potior sit heredibus, etiamsi liberos habebunt.[1]

> Ulp. xvii. 3: Caduca autem cum suo onere fiunt: ideoque libertates et legata vel fideicommissa ab eo data, ex cuius persona hereditas caduca facta est, salva sunt.[2]

The earlier right of accrual only remained for ascendants and descendants to the third degree instituted in the testament.

> Id. xviii.: Item liberis et parentibus testatoris usque ad tertium gradum lex Papia ius antiquum dedit, ut heredibus illis institutis, quod quis ex

---

[1] And although in claiming lapses, one primary right is that of the heirs who have children, and then, if the heirs have no children, the right belongs to the legatees that have children, yet it is expressly stated in the *l. Papia* itself that a conjoint co-legatee, if he have children, is preferred to heirs, even though they shall have children.

[2] Now lapses ensue with their own burdens; and therefore gifts of freedom, legacies, or bequests in trust, charged upon him in whose person the inheritance has lapsed, are not affected.

eo testamento non capit, ad hos pertineat aut totum aut ex parte, prout pertinere possit.[1]

In default of such, and previously also of persons entitled to the 'caducorum vindicatio,' the caducum fell to the Treasury.

Id. xvii. 2: Hodie ex constitutione imperatoris Antonini **omnia** caduca fisco vindicantur, sed servato iure antiquo liberis et parentibus.[2]

The escheat was defeated by substitutions.

Imp. Iust.: Sed et ipsis testamentorum conditoribus sic gravissima caducorum observatio visa est, ut et substitutiones introducerent, ne fiant caduca, et si facta sint, ad certas personas recurrere disponerent, vias recludentes, quas lex Papia posuit in caducis.—C. 6, 51, l. un. pr.[3]

Mod.: In tempus capiendae hereditatis institui heredem posse, benevolentiae est, veluti 'Lucius Titius, cum capere poterit heres esto'; idem et in legato.—l. 63 (62) pr., D. de her. inst.[4]

3. Justinian, by a Constitution of the year 534 (l. un. C. 6, 51), abolished the whole law of the caducorum vindicatio, and re-established the earlier law of accrual (ius antiquum) in its full extent.

---

[1] The *l. Papia* has likewise granted the ancient right to descendants and ascendants of the testator as far as the third degree; so that when such have been appointed heirs, anything which another person does not take under the testament belongs to them in whole or in part, according as it can belong.

[2] At the present day, by virtue of a constitution of the Emp. Antonine, all lapses are claimed for the Treasury, but with a reservation of the old rule for the benefit of descendants and ascendants.

[3] But also as regards testators themselves, the practice as to lapses seemed so very onerous that they introduced substitutions, to avoid lapses, and if they did occur, arranged them so as to fall back upon certain persons, defeating the methods established by the *l. Papia* in respect of lapses.

[4] That an heir can be instituted for the period when he can take the inheritance, is a mark of leniency, for example: 'L. T. shall be heir when he is able to take.' The like also in respect of a legacy.

Book III. Part III.

There is finally a series of cases in which the inheritance—or a legacy—has devolved ab intestato or is again taken away ex testamento from the successor, capable of inheritance and acquisition, because of unfitness (indignitas). What is thus taken away (ereptorium s. erepticium) passes as a rule to the Treasury, in certain cases to other persons.[a]

[a] Cf. D. 28, 4, l. 1, § 3, l. 4; 38, 6. 1. 8.

Pap.: Cum heredis nomen mutata voluntate paterfamilias incisis tabulis induxisset atque ideo fisco portionis emolumentum adiudicatum fuisset, eam rem legatariis non obesse, qui retinuerunt voluntatem, D. Marco placuit, et ideo cum suo onere fiscum succedere.—D. 34, 9, 16, 2.[1]

Marc.: Aufertur hereditas ex asse et ad fiscum pertinet, si emancipatus filius contra tabulas bonorum possessionem patris ut praeteritus petierit et ex substitutione impuberis adierit hereditatem.—Indignum esse D. Pius illum decrevit, qui manifestissime comprobatus est id egisse, ut per negligentiam et culpam suam mulier, a qua heres institutus erat, moreretur.—l. 2 pr., l. 3 eod.[2]

§ 176. Protection of the Right of Inheritance.

The action with which the heir makes good his right of inheritance is the 'hereditatis petitio,' an actio arbitraria.

---

[1] When the *pat. fam.* shall have altered his intention, struck out the name of the heir and cut through the tablets, and the amount of his share has accordingly been confiscated to the Treasury, the late Emp. Marcus decided that such circumstance does not prejudice the legatees, who have retained the disposition made to them, and therefore the Treasury succeeds with the heir's own burden.

[2] If an emancipated son, who has been passed over, has laid claim to the possession of the father's goods in opposition to his testament, and upon the ground of substitution for a minor has entered upon the inheritance, the whole inheritance is taken from him, and devolves upon the Treasury.—The late Emp. Pius has pronounced such person unworthy as has been quite clearly proved to have brought about by his negligence and fault the death of a woman by whom he was appointed heir.

This lies against every one who possesses an object belonging to the inheritance 'pro herede' (*i.e.*, assuming to itself a right of inheritance), or 'pro possessore' (without appeal to a ground of law). The fictus possessor, as in the case of rei vindicatio, is on a par with the actual possessor.[a]

[a] § 90.

> Regulariter definiendum est eum demum teneri petitione hereditatis, qui vel ius pro herede vel pro possessore possidet vel rem hereditariam—licet minimam. Itaque qui ex asse vel ex parte heres est, intendit quidem hereditatem suam esse totam vel pro parte, sed hoc solum ei officio iudicis restituitur quod adversarius possidet, aut totum, si ex asse sit heres, aut pro parte ex qua heres est.—Pro herede possidet, qui putat se heredem esse; sed an et is, qui scit se heredem non esse, pro herede possideat, quaeritur: et Arrianus putat teneri, quo iure nos uti Proculus scribit. . . . Pro possessore vero possidet praedo,—qui interrogatus cur possideat, responsurus sit 'quia possideo,' nec contendet se heredem vel per mendacium,—nec ullam causam possessionis possit dicere: et ideo fur et raptor petitione hereditatis tenentur.—l. 9 (Ulp.), l. 10 (Gai.), l. 11–l. 13 pr. (Ulp.), D. h. t. (de H. P. 5, 3).[1]

---

[1] One can as a rule state that he alone is liable to the inheritance action who commands a right, or an inheritance as heir or as possessor,—although it be of the least extent. He therefore that is universal or partial heir does in fact claim the inheritance as his wholly or partially, but by the aid of the *iudex* that alone is restored to him which the opponent possesses, either the whole, if he be universal heir, or according to the share for which he is heir.—He possesses as heir who considers himself to be the heir.—But the question arises whether he who knows he is not heir, does possess as heir: Arrian is of opinion that he is liable, and Proculus writes that this is our law. . . . A robber occupies as possessor,—who when asked the reason of his possession can only answer, 'Because I possess,' and will not, or only by means of a falsehood, maintain that he is heir—and can allege no ground of his possession; and therefore the thief and the robber are liable to the inheritance action.

Book III. Part III.

Ulp.: Item a debitore hereditario, quasi a iuris possessore, . . . posse hereditatem peti constat.—Item qui a debitore hereditario exegit, petitione hereditatis tenetur.—Ulp. l. 13, § 15, l. 16, § 1 eod.[1]

[a] D. 5, 3, 50 pr. The object of the action is the inheritance itself;[a] it is an 'hereditatis vindicatio (s. in rem actio de universitate)' which, however, comprises also personal performances. Its purpose is, judicial recognition of the right of inheritance and restitution of the objects of inheritance 'cum omni causa,' and after deduction of the outlay, with discrimination between the bonae and malae fidei possessor.[b]

[b] § 90.

Id.: Petitio hereditatis, etsi in rem actio sit, habet tamen praestationes quasdam personales, ut puta eorum quae a debitoribus sunt exacta.—l. 25, § 18 eod.[2]

Gai. iv. § 133: Olim quaedam (praescriptiones) et pro reo opponebantur, qualis illa erat praescriptio: EA RES AGATVR, SI IN EA RE PRAEIVDICIVM HEREDITATI NON FIAT, quae nunc in speciem exceptionis deducta est et locum habet, cum petitor hereditatis alio genere iudicii praeiudicium hereditati faciat, veluti cum res singulas petat.[3]

---

1 It is well known that an inheritance can likewise be sued for from a debtor of the inheritance as if from the possessor of a right.—Likewise a person that has recovered from a debtor of the inheritance is liable to the inheritance action.

2 The inheritance action, although it is a real action, nevertheless embraces certain personal performances, as for example, of that which has been recovered from debtors.

3 Formerly some (prescriptions) were set up on behalf of the defendant; as was such a prescription as this: 'That matter may be the subject of the action, provided it does not involve a prior decision as to the inheritance,' which is now thrown into a kind of plea, and is employed when a claimant of the inheritance, by another sort of action, may get a prior decision as to the inheritance; for example, when he sues for particular things.

According to a SC. Iuventianum (under Hadrian), not merely all that belongs to the heritage, but every accretion in general that he has made from the inheritance has to be taken away from the defendant—'res succedit in locum pretii et pretium in locum rei'[a]—but, on the other hand, the bonae fidei possessor has to be liable also alone to the extent of the enrichment still subsisting.

[a] This is questionable as a general rule.

> Paul.: Post senatusconsultum omne lucrum auferendum esse tam bonae fidei possessori quam praedoni dicendum est.—l. 28 eod.[1]
>
> Ulp.: Ait senatus: '**placere, a quibus petita hereditas fuisset, si adversus eos iudicatum esset, pretia, quae ad eos rerum ex hereditate venditarum pervenissent, etsi eae ante petitam hereditatem deperissent deminutaeve essent, restituere debere; . . . eos autem, qui iustas causas habuissent, quare bona ad se pertinere existimassent, usque eo dumtaxat (condemnandos), quo locupletiores ex ea re facti essent.**'—Bonae fidei possessor si vendiderit res hereditarias, sive exegit pretium sive non, quia habet actionem, debebit pretium praestare: sed ubi habet actionem, sufficiet eum actiones praestare.—l. 20, §§ 6, 17 eod.[2]

---

[1] For since the *SCtum* it will have to be stated that all profit must be taken away from both the *bon. fid.* possessor and the robber.

[2] The Senate says: 'that it decides that those from whom an inheritance is claimed, if judgment have been given against them, must restore the purchase-money which has come to their hands for the sale of things belonging to the inheritance, although they should have perished or been diminished before the inheritance action was brought; . . . but those who shall have had a lawful reason for thinking that goods belonged to them (are to be condemned) only so far as they shall have been enriched by such thing.'—If a *bon. fid.* possessor have sold things belonging to an inheritance, he must account for the purchase-money, whether he has recovered the price or not, because an action is at his command. But when he has the action, it will be enough for him to make over the right of action.

[a] Sc. bonae fidei possessores.

Id.: Quemcumque sumptum fecerint [a] ex hereditate, si quid dilapidaverunt perdiderunt, dum re sua se abuti putant, non praestabunt.—l. 25, § 11 eod.[1]

Id.: Item veniunt in hereditatis petitionem etiam ea quae hereditatis causa comparata sunt, ut puta mancipia pecoraque et si qua alia necessario hereditati sunt comparata. Et si quidem pecunia hereditaria sint comparata, sine dubio venient; si vero non pecunia hereditaria, videndum erit: et puto etiam haec venire, si magna utilitas hereditatis versetur, pretium scilicet restituturo herede.—l. 20 pr. eod.[2]

The bonorum possessor has for the enforcement of his Praetorian right of inheritance—

[b] Cf. § 154

[c] Sc. possessoriam.

(1) the 'hereditatis petitio' as utilis actio.[b]

Gai.: Per hereditatis petitionem [c] tantumdem consequitur bonorum possessor, quantum superioribus civilibus actionibus heres consequi potest. —l. 2, D. de poss. H. P. 5, 5.[3]

(2) The interdictum adipiscendae possessionis '*quorum bonorum*.'

Ait praetor: QVORVM BONORVM EX EDICTO MEO

---

[1] Whatever outlay they (*i.e.*, possessors in good faith) have incurred by reason of the inheritance, when they have allowed anything to decay or have lost it, whilst supposing that they consumed their own property, they will not make good.

[2] There likewise come into account in the inheritance action such things as have been purchased for the benefit of the inheritance, for example, slaves and cattle, and any other thing of necessity purchased for the inheritance. And if in fact it has been purchased with money of the inheritance, it will undoubtedly belong to that. But if the purchase have not been made with money of the inheritance, it will require consideration. I am of opinion that such things also belong to it, when great advantage to the inheritance depends upon them, although the heir must of course restore the price.

[3] The occupant of the goods by this action of inheritance obtains the same as the heir can obtain by the above-mentioned civil actions.

ILLI POSSESSIO DATA ESSET, QVOD DE HIS BONIS PRO HEREDE AVT PRO POSSESSORE POSSIDES POSSIDERESVE, SI NIHIL VSVCAPTVM ESSET, QVODQVE DOLO MALO FECISTI, VTI DESINERES POSSIDERE, ID ILLI RESTITVAS.—l. 1 pr., D. quor. bon. 43, 2.[1]

Gai. iv. § 144: Ideo autem adipiscendae possessionis vocatur interdictum, quia ei tantum utile est, qui nunc primum conatur adipisci rei possessionem; itaque si quis adeptus possessionem amiserit, desinit ei id interdictum utile esse.[2]

§ 177. Succession without an Heir. *Bonorum Addictio Libertatum Servandarum Causa.*

Property left behind without an heir (bona vacantia)[a] according to the lex Iulia et Papia Poppaea (caducaria) fell to the Treasury, which is responsible to the creditors and legatees, as an heir, but not beyond the value of the heritage.

[a] Cf. Paterson, s. 10.

Ulp. xxviii. 7: Si nemo sit, ad quem bonorum possessio pertinere possit, aut sit quidem sed ius suum omiserit, populo bona deferentur ex lege Iulia caducaria.[3]

Callist.: D. Pius rescripsit, vacantium bonorum nuntiationem quadriennio finiri idque tempus ex die, quo certum esse coepit neque heredem neque bonorum possessorem exstare,

---

[1] The Praetor says: 'Of whatever goods possession has been granted to so and so by my edict, that which you possess of such goods as heir or occupant, or would possess if nothing had been acquired by use, and that of the possession of which you have divested yourself by a fraudulent act, deliver up to so and so.'

[2] Now the interdict is said to be for obtaining possession, because it is only of use to a man who is now for the first time endeavouring to obtain possession; and therefore, if after obtaining it he lose it, such interdict ceases to be of use to him.

[3] If there be no one to whom the *bon. poss.* can belong, or if there in fact be such, but he has abandoned his right, the property passes to the People by virtue of the *l. Iulia* upon escheats.

Book III. Part III.

computari oportere.—l. 1, § 2, D. de I. F. 49, 14.[1]

Iul.: Quotiens lege Iulia bona vacantia ad fiscum pertinent, et legata et fideicommissa praestantur, quae praestare cogeretur heres, a quo relicta erant.—l. 96, § 1, D. de leg. 1 (30).[2]

An bona, quae solvendo non sint, ipso iure ad fiscum pertineant, quaesitum est. Labeo scribit ea quae solvendo non sint, ipso iure ad fiscum pertinere; sed contra sententiam eius edictum perpetuum scriptum est, quod ita bona veneant si ex his fisco adquiri nihil possit.—l. 1, § 1, D. de I. F.[3]

[a] § 78.

By the sale of the heritage in the mass,[a] the title of the Treasury passes to the purchaser.

Iul.: Ei, qui partes hereditarias vel totam a fisco mercatus fuerit, non est iniquum dari actionem, per quam universa bona persequatur. —D. 5, 3, 54 pr.[4]

Ulp.: Item si quis a fisco hereditatem quasi vacantem emerit, aequissimum erit utilem actionem [b] adversus eum dari.—l. 13, § 9 eod.[5]

[b] Sc. hereditatis petitionem.

---

[1] By a rescript of the late Emp. Pius, notice of a void inheritance terminates after four years, and that time must be reckoned from the day when it is first certain that neither an heir nor a *bonorum possessor* is forthcoming.

[2] Whenever void goods by the *l. Iulia* devolve upon the Treasury, both legacies and bequests in trust are paid which the heir, upon whom they were charged, would have had to pay.

[3] The question was mooted whether an insolvent estate devolves *ipso iure* upon the Treasury. Lab. writes, that an insolvent estate does devolve upon the Treasury, but the perpetual Edict has decided against his view; according to which the estate is sold in case nothing is to be acquired from it for the Treasury.

[4] To a person who has purchased parts of a heritage from the Treasury it is not unreasonable that an action should be given by which he may pursue the whole estate.

[5] Likewise if a man has purchased from the Treasury a heritage as if void, it will be quite fair that an analogous action should be given against him.

If the Treasury will not accept the heritage, bankruptcy proceedings are taken (sale by the creditors of the inheritance).

> Gai. iii. § 78: Mortuorum bona veneunt velut eorum, quibus certum est neque heredes neque bonorum possessores neque ullum alium iustum successorem existere.[a] [1]

[a] Cf. § 204.

According to a Constitution of Marcus Aurelius, the Treasury is excluded in respect of property left without an heir by the 'bonorum addictio libertatum servandarum causa,' which is given under certain conditions to slaves enfranchised in the testament, or by an intestate codicil.

> Inst. iii. 11 pr.: Accessit novus casus successionis ex constitutione D. Marci. Nam si hi, qui libertatem acceperunt a domino in testamento, ex quo non aditur hereditas, velint bona sibi addici libertatum conservandarum causa, audiuntur: et ita rescripto D. Marci at Popilium Rufum continetur.[2]
>
> Ulp.: (Constitutio D. Marci) iubet libertatem competere servo et bona ei addici, si idonee creditoribus caverit de solido, quod cuique debetur, solvendo;—in quem etiam utiles actiones plerumque creditoribus competunt.—D. 40, 5, ll. 2 and 3.[3]

---

[1] The goods of deceased persons are sold, for instance, of those to whom it is certain that there are no heirs forthcoming, or possessors of the property, or any other lawful successor.

[2] A new case of succession was introduced by a constitution of the late Emp. Marcus. For if those who have received a grant of liberty from their master, in a testament under which no entry is made upon the inheritance, desire that the property should be assigned to them for the purpose of maintaining their liberty, their claim is heard. And this is contained in the rescript of the late Emp. Marcus to Pop. Ruf.

[3] (A constitution of the late Emp. Marcus) directs that liberty belongs to a slave, and the goods must be adjudged to him, if he has given the creditors ample security for the payment of

CHAPTER IV.

BEQUESTS AND *MORTIS CAUSA DONATIONES*.

§ 178. NATURE AND OBJECT OF BEQUESTS.

BOOK III. Part III.

BEQUEST (legatum in the wider sense) is in general the appropriation by last will of a single portion of property to a third person, diminishing the heritage in its character as the object of universal succession, whether direct or indirect, *i.e.*, according to its value. The taker of the bequest (legatee) is called 'honoratus'; he that has to discharge it, the 'oneratus.' The validity of a bequest is conditioned by the commencement of universal succession.[a]

[a] § 153, ad init.; D. 26, 2, 9.

Flor.: Legatum est delibatio hereditatis, qua testator ex eo, quod universum heredis foret, alicui quid collatum velit.—l. 116 pr., D. de leg. I.[1]

Mod.: Legatum est donatio testamento relicta. —l. 36 eod. II.; cf. Inst. ii. 20, 1.[b] [2]

[b] See Markby, p. 382, note.

The general requisites of a bequest are the following—

(1) The honoratus must possess testamenti factio.

Legari autem illis solis potest, cum quibus testamenti factio est.—§ 24, I. h. t. (de legat. 2, 20).[3]

(2) He must be a certa persona.[c]

[c] § 159.

Ulp. xxiv. 18: Incertae personae legari non potest, veluti: 'Quicumque filio meo filiam suam

---

what is owing to each. Against him also the creditors have generally command of analogous actions.

[1] A bequest is a deduction from the inheritance by which the testator desires to appropriate something to any person from the whole that would belong to the heir.

[2] A bequest is a gift left by testament.

[3] Now a bequest can be made alone to those with whom there is *testamenti factio*.

in matrimonium collocaverit, ei heres meus tot milia dato'; sub certa vero demonstratione incertae personae legari potest, velut: 'Ex cognatis meis qui nunc sunt, qui primus ad funus meum venerit, ei heres meus illud dato.'[1]

(3) By ante-Justinianean Law, the bequest cannot merely take the form of a penalty imposed upon the oneratus (poenae nomine relictum).

Ib. § 17: Poenae causa legari non potest; poenae autem causa legatur, quod coercendi heredis causa relinquitur, ut faciat quid aut non faciat, non ut ad legatarium pertineat, ut puta hoc modo: Si filiam tuam in matrimonium Titio collocaveris, decem milia Seio dato.'[2]

At huiusmodi scrupulositas nobis non placuit, et generaliter ea quae relinquuntur, licet poenae nomine fuerint relicta vel adempta vel in alios translata, nihil distare a ceteris legatis constituimus.—§ 36, I. h. t.[3]

In general, everything that confers any proprietary advantage upon the beneficiary can be the object of the bequest. And so, both corporeal things—whether single (determined individually or generically, especially money), or collective wholes, *e.g.*, grex, suppellex, or

---

[1] A bequest cannot be left to an uncertain person; for example, thus: 'Whosoever shall have given his daughter in marriage to my son, let my heir give him so many thousand sesterces.' A bequest can, however, be made to an uncertain person under a definite description; for example, thus: 'Let my heir give such and such a thing to him of my present kinsmen who shall first come to my funeral.'

[2] A bequest cannot be made by way of penalty; and a bequest is by way of penalty when something is left for the purpose of obliging the heir to do or forbear from doing any act, and not with the view of its belonging to the legatee; as for example, in this way: 'If you give your daughter in marriage to Titius, give Seius 10,000 sesterces.'

[3] But we have not approved of exactitude of this kind, and have settled in general terms that whatever is left, although left, revoked, or transferred to different persons by way of penalty, shall not differ from other bequests.

Book III. Part III.

totalities of property, *e.g.*, peculium, or further, performances solitary or repeated (rents, alimony)—and rights (iura in re aliena,[a] and claims). Claims can in different ways form the object of a bequest: legatum *nominis*,[b] legatum *liberationis*, legatum *debiti*.

[a] § 96.
[b] C. 6. 37. 18.

Paul. iii. 6, § 17: Ususfructus uniuscuiusque rei legari potest, et aut ipso iure constituetur aut per heredem praestabitur: ex causa damnationis per heredem praestabitur, ipso iure per vindicationem.[c] [1]

[c] § 179.

Tam autem corporales res quam incorporales legari possunt; et ideo et quod defuncto debetur, potest alicui legari, ut actiones suas heres legatario praestet, nisi exegerit vivus testator pecuniam: nam hoc casu legatum extinguitur. Sed et tale legatum valet: 'Damnas esto heres domum illius reficere,' vel 'illum aere alieno liberare.'—§ 21, I. h. t.[2]

Si quis debitori suo liberationem legaverit, legatum utile est et neque ab ipso debitore neque ab herede eius potest heres petere, nec ab alio qui heredis loco est: sed et potest a debitore conveniri, ut liberet eum. Potest autem quis vel ad tempus iubere, ne heres petat.—Ex contrario si debitor creditori suo quod debet legaverit, inutile est legatum, si nihil plus est in legato quam in debito, quia nihil amplius habet per legatum: quodsi in diem vel sub condicione

---

[1] The usufruct can be bequeathed of anything whatsoever, and will either be determined by operation of law, or will be made over by the heir: it will be made over by the heir on the ground of *damnatio*, and by operation of law through *vindicatio*.[d]

[d] § 179.

[2] Now a bequest can be made of both corporeal and incorporeal things; and therefore even that which is due to the deceased may be bequeathed to a person, so that the heir make over to the legatee his rights of action, unless the testator has got in the money during his lifetime; for in this case the legacy lapses. But a legacy of the following kind also holds good: 'Let my heir be bound to repair the house of so and so,' or 'to release so and so from his debts.'

debitum ei pure legaverit, utile est legatum propter repraesentationem.—§§ 13–14, I. eod.[1]

Iul.: Respondit, quotiens debitor creditori suo legaret, ita inutile esse legatum, si nihil interesset creditoris, ex testamento potius agere, quam ex pristina obligatione.—D. 34, 3, 11 pr.[2]

Like as in succession is exhibited the opposition of ius civile and ius praetorium, so in Hereditas and Bonorum Possessio does that of Civil Law, which is more strict, and that which is more equitable—rooted in ius gentium—display its operation in respect of bequests: upon this is grounded the distinction of 'legatum' and 'fideicommissum.' The former is the older, more stringent and narrow, the latter the more modern, more liberal and broad form of bequest.—The assimilation of the two forms—as in respect of universal succession, the fusion of the Civil and the Praetorian system of succession—was first accomplished in the Justinianean Law.

Ulp. xxiv. 1: **Legatum** est quod legis modo id est imperative testamento relinquitur: nam ea quae precativo modo relinquuntur, **fideicommissa** vocantur.[3]

---

[1] If a man have bequeathed to his debtor a release of the debt, the bequest is operative, and his heir cannot claim payment from the debtor himself, his heir, or other person in the place of heir. But he may himself be sued by the debtor to give him a release. Now a man may direct his heir not to sue for a certain time.—On the other hand, if a debtor bequeath to his creditor the debt due to him, such bequest is ineffectual, if there be nothing more in the bequest than in the debt, because he receives nothing more by the bequest. But if he make an absolute bequest of a debt due at a future time or conditional, the bequest is valid on account of its earlier payment.

[2] He answered: Whenever the debtor makes a bequest to his creditor, such bequest is invalid, if it should be of no advantage to the creditor rather to sue upon the testament than upon the original obligation.

[3] A Bequest is that which is left by testament in the form of a *lex*, that is, imperatively; for those bequests which are made in the form of a request are called *fideicommissa*.

Book III. Part III.

Id. xxv. 1: Fideicommissum est quod non civilibus verbis, sed precative relinquitur; nec ex rigore iuris civilis proficiscitur, sed ex voluntate datur relinquentis.[1]

SPECIES OF BEQUESTS.

§ 179. Legata.

The person to make a testament can leave a legatum only if he make a testament; and indeed by older Law it had always to be provided for in the testament itself, by classical Law it could also be in 'codicilli testamento confirmati.'[a]

[a] § 180, ad fin.

Gai. ii. § 270[a]: Legatum codicillis relictum non aliter valet, quam si a testatore confirmati fuerint, id est nisi in testamento caverit testator, ut quidquid in codicillis scripserit, id ratum sit.[2]

Moreover, the disposition can only obtain after the institution of heir,[b] and the legacy can only be imposed upon a testamentary heir.

[b] Ulp. xxiv. 15.

Ulp. xxiv. §§ 20–21: A legatario legari non potest.—Legatum ab eo tantum dari potest, qui heres institutus est: ideoque filiofamiliae herede instituto vel servo, neque a patre neque a domino legari potest.[3]

Ib. § 16: Etiam post mortem heredis legari non potest, ne ab heredis herede legari videatur, quod iuris civilis ratio non patitur; in mortis autem

---

[1] A *fideicommissum* is a bequest expressed not in the language of the *ius civile*, but by way of request; and does not take effect by force of civil law, but is given in agreement with the wish of the person leaving it.

[2] A legacy left by a codicil is not valid unless it has been confirmed by the testator, that is, unless the testator has provided in his testament that whatever he shall have written in his codicil is to be ratified.

[3] A legacy cannot be charged upon a legatee.—A legacy can only be charged upon him who has been instituted heir; and therefore, if it be a *fil. fam.* or a slave that is instituted heir, a legacy cannot be charged upon his father or his master.

heredis tempus legari potest, velut CVM HERES MORIETVR.[1]

As the institution of heir, so also must the disposition of a legacy be accomplished in a definite, solemn formula (verba civilia).[a]—There are four forms of legacy, very diverse as regards their operation.

[a] § 178, ad fin.

(1) legatum *per vindicationem* ('do lego' legatum).

Ulp. xxiv. 3 : Per **vindicationem** his verbis legamus: DO LEGO, CAPITO, SVMITO, SIBI HABETO.—§ 7 : Per vindicationem legari possunt res, quae utroque tempore ex iure Quiritium testatoris fuerunt, mortis et cum testamentum faciebat, praeterquam si pondere numero mensura contineantur : in his enim satis est, si vel mortis dumtaxat tempore testatoris fuerint ex iure Quiritium.[2]

Gai. ii. § 194: Ideo autem per vindicationem legatum appellatur, quia post aditam hereditatem statim ex iure Quiritium res legatarii fit; et si eam rem legatarius vel ab herede vel ab alio quocumque, qui eam possidet, petat, vindicare debet, i.e. intendere 'eam rem suam ex iure Quiritium esse.'[3]

---

[1] Also no legacy can be bequeathed (to take effect) after the death of the heir, lest there should seem to be a legacy charged upon the heir of the heir, which the principle of the Civil Law does not allow ; but a legacy can be bequeathed (to take effect) at the time of the heir's death, as 'When my heir shall be dying.'

[2] We bequeath a legacy by vindication in the following words : 'I give and bequeath,' 'acquire,' 'take,' 'have for himself.'—By vindication those things can be bequeathed which belonged to the testator by Quiritarian Law at both times, *i.e.*, at the time of his death, and at the time when he made his testament, unless they are things which pass by weight, number or measure ; for as to these it is sufficient if they belonged to the testator by Quiritarian Law at the time of his death alone.

[3] Now the legacy *per vindicationem* is so called because, after the inheritance has been taken up, the thing forthwith becomes the property of the legatee by Quiritarian Law ; and if the legatee claim the thing, either from the heir or from any other

BOOK III. Part III.

(2) legatum *per damnationem*.

Ulp. xxiv. 4: Per **damnationem** (legamus) his verbis: HERES MEVS DAMNAS ESTO DARE, DATO, FACITO, HEREDEM MEVM DARE IVBEO.—8: Per damnationem omnes res legari possunt, etiam quae non sunt testatoris, dummodo tales sunt, quae dari possint.[1]

The two following are varieties thereof.

(3) legatum *per praeceptionem*.

Gai. ii. §§ 216–7: Per **praeceptionem** hoc modo legamus: LVCIVS TITIVS HOMINEM STICHVM PRAECIPITO. § Sed nostri quidem praeceptores nulli alii eo modo legari posse putant, nisi ei qui aliqua ex parte heres scriptus esset: 'praecipere' enim esse praecipuum sumere; quod tantum in eius persona procedit, qui aliqua ex parte heres institutus est, quod is extra portionem hereditatis praecipuum legatum habiturus sit. § 221: Sed diversae scholae auctores putant etiam extraneo per praeceptionem legari posse, proinde ac si ita scribatur: TITIVS HOMINEM STICHVM CAPITO, supervacuo adiecta PRAE syllaba, ideoque per vindicationem eam rem legatam videri: quae sententia dicitur D. Hadriani constitutione confirmata esse.[2]

---

person who has possession of it, he must do so by vindication, *i.e.*, claim that 'the thing is his by Quiritarian Law.'

[1] (We bequeath a legacy) *per damnationem* in these words: 'Let my heir be bound to give,' 'give,' 'do,' 'I direct my heir to give.'—All things can be bequeathed *per damnationem*, even those which do not belong to the testator, provided they are such as can be given.

[2] We bequeath *per praeceptionem* in this manner: 'Let Luc. Tit. take the slave Stichus by preference.' But our teachers think that a bequest cannot be made in this form to any other than one instituted heir to some part: for *praecipere* means to take by preference; and this is only possible in the case of one who is instituted heir to some part, because he can have the legacy by preference, over and above his share of the inheritance. But the authorities of the other school think that a legacy may be left *per praeceptionem* even to an outsider, just as if the bequest

Ulp. xxiv. 11: Per praeceptionem legari possunt res, quae etiam per vindicationem.[1]

(4) legatum *sinendi modo relictum.*

Ib. § 5: **Sinendi modo** ita (legamus): HERES MEVS DAMNAS ESTO SINERE LVCIVM TITIVM SVMERE ILLAM REM SIBIQVE HABERE.—§ 10: Sinendi modo legari possunt res propriae testatoris et heredis eius.[2]

(5) But according to a SC. Neronianum, every legacy which would stand as a legacy per damnationem—in whatever form it has been left—must be upheld, so that henceforth an actio in personam could arise against the heir upon every valid legacy (even that per vindicationem).

Ib. § 11[a]: Si ea res, quae non fuit utroque tempore testatoris ex iure Quiritium, per vindicationem legata sit, licet iure civili non valeat legatum, tamen senatusconsulto Neroniano confirmatur, quo cautum est, ut quod minus ratis verbis legatum est, perinde sit ac si optimo iure legatum esset: optimum autem ius legati per damnationem est.[3]

---

were thus written: 'Let Tit. take the slave Stichus,' the addition of the syllable *prae* being superfluous; and therefore that such a legacy appears to be one *per vindicationem*, an opinion which is said to have been confirmed by a constitution of the late Emp. Hadrian.

[1] Things admit of being bequeathed *per praeceptionem* which can also be bequeathed *per vindicationem.*

[2] By way of sufferance thus: 'Let my heir be bound to suffer Luc. Tit. to take such or such a thing, and to have it for himself.'—By way of sufferance such things can be bequeathed as belong to the testator or his heir.

[3] If a thing that was not the testator's property by Quiritarian Law at both dates has been bequeathed *per vindicationem*, although by civil law the legacy is not valid, yet it is confirmed by the *SCtum Neronianum;* in which it was provided that when a legacy is given by inappropriate words, it shall be the same as if it had been given in the most advantageous form; and the most advantageous form of legacy is that *per damnationem.*

Book III.
Part III.

§ 180. Fideicommissa.

Fideicommissum is the informal bequest to a third person (fideicommissarius) imposed by way of request upon the heir or else an honoratus (fiduciarius).[a]

[a] For the English *trustee*, see Blackst. ii. 327-8 (Steph. i. 357-8). Cf. Digby, p. 273; H. A. Smith, 'Principles of Equity,' pp. 18-19.

Ulp. xxv. 2: Verba fideicommissorum in usu fere haec sunt: FIDEI COMMITTO, PETO, VOLO DARI et similia.—§ 9: Item Graece fideicommissum scriptum valet, licet legatum Graece scriptum non valeat.[1]

Paul. iv. 1, § 5: Qui fideicommissum relinquit, etiam cum eo, cui relinquit, loqui potest, velut: PETO, GAI SEI, CONTENTVS SIS ILLA RE, aut VOLO TIBI ILLVD PRAESTARI.[2]

These fideicommissa were not binding according to the older civil Law, and their fulfilment depended alone on the piety of the oneratus. It was first under Augustus that regard was in particular cases paid to the will of the testator by means of the extraordinaria cognitio[b] of the consuls, and the fiduciarius was held to the performance of the fideicommissum.[c] From this was gradually developed in constant practice normal legal enforcement of all fideicommissa—(praetor fideicommissarius)—and so the recognition of fideicommissa as a regular legal institute of the Civil Law, although they could always alone be made available extra ordinem.[d]

[b] § 187.

[c] *Infra.*

[d] D. 50, 16, 178, 2.

Inst. ii. 23, §§ 1, 12: Sciendum itaque est omnia fideicommissa primis temporibus infirma esse, quia nemo invitus cogebatur praestare id de quo rogatus erat. Quibus enim non poterant

[1] The language of bequests in trust which is commonly used is this: 'I commit to your trust,' 'I ask,' 'I wish to be given' and the like.—§ Likewise a *fideicommissum* written in Greek is valid, though a legacy written in Greek is not.

[2] He that leaves a *fideicommissum* can also parley with the legatee thus: 'I beg, G. S., that you will be satisfied with that thing,' or 'I desire that such and such a thing be made over to you.'

hereditates vel legata relinquere, si relinquebant, fidei committebant eorum qui capere ea testamento poterant: et ideo fideicommissa appellata sunt, quia nullo vinculo iuris, sed tantum pudore eorum qui rogabantur continebantur. Postea primus D. Augustus semel iterumque gratia personarum motus (vel quia per ipsius salutem rogatus quis diceretur, aut ob insignem quorundam perfidiam) iussit consulibus auctoritatem suam interponere. Quod quia iustum videbatur et populare erat, paulatim conversum est, in adsiduam iurisdictionem: tantusque favor eorum factus est, ut paulatim etiam praetor proprius crearetur, qui fideicommissis ius diceret, quem fideicommissarium appellabant.—Prima fideicommissorum cunabula a fide heredum pendent et tam nomen quam substantiam acceperunt, et ideo D. Augustus ad necessitatem iuris ea detraxit.[1]

Ulp. xxv. 12: Fideicommissa non per formulam petuntur, ut legata, sed cognitione Romae

---

[1] It must, then, be observed that in the earliest times all bequests in trust were invalid, because no one was compelled against his will to perform that which he was only requested to do. For when people left anything to those to whom they could not leave an inheritance or legacies, they entrusted them to the good faith of such as could take under the testament; and therefore what was left was called gifts in trust, because it rested on no legal obligation, but only on the conscientiousness of those who were asked to carry them out. Afterwards, the Emp. Augustus, being repeatedly moved by personal consideration (or because some one was asked, 'by the Emperor's safety,' or on account of some notable cases of perfidy), ordered the consuls to interpose their authority. As this seemed equitable, and in the general interest, it was gradually turned into a regular jurisdiction; and so great became the popularity of bequests in trust that in time a special Praetor was appointed to adjudicate upon *fideicommissa*, and he was called the Praetor for bequests in trust.—The first beginning of bequests in trust depended on the good faith of heirs, and so derived their name and essence, and for this reason the Emp. Augustus rendered them binding in law.

quidem consulum aut praetoris, qui fideicommissarius vocatur, in provinciis vero praesidis provinciae.[1]

Like the legatum, the fideicommissum requires testamenti factio of the testator and of the beneficiary.

> Ulp. xxv. § 4 : Fideicommissum relinquere possunt, qui testamentum facere possunt.—§§ 6–7 : Fideicommissa dari possunt his, quibus legari potest.—Latini Iuniani fideicommissum capere possunt, licet legatum capere non possint.[2]

But it is fettered by none of the prescribed forms that are operative in the case of the legatum.

> Ib. § 8 : Fideicommissum et ante heredis institutionem et post mortem heredis et codicillis etiam non confirmatis testamento dari potest, licet ita legari non possit.[3]

And further, it can be imposed upon not merely the testamentary heir, but a legatee also or fideicommissary, even an heir in intestacy.

> Gai. ii. § 271 : Item a legatario legari non potest, sed fideicommissum relinqui potest ; quin etiam ab eo quoque, cui per fideicommissum relinquimus, rursus alii per fideicommissum relinquere possumus.[4]

---

[1] *Fideicommissa* are not, like *legata*, sued for by formula, but at Rome upon investigation by the consuls or the so-called Fideicommissary Praetor, in the provinces upon investigation by the President.

[2] Those can leave a fideicommissum who can make a testament.—*Fideicommissa* can be given to those persons to whom a bequest can be made. Junian Latins can take a *fideicommissum*, though they cannot take a *legatum*.

[3] A *fideicommissum* can be given both before the appointment of the heir and (to take effect) after the death of the heir, and even by a codicil unconfirmed in a testament, although legacies cannot be so left.

[4] Likewise a legacy cannot be charged upon a legatee, but a *fideicommissum* can be so left ; nay more, we can again charge him to whom we have left a *fideicommissum* with a *fideicommissum* in favour of a third party.

Ulp. cit. § 4: Etiam intestato quis moriturus fideicommissum relinquere potest.[1]

Also in respect of the disposition itself, the fideicommissum is under no restriction as to form. It can be legally left not only in the testament, but also, at discretion, in any writing by way of last will, codicilli (that is, strictly a letter to the future heir)—and it is immaterial whether this is confirmed by a testament or not (codicilli testamento confirmati),[a] indeed whether a testament is made or not (intestate codicil)[b]—or by word of mouth without any form:[c] the mere certainty of the testator's will suffices for this.

> Inst. ii. 25 pr., § 1: Ante Augusti tempora constat ius codicillorum non fuisse, sed primus Lucius Lentulus, ex cuius persona etiam fideicommissa coeperunt[d] codicillos introduxit. Nam cum decederet in Africa scripsit codicillos testamento confirmatos, quibus ab Augusto petiit per fideicommissum, ut faceret aliquid; et cum D. Augustus voluntatem eius implesset, deinceps reliqui auctoritatem eius secuti fideicommissa praestabant et filia Lentuli legata, quae iure non debebat, solvit. Dicitur Augustus convocasse prudentes, inter quos Trebatium quoque, cuius tunc auctoritas maxima erat, et quaesiisse, an possit hoc recipi nec absonans a iuris ratione codicillorum usus esset: et Trebatium suasisse Augusto, quod diceret utilissimum et necessarium hoc civibus esse propter magnas et longas peregrinationes, . . . ubi si quis testamentum facere non posset, tamen codicillos posset. Post quae tempora cum et Labeo codicillos fecisset, iam nemini dubium erat, quin codicilli iure optimo admitterentur.—Sed cum ante testamentum factum codicilli facti erant, Papinianus ait non aliter

[a] *Supra*, and § 179, ad init.

[b] See last extract above.

[c] Cf. § 181, and Brown, s. Codicil.

[d] Cf. ib. ii. 23. 1 (*sup.*).

---

[1] Even a man about to die intestate can leave a *fideicommissum*.

vires habere, quam si speciali postea voluntate confirmentur; sed D. Severus et Antoninus rescripserunt, ex his codicillis qui testamentum praecedunt posse fideicommissum peti, si appareat eum, qui postea testamentum fecerat, a voluntate quam codicillis expresserat non recessisse.[1]

Paul.: Conficiuntur codicilli quattuor modis: aut enim in futurum confirmantur, aut in praeteritum, aut per fideicommissum testamento facto, aut sine testamento.—D. 29, 7, 8 pr.[2]

---

[1] It is well known that no law of codicils existed before the time of Augustus, but Luc. Lent. was the first to introduce codicils, through whom also gifts in trust originated. For when he died in Africa, he wrote a codicil confirmed by his testament, in which he begged Augustus by way of *fideicommissum* to perform something; and when the Emperor Augustus had fulfilled his wish, the rest thereupon, following his example, paid the gifts in trust, and the daughter of Lent. discharged legacies which she was under no legal obligation to do. It is said that Augustus called together those learned in the law, and amongst them Trebatius, whose reputation then was the greatest, and inquired whether this could be allowed, and whether the employment of codicils did not conflict with legal principle; and then Treb. persuaded Augustus by saying that it was most useful and necessary for the citizens, on account of great and distant journeys, when a man, if unable to execute a testament, should still be able to make a codicil.—After this time, when Labeo also had made a codicil, no one had a doubt any longer that codicils should be allowed with perfect right.—But when a codicil has been made before the execution of the testament, Papin. asserts that it cannot be valid unless afterwards confirmed by express declaration; but the Empp. Severus and Antonine settled by rescript that a gift in trust under a codicil preceding a testament might be enforced if it should appear that he who afterwards made a testament had not departed from the wish which he had expressed in the codicil.

[2] Codicils are made in four ways; for they are either confirmed for a future time, or for past time, or by testament made by way of *fideicommissum*, or without a testament.

§ 181. Assimilation of *Legata* and *Fideicommissa*.

From the time that dispositions could be validly made by legata, not merely in the testament, but also in codicilli testamento confirmati, and later on—when already by the SC. Neronianum[a] the rules as to form had been relaxed—according to a constitution of Constantine, even without any observance of solemn forms, the difference between legata and fideicommissa was confined practically to the fact that the former were the bequests charged upon a testamentary heir, the latter such as were charged upon a legatee or fideicommissary and those left ab intestato.

[a] § 179, ad fin.

> Imp. Const.: In legatis vel fideicommissis verborum necessaria non sit observantia, ita ut nihil prorsus intersit, quis talem voluntatem verborum casus exceperit aut quis loquendi usus effuderit.—C. 6, 37, 21.[1]

Justinian, finally, assimilated legata and fideicommissa in such way, that henceforth the most favourable legal propositions for the one shall also avail for the other.

> Cum antiquitatem invenimus legata quidem stricte concludentem, fideicommissis autem, quae ex voluntate magis descendebant defunctorum, pinguiorem naturam indulgentem, necessarium esse duximus omnia legata fideicommissis exaequare, ut nulla sit inter ea differentia, sed quod deest legatis hoc repleatur ex natura fideicommissorum, et si quid amplius est in legatis, per hoc crescat fideicommissorum natura.—§ 3, I. de leg. 2, 20.[2]

---

[1] In legacies or bequests in trust there can be no necessary rule as to words, so that it is altogether immaterial what form of words a man uses in order to such a declaration of his will, or in what manner of speech he has expressed himself.

[2] Having observed that the ancients confined legacies in fact within narrow compass, but accorded a more comprehensive character to gifts in trust, as arising more from the wishes of

[a] Iust.

Ulp.: Per omnia[a] exaequata sunt legata fideicommissis.—l. 1, D. eod. 1 (30).[1]

On the other hand, the previous informality of codicilli (not merely of testamento non confirmati) was not kept up; from the time of Theodosius the Great and Justinian they can be made only in the presence of five witnesses, in writing or by word of mouth.

Imp. Constantin.: In codicillis, quos testamentum non praecedit, . . . septem testium vel quinque interventum non deesse oportet, . . . ut testantium successiones sine aliqua captione serventur.—C. Th. 4, 4, 1.[2]

[b] Iust.

Imp. Theod.[b]: In omni ultima voluntate, excepto testamento, quinque testes . . . in uno eodemque tempore debent adhiberi, sive in scriptis sive sine scriptis voluntas conficiatur, testibus videlicet, quando scriptura voluntas componitur, subnotationem suam accommodantibus.—C. 6, 36, 8, 3.[3]

He that makes a testament can direct that it shall be treated as a codicil, in case it should not stand good as a testament:—codicillary clause (clausula codicillaris). In this case institutions of heir, and other provisions by last will met with in the testament, have

---

the deceased, we have deemed it necessary to make all legacies equal to gifts in trust, so that there be no difference between them, but that what is defective in legacies be made up from their character as gifts in trust, and if legacies possess any advantage, gifts in trust will acquire an extended character.

[1] Legacies have in all respects been assimilated to bequests in trust.

[2] In codicils not preceded by a testament . . . the intervention of seven or five witnesses must not fail, . . . so that testamentary successions be preserved without prejudice.

[3] In every disposition by last will, save a testament, five witnesses ought to be called in at one and the same time, whether the declaration be made in writing or without writing; the witnesses of course adding their subscription when the declaration is made in writing.

the signification of fideicommissa—universal or singular —imposed upon the heir in intestacy.

> Ulp.: Plerique solent, cum testamenti faciunt perscripturam, adiicere velle hoc etiam vice codicillorum valere.—D. 29, 1, 3.[1]
>
> Paul.: Ex ea scriptura, quae ad testamentum faciendum parabatur, si nullo iure testamentum perfectum esset, nec ea, quae fideicommissorum verba habent, peti posse. § Ex his verbis, quae scriptura paterfamilias addidit: 'ταύτην τὴν διαθήκην βούλομαι εἶναι κυρίαν ἐπὶ πάσης ἐξουσίας = [hoc testamentum volo esse ratum, quacumque ratione poterit],' videri eum voluisse omnimodo valere ea quae reliquit, etiamsi intestatus decessisset.—D. 28, 1, 29.[2]

§ 182. Limitation of Bequests; the *Quarta Falcidia* in particular.

The unrestrained freedom of bequest[a] originally appertaining to every testator often resulted in the testament becoming 'destitutum,' and dissipation of the heritage: an impropriety which legislation endeavoured to meet by restrictions as to the extent of legacies.

[a] Cf. D. 50, 16, 120.

> Gai. ii. § 224: Sed olim quidem licebat totum patrimonium legatis atque libertatibus erogare, nec quidquam heredi relinquere praeterquam inane nomen heredis; idque lex XII tabularum permittere videbatur, qua cavetur, ut quod quisque de re sua testatus esset id ratum haberetur, his

---

[1] Very many in their written testament are wont to add that, it is their will that this shall also pass as a codicil.

[2] Upon such a document as was intended to constitute a testament if the testament was altogether imperfect, one cannot either lay claim to *fideicommissa* which are contained in it. § From the following words, which a *pat. fam.* added in writing, 'My will is that this testament shall be valid in whatever way it can,' it appears to have been his will that his bequests should stand good in all events, although he should have died intestate.

Book III. Part III.

verbis VTI LEGASSIT SVAE REI, ITA IVS ESTO: quare qui scripti heredes erant, ab hereditate se abstinebant et idcirco plerique intestati moriebantur.[1]

First of all, the lex Furia (a lex minus quam perfecta)[a] fixed as maximum for every legacy—as well as mortis causa donatio—the sum of 1000 *asses*, with the exception of legacies left to certain near relations.[b]

[a] See § 4, ad fin.

[b] Cf. Vat. fgm. 216, 218; D. 38, 8, 1. 3.

Ulp. fgm. 2: Minus quam perfecta lex est, quae vetat aliquid fieri, et si factum sit, non rescindit, sed poenam injungit ei, qui contra legem fecit: qualis est lex Furia testamentaria, quae plus quam mille asses legati nomine mortisve causa prohibet capere praeter exceptas personas, et adversus eum, qui plus ceperit, quadrupli poenam constituit.[2]

Vat. fgm. 301 (Paul.): Lex Furia sex gradus et unam personam ex septimo gradu excepit, sobrino natum.[3]

Gai. ii. § 225: Sed haec lex non perfecit quod voluit: qui enim verbi gratia quinque milium aeris patrimonium habebat, poterat quin-

---

[1] But of old it was in fact lawful to expend the whole of a patrimony in legacies and gifts of freedom, and to leave nothing to the heir save the empty title of heir; and a law of the Twelve Tables was considered to permit this, in which it is provided that the disposition made by a man of his estate should be valid in these words: 'As a man shall have bequeathed a legacy of his property, so let it be law.' Wherefore those who were appointed heirs kept aloof from the inheritance, and thus many persons died intestate.

[2] A law less than perfect is one that forbids something to be done, and if it have been done, does not rescind it, but imposes a penalty on him who has acted contrary to the law: such is the *l. Furia Testamentaria*, which forbids persons, other than those exempted, from taking more than a thousand *asses* as a legacy or gift in view of death, and appoints a fourfold penalty against a person that has taken more.

[3] The *l. Furia* excepted six degrees, and one person from the seventh degree, the child of a cousin-german.

que hominibus singulis millenos asses legando totum patrimonium erogare.[1] Book III. Part III.

As this limitation proved to serve the purpose little, the lex Voconia[a]—which in general made a great inroad upon freedom of testation—provided in respect of the testaments of all citizens enrolled in the first class, that no legacy (or mortis causa donatio) should exceed the amount of the share of the property remaining to the heir (or of the hereditary portions of all the heirs)[b] and that it should be inoperative beyond that.

[a] Gai. ii. 274.

[b] Cf. § 185.

Ib. § 226: Ideo postea lata est lex Voconia, qua cautum est, ne cui plus legatorum nomine mortisve causa capere liceret quam heredes caperent; ex qua lege plane quidem aliquid utique heredes habere videbantur; sed tamen fere vitium simile nascebatur: nam in multas legatariorum personas distributo patrimonio poterat testator adeo heredi minimum relinquere, ut non expediret heredi, huius lucri gratia totius hereditatis onera sustinere.[2]

Effectual relief was finally afforded by the lex Falcidia (A.U. 714), according to which there should remain undiminished by legacies to each heir one-fourth of the heritage; in the case of several heirs, to each one-fourth of his hereditary share:—QUARTA FALCIDIA.

Gai. ii. § 227: Lata est itaque lex Falcidia,

---

[1] But this *lex* did not accomplish its object. For he who had, for example, a patrimony of 5000 *asses*, could expend his whole patrimony by bequeathing 1000 *asses* to each of five persons.

[2] Hence, the *l. Voconia* was afterwards passed, by which it was provided that no one should be allowed to take more by way of legacy or gift in contemplation of death than did the heirs. By this *lex* it seemed clear that the heirs must have something in any case; but a defect almost of the same kind arose; for by a distribution of the patrimony amongst a considerable number of legatees, testators could leave so very little to the heir, that it did not answer his purpose for the sake of this profit to undertake the burdens of the entire inheritance.

qua cautum est, ne plus ei legare liceat, quam dodrantem; itaque necesse est, ut heres quartam partem hereditatis habeat: et hoc nunc iure utimur.[1]

Paul.: Lex Falcidia lata est, quae primo capite liberam legandi facultatem dedit his verbis: QVI CIVES ROMANI SVNT, QVI EORVM POST HANC LEGEM ROGATAM TESTAMENTVM FACERE VOLET, VT EAM PECVNIAM EASQVE RES QVIBVSQVE DARE LEGARE VOLET, IVS POTESTASQVE ESTO, VT HAC LEGE LICEBIT. Secundo capite modum legatorum constituit his verbis: QVICVMQVE CIVIS ROMANVS POST HANC LEGEM ROGATAM TESTAMENTVM FACIET; IS QVANTAM CVIQVE CIVI ROMANO PECVNIAM IVRE PVBLICO DARE LEGARE VOLET, IVS POTESTASQVE ESTO, DVM ITA DETVR LEGATVM, NE MINVS QVAM PARTEM QVARTAM HEREDITATIS EO TESTAMENTO HEREDES CAPIANT. EIS QVIBVS QVID ITA DATVM LEGATVMVE ERIT, EAM PECVNIAM SINE FRAVDE SVA CAPERE LICETO; ISQVE HERES, QVI EAM PECVNIAM DARE IVSSVS DAMNATVS ERIT, EAM PECVNIAM DEBETO DARE, QVAM DARE DAMNATVS EST.—l. 1 pr., D. ad l. Falc. 35, 2.[2]

---

[1] Therefore the *l. Falcidia* was passed, by which it was provided that it should not be lawful to bequeath more than three fourths; and therefore the heir must needs have a fourth of the inheritance, and this is the law we now observe.

[2] The *l. Falcidia* was passed, which in its first chapter gave free power of bequest in the following words: 'Those who are Roman citizens, whichever of such shall after the introduction of this *lex* desire to make a testament, shall have right and power to give and bequeath money and things to every one as he will, as shall be allowed by this statute.' In the second chapter it prescribes the quantity of bequests in the following words: 'Whatever Roman citizen shall make a testament after the introduction of this statute shall have right and power to give and bequeath according to public law as much as he likes to any Roman citizen, provided that the bequest shall be given in such form that the heirs take by the testament not less than the fourth part of the inheritance. Those to whom anything shall have been given or bequeathed shall be at

Gai.: In singulis heredibus rationem legis Falcidiae componendam esse non dubitatur: et ideo si Titio et Seio heredibus institutis semis hereditatis Titii exhaustus est, Seio autem quadrans totorum bonorum relictus sit, competit Titio beneficium legis Falcidiae.—l. 77 eod.[1]

The lex Falcidia, which originally was applicable only to legata, was by the SC. Pegasianum (under Vespasian A.D. 75) extended also to fideicommissa,[a] but the heir always retained only claim to the fourth part.

[a] Gai. ii. 254, *sqq.*

Ulp.: Numquam legatarius vel fideicommissarius, licet ex Trebelliano senatusconsulto restituitur ei hereditas, utitur legis Falcidiae beneficio. —l. 47, § 1, D. eod.[2]

Paul.: Dixi legem Falcidiam inductam esse a D. Pio etiam in intestatorum successionibus propter fideicommissa.—l. 18 pr. eod.[3]

The extent of the heritage at the time of the death of the testator, after abstraction of the debts of the inheritance, is made the basis for calculating the Falcidian fourth; the abatement of the legacies follows pro rata.

Gai.: In quantitate patrimonii exquirenda visum est mortis tempus spectari. Qua de causa si quis centum in bonis habuerit et tota ea

liberty to accept it without prejudice to themselves, and the heir upon whom the payment of such money has been charged shall be obliged to pay such money the payment of which has been imposed upon him.'

[1] There is no doubt that the *l. Falcidia* is to be applied in respect of the individual heirs; and therefore, if when Tit. and Sei. have been appointed heirs, one half of the inheritance of Tit. has been exhausted, but one fourth of the whole estate has been left to Sei., the benefit of the *l. Falcidia* belongs to Tit.

[2] The legatee or fideicommissary never has the benefit of the *l. Falcidia*, although by the *SCtum Trebellianum* the inheritance is restored to him.

[3] I have said that the *l. Falcidia* was by the late Emp. Pius applied also to the inheritance of intestates because of *fideicommissa*.

BOOK III.
Part III.

legaverit, nihil legatariis prodest, si ante aditam hereditatem per servos hereditarios aut ex partu ancillarum hereditariarum aut ex fetu pecorum tantum accesserit hereditati, ut centum legatorum nomine erogatis habiturus sit heres quartam partem; sed necesse est, ut nihilominus quarta pars legatis detrahatur. Et ex diverso, si ex centum septuaginta quinque legaverit et ante aditam hereditatem in tantum decreverint bona, incendiis forte aut naufragiis aut morte servorum, ut non plus quam septuaginta quinque vel etiam minus relinquatur, solida legata debentur; nec ea res damnosa est heredi, cui liberum est non adire hereditatem: quae res efficit, ut necesse sit legatariis, ne destituto testamento nihil consequantur, cum herede in portionem legatorum pacisci.—l. 73 pr., D. eod.[1]

Cum autem ratio legis Falcidiae ponitur, ante deducitur aes alienum, item funeris impensa et pretia servorum manumissorum, tunc deinde in reliquo ita ratio habetur, ut ex eo quarta pars

---

[1] As regards the ascertainment of the extent of a patrimony, it has been considered that we must look to the time of the death. If any one, accordingly, had one hundred *sestertia* in his estate, and has entirely exhausted that in legacies, it is of no avail to the legatees if, before entry upon the inheritance, so great an increase to it has accrued through slaves of the inheritance, or by virtue of offspring of slave-women belonging to the inheritance, or from young of cattle, that the heir, although one hundred (*sestertia*) should have been exhausted in legacies, will notwithstanding receive the fourth part, but the fourth part must none the less be deducted from the legacies. And on the other hand, if of one hundred he has bequeathed seventy-five (*sestertia*) and the estate before entry has so dwindled, it may be by fires, or shipwrecks, or the death of slaves, that not more than seventy-five, or even less, are left, the legacies must be discharged in full. And this is not disadvantageous to the heir, who is at liberty not to enter upon the inheritance; the result of which is that it is necessary for the legatees, lest they obtain nothing from an abandoned testament, to bargain with the heir for a share of their legacies.

apud heredes remaneat, tres vero partes inter legatarios distribuantur, pro rata scilicet portione eius, quod cuique eorum legatum fuerit.—§ 3, I. eod. (2, 22).[1]

Marc.: In quartam hereditatis, quam per legem Falcidiam heres habere debet, imputantur res quas iure hereditario capit, non quas iure legati vel fideicommissi vel implendae condicionis causa accipit.—l. 91 pr., h. t.[2]

§ 183. Acquisition and Protection of Bequests.

In the acquisition of the bequest there are two points of time to distinguish—

(1) The legacy *vests*—that is, the claim to the bequest, and so the right to the acquisition of the right bequeathed in the entry upon the inheritance, has been definitely originated for the beneficiary—(dies legati *cedit*) as a rule at the moment of the testator's death,[a] provided that it was left unconditionally; according to the direction of the lex Papia Poppaea, repealed by Justinian, first at the moment of the opening of the testament. Upon the death of the oneratus 'post diem cedentem,' the bequest is transmitted to his heirs.

[a] D. 34, 7, 3.

Ulp. xxiv. 31: Legatorum, quae pure vel in diem certum relicta sunt, dies cedit antiquo quidem iure ex mortis testatoris tempore, per

---

[1] Now when the calculation is made under the *l. Falcidia*, debts, funeral expenses and the value of freed slaves are first deducted, and then the residue is reckoned in such a way that the fourth part thereof remains in the hands of the heirs, whilst the other three parts are distributed amongst the legatees, in proportion of course to the share bequeathed to each of them.

[2] Now the fourth part of the inheritance by the *l. Falcidia*, which the heir must retain, are things reckoned which he acquires by right of inheritance, not those which he obtains by virtue of a legacy, a gift in trust, or by reason of the fulfilment of a condition.

BOOK III. Part III.

legem autem Papiam Poppaeam ex apertis tabulis testamenti: eorum vero quae sub condicione relicta sunt, cum condicio exstiterit.[1]

Id.: Si post diem legati cedentem legatarius decesserit, ad heredem suum transfert legatum.—l. 5 pr., D. quando di. leg. 36, 2.[2]

Si cum dies legati cedere inciperet, alieni quis iuris est, deberi his legatum, quorum iuri fuit subiectus: et ideo, si post diem legati cedentem liber factus est, apud dominum legatum relinquet. Sed si usufructus fuerit legatus, licet post mortem testatoris ante aditam tamen hereditatem sui iuris efficiatur, sibi legatum adquirit.—l. 5, § 7 eod.[3]

Ulp.: Dies ususfructus, item usus non prius cedet, quam hereditas adeatur.—D. 7, 3, l. un. § 2.[4]

(2) The bequest becomes due (dies legati *venit*)—that is, the right bequeathed itself is acquired, and the bequest can be claimed by the beneficiary—as soon as entry has been made upon the inheritance, unless the testator have still further postponed the point of time for the fulfilment.[a]

[a] D. 50, 16, 213 pr.

---

[1] Legacies left unconditionally, or until a certain day, by the old Law vested at the testator's death, but by the *l. Papia Poppaea* at the opening of the tablets of the testament. Those, however, which have been left conditionally vest when the condition is fulfilled.

[2] If a legatee have died after the vesting of the legacy, he transfers the legacy to his heir.

[3] If at the time from which a legacy begins to vest a man is subject to the authority of another, the legacy is due to those to whose authority he has been subject; if therefore the legacy was unconditional, and (the party interested) has become free after the vesting of the legacy, he will leave the legacy in the hands of his master. But if a usufruct have been bequeathed, he acquires the legacy for himself, although it is after the testator's death that he becomes independent, but before entry on the inheritance.

[4] The usufruct as well as the use will not vest before the inheritance is taken up.

Mod.: Omnia, quae testamentis sine die vel condicione adscribuntur, ex die aditae hereditatis praestantur.—l. 32 pr., de leg. II. (31).[1]

Paul.: Si dies apposita legato non est, praesens debetur aut confestim ad eum pertinet cui datum est; adiecta, quamvis longa sit, si certa est, veluti Kalendis Ianuariis centesimis, dies quidem legati statim cedit, sed ante diem peti non potest.—l. 21 pr., D. quando di. leg.[2]

Ulp.: Heredis aditio moram legati quidem petitioni facit, cessioni diei non facit.—Interdum aditio hereditatis legatis moram facit, ut puta si forte servo manumisso . . . aliquid legatum sit: nam servo legati relicti ante aditam hereditatem dies non cedit.—l. 7 pr., § 6 eod.[3]

The effect of acquisition takes shape differently according to the object and the form of the legacy.

(1) The legatum per vindicationem makes the legatee the immediate owner of the thing bequeathed, and forthwith confers upon him the rei vindicatio.[a] The acquisition takes place without the knowledge and consent of the beneficiary, but subsequent repudiation again annuls the acquisition retrospectively.

[a] Gai. ii. 194.

Gai. ii. § 195: In eo solo dissentiunt prudentes, quod Sabinus quidem et Cassius ceterique nostri praeceptores quod ita legatum sit, statim post

[1] Everything that is added in testaments without limit of time or condition is performed from the date of entry upon the inheritance.

[2] If no date have been attached to a legacy, it is an immediate debt, or belongs at once to the person to whom it has been given; if a date have been added, however remote, if it be certain, for example, Jan. 1 after one hundred years, the legacy in fact vests at once, but it cannot be claimed before the day appointed.

[3] The entry of the heir causes a delay in the claim of a legacy, but does not to its vesting.—Sometimes entry upon the inheritance subjects legacies to delay, for example, if anything has been bequeathed to a freed slave; for before entry upon the inheritance there is no vesting of a legacy left to a slave.

Book III. Part III.

aditam hereditatem putant fieri legatarii, etiamsi ignoret sibi legatum esse, et posteaquam scierit et repulerit legatum, proinde esse atque si legatum non esset; Nerva vero et Proculus ceterique illius scholae auctores non aliter putant rem legatarii fieri, quam si voluerit eam ad se pertinere: sed hodie ex D. Pii Antonini constitutione hoc magis iure uti videmur, quod Proculo placuit (?).—§ 200: Illud quaeritur quod sub condicione per vindicationem legatum est, pendente condicione cuius esset: nostri praeceptores heredis esse putant exemplo statuliberi, . . . quem constat interea heredis servum esse; sed diversae scholae auctores putant nullius interim eam rem esse: quod multo magis dicunt de eo, quod sine condicione legatum est, antequam legatarius admittat legatum.[1]

Iul.: Cum servus legatur, et ipsius servi status et omnium, quae personam eius attingunt, in suspenso est; nam si legatarius repulerit a se legatum, numquam eius fuisse videbitur, si non

[1] On the following point alone the jurists disagree, for Sabin. and Cass. and the rest of our teachers think that what has been bequeathed in this way becomes the property of the legatee immediately after the inheritance has been entered upon, even if he be ignorant that the bequest has been made to him; and that after he has become aware of it and refused it, it is as though nothing had been bequeathed; whilst Nerva and Proculus and the other authorities of that school think that the thing does not become the legatee's, unless he wish that it should belong to him. But at the present day, according to a constitution of the late Emp. Pius Antoninus, we seem rather to follow the rule of Proculus.—The question arises, whose is a legacy left *per vindicationem* under a condition, whilst the condition is unfulfilled? Our teachers think that it belongs to the heir, by the analogy of the *statuliber* . . . who, it is allowed, is the slave of the heir for the meantime; but the authorities of the opposite school are of opinion that the thing belongs to no one meanwhile; and they assert this much more of a thing bequeathed without condition, before the legatee accepts the legacy.

repulerit, ex die aditae hereditatis intelligitur.—l. 86, § 2, D. de leg. I (30).[1]

Ulp.: Ubi legatarius non repudiavit, retro ipsius fuisse videtur, ex quo hereditas adita est; si vero repudiaverit, retro videtur res repudiata fuisse heredis.—l. 44, § 1 eod.[2]

Ner.: Quae legantur, recta via ab eo, qui legavit, ad eum cui legata sunt, transeunt.—D. 47, 2, l. 65 (64).[3]

Ulp.: —(res sub condicione legata) interim heredis est, existente autem condicione ad legatarium transit.—D. 7, 1, 12, 5.[4]

(2) The legatum *per damnationem* and the legatum *sinendi modo* engender only an obligatio quasi ex contractu[a] between the heir and the legatee, which has to be enforced by condictio certi, or actio incerti ex testamento.[b]

[a] § 135.

[b] Cf. § 116.

Gai. ii. § 204: Quod autem ita[c] legatum est, post aditam hereditatem, etiamsi pure legatum est, non ut per vindicationem legatum, continuo legatario adquiritur, sed nihilominus heredis est: et ideo legatarius in personam agere debet, id est intendere 'heredem sibi dare oportere,' et tum heres rem, si mancipi sit, mancipio dare aut in iure cedere possessionemque tradere debet.—

[c] Sc. per damnationem.

[1] When a slave is bequeathed, the status of the slave himself, and of all that which concerns him personally, is in uncertainty; for if the legatee shall decline the legacy, it will be considered never to have belonged to him, but if he shall not decline it, it is considered to be his property from the date of entry upon the inheritance.

[2] When a legatee has not renounced, the thing is considered to have belonged to him retrospectively at the time of entry upon the inheritance; but if he has renounced, the thing renounced is considered to have been the heir's property retrospectively.

[3] Things bequeathed pass directly from the testator to the legatee.

[4] —(A thing bequeathed conditionally) for the time being belongs to the heir, but passes to the legatee on the fulfilment of the condition.

Book III. Part III.

§§ 213–4: Ita et in sinendi modo legato iuris est: et ideo huius quoque legati nomine in personam actio est QVIDQVID HEREDEM EX TESTAMENTO DARE FACERE OPORTET.—Sunt tamen qui putant ex hoc legato non videri obligatum heredem, ut mancipet aut in iure cedat aut tradat, sed sufficere, ut legatarium rem sumere patiatur; quia nihil ultra ei testator imperavit, quam ut sinat i.e. patiatur, legatarium rem sibi habere.[1]

[a] § 179.

(3) The effect of the legatum *per praeceptionem*[a] was matter of dispute amongst the schools.

[b] Sc. per praeceptionem.

Ib. § 219: Item nostri praeceptores quod ita[b] legatum est, nulla alia ratione putant posse consequi eum, cui ita fuerit legatum, quam iudicio familiae erciscundae, quod inter heredes de hereditate erciscunda i.e. dividunda accipi solet; officio enim iudicis id contineri, ut et quod per praeceptionem legatum est adiudicetur.—§ 222: Secundum hanc opinionem[c] si ea res[d] ex iure Quiritium defuncti fuerit potest a legatario vindicari, sive is unus ex heredibus sit sive extraneus; quod si in bonis tantum testatoris fuerit, extraneo quidem ex senatusconsulto[e] utile erit

[c] Sc. diversae scholae auctorum, ibid. § 221.

[d] Sc. per praeceptionem legata.

[e] Sc. Neroniano.

---

[1] But that which is thus bequeathed, after entry upon the inheritance, and although it be bequeathed absolutely, nevertheless belongs to the heir; and therefore is not, like a legacy, *per vindicationem*, at once acquired by the legatee; and therefore the legatee must sue by a personal action, *i.e.*, plead that 'the heir ought to give it to him'; and then, if it be a *res mancipi*, the heir must make it over by mancipation or by surrender in court, and deliver up possession.—So also is the rule in respect of a legacy *sinendi modo;* and therefore in respect of such legacy also the action is personal, running thus: 'whatever the heir ought to give or do according to the testament.'—There are, however, those who think that the heir is not to be considered bound by a legacy of this sort to mancipate, make surrender in court, or deliver, but that it is enough for him to permit the legatee to take the thing; because the testator laid no injunction upon him further than that he should allow, *i.e.*, suffer, the legatee to have the thing for himself.

legatum, heredi vero familiae erciscundae iudicis officio praestabitur.[1] Book III Part III.

(4) In the Law of Justinian, it always depends alone upon the object of the legacy whether, according to the nature thereof, the honoratus has merely a personal or a real action[a] besides, in case something belonging to the testator has been bequeathed. [a] l. 44, 1; D. de leg. 1, l. 30 47, 2, 65 (64) (sup.).

> Imp. Iust.: Rectius esse censemus . . . omnibus tam legatariis quam fideicommissariis unam naturam imponere et non solum personalem actionem praestare, sed etiam in rem, quatenus eis liceat easdem res, vel per quodcumque genus legati vel per fideicommissum fuerint derelictae, vindicare in rem actione instituenda, et insuper utilem Servianam i.e. hypothecariam super his, quae fuerint derelicta, in res mortui praestare.—C. 6, 43, 1, 1.[2]

If the same thing have been bequeathed to several, there was, before the lex Papia,[b] accrual— [b] § 175.

---

[1] Moreover, our teachers are of opinion that a legacy of this sort can be sued for by the legatee by no other means than the action for the partition of an inheritance, which is usually employed amongst heirs for the purpose of 'erciscating,' that is, dividing the inheritance; for included in the functions of the *iudex* is the assignment of a legacy *per praeceptionem*.—According to this view, if such thing belonged to the deceased by Quiritarian Law, the legatee can sue for it by *rei vindicatio*, whether he be one of the heirs or a stranger; but if it belonged to the testator only as *in bonis*, the legacy will be effectual to a stranger, by the *SCtum*, but to the heir will be paid over by the authority of the *iudex*, in an action for the partition of the inheritance.

[2] We consider it more suitable . . . to impart a single character to all, as well legatees as fideicommissaries, and not only to give them a personal action but a real action also, so that they shall be at liberty to lay claim to the same things by bringing a real action, whether they have been left to them by some kind of legacy or by a bequest in trust; and further our will is to accord them an analogous Servian action, that is, a hypothecarian action against the estate of the deceased in respect of the things which shall have been left.

Book III. Part III.

(1) of the share that lapsed, always to the co-legatee in the case of a legacy *per vindicationem* and *per praeceptionem*.[a]

[a] l. 80, D. de leg. III (32).

Ulp. xxiv. 12: Si duobus eadem res **per vindicationem** legata sit, sive **coniunctim**, velut TITIO ET SEIO HOMINEM STICHVM DO LEGO, sive **disiunctim**, velut TITIO HOMINEM STICHVM DO LEGO, SEIO EVNDEM HOMINEM DO LEGO, concursu partes fiunt: non concurrente altero pars eius iure civili alteri adcrescebat, sed post legem Papiam Poppaeam non capientis pars caduca fit.[1]

(2) In the case of a legacy *per damnationem*, there was no right of accrual between the co-legatees; if the same thing were left separately to several, each could claim it (or its aestimatio) entirely.

Ib. § 13: Si per **damnationem** eadem res duobus legata sit, si quidem **coniunctim**, singulis partes debentur (et non capientis pars iure civili in hereditate remanebat; nunc autem caduca fit): quodsi **disiunctim**, singulis solidum debetur.[2]

(3) The legal relation of the co-legatees in the case of legatum *sinendi modo* was a subject of dispute.

Gai. ii. § 215[b]: Maior illa dissensio in hoc[c] legato intervenit, si eandem rem duobus pluribusve disiunctim legasti; quidam putant utrisque

[b] §§ 213-4 (*sup.*).

[c] Sc. sinendi modo.

[1] If the same thing have been bequeathed to two persons *per vindicationem*, whether jointly, as, 'I give and bequeath to Tit. and Sei. the slave Stichus,' or severally, as for example, 'I give and bequeath to Tit. the slave Stichus, I give and bequeath the same slave to Sei.,' if they together accept, shares are created, while if one did not accept, his share used to accrue to the other according to civil law; since the *l. Papia Poppaea*, however, the share of him who does not take becomes a lapse.

[2] If the same thing have been bequeathed to two persons *per damnationem*, and that jointly, a share is due to each (and the share of the one who did not take used to remain in the inheritance according to civil law, but now becomes a lapse); but if it have been bequeathed severally, the whole is due to them individually.

solidum deberi, sicut per damnationem: nonnulli occupantis esse meliorem condicionem aestimant, quia cum in eo genere legati damnetur heres patientiam praestare, ut legatarius rem habeat, sequitur, ut si priori patientiam praestiterit et is rem sumpserit, securus sit adversus eum, qui postea legatum petierit, quia neque habet rem, ut patiatur eam ab eo sumi, neque dolo malo fecit, quominus eam rem haberet.[1]

(4) In the Justinianean Law division and accrual obtain between all co-legatees who are 're coniuncti.'

Imp. Iust.: Ubi autem legatarii vel fideicommissarii duo forte vel plures sunt, quibus aliquid relictum sit, si quidem hoc **coniunctim** relinquatur et . . . pars quaedam ex his deficiat, sancimus eam omnibus, si habere maluerint, pro civili portione cum omni suo onere adcrescere, vel si omnes noluerint, tunc apud eos remanere, a quibus derelictum est; cum vero quidam voluerint quidam noluerint, volentibus solummodo id totum accedere. Sin autem **disiunctim** fuerit relictum, si quidem omnes hoc accipere et potuerint et maluerint, suam quisque partem pro virili portione accipiat: . . . sin vero non omnes legatarii, quibus separatim res relicta est, in eius adquisitionem concurrant, sed unus forte eam accipiat, haec solida eius sit quia sermo testatoris omnibus prima facie solidum adsignare videtur,

---

[1] The following more important difference of view arises in respect of this kind of legacy, if you have bequeathed the same thing to two or more severally; some are of opinion that the whole is due to each, as in a legacy *per damnationem;* some think that the condition of the one who first appropriates it is the better, because since in that kind of legacy the heir is obliged to suffer the legatee to have the thing, it follows that if he extend toleration to the first legatee and he have taken the thing, he is safe against the other who afterwards demands the legacy, because he neither has the thing, so as to permit it to be taken from him, nor has he acted fraudulently, so as not to have it.

Book III. Part III.

aliis supervenientibus partes a priore abstrahentibus, ut ex aliorum quidem concursu prioris legatum minuatur.—C. 6, 51, l. un. § 11.[1]

§ 184. Lapse of Bequests.

The grounds of the lapse of a bequest can be:

(1) its original invalidity or inefficacy;[a] and here we have to make special mention of the 'regula Catoniana.'[b]

[a] §§ 178, 181. Cf. § 161.

[b] Brown, s. vv.

Cels.: Catoniana regula sic definit: quod, si testamenti facti tempore decessisset testator, inutile foret, id legatum, quandocumque decesserit, non valere; quae definitio in quibusdam falsa est.—l. 1 pr., D. de reg. Cat. 34, 7.[2]

Inst. ii. 20, § 10: Si rem legatarii quis ei legaverit, inutile legatum est, quia quod proprium est ipsius, amplius eius fieri non potest; et licet alienaverit eam, non debetur nec ipsa nec aestimatio eius.[3]

---

[1] But when there are two, it may be, or several legatees or fideicommissaries, to whom something has been left, and it is left to them jointly, and a certain part thereof falls through, we enact that if they all prefer to have it, it shall accrue to all with its burdens, in the proportions prescribed by civil law, or if all decline it, it shall remain with those by whom it has been bequeathed; but when some wish for it, and some decline it, the whole accrues alone to those who care for it. If, however, anything shall be left severally, and all shall both be able and prefer to receive it, let each receive a single share; . . . but if not all the legatees to whom the property has been left severally agree upon the acquisition thereof, but perhaps only one will accept it, it shall wholly belong to him, because the language of the testator seems at first sight to assign the whole to all, when others coming in besides subtract shares from the first, so that by the joint action of the later ones the legacy of the first is diminished.

[2] The Catonian rule is in the following terms: Such legacy as, if the testator had died at the time of making the testament would have been void, is of no effect, whensoever the testator shall have died. This definition in certain cases is erroneous.

[3] If a man have bequeathed to a legatee the property of such,

Pap.: Catoniana regula non pertinet ad ea legata, quorum dies non mortis tempore, sed post aditam cedit hereditatem.—l. 3, D. de reg. Cat.[1]

Ulp.: Sed si sub condicione (res mea mihi) legetur, poterit legatum valere, si existentis condicionis tempore mea non sit . . . quia ad condicionalia (legata) Catoniana non pertinet.—l. 41, § 2, D. de leg. I.[2]

Id. xxiv. 23: Ei, qui in potestate manu mancipiove est scripti heredis, sub condicione legari potest, ut requiratur, an quo tempore dies legati cedit, in potestate heredis non sit.[3]

(2) Revocation (ademptio legati),[a] which can occur either expressly or tacitly.

[a] See Brown, s. *Ademptio*.

Ulp. xxiv. 29: Legatum quod datum est adimi potest vel eodem testamentum, vel codicillis testamento confirmatis: dum tamen eodem modo adimatur, quo modo datum est.[4]

Inst. ii. 20, § 12: Si rem suam legaverit testator posteaque eam alienaverit, Celsus existimat, si non animo adimendi vendidit, nihilominus deberi, idque divi Severus et Antoninus rescripserunt.[b] [5]

[b] Cf. Story, § 1114 (Grigsby, p. 772).

---

the legacy is void, because what is a man's own cannot be made still more his property; and although he have alienated it, neither the thing itself nor its value is due.

[1] The Catonian rule does not apply to those legacies the vesting of which takes place, not at the time of death, but after entry upon the inheritance.

[2] But if (my property) is bequeathed (to me) conditionally, the legacy can stand good so far as the thing is not my property upon the fulfilment of the condition . . . because the Catonian rule does not apply to conditional legacies.

[3] A legacy can be given conditionally to a person who is under the *potestas*, *manus*, or *mancipium* of the appointed heir; so as to require his not being under the *potestas* of the heir at the time the legacy vests.

[4] A legacy that has been given can be revoked either by the same testament, or by a codicil confirmed by the testament, provided, however, that it is revoked in the same mode in which it was given.

[5] If a testator shall have bequeathed his own property, and afterwards have alienated it, Cels. thinks that the legacy is

BOOK III. Part III.

Ulp.: Non solum autem legata, sed et fideicommissa adimi possunt et quidem nuda voluntate. Unde . . . si capitales vel gravissimae inimicitiae intercesserint, ademptum (fideicommissum) videri. Secundum haec et in legato tractamus doli exceptione opposita.—D. 34, 4, 3, 11.[1]

The revocation can also be accomplished by means of alteration or transfer of the legacy (translatio egati).

Paul.: Translatio legati fit quattuor modis: aut enim a persona in personam transfertur; aut ab eo qui dare iussus est transfertur, ut alius det; aut cum res pro re datur, ut pro fundo decem aurei; aut quod pure datum est transfertur sub condicione.—l. 6 pr. eod.[2]

(3) If the testament itself become invalid, or 'destitutum,' the bequests together collapse.[a] But the Praetorian edict ('si quis omissa causa testamenti ab intestato possidet hereditatem') protects the legatees, if the person instituted in the testament, to nullify the bequests, craftily does not enter upon the inheritance ex testamento, in order thus either himself to acquire it ab intestato or to appropriate it to another (intestate heirs or substitutes).[b]

[a] D. 26, 2, 9; § 181, ad fin.; D. 29, 4, 17.

[b] § 168.

Ulp.: Praetor voluntates defunctorum tuetur et eorum calliditati occurrit, qui omissa causa

still due, if the testator did not sell it with the intention of adeeming the legacy; and the late Empp. Severus and Antoninus have so decided by rescript.

[1] Now not only legacies but gifts in trust can be revoked, and that by mere declaration. We must therefore consider that (a gift in trust) has been revoked if a mortal or very violent feud has arisen. We deal with a legacy according to the same rule when a plea of fraud has been set up.

[2] The transfer of a legacy comes about in four ways; for it is either transferred from one person to another; or the transfer is made by him who is directed to convey, in order that another may convey; or if instead of one thing another is given, for example, instead of an estate, ten gold-pieces; or if anything given absolutely is transferred conditionally.

testamenti ab intestato hereditatem partemve eius possident ad hoc, ut eos circumveniant, quibus quid ex iudicio defuncti deberi potuit, si non ab intestato possideretur hereditas, et in eos actionem pollicetur.—Si quis per fraudem omiserit hereditatem ut ad legitimum perveniat, legatorum petitione tenebitur.—D. 29, 4, l. 1 pr., § 13.[1]

Id.: —ubi pecunia accepta repudiavit, ibi dicamus eum qui omisit conveniendum, ubi vero gratis, in fraudem tamen eorum quibus quid relictum est, possessorem debere conveniri utili actione.—l. 4, § 1 eod.[2]

On the other hand, if merely the oneratus fail, the burden of the bequests passes with the hereditary portion to the joint-heirs,[a] or substitutes, acquiring such by accrual. [a] § 175.

Id.: —post rescriptum Severi, quo fideicommissa ab instituto relicta a substitutis debentur, et hic [b] quasi substitutus cum suo onere consequetur adcrescentem portionem.—l. 61, § 1, D. de leg. II. (31).[3] [b] Sc. coheres.

---

[1] The Praetor protects the dispositions of deceased persons, and counteracts the craft of those who, ignoring the testamentary title, have possession of the inheritance or a part thereof as heirs by intestacy, with the object of depriving those to whom something would have been due according to the judgment of the deceased, were not the inheritance possessed *ab intestato;* and he promises an action against them.—If a man have fraudulently forborne to take up an inheritance, in order that it may devolve upon the heir-at-law, he will be liable to a claim for legacies.

[2] —when he received money for his renunciation, we shall say that a person who has ignored the title should be sued, but even when it has been without reward, yet in fraud of those to whom anything has been bequeathed, the possessor ought to be sued by an equitable action.

[3] —since the rescript of Severus, whereby *fideicommissa* charged upon the heir are a debt from the after-heirs, he (*i.e.*, the co-heir) also, in the character of after-heir, will acquire the accrued inheritance with its incumbrances.

BOOK III. Part III.

§ 185. *PARTITIO LEGATA* AND UNIVERSAL TESTAMENTARY TRUST.

Not merely a single object of property, but also a share of the Inheritance itself can be the object of the legacy, so that the heir has to divide the latter with the legatee: this is the *PARTITIO LEGATA*, the origin of which is connected with the lex Voconia.[a]

[a] Gai. ii. 274 and 226.

> Ulp. xxiv. 25: Sicut singulae res legari possunt, ita universarum quoque summa id est pars legari potest, quae species **partitio** appellatur; ut puta hoc modo: HERES MEVS CVM TITIO HEREDITATEM MEAM PARTITO DIVIDITO; quo casu dimidia pars bonorum Titio legata videtur: potest autem et alia pars velut tertia vel quarta legari.[1]
>
> Pomp.: Cum bonorum parte legata dubium sit, utrum rerum partes, an aestimatio debeatur, Sabinus quidem et Cassius aestimationem, Proculus et Nerva rerum partes esse legatas existimaverunt. Sed oportet heredi succurri, ut ipse eligat, sive rerum partes sive aestimationem dare maluerit.—l. 26, § 2, D. de leg. I. 30.[b][2]

[b] Cf. ibid. (§ 73).

The taker of the bequest (legatarius partiarius) remains singular successor, to whom pass neither claims nor debts of the inheritance; therefore special, reciprocal 'stipulationes partis et pro parte' were commonly concluded between him and the heir, as to proportional

---

[1] Just as single articles can be bequeathed, so can an aggregate of things, that is, a share, which kind of legacy is called a 'partition'; as for example, in this way: 'Let my heir share and divide my inheritance with Tit.' In this case half of the estate is considered as bequeathed to Tit.; but yet other shares can be bequeathed, as a third or fourth.

[2] When as regards the bequest of a part of the estate it is doubtful whether shares of the property or their value ought to be rendered, Sab. and Cass. thought that it was the value, but Proc. and Nerva that it was the shares which were bequeathed. But we must aid the heir, that he himself may choose whether he prefer to give shares of the property or their value.

participation in the 'activa' and 'passiva' of the inheritance,—by enjoyment of the heir's revenues and share in the burden of the payments to be made by him in respect of the inheritance, pro rata.

> Ulp. xxv. 15: Partis autem et pro parte stipulationes proprie dicuntur quae de lucro et damno communicando solent interponi inter heredem et legatarium partiarium, id est cum quo partiri iussus est heres.[1]

Besides the 'legatum partitionis,' there arose later on the Universal Testamentary Trust (fideicommissum hereditatis, fideicommissaria hereditas) which gradually supplanted the former.

The testator can, that is, by fideicommissary directions impose upon the testamentary heir, or the one under an intestacy (fiduciarius heres), the restoration of the inheritance or a share thereof to a third person (fideicommissarius heres).

> Gai. ii. § 250: Cum igitur scripserimus: LVCIVS TITIVS HERES ESTO, possumus adiicere: ROGO TE LVCI TITI PETOQVE A TE, VT CVM PRIMVM POSSIS HEREDITATEM MEAM ADIRE, GAIO SEIO REDDAS RESTITVAS; possumus autem et de parte restituenda rogare; et liberum est, vel sub condicione vel pure relinquere fideicommissa vel ex die certa.[2]

At first the fiduciary was in all portions treated as heir even after restoration had taken place; and a

---

[1] Now those stipulations are properly called 'of and for a part' which are commonly interchanged for the purpose of dividing gain and loss, between the heir and a partiary legatee, that is, a person with whom the heir is directed to share the inheritance.

[2] When, therefore, we have written 'Let Luc. Tit. be heir,' we can add, 'I ask you, Luc. Tit., and request you, that as soon as you are able to enter upon my inheritance, you will give it up and deliver it to Gaius Seius.' We can also ask him to deliver a portion; and we are at liberty to leave gifts in trust either conditionally, or absolutely, or from a certain date.

Book III. Part III.

transfer of the claims and debts of the inheritance to the fideicommissary here no more obtained than in respect of the partitio legata; and therefore a nominal sale of the inheritance to the latter and conclusion of reciprocal 'stipulationes quasi emptae venditae hereditatis' were requisite to bring about the practical result of Universal Succession.

> Ib. §§ 251–2: Restituta autem hereditate is qui restituit nihilominus heres permanet: is vero qui recipit hereditatem, aliquando heredis loco est, aliquando legatarii. § Olim autem nec heredis loco erat nec legatarii, sed potius emptoris: tunc enim in usu erat ei, cui restituebatur hereditas, nummo uno eam hereditatem dicis causa venire; et quae stipulationes inter venditorem hereditatis et emptorem interponi solent, eaedem interponebantur inter heredem et eum cui restituebatur hereditas, id est hoc modo: heres quidem stipulabatur ab eo, cui restituebatur hereditas, ut quidquid hereditario nomine condemnatus fuisset sive quid alias bona fide dedisset, eo nomine indemnis esset, et omnino si quis cum eo hereditario nomine ageret, ut recte defenderetur; ille vero, qui recipiebat hereditatem, invicem stipulabatur, ut si quid ex hereditate, ad heredem pervenisset, id sibi restitueretur, et ut etiam pateretur eum hereditarias actiones procuratorio aut cognitorio nomine exsequi.[1]

[1] But upon restitution of the inheritance, he who has made restitution remains heir notwithstanding; whilst he who receives the inheritance is sometimes in the place of heir, sometimes in that of legatee. § But formerly he used to be neither in the place of heir nor of legatee, but rather in that of purchaser; for it was then the custom that the inheritance, as a matter of form, should be sold for a single coin to him to whom it was given up; and those stipulations which are generally entered into between the vendor and the purchaser of an inheritance were entered into between the heir and the person to whom the inheritance was restored, in the following manner. The heir took a stipulation from him to whom the inheritance

Later on, however, the SC. Trebellianum, under Nero (A.D. 62) directed that after restoration had been accomplished, the actions of inheritance should as utiles actiones be given to and against the universal fideicommissary.

> Factum est SCtum temporibus Neronis Annaeo Seneca et Trebellio Maximo consulibus, cuius verba haec sunt: . . . 'PLACET, VT ACTIONES QVAE IN HEREDES HEREDIBVSQVE DARI SOLENT, EAS NEQVE IN EOS NEQVE HIS DARI, QVI FIDEI SVAE COMMISSVM SIC VTI ROGATI ESSENT RESTITVISSENT, SED HIS ET IN EOS, QVIBVS EX TESTAMENTO FIDEICOMMISSVM RESTITVTVM FVISSET, QVO MAGIS IN RELIQVVM CONFIRMENTVR SVPREMAE DEFVNCTORVM VOLVNTATES.'—l. 1, §§ 1, 2, D. h. t. (ad SC. Treb. 36, 1).[1]
>
> Gai. ii. § 253: —post quod senatusconsultum desierunt illae cautiones in usu haberi; praetor enim utiles actiones ei et in eum, qui recepit hereditatem, quasi heredi et in heredem dare coepit eaeque in edicto proponuntur.[2]

---

was restored that he should be saved harmless in respect of all that he should give as heir, or for anything which he might give otherwise *bona fide*, and that in any case, if any one took proceedings against him in respect of the inheritance, he should be duly defended; whilst the receiver of the inheritance in his turn took a stipulation, that if anything should come to the heir from the inheritance, it should be delivered to him; and that the heir would also suffer him to bring actions in respect of the inheritance, as *procurator* or *cognitor*.

[1] This *SCtum* was made in the time of the Emp. Nero, in the consulship of Annaeus Seneca and Trebellius Maximus. Its language is as follows: '. . . it is decided that all actions, which are generally granted to and against the heir shall be granted neither to them nor against those who, as they were enjoined, have made over a *fid. comm.* laid upon them, but to those and against them to whom a *fid. comm.* shall have been made over in accordance with a testament, in order that the last declarations of deceased persons may for the future be the more confirmed.'

[2] After this *SCtum* those securities ceased to be used; for the Praetor began to allow equitable actions for and against

BOOK III. Part III.

[a] § 182.

Finally, the SC. Pegasianum[a] gave the fiduciarius heres the quarta Falcidia; when he restored the inheritance after deduction of the one-fourth (ex SC. Pegasiano), the SC. Trebellianum did not come into application, and the universal fideicommissary assumed the position of a legatarius partiarius.

Gai. ii. §§ 254–7: Sed rursus quia heredes scripti, cum aut totam hereditatem aut paene totam plerumque restituere rogabantur, adire hereditatem ob nullum aut minimum lucrum recusabant atque ob id extinguebantur fideicommissa, Pegaso et Pusione consulibus senatus censuit, ut ei, qui rogatus esset hereditatem restituere, proinde liceret quartam partem retinere, atque e lege Falcidia in legatis retinendi ius conceditur: ex singulis quoque rebus, quae per fideicommissum relinquuntur eadem retentio permissa est. Per quod Senatusconsultum ipse heres onera hereditaria sustinet: ille autem, qui ex fideicommisso reliquam partem hereditatis recipit, legatarii partiarii loco est: . . . unde effectum est, ut quae solent stipulationes inter heredem et partiarium legatarium interponi, eaedem interponantur inter eum qui ex fideicommissi causa recipit hereditatem, et heredem. § Ergo si quidem non plus quam dodrantem hereditatis scriptus heres rogatus sit restituere, tum ex Trebelliano senatusconsulto restituitur hereditas et in utrumque actiones hereditariae pro rata parte dantur, in heredem quidem iure civili, in eum vero, qui recipit hereditatem, ex senatusconsulto Trebelliano.—§ At si quis plus quam dodrantem vel etiam totam hereditatem restituere rogatus sit, locus est Pegasiano senatusconsulto. § Sed is qui semel adierit . . . sive retinuerit quartam partem sive noluerit retinere, ipse universa onera hereditaria sustinet; . . . si vero totam heredi-

---

the person who received the inheritance, as if to and against the heir, and these are set forth in the Edict.

tatem restituerit, ad exemplum emptae et venditae hereditatis stipulationes interponendae sunt.[1]

If the heir decline to enter upon the inheritance, by the SC. Pegasianum he can be compelled to make entry and restitution without deduction of the one-fourth, and the restitution has then the effect prescribed by the SC. Trebellianum.

Ulp. xxv. 16: Si heres damnosam hereditatem dicat, cogitur a praetore adire et restituere totam, ita ut ei et in eum, qui recipit hereditatem, actiones dentur, proinde atque si ex Trebelliano senatusconsulto restituta fuisset: idque ut ita fiat, Pegasiano senatusconsulto cautum.[2]

---

[1] But again, inasmuch as the instituted heirs, when generally asked to make over the whole or almost the whole of the inheritance, declined to enter upon it because of the little or no profit, and thus *fid. comm.* were extinguished, therefore in the consulship of Pegasus and Pusio the Senate decreed, that he who was asked to make over the inheritance should be entitled to retain a fourth part, just as retention is permitted by the *l. Falcidia* in respect of legacies (and the same retention was also allowed in the case of single things bequeathed in trust). By this *SCtum* it is the heir himself that sustains the burdens of the inheritance, whilst he that receives the residue of the inheritance by virtue of the *fid. comm.* is in the position of a legatee in part. The result of this is, that the same stipulations which commonly pass between the heir and the partiary legatee are also exchanged between him who receives the inheritance by reason of a *fid. comm.* and the heir. § If, therefore, the instituted heir be asked to restore no more than three-fourths of the inheritance, the inheritance is thereupon restored in accordance with the *SCtum Trebell.*, and actions relating to the inheritance are granted against both according to their respective shares: against the heir by civil law, and against him that receives the inheritance by the *SCtum Trebell.* § But if a man is asked to make over more than three-fourths, or even the entire inheritance, the *SCtum Pegas.* comes into operation. § But he who has once entered on the inheritance, whether he has retained or do not care to retain the fourth part, takes upon himself all the burdens of the inheritance . . . whilst if he have made over the whole inheritance, stipulations after the analogy of those in respect of a bought and sold inheritance must be exchanged.

[2] If an heir declare the inheritance to be ruinous, he is com-

Gai.: —quod beneficium his, quibus singulae res per fideicommissum relictae sint, non magis tributum est quam legatariis.—D. 29, 4, 17.[1]

Finally, both senatus-consulta were blended together in the Law of Justinian in such way that henceforth restitution, even deducta quarta, always has the result appointed in the SC. Trebellianum, but the SC. Pegasianum was in name completely abolished.

Inst. ii. 23, § 7: Omnibus modis suggestis tam similitudinibus quam differentiis utriusque senatusconsulti placuit, exploso senatusconsulto Pegasiano, . . . omnem auctoritatem Trebelliano senatusconsulto praestare, ut ex eo fideicommissariae hereditates restituantur, sive habeat heres ex voluntate testatoris quartam sive plus sive minus sive penitus nihil, ut tunc, quando vel nihil vel minus quarta apud eum remaneat, liceat ei vel quartam vel quod deest ex nostra auctoritate retinere, quasi ex Trebelliano senatusconsulto pro rata portione actionibus tam in heredem quam in fideicommissarium competentibus: si vero totam hereditatem sponte restituerit, omnes hereditariae actiones fideicommissario et adversus eum competunt. Sed etiam id quod praecipuum Pegasiani senatusconsulti fuerat, ut quando recusabat heres scriptus sibi datam hereditatem adire, necessitas ei imponeretur totam hereditatem volenti fideicommissario restituere et omnes ad eum et contra eum transirent actiones, et hoc transposuimus ad senatusconsultum Trebellianum, ut ex hoc solo et necessitas heredi imponatur, si ipso nolente adire fideicommissarius desiderat restitui sibi heredita-

---

pelled by the Praetor to make entry and to restore the whole, so that actions may be granted for and against the person who receives the inheritance, just as though restitution had been made under the *Sctum Trebellianum*; and provision to that effect has been made by the *Sctum Pegasianum*.

[1] This benefit is granted to those to whom single things have been bequeathed by *fid. comm.* just as little as by legatees.

tem, nullo nec damno nec commodo apud heredem manente.[1]

For the protection of his right, the universal fideicommissary has at his command the fideicommissaria hereditatis petitio.

Ulp.: Hanc actionem sciendum est adversus eum, qui restituit hereditatem, non competere.—D. 5, 6, 3, 1.[2]

A disposition can be made by universal fideicommissum also as successive, and further, in the form of the so-called fideicommissary, substitution.[a]

[a] Cf. § 160.

Gai. ii. § 277: Quamvis non possimus post mortem eius, qui nobis heres exstiterit, alium in locum eius heredem instituere, tamen possumus eum rogare, ut **cum morietur**, alii eam hereditatem totam vel ex parte restituat; et quia **post**

---

[1] Having considered all the points of agreement and difference in both *Scta*, we have decided to repeal the *Sctum Pegasianum* . . . and to give all legal force to the *Sctum Trebellianum*, so that inheritances bequeathed in trust shall be made over by virtue of the latter, whether the heir by desire of the testator have a fourth, or more, or less, or nothing whatever; but so that when either nothing or less than a fourth is left to him, he may by our authority retain a fourth part, or the amount of the deficiency, or demand repayment of it if he has paid it, as though under the *Sctum Trebellianum*, whilst actions shall lie both against the heir and the beneficiary, according to their respective shares. But should the heir of his own accord make over the entire inheritance, all actions in respect of the inheritance lie for and against the fideicommissary. But that which is peculiar to the *Sctum Pegasianum*, viz., that when the appointed heir refused to enter upon the inheritance which had been given him, the necessity was imposed upon him of making over the whole inheritance to the beneficiary at his request, and of transferring actions both for and against him,—this provision we have added to the *Sctum Trebellianum*, so that by the latter alone is the obligation imposed upon the heir, when he declines to make entry, and when the beneficiary desires that the inheritance should be made over to him, the heir experiencing neither gain nor loss.

[2] It must be noted that this action does not attach against him who has restored an inheritance.

Book III. Part III.

mortem quoque heredis fideicommissum dari potest, idem efficere possumus, et si ita scripserimus; CVM TITIVS HERES MEVS MORTVVS ERIT, VOLO HEREDITATEM MEAM AD PVBLIVM MAEVIVM PERTINERE; utroque autem modo, tam hoc quam illo, Titius heredem suum obligatum relinquit de fideicommisso restituendo.[1]

§ 186. *Mortis Causa Capiones* and *Donationes.*

'Mortis causa *capio*' in the narrow sense is, according to classical usage, every acquisition that any one makes by occasion of the death of another, whether from the property of the deceased or of a third person, with the exception of succession, of legacies and fideicommissa.

> Gai.: Mortis causa capitur, cum propter mortem alicuius capiendi occasio obvenit, exceptis his capiendi figuris, quae proprio nomine appellantur: certe enim et qui hereditario aut legati aut fideicommissi iure capit, ex morte alterius nanciscitur capiendi occasionem, sed quia proprio nomine hae species capiendi appellantur, ideo ab hac definitione separantur.—(Mortis causa) capitur veluti pecunia, quam statuliber aut legatarius alicui condicionis implendae gratia numerat, sive extraneus sit qui accepit sive heres. Eodem numero est pecunia, quam quis in hoc accipit ut vel adeat hereditatem vel non adeat, quique in hoc accipit pecuniam, ut legatum omittat.—l. 31 pr., § 2, D. h. t. (de mort. c. don. 39, 6).[2]

---

[1] Although we cannot appoint another as heir after the death of him who has become our heir, yet we can ask him at death to make over to another the whole or part of the inheritance, and as a *fid. comm.* can also be given after the death of the heir, we can also produce the same effect by expressing ourselves thus: 'When Tit., my heir, is dead, I wish my inheritance to belong to Publ. Maev.' Now in both ways, as well the latter as the former, Tit. leaves his heir bound to restore a *fid. comm.*

[2] A gift *mortis causa* is acquired when opportunity is afforded of acquiring by reason of some one's death, with the exception

To mortis causa capiones belong also in particular—unquestionably again distinguished from them—mortis causa *donationes*,[a] *i.e.*, the gifts that any one makes in contemplation of his death before the donee, and which regularly do not become perfect until such death.[b]

[a] Inst. ii. 7, 1. Cf. A. A. Smith, 'Equity,' pp. 527-532.

[b] Cf. Blackstone, ii. 514 (Steph. ii. 46-7).

Mod.: Mortis causa donatio est, cum quis magis habere se vult, quam eum cui donat, magisque eum cui donat, quam heredem suum.—l. 1 pr., D. h. t.[1]

Paul.: Mortis causa donatio fit multis modis: alias extra suspicionem ullius periculi a sano et in bona valetudine posito, cui ex humana sorte mortis cogitatio est; alias ex metu mortis, aut ex praesenti periculo aut ex futuro, si quidem terra marique, tam in pace quam in bello, et tam domi quam militiae, multis generibus mortis periculum metui potest. . . . Et sic donari potest, ut non aliter reddatur, quam si prior ille qui accepit decesserit.—l. 35, § 4 eod.[2]

---

of those species of acquisition which are designated by a special name, for it is certain that a person who takes by right of inheritance, or legacy, or bequest in trust, also acquires opportunity of taking by the death of another; but inasmuch as these species of acquisition are designated by a special name, they are accordingly excluded from this definition.—We take (*mortis causa*) for example, money which a *statuliber* or a legatee pays to some one for the fulfilment of a condition, whether the recipient be a stranger or the heir. In the same category is money which a man receives for the purpose either of making entry upon an inheritance or of forbearing to do so, and he that receives money in consideration of his not claiming a legacy.

[1] There is a gift *mortis causa* when some one prefers rather that he should himself have possession of the thing than the person to whom he gives it, and that the latter should have it in preference to his own heir.

[2] A gift *mortis causa* obtains in many ways: at one time, without apprehension of any danger, by a man endowed with sound mind and good health, who contemplates death in the course of nature; at another time, from fear of death, because of either immediate or future danger, since there can be many descriptions of apprehended danger of death, by land and by

Book III. Part III.

Ulp.: Non videtur perfecta donatio mortis causa facta, antequam mors insequatur.—l. 32 eod.[1]

Id.: Qui mortis causa donavit, ipse ex poenitentia condictionem vel utilem actionem habet.—l. 30 eod.[2]

Id.: Si mortis causa res donata est et convaluit qui donavit, videndum, an habeat in rem actionem. Et si quidem quis sic donavit, ut, si mors contigisset, tunc haberet cui donatum est, sine dubio donator poterit rem vindicare; mortuo eo tunc is cui donatum est. Si vero sic, ut iam nunc haberet, redderet, si convaluisset vel de proelio vel peregre rediisset, potest defendi in rem competere donatori, si quid horum contigisset, interim autem ei cui donatum est.—l. 29 eod.[3]

Mortis causa donationes were step by step assimilated to bequests, especially as regards capacity and the quarta Falcidia—as to which in detail many controversies existed—from the time of Justinian also in respect of the form of disposition, in case the donation generally required a form.[a]

[a] § 129, ad fin.

Senatus censuit placere mortis causa donationes factas in eos, quos lex prohibet capere, in eadem

water, both in peace and in war, at home and on service. . . . And so a gift can be made in such way that it shall not be returned unless the donee be the first to die.

[1] A gift made *mortis causa* is not considered complete before death ensues.

[2] He that has made a donation in view of death has, in case of regret, a personal or equitable action.

[3] If a thing was given in contemplation of death, and the donor has recovered, we have to consider whether he has the proprietary action. And if in fact a man has made a donation in such way that, if his death should have happened, then the donee shall have the thing, the donor will without doubt be able to recover the ownership; but if he have died, then the donee. But if it have been given in this way, that he shall now already have the thing, but shall restore it if the donor recover, or shall have returned from battle, or from a journey, it may be maintained that the donor has the proprietary action after that one of these conditions has been fulfilled, but, on the other hand, the donee in the meantime.

causa haberi, in qua essent, quae testamento his legata essent, quibus capere per legem non liceret. —l. 35 pr. eod.[1]

Imp. Iust.: —sancimus omnes mortis causa donationes . . . actis minime indigere neque exspectare publicarum personarum praesentiam . . . : sed ita res procedat, ut si quinque testibus praesentibus vel in scriptis vel sine litterarum suppositione aliquis voluerit mortis causa donationem facere, et sine monumentorum accessione res gesta maneat firmitate vallata, . . . et omnes effectus sortiatur, quos ultimae habent liberalitates, nec ex quacumque parte absimilis eis intelligatur. —l. 4, C. h. t. 8, 56 (57).[2]

The most important difference between the two lies in this, that mortis causa donationes have a donative character as of a contract, whence they are also operative even without the existence of an heir; and some differences besides remained which are explained by the contractual nature of this species of gifts.

Marc.: Filiusfamilias qui non potest facere testamentum nec voluntate patris, tamen mortis causa donare patre permittente potest.—l. 25, § 1, D. h. t.[3]

---

[1] The Senate decided that gifts in contemplation of death made to those whom the statute does not allow to acquire should be regarded as in the same position as if they were legacies that had been given by testament to those who are not allowed by the statute to acquire.

[2] We enact that all gifts in view of death . . . shall need no judicial proceedings, and not require the presence of public persons; but let the matter so proceed that if a man shall desire to make a gift *mortis causa* in the presence of five witnesses in writing, or without the support of documents, and without the addition of records, the transaction shall remain adequately protected . . . and shall acquire all those effects which last bounties have, and shall be regarded in no particular as different from them.

[3] A *fil. fam.*, who cannot make a testament, not even with his father's consent, can however make a gift *mortis causa*, if the father allow him.

BOOK IV. (APPENDIX).

THE JUDICIAL ENFORCEMENT OF RIGHTS ('ACTIONES').[a]

[a] Cf. Puchta, ii. §§ 149-188; Rivier, pp. 221-266, 379-402, 529-539; Moyle, Excursus x.

CHAPTER I.

THE CONSTITUTION OF THE COURT.

§ 187. Form of Roman Civil Procedure.

Book IV. Chapter I.

ROMAN Civil Procedure (ordo iudiciorum privatorum) is characterised by the division of judicial functions between the functionary entrusted with the administration of the Law (magistratus iuri dicundo) and the judge (iudex). All regular proceedings were divided into two departments, already externally separated from each other: into proceedings *in iure* (*i.e.*, at the Court) before the 'magistratus iuri dicundo,' and those *in iudicio* before private persons as jurors. The object and purpose of proceedings 'in iure' was: Instructions as to the action and disposal of the processual presumptions (as legitimation of the parties and allowance of the action generally), confirmation of the suit, *i.e.*, the formulating of the claims enforced, nomination of the iudex (ordinatio iudicii); it found its conclusion in the 'litis contestatio,' which originally consisted in a ceremonial summoning of witnesses as to the proceedings arranged. The further proceedings, investigation and establishment of the actual conditions of the legal claim (taking the evidence), as well as discussion and consideration of its legal elements—not the mere question of fact—formed the object of procedure 'in iudicio,' closing with the judgment (sententia).

Paul. Diac. ex Festo h. v. (p. 57 Müll.): **Contestari litem** dicuntur duo aut plures adversarii, quod ordinato iudicio utraque pars dicere solet: 'testes estote.'[1]

Besides the 'ordo iudiciorum privatorum,' there still existed proceedings 'extra ordinem,'—'extraordinaria cognitio.' That is, in certain cases the magistrate arranged for no iudicium, but himself investigated and decided the suit.[a] Cases of this extraordinaria cognitio multiplied in the course of time, and became always increasingly the rule, until at last Diocletian[b] abolished the ancient 'ordo iudiciorum privatorum.'

[a] D. 50, 16, 178, 2.

[b] A.D. 294?

§ 188. Jurisdiction. Competence.

Since a sharp separation between government and administration of justice, and corresponding comprehensive division of administrative and judicial magistracy, is foreign to the Law of the Roman State, jurisdiction appears as an ingredient of superior official authority in general. Originally it belonged in Rome to the Consuls, later on as a special function to the Praetors, and in matters of the market to the Curule Aediles. In Italy, with the exception of the urbica diocesis (Rome and environs), it was transferred by Hadrian to four 'consulares,' by Marcus Aurelius to several 'iuridici.' In the Provinces, the control of the administration of justice devolved upon the governors (praesides provinciae). Moreover, there was still in the imperial period an extensive series of special jurisdictions for certain legal matters, as for example, matters of fideicommissum, police and finance, in which latter especially a comprehensive jurisdiction belonged to the officers of the Revenue. The municipal magistrates possessed only a limited, inferior jurisdiction, in matters of small debts.

[1] Two or more opponents are said *contestari litem* (to join issue) because upon the constitution of the tribunal both sides commonly say, 'Ye shall be my witnesses.'

Book IV. Chapter I.

In the judicial authority of the magistrates entrusted with the administration of the Law (officium ius dicentis) are distinguished—

(*a*) 'iurisdictio' in the narrower sense, that is, the ordinary administration of the Law, as a rule amounting to arrangement of a iudicium in formal suits under Private Law (iudicem iudicare iubere);

(*β*) 'imperium' (mixtum), that is, the higher magisterial arbitrary authority of command and executive — cautiones, missiones (including the bonorum possessio), in integrum restitutio[a]—which belongs to the municipal magistrates only in a limited degree;

(*γ*) 'legis actio s. iurisdictio voluntaria,' that is, formal magisterial co-operation for legalisation of certain transactions (manumissio, adoptio, in iure cessio), which the municipal magistrates do not as a rule possess.

In respect of their significance and operation in Procedure, the Courts presided over by a Roman magistrate in formulary proceedings are divided into:

'*legitima* iudicia,' Courts conformable to the purposes of the old ius civile, and dependent upon the old Roman procedure, and 'iudicia *imperio continentia*,' which were Courts resting upon the absolute power of magistrates. The practical significance of this consists principally:

(1) in the latter iudicia being naturally determined with the office (year of office) of the magistrate who had instituted them, whilst the originally unlimited continuance of the legitima iudicia was first limited by the lex Iulia iudiciaria (so-called Limitation of Actions);

(2) In their different operation as regards the litis contestatio.[b]

Gai. iv. §§ 104–5: Legitima sunt iudicia, quae in urbe Roma vel intra primum urbis Romae miliarium inter omnes sives Romanos sub uno

[a] § 30.

[b] Gai. iv. 106-7. Cf. ib. iii. 83; i. 184; Ulp. xi. 27; § 78; and Vat. fgm. 47.

iudice accipiuntur; eaque e lege Iulia iudiciaria, nisi in anno et sex mensibus iudicata fuerint, exspirant: et hoc est quod vulgo dicitur, e lege Iulia litem anno et sex mensibus mori. § Imperio vero continentur recuperatoria et quae sub uno iudice accipiuntur interveniente peregrini persona iudicis aut litigatoris; in eadem causa sunt, quaecumque extra primum urbis Romae miliarium . . . accipiuntur: ideo autem imperio contineri iudicia dicuntur, quia tamdiu valent, quamdiu is qui ea praecepit, imperium habebit.—§ 109: Ceterum potest ex lege quidem esse iudicium, sed legitimum non esse; et contra ex lege non esse, sed legitimum esse:[a] nam . . . si ex ea causa, ex qua nobis edicto praetoris datur actio, Romae sub uno iudice inter omnes cives Romanos accipiatur iudicium, legitimum est.[1]

[a] This shows '*legitimum* iudicium' to be 'almost untranslatable': Muirhead on Gai. iii. § 180.

The competence of the Court in the particular case is governed by the personality of the defendant. The personal competence of the Court is decided—

(1) by the muncipal Law of the person in a

---

[1] *Iudicia* are *legitima* which are heard before a single *iudex* in the city of Rome, or within the first milestone from the city of Rome, being between Roman citizens; and these, according to the *l. Iulia iudiciaria*, come to an end unless they have been decided within a year and six months. This is what is meant by the common saying, that by the *l. Iulia iudiciaria* an action dies in a year and six months. § Depending upon the *imperium* (of the Praetor) are those before *recuperatores*, and those which are heard before a single *iudex*, in which the *iudex* or a litigant is a foreigner. In the same position are all actions which are heard beyond the first milestone from the city of Rome. The actions are said to depend upon the *imperium*, because they are effectual only so long as the Praetor who authorised them shall retain office.—§ Moreover, an action may indeed be derived from a *lex* and yet not be *legitimum*, and conversely, it may not be derived from a *lex* and yet be *legitimum*; for . . . if in a case where an action is allowed us by the Praetor's edict the trial be at Rome before a single *iudex* and all the parties are Roman citizens, the action is *legitimum*.

Book IV. Chapter I.

community (forum *originis*); after conferment of citizenship upon all Italy the citizens of the municipia had a double forum originis, at home and in Rome, where however an action could alone be maintained in the case of absence (ius revocandi domum).[a]

[a] See Westlake, pp. 25, 192, *sqq.*

Ulp.: Municipem aut nativitas facit, aut manumissio, aut adoptio.—l. 1 pr., ad munic. 50, 1.[1]

Mod.: Roma communis nostra patria est.—l. 33 eod.[2]

(2) By continuous residence in a community (forum *domicilii*).[b]

[b] Ibid. pp. 259, *sqq.*

Imp. Diocl.: Cives quidem origo manumissio adlectio adoptio, **incolas** vero domicilium facit. Et in eo loco singulos habere **domicilium** non ambigitur, ubi quis larem rerumque ac fortunarum suarum summam constituit, unde rursus non sit discessurus, si nihil avocet, unde cum profectus est, peregrinari videtur, quo si rediit, peregrinari iam destitit.—C. 10, 40 (39), 7.[3]

Gai.: Incola et his magistratibus parere debet apud quos incola est, et illis apud quos civis est; . . . municipali iurisdictioni in utroque municipio subiectus est.—l. 29, ad munic.[c] [4]

[c] Cf. Bluntschli, 'Theory of the State,' pp. 195, *sqq.* (E. Tr.).

---

[1] A man is made a burgher either by birth, or enfranchisement, or adoption.

[2] Rome is our common fatherland.

[3] Citizens are constituted by origin, manumission, election or adoption, but inhabitants by residence. And there is no doubt that every one has his residence where he has set up his altar and his establishment, with the intention of not again departing therefrom, if nothing call him away; and when he has left such place, he is considered to be a foreigner, and when he has returned, he has ceased to be a foreigner.

[4] An inhabitant must both render obedience to that magistracy amidst which he is an inhabitant, and to that amidst which he is a citizen; and in both municipalities he is subject to the municipal jurisdiction.

§ 189. Iudices.

In Rome either standing colleges of judges, or, as was the rule, single judges whom the magistrate appointed as jurors for the particular suit, acted as judges *in iudicio*.[a] [a] § 187.

The former are—

(1) The 'Decemviri iudices s. litibus iudicandis magistratus' (since the seventh century elected by the People) who were originally competent for actions of freedom,[b] but to whom was transferred by Augustus the conduct of the Centumviral court (centumviralem hastam cogere). [b] §

(2) The primeval Court of the Centumviri had in republican times consisted of 105 persons, three chosen out of each of the 35 tribes. It is questionable whether in the most ancient time it was not out of the 30 curiae, to which had to be added 10 members of the Senate, by lot as decemviri, and at the same time 'decem primi' of the collegium. From the time of Augustus, however, it consists of 180 members, and is divided into four independent sections (hasta, consilium, tribunal, iudicium). They were at first competent for the *Vindicationes*[c] but principally, and later on exclusively, for suits of inheritance, especially upon the validity or affirmation of testaments.[d]

[c] Perhaps with restriction to *res mancipi*.

[d] *Querela inofficiosi*; § 169.

The single judges appointed by the magistrate are—

(1) IUDICES (privati) or ARBITRI. These were in the beginning taken from the Senators, then indeed from the Knights; but in civil causes a list of jurors had to be set up by the Praetor (album iudicum selectorum) from the time of Augustus, who by his *leges Iuliae iudiciariae* transferred the judicial office (munus iudicandi) to three 'decuriae iudicum,' formed for criminal and civil causes, possessed of an equestrian fortune (quatringenarii), and a fourth decuria of the 'ducenarii' appointed for minor

civil causes, to which Caligula further added a fifth decuria. The selection of jurors in the particular case as a rule was effected by agreement of the parties, in which the proposal (iudicem ferre) belonged to the plaintiff, whilst the defendant possessed the rejection upon oath of the person proposed (iniquum eiurare). The person chosen was appointed judge by the magistrate (iudicis datio s. addictio) and was sworn.

[a] § 7.

(2) *RECUPERATORES* are originally the arbitrators in courts of foreigners[a] constituted by international agreement; later on they appear in the most diverse legal matters of Roman citizens amongst themselves. Three or five were regularly appointed, and in the particular case were chosen by lot (sortitio) and presentation by the magistrate, rejection (reiectio) by the parties being permitted.

> Fest. h. v. (p. 274^{m}): **Reciperatio** est, ut ait Gallus Aelius, cum inter populum et reges nationesque et civitates peregrinas lex convenit, quomodo per reciperatores reddantur res reciperenturque, resque privatas inter se persequantur.[1]

In the Provinces the judges were chosen by the governor, as a rule, from the Roman citizens domiciled at the place of the Court (conventus civium Romanorum), but also in certain cases, according to the provincial constitution, from the provincials.

§ 190. Court-days.

As regards the days appointed in Rome for judicial proceedings, we have to distinguish for republican times—

[1] A *reciperatio*, according to G. A., is when a *lex* is agreed upon between a people and kings and nations and foreign States, as to the manner in which things shall be given and received back through *reciperatores*, and how they shall conduct private matters between themselves.

(α) days on which a proceeding could take place 'in iure' before the magistrate, which were the dies *fasti* appointed by the Calendar (in the Julian Calendar 55–56): standing court-days, originally the days upon which a legis actio could be entertained, conformably with the fas; in contrast, on the one hand, to the dies *nefasti* (upon which such a transaction contains a nefas, but other acts of jurisdiction appertaining to the imperium were allowed); on the other, with the dies *comitiales*, which were free for jurisdiction only if no assembly of the People took place.

(β) For proceedings 'in iudicio' there were no established court-days, but they were restricted as to time by festivals and holidays.

(2) After the judicial year (actus rerum) had been further settled by Augustus, in respect of the services of jurors,[a] it was afresh regulated by Marcus Aurelius, both for the magistrates with jurisdiction and for the iudices, in such way that it henceforth contained 230 court-days (dies iudiciarii). Upon the 'dies feriati' a valid judicial proceeding could take place alone exceptionally in certain pressing cases (causae exceptae), or by consent of the parties.

[a] § 189.

In the Provinces a court was held (forum, conventum agere) by the governor, or his legatus, or quaestor delegated by him, in the chief places within the limits of his jurisdiction that were most visited by him (conventus), where at times appointed every year assemblies (conventus) took place.

CHAPTER II.

THE PROCEEDINGS.

§ 191. THE COMMENCEMENT OF THE SUIT.

BOOK IV. Chapter II.

THE opening of the suit required the presence of the parties before the Court. As a rule—in ordinary proceedings—it was the business of the plaintiff to bring the defendant to the Court, in order judicially to make good his claim.

For this purpose, according to the Twelve Tables—with certain exceptions—where he met with the opponent, and without alleging his legal claim, he possessed the *in ius vocatio* (in case of necessity, accompanied by the employment of force—manus iniectio), with which the party summoned must at once comply, and he could only avoid it by furnishing a *Vindex*, who took the action upon himself (but cum poena dupli). The Praetorian Edict assured operation to the in ius vocatio by penal actions against the opponent who was unsubmissive, or furnished no vindex, as well as against him that by force withdrew the latter from the in ius vocatio.[a]

[a] Gai. iv. 46.

> Lex XII tabularum : SI IN IVS VOCAT, ITO ; NI IT, ANTESTAMINO : IGITVR EM CAPITO. SI CALVITVR PEDEMVE STRVIT, MANVM ENDO IACITO. SI MORBVS AEVITASVE VITIVM ESCIT, IVMENTVM DATO; SI NOLET ARCERAM NE STERNITO. ADSIDVO VINDEX ADSIDVVS ESTO ; PROLETARIO (CVI ? IAM CIVI ?) QVIS VOLET VINDEX ESTO.[1]

---

[1] A man when summoned before a magistrate, shall go ; in default of his going, let the plaintiff call bystanders to witness : then shall he take him. If he shirks or runs away, the plaintiff shall lay hands on him. If illness or age be an impediment, the plaintiff shall provide a beast of burden ; if the defendant refuse, the plaintiff need not provide a carriage. The protector of a landowner must be a landowner ; whosoever likes shall be protector to a citizen that is a *proletarius* (of the lowest class).

Ulp.: In ius vocari non oportet . . . magistratus qui imperium habent. . . . Praeterea in ius vocari non debet qui uxorem ducat aut quae nubat, nec iudicem dum de re cognoscat, nec eum dum quis apud praetorem causam agit, neque funus ducentem familiare.—D. 2, 4, 2.[1]

Praetor ait: PARENTEM, PATRONVM PATRONAMVE, LIBEROS PARENTES PATRONI PATRONAE IN IVS SINE PERMISSV MEO NE QVIS VOCET.—l. 4, § 1 eod.[2]

Plerique putaverunt nullum de domo sua in ius vocari licere.—Sed si aditum ad se praestet aut ex publico conspiciatur, recte in ius vocari eum Iulianus ait.—Sed . . . de domo sua nemo extrahi debet.—l. 18 (Gai.), ll. 19, 21 (Paul.) eod.[3]

In place of the in ius vocatio, later on the private and voluntary promissio offered to the plaintiff (with or without giving security or a penal promise) by the defendant, or by another for him—upon a certain day to present himself in iure (*vadimonium* = 'cautio s. satisdatio iudicio sisti ')[a] became increasingly customary and acquired recognition in the Praetorian Edict.[b]

[a] See Brown, s. *Satisdatio;* Paterson, sect. 1140.

[b] *Infra.*

In the Provinces a simple notification of the suit by the plaintiff to the defendant (litis denuntiatio), with the summons to appear at the next 'conventus,' took the place of the in ius vocatio, which here indeed was not applicable.

In the later Law—although from the time of Marcus

---

1 There must be no summoning to court of magistrates having public authority. . . . Moreover, a bridegroom or bride ought not to be summoned, nor a *iudex* whilst engaged in trying a cause, nor any person so long as he is engaged in proceedings before the Praetor, nor he that conducts the funeral of one of his family.

2 The Praetor says: 'Let no one without my permission summon a parent, a patron or patroness, the children or parents of a patron or patroness.'

3 Very many have been of opinion that it is unlawful to summon a man from his own house.—But if he afford access to his person, or be seen in public, Julian says it is lawful for him to be summoned.

Book IV. Chapter II.

Aurelius, but this is very doubtful—the general formality for commencing the suit was the litis denuntiatio (in the beginning by private testatio, from the time of Constantine by declaration upon record in the presence of a magistrate), the place of which finally, in the Law of Justinian, was taken by the delivery of a bill of complaint (libellus conventionis) before the competent judge, to ground issue of a summons against the defendant.

If the in ius vocatio or summons 'vadimonium promittere' was impossible because of an obstacle affecting the opponent personally, or if he, notwithstanding the giving of vadimonium, did not appear in iure (vadimonium desertum), he was accounted 'indefensus,' and according to the Praetorian Edict, execution attached against his property (missio in possessionem, and further, according to circumstances, bonorum venditio).[a]

[a] Cf. § 204.

Cic. p. Quinctio 19, 60: Edictum: QVI FRAVDATIONIS CAVSA LATITARIT.—CVI HERES NON EXTABIT.—QVI EXILII CAVSA SOLVM VERTERIT.—QVI ABSENS IVDICIO DEFENSVS NON FVERIT.[1]

Praetor ait: QVI FRAVDATIONIS CAVSA LATITABIT, SI BONI VIRI ARBITRATV NON DEFENDETVR, EIVS BONA POSSIDERI VENDIQVE IVBEBO.—D. 42, 4, 7, 1.[2]

Ulp.: Praetor ait: IN BONA EIVS, QVI IVDICIO SISTENDI CAVSA FIDEIVSSOREM DEDERIT, SI NEQVE POTESTATEM SVI FACIET NEQVE DEFENDETVR, IRI IVBEBO.—Quid si non latitet, sed absens non

---

1 The Edict (runs): 'He that with fraudulent intent shall have absconded.'—'He that shall be without an heir.'—'He that shall have quitted the country by reason of exile.'—'He that by failing to appear before the *iudex* shall be unrepresented.'

2 The Praetor says: 'If a man shall keep out of the way with fraudulent intent, and in the opinion of an honourable man be not represented, I will order possession and sale of his goods.'

defendatur? Nonne videtur potestatem sui non facere?—l. 2 pr., § 2 eod.[1]

Paul.: Cum dicitur: ET EIVS, CVIVS BONA POSSESSA SVNT A CREDITORIBVS, VENEANT, PRAETERQVAM PVPILLI ET EIVS, QVI REI PVBLICAE CAVSA SINE DOLO MALO ABFVIT, intelligimus eius qui dolo malo abfuerit posse venire. § Si ab hostibus quis captus sit, creditores eius in possessionem mittendi sunt, ut tamen non statim bonorum venditio permittatur, sed interim bonis curator detur.—l. 6, §§ 1, 2 eod.[2]

Ulp.: Haec autem locum habent, quotiens pupillus non defendatur a quocumque, sive habeat tutorem pupillus sive non habeat.—l. 5 pr. eod.[3]

If the formal opening of the suit could not take place already upon the first appearance in iure, or if the proceedings by way of instructions could not be finished (*e.g.*, because of insufficient legitimation of the parties, or because the defendant refused immediate confession upon justifiable grounds), so as to avoid a repeated in ius vocatio, already according to the Twelve Tables, but further developed by the Praetorian Edict, the duty devolved upon the defendant, as ordered by the magistrate, to give vadimonium (limited to a

[1] The Praetor says: 'I will order seizure of the goods of him that shall have given security for his appearance before the court, if he shall neither himself appear nor be represented.' What if he do not keep out of the way, but is not represented in his absence? Does he not also seem not to be available?

[2] When it is said, 'And let them sell such person's goods of which the creditors have taken possession, except such as belong to a ward or a person who without bad intention was absent on state affairs,' the meaning is, that the property of one who shall be absent with evil intention can be sold. § If a man has been captured by the enemy, his creditors must be put in possession, but so that the sale of the property must not be allowed immediately, but a curator be appointed over it for the meantime.

[3] Now these rules apply whenever a ward is not represented by some one or other, whether he have a guardian or not.

Book IV. Chapter II.

maximum) for his reappearance upon the subsequent day appointed.[a]

[a] Gai. iii. 224.

Gai. iv. §§ 184–6: Cum in ius vocatus fuerit adversarius neque eo die finiri potuerit negotium, vadimonium ei faciendum est, i.e. ut promittat se certo die sisti. § Fiunt autem vadimonia quibusdam ex causis **pura**, i.e. sine satisdatione, quibusdam **cum satisdatione,** quibusdam iureiurando, quibusdam recuperatoribus suppositis, i.e. ut qui non steterit is protinus a recuperatoribus in summam vadimonii condemnetur: eaque singula diligenter praetoris edicto significantur. § Et siquidem iudicati depensive agetur, tanti fiet vadimonium, quanti ea res erit, si vero ex ceteris causis, quanti actor iuraverit non calumniae causa postulare sibi vadimonium promitti: nec tamen pluris quam partis dimidiae, nec pluribus quam sestertium C milibus fit vadimonium.[1]

COURSE AND FORMS OF PROCEEDINGS *IN IURE.*

§ 192. THE *LEGIS ACTIONES.*

In the most ancient time the parties had in iure to summarise their legal claims in definite formulae—'legis actiones'—that were legally established and in

[1] When the defendant has been summoned into court, and the matter cannot be concluded on that day, security must be given by him, that is, he must undertake to appear on a certain day. § Now in some cases the *vadimonia* are simple, that is, without sureties, in some they are with sureties, in some an oath is taken, in some *recuperatores* are introduced, *i.e.*, that a man failing to appear will be summarily condemned by the *recuperatores* in the amount of his security; and each of these matters is carefully explained in the Praetor's Edict. § And if the action be upon a judgment, or for money paid by a guarantor, the amount of security will be that sued for; but if upon other grounds, the security will be for such amount as the plaintiff shall swear that he does not demand vexatiously as a promise of security to himself, but its amount cannot be fixed higher than half that sued for, or than 100,000 sesterces.

exact conformity with the tenor of the laws,[a] and consisted of a solemn address and reply, accompanied by corresponding ritual and symbolic acts.

[a] § 7.

> Gai. iv. § 11: Actiones, quas in usu veteres habuerunt, legis actiones appellabantur, vel ideo quod legibus proditae erant, . . . vel ideo quia ipsarum legum verbis accommodatae erant et ideo immutabiles proinde atque leges observabantur: unde eum, qui de vitibus succisis ita egisset, ut in actione vites nominaret, responsum est rem perdidisse, quia debuisset arbores nominare, eo quod lex XII tabularum, ex qua de vitibus succisis actio competeret, generaliter de arboribus succisis loqueretur.[1]

The parties, with the assistance of the Praetor, had to maintain the suit in their own person; representation was as a rule inadmissible.

> Ulp.: Nemo alieno nomine lege agere potest (D. 50, 17, 123 pr.). —nisi pro populo, pro libertate, pro tutela (Inst. iv. 10 pr.).[2]

There were five of these legis actiones.

(1) The legis actio *sacramento*, the ordinary and regular form of proceedings, the drift of which was that each party called upon the other to appoint a wagering[b] and penal sum in the event of the contention in Law which they had set up being

[b] It is questionable whether it was upon oath.

---

[1] The actions which the ancients were accustomed to use were called *legis actiones*, either from the fact that they were created by *leges*, for at that time the Praetor's Edicts, whereby very many actions have been introduced, were not yet put forth; or because they were adapted to the words of the *leges* themselves, and so were regarded as unchangeable as *leges*. Hence, when a person who had taken proceedings for vines cut down used the word 'vines,' the opinion was given that he had lost the case, because he ought to have used the word 'trees,' inasmuch as the law of the Twelve Tables, on which lay the action for vines cut down, spoke in general terms of 'trees.'

[2] No one can proceed by *legis actio* in the name of another—save on behalf of the People, of freedom, of guardianship.

Book IV. Chapter II.

unjustified, and upon which a decision was then taken in iudicio (at the same time, accordingly, indirectly upon the claim in dispute)—'utrius sacramentum iustum, utrius iniustum.' In the legis actio in rem with vindicatio and contravindicatio (manum conserere)—as especially in proprietary litigation [a]—each party was at the same time plaintiff and defendant, and when maintaining his right, had to adduce proof thereof.[b] The possession for the time being was here adjudged by the magistrate to one party (vindicias dicere) in consideration of his giving cautio for the eventual delivery up of the thing cum omni causa (praedes litis et vindiciarum); in proceedings for freedom,[c] the vindiciae were always given secundum libertatem.[d]

[a] § 90.

[b] Which may perhaps be called the twofold aspect of the proceedings.

[c] § 40.

[d] Comp. also §§ 27, 37; Gai. i. 134; and § 79.

Gai. iv. §§ 13–4: **Sacramenti** actio generalis erat: de quibus enim rebus ut aliter ageretur, lege cautum non erat, de his sacramento agebatur; eaque actio . . . periculosa erat . . . , nam qui victus erat, summam sacramenti praestabat poenae nomine, eaque in publicum cedebat **praedesque** eo nomine praetori dabantur. . . . § Poena autem sacramenti aut quingenaria erat aut quinquagenaria: nam de rebus mille aeris plurisve quingentis assibus, de minoris vero quinquaginta assibus sacramento contendebatur; nam ita lege XII tabularum cautum erat. At si de libertate hominis controversia erat, . . . ut quinquaginta assibus contenderetur eadem lege cautum est, favore scilicet libertatis, ne onerarentur adsertores.[1]

[1] The sacramental action was the general one; for in cases where there was no provision made in any *lex* for proceeding in another way, the form was by *sacramentum;* and this action was risky . . . for he that was defeated forfeited the amount of the deposit by way of penalty, another went to the Treasury, and sureties were given in that behalf to the Praetor. . . . § Now the sacramental penalty was either five hundred or fifty (*asses*). For when the suit was for things of the value of a thousand *asses* or more, the deposit would be five hundred, but when for less, it would be fifty; for thus it was provided by a

Probus de notis iur. § 4: AIO TE MIHI DARE OPORTERE.—QVANDO NEGAS, TE SACRAMENTO QVINGENARIO PROVOCO.[1]

Gai. iv. § 16: Si in rem agebatur, mobilia quidem et moventia, quae modo in ius adferri adducive possent, in iure vindicabantur in hunc modum. Qui vindicabat festucam tenebat; deinde ipsam rem adprehendebat, veluti hominem, et ita dicebat: HVNC EGO HOMINEM EX IVRE QVIRITIVM MEVM ESSE AIO: SECVNDVM SVAM CAVSAM SICVT DIXI, ECCE TIBI, VINDICTAM IMPOSVI, et simul homini festucam imponebat. Adversarius eadem similiter dicebat et faciebat. Cum uterque vindicasset, praetor dicebat: MITTITE AMBO HOMINEM. Illi mittebant. Qui prior vindicaverat, ita adversarium interrogabat: POSTVLO ANNE DICAS QVA EX CAVSA VINDICAVERIS? Ille respondebat: IVS FECI SICVT VINDICTAM IMPOSVI. Deinde qui prior vindicaverat, dicebat: QVANDO TV INIVRIA VINDICAVISTI, D AERIS SACRAMENTO TE PROVOCO; adversarius quoque dicebat: SIMILITER ET EGO TE. . . . Postea praetor secundum alterum eorum **vindicias dicebat,** id est interim aliquem possessorem constituebat eumque iubebat **praedes** adversario dare **litis et vindiciarum,** is est rei et fructuum. . . . Festuca autem utebantur quasi hastae loco, signo quodam iusti dominii, quod maxime sua esse credebant, quae ex hostibus cepissent; unde in centumviralibus iudiciis hasta praeponitur.[2]

---

law of the Twelve Tables. But if the suit related to the liberty of a slave . . . it was provided that the suit should be carried on with a deposit of fifty *asses*, with the view of course of favouring liberty, that the defenders of liberty should not be burdened.

[1] 'I affirm that you ought to give it to me. Since you deny this, I sue you with a deposit of five hundred (*asses*).'

[2] If the proceedings were *in rem*, movable and self-moving things that could be carried or brought into court were claimed in the following way. The claimant held a rod in his hand; then he laid hold of the actual thing, a slave for example, and

Book IV.
Chapter II.

Ib. § 17: Si qua res talis erat, ut sine incommodo non posset in ius adferri vel adduci, veluti si columna aut grex alicuius pecoris esset, pars aliqua inde sumebatur, deinde in eam partem quasi in totam rem praesentem fiebat vindicatio; . . . similiter si de fundo vel de aedificio controversia erat, pars aliqua inde sumebatur, . . . veluti ex fundo gleba et ex aedibus tegula.[1]

(2) The legis actio per *manus iniectionem* was a strictly executive action, in its final result originally introducing the destruction of the caput; in which the debtor could not conduct the proceedings in his own person, but he required a *Vindex* to undertake such proceedings for him, at the risk of condem-

spoke as follows: 'I affirm that this slave is mine by Quiritarian Law, according to the title I have declared. Behold, I have laid my rod upon him'; and at the same time he laid the rod on the slave. His opponent then spoke and acted in like manner; and when each had made his claim, the Praetor said: 'Let go the slave, both of you.' They did so. The first claimant said: 'I ask you whether you will state the ground of your claim.' To that the other replied: 'I exercised my right when I touched him with my rod.' Then the first claimant said: 'Since you have made a wrongful claim, I challenge you in a deposit of five hundred *asses*.' His opponent also said likewise: 'I challenge you.' Next the Praetor used to assign the *vindiciae* to one or other of the parties, that is, he gave interim possession of the thing sued for to one of them, and ordered him at the same time to provide his adversary with sureties *litis et vindiciarum*, *i.e.*, of the thing and its profits. . . . Now they made use of a rod instead of the spear, which was the symbol of lawful ownership, for men considered those above all things to be their own which they had taken from the enemy; and this is the reason why a spear is set up in front of the Centumviral Courts.

[1] When anything was of such a nature that it could not without inconvenience be carried or brought into court, for example, if it were a pillar, or a herd of cattle of some sort, some portion of it was taken, and the claim was made upon that portion, as though the whole thing were there. . . . Similarly, if the dispute was about a field, or a building, some part was taken from it, . . . for example, a clod was taken from the field, and a tile from the house.

nation in double the amount, in order to escape the addictio and being carried away into servitude for debt. Originally introduced against the iudicatus, confessus[a] and nexus,[b] it was also in the fifth century transferred to other liquidated claims, but at the same period its stringency was relaxed. (Manus iniectio 'pro iudicato'—'pura.'[c])

[a] § 27.

[b] § 116.

[c] Cf. Gai. iii. 127; §§ 133 182, 204.

Gai. iv. §§ 21–5: Per **manus iniectionem** de his rebus agebatur, de quibus ut ita ageretur, lege aliqua cautum est, velut iudicati lege XII tabularum; quae actio talis erat: qui agebat, sic dicebat: QVOD TV MIHI IVDICATVS (sive DAMNATVS) ES SESTERTIVM X MILIA, QVANDO NON SOLVISTI, OB EAM REM EGO TIBI SESTERTIVM X MILIVM IVDICATI MANVM INICIO, et simul aliquam partem corporis eius prendebat; nec licebat iudicato manum sibi depellere et pro se lege agere, sed vindicem dabat qui pro se causam agere solebat; qui vindicem non dabat, domum ducebatur ab actore et vinciebatur. § Postea quaedam leges ex aliis quibusdam causis pro iudicato manus iniectionem in quosdam dederunt, sicut lex Publilia in eum, pro quo sponsor dependisset, si in sex mensibus proximis, quam pro eo depensum esset, non solvisset sponsori pecuniam; item lex Furia de sponsu adversus eum, qui a sponsore plus quam virilem partem exegisset. . . . § Sed aliae leges in multis causis constituerunt quasdam actiones per manus iniectionem, sed **puram,** i.e. non **pro iudicato,** veluti lex Furia testamentaria. . . . § Ex quibus legibus cum agebatur manum sibi depellere et pro se lege agere reo licebat; nam et actor in ipsa legis actione non adiiciebat hoc verbum PRO IVDICATO, sed nominata causa, ex qua agebat, ita dicebat: OB EAM REM EGO TIBI MANVM INICIO. . . . § Sed postea lege Vallia[d] excepto iudicato et eo pro quo depensum est, ceteris omnibus, cum quibus per manus iniectionem

[d] ? Valeria. But see Muirhead on Gai. iii. 121.

agebatur, permissum est, sibi manum depellere et pro se lege agere.[1]

Gell. xx. 1, §§ 42–49: Confessi aeris ac debiti iudicatis triginta dies sunt dati conquirendae pecuniae causa . . . eosque dies decemviri iustos appellaverunt, velut quoddam iustitium, i.e. iuris inter eos quasi interstitionem quandam et cessationem, quibus diebus nihil cum his agi iure posset. Post deinde nisi dissolverent, ad praetorem vocabantur et ab eo quibus erant iudicati addicebantur, nervo quoque et compedibus vincie-

[1] Similarly an action by way of arrest lay for those cases in respect of which this remedy was provided by any *lex*, as in the case of an action upon a judgment resulting from the Law of the Twelve Tables, and that action was of the following nature. The party suing spoke as follows: 'Whereas you have been adjudicated (or condemned) to pay me 10,000 sesterces, and seeing that you have made default in payment, I therefore lay hands upon you for the judgment-debt of 10,000 sesterces,' and at the same time he laid hold of some part of his body. The person against whom judgment had been given was not allowed to remove the hand and act for himself in the suit, but he furnished a protector, who, as the custom was, conducted the case for him. He that did not furnish a protector was led away by the plaintiff to his house and put in chains. § Afterwards certain *leges* allowed the action *per manus iniectionem* upon a judgment against some specified persons under other particular circumstances; for example, the *l. Publilia*, against him for whom a surety had paid money, if he had not repaid it to the surety within six months next after it was paid on his behalf; so, again, the *l. Furia de sponsu* against him who had exacted from a surety more than his proportion. . . . § But other *leges* in many cases established actions *per man. iniect.*, but *pura* (simple), *i.e.*, not 'as upon a judgment'; for example the *l. Furia testamentaria*. . . . § When an action was brought upon these and other similar *leges*, the defendant was at liberty to remove the hand of the plaintiff, and conduct the action for himself; for the plaintiff did not in the *legis actio* add the phrase 'pro iudicato,' but stating the case, went on thus: 'On that account I lay my hand on you.' . . . § But afterwards leave was given by the *l. Vallia* to all other persons, save a judgment-debtor and him for whom money had been paid when sued *per man. iniect.*, to remove the hand and conduct the action for themselves.

bantur.—Sic enim sunt, opinor, verba legis[a]: AERIS CONFESSI REBVSQVE[b] IVRE IVDICATIS TRIGINTA DIES IVSTI SVNTO. POST DEINDE MANVS INIECTIO ESTO: IN IVS DVCITO. NI IVDICATVM FACIT AVT QVIS ENDO EO IN IVRE VINDICIT, SECVM DVCITO.—Erat autem ius interea paciscendi ac nisi pacti forent habebantur in vinculis dies sexaginta. Inter eos dies trinis nundinis continuis ad praetorem in comitium producebantur, quantaeque pecuniae iudicati essent, praedicabatur. Tertiis autem nundinis capite poenas dabant aut trans Tiberim peregre venum ibant.—Si plures forent, quibus reus esset iudicatus, secare, si vellent, atque partiri corpus addicti sibi hominis permiserunt. Et quidem verba ipsa legis dicam: TERTIIS NVNDINIS PARTIS SECANTO; SI PLVS MINVSVE SECVERVNT, SE FRAVDE ESTO.[1]

[a] Sc. XII tabularum.

[b] AERISQVE

[1] Parties against whom judgment was given for an admitted debt were granted thirty days for the purpose of raising the money . . . and those days were by the decemvirs called 'lawful,' as a sort of *iustitium*, *i.e.*, a certain interval and cessation of law between them, so to speak, during which days no proceedings could be taken against them. After that, if payment were not made, the debtors were summoned before the Praetor and by him delivered to those to whom they had been adjudged, and were bound in stocks and fetters. The words of the *lex* [*i.e.*, of the Twelve Tables] are, 'Thirty days shall be the lawful limit of an acknowledged debt, and for matters decided in court in respect of an admitted debt. After that, let his person be seized, let him be brought before the magistrate. Unless he satisfy the judgment-debt, or some one appears in court on his behalf as *vindex*, let the creditor take him home.' —But there was power in the meantime to compromise the matter; and unless such compromise were made by them, the debtors were held in chains for sixty days. During such period, upon every third consecutive market-day, they were exhibited before the Praetor in the *comitium*, and proclamation was made of the amount of the judgment-debt against them. On the third market-day they were put to death, or sold into slavery beyond the Tiber. If there were several persons to whom the defendant was adjudged, they were allowed, if they chose, to cut and divide the body of the man adjudged to them. Indeed I will mention the very words of the lex: 'Let them on

BOOK IV. Chapter II.

[a] Cf. 'Early History of Institutions,' pp. 258, *sqq.*

(3) The anomalous legis actio per *pignoris capionem*[a] was a solemn private distraint introduced for certain claims privileged because of their sacral or public nature, upon the further course of which we possess no information.

Gai. iv. §§ 26–9: Per **pignoris capionem** lege agebatur de quibusdam rebus moribus, de quibusdam lege. § Introducta est **moribus** rei militaris: nam et propter stipendium licebat militi ab eo qui id distribuebat, nisi daret, pignus capere (dicebatur autem ea pecunia . . . **aes militare**); item propter eam pecuniam licebat pignus capere, ex qua equus emendus erat, quae pecunia dicebatur **aes equestre**; item propter eam pecuniam, ex qua hordeum equis erit comparandum, quae pecunia dicebatur **aes hordiarium.** § **Lege** autem introducta est pignoris capio veluti lege XII tabularum adversus eum qui hostiam emisset nec pretium redderet, . . . item lege censoria data est pignoris capio publicanis vectigalium publicorum populi Romani adversus eos, qui aliqua lege vectigalia deberent. § Ex omnibus autem istis causis certis verbis pignus capiebatur et ob id plerisque placebat, hanc quoque actionem legis actionem esse; quibusdam autem placebat legis actionem non esse, primum quod pignoris capio extra ius peragebatur, i.e. non apud praetorem, plerumque etiam absente adversario, cum alioquin ceteris actionibus non aliter uti possent, quam apud praetorem praesente adversario, praeterea quod nefasto quoque die, i.e. quo non licebat lege agere, pignus capi poterat.[1]

---

the third market-day divide their shares; if they have cut too much or too little, it shall not[b] prejudice them.'

[b] Se = sine.

[1] The *legis actio* by *pignoris capio* (distress) originated from custom in respect of some matters, from statute in respect of others. § That which dealt with matters affecting the army was brought in by custom. For a soldier was allowed to distrain upon the paymaster in respect of his pay. (Such money

(4) The legis actio per *iudicis arbitrive postulationem*, which is scarcely known more than by name, it is supposed, was intended for such matters as, according to their nature, required a more independent position and a more arbitrary opinion in the judge, as especially matters of partition (*e.g.*, arbitrium familiae erciscundae, actio aquae pluviae arcendae,—actio rei uxoriae).[a]

(5) The legis actio per *condictionem* was a new and more simple form of procedure which took the place of the unwieldy sacramenti actio, for strictly unilateral claims relating to a 'certum,' and introduced the transition to proceedings 'per formulas.' It consisted in a summons to the defendant, which probably connected itself with the claim and denial of debt in iure—unless the plaintiff preferred to tender an oath to the defendant upon the debt;[b] this was, to appear again on the thirtieth day for the appointment of a iudicium, to which, it is supposed, attached a penal[c] 'sponsio et restipulatio tertiae partis' of the sum in dispute.[d]

[a] The *a. r. u.* is questionable.

[b] § 27.

[c] Whether one in pecuniary claims was at the same time pre-judicial is very doubtful.

[d] Cf. § 206

---

was called 'aes militare.') So, too, it was lawful for a soldier to distrain for payment of the sum required for the purchase of a horse; and this money was called 'aes equestre.' So again, he could take a pledge for the money to be provided for the purchase of forage for his horse, and this was called 'aes hordiarium.' § *Pignoris capio* was introduced by statute; as for instance, by a law of the Twelve Tables, against a man who bought a victim for sacrifice and failed to pay the price. So also a *pign. cap.* was given by a *lex censoria* to farmers of the public revenues of the Roman people against those who were liable for taxes under any statute. § In all these cases the pledge was seized with a set form of words; and hence a majority held that this was a *leg. act.* too; but some thought that it should not be so regarded: first, because the *pign. cap.* took place out of court, *i.e.*, not before the Praetor, and besides generally in the absence of the opponent, whereas the plaintiff could not put actions of the law in operation except before the Praetor and in the presence of his opponent; and further, because the pledge might be seized even on a *dies nefastus*, that is, on a day when it is not lawful to proceed by an action at law.

Book IV. Chapter II.

Gai. iv. §§ 18–19: —**condicere** autem denuntiare est prisca lingua. Itaque haec quidem actio proprie **condictio** vocabatur: nam actor adversario denuntiabat, ut ad iudicem capiendum die trigesimo adesset. . . . § Haec autem legis actio constituta est per legem Siliam et Calpurniam, lege quidem Silia certae pecuniae, lege vero Calpurnia de omni certa re.[1]

PROCEEDINGS *PER FORMULAS.*

§ 193. In General.

At a later period, as its solemnities were given up, the place of procedure by legis actio was by gradual development (lex Aebutia *circ.* 550 U.C., leges Iuliae Augusti) taken by the so-called FORMULARY PROCESS, in which the parties by free discussion laid their claims in iure before the magistrate, and he, accordingly, briefly cast the object of the suit in a formula (concepta verba), that is, a written instruction to the judge to whom the matter was referred for decision, which was furnished with a hypothetical injunction to condemn and absolve. The Praetors accordingly acquired, on the one hand, an influence they had not before had upon the shape of the suit, and the form of the judicial prosecution of the claim in the particular case; on the other, the power to operate upon positive law itself by modification and development, because, in the exercise of their power of jurisdiction, they granted actiones and composed formulae for their enforcement by proceedings, not merely for claims founded iure civili—previously participating in a legis actio—but

[1] Now *condicere* in the ancient language means *denuntiare* (to give notice). This action, therefore, was properly called *condictio;* for the plaintiff warned his opponent to appear on the thirtieth day for the appointment of a *iudex*. . . . § This form of *legis actio* was established by the *leges Sil. et Calp.;* by the *l. Silia* in respect of the recovery of a liquidated sum, by the *l. Calpurnia* in respect of any certain thing.

also for those which, according to later legal opinion, appeared to require legal protection through the absolute power of the magistrate.[a] Thus for most claims the Praetorian jurisdiction developed fixed formulae, which the edict (album praetoris) contains for every one's information in the shape of formularies.

[a] Cf. §§ 7, 24, 200.

> Gai. iv. §§ 30–1: Sed istae omnes legis actiones paulatim in odium venerunt: namque ex nimia subtilitate veterum, qui tunc iura condiderunt, eo res perducta est, ut vel qui minimum errasset, litem perderet; itaque per legem Aebutiam et duas Iulias sublatae sunt istae legis actiones effectumque est, ut per concepta verba, i.e. per formulas litigemus. § Tantum ex duabus causis permissum est lege agere, damni infecti et si **centumvirale iudicium** futurum est.[1]

Independent formulae did not immediately arise for all claims. Thus in the beginning a iudicium for legal claims was besides often brought about by a necessary 'sponsio praeiudicialis,' to be agreed between the parties in iure, under the authority of the Praetor, upon the subject-matter of the claim in question, which then was referred to the judge for decision, by means of formula 'certae pecuniae creditae': as in particular occurred with actiones in rem. Moreover, for a long time proceedings per sponsiones continued to exist for many claims alongside of those per formulas.[b]

[b] Cf. § 201.

[1] But all those *legis actiones* gradually fell into discredit; for through the overdrawn subtlety of the old jurists, who then arranged the law, matters were carried so far, that a suitor who made the slightest mistake lost the cause. And so these *legis actiones* were abolished by the *l. Aebutia* and the two *leges Iuliae*, and the result has been that we now maintain an action by a fixed form of words, that is to say, by *formulae*. § In two cases alone have suitors been allowed to employ a *legis actio*, viz., in respect of *damnum infectum*, and if the case had to come before the Centumviral Court.

Book IV. Chapter II.

Gai. iv. §§ 91, 93-5: . . . in rem actio duplex (est), aut enim per formulam petitoriam agitur, aut per sponsionem. . . . § Per sponsionem hoc modo agimus: provocamus adversarium tali sponsione SI HOMO QVO DE AGITVR EX IVRE QVIRITIVM MEVS EST, SESTERTIOS XXV NVMMOS DARE SPONDES? deinde formulam edimus, qua intendimus sponsionis summam nobis dari oportere; qua formula ita demum vincimus, si probaverimus rem nostram esse. § Non tamen haec summa sponsionis exigitur: non enim poenalis est, sed praeiudicialis et propter hoc solum fit, ut per eam de re iudicetur; unde etiam is cum quo agitur non restipulatur. . . . § Ceterum si apud centumviros agitur, summam sponsionis non per formulam petimus, sed per legis actionem: sacramento enim reum provocamus; eaque sponsio sestertium CXXV nummum fieri solet propter legem Crepereiam (?).[1]

Cic. in Verr. 1, 45, 115: Si quis testamento se heredem esse arbitraretur, lege ageret in hereditatem aut 'pro praede litis vindiciarum' cum satis accepisset, sponsionem faceret et ita de

---

[1] The real action is twofold, for proceedings are taken either by a petitory formula or by a sponsion. . . . § By sponsion we proceed as follows. We challenge our opponent by a sponsion of this sort: 'If the slave in question be mine by Quiritarian Law, do you undertake to give me twenty-five sesterces?' Then we put forth a formula, in the *intentio* of which we state that the amount of this sponsion is due to us; and under this formula we are successful only as we prove that the thing is ours. § The amount of this sponsion, however, is not exacted; for it is not penal, but pre-judicial,[a] and only introduced to obtain thereby a decision as to the property; for which reason also the defendant enters into no counter-stipulation. . . . § But when the action is brought before the centumvirs, we do not sue for the amount of the sponsion by a formula, but by a *legis actio;* for we challenge the defendant by the sacramental wager; and such sponsion is commonly fixed at 125 sesterces, in pursuance of the *l. Crepereia.*

[a] *I.e.*, preliminary: cf. *supra*, p. 208.

hereditate certaret. Hoc iure et maiores nostri et nos semper usi sumus.[1] Book IV. Chapter II.

And further, a formal linking of the formula to the corresponding legis actio by means of a fiction,[a] contained in the formula, of the actual undertaking of such legis actio, seems in the beginning to have obtained for certain claims.

[a] See 'Anct. Law,' pp. 25-26.

Gai. iv. § 10: Quaedam sunt actiones, quae ad legis actionem exprimuntur, quaedam sua vi ac potestate constant.—§ 32: In ea formula, quae publicano proponitur, talis fictio est, ut 'quanta pecunia olim si pignus captum esset, id pignus is a quo captum erat luere deberet,' tantam pecuniam condemnetur.[2]

§ 194. Instructions for the Suit. (Assignment of the Formula.)

The drift of the proceedings before the magistrate is, the assignment of a formula to be moulded by him according to the applications (*postulare*)[b] made by the parties—in person or by their legal assistant (patronus, advocatus)—which the magistrate has considered admissible, and accordingly, the appointment of a 'iudicium' for the actual suit. The setting on foot of the action (actionis editio) is effected by signification of the claim in question, with reference to the actio proposed in the Edict, and the appropriate standing

[b] Cf. § 57, ad fin.

[1] Whosoever considered himself to be heir by a testament should proceed by *legis actio* against the inheritance, or upon having received security *p. p. l. v.*, should enter into a *sponsio*, and so sue for the inheritance. This law has ever been in use by our ancestors and ourselves.

[2] Moreover, there are some actions which are framed by reference to a *legis actio*, whilst others depend upon their own force and power.—§ In that formula which is announced in behalf of a collector of taxes, there is a fiction of this sort, that the defendant shall be condemned in such a sum as, in olden time when a pledge was seized, he from whom the distraint had been made would have had to give by way of ransom.'

formula, perhaps contained in it, to the grant of which action, or filling up of the formula—or even alteration with respect to the concrete circumstances—the plaintiff's application is directed; in return for which the defendant is permitted to move for the rejection of the plaintiff's application, or modification of the formula, by acceptance of the legal elements established by him. By decree of the magistrate—against which an appeal lies—a decision is given upon these applications, as well as upon the allowance, or entire refusal, of the action in general (*dare—denegare* actionem, *e.g.*, in case of defective legitimation of a party, inadmissibility of the action in itself),[a] and the formula as made out is handed to the parties, with which the Litis Contestatio[b] is commenced. The contents of the formula, in its material relation unchangeable, and binding both the parties and the judge, which exactly determines and fixes the disputed relation of the parties in its legally important elements, governs the further judicial investigation and final judgment.

[a] § 198.
[b] § 26.

> Ulp.: [Praetor] tres fecit ordines, nam quosdam in totum prohibuit postulare, quibusdam vel pro se permisit, quibusdam et pro certis dumtaxat personis et pro se permisit.—D. 3, 1, 1, 1.[1]

In order to enable the plaintiff to make good his claim against the person legally liable, and to secure him against the disadvantages of fruitless procedure, or such as imperils his claim against a wrong opponent—not merely for establishment of so-called passive legitimation—in certain cases the Praetor required the defendant to give a definite answer, in agreement with the truth, and formally binding him, to the *interrogatio in iure* which issues against him; that is, whether and how far there exists in his person the relation

[1] [The Praetor] has made three classes; for some he has entirely forbidden to make applications, some he has allowed to do so only for themselves, some to do so both for others, but only certain persons, and for themselves.

presumed by the plaintiff and required for carrying through the action in question. By a declaration in the affirmative sense, the defendant unconditionally undertook the defence to the extent covered by his statement; a traverse of the declaration, and false denial in general of the relation in question, or to the extent actually existing, made him liable to 'defensio in solidum' (Actiones interrogatoriae).[a] [a] § 171.

Callistr.: Totiens heres in iure interrogandus est, . . . quotiens adversus eum actio instituitur et dubitat actor, qua ex parte is, cum quo agere velit, heres sit. Est autem interrogatio tunc necessaria, cum in personam sit actio et ita, si certum petetur, ne dum ignoret actor, qua ex parte adversarius defuncto heres exstiterit, interdum plus petendo aliquid damni sentiat.—D. 11, 1, 1 pr.[1]

Ulp.: Voluit praetor adstringere eum qui convenitur ex sua in iudicio responsione, ut vel confitendo vel mentiendo sese oneret.—l. 4 pr. eod.[2]

Gai.: Qui interrogatur, an heres vel quota ex parte sit, vel an in potestate habeat eum, cuius nomine noxali iudicio agitur, ad deliberandum tempus impetrare debet.—l. 5 eod.[3]

Paul.: Si quis interrogatus de servo qui damnum dedit, respondit suum esse servum,

---

[1] The heir must always be interrogated before the Court when an action is being brought against him and the plaintiff is uncertain for what portion the person is heir whom he desires to sue. Now the interrogatory is necessary when the action is a personal one, and that if the subject of the action is definite, lest the plaintiff, whilst not knowing for what share his opponent has become heir to the deceased, sometimes should experience loss by claiming too much.

[2] The Praetor aimed at binding the person sued by his answer before the tribunal, so that he might be weighted with his admission or his denial.

[3] He that is asked whether he is heir, or for what part, or whether he has the person under his power on account of whom he is sued in a noxal action, ought to demand time for deliberation.

Book IV.
Chapter II.

tenebitur lege Aquilia quasi dominus.—l. 8 eod.[1]

Ulp.: Si quis, cum heres non esset, responderit ex parte heredem esse, sic convenietur, atque si ex ea parte heres esset: fides enim ei contra se habebitur.—l. 11, § 1 eod.[2]

Si, cum esset quis ex semisse heres, dixerit se ex quadrante, mendacii hanc poenam feret, quod in solidum convenitur.—Qui tacuit quoque apud praetorem, in ea causa est, ut instituta actione in solidum conveniatur, quasi negaverit se heredem esse: nam qui omnino non respondit, contumax est.—Ibid. §§ 3, 4.[3]

Paul.: Si negavit dominus in sua potestate esse servum, permittit praetor actori arbitrium, utrum iureiurando id decidere an iudicium dictare sine noxae deditione velit, per quod vincet, si probaverit eum in potestate esse vel dolo eius factum, quo minus esset.—D. 9, 4, 22, 4.[4]

Ulp.: 'In potestate' sic accipere debemus, ut facultatem et potestatem exhibendi eius habeat: ceterum si in fuga sit vel peregre, non videbitur esse in potestate.—l. 21, § 3 eod.[5]

---

[1] If a man, when asked concerning a slave who has inflicted damage, answers that he is his slave, he will be liable by the *l. Aquilia*, as if he were the master.

[2] If any one, without being heir, shall answer that he is part heir, he will be sued in such way as if he were actually heir for a part; for credit will be given against himself.

[3] If, when a man was heir for a half, he said he was heir for a fourth, he will suffer punishment for his falsehood, by being sued for the whole.—He that has maintained silence also before the Praetor is in this position, that by an action brought he is sued for the whole, as if he denied that he was heir; for a person that makes no answer commits contempt of court.

[4] If the master has denied that a slave is under his power, the Praetor affords the plaintiff choice whether he will make the decision rest upon oath, or bring an action without noxal surrender, by means of which he will succeed if he shall prove that such slave is under the defendant's power, or that it is by a fraudulent act of his that he is not.

[5] We must understand 'under power' thus: that the

The defendant who without cause refuses to be subjected to the action, or does not to the full extent comply with the duty of defence which devolves upon him—including the cautiones[a] or sponsiones[b] he has to give—is treated as a *confessus*,[c] like the 'iudicatus.'[d]

[a] § 195.
[b] § 193.
[c] § 27.
[d] Cf. Ulp inst. fgm. iv. (vi.); D. 6, 1, l. ult. § 113.

> Ulp.: Non defendere videtur . . . et is qui praesens negat se defendere, aut non vult suscipere actionem.—D. 50, 17, 52.[1]
>
> Lex Rubria, cap. 21: A QVOQVOMQVE PECVNIA CERTA CREDITA [A QVO QVID PRAETER PECUNIAM CERTAM CREDITAM. Cap. 22] . . . PETETUR, SEI IS EAM PECVNIAM IN IVRE . . . CONFESSVS ERIT, . . . SEIVE IS IBEI DE EA RE IN IVRE NON RESPONDERIT NEQVE DE EA RE SPONSIONEM FACIET NEQVE IVDICIO VTEI OPORTEBIT SE DEFENDET: TVM SIREMPS RES LEX IVS ESTO, ATQVE . . . SEI IS . . . IVRE LEGE DAMNATVS ESSET.[2]

§ 195. *Cautiones* in Procedure.

For the guarantee of the possibly successful plaintiff, the defendant can be obliged in iure forthwith to give cautio to the former by way of security in the event of his condemnation—'stipulatio (satisdatio) *iudicatum solvi*.'[e]

[e] Cf. Paterson, s. 1140.

This duty of cautio devolves upon the defendant—as the possessor—as a rule in the case of, in rem,

---

defendant has the capacity and power to produce him; but if he is a fugitive or abroad, he will not be regarded as under power.

[1] He too is considered to have no defence who is present and declines to defend the action, or does not care to expose himself to it.

[2] 'Whosoever shall be sued for a fixed sum of money owing [by whom aught save a fixed etc.] . . . if he shall confess such amount in court . . . or if he shall not make answer there in court concerning such matter, and shall enter into no engagement as to such matter, nor make a defence before the *iudex* in manner required, then precisely shall the proceeding be binding as statute or law, . . . as if he . . . had been condemned by law or statute.'

BOOK IV. Chapter II.

actiones, especially the 'rei vindicatio' and the 'hereditatis petitio.'[a]

[a] Gai. iv. 16; Cic. in Verr. i. 45, 115; Ulp. inst. fgm. iv. (vi.); D. 6, 1, l. ult.

Ulp.: **Iudicatum solvi** stipulatio tres clausulas in unum collatas habet: de re iudicata, de re defendenda, de dolo malo.—D. 46, 7, 6.[1]

Gai. iv. § 89: Si in rem tecum agam, satis mihi dare debes: aequum enim visum est te ideo quod interea tibi rem, quae an ad te pertineat dubium est, possidere conceditur, cum satisdatione mihi cavere, ut si victus sis nec rem ipsam restituas nec litis aestimationem sufferas, sit mihi potestas aut tecum agendi aut cum sponsoribus tuis. § 91: Ceterum . . . si quidem per formulam petitoriam agitur, illa stipulatio locum habet quae appellatur 'iudicatum solvi,' si vero per sponsionem, illa quae appellatur 'pro praede litis et vindiciarum.'[2]

Paul. i. 11, § 1: Quotiens hereditas petitur . . . si satis non detur, in petitorem hereditas transfertur; si petitor satisdare noluerit, penes possessorem possessio remanebit: in pari enim causa potior est possessor.[3]

---

[1] The stipulation that the judgment shall be satisfied has three clauses united in one; concerning the judgment given, concerning defence of the matter, concerning fraudulent conduct.[b]

[b] See Hunter, p. 1026.

[2] If I sue you by an action *in rem*, you must give me security. For it has seemed fair that you should find me security in respect of such thing as you are allowed to have possession of meanwhile, your ownership of which is doubtful, so that if you are defeated, and neither restore the property itself nor pay the assessed damages, I may have power to sue either you or your sureties. § But if proceedings be taken by means of a petitory formula, that stipulation called 'iudicatum solvi' is employed; but if by means of sponsion, that stipulation called 'pro praede litis et vindiciarum.'

[3] Whenever claim is made to a heritage, . . . if security be not given, the heritage is made over to the claimant; if the claimant refuse to give security, possession will remain with the occupier, for in parity of circumstances the occupier is preferable.

It is the same in respect of actiones 'in personam' in certain cases only and upon special grounds. Book IV. Chapter II.

Gai. iv. § 102: Quodsi proprio nomine aliquis iudicium accipiat in personam, certis ex causis satisdare solet, quas ipse praetor significat; quarum satisdationum duplex causa est, nam aut propter genus actionis satisdatur, aut propter personam, quia suspecta est: propter **genus actionis**, velut iudicati depensive . . . ; propter **personam**, veluti si cum eo agitur qui decoxerit cuiusve bona a creditoribus possessa proscriptave sunt, sive cum eo herede agatur quem praetor suspectum aestimaverit.[1]

§ 196. Representation.

Representation in the formulary procedure is admissible to the widest extent.[a] The representative, who judicially enforces the claim of another—whether upon another's or his own account (procurator in rem suam)[b] —or defends the claim that is raised against a third party, becomes by the Litis Contestatio himself party to the proceedings.[c]

[a] Cf. I. 4, 10 pr.

[b] Cf. § 144.

[c] Upon the expression of representation in the formula, see § 200.

Gai. iv. § 82: Nunc admonendi sumus agere nos aut nostro nomine aut alieno, veluti cognitorio procuratorio tutorio curatorio.[2]

Mac.: —procurator lite contestata **dominus litis** efficitur (D. 49, 1, 4, 5). —litis contestatione res

[1] But if any one be defendant on his own account in a personal action, it is usual to give security in certain cases indicated by the Praetor himself. There are two reasons for giving security; for it is either given on account of the nature of the suit, as in that upon a judgment, or for money paid by a surety . . . on account of the person, as when the defendant has incurred fraudulent bankruptcy, or possession of his goods has been taken, or they have been advertised for sale by his creditors, or when the proceedings are against an heir whose conduct the Praetor has deemed suspicious.

[2] It is to be observed that we sue either in our own or another's name, as that of a *cognitor*, *procurator*, *tutor*, *curator*.

procuratoris fit eamque suo iam quodammodo nomine exsequitur.—D. 44, 4, 11 pr.[1]

In the classical Law two kinds of representatives in procedure continue to be distinguished.

(1) The 'Cognitor,' formally appointed in iure, is the authorised representative of the plaintiff in his original character.

Gai. iv. § 83: **Cognitor** certis verbis in litem coram adversario substituitur, nam actor ita cognitorem dat: QVOD EGO A TE verbi gratia FVNDVM PETO, IN EAM REM LVCIVM TITIVM TIBI COGNITOREM DO; adversarius ita: QVOD TV A ME FVNDVM PETIS, IN EAM REM TIBI PVBLIVM MAEVIVM COGNITOREM DO. Potest, ut actor ita dicat: QVOD EGO TECVM AGERE VOLO, IN EAM REM COGNITOREM DO; adversarius ita: QVOD TV MECVM AGERE VIS, IN EAM REM COGNITOREM DO. Nec interest praesens, an absens cognitor detur; sed si absens datus fuerit, cognitor ita erit, si cognoverit et susceperit officium cognitoris.[2]

(2) The 'Procurator'—at first indeed as 'pro-

---

[1] A *procurator* (attorney) is rendered master of the suit upon joinder of issue.—By commencement of the suit, the matter vests in the *procurator*, and he carries it on as it were in his own name.

[2] A *cognitor* is by certain words substituted for oneself in a cause, and in the opponent's presence. For the way in which the plaintiff appoints a *cognitor* is as follows: 'Whereas I am suing you for land,' for example, 'I appoint Luc. Tit. to be my *cognitor* against you for such matter.' The opponent appoints thus: 'Whereas you are suing me for the land, I appoint Publ. Maevius as my *cognitor* for such matter.' The plaintiff may say as follows: 'Whereas I am desirous of bringing an action against you, I appoint a *cognitor* for such matter'; and the defendant may say: 'Whereas you desire to bring an action against me, I appoint a *cognitor* for such matter.' The presence or absence of the *cognitor* at the time of his appointment is of no importance; but if he be absent at the time of his appointment, he will become *cognitor* only upon notice of the duty and acceptance thereof.

curator omnium rerum,' then also as 'procurator litis'—who was informally charged with the conduct of the proceedings, which (especially for the absent defendant) he could undertake even without a commission, but was always, in case of proceedings being brought, liable to defend the represented party even in opposition to claims enforced against him.[a]

[a] Cf. § 50, ad fin.

Ibid. § 84: **Procurator** vero nullis certis verbis in litem substituetur, sed ex solo mandato et absente et ignorante adversario constituitur: quin etiam sunt, qui putant eum quoque procuratorem videri, cui non sit mandatum, si modo bona fide accedat ad negotium et caveat, ratam rem dominum habiturum.[1]

Ulp.: —personae . . . quibus sine mandatu agere licet: ut puta liberi (licet sint in potestate), item parentes et fratres et adfines et liberti.—D. 3, 3, 35 pr.[2]

Ait praetor: CVIVS NOMINE QVIS ACTIONEM DARI SIBI POSTVLABIT, IS EVM VIRI BONI ARBITRATV DEFENDAT.—l. 33, § 3 eod.[3]

Vat. fgm. 330: Papinianus respondit, si procurator absentis aliquam actionem absentis nomine inferre velit, cogendum eum adversus omnes absentem defendere.[4]

---

[1] But a *procurator* is substituted in view of the action by no special form of words, but by mere commission, even in the absence or without the privity of the opponent. Nay more, some hold that if he have received no commission a person may still be considered a *procurator*, provided only he enter upon the business in good faith, and give security that transactions shall be ratified by his principal.

[2] —persons . . . who are allowed to sue without a commission; for example, children (although they are under power), parents too, and brothers, connections and freedmen.

[3] The Praetor says: 'In whosesoever name a man shall apply for an action to be given to him, he shall protect such person in conformity with the judgment of an honourable man.'

[4] Pap. gives as his opinion, that if the attorney of an absent party desire to bring any action in the name of such absent

Book IV. Chapter II.

(3) The late classical 'Procurator praesentis' and 'apud acta factus' was in many respects on the same footing as the Cognitor.

In respect of the processual effect of representation, and the cautionary obligation connected with it, the following distinctions have to be made.

If representation occurs on the part of the defendant (defensio), there is always need of the 'cautio iudicatum solvi,' since the plaintiff loses his claim against the original opponent in consequence of consumption of the proceedings.[a]

[a] § 26.

Pomp.: Solutione vel iudicium pro nobis accipiendo et inviti et ignorantes liberari possumus. —D. 46, 3, 23.[1]

Ulp.: —adversus defensorem qui agit, litem in iudicium deducit.—D. 44, 2, 11, 7.[2]

Gai. iv. § 101: Ab eius vero parte cum quo agitur, siquidem alieno nomine aliquis interveniat, omnimodo satisdari debet: **quia nemo alienae rei sine satisdatione defensor idoneus** intelligitur; sed siquidem cum **cognitore** agatur, dominus satisdare iubetur, si vero cum **procuratore,** ipse procurator; idem et de tutore et de curatore iuris est.[3]

[b] Paulus?

Vat. fgm. 317[b]: Quae satisdatio adeo neces-

---

party, he must be compelled to conduct the defence of the absent party against all persons.

[1] By payment, or the undertaking of an action on our behalf, we can be discharged even without our consent and without our knowledge.

[2] —the plaintiff carries the suit before the *iudex* against the representative.

[3] But in respect of a defendant, if a man intervenes in another's name, security must be given in all cases, because no one is considered a competent defendant in another man's cause without security; but if the proceedings are against a *cognitor*, the principal is ordered to give security; if, however, they are against a *procurator*, the *procurator* himself must give it. The same rule further holds in respect of a tutor or curator.

saria est, ut eam remitti non posse, etiamsi apud acta procurator constituatur, D. Severus constituerit.[1]

In the case of representation upon the part of the plaintiff there arises—

(1) as a rule, no obligation of cautio in respect of the Cognitor, since the defendant, by the nature of the representative's commission, is here already always naturally protected against a revival of the action by the party represented (dominus).

Gai. iv. § 97: Nec si per cognitorem quidem agatur ulla satisdatio vel ab ipso vel a domino desideratur: cum enim certis et quasi solemnibus verbis in locum domini substituatur cognitor, merito domini loco habetur.[2]

(2) Every other representative had, at first indeed invariably, to provide *cautio de rato*.[a] But later on the giving of cautio was made dependent upon whether or not the right of action of the principal is itself destroyed by the representative's proceedings—which was accepted in the case of actual authorisation (*verus* procurator)—and, in the case of its being so destroyed, for the security of the defendant established the obligation to give cautio only when the authority or legitimation for taking proceedings was doubtful. Thus as a rule was the finding of cautio dispensed with particularly in respect of the 'procurator praesentis, ad acta factus,' and of an official representative.[b]

[a] 'Ratam rem dominum habiturum,' 'amplius eo nomine neminem petiturum.'

[b] For the 'actio iudicati,' see § 204.

Ibid. § 98: Procurator vero si agat, satisdare jubetur ratam rem dominum habiturum: periculum

---

[1] And this security is so indispensable, that the late Emp. Severus enacted that it cannot be waived, even if the *procurator* be appointed in the course of the proceedings.

[2] And if proceedings be taken by means of a *cognitor*, no security is required either from him or from his principal. For since the *cognitor* is substituted for his principal by certain and, as it were, solemn words, he is rightly regarded as occupying the position of the principal.

Book IV. Chapter II.

enim est, ne iterum dominus de eadem re experiatur; quod periculum non intervenit, si per cognitorem actum fuerit, quia de qua re quisque per cognitorem egerit, de ea non magis amplius actionem habet quam si ipse egerit.[1]

[a] Cf. *supra*.

Ibid. § 84[a]:—quamquam et ille, cui mandatum est, plerumque satisdare debet, quia saepe mandatum initio litis in obscuro est et postea apud iudicem ostenditur.[2]

Vat. fgm. 333 (Pap.): Absentis procuratorem satisdare debere de rato habendo, recte responsum est: multis enim casibus ignorantibus nobis mandatum solvi potest, vel morte vel revocato mandato. Cum autem certum est mandatum perseverare, i.e. cum praesens est dominus, satisdationis necessitas cessat.[3]

[b] Ulpian?

Ibid. 317[b]: [Apud acta facto] procuratori haec satisdatio remitti solet: nam cum apud acta nonnisi a praesente domino constituatur, cognitoris loco intelligendus est.[4]

---

[1] But if a *procurator* is suing, he is ordered to give security for his principal's ratification of his acts; for there is a danger of the principal proceeding afresh in respect of the same matter: this danger does not arise if proceedings have been taken through a *cognitor;* for a man who is sued through a *cognitor* has no further action in respect of the same matter than if he sued in person.

[2] —although even he who holds a commission must generally give security, because often a commission is not disclosed at the beginning of a suit, and is afterwards brought forward before the *iudex*.

[3] An opinion was correctly given that the *procurator* of an absent party ought to give security for confirmation of his acts by his principal; for in many cases without our knowledge a commission can be determined, either by death or by the revocation thereof. But when it is certain that the commission continues, *i.e.*, when the principal is present, the need for security is over.

[4] The *procurator* [appointed at the hearing] is commonly excused this security; for since he is appointed at the proceedings only by the principal when present, he is to be regarded as in the position of a *cognitor*.

Imp. Ant. Pius: Cautio ratihabitionis tunc exigitur a procuratore, quotiens incertum est, an ei mandatum est.—C. 2, 12, 1.[1]

Ulp.: —ex parte actoris in iudicium deducunt . . . procurator cui mandatum est, tutor, curator furiosi vel pupilli, actor municipum.—D. 44, 2, 11, 7.[2]

Gai. iv. § 99: Tutores et curatores eo modo quo et pro curatores satisdare debere, verba edicti faciunt; sed aliquando illis satisdatio remittitur.[3]

Ulp.: Vulgo observatur, ne tutor caveat ratam rem pupillum habiturum, quia rem in iudicium deducit.—D. 26, 7, 23.[4]

Id.: Licet verum procuratorem in iudicio rem deducere verissimum est, tamen et si quis, cum procurator non esset, litem sit contestatus, deinde ratum dominus habuerit, videtur retro res in iudicium recte deducta.—D. 5, 1, 56.[5]

Moreover, the defendant could by a plea (exceptio cognitoria, procuratoria) rebut the representative that was not qualified,[a] or was not authorised (falsus procurator)—as in fact not having 'legitimatio ad causam'—without in the latter case prejudice being done to the claim of the party entitled to the action (dominus) by the absolution of the defendant.[b]

[a] §§ 57, 194.

[b] Cf. Gai. iv. § 123.

[1] Security for ratification is required from a *procurator* whenever it is doubtful whether he has a commission.

[2] On the part of the plaintiff, the matter is carried before the *iudex* by a *procurator* with a commission, a tutor, a curator of a madman or ward, the representative of a municipality.

[3] The words of the Edict require that tutors and curators should give security in the same manner as *procuratores*, but sometimes security is waived in their case.

[4] It is commonly ruled that a guardian need not give security for the ward's ratification of his acts because of his taking proceedings.

[5] Although it is perfectly true that one who is really a *procurator* can carry a suit before the *iudex*, yet if any one, not a *procurator*, has raised the issue, and the principal has subsequently given his ratification, it is considered retrospectively that the matter was rightly carried before the *iudex*.

BOOK IV. Chapter II.

Gai. iv. 124: Non solum autem ex tempore, sed etiam ex persona dilatoriae exceptiones intelliguntur, quales sunt cognitoriae veluti si is qui per edictum cognitorem dare non potest, per cognitorem agat, vel dandi quidem cognitoris ius habeat, sed cum det cui non licet cognituram suscipere: nam si obiiciatur exceptio cognitoria, si ipse talis erit, ut ei non liceat cognitorem dare, ipse agere potest; si vero cognitori non liceat cognituram suscipere, per alium cognitorem aut per semet ipsum habet agendi potestatem, et tam hoc vel illo modo evitare potest exceptionem; quodsi dissimulaverit eam et per cognitorem egerit, rem perdit.[1]

THE *PARTES FORMULAE*.

§ 197. THE ORDINARY CONSTITUENTS.

Every normal formula necessarily consisted of two parts: the *intentio*, that is, the statement of the plaintiff, which has to be confirmed by the judge—sometimes the signification of the legal claim in dispute, at other times the assertion of a definite fact that originates a right [a]—as the condition of the condemnation of the defendant; and the *condemnatio*, the conditional instructions for condemnation (and absolution), which at the same time gives precision to the object of the condemnation. According as the intentio relates

[a] Cf. § 200.

[1] Dilatory pleas are regarded as relating not merely to time, but also to the person, of which sort are those affecting *cognitores*, as in the case of a person who by the Edict cannot nominate a *cognitor*, and yet takes proceedings by one, or in the case of a man who has the right of nominating a *cognitor*, but nominates a person unsuitable for the office: for if an *exceptio cognitoria* is raised, and the principal is not entitled to nominate a *cognitor*, he can sue in person; whilst if the *cognitor* cannot lawfully undertake the office, the principal has full power to sue either by means of another *cognitor* or in person. By either of these ways he can avoid the plea; but if he make light of it and sue by the *cognitor*, he loses the cause.

to a real right belonging to the plaintiff, or the delivery of a certain thing or sum of money, or to a performance to be ascertained by the judge [a]—a distinction is made between a 'certa' and an 'incerta' formula. The latter, besides the intentio, contained a demonstratio setting forth the legal ground of the claim (*i.e.*, the juristic fact originating the claim). The intentio—associated with the demonstratio, which with it constitutes a united whole—as the adequate formal expression for the right maintained by the plaintiff, and to be proved in iudicio, formed the basis of the whole system of Procedure and was decisive for the result of the proceedings.[b] In respect of the so-called 'iudicia divisoria,' an *adiudicatio* was associated with the condemnatio.

[a] Cf. § 105.

[b] Cf. § 202.

Gai. iv. §§ 39–44: Partes autem formularum hae sunt: demonstratio, intentio, adiudicatio, condemnatio. § **Demonstratio** est ea pars formulae, quae ideo inseritur, ut demonstretur res de qua agitur, velut haec pars formulae: QVOD AVLVS AGERIVS NVMERIO NEGIDIO HOMINEM VENDIDIT— § **Intentio** est ea pars formulae, qua actor desiderium suum concludit, velut haec pars formulae: SI PARET NVMERIVM NEGIDIVM AVLO AGERIO SESTERTIVM X MILIA DARE OPORTERE; item haec: QVIDQVID PARET NVMERIVM NEGIDIVM AVLO AGERIO DARE FACERE OPORTERE; item haec: SI PARET HOMINEM STICHVM EX IVRE QVIRITIVM AVLI AGERII ESSE. § **Adiudicatio** est ea pars formulae, qua permittitur iudici rem alicui ex litigatoribus adiudicare, velut si inter coheredes familiae erciscundae agatur, aut inter socios communi dividundo, aut inter vicinos finium regundorum; nam illic ita est: QVANTVM ADIVDICARI OPORTET, IVDEX TITIO ADIVDICATO. § **Condemnatio** est ea pars formulae, qua iudici condemnandi absolvendive potestas permittitur, velut haec pars formulae: IVDEX NVMERIVM NEGIDIVM AVLO AGERIO SESTERTIVM X MILIA CONDEMNA; SI NON PARET,

BOOK IV. Chapter II.

[a] Sc. in formulis.

ABSOLVE.—§ Non tamen istae omnes partes simul inveniuntur,[a] sed quaedam inveniuntur quaedam non inveniuntur: certe intentio aliquando sola invenitur, sicut in **praeiudicialibus formulis,** qualis est qua quaeritur, aliquis libertus sit, vel quanta dos sit, et aliae complures; demonstratio autem et adiudicatio et condemnatio nunquam solae inveniuntur.[1]

When condemnation ensued, it was always for a sum of money. According as its extent was alleged in the condemnatio as part of the formula itself, or was left to the finding and settlement by the judge, a

[1] Now the parts of a formula are these: the 'demonstratio,' the 'intentio,' the 'adiudicatio' and the 'condemnatio.' § The *demonstratio* is that part of a formula which is inserted for the purpose of setting forth what is the matter in issue; as for instance, this part of a formula: 'Whereas Aul. Ager. sold a slave to Numer. Negid.'—§ The *intentio* is that part of a formula in which the plaintiff embodies his demand; as for instance, this part of a formula: 'If it appear that Num. Neg. ought to give to Aul. Ag. 10,000 sesterces.' Or this: 'Whatever it appears that Num. Neg. ought to give or do for Aul. Ag.' Or this: 'If it appear that the slave Stichus belongs to Aul. Ag. by Quiritarian Law.' § The *adiudicatio* is that part of a formula in which the *iudex* is empowered to adjudge something to one of the litigants; as for example, in the suit between co-heirs for partition of the inheritance, or between partners for a division of the partnership property, or between neighbours for a settlement of boundaries. For here the formula runs thus: 'Let the *iudex* adjudge to Tit. as much as ought to be adjudged.' § The *condemnatio* is that part of a formula in which the *iudex* is empowered to condemn or acquit, as for example, this part of a formula: '*Iudex*, condemn Num. Neg. to pay 10,000 sesterces to Aul. Ag.; if it do not appear (that the case is proven) acquit him.' § But all these parts are not constantly found together in the same formula, but some are found and some are not. The 'intentio' is certainly sometimes found alone, as in pre-judicial formulae; such, for instance, as that wherein the question is whether a person is a freedman, or what is the amount of a marriage portion, and many others. But the 'demonstratio,' the 'adiudicatio' and the 'condemnatio' are never found alone.

distinction was made between condemnatio *certae* and *incertae* pecuniae.[a]

Gai. iv. §§ 48–52: Omnium autem formularum, quae condemnationem habent, ad **pecuniariam aestimationem** condemnatio concepta est; itaque et si corpus aliquod petamus, veluti fundum hominen vestem aurum argentum, iudex non ipsam rem condemnat eum, cum quo actum est, sicut olim fieri solebat, sed aestimata re pecuniam eum condemnat. § Condemnatio autem vel certae pecuniae in formula ponitur vel incertae. § **Certae pecuniae** in ea formula qua certam pecuniam petimus—[v. § 43]. § **Incertae** vero condemnatio pecuniae duplicem significationem habet: est enim una cum aliqua praefinitione, quae vulgo dicitur **cum taxatione**, velut si incertum aliquid petamus; nam illic ima parte formulae ita est: IVDEX NVMERIVM NEGIDIVM AVLO AGERIO DVMTAXAT X MILIA CONDEMNA; SI NON PARET, ABSOLVE. Vel incerta est **et infinita,** velut si rem aliquam a possidente nostram esse petamus i.e. si in rem agamus vel ad exhibendum; nam illic ita est: QVANTI EA RES ERIT, TANTAM PECVNIAM, IVDEX, NVMERIVM NEGIDIVM AVLO AGERIO CONDEMNA; SI NON PARET, ABSOLVE.—§ Quid ergo est? iudex si condemnet, certam pecuniam condemnare debet, etsi certa pecunia in condemnatione posita non sit; debet autem iudex attendere, ut cum certae pecuniae condemnatio posita sit, neque maioris neque minoris summa posita condemnet, alioquin litem suam facit.[1]

[a] Cf. § 112; Gai. iii. 224; §§ 137, 139, 176.

[1] Now the *condemnatio* of all formulae that have a condemnatory clause is framed by reference to a pecuniary valuation; therefore, although we are suing for some specific thing, as for instance, land, a slave, a garment, gold, silver, the *iudex* does not condemn the defendant in the thing itself, as was formerly the custom, but condemns him to pay money according to the valuation of the thing. § The *condemnatio* is inserted in the formula for a liquidated sum, or for a sum uncertain. § It is for a liquidated sum in the formula by which we sue for a

Book IV. Chapter II.

EXTRAORDINARY CONSTITUENTS.

§ 198. *Exceptiones* and *Replicationes*.

[a] See in general § 28.

The 'exceptio'[a] contains—in contrast with the denial of the plaintiff's intentio—an exception to the condemnation, made good by the defendant. It therefore constitutes in the formula an additional defence to the intentio, conceived in the form of a negative condition of the instructions for condemnation, as the positive condition of the condemnatio. 'Denegatio actionis' occurred in the case of the exceptio admitting of proof already in iure, if not in turn met by a 'replicatio.'

Ulp.: Exceptio dicta est quasi quaedam **exclusio**, quae opponi actioni cuiusque rei solet ad excludendum id, quod in intentionem condemnationemve deductum est.—D. 44, 1, 2 pr.[1]

Gai. iv. § 119: Omnes autem exceptiones in **contrarium** concipiuntur, quam adfirmat is cum

---

liquidated sum.—§ But a *condemnatio* for an uncertain sum has a twofold meaning. For there is one form with a definite limitation, and this form is generally called *cum taxatione;* for example, when we make an uncertain claim, for then the final part of the formula is as follows: 'Do you, *iudex*, condemn Num. Neg. to pay to Aul. Ag. not more than 10,000 sesterces: if it do not so appear, acquit him.' Or it is one uncertain and unlimited; for instance, when we claim something as ours from one in possession of it, that is, if we sue by a real action, or for production; for then the *condemnatio* runs: 'Do you, *iudex*, condemn Num. Neg. to pay to Aul. Ag. the value of the thing: if it do not so appear, acquit him.' § What is the result of this? That a *iudex*, if he condemn, must do so in a fixed sum, even though no fixed sum has been inserted in the *condemnatio*. But the *iudex* must take care, when the *condemnatio* is limited to a fixed sum, not to condemn for an amount larger or smaller than that inserted, otherwise he makes the cause his own.

[1] By 'exceptio' is meant an exclusion, as it were, which is commonly set up in opposition to an action in respect of any matter, to exclude that which has been submitted in the *intentio* or the *condemnatio*.

quo agitur. Nam si verbi gratia reus dolo malo aliquid actorem facere dicat, qui forte pecuniam petit, quam non numeravit, sic exceptio concipitur: SI IN EA RE NIHIL DOLO MALO AVLI AGERII FACTVM SIT NEQVE FIAT; item si dicatur contra pactionem pecuniam peti, ita concipitur exceptio: SI INTER AVLVM AGERIVM ET NVMERIVM NEGIDIVM NON CONVENIT, NE EA PECVNIA PETERETVR. Et denique in ceteris causis similiter concipi solet: ideo scilicet quia omnis exceptio obiicitur quidem a reo, sed ita formulae inseritur, ut **condicionalem faciat condemnationem,** i.e. ne aliter iudex eum cum quo agitur condemnet, quam si nihil in ea re, qua de agitur, dolo actoris factum sit; item ne aliter iudex eum condemnet, quam si nullum pactum conventum de non petenda pecunia factum fuerit.[1]

The defendant had, as a rule, to present his plea 'in iure' and to see that it was inserted in the formula, should it obtain consideration by the iudex.—According to their formal, external nature, exceptiones can be designated as those objections of the defendant which the iudex might take into consideration, not *ex*

---

[1] Now all pleas are formulated negatively. For if, by way of example, the defendant allege that the plaintiff is doing something fraudulently, suing, it may be, for a sum which he has never advanced, the plea is worded thus: 'if nothing fraudulent has been done or is being done in such matter on the part of Aul. Ag.' Again, if it be asserted that money is claimed contrary to agreement, the plea is framed thus: 'if there have been no agreement between Aul. Ag. and Num. Neg. that such money shall not be sued for.' And, in fine, a like mode of expression is usual in all other cases; because, of course, every plea is set up by the defendant, but incorporated in the formula in such way as to render the *condemnatio* conditional, that is to say, that the *iudex* is only to condemn the defendant if nothing fraudulent have been done on the part of the plaintiff in such matter; and further, that the *iudex* is only to condemn him if there has been no agreement made that the money should not be sued for.

officio, but only in pursuance of the Praetor's instructions.—But in respect of the 'bonae fidei iudicia,'[a] in which bona fides forms an essential element of the intentio itself, the iudex had already *ex officio* to entertain every plea giving to the plaintiff's claim the appearance of contravening bona fides;[b] so that here exceptiones were in processual significance only requisite in case either, notwithstanding the plea, the plaintiff's claim was consistent with aequitas, or no certain expectation could be entertained that it would be considered by the iudex.

[a] § 24.

[b] As the *doli exceptio*: D. 44, 4, 2, 5.

Iul.: —iudicium fidei bonae . . . continet in se doli mali exceptionem.—l. 84, § 5, D. de leg. I. 30.[1]

Paul.: Bonae fidei iudicio exceptiones pacti insunt.—D. 18, 5, 3.[2]

Exceptiones are divided:—

(*a*) according to the law-source from which they are derived, into 'civiles'[c] and 'praetoriae,'[d] so that with the former the respective rule of civil law was actualised through the legal aid of the Praetor, by means of an exceptio given to the defendant;

(β) according to their conception, or wording, into exceptiones 'vulgares' and 'in factum';[e]

(γ) according to the scope of their operation, into exceptiones 'peremptoriae' and 'dilatoriae.'[f]

[c] §§ 30, 120, 129, 145.

[d] Where, however, it must be observed that all *exceptiones* are Praetorian in form.

[e] Cf. § 200.

[f] § 28.

Gai. iv. § 118: Exceptiones autem alias in edicto praetor habet propositas, alias causa cognita accommodat; quae omnes vel ex legibus vel ex his, quae legis vicem obtinent, substantiam capiunt, vel ex iurisdictione praetoris proditae sunt.[3]

---

[1] A *bon. fid.* action embraces a plea of fraud.

[2] In a *bon. fid.* action are comprised pleas derived from an agreement.

[3] Some pleas have been put forth by the Praetor in his Edict, some he vouchsafes after investigating the matter. All of them are derived either from *leges*, or enactments that acquire the force of *leges*, or are derived from the Praetor's jurisdiction.

The plaintiff's replicatio contains the assertion of an exception as concerns the exceptio, and thus appears in the formula as a rule—but not without exception—in the affirmative style, and so in the form of a positive condition of the condemnatio.

> Gai. iv. § 126: Si verbi gratia pactus sim tecum, ne pecuniam quam mihi debes a te peterem, deinde postea in contrarium pacti simus, i.e. ut petere mihi liceat, et, si agam tecum, excipias tu, ut ita demum mihi condemneris, SI NON CONVENERIT NE EAM PECVNIAM PETEREM, nocet mihi exceptio pacti conventi: namque nihilominus hoc verum manet, etiam si postea in contrarium pacti simus; sed quia iniquum est, me excludi exceptione, replicatio mihi datur ex posteriore pacto hoc modo: SI NON POSTEA CONVENERIT, VT EAM PECVNIAM PETERE LICERET.[1]

§ 199. Praescriptiones.

'Praescriptio' designates in general an addition to the formula in the form of a preliminary note; thus in the older Law some pleas also had the form of a praescriptio.[a] In later times 'praescriptio' in the wider sense is often synonymous with 'exceptio.'[b] The following are praescriptiones in the strict sense.

[a] Gai. iv. 133.
[b] § 25.

(1) The praescriptiones *pro actore*. By these is understood a proviso annexed to the formula, which

[1] If, for example, I have agreed with you not to proceed against you for money you owe me, and afterwards we make an agreement to the contrary, that is, that I shall be at liberty to sue you, and if on my taking proceedings against you, you meet me with a plea that you ought to be condemned to pay me only 'if there have been no agreement that I should not sue for the money,' this plea of agreement made is to my prejudice; for this agreement none the less remains a fact, even if we have subsequently agreed to the contrary. But as it is unfair for me to be defeated by the plea, a replication is allowed me upon the later agreement, thus: 'if there have been no later agreement enabling me to sue for the money.'

it required in the enforcement of a particular claim—especially now arising for the first time—from an incerti obligatio, in order that the action should be kept up for the remaining performances—or such as become due later on—arising from the same obligatio; these would otherwise be consumed by Litis Contestatio,[a] since the 'una et incerta obligatio' itself is brought *in iudicium* by the intentio, which comprises its whole content.

[a] § 26; D. 4, 34, 4.

Gai. iv. §§ 130–131[a]: Videamus etiam de **praescriptionibus,** quae receptae sunt **pro actore.** § Saepe enim ex una eademque obligatione aliquid iam praestari oportet, aliquid in futura praestatione est, veluti cum in singulos annos vel menses certam pecuniam stipulati fuerimus: nam finitis quibusdam annis vel mensibus huius quidem temporis pecuniam praestari oportet, futororum autem annorum sane quidem obligatio contracta intelligitur, praestatio vero adhuc nulla est; si ergo velimus id quidem, quod praestari oportet, petere et in iudicium ducere, futuram vero obligationis praestationem in integro relinquere, necesse est, ut cum hac praescriptione agamus: EA RES AGATVR CVIVS REI DIES FVIT: alioquin si sine hac praescriptione egerimus, ea scilicet formula qua incertum petimus, cuius intentio his verbis concepta est: QVIDQVID PARET NVMERIVM NEGIDIVM AVLO AGERIO DARE FACERE OPORTERE, totam obligationem id est etiam futuram in hoc iudicium deducimus. § Item si verbi gratia ex empto agamus, ut nobis fundus mancipio detur, debemus hoc modo praescribere: EA RES AGATVR DE FVNDO MANCIPANDO, ut postea si velimus vacuam possessionem nobis tradi, . . . [rursus ex empto agere possimus; nam si praescribere obliti] sumus, totius illius iuris obligatio illa incerta actione QVIDQVID OB EAM REM NVMERIVM NEGIDIVM AVLO AGERIO DARE FACERE OPORTET per intentionem consumitur, ut postea nobis agere valentibus de vacua possessione tradenda nulla supersit actio.[1]

Cic. de or. 1, 37, 168: —homo ex numero disertorum postulabat, ut illi unde peteretur vetus atque usitata exceptio daretur **'cuius pecuniae dies fuisset;'** quod petitoris causa comparatum esse non intelligebat: ut, si ille infitiator probasset iudici ante petitam esse pecuniam, quam esset coepta deberi, petitor rursus cum peteret, ne exceptione excluderetur **'quod ea res in iudicium ante venisset.'**[2]

---

[1] Let us also consider the subject of the *praescriptiones* which are admissible on behalf of the plaintiff. § For often, in consequence of one and the same obligation, there is something to be furnished at once and something at a future time. For instance, when we have stipulated for a certain payment every year or every month; for then upon the completion of a certain number of years or months, the money for that period must be paid, but whilst an obligation is held to have been certainly contracted in respect of future years, yet there is no need for payment. If, therefore, we wish to sue for that which is actually payable and to carry the matter before the *iudex*, but to leave the future discharge of the obligation untouched, it is necessary to sue with this praescription: 'Let that be the matter of action, the time for performance of which is past'; otherwise, if we have proceeded without this praescription, that is, with the formula by which we sue for an uncertain thing, and the *intentio* is couched in these words: 'Whatever it appears that Num. Neg. ought to give or do to Aul. Ag.,' we have included the whole obligation, that is, even the future part of it, in this action. § Likewise if, for instance, we bring an action upon a purchase, for the conveyance to us of land by mancipation, we ought to employ a praescription thus: 'Let the matter of action be the conveyance of the land by mancipation'; so that if we afterwards wish to have vacant possession delivered to us . . . [we may be able to sue again upon the purchase; for if we have forgotten to prescribe,] the obligation in respect of the entire right is destroyed by the *intentio* in the uncertain action: 'Whatever on account of such thing Num. Neg. ought to give or do to Aul. Ag.'; so that if we afterwards wish to sue for the delivery of vacant possession, there is no action remaining.

[2] An advocate applied for the allowance to the defendant of the old and accustomed plea: 'for such sum as was already due'; from not being aware that the plea was provided on

Book IV. Chapter II.

Paul.: Cum stipulamur 'quidquid te dare facere oportet,' id quod praesenti die dumtaxat debetur in stipulationem deducitur, non, ut in iudiciis, etiam futurum.—D. 45, 1, 76, 1.[1]

Iavol.: Non quemadmodum obligatio in pendenti potest esse et vel in futurum concipi, ita iudicium in pendenti potest esse, vel de his rebus quae postea in obligationem adventurae sunt.—D. 5, 1, 35.[2]

In respect of the action against the surety, the relation of suretyship was set forth in the form of a praescriptio.

Gai. iv. § 137: Si cum sponsore aut fideiussore agatur, praescribi solet in persona quidem sponsoris hoc modo: EA RES AGATVR QVOD AVLVS AGERIVS DE LVCIO TITIO . . . incertum . . . STIPVLATVS EST, QVO NOMINE NVMERIVS NEGIDIVS SPONSOR EST, CVIVS REI DIES FVIT; in persona vero fideiussoris: EA RES AGATVR QVOD NVMERIVS NEGIDIVS PRO LVCIO TITIO . . . incertum . . . FIDE SVA ESSE IVSSIT, CVIVS RES DIES FVIT; deinde formula subiicitur.[3]

---

behalf of the plaintiff—so that, if the party repudiating should have proved to the *iudex* that the proceedings had been taken before the money became due, when the plaintiff again sued, he should not be estopped by the plea that 'such matter had been already before the *iudex*.'

1 When we stipulate for 'whatever it is incumbent upon you to give or to do,' that alone which is due at the time being is made the subject of the stipulation, not, as in judgments, future liability also.

2 A judgment cannot remain in suspense as an obligation, which may perhaps be framed in view of the future, even concerning those points which are in the future to come within the range of the obligation.

3 If proceedings are taken against a *sponsor* or *fideiussor*, the praescription in the case of the *sponsor* is usually in this form: 'Let the matter of action be the amount now due upon the stipulation which Aul. Ager. took for something indefinite from Luc. Tit., on whose behalf Num. Neg. was *sponsor*, the time for

Occasionally also a praescriptio takes the place of the demonstratio.[a]

[a] § 200.

§ 200. Variety of Actions in Respect of their Formulation.

The Praetor frequently gave facilities for the legal prosecution of claims recognised in the Edict, by the grant of 'actiones ficticiae,'[b] through which such claims were made to depend upon the ius civile.[c] In these cases the formula contained the fiction of a certain presumption of fact appertaining to the action which was required by the Civil Law, so that the iudex was instructed to decide as if a certain actual or legal preliminary had or had not occurred—'actio rescissoria'; or as if a certain legal requirement of the action were present, which in reality was absent.[d]

[b] Gai. iv. 32.

[c] § 24.

[d] Cf. D. 4, 5, 2 1; 4, 4, 13, 1; Gai. iii. 84 and iv. 38; ib. 4, 36; D. 39, 5, 21, 1; Gai. iv. 34; ib. 35.

> Gai. iv. § 37: Civitas Romana peregrino fingitur, si eo nomine agat aut cum eo agatur, quo nomine nostris legibus actio constituta est, si modo iustum sit, eam actionem etiam ad peregrinum extendi; veluti si furti nomine agat peregrinus aut cum eo agatur, formula ita concipitur: I.E. SI PARET [A DIONE HERMAEI FILIO FVRTVM FACTVM ESSE L. TITIO aut SI PARET] OPE CONSILIO DIONIS HERMAEI FILII FVRTVM FACTVM ESSE PATERAE AVREAE, QVAM OB REM EVM, SI CIVIS ROMANVS ESSET, PRO FVRE DAMNVM DECIDERE OPORTERET et reliqua; item si peregrinus furti agat, civitas ei Romana fingitur; similiter, si ex lege Aquilia peregrinus damni iniuriae agat aut cum eo agatur, ficta civitate Romana iudicium datur.[1]

---

payment of which is past.' And in the case of a *fideiussor*: 'Let the matter of action be the amount now due that Num. Neg. undertook as surety on behalf of Luc. Tit. in respect of something indefinite, the time for payment of which is past.' Then follows the formula.

[1] Roman citizenship is also fictitiously ascribed to a foreigner, if he sues or is sued in a case for which an action has been granted by our laws, provided only it be reasonable that such

Book IV. Chapter II.

An action could also be transferred to other persons than those for whom it was originally intended, by a change of the subjective relation in the formula (transference of the condemnatio to another) actively or passively, whether by or contrary to the desire of the person entitled to the action (as utilis actio). So in the case of representation in procedure.[a]

[a] Cf. §§ 119, 112, 114, 185; Gai. iv. 35.

Gai. iv. §§ 86–7: Qui autem alieno nomine agit, intentionem quidem ex persona domini sumit, condemnationem autem in suam personam convertit; nam si verbi gratia Lucius Titius pro Publio Maevio agit, ita formula concipitur: SI PARET NVMERIVM NEGIDIVM PVBLIO MAEVIO SESTERTIVM X MILIA DARE OPORTERE, IVDEX NVMERIVM NEGIDIVM LVCIO TITIO SESTERTIVM X MILIA CONDEMNA. SI NON PARET, ABSOLVE; in rem quoque si agat, intendit PVBLII MAEVII REM ESSE EX IVRE QVIRITIVM et condemnationem in suam personam convertit. § Ab adversarii quoque parte si interveniat aliquis, cum quo actio constituitur, intenditur 'dominum dare oportere,' condemnatio autem in eius personam convertitur, qui iudicium accepit; sed cum in rem agitur, nihil in intentione facit persona eius cum quo agitur, sive suo nomine sive alieno aliquis iudicio interveniat: tantum enim intenditur '**rem actoris esse**.'[1]

---

action should be extended to a foreigner; for example, if upon the ground of theft a foreigner sues or is sued, the formula is framed thus: 'Let so and so be *iudex*. Should it appear [that a theft was committed on Luc. Tit. by Dion son of Herm., or if it appear] that by the aid and advice of Dion son of Herm. a theft was committed on Tit. of a golden goblet, for which matter, if he were a Roman citizen, he would have to make satisfaction for the loss as a thief,' etc. Again, if a foreigner sues for theft, Roman citizenship is by fiction ascribed to him. So again, if a foreigner sues or is sued under the *l. Aquilia* for wrongful damage, an action is granted upon the fiction that he possesses Roman citizenship.

[1] Now a person that sues in another's name lays the *intentio* in the name of his principal, but turns the *condemnatio* into his own name. For if, for example, Luc. Tit. sues for Publ. Maev.,

The significance of actiones 'in factum' is determined sometimes by the manner of conception of the formula, at other times by its position in the Praetorian Edict. We have accordingly to distinguish—

(1) Actiones with formula *in ius*, and with formula *in factum concepta*. The former are the actions with an intentio iuris civilis, which formulates a legal claim belonging to the plaintiff according to ius civile; the latter are the (Praetorian) actions, in respect of which the instructions to condemn are annexed in the intentio to the existence of a definite fact, instead of to that of a right; which is set forth in greater detail in the formula,—a fact which is sometimes simple, at other times juristic, and so in its legal meaning and importance to be established judicially.

Gai. iv. §§ 45–6: Sed eas quidem formulas, in quibus de iure quaeritur, **in ius conceptas** vocamus, quales sunt, quibus intendimus NOSTRVM ESSE ALIQVID EX IVRE QVIRITIVM, aut NOBIS DARI OPORTERE, . . . in quibus iuris civilis intentio est. § Ceteras vero **in factum conceptas** vocamus, i.e. in quibus nulla talis intentio concepta est, sed initio formulae nominato eo quod factum est, adiciuntur ea verba, per quae iudici damnandi absolvendive potestas datur; qualis est

---

the formula is thus drawn up: 'If it appear that Num. Neg. is bound to give 10,000 sesterces to Publ. Maev., do you, *iudex*, condemn Num. Neg. to pay the 10,000 sesterces to Luc. Tit.; if otherwise, acquit him.' If, again, the action is *in rem*, his claim is that such and such a thing is the property of Publ. Maev. by Quiritarian Law,' and he turns the *condemnatio* into his own name. § So, if some one appears on the part of the defendant against whom the suit is laid, the claimant's allegation is that 'The principal ought to give'; but the *condemnatio* is changed into the name of the person that has undertaken the action. But when the proceedings are *in rem*, the name of the person against whom the action is brought has no effect on the *intentio*, whether such person defends on his own account or on that of another; for by the statement of claim it is simply alleged that 'the thing belongs to the plaintiff.'

Book IV. Chapter II.

formula qua utitur patronus contra libertum, qui eum contra edictum praetoris in ius vocavit; nam in ea ita est: RECVPERATORES SVNTO. SI PARET illum PATRONVM AB illo illius PATRONI LIBERTO CONTRA EDICTVM illius PRAETORIS IN IVS VOCATVM ESSE, RECVPERATORES illum LIBERTVM illi PATRONO SESTERTIVM X MILIA CONDEMNATE S. N. P. A. Ceterae quoque formulae, quae sub titulo '**de in ius vocando**' propositae sunt, in factum conceptae sunt, velut adversus eum qui in ius vocatus neque venerit neque vindicem dederit;—et denique innumerabiles eiusmodi aliae formulae in albo proponuntur.[1]

Ib. § 47: Sed ex quibusdum causis praetor et in ius et in factum conceptas formulas proponit, veluti depositi et commodati. Illa enim formula, quae ita concepta est: IVDEX ESTO. QVOD AVLVS AGERIVS APVD NVMERIVM NEGIDIVM MENSAM ARGENTEAM DEPOSVIT, QVA DE RE AGITVR, QVIDQVID OB EAM REM NVMERIVM NEGIDIVM AVLO AGERIO

---

[1] But those formulae in which is raised a question of law we call *in ius conceptae*. Such are those in which we allege that something is ours by Quiritarian Law, or that it ought to be given to us . . . in which the *intentio* appertains to civil law. § But other formulae we call *in factum conceptae;* those, namely, in which no such *intentio* is drawn up, but at the beginning of the formula, after a specification of what has been done, words are added by which power is given to the *iudex* to condemn or acquit. Of this kind is the formula used by the patron against his freedman who has summoned him into court contrary to the Praetor's Edict, for it contains the following words: 'Let so and so be *recuperatores*. If it appear that such and such a patron has been summoned into court by such and such a freedman of that patron contrary to the edict of such and such a Praetor, do you, the *recuperatores*, condemn that freedman to pay to such patron 10,000 sesterces; and if it do not so appear, acquit him.' The other formulae also which are set forth under the title *de in ius vocando*, are framed *in factum;* as for example, that against him who when summoned into court has neither appeared nor furnished a protector;—and there are, in fine, innumerable other formulae of the same kind set forth in the Edict.

DARE FACERE OPORTET EX FIDE BONA EIVS, IVDEX, NVMERIVM NEGIDIVM AVLO AGERIO CONDEMNATO [NISI RESTITVAT]; SI NON PARET, ABSOLVITO, in ius concepta est. At illa formula, quae ita concepta est: I.E. SI PARET AVLVM AGERIVM APVD NVMERIVM NEGIDIVM MENSAM ARGENTEAM DEPOSVISSE EAMQVE DOLO NVMERII NEGIDII AVLO AGERIO REDDITAM NON ESSE, QVANTI EA RES ERIT, TANTAM PECVNIAM IVDEX NVMERIVM NEGIDIVM AVLO AGERIO CONDEMNATO; S. N. P. A., in factum concepta est.[1]

(2) Actiones *in factum*, in contrast with the actiones *vulgares*. By the latter are understood the actions for which definite, established formulae (conceived in ius or in factum) were set up in the Edict; by the former, those actions which—in the Edict generally only promised—did not possess a typical formula, so that the formula was specially composed for the particular case, according to its individuality. Moreover, the formula for this itself could again either be conceived in factum, or contain a iuris civilis intentio ('quidquid paret d. f. o.').[a] [a] § 133.
The latter was the case in respect of actiones (incerti) in factum *civiles* (s. *praescriptis verbis*) that is, actions which spring from transactions recognised in the Civil Law, but not provided with a special name, the formulae for which therefore

[1] But in respect of certain causes the Praetor puts forth both *formulae in ius conceptae* and *formulae in factum conceptae*; for example, in the actions on a deposit and on a loan. For that formula is *in ius concepta* which is drawn up thus: 'Let so and so be *iudex*. Whereas Aul. Ager. has deposited with Numer. Negid., the silver table in question, whatever on account of this Num. Neg. ought in good faith to give or to do to Aul. Ag., do thou, *iudex*, condemn Num. Neg. to give or to do to Aul. Ag., unless he make restoration. If it do not so appear, acquit him.' But that is a formula *in factum concepta* which is drawn up thus: 'Let so and so be *iudex*. If it appear that Aul. Ag. has deposited with Num. Neg. a silver table, and that this through the fraud of Num. Neg. has not been restored, do thou, *iudex*, condemn Num. Neg. to pay to Aul. Ag. such amount as the thing shall be worth. If it do not so appear, acquit him.'

BOOK IV. Chapter II.

contained a representation of the essential *de facto* elements of the legal matter concerned (praescripta verba), in lieu of the demonstratio technically setting forth the ground of action, and had therefore to be differently framed for each concrete case.[a]

[a] See § 126.

Pap.: Nonnumquam evenit, ut cessantibus **iudiciis proditis et vulgaribus actionibus**, cum proprium nomen invenire non possumus, facile descendamus ad eas, quae **in factum** appellantur. —D. 19, 5, 1 pr.[1]

Pomp.: Quia actionum non plenus numerus esset, ideo plerumque **actiones in factum** desiderantur. Sed et eas actiones, quae legibus proditae sunt, si lex iusta et necessaria sit, supplet praetor in eo quod legi deest: quod facit in lege Aquilia reddendo actiones in factum accommodatas legi Aquiliae, idque utilitas eius legis exigit.—l. 11 eod.[2]

Actiones 'stricti iuris,' 'bonae fidei' (which in the intentio incerti had the addition 'ex fide bona') and 'arbitrariae' have already been considered.[b]

[b] See § 24.

§ 201. INTERDICTA.

The further judicial proceedings required in the event of non-compliance with the Interdictum issued by the magistrate,[c] in the Restitutory and Exhibitory interdicts were associated either immediately with the

[c] § 29.

---

[1] It sometimes happens that if the actions which have been created by the courts and are in common use do not suffice, since we can find no special name, we readily resort to those which are called 'upon the case.'

[2] From the fact that the number of actions is not complete, actions *in factum* are therefore generally wanted. But those actions also which have been created by statutes, if the statute is reasonable and necessary, are completed by the Praetor in respect of that which is lacking in the statute. This he does in respect of the *l. Aquilia* by granting actions *in factum* formed after the analogy thereof; and the usefulness of the statute demands it.

issue of the interdict (formula arbitraria), or they were accomplished by a 'sponsio et restipulatio poenalis' to be given by one of the parties (*i.e.*, promise and counter-promise of a penal sum in the event of the Praetor's order being contravened, or of its not being contravened); concerning which an ordinary *iudicium* obtained,—and to these, in case the plaintiff had succeeded, was then further annexed an *arbitrium* affecting the thing itself, with eventual condemnation of the defendant in damages (secutorium iudicium).

Gai. iv. § 141: Nec tamen cum quid iusserit fieri aut fieri prohibuerit, statim peractum est negotium, sed ad iudicem recuperatoresve itur et ibi editis formulis quaeritur, an aliquid **adversus praetoris edictum** factum sit, vel an factum non sit, quod is fieri iusserit.[1]

Ibid. §§ 162–4: Si igitur restitutorium vel exhibitorium interdictum redditur, velut ut restituatur ei possessio qui vi deiectus est, aut exhibeatur libertus cui patronus operas indicere vellet, modo sine periculo res ad exitum perducitur, modo cum periculo. § Namque si arbitrium postulaverit is cum quo agitur, accipit formulam quae appellatur **arbitraria**; et iudicis arbitrio si quid restitui vel exhiberi debeat, id sine periculo exhibet aut restituit, et ita absolvitur; quodsi nec restituat neque exhibeat, quanti ea res est condemnatur; sed et actor sine poena experitur cum eo, quem neque exhibere neque restituere quicquam oportet.—§ Observare autem debet is qui vult arbitrum petere, ut statim petat, antequam ex iure exeat, i.e. antequam a praetore discedat.[2]

---

[1] The matter is not, however, immediately concluded when he has ordered or forbidden the doing of something, but it goes before a *iudex* or *recuperatores*, and there, upon the issuing of formulae, the question is raised whether anything has been done contrary to the Praetor's Edict, or whether what he ordered to be done has not been done.

[2] If, therefore, a restitutory or exhibitory interdict be granted, for example, that possession shall be restored to a person who

Book IV. Chapter II.

Ib. § 165: Itaque si arbitrum non petierit, sed tacitus de iure exierit, cum periculo res ad exitum perducitur: nam actor provocat adversarium sponsione, ni contra edictum praetoris non exhibuerit aut non restituerit, ille autem adversus sponsionem adversarii restipulatur; deinde actor quidem sponsionis formulam edit adversario, ille huic invicem restipulationis: sed actor sponsionis formulae subiicit et illud iudicium de re restituenda vel exhibenda, ut si sponsione vicerit, nisi ei res exhibeatur aut restituatur, [quanti ea res erit, adversarius ei condemnetur].[1]

Ib. § 169: . . . **Cascelliano** sive **secutorio** iudicio de possessione reciperanda experitur;

---

has been forcibly ejected, or that a freedman shall be produced upon whom a patron desires to impose services, the matter is sometimes brought to an issue without risk, sometimes with risk. § For if the defendant has demanded an arbitrator, he receives a so-called *formula arbitraria;* and if by the award of the *iudex* he has to restore or produce something, he restores or produces it without any penalty, and so is discharged from liability; but if he do not restore or produce it, he is condemned to pay its value. But the plaintiff also sues a man who is not under obligation to produce or restore anything, without making himself liable to any penalty.—§ Now he who wishes to claim an arbitrator should make his claims before going out of court, that is, before he leaves the Praetor's presence.

[1] Hence, if he have not claimed an arbitrator, but have left the court in silence, the matter is carried on to its issue at his risk. For the plaintiff challenges his opponent with a wager: 'Unless in defiance of the Praetor's Edict he shall have failed to produce or to restore,' and the latter takes a counter-stipulation as against the wager of his opponent. Next, the plaintiff delivers to his opponent the formula of his wager, and the defendant in his turn delivers to the other the formula of the counter-stipulation. But the plaintiff joins to the formula of the wager another action for restitution or production of the thing, so that if he succeed on his wager, and the thing is not produced or restored, [his opponent shall be condemned for the value of the thing].

. . . dicitur autem hoc iudicium secutorium, quod sequitur sponsionis victoriam.[1] Book IV. Chapter II.

Proceedings always required the interposition of a penal sponsio in respect of the Prohibitory interdicts. The shape taken by interdicta duplicia is diffuse,[a] especially the 'uti possidetis,' in case the question here be not of one-sided frivolous disturbance of possession, but of usurpation of possession, and each party ascribe the possession to himself, especially if there be primarily need of a speedy decision of the question of possession, in order to pave the way for the proprietary action and to determine which of them was to be plaintiff or defendant.[b] Here the parties did not need to await a real disturbance of possession (vis) of any kind taking place after the issue of the interdict, but they could compel one another in iure to a formal and symbolic disturbance (vis ex conventu). With this were associated reciprocal 'sponsiones et restipulationes poenales.' The provisional position of the possession during the proceedings by interdict was settled in the case of immovables by way of biddings between the parties (fructus licitatio—fructuaria stipulatio). The decision of all these claims resulting from the preliminary legal acts, and, accordingly, of the question of possession itself, was committed to the iudex appointed by a corresponding formula. If the opponent refused to undertake such acts as conditioned the further conduct and carrying through of the possessory suit, special interdicta secundaria attached.

[a] § 29.

[b] §§ 76, 91.

Gai. iv. §§ 166[a], 167: —iudex . . . illud requirit quod praetor interdicto complexus est, i.e. uter eorum eum fundum easve aedes per id tempus, quo interdictum redditur, nec vi nec clam nec precario[c] possederit. Cum iudex id exploraverit et forte secundum me iudicatum sit,

[c] Sc. ab adversario.

[1] . . . he proceeds for the recovery of possession by the Cascellian or Secutorian action . . . now this action is called 'secutory' because it follows success in the wager.

Book IV.
Chapter II.

adversarium mihi et sponsionis et restipulationis summas quas cum eo feci condemnat, et convenienter me sponsionis et restipulationis quae mecum factae sunt absolvit; et hoc amplius si apud adversarium meum possessio est, quia is fructus licitatione vicit, nisi restituat mihi possessionem, **Cascelliano** sive **secutorio** iudicio condemnatur. § Ergo is qui fructus licitatione vicit, si non probat ad se pertinere possessionem, sponsionis et restipulationis et fructus licitationis summam poenae nomine solvere et praeterea possessionem restituere iubetur, et hoc amplius fructus quos interea percepit, reddit: summa enim fructus licitationis non pretium est fructuum, sed poenae nomine solvitur, quod quis alienam possessionem per hoc tempus retinere et facultatem fruendi nancisci conatus est.[1]

Ib. § 170: Sed quia nonnulli interdicto reddito cetera ex interdicto facere nolebant, atque ob id non poterat res expediri, praetor in eam rem prospexit et comparavit interdicta, quae

[1] —the *iudex* investigates the point which the Praetor dealt with in his interdict, viz. which of them at the time when the interdict was issued was in possession of the land or house neither by violence, nor secretly, nor upon sufferance. When the *iudex* has ascertained this and judgment has been given, it may be, in my favour, he condemns my opponent to pay the amounts of the wager and of the counter-stipulation which I entered into with him, and consequently releases me from the wager and counter-stipulation which he entered into with me. And further, if possession be with my opponent, from overbidding me in the *fructus licitatio*, he is condemned in a Cascellian or Secutorian action, if he do not restore the possession to me. § And so, if the successful bidder for the fruits does not prove that the possession belongs to him, he is ordered by way of penalty to pay the amount of the wager and counter-stipulation and of his bid for the fruits, besides giving up possession; and besides this, he restores the fruits which he has gathered in the meanwhile. For the sum bid for the fruits is not the price of the fruits, but is paid by way of penalty for the attempt to retain during such time the possession and the power of enjoyment which belonged to another.

secundaria appellamus, quod secundo loco redduntur: quorum vis et potestas haec est, ut qui cetera ex interdicto non faciat (veluti qui vim non faciat aut fructum non liceatur aut qui fructus licitationis satis non det, aut si sponsiones non faciat sponsionumve iudicia non accipiat), sive possideat, restituat adversario possessionem, sive non possideat, vim illi possidenti ne faciat.[1]

THE FURTHER PROCEEDINGS (JUDGMENT, EXECUTION, LEGAL REMEDIES).

IUDICIUM.

§ 202. Subject-matter and Pre-requisites of the Judicial Sentence.

The 'iudicium' is concluded and the official function of the judge ended by the judgment (sententia iudicis), in which the judge, upon the ground of knowledge of the case derived from the discussions of the parties and from the reception of evidence, in agreement with his conviction, as a rule verbally pronounces the condemnation (for a certain sum of money) decisive of the suit, or absolution of the defendant.[a] In the classical Law there was no limitation as to time of discussion in iudicio, as there had been by the Twelve Tables.

[a] § 27.

Imp. Alex.: Praeses provinciae non ignorat, **definitivam sententiam**, quae condemnationem vel

[1] But as some persons, on the interdict being issued, used to refuse to do the other things arising out of the interdict, and thus a matter could not be forwarded, the Praetor gave his attention to this and provided interdicts which we call secondary, because they are granted in the second instance. Their force and effect is this, that a person who does not perform the other things arising out of the interdict, as for example, if he will not do conventional violence, or does not bid for the fruits, or does not give security in respect of the *fructus licitatio*, or will not engage in wagers, or will not defend the actions arising therefrom if he is in possession, has to deliver over the possession to his opponent; if he does not possess, he has to do no violence to the possessor.

Book IV. Chapter II.

absolutionem non continet, pro iusta non haberi. —C. 7, 45, 3.[1]

Ulp.: Iudex posteaquam semel sententiam dixit, iudex esse desinit; et hoc iure utimur, ut iudex qui semel vel pluris vel minoris condemnavit, amplius corrigere sententiam suam non possit: semel enim male seu bene officio functus est.—D. 42, 1, 55.[2]

Gell. xvii. 2, 10: In XII tabulis ita scriptum est: ANTE MERIDIEM CAVSAM COICIVNTO, CVM PERORANTO AMBO PRAESENTES POST MERIDIEM PRAESENTI LITEM ADDICITO. [SI AMBO PRAESENTES] SOL OCCASVS SVPREMA TEMPESTAS ESTO.[3]

In order to have legal effect, the judgment must as a rule be pronounced in the presence of the parties. But inexcusable absence of the defendant (iudicium desertum) led to proceedings for contumacy[a] and, in case the plaintiff succeeded in proving his claim, to judgment by default (in eremodicio) against the absent party, against which upon subsequent proof of sufficient grounds of excuse for non-appearance before the judge, there was open to him the in integrum restitutio alone. If cautio iudicatum solvi had been given, the plaintiff, in the event of the defendant's absence—because of having no defence—could forthwith make his claim

[a] Cf. Gell. *sup.*

1 The provincial president is well aware that a final judgment which contains no condemnation or absolution is not regarded as legal.

2 After that the *iudex* has once delivered judgment, he ceases to be *iudex*, and our rule is that a *iudex* who has condemned either for too much or for too little cannot further amend his judgment; for he has discharged his functions, whether it be badly or well.

3 In the Twelve Tables is found written: 'Let them state each his case in the forenoon. Let them then conclude, both being present. In the afternoon let the officer give judgment in favour of the party present. [If both be present] the trial may last till sunset, as the extreme limit of time.'

upon the surety, against whom, however, the judgment of contumacy had no effect.

Book IV. Chapter II.

The contents of the judgment are governed by the formula, to which the judge is strictly bound. This yields the following results.

(1) In the case of an intentio relating to a certum—as the condition of the condemnatio—if the maintenance thereof either contains more than the plaintiff has to claim, or at the time is unfounded (plus or pluris petitio), absolution of the defendant must ensue, and furthermore, by virtue of consumption of the proceedings, entire loss of the whole claim (defeat in the suit, causa cadere).[a]

[a] Cic. pro Rosc. Com. 4; Gai. iv. 55.

Gai. iv. § 53[a]: Si quis intentione plus complexus fuerit, causa cadit id est rem perdit, nec a praetore in integrum restituitur exceptis quibusdam casibus.[1]

—nisi minor erat XXV annis.—Sane si magna causa iusti erroris interveniebat, . . . etiam maiori XXV annis succurrebatur: veluti si quis totum legatum petierit, post deinde prolati fuerint codicilli, quibus pars legati adempta sit.—§ 33, J. de act. 4, 6.[2]

Plus autem quattuor modis petitur; re, tempore, loco, causa. **Re**: veluti si quis pro decem aureis, qui ei debebantur, viginti petierit, aut si is cuius ex parte res est, totam eam vel maiore ex parte suam esse intenderit. **Tempore**: veluti si quis ante diem vel ante condicionem petierit. . . .

---

[1] If a man has embraced too much in his *intentio*, his action falls to the ground, *i.e.*, he loses the thing sued for, and he is not reinstated by the Praetor, except in certain cases.

[2] —unless he was under 25 years of age. If indeed there was so important a ground for an excusable mistake . . . relief was afforded even to one of more than 25 years of age: as for instance, if a man claimed the whole of a legacy, and afterwards a codicil was produced in which a part of the legacy was adeemed.

Book IV. Chapter II.

Loco plus petitur, veluti cum quis id, quod certo loco sibi stipulatus est, alio loco petit sine commemoratione illius loci, in quo sibi dari stipulatus fuerit: verbi gratia si is qui ita stipulatus fuerit: 'Ephesi dari spondes?' Romae pure intendat 'dari sibi oportere' . . . , quia utilitatem quam habuit promissor, si Ephesi solveret, adimit ei pura intentione . . . § 33, J. cit.[1]

Gai. iv. § 53[a]: **Causa** plus petitur, velut si quis in intentione tollat electionem debitoris, quam is habet obligationis iure, velut si quis ita stipulatus sit: **'sestertium x milia aut hominem Stichum dare spondes?'** deinde alterutrum solum ex his petat; nam quamvis petat quod minus est, plus tamen petere videtur, quia potest adversarius interdum facilius id praestare, quod non petitur. . . . Idem iuris est, si quis generaliter hominem stipulatus sit, deinde nominatim aliquem petat, velut Stichum, quamvis vilissimum. Itaque **sicut ipsa stipulatio concepta est, ita et intentio formulae concipi** debet.[2]

---

[1] Now too much is sued for in four ways: in respect of the thing, time, place, cause. In respect of the thing, as where a man has sued for twenty *aurei* instead of the ten that were due to him, or when he that has a share in a thing has claimed as his property the whole or too large a part of it. In respect of time, as when a man has sued before the date for performance, or before the fulfilment of a condition. . . . Too much is sued for in respect of place, as where a person who has stipulated for something to be given him at a fixed place sues for it elsewhere without mention of that place at which he stipulated for the transfer; for example, if a person who has stipulated thus: 'Do you undertake to give me the thing at Ephesus?' shall claim unconditionally that the gift ought to be made to him at Rome . . . because by the unconditional claim he takes away the advantage which the promisor would have had if he paid at Ephesus.

[2] Too much is sued for in respect of the cause, as when a man in his *intentio* deprives his debtor of the election which he has by virtue of the obligation, as when a person has stipulated thus: 'Do you undertake to give 10,000 sesterces or the slave Stichus?' and afterwards the creditor claims one or

(2) On the other hand, asking too little in the intentio does not prejudice the remainder of the plaintiff's claim; he was only obliged to postpone the action to the next year's term for the residue of his demand—as though there were a tacit delay contained in it—by reason of the 'exceptio *litis dividuae*,' which here belonged to the defendant.

Ibid. § 56: —minus autem intendere licet; sed de reliquo intra eiusdem praeturam agere non permittitur: nam qui ita agit per exceptionem excluditur, quae exceptio appellatur **litis dividuae.**[1]

Ib. § 122: Item si is qui cum eodem plures lites habebat, de quibusdam egerit, de quibusdam distulerit, ut ad alios iudices agantur, si intra eiusdem praeturam de his quas distulerit, agat, per hanc exceptionem, quae appellatur **rei residuae** summovetur.[2]

If the demonstratio—as the groundwork of the intentio incerti—contain more or less than the plaintiff can prove, this exercises no influence upon his claim.

Ib. 54: Illud satis apparet in incertis formulis plus peti non posse, cum certa quantitas non pe-

other only of these; for although he may sue for that which is less in value, yet he is considered to sue for more, because one's opponent can sometimes more easily give that which is not claimed. . . . The rule is the same when a person has stipulated for a slave in general terms and afterwards sues for a particular slave, as Stichus, although of the least value. Therefore the *intentio* of the formula ought to be drawn up in conformity with the wording of the stipulation.

[1] A statement of claim for too little is, however, admissible; but proceedings cannot be had for the rest of the claim during that praetorship. For a person suing is defeated by the so-called *exceptio litis dividuae* (plea of divided suit).

[2] Likewise, if he who had several actions against the same person has proceeded in some but postponed others, in order that they may go before other *iudices*, and then within the same praetorship proceeds in those which he postponed, he is met by the so-called *exceptio rei residuae* (plea of claim standing over).

BOOK IV. Chapter II.

tatur, sed 'quidquid adversarium dare facere oportet' intendatur.[1]

Ib. §§ 58–9: Si in demonstratione plus aut minus positum sit, nihil in iudicium deducitur et ideo res in integro manet; et hoc est quod dicitur, falsa demonstratione rem non perimi. § Sed sunt qui putant minus recte comprehendi, ut qui forte Stichum et Erotem emerit, recte videatur ita demonstrare 'quod ego de te hominem Erotem emi,' et si velit, de Sticho alia formula agat, quia verum est eum qui duos emerit, singulos quoque emisse: idque ita maxime Labeoni visum est. Sed si is qui unum emerit, de duobus egerit, falsum demonstrat. Idem et in aliis actionibus est, veluti commodati et depositi.[2]

[a] § 197 ad fin.

The damage to the defendant arising from an erroneous condemnatio—which, however, binds the judge[a]—is removed by in integrum restitutio, though not invariably.

Ib. § 57: At si in condemnatione plus petitum sit quam oportet, actoris quidem periculum nullum est, sed reus cum iniquam formulam acceperit, in integrum restituitur, ut minuatur condemnatio; si vero minus positum fuerit quam oportet, hoc solum actor consequitur quod posuit: nam tota

[1] It is clear enough that in uncertain formulae one cannot sue for too much, since a definite amount is not sued for, but the claim is made for whatever one's opponent ought to give or do.

[2] If too much or too little is set down in the *demonstratio*, there is nothing submitted to the *iudex*, and the matter remains intact; and this is what is meant by the saying that a matter is not extinguished by a false *demonstratio*. Some, however, think that less may be included, so that, for instance, a person who has purchased Stichus and Eros may be considered to have drawn his *demonstratio* correctly thus: 'Whereas I have bought the slave Eros of you,' and, if he like, he may claim Stichus by another formula; because it is a fact that he who has purchased two slaves is also the purchaser of each of them; and this was certainly Labeo's opinion. But if the purchaser of one thing should sue for two, his *demonstratio* is false. This rule holds in other actions also, as those of loan and deposit.

quidem res in iudicium deducitur, constringitur autem condemnationis fine, quam iudex egredi non potest; nec ex ea parte praetor in integrum restituit, . . . exceptis minoribus XXV annorum.[1]

§ 203. Translatio Iudicii.

Although the formula once given is, as the rule of proceedings in iudicio, unchangeable according to its material contents, yet a change in personal relations may be rendered necessary by circumstances.

Thus, there is need of the transfer of the formula to another judge, if the one appointed die or become incapable (mutatio iudicis).

And further, transfer to another person as party to the proceedings (translatio iudicii in the narrower sense) is requisite, or permissible, in the following cases.

Upon the death of a party, since an intentio as well as a condemnatio placed to the name of the deceased would be absurd, and judgment going for or against him would be void;[a] in which case the formula is recast for the heir. (Resumption of the proceedings.)

[a] D. 5, 1, 74, 2.

> Paulus respondit, eum qui in rebus humanis non fuit sententiae dictae tempore, inefficaciter condemnatum videri.—D. 49, 8, 2 pr.[2]
>
> Ulp.: Si operarum iudicio actum fuerit cum liberto et patronus decesserit, convenit trans-

---

[1] But if too much has been stated in the *condemnatio*, the plaintiff is at no risk; but when the defendant has received an unfair formula, he is restored to his former position. But if too little has been stated, the plaintiff only obtains what he has stated; for whilst the whole matter is brought before the *iudex*, it is controlled by the last clause of the *condemnatio*, beyond which the *iudex* must not go; nor does the Praetor upon such part of the formula allow *in integrum restitutio* . . . except in respect of persons under 25 years of age.

[2] Paul. answers, that the condemnation is considered void of a party who was not alive at the time judgment was pronounced.

Book IV. Chapter II.

lationem heredi extraneo non (?) esse dandam; filio autem, et si heres non exstat, et si lis contestata non fuerat, tamen omnimodo competit, nisi exheredatus sit.—D. 38, 1, 29.[1]

Id.: Mortuo filio post litis contestationem, transfertur iudicium in patrem dumtaxat de peculio et quod in rem eius versum est.—D. 5, 1, 57.[2]

Id.: Plures heredes rei necesse habebunt unum dare procuratorem, ne defensio per plures scissa incommodo aliquo afficiat actorem; aliud est in heredibus actoris, quibus necessitas non imponitur, ut per unum litigent.—D. 46, 7, 5, 7.[3]

In certain cases of a change of status, as in the person of the plaintiff by arrogation, of the defendant in
[a] § 113. noxal actions, by emancipation or manumission,[a] and
[b] D. 44, 7, 9. the like.[b]

Id.: Sed si pater lite contestata coeperit abesse vel etiam negligere executionem pater vilis, dicendum est causa cognita translationem filio competere; idem et si emancipatus filius esse proponatur.—D. 47, 10, 17, 14.[4]

A translatio ensues also 'causa cognita'—

---

[1] If an action have been brought against a freedman for services, and the patron is dead, it is agreed that no transfer shall be given to a stranger heir; but that even if he have not become heir, and there was no joinder of issue, it belongs, however, in any case to the son, unless he have been disinherited.

[2] Upon the death of a son after joinder of issue, an action is transferred against the father only so far as it concerns *peculium*, and what was converted into his property.

[3] Several heirs of the defendant will have to furnish a single representative, that the defence divided amongst several may place the plaintiff at no disadvantage. It is otherwise in respect of the plaintiff's heirs, upon whom no necessity is laid of suing by a single procurator.

[4] But if the father upon joinder of issue began by being absent, or a bad father has neglected to follow up the case, we shall have to say that when the case is heard a transfer attaches to the son. The same holds also if it be alleged that the son has been enfranchised.

(α) if a change occur in the existing vicarious relation in the proceedings.

Paul.: Ante litem contestatam libera potestas est vel mutandi procuratoris, vel ipsi domino iudicium accipiendi.—Post litem autem contestatam reus qui procuratorem dedit, mutare quidem eum vel in se litem transferre . . . potest, causa tamen prius cognita.—D. 3, 3, ll. 16 and 17.[1]

Item si suspectus sit procurator aut in vinculis aut in hostium praedonumve potestate,—vel iudicio publico privatove vel valetudine vel maiore re sua distringatur—vel si . . . inimicus postea fiat—aut adfinitate aliqua adversario iungatur—aut longa peregrinatio et aliae similes causae impedimento sint,—mutari debet; vel ipso procuratore postulante.—Ulp., Gai. and Paul. ll. 19–24 eod.[2]

(β) if representation becomes necessary after the Litis Contestatio.

Gai.: Qui proprio nomine iudicium accepisset, si vellet procuratorem dare, in quem actor transferat iudicium, audiri debet solemniterque pro eo iudicatum solvi satisdatione cavere.—l. 46 pr. eod.[3]

---

[1] Before joinder of issue there is full liberty either to change the *procurator*, or for the principal himself to undertake the action.—But after *lit. cont.* a defendant who has furnished a *procurator* can in fact change him or transfer the suit to himself, but upon the case being first investigated.

[2] Likewise if the *procurator* be under suspicion, or in chains, or in the power of the enemy or robbers,—or be hindered by a public or a private action, or by sickness, or by some important concern of his own,—or shall afterwards become hostile (to the principal), or be connected by some affinity with the opponent—or a long journey, and other like reasons obstruct—he ought to be changed; even upon the application of the *procurator* himself.

[3] If he that had submitted to an action in his own name should wish to appoint a *procurator*, to whom the plaintiff shall transfer the action, he must be heard, and shall give formal security with sureties on his behalf for satisfaction of the judgment.

Book IV. Chapter II.

§ 204. Execution of the Judgment.

From the legal condemnatory judgment springs the 'actio iudicati,' for payment of the sum of money forming the object of the condemnation.[a] In the case of representation in the proceedings—

[a] § 27.

(1) in respect of the conduct of such proceedings by a cognitor (or procurator praesentis), the actio iudicati is actively and passively transferred to the person represented; but not so in the case of the procurator absentis.[b]

[b] § 196.

Vat. fgm. 317: Cognitore interveniente iudicati actio domino vel in dominum datur—non alias enim cognitor [iudicati actione] experietur vel ei actori subiicietur, quam si in rem suam cognitor factus sit—; interveniente vero procuratore iudicati actio ex edicto perpetuo ipsi et in ipsum, non domino vel in dominum competit.[1]

Pap.: Quoniam praesentis procuratorem pro cognitore placuit haberi, domino causa cognita dabitur et in eum iudicati actio. —nec iudicati actio post condemnatum procuratorem[c] in dominum datur, aut procuratori qui vicit denegatur.—Ibid. §§ 331–2.[2]

[c] Sc. absentis.

Ulp.: Si procurator meus iudicatum solvi satisdederit, in me ex stipulatu actio non datur; sed et si defensor meus satisdederit, in me ex

---

[1] Where a *cognitor* intervenes, the action upon a judgment is given to the principal or against the principal—for the *cognitor* will conduct [the *iud. act.*], or the matter will be under his control as so conducting it, only if he have been made *cognitor* in his own cause—; but if a *procurator* intervene, the *iud. act.* according to the *edict. perp.* attaches to him and against him, not to the principal or against the principal.

[2] Since it was decided that the *procurator* of a party present should be regarded as a *cognitor*, upon the hearing of the cause the *iud. act.* will be given to the principal, and against him.—Neither is the *iud. act.* given against the principal after the condemnation of a *procurator* (*i.e.*, of an absent party) nor is it refused to the successful *procurator*.

stipulatu actio non datur, quia nec iudicati mecum agi potest.—D. 3, 3, 28.[1]

(2) The actio iudicati is likewise given upon the ground of proceedings conducted by the guardian for his ward (at any rate after termination of the guardianship) to and against the latter.[a] [a] § 112.

Ulp.: Si tutor condemnavit sive ipse condemnatus est, pupillo et in pupillum potius actio iudicati datur . . . ; et hoc etiam D. Pius rescripsit et exinde multis rescriptis declaratum est in pupillum dandam actionem iudicati semper tutore condemnato.—D. 26, 7, 2.[2]

Pap.: Post mortem furiosi non dabitur in curatorem qui negotia gessit iudicati actio, non magis quam in tutores [post depositum officium ?].—D. 26, 9, 5 pr.[3]

The carrying out of the judgment—*i.e.*, in ordinary proceedings, prosecution of the recognised claim by the plaintiff, in proceedings by cognitio, execution of the judicial sentence through official interference by the magistrate—takes place by way of execution against the person and the property.

(1) Execution against the person according to ius civile—but without manus iniectio—continued in the classical Law in a milder form,[b] whereby the [b] § 192. plaintiff took into custody the debtor adjudged to

[1] If my *procurator* have given security for satisfaction of the judgment, an action upon the stipulation is not given against me; but if my defender also shall have given security, no action on the stipulation is given against me, because I cannot be sued upon a judgment either.

[2] If an action has been decided for or against a guardian, the action upon the judgment is given rather to the ward and against the ward; . . . and this was the subject also of a rescript by the late Emp. Pius, and by many subsequent rescripts has it been declared that the action must always be given against the ward when the suit has gone against the guardian.

[3] After the death of a madman the action upon a judgment will not be given against the curator who managed the business, any more than against tutors [upon laying down their office].

Book IV. Chapter II.

him by the Praetor, served only still as an indirect compulsory remedy to obtain payment.

(2) Universal execution against the property, introduced by the Praetorian Edict—after the analogy of the auction of goods that had fallen to the State[a] —was at the same time the form for bankruptcy, if several creditors raised a claim for satisfaction from the property of the common insolvent debtor (decoctor, defraudator).

Proceedings in bankruptcy were begun by the grant, for the security of claims, of 'missio in bona debitoris,'[b] upon the application of even only one creditor, by decree of the Praetor without causae cognitio; and by the proscriptio bonorum, which was associated with it, and issued from the person installed (*i.e.*, public notification of the grant of immissio and eventual offer for sale of the goods) during the legal interval.[c] Consequently, after a certain interval the public sale followed by the Magister, chosen upon the decree of the Praetor from amongst the creditors, after preliminary settlement and publication of the conditions of sale (leges venditionis) and adjudication (addictio)[d] of the property in the bulk to the bidder offering to the creditors the highest percentage as purchase-money (bonorum emptor), who became universal successor[e] of the common debtor, and had to satisfy the creditors pro rata,[f] whilst he managed the retail sale upon his own account.[g]

Gai. iii. §§ 78–9: Bona autem veneunt aut vivorum aut mortuorum: vivorum, velut eorum qui fraudationis causa latitant, nec absentes defenduntur; item eorum qui ex lege Iulia bonis cedunt; item iudicatorum post tempus, quod eis partim lege XII tabularum, partim edicto praetoris ad expediendam pecuniam tribuitur.—§ Si quidem vivi bona veneant, iubet ea praetor per dies continuos XXX possideri et proscribi, si vero mortui per dies XV; postea iubet convenire creditores et ex eo numero magistratum creari, id est eum per

[a] § 78.

[b] D. 42, 4, 12.

[c] Gell. xx. 1, §§ 42, *sqq.*; § 195; Gai. iii. 120.

[d] It is questionable whether confirmed by the Praetor.

[e] § 77.

[f] Gai. iv. 65, *sqq.*

[g] Comp. also Lex Iul. municip. c. 25; Gai. ii. 154-5.

quem bona veneant; . . . itaque vivi bona die XXX, mortui vero die XX [a] emptori addici iubet.[1]

Ulp.: —missus in possessionem nunquam pro domino esse incipit; nec tam possessio rerum ei quam custodia datur . . . sed simul cum eo[b] possidere iubetur.—D. 36, 4, 5 pr.[2]

[a] XV?

[b] Sc. domino.

—cum creditores rei servandae causa mittuntur in possessionem, is qui possidet, non sibi sed omnibus possidet.—l. 5, § 2 eod.[3]

Paul.: Cum unus ex creditoribus postulat in bona debitoris se mitti . . . et praetor permisit, . . . commodius dicitur, non tam personae solius petentis, quam creditoribus et in rem permissum videri.—D. 42, 5, 12 pr.[4]

Gai. iii. § 80: Neque autem bonorum possessorum neque bonorum emptorum res pleno iure

---

[1] Now the goods which are sold may belong either to the living or the dead: the living, for example, when men keep out of the way with fraudulent intent, and being absent are not defended; likewise, when men make a surrender of their effects under the *l. Iulia;* likewise the goods of judgment-debtors after lapse of the time which is granted them, partly by a law of the Twelve Tables, partly by the Praetor's Edict, for the purpose of raising the money.—§ If the goods of a living person be sold, the Praetor orders seizure and an advertisement for sale for thirty successive days, but if those of a dead person, for fifteen days; afterwards he makes an order for a creditor's meeting and the appointment from their number of a *magister*, *i.e.*, a person by whom the goods shall be sold. . . . And so he directs that the goods of a living person shall be adjudicated after thirty, but those of a dead person after twenty days.

[2] He that is installed in possession never becomes owner, and not so much the possession of the goods as the care-taking is given to him . . . but he is bidden to occupy at the same time as the owner.

[3] —when creditors are put in possession with the view of preserving the property, the person who has possession possesses not for himself but for all.

[4] When one of the creditors applies to be put in possession of the debtor's goods . . . and the Praetor has allowed this . . . it is more to the purpose to say that such consent relates not so much to the claimant alone personally as to the creditors and the property itself.

Book IV. Chapter II.

fiunt, sed **in bonis** efficiuntur ; ex iure Quiritium autem ita demum adquiruntur, si usuceperunt.[1]

Id. iv. § 145 : Bonorum emptori proponitur interdictum quod[a] quidam 'possessorium' vocant.[2]

[a] Sc. adipiscendae possessionis.

Ibid. § 35 : Bonorum emptor ficto se herede agit, sed interdum et alio modo agere solet : nam ex persona eius cuius bona emerit, sumpta intentione, convertit condemnationem in suam personam, id est ut quod illius esset vel illi dari oporteret, eo nomine adversarius huic condemnetur ; quae species actionis appellatur **Rutiliana,** quia a praetore P. Rutilio, qui et bonorum venditionem introduxisse dicitur, comparata est ; superior autem species actionis, qua ficto se herede bonorum emptor agit, **Serviana** vocatur.[b] [3]

[b] Comp. Brown, s. 'Fictions.'

Pap.[c] : Imperatores Antoninus et Verus rescripserunt eos, qui bona sua negant iure venisse, praeiudicio experiri debere.—D. 42, 5, 30.[4]

[c] Iust.

Mod. : Si debitoris bona venierint, postulantibus creditoribus permittitur rursum eiusdem

---

[1] Now neither *bon. possessores* nor the purchasers of a bankrupt's estate become owners by a fully legal, but it is an equitable title that they acquire, and it is only by their completion of *usus* that it becomes theirs by Quiritarian Law.

[2] An interdict (*i.e.*, to obtain possession) is set forth in the Praetor's Edict in favour of the purchaser of an insolvent's goods, which some call 'possessory.'

[3] The purchaser of a bankrupt's estate sues under the fiction that he is heir. But sometimes he sues in another way. For, making out the *intentio* in the name of the person whose property he has purchased, he turns the *condemnatio* into his own name ; that is to say, that his opponent is to be condemned to make payment to him in respect of what belonged to, or what ought to have been given to, the bankrupt. This form of action is called 'Rutilian,' because it was provided by the Praetor Rutilius, who is also said to have introduced the *bonorum venditio.* The form of action first mentioned, in which the purchaser of the bankrupt's effects sues under the fiction of heirship, is called 'Servian.'

[4] The Empp. Antonine and Verus by rescript directed that persons who dispute the legality of the sale of their property must proceed by a pre-judicial action.

bona distrahi, donec suum consequantur.—D. 42, 3, 7.[1]

According to later Law, however, the bona debitoris are sold in parcels by a 'curator bonorum,' and the creditors are satisfied out of the purchase-money, according to the ratio of their claims; but there is also a set of privileged claims which have precedence over all others.

Gai.: Curator ex senatusconsulto constituitur, cum clara persona (veluti senatoris vel uxoris eius) in ea causa sit, ut eius bona venire debeant: nam ut honestius ex bonis eius quantum potest creditoribus solveretur, curator constituitur distrahendorum bonorum gratia vel a praetore vel in provinciis a praeside.—D. 27, 10, 5.[2]

Pap.[a]: Imperatores Antoninus et Verus rescripserunt bonis per curatorem ex senatusconsulto distractis, nullam actionem ex ante gesto fraudatori competere.—D. 42, 7, 4.[3]

[a] Iust.

Inst. iii. 12 pr.: Erant . . . olim et aliae per universitatem successiones; qualis fuerat bonorum emptio, quae de bonis debitoris vendendis per multas ambages fuerat introducta: . . . sed . . . bonorum venditiones exspiraverunt et tantummodo creditoribus datur officio iudicis bona possidere et, prout eis utile visum fuerit, ea disponere.[4]

---

[1] If a debtor's goods have been sold, upon the application of the creditors, further sales are allowed of the same person's goods, until they realise their own claims.

[2] By virtue of a *Sctum*, a curator is appointed if a notable person (a senator, for example, or his wife) be in such a position that his property has to be sold; for in order that so much as can should be paid to the creditors from the property in a more honourable way, a curator is appointed to sell the property, either by the Praetor or in the provinces by the President.

[3] The Empp. Antonine and Verus by rescript directed that after a sale by the curator in accordance with the *Sctum*, no action upon what has before been done is available to a fraudulent debtor.

[4] There were formerly also other kinds of succession to the

Book IV. Chapter II.

In pursuance of a lex Iulia, the debtor by voluntary surrender of property (cessio bonorum)[a] escapes the infamy that otherwise befalls him—as well as execution against the person—and acquires the 'beneficium competentiae'[b] in respect of after-acquired property.

[a] Cf. Blackst. ii. 472-3 (Steph. ii. 147, note); Bell, Dict. s. vv.; Paterson, s. 1186.

[b] § 139.

Imp. Alex.: Debitores qui bonis cesserint, licet ex ea causa bona eorum venierint, infames non fiunt.—C. 2, 11 (12), 11.[1]

Id.: Qui bonis cesserint, nisi solidum creditor receperit, non sunt liberati: in eo enim tantum hoc beneficium eis prodest, ne iudicati detrahantur in carcerem.—C. 7, 71, 1.[2]

Ulp.: Is qui bonis cessit, si quid postea adquisierit, in quantum facere potest convenitur.—D. 42, 3, 4 pr.[3]

Paul.: Quem poenitet bonis cessisse, potest defendendo se consequi, ne bona eius veneant.—l. 5 eod.[4]

Special execution, in opposition to the old Roman spirit, by means of distraint and public sale of single portions of property by subordinates of the magistrate (apparitores), first acquired recognition and development in imperial times,[c] whilst natural execution in actions for restitution, inconsistent with the charac-

[c] Cf. § 192.

---

aggregate. Such was the *bonorum emptio*, which was introduced for selling by a roundabout way the property of debtors; . . . but . . . *bon. vend.* have disappeared, and creditors are only allowed to take possession of the goods under the authority of a *iudex*, and dispose of them as seems to them expedient.

[1] Debtors who have made a surrender of their property do not fall under infamy, although in consequence thereof a sale have taken place of their property.

[2] Persons that have made a surrender of their goods are not released unless the creditor has received full satisfaction; for they enjoy this unique benefit, that insolvents are not to be cast into prison.

[3] He that has made a surrender of his goods, if he shall afterwards acquire anything, is sued for as much as he can render.

[4] He that regrets having made a surrender of his goods, can by showing cause succeed in stopping a sale thereof.

ter of ordinary proceedings,[a] only indeed belongs to the post-classical period.

Call.: D. Pius in haec verba rescripsit: 'His qui fatebuntur debere aut ex re iudicata necesse habebunt reddere, tempus ad solvendum detur...; eorum, qui intra diem . . . non reddiderint, pignora capiantur eaque, si intra duos menses non solverint, vendantur; si quid ex pretiis supersit, reddatur ei, cuius pignora vendita erant.'—D. 42, 1, 31.[1]

[a] 197.

Ulp.: —primo quidem res mobiles et animales pignori capi iubent, mox distrahi; quarum pretium si . . . non suffecerit, etiam soli pignora capi iubent et distrahi: quodsi nulla moventia sint, a pignoribus soli initium faciunt; quodsi nec quae soli sunt sufficiant vel nulla sint soli pignora, tunc pervenietur ad iura: exsequuntur itaque rem iudicatam praesides isto modo. § Si pignora quae capta sunt emptorem non inveniant, rescriptum est ab imperatore nostro et divo patre eius, ut addicantur ipsi, cui quis condemnatus est, . . . utique ea quantitate quae debetur.—l. 15, §§ 2, 3 eod.[2]

---

[1] The late Emp. Pius issued a rescript in the following terms: 'Those who shall confess their indebtedness, or shall have to make restitution by virtue of a legal judgment, shall be allowed time for payment; . . . let pledges be taken from those who shall not pay within the term, and, in default of payment within two months, let such things be sold; if there be any surplus from the purchase-moneys, let it be delivered up to him whose pledges were sold.'

[2] —in the first place they order movables and live stock to be taken in pledge, and then sold; and if the proceeds of the sale of such shall not suffice, they order distraint and sale of lands: but if there are no movables, they begin with a pledge of the land; but if those of the immovable estate do not suffice or none exist, then they will resort to rights; and the presidents, therefore, in that manner execute a judgment. § If the pledges that have been taken do not find a purchaser, by a rescript of our Emp. and his deceased father, the debtors themselves shall be adjudicated to the person in whose favour the condemna-

Book IV. Chapter II.

[a] ? Iust.

Ulp.[a]: Qui restituere iussus iudici non paret contendens non posse restituere, si quidem habeat rem, manu militari officio iudicis ab eo possessio transfertur.—D. 6, 1, 68.[1]

§ 205. Legal Remedies.

[b] It is questionable whether with restriction to *extraordinariae cognitiones*.

An appeal (appellatio, provocatio), with regulated series of instances and of reformatory character, first obtained in the sphere of the 'ius extraordinarium,' in imperial times.[b] It went—except as to special jurisdictions—from the *iudex* to the magistrate with jurisdiction, to the judge delegated by the Emperor, and, so far as an appeal lay from such judge (as the praefectus praetorio), to the Emperor himself.

Ulp.: Appellandi usus quam sit frequens quamque necessarius, nemo est qui nesciat, quippe cum **iniquitatem iudicantium vel imperitiam recorrigat**: licet, nonnumquam bene latas sententias in peius reformet.—D. 49, 1, 1 pr.[2]

The putting in of an appeal

(1) must take place at once verbally, or within a short interval (dies fatales) in a written form (libelli appellatorii); it has a suspensive effect as regards the judgment pronounced, and is attended by a penalty for vexatious litigation.

Ulp.: Biduum vel triduum appellationis ex die sententiae latae computandum erit.—In propria causa biduum accipitur.—Quare procura-

---

tion was, . . . at any rate for such an amount as he has to claim.

[1] When a person does not comply with the order of the *iudex* to make restitution, and maintains that he cannot make restitution, if he in fact have the thing, the possession is by armed force transferred from him by the authority of the *iudex*.

[2] Every one is aware how common and how needful is the custom of appeal, from the fact that it repairs the unfairness or unskilfulness of judges, although sometimes it alters for the worse judgments well pronounced.

Pomp.: Furioso sententia a iudice dici non potest.—l. 9 eod.[1]

(3) If it have been pronounced in the absence of a party.[a]

[a] But comp. § 202.

Paul. v. 5ª, § 6: Ea quae altera parte absente decernuntur, vim rerum iudicatarum non obtinent.[2]

(4) If it violate a valid decision, or directly negative an established rule of law; but not indeed if the decision do not agree with positive law: if, for instance, a rule of law is falsely applied.[b]

[b] Cf. *inf.* D. 5, 1, 74, 2; 10, 2, 36; and § 203.

Mod.: Si expressim sententia contra iuris rigorem data fuerit, valere non debet, et ideo et sine appellatione causa denuo induci potest; non iure profertur sententia, si specialiter contra leges vel senatusconsultum vel constitutionem fuerit prolata.—D. 49, 1, 19.[3]

Mac.: Contra constitutiones autem iudicatur cum de iure constitutionis non de iure ligatoris pronunciatur.—D. 49, 8, 1, 2.[4]

Call.: Cum prolatis constitutionibus contra eas pronuntiat iudex, eo quod non existimat causam, de qua iudicat, per eas iuvari, non videtur contra constitutiones sententiam dedisse.—D. 42, 1, 32.[5]

The invalidity of the judgment can form the subject of further proceedings, in which a decision is given

---

[1] Sentence cannot be given by a *iudex* for a madman.

[2] Matters that are decided in the absence of one of the two parties do not obtain the force of *res iudicatae*.

[3] If judgment has been expressly given in opposition to the rigour of the law, it shall be invalid, and the cause can therefore be retried even without appeal. A sentence is not passed in accordance with law, if it have expressly been passed in opposition to statutes, or a decree of the Senate, or a constitution.

[4] Now judgment is given in opposition to constitutions when sentence is passed against the law of the constitution, not against the right of the litigant.

[5] When appeal is made to constitutions, and yet the *iudex* pronounces against them, because he does not consider that the case in which he gives judgment is supported by them, he is not regarded as having delivered judgment in opposition to the constitution.

Book IV. Chapter II.

upon the legal existence of the judgment. The nullity of the judgment is established either

(*a*) defensively, on the part of the defendant, by denial of the ground of the actio iudicati brought against him,[a] or on the part of the plaintiff, who repeatedly prosecutes his claim, by resisting the defendant's appeal to the res iudicata (exceptio rei iudicatae); or

[a] § 195.

(*β*) aggressively, on the part of a party condemned, by recalling—cum poena dupli—the performance rendered in consequence of the judgment, by means of 'revocatio in duplum,' but not by means of 'condictio indebiti.'

Mac.: Si quaeratur, iudicatum sit nec ne, et huius quaestionis iudex non esse iudicatum pronuntiaverit: licet fuerit iudicatum, rescinditur, si provocatum non fuerit.—D. 49, 8, 1 pr.[1]

Iul.: Respondi: iudicium quod iam mortuo debitore per defensorem eius accipitur nullum esse, et ideo heredem non liberari: defensorem autem si ex causa iudicati solverit, repetere non posse.—D. 5, 1, 74, 2.[2]

Paul.: Non est iudicium familiae erciscundae nisi inter coheredes acceptum: sed quamvis non sit iudicium, tamen sufficit ad impediendam repetitionem, quod quis se putat condemnatum.—D. 10, 2, 36.[3]

Ulp.: . . . si ex condemnatione fuerit pecunia

---

[1] If inquiry be made whether judgment has been given or not, and the *iudex* has replied to this question, that judgment has not been given, although it have been, yet such judgment is rescinded, if no appeal have been made.

[2] I replied: An action which, whilst the debtor was already dead, is undertaken by his representative, is of no effect, and therefore the heir is not discharged, but the representative, if he has paid upon the ground of the judgment, cannot recover.

[3] The action for partition of an inheritance only obtains between actual co-heirs, but although there was no action, yet it is still enough to hinder recovery that a man thinks he was condemned.

soluta, . . . propter auctoritatem rei iudicatae repetitio cessat.—D. 17, 1, 29, 5.[1]

And finally, against an already valid judgment, in the presence of a ground of restitution,[a] 'in integrum restitutio' can be given by the higher (or a like) judge, by which it is rescinded, and it is replaced by fresh proceedings; to be distinguished from restitution as against delay in appeal. Likewise, a judgment obtained by deceit may be contested by ordinary remedies for dolus.

[a] § 30.

Mac.: Inter minores XXV annis et eos qui reipublicae causa absunt hoc interest, quod minores etiam qui per tutores curatoresve suos defensi sunt, nihilo minus in integrum contra rem iudicatam restituuntur cognita scilicet causa: ei vero qui reipublicae causa absit, ceteris quoque qui in eadem causa habentur, si per procuratores suos defensi sunt, hactenus in integrum restitutione subveniri solet, ut appellare his permittatur. —D. 4, 1, 8.[2]

Herm.: Appellatio iniquitatis sententiae querelam, in integrum vero restitutio erroris proprii veniae petitionem vel adversarii circumventionis allegationem continet.—D. 4, 4, 17.[3]

Ulp.: Quod appellatio interposita maioribus

---

1 —if money has been paid by virtue of a judgment . . . recovery is lost, because of the binding force of the decision.

2 Between those who are less than 25 years of age and persons that are absent on State business there is this difference, that minors even who have been defended by tutors or curators are none the less reinstated in their former position in spite of the decision, of course after investigation of the case; but a person who is absent on State business, as also others that are regarded as in the same position, if they have been defended by their *procuratores*, are so far relieved by reinstatement in their former position that they are allowed to appeal.

3 Appeal embraces a complaint against the unfairness of a sentence; but reinstatement in the former position, either a petition for pardon because of one's own mistake, or the allegation of fraud upon the part of the opponent.

Book IV. Chapter II.

praestat, hoc beneficio aetatis consequuntur minores.—l. 42 eod.[1]

Paul.: Cum a te pecuniam peterem eoque nomine iudicium acceptum est, falso mihi persuasisti, tamquam eam pecuniam servo meo aut procuratori solvisses, eoque modo consecutus est, ut consentiente me absolvereris: . . . ex integro agere possum et si obiiciatur exceptio rei iudicatae replicatione[a] iure uti potero.—D. 4, 3, 25.[2]

[a] Sc. doli.

§ 206. Processual Penalties.

To malicious and rash, as well as in general unfounded proceedings, pecuniary damages and forensic penalties are attached in certain cases for the part subject thereto (poenae temere litigantium).[b] To these belong the following.

[b] Cf. §§ 192, 205.

(1) The cases of so-called 'lis crescens' ('lis infitiando crescit in duplum'[c]) in which condemnation for twice the amount falls upon the defendant subject thereto.

[c] Gai. iv. 9; C. 4, 5, 4.

(2) The 'sponsio et restipulatio poenalis.'[d]

[d] Cf §§ 128, 194, 201.

Gai. iv. § 171: Ex quibusdam causis sponsionem facere permittitur, veluti de pecunia certa credita et pecunia constituta; sed certae quidem creditae pecuniae tertiae partis, constitutae vero pecuniae partis dimidiae.[3]

(3) Apart from the previous cases, each party can

---

[1] That which is assured to persons of full age by the bringing of an appeal, minors obtain by virtue of favour shown to their age.

[2] When I sued you for the money, and the action was accepted in that behalf, you falsely led me to think as though you had paid this money to my slave or *procurator*, and in this way managed that, with my consent, you were acquitted. . . . I can bring a fresh action, and if the plea of *res iudicata* be set up against me, I shall have the law on my side in employing the replication (*i.e.*, of fraud).

[3] In some cases one is allowed to make a wager, as for example, in an action upon the loan of a sum certain, and for

require from the other the 'iusiurandum calumniae' which operates as a moral means of deterring from unjustified proceedings.

Ibid. § 172: Quodsi neque sponsionis neque dupli actionis periculum ei cum quo agitur iniungatur, ac ne statim quidem ab initio pluris quam simpli sit actio, permittit praetor iusiurandum exigere 'non calumniae causa infitias ire': unde quamvis heredes . . . item feminae pupillique eximantur periculo sponsionis, iubet tamen eos iurare.[1]

Paul.: Qui familiae erciscundae et communi dividundo et finium regundorum agunt, et actores sunt et rei: et ideo iurare debent, 'non calumniae causa litem intendere' et 'non calumniae causa infitias ire.'—D. 10, 2, 44, 4.[2]

(4) The calumniae iudicium concurs with the last-mentioned for the defendant at his option.

Gai. iv. § 175: Calumniae iudicium adversus omnes actiones locum habet et est decimae partis (rei; sed) adversus adsertorem tertiae partis est.—§ 178: Calumniae iudicio nemo damnatur nisi qui intelligit non recte se agere, sed vexandi adversarii gratia actionem instituit.[3]

---

an agreed amount; but in the case of an ascertained loan the wager is allowed for a third part, in that of an agreed amount it is for a half.

[1] But if the risk neither of a wager nor of an action for double the amount is laid upon the defendant, and if the action, to begin with, is not for more than the simple sum demanded, the Praetor allows an oath to be required 'that he is not denying the claim vexatiously.' Hence, although heirs, . . . and again, women and wards are exempted from the risk of a wager, the Praetor orders them to take the oath.

[2] Persons that bring the actions for partition of an inheritance, for division of joint property, and for the settlement of boundaries are both plaintiffs and defendants; and, accordingly, must swear that 'they do not bring the action for a vexatious claim,' and 'that they will not make denial vexatiously.'

[3] The action for vexatious litigation is employed in opposition to all actions, and is for a tenth part of (the thing; but)

Book IV.
Chapter II.

(5) Likewise, with the previous means of defence a 'contrarium iudicium' is in certain actions given to the successful defendant at his option.

Ib. §§ 177–8 : Contrarium autem iudicium ex certis causis constituitur, veluti si iniuriarum agatur, et, . . . decimae partis datur.—§ Contrario iudicio omnimodo damnatur actor, si causam non tenuerit, licet aliqua opinione inductus crediderit se recte agere.[1]

---

against an *adsertor libertatis* it is for the third part.—§ No one is condemned in the action for vexatious litigation unless he knows that his proceedings are wrongful, but has brought the action with the view of annoying his opponent.

[1] Now the cross-action is established for certain cases (alone); thus, for that of the action for injury, and . . . is granted for the tenth part.—§ For a cross-action the plaintiff is always condemned, if he has been unsuccessful in his proceedings, even though he was led by some notion to believe that he was right in bringing his action.

INDEX TO THE LATIN PASSAGES.

(The figures enclosed in brackets denote the number of the page.)

I. JURISTIC SOURCES.

A. JUSTINIANEAN SOURCES.

(a) Institutiones.

INSTITUTIONES.

INSTITUTIONES.

(*b*) DIGESTA.

DIGESTA.

DIGESTA.

GAII INSTITUTIONES.

LEX IULIA MUNICIPALIS.

LEX MALACITANA.

LEX RUBRIA DE GALLIA CISALPINA.

PAULI SENTENTIAE.

ULPIANI FRAGMENTA.

C. POST-JUSTINIANEAN SOURCES.

II. NON-JURISTIC AUTHORS.

GENERAL INDEX.

(*The numbers are those of the pages.*)

A

J

K

L

M

T

U

V

W

PRINTED BY BALLANTYNE, HANSON AND CO.
LONDON AND EDINBURGH